A Reference Guide to
Latin American History

A REFERENCE GUIDE TO LATIN AMERICAN HISTORY

JAMES D. HENDERSON
HELEN DELPAR
MAURICE P. BRUNGARDT

RICHARD N. WELDON
TECHNICAL EDITOR

M.E.Sharpe
Armonk, New York
London, England

Library of Congress Cataloging-in-Publication Data

A reference guide to Latin American history / James D. Henderson.
General Editor ... [et al.].
    p.   cm.
Includes bibliographical references and index.
ISBN 1-56324-744-5 (alk. paper)
  1. Latin America—History Chronology. 2. Latin America—Biography
Dictionaries. I. Henderson, James D., 1942–
F1410.R395   1999   99-28766
980′.002′02—dc21   CIP

Printed in the United States of America

The paper used in this publication meets the minimum requirements of
American National Standard for Information Sciences
Permanence of Paper for Printed Library Materials,
ANSI Z 39.48-1984.

⊗

BM (c)   10   9   8   7   6   5   4   3   2   1

CONTENTS

PART II
TOPICAL CHRONOLOGY

A Reference Guide to
Latin American History

INTRODUCTION

A *Reference Guide to Latin American History* presents significant events of Latin American history through the year 1999. The *Reference Guide* is the collaborative work of three specialists in the field: Maurice P. Brungardt of Loyola University New Orleans, who wrote on the pre-Columbian and colonial periods; Helen Delpar of the University of Alabama-Tuscaloosa, who wrote on the independence era and the nineteenth century; and James D. Henderson of Coastal Carolina University, who wrote on twentieth-century Latin America.

This book was inspired by a one-volume reference to United States history, the *Encyclopedia of American History* (1953) by Richard B. Morris. Following Morris, it employs a tripartite organization. PART ONE, constituting approximately half the work, is a chronology of significant events in Latin American history from the arrival of the first humans in the Americas through July 1999. PART ONE is divided into several sections, each of which encompasses a distinct era in Latin American history, with emphasis on the twentieth century. Each section is further divided on the basis of regional geography. For example, each of the sections covering events after 1826 is divided into the following subsections: International Developments; Mexico, Central America, and the Caribbean; the Bolivarian Republics; Southern Cone; and Brazil.

PART TWO is a topical chronology. It traces significant events and trends in the region on the basis of themes running from politics and economics to fine arts and popular culture. PART THREE consists of biographical sketches of three hundred significant figures of Latin American history.

Boldface is used in the chronological and topical sections, and in the index, to alert the reader that the person mentioned is included among the three-hundred biographical sketches. Our general policy is to translate titles of Spanish- or Portuguese-language literary works only when the volume exists in English translation. For the names of paintings, pieces of music, and films, an English translation is usually provided.

The authors of *A Reference Guide to Latin American History* collaborated closely during its preparation, proofreading one another's contributions. Richard N. Weldon of Coastal Carolina University, the book's technical editor, was in charge of formatting the work and proofreading it, as well as producing all of the maps.

The *Reference Guide* contains a select bibliography of works dealing with Latin America.

The authors welcome readers' responses to their treatment of Latin America's history. They can be contacted at their respective e-mail addresses: *brungard@loyno.edu* (Maurice P. Brungardt), *hdelpar@tenhoor.as.ua.edu* (Helen Delpar), *henderj@coastal.edu* (James D. Henderson).

Part I

General Chronology

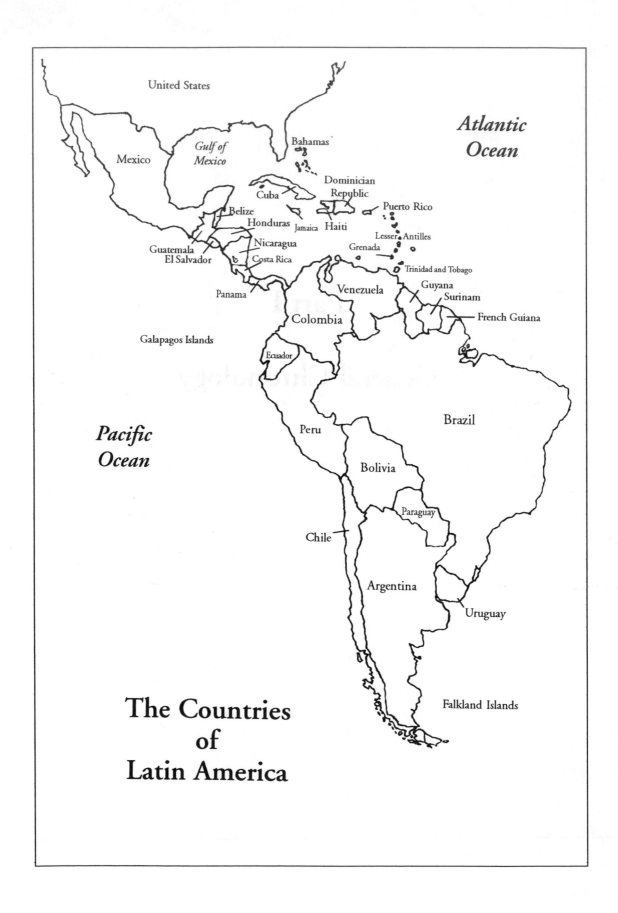

United States

Atlantic Ocean

Mexico

Gulf of Mexico

Bahamas

Cuba

Dominician Republic

Puerto Rico

Belize

Honduras

Jamaica

Haiti

Lesser Antilles

Guatemala

Nicaragua

Grenada

El Salvador

Costa Rica

Trinidad and Tobago

Panama

Venezuela

Guyana

Surinam

Colombia

French Guiana

Galapagos Islands

Ecuador

Pacific Ocean

Peru

Brazil

Bolivia

Paraguay

Chile

Argentina

Uruguay

Falkland Islands

The Countries of Latin America

THE AMERICAS: Pre-Columbian to European Contact

The Beginnings
c. 40,000- c. 8000 B.C.E.

Humans appeared late in the Americas. Scholars now list Monte Verde in southern Chile as the oldest settlement in the New World, dating it from c. 12,500 years ago, or 10,500 B.C.E. (B.C.E., before the common era, and C.E., common era, are now used to designate dates instead of the Eurocentric B.C., before Christ, and A.D., *anno domini*, the year of our Lord. The abbreviation c. used with dates, from the Latin *circa*, means an approximate rather than an exact date.) The oldest human skeletal remains are of *Homo sapiens*. No other hominid species has been found, reinforcing scholars' assumptions that in the New World there was not an evolution from earlier forms but rather a migration of modern beings from the Old to the New World. Most authorities point to the Bering Strait between Siberia and Alaska as the logical crossing point.

The formation of glaciers during the Ice Age (Pleistocene period) lowered sea levels and left a land bridge, which scholars call Beringea, over which immigrants traveled, perhaps beginning in the period 40,000 to 30,000 B.C.E. The end of the Ice Age brought rising temperatures and water that covered the bridge between 10,000 and 9000 B.C.E. and virtually ended contact with the Old World. From here the peoples of the Americas evolved and developed their culture independently of the rest of the world until 1492 C.E. when **Christopher Columbus** mistakenly discovered and named them "Indians." This rules out Euro- and Afrocentric explanations, which posit outside influences for development in the Americas and which fail to credit ancient Americans for their native genius and cultural achievements. Since 1492 various theologians, scholars, and dilettantes have concocted preposterous theories on flimsy

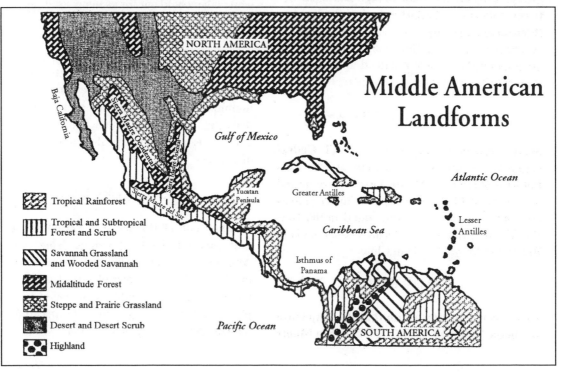

7

evidence that run the gamut from the native Americans being one of the lost tribes of Israel to their being visited by ancient astronauts from distant galaxies.

The earliest evidence for human presence in the Americas is the archaeological remains of primitive stone tools from temporary campsites of nomadic hunter-gatherers that have been found in the United States, Mexico, Peru, Chile, and Brazil. The earlier the site, the thinner, the more scattered, the more ambiguous, and the more hotly debated the evidence. The radiocarbon dates of the various sites are claimed to run anywhere from 31,000 to 12,000 B.C.E. The more conservative scholars accept later dates and assume people migrated sometime after 20,000 B.C.E., while others are more open to the evidence and would accept sometime before 20,000 B.C.E. Whatever the case, by the end of this period human presence is irrefutable, and by 10,000 B.C.E. *Homo sapiens* certainly had spread over most of the Americas.

c. 31,000- c. 12,000 B.C.E.

Homo sapiens **first appeared in the Americas as groups crossed the land bridge Beringea between Siberia and Alaska during the Ice Age (Pleistocene period).** No other hominid type has ever been found in the New World, reinforcing the assumption that people migrated to the Western Hemisphere and did not evolve there.

c. 30,000- c. 20,000 B.C.E.

Some archaeologists claim that El Cedral campsite in the Mexican state of San Luis Potosí is older than Monte Verde. Its stone and bone tools establish the presence of hunter-gatherers. Other similar campsites found in the New World producing like results are Pedra Furada in Brazil and Monte Verde in Chile.

c. 19,000 B.C.E.

Some archaeologists claim that the Tlapacoya site in the Valley of Mexico is older than Monte Verde. Its stone and bone tools and an obsidian blade were used by hunter-gatherers as crude choppers, scrapers, and knives.

c. 12,000- c. 9000 B.C.E.

Throughout the Americas from Canada to Tierra del Fuego are found Clovis projectile points that were used in the hunting of big game such as mammoths and mastodons. These animals disappeared with the end of the Ice Age and forced humans to adapt to the changes in climate. Some projectile points are found with the skeletal remains of the animals killed.

Monte Verde, Chile, is presently identified as the oldest site (c. 10,500 B.C.E.) verified by stratigraphy. Its location at the southern end of South America suggests that *Homo sapiens'* presence must have begun thousands of years earlier in order to have migrated this far south from Alaska. The trek would have required millennia in order to cross formidable barriers, overcome new diseases, and adapt to different plants and climatic conditions. Some scholars argue for as few as 2,000 years for this migration while others hold out for as many as 20,000.

c. 9000 B.C.E.

Butchering site of Santa Isabel Iztapan in the Valley of Mexico contains the remains of two mammoths and the tools for their killing and dressing. "Tepexpan Man," found at a nearby village, has turned out to be the complete skeleton of a female.

c. 10,000- c. 8000 B.C.E.

Gradual end of the Ice Age raised sea levels that covered the land bridge from Asia to America. Asian migration ended and humans in the Western Hemisphere evolved independently of the rest of the world until the arrival of **Christopher Columbus.** Big game disappeared and humans began to rely more on plant food.

Domestication of Plants and Animals in the Americas
c. 8000- c. 1500 B.C.E.

The end of the Ice Age brought climatic changes and, if species were to survive, necessary adaptation. It spelled the demise of the mammoths that roamed much of the North American continent. Adaptation resulted in an increased reliance on plant foods and their domestication. As native Americans selected plants for traits based on their utility, they gradually domesticated plants and eventually raised them as crops. Some of the plants domesticated were maize, beans, squash, potatoes, manioc, tomatoes, avocados, cacao, papaya, guava, vanilla, cacti, cotton, chilies, and indigo. Beans were one of the earliest crops (7000-5000 B.C.E.) and appeared independently in Mexico and Peru. Maize originated in Mexico (5000-3600 B.C.E.) and spread to Peru by perhaps 4000 B.C.E. The domesticated potato dates from c. 5000 B.C.E. and came from Peru. Manioc, also called *yuca* or cassava, is thought to have originated in Brazil or Central America. Animals were less important than in the Old World, but Peruvians domesticated the llama and alpaca between 4000 and 3000 B.C.E. Each major region had a particular ecology, and domestication proceeded down distinctive paths, frequently with widely different results. Millennia of evolution were needed before plants yielded enough food for storage and to sustain a fully agrarian lifestyle. But when the process was complete, it made far-reaching changes possible, such as social ranking, craft specialization, and other elements of social complexity that are the essence of civilization. Village agriculture, ceramics, public buildings, ceremonial structures, irrigation works, fortified towns, and eventually cities appeared in South and Mesoamerica (Mexico and Central America).

c. 7000- c. 5000 B.C.E.

Caves in Tamaulipas, Mexico, yield early variety of beans and bottle gourds that were used as receptacles. Caves in Tehuacán Valley, Puebla, contain chilies, avocado, squash, and amaranth. Both are clear evidence that ancient Americans were selecting and raising plants. At least five millennia were required before the yield was sufficient for humans to depend solely on agriculture. The process is frequently called the Agrarian or Neolithic Revolution.

c. 5000- c. 3500 B.C.E.

The domestication of maize is thought to have taken place in southwestern Mexico in the Balsa River Basin and to have come from a subspecies of the wild grass teosinte. It may have reached the Peruvian highlands by 4000 B.C.E. and Chile soon after.

c. 5000- c. 4500 B.C.E.

Plant remains of the domesticated potato near Lake Titicaca. Evidence of domestication of beans in Peru's highland Callejón de Huaylas Valley.

    Earliest pottery in the Americas appeared at Taperinha on the Amazon River. The use of pottery by this ancient fishing village has suggested to some scholars that pottery may have arisen before agriculture, and that the two did not necessarily appear together. The same debate has sprung up in Colombia and Ecuador, where pottery appeared a millennium later in village communities with an aquatic resource base.

c. 4000- c. 3000 B.C.E.

Llama and guinea pig began to appear as domesticated animals in Peru.

c. 3500- c. 1500 B.C.E.

Pottery appeared at the Valdivia archeological site in the Ecuadorian coastal province of Guayas.

c. 3100- c. 2500 B.C.E.

Pottery evident at Puerto Hormiga in the lowlands of northern Colombia.

c. 2800- c. 2000 B.C.E.

Public structures at preceramic highland Peruvian site of Kotash contained sunken fire

pits used to burn ritual offerings. Findings suggest highland people shared a common religious tradition that archaeologists call the Kotash religious tradition.

c. 2000 B.C.E.

Pottery began to appear in Peru.

1785 B.C.E.

Oldest archaeological evidence of manioc in Casma Valley of Peru, although it probably originated in Central America or Brazil.

Native American Civilizations in Mesoamerica
c. 2000 B.C.E.-1521 C.E.

Scholars divide Mesoamerican history before the Spanish conquest into four major periods:

Archaic	8000-2000 B.C.E.
Pre-Classic (or Formative)	2000 B.C.E.-150 C.E.
Classic	150-900 C.E.
Post-Classic	900-1521 C.E.

The designation "Classic" comes from a European historical model and its association with ancient Greece and the high point of its civilization. It also parallels the time when the Maya wrote and dated their stone monuments, but the Classic period should not be seen as the high point of ancient American civilizations.

Between 1500 and 400 B.C.E., Mexico's southern Gulf Coast witnessed the rise and fall of the Olmec, whose culture embodied many of Mesoamerica's first achievements. In the pre-Classic period the Olmec, often said to be the mother culture of Mexico, produced major ceremonial centers, a well-defined artistic style, a ritual ball game, and calendar and writing systems that they shared with other contemporary societies of Mesoamerica. A network of trade and interaction tied them with Oaxaca and Central Mexico and with places as far away as El Salvador. Their most spectacular artistic creations were colossal heads of basalt weighing as much as fifty tons

brought from sixty miles away without benefit of beasts of burden. The mobilization of labor necessary for such transportation was in itself evidence of a new social order.

Other complex societies appeared about the same time as the Olmec, or shortly thereafter. Contact, trade, war, and exchange brought cross-acculturation, although in exactly what order is and will be the subject of much scholarly research. All present accounts are tentative. Especially noteworthy were the beginnings of the Maya in the Yucatán Peninsula and Belize and of the Zapotec in Oaxaca. In Central Mexico two rivals for control of the valley of Mexico were Cuicuilco, with its circular-step pyramid, and Teotihuacán, with its massive urban complex that would eventually house 150,000. Cuicuilco was removed from competition in the first century C.E. when the volcano Xitle erupted and entombed it under twenty feet of lava and opened the way for the rapid expansion of Teotihuacán. Only a strongly centralized state could have managed the subsequent growth, size, and complexity of this precocious city-state. Politically it controlled highland Central Mexico; economically its merchants traded as far as Honduras; and ideologically its religious icons and symbols predominated in Mesoamerica and even penetrated Maya belief structures and artistic forms. The collapse of Teotihuacán came suddenly in the seventh century C.E. when its occupants, apparently in an internal revolt, selectively burned the most important religious and administrative buildings. Perhaps the elite demanded too much from an overburdened populace. Future success from social management would require greater consensus that would possibly come from a more integrative ideology and religion, increased social mobility and freedom at least for some, population control, and better planning and use of scarce resources. Such objectives were difficult if not impossible to reconcile. All native American civilizations faced these problems, some with more success than others.

It was Maya civilization that was most striking in its rise and fall. Competing city-states, mainly in the lowlands of southern Mexico and Guatemala, flowered in the Classic period (150-

900 C.E.). Maya achievements were elaborate astronomical, mathematical, and calendar systems, which included place notation (the use of zero), linear dating, and base-20 numbering; writing; and monumental architecture with a wide variety of styles and innovative techniques. Maya civilization manifested itself in the up-and-down fortunes of its many city-states as war, conquest, diplomacy, building, and commerce ruined some and rewarded others. The most renowned cities were Tikal in the Petén jungle of Guatemala, Palenque in the hills of Chiapas, and Copán in Honduras. The bloom of Maya civilization withered between 800 and 900 C.E. as city-states were abandoned and writing stopped. The last date recorded by the Mayas on their stone stelae was 909. Here the written historical record ends. The collapse is not completely understood, but archaeological findings reveal demographic and ecological pressures. An exploding population required more food. In addition to slash-and-burn agriculture the Maya used raised fields, canals, terracing, and kitchen agriculture. The more intensive exploitation might have upset fragile tropical ecosystems. Skeletal remains reveal the inhabitants as malnourished and chronically ill. The rapid expansion in construction obviously required a greater collective effort and might have overburdened society's productive capacity and undermined elite control. Ecological and economic collapse may have been hastened by increasing militarism of Maya society that concentrated population in urban centers to the detriment of agricultural production. Maya cities continued but without the writing and numbering systems and sophisticated achievements of the Classic era. In the post-Classic period (900-1521 C.E.), Chichén Itzá emerged after 1000 as the most powerful Maya city-state, but was sacked and replaced by Mayapan shortly before 1200. Mayapan suffered the same fate in 1441.

In Central Mexico the abundant resources and

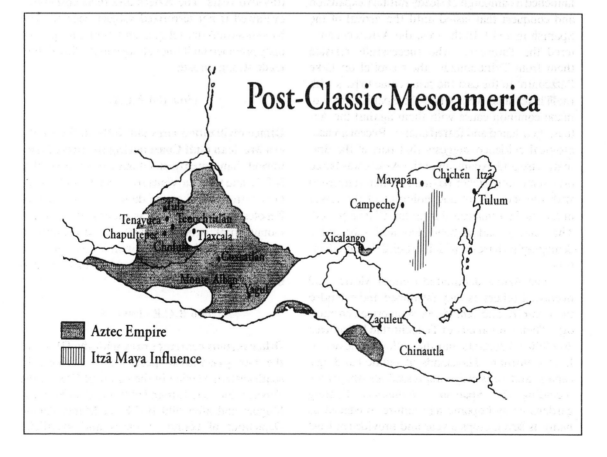

Post-Classic Mesoamerica

Tula
Tenayuca · Tenochtitlán
Chapultepec · · Cholula · Tlaxcala
Coxcatlán
Monte Albán · Yagul
Mayapán · Chichén Itzá
Campeche ·
Xicalango · Tulum
Zaculeu
Chinautla

▨ Aztec Empire
||||| Itzá Maya Influence

propitious location did not tolerate a power vacuum for long. Tula appeared in the tenth century
C.E. as the largest urban center since Teotihuacán, but evidence about its inhabitants, the Toltec,
and the relationship of their artistic styles with
those of the post-Classic Maya, with whom they
shared some common motifs, is ambiguous. At
issue is who came first and how the one influenced the other. The Toltec abandoned Tula about
1150, but the reasons are again unclear. The way
was now open for the rise of the Nahuatl-speaking
Aztecs.

Migrating from the "barbaric" and nomadic
north and settling in the valley of Mexico in the
twelfth and thirteenth centuries, competing Aztec
groups established themselves on the shores of
Lake Texcoco and evolved into rival city-states,
the most important being Azcapotzalco, Texcoco,
Tlacopán, and Tenochtitlán. The last three banded
together in 1428 under the leadership of
Tenochtitlán, overthrew Azcapotzalco, and
launched a campaign of steady military expansion
and conquest that lasted until the arrival of the
Spanish in 1519. In the west the Aztecs encountered the Tarascans, who successfully resisted
them from Tzintzuntzán, their capital on Lake
Pátzcuaro. In the east the same came to pass with
the Tlaxcalans, who, when the Spanish arrived,
made common cause with them against the Aztecs, their hated and feared enemy. Recent archaeological evidence suggests that part of the dramatic rise and expansion of the Aztecs was based
on a materially richer peasantry when contrasted
with the meager lot and holdings of the lower
orders of Teotihuacán during the Classic period.
The Aztecs had a better-fed and substantive
demographic base on which to build their civilization.

The Aztecs dominated Central Mexico and
overawed others as they fashioned and extended
their empire and remade Mesoamerican cosmology. Their capital city of Tenochtitlán had at least
200,000 inhabitants and the valley of Mexico at
least a million. Thousands of public buildings,
canals, and causeways impressed all who came,
including the Spanish. *Chinampas*, floating
gardens or hydroponic agriculture, produced as
many as seven crops a year and provided at least

half of Tenochtitlán's requirements with the rest
being supplied by tribute-paying provinces. The
agrarian surplus sustained craftsmen, merchants
(*pochteca*), soldiers, priests, and nobles. Artisans
(*tolteca*) embellished Tenochtitlán and enriched
the nobility (*pipiltin*) and other state functionaries.
Hereditary commoners (*macehualtin*) paid tribute
and supplied labor for public projects. People
could sell themselves or their children as slaves
(*tlacotin*) or fall into servitude as a result of a
crime or capture in warfare. Merchants and
artisans also paid tribute.

The supreme ruler of the Aztecs was the
emperor (*tlatoani*), who was more of a military
leader than a religious one, but secular goals were
always subsumed under an ideology that was
overwhelmingly religious. The Aztecs reworked
Mesoamerican cosmology to justify their expansion and imperial mission. For them human
sacrifice propitiated the gods and postponed the
end of the world, which was threatened every
fifty-two years. The Aztecs and their cosmology
overawed if not terrorized subject peoples. The
harshness of Aztec religion and its gloomy philosophy provided fault lines along which Christianity
made strong inroads.

1500-400 B.C.E.

**Olmec civilization rises and falls on the south-
ern Mexican Gulf Coast during the pre-Classic
period.** San Lorenzo stood out from 1350 to 900
B.C.E. and then La Venta from 900 to 400 B.C.E.
Other sites were Laguna de los Cerros and Tres
Zapotes. Symmetrical plazas, platforms, and other
monumental structures, such as ball courts, a
distinctive artistic style, colossal heads, and trade
in jade and obsidian characterized Olmec civilization.

600 B.C.E.-150 C.E.

**Other regions contemporary with the Olmec of
the late pre-Classic period also thrived.** In
southwestern Mexico in the valley of Oaxaca the
Zapotec flourished around 600 B.C.E. at San José
Mogote and after 500 B.C.E. at Monte Albán.
Depictions of bound prisoners and sacrificial

victims carved on stone monuments suggest violence, warfare, and the ritual human sacrifice that would be a characteristic of later Mesoamerican civilizations. The earliest evidence of writing and the Mesoamerican calendar also appeared. The hieroglyphs came from a 260-day cycle. Later glyphs included a second cycle based on a solar year of 365 days. Combining the two cycles produced the fifty-two-year "century" that was common throughout Mesoamerica.

In Belize, Yucatán, southern Mexico, and the Petén, the Maya began to come to cultural life about 300 B.C.E. The lowlands witnessed the beginnings of monumental architecture, stucco masks, and irrigation.

In the valley of Mexico, Cuicuilco and Teotihuacán began their rise to power. But the former was snuffed out by the volcano Xitle in the first century C.E., and Teotihuacán proceeded to dominate all of Central Mexico.

150-750 C.E.

Teotihuacán continued its explosive urban growth, peaking by 500 C.E. Its 2,000 residential structures housed at least 150,000 persons, at the time the largest city in the world outside of China. Commensurate with its size was its influence throughout Mesoamerica. It dominated most of the highlands of Central Mexico by conquest. The conquered populations laid out their cities along the same cardinal axis (16 degrees east of north) as Teotihuacán. Its distinctive architectural style appeared in structures at Kaminaljuyú in highland Guatemala, and its pottery and obsidian artifacts were traded as far south as Honduras.

150-900 C.E.

Maya civilization rose phoenix-like in southern Mesoamerica. While all ancient Mesoamerican civilizations were literate, the Maya inscribed their glyphs on far more imperishable materials like stone stelae, staircases, door lintels, facades, and pottery. As a result, more specific detail and chronology on dynastic histories, political alliances, warfare, and ritual exist for the Maya than

for any other pre-Spanish New World civilization. The historical record deciphered to date shows competing city-states, among which Tikal, Palenque, and Copán stand out in greatest detail. Between 800 and 900 C.E. Classic Maya civilization in the southern lowlands came to an end.

378 C.E.

Conquest of Uaxactún by Jaguar Paw, Maya ruler of Tikal.

426 C.E.

Founding date of Copán's ruling dynasty. Yax-Kuk-Mo' (Blue Quetzal Macaw) was the first of sixteen successive dynastic rulers.

431 C.E.

Recorded date of the beginning of Palenque's dynastic history.

c. 550-650 C.E.

Hundred-year hiatus when little new construction occurred in Maya lowlands. Tikal lost its influence and was probably defeated by Caracol.

615-683 C.E.

Reign of Lord Pacal (Shield), Palenque's greatest ruler. His pyramid-tomb has yielded some of the greatest archaeological treasures of the Classic Maya as well as a list of Palenque's dynastic rulers back to mythical times, including Pacal's mother, Lady Zac Kuk (r. 612-640), and his great-grandmother, Lady Kanal Ikal (r. 583-604).

682-723? C.E.

Reign of Al Cacaw, who restored Tikal's former power and prosperity.

738 C.E.

18 Rabbit, Copan's thirteenth ruler, was captured and executed by forces from the city of

Quirigua. All of the stelae in Copán's great plaza were erected during the reign of 18 Rabbit.

763-820? C.E.

Reign of Yax-Pac (First Dawn), the last dynastic ruler of Copán. The latest date on the surviving structures at Copán is 820.

769-? C.E.

Reign of Chitam, last of the thirty-nine rulers of the dynasty that had been in power in Tikal since the third century C.E.

799 C.E.

Erection of Palenque's last dated monument.

840 C.E.

Erection of last dated monument along the Usumacinta River.

869 C.E.

Erection of Tikal's last dated monument.

900-1519 C.E.

The post-Classic period failed to produce a strong centralizing power until very late when the Aztecs appeared. With power fragmented states were small and increasingly militaristic, although trade and markets continued to expand. In the valley of Oaxaca the Zapotecs and Monte Albán gave way to the Mixtecs and Mitla as the dominant power.

c. 900- c. 1150 C.E.

In Central Mexico the Toltecs developed and abandoned Tula. The written and archaeological records diverge as to Tula's importance. Also unclear is whether it or Maya Chichén Itzá, with which it shared common stylistic motifs, influenced the other.

987 C.E.

Topiltzín Quetzalcoatl, high priest, supposedly expelled from Tula in a power struggle with Tezcatlipoca. Native histories have him arriving in Chichén Itzá in Yucatán in the same year, thus explaining the similarities in artistic styles between the two cities. But the different authors of these native histories, especially the Aztecs, sought their genealogical validation in the Toltecs and tended to glorify Tula. The archaeological record, on the other hand, suggests the Toltecs had a materially poor culture and were unlikely to have exercised such a strong influence. The post-Classic Maya continued to be dominated by Chichén Itzá until late in the twelfth century when it was sacked by Mayapan, which in turn suffered the same fate in 1441 C.E. Thereafter, until the arrival of the Spanish, various petty Maya city-states, sixteen initially, fought for control without any gaining ascendancy.

1111 C.E.

Mythical date when the Aztecs began their sojourn south. According to their official history, the Mexica, as they called themselves, started their trek from their legendary homeland Aztlán (Azteca is the Nahua word meaning "House of Aztlán"), which is sometimes identified as one of the small islands on the Pacific coast of the state of Nayarit.

c. 1240s-70s C.E.

Aztecs settled in the valley of Mexico. As nomadic barbarians from the north, the Aztecs had the necessary fighting skills to gain some acceptance among rival city-states when they served as mercenaries.

1324-25 C.E.

Aztecs occupied the site of their future great city Tenochtitlán. Rejected and expelled from various city-states in the valley of Mexico for their cruel warfare, the Aztecs took control of some lake islands in the year 2 Calli (House) but as subjects of the neighboring city of Azcapotzalco. As told by their official history, they were to locate their city where they would find an eagle perched on a cactus with a snake in its beak. When the circumstances of the oracle came together on a rock outcropping in the middle of Lake Texcoco, the foundation seemed problematic in such a seemingly inhospitable aquatic setting. But the icon has since become the national symbol of Mexico and the city the world's largest.

1427-28 C.E.

Triple Alliance formed. The city-states of Texcoco, Tlacopán (Tacuba), and Tenochtitlán forged a military alliance and defeated the latter's nominal overlord, Azcapotzalco. Led by Tenochtitlán's ruler Itzcóatl (Obsidian Snake, r. 1427-40) and Texcoco's brilliant Nezahualcóyotl (r. 1431-72), the Aztecs turned their Nahua-speaking city-states into a great power that quickly dominated the valley of Mexico and put them on the road to imperial greatness. Tenochtitlán's ascendancy in the alliance grew until it was the dominant force. Itzcóatl had manuscripts burned that differed from the official Aztec accounts which upgraded their past and associated them with the now legendary Toltecs.

1450-51 C.E.

Famine swept Central Mexico. Native histories reported unseasonably cold and wet weather leading to widespread crop failure. The military conquest of Moctezuma I (r. 1440-68), the Aztecs' greatest expansionist, slowed, but, in an attempt to placate the gods, human sacrifice increased.

1473

Tlatelolco, the northern half of the Aztec capital of Tenochtitlán, rebelled. The warrior and priestly elite easily subdued Tlaltelolco, the home of the Aztec merchant class, and had its ruler killed and replaced with one of their own.

1502

Upon the death of Ahuitzotl (r. 1486-1502), Moctezuma II (r. 1502-20) was chosen to be- come the new Aztec emperor (*tlatoani*). Moctezuma's seventeen-year reign before the arrival of the Spanish revealed the strengths and weaknesses of Aztec polity. The empire was loosely organized and lacked the necessary integrative functions to resist the Spanish. Native enemies like the Tlaxcalans, who had been left unconquered in a strategic province, would join the Spanish. Many subject peoples had not been integrated into the Aztec system. They resented Aztec rule and also deserted to the Spanish. Aztec control over the entry and exit points of their empire was weak. Once inside, the Spanish could bring to bear the corrosive effects of superior weaponry, mobility, and a mind-set that transcended the gloomy and obsessive perspective of the Aztecs.

Native American Civilizations in Andean South America c. 2000 B.C.E.- c. 1532 C.E.

In comparison with Mesoamerica, far less archaeological work of a systematic nature has been done on South America and the Caribbean, and the scattered evidence found makes conclusions about chronology, patterns, and connections subject to extensive future revision. General chronological divisions have only been accepted for Andean South America, although they are sometimes applied to Brazil, northern South America, and the Caribbean. Currently Andean civilization is divided into seven periods:

Pre-Ceramic	c. 3000-c. 2000 B.C.E.
Initial	c. 2000-c. 1400 B.C.E.
Early Horizon (Chavín)	c. 1400-c. 200 B.C.E.
Early Intermediate	c. 200 B.C.E.-c. 400/600 C.E.
Middle Horizon	c. 400/600 C.E.-c. 800/1100 C.E.
Late Intermediate	c. 800/1100-c. 1475
Late Horizon (Inca Empire)	c. 1475-1532

The Early, Middle, and Late Horizon periods saw a homogeneous art style spread over a wide area, while the Intermediate periods witnessed regional stylistic diversity.

Andean South America—mainly Peru and Bolivia—is a region of dramatic contrasts, a narrow desert coastal strip, a humid area of tropical rain forest that slopes toward the Amazon, and between, the towering Andes that rise and fall forming intermontane basins and a wide variety of climatic and ecological zones. As civilization developed in the Andes, these zones had to be bridged in order to be effectively exploited. Distinctive labor institutions and social management were developed to overcome the uniqueness of Andean geography, which scholars have termed *verticality*.

It was in the Peruvian highlands (*sierra*) that a geographically more extensive material culture with a distinctive style first made its appearance in South America. This pan-Andean manifestation was centered on Chavín de Huántar. The Chavín style acquired special prominence in the period c. 1400 to c. 400 B.C.E. Whether political control went with its cultural domination is unclear. What is evident is that pan-Andean movements in general originated in the highlands and the *altiplano* (high plateau) that starts just north of

South American Landforms

Tropical Rainforest

Tropical and Subtropical Forest and Scrub

Savannah Grassland and Wooded Savannah

Midaltitude Forest

Steppe and Prairie Grassland

Desert and Desert Scrub

Highland

Lake Titicaca and runs south for 500 miles at an average elevation of 13,000 feet. The altiplano provided its inhabitants with rich grazing lands for their wool- and meat-producing llamas and alpacas and fertile soil for their potatoes and other nutritional root crops. But maize—which could not be grown above 10,000 feet–as well as coca, cotton, and fruits, had to be gotten elsewhere. It was highland inhabitants (*serranos*) who were most in need of exchange, trade, commerce, expansion, or conquest in order to obtain those commodities they could not produce. This need probably also accounts for why so much of the thrust for unification came from the sierra.

The next expression of a pan-Andean identity was found in the lands surrounding Lake Titicaca where Tiwanaku (Tiahuanaco) in Bolivia held sway from c. 100 to c. 1200 C.E. After 400 their material culture spread to the coasts of Peru and Chile. In the 500s the Huari at Ayacucho transformed the Tiwanaku style into their own as its expansion across the highland and littoral demonstrated. With the decline of the Huari around 800 and of Tiwanaku about 1000, the coast had an independent existence until the Inca reasserted sierra control. On the coast a series of expanding states succeeded one another, some even before the demise of the Huari. The Moche arose as early as 100 B.C.E. and eventually controlled over 300 miles of the northern Peruvian coast until their collapse between 600 and 750 C.E. The Sicán replaced them between 700 and 900 and controlled a luxury goods trade stretching from southern Colombia to Chile with links over the Andes to the upper Amazon as well. The trade included emeralds, gold nuggets, and tropical shells. After the Sicán came the Chimú, who united a 600-mile stretch of the Peruvian littoral into a coastal empire as they ruled from their capital, Chan Chan, from c. 900 to c. 1460 when they were conquered by the Inca. In the altiplano regional powers also held sway as at least twelve Aymara-speaking kingdoms controlled the area from Cuzco to Potosí between 1200 and 1500.

But the time was ripe for a more unifying force to take hold in the Andes, and it was the Inca who filled this role in a way similar to that of the Romans. The Inca were an obscure people who, so their history relates, settled in the valley of Cuzco in about 1200 and who through military raids and intermarriage gradually took control only to suffer near defeat in the great war against the Chanca Confederation in the 1430s. Their victory under the leadership of their greatest emperor, Pachacuti, had obvious parallels with the story of the modest beginnings of the Romans and the dramatic victories of Cincinnatus thus making the early historiography of the Inca suspect. Nevertheless, Pachacuti was an actual historical figure. Scholars are aware that the Inca and the Spanish retold and rewrote the pre-Columbian history of the Andes from the point of view of their own oral, literary, and historical traditions, and that much of what has traditionally been accepted as the preconquest history of the area has been colored by these perspectives.

The Inca, when compared with Aztec society, appeared more stratified, structured, and organized. At the top were the emperor and the nobility, who literally owned the empire. They were so few in number that outsiders had to be brought in to staff some posts. Neighboring peoples were made Inca by adoption and given important positions. Local elites who helped their people submit peacefully to Inca overlordship were confirmed in positions of authority and left with their private lands and individual workers. The children of provincial rulers were sent to Cuzco where they were instructed in Inca culture and taught Quechua. Despite the large-scale Quechuanization of much of the empire, the separate privileges for some and the short time remaining before the arrival of the Spanish left many heterogeneous elements that rivaled the cultural mosaic in Mesoamerica. Even today, 30 percent of the people of Bolivia speak Aymara rather than Quechua.

As has already been suggested, the way the Andes divided, separated, and walled off valleys and regions from one another had major ramifications in the development of Andean civilizations and their societies. What one community produced from its ecosystem, another frequently wanted but could not have without some sort of exchange. These commodities were not always acquired in the same time-honored ways of trade and commerce with which Western Europe was familiar. The uniqueness of Andean geography has been expressed as *verticality*, in which commodities whose production was limited to certain elevations were exchanged for those from other elevations. While verticality would to a Western mind seemingly promote barter and markets, and did, there were other ways to effect these exchanges. One of them was for individual communities to occupy the different elevation zones with groups of individuals from their own community. People as a labor force were rotated up or down the Andes depending on the requirements of the community. Sometimes their rotation out was permanent; in other instances it was for a limited period of time. Local *curacas* (caciques, leaders, chiefs) and other elite figures probably made the assignments and distributed what was produced. The evolution of this system took place over a long period of time. It had certainly been in existence long before the Inca appeared on the scene and developed it into their *mita* (rotary-draft system of labor), which the Spanish continued in a variety of different forms and which in the infamous case of the Potosí silver mountain became synonymous with extreme exploitation. From the point of view of the Inca, when organized by them and for their benefit, the mita would seem to take on the benign appearance of group solidarity working for the well-being of all. At least this is the way scholars present the subject. The reality, however, is that under both the Inca and the Spanish, the mita probably involved a significant amount of force, inequality, and exploitation. The main point is that the verticality of the Andes posed special problems whose solution led to the development of structures for integration but which also involved a significant element of social control. In addition, those Andean societies that arose in the desert coastal strip developed social structures that, while different from those of the sierra, were similarly hierarchical and rigid. The complex irrigation systems required a high degree of social management from an elite directing–class. In general, therefore, Andean societies were more hierarchical and socially rigid than their Mesoamerican counterparts.

c. 1400-c. 200 B.C.E.

First pan-Andean cultural style--Chavín--appeared and spread throughout much of the Andes. Named after the Peruvian highland site of Chavín de Huántar, the style--which really appeared elsewhere half a millennium earlier than its namesake--included bilateral symmetry, double imaging, and icons representing animals from the Amazon. Sitting astride a trade route between the coast and the lowland rain forest, Chavín became an important center of exchange. By 1200 B.C.E. temples with its stylistic signature appeared on the Peruvian north coast and highlands. By 1000 B.C.E. the style had reached as far south as Lima and by 500 B.C.E. as far as modern Cajamarca in the north and Ayacucho in the south.

c. 370 B.C.E.- c. 540 C.E.

Nasca culture flourished on the southern Peruvian coast during the Intermediate period until absorbed by the pan-Andean Huari. This regional culture exploited underground rivers and streams to irrigate their fields. Its capital, Cahuachi, was really a ceremonial center that was empty much of the time. Trophy heads depicted on pottery and mummified real ones found in tombs undoubtedly suggest the warfare and human sacrifice prevalent at the time. Nasca icons with their geometric, human, feline, and serpent characteristics captured something of the supernatural. They appeared on ceramics and on a gigantic scale on the dry desert where some correlated with the location of water.

c. 100 B.C.E.-c. 540 C.E.

Moche culture blossomed during the Intermediate period. This regional culture controlled over 300 miles of the northern Peruvian coast during its maximum extension. The Moche constructed fortifications, roads, and canals and elaborated a complex system of irrigation. Their realistic art style is our chief source of knowledge about their society, since a wide spectrum of human life and activity was depicted.

c. 400-c. 1100 C.E.

Middle Horizon was the period in which Tiwanaku (Tiahuanaco) and closely related Huari (Wari) cultures became pan-Andean and spread throughout much of Peru and Bolivia. At 12,600 feet, Tiwanaku was located near Lake Titicaca and had a population estimated between 20,000 and 40,000. Stone for massive structures was hauled in from elsewhere. This and the agrarian surplus needed to feed people at that elevation required extensive social management and control. Huari, farther north near modern Ayacucho, was about the same size. The exact chronology and relationship between the two are much debated. Both shared common artistic styles, such as interlocked tapestry tunics and knotted hats, and similar public monuments and icons. Tiwanaku appeared first, expanding (c. 400-c. 600) to coastal areas of Chile and Peru, but the Huari performed certain functions, such as building roads, that suggest the Inca inherited many of their traditions. The Huari also had *quipu*, or stringed record-keeping devices, made of different colors while the Inca used knotted ones.

c. 700-c. 1375 C.E.

Sicán culture emerged on the northern Peruvian coast in the void left by the earlier Moche. Sicán iconography showed a cosmology of duality that rested on natural and supernatural worlds ruled by a lord in the first case and a deity in the second. The numerous temples and monuments manifested a theocratic society requiring a rigid social structure to compel so much building on such a limited demographic base. Sicán's superior metallurgical skills and control of a luxury-goods trade of gold, emeralds, and sea shells made its influence felt from southern Colombia and the upper Amazon to the Peruvian-Chilean border. Its cultural horizon was indeed extensive. Its influence diminished after its capital, of the same name, was burned about 1075. Its conquest by the Chimú around 1375 marked its demise.

c. 900-c. 1460 C.E.

The Chimú built an empire along 600 miles of the Peruvian north coast. From its capital, Chan Chan, the Chimú had two periods of expansion.

The first began about 1350 and absorbed the Moche. The second was undertaken by the Chimú ruler, Minchancaman, and terminated about 1450. Two decades later the Inca conquered the Chimú and transported Minchancaman to Cuzco as a hostage. Noted for their metallurgical skills, especially gold-working, the Chimú put together an empire with enormous irrigation works, an extensive system of roads, and elaborate public structures, all based on a rigidly stratified society.

c. 1200 C.E.

Mythical beginnings of the Inca when, according to different indigenous accounts, they either migrated or fought their way into the valley of Cuzco.

c. 1200-c. 1500

Rival Aymara-speaking polities established control over the altiplano around Lake Titicaca north and especially south. About 1440 the Inca began their expansion south and their incremental absorption of the Aymara into their state system.

c. 1438-71

Reign of Pachacuti, the greatest of the Inca emperors. In c. 1438 Pachacuti rallied the Inca from near defeat by the Chanca Confederation. As the story goes, only the superhuman efforts of the Inca Yupanqui, the son of the cowardly ruler Viracocha, turned the tide and saved Cuzco and the Inca. In celebration he seized his father's throne, changed his name to Pachacuti, Quechua for "he who shakes the earth," and began a series of campaigns that transformed the Inca into the lords of Cuzco and the rulers of an empire that stretched from the central Peruvian highlands to the shores of Lake Titicaca by the time of his death c. 1471. He launched the Inca on their greatest period of expansion and state building, creating requisite bureaucracies, codifying Inca law, and designing and rebuilding the capital, Cuzco. In addition he established a network of paved highways, storehouses (*qolpa*), and inns (*tambos*) at which imperial runner-mailmen (*chasqui*) rested. Finally, he had the famous Machu Picchu built as his private estate and personal retreat in a mountainous setting so dramatic for its aesthetic beauty that it has become a world-famous tourist attraction as the "Lost City of the Incas" as it seemingly hovers in mid-air, an emerald-framed jeweled city set in the middle of the cloud-draped Andes.

c. 1471-93

Reign of Inca Emperor Topa Inca. The son of Pachacuti, Topa Inca conquered the last great rival of the Inca, the Chimú, in 1475-76 and pushed the outer limits of the empire into Ecuador in the north and into Chile and Argentina in the south.

c. 1493-c. 1527

Reign of the Inca emperor Huayna Capac. He successfully incorporated most of Ecuador into the Inca empire. His absence from the capital Cuzco for almost two decades set the stage for the civil war between his two sons, Huascar and **Atahualpa**, as rival claimants to the throne.

c. 1524-32

Smallpox epidemic raced ahead of the arriving Spanish (1532) and devastated the Inca Empire. It carried off millions, including the emperor **Huayna Capac.**

Other Native American Civilizations and Cultures 2000 B.C.E. -1537 C.E.

The tendency toward state formation and political control over a wide area observed in Mesoamerica and the Peruvian and Bolivian Andes was not as strong elsewhere in South America or the Caribbean. No pan-movements comparable to those of Teotihuacán, Chavín, Tiwanaku, Huari, the Maya, Aztec, and Inca are evident. Nevertheless, the Muisca in the Cordillera Oriental of Colombia were on the verge of state formation when the Spanish arrival interrupted the process in 1536. Population growth, greater social complexity, more efficient tribute mechanisms, and greater political control centered on the leaders known as the *zipa* at Bogotá and the *zaque* at Tunja probably made urban growth, state consolidation, and expansion inevitable.

More urban and technically and artistically superior, but demographically far fewer than the Muisca, were the Tairona on the Colombian coast near Santa Marta. Both the Muisca and Tairona spoke Chibcha and produced distinctive gold pieces by the lost-wax method. These metallurgical skills were common to many of the Chibcha-speaking groups from Ecuador to Costa Rica, and it was probably via these groups that the metal-working came to be known and practiced in Mexico.

Both the Muisca and the Tairona were vibrant civilizations when the Spanish arrived in the sixteenth century. Long since disappeared were the obscure and little-understood people associated with the archaeological site of San Agustín in Colombia's upper Magdalena River Valley. They produced huge monolithic statues whose stylized forms still fascinate today.

Also present in Colombia, as well as in Venezuela and the Caribbean Islands, were usually divided into the Arawak-speaking Taíno (frequently simply called Arawaks) and the Caribs. At the time of **Columbus**'s arrival the Arawaks lived in permanent agricultural settlements, raised manioc as their main staple, made pottery, were led by caciques (political leaders or chiefs) and priests, had nobles or an upper class (*nitainos*), and a retainer or servant group (*naboría*). The Caribs lived from the sea and tended to reside on the Lesser Antilles, or Leeward Islands, and raided the Arawaks to the north on the islands of Hispaniola and Cuba. It was the Spanish who emphasized the difference between the so-called peace-loving, compliant, easily conquered Arawaks and the wild, untamed, savage Caribs. It is not clear how valid the distinction is, since they both spoke Arawak, and the Spanish tended to call any Native Americans on the Colombian or Venezuelan coast who resisted, Caribs. Whatever the case, Arawak-speaking groups had penetrated much of the Colombian and Venezuelan coast and rivers leading up to the interior highlands and thus had separated many of the original Chibcha-speaking communities, some of which are still found in Panama and Costa Rica. Before the Arawaks and the Caribs island-hopped their way across the Caribbean, they may have migrated from Brazil through Venezuela.

Also from Brazil were those Native Americans speaking the Tupi languages. There are seven different language branches in the Tupi linguistic family. The most notable are Tupi-Guaraní and Tupinambá. At the time of the conquest, semi-sedentary Indian groups from Argentina, Paraguay, most of Brazil, and the Amazon lowlands of Peru, Colombia, and Venezuela belonged to this linguistic family, but none of them manifested the same degree of class distinction, social differentiation, artisan skills, and monumental architecture as the Aztec, Maya, and Inca. As a result, chronology is provided only for San Agustín, the Tairona, and the Muisca. Future archaeological discoveries may well change the above summary.

c. 1500-1400 B.C.E.

First evidence of human occupation of the archaeological site of San Agustín in Huila, Colombia.

c. 400 B.C.E.-900 C.E.

Scholars designate this as the Classical period for the Native American culture associated with San Agustín. Monolithic statues, burial monuments, terraced land, and roads characterized this culture, which geographically occupied the area where Colombia's Cordillera Central and Oriental come together and form the headwaters of the Magdalena River.

c. 300-c. 200 B.C.E.

Approximate date of the oldest native American gold ornament found in Colombia. It was discovered near Tumaco on the southern Pacific coast near the Ecuadorian border.

c. 300-1500 C.E.

Dates assigned by archaeologists to the Tairona civilization. The Tairona were located on the slopes and Atlantic coast of Colombia's Sierra Nevada de Santa Marta. While the area they occupied was geographically minuscule, the Tairona had paved roads, stone stairs, and retaining walls; terraced land; and elaborate canals, aqueducts, and drainage systems. Many scholars consider them to be Colombia's most advanced Native American civilization.

c. 700-c. 800 C.E.

The Muisca culture first appeared in the Cordillera Oriental. Archaeologists have arrived at this conclusion based on the replacement of pre-Muisca incised pottery with the painted ceramics that were characteristic of the Muisca.

1470-1537

Muisca state formation began but was interrupted by the Spanish conquest. By the beginning of the sixteenth century the four native American chiefdoms of Bogotá, Duitama, Sogamoso, and Tunja had emerged as the most important and as the main contenders for further political consolidation as they fought over who would be the *zipa* and the *zaque*.

1470-90. As the first *zipa*, Saguanmachica ruled the southern half of the Muisca territory, an area associated with the Sabana de Bogotá and the highlands of the present-day department of

Indians of South America

Cundinamarca. His capital was located on the Sabana de Bogotá. Organized around the *zipa* was a cult associated with the moon, from which he was believed to have descended.

1482-87. As the first *zaque*, Unsahúa ruled the northern half of the Muisca territory, an area associated with the highlands of the present-day department of Boyacá. His capital was centered on Hunza (Tunja). Associated with the *zaque* was a cult of the sun, from which he was believed to have descended.

1490-1522. Nemequene ruled as the *zipa* after overthrowing Saguanmachica, whose confederation of Bacatá was opposed by the *zaque*.

1522. Battle of Arroyo de las Vueltas near Chocontá between the *zipa* Nemequene and the *zaque* Quemuenchatocha ended in the death of Nemequene, who was succeeded by Tisquesusa.

1537. Tisquesusa was killed near Facatativá by one of **Gonzalo Jiménez de Quesada**'s soldiers.

August 20. Battle of Hunza (Tunja) between the forces of Jiménez de Quesada and the *zaque* Quemuenchatocha in which the latter was defeated and made a prisoner of the Spanish.

COLONIAL LATIN AMERICA

Iberian Expansion and International Developments 1402-1803

Spain and Portugal's presence in the Americas, as the first of the European powers, is explained by their geopolitical setting, early nation-state formation and identity, and advantageous use of contemporary technology. In the southwestern corner of Europe, both Spain and Portugal were well placed to exploit those parts of the world whose cosmologies and technology were constrained by the particularities of their individual mini-worlds and micro-visions.

Portugal could not expand to the north or east without risking war with Castile. South and down the African coast was the obvious route of conquest for the kingdom. With the Azores, Madeira, Cape Verde, and São Tomé islands acquired in the course of their initial expansion, the Portuguese had an advantage over everyone else. They also possessed the necessary experience and infrastructure to continue around the Cape of Good Hope to capture the luxury-goods trade in spices from the Far East, which they did with the successful voyage of Vasco da Gama (1497-99). The Portuguese tradition of maritime trade from a series of fortified trading posts, rather than full-scale territorial conquest, became their trademark and was consistent with their limited demographic base. Nevertheless, the sugar plantation economy based on slave labor that they developed on the Atlantic islands off the coast of Africa gave them a more substantive model for occupation and conquest in the New World. When they finally grasped the possibilities inherent in their newly discovered Brazil, which took them at least forty years, they already had the necessary experience and resources in tropical areas to transfer the sugar plantation economy model across the Atlantic to parallel latitudes in Brazil. Portugal's inclusion in the Spanish empire (1580-1640) also probably bought them time initially and shielded them from the attacks of other European powers. But when Spain weakened, the association became a liability, and the Portuguese revolted ending the relationship.

Castile and Aragon's fortuitous unification with the marriage of **Isabella** and **Ferdinand** (1469) brought a national identity to Spain. While this initially gave Spain a head start over other potential European rivals, it also saddled the country with excess baggage on the road to solid nation-state formation and modernization. Ferdinand's diplomatic policy of marrying his children into the royal houses of Europe produced spectacular additions to the Spanish patrimony. But as the new kingdoms were ruled separately, they resisted integration into Spain's empire. Opposition and resistance eventually proved costly and hindered competition with other European powers.

Spain like Portugal found it easier to expand into the non-European world. But save for the Canary Islands it had already assigned Portugal its rights in the south Atlantic by the Treaty of Alcáçovas (1479). As a result, Spain's support of **Christopher Columbus**'s western voyage made good sense. Only the west held the promise of easy conquests. When **Columbus** returned with news of his discovery, Spain immediately funded a second voyage of seventeen ships with twelve hundred people to control whatever had been discovered. Ships, guns, steel, and disease eased the Spanish conquest of the New World. Acculturation of the native Americans gave Spain demographic superiority over its European rivals. This initial advantage of position and numbers allowed Spain to resist most challenges over the next three hundred years. Only in isolated places--Belize, the Guianas, the southwestern United States, some Caribbean islands, and the Malvinas (Falkland Islands)--were the Iberians dislodged.

The gold and silver flowing back to Spain from the booty and treasure collected during the conquest, and the great mining strikes of the 1540s, gave Spain control over much of Europe's monetary supply. With this, Spain during the reign of Emperor **Charles V** (1516-56), became the most powerful state in Western Europe and sought ascendancy over the Atlantic trade and the exclusion of other European powers. Spain developed a fleet system to protect the transfer of American treasure and institutional mechanisms to limit exchanges with the other European powers whose positive trade balances siphoned away much Spanish bullion.

The system served Spain well, but in the long term favored that country's enemies. The latter's technological and industrial superiority gradually moved them to the fore in Western Europe. Meanwhile Spain was drawn into a series of Atlantic-wide conflicts with the Netherlands, France, and England that were usually fought in religious and nationalistic terms. Those struggles, which engaged Spain from the reign of **Philip II** (1556-98) to the Wars of Independence (1808-25), determined who would predominate in international trade and commerce. As early as the seventeenth century they had weakened Spain to the extent that it was no longer Europe's leading power.

Spain saw its success and even its survival as requiring control over the sources of its bullion as well as fidelity to Catholicism. Its enemies found it difficult to breach Iberian domination in the Indies and at first had to content themselves with pirate raids and the support of Protestants and other groups unhappy with Spanish rule. Among the latter were the Dutch, Portuguese, and Catalans. Later, especially in the eighteenth century, contraband and direct trade with Spain and Portugal's New World colonies would further undermine imperial control. Nevertheless, it was not until the seventeenth century that other European powers--the French, English, and Dutch--were able to establish permanent settlements in the New World, but only in North America and the Caribbean. The bulk of Spain and Portugal's subject population, sufficiently accustomed to Iberian ways, remained intact. This Iberian demographic superiority in the New World effectively withstood the challenges and blandishments of others until the independence movement of the early nineteenth century definitively ended Iberian ascendancy in the New World.

1402

Tentative efforts were undertaken to colonize Lanzarote, the most easterly of the Canary Islands, in the south Atlantic, by the French and Castilians.

1415

August 24. **João I, king of Portugal (1385-1433), occupied Ceuta on the African side of the Strait of Gibraltar.** This began a policy of expansion on the African mainland.

1419

The Portuguese began reconnaissance of the island of Madeira.

1420

The Portuguese, led by Bartolomeu Perestrelo, attempted the settlement of Porto Santo, a small island near Madeira. His granddaughter married **Christopher Columbus**.

1437

Prince Henry the Navigator (1394-1460), who promoted the voyages of exploration giving Portugal an overseas empire, failed to take Tangiers. He planned the southern expansion of the Portuguese in the hopes of capturing the source of the gold that crossed the Sahara Desert in the caravans organized by Muslim traders. His failure to take Tangiers led him to expand in the south Atlantic down the African coast to outflank the Muslims rather than confront them directly.

1440s

Portugal began the production of sugar on Madeira.

1443

Portugal imported African slaves to Madeira to labor on their plantations and sugar-refining operations.

1444

The first large-scale shipment of African slaves landed in Lisbon.

1469

October 19. **The marriage of Isabella and Ferdinand** set the stage for the potential unification of Spain. The success of that endeavor depended upon whether they succeeded to their respective thrones of Castile and Aragon.

1470-72

Portugal began exploitation of the West African coast for pepper, gold, and ivory, from which the Gold and Ivory coasts took their names. The Portuguese crossed the equator into the southern hemisphere.

1474

December 11. **Isabella claimed the throne of Castile on the death of her half brother, Henry IV.** Conflict over the succession plunged the Iberian peninsula into a civil war that lasted until 1479.

1479

January 19. **Ferdinand II of Aragon succeeded to the throne on the death of his father, John II.**
September 4. **The Treaty of Alcáçovas ended the war between the Portuguese and the Spanish** and confirmed the succession of **Isabella** to the throne of Castile. The Castilians got the Canaries but were excluded from the rest of the African South Atlantic, which was reserved for the Portuguese, who in addition received the Azores, Madeira, and Cape Verde islands.

1482

February. **The reconquest of Granada was begun.** It was aimed at driving the Moors from their last stronghold on the Iberian Peninsula.
Pope Sixtus IV approved the Spanish request to establish the Inquisition in all their kingdoms.

1486-1512

Various popes in a series of papal bulls transferred power over the church in Granada and the New World to the Spanish monarchs. This power was collectively known as the *patronato real* (royal patronage) and included everything from royal appointments to the establishment of church sees as well as what papal pronouncements would be disseminated. It was given in view of the monarchy's willingness to subsidize the church's mission by building churches and funding the work of missionaries.

1487-88

August. **The Portuguese Bartolomeu Dias and his three-ship expedition sailed from Lisbon.** They rounded the Cape of Good Hope without actually seeing it, going up the east African coast as far as the Great Fish River. The route to India was now evident. It took another decade to amass the capital and carry out the organization and proper execution of the plan. The expedition returned to Lisbon in December 1488.

1492

January 2. **The Moorish kingdom of Granada surrendered.** This brought the Christian Reconquest of the Iberian Peninsula to a close.
March 30. **A royal edict was issued expelling the Jews from Spain unless they converted to Christianity.**
April 30. **Ferdinand and Isabella authorized Columbus's voyage of discovery in the western Atlantic.**
August 3. **Christopher Columbus sailed from Palos, Spain.**
Antonio de Nebrija's *Gramática castellana* appeared. The first published grammar of a modern European language, it formed the basis for the linguistic unification of the Hispanic world.

1493

March 15. **Columbus returned to Palos from his first voyage to the New World.**
April. **Columbus** was received by **Ferdinand** and **Isabella** in Barcelona.

1494

June 7. **The Treaty of Tordesillas was concluded between Portugal and Castile.** It revised a papal demarcation (1493) of newly discovered lands. The treaty assigned to Castile lands west of a line drawn 370 leagues west of the Cape Verde Islands. Lands east of the line were recognized as belonging to the Portuguese. This would place Brazil in the Portuguese sphere when it was later discovered by them in 1500.

1497-99

Portuguese navigator Vasco da Gama traveled to the Far East.

July 8. Da Gama's four-ship expedition departed from Lisbon.

November 22. Da Gama's group rounded South Africa at the Cape of Good Hope.

March 2, 1498. The expedition reached Mozambique.

April 24. With a Muslim pilot, da Gama began his crossing of the Indian Ocean.

May 20. The da Gama expedition reached Calicut, India.

October 5. The expedition began its return voyage.

March 20, 1499. Da Gama's group rounded the Cape of Good Hope.

July 10. The first ship home to Lisbon was the *Berrio*. Da Gama arrived in late August, or the first weeks of September. Windfall profits from the spices brought back repaid the cost of the expedition and broke the Italian monopoly over those commodities. The Portuguese *carreira da India* (maritime route to India) would endure for over three hundred years (1497-1863), but in the seventeenth century the Dutch, British, and French presence in the Far East would become more important.

1500

June 20. **The Spanish monarchy issued an edict declaring native Americans to be free vassals.**

1503

February 14. **The Casa de Contratación (House of Trade) was established at Seville to regulate trade, commerce, and shipping with America.** Its role was to oversee the provisioning of the fleets, the registering of American treasure, and the keeping of essential accounts and records.

December 20. **The Spanish crown issued an edict permitting the allotment of native Americans to Spanish settlers.** Called *repartimiento*, the institution became the basis for the forced labor institution known as the *encomienda*.

1504

November 26. **Death of Isabella I of Castile.**

1507

April 25. **In the monastery of Sainte-Dié in Lorraine, Martin Waldseemüller printed his world map.** It outlined the contours of the New World and named it "America" after **Amerigo**

Iberian Peninsula, circa 1480

Vespucci, whose letters had disseminated so much information about the discoveries in European commercial circles.

1513

The *requerimiento* was drawn up. That legal document was to be read to native Americans by interpreters before hostilities could begin. It traced the history of the world, related the donation of the New World by the pope to the Spanish crown, and invited the Indians to accept Christianity and Spanish rule. If they refused, they could be conquered by force. The first recorded use of the requerimiento was on June 14, 1514.

1516

January 23. **Death of Ferdinand II of Aragon.**

1517

November 4. **Charles of Ghent and his mother, Juana La Loca (the madwoman), met at Tordesillas, Spain.** They agreed to his assumption of royal power as Charles I, king of Spain.

1519

June 28. **Charles I was elected Holy Roman Emperor as Charles V.** Charles's extensive dynastic inheritances burdened Spain with territories that were difficult to defend.

1519-1522

Magellan's expedition circumnavigated the globe.
September 20, 1519. The Portugese navigator Ferdinand Magellan's five-ship expedition departed Sanlúcar, Spain. Commissioned by Spanish King **Charles V** to find a westward route to Asia, Magellan successfully executed the commission and made good Spanish claims to the Far East.

January 1520. Magellan explored the Río de la Plata estuary. His group wintered farther south on the Patagonian coast.

October 21-November 28. Magellan's group entered the strait that would bear his name and emerged in the Pacific thirty-nine days later.

March 6, 1521. After crossing the Pacific, Magellan's expedition encountered inhabitants on the island of Guam.

April 27. In the Philippines Magellan involved himself in a local war and was killed on the island of Mactam. Juan Sebastián de Elcano took command of the expedition.

September 8, 1522. Elcano arrived in Spain with the remaining ship, thus at last completing the circumnavigation of the globe. The event countered Portuguese expansion in Asia and provided the Spanish with the basis for their claim to a presence in the Far East.

1524

The Council of the Indies (Consejo de Indias) was chartered.

1525-83

The Spanish undertook colonization efforts in Asia. After Magellan's voyage and the discovery of the Philippines, the Spanish established a presence in the Far East to counter Portuguese settlement there. The terms of their Alcáçovas treaty agreement (1479) precluded them from using the Portuguese route around Africa. They established a colony in the Philippines and supplied and sustained it from New Spain (Mexico). But it took them four decades to master the complicated logistics of that venture.

1525-26. **Charles V** ordered a second circumnavigation of the globe via the Strait of Magellan. Juan García Jofre de Loaysa headed the expedition to the Philippines, but it failed to establish a colony there. Andrés de Urdaneta served as a young page and ended up shipwrecked in the Moluccas before returning to Spain.

1527-28. In New Spain **Hernán Cortés** helped sponsor the expedition of Álvaro de Saavedra Cerón across the Pacific. It sailed from Zihuatanejo but failed to establish a colony or to survive the return trip to New Spain.

1529. Treaty of Zaragoza signed between Spain and Portugal extended the Tordesillas line of 1494 in the Atlantic around the globe into the Pacific, and while this technically placed the Philippines in the Portuguese sphere, the Spanish claimed prior discovery. After several failed attempts in the first half of the century, they effectively consolidated their claim when they finally established a viable route between the Philippines and New Spain in the 1560s.

1540-41. **Pedro de Alvarado** and his rustic fleet left Guatemala for an attempted trans-Pacific crossing via New Spain. But Alvarado's death (June 29, 1541) aborted the expedition.

1542-44. **Antonio de Mendoza**, the viceroy of New Spain, seized Alvarado's make-shift fleet and dispatched Ruy López de Villalobos across the Pacific to colonize the Philippines. Villalobos failed as a result of his capture by the Portuguese.

1564-65. The Spanish colonized the Philippines once they perfected the round-trip crossing of the Pacific from New Spain. On November 21, 1564, Miguel López de Legazpi and his expedition of five ships and 379 persons, among whom was his missionary-pilot, Andrés de Urdaneta, departed from Navidad, Jalisco, New Spain, for the Philippines. Upon arrival (February 13, 1565) they began the occupation and conquest of the islands with the help of Philippine allies. On June 1, the cleric-pilot Urdaneta began the return voyage to New Spain leaving Cebu in the fastest ship available, provisioned for an eight-month voyage. He followed a more northerly route than was taken in previous attempts, taking advantage of the westerlies and the Japan current to become

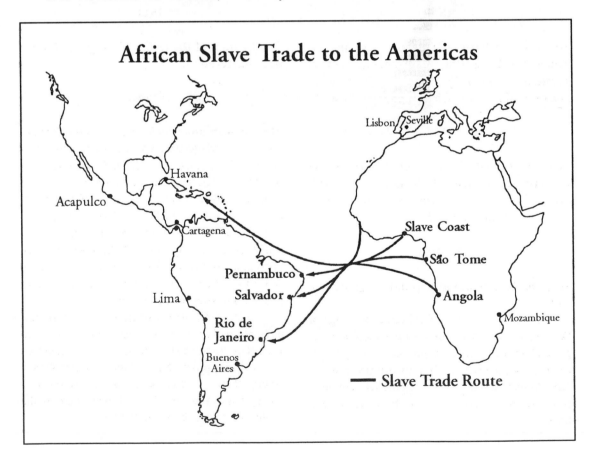

African Slave Trade to the Americas

the first European to cross the Pacific from west to east. Even though the arrival in New Spain (October 8) was accomplished in a little over four months, the human cost was high, as sixteen of Urdaneta's forty-four man crew had died.

1571. López de Legazpi dispatched the first Manila galleons loaded with Chinese silks and fine ceramics to New Spain. Thereafter one or two ships a year crossed the Pacific between Acapulco and Manila carrying Mexican silver in exchange for Chinese silks and other Asian products. Fabulous profits could be made in the Manila trade, and sometimes a single galleon carried as much as 4 million silver pesos to acquire the Asian goods that were then resold in the New World at tremendous markups. That trade maintained Spain's presence in Asia.

1583. An audiencia (subdivisions of viceroyalties; see Political Develoments, Colonial Period, below) was established at Manila subordinate to New Spain.

1540

September 27. **Pope Paul III approved the establishment of the Jesuits as a religious order.** Their founder was Ignatius of Loyola (1491-1556), a Spanish Basque, whose spiritual vision and discipline drew from founts of Spanish religious zeal and nationalism. Although the Jesuits arrived in the New World after most of the conquest had taken place, they quickly became the most important regular order in the Americas.

1542

November 20. **The New Laws were promulgated.** These royal ordinances outlined procedures to be followed by the Council of the Indies, and reformed Spanish government in the New World. They also banned the enslavement of Indians and regulated the *encomienda.* The most controversial provision ended the granting of new

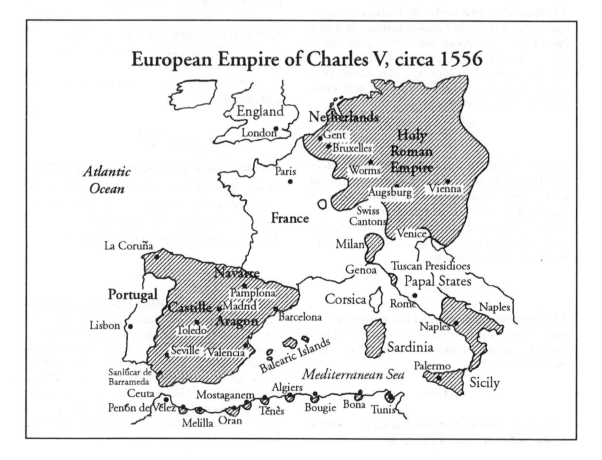

European Empire of Charles V, circa 1556

encomiendas and stated that existing *encomiendas* were to revert to the crown upon the death of the holder, but it was revoked on October 20, 1545.

1543

The Consulado of Seville (Universidad de los Cargadores de las Indias), a merchants' guild, was chartered by the crown. Its members regulated the fleet sailing annually between Seville and Spanish America.

1545-64

The Council of Trent met to approve an agenda for reform of the Catholic Church and to counter the effects of the Protestant Reformation. Its reforms were implemented throughout the Spanish empire.

1549

The Spanish crown prohibited *servicio personal* (personal service, indiscriminate use of Indian labor) in its American colonies. Native Americans held in *encomienda* were not to be worked at the discretion of colonists. But where royal government was weak enforcement was either delayed or not carried out.

1550

August. **A debate was held between the cleric Bartolomé de las Casas, protector of the Indians, and Spanish jurist Juan Ginés de Sepúlveda.** The Valladolid Interlocutory, as it came to be known, centered on the treatment of native Americans and the question of whether the Indians were fully human.

1551

The Spanish again banned the enslavement of native Americans. Nevertheless, legal exceptions existed in frontier areas like northern New Spain and southern Chile.

1556

January 16. **Abdication of Charles V as king of Spain and accession of Philip II.**

1558

November 17. **The death of Mary Tudor, queen of England and Philip II's wife, dissolved the union between Spain and England.**

1559-1687

Sale of public office became a long-standing abuse under the Spanish Hapsburgs. The practice intensified with each declaration of bankruptcy by the crown, greatly undermining the effectiveness of imperial administration. The practice was not eliminated until the Bourbon Reforms of the eighteenth century. The Spanish monarchy declared bankruptcy in 1557, 1575, 1596, 1607, 1627, 1647, 1653, and 1680.

1559. The crown approved the sale of notarial positions in Spanish America.

1606. The crown approved the sale of most public offices in Spanish America.

1633. The sale of treasury positions was permitted throughout Spanish America.

1677. The sale of *corregimientos* and *alcaldías mayores* was approved.

1687. The sale of audiencia positions was authorized.

1564

The Spanish fleet system took its definitive form. Ideally there were two convoys sailing from Seville annually. The first was the *flota*, in April, bound for Veracruz. The second, the *galeones*, in August, sailed for the Isthmus of Panama.

1566

The Netherlands rebelled against Spanish rule. The Netherlands, Europe's richest provinces, wanted autonomy and resented imposition of the decrees of the Council of Trent. Their rebellion lasted until the independence of the northern provinces was recognized in the Treaty of Westphalia (1648). That struggle, more than any, sapped Spanish strength, consumed precious resources, and frustrated Spain's imperial ambitions.

1569

Philip II authorized offices of the Inquisition in Lima and Mexico City.

1570

October 7. **Spain defeated the Turks in the Battle of Lepanto.** The Spanish-led fleet of 208 ships defeated a Turkish fleet of 230 vessels. The Turks lost 195 ships, 30,000 were killed or wounded, and 3,000 taken prisoner; the allies 12 ships; with 9,000 dead and 21,000 wounded. Many of the ships and their crews had been called away from the Indies fleets. While the victory halted the Turkish advance in the Mediterranean, it increased Spain's exposure in the Indies, making possible the raids of John Hawkins, Francis Drake, and other freebooters.

1573

July 13. **Philip II promulgated a new set of regulations to govern future discoveries.** The emphasis was on the peaceful conversion and subjugation of the Indians, and the word "conquest" was eschewed in favor of "pacification."

1580

January 31. **The death of Cardinal Henry, king of Portugal (1578-80), brought forth seven claimants to the throne.** The most powerful was **Philip II** of Spain. His forces, under the duke of Alba, invaded Portugal (August 25) and won the Battle of Alcántara near Lisbon. Portugal and its empire, extending from Brazil to the Far East, were ruled by the king of Spain for the next sixty years.

1587

April. **Francis Drake raided Cádiz.** He caught and destroyed the Spanish fleet and its cargo bound for New Spain.

1588

The Spanish Armada. The Spanish completed plans for the invasion of England in response to the latter's support of Dutch rebels and freebooter attacks on Spanish ports and treasure shipments throughout the empire. Gradually an armada was assembled at Lisbon.

May 28. The armada, 131 ships and 30,000 men strong, sailed from Lisbon.

July 25-August 8. The armada entered the English Channel and suffered a series of storms and several naval engagements with the quicker English ships. Without a secure port or the channel cleared of English and Dutch ships, an invasion of England aborted. With supplies running low, the decision was made to return the armada to Spain by sailing into the North Sea and around northern Scotland and Ireland rather than going back through the channel.

September 19-21. The remnants of the armada made port in northern Spain. Spanish losses had been thirty to forty ships and 15,000 men. Half of the Atlantic fleet had been lost. An extreme shortage of ships and seamen raised shipping rates. The government's own *avería* tax to organize the annual fleet to America climbed from 1.7 percent in 1585 to 8 percent in 1591.

1596

June 29-July 15. **An Anglo-Dutch naval expedition of 128 ships sacked Cádiz.** It destroyed thirty-four Spanish ships and 4 million ducats worth of cargo bound for the New World.

1598

September 13. **The death of Philip II brought Philip III to the Spanish throne.**

1609

A truce was signed between Spain and the Netherlands. War broke out again in 1621.

1621

March 31. **The death of Philip III brought Philip IV to the Spanish throne**.

1628

Spain's treasure fleet was captured near Matanzas, off the northern coast of Cuba, by the Dutch privateer Piet Heyn.

1640-59

The Catalans revolted against Spanish rule. The reform and centralizing policies of the Count-Duke **Olivares**, Philip IV's (1621-65) *privado* or principal advisor (1622-43), provoked a rebellion in Catalonia.

February–March 1640. Clashes occurred between troops and civilians over the billeting of Castilian soldiers in Catalan households.

June 7. Riots in Barcelona broke out and a roaming mob murdered the viceroy of Catalonia.

January 23, 1641. Catalonia placed itself under the king of France in exchange for French military protection.

1650-54. Plague swept Catalonia and carried off 36,000 in Barcelona alone.

October 13, 1652. Barcelona was retaken by Castilian soldiers.

November 7, 1659. Peace Treaty of Pyrenees was signed between Spain and France. Spain--and Catalonia--lost both Roussillon and Conflans, but Catalonia and Spain were reconciled, with Catalonia keeping its special laws and privileges.

1640

December 1. **The revolt of Portugal began**. While Spain was occupied with the rebellion of the Catalans and war with France, the Portuguese proclaimed João IV, the duke of Braganza, their king. The union of Spain and Portugal, which began in 1580, thus ended.

1665

September 17. **The death of Philip IV brought Charles II to the Spanish throne**.

1700

October 3. **Charles II, the last Hapsburg ruler of Spain, named Philip of Anjou, grandson of Louis XIV of France, heir to his dominions**.

November 1. **The Spanish king Charles II died**. Shortly thereafter Philip of Anjou was proclaimed as Philip V in Castile but opposed in Catalonia, Aragon, and Valencia, where a rival claimant was supported.

1701-13

The War of the Spanish Succession. The accession of **Philip V** (1700-46), a potential successor to the throne of France, affected the balance of power in Europe and produced an armed conflict in which Great Britain, Holland, Austria, and other states were allied against Spain and France. By the terms of the Treaty of Utrecht (1713), Philip renounced his claim to the French throne. He was able to keep his American and Asian possessions but lost Minorca and Gibraltar to Britain, Sicily to Savoy, and Flanders, Naples, Milan, and Sardinia to Austria. The British also won the exclusive right (*asiento de negros*) to sell African slaves in Spanish America for thirty years and to send a ship of 500 tons to the annual trade fairs in Panama. The new Bourbon dynasty in Spain developed new policies that were intended to reverse the general decline that had set in under the Hapsburgs. These changes are known as the Bourbon Reforms and took place in the course of the eighteenth century. They are most commonly associated with the reforms of **Charles III** (1759-88).

1714

The Ministry of the Indies was established. The Spanish crown ended Hapsburg government-by-council, replacing it with cabinet-style rule. Thus a new Ministry of the Indies was assigned the duties of the Council of the Indies. The latter body continued to exist as an advisory body. It also heard cases appealed from the audiencias.

1717

Casa de Contratación was transferred from Seville to Cádiz. That put the House of Trade closer to the port of embarkation and facilitated its watchdog function in overseeing the re-export of foreign merchandise to America, since the ships were already departing from Cádiz rather than Seville.

1739-48

The War of Jenkins's Ear. Britain waged war on Spain in response to what it saw as an overzealous Spanish attempt—cutting off the ear of Captain Jenkins—to limit British contraband in the Caribbean.

1743

Publication of José del Campillo y Cossio's *Nuevo sistema de gobierno para la América* (New System of Economic Government for America). In his treatise, the former minister of finance indicted the economic structure of the Spanish empire as too restrictive and too dependent on precious metals. He argued that only a reform of economic attitudes and policies would lead to economic growth and a restoration of Spanish power. Much of Spain's later movement toward freer trade within the empire was based on principles articulated in Campillo's work.

1746

July 9. **Spanish king Philip V died, and was succeeded by Ferdinand VI**.

1756-63

The Seven Years' War. The war between France and Great Britain laid bare Spanish imperial weakness and led it to undertake serious reform. Spain entered on the side of France against Britain in 1762. The British occupied Havana and the Philippines and dealt France a stunning series of defeats around the world. While Cuba and the Philippines were returned to the Spanish and the French gave Louisiana to them as well, in compensation for their loss of East and West Florida, changes had to be made if Spain was going to compete effectively. Freer trade and the intendancy system were introduced in Cuba (1764) and later extended to other parts of the Spanish empire.

1759

August 10. **Spanish king Ferdinand VI died and was succeeded by Charles III**.

September 3. **The Jesuits were ordered expelled from the Portuguese empire**.

1767

March 1. **The Jesuits were ordered expelled from the Spanish empire**.

1773

July 21. **Pope Clement XIV suppressed the Jesuit order in response to pressure applied by the French and Spanish monarchies**.

1776

The *flota* to New Spain as part of the fleet system was abolished.

1776-83

War of United States Independence.
June 1779. Spain joined France in the war of American Independence against Britain.
1782. Spain captured Florida, Belize, and Minorca but failed to take Gibraltar.
September 3, 1783. The Treaty of Versailles approved Spain's recovery of Florida and Minorca.

1778

October 12. **"Free trade" decree promulgated.** Except for Venezuela and New Spain, direct trade was allowed between the different regions of Spanish America and thirteen Spanish peninsular ports. Those New World ports, however, that were not specifically designated could not legally participate.

1788

December 14. **Spanish king Charles III died and was succeeded by Charles IV.**

1790

The Casa de Contratación (House of Trade) was abolished as unnecessary in light of free trade within the Spanish empire.

1793-1802

French Revolutionary and Napoleonic Wars. Spain became involved in the global struggle between Britain and France as a result of the French Revolution and the rise of Napoleon.

March 7, 1793. France declared war on Spain, which allied itself with Britain (March 13) and invaded French Roussillon and Navarre. The French responded and successfully occupied Catalonia and Guipúzcoa (1794-95).

June 19, 1795. By the Treaty of Basel, Spain recovered Catalonia and Guipúzcoa but had to give up Santo Domingo, her oldest colony in the New World, so that the French could attempt a reconquest of Saint Domingue.

October 1, 1800. By the Second Treaty of San Ildefonso Spain returned Louisiana to France.

March 1802. By the Treaty of Amiens, Spain recovered Minorca but lost Trinidad to Britain, which had occupied it in 1797.

1798

Spain confiscated church wealth. The crown seized the church's endowments for chantries and pious foundations. The decree was applicable only in Spain but was a forerunner to the 1804 (December 26) *ley de consolidación,* which extended the appropriation measure to Spanish America. Both measures were an attempt to raise critically needed funds to wage war and to consolidate the Spanish national debt.

The Caribbean and Central America, 1492-1803

The Caribbean initially became the main focus of Spanish activity in the New World. It was there that Spanish values, attitudes, and social, economic, and political structures and institutions crystallized suddenly in the first years of the conquest and were then passed on to the rest of Spanish America. The Caribbean became the launching point for the discovery and occupation of the mainland. Afterward it became the front line of defense against the encroachment of other European powers.

What **Christopher Columbus** had discovered on his first voyage to the west was not immediately evident. Until the day he died he thought it was a route to the Far East, the "Indies," and not a New World. The Spanish quickly suspected otherwise. Whatever was out there, they immediately moved to claim it as theirs and backed their ambitions with a seventeen-ship, 1,200-person expedition for **Columbus**'s second voyage. The Spanish gave **Columbus** extensive political authority. But steeped in a Portuguese and Italian maritime tradition of exploration and trade, **Columbus** was more interested in discovering than in governing. He set a singular record of discovery in the western Atlantic, making new additions to European geographical knowledge with every voyage. He discovered Cuba and Hispaniola on the first voyage; Dominica, Puerto Rico, and Jamaica on the second; the Orinoco River, Trinidad, and Margarita on the third; and the Central American coast from Honduras to Panama on the fourth. But as far as government was concerned he quickly allowed the Spanish to displace him. He was forced to deal with a revolt when Francisco Roldán led other Spanish settlers in western Hispaniola to declare their independence of his authority in 1497.

The monarchy replaced **Columbus** as governor in 1499 when they appointed Francisco de Bobadilla in his place. Overseeing crown interests and developing its New World policy was Juan Rodríguez de Fonseca, the royal chaplain and archdeacon of the cathedral of Seville, who quickly licensed others to trade, discover, and govern. The discovery of pearl beds off the Venezuelan coast and a profitable trade in gold ornaments and native American slaves farther west along the Colombian coast focused attention on the mainland and led to the first settlement (1510) on the Panamanian side of the Gulf of Urabá. That led to the discovery of the Pacific Ocean (1513) and the conquest of Peru (1532-40) and of southern Central America (1522-27). In the meantime the occupation of Caribbean islands other than Hispaniola began with the conquest of Puerto Rico (1508) and Cuba (1511-15). In all three an ephemeral gold boom fueled the initial occupation. But it was enough to support occupation of the mainland, with Cuba being the point of departure for the conquest of Mexico (1519-22).

When the great wealth of Mexico and Peru became known, the role of the Caribbean and of Central America (Panama) changed. They were no longer the main focus of Spanish settlement in the New World but instead became strategic points in the Spanish pipeline through which precious metals and merchandise flowed to and from Spain. They became the front line of defense as the English, Dutch, and French tried to seize this bullion by interdicting shipments or by raiding coastal settlements. The Spanish responded with the convoy (*flota*) system of regular shipping and a program of building fortifications at Havana, Santo Domingo, San Juan de Puerto Rico, Cartagena, Portobelo, and San Juan de Ulúa. While individual coastal cities fell to freebooters from time to time, an ever more elaborate system of fortifications usually delayed the attackers long enough for yellow fever, malaria, and dysentery to overwhelm them. Rival European powers, however, made inroads by establishing settlements on the periphery of the Spanish empire, especially in the Lesser Antilles and on the Caribbean coast of Central America. These settlements sustained themselves initially through piracy and the cutting of brazilwood, but by the eighteenth century the more successful ones had developed a flourishing contraband trade with the Spanish and a sugar plantation economy based on slave labor. The Spanish responded by implementing freer trade and administrative reform. These changes were frequently implemented first in the Caribbean, where the challenge of rival European powers was the greatest.

1492-93

First voyage of Christopher Columbus to the New World.

Early 1486. **Columbus** first presented his plan of a western voyage to Asia to **Ferdinand** and **Isabella** at Alcalá de Henares, Spain.

April 30, 1492. Ferdinand and Isabella authorized Columbus's voyage of discovery.

August 3. Columbus departed from Palos, Spain, with ninety men on board the *Santa María*, *Niña*, and *Pinta*.

August 10. Arrival in the Canaries.

September 6. Departure from the Canaries.

October 12. 2 A.M. After a crossing of thirty-three days, land was sighted in the Bahamas, and the fateful discovery of the "Indies" was made. Columbus's first landfall was an island called Guanahaní, which he renamed San Salvador.

October 28. Exploration along the north coast of Cuba was begun.

December 6. Arrival off the north coast of Hispaniola.

December 24. When the *Santa María* ran aground, Columbus, believing God wanted a town there, founded Navidad. During the same month, Martín Alonso Pinzón, the captain of the *Pinta*, discovered placer gold in the stream beds of the mountainous interior of Hispaniola.

January 16, 1493. The return voyage to Spain was begun with thirty-nine men of the shipwrecked *Santa María* staying behind at Navidad.

February 14. A storm separated the *Pinta* and *Niña* near the Azores.

March 4. Columbus arrived in Portugal. A few days later he was received by King João II. Meanwhile, Pinzón and the *Pinta* had landed at Bayona in Galicia.

March 13. Columbus sailed from Lisbon.

March 15 The *Pinta* and *Niña* arrived at Palos on the same day.

April. Columbus was received by Ferdinand and Isabella in Barcelona.

1493-96

Second voyage of Columbus.

September 25. Seventeen ships with upward of twelve hundred men but no women sailed from Cádiz.

October 13. Expedition departed from the Canaries.

November 3. Crossing in twenty days, Columbus made landfall at Dominica in the Lesser Antilles.

November 19. Columbus landed on Puerto Rico.

November 28. The group arrived at Navidad on the north coast of Hispaniola after sailing through the Lesser Antilles. There were no survivors of the thirty-nine left the previous year at Navidad.

January 2, 1494. Columbus established the town of Isabella on the north coast of Hispaniola, but its poor location—scanty resources, lack of water, and small number of native Americans—led to its abandonment several years later in favor of Santo Domingo. Continued interest in the gold discovered on the first expedition led to more strikes and the first gold boom in the New World.

March 12. Columbus left the coast for the first time and explored the gold fields in the interior.

April 24. Columbus sailed from Isabella for further exploration in a five-month three-ship expedition that followed the southern coastline of Cuba and Hispaniola and coasted Jamaica twice.

May 5. Columbus went ashore at Jamaica.

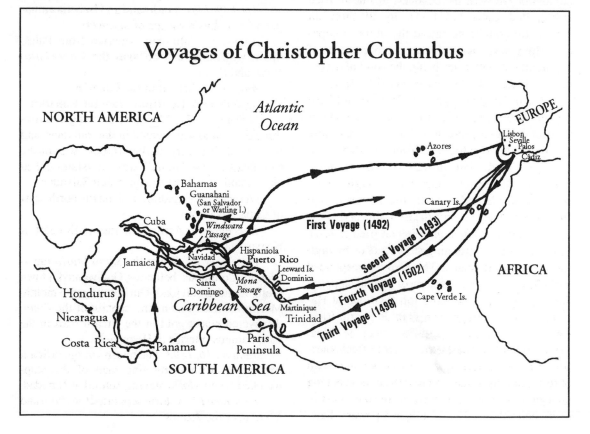

Voyages of Christopher Columbus

June 24. Ships arrived from Spain with supplies and Columbus's brother, Bartolomé Colón.

September 29. Columbus's expedition returned to Isabella.

Late 1494. First native American revolt against the Iberians occurred on Hispaniola when ten Spaniards were killed in the burning of a fort called Magdalena, on the Yaque River.

February 24, 1495. Four ships captained by Antonio de Torres sailed from Hispaniola for Spain with disgruntled Spaniards and five hundred native Americans as slaves.

March 24. Columbus marched inland for a second time, but to subdue the native Americans.

October. Juan Aguado, a royal agent sent to investigate Columbus, arrived at Hispaniola.

March 10, 1496. Columbus sailed for Spain to defend his government.

June 11. Columbus arrived in Cádiz.

1496

August 4. **Bartolomé Colón founded Santo Domingo, and Isabella was gradually abandoned.** Santo Domingo had an excellent harbor and more resources. It was also better located to receive those ships making the preferred landfall in the New World near Dominica in the Lesser Antilles as well as better situated to explore and settle the southern Caribbean and northern coasts of Venezuela and Colombia.

1497

Francisco Roldán seized the arms at Isabella and challenged the rule of Columbus and his brothers. He and his followers lived in western Hispaniola independent of the government of Columbus. They parceled out the native Americans to individual Spaniards. This practice was a forerunner to the *encomienda*, the forced labor institution that later took hold on the mainland.

1498-1500

Third voyage of Columbus.

May 30. Columbus and his fleet of six ships with three hundred men and thirty women de-

parted Spain. In the Canaries he dispatched three caravels to Santo Domingo via the Dominica passage and with the rest he took a more southerly route via the Cape Verde Islands. He made landfall at Trinidad (July 31), set foot on the South American continent (August 5), noting the large discharge of the Orinoco River, and passed Margarita before turning north and sailing directly to Santo Domingo.

August 31. Columbus arrived in Santo Domingo.

May 21, 1499. The monarchy appointed Francisco de Bobadilla to investigate and replace Columbus as governor in the New World. The deterioration of affairs in Hispaniola--Roldán's revolt, the lack of revenues from suspected great wealth, the reported ill-treatment of the native Americans--had led to the crown's decision to replace Columbus.

June 1500. Bobadilla sailed from Spain.

August 23. Bobadilla arrived in Santo Domingo.

September. Bobadilla imprisoned Columbus and his two brothers and shipped them back to Spain in October.

1499

Juan Rodríguez de Fonseca ended Columbus's exclusive privilege to trade and discover in the New World. The royal chaplain and archdeacon of the cathedral of Seville, who had been representing the monarchy's interests in the Indies since 1493 when he oversaw the organization of Columbus's second voyage to the New World, issued licenses to trade, discover, and govern to Alonso de Hojeda, Peralonso Niño, Vicente Yáñez Pinzón, and Diego de Lepe. The latter two explored the Guiana and Brazilian coastlines outside of the Caribbean. (See Northern South America, 1499.)

1502

April. **Nicolás de Ovando, the new governor appointed to replace Bobadilla, arrived in Hispaniola.** His large fleet with 2,500 settlers, among whom was **Bartolomé de las Casas**, the future defender of the rights of native Americans, represented new efforts on the part of the monarchy to consolidate and expand on their New World discoveries.

1502-4

Fourth voyage of Columbus.

March 14. **Ferdinand** and **Isabella** approved **Columbus**'s fourth voyage.

May 11. Columbus departed from Spain with only four ships.

May 25. Columbus sailed from the Canaries.

June 15. Crossing in twenty-two days, Columbus made landfall at Martinique.

June 29. Columbus arrived at Santo Domingo and warned Governor Ovando of an approaching hurricane and then fled west before it sank the imperial fleet that had planned to return to Spain in July.

July–October. Regrouping off the coast of Honduras, Columbus spent the next four months exploring the Central American coast down to Panama, fighting contrary winds and currents most of the way.

November 26. **Columbus** reached Retrete, twenty miles east of the future Nombre de Dios, the farthest point in his Central American exploration.

April 16, 1503. After five months of trying to establish a viable settlement in Panama, Columbus gave up and sailed off toward Jamaica.

June 25. Columbus's worm-eaten ships left him marooned on Jamaica for the next fourteen months.

November 7, 1504. Columbus finally arrived in Seville, his health broken. He never returned to America, and continued to believe that he had found a route to the "Indies" or Asia, rather than having discovered a New World.

1503

First sugar mill began operations in the New World on Hispaniola.

April. The monarchy appointed Juan de la Cosa *alguacil mayor* (high sheriff) of Urabá on the mainland near the present-day border of Panama and Colombia.

October 30. Queen **Isabella** issued an edict that allowed the enslavement of "rebellious" native Americans of Tierra Firme who resisted Spanish acculturation.

Autumn. Governor Ovando orchestrated the massacre of eighty-four native American caciques (chiefs) in western Hispaniola and left Diego Velázquez, the future conqueror and governor of Cuba, in charge.

December 20. The monarchy issued the edict that was the basis for Governor Ovando's distribution (*repartimiento*) of native Americans on Hispaniola among the Spaniards. Later, on the mainland, this forced labor mechanism was known as the *encomienda*.

1508

In Hispaniola Governor Ovando dispatched Sebastián de Ocampo on a geographical survey that circumnavigated Cuba.

Vicente Yáñez Pinzón and Juan Díaz de Solís, looking for a way through or around the mainland, explored the coast of Mesoamerica from the Gulf of Honduras to as far north as present-day Tampico, Mexico.

Juan Ponce de León and forty-two settlers founded the town of Caparra, near present-day San Juan, and began the conquest of Puerto Rico. In 1521 the city was moved and renamed San Juan Bautista.

June. **The crown divided the mainland into two spheres.** The area west of the Gulf of Urabá and north into Central America (Veragua) went to Diego de Nicuesa while the area to the east, the northern Colombian coast, went to Alonso de Hojeda. The latter's two partners in this venture were Martín Fernández de Enciso and Juan de la Cosa.

1509

Diego Colón, the eldest son of Christopher Columbus, replaced Ovando as governor in Hispaniola. Not wishing to see Jamaica included in the concessions made to Nicuesa and Hojeda on the mainland, he sent Juan de Esquivel to occupy the island.

1510

Spring. **Hojeda occupied the east side of the Gulf of Urabá but returned to Hispaniola sick,** leaving **Francisco Pizarro**, the future conqueror of Peru, in charge of the sixty survivors of the original three hundred. They pulled out too, but reconsidered when they met Fernández de Enciso's supply ship near Cartagena, and, with Enciso in command, they returned to Urabá.

Nicuesa failed in his attempt to colonize Central America. After arriving in Veragua (Panama), he split his fleet and ended up lost off the Mosquito Coast of Nicaragua.

November. **Vasco Núñez de Balboa**, the future European discoverer of the Pacific Ocean, convinced Enciso's starving group to move across the Gulf of Urabá and occupy the native American town of Darién, on the west bank. Nicuesa's group of two hundred survivors joined Enciso's at Darién which was appropriated and chartered as the Spanish settlement of Santa María la Antigua.

1511

October 5. **Royal decree issued establishing the first audiencia in the New World at Santo Domingo.**

First dioceses erected in the New World at Santo Domingo in Hispaniola and Caparra in Puerto Rico.

December 21. **The Dominican priest Antonio de Montesinos became the first to condemn publicly Spanish treatment of the native Americans** in his Christmas Sunday sermon in Santo Domingo.

1511-15

The conquest of Cuba took place.

1511. The monarchy approved the agreement between Diego Colón and Diego Velázquez for the occupation of Cuba, and Velázquez departed from Spain with three hundred men. He and **Pánfilo de Narváez** worked in tandem as their separate forces moved across the island.

1512. The discovery of gold brought a rush of settlers and fueled the rapid conquest of the island.

1514. Havana was founded but relocated to its present site on the northwest coast in 1519. Its natural harbor, defensive location, and position on the Gulf Stream made it a logical stopover and resupply point for the return trip across the Atlantic for the rest of the colonial period.

1515. On the southeast coast Santiago de Cuba was founded and became Velázquez's residence and capital.

1511-19

Colonization of the mainland. The initial settlement of the mainland began to take form in Panama, setting the stage for the European discovery of the Pacific Ocean and the conquest of Peru and, from the south, of Central America.

April 1511. **Vasco Núñez de Balboa** emerged as the leader of the colony on the mainland at Santa María la Antigua, having expelled Nicuesa and Enciso on two separate ships along with other disgruntled Spaniards. Balboa successfully organized the colony by forging mutually beneficial alliances with native Americans who supplied the Spanish with food and gold ornaments in return for help against their traditional enemies.

Fall. Balboa learned of the existence of the Pacific Ocean from native informants.

1512. Balboa explored south into Colombia, moving up the Atrato River, and looking for "Dabeiba," the presumed source of the gold for the native American ornaments. His group came within sight of the Cordillera Occidental.

January 1513. Having returned to his base at Santa María, Balboa made plans to find the Pacific Ocean.

July 27. In Spain royal officials appointed **Pedro Arias de Ávila (Pedrarias)** captain general and governor of Castilla de Oro. At the time, except for the ill-defined Veragua, this included those areas of the mainland organized by Balboa and the concessions of Nicuesa and Hojeda.

September 1. Balboa's trans-isthmian expedition of 190 Spaniards and one thousand native Americans departed from Santa María.

September 27. Balboa climbed a mountain alone to become the first European to view the eastern shore of the Pacific. He took possession of the ocean on behalf of Spain on September 29.

January 1514. Balboa's force returned to their base at Santa María.

April. Financed by 40,000 ducats from the Spanish treasury, Pedrarias's fleet of fifteen hundred sailed from Spain and included **Hernando de Soto** and the future historians Gonzalo Fernández de Oviedo y Valdés and **Bernal Díaz del Castillo**.

Late June. Pedrarias's expedition arrived in Darién.

Late 1515. Pedrarias founded Acla and the Spanish presence in Panama shifted west away from Balboa's Santa María.

January 1519. Pedrarias had **Francisco Pizarro** arrest Balboa and then tried and executed the latter on a spurious charge of treason.

August 15. Pedrarias founded the town of Panama on the west coast of the isthmus.

1512

December 27. **The Laws of Burgos were promulgated.** Enacted after a debate sparked by the complaints of **Antonio de Montesinos** and other Dominicans on Hispaniola, the laws were intended to govern relations between Spaniards and Indians. They retained the *encomienda* and other forms of forced labor, but *encomenderos* were ordered to build churches, provide instruction in reading, writing, and Christianity to boys, and refrain from beating Indians and calling them dogs. The laws had little effect on conditions in Hispaniola.

1513-65

Spanish exploration of the southeastern United States. Various Spanish conquistadors attempted to strike it rich on the mainland north of Cuba in what is today the United States. All failed. The Spanish settlement at Saint Augustine was defensive and protected the northern flank of the Spanish empire and the entrance to the Gulf of Mexico and the Caribbean.

1513. **Juan Ponce de León**, the conqueror and governor of Puerto Rico, received a license to lead an expedition to Florida, an area that included much more than the present-day state of the same name. On Easter Sunday his expedition made the first Spanish landing in the United States but failed to establish a colony.

1521. **Ponce de León** returned to Florida with a second expedition but was wounded and again failed to establish a settlement.

1523-26. Lucas Vázquez de Ayllón, a judge in the audiencia of Santo Domingo, received a license in 1523 to establish a colony in Florida and did so in 1526, probably somewhere on the Carolina coast. Vázquez de Ayllón and most of the colony of six hundred died, and the colony was abandoned after only three months.

1526-36. **Pánfilo de Narváez** was licensed (1526) to lead an expedition to Florida. On June 17, 1527, Narváez's force of five ships with upward of six hundred personnel sailed from Sanlúcar, Spain, and arrived in Hispaniola in mid-August. They spent the winter of 1527-28 in Cuba, adding supplies and more participants after losing two ships and fifty men to a hurricane, and other members to better offers from other Spanish captains. On April 14, 1528, the expedition of four hundred arrived in Florida and went ashore near Tampa Bay. Narváez and **Alvar Núñez Cabeza de Vaca** led three hundred across the Florida panhandle while the others followed along the coast in ships. Unfortunately, the ships went on to New Spain, leaving the land forces stranded near present-day Tallahassee. Here the few remaining fashioned crude ships and tried to cross the Gulf of Mexico. At length the party made its way to the Texas coast. Only four survived, among them Cabeza de Vaca. They spent the next eight years moving westward toward New Spain thanks to the help of native Americans who supplied them with food in exchange for their work as shamans. On April 1, 1536, Cabeza de Vaca and his companions encountered a party of Spaniards on the Pacific coast near Culiacán in northern New Spain.

1537-42. **Hernando de Soto** was made governor of Cuba and given a license (April 1537) to conquer Florida. His expedition of more than five hundred landed near Tampa Bay (May 1539) and began their trek across the southeastern part of the United States. Soto died on May 21, 1542, in Louisiana, and was buried in the Mississippi River to hide his death from native Americans hostile to the Spanish presence. The remaining Spaniards built ships and floated down the Mississippi and across the Gulf of Mexico to New Spain.

1565. The Spanish, under the leadership of Pedro Menéndez de Avilés, cleared Florida of French settlements and forts, killing most of their inhabitants. On September 8, Menéndez founded Saint Augustine, the oldest permanent European settlement in the United States.

1522-27

Exploration and conquest of Central America.

1522. Gil González Dávila, a rival of Pedrarias, sailed from Panama and explored the Pacific coast of Costa Rica. Moving inland, he discovered Lake Nicaragua. His expedition set off a frenzied competition for control of Central America, with claimants coming from Mexico, Panama, and Santo Domingo.

1523. Gil González Dávila returned to Panama but trouble with Pedrarias caused him to flee to Hispaniola with over 100,000 gold pesos and organize his return to Nicaragua a year later.

December. **Pedro de Alvarado** left Mexico with a large army bound for Guatemala. A smallpox epidemic had preceded him, decimating the native population.

1524. **Pedrarias** moved to occupy Nicaragua by despatching a large force under Francisco Fernández de Córdoba, who founded the towns of Granada and León, claimed Honduras, and intimidated González Dávila into abandoning Nicaragua. He next tried to create a kingdom independent of Pedrarias.

April. Alvarado arrived in Guatemala and found the native Americans locked in a civil war. Alvarado sided with the Cakchiquel and the allies defeated the Quiché.

May 12. In Honduras Cristóbal de Olid, one of **Hernán Cortés**'s most trusted captains, was arrested, tried, and executed on a spurious treason charge after declaring his independence from his master.

1525. Cortés marched across Petén into Honduras and claimed the area.

1526. In Nicaragua, Pedrarias executed his rebellious captain Fernández de Córdoba.

1527. Pedrarias and Alvarado were made captain general and governor of Nicaragua and Guatemala, respectively.

1535

February. **The monarchy issued a decree creating the audiencia of Panama.**

1537-97

Spanish defense of the Caribbean. French, English, and Dutch attacks led the Spanish to develop the trans-Atlantic convoy system (*flota*) and to build fortifications to protect Havana, Santo Domingo, San Juan de Puerto Rico, and Portobelo. A permanent military presence was established. In Havana it fluctuated between 400 and 1,000 soldiers.

1537. A French fleet occupied Havana.

1538-40. French corsairs harassed Santiago de Cuba.

1554. A French squadron sacked Santiago de Cuba.

1555. A French naval force led by Jacques de Sores burned Havana.

1558. The French attacked Santiago de Cuba.

Summer 1572. Francis Drake raided Nombre de Dios and captured 450,000 pesos of the Peruvian silver shipment crossing the isthmus on mules.

1577. La Fuerza fortification was completed at Havana.

1585. The Italian military engineer Juan Bautista Antonelli recommended that the Spanish transfer their Atlantic isthmian port to Portobelo.

1585-86. Sir Francis Drake captured Santo Domingo and Cartagena.

1595. Combined forces of John Hawkins and Drake were defeated at San Juan de Puerto Rico, Cartagena, and Panama City with Drake dying (January 28, 1596) off the coast of Panama.

1597. The fortresses of El Morro and La Punta were completed at Havana.

1538

October 22. **In Spain Pedro de Alvarado was absolved of "bad government" charges and reappointed governor of Guatemala.**

1541

September 9. **Upon learning of the death of Pedro de Alvarado in Mexico**, the *cabildo* of Santiago de Guatemala made his widow, Beatriz de la Cueva, interim governor, but two days later she died as an earthquake destroyed the city with great loss of life. Her brother, Francisco de la Cueva, became the next governor.

1542

November 20. **In addition to protecting the native Americans, the New Laws called for the establishment of the Audiencia de los Confines in Central America.** It was to replace the audiencia of Panama and have jurisdiction over the territory of Tabasco, Chiapas, and Yucatán through Panama.

1543

Annual fleet system between Seville and the Caribbean established with one sailing each year.

1544

May. **Audiencia de los Confines held its first session at Gracias a Dios, Honduras.**

1546

First archdioceses erected in the New World at Santo Domingo, Mexico City, and Lima.

1549

Audiencia de los Confines moved from Gracias to Santiago de Guatemala (Antigua). It was later moved to Panama in 1563.

1553

Havana became nominal capital of Cuba.

1563

Juan Vázquez de Coronado founded Cartago as the capital of Costa Rica.

1564

The Spanish fleet system took its definitive form, with two convoys each year sailing from Seville: the first, the *flota*, in April, bound for Veracruz, and the second, the *galeones*, in August, bound for the Isthmus of Panama.

1567

An audiencia was reestablished for Santiago de Guatemala. It began to function in 1570 as the audiencia of Guatemala with jurisdiction from Chiapas through Costa Rica.

1578

Silver strikes in Honduras fueled the growth of Tegucigalpa.

1582

First Jesuits arrived in Guatemala.

1597

March 20. **Portobelo (Puerto Bello) was established as the principal Caribbean terminus for the South American fleets (*galeones*).** It replaced an earlier site, Nombre de Dios, which was considered unhealthful and vulnerable to Indian attacks. During the heyday of the fleets, large fairs were held in Portobelo where European goods were traded for South American products. Because of its commercial importance, Portobelo was frequently attacked by buccaneers and other enemies of Spain, such as Henry Morgan (1668). It declined with the demise of the fleet system in the eighteenth century.

1604-65

European rivals of Spain established a presence in the Caribbean. On the periphery of the Spanish empire the Dutch, English, and French planted permanent colonies in the Lesser Antilles, the Guianas, and Central America. (See also Northern South America.) Piracy, sugar production based on slave labor, brazilwood, and contraband trade with the Spanish became the mainstays of their colonies.

1621. Dutch formally chartered the West India Company.

1624. English occupied St. Kitts (St. Christopher).

1625. English and Dutch settled St. Croix.

1627. Eighty English planters and some slaves began the colonization of Barbados.

1628. English occupied Nevis. Returning Spanish treasure fleet captured near Matanzas off the northern coast of Cuba by the Dutch privateer Piet Heyn.

1630. The British settled Providence Island, off the coast of Nicaragua, and began to target Spanish control of the Caribbean coast of Central America.

1630-40. Dutch settled Curaçao, Saba, St. Martin, and St. Eustatius. English occupied Antigua, Montserrat, and St. Lucia. French settled Martinique and Guadeloupe.

1638. British logcutters and buccaneers began to operate from Belize.

1640. Population of English colony of Barbados approximated 30,000.

1642. The British successfully occupied Roatán Island in the Bay of Honduras.

1643. A Dutch raid on Trujillo led the Spanish to abandon this Honduran port until 1789.

1647. First shipment of sugar from Barbados sent to England.

1655. The English under Admiral William Penn and General Oliver Robert Venables attacked and occupied Jamaica after being repelled at Santo Domingo.

1656. Only 400 of the 1,600 arriving English settlers survived the year in the colonization of Jamaica. The island became one of the main bases for contraband trade with Spanish America.

1665. French dispatched a governor to Tortuga Island and began the colonization of Saint Domingue (Haiti).

1607

Official capital of Cuba moved from Santiago to Havana. A captain-general was to exercise judicial authority over the entire island but Santiago was to retain administrative independence.

1660

José Pineda Ibarra installed the first printing press in Central America at Santiago de Guatemala.

1671

January–February. **With a commission from the governor of Jamaica, Henry Morgan and his men attacked the Isthmus of Panama**. They began by assaulting the fort of San Lorenzo at the mouth of the Chagres River and later captured and looted the city of Panama, which was destroyed by fire. This was the last great buccaneering raid against Spanish possessions as the British pledged to reduce piracy by the Treaty of America (1670), which also provided for Spanish recognition of British possessions in the New World. On January 21, 1673, a new Panama City was founded on the site of the modern capital of that name.

1676

Spain authorized the establishment of the first university in Central America. The University of San Carlos in Guatemala began to function in 1681.

1697

September 20. **By the Treaty of Ryswick, which ended the War of the League of Augsburg, Spain ceded the western third of Hispaniola to France.** French pirates and settlers had occupied Tortuga Island and the adjacent north coast since the early seventeenth century. Under French rule, the colony (now known as Saint Domingue) became a leading producer of sugar. Large numbers of slaves were imported to man the plantations and accounted for about 90 percent of the population in 1789.

1698-1700

Failure of British colony in Panama. William Paterson, founder of the Bank of England and director of the African Company, unsuccessfully tried to establish a Scottish colony in Panama at Darién.
November 4, 1698. Expedition of 1,200 settlers arrived and founded New Saint Andrew.
June 1699. Colony abandoned the first time.
November. Some colonists returned.
February 23-March 17, 1700. Repeated Spanish attacks on the colony occurred.
April 11. Colony definitively abandoned.

1717-23

Tobacco monopoly introduced in Cuba.
August 1717. Five hundred armed tobacco farmers occupied Havana and compelled the resignation of Governor General Vicente Raxa and the suspension of the monopoly.
1720. One thousand additional soldiers strengthened the Havana garrison and the monopoly was reinstated.
1723. Revolt of one thousand tobacco farmers quashed, with scores of them killed or executed.

1728

University of Havana established.

1729

November. **Central America's first newspaper, *Gaceta de Guatemala*, appeared.** It ceased publication in 1731, but was revived as a weekly in 1794.

1731

Spain approved the establishment of a mint in Guatemala; the first coins were issued in 1733.

1733

Santiago's administrative independence terminated and Havana ruled Cuba as one for the first time.

1736

San José, the future capital of Costa Rica, was established.

1740

Havana Trading Company (Real Compañía de Comercio) chartered to monopolize trade and commerce with Cuba.

1751

Audiencia of Panama abolished.

1752

Crown monopoly over liquor established in Guatemala.

1755

Barcelona Trading Company chartered to trade with Santo Domingo, Puerto Rico, and Margarita.

1762

August 14. **British occupation of Cuba**. The British captured Havana for a ten-month occupation as a result of Spain's entry into the Seven Years' War between Great Britain and France. The British threw the port open to world trade and the Cuban economy boomed with slave imports fueling the expansion of the sugar industry. In order to hold Cuba, the Spanish introduced the intendancy system and freer trade. These reforms in Cuba were later extended to other parts of the empire.

1764

The intendancy system was introduced for the first time in the New World in Cuba. It was meant to improve efficiency in administration, augment revenues, and increase centralization at the regional level.

1765

October 16. **Freer trade for the Spanish Caribbean**. The main ports on the Spanish Caribbean islands of Cuba, Santo Domingo, Puerto Rico, Margarita, and Trinidad were authorized to trade directly with the nine Iberian ports of Alicante, Barcelona, Cádiz, Cartagena, Gijón, La Coruña, Málaga, Santander, and Seville. Thus, trade with America no longer had to be channeled exclusively through Cádiz.

1773

June–July. **A series of earthquakes destroyed much of Santiago de Guatemala (now known as Antigua)**. As a result, in 1776 the capital of the captaincy was moved to the site of modern Guatemala City.

1774

Spain rescinded all duties on Cuban imports.

1776

Spain allowed Cuban ports to trade directly with the British North American colonies in order to support their rebellion against Great Britain.

1778-1803

Expansion of free trade in the Spanish Caribbean. Cuban ports—Santiago de Cuba, Trinidad, Batabanó (1778), Nuevitas (1784), Matanzas (1793), Caibarién (1794), Manzanillo (1802), and Baracoa (1803)—other than Havana were authorized to trade directly with selected Spanish peninsular ports and the other Spanish American colonies.

1786

Intendancies were created for Nicaragua, Honduras, El Salvador, and Chiapas.

1789

February 28. **In response to pressure from Cuban sugar producers the monarchy authorized free trade in slaves without restriction**.

1791

August 22. **Slave revolt in Saint Domingue (the future Haiti)**. A major uprising by slaves began in the northern plains region and convulsed the French colony, already in turmoil as a result of the 1789 revolution in France. Led by **Toussaint L'Ouverture, Jean-Jacques Dessalines**, and others, the slaves eventually won their freedom and ended French rule over the colony. Meanwhile, most of the whites fled or were killed, and the colony's sugar industry was destroyed. The rebellion enhanced sugar production in the rest of the Caribbean, especially in Cuba, as the price of sugar increased 300 percent between 1790 and 1795.

1794

Consulado of Havana (merchants' guild) created.

1801

January. **Eight thousand black solders from Saint Domingue conquered Santo Domingo**, which had remained under Spanish control despite the Treaty of Basel. Thus, the entire island of Hispaniola was under the rule of **Toussaint L'Ouverture** until early 1802, when his troops were repelled by French forces with the help of Spanish-speaking residents. Meanwhile, the Audiencia was transferred to Cuba from Santo Domingo as a result of the invasion, and Cuba now had jurisdiction over Puerto Rico, Louisiana, and Florida.

1803

The monarchy transferred jurisdiction over San Andrés Island and the Mosquito Coast to the Viceroyalty of New Granada (present-day Panama, Colombia, and Venezuela).

November 30. **The last French troops left Saint Domingue.** Under Napoleon I, the French had attempted to regain control of the colony, which had been virtually independent under **Toussaint L'Ouverture**, and to restore slavery. However, the resistance of **Jean-Jacques Dessalines** and other black leaders, coupled with the ravages of yellow fever and the resumption of war against Great Britain, led to the abandonment of Napoleon's project. More than 40,000 French troops were lost in Saint Domingue.

Mexico
1517-1803

Mexico became the jewel of Spain's New World empire from the moment **Hernán Cortés** overcame Aztec resistance at Tenochtitlán in 1521.

Almost immediately construction got under way on the new Spanish capital of Mexico City, even as Cortés and other Spaniards fanned out to the north and south to subjugate outlying regions. Mexico also became the base for the conquest of Honduras and Guatemala, the latter under **Pedro de Alvarado**. Although the crown bestowed generous economic rewards on Cortés, it moved quickly to establish royal authority over the new colony with the creation of an audiencia and the appointment of a viceroy, **Antonio de Mendoza**, who arrived in 1535. Mexico City thus became the capital of the Viceroyalty of New Spain, which embraced not only Mexico but also Central America, the Caribbean, and the Philippines. Governors of these provinces, however, enjoyed considerable freedom of action.

The discovery of another rich and advanced indigenous civilization in Andean South America did not dim the luster of Mexico. Silver deposits were found in various locations in central and northern Mexico in the mid-1540s and later. After a decline in production in the mid-seventeenth century, owing mainly to a shortage of the

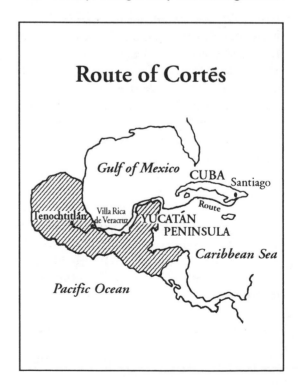

Route of Cortés

mercury needed for refining, output rose gradually, reaching a peak in the late eighteenth century. A complex and diversified economy developed in Mexico, producing agricultural commodities for both domestic consumption and export to Spain and to Cuba, Venezuela, and other colonies. Also important was a vast livestock industry that produced cattle and sheep as well as horses, mules, and oxen. Demand for textiles and most manufactured goods was met by artisanal production and by factories known as *obrajes*. In the seventeenth century, as Spain experienced political and economic decline, the colony continued to grow.

As in other colonies, the Spanish looked to the Indians to provide the bulk of the labor, initially through the institution of the *encomienda*, which provided a deserving Spaniard (the *encomendero*) with the labor and tribute of a designated group of Indians. After the mid-sixteenth century, however, encomenderos could no longer exact labor from their Indians. As a result, a system of rotational forced labor, known as the *repartimiento* (also called *cuatequil* in Mexico) was introduced. Indians assigned in *repartimiento* labored on plantations and mines for approximately forty-five days per year under harsh conditions and were often cheated out of their pay. The viceroy ordered an end to the agricultural repartimiento in 1632, and free wage labor became increasingly dominant in mining as well. In some areas agricultural workers were bound to estates by debt. Workers of African origin, both slave and free, were also found in small numbers.

During the eighteenth century the increase in silver production, which now outpaced that of Peru, and the growth of other exports, such as cochineal dye, made Mexico the most prosperous colony in Spanish America. Economic growth was accompanied by demographic expansion. The Indian population, which declined drastically after the conquest and reached its lowest point in the first half of the seventeenth century, recovered somewhat and numbered about 2.5 million in 1793, or 52 percent of the total of 4.8 million. Persons of mixed racial ancestry accounted for about 25 percent of the remainder, and whites for about 22 percent.

By this time, however, the divisions among whites between native-born creoles and Spaniards (known as *peninsulares* or, more negatively, as *gachupines*) were quite sharp. Mexico had attained substantial economic autonomy from Spain, yet it was drained of its resources because of the financial and military needs of the mother country. Moreover, the Spanish routinely denigrated the character and abilities of creoles while attempting to monopolize the chief offices in state and church. Creoles increasingly felt a sense of incipient nationalism, reflected in the widespread cult of the Virgin of Guadalupe.

1517

February 8. **Sailing from Cuba, Francisco Hernández de Córdoba explored the coast of the Yucatán peninsula.** The expedition ended after Hernández de Córdoba was badly wounded in an encounter with Indians.

1518

May 3. **Juan de Grijalva arrived in Cozumel at the head of a large expedition dispatched from Cuba to follow up on the discoveries of Hernández de Córdoba.** Grijalva's expedition sailed along the coast of Yucatán and up the Mexican coast as far as the Pánuco River. Grijalva thus entered the dominions of **Moctezuma**, the Aztec (Mexica) emperor, and obtained evidence of the advanced civilizations and riches to be found on the mainland.

1519

February. **The Spanish invasion of central Mexico. Hernán Cortés** set out from Cuba in defiance of Governor Diego de Velázquez. The expedition began with some 500 men, 16 horses, and 11 small ships. After arriving at Cozumel, they encountered two Spaniards, Gerónimo Aguilar and Gonzalo Guerrero, shipwrecked since 1511. Guerrero had been assimilated into indigenous society and chose to remain, but Aguilar joined the expedition and served as an interpreter.

March 25. **The Spanish won a victory over Indian warriors at Cintla in Tabasco.** Soon afterward the Tabasco chiefs presented Cortés with twenty women. One of them, **Malinche**, would become his mistress and interpreter. After landing at San Juan de Ulúa, Cortés founded a settlement called Villa Rica de la Vera Cruz (Veracruz). With this action, he attempted to cast off the authority of Velázquez and asserted his right to govern the newly discovered territories. Even so, fearing mutiny by partisans of Velázquez, Cortés blocked all avenues of retreat by scuttling his ships.

August 16. **The Spanish began marching inland to the Aztec capital of Tenochtitlán.** At Cholula, the Spanish and Indian allies from Tlaxcala cut down thousands of warriors who had planned to attack them under orders from **Moctezuma**.

November 8. **Cortés and Moctezuma greeted each other in Tenochtitlán.** Although the meeting was ostensibly friendly, Cortés mistrusted the emperor's intentions and seized him a few days later. Moctezuma was well treated but remained a prisoner.

1520

Spanish disaster at Tenochtitlán.

May 4. **Leaving Pedro de Alvarado in charge at Tenochtitlán, Cortés** left for Veracruz to repel **Pánfilo de Narváez**, an agent of Velázquez, who had recently arrived with nine hundred Spaniards. A member of the Narváez expedition carried smallpox, which soon ravaged the Indian population. Cortés easily defeated Narváez but quickly returned to Tenochtitlán, where the Aztecs had risen against the Spanish after Alvarado had ordered an attack on Aztec leaders during a religious ceremony. **Moctezuma** was killed during the fighting that followed, probably by his own people.

June 30-July 1. **During their "night of sorrow" (*noche triste*) the Spanish attempted to escape from Tenochtitlán but were ambushed by the Indians, who inflicted heavy casualties.** Having found refuge among the still loyal Tlaxcalans, Cortés laid plans to regain control of Tenochtitlán.

December 31. **Cortés arrived in Texcoco,** which he found deserted and which became the base for a planned siege of Tenochtitlán.

1521

Fall of the Aztec Empire.

May. **The Spanish attack on Tenochtitlán began.** Cortés had under his command approximately one thousand Spanish soldiers as well as many Indian auxiliaries. In addition, the Spanish had built thirteen brigantines which were floated on Lake Texcoco, where Tenochtitlán was located. The Aztecs, led by their new emperor, **Cuauhtémoc**, resisted fiercely.

August 31. **Tenochtitlán fell to the Spanish, and Cuauhtémoc surrendered.** Cortés now began to erect a new Spanish settlement—the future Mexico City—on the ruins of Tenochtitlán.

1522

October 15. **Charles V appointed Hernán Cortés governor and captain-general of the territory he had conquered.** Later (July 6, 1529), he was named marqués del Valle de Oaxaca. Cortés thereby received the right to collect tribute from 23,000 Indians in 22 towns in central Mexico, Oaxaca, and Tehuantepec. The grant, which was to pass to Cortés's descendants in perpetuity, also included judicial powers.

1524

May. **Twelve Franciscans arrived in Veracruz to undertake conversion of the indigenous population.** Two other Franciscans and the lay brother Pedro de Gante had preceded them, but their arrival marked the beginning of organized missionary activity in Mexico. Led by Martín de Valencia, the barefoot friars walked all the way from Veracruz to Mexico City.

1527

December 12. **Juan de Zumárraga, a Franciscan, was appointed the first bishop of Mexico.**

When an archbishopric was created in 1546, embracing the dioceses of Mexico, Michoacán, Tlaxcala, Guatemala, and Chiapas, **Zumárraga** was named to the post, but died soon afterward.

1528

December. **The judges (*oidores*) of Mexico's first high court, or audiencia, arrived in Veracruz, along with its president, Nuño de Guzmán.** The creation of the audiencia reflected the crown's desire to weaken the political influence of **Cortés** and to assert its control over the colony. The audiencia and Guzmán became notorious for their corruption and mistreatment of the Indians, prompting complaints by Bishop **Zumárraga** and others. Guzmán also gained notoriety for his cruelty in the conquest of the region in west-central Mexico known as New Galicia. Members of a second audiencia, which replaced the first, arrived in Mexico in 1530.

1531

April 16. **Puebla de los Ángeles (now Puebla de Zaragoza) was founded.** However, flooding soon destroyed the new settlement, which was refounded in nearby Atlixco in 1532.

December 9-12. **According to legend, the Virgin Mary appeared three times to a Christianized Indian called Juan Diego at Tepeyac near Mexico City.** At her direction, Juan Diego gathered roses in his cloak to show to bishop Zumárraga. When the cloak was opened, the image of the Virgin was imprinted on it. The first written accounts of the miracle date only from the mid-seventeenth century, but the image on the cloak is believed by many to be preserved at the present basilica of the Virgin of Guadalupe near Mexico City. In 1754 Pope Benedict XIV recognized the Virgin of Guadalupe as the patroness of New Spain and set December 12 as her feast day. Juan Diego was beatified in 1990.

1535

May 3. **Hernán Cortés landed in La Paz Bay in Baja California, where he attempted unsuccess-**

fully to establish a colony. Cortés returned to Mexico City in 1536, but in 1539-40 he sponsored a voyage by Francisco de Ulloa which proved that California was not an island.

October. **Mexico's first viceroy, Antonio de Mendoza, arrived in Veracruz.** During his fifteen years of service there he established royal authority and laid the institutional foundation for the future administration of the colony. He also encouraged exploration.

1539

November 30. **Don Carlos Chichimecatecuhti, lord of Texcoco, was executed in Mexico City after being convicted of heresy and idolatry.** He had been denounced earlier in the year to Bishop **Juan de Zumárraga**, who also held the position of Inquisitor. Don Carlos was accused of publicly attacking Christianity and the conduct of the clergy and of questioning the legitimacy of Spanish rule over Mexico. A search of his home revealed a cache of pre-Columbian idols. Although he denied the charges, he was found guilty, and because he refused to acknowledge his guilt, he was turned over to the secular authorities for execution. The fate of Don Carlos produced much criticism in Spain and contributed to the decision to exempt Indians from the jurisdiction of the Holy Office of the Inquisition after its establishment in 1571. They were to remain under the control of bishops in matters of faith and morals.

1540

April 22. **Francisco Vázquez de Coronado left Culiacán, Mexico, to find a city called Cíbola,** described as rich and populous by a Franciscan friar, Marcos de Niza, who claimed to have seen it. During the next two years **Coronado** and his companions traveled extensively in the future New Mexico, Arizona, Texas, Oklahoma, and Kansas but found no riches.

1540-41

The Mixtón War. Unpacified Indians known as Chichimecas launched a major uprising against the Spanish in the province known as New Galicia, also sparking rebellion among the exploited *encomienda* Indians of the region. Rebel leaders promised their followers that victory would bring material abundance and the restoration of their ancient gods. **Pedro de Alvarado** was fatally injured while leading an unsuccessful attack against the Indians. The spread of the revolt, which was fed by Spanish defeats, led Viceroy **Mendoza** to go to New Galicia himself, accompanied by several hundred Spanish horsemen and thousands of loyal Indians. He inflicted a decisive defeat on the rebels at their hilltop fortress at Mixtón.

1542

January 6. **Francisco de Montejo the Younger founded the city of Mérida on a Maya site called T'Hoo in Yucatán.** Montejo's father, also called Francisco, had begun the conquest of the Yucatán peninsula in 1527 but had been unsuccessful because of Maya resistance. While the elder Montejo was occupied elsewhere, his son renewed the campaign in 1540. Although the Maya mounted a large-scale uprising in 1547, the Spaniards won control of most of the peninsula. However, the last group of independent Maya, who lived near Lake Petén Itzá in present-day Guatemala, were not conquered until 1697.

February. **The city of Guadalajara was established at its present site south of the Santiago River.** The town had been moved from other locations several times since its initial foundation in 1531.

June 27. **Juan Rodríguez Cabrillo left the Mexican port of Navidad to explore the coast of Upper California.** On September 2 he put in at a harbor he called San Miguel (modern San Diego) and later sailed northward to the Santa Barbara Channel islands. Cabrillo died on January 3, 1543, but his chief pilot and second-in-command, Bartolomé Ferrer, sailed as far north as the Rogue River.

1544

March 8. **The inspector (*visitador*) Francisco Tello de Sandoval reached Mexico City.** He was authorized to conduct a judicial review (*residen-* *cia*) of all the royal officials in the viceroyalty and to put the New Laws into effect there. But there was so much opposition to the New Laws that Sandoval, heeding the advice of Viceroy Mendoza, delayed their enforcement until appeals could be made to Spain. Sandoval remained in Mexico until 1547.

1545-48

A great epidemic swept central Mexico, causing high mortality among the Indians. It was characterized by fever and bleeding, especially from the nose. The cause of the epidemic may have been typhus, which is also blamed for major epidemics in 1576-80 and 1736-37.

1546-48

September 8. **Juan de Tolosa and a party of Spaniards and Indians discovered silver in Zacatecas.** According to tradition, the town of Zacatecas was founded on January 20, 1548. In that year even richer deposits of silver were found in the region. In the 1550s silver deposits were also found in Guanajuato, Pachuca, and Sombrerete.

1548

February 13. **A royal decree ordered the establishment of an audiencia with jurisdiction over the province of New Galicia.** Its seat was initially located in Compostela but was moved to Guadalajara in 1560. The audiencia was subordinate to that of Mexico.

1551

September 21. **The crown ordered the establishment of a university in Mexico City.** It was formally inaugurated on January 21, 1553.

1562

May. **Reports of hidden Maya idols and human remains in Yucatán led to an investigation by**

Diego de Landa, head of the Franciscan order on the peninsula. **Landa** became convinced that the Maya were secretly practicing their traditional religion and were even engaged in human sacrifice. His widespread use of torture to elicit confessions produced criticism from the newly arrived bishop of Yucatán, Francisco de Toral, and from Spanish settlers, who disliked disruptions in the lives of their Indian laborers. Toral prohibited the use of torture and freed imprisoned Indians. Landa himself became bishop of Yucatán in the early 1570s but was instructed to refrain from imprisoning or flogging Indians. The events in Yucatán, like the case of Don Carlos in 1539, contributed to the exemption of Indians from the jurisdiction of the Holy Office of the Inquisition.

1563

July 8. **Francisco de Ibarra founded the town of Durango, which became the capital of the large northern frontier region known as New Vizcaya.** The administrative seat of New Vizcaya was moved to San José del Parral (now Hidalgo del Parral) after a major silver strike in 1631. The discovery of silver at Santa Eulalia (now Aquiles Serdán) led to the establishment (1718) of another important town nearby, San Felipe el Real de Chihuahua (the modern city of Chihuahua).

1566

July 16. **Martín Cortés, the only legitimate son and heir of Hernán Cortés, was arrested in Mexico City.** He was accused of conspiring with two brothers, Alonso and Gil González de Ávila, and others to overthrow royal authority in Mexico and set himself up as king. The Ávila brothers were both executed, but Cortés, who probably did not play an active role in the alleged conspiracy, was sent to Spain, where he was eventually pardoned. The Ávila brothers are usually considered representative of the *encomendero* class, unhappy because the crown refused to confer their grants of Indians in perpetuity.

1568

September. **The English seaman John Hawkins and his fleet of five ships were forced by bad weather to seek refuge in the fort of San Juan de Ulúa in the harbor of Veracruz.** In this, as in two previous voyages to the Indies, Hawkins had been engaged in the sale of African slaves to colonists in the Caribbean and northern South America in defiance of the Spanish monopoly on commerce. When the Spanish fleet (*flota*) arrived the next day bearing the new viceroy, Martín de Enríquez, Hawkins, who now controlled the harbor, allowed it to enter. Both sides promised to avoid hostilities, but Enríquez attacked the English, many of whom were killed or captured. One of those who escaped was Hawkins's kinsman, Francis Drake.

1571

November 4. **A tribunal of the Holy Office of the Inquisition was established in Mexico City.** Like other such bodies, it investigated cases of suspected heresy, blasphemy, sorcery, and bigamy; it also censored books. Among its first victims were some thirty-six Englishmen, survivors of the John Hawkins expedition, who were prosecuted as Protestant heretics.

1592

June 15. **The crown ordered the establishment of a consulado (merchants' guild and court) in Mexico City.** Modeled on those of Spain, the Mexican consulado served the city's mercantile elite, who in turn had ties with the merchants of Seville. Consulados were established in Guadalajara and Veracruz in 1795.

1596

September 20. **The city of Monterrey in northern Mexico was founded by Diego de Montemayor.** It was named in honor of the viceroy of

Mexico, Gaspar de Zúñiga y Acevedo, conde de Monterrey. Two towns had earlier been founded nearby (1577, 1582), but both were abandoned.

1598

April 30. **Juan de Oñate formally took possession of the future New Mexico in a ceremony on the Río Grande.** After crossing the river near modern El Paso, Oñate and his party moved northward among communities of Tewa-speaking Pueblo Indians. On July 11 he reached San Juan, which became his base, though in 1599 he moved across the river to San Gabriel. Over the next few years Oñate and his companions made extensive explorations throughout the region but found no ready sources of wealth. The colony's lack of material and human resources, disaffection among the Spanish, and Indian hostility led Oñate to resign his governorship in 1607. But the crown retained the colony, primarily as a mission field. Its new capital was Santa Fe, founded about 1607.

1624

January 15. **Rioting in Mexico City forced the viceroy, Diego Carrillo de Mendoza y Pimentel (conde de Gelves), to flee.** The disturbance has been attributed to apparent food shortages and to tensions arising from conflict between the viceroy and the archbishop, Juan Pérez de la Serna. This was the first time that a viceroy was deposed in such a fashion. He was not reinstated by the crown, which named Rodrigo Pacheco y Osorio (marqués de Cerralvo) as his successor.

1629

September. **Mexico City was flooded in the most serious inundation of the colonial period.** Hundreds died, and many were forced to leave the city. The waters did not fully recede until 1634. The immediate cause of the flood was unusually heavy rainfall at the start of the rainy season, but it can also be attributed to the failure of government efforts to control the waters of Lake Texcoco.

1640-49

Palafox in Mexico. Juan de Palafox y Mendoza, a protégé of the powerful count-duke of **Olivares**, arrived in Mexico on October 12, 1640, to serve as bishop of Puebla and inspector-general (*visitador*) of the viceroyalty. Moralistic and puritanical, he soon became embroiled in a conflict with the Franciscans and other mendicant orders over control of their Indian parishes in Puebla. He also quarreled with the viceroy, Diego López Pacheco y Bobadilla (duque de Escalona), whom he accused of pro-Portuguese sympathies after the revolt of Portugal against Spanish rule in 1640. In 1642 he was authorized by Olivares to remove the viceroy and to assume the office himself temporarily. During his brief reign (June–November 1642), Palafox unleashed a crusade against prostitution and other sinful conduct while the Inquisition moved against suspected Jews. Palafox later clashed with his successor as viceroy, García Sarmiento de Sotomayor (conde de Salvatierra), and with the Jesuits of Puebla over their refusal to pay the tithe on the products of their estates. The latter conflict reached a climax on March 10, 1647, when Palafox prohibited Jesuits from exercising their priestly functions in the diocese of Puebla. As the viceroy prepared to move against him, Palafox went into hiding (June 14, 1647), but he returned to his diocese in triumph the following November after the crown removed Salvatierra, dispatching him to Peru as viceroy. Palafox's dispute with the Jesuits continued unabated until, having lost favor in Spain, he was ordered to leave Mexico (June 10, 1649). Palafox's stormy career in Mexico illustrates the tensions that often arose between ecclesiastics and lay officials and between members of the secular clergy and the religious orders.

1680

August 10. **A massive rebellion of Pueblo Indians began in New Mexico.** Resentful of Spanish demands for their labor and of the religious practices imposed by missionaries, the Pueblo killed 21 of the 32 Franciscans in the region and approximately 400 settlers and officials. The survivors were forced to abandon the colony. In 1692 Diego de Vargas began a successful reconquest of New Mexico.

1683

May. **Some eight hundred buccaneers led by a Frenchman called Laurent Graff (known as Lorencillo in Spanish) seized control of Veracruz by a stratagem.** The inhabitants were dragged out of their homes and confined to churches, where they were kept without food and water while the buccaneers raped the women and looted the town. Leading citizens were then taken to a nearby island and held as hostages until a ransom was paid. The buccaneers left without hindrance.

1687

March. **Jesuit Father Eusebio Kino began his mission to the Pima Indians,** who occupied a little known region known as Pimería Alta, now included in northwestern Sonora and southwestern Arizona. Establishing his base at a mission called Nuestra Señora de los Dolores, Kino remained in Pimería Alta until his death in 1711. He explored the region thoroughly and convinced other Jesuits to undertake missionary work there as well as in California. In 1708 he claimed to have personally baptized more than four thousand Indians.

1692

June 6. **Driven by a shortage of food, rioters in Mexico City burned the viceregal palace, demolished the buildings of the city government, and looted dozens of shops.** Many persons were also killed or wounded.

1712

August. **Inhabitants of twenty-one Maya-speaking communities in highland Chiapas rose in rebellion against Spanish authorities to defend a new and unrecognized cult of the Virgin Mary.** Numerous Spanish and mestizo priests and settlers were killed before the revolt was crushed the following February.

1716-21

Spanish colonization of Texas. While the Spanish had explored Texas and missions had been founded there in the sixteenth and seventeenth centuries, French encroachments from Louisiana led the government to establish more permanent settlements there. An expedition in 1716-17 headed by Captain Domingo Ramón resulted in the establishment of six missions in East Texas as well as a presidio, or fort, on the Neches River. Hoping to establish a way station between East Texas and the Río Grande, Martín de Alarcón brought a party of seventy-two persons, horses, mules, and other livestock to Texas in 1718. The mission San Antonio de Valero (the chapel of which would become known as the Alamo) was founded on May 1, 1718, and four days later Presidio San Antonio de Béxar was established nearby. The civilian community that grew up around the fort formed the nucleus of Villa de Béxar, the most important Spanish town in Texas. After a French incursion led to the abandonment of the East Texas missions and fort, a 500-man expedition led by the Marqués de Aguayo reestablished them in 1720-21.

1722

June. **The *Gaceta de México*, the first newspaper to be published in Latin America, appeared in Mexico City.** The eight-page newspaper contained official notices as well as news about religion, trade, society, and new books. Only six numbers were issued in 1722, but the newspaper was revived in January 1728 and was published under that name until 1739.

1761

November. **An anti-Spanish rebellion began in the small town of Quisteil in Yucatán.** Little is known about the origins and extent of the uprising, but Spanish officials feared that a large-scale revolt was planned. The rebel leader, an Indian called Jacinto Uc, took the name of Canek, ruler of the Maya enclave conquered in 1697, and reportedly crowned himself king. He was soon captured and executed (December 14, 1761), but has become a symbol of indigenous resistance.

1765

July 18. **José de Gálvez arrived in Veracruz to begin his six-year inspection of Mexico.** Gálvez traveled extensively, directed the expulsion of the Jesuits (1767), and recommended numerous reforms to increase revenues and improve colonial defenses, especially in the northern frontier areas. Some of the reforms advocated by Gálvez, such as the establishment of the intendancy system, were not introduced until after he became minister of the Indies in 1776.

1767

June 25. **The order for expulsion of the Jesuits was promulgated in Mexico.** The viceroy, Francisco de Croix, entrusted the execution of the order to the inspector-general, **José de Gálvez**. Riots over the order occurred in San Luis Potosí, Guanajuato, and other places, though grievances over taxes also contributed to the disturbances. Gálvez dealt harshly with the ringleaders, and dozens were executed, imprisoned, or banished. About 680 Jesuits were forced to leave Mexico.

1769

Spanish colonization of Upper California. Concerned about possible Russian encroachments in the region, **José de Gálvez** dispatched a large expedition by land and by sea to occupy Upper California. Commanded by Gaspar de Portolá, the expedition founded a settlement and mission at San Diego. In addition, a trail to the north was opened, San Francisco Bay was visited, and a fort (presidio) and mission were founded at Monterey. Junípero Serra, a Franciscan missionary, was the religious leader of the expedition and founded nine missions in Upper California before his death in 1784.

1776

August 22. **A royal order called for the incorporation of the provinces of Coahuila, Texas, New Mexico, New Vizcaya, Sinaloa, Sonora, and California into a new administrative unit called the Provincias Internas.** It was to be headed by a commander-general who was to be virtually independent of the viceroy and was to concentrate on military matters. The creation of the new unit was a result of increased pressure from Apaches and other Indians against Spanish frontier settlements as well as threats from other European powers. The first commander-general was Teodoro de Croix (1777-83). In 1786 the Provincias Internas were divided into western and eastern zones.

1777

May 24. **The Cuerpo de Minería, or miners' guild, was formally organized.** Its purpose was to promote the interests of Mexico's mining industry and to adjudicate disputes involving the industry. In 1783 a detailed and comprehensive mining code that served as the guild's charter was adopted. The code was later adopted in New Granada and other colonies. Under the leadership of Fausto de Elhuyar, who was appointed director-general of the guild in 1786, a School of Mines was established (1792) to improve technical and metallurgical expertise.

1786

October 11. **A royal decree divided Mexico into twelve intendancies:** Mexico, Puebla, Guadalajara, Guanajuato, Oaxaca, San Luis Potosí, Veracruz, Valladolid, Mérida, Zacatecas, Durango, and Arizpe.

1789

February 28. **The crown extended free trade to New Spain and to Venezuela.** This meant that these regions could now trade freely with Spanish ports besides Cádiz and that the fleet system had come to a definitive end.

Northern South America
1498-1803

Northern South America embraces the present-day countries of Venezuela, Colombia, and Ecuador, the latter two being known respectively as New Granada and Quito during the colonial period. Many historians would also include Panama, since while under Spanish rule it was part of the Viceroyalty of Peru and in the national period part of Colombia (until 1903). Of all of the major regions of the Iberian world, Northern South America is probably the most diverse and complex and the most difficult to generalize about. Its range of climates, cultures, and ethnic groups runs the gamut from the Caribbean world of the Colombian and Venezuelan coasts to the Pacific coast communities of Colombia and Ecuador. In the interior the Andean world thrusts up in a north-south line of volcanic peaks and intermontane valleys in Ecuador and southern Colombia before splitting into the Western, Central, and Eastern Cordilleras, which are in turn separated by the Cauca and Magdalena river valleys. Near the Venezuelan border the Eastern Cordillera divides again to form the Lake Maracaibo basin and the northeasterly run of the Venezuelan Andes. On the Amazonian side of the Andes the Colombian and Venezuelan *llanos* (plains) and the Ecuadorian Amazon face Portuguese America. This geographical diversity lacks a central organizing feature, accounting for the extreme regionalism of northern South America. It also explains why it has been difficult to unify not only the area but the individual countries, and why administrative and jurisdictional boundaries have changed frequently.

While it is said that Ecuador is more Indian, Colombia more mestizo, and Venezuela more mulatto than the others, each in turn has regions where the ethnic mix is the reverse. Nevertheless, highland Ecuador was conquered by the Inca and approximates a Peruvian reality more so than do Colombia and Venezuela, while the latter two have a Caribbean component that Ecuador does not. The native Americans were always more numerous in the interior in the highlands in all three countries and survived the Spanish conquest and colonial period to a much greater extent than on the coast and along the river systems, where African slaves became the dominant labor force, especially on the Venezuelan cacao plantations and in the New Granadan gold fields.

Northern South America historically has been pulled in contrary directions by the different traditions of its coast and interior. This tension between the lowlands and the highlands was resolved in favor of the latter in Ecuador and Colombia, where their respective capitals of Quito and Bogotá and other major cities were located deep in the Andean interior. The contrary took place in Venezuela, where the Andes were much lower in elevation and the capital of Caracas, while in the mountains, was not far from the coast. The coast was exposed and open to the outside world and was synonymous with trade, commerce, and change while the Andean interior was isolated and traditional and resistant to innovation from both within and without.

Northern South America's role in the Spanish empire changed over the course of the colonial period. Initially it served as a staging area for the discovery and conquest of Peru. The three expeditions of **Francisco Pizarro** that were needed to verify the existence and extent of the Inca empire and then to conquer it were launched from Panama, which had in turn been settled as an outgrowth of Spanish activity along the northern coast of New Granada and Venezuela. As the magnitude of the precious metals available in Peru became known, it became imperative for the Spanish to create an infrastructure capable of protecting the source of this bullion whose stream was essential to Spanish power. Northern South America was a key part of this infrastructure and linked Spain with Peru. It also served as a defensive bulwark against which Spain's rivals would have to expend their forces in order to get at the precious metals streaming back to Spain.

To protect and maintain the flow of bullion and merchandise to the Old and New World, Spain developed a convoy system of shipping, half of which departed from Spain for Veracruz, ideally in April, with the rest to follow in August bound for Cartagena-Panama, where they had a trade fair and picked up the silver coming north from Peru and crossing the isthmus. This half of the fleet would anchor, sometimes for several months, in Cartagena's interior harbor on the New Granadan coast until word arrived that the silver from Peru was transiting the isthmus, at which time the fleet sailed to Panama. The fleet was composed of royal warships and private merchant vessels. Sometimes a separate contingent of warships made the run to the New World just to pick up the silver at Panama, but ideally all sailed together and combined a trade fair in Panama with the securing of the king's share of the bullion. After the three- to four-week trade fair at Nombre de Dios or, after 1597, Portobelo, the fleet returned to Cartagena for provisioning before sailing to Havana and joining the Mexican-based half of the fleet for the return to Spain.

As the New World terminus for the South American fleet, Cartagena assumed a position of strategic importance within the Spanish empire. Without Cartagena the shipment of bullion from Peru was in jeopardy, and without precious metals the Spanish economy could not function. Ideally the trade system was supposed to work smoothly, but many things could go wrong in Peru, Panama, Cartagena, the Caribbean, and Spain, sometimes delaying the fleet for several years. Nevertheless, there always seemed to be enough bullion en route to Spain to warrant another sailing. The provisioning of the fleet for its long stay at Cartagena generated a demand that was supplied from all over the Caribbean. Cartagena also served as an entry point through which merchandise and slaves were introduced into much of South America. Spain built great fortifications around Cartagena and continued to expand its defensive perimeter throughout the colonial period. Without doubt, Cartagena was the most important Iberian port in the New World in the sixteenth century. In the seventeenth only Havana and Buenos Aires rivaled it, though by the eighteenth they would

surpass it.

By the eighteenth century the relative importance of Peru in the Spanish empire had shrunk considerably while northern South America as a whole had become more diversified and self-sufficient. Over the course of the colonial period northern South America developed regional economies and societies that gave the area its most distinctive characteristic. Venezuela had pearl beds, and the provisioning of the fleet at Cartagena with wheat brought development to Andean valleys around Caracas. In exchange for their grain, Caraqueños bought African slaves in Cartagena to replace their rapidly diminishing native American laborers supplied through the *encomienda* and *mita*. An even more suitable and profitable commodity than grain was cacao, which by the seventeenth century had become Venezuela's chief export, mainly to New Spain. It remained so throughout the colonial period. Cacao brought in the specie necessary for Venezuelans to pay for imports. It also fueled the ethnic transformation of Venezuela.

Gold deposits made New Granada the object of Spanish interest throughout the colonial period. The diffuseness of the New Granadan gold fields, however, prevented them from becoming mining centers such as Potosí or Zacatecas. What developed were the regional cities of Popayán, Cali, and Medellín, which organized the exploitation of nearby gold fields. By the seventeenth century a shortage of native American laborers in the gold producing areas led to their replacement with African slaves, especially in Antioquia, the Cauca Valley, and the Chocó, all in western New Granada. Ethnic change followed these economic developments.

Ecuador, like Venezuela, lacked significant mining production. In the colonial period its main export was textiles, primarily to Peru and secondarily to New Granada.. Two regional economies emerged in the Ecuadorian sierra, or highlands. First to appear was the north-central sierra running from Ibarra through Quito to Riobamba, which produced woolen textiles in *obrajes* (mills or sweatshops) using *encomienda* laborers. The second emerged later in the south sierra and was centered in Cuenca. It produced cotton textiles in a putting out or cottage industry, especially among the native Americans who had migrated there from the more depressed north. The north-central sierra market of Quito had fallen into a state of decline by 1690 and was being overtaken by the Cuenca market of the south sierra, which entered its own period of decline a century later when freer trade allowed through the Bourbon Reforms brought a flood of cheap European textiles. Guayaquil, as Ecuador's premier port and as Spain's main ship building center in the Pacific, constituted a third regional market. But it was the exceptional fertility of Guayaquil's rich hinterland, drained by the Guayas River, and the freer trade allowed by the Bourbon Reforms between 1778 and 1789, that launched Ecuador's cacao boom and marked the rise of a coastal economy and society that eventually rivaled that of the sierra.

Northern South America's growing importance led the Spanish to try to unify the entire area in 1717 and again in 1739 under the viceroy of New Granada, the first new viceroyalty in Spanish America since 1542. Whether the new viceroy was to man the coastal defenses at Cartagena or develop interior provinces depended on the state of belligerency with Spain's European rivals. Both were officially stated, but difficult-to-achieve, objectives. For northern South America Spain made and unmade audiencias and administrative, judicial, and ecclesiastical boundaries in stop-and-go attempts at restructuring. Overall there was a drive toward bringing Quito (Ecuador), New Granada (Colombia), Panama, and Venezuela under one authority, but with Venezuela manifesting the greatest amount of independence and autonomy. Spanish attempts to bring in more revenues with new taxes and a more efficient collection of old ones produced widescale resentment and opposition in many regions. This, coupled with a bureaucracy that was increasingly Spanish born, provoked rebellion in Venezuela (1749-51), Quito (1765), and New Granada (1781), but no distinct call for independence. It was clear that regional issues predominated over larger imperial concerns.

1498

August. **During his third voyage Christopher Columbus made landfall near the mouth of the Orinoco River** and passed through the Dragon's Mouth, a narrow entrance into the Gulf of Paria between Venezuela and Trinidad. There a landing party amassed pearls through trade with the native Americans.

1499

Juan Rodríguez de Fonseca ended Columbus's monopoly in the New World, and the exploration of the coast of northern South America was opened to others. The royal chaplain and architect of Spanish policy in the Atlantic issued licenses to new participants for trade and discovery. The recipients were Peralonso Niño and Alonso de Hojeda. The pearl beds found the year before by **Columbus** were the logical choice for quick profits.

May–June. Niño and Hojeda sailed from Spain within a few weeks of each other. Niño's one-ship expedition arrived first and began the exploitation of the pearl fisheries on the island of Cubagua between Cumaná and Margarita. His group returned to Spain the next year with significant profits.

Late June. Hojeda and his partner Juan de la Cosa made landfall near Guiana. They explored the Venezuelan coast as far as the Guajira Peninsula during July and August. They turned north and arrived in Hispaniola September 5.

1500

Juan de la Cosa mapped the coast of northern South America based on his voyage of the previous year. "Venezuela" first appeared on this map; Cosa had seen a native American settlement on stilts in Lake Maracaibo, and it reminded him of Venice.

The success of the Niño and Hojeda expeditions moved the crown and Spanish capitalists to agree to terms for three new voyages. The Guerra brothers—the financial backers of Niño—Rodrigo de Bastidas, and Hojeda got the licenses. It was Cristóbal Guerra rather than Niño who returned to exploit the pearl fisheries and hunt slaves along the Venezuelan and Colombian coasts. Bastidas signed his concession June 8, and , along with his partner, Juan de la Cosa, agreed to stay away from the pearl fisheries and to explore farther west along the Colombian coast; they sailed from Spain in October.

1501

Bastidas and Cosa spent most of the year exploring the length of the Caribbean coast of Colombia. They noted the excellent harbor sites at Cartagena and the Gulf of Urabá. They accumulated significant amounts of gold through trade with the native Americans and arrived back in Spain in September, 1502.

1502

May–June. **Hojeda's second expedition reexplored the Venezuelan coast** from Margarita to the Guajira penisula. Hojeda, as governor of Coquibacoa—an ill-defined area of the western Venezuelan coast—established the first administrative subdivision on the American mainland on the Guajira Penisula, a desolate stretch and bad choice for settlement. Administratively it did not endure, and economically the expedition netted meager returns from the enslavement of native Americans.

1504-6

A new expedition led by Juan de la Cosa reexplored the northern South American coast from Margarita to the Gulf of Urabá. Dispatching brazilwood and native Americans back to Spain from Cartagena, Cosa went on to the protected waters of the Gulf of Urabá where his worm-eaten ships left his expedition stranded for

eighteen months. The gold from the appropriated native ornaments made the Gulf of Urabá a logical choice for future expeditions.

1508-10

The exploration and colonization of Urabá and Veragua. Hojeda had received a license to lead his third expedition to Tierra Firme in September of 1504 in spite of his lack of success on his previous ventures. His patron was Juan Rodríguez de Fonseca, the royal chaplain and architect of Spanish policy in the New World. Hojeda was late getting started again, and by 1508 Fonseca had divided the mainland into two spheres. The area west of the Gulf of Urabá and into Panama and Central America, the area Columbus had named Veragua and had explored on his fourth voyage, was licensed to Diego de Nicuesa. East of Urabá, the northern Colombian coast, was given to Hojeda. His two partners in this venture were Martín Fernández de Enciso and Juan de la Cosa. Both Nicuesa and Hojeda sailed from Hispaniola in December 1509, and headed for the harbor at Cartagena. The first off were Hojeda and Cosa with three hundred men, while Nicuesa followed with 785 in five ships. (For the results of the two expeditions, see Caribbean and Central America, 1510.) Cosa was killed by an Indian arrow (February 28, 1510). The expeditions resulted in settlement in the Gulf of Urabá area. (See Caribbean and Central America, 1511-19.)

1510

Spanish settlement in eastern Venezuela. The richness of the pearl beds on the island of Cubagua led the Spanish to establish the town of Nueva Cádiz there. The Spanish had now occupied the western and eastern fringes of northern South America but nothing in between.

1511-19

Colonization of the mainland. The initial attempts at settlement of the mainland began to take form in Panama setting the stage for the European discovery of the pacific Ocean and the conquest of Peru and, from the south, of Central America (see Caribbean and Central America, 1511-19).

1520

Native Americans and Spanish clashed on the Venezuelan coast. Reacting against Spanish slaving expeditions and forced labor in the pearl fisheries of Cubagua, the native Americans rebelled against the Spanish. The punitive expedition of Jácome Castellón followed in retaliation, and he began building a fort at the future site of Cumaná.

May 19. The Dominican priest **Bartolomé de las Casas**, defender of the rights of native Americans, was licensed to colonize Venezuela. Obligated to establish three towns with forty residents each, las Casas failed in this and in his attempt to convert the natives. His order's mission of Chichirivichi was destroyed by the natives in October.

1521

More Spanish expeditions punished the natives along the Venezuelan coast. Captain Gonzalo de Ocampo's imposed peace allowed both Dominicans and Franciscans to return to proselytize among the native Americans.

1522

Spanish first attempted to reach Peru. Pedro Arias de Ávila (Pedrarias), captain-general and governor of Panama, agreed to allow Pascual de Andagoya to explore southeast from Panama down the Pacific coast. Andagoya got as far as the Baudó River in the Colombian Chocó before falling ill.

1523

Cumaná was established. With Castellón's fort finally finished, it was officially chartered as Nuevo Toledo (Cumaná), thus securing the first mainland settlement of Venezuela.

1524-26

Francisco Pizarro's first expedition failed to reach Peru. Andagoya's illness led Pedrarias to put **Francisco Pizarro** in charge of a second expedition to Peru, Pizarro's first. Departing from Panama in November, Pizarro pushed even farther south than Andagoya and discovered the San Juan River just north of present-day Buenaventura. He spent more than a year exploring the Colombian coast before returning to Panama in the spring of 1526 without reaching Peru.

1525

March 18. **Margarita became a governorship**. By royal decree the island became a separate administrative entity, and Marcelo de Villalobos, *oidor* of the audiencia of Santo Domingo, was made its first governor.

1526-27

Colonization of western Venezuela and eastern Colombia begun.

May 28, 1526. Rodrigo de Bastidas sailed from Santo Domingo with his expedition of 500 and soon afterwards established Santa Marta. Bastidas had received his license November 6, 1524, at which time he had also been named governor of Santa Marta.

November 1526. Juan de Ampiés was appointed governor of Tierra Firme and licensed to colonize the mainland and islands of western Venezuela (Curaçao, Aruba, and Bonaire).

April 1527. Bastidas was wounded in a botched assassination attempt but died July 8 in Santiago de Cuba.

July 26, 1527. Ampiés expedition founded Coro, Venezuela.

1528

March 27. **The Welsers were authorized to conquer western Venezuela**. The German banking house acquired the right to colonize the Lake

Maracaibo region from Coro to the Guajira Peninsula. They named the German Ambrosio Alfinger as governor. When Alfinger arrived February 24, 1529, he ordered Ampiés out and organized the export of native Americans as slaves to the Caribbean islands. He also undertook three expeditions from Coro, all to find the "South Sea" or Pacific Ocean. One charted the Lake Maracaibo basin, another explored westward into eastern Colombia, perhaps as far as the Magdalena River and the present-day department of Santander. On the return through Norte de Santander Alfinger was wounded by natives and died near Pamplona in 1533.

1531

September 9. **The crown petitioned Rome to make Santa Marta a bishopric.** Pope Clement VII complied January 10, 1534.

1533

June 1. **Pedro de Heredia, who had been authorized to colonize Nueva Andalucía, or western Colombia, officially founded Cartagena.** Cartagena's port made it a logical choice for settlement. Heredia had great success in Cartagena, overseeing expeditions to surrounding areas in 1533-37 and after 1540, the most important of which found the gold-laden Sinú burial grounds. Heredia was unusual in being able hold on to his settlement even though it was not the basis of further conquests in the interior. He drowned in 1554 on his way to Spain to answer charges against his government. In October of 1533, Spain petitioned Rome to make Cartagena a bishopric, which Pope Clement VII ratified in his bull of April 24, 1534.

1534-36

Sebastián de Belalcázar explored and conquered Ecuador and southern Colombia. Organizing an expedition from his lieutenant-governorship of Piura in Peru, Belalcázar carried out the conquest of the area around Quito. He did not have permission from his chief **Francisco Pizarro** and his independent action brought about his eventual dismissal by the latter. When **Pedro de Alvarado** and **Diego de Almagro** appeared in Quito and made a separate pact, Belalcázar had to subordinate himself again to Pizarro. In order to escape Pizarro's authority and control, Belalcázar kept moving north and eventually carved out a place for himself in southern Colombia.

February–March 1534. Belalcázar began the conquest of Ecuador. The Cañaris joined forces with Belalcázar against their Inca overlords.

May 3. The Battle of Tiocajas scattered the native American resistance and left Belalcázar's forces in control of Quito.

August 15. Diego de Almagro chartered the foundation of Santiago de Quito on the site of present-day Riobamba. His precipitous arrival and assumption of command from Belalcázar was intended to block Alvarado's participation in the conquest of Peru, that is, to leave this project in his and Francisco Pizarro's hands. Alvarado reached an appropriate settlement with Almagro and returned to Guatemala much richer. Many of his men, however, remained and went on to participate in the conquest of southern Colombia by Belalcázar.

December 6. Belalcázar chartered a second Quito, at a more appropriate site than the first. Earlier, on August 28, while in Riobamba, Alvarado ordered the foundation of San Francisco de Quito in honor of Francisco Pizarro. He designated the town councilmen. But the actual on-site foundation and inscription of the 204 *vecinos* (Spanish residents) was carried out in December by Belalcázar on the site of what had been **Atahualpa**'s northern capital.

February–June 1535. Belalcázar dispatched Pedro de Añasco and then Juan de Ampudia north into southern Colombia to prepare the way for his forthcoming expedition.

August. Belalcázar founded Santiago de Guayaquil as the appropriate port for the entrance of people and merchandise on their way to Quito and the highlands.

Early 1536. Belalcázar departed Quito on his

expedition of conquest to southern Colombia.

July 25. Traditional date given for Belalcázar's foundation of Cali.

December 24. Belalcázar founded Popayán. The distribution of lots and assignment of councilmen, however, was carried out January 13, 1537, by his subordinate, Juan de Ampudia.

1535-39

The conquest of the Muisca. This span of years marks the uncoordinated but concurrent exploration and conquest of much of the highland interior of Colombia. Three separate expeditions went out almost simultaneously to subdue the last major undiscovered native American civilization, the Muiscas of Colombia's Eastern Cordillera.

1535. In Santa Marta Pedro Fernández de Lugo, the new governor, arrived with a large contingent that strained local resources. An expedition to the interior was a logical solution, and **Gonzalo Jiménez de Quesada** was given command. In Coro, Venezuela, **Nicolás Féderman** and Jorge Espira began a two-pronged conquest of the highland interior. Féderman proceeded west and then planned to ascend the Magdalena River, but he found his way blocked by the Spanish at Santa Marta. He returned to Coro. Espira headed south and then southwest across the Venezuelan and Colombian *llanos.* He and a few survivors struggled back to Coro in 1538 without much to show for their effort.

1536. With a *residencia* or judicial review of his term in office looming, Féderman fled and led his followers across the *llanos* in the direction of Espira's expedition. They crossed paths without ever meeting.

April 5. Jiménez de Quesada's expeditionary force departed Santa Marta. They spent the next eleven months struggling up the Magdalena River before reaching the highlands near present-day Vélez. Only 200 of the original 670 Spaniards survived the march.

August 20, 1537. Jiménez's forces routed the Muisca in the Battle of Hunza near Tunja. The zaque or Muisca overlord, Quemuenchatocha, was made prisoner.

August 6, 1538. Traditional date for the founding of Santa Fé de Bogotá. Jiménez named the region he had conquered the kingdom of New Granada after his home province. During the conquest Jiménez's group gathered up 200,000 pesos in gold and 1,815 large emeralds.

February 1539. Both the Féderman and Belalcázar expeditions arrived in Bogotá to find that Jiménez had arrived almost two years earlier. Féderman had followed the curve of the Eastern Cordillera as he worked his way across the Venezuelan and Colombian *llanos.* When he encountered gold ornaments among the native Americans, he turned west and ascended the Andes toward the presumed source. From Popayán Belalcázar had crossed the Central Cordillera and descended the upper Magdalena River Valley on its west bank. Belalcázar arrived on the Sabana de Bogotá a few days after Féderman. With a parity of forces, the leaders of the three groups decided not to fight but to travel together to Spain to plead their individual cases before royal officials.

April 27. The three conquistadors rechartered Bogotá as a city and assigned positions and lots to those of their followers who wished to remain. Most of Jiménez's and Férderman's followers stayed, but far fewer of Belalcázar's did.

1538

Audiencia of Panama began to function. It included everything south of Nicaragua and the coast of Cartagena to the Río de la Plata. Venezuela remained under the audiencia of Santo Domingo. A reorganization occurred in 1542.

1540

Francisco Pizarro named his brother Gonzalo governor of Quito.

1541-43

Gonzalo Pizarro began an expedition to explore east of Quito in a search of a rumored "Land of Cinnamon." After descending the eastern slope of the Andes by way of the Napo River, Pizarro dispatched **Francisco de Orellana** in a brigantine with orders to return to the base camp after twelve days. But he found it impossible to retrace his route. Continuing downstream, Orellana entered the Amazon on February 11, 1542, and finally reached the Atlantic on August 26, 1542. Pizarro retraced his steps arriving in Quito June 1543.

1544-89

Period of Venezuelan Town Foundation. The movement of settlers into the Segovian Highlands away from Coro on the coast led to the establishment of Venezuela's most important Andean towns.

1545. Juan de Carvajal founded El Tocuyo.

1552. Barquisimeto was established.

1555. Valencia was chartered.

1558. Mérida and Trujillo were settled.

1567. Diego de Losada founded Caracas, and Alonso Pacheco established Maracaibo.

1589. Caracas's port was located at La Guaira.

1544-95

Spanish defense of northern South America. French, English, and Dutch attacks led the Spanish to develop the trans-Atlantic convoy (*flota*) system and to build fortifications to protect Havana, Santo Domingo, San Juan de Puerto Rico, Cartagena, Portobelo, and San Juan de Ulúa.

1544. The French corsair Roberto Val sacked Cartagena.

1559. The French sacked Cartagena.

1567. The French plundered Coro, Venezuela.

1568. During his third slave-trading voyage to the Caribbean, John Hawkins captured Riohacha, site of a pearl fishery, and coerced the citizens into purchasing some of his slaves. After threatening to attack Santa Marta, he sold additional slaves there.

February 9-11, 1586. Sir Francis Drake captured Cartagena. He left in mid-April after burning part of the city and exacting a large

ransom.

May 29, 1595. The English corsair Amyas Preston entered Caracas, which was plundered and burned. He burned Coro in mid-June.

December 1, 1595. During his last, ill-fated expedition to the Caribbean, Drake captured Riohacha. After burning the city, he occupied Santa Marta but left (December 21) after finding nothing of value.

1546-1606

Ecuadorian Town Foundation.

1546-48. Alonso de Mercadillo founded Loja.

April 12, 1557. Gil Ramírez Dávalos established Cuenca in response to the orders of the Marqués de Cañete, the third viceroy of Peru.

1588-89. Riobamba was given municipal status.

December 8, 1595. Damián Meneses settled the gold mining town of Zaruma. Gold strikes quickly followed at Zamora and Gualaceo.

September 18, 1606. Cristóbal de Troya chartered Ibarra at the request of the audiencia of Quito.

1546

August 22-27. **In response to Spain's request Pope Paul III made Popayán a bishopric.**

1549

The audiencia of New Granada was established with its capital at Bogotá. It embraced the coast of Cartagena, the Magdalena and Cauca river valleys, and the Colombian *llanos.* Large areas of the audiencia remained unsettled and unconquered until the eighteenth century.

1563

Northern South America underwent administrative reorganization. New audiencias were decreed for Panama and Quito. The latter's jurisdiction covered an area much larger than modern Ecuador. In addition, it included southern Colombia--Buga, Cali, Popayán, Pasto, and the Pacific Coast to Buenaventura--and northern Peru to the Marañón River. New Granada received a captain-general who was independent of the viceroy in Lima. Andrés Diez Venero de Leiva was the first, and he served a decade in Bogotá before advancing to a position on the Council of the Indies. Venezuela continued under the audiencia of Santo Domingo. This administrative arrangement endured until the eighteenth century. Bogotá also became an ecclesiastical see and was from the start an archbishopric.

1564

February 14. **Andrés Diez Venero de Leiva, New Granada's first captain general and president, arrived in Bogotá.** He was the first in a succession of sixteenth-century *presidentes letrados* (lawyer-presidents) whose legal training enabled them to limit *encomendero* power and influence and establish royal authority.

1570

Shipwreck along Ecuadorian north coast freed a cargo of African slaves. They conquered much of the province of Esmeraldas, and their *zambo* (Spanish for African/Indian mixture) descendants controlled much of the province years later.

1593

First *corregidores de indios* appointed in New Granada. These newly created royal officials were to collect tribute from the native Americans in place of the encomenderos. This interposition was one of the ways the crown gradually asserted control and limited the power of the encomenderos.

1595

March 22. **Sir Walter Raleigh arrived in Trinidad to begin a search for a wealthy kingdom called Manoa believed to exist in northern South America.** In Trinidad he captured Antonio de Berrío, governor of the island, who had engaged in a similar quest and provided additional information to the Englishman. With five boats and about one hundred men, Raleigh sailed up the Orinoco River to its confluence with the Caroní. Soon afterward, his supplies nearly exhausted, Raleigh ended his search. A second expedition by Raleigh to the region in 1617 also ended in failure.

1596-1697

European rivals of Spain established a presence in northern South America. On the periphery of the Spanish empire the Dutch, English, and French planted permanent colonies in the Lesser Antilles, the Guianas, and Central America. Piracy, sugar production based on slave labor, brazilwood, and contraband trade with the Spanish became the mainstays of their colonies.

1596-1620. The Dutch settled what in 1790 would become Georgetown, attempted settlements elsewhere in the Guianas, and developed the salt industry at Araya on the Venezuelan coast.

1616. The Dutch occupied Essequibo.

1630. The British settled Providence Island, off the coast of Nicaragua, and began to target Spanish control of the Caribbean coast of Central America.

1648. Under the terms of the Treaty of Munster, Spain recognized the Dutch occupation of Guiana east of the Essequibo River.

1668. In Venezuela the French pirate Gramont sacked and burned Trujillo and attacked Maracaibo, Gibraltar, and La Guaira.

1670. Henry Morgan sacked Santa Marta and Riohacha. Other buccaneers plundered Panama and Maracaibo.

1695. The French corsair Jean Bautista Ducasse sacked Cartagena.

May 6, 1697. Jean Bernard Desjeans, Baron de Pointis, and Ducasse, with a fleet of sixty ships, conquered Cartagena and made off with 10 million pesos in booty.

1605-28

Juan de Borja served as captain-general of New Granada and president of the audiencia of

Bogotá. The first in a long line of *capa y espada* (military) captains-general and presidents in New Granada, Borja was energetic and effective. He established the Tribunal de Cuentas (1605) for the proper auditing of royal income and expenses, got the royal mint operating in Bogotá (1620), and put an end to the rebellion of the fierce Indians known as the Pijao (1557-1612). Borja's war (1608-12) against them in the Central Cordillera reestablished communication between Bogotá and Popayán and points south to Quito.

1605

September 26. **A tribunal of the Holy Office of the Inquisition was established in Cartagena.** It was given jurisdiction over New Granada, Venezuela, Panama, and the islands of the Caribbean.

1612

Neiva was re-founded. As the war with the Pijao drew to a close, Diego de Ospina re-established the town of Neiva in the Upper Magdalena River Valley.

1615-36

Antonio de Morga served as president of the audiencia of Quito. The exceptionally long government of activist president Morga paralleled the strong administration of Juan de Borja (1605-28) in New Granada. Morga floated various schemes to organize coastal defenses and to plant colonies north of Quito, but without much support from the viceroy in Lima.

1624

August 25-26. **The Dutch sacked and burned Guayaquil before being repelled by its Spanish defenders.** The event led Spanish officials to attempt the conquest of Esmeraldas, the Ecuadorian province north from Guayaquil along the

coast, which was strongly resisted by the Malaba, a small indigenous group.

1675

November 2. **Medellín was formally established in the valley of Aburrá.** A town had been founded nearby in 1616, and about 3,000 settlers were living in the fertile valley when Medellín, destined to become Colombia's second largest city, was founded.

1695

The Consulado of Bogotá was established. The twenty founding merchants were allowed to regulate trade to the interior from Cartagena in exchange for paying a tax on the merchandise off-loaded by the Spanish fleet. The War of the Spanish Succession, however, disrupted the sailing of the annual fleets and the consulado was suppressed in 1713.

1717-23

The Viceroyalty of New Granada was erected with its capital in Bogotá. Except for the audiencia of Panama, all of northern South America came under the jurisdiction of the new viceroy. The audiencia of Quito was suppressed. But high administrative costs led to abolition of the viceroyalty. Quito's audiencia was re-established.

1728

The Caracas Company was chartered. It was given a monopoly over the cacao trade between Venezuela and Spain in exchange for defending the Venezuelan coast, preventing contraband, and increasing cacao production and the number of slaves. It lost its trade monopoly in 1784.

1739

New Granada was again raised to the rank of a viceroyalty. Venezuela and the audiencias of

Panama and Quito came under its jurisdiction, although Venezuelan judicial cases went to Santo Domingo, and Caracas was no longer dependent on Bogotá after 1742.

1741

March 20. **A large British fleet, commanded by Admiral Edward Vernon, began a bombardment of Cartagena.** The British expedition also consisted of more than 10,000 British and colonial soldiers and marines. Led by the newly arrived viceroy, Sebastián de Eslava, and by a veteran naval officer, Blas de Lezo, the Spanish defenders were able to repel the British attackers, who had withdrawn by early May. The attack on Cartagena had been preceded by the capture of Portobelo, Panama, in November 1739. Both engagements took place during the War of Jenkins' Ear.

1749-51

Venezuelans rebelled against the policies of the Caracas Company. Losing his government position in Panaquire to a Caracas Company official, Juan Francisco de León organized a march on Caracas where royal officials went through the motions of accepting his demands, ending the Company's monopoly privileges and semi-government functions. León marched on Caracas again when the accord was not honored, but a new governor and 1,500 soldiers easily defeated León's force.

1765

May–June. **Riots broke out in Quito.** Introduction of the *aguardiente* (liquor) monopoly and the institution of a more efficient collection of *acabala* (sales) taxes by the viceroy of New Granada aroused elite groups as well as the masses. The measures were suspended. A divergence between the elite and the lowborn, however, led to a gradual re-assertion of royal control and the implementation of the measures. With the audiencia of

Quito purged of opposition members, and the arrival of soldiers on September 1, 1766, the *aguardiente* monopoly was reinstated on February 14, 1767.

1776

Intendancy of Venezuela created. Six provinces—Caracas, Barinas, Maracaibo, Guyana, Cumaná, and Margarita/Trinidad—were brought together under one fiscal administrator residing in Caracas. The reorganization foreshadowed further centralization when the captaincy-general and audiencia were created in 1777 and 1786.

1776-77

Trade was opened between Santa Marta and Riohacha and numerous Spanish ports from which it had formerly been barred. The rest of the viceroyalty of New Granada, except for Venezuela, was incorporated into the system of free trade with Spain by a decree of October 12, 1778. Free trade for Venezuela, as well as New Spain, was authorized in 1789.

1777

Venezuela was made a captaincy-general. Political and military authority over the provinces of Guyana, Cumaná, and Maracaibo, and the islands of Trinidad and Margarita, was added to the jurisdiction of the captain-general of Caracas, who became the captain-general of Venezuela.

1778-82

The Comunero Rebellion convulsed New Granada. Regent and Visitor-General Juan Francisco Gutiérrez de Piñeres began the implementation of changes associated with the Bourbon Reforms--tax increases, new assessments, more restrictive tobacco and liquor monopolies, and a preference for peninsulars over creoles in government positions. The measures aroused a broad-based opposition movement that began in the

Socorro–San Gil region and rapidly spread through much of New Granada.

January 1778. Gutiérrez de Piñeres arrived in Bogotá and began his review of royal government. His administrative and fiscal restructuring alarmed a wide spectrum of interest groups.

October 20, 1780. Violent protests took place in Mogotes.

March 16, 1781. Riots broke out in Socorro. Royal liquor and tobacco monopoly offices were sacked.

Late May. The rebellion spread throughout the Eastern Cordillera and culminated in a march of 20,000 armed protesters on Bogotá. Camped out at Zipaquirá, they awaited discussions and a satisfactory settlement with royal officials, most of whom had fled.

June 4-8. Juan Francisco Berbeo and Archbishop Antonio Caballero y Góngora, Comunero leader and royal representative respectively, drafted capitulations suspending the onerous measures.

Summer. Caballero y Góngora toured the main centers of protest and preached peace and obedience to royal authority. He gradually reintroduced some of the offending fiscal measures but suspended several others. He chose not to prosecute those participants who accepted royal authority, thereby splitting the Comunero coalition. A rump group led by José Antonio Galán continued the rebellion.

October 13. Galán was captured in Onzaga and executed on February 1, 1782.

June 1782. Caballero y Góngora became viceroy of New Granada.

1782-89

Antonio Caballero y Góngora served as viceroy of New Granada. His finesse in ending the Comunero Rebellion earned Caballero y Góngora the unusual appointment—as a cleric in the secular age of the late Bourbon period—of viceroy. He undertook reforms that would win the support of creoles, and refused to introduce the intendancy system, which would have tightened

fiscal administration in New Granada. He sponsored the Botanical Expedition of José Celestino Mutis, as well as the engineering missions of Juan Antonio Mon y Velarde and Juan José D'Elhuyar to Antioquia and Tolima. Nevertheless, he increased the Spanish military presence in the interior and reorganized the military in the event armed force became necessary.

1784

The Caracas Company was abolished. Its inability to supply needed goods and slaves along with the move toward freer trade within the Spanish empire ended its exclusive monopoly over the Venezuelan cacao trade to Spain.

1786

The audiencia of Caracas was created. Its judicial authority extended over the captaincy-general of Venezuela.

1787-88

In Quito royal authorities arrested Eugenio de Santa Cruz y Espejo on charges of subversion. Ecuador's most famous intellectual from the colonial period was shipped to Bogotá where his trial resulted in his acquittal. His friendship there with **Antonio Nariño** and Francisco Antonio Zea further radicalized him. On his return to Quito in 1791 he published Ecuador's first newspaper and became director of its library.

1793

Antonio Nariño published a Spanish version of the French *Declaration of the Rights of Man* in Bogotá. Imprisoned in 1794 and shipped to Spain, Nariño escaped and returned to New Granada in 1797 and later participated in the wars of independence.

1793-95

Commercial consulados were established in Caracas and Cartagena in 1793 and 1795

respectively. Made up of an elite group of merchants, the consulado was a court of first instance to settle commercial matters—last wills of members, contracts, establishing and liquidating companies, insurance, bankruptcy, and shipping—and to stimulate economic development. The Caracas consulado had representatives in the ports of Cumaná, Barcelona, La Guaira, Puerto Cabello, and Maracaibo, while Cartagena's had twenty-one agents in the towns in the interior of New Granada as well as in Panama and Guayaquil.

1795

May 10. **A revolt of blacks and mulattoes erupted in Coro, center of Venezuela's sugar industry.** The uprising was led by Leonardo Chirinos, a free *zambo*, and José Caridad González, a free black, and reflected the influence of the ideas of the French and Haitian revolutions. Approximately three hundred slaves and free blacks sacked haciendas and killed landowners, but the revolt was quickly suppressed.

1797

July 12. **Authorities discovered a conspiracy in La Guaira, Venezuela.** Led by Manuel Gual, a retired army captain, and José María España, a magistrate in Macuto, the plotters envisioned the establishment of a republican government, the abolition of slavery and Indian tribute, freedom of trade, and tax reform. However, the plotters' call for racial equality and appeals to the rights of man alarmed creole property-owners, who asserted their loyalty to the crown. Gual fled Venezuela and died, probably of poison, in 1800. España also fled but returned to Venezuela, where he was betrayed and hanged (May 8, 1799).

1799-1804

Alexander von Humboldt's five-year scientific mission to Spanish America brought the region international attention. In northern South America Humboldt visited Caracas, the Orinoco, Cartagena, Bogotá, and Quito during the years 1799–1803. His other stops included Cuba, Lima, Acapulco, Mexico City, and Veracruz.

Peru
1522-1803

Since the time of **Balboa's** discovery of the Pacific Ocean in 1513, the Spanish in Panama had reports from native informants of a rich kingdom to the southeast called "Biru." But the difficulties in getting there delayed the conquest for two decades. The contrary winds and currents and the geographical barriers of the lands in between required greater financial resources and organizational skills than were initially available. Nevertheless, the early expeditions carried back enough evidence to warrant follow-up ventures. The elements necessary for success were finally in place by the time of **Francisco Pizarro's** third expedition (1531). He had assembled a company of men with exceptional cohesion and focus that overcame the obstacles. During his return to Spain in 1528-30 he had recruited partisans from his home town of Trujillo and province of Extremadura, including his three brothers. He had concluded a *capitulación* or agreement with the crown, which gave his and **Diego de Almagro's** companies exclusive rights over the venture and which promised aid in the acquisition of horses, guns, and supplies. The hoped-for titles, rents, annuities, and income would come, but only if they were successful in finding and taking the riches they said existed. With the Spaniards' capture of the Inca emperor **Atahualpa** at Cajamarca in 1532, they complied with their part of the bargain with the crown and forever changed the world of Andean South America. In exchange for his promised freedom, Atahualpa ordered that his kingdom's gold and silver be sent to Cajamarca, and precious metals flowed in from all directions. The Spanish had found the linchpin that would bring them their richest prize in the New World. Mexico's precious metal production would not exceed Peru's until the end of the seventeenth century.

Atahualpa's treasure made the 168 Spaniards

at Cajamarca singularly wealthy and brought a stampede of others who wanted to share in the good fortune. It also increased the envy and ill-will of those left out, among whom were those in Almagro's company. While Almagro had helped organize and finance Pizarro's three expeditions, his group had arrived at Cajamarca late and did not share in the distribution of the booty. Most of Peru's best encomiendas and newly created positions in the recently founded towns went to Pizarro and his company. Nevertheless, Almagro's forces were initially satisfied to undertake the conquest of Chile in the expectation of repeating Pizarro's exploits there, which was not to be. They returned empty handed, after suffering great hardship, and were determined to fight to get what they saw as their fair share of Peru's wealth. Although they helped break the Inca siege of the Spanish trapped at Cuzco, they lost the Battle of Salinas to the Pizarros, and **Hernando Pizarro** had Almagro executed. Without their leader the forces of Almagro lost their power and legitimacy to enforce their claims to Peru's wealth. In a fit of desperation that precipitated a new order in Peru, Almagro's mestizo son avenged his father's death when he assassinated the Pizarro clan-leader Francisco in Lima in 1541. With Juan already dead, Hernando away in Spain, and **Gonzalo** in Quito, there were no Pizarros present to counterattack. Representatives of the monarchy quickly asserted royal authority and filled the vacuum. They worked to displace the Pizarro group by redistributing its encomiendas and positions to others. When the New Laws were issued in 1542 to limit the power of encomenderos, the stage was set for a rebellion. Gonzalo, who had been designated by Francisco in his will as the successor to the governorship of Peru, but who was denied that office and banished to his estates in Charcas, became the natural leader of those rebelling against crown authority. While Gonzalo was initially successful, and even defeated and executed the Viceroy **Blasco Núñez de Vela** in 1546, royal authority gradually undermined and overcame the group's solidarity. Without royal valida-

tion no group could hold its power and position from the push of outsiders and the defection of insiders.

As crown officials extended royal authority over Peru, they organized the kingdom, including its native population, for the benefit of themselves and their king. The presence of a highly disciplined native population already effectively organized by the Inca to deliver labor and services, coupled with the discovery of a mountain of silver at Potosí in 1545, largely determined Peru's role in the Spanish empire for the rest of the colonial period. Its function was to supply the mother country with bullion. That river of precious metals was the lifeblood of the Spanish empire. The key administrative problem was making sure the bullion got back to Spain. As far as Peru was concerned, this involved maintaining control over the Pacific coast of South and Mesoamerica and the Isthmus of Panama, and having a fleet system that could transport the bullion back to Spain. Peru was geographically self-contained, isolated, and easily defended as long as Spain controlled the isthmus, the Philippines, Chile, and Argentina. This guaranteed that the Pacific would be a Spanish lake even though buccaneers of various European powers occasionally made their way through the Straits of Magellan and raided there. But without permanent settlements or bases on the Pacific coast they were condemned to flee westward and to return to their home base by sailing around the world, a daunting proposition keeping most at bay. Even when Spain declared bankruptcy, American treasure constantly flowed back and replenished Spanish coffers. This never-ending stream, although occasionally interrupted, guaranteed the Spanish empire exceptional leverage in its imperial operations.

Peru's wealth and organized native population offered vast possibilities for individual Spanish enrichment. Spanish bureaucrats eagerly sought government positions there, especially as governors and *corregidores de indios*. Great fortunes were made distributing merchandise to native American communities at inflated prices.

Spanish administration stamped out native resistance and regularized native American labor during the viceregal reign (1569-81) of **Francisco de Toledo**. He captured and executed **Túpac Amaru**, the last Inca emperor, in 1572 and reinstated the *mita*, the Inca system of draft labor. This solved the labor shortage at Potosí by making thousands available annually for work there, many of whom traveled hundreds of miles with their families to work in the mine. Other than the rebellion of 1780-81, when some native Americans again rallied under the name Túpac Amaru, and the imperial reorganization of the late eighteenth century, there were not many dramatic changes after the sixteenth century.

1522

First Spanish attempt to reach Peru. Pedro Arias de Ávila (Pedrarias), captain-general and governor of Panama, agreed to allow Pascual de Andagoya to explore southeast from Panama down the Pacific coast. Andagoya got as far as the Río Baudó in the Colombian Chocó before falling ill.

1524-26

Francisco Pizarro's first expedition failed to reach Peru. Andagoya's illness led Pedrarias to put **Francisco Pizarro** in charge of a second expedition to Peru, Pizarro's first. Departing from Panama in November, Pizarro pushed even farther south than Andagoya and discovered the San Juan River just north of present-day Buenaventura. He spent more than a year exploring the Colombian coast before returning to Panama in the spring of 1526 without reaching Peru.

1526

Summer. **Pizarro launched his second expedition.** In company with **Diego de Almagro** he sailed from Panama in two small ships with a force of 160 men and a few horses.

Fall. Pizarro's force seized gold figurines from the native population at the mouth of the San Juan River. Almagro returned to Panama with the gold in the hopes of attracting more participants. Pizarro's force continued south in the one remaining ship and occupied the Colombian island of Gallo in the Gulf of Tumaco while Bartolomé Ruiz, the ship's pilot, reconnoitered south down the Ecuadorian coast.

1527

Pizarro reached Peru. About the same time that Ruiz returned from his reconnaissance and reported that there was an advanced native American civilization to the south, two more ships arrived from Panama with orders from Pedro de los Ríos, governor of Castilla de Oro (Panama), for all to return. The Gallo Island climate and lack of supplies had taken their toll. Many had died and others had become ill. Most had had enough hardship and were ready to comply. But Pizarro and twelve others ignored the orders to return. After relocating the thirteen to the more promising island of Gorgona farther north, Pizarro dispatched Ruiz back to Panama for more supplies and reinforcements. Seven months later Ruiz returned to Gorgona with provisions but with no additional participants. Nevertheless, Pizarro sailed on to Peru, landing at Túmbez, where he exchanged presents with the local cacique before reconnoitering the northern third of the Peruvian coast. He took three native American boys with him, so they could learn Spanish and serve as interpreters if and when a third expedition took place. He and his company returned to Panama at the beginning of 1528.

1528

Pizarro failed to convince Governor Ríos to approve his third expedition to Peru. As a result, he decided to seek approval at the Spanish court. He took with him some native Americans, three llamas, gold and silver ornaments, and cloth, all from Peru and all designed to win support and funding for the undertaking. Upon arrival in Seville, Pizarro was jailed for the collective debts of the Panamanian colony but then was freed by orders of the Royal Council. Later at Toledo Pizarro briefed Emperor **Charles V** on Peru and plans for a third expedition.

1529

July 26. **At Toledo the crown and Pizarro reached an agreement for the conquest of Peru.** While dated July 26, the *capitulación* was not signed until August 17. Its many clauses offered extensive possibilities for Pizarro's future enrichment but only if the conquest was successful.

1530

January. **Pizarro recruited participants for his third expedition in his native province.** This core group of regional followers brought to the enterprise an usual amount of solidarity that accounted for much of its future success. It was the culmination of the Mediterranean mercantile partnership or company adapted to the possibilities of the military conquest of the New World. Shortly thereafter Pizarro's company sailed for Panama.

1531

January. **Pizarro's third expedition began.** Pizarro readied three ships with 180 men and 27 horses and sailed from Panama for Peru but landed on Puná Island, off the Gulf of Guayaquil, where he and his group suffered through several months of attacks from native Americans. Almagro remained in Panama to recruit more participants.

November. **Sebastián de Belalcázar** and his company of 12 horses and 30 men arrived from Nicaragua and augmented Pizarro's numerically thin forces. As a result, he entered the expedition as a captain or leader with rights to a larger share

of any booty acquired.

December 1. **Hernando de Soto** also arrived at Puná at a critical juncture. His company of about 100 men and 25 horses in two ships helped Pizarro's forces repel the attacks of native Americans. Soto also was made a captain or principal in the expedition.

1532

April. **Pizarro's expedition finally reached the Peruvian mainland**, entering Inca territory near Túmbez.

May 16. The expedition began its move south.

November 16. The Spanish captured the Inca emperor **Atahualpa**. **Francisco Pizarro**'s force of 168 men overwhelmed Atahualpa's entourage at Cajamarca. The standard Spanish practice of holding a leader hostage and making him do their bidding unfolded according to plan. The imprisoned Atahualpa agreed to Spanish ransom demands and his orders to bring in Inca gold circulated throughout the Inca empire. The Spanish waited eight months at Cajamarca for reinforcements and for the ransom to arrive. In the meantime they exploited divisions among the Andeans, especially between the followers of Huascar and Atahualpa. The latter, fearful the Spanish would replace him with Huascar, his half-brother, secretly had Huascar executed.

1533

January. **For the next six months Francisco Pizarro dispatched scouting parties.** His brother **Hernando** oversaw the inspection of the sacred Inca shrine of Pachacámac near present-day Lima. There he took an active role in the collection of Inca treasure, and with others he desecrated the wooden statue, representing the deity, before shocked natives.

April 14. **Diego de Almagro**'s force of some 200 men arrived in Cajamarca from Panama. They would not share in the division of **Atahualpa**'s treasure, and this estranged them from the followers of Pizarro.

Mid-May. The Spanish began melting down and assaying Atahualpa's treasure.

July 16. The smelting operation was completed and its distribution among the 168 who captured Atahualpa was begun.

July 25. The distribution of the treasure among the 168 was completed. Rich beyond compare, they became models for all others who came to the New World in search of wealth.

July 26. The Spanish executed Atahualpa, spurred by rumors of large-scale native troop movements and by the Inca ruler's bestowal of gifts to rivals of the Pizarros.

August 11. **Francisco Pizarro**'s force left Cajamarca to begin their conquest of the rest of the Inca empire.

October 12. The Spanish reached Jauja in the central highlands east of present-day Lima. It now had its first dedication as a Spanish city.

October 28. Francisco Pizarro's contingent departed from Jauja for the Inca capital of Cuzco.

November 8. **Hernando de Soto**'s advance party of mounted Spaniards was ambushed at Vilcaconga. Several Spaniards lost their lives to boulders pushed down from on high; others died in hand-to-hand fighting.

November 15. The Spanish entered Cuzco.

December. The Spanish installed Manco Inca from the Huascar faction as the new Inca ruler.

1534

February 22. **The gold and silver collected at Cuzco was distributed.** The Spanish had begun the process of smelting and assaying the precious metals collected in and around Cuzco.

March 23. Cuzco was chartered as a Spanish city.

April 25. Returning from Cuzco, **Francisco Pizarro** rededicated the centrally located Jauja with an eye to making it his capital.

May 21. In Spain **Hernando Pizarro** signed a *capitulación* for **Diego de Almagro** to conquer 200 leagues beyond Francisco Pizarro's Peruvian

conquest. This became the basis for Almagro's unsuccessful expedition to Chile (1535-37).

1535

January 18. **Francisco Pizarro formally founded Lima, Ciudad de los Reyes (City of the Kings), as the Spanish capital of Peru**. He located it on the coast rather than in the highlands because it was easily defended there and accessible from Panama.

March. Farther north, also on the coast, Pizarro formally established the town of Trujillo, named after his hometown. Diego de Almagro had actually chosen the site and laid it out near the old Chimú capital of Chan Chan in 1534. Trujillo

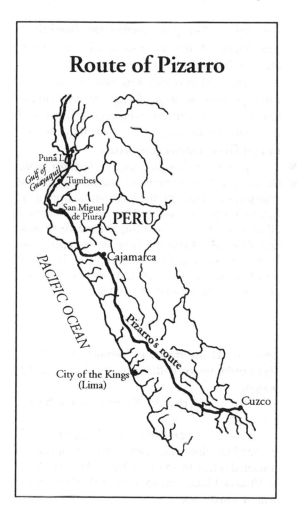

Route of Pizarro

became the dominant city in northern Peru and an obligatory stopover on the overland route to and from Lima.

1536

May. **The Inca rebelled**. When Manco Inca perceived that the Spanish wanted him only as a puppet ruler and not as an ally, he moved his people to fight, besieging Cuzco with upward of 200,000 for ten months. The 190 Spaniards trapped there were cut off until reinforcements arrived from Lima, Almagro's expedition returned from Chile, and harvest time depleted Inca forces.

1537

January 8. **The pope named the Dominican friar Vicente Valverde bishop of Cuzco**. It was the first diocese created in Peru.

March. Manco Inca and some of his forces withdrew from the siege of Cuzco to the mountain fortress of Vilcabamba, where an independent Inca state continued until 1572 when the viceroy **Francisco de Toledo** destroyed it.

April 18. About the time the Spanish broke the siege at Cuzco, Almagro and his disgruntled veterans marched into the Inca capital from their failed Chilean expedition. They seized it, claimed all of southern Peru, and imprisoned **Hernando** and **Gonzalo Pizarro**. Gonzalo escaped, and Hernando was freed on condition that he would return to Spain. Once freed he did not keep his promise, to the chagrin of Almagro.

1538

April 26. **At the Battle of Salinas**, near Cuzco, **Hernando Pizarro** defeated the forces of **Almagro**.

July 8. Hernando Pizarro had Almagro executed.

Mid-year. Pedro Anzures de Campo Redondo founded La Plata (sometimes called Chuquisaca; renamed Sucre in 1839) in Upper Peru (Bolivia) as Villa de Plata. It would later (1552) become the seat of a bishopric.

1539

January 9. **Francisco Pizarro established Ayacucho (Huamanga) as San Juan de la Frontera in the highlands of south central Peru**. Alonso de Alvarado moved it to its present location on April 25, 1540. Halfway between Cuzco and Lima, Ayacucho functioned as a stopover between the two. In the colonial period it was an important administrative center and the residence for miners from Huancavelica.

1540

August 15. **The Spanish established Arequipa** in southern Peru, the country's most important city after Lima. During the colonial period its wines dominated the market of Upper Peru (Bolivia).

1541

May 13. **Lima was designated the second bishopric in Peru**.

June 26. In Lima, partisans of **Diego de Almagro's** mestizo son, Diego the Younger, assassinated the Pizarro clan-leader **Francisco**. That opened the way for royal officials to redistribute the wealth and power, and to assert royal authority in a more thoroughgoing fashion. It also set the stage for a full-scale rebellion against the crown on the part of those displaced.

1542

September 16. **Battle of Chupas**. Near Huamanga, Governor Cristóval Vaca de Castro defeated the forces of Diego de Almagro the Younger.

1543

Lima audiencia created.

1544

March 4. **Viceroy Blasco Núñez de Vela arrived in Peru at Túmbez**. He began enforcement of the New Laws (1542), which reduced the power of the encomenderos. Suddenly he faced a full-scale rebellion against crown authority. **Gonzalo Pizarro** emerged as its leader.

September 18. The *oidores* of the audiencia arrested and imprisoned the viceroy Núñez de Vela.

October. The *oidores* had the viceroy forcibly shipped out of Lima with a presumed destination back to Spain. But the ship's captain freed Núñez de Vela at Túmbez, where the latter began to amass men and material to retake the viceroyalty.

1545

April. **Silver strike at Potosí.** A mountain of silver was discovered at El Cerro Rico (Rich Hill) de Potosí, the site of the single greatest source of precious metals in the Spanish empire. Potosí as an urban nucleus at the base of the mountain became the Villa Imperial (Imperial Town), with 100,000 people by the beginning of the seventeenth century. Half of all the silver produced in the New World before 1650 came from the sole district of Potosí. At nearly 14,000 feet, the town had its provisions hauled in on hundreds of mule trains. Potosí was the reason for the Spanish presence in the Río de la Plata region during the sixteenth and seventeenth centuries. Towns in the northwest like Mendoza, Jujuy, Salta, Tucumán, and Córdoba owed their existence to the market they supplied in Potosí. Buenos Aires, as Potosí's back door, was refounded in 1580 and had to be held against all enemies. The easiest way for Spain's enemies to get Potosí's silver, however, was along contraband routes that snaked their way through the port, across the pampas, and into the Andes.

Manco Inca was treacherously murdered by some of Diego de Almagro's followers who had been given refuge in the Inca's stronghold of Vilcabamba.

1546

January 18. **At the Battle of Añaquito near Quito**, Ecuador, **Gonzalo Pizarro** defeated Núñez

de Vela and then had him executed.

1547

June 30. **The royal emissary Pedro de la Gasca arrived in Túmbez, Peru.** He was sent to crush the encomendero rebellion.

1548

April 9. **Gasca defeated the rebels at Jaquijahuana, near Cuzco.** The rebel leader Gonzalo Pizarro was executed the following day.

October 20. Alonso de Mendoza founded La Paz—the future capital of modern Bolivia—to protect the road connecting Spanish Peru with the mining cities of Potosí, Porco, and La Plata in Upper Peru.

1551

May 12. **The crown ordered the creation of a university in Lima.** This decree was the genesis of the Universidad de San Marcos, but the institution languished until the late sixteenth century.

1552

Mining district in Upper Peru seized by rebels. Sebastián de Castilla, son of the Count of Gomera, became the nominal leader of those angered by their inability to acquire encomiendas. The revolt quickly spread to other sectors of Peruvian conquest society.

1553-54

Peru's civil wars came to an end. The discontent of the previous year blossomed into a full-scale rebellion as Francisco Hernández Girón, a dissatisfied encomendero, led the last major revolt against royal authority associated with the so-called civil wars. He inspired other malcontents to join and even organized a company of 300 to 400 black slaves, promising them freedom if they won. His forces dominated much of the Peruvian highlands for a year, and even threatened Lima. His defeat effectively ended early Peru's turbulent period.

1559

La Plata (Sucre today, sometimes called Chuquisaca in the colonial period) became the capital of the province and audiencia of Charcas. It oversaw much of the mining activity of Upper Peru. Officials preferred its climate and lower elevation to that of the mining sites of Potosí and Porco. The audiencia was the largest in South America until its partial dismemberment in favor of Río de la Plata in 1783.

1561

Ñulfo de Chávez founded Santa Cruz de la Sierra in the lowlands of Upper Peru (Bolivia).

1568

April 1. **The first Jesuits to serve in Spanish America arrived in Lima.**

1569

November 30. **Francisco de Toledo arrived in Lima.** Like **Antonio de Mendoza**, Mexico's first viceroy, Toledo put much of Peru's colonial administration in place during his twelve-year reign as viceroy. He had orders to introduce the amalgamation or mercury process into the Peruvian mining system, which he did with spectacular results. Potosí's silver output jumped 670 percent from 1572 to 1582.

1570

January 29. **The first New World tribunal of the Inquisition was established in Lima.**

1571

August 4. **Huancavelica was established as La Villa Rica de Oropesa.** Named in honor of Peru's new viceroy, **Francisco de Toledo**, whose father was the third count of Oropesa, Huancavelica

revitalized Peru's silver production. Huancavelica's newly discovered mercury mines had been in operation since 1563, but silver refining through amalgamation did not start at Potosí until 1571. The Huancavelica mines became essential to the refining process in Peru, supplying it with mercury and sometimes providing for New Spain's needs as well. Labor requirements at Huancavelica were met through the *mita*. Mercury poisoning resulted in the death of many workers until a new ventilation shaft was opened in 1642.

1572

September 25. **The Inca ruler Túpac Amaru was beheaded in Cuzco.** He had been captured several weeks earlier after **Viceroy Francisco de Toledo** determined to destroy the Inca enclave at Vilcabamba, which he considered a threat to Spanish authority.

October 5. **The viceroy Toledo left Cuzco for Upper Peru.** He remained until mid-1575, organizing the labor and mining system that would exploit Potosí for the next 250 years. The first silver mills in Peru specifically designed to use the amalgamation refining process were built in Potosí in this year. A royal mint was also opened in Potosí.

1574

Sebastián Barba de Padilla founded Cochabamba as Villa de Oropesa. Established on the recommendation of the viceroy **Toledo**, Cochabamba was to serve as a bulwark against a possible invasion of the highlands by the Chiriguanos. It quickly found an outlet in Potosí for its temperate climate products.

1579

February 13. **Francis Drake attacked Spanish shipping in Callao.** Earlier he had raided Valparaiso, Chile. On March 1, 1579, off the coast of Ecuador, he captured a Spanish vessel, *Nuestra*

Señora de la Concepción, laden with silver, gold, and jewels. He later crossed the Pacific and Indian oceans before arriving in England as a national hero.

1592

The Inca sculptor Tito Yupanqui finished the statue of the Virgin of Copacabana. Named after a place just south of Lake Titicaca, the statue was a good representation of the newly emerging Cuzco style among native and mestizo artisans.

1600-1604

Volcanic eruptions and earthquakes seriously damaged Arequipa and its surrounding valley.

1605

July 5. **New bishoprics were created at La Paz and Santa Cruz de la Sierra in Upper Peru.**

1606

November 1. **The city of Oruro in Upper Peru was founded. It had been a mining center since the late sixteenth century.**

1613

The Consulado (merchants' guild) of Lima was created.

1624

The Jesuits opened the University of San Francisco Xavier in La Plata.

1629

January 14. **Luis Gerónimo Fernández de Cabrera, Conde de Chinchón, assumed his duties in Lima as viceroy of Peru.** He introduced new taxes on the salary of government and church officials (*media añata, mesada eclesiástica*) and on drinking establishments (*composición de pulperías*).

1661

A tax revolt led by Antonio Gallardo broke out in La Paz.

1677

The University of San Cristóbal de Huamanga began operations in Ayacucho.

1683

October 1. Date on which a Peruvian-wide census was undertaken.

1687

October 20. **An earthquake destroyed Lima and its port Callao.** Tremors continued until December 2. Many citizens fled in panic, and the viceroy, the Duque de la Palata, was forced to camp out in the main square of Lima for more than two months. With its irrigation system also devastated, Lima had to be fed by foodstuffs, especially wheat, imported from Chile. The event marked a turning point in Chile's economic development.

1710

Potosí was overtaken by Zacatecas, Mexico, in silver production.

1730

November. **In Cochabamba the *castas* revolted against Spanish attempts to collect tribute from mestizos, who had traditionally been exempt.**

1736

The Spanish reduced the *quinto* tax on silver

produced at Potosí from a fifth to a tenth. This incentive plus increased demands on *mita* labor brought a slight increase in precious metal production.

1739

Tax revolt broke out in Oruro. Juan Vélez de Córdoba, the leader, and others plotted to restore the Inca monarchy and abolish tribute payments, the *mita*, and the forced sale of merchandise (*reparto*) to native Americans.

1742

An indigenous rebellion broke out in the jungles and mountain passes and valleys of east-central Peru. Led by Juan Santos, who claimed the name and direct ancestry of **Atahualpa**, the movement destroyed Franciscan missions in the lowlands and raided into the highlands from 1742 to 1752.

1756

The forced sale of merchandise (*reparto*) to native American communities was legalized.

1776

July 27. **Lima lost its jurisdiction over Upper Peru, Paraguay, and Buenos Aires** with the creation of the Viceroyalty of Río de la Plata.

1777

June. **The inspector general José Antonio de Areche arrived in Lima**. His program of tax increases and greater administrative control and efficiency and the failure to resolve long-standing abuses produced uprisings in the Andes that eventually culminated in the pan-Andean **Túpac Amaru** revolt (1780-82). Beginning as early as 1777 in Chayanta in Upper Peru, Tomás Catari preached a messianic message of resistance to his Aymara followers. **José Gabriel Condorcanqui**, a mestizo *curaca* (chief) and direct descendant of the Inca, represented various caciques and other native Americans. He spent much of the year in Lima trying to get the *mita* abolished as well as trying to correct other flagrant abuses.

1778-79

Condorcanqui opted for rebellion. Rebuffed by Areche and other Spanish administrators, Condorcanqui returned to the highlands and made the necessary preparations for a wide-scale revolt.

1780

Rebellion engulfed Andean Peru.
   November 4. Traditional starting date of the great revolt in highland Peru was marked by Condorcanqui's publicly taking the name of **Túpac Amaru**, the last Inca emperor, executed by the Spanish in 1572, and by his arrest of Antonio de Arriaga, the *corregidor* of Tinta, notorious for abusing and exploiting native Americans.
   November 10. The *corregidor* Arriaga was judged corrupt and coercive in forcing native Americans to buy overpriced merchandise distributed in the hated *reparto* and was hanged at Tungasuca.
   November 16. Trying to broaden the base of his movement, Túpac Amaru decreed all slaves to be free.
   December. The rebellion spread and encompassed the Lake Titicaca region in the south and the Cuzco area in the north.

1781

A new native insurrectionary movement appeared in the provinces of Sicasica, Yungas, and Pacajes. Julián Apaza, its leader, took the name Túpac Catari and associated himself with Tomás Catari and **Túpac Amaru**. Some native Americans saw their leaders as messiahs. When the rebel leader Tomás Catari was killed in January 1781, some thought that like Jesus Christ he would rise again. They clearly believed in an Inca restoration that would expel all the Spanish.

Perhaps as many as 100,000 died in the conflict. In spite of the mushrooming rebellion, government mobilization and ethnic and class rivalries doomed the revolt.

January 2-9. Túpac Amaru's rebel force of 40-60,000 besieged Cuzco, but growing opposition from royalist caciques forced him to lift the siege. Increasing violence led mestizos and creoles to withdraw their support.

February–April. Creoles in Oruro rose against European-born whites. When large numbers of Indians invaded the city, however, creoles and Europeans joined forces to resist them.

March 14. Túpac Catari's combined Aymara- and Quechua-speaking force of 10-40,000 began a six- month siege of La Paz.

April 6. Betrayed, Túpac Amaru was captured in Langui.

May 18. In Cuzco Túpac Amaru was forced to witness the torture and execution of his wife and other relatives and was then himself torn apart by horses attached to his four limbs.

July 18. The siege of La Paz was temporarily broken with the arrival of General Ignacio Flores's army, which quickly had to withdraw.

September–October. The siege was definitively ended with the arrival of José de Reseguín's force.

November 9. Betrayed by Tomás Inga Lipe, a one-time ally, Túpac Catari was captured, tried, and condemned to death.

November 14. Túpac Catari's sentence was carried out as four horses attached to his limbs were driven in different directions.

1784

July 7. **The intendancy system was introduced into Peru.** *Corregimientos* and their venal *corregidores* were abolished and replaced with the seven intendancies of Lima, Tarma, Trujillo, Arequipa, Cuzco, Huamanga, and Huancavelica.

1787

February 26. **The Spanish established their last audiencia in the New World at Cuzco.** Its creation was in response to the discontent revealed by the rebellions that had shaken Andean Peru. It was an attempt to provide a speedier and more efficient system of justice and to resolve some of the problems that provoked the rebellion. Nevertheless, the audiencia remained largely a judicial entity and had little administrative impact upon problem-solving.

1790

October. **Latin America's first daily newspaper, the *Diario de Lima*, appeared.** It was published until September 1793.

Chile
1535-1803

The story of Chile's discovery, conquest, and settlement by the Spanish was unlike that of Peru's. Closure was a long and arduous process. **Diego de Almagro**'s Chilean expedition (1535-37) was a failure. His vision of wealth and treasure and a native population as pliant as the Inca was shattered by freezing mountain passes, burning deserts, and hostile attacks of peoples the Spanish generically called Araucanians. The Mapuches, as their descendants are known today, had long resisted Inca incursions and were thoroughly ready to resist those of another empire as well. Almagro's return to Peru in 1537 gave the Mapuches a brief respite before the expedition of **Pedro de Valdivia** (1540-41). Valdivia's contest with the Araucanians was perhaps the bloodiest in the New World, excessive in its brutality. The clash was immortalized in Alonso de Ercilla y Zúñiga's epic poem *La Araucana* (Part 1, 1569; Part 2, 1578; Part 3, 1589).

In Chile the Spanish--whether as ranchers, farmers, miners, or merchants--forged a frontier society whose elite lived from Indian labor as *encomenderos* and as slavers. In the Central Valley the fertile land and closeness to the coast eventually allowed for the production of cheap provisions for Peru, especially wheat for Lima. In Chilean mining areas, particularly in the south, the Spanish enslaved native Americans and mined gold, over 7 million pesos before 1569. In Chile, Indian tribute was excessive, and was usually fixed in gold. The Araucanians resisted Spanish pretensions and repeatedly destroyed their settlements. By the end of the sixteenth century they had learned to ride Spanish horses, use firearms, and make gunpowder. As guerrillas they adopted hit-and-run and scorched-earth tactics. Among the Spanish a long debate broke out over how the Araucanians should be tamed, and while most were of a mind to kill, maim, or enslave those who resisted, there were those who urged restraint, defensive warfare, and peaceful conversion by missionaries. Meanwhile, the Araucanians continued to resist. In 1598 all Spanish influence south of the Bío-Bío River, near modern Concepción, was swept away and reverted to Araucanian control. The Araucanians beheaded Valdivia in 1553 and Martín García Oñez de Loyola in 1599, the latter's head only being returned to the Spanish nine years later. In 1608 the Spanish received crown authority to enslave the Araucanians, something they had been doing for some time. The Spanish continued to alternate between draconian and peaceful measures. Between 1541 and 1664 they lost more than 20,000 soldiers and settlers and spent more than 17 million pesos trying to subdue the Araucanians.

Chile could not be held solely through the riches gained there. A permanent subsidy (*situado*) from Peru was necessary in order to maintain forts along the southern frontier. From a strategic point of view they kept the Araucanians at bay and rival European powers out. Freed from paying for its own defense, receiving an annual subsidy from Peru, and a growing demand from Lima for its agrarian products, Chile prospered. Late in the colonial period Chile coalesced and showed the signs of vitality that would foreshadow its rise as the most successful Latin American country in the nineteenth century in terms of its national development. The long period of continuous frontier warfare during the colonial period had forged a mestizo society that was more homogeneous than the rest of Latin America. As a result Chile was ripe for national unification. Chile's colonial governors and higher administrators found the province to be a stepping-stone in their careers to higher office, especially late in the colonial period when several were promoted to the position of viceroy of Río de la Plata or of Peru.

1535-37

Diego de Almagro failed to find riches in Chile.
July 3. **Diego de Almagro**'s expeditionary force to Chile departed from Cuzco. It traversed southern Bolivia and northern Argentina before crossing the Andes and entering Chile through the pass of San Francisco. It then traveled the length of the Central Valley and reached as far south as present-day Concepción before retracing its steps as far north as modern Copiapó. The expedition stayed in Chile until late 1536, when it crossed the Atacama Desert and re-entered Peru, reaching present-day Arequipa early in 1537.

1540

Pedro de Valdivia began the conquest of Chile.
Mid-January. **Valdivia**'s expedition to Chile left Cuzco.
December. Valdivia's group reached the Copiapó Valley.

1541

February 12. **Valdivia founded Santiago.**
September 11. Araucanian Indians attacked Santiago and nearly destroyed it.

1544

August. **Valdivia's lieutenant Juan Bohón founded La Serena to protect the route to southern Peru.**

1549

January 21. **Valdivia returned to Chile from Peru**, where he took part in the suppression of the revolt led by **Gonzalo Pizarro.**

1550

October 5. **Valdivia founded Concepción to protect the southern frontier from Araucanian attack.**

1552

Valdivia pushed south and set up outposts at La Imperial, Valdivia, and Villarica.

1553

December 25. **Valdivia and fifty of his company were killed** at a fort called Tucapel south of Concepción. **Lautaro**, the leader of the Araucanians, ambushed his former master and forced the Spanish to abandon various settlements.

1557-61

García Hurtado de Mendoza successfully ruled as governor of Chile. Sent out by his father, the marquis of Cañete and viceroy of Peru, Hurtado de Mendoza was only twenty-one. His government was aided by funds from the Peruvian treasury. He despatched expeditions to retake lost territory, establish new towns, and explore south to the Straits of Magellan. Alonso de Ercilla y Zúñiga accompanied the governor and witnessed many of the events described in his epic poem *La Araucana.*
April 29, 1557. The Spanish defeated the Araucanians at Peteroa, and **Lautaro** was killed.
1558. Osorio was founded. Concepción was rebuilt and resettled for the third time.

1561

May 18. **The diocese of Santiago was created.**

The first bishop was Bartolomé Rodrigo González Marmolejo.

1563

March 22. **The diocese of La Imperial was established.** It was transferred to Concepción in 1603.

1598

December 23. **Pelantaru led the largest Araucanian uprising to date.** Governor Martín García Oñez de Loyola was captured and beheaded at Curalava. Spanish settlements south of the Bío-Bío River were overrun and abandoned.

1600

An annual subsidy (*situado*) from Peru, although not always paid on time, was set aside for Chile. It supplied the necessary support to hold the colony against the Araucanians. The subsidy established a precedent. Other frontier provinces of the Spanish empire would also receive *situados* from the more lucrative and settled ones to pay for necessary defense.

1608

Philip III (r. 1598-1621) authorized perpetual slavery for the Araucanians. Pope Paul V sanctioned a Spanish holy war against them as well.

1609

At the Spanish court the Jesuit Luis de Valdivia argued the case for a defensive war against the Araucanians.
An audiencia for Chile was located at Santiago.

1610

December 8. **The crown reversed itself and made defensive warfare official policy in Chile.**

The decision was based on the arguments of Luis de Valdivia. To implement the policy the Jesuit Valdivia was named *visitador general* (chief inspector) to Chile.

1612

December 14. **The Araucanians assassinated three Jesuits at Elicura.** Warfare against the Araucanians was resumed.

1619

November. **Luis de Valdivia quit Chile.** His policy of defensive warfare was largely abandoned.

1645-46

The viceroy of Peru resettled Valdivia with 1,800 men, artisans, and 188 cannons transported in 12 ships. The purpose was to keep the Araucanians occupied in the south and to relieve pressure on Spanish settlements farther north. It also helped prevent European rivals from establishing colonies there.

1647

May 13. **Santiago was destroyed by an earthquake.**

1655

February. **An Indian uprising temporarily drove the Spanish from towns and forts south of the Bío-Bío River as well as from territory as far north as Chillán.**

1680

December 13. **Pirates under the English buccaneer Bartholomew Sharp plundered La Serena.**

1730

July 2. **An earthquake devastated Santiago.**

The resulting tidal wave seriously damaged Valparaíso.

1737-45

José Antonio Manso de Velasco successfully administered Chile as governor. His policies led to the establishment of new settlements in the Central Valley and mining areas, such as San Felipe (1740), Canquenes, Los Angeles, San Fernando (1742), Curicó, Melipilla, and Rancagua (1743). As a reward he was made viceroy of Peru.

1749

La Moneda mint was opened for operation in Santiago.

1751

May 25. **An earthquake and tidal wave destroyed Concepción.** In 1764 the city was relocated to the north side of the Bío-Bío River.

1778-95

The empire-wide Bourbon Reforms hastened change and restructuring in Chile.
   1778. The first detailed census was taken. Chile was opened to free trade within the Spanish empire.
   1786-87. Chile was divided into two intendancies, Santiago and Concepción, with the governor being the senior intendant.
   1795. A *consulado* was established at Santiago for the area's leading merchants.

1787-96

Ambrosio O'Higgins--father of future independence leader Bernardo O'Higgins--successfully administered Chile as governor. He was advanced to the position of viceroy in Peru.

1796-99

Gabriel de Avilés ruled as governor. He was promoted to viceroy in Buenos Aires (1799-1801) and then in Lima (1801-06).

Río de la Plata
1514-1803

The Spanish discovery and conquest of Río de la Plata, the area associated with the modern-day countries of Argentina, Paraguay, and Uruguay, initially came about as a result of attempts to find a shorter route to Asia and to secure the southern frontier against European interlopers following the conquest of Peru (1532-38) and the silver strike at Potosí (1545). Protecting the stream of precious metals that poured out of Upper Peru was of overriding concern. Three separate provinces—Tucumán, Paraguay, and Buenos Aires—emerged and served as a bulwark against foreign attacks on Peru. Over time each developed its own separate existence and rationale. By the end of the colonial period Buenos Aires's precocious development had transformed it into the administrative center of not only Paraguay and Uruguay, but of Upper Peru (including Potosí) as well. Lima thus lost its long-standing jurisdiction over Upper Peru.

In the sixteenth century the need to supply Potosí--a city at nearly 14,000 feet, with over 100,000 inhabitants by 1600, and one of the largest cities in the world--spawned a series of settlements in Chile and in the province of Tucumán (northwestern Argentina).

On the Río de la Plata coast Spanish control precluded other European powers from establishing settlements there. As long as Spain's rivals were denied bases there and in Chile, the southern flank of the Spanish empire was protected and the Pacific remained a Spanish lake. Buenos Aires controlled the entrance to the Río de la Plata and was the logical point from which to patrol the coast. But it was not until 1580 that the Spanish were able to maintain a permanent presence there. The native Americans were too nomadic to submit to the Spanish, who were forced to go upriver to Paraguay where they became masters of the semi-sedentary Guaraní. From their provincial capital of Asunción, the Spanish eventually refounded Buenos Aires in 1580.

That same year found Portugal and its empire becoming part of Spain's. When the Portuguese revolted in 1640, and successfully took themselves out of the Spanish empire, the frontier between Brazil and Río de la Plata became an important factor in the history of Buenos Aires, Paraguay, and Brazil. The Jesuit *reducciones* (missions) in Paraguay, and incursions against them by slave hunters from São Paulo, became part of the dynamics, determining who would control that common space. Farther south similar friction between the two empires developed over whether the Spanish or the Portuguese would occupy the Banda Oriental (eastern bank) of the Río de la Plata in what would become Uruguay.

Initially Buenos Aires was Potosí's back door. But Buenos Aires offered a far more direct and less expensive route to Europe than the legally prescribed Panamanian one. It avoided the isthmus crossing, the contrary winds and currents of the Pacific, and the Andean trek. Traffic and commerce, increasing amounts of it contraband, gradually began to make its way through the port to Potosí to absorb bullion. By the second half of the eighteenth century the contraband trade had become torrential. The shift in importance away from Panama and Lima and toward the Southern Cone was officially recognized in 1776. That year the viceroyalty of Río de la Plata was created, with Buenos Aires granted jurisdiction over the Río de la Plata, Paraguay, and Upper Peru (including Potosí).

During the late eighteenth century an ancillary development took place around Buenos Aires on the pampas, one of the most fertile areas in the world. The livestock that had escaped from sixteenth-century Spanish expeditions had multiplied to the extent that there were millions roaming the pampas by the eighteenth century. While initially oriented toward the Potosí market, by the late eighteenth century the pampas had developed exports of leather for the belts and pulleys of the European Industrial Revolution, as well as salted beef consumed on the slave plantations of Brazil and Cuba.

1514

The first European reconnaissance of the Río de la Plata was undertaken. The Portuguese navigators Nuño Manuel and Juan de Haro explored the Río de la Plata estuary.

1515-16

October 5. **The Juan Díaz de Solís expedition sailed from Sanlúcar, Spain, in search of a new and shorter passage to the Far East around South America.** They arrived in the Río de la Plata estuary the following January. Upon disembarkation on the future Uruguayan coast, Solís was captured and executed by the Charrúa. Solís had been Spain's *piloto mayor* (chief pilot) since the death of **Amerigo Vespucci** in 1512.

1519-20

Ferdinand Magellan's expedition sailed around the world, with its longest stopover in the Argentine littoral.

September 20, 1519. Ferdinand Magellan's five-ship expedition to find a westward route to Asia departed Sanlúcar, Spain.

January 1520. Magellan explored the Río de la Plata estuary. As the colder months approached, his group wintered on the Patagonian coast.

October 21-November 28, 1520. Magellan's group entered the strait that would bear his name and emerged in the Pacific thirty-nine days later.

1526-30

April 3, 1526. **Sebastian Cabot was dispatched on a follow-up, round-the-world expedition.** Upon arriving in the Río de la Plata (February 21, 1527), however, persistent rumors about extraordinary silver deposits led him to seek riches on the mainland in vain. Upon his return to Spain in 1530 he suffered a two-year banishment to Africa. The settlement he founded on the lower Paraná River at its confluence with the Carcarañá did not endure.

1534-37

The Pedro de Mendoza expedition failed to colonize Buenos Aires.

May 21, 1534. A *capitulación* (contract) signed between the crown and **Pedro de Mendoza** made him *adelantado* (frontier military com-

mander), governor, and captain-general of Río de la Plata.

August 24, 1535. Mendoza's force sailed from Spain. With **Sebastian Cabot**'s visions of fabulous silver strikes still fueling Spanish expectations, and the finds in Peru requiring that the Spanish southern flank be secured, the crown dispatched a fourteen-ship fleet with over 1,500 participants. This was the largest Spanish expedition to the New World since **Christopher Columbus**'s second voyage.

February 3, 1536. First foundation of Buenos Aires as Santa María del Buen Aire. With hostile natives pressing in and no one to carry their baggage, the Spanish nearly starved. They gradually retreated up river into Paraguay where the semi-sedentary Guaraní sustained the Spanish.

June 23, 1537. Mendoza, sick and on his way back to Spain, died at sea, probably of syphilis.

1537

August 15, 1537. **Asunción, Paraguay, was founded by Juan de Salazar de Espinosa**, and settled by survivors of the ill-fated Mendoza expedition. Asunción thus replaced Buenos Aires as the springboard for Spanish occupation and colonization of the area drained by the rivers (Paraná, Paraguay, and Uruguay) making up the Río de la Plata system. The diocese of Asunción was created in 1547.

1540-48

Domingo Martínez de Irala replaced Alvar Núñez Cabeza de Vaca as the governor of the Río de La Plata colony.

March 18, 1540. In Spain **Cabeza de Vaca** was appointed the second *adelantado* and governor of Río de la Plata. The purpose of his expedition was to revitalize the failed **Mendoza** expedition and put the colony on a sounder footing.

March 29, 1541. Cabeza de Vaca's expedition of three ships arrived in Río de la Plata. There he rescued the few remaining survivors from the Mendoza expedition, still beseiged in Buenos Aires and moved upriver to Asunción.

March 11, 1542. Cabeza de Vaca arrived in

Asunción and assumed command there.

April 25-26, 1544. With the support of most of the colony, Domingo Martínez de Irala overthrew and imprisoned Cabeza de Vaca for ineffective leadership.

August 15, 1545. Cabeza de Vaca reached Spain after being forcibly returned by Irala.

Late 1547-early 1548. Faced with a revolt by some of Cabeza de Vaca's former cohorts, Irala placated the rebels by marrying four of his mixed-blood daughters to the leaders.

1555

Irala, de facto ruler since Cabeza de Vaca's departure, was made governor of Paraguay.

1553-82

The Spanish colonized Tucumán (northwestern Argentina) from Chile and Upper Peru (Bolivia). Throughout the colonial period the main orbit of those colonies was the Andes, especially Potosí, and the Pacific, rather than the Atlantic and Buenos Aires.

1553. The first permanent Spanish town in present-day Argentina was established at Santiago del Estero by settlers from Peru.

March 2, 1561. Mendoza, in western Argentina, was founded and colonized from Chile by Captain Pedro del Castillo. Sent out by the governor of Chile, García Hurtado de Mendoza, the colonizers refounded the settlement on March 28, 1562, "two arquebus shots towards the southeast." Mendoza initially functioned as the easternmost frontier settlement for Chile and Argentina and as a possible way station for troops sent to Chile via Río de la Plata. Its encomenderos lived in Santiago and regularly brought their charges across the Andes to work in Chile. The agricultural potential of Mendoza was gradually exploited. By the seventeenth century it began to supply Potosí on a regular basis with wine, livestock, and wheat.

1562. Captain Juan de Jofré founded San Juan de la Frontera just north of Mendoza on the orders of the governor of Chile. It was moved to its present location in 1593.

1563. The governorship of Tucumán was created with the governor residing at Santiago del Estero and under the jurisdiction of the audiencia of Charcas in Upper Peru.

1565. Tucumán, a city in northwestern Argentina, was founded from Peru by Captain Diego de Villaroel. It was moved to its present location in 1685. It served as a transit and supply center for Potosí, sending wheat, sugar, and livestock.

April 30, 1570. The bishopric of Tucumán was created, the first in Argentina, with the bishop residing at Santiago del Estero.

July 6, 1573. Córdoba, a city in northwestern Argentina, was founded by Jerónimo Luis de Cabrera, governor of Tucumán. The settlement served as obligatory stopping and resupply point for goods and travelers on their way to the Andes, Chile, and Upper Peru.

1582. Salta, in northwestern Argentina, was established by Hernando de Lerma. Wheat, sugar, corn, and wine and European goods from Tucumán, Mendoza, and Córdoba passed through Salta on their way to Potosí. Salta itself raised and conditioned mules for the Upper Peru trade whose sale at Salta's annual fair reached 50,000 by the late seventeenth century.

1573-88

As the Spanish community at Asunción stabilized and strengthened, it sent settlers downstream to re-establish control over the Argentine littoral.

November 15, 1573. Juan de Garay, having moved downriver from Asunción, founded Santa Fé. It was relocated in the 1650s.

June 11, 1580. Continuing colonization southward from Asunción, Garay refounded Buenos Aires.

April 3, 1588. Corrientes was formally founded by Juan Torres de Vera and Alonso de Vera y Aragón. On the Paraná River, it served as a way station between Buenos Aires and Asunción.

1605

March 3. **The *cabildo* (city council) of Mendoza levied quotas** of 3,000 *fanegas* (4,500 bushels) of wheat, 684 cattle, and 50 *arrobas* of wine on area landowners to sustain the one thousand Spanish soldiers wintering there before they could proceed through the snowed-in mountain passes to put down the Araucanian rebellion in Chile.

1609

The Jesuits began their missionary work among the Guaraní. Of the thirty-two missions the Jesuits established among the Guaraní, ten were in the province of Paraguay. Acculturating and concentrating the Guaraní in mission communities, the Jesuits unintentionally made the native Americans apt targets for Portuguese slavers from São Paulo who coveted their labor. They also animated the covetous designs of the labor-hungry Paraguayan settlers. The dispute over who would control this labor involved the Jesuits in long-term controversies with both parties that eventually created much of the anti-Jesuit sentiment and led to their expulsion from the Portuguese and Spanish empires in 1759 and 1767, respectively.

1617

The governorship of Buenos Aires was created. Recognizing Buenos Aires's growing importance, the Spanish gave it a governor separate and independent of Asunción. The bishopric of Buenos Aires was created in 1620.

1622

The contraband trade with Potosí was attacked. In response to the increasing flow of contraband goods from Europe to Potosí via Buenos Aires, the Spanish outlawed trade with Brazil and established an inland customshouse at Córdoba.

1623

Bishop Fernando Trejo y Sanabria made the Jesuit *colegio* at Córdoba the first university in the Río de la Plata area.

1630

The first notice of the Virgin of Luján ap-

peared. A cart stuck in the mud was miraculously dislodged. The resulting shrine to the Virgin of Luján was transformed into a basilica and the site of Argentina's most revered religious pilgrimage.

1642-50

Bishop Bernardino de Cárdenas challenged the autonomy of the Jesuit missions.

1642. Bernardino de Cárdenas, the newly consecrated bishop of Paraguay, arrived in Asunción to administer his see. He insisted on visiting all parishes and religious centers under his jurisdiction, but the Jesuits challenged his right to inspect their Guaraní missions and disputed the validity of his consecration and his right to be bishop.

1644. Gregorio de Hinestrosa, governor of Paraguay and an ally of the Jesuits, expelled Cárdenas, who had allied himself with the labor-hungry Paraguayan settlers.

1647. Cárdenas arrived again in Asunción after the audiencia of Charcas had reinstated him and faced a new governor, Diego de Escobar Osorio.

1649. Governor Escobar died, and the cabildo of Asunción named Bishop Cárdenas the new governor, who then expelled the Jesuits from Asunción.

1650. The Jesuits organized their mission charges into an army. They then defeated the Paraguayan militia near San Lorenzo, occupied and plundered Asunción, and expelled Cárdenas once again. Although reinstated as bishop by Philip IV in 1660, Cárdenas had given up the fight and preferred to accept the bishopric of Santa Cruz de la Sierra in Upper Peru. The anti-Jesuit sentiment, nevertheless, continued to persist in many circles.

1671

The Spanish relocated the customshouse of Córdoba to Salta. The inability or unwillingness of authorities in Upper Peru to stop the flow of contraband was recognized by this move. Córdoba was now put under the control of Buenos Aires, whose jurisdiction had been considerably enlarged with this move westward.

1680

The Portuguese established the settlement of Colônia do Sacramento. With this base across the estuary from Buenos Aires, the Portuguese challenged Spanish control over the Río de la Plata. Thus began the long-running contest over whether the Banda Oriental (eastern bank) of the Río de la Plata would be Portuguese or Spanish. The competition between Argentina and Brazil continued in the nineteenth century and culminated in the creation of the buffer state of Uruguay.

1699

The see of the bishop of Tucumán was transferred from Santiago del Estero to Córdoba.

1702

Spanish forces from Buenos Aires captured Colônia do Sacramento. As a result of their alliance with the English during the War of the Spanish Succession (1701-13), the Portuguese made their holdings fair game for the Spanish, who crossed the bay and took control of Colônia. Nevertheless, the Treaty of Utrecht (1713) returned the settlement to the Portuguese.

1724

August. **José de Antequera y Castro, governor (1721-25) of Paraguay, and his force of 3,000 annihilated the Jesuit-led Guaraní militia on the Tebicuary River**. He then expelled the Jesuits from Asunción. Antequera had involved himself in the long-standing dispute over whether the Jesuits or the Paraguayan settlers would control the labor of the Guaraní living in the missions. While Antequera had the support of the audiencia of Charcas, the viceroy, José de Armendáriz, was a partisan of the Jesuits. With so many dead from the victory, Antequera had to flee to Córdoba and then to Charcas, where he was arrested and remitted to Lima in 1726.

November 9. Bruno Mauricio de Zavala, the governor of Buenos Aires, ordered the establishment of Montevideo. This was the first Spanish settlement on the Banda Oriental of the Río de la Plata across the bay from Buenos Aires. Located farther east than the Portuguese settlement of Colônia do Sacramento, it challenged contraband shipping before it could be off loaded in the Portuguese port. In 1726 some of the town's first settlers arrived from Tenerife, Santa Fé, and Buenos Aires.

1730-35

Comunero Rebellion ran its course in Paraguay. This was the result of the long-standing dispute between the Jesuits and the Paraguayan settlers, which had been ongoing since the controversy with Bishop Cárdenas in the 1640s, fueled by the more recent one with Governor Antequera in 1724.

1730. The pro-Jesuit viceroy of Peru, José de Armendáriz, appointed Ignacio de Soroeta as governor of Paraguay.

1731. Paraguayan settlers expelled Governor Soroeta.

July 5. In Lima the viceroy-instructed *audiencia* (court) found the former governor of Paraguay, Antequera, guilty of treason and heresy and condemned him to death. A riot ensued over the sentence and Antequera was shot by the viceroy's troops before he reached the gallows.

July 1733. In Asunción the new appointee of Viceroy Armendáriz, Governor Manuel Agustín de Ruiloba y Calderón, arrived and was shot by Paraguayan settlers.

1735. Bruno Mauricio de Zavala, the governor of Buenos Aires, arrived and put down the revolt, executing four leaders and exiling and removing from office other principals.

1762

The Spanish from Buenos Aires crossed the Río

de la Plata and once again captured Colônia de Sacramento. Nevertheless, in the Treaty of Paris (1763) the town was returned to Portuguese control.

1766-74

England and Spain posted rival claims to control over the Malvinas, or Falkland Islands. Spain claimed its discovery occurred in 1520, while England asserted its discovery took place in 1592. Whalers of various nationalities used the islands as their base during the second half of the eighteenth century. The English abandoned attempts at a permanent settlement in 1774 and did not reoccupy the islands until 1833.

1767

The expulsion of the Jesuits took place. This adversely affected the University of Córdoba and

the Jesuit missions, especially those in Paraguay and along the border with Brazil.

1776

July 27. **A decree was issued creating the viceroyalty of Río de la Plata.** The viceroyalty included Argentina, Paraguay, and Upper Peru (Bolivia). Its creation was a manifestation of a structural shift that had occurred in the Spanish empire. Atlantic areas had grown in importance as more direct routes were found to conduct commerce between the Old and New Worlds. With Buenos Aires rather than Lima having jurisdiction over Potosí, the shift was patently evident. Another factor was the growing export trade in hides from the pampas that went to Europe rather than to the Potosí market.

1777

Pedro Antonio de Ceballos, the newly appointed first viceroy of Río de la Plata, ousted the Portuguese from Colônia do Sacramento. This time the Banda Oriental of the Río de la Plata remained in Spanish hands, since it was confirmed by the Treaty of San Ildefonso (1777). Ceballos promulgated Spanish free-trade ordinances in the same year.

1782

January 28. **Administrative reorganization of the viceroyalty of La Plata came with the introduction of the intendancy system.** Three intendancies were created for Argentina—Buenos Aires, Córdoba, and Salta; one for Paraguay—Asunción; and five for Upper Peru—Charcas, Potosí, Cochabamba, La Paz, and Puno (1784-96). The frontier area with Brazil was beefed up with four military governors, one each for Montevideo, Misiones, Mojos, and Chiquitos.

1790s

The *saladeros* as an organized "factory" system appeared on the eastern bank of the Río de la Plata. Individual *estancieros*, large-scale land-owners, began to make use of the carcasses of the livestock that were previously left to rot after being stripped for their hides for export. The meat was salted for preservation and then exported as jerky to the slave plantations in Brazil and Cuba. It represented the beginnings of a more intensive exploitation of the pampas that would eventually transform the Río de la Plata area in the course of the nineteenth century.

Brazil
1500-1803

Pedro Álvares Cabral's accidental discovery of Brazil on his way to India was symptomatic of Portugal's initial relationship with what proved to be its most enduring colonial legacy. Asia and Africa were the primary foci of Portugal's imperial ambitions well into the seventeenth century. This was appropriate since in the sixteenth century Brazil never accounted for more than 3 percent of royal income while India always brought in more than 25 percent. Brazil was therefore not really neglected, but seen from the vantage point of its significance today, it certainly seemed to be an afterthought. As Portugal lost ground in Asia and Africa, however, and the Spanish created their New World empire, it looked more and more to its American colony. Being part of the Spanish empire from 1580 to 1640 also led Portugal to focus more attention on its American territory. In Brazil this imperial union produced the first faint stirrings of a distinctive identity as its colonists struggled to differentiate themselves from Spanish Americans.

For the Portuguese monarchy in 1500 the first order of business concerning Brazil was to determine what had been discovered, its value, and how best to exploit it, given Portugal's limited population and resources. Follow-up expeditions to Cabral's discovery quickly charted the Brazilian coastline and showed that Brazil clearly fell within the Portuguese sphere of influence as defined by the Treaty of Tordesillas (1494). A north-south line drawn 370 leagues west of the Cape Verde Islands intersected Brazil at the mouth of the Amazon River in the north and stretched toward the Río de la Plata estuary in the south. In accordance with the treaty, all territory east of the line fell within the Portuguese sphere, and it was here that Portugal's role in the New World was played out.

At first Brazil offered no immediate return on capital invested in the always expensive voyages of discovery. The only commodity found for which there was any demand was brazilwood, from which a red dye was extracted in Europe for use in making textiles. That determined the limited interest and meager results of the first fifty years of Portugal's presence in Brazil. Initially the crown leased part of Brazil to a group of Lisbon merchants prominent in the trade to Africa and India. The lease reverted to the crown when its three years were up in 1505. Meanwhile, *feitorias* (fortified trading posts) were being established along the Brazilian coast. In exchange for food for the *feitorias* and dressed brazilwood for conveyance to Europe, the Portuguese provided the native Americans with goods such as highly prized metal tools that increased the productivity of their traditional economy. The French, whose textile industry consumed many of the logs, took an immediate interest in Brazil. They rarely attempted permanent settlements like the Portuguese, preferring instead to trade with the native Americans in exchange for brazilwood. French privateers also raided Portuguese ships and sites where logs were stacked. Suddenly the European market was flooded, and the price of brazilwood fell dramatically. Both the Portuguese crown and Lisbon merchants suffered as a result. The French seized an average of twenty Portuguese ships a year between 1520 and 1530 if those taken near the Azores are counted. Attempts by the Portuguese to patrol the Brazilian coast came to naught; it was too long and open, and Portugal lacked the necessary resources. A change in policy from the fortified trading posts was necessary if the Portuguese were to hang on to Brazil.

The new policy adopted in 1534 was based on the division of Brazil into fifteen territories (captaincies), which were awarded to twelve captains (*donatários*). These hereditary grants conveyed many judicial and fiscal powers to the captain-donatary, who in turn was to attract settlers to his captaincy and to spell out his relationship to them in a charter (*foral*). A major advantage to the crown was that all costs were the responsibility of the captain, while the crown retained some control and shared in revenues generated in the captaincies. Only ten of the twelve captains actually tried to develop their captaincies, and only Pernambuco and São Vicente could be said to be successes by 1550; the principal problem was that colonization produced more conflict with the native Americans than did fortified trading posts. Between 1548 and 1791 the crown gradually regained control of all of the hereditary captaincies.

Despite the limited results of the donatary captaincies, the Portuguese had established a spotty presence up and down the Brazilian coast, won over some native Americans as allies, and gained valuable time and experience. Nevertheless, the French still kept coming and the geopolitical situation was changing. The fabulous riches evident in Peru and the mining strike at Potosí (1545) made the Portuguese ever more aware of the possible value of their Brazilian territories. It was therefore essential that the French be expelled once and for all. In addition, now that the Spanish had struck it rich in Peru, they could not be allowed to encroach on Portugal's Brazilian territories. This required a presence in Brazil beyond that of the captain-donataries, whose authority extended only to the borders of their individual captaincies.

The change came in 1549 when King João III (1521-57) implemented a plan to increase the Portuguese presence in Brazil and to assert royal authority there. In 1549 Bahia was chosen as the seat of the future royal government, and **Tomé de Sousa** was named the first governor-general. João III instructed him to help the captain-donataries, build towns and forts, administer justice, and increase his revenues. Accompanying Sousa's expedition to the New World were six Jesuits, the first in Latin America. Their close association with the new governor and with the government in general gave them a key role in Portuguese interaction with the native Americans. The Jesuits' role in acculturating the Indians to Portuguese ways was fundamental in Brazil's remaining under Portuguese control.

Also important in this regard were those

Portuguese who had lived among the native Americans and been acculturated in the opposite direction, becoming valued members of indigenous society. The most famous were **Caramurú** in Bahia and João Ramalho in São Vicente and São Paulo. Either as shamans with magical powers or as warriors with superior fighting skills or both, these Portuguese learned the secrets of native society and advised the Portuguese on how best to proceed. As wizards or frontier fighters, they had many wives and sired many *mameluco* (mestizo, or mixed-race) children who inherited the skills of both cultures. They were responsible for creating a population numerous enough and sufficiently steeped in Portuguese values that Brazil remained Portuguese.

The new royal government was successful in expelling the French from a foothold in Guanabara Bay. More serious was the seventeenth-century effort of the Dutch to seize Brazil by force. The Dutch campaign was an outgrowth of the larger drama involving the Spanish empire. The Netherlands and Spain had been linked dynastically from the time Charles I, a native of Ghent, became king of Spain in 1516. By the late sixteenth century the Dutch no longer wanted the king of Spain as their ruler, yet much of their livelihood depended on their trade within the Spanish empire. Determined to have both their independence and their trade, the Dutch rebelled against Spain in 1566; the war continued fitfully until the independence of the northern provinces of the Netherlands was recognized in the Treaty of Westphalia (1648). With the union of the Portuguese and Spanish empires under the king of Spain from 1580 until 1640, the Dutch found themselves excluded more and more from the Portuguese carrying trade, especially from Brazil, where they provided more than half the ships. Deciding to conquer those areas they considered vital to their prosperity, they founded the Dutch East India and Dutch West India companies in 1602 and 1621, respectively. For Brazil the ensuing world-wide struggle was devastating and brought the destruction of their plantations and sugar mills. These areas eventually recovered, but meanwhile the center of the world's sugar production had moved from Brazil to the Caribbean.

The discovery of gold in Minas Gerais and other locations starting in the 1690s brought a new source of revenue for the government and transformed the districts in the interior where the precious metals were found. Towns such as Vila Rica de Ouro Prêto grew up around the mining camps, and roads and water routes linked these areas with the coastal settlements. The increasing economic importance of central and southern Brazil was reflected in the transfer of the colonial capital from Salvador da Bahia to Rio de Janeiro in 1763.

Declining gold production brought an economic slump after 1760, but by the end of the century, sugar and other agricultural exports were expanding, partly because of international conditions, notably the turmoil in Saint Domingue (Haiti), which had disrupted sugar production there. Under the leadership of the **Marquês de Pombal**, the government also attempted to modernize and stimulate the economies of both Portugal and Brazil.

By 1800 Brazil had expanded far beyond the boundaries mandated by the Treaty of Tordesillas, a fact recognized by Spain in the late eighteenth century, though conflict for control of the lands surrounding the Río de la Plata system continued well into the nineteenth century. As the century began, Brazil's population remained relatively small, totaling some 2 million, of whom about two-thirds, both slave and free, were of African origin. Native Americans in the areas settled by the Portuguese accounted for only 5 percent of the population. These figures reflect the increasing importance of African slavery as the indigenous population declined because of disease, exploitation, and other traumas associated with the Portuguese settlement of Brazil. The population was scattered among eleven captaincies and seven subordinate captainies, which were subject to the former. Since 1720 the governor-general had held the title of viceroy, but in reality he exerted little authority beyond his captaincy of residence.

Colonial Brazil remained overwhelmingly

rural, and the principal cities were small in comparison with Mexico City or Lima. In 1800 the population of Rio de Janeiro was about 80,000, and that of Salvador about 70,000. No university was ever established in colonial Brazil, nor was a printing press permanently located there. But, colonial elites were not ignorant of the ideas of the Enlightenment, which were introduced through imported books and by students who had traveled to Portugal or France for higher education. Thus, an intellectual awakening can be discerned by the late eighteenth century which contributed to the independence movement after 1808.

1500

April 22. **Pedro Álvares Cabral accidentally discovered Brazil.** On its way to India, his thirteen-ship fleet sailed far out into the Atlantic to catch the currents and winds necessary to carry it around the tip of South Africa. The fleet made landfall near present-day Pôrto Seguro. After restocking the fleet and dispatching a ship back to Lisbon with news of the discovery, **Cabral** weighed anchor on May 1 and continued his voyage to India. At the Portuguese court Brazil was initially seen as a way-station on the route to India. At least two Spanish expeditions—one led by Alonso de Hojeda in 1499 and the other led by Vicente Yáñez Pinzón in 1500—had visited Brazil before Cabral. But neither had any long-term significance in terms of colonization because Brazil fell into the territory assigned to Portugal by the Treaty of Tordesillas.

1501

May 13. **A three-caravel expedition of exploration sailed from Lisbon to determine the extent of the land discovered by Cabral.** Captained by Gonçalo Coelho and later described by on-board chronicler **Amerigo Vespucci**, the expedition ran out 2,000 miles of the Brazilian coastline from Cape São Roque in the north to Cananéia in the south and returned to Portugal in 1502.

1502-5

The crown leased Brazil for three years to a consortium of Lisbon merchants led by Fernão de Noronha. The terms gave an ever higher annual percentage of potential profits to the crown and obligated the consortium to send out three ships a year and establish a *feitoria*, or fortified trading post. The expedition sent out at least two expeditions.

August 1502–April 1503. The first expedition sailed from Lisbon, made landfall near Cape São Roque, reconnoitered as far as Pôrto Seguro, and returned with a boatload of brazilwood and native American slaves.

May 10, 1503. The second expedition, better known because **Amerigo Vespucci** captained one of the six ships and described his experience in his letter to Soderini, departed from Lisbon. Running into foul weather near the island of Fernão Noronha (named in honor of the leader of the consortium) off the northeast coast of Brazil, Vespucci and one other captain were separated from the fleet. They sailed south to Cabo Frio. There they met one of the conditions of the lease by building a *feitoria*, where they left a garrison of twenty-four men. In June 1504 they arrived back in Lisbon with another cargo of brazilwood.

1504-5

The French made their first appearance in Brazil. While trying to sail to India, Binot Paulmier de Gonneville, captain of the *Espoir*, was, much like **Cabral**, accidentally carried by winds and currents to Brazil, where he loaded brazilwood for his return voyage.

1506-34

During the trading post era, the Portuguese exploited stands of brazilwood closest to the coast and countered French and Spanish activity. Although the evidence is indirect, the Portuguese probably established *feitorias* at Pernambuco, Bahia, Pôrto Seguro, Cabo Frio, and São Vicente. Ships sailing from Lisbon delivered supplies and the trading goods used to motivate native Americans to cut down and dress the trees for easy shipment. One well-documented expedition involved the 1511 voyage of the *Bretoa*, whose cargo of 5,000 logs, each one weighing 44 to 66 pounds, paid a tax of 30 percent on its assessed value when it landed in Lisbon.

Spanish interest in Brazil stemmed from their desire to find a passage to the Far East through or around South America. The Spanish voyages of Juan Díaz de Solís (1515-16), Ferdinand Magellan (1519-22), Juan García Jofre de Loaysa (1525-26), Diego García (1526-30), and **Sebastian Cabot** (1526-30) all had this purpose and touched the Brazilian coast. These voyages underscored the difficulties of a westerly route to Asia and turned Spanish attention toward exploring the Río de la Plata estuary and limiting Portuguese claims in South America.

French interest lay in exploiting the commercial possibilities of brazilwood. With a ready market in the French textile industry in such ports as Dieppe and Rouen, French ship captains returned repeatedly to Brazil in the sixteenth century. Hugues Roger came to Brazil in 1521; Jean Parmentier, the poet from Dieppe, came between 1520 and 1525; and the Normans appeared in Guanabara Bay in 1525.

1516-19

The Portuguese dispatched the first squadron to patrol the Brazilian coast against the French. Captained by Cristovão Jacques, it established a *feitoria* at Pernambuco, where its residents planted the first sugar cane in Brazil. More Portuguese patrols were sent out in the 1520s to counter the growing French presence.

1526

Sugar was first produced in Brazil. Lisbon customs records show that sugar from Pernambuco was shipped to Portugal at least as early as 1526.

1527

Cristovão Jacques's Portuguese squadron of six

ships captured three French vessels loading brazilwood at Bahia. The French crew was hanged or buried alive.

1530-33

Martim Afonso de Sousa's expedition to Brazil marked the transition from the trading post era to one of direct grants to individuals. Several great lords offered to explore, settle, and defend Portugal's New World territories, but King João III first tried financing his own expedition and in 1530 chose Sousa to lead the undertaking. **Sousa** was directed to explore the Amazon River and the Río de la Plata, drive the French out, and establish a *feitoria* and a permanent settlement. Out of his expedition would come one of the few success stories in the early colonization of Brazil, the colony of São Vicente, which came to anchor Portugal's developing presence in southern Brazil.

January 1531. **Sousa's fleet of five ships and some 500 men reached Pernambuco** and encountered a French force of three ships that had seized the *feitoria*. Sousa defeated them and took their ships, dispatching two to explore the Amazon and the third to Lisbon with a load of brazilwood.

February. Sousa left Pernambuco and sailed south to the Bay of All Saints (Bahia de Todos os Santos), site of the future Salvador da Bahia. There he found the Portuguese Diogo Álvares, known as **Caramurú**, living among the native Americans. His knowledge of native lore served a succession of Portuguese colonists, clerics, and royal officials.

August 12-September 25. After three months in Guanabara Bay, Sousa's force moved south and spent forty-four days at Cananéia, where they found survivors of the Solís and **Cabot** expeditions living among the native Americans. Their stories about a kingdom in the west rich in gold and silver convinced Sousa of its existence. He organized a party of eight men under the command of Pêro Lobo Pinheiro to search for it. They departed on September 1 and were never heard from again.

January 22, 1532. Sousa chose the island of São Vicente (near modern Santos) as the site for the new colony. He organized the community on a sound footing, planted sugar cane, and worked to establish a viable relationship with the native Americans. For this latter purpose he approved a second settlement, which was erected in the highlands at the Indian community of Piratininga, not far from the future São Paulo. Here he put the experienced João Ramalho in charge as *capitão mor* (chief captain).

May 22. While Sousa remained behind in São Vicente, the fleet sailed from São Vicente to return to Portugal under the command of his brother, Pêro Lopes. In Pernambuco, Pêro Lopes captured two French ships and retook the *feitoria* the French had again captured. He hanged the French commander and twenty of his men, and let his native American allies eat another two.

September. News arrived from Portugal that King João III had decided to parcel out Brazil to various captains. Martim Afonso de Sousa was to receive two captaincies, São Vicente and Rio de Janeiro, and his brother Pêro Lopes another three, Santo Amaro, Santa Ana, and Itamaracá.

1534-49

The era of the donatary captaincies. The difficulties involved in developing Brazil led the king to shift the burden of colonization to those who accepted his fifteen captaincies (*donatários*). The fifteen captaincies from south to north were Santa Ana, São Vicente, Santo Amaro, Rio de Janeiro (or Guanabara Bay), São Tomé, Espíritu Santo, Pôrto Seguro, Ilhéus, Bahia, Pernambuco, Itamaracá, Rio Grande do Norte, Piauí, Maranhão, and Pará. Four of the twelve donatários never attempted to settle their captaincies, and four others soon succumbed to hostile Indians. Four—São Vicente, Pernambuco, Pôrto Seguro, and Ilhéus—survived beyond 1549.

São Vicente. Of the four southern captaincies, São Vicente was the only success. Although its captain, **Martim Afonso de Sousa**, left Brazil

in 1533 and never returned, he laid the basis for its success by planting sugar cane and developing a viable relationship with the native Americans. His deputy, Brás Cubas, relocated São Vicente and began the construction of a church and hospital, O Hospital de Todos os Santos, which gave its name to the present-day city of Santos. By 1548 São Vicente had six sugar mills (*engenhos*), 600 inhabitants, and 3,000 slaves, mainly native Americans. But its growth was restricted by its location on a narrow coastal strip and its distance from European markets for sugar.

Pôrto Seguro. This captaincy was granted to Pêro do Campo Tourinho, a rich landowner from

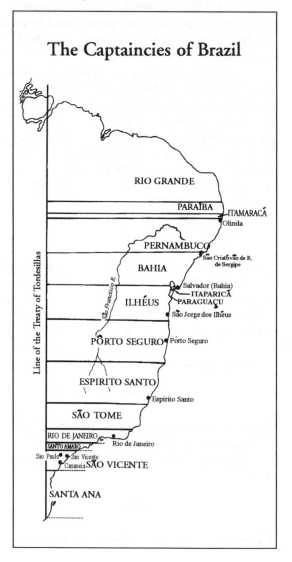

The Captaincies of Brazil

northern Portugal, on May 24, 1534. Some 600 settlers arrived in late 1534 or early 1535. After eleven years, six or seven settlements were functioning, but Tourinho aroused opposition because of his strict work ethic and irreverent attitude toward the church. In 1546 conspirators had him arrested and shipped back to Portugal, where he was eventually exonerated. He never returned to Brazil.

Ilhéus. This captaincy was granted to Jorge de Figueiredo Correia on July 26, 1534. As secretary of the royal treasury, he was obliged to remain in Portugal and appointed the Castilian Francisco Romero to carry out colonization of the captaincy. Drawing on Figueiredo's great wealth, Romero put together a substantial expedition of settlers and founded São Jorge de Ilhéus as the capital of the colony. Sugar was planted, and engenhos were built. Relations with the native Americans were peaceful.

Pernambuco. The most successful captaincy was Pernambuco, which was granted to **Duarte Coelho** on March 10, 1534, as a reward for his exploits as a navigator and soldier in Asia, North Africa, and France. His success in Pernambuco is attributed to the region's prior economic development as the site of one of the first *feitorias* in Brazil and the place where sugar was first produced. The long Portuguese presence produced a substantial number of *mamaluco* children before Coelho arrived, and he could build his captaincy around this seasoned nucleus.

March 1535. **Coelho and his colonists landed in Pernambuco.** Paulus Nunes, the local commander, turned the fort and feitoria over to him. Coelho named the colony Nova Lusitânia and made Recife its capital.

1537. **Coelho founded Olinda north of Recife.** Olinda eventually became the preferred home of the sugar planters, and tension developed between them and the merchants based in Recife.

1542

February 11-August 26. **Francisco de Orellana, a Spaniard, and his companions became the first Europeans to sail down the Amazon River to its mouth.** A member of the **Gonzalo Pizarro** expedition which vainly sought cinnamon and gold in eastern Ecuador, Orellana headed a party of 50 to 60 that struck out in search of food but instead explored the Amazon and its tributaries. Gaspar de Carvajal, a Dominican friar who accompanied Orellana, reported that the Spanish had skirmished with women warriors, or Amazons, who lived along the river.

1549

March 29. **Tomé de Sousa, Brazil's first governor-general, landed in Bahia.** With the creation of this position, João III raised Brazil to new importance in the Portuguese empire. The year before, the crown had purchased Bahia from the heirs of its captain-donatary, Francisco Pereira Coutinho, and made it a crown captaincy. Sousa's fleet of six ships carried other royal officials, 600 soldiers, 400 convicts (*degregados*), artisans, and six Jesuits, the first in the New World, who were led by **Manuel da Nóbrega.** Sousa immediately began the construction of the city of Salvador da Bahia on a high bluff overlooking the Bay of All Saints. It remained the seat of royal government until the capital was moved to Rio de Janeiro in 1763.

1552

June 22. **Brazil's first bishop, Pêro Fernandes Sardinha, landed in Bahia to occupy his see in Salvador.** Differences quickly appeared between him and the Jesuits over how best to christianize the native Americans. The Jesuits preferred to learn native ways and languages while the bishop wanted the Indians to learn Portuguese ways before being accepted as Christians. After a shipwreck near the São Francisco River in 1556, the bishop was killed and eaten by Caeté Indians.

1553

Sousa's successor as governor-general, **Duarte da Costa,** arrived in Salvador. He was accompanied by seven more Jesuits, among them the great linguist and teacher **José de Anchieta**.

1554

January 25. **Manuel da Nóbrega and other Jesuits consecrated a combined school and mission named in honor of Saint Paul (São Paulo).** The mission was located on the plain of Piratininga near the settlement established in 1532 by **Martim Afonso de Sousa**. This was the origin of the modern city of São Paulo. It grew slowly, hampered by its location on a plateau that could only be reached by ascent of the 2,400-foot coastal range.

1555

November 14. **A French colonizing expedition arrived in Guanabara Bay.** Led by Nicolas Durand de Villegagnon, a knight of Malta and vice admiral of Brittany, the eighty-man expedition founded a colony called Antarctic France on an island in the bay. Three hundred Protestant settlers arrived in 1557. Villegagnon returned to France in 1559.

1560

March. **Brazil's third governor-general, Mem de Sá, destroyed the French colony in Guanabara Bay.** Survivors, however, established themselves on the mainland, where they encouraged their Indian allies to attack the Portuguese.

1565

March 1. **Eustácio de Sá, a nephew of Mem de Sá, founded Rio de Janeiro as a base for fighting the French and their indigenous allies, the Tamoio.** The city was initially called São Sebastião in honor of King Sebastian (1557-78).

1567

January 20. **Mem de Sá and his nephew, Eustá-**cio de Sá, launched a successful offensive against the Tamoio and the French near Rio de Janeiro. Eustácio was mortally wounded by an arrow, and surviving Tamoio were enslaved.

1570

March 20. **King Sebastian issued a law banning the enslavement of native Americans.** But it allowed the enslavement of Indians captured in just wars, and this exception created a loophole that made the law ineffective.

1591

June 9. **Heitor Furtado de Mendonça arrived in Bahia to conduct a visitation for the Portuguese Inquisition.** Moving to Pernambuco in 1593, Mendoça remained in Brazil until 1595. No permanent tribunal of the Inquisition was ever established in Brazil, but some clergymen there were invested with inquisitorial powers, and investigators were again dispatched in 1618 and 1763. Inquisitors in Brazil were especially active in investigating people accused of secretly practicing Judaism; those denounced might be sent to Portugal for trial and punishment.

1598

December 25. **The Portuguese founded Natal.** This was the first of a series of settlements established by the Portuguese ever closer to the Amazon to counter the presence of foreigners. Today it is the capital of the state of the Rio Grande do Norte.

c. 1600-94

The African state of Palmares flourished in the backlands of the captaincy of Pernambuco. Palmares was the largest and most long-lived of the many *mocambos* or *quilombos*, settlements of fugitive slaves, that were founded in colonial Brazil. Its population may have numbered as many as 30,000 in the late seventeenth century.

During the early and mid-seventeenth century the Portuguese and Dutch conducted several unsuccessful expeditions against Palmares. Settlers complained that they lost servants and field hands to Palmares through raids or flight, while the Portuguese authorities were unwilling to allow a separate state to exist within Brazil. Starting in the 1670s, more systematic efforts were made to destroy Palmares. In 1694 a force of Paulistas and local fighters captured Palmares after a twenty-day siege.

1609

March 7. **A High Court of Appeals (*relação*) was established in Bahia.** It was suppressed in 1626 but reinstated in 1652. The court was primarily a judicial body but also advised the governor-general and reviewed the conduct of officials at the end of their terms. A second *relação* was established in Rio de Janeiro in 1751.

July 30. **The crown declared that all the indigenous inhabitants of Brazil were to be free.** According to the law, Indian slaves were to be freed, no Indian was to be compelled to labor, and all native workers were to receive wages like other free persons. The task of protecting and acculturating the Indians was entrusted to the Jesuits. This law produced such intense opposition from settlers in Brazil that it was soon repealed. A new measure (September 10, 1611) restored slavery for prisoners captured in just wars and for captives ransomed from the Indians themselves. The Jesuits also lost their civil powers over mission villages.

1612

September 8. **The Frenchman Daniel de La Touche (de La Ravardière) founded Saint Louis, named in honor of the French king, Louis XIII.** When the Portuguese drove the French out in 1615, it became São Luís do Maranhão.

1616

January 12. **Francisco Caldeira Castelo Branco**

founded Belém. Located near the mouth of the Amazon River, Belém served the Portuguese as a staging area for their drive to expell foreigners from northern Brazil. It also helped the Portuguese control and stimulate the development of the Amazon basin.

1621

The State of Maranhão was created. It combined several northern territories, including the captaincies of Maranhão and Pará, while the rest of the colony was included in the State of Brazil. The creation of the northern state was partly intended to counter the colonization efforts of various European powers. Because of contrary winds and currents, it was frequently easier to communicate directly with Lisbon than with Bahia. At first its capital was São Luís do Maranhão; in 1737 Belém became the capital. The two states were reunited into a single entity in 1772.

1624-54

The Dutch occupation of Brazil. With the renewal of war between Spain and the Netherlands in 1621, the Dutch moved to conquer those areas of the New World they saw as essential to their continued prosperity as the world's leaders in trade and commerce. A logical target was Brazil, where the Dutch also dominated the carrying trade between it and Europe. In the ensuing struggle—the most costly European conflict in the New World of the colonial era—thousands of people lost their lives, thousands more were uprooted, and property losses were enormous. The war continued even after the Portuguese threw off Spanish rule on December 1, 1640.

May 8-10, 1624. A Dutch fleet of twenty-six ships carrying 3,300 men captured Salvador da Bahia. The Dutch were themselves besieged by those who had fled the city.

May 1, 1625. A combined Spanish-Portuguese armada of fifty-two ships and 12,500 men led by Fadrique de Toledo y Osorio recaptured Salvador.

February 1630. The Dutch next targeted sugar-rich Pernambuco. The Dutch West India Company financed a fleet of sixty-seven ships and 7,000 men commanded by Henrick Corneliszoon Loncq that captured Olinda, Recife, and the island of Antônio Vaz. The Dutch, however, were again confined to their coastal positions and were harassed by those who had fled to the interior.

May 1631. Another Spanish-Portuguese fleet sailed from Portugal to attack the Dutch. Although it fought the Dutch fleet to a draw, it failed to supply needed reinforcements (only 700 men got through) and left the Dutch in control of the Brazilian coast. Nevertheless, the local Portuguese resistance kept the Dutch bottled up in Recife and forced them to abandon Olinda in November.

1632-35. The Pernambucan-born Domingos Fernandes Calabar turned coat, joined the Dutch, and provided them with key information about terrain and local conditions (April 20, 1632). Having received reinforcements, the Dutch expanded their control of Pernambuco, and by 1635 they controlled the coast as far north as Rio Grande do Norte. As more and more colonists in Dutch-controlled areas went over to their side, the Iberian response was the despatch of 2,500 troops, who arrived in November. They adopted the guerrilla tactics of the now famous Antônio Filipe Camarão, a native American, and **Henrique Dias**, a black, both of whom were allies of the Portuguese.

January 23, 1637. Johan Maurits, count of Nassau-Siegen and newly appointed governor-general of Dutch Brazil, arrived in Recife. He rebuilt and expanded the town, pushed Dutch control south to the São Francisco River, raided Ilhéus and Bahia even farther south, and captured Ceará in the north. He also dispatched a fleet to Africa that captured the Portuguese fortress and trading center of São Jorge de Mina.

May 1638. Maurits failed to capture Bahia. Late in the year an Iberian fleet of forty-six ships and 5,000 soldiers led by Fernão de Mascarenhas sailed with the purpose of retaking the Brazilian Northeast, but 3,000 died during its slow Atlantic crossing.

June 12, 1641. In Europe, the Netherlands and the new Portuguese monarchy signed a ten-year truce, but in Brazil Maurits occupied Sergipe del Rey and São Luís, the capital of Maranhão. This was the maximum extent of the Dutch occupation of Brazil. In addition, Maurits dispatched a fleet of twenty-one ships and 3,000 men across the Atlantic to Africa and captured Angola, Benguela, São Tomé, Ano Bom, and Axim. He returned to Europe in 1644.

June 13, 1645. Portuguese colonists under Dutch control revolted and defeated the Dutch at Monte das Tabocas thirty miles outside Recife (August 3). Other land victories followed, but at sea the Portuguese-led fleet of **Salvador de Sá** was destroyed by the Dutch force of Jan Corneliszoon Lichthart.

April 19, 1648. A Portuguese force of fewer than 3,000 led by Francisco Barreto defeated 5,000 Dutch and their Amerindian allies at Guararapes in Pernambuco. The Dutch abandoned Olinda.

August 24, 1648. Having sailed to Africa from Rio de Janeiro, Salvador de Sá and his 15-ship fleet and 2,000 men recaptured Luanda in Angola as well as Benguela and São Tomé soon after.

February 6, 1649. King João IV chartered the Brazil Company. This private company, founded on the initiative of the Jesuit priest **Antônio Vieira**, was given extensive trading privileges in Brazil and was authorized to fit out a naval force to convoy all ships sailing to and from Brazil. The company was founded in response to continued Dutch seizures of Portuguese shipping in the South Atlantic despite the existence of the ten-year truce.

February 17, 1649. The second battle of Guararapes again brought Portuguese victory over a Dutch force of 3,500. Nevertheless, the Dutch still retained control of Brazilian waters.

December 20, 1653. The Brazil Company's force of seventy-seven ships, their fourth armada to Brazil since 1649, arrived in Pernambuco to begin a blockade of Recife. The Dutch, overextended as a result of the First Anglo-Dutch War (1652-54), no longer controlled Brazilian waters.

January 26, 1654. The Dutch capitulated and

signed away all of their Brazilian holdings in the agreement of Taborda. Two days later the Portuguese entered Recife, and the Dutch empire in Brazil disappeared.

1628-41

Slave-hunting expeditions (*bandeiras*) from São Paulo were at their height. Residents of São Paulo, most of them *mamalucos*, and their Indian auxiliaries conducted many raids on Jesuit missions in Paraguay and other Spanish-held territories. The expeditionaries (known as *bandeirantes*) seized thousands of Indians, most of whom were shipped to other parts of Brazil. Condemnations of the raids by the governor-general and the pope were ignored. Many missions were abandoned, but the Jesuits began to arm their Indian charges, who defeated the Paulistas along the Mbororé River, a tributary of the Uruguay, in 1641. This engagement marked the end of the expeditions directed against the missions. Other factors in their decline were the increasing availability of African slaves and the greater impermeability of the boundaries between Spanish territory and Brazil after the accession of the Braganzas in 1640. The expeditions of the bandeirantes contributed to eventual Portuguese domination of the territory traversed.

1643

December 2. **The Overseas Council (Conselho Ultramarino) was formally inaugurated.** The new council was the successor of the India Council (1604-14), which was itself modeled on the Spanish Council of the Indies. Composed of a president and 36 councillors, it was the chief administrative organ overseeing most of Portugal's overseas possessions, including Brazil. It also advised the king. In the late eighteenth century, however, it increasingly lost power to government ministers.

1680

January 20. **A Portuguese expedition headed by Manuel de Lobo, governor of Rio de Janeiro, began construction of a fort and settlement at Colônia do Sacramento on the northern bank of the Río de la Plata estuary.** The Spanish destroyed Colônia soon after (August 7, 1680), but it was rebuilt three years later. The establishment of Colônia represented an important step in Portugal's advance into territories in the Río de la Plata area that were claimed by Spain, which vigorously resisted Portuguese ambitions. Meanwhile, Portuguese settlers had been moving into Paraná, Santa Catarina, and Rio Grande do Sul provinces, which eventually became part of southern Brazil.

April 1. **The crown ordered an end to the slavery of native Americans in the State of Maranhão.** This law, inspired by the Jesuit priest **Antônio Vieira**, was the culmination of decades of conflict over Indian labor in the Amazon basin. Colonists in the region, too poor to afford African slaves, demanded easy access to Indian labor while the Jesuits sought to gather native Americans into mission villages (*aldeias*) under their control and prevent their enslavement. Tempers had flared to such a point that in 1661 colonists in São Luís rose up against the Jesuits in Maranhão and expelled many of them, including Vieira. The 1680 law ordered that enslaved Indians be set free, and that henceforth no Indian was to be enslaved under any circumstances. The legislation also regulated the labor of Indians for wages and proposed that African slaves be made available at moderate prices. Settlers complained about the law, and in February 1684 malcontents in São Luís seized the governor and the Jesuits. The crown crushed the rebellion, but allowed Indian slavery again in 1688 for prisoners taken in just wars.

1693-95

Prospectors from São Paulo discovered alluvial gold in various places in Minas Gerais. News of the strikes touched off a gold rush that threatened to depopulate other sections of the colony. Paulistas also discovered gold in Cuiabá, Mato Grosso (1718), Goiás (1725), and Guaporé in present-day Rondônia (1734). As a result, gold production in Brazil rose steadily during the first half of the eighteenth century, reaching a peak in the early 1750s and declining thereafter.

1708

November. **Fighting broke out in Minas Gerais between Paulistas and men from Portugal and other sections of Brazil.** The Paulistas, who had been responsible for the discovery of gold in the region, believed that they should dominate the mining areas and resented the presence of the latter, whom they referred to with the derogatory epithet *emboabas*, which may be derived from the name of a local bird. The emboabas defeated the Paulistas, but the royal government stepped in to restore order in 1709. In that year the new captaincy of São Paulo and Minas de Ouro was created to facilitate royal control over the mining areas.

1710

February 14-15. **A stone column (*pelourinho*), symbolic of municipal status, was erected in Recife, touching off the "War of the Mascates."** Tensions had arisen between the Brazilian-born planters of Olinda and the inhabitants of Recife, which had been an insignificant village until the Dutch made it their capital. The town was dominated by merchants, usually natives of Portugal. The latter were derisively called *mascates*, or peddlers, by the planters who were often indebted to them. The planters and their supporters, angry over Olinda's loss of status with the elevation of Recife to urban rank, reacted violently. They attacked Recife, tore down the *pelourinho*, and forced the governor of Pernambuco, considered sympathetic to the peddlers, to flee. Peace was not restored for several years, but Recife remained a municipality. The conflict is sometimes seen as symptomatic of developing hostility to Portugal and of embryonic nationalism in Pernambuco.

September 19. **Jean François Duclerc, a French privateer, attacked Rio de Janeiro.** He had sailed from Brest the previous May with six ships and 1,500 men. This new French assault on Brazil came after Portugal had joined Great Britain, an enemy of France, in the War of the Spanish Succession. The attack failed, however,

and Duclerc surrendered, only to be murdered the following March by a party of masked men.

1711

September 12. **A French privateering fleet of sixteen ships carrying 5,500 men sailed into the harbor of Rio de Janeiro.** Commanded by René Duguay-Trouin, the expedition sought satisfaction for the defeat inflicted on Jean Duclerc the year before. After a heavy bombardment from the ships' guns, most of the residents fled, and the city surrendered. Duguay-Trouin demanded and received a large ransom of gold, sugar, and cattle, and left the city on November 13.

1720s

Diamonds were discovered in Minas Gerais. The date and circumstances of the discovery are not known as the stones were not recognized as diamonds at first. Later there were efforts to keep the discovery a secret. After it was informed of the discovery in 1729, the crown strictly regulated diamond mining in an attempt to prevent smuggling and to limit supply in order to maintain price levels in Europe.

1750

January 13. **The Treaty of Madrid attempted to fix the boundaries between Spanish and Portuguese territory in South America.** Portugal renounced its claims to Colônia do Sacramento, acknowledging Spanish supremacy in the Río de la Plata, while Spain accepted the Portuguese claim to much of Amazonia and ceded to Portugal the territory east of the Uruguay River and north of the Ibicuí occupied by seven Jesuit missions. In general, the treaty accepted the principle of possession (*uti possidetis*) as the basis for territorial claims and represented Spain's recognition of Portuguese expansion beyond the limits set by the Treaty of Tordesillas.

July 31. **The death of King João V and the accession of his son José I brought the ascen-**

dancy of the **Marquês de Pombal, who became secretary of state for war and foreign affairs.** After a disastrous earthquake in Lisbon on November 1, 1755, **Pombal** took charge of relief operations and became a virtual dictator. He introduced wide-ranging but controversial administrative and economic changes in both Portugal and Brazil.

1754-58

Spanish and Portuguese forces compelled the Guaraní Indians of the seven missions east of the Uruguay River to abandon their missions. By the Treaty of Madrid (1750) this Spanish-held territory was to be ceded to Portugal, and the Guaraní inhabitants were to move to new sites west of the Uruguay. The Indians, however, defied the authorities and bowed only to superior force. Accusations that their Jesuits mentors encouraged their defiance may be unfounded.

1755

June 6. **The royal government declared the native Americans of Maranhão and Pará to be free citizens who could live and work wherever they wished.** Moreover, mission villages were to become towns controlled by the Indians themselves, not the Jesuits. The law was partly abrogated in 1757 when non-Indian directors were put in charge of Indian towns. A related decree of 1755 encouraged intermarriage between Indians and whites and removed all legal disabilities against children born of such unions.

June 7. **The Portuguese government created the General Company of Commerce of Greater Pará and Maranhão to encourage the importation of African slaves to northern Brazil.** Anticipating settler complaints about the lack of indigenous workers in light of the law of June 6, the government gave the company the exclusive right to supply the region with African slaves as well as other privileges. As a result of its efforts, more than 25,000 slaves were imported before it was abolished in 1778. The company

also promoted the cultivation of cotton, rice, and other crops.

1759

September 3. **The Portuguese government suppressed the Society of Jesus and ordered all Jesuits to leave Portugal and its possessions.** The action was due in part to the strong dislike of the **Marquês de Pombal** for the order, which he implicated in an unsuccessful plot to murder the king (1758). It is believed, however, that Pombal's main motive was to seize the Jesuits' properties and to eliminate them as a force in the economy. More than six hundred Jesuits were forced to leave Brazil, where they were by far the wealthiest religious order.

1761

February 12. **The Treaty of Pardo nullified the Treaty of Madrid (1750).** The demarcation of borders called for by the latter was not carried out because of the recalcitrance of the Indians in the seven missions and other problems. As a result, the Portuguese retained Colônia do Sacramento, which was seized by Spain in 1762. Spain returned Colônia at the conclusion of the Seven Years' War, during which Spain and Portugal were on opposite sides.

1777

March 1. **The Marquês de Pombal submitted his resignation to Queen Maria I.** Maria, who had succeeded to the throne upon the death of her father, José I, on February 24, accepted Pombal's resignation and reversed many of his policies.

October 1. **The Treaty of San Ildefonso was signed.** The treaty again defined the boundaries between Portuguese and Spanish territory in South America. The territorial arrangements were generally similar to those of the failed Treaty of Madrid (1750). However, Spain kept the seven missions territory while acknowledging Portuguese control of disputed lands in Santa Catarina and Rio Grande do Sul. In a secret article, Portugal also ceded to Spain the west African islands of Ano Bom and Fernando Po.

1788-89

The Conspiracy of Minas Gerais (Inconfidência Mineira). Members of the elite in Minas Gerais launched a conspiracy against the government that was foiled when it was denounced to the authorities. The principal conspirators were motivated by the government's plan to collect back taxes in the captaincy and impose other objectionable policies. However, some conspirators, inspired by the United States example, looked for the establishment of an independent republic. Only one person, **Joaquim José da Silva Xavier**, was executed. A low-ranking army officer, he was known as Tiradentes (Tooth-puller) because he had once practiced dentistry. The abortive plot is often considered a precursor of Brazil's movement for independence in the early nineteenth century.

1798

The Conspiracy of the Tailors (Inconfidência dos Alfaiates). In Salvador da Bahia a group of conspirators, many of whom were non-white, plotted to separate Brazil from Portugal. Tailors and other artisans, as well as army enlisted men, were prominent among the conspirators. They were motivated by unhappiness over the high cost of living, but their manifestoes, influenced by the French Revolution, also called for an end to slavery, the abolition of racial distinctions, and the establishment of a republic. Regional elites, however, had little interest in supporting the social revolution envisioned. The plot proved abortive and four persons, all mulattoes, were eventually executed.

Brazil at the End of the Colonial Era

THE STRUGGLE FOR INDEPENDENCE
1804-1825

The struggle for independence in Latin America was long, complex, and, in many places, violent. It was partly an outgrowth of developments within the colonies and partly the result of events in Europe. Each colony's experience was unique. By 1825, however, Brazil and all but two of the Spanish colonies—Cuba and Puerto Rico—had become independent nations. Haiti threw off French rule even earlier.

By 1800 many creoles had grievances against the Spanish regime. Although commercial restrictions had been loosened in the late eighteenth century, creoles still resented Spain's continued monopoly of colonial trade. Influenced by the principles of the Enlightenment and the American Revolution, some creoles questioned the power of the monarchy and the church. There was also a widespread feeling that colonial interests were being sacrificed for Spanish ends, a sentiment that bred an embryonic nationalism in many places. Despite dissatisfaction, most creoles were fearful of any social upheaval that might threaten the existing social and economic order.

Spain's participation in the European wars that broke out after the French Revolution of 1789 disrupted its relations with its colonies, in particular damaging its monopoly of trade. The crucial event was Napoleon Bonaparte's invasion of the Iberian Peninsula in 1807-8. The departure of the Portuguese royal family for Brazil in 1807 set that colony on the road to independence. After his troops had overrun Portugal, Napoleon moved against Spain, imprisoning the king, **Ferdinand VII**, and installing his own brother Joseph on the throne. In the colonies creoles used Ferdinand's captivity as a pretext to move against Spanish officials and to claim the right to govern themselves in the absence of the legitimate monarch.

Many Spaniards resisted French rule, led first by a central junta based in Seville, then by a Regency, and finally by a *cortes* (parliament). The Spanish anti-French forces, though often liberal in domestic matters, had little sympathy with creole pretensions and declared the colonies to be an integral part of Spain. Ferdinand, who was restored to his throne in 1814, was also determined to subdue the rebellious colonists. In Mexico, Venezuela, and other colonies, many creoles actively supported the Spanish forces because of their fear of social revolution, and contributed significantly to the Spanish reconquest of most of the colonies by 1816. But the refusal of Ferdinand to make concessions to the colonists and the repressive policies of the restored Spanish authorities alienated even more creoles and brought them to the side of independence. If support for independence increased over the years, there was little consensus on the new states to be established. Monarchy and republicanism each had supporters. Provincial leaders sought independence not only from Spain but also from the old viceregal capitals. As a result, internal quarrels often impeded the struggle against Spain.

1804

January 1. **The independence of Haiti was proclaimed by Jean-Jacques Dessalines, who became emperor of the new nation.** The independence of the former French colony of Saint Domingue came after the final withdrawal of French troops in 1803. Napoleon had dispatched a large force to Saint Domingue in 1801 to subdue the colony and to restore slavery, but armed resistance by blacks and the ravages of yellow fever led him to abandon the effort.

December 26. **A Spanish decree ordered the secuestration of the charitable funds of the church in the colonies** (*consolidación de vales*). This decree, issued soon after Spain went to war against Great Britain, meant that landowners, merchants, and others who had borrowed from the funds now had to pay their debts so that the sums collected could be sent to Spain. In Mexico, about 12 million pesos were collected before the decree was suspended by the viceroy in 1808. This unpopular measure alienated many creoles.

1806

June 27. **A British expeditionary force of 1,700 men occupied Buenos Aires. Great Britain was then at war with Spain and viewed its colonies as possible markets for British products.** Although the viceroy of the Río de la Plata, the Marquis of Sobremonte, fled to Córdoba, creoles prepared to resist under the leadership of Santiago Liniers, a French officer in Spanish service. The hastily organized militia defeated the British force on August 12, 1806. Liniers was later named temporary viceroy.

October 17. **Dessalines, the emperor of Haiti, was assassinated in an army ambush.** Haiti was now divided into a northern state ruled by **Henri Christophe**, who proclaimed himself King Henry in 1811, and a southern republic headed by **Alexandre Pétion**.

1807

June 23. **A 9,000-man British force under General John Whitelocke disembarked near Buenos Aires and attacked the city.** The British had captured Montevideo on February 3, 1807, but were unsuccessful in Buenos Aires. The events of 1806 and 1807 stimulated the self-confidence and nationalism of Buenos Aires creoles, who had defeated the British invaders without Spanish assistance.

1808

March 7. **The Portuguese royal family arrived in Rio de Janeiro**, having left Lisbon the previous November to escape invading French forces. Thousands of courtiers and officials accompanied the royal family, which was headed by João, the prince regent, who governed on behalf of his demented mother, Queen Maria I. The Portuguese fleet was escorted by a British squadron.

September 15. **Spanish elites in Mexico City deposed the viceroy, José de Iturrigaray**, whom they considered overly partial to the creoles. The Spaniards installed a more compliant viceroy, Pedro Garibay, and created a private army, the Volunteers of Ferdinand VII, to defend their interests. Creole resentment over these actions was exacerbated by drought and economic recession, especially in the Bajío region of west-central Mexico.

1809

January 1. **A Spanish conspiracy in Buenos Aires to depose the acting viceroy, Liniers, proved unsuccessful.** The Spaniards distrusted Liniers as a foreigner and considered him too favorably disposed to the creoles. In July he was removed by Spain's central junta and replaced by Baltasar Hidalgo de Cisneros.

July 16. **Creole radicals in La Paz seized the intendant and the bishop.** Shortly afterward they formed a governing junta that openly demanded independence from Spain. The viceroy of Peru, José de Abascal, dispatched troops to quell the rebels, who were defeated in October. Nine were executed, and many others exiled. A more moderate uprising in Chuquisaca on May 25, 1809, had also failed.

August 10. **Creoles in Quito overthrew the audiencia and formed a governing junta.** They claimed to be acting in defense of the rights of the imprisoned **Ferdinand VII**, but they denounced the Spanish monopoly of power in government. The viceroy of Peru forced the junta to surrender on October 28, 1809, and restored the audiencia to power.

1810

April 19. **Creoles in Caracas, Venezuela, deposed the Spanish authorities** and established a governing junta that claimed to rule on behalf of Ferdinand.

May 25. **Creole revolutionaries in Buenos Aires deposed Viceroy Cisneros and installed a four-man junta.** The junta claimed to govern on behalf of Ferdinand but acted as if it were independent of Spain. Other sections of the viceroyalty, however, refused to acknowledge the authority of the junta. Provincial leaders feared that their economic interests would suffer under the hegemony of Buenos Aires. This conflict would provoke upheaval in the region for decades.

July 20. **Creole revolutionaries in Santa Fe de Bogotá, capital of the viceroyalty of New Granada, deposed the viceroy and formed a junta to govern the colony.** These events occurred after a Spanish merchant made an insulting remark about Americans. But conflict soon developed between federalists and centralists over the amount of autonomy the various provinces would have in any new government.

August 2. **Mobs attacked a Quito jail in an effort to free prisoners who had been convicted for their role in the 1809 uprising.** In the ensuing melee royalist troops from Peru killed seventy of the prisoners and three hundred others. This massacre led to the formation of another junta on September 22, 1810, which ruled until it was crushed by royalist forces in 1812. Ecuador then remained under the control of the viceroy of Peru, but a pro-independence revolt was launched in Guayaquil on October 9, 1820.

September 16. **Miguel Hidalgo, a creole priest, publicly denounced Spanish misrule** in Dolores, Guanajuato, the parish in the Bajío region of Mexico to which he was assigned. Hidalgo had joined other creoles in the region in planning an uprising but was forced to act prematurely when the conspiracy was discovered. Hidalgo soon attracted thousands of Indians and mestizos to his cause but failed to control their actions. The massacre of Spaniards who had entrenched themselves in the granary (*alhóndiga*) of Guanajuato and the sack of the city (September 28, 1810) shocked creoles as well as Europeans.

September 18. **Chilean creoles removed Spanish officials and established a governing junta in Santiago.** It was ostensibly loyal to Ferdinand, but some creoles already favored independence.

1811

February 26. **Rural leaders in the Banda Oriental (later the Republic of Uruguay) began an anti-Spanish campaign with the help of Buenos Aires.** José Gervasio Artigas soon became commander of these forces and inflicted a serious defeat on the Spaniards at Las Piedras. The situation became more complicated with the invasion of Portuguese troops from Brazil, which had long coveted the province. Fearing the Portuguese more than the Spaniards, Buenos Aires signed an armistice with the viceroy, Francisco Xavier de Elío, on October 20, 1811. Under British pressure, the Portuguese withdrew in 1812. Meanwhile, **Artigas** had concluded that the Banda Oriental must seek independence both from Buenos Aires and from Spain and withdrew temporarily from the scene.

May 14-15. **Creole leaders in Asunción, Paraguay, launched a movement to end Spanish power in the province and asserted their independence from Buenos Aires as well.** The Paraguayans had already shown their desire for self-rule by defeating armies sent from Buenos Aires at the battles of Paraguarí (January 9, 1811) and Tacuarí (March 9, 1811). A three-man junta was established to govern Paraguay. One of its members, **José Gaspar Rodríguez de Francia**, soon became Paraguay's dictator and ruled the country until his death in 1840.

July 5. **A national congress dominated by creoles declared Venezuela's independence from Spain and established a republic.** However, royalists fought to preserve Spanish rule, often backed by blacks and mulattoes who felt little motivation to support independence.

July 30. **Miguel Hidalgo was executed by Spanish officials** in the northern Mexican city of Chihuahua. He and other insurgents had been captured on January 17, 1811, after being defeated at the Battle of Calderón, near Guadalajara.

Hidalgo's failure is usually attributed partly to his military errors but mainly to the fact that most Mexican creoles remained aloof from his movement. They feared that the victory of his Indian and mestizo forces would bring social revolution.

1812

March 26. **A major earthquake struck Venezuela.** It inflicted severe damage on Caracas, La Guaira, and other towns and killed many pro-independence soldiers in those places. Royalist clergymen called the earthquake, which occurred on Holy Thursday, God's punishment on those who had disavowed the king. The pro-independence forces suffered reverses in the ensuing months, and **Francisco de Miranda**, the supreme commander, capitulated to the Spaniards on July 25, 1812. Angered by Miranda's capitulation, **Simón Bolívar** prevented his departure from Venezuela. That allowed Miranda's arrest and imprisonment by royalists. The incarcerated Miranda died in Cádiz, Spain, July 14, 1816.

1813

August 6. **Simón Bolívar, the new leader of Venezuela's patriot forces, entered Caracas in triumph.** Establishing Venezuela's second republic, he held dictatorial powers but was unable to prevail against the royalist leader, José Tomás Boves, whose army was made up largely of cowboys from Venezuela's *llanos*, or plains, region. By the end of 1814 the second republic had been crushed, and Bolívar went into exile.

November 6. **Mexico's independence was declared by a congress meeting at Chilpancingo, Guerrero.** The congress was convened by **José María Morelos**, a priest who had emerged as **Hidalgo**'s successor in the anti-Spanish struggle. Military reverses later forced the congress to move to Apatzingán, Michoacán, where they issued Mexico's first constitution (October 22, 1814).

1814

August 2. **Creole reformers in Cuzco, Peru, took control of the city from Spanish officials.** To widen the movement's appeal, the creoles obtained the support of Mateo García Pumacahua, an Indian leader hitherto loyal to Spain. The insurgents sought independence from Lima as well as Spain, and the movement soon spread to Arequipa and other cities in southern Peru. However, the prospect of Indian rebellion alarmed many creoles, and Spain had subdued the revolt by mid-1815. Peru remained a royalist bastion until 1821.

October 1-2. **Chilean forces led by Bernardo O'Higgins suffered a decisive defeat at the hands of Spanish forces at Rancagua.** This victory restored Spanish rule to Chile, but the repressive policies of the authorities alienated most Chileans and increased pro-independence sentiment.

1815

December 6. **The Spanish general Pablo Morillo occupied Cartagena, New Granada, after a destructive siege of 100 days.** Morillo had arrived in Venezuela in April 1815 with 10,000 troops. After consolidating Spanish power there, he moved successfully against revolutionary forces in New Granada. In both places he executed or exiled hundreds of revolutionaries and confiscated their property.

December 17. **João issued a decree elevating Brazil to the status of a kingdom equal to Portugal.** Although the French no longer ruled Portugal, João was reluctant to return. The decree was designed to correct the anomaly of his continued residence in a colony. The prince regent became King **João VI** in 1816 upon the death of Queen Maria.

December 22. **Morelos was executed by Spanish forces near Mexico City.** After waging successful campaigns in west-central Mexico from 1811 to 1813, **Morelos** suffered a serious defeat late in 1814 while trying to capture Valladolid (now Morelia, Michoacán). He was taken prisoner on November 5, 1815. Like **Hidalgo**, Morelos failed to win significant creole support.

1816

July 9. **Delegates to a congress in Tucumán formally declared the independence of Buenos Aires and other provinces that later comprised**

Argentina. The congress also drew up a constitution for the United Provinces of South America. But, the absence of delegates from Santa Fe, Entre Ríos, and other provinces of the old Viceroyalty of the Río de la Plata revealed their continued resistance to domination by Buenos Aires.

August 28. **Portuguese forces again invaded the Banda Oriental**, which had been abandoned by Spain in 1815. **Artigas**, who had governed the province since then, was forced to evacuate Montevideo in January 1817. Waging a guerrilla campaign against the Portuguese in the interior, he suffered a serious defeat at Tacuarembó (January 22, 1820).

December 31. **Bolívar returned to Venezuela to renew the struggle against Spain.** Instead of staying near the coast, he headed for the *llanos*. After the fall of Angostura (now Ciudad Bolívar) in July 1817, he established his headquarters in that city. With the help of **José Antonio Páez**, a major regional chieftain, he forged a new army.

1817

January 9. **A 5,000-man army organized by José de San Martín began its epic march across the Andes to Chile.** San Martín, convinced that the independence of the Río de la Plata would not be secure until the Spaniards were removed from Chile and Peru, had begun to organize his army in Mendoza (Argentina) in 1814, joined by **Bernardo O'Higgins** and other Chilean exiles.

February 12. **A victory at Chacabuco gave San Martín and O'Higgins control of the Chilean capital of Santiago,** though the Spaniards remained a threat. A few days later **O'Higgins** became supreme director of Chile.

March 6. **A republican revolt erupted in the captaincy of Pernambuco, Brazil.** The rebels, many of them associated with Masonic lodges, were influenced by anti-Portuguese sentiment, by the ideology of the Enlightenment, and by the contemporary Spanish American revolutions. The revolt found little support in other regions and was crushed in May.

1818

April 5. **José de San Martín defeated a Spanish army at Maipú near Santiago, assuring Chilean independence.** Bernardo O'Higgins had formally proclaimed Chile's independence on February 12, 1818.

1819

February 15. **A national congress called by Bolívar met at Angostura, Venezuela.** Although most of Venezuela still remained under Spanish control, the congress adopted a constitution for a new republic embodying principles set forth by **Bolívar** and elected him president.

August 7. **Bolivar's army defeated royalist forces at the Battle of Boyacá,** near Santa Fe de Bogotá, effectively ending Spanish control of New Granada. Bolívar's forces had reached the battle site after a grueling trek across the plains of Venezuela and New Granada, followed by an equally arduous passage over the Andes.

December 17. **The congress of Angostura decreed the union of New Granada and Venezuela** in the republic of Colombia, usually referred to as Gran, or Greater, Colombia.

1820

October 8. **Henri Christophe, suffering from poor health, committed suicide.** This event allowed **Jean-Pierre Boyer**, who had succeeded **Alexandre Pétion** in southern Haiti, to reunite the country under a single ruler.

1821

February 24. **Agustín de Iturbide, a creole and head of the royalist army, issued the Plan de Iguala, which called for Mexico's independence from Spain.** It also called for the establishment of a monarchy, preservation of the status of the church and the military, and unity between Spaniards and Mexicans. The plan quickly won adherents among insurgents and conservative creoles as well as the bulk of the royalist forces. Its success is usually attributed to its conservative supporters who feared the liberalism of the Spanish Constitution of 1812—which was forced on Spanish king **Ferdinand VII** in 1820 and was supposed to go into effect in Mexico—and who opted for the Plan of Iguala and its promise of social stability. On August 24, 1821, Juan O'Donohú, Spain's newly arrived emissary, signed the Treaty of Córdoba recognizing Mexico as an independent nation. Spain repudiated the treaty but by 1822 it controlled only the fortress of San Juan de Ulúa in the harbor of Veracruz. The Spaniards left the fortress in 1824.

April 26. **King João VI returned to Portugal** in an effort to preserve the monarchy, the survival of which was threatened by a liberal revolution there (1820). He left his son **Pedro** to act as regent of Brazil.

June 24. **Bolívar's forces defeated the Spanish army at Carabobo,** southwest of Valencia, Venezuela. This battle marked the final triumph of patriot forces in Venezuela.

July 9. **Patriot troops under the command of José de San Martín entered Lima after the city had been evacuated by Spanish forces.** San Martín's army of 4,500 had sailed from Chile on August 20, 1820, escorted by warships commanded by **Thomas Cochrane**, a British naval officer in Chilean service. Once in Lima, San Martín declared the independence of Peru (July 28, 1821), and he was named protector with supreme civil and military power (August 3, 1821). His position remained insecure, however, because Spanish forces still controlled the interior.

July 12. **A congress meeting in Cúcuta, New Granada, adopted a constitution for Gran Colombia,** now comprising New Granada, Venezuela, and Ecuador. It provided for a highly centralized state and for the gradual abolition of slavery. On September 7, 1821, the congress elected **Simón Bolívar** president and **Francisco de Paula Santander** vice president. As Bolívar remained preoccupied by the war against Spain, effective power devolved upon Santander.

September 15. **Guatemalan elites, reacting to events in Mexico, declared the independence of Central America from Spain.** The top Spanish official in the region, Gabino Gainza, did not oppose the action. Facing military pressure from **Iturbide**'s Mexico and desirous of preserving stability, Guatemalan leaders decided that Central America should unite with Mexico. Over 100 towns in Central America endorsed the move, but localist sentiment remained strong.

November 28. **Creoles in the city of Panama declared Panamanian independence** from Spain and voted to become part of Gran Colombia.

1822

January 12. **President Boyer announced that Santo Domingo would be annexed to Haiti** and prepared to invade Dominican territory, marking the beginning of twenty-two years of Haitian rule over the entire island of Hispaniola. These actions occurred after the Dominicans had declared independence from Spain on November 30, 1821.

May 19. **Iturbide was proclaimed emperor of Mexico.** This action was taken by the Mexican congress in response to military pressure. But **Iturbide** lacked deep-seated support, faced serious financial problems, and was criticized for dictatorial methods. In the face of widespread military defections, he abdicated on March 19, 1823.

May 24. **Forces under Antonio José de Sucre defeated Spanish troops on the slopes of Mount Pichincha, overlooking Quito, Ecuador.** **Bolívar** had sent Sucre to Ecuador to assist revolutionaries in the port of Guayaquil and to win the province for Gran Colombia. Although the Battle of Pichincha marked the end of Spanish rule in Ecuador, the disposition of Guayaquil remained unclear as it was claimed by Peru as well as Gran Colombia.

June 19. **U.S. president James Monroe formally received Manuel Torres,** chargé d'affaires of Gran Colombia, thereby conferring United States recognition on the new republic. The United States was the first non–Latin American country to recognize the newly independent states. In a message to Congress the previous March, Monroe had stated that the Latin American nations deserved recognition and asked that funds be appropriated for this purpose. The second country to be recognized was Mexico (December 12, 1822).

July 26-27. **San Martín and Bolívar met in Guayaquil.** During the famous meeting, the two liberators discussed the prosecution of the war in Peru as well as the future of Guayaquil. Concluding that Bolívar was in a better position to expel the remaining Spanish forces from Peru, San Martín decided to withdraw from the scene. Upon returning to Lima, he resigned as protector and left Peru. Guayaquil was incorporated into Gran Colombia.

September 7. **Pedro declared the independence of Brazil from Portugal.** He took this action on the banks of the Ypiranga, a small river near São Paulo. It came as a result of Portuguese efforts to reduce Brazil to colonial status again.

On October 10, 1822, **Pedro** was crowned emperor of Brazil.

1823

January 28. **Bernardo O'Higgins was forced to resign as supreme director of Chile.** His efforts at reform had alienated both large landowners and the church, and he lacked a strong political base.

June 24. **A constituent congress met in Guatemala and declared the independence of Central America from Mexico.** A federal republic called the United Provinces was created, comprising the provinces of Guatemala, El Salvador, Honduras, Nicaragua, and Costa Rica. Manuel José Arce of El Salvador was chosen as president. The federation's capital was initially located in Guatemala City but was moved to San Salvador in 1834.

August 18. **José Francisco Lemus, a Cuban veteran of Bolívar's army, was arrested** and jailed for plotting the overthrow of Spanish rule on the island and the establishment of an independent republic. This conspiracy, known as the Soles y Rayos de Bolívar, was but one of several unsuccessful anti-Spanish plots during the independence era. Several factors inhibited the development of pro-independence sentiment in Cuba, among them the presence of thousands of royalist exiles from the former colonies. Most important was fear on the part of Cuban planters that anti-Spanish agitation might result in an uprising of slaves, as had occurred in Saint Domingue.

September 1. **Bolívar arrived in Lima** at the invitation of Peruvian creoles, who had been unable to establish an effective government after the departure of **José de San Martín**. He was granted dictatorial powers to prosecute the war against Spain.

December 2. **President Monroe asserted the principles known as the Monroe Doctrine in a message to congress.** His statement, which declared that the Americas were no longer open to European colonization and the United States would regard any intervention of a European power in the Americas as an unfriendly act against the United States, was spurred in part by the fear (later shown to be unfounded) that France might join Spain in trying to subdue the rebellious colonies of Spanish America. Monroe stated that the United States would regard any such effort as "dangerous" to its "peace and safety."

1824

March 25. **Pedro I promulgated a constitution for Brazil.** The constitution was written by a 10-man council of state after **Pedro** had disbanded a constituent assembly with which he had quarreled. The constitution provided for a centralized government and gave the emperor extensive powers, including a "moderating power," which made him the arbiter of the political system. The constitution remained in force until 1889.

July 2. **Rebels in Recife proclaimed the independence of Pernambuco** and called upon other provinces of northeast Brazil to join in a new Confederation of the Equator. Only Ceará heeded the call, though there was some support in Piauí. The rebellion arose out of opposition to the emperor's dissolution of the constituent assembly and to his newly appointed governor for Pernambuco. A naval bombardment of Recife and the landing of troops there ended the revolt in Pernambuco in September 1824 and in Ceará in October.

August 6. **Troops led by Bolívar and Sucre defeated Spanish forces on the high mountain plain of Junín, near Jauja, Peru.** No shots were fired during the hour-long battle, which was fought with swords and lances.

October 4. **A constituent congress formally published a new constitution for Mexico.** It created a federalist republic and established Catholicism as the national religion. Guadalupe Victoria, a veteran of **José María Morelos**'s campaign against Spain, became the first president.

December 9. **Troops under Sucre decisively defeated Spanish forces at Ayacucho, Peru, in** the last major battle of the wars for independence. Viceroy José de La Serna was taken prisoner and agreed to evacuate Peru.

1825

April 19. **Juan Antonio Lavalleja and thirty-two companions invaded the Banda Oriental in an attempt to expel the occupying Portuguese forces.** His campaign received aid from the United Provinces of South America, which wished to incorporate the Banda Oriental.

August 6. **An assembly meeting in Chuqui-** saca declared the independence of Upper Peru, which was named Bolivia, in honor of **Simón Bolívar.** Royalist sentiment in the region had remained strong until Spanish defeats in Peru made continued adherence to Spain unfeasible. The arrival of **José Antonio de Sucre** late in 1824 and his subsequent victory over the last royalist forces finally decided the issue.

December 22. **Brazil declared war on the United Provinces of South America** in an effort to retain control of the Banda Oriental. Brazil's action marked the beginning of the Cisplatine War (1825-28).

Political Organization of Colonial Latin America

Disputed by England, Russia, and Spain

Effective Frontier of Spanish Settlement

New France

English Colonies

Viceroyalty of New Spain

Mexico City

Haiti (French from 1697) and Santo Domingo

Jamaica (conquered by English, 1655)

Original boundary between viceroyalties of New Spain and Peru

Guiana

Viceroyalty of New Granada (established 1717, 1739)

Bogotá

Pernambuco (held by Dutch, 1630-54)

Grão Pará

Maranhao

Atlantic Ocean

Viceroyalty of Peru

Lima

Mato Grosso

Goias

Bahia

Minas Gerais

Pacific Ocean

Sao Paulo

Rio de Janeiro

Viceroyalty of La Plata (established 1776)

Santiago

Buenos Aires

Rio Grande do Sul

1494 Line of Tordesillas

Spanish America: Viceroyalties

Portuguese America (viceroyalty of Brazil): Captaincies-general

CAUDILLOS AND CONFLICT
1826-1870

The reverberations of the wars of independence and the breakup of the Spanish and Portuguese empires in America were felt during most of the period 1826-70. **Simón Bolívar** and other independence leaders hoped to reconstitute the old viceroyalties, but centrifugal tendencies proved too strong. As a result, many new nations emerged, often embracing territories once under the jurisdiction of the old audiencias (high courts). Within the new nations there were bitter conflicts over the form of government that should be adopted, the role of the Catholic Church, and other issues. Adding to the turmoil were the pretensions of veteran military leaders, who asserted, often by force, their right to rule the nations they had helped create. They were the first *caudillos*, or strongmen, of the postindependence era. Only Brazil, whose path to independence had diverged from that of Spanish America, avoided serious disarray. Regional revolts erupted in the 1830s and 1840s, but major challenges to the monarchy or to its territorial integrity failed to materialize.

As the period drew to a close, a greater degree of stability became evident in Spanish America, especially in Chile, Argentina, and Mexico, as well as in Brazil. As a result, economic growth linked to the expansion of exports for North Atlantic markets quickened. Railroads and telegraph lines were constructed, foreign capital entered the region, and in general modernization got under way.

International Developments

On several occasions before 1870, representatives from various countries met to discuss threats to Latin American independence. None of the treaties produced at these meetings ever went into effect. However, these conferences laid the foundations for the Pan American movement of the twentieth century.

1826

June 22. **The First Panama Congress**. Delegates from Gran Colombia, Central America, Peru, and Mexico met in Panama to consider plans for continental unity. An official observer from Great Britain was also present. The congress, the brainchild of **Simón Bolívar**, drew up agreements providing for mutual defense in case of attack by a foreign power, the peaceful settlement of disputes, reciprocal rights of citizenship, and repudiation of the slave trade. Only Gran Colombia ratified the treaties, but the congress set a precedent for later meetings.

1847

December 11. **The First Lima Conference.** Delegates from Bolivia, Chile, Ecuador, New Granada (Colombia), and Peru attended this meeting, which was convened at a time of mounting foreign threats to Latin America. The most serious was the effort of **Juan José Flores** to organize an armed expedition from Spain to install a Spanish prince as ruler of Ecuador. In addition, the United States had invaded Mexico, and France and Great Britain were blockading Buenos Aires. The delegates approved several treaties, including one creating a defensive alliance among the five republics, but none was ever ratified. The Flores expedition also proved abortive.

1864

October 15. **The Second Lima Conference.** Delegates from Bolivia, Chile, Colombia, Ecuador, Guatemala, and Venezuela convened as Peru was embroiled in a serious dispute with Spain (see Bolivarian Republics, 1864). The delegates attempted without success to act as mediators in the dispute. They also drafted a treaty providing for a defensive alliance, but it was never ratified.

Mexico, Central America, and the Caribbean

Mexico, Central America, and the Caribbean experienced the tribulations of the post-independence era perhaps to a greater degree than any other region of Latin America. Conflicts between Conservatives and Liberals in Mexico and Central America were intense and violent. By 1870 Liberals had triumphed in Mexico and were on the verge of victory in Central America. Throughout the region, authoritarian rulers—such as **Antonio López de Santa Anna** in Mexico and **Rafael Carrera** in Guatemala—were the norm.

The countries of this region were unique in the precariousness of their nationhood and their vulnerability to stronger powers, notably Great Britain and the United States, which began its rise to regional hegemony during this period. Mexico was invaded by France and by the United States and lost half its territory to the latter. The British attempted to establish a protectorate on the Mosquito Coast of eastern Nicaragua, and a United States citizen, **William Walker**, briefly served as president of that country. The United States played an increasingly prominent role in Panama, which was part of the territory of Colombia (New Granada). Leaders in the Dominican Republic accepted a brief restoration of Spanish rule and later sought annexation to the United States. Cuba and Puerto Rico remained Spanish colonies. Many Cubans favored independence, but others preferred annexation to the United States.

1826

September 26. **Conflict in Central America.** José Manuel de Arce, president of the Central American Federation, arrested Juan Barrundia, head of the Guatemalan state government. Arce, once a moderate Liberal, now allied himself with Guatemalan Conservatives led by Mariano Aycinena. As a result, civil war soon raged throughout Guatemala, El Salvador, and Honduras. **Francisco Morazán**, a Honduran, became head of the Liberal forces in 1827.

1829

April 12. **Civil war in Central America ended** with the capitulation of Guatemala City after Liberal forces under **Morazán** won a decisive victory at Hacienda Las Charcas (March 15, 1829). He now became president of the Central American Federation, and Liberals came to power in Guatemala and the other Central American states.

July 27-29. **About 2,800 Spanish soldiers landed on Mexico's gulf coast and occupied Tampico.** Their commander, Brigadier General Isidro Barredas, proclaimed the restoration of the viceroyalty of New Spain, expecting that Mexicans would flock to the Spanish standard. After **Antonio López de Santa Anna** began a siege of the city, the Spaniards, weakened by the lack of provisions and the ravages of yellow fever, were forced to surrender (September 11, 1829).

December 4. **Revolt in Mexico.** Vice President Anastasio Bustamante of Mexico launched a successful rebellion against President **Vicente Guerrero**, who had himself taken office the previous April in irregular circumstances.

1831

August. **Liberal Mariano Gálvez became chief of the state of Guatemala.** He advanced an ambitious but controversial program that included educational reform, anticlericalism, large land grants to foreigners, tariff reductions harmful to domestic industry, a new head tax, and the introduction of a new judicial system (the Livingston Codes). These measures were resisted by Conservatives, peasants, and others who opposed changes in Guatemalan life.

1833

April 1. **Santa Anna became president of Mexico after leading a revolt against the Bustamante regime.** However, **Santa Anna** left the government in the hands of his vice president, Valentín Gómez Farías, who proceeded to carry out a program of Liberal reform that alienated the military and the clergy.

1834

April 24. **Santa Anna reassumed the presidency of Mexico** after deposing Vice President Gómez Farías. Now acting as the champion of Conservative forces, Santa Anna ended most of Gómez Farías's Liberal reforms. A new centralist constitution was adopted in 1836.

1835

May 5. **Braulio Carrillo became chief of the state of Costa Rica.** After stepping down in 1837, he was restored to power by a military coup (May 27, 1838). He established a harsh dictatorship but avoided entanglement in the conflicts taking place elsewhere in Central America. He encouraged coffee cultivation, promoted education, and definitely established the capital at San José. He remained in power until 1842.

November 3. **Texas declared its independence from Mexico.** For years there had been growing antagonism between the Mexican government and Texans, who were mainly immigrants from the United States. It was exacerbated by the **Santa Anna** administration's centralizing tendencies, which limited local self-government. Santa Anna led Mexican forces in an attempt to crush the rebels, but suffered a decisive defeat at the Battle of San Jacinto (April 21, 1836). Santa Anna, who was taken prisoner two days later, pledged to seek Mexican recognition of the Texas Republic but the agreement was not implemented.

1837

March–May. **Guatemalan peasants rose in revolt against the Gálvez government.** The peasants, already hostile because of the government's Liberal policies, were further alienated when a cholera epidemic broke out. The government quarantined affected areas and took other steps to contain the epidemic, but the peasants did not understand them and believed priests who told them that the government had poisoned the water.

The insurgency led to the rise of **Rafael Carrera**, who brought about the demise of the Liberal regime and allied himself with the Conservatives in 1838.

1838

July 7. **Disintegration of the Central American Federation.** The federal congress of Central America declared its constituent states to be "sovereign, free and independent political bodies." This declaration reflected waning commitment to the federation as Nicaragua, Honduras, and Costa Rica seceded and as Conservatives gained ascendancy throughout the region. President **Francisco Morazán** fought unsuccessfully to preserve the federation and the Liberal cause.

July 16. **Juan Pablo Duarte of the Dominican Republic formed a secret society, La Trinitaria,** to oppose Haitian rule.

November 27. **Mexico's "Pastry War."** A French fleet bombarded Veracruz, forcing Mexican troops to evacuate the fortress of San Juan de Ulúa. French forces had arrived in Mexican waters in March 1838 to demand payment of money owed to French nationals who had suffered losses during Mexico's internal disorders. Among them was a baker whose claims led to the naming of the conflict as the Pastry War. On December 5, 1838, French troops were landed in Veracruz, but Mexican forces under **Santa Anna** drove them back toward the coast. A treaty signed on March 19, 1839, provided for Mexico's payment of $600,000 and for French withdrawal.

1840

March 18-19. **Carrera decisively defeated Morazán in Guatemala City, ending the Central American Federation.** Carrera, now dominant in Guatemala, was also able to install friendly regimes in El Salvador and Honduras.

November 18. **Panama declared its independence from New Granada (Colombia)** during the War of the Supremes (see Bolivarian

Republics, 1840). A sovereign state was created that envisioned rejoining Colombia only if a federalist form of government was established in the latter. After crushing the revolt, the Colombian government secured the reintegration of Panama on December 31, 1841.

Mexico's president after leading a revolt against Anastasio Bustamante. **Santa Anna** moved toward dictatorship and sponsored the writing of another constitution, the *Bases Orgánicas* (1843). A rebellion in 1844 drove him from office and into exile (June 3, 1845).

1841

January 1. **Francisco Ferrera was inaugurated as Honduras's first president.** An ally of Guatemala's **Carrera**, he served as president until 1847. His administration marked the beginning of thirty-five years of Conservative rule in Honduras.

October 19. **Santa Anna was sworn in as**

1844

La Escalera conspiracy in Cuba. Following slave revolts in Cárdenas and Matanzas in 1843 and reports of a projected uprising in Sabanilla, Spanish authorities in Cuba became convinced that a large conspiracy was being planned. From January through March 1844, government agents aided by planters interrogated and tortured thou-

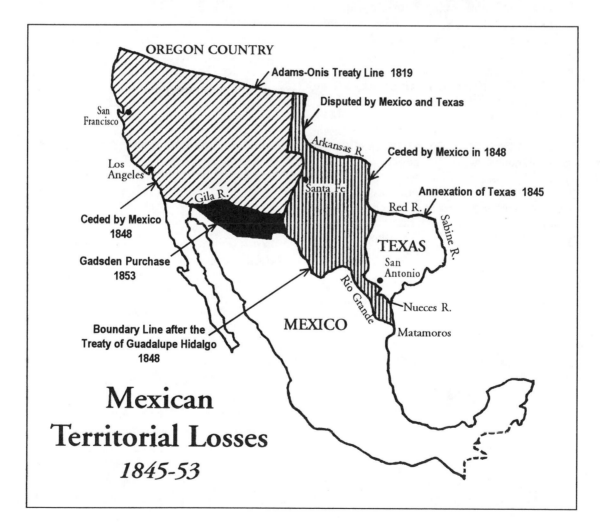

Mexican Territorial Losses 1845-53

sands of slaves and free blacks in the sugar-growing regions of western Cuba. The affair derives its name from the ladder (*escalera*) to which torture victims were tied to be lashed. Some historians doubt that a conspiracy existed, but others assert its reality. Thousands, including some whites, were executed, imprisoned, or banished. Among those executed was Gabriel de la Concepción Valdés (known as Plácido), a free mulatto and well-known poet. David Turnbull, an outspoken abolitionist who had served as British consul in Havana from 1840 to 1842, was named as the prime mover of the conspiracy and was condemned *in absentia*. As a result of the alarm produced by reports regarding the conspiracy, efforts were made to curb the slave trade, which declined significantly in the following years.

February 27. **The Dominican Republic gained independence from Haiti** after revolutionaries seized a fortress in Santo Domingo and forced the Haitian commander to surrender.

March 19. **Expanded British presence on the Mosquito Coast.** Having decided to establish a protectorate over the Mosquito Coast in 1843, the British foreign minister, Lord Aberdeen, named Patrick Walker to the position of British agent and consul-general to the Mosquito nation. The Mosquito shore, stretching south from Cape Gracias a Dios along the eastern coast of Nicaragua, was populated by various indigenous groups, including the Mosquitos. During the eighteenth century the Mosquitos became allied with the British, who moved to expand their influence over the area in the 1840s.

November 3. **Pedro Santana became the first president of the Dominican Republic.** For the next three decades he and his chief rival, Buenaventura Báez, would dominate the political life of the nation.

December 14. **Carrera took office as president of Guatemala.** He resigned in August 1848 amid a Liberal uprising but defeated the Liberals the following year and became president again on November 6, 1851, ruling until his death in 1865.

1846

May 13. **The United States Congress declared war on Mexico.** Relations between the United States and Mexico had worsened after United States annexation of Texas (March 1, 1845). Aggravating the tension was a dispute over whether the western boundary of Texas was the Nueces River or the Rio Grande. John Slidell, President James Polk's special envoy to Mexico, was instructed to resolve this dispute and to purchase additional territory from Mexico, but when his instructions became public, President José Joaquín Herrera refused to receive him. Polk had already decided to seek a declaration of war when news of a skirmish (April 25, 1846) between U.S. and Mexican troops in the disputed territory allowed him to claim that Mexico had invaded the United States and "shed American blood on American soil." In Mexico **Santa Anna** was named commander of the country's forces; Mexico's Congress appointed him president in December.

December 12. **The Bidlack-Mallarino Treaty was signed.** Under its terms Colombia pledged that the right of way across the Isthmus of Panama would be "open and free" to United States citizens. The United States guaranteed the "perfect neutrality" of the isthmus as well as Colombia's sovereignty over it. This treaty paved the way for the construction of an isthmian railroad by United States investors and for deepening United States interest in Panama.

1847

March 1. **Faustin Soulouque became president of Haiti.** He proclaimed himself Emperor Faustin I in 1849. Fearing foreign domination of the Dominican Republic, he invaded that country in 1849 and 1850, but his ambitions were blocked by Great Britain and France. A black nationalist, Soulouque weakened the power of Haiti's mulatto elite.

July 30. **Mexico's Caste War.** Mayas under Cecilio Chi attacked the town of Tepich in Mexico's Yucatán state. This event is usually seen as the beginning of the Caste War, a major revolt by Mayas that nearly succeeded in driving non-Indians, or *ladinos*, from Yucatán. The revolt occurred during Mexico's war with the United States and at a time when ladinos were divided and the relationship between Mexico and Yucatán was in dispute. The revolt is often linked to economic changes that threatened Maya land-holdings and culture. Mayas in northwestern Yucatán were less affected by these changes and remained peaceful.

September 13. **United States troops success-fully stormed Chapultepec Castle to complete their conquest of Mexico City.** After the start of hostilities in 1846, the United States had captured New Mexico and California and won control of northeastern Mexico. U.S. forces then began an invasion of central Mexico with a landing in Veracruz on March 27, 1847. The battle for Mexico City began in August. After the United States occupation of the capital, **Santa Anna** resigned the presidency and went into exile but returned to power in 1853.

1848

January 1. **Anglo-Mosquitian forces seized San Juan, Nicaragua, and renamed it Greytown.** This attack and the subsequent destruction of the Nicaraguan fort at Serapaqui (February 8, 1848) were intended to establish the San Juan River as the southern boundary of Mosquitia. The incident also reflected current British interest in dominating Central America and controlling any interoceanic route that might be constructed there.

February 2. **The Treaty of Guadalupe-Hidalgo was signed, ending Mexico's war with the United States.** The treaty recognized United States possession of Texas with the boundary set at the Rio Grande and ceded New Mexico and Upper California to the United States. The United States was to pay Mexico $15 million and to assume $3.23 million in claims against Mexico by U.S. citizens. Although the United States negotiator, Nicholas P. Trist, had not been authorized to sign the treaty, President Polk decided to submit it to the U.S. Senate, which ratified it on March 10, 1848.

Crisis of the Caste War. Yucatán's rebellious Mayas made major gains, capturing Valla-

dolid (March 19, 1848) and other important towns. As Maya fighters returned to their homes to plant corn, *ladinos* went on the offensive and, strengthened by aid from Mexico, gradually recovered lost territory. Unpacified Maya settled in Chan Santa Cruz, which was not conquered until 1901.

1850

April 19. **The Clayton-Bulwer Treaty was signed in Washington.** A product of U.S.-British rivalry for influence in Central America, the treaty provided that neither country would seek exclusive control of any trans-isthmian canal that might be built. It also stated that neither would seek domination of Nicaragua, the Mosquito Coast, or any other part of Central America.

1851

August 11. **Filibusters in Cuba.** An expedition led by Narciso López, a Venezuelan-born opponent of Spanish rule, landed near Havana after sailing from New Orleans on August 9. Many of his followers were Southerners who favored United States annexation of Cuba. This was López's third attempt at revolutionizing the island. The first (1849) was halted by United States authorities; the second (1850) ended in failure after a landing near Cárdenas. In 1851 the Spanish authorities soon captured the expeditionaries, and many Americans were executed or imprisoned. López was publicly garroted (September 1, 1851).

1853

April 20. **Santa Anna was inaugurated as president of Mexico.** He soon established a Conservative dictatorship with monarchical trappings.

December 30. **Gadsden Purchase. Santa Anna** sold the Mesilla Valley in northern Mexico to the United States for $10 million in a transaction known as the Gadsden Purchase. The United States considered the land, now the southern part of New Mexico and Arizona, desirable for a projected railroad route to California. The transaction alienated many Mexicans and contributed to a Liberal revolt against the **Santa Anna** government.

1854

March 1. **Mexican Liberals in revolt against the Santa Anna government set forth their goals in the Plan de Ayutla.** Led by Juan Álvarez, the revolution quickly spread throughout the country.

July 13. **The *U.S.S. Cyane* bombarded and burned Greytown, destroying the city.** The bombardment climaxed years of friction between British officials there and United States citizens, especially Cornelius Vanderbilt, whose Accessory Transit Company transported passengers across Nicaragua.

October 18. **The Ostend Manifesto.** Three United States diplomats--Pierre Soulé, John Y. Mason, and James Buchanan, respectively ministers to Spain, France, and Great Britain--met in Ostend, Belgium, and Aix-La-Chappelle, France, at the suggestion of Secretary of State William L. Marcy to discuss measures to further United States plans to acquire Cuba. The United States was interested in purchasing Cuba, for which it was prepared to pay as much as $130 million. The ministers' confidential report to Marcy soon became public and became known as the Ostend Manifesto. It emphasized the island's importance to the United States and asserted that, if Spain refused to sell the island, the United States would be justified "in wresting it from Spain." Marcy repudiated the report, which intensified Spanish opposition to United States ambitions in Cuba.

1855

January 27. **Work was completed on the Panama Railroad.** The railroad, the first to be built on the territory of New Granada (Colombia), stretched for forty-seven miles from Colón (also known as Aspinwall) on the Atlantic to the city of Panama on the Pacific. It was built by three Americans—businessmen William H. Aspinwall and Henry Chauncey and explorer-archaeologist John Lloyd Stephens—and quickly proved profitable.

February 27. **The state of Panama was created through an amendment to the constitution of New Granada (Colombia).** Panama remained a self-governing state until 1886 when Colombia adopted a new centralist constitution.

June 16. **William Walker arrived in Nicaragua to assist Liberals there.** Originally accompanied by fifty-seven other Americans, **Walker** soon became the dominant force in Nicaragua and assumed the presidency in July 1856.

Mexico's Liberal Reform (La Reforma). The resignation of **Santa Anna** (August 12, 1855) signaled the triumph of the Ayutla revolution. The reformers, many of them middle-class provincials who represented a new generation of Liberals, set about weakening the pillars of Mexican conservatism, the army and the church. The Ley Juárez (November 23, 1855) drastically restricted military and ecclesiastical privileges. The Ley Lerdo (June 25, 1856) was designed to force the church and civil corporations to divest themselves of their landholdings. A new constitution (February 5, 1857) restored federalism, emphasized individual rights, and failed to declare Roman Catholicism to be the religion of the nation. These and other measures produced bitter opposition from the clergy and lay Conservatives.

1856

April 15. **Panama's Watermelon Riot.** Rioting began in the city of Panama after an American traveler refused to pay a Panamanian vendor for a slice of watermelon. This dispute soon escalated into a major disturbance that resulted in the deaths of about eighteen U.S. citizens and two Panamanians. In addition, the rioters destroyed property belonging to the United States–owned Panama Railroad. The high toll of United States lives and property reflected growing anti-American feeling in Panama. The recently opened railroad, which quickly transported passengers across the isthmus to waiting steamers, had displaced many Panamanian workers. There were also fears of an invasion by United States filibusters associated with **William Walker**. United States officials maintained that the riot had been premeditated and that Panamanian authorities had taken part in the violence. In 1857 Colombia accepted liability for the riot and eventually paid approximately $412,000 to United States claimants.

1857

May 1. **William Walker yielded power in Nicaragua and left the country aboard a United States naval vessel.** He had been defeated by a coalition of Central Americans led by Juan Rafael Mora, president of Costa Rica, who also received British assistance.

November 15. **Tomás Martínez became president of Nicaragua.** His administration, which ended in 1867, initiated a thirty-six-year period of Conservative rule in Nicaragua.

1858

January 11. **Conservatives regained power in Mexico.** Conservative general Félix Zuloaga became president of Mexico after forcing the resignation of Ignacio Comonfort, a moderate Liberal, who left the country. In the ensuing War of the Reform, leadership of the Liberals fell to **Benito Juárez**, who as chief justice of the Supreme Court was next in line for the presidency.

December 23. **Fabre Nicholas Geffrard became president of Haiti.** Geffrard came to power after ousting Faustin Soulouque. Geffrard restored the republic, encouraged trade, and promoted education. In 1860 relations with the Vatican were established with the signing of a concordat giving the Catholic Church special powers in Haiti. Relations with the United States were established in 1862. Geffrard ruled dictatorially and was ousted in 1867.

1859

April 30. **The Wyke-Aycinena Treaty was signed.** Under the treaty Guatemala recognized British sovereignty over Belize (British Honduras) provided that the British build a road linking the city of Guatemala with the Caribbean coast. As the road was not built, the Guatemalans later abrogated the treaty and disavowed British rights in Belize.

July 12. **Mexican anticlerical decrees.** The Liberal government headed by **Benito Juárez**, who was based in Veracruz, issued several anticlerical measures intended to punish the clergy for aiding the Conservatives in the War of the Reform and to raise funds to prosecute the war. Provisions of the decrees included separation of church and state, confiscation of ecclesiastical properties, and the suppression of religious orders.

1860

January 28. **The Treaty of Managua was signed, ending the British protectorate over the Mosquito Coast.** Under the terms of the treaty, Great Britain recognized Nicaraguan sovereignty over Greytown and the Mosquito Coast. In exchange the Nicaraguans promised to grant autonomy to the Mosquito Indians and to pay them an annuity for ten years.

1861

January 11. **Juárez entered Mexico City in triumph after the defeat of the Conservatives.**

March 18. **Pedro Santana proclaimed the annexation of the Dominican Republic to Spain.** Santana had long been convinced that the Dominican Republic needed a foreign protector, but the Spanish restoration was unpopular from the start, and armed opposition had developed by 1863.

December. **European intervention in Mexico.** Facing acute fiscal problems, **Juárez** announced a two-year moratorium on payments on Mexico's foreign debt. As a result, Spain, Great Britain, and France agreed (October 31, 1861) to occupy Veracruz in order to use its customs revenue for service of the debt. Approximately 9,000 troops began arriving in December, but the Spanish and British withdrew after they realized that the French intended a permanent conquest of Mexico.

1862

May 5. **Mexican armies under General Ignacio Zaragoza defeated French forces at Puebla.** After the arrival of reinforcements, however, the French were able to occupy most of the country and **Juárez** was forced to leave Mexico City on May 31, 1863.

1863

October. **A Guatemalan army occupied San Salvador as Rafael Carrera drove Gerardo Barrios from power.** Barrios, who had been president of El Salvador since 1859, was a Liberal but had initially worked in concert with Salvadoran Conservatives and **Carrera**. But he began an anticlerical campaign that offended Carrera, who also accused him of interfering in Honduran affairs. After the ouster of Barrios, Carrera installed Francisco Dueñas as president of El Salvador.

1864

May 29. **Maximilian, archduke of Austria, arrived in Veracruz to serve as emperor of Mexico.** Maximilian had been offered the crown by Mexican Conservatives, who hoped to undo the Liberal reform, and was supported by Napoleon III, who hoped to re-establish French influence in the Western Hemisphere. Once in Mexico City, Maximilian disappointed some Conservatives by following a generally moderate course, but Liberals under **Juárez** were determined to unseat him. The United States government was also opposed to Maximilian.

1865

July 20. **The last Spanish troops left the Dominican Republic.** Mounting opposition had led the Spanish government to abandon its efforts to regain control of its former colony.

1867

June 19. **Maximilian was executed by a firing squad near Querétaro.** He had surrendered to Liberal forces the previous month. Maximilian's position had become untenable as a result of Liberal military advances, the withdrawal of French troops, and United States opposition. Many urged **Juárez** to spare Maximilian's life, but remembering the execution of Liberal prisoners during the recent conflict, he was not disposed to be merciful.

December 19. **The Mexican Congress declared Juárez the winner of a presidential election held in October.** **Juárez** had defeated the Liberal general **Porfirio Díaz** by a wide margin. After taking office on December 25, Juárez promoted economic reform and the expansion of primary education.

1868

September 23-24. **Grito de Lares.** A small group of Puerto Rican coffee growers, laborers, and slaves rose against Spain in the town of Lares and a declared a republic. However, they were soon routed by Spanish forces. The rebellion in Puerto Rico followed a military revolt in Spain and the flight of Queen Isabella II.

October 10. **Grito de Yara.** Revolutionaries in the town of Yara in eastern Cuba rebelled against Spanish rule. Led by Carlos Manuel de Céspedes, the revolt marked the beginning of Cuba's Ten Years' War for independence. It was supported mainly by native-born Cubans from the eastern half of the island, including large sugar planters, small landholders, and free blacks.

1869

March 29. **A treaty providing for United States annexation of the Dominican Republic was signed in Santo Domingo.** The treaty was engineered by Dominican president Buenaventura Báez, who also arranged a plebiscite approving it by a wide margin (February 19, 1870). In reality, the treaty was unpopular in the Dominican Republic. Despite strong support from President Ulysses S. Grant, the treaty failed of ratification in the United States Senate.

1870

April 27. **Tomás Guardia came to power in Costa Rica.** After deposing President Jesús

Jiménez, Guardia dominated Costa Rica until his death in 1882. Guardia broke the power of the country's Conservative landowners, established a Liberal dictatorship, and in 1871 began a railroad to link San José with the Caribbean port of Limón.

July 4. **Spain decreed the gradual abolition of slavery in Puerto Rico and Cuba in the Moret Law.** It provided that all children born to slave parents were to be free, though attached to their owners by a system of tutelage until the age of 18. Slaves over age 60 were also freed.

Bolivarian Republics: Bolivia, Colombia, Ecuador, Peru, Venezuela

The early history of the five Bolivarian republics—Bolivia, New Granada (known as Colombia after 1863), Ecuador, Peru, and Venezuela—was shaped by their experiences in the struggle for independence and by the leadership of **Simón Bolívar** and his lieutenants. Bolívar attempted to recreate the viceroyalty of New Granada by uniting New Granada, Ecuador, and Venezuela in the nation known as Gran, or Greater, Colombia, of which he was president until 1830. Regional loyalties and interests, however, aggravated by obstacles to communications, led to the breakup of Gran Colombia in 1830. Bolívar also held the title of dictator of Peru from 1823 to 1827 and briefly wielded power in Bolivia as well. Subsequent efforts to unite these two countries also proved unsuccessful.

In each of the five republics the first leaders were veterans of the independence movement whose military triumphs at Ayacucho and other battlefields allowed them not only to claim commanding roles in the new nations but also to ignore constitutional prescriptions and unseat rivals. Meanwhile, Liberal and Conservative movements or parties arose to shape the content of public discourse. Despite debate over federalism versus centralism and other issues, politics was generally driven by personalism and opportunism rather than ideology.

The ravages of the independence wars, constant political upheaval, and the impoverished state of the new national treasuries initially hindered sustained economic growth. By 1870, however, the five republics had begun to be more fully integrated into the North Atlantic economy through the modest expansion of exports such as tobacco in Colombia, coffee in Venezuela, and guano in Peru. Guano, the droppings of birds which nested off Peru's coasts, became highly prized in Europe and the United States as a fertilizer. In Bolivia the long-stagnant silver mining industry experienced a revival after 1850. Improvements in infrastructure also took place, usually with foreign capital and know-how. Especially important was the construction of railroads and highways that linked the highland areas of Peru and Ecuador with the Pacific coast. The introduction of steam navigation on New Granada's Magdalena River in the 1840s was equally important.

1826

April 27. **Separatist movement in Venezuela.** The municipal council of Valencia deplored the recent suspension of **José Antonio Páez** from his position as commanding general of the department of Venezuela. This action was taken by the government of Gran Colombia after it received complaints regarding Páez's conduct while recruiting soldiers in Caracas. On April 30 Páez reassumed his position, thereby defying the central government in Bogotá, which declared him to be a rebel. These events underlined the dissatisfaction in Venezuela with the existing constitutional system and made Páez the rallying point for separatists.

August 6. **Antonio José de Sucre became president of Bolivia** under a constitution drafted by **Bolívar**. Although the constitution provided for a lifetime presidency, **Sucre** stated that he would serve for only two years.

September 4. **Bolívar sailed from Peru,** where he had been wielding dictatorial power for more than two years. He traveled to Gran Colombia to confront the rebellion of **Páez** and other serious threats to the nation's existence.

1827

January 1. **Páez was amnestied by Bolívar.** Having returned to Venezuela, Bolívar also reinstated **Páez** as military governor of Venezuela. As a result, Páez's position was strengthened, and separatist tendencies allayed, but only temporarily.

August 22. **José de la Mar took office as president of Peru** after being elected by a constituent congress.

1828

April 18. **Sucre surrendered his presidential powers to his cabinet** after being wounded in an unsuccessful military rebellion in Chuquisaca. On August 3, 1828, he resigned the presidency of Bolivia. **Sucre** had attempted to lessen the influence of the Catholic Church, reform the tax system, and revive the mining industry, but had met with little success.

September 25. **Bolívar narrowly escaped assassination in Bogotá.** The would-be assassins were New Granadans opposed to the dictatorship assumed by Bolívar in June 1828. Several alleged plotters were executed. **Francisco de Paula Santander**, vice president of Gran Colombia and leader of the opposition to Bolívar, was accused of complicity in the plot and was exiled.

1829

February 27. **Gran Colombian forces defeated Peru at the Battle of Tarqui.** Hostilities between the two countries began in 1828 over several issues, notably the disposition of Guayaquil, which was occupied by Peru on February 1, 1829, after a naval bombardment and blockade. A Peruvian army led by President la Mar and Agustín Gamarra invaded Ecuador but was repelled by Gran Colombian forces under **Sucre** at Tarqui, near Cuenca. The Peruvians evacuated Guayaquil, but the boundary between Peru and Ecuador was not definitively settled.

May 20. **Andrés Santa Cruz became president of Bolivia.** During his ten-year tenure Bolivia enjoyed political stability while the government undertook important administrative reforms, such as enactment of a new civil and commercial code.

December 20. **Agustín Gamarra took office as president of Peru.** He was elected chief executive after he and other army officers deposed José de La Mar, whose prestige had suffered after the Peruvian defeat at Tarqui.

1830

March 1. **Bolívar took a leave of absence** from the presidency of troubled Gran Colombia, already in the throes of disintegration. He refused to serve as chief executive under a new constitution and left for Europe. He died of tuberculosis in Santa Marta on December 17, 1830.

May 6. **A constituent assembly met in Venezuela.** This body drew up a constitution for an independent Venezuela.

May 13. **The independence of Ecuador was declared by an assembly in Quito.** The assembly also named **Juan José Flores** to head Ecuador's government. Later in 1830 he was elected to a four-year term as president.

1831

April 11. **José Antonio Páez became president of Venezuela.** Páez, who had been serving as provisional president since 1830, was the dominant figure in what is known as the Conservative Oligarchy (1830-47). During this period he served twice as president (1831-35, 1839-43) while remaining a powerful influence during the administrations of José María Vargas (1835-37) and Carlos Soublette (1837-39, 1843-47). Despite the era's name, the various administrations tended to follow policies in accordance with nineteenth-century economic liberalism.

1832

October 7. **Francisco de Paula Santander became provisional president of New Granada.**

He was later elected to a four-year term beginning in 1833. A new centralist constitution for New Granada had been promulgated in March 1832.

1834

April 10. **Venezuela's law on the liberty of contracts.** This measure represented a move away from colonial economic regulation and practices and toward liberal policies. It removed all limits on interest rates and facilitated foreclosure of debtors' properties. It alienated landowners whose economic fortunes fluctuated in accordance with market prices for coffee, cacao, and other commercial crops and contributed to political divisiveness in the country.

1835

August 2. **Vicente Rocafuerte was elected president of Ecuador** by a constitutional convention in Ambato. **Rocafuerte**, a Liberal, had rebelled against the government of **Juan José Flores** and had been captured by Flores in 1834. The two leaders made peace with each other and apparently agreed to alternate in the presidency.

1836

October 28. **The Peru–Bolivia Confederation was established.** The union of the two nations had long been a dream of **Andrés Santa Cruz**, who became head of the new state. Many, especially in northern Peru, were unenthusiastic about the confederation, and Chile perceived it as a threat to its commercial interests on the Pacific. Chile declared war on the confederation in December 1836.

1837

April 1. **Santander surrendered the presidency of New Granada to José Ignacio de Márquez,** who had been chosen by Congress after winning a plurality in the electoral college. He was not **Santander**'s choice to succeed him, partly because he was endorsed by the surviving Bolivarians.

1839

January 20. **Demise of the Peru–Bolivia Confederation.** Confederation forces led by **Andrés Santa Cruz** were defeated by a combined force of Chileans and Peruvians led by **Manuel Bulnes** at Yungay, north of Lima. After his defeat, Santa Cruz was also deposed as head of the Bolivian government (February 20).

January 31. **Juan José Flores was re-elected president of Ecuador** by the Congress, succeeding **Vicente Rocafuerte**.

1840

January 18. **New Granada's "War of the Supremes" began** when José María Obando rebelled against the government of José Ignacio de Márquez. Obando, whom Márquez had defeated for the presidency in 1836, was soon joined by other army officers and opponents of Márquez. Their common goal was greater regional autonomy. The government had crushed the revolt by 1842. The divisions generated by the war laid the foundation of New Granada's two political parties—the Conservatives and the Liberals—which emerged during the 1840s.

1841

November 18. **The Battle of Ingavi.** In October 1841 Agustín Gamarra, again serving as president of Peru, invaded Bolivia in the hope of annexing part of its territory to Peru. At Ingavi, south of La Paz, Bolivian forces under President José Ballivián defeated the Peruvians, and Gamarra himself was killed. This battle put an end to plans to unite Peru and Bolivia. Ballivián ruled Bolivia until 1847.

1845

March 6. **A revolution against Flores of Ecuador began in Guayaquil.** Instigated by **Vicente Rocafuerte**, the revolution was a response to

Flores's decision to perpetuate himself in office. In addition, the Roman Catholic clergy objected to a new constitution (1841) that gave the government control of church appointments. Clergy were also required to swear to uphold the constitution. Flores was forced to make peace with the revolutionaries and left for Europe (June 25, 1845).

April 1. **Tomás Cipriano de Mosquera was inaugurated as president of New Granada.** Associated with the embryonic Conservative party, **Mosquera** undertook a series of reforms, aimed at liberalizing the economy, such as the reduction of tariffs and the abolition of the colonial-era tobacco monopoly.

April 20. **Ramón Castilla took office as president of Peru.** **Castilla** had emerged as the dominant leader in the revolutionary movement directed against Manuel I. Vivanco. During Castilla's six-year term, guano exports rose significantly, and the increased revenue allowed improvements in national finances and education.

1848

January 24. **Liberal oligarchy in Venezuela (1848-58).** A mob invaded the Chamber of Deputies and forcibly prevented it from proceeding with the impeachment of President José Tadeo Monagas. Although he had been elected in 1846 with the support of **José Antonio Páez** and the Conservatives, Monagas had moved toward the new Liberal party after becoming president. The Conservatives then sought his removal, but Monagas remained in the presidency, now supported mainly by Liberals. He was succeeded by his brother, José Gregorio Monagas (1851-55).

December 8. **Manuel I. Belzú became president of Bolivia** after a victory over the incumbent government at Yamparáez near Sucre (formerly Chuquisaca). Belzú was hostile to Bolivia's commercial and mining elite and tried to defend the interests of urban artisans. He retired from the presidency in 1855.

1849

April 1. **José Hilario López, a Liberal, became president of New Granada.** His administration, which set the stage for twenty-six years of Liberal hegemony, continued the reformist thrust begun under **Tomás C. Mosquera.** Important measures included the abolition of slavery and an end to restriction on the alienation of Indian lands (*resguardos*). Other measures, such as the expulsion of the Jesuits and the abolition of academic degree requirements for the exercise of professions, proved very controversial.

1851

April 20. **José Rufino Echenique succeeded Ramón Castilla as president of Peru.** During his administration a program to pay off the internal debt, begun under **Castilla**, created great controversy as critics charged that the operation (known as the consolidation) was riddled with fraud and corruption. Criticism was also directed at an arrangement whereby part of the internal debt was converted to foreign debt.

1854

January 7. **Revolution in Peru.** Dissatisfaction over the financial policy of the José Rufino Echenique administration led to a major insurrection beginning in Arequipa. **Ramón Castilla** became head of the Liberal-oriented movement, during which he decreed an end to the payment of tribute by Indians (July 5, 1854) and the abolition of slavery (December 5, 1854). Echenique stepped down after being decisively defeated in an engagement near Lima on January 5, 1855. Castilla ruled Peru until 1862, adopting a middle position between Liberals and Conservatives.

April 17. **General José María Melo staged a coup against New Granada's president, José María Obando**, and established a military dictatorship. The coup occurred amid conflict between two factions within the Liberal party: the Gólgotas, who favored continued reform, and the more moderate Draconianos, who were supported by the armed forces and politically active artisans. Both Melo and Obando were allied with the Draconianos, and some implicated the president in the coup. A coalition of Gólgotas and Conservatives succeeded in driving Melo from power by December. Obando did not return to the presidency, and a Conservative, Manuel María Mallarino, completed his term.

1855

February 27. **New Granada moved toward federalism.** Legislation establishing the self-governing state of Panama, which was then part of the territory of New Granada, was followed by the passage of similar bills, creating a total of nine states by 1861.

1858

March 15. **End of Venezuela's Liberal Oligarchy.** José Tadeo Monagas, who had returned to the presidency in 1855, was forced to resign. He and his brother José Gregorio had enacted several measures endorsed by Liberals, such as modification of the 1834 law on contracts and the abolition of slavery (March 22, 1854). However, José Tadeo's return to the presidency and constitutional changes extending the presidential term and strengthening the executive led both Liberals and Conservatives to accuse him of dictatorial tendencies. A revolution led by Julián Castro, governor of Carabobo, brought about Monagas's departure.

1859

February 20. **Venezuela's Federal War began.** Liberals under General Ezequiel Zamora rose in rebellion in the state of Coro against the against the Conservative-dominated regime of Julián Castro. The establishment of a federation was the major Liberal goal in this bloody conflict, which is sometimes seen as a class war.

1860

May 8. **Liberal revolution in Colombia. Tomás Cipriano de Mosquera**, governor of the state of Cauca, disavowed the central government, headed by Conservative Mariano Ospina Rodríguez, and in effect withdrew Cauca from the confederation. Although Mosquera had ties with the Conservative party, he now allied himself with the Liberals to launch a nationwide revolt against Ospina.

1861

April 2. **Inauguration of García Moreno in Ecuador. Gabriel García Moreno** would rule Ecuador, except for a four-year interval (1865-69), until his assassination in 1875. He was a committed Conservative and strong partisan of the Catholic Church, which gained a uniquely privileged position in the concordat of 1862. The García Moreno regime is also noteworthy for construction of a road between Quito and Guayaquil and for the promotion of education.

July 18. **Liberal forces under Mosquera captured Bogotá.** The Conservative government of Mariano Ospina Rodríguez disintegrated, and **Tomás Mosquera** became provisional president of New Granada. In this capacity he enacted several anticlerical measures, including decrees nationalizing church property, suppressing religious orders, and authorizing government supervision of all religious sects.

1863

May 8. **A constitution creating the United States of Colombia was drafted.** The work of Liberals victorious in the recent civil war, the constitution established a federal union comprised of nine sovereign states: Antioquia, Bolívar, Boyacá, Cauca, Cundinamarca, Magdalena, Panama, Santander, and Tolima. The weak central government was headed by an executive who served a two-year term.

May 22. **The Treaty of Coche ended Venezuela's Federal War.** The treaty, though negotiated with the government of **José Antonio Páez**, who had become dictator in 1861, marked the triumph of the federalist cause. In July 1863, the federalist leader Juan C. Falcón became president, but his vice president, **Antonio Guzmán Blanco**, was the effective ruler. A new constitution in

1864 provided for the federal organization of the country.

December 7. **Colombian victory over Ecuador at Cuaspud.** Tensions had arisen between Colombia, then under a Liberal, anticlerical administration, and the Conservative, proclerical government of **Gabriel García Moreno.** An Ecuadorian army commanded by **Juan José Flores** crossed the Colombian border in the hope of aiding Conservatives there. This hope was not realized, and Colombian forces under **Tomás Mosquera** routed the Ecuadorians at Cuaspud, an hacienda near the border. A peace treaty was signed soon afterward.

1864

April 14. **Spain occupied Peru's Chincha Islands.** Relations between the two governments had become strained after an altercation (1863) between a Peruvian landowner and Spanish colonists, during which several of the latter had been killed or wounded. The Peruvians suspected that Spain wanted to use revenue from the islands, which yielded most of Peru's guano, to pay Spanish claims against Peru. They might even serve as a base for the reconquest of the entire nation.

December 28. **Mariano Melgarejo took power in Bolivia** after overthrowing the government of José María Achá. As dictator of Bolivia, Melgarejo became notorious for his arbitrary conduct and for a decree (1866) divesting Indian communities of their lands.

1866

January 14. **Peru declared war on Spain.** Although a treaty had been signed on January 27, 1865, resolving the differences between the two countries, many Peruvians found it objectionable. After the Peruvian Congress adjourned without ratifying the treaty, President Juan Antonio Pezet declared it in force, and Spain returned the Chincha Islands to Peru. As a result, Pezet was denounced as a traitor and ousted late in 1865.

The new government rejected the treaty and allied itself with Chile, already at war with Spain (see Southern Cone, 1865). Bolivia and Ecuador also joined the alliance.

May 2. **Spain bombarded Callao.** Seven Spanish warships bombarded the port city, but Peruvian artillery responded effectively, damaging several vessels and forcing withdrawal of the fleet. The Peruvians therefore claimed a great victory. After lengthy negotiations an armistice was reached on April 11, 1871.

1867

May 23. **Tomás Mosquera was deposed as president of Colombia** three weeks after he had closed Congress and declared the republic to be in a state of war. These events stemmed from a clash between **Mosquera** and his Liberal critics, who suspected him of dictatorial tendencies. They were also outraged by news of a secret treaty making Colombia an ally of Peru in its war with Spain. Colombia's official policy was one of neutrality in the conflict. Santos Acosta completed the remaining ten months of Mosquera's term.

1869

July 5. **Peru signed the Dreyfus Contract.** By the terms of the contract, the Paris firm headed by August Dreyfus was to receive 2 million tons of guano from Peru along with the exclusive right to sell guano in Europe and its colonies. The firm was to pay Peru 2 million soles (about $2 million) as well as make monthly payments of 700,000 soles until March 1871 and service Peru's foreign debt. The administration of José Balta negotiated the contract in the hope of ending dependence on the multiple consignees to whom guano had hitherto been sold, obtaining funds for railroad development, and in general improving Peruvian finances. However, the government proceeded to borrow large sums from Dreyfus, and when Balta's term ended in 1872, the foreign debt was ten times larger than when he took office.

1870

April 27. **Triumph of Guzmán Blanco over Venezuelan Conservatives.** **Antonio Guzmán Blanco** entered Caracas, ousting Conservatives who had deposed President Falcón in 1868 in the "Blue Revolution," so called for the color of the Conservative flag. Guzmán would rule Venezuela directly or indirectly until 1888.

Southern Cone: Argentina, Chile, Paraguay, Uruguay

In the decades after independence, the history of Chile diverged from that of the rest of the Southern Cone. By the 1830s Conservatives, backed by the landowning class, were in control and established an authoritarian regime that provided order and stability. Periodic revolts and pressures for liberalization had little impact on the system. Meanwhile, though subject to the vagaries of international markets, Chile prospered through the export of agricultural and mineral products.

By contrast, in the former viceroyalty of Río de La Plata, chaos appeared to reign during much of the period. The seeming desire of the province of Buenos Aires to reconstitute the viceroyalty under its hegemony produced resistance among the various outlying provinces and in Paraguay and the Banda Oriental (Uruguay), which was also coveted by Brazil. Related to this conflict was the division between Federalists, who favored a high degree of provincial autonomy in any nation that might emerge, and Unitarians, who favored a centralized form of government. **Juan Manuel de Rosas**, who governed in Buenos Aires province from 1829 to 1852, dominated a loosely drawn Argentine Confederation, but it was not until after his fall that an Argentine nation was definitively organized. By 1870, as relative stability returned to the region, Argentina was poised to begin an era of remarkable social and economic changes. Uruguay, meanwhile, had attained independence from both Argentina and Brazil, as had Paraguay. In 1870, however, the latter lay prostrate as a result of its defeat by Brazil, Argentina, and Uruguay in the Paraguayan War (also known as the War of the Triple Alliance).

1826

February 7. **Bernardino Rivadavia was named president of the United Provinces of the Río de La Plata.** He was elected to the post by a constituent congress that drafted a new constitution for the Argentine provinces. But the provinces did not ratify the constitution and considered themselves independent states.

1827

June 27. **Rivadavia resigned as president of the United Provinces.** He had been opposed by Federalists and landowners in Buenos Aires province who disapproved of his economic liberalism and modernizing policies. His failure to win the ongoing Cisplatine War with Brazil also drew criticism.

1828

August 27. **Brazil and the United Provinces signed a treaty ending the Cisplatine War and creating the nation of Uruguay.** This agreement was reached with the help of British mediation after the two belligerents had reached a stalemate on the battlefield. Meanwhile, the desire for nationhood had grown among the inhabitants of the region.

1829

December 6. **Juan Manuel de Rosas was elected governor of Buenos Aires province for a three-year term by the provincial assembly.** The leader of the Federalist party in the province, he had recently defeated the Unitarian chieftain Juan Lavalle. Seen by the landed class as a guarantor of order and security, he was given extraordinary powers to govern the province.

1830

April 17. **Chilean Conservatives triumphed at the Battle of Lircay.** Their victory over the forces of the Liberal general Ramón Freire ended the political unrest that had followed the resignation of **Bernardo O'Higgins** in 1823. It also marked the beginning of three decades of Conservative rule in Chile. The architect of Chile's new order was **Diego Portales**, chief minister of President Joaquín Prieto (1831-41). At this time Conservatives were often referred to as *pelucones* (bigwigs), and their Liberal opponents as *pipiolos* (novices). These groups were the forerunners of the Conservative and Liberal parties that emerged in the 1840s and 1850s.

November 6. **Fructuoso Rivera took office as president of Uruguay.** A constitution establishing the Estado Oriental del Uruguay had been adopted the previous July. It provided for a centralized republic and for a president who was to be elected by the General Assembly for a four-year term. The constitution remained in force until 1919.

1831

January 4. **The Federal Pact was signed by the provinces of Buenos Aires, Santa Fe, and Entre Ríos.** In the Federal Pact the signatories organized themselves into a loose Argentine Confederation and delegated the conduct of foreign affairs to Buenos Aires. As other provinces came under the rule of allies of **Juan Manuel de Rosas**, they too joined the confederation.

1833

January 3. **Great Britain asserted its sovereignty over the Falkland Islands (known in Argentina as the Malvinas).** This action was accomplished by a British naval officer, J.J. Onslow of *H.M.S. Clio*, who raised the Union Jack at Puerto Soledad, ignoring Argentine protests. Both Spain and Great Britain claimed discovery of the islands in the sixteenth century, and settlers from the two countries, as well as France, moved

there in the eighteenth century. The islands were also visited by United States seal hunters.

May 25. **A new Chilean constitution was promulgated.** Reflecting the Conservative principles dominant at the time, the constitution provided for a strong executive who could be elected to two consecutive five-year terms. Suffrage was restricted to males over twenty-five who could meet literacy and property requirements. Roman Catholicism was declared the official religion, and no other might be publicly observed. The constitution, though substantially modified, remained in force until 1925.

1835

April 13. **Juan Manuel de Rosas was elected governor of Buenos Aires province for a second time.** Having demanded and received dictatorial powers, Rosas ruled the province until 1852.

1837

June 6. **Diego Portales of Chile was assassinated.** Having received extraordinary powers to wage war against the Peru–Bolivia Confederation, **Portales** went to Quillota to review troops. Mutinous soldiers seized and later executed him.

1838

March 28. **French naval forces blockaded Buenos Aires.** Conflict with the **Rosas** government had arisen over the desire of France to advance its economic interests in the region and complaints of mistreatment of French citizens in Argentina. The French also gave support to Rosas's enemies in Argentina and Uruguay. The blockade damaged the Buenos Aires economy and gave Rosas justification for a wave of terror against his domestic foes. A convention signed on October 29, 1840, provided for the lifting of the blockade and the granting of most-favored-nation treatment to France.

1839

March 1. **Fructuoso Rivera was elected president of Uruguay.** Rivera gained power a second time after launching a successful revolt in 1836 against his successor, Manuel Oribe, who resigned on October 24, 1838. During the conflict, Oribe's supporters came to be known as Blancos (Whites), while Rivera's partisans were called Colorados (Reds). Shortly before Rivera's election, Uruguay declared war on **Rosas**, who had assisted Oribe and now sought to restore him to power. The ensuing conflict (1839-51) is known was the Guerra Grande (Great War). It eventually drew in not only Uruguay and the Argentine provinces but also Brazil, France, and Great Britain.

1840

September 20. **José Gaspar de Francia, Paraguay's long-time dictator, died.** **Francia** had ruled Paraguay singlehandedly since 1814. He had created a strong, self-sufficient nation which had maintained its independence despite the ambitions of Argentina.

1843

February 16. **Montevideo besieged.** After defeating the forces of **Fructuoso Rivera** at Arroyo Grande (December 6, 1842), Oribe gained control of most of the Uruguayan countryside. Based at Restauración, he besieged Montevideo, which was also blockaded by sea by the **Rosas** government. The defenders of Montevideo included thousands of anti-Rosas exiles. The siege of Montevideo ended after peace was restored between the Uruguayan parties in 1851.

May 21. **An expedition asserted Chilean sovereignty in the Strait of Magellan.** Chile took this action because of fears that the British or French might establish colonies there. To strengthen their claims to the region, the Chileans built Fort Bulnes on the Brunswick Peninsula in the strait. This fort was soon abandoned for Punta Arenas, established in 1848 thirty miles to the north in a better location.

1844

March 13. **Carlos Antonio López was elected president of Paraguay for a ten-year term by the congress.** Since 1841 **López** had shared power with Mariano Roque Alonso in a two-man consulate. As president, he began the modernization of the landlocked nation.

1845

September 17. **Anglo-French forces declared a blockade of Buenos Aires.** The previous month they had seized the Argentine fleet blockading Montevideo. Although Great Britain had previously had good relations with the **Rosas** government, British officials feared that Rosas's intervention in Uruguay's civil war might threaten that country's independence. In addition, the British sought free navigation of the Paraná River, which Rosas refused. In November an Anglo-French fleet forced its way into the Paraná and escorted a group of merchantmen to Entre Ríos and Corrientes provinces. The British ended their blockade in 1847, the French a year later. Agreements between the Rosas government and the two European powers were reached in 1849 and 1850. Since Rosas conceded little in these, he became a hero to Argentine nationalists.

1850

April 14. **The Society of Equality was founded in Chile.** Its founder was Francisco Bilbao, a radical who had witnessed the French Revolution of 1848 and sought a more egalitarian society in Chile. He hoped to use the society to educate workers about their rights, but it soon became embroiled in presidential politics, opposing **Manuel Montt**, the candidate favored by the government. The society was suppressed in November 1850.

1851

May 29. **Alliance against Rosas.** Representatives of Brazil, Montevideo, and the province of Entre Ríos signed a treaty committing themselves to war against the Argentine dictator and Manuel Oribe, his Uruguayan ally. The governor of Entre Ríos, **Justo José de Urquiza**, had long been a

Rosas supporter but had concluded that the economic interests of his province required **Rosas's** removal. Brazil resented Rosas's efforts to dominate Uruguay and Paraguay and sought free navigation of Argentine rivers, which Rosas denied.

September 18. **Manuel Montt was inaugurated as Chile's president amid a Liberal uprising.** Liberals, who had backed the candidacy of José María de la Cruz, claimed that Montt's election had been fraudulent and had risen in revolt in La Serena and Concepción. The revolutionaries suffered a decisive defeat at the hands of government forces led by **Manuel Bulnes** at the Loncomilla River (December 8, 1851).

October 8. **Oribe capitulated to Urquiza and Brazil.** Starting in July 1851, Brazilian forces and an army led by **Urquiza** invaded Uruguay, promising conciliation. Oribe in effect betrayed **Rosas** by surrendering to the invaders. The siege of Montevideo was lifted soon afterward.

1852

February 3. **Rosas's forces were defeated at the Battle of Caseros.** A 24,000-man army led by **Urquiza** decisively defeated **Rosas**'s forces near Buenos Aires. Rosas resigned the governorship of the province and fled to England.

July 17. **Argentina formally recognized Paraguayan independence.** It had previously treated Paraguay as a breakaway province. Recognition of Paraguay by Great Britain, France, and other countries soon followed.

1853

May 25. **Urquiza proclaimed the constitution of the newly organized Argentine Confederation.** The province of Buenos Aires refused to accept the constitution and remained outside of the confederation, which established its capital at Paraná. **Urquiza** became president of the confederation in 1854.

1856

January. **Chile's sacristan question.** After a senior sacristan of the cathedral of Santiago dismissed a servant, two canons who disagreed with this decision were suspended. They appealed their suspension to the Supreme Court, which reinstated them. To the archbishop of Santiago, Rafael Valentín Valdivieso, the Supreme Court action was an intrusion of the state into the spiritual affairs of the church. The two canons soon submitted, but the episode sparked tension between the Catholic Church and the **Montt** administration. As a result, proclerical Conservatives formed a coalition, or fusion, with Liberals in 1858.

1859

January 5. **Unsuccessful revolt in Chile.** Pedro León Gallo, a wealthy miner, rebelled against the **Montt** administration in Copiapó. The revolt occurred at a time of mounting opposition against Montt's repressive policies and his choice of Antonio Varas as his successor. Uprisings also occurred in San Felipe, Talca, and other towns, but the insurgents were crushed at Cerro Grande, near La Serena, on April 29, 1859. Varas later withdrew from the presidential contest, and Montt was succeeded by José Joaquín Pérez.

October 23. **The Battle of Cepeda.** In this engagement the army of the Argentine Confederation led by **Justo José de Urquiza** forced the withdrawal of the forces of Buenos Aires province. The battle led to the formal incorporation of the province into the confederation. But tensions between provincial and confederation leaders remained strong.

1861

September 17. **The Battle of Pavón.** This clash took place between forces of the Argentine Confederation and those of Buenos Aires province as a result of continuing differences over terms of the province's incorporation into the confederation.

BOLIVIA

BRAZIL

Paraguay River

Branco River

PARAGUAY

Apa River

Paraná River

Concepción

Pilcomayo River

Bermejo River

Paraguayan War
1864-70

Asunción

Iguaçu River

Corrientes

ARGENTINA

Paraná River

Uruguay River

BRAZIL

━━━ Present Boundary

▐▐▐ Awarded to Argentina

▨▨▨ Awarded to Brazil

Urquiza, commanding the confederation army, withdrew from the battlefield. He had not been defeated but may have despaired of the final outcome. The confederation government now collapsed, and **Bartolomé Mitre**, governor of Buenos Aires, became president of Argentina in 1862.

1862

October 16. **Francisco Solano López was named president of Paraguay for a ten-year term.**

López was elected to the presidency by the Paraguayan congress upon the death of his father, **Carlos Antonio López**.

1863

April 19. **Venancio Flores launched a revolution in Uruguay.** The Colorado chieftain and former president sought to overthrow the Blanco governments of Bernardo P. Berro (1860-64) and Atanasio C. Aguirre (1864-65). In this effort he had the backing of the Argentine president, **Bartolomé**

Mitre, and of Brazil. Flores won power in Uruguay early in 1865.

1864

November 12. **Start of the Paraguayan War (War of the Triple Alliance).** The Paraguayan gunboat *Tacuarí* fired on the Brazilian steamer *Marquês de Olinda* as it sailed up the Paraguay River to Mato Grosso. The Paraguayans seized the ship and severed diplomatic relations with Brazil. **Francisco Solano López**, Paraguay's president, objected to Brazil's overt military intervention in Uruguay's civil war, which he considered disruptive of the regional balance of power and an indirect threat to Paraguay. In December 1864 Paraguayan forces successfully invaded Mato Grosso.

1865

March-April. **Paraguay and Argentina at war.** In order to dispatch troops to Uruguay and southern Brazil, President **Francisco Solano López** asked **Mitre** of Argentina to allow them to cross Argentine territory. When Mitre refused, the Paraguayans declared war (March 18) and attacked the Argentine river town of Corrientes (April 13).

May 1. **The Triple Alliance was signed.** Brazil, Argentina, and Uruguay concluded a treaty uniting them in a war against the **López** government of Paraguay. The treaty guaranteed the future independence of Paraguay but also indicated that Argentina and Brazil intended to acquire long-disputed territory from Paraguay. As a result, the Paraguayans feared that an Allied victory would mean the dismemberment of their country. The Allied forces were made up mainly of Brazilians and were led initially by **Mitre** of Argentina and later by two Brazilians, the **Duque de Caxias** and the Conde d'Eu, the emperor's son-in-law.

September 24. **Chile declared war on Spain.** Tensions had arisen because of public sympathy for Peru in its conflict with Spain (see Bolivarian Republics, 1864) and because of Chilean unwillingness to supply the Spanish fleet with coal.

When the Spanish commander issued an ultimatum demanding a twenty-one-gun salute, the Chilean Congress responded by unanimously declaring war.

1866

March 31. **Spain bombarded Valparaíso.** The Spanish fleet, which had been blockading Valparaíso, bombarded the defenseless port for three hours. The customshouse was destroyed and other buildings were damaged, but there were few casualties. An armistice was reached in 1871, and a peace treaty signed in 1883.

September 22. **Paraguayan victory at Curupaití.** On the offensive since late 1865, the Allies had moved into southern Paraguay. At Curupaití on the Paraguay River, Allied forces suffered heavy casualties as they hurled themselves against well-entrenched Paraguayan defenders. Paraguayan casualties totaled only about fifty while the Allies lost an estimated 9,000 men before **Bartolomé Mitre** gave the order for withdrawal.

1868

July 24. **Fall of Humaitá.** After a period of relative inactivity following their defeat at Curupaití, the Allies continued their slow advance against the Paraguay River strongholds of the **López** government. The most famous of these was Humaitá, known as the Sebastopol of South America. The fort was evacuated on July 24 after a thirteen-month siege, and the surviving defenders surrendered on August 5. The Paraguayans suffered additional reverses during the Lomas Valentinas campaign of December 1868.

October 12. **Domingo F. Sarmiento became president of Argentina.** During his six-year term he encouraged immigration and promoted public education.

1870

March 1. **Death of Francisco Solano López and end of the Paraguayan War.** Despite the near-annihilation of the Paraguayan army and the Allied occupation of Asunción in January 1869,

López was able to continue his resistance. He was killed by a Brazilian cavalry unit at Cerro Corá in northeastern Paraguay. A preliminary accord ended the war on June 20, 1870. Estimates of Paraguay's wartime deaths from combat, cholera, and other causes range from 8.7 percent to 50 percent of the prewar population. Brazil and Argentina eventually acquired approximately 55,000 square miles of Paraguayan territory. The last of their troops left Paraguay in 1876, but both countries continued to exercise great influence on Paraguayan affairs.

March. **"Revolution of the Lances" in Uruguay.** The Blanco party launched a major uprising against the government of Lorenzo Batlle (1868-72), a strong Colorado partisan. The conflict ended after an agreement was reached on April 6, 1872, in which the government promised to appoint Blancos to four of the nineteen departments into which Uruguay was divided.

Brazil

Brazil's relative stability in the decades after independence is usually attributed to the existence of the monarchy, which provided continuity and legitimacy of political leadership. Even so, there was much unrest in the 1830s as **Pedro I** was forced to abdicate and revolts broke out in several provinces, often reflecting racial and social tensions. By 1850, however, peace had been restored throughout the empire. For nearly fifty years **Pedro II** ruled benignly, exercising to the fullest the extensive powers granted him by the constitution of 1824. Liberal and Conservative parties took shape, but only a small minority of the population participated in politics.

Brazil experienced substantial economic change during these decades as coffee replaced sugar as the leading export, enhancing the wealth and influence of landowners in Rio de Janeiro and other coffee-growing provinces. The 1850s brought improvements in communications and transportation with the introduction of the telegraph and the construction of Brazil's first rail-roads. The end of Brazil's participation in the international slave trade hurt plantation owners but weakened the institution of slavery and freed capital for investment in other enterprises.

Brazil bore the burden of the war against Paraguay between 1864 and 1870 (see Southern Cone, 1864) and was affected by the conflict in various ways. The war left Brazil with a large foreign debt and depreciated currency. Because thousands of slaves were freed when they agreed to join the army, the war further weakened slavery.

1826

March 10. **Death of King João VI of Portugal.** Upon King João VI's death a regency proclaimed **Pedro I** of Brazil as king of Portugal. Realizing that he could not rule both countries, Pedro surrendered the Portuguese crown to his eight-year-old daughter, Maria da Glória. Pedro's younger brother, Miguel, was to act as regent of Portugal during the queen's minority and later marry her. In 1828, however, Miguel usurped the Portuguese throne and a civil war ensued.

November 23. **Brazil signed a slave trade treaty with Great Britain.** Under the terms of the treaty, which went into effect in 1827, Brazil committed itself to end the slave trade in three years. After that date slave trafficking was to be treated as piracy, and British ships would be authorized to stop and search Brazilian-flag vessels in international waters if they were suspected of carrying slaves.

1828

June 9-13. **Mutiny of mercenaries in Rio de Janeiro.** German and Irish troops recruited to fight in the war against Argentina rioted in Rio de Janeiro after a German soldier was whipped for insubordination. They looted taverns and stores, attacked police stations, and destroyed private houses. Brazilian regular and militia forces and civilian volunteers, including slaves, forced the mutineers to surrender, but the loss of the foreign soldiers made it difficult for Brazil to continue the war.

1831

April 7. **Pedro I abdicated the throne of Brazil.** Several factors led to mounting criticism of **Pedro I** after 1828: the loss of Uruguay, animosity between native-born Brazilians and the Portuguese community, and accusations that Pedro was a tyrant and that he was overly preoccupied with Portuguese affairs. In the face of popular and military opposition to his cabinet appointees, Pedro decided to step down in favor of his five-year-old son, the future **Pedro II**. As required by the constitution, a three-man regency was named to govern on behalf of young Pedro.

1834

August 12. **Promulgation of the Additional Act.** This set of amendments to the constitution of 1824 represented a concession to regionalist sentiment by creating elected provincial assemblies. The council of state, associated with **Pedro I**, was also abolished. In addition, the three-man regency was replaced by a single regent. Diogo Antônio Feijó was elected to this post in 1835. The powers of the provincial assemblies were later restricted, and the council of state was revived in 1841.

1835

January 6. **The bloody Cabanagem Revolt broke out in Belém,** capital of the province of Pará. The revolt derives its name from the word *cabanas*, or shanties, which were associated with the Indians, people of color, and other lower-class elements who supported it. The uprising began after years of dissension among provincial elites, many of whom were Portuguese. Quickly capturing Belém, the rebels killed the provincial president (governor), released prisoners, and engaged in widespread looting. The revolt later spread to Manaus, which the rebels seized in March 1836. However, the insurgents suffered from internal dissension and lack of direction. Imperial troops crushed the movement with great brutality, though some fighting continued until 1840.

January 24-25. **African rebels captured parts of the city of Salvador (Bahia).** Authorities had been forewarned of the conspiracy and quickly regained control. More than 200 persons were tried for complicity in the uprising, and four were executed. Since many of the slaves and ex-slaves involved were African-born Muslims (known as Malês in Bahia), it was believed that they hoped to establish a Muslim state.

September 20. **Beginning of the Farroupilha Revolt in Rio Grande do Sul.** The movement's name comes from the word *farrapos*, or ragmuffins, used to describe the rebels. The conflict arose out of federalist sentiment in Rio Grande do Sul, Brazil's most southerly province, and the belief that its interests were ignored by the central government. After capturing and briefly holding the provincial capital of Pôrto Alegre, the rebels set up an independent republic in the interior, much of which they controlled. Aided by the Uruguayan leader **Fructuoso Rivera**, the rebels resisted imperial troops until the arrival in 1842 of Luís Alves de Lima e Silva (the future **Duque de Caxias**), who had pacified the region by 1845.

1837

November 17. **Army officers in Salvador (Bahia) took control of the city,** launching the revolt known as the Sabinada. It is named after one of its civilian leaders, Francisco Sabino Álvares da Rocha Vieira. After capturing the city, the rebels gained adherents from the ranks of slaves and the free colored population. The officers had numerous grievances, including low salaries and limited opportunities for promotion. Hostility to Portuguese residents was also strong among the rebels, who proclaimed their loyalty to the emperor. After a four-month siege, government forces regained control of the city in mid-March 1838.

1838

December 13. **The Balaida Revolt in Maranhão began** with an assault on the jail in the town of Manga. Led by a cowboy, Raimundo Gomes, the assailants attracted many followers, mainly slaves, peasants, and other members of the lower classes of Maranhão and the province of Piauí. They resented the continued influence of the Portuguese and forced recruitment for the army. One of the leaders, nicknamed Balaio because he sold baskets (*balaios*), gave his name to the movement. On August 1, 1839, the rebels captured the important town of Caxias. Having been named provincial president, Luís Alves de Lima e Silva (later the **Duque de Caxias**) successfully moved against the rebellion, which had been crushed by early 1841.

1840

July 22. **The majority of Pedro II was declared.** Amid continuing provincial disturbances and fears that Brazil might disintegrate, Liberals in the General Assembly began to call upon **Pedro** to rule despite the fact that he had not reached the age of eighteen as required by the constitution. When the fourteen-year-old Pedro was asked by a parliamentary delegation whether he wished to rule, he replied affirmatively. On July 23 he appeared before the parliament and swore to uphold the constitution. He was crowned in 1841.

1848

November 7. **A republican revolt erupted in Olinda, Pernambuco.** It is known as the Praiera Revolt after the name of a street (Rua da Praia) in Recife where the offices of a Liberal newspaper were located. Inspired by the French Revolution of 1848, the insurgents were motivated by resentment toward the powerful landowners of the province and Portuguese control of urban commerce. After an unsuccessful attempt to capture Recife in February 1849, the revolt was crushed, though guerrillas remained active until 1851. This was the last republican revolt until 1889.

1850

September 4. **The Queiroz Law ending the slave trade was approved.** Although Brazil had committed itself to ending the slave trade in 1830,

large numbers of slaves continued to enter the country, to the great indignation of the British. When the 1826 treaty with Great Britain expired in 1845 and the Brazilian government refused to renew it, the British responded with the Aberdeen Act (August 8, 1845), which authorized the British to act against Brazilian slavers unilaterally. In 1850 British cruisers were sent into Brazilian territorial waters in pursuit of slave traders. This British pressure and growing doubts in Brazil about the institution of slavery contributed to the passage of the 1850 law, which declared slave trading to be piracy and provided that violators were to be judged by Brazilian admiralty courts rather than local juries. Named after Eusebio de Queiroz, the minister of justice, the law was effectively enforced, and the importation of slaves to Brazil soon ended.

1863

June 4. **Brazil severed diplomatic relations with Great Britain.** The dispute between the two countries began in 1861 when Brazilians looted a British ship wrecked on the shores of Rio Grande do Sul. In 1862 Brazilian authorities arrested three drunken British naval officers who were not in uniform, but released them upon learning their identity. The British minister, William D. Christie, demanded compensation for the looting of the ship and satisfaction for the insult to the officers. Another source of conflict between Christie and Brazil was the former's campaign on behalf of *emancipados*, technically free Africans who were kept in servitude. When Brazil rejected Christie's demands, he ordered a blockade of Rio de Janeiro (December 31, 1862). During the blockade the British seized five merchant vessels flying the Brazilian flag. Brazil agreed to pay for damages to the looted ship but disagreement over the seizure of the Brazilian vessels led the Brazilian minister in London to ask for his passport. Relations were restored in 1865.

1867

September 7. **Brazil opened the Amazon River to the ships of all nations.** British and United States officials and scientists had urged such action since the 1850s, but the Brazilian government, suspicious of United States intentions, initially insisted on keeping the river closed to foreign vessels. By the mid-1860s many Brazilians had altered their views on the matter, and the government issued a decree changing the policy (December 7, 1866).

1868

July. **Fall of the Zacharias Ministry.** The most serious political crisis in the reign of **Pedro II** occurred when the emperor disagreed with the prime minister, Zacharias de Goes e Vasconcelos, over an appointment to the Senate. Zacharias, a Liberal, resigned, whereupon the emperor selected a Conservative to succeed him, dissolved the General Assembly, and called for new elections, which were won by the Conservatives, who controlled the electoral machinery. In 1869 the Liberals, infuriated by their loss of power, issued manifestoes calling for curbs on the emperor's power, electoral reform, and the gradual abolition of slavery. The crisis also spurred the re-emergence of republicanism.

1870

November 3. **A Republican club was formed in Rio de Janeiro.** In December it issued a manifesto calling for the abolition of the monarchy and the establishment of a federal republic. The republican movement gradually gained strength in Rio de Janeiro, São Paulo, and other cities.

INCIPIENT MODERNIZATION AND SOCIAL CHANGE
1871-1929

After 1870 the political instability that had characterized much of Latin America in the post-independence decades abated, and military-dominated governments became less common. Regimes were frequently authoritarian, however, and political democracy made only limited gains. Such an outcome was satisfactory to many intellectuals who embraced positivism in the late nineteenth century. Developed by the Frenchman Auguste Comte (1798-1857), positivism upheld elitist, technocratically oriented political regimes as the best guarantors of order and progress.

The political stability of the post-1870 era created an environment conducive to the rapid expansion of exports of minerals and agricultural products for the markets of Western Europe and the United States. In Argentina, Brazil, Mexico, and Colombia there was also growth in the industrial sector, still confined mainly to the production of consumer goods for the small domestic market. Foreign investment, especially from Great Britain, poured into Latin America and contributed significantly to improvements in transportation, communications, and financial services. In short, the Latin American economies became more fully integrated into the North Atlantic economic system.

The years 1871-1929 were also characterized by substantial social change. Millions of immigrants were attracted to Brazil and the Southern Cone countries and often settled in cities such as São Paulo and Buenos Aires, which grew dramatically. Advances in education, coupled with economic expansion and the growth of government bureaucracies, created a new middle class that demanded a larger voice in policymaking. The changing economy also created a new labor force of mining, transportation, and factory workers who pressed for better wages and working conditions. Labor militance, sometimes inspired by anarchist and socialist doctrines, alarmed the upper classes and government leaders fearful of social conflict.

The rural poor, who still comprised the majority of Latin Americans, fared badly in the post-1870 era. The expansion of commercial agriculture came at the expense of the landholdings of indigenous communities in Mexico, Guatemala, Bolivia, and other countries. As haciendas incorporated these newly available lands, the dispossessed peasantry became a source of inexpensive labor. Rural rebellions were frequent after 1871, and the great Mexican Revolution of 1910 was sparked in part by demands for agrarian reform.

World War I disrupted patterns of trade and investment, and after the war the United States played a more important role in the economies of the region, especially as a source of loans and direct investment in manufacturing. United States influence is illustrated by the work of economist Edwin Kemmerer, who between 1917 and 1934 helped reform the monetary and banking systems of Chile, Colombia, Peru, and other countries. As United States loans dried up and commodity prices collapsed with the start of the Great Depression, most Latin American economies were thrown into disarray, and political upheaval followed.

Over the first three decades of the twentieth century, Latin American political elites struggled to modernize their nations. In most places lucrative exports paid for long-delayed railroad and highway-building projects, the improvement of port facilities, and a host of other public works programs. Only Mexico witnessed a thoroughgoing protest against the path charted by elite modernizers. There, in 1910, a populist revolution erupted presaging a cycle of social protest in Latin America that gained in intensity over ensuing decades.

The United States exercised great dominance over Central America and the Caribbean during early decades of the twentieth century. Cuba's early years as an independent nation were closely monitored by the United States, American forces occupied Haiti and Nicaragua for extended periods of time, and the United States assisted Panama in gaining independence from Colombia. During World War I and afterward, America's military intervention gave way to commercial and political dominance.

International Developments

The principal international theme in the six decades after 1870 was the growth of U.S. economic and political influence in Latin America, especially in Mexico, Central America, and the Caribbean. Citing the Monroe Doctrine, President Theodore Roosevelt and other leaders justified military and economic intervention to ensure political and financial stability in Latin America and thereby forestall possible European inroads in the region. U.S. dominance was also evident in the Pan American movement, launched in 1889 with the first of a series of conferences dealing with inter-American issues. After 1900 these conferences increasingly became forums where Latin American delegates criticized U.S. armed intervention in their countries. Throughout the period, however, the United States continued to assert the right of intervention, even though instances of armed intervention became less frequent after World War I with the demise of any credible European threat to the hemisphere.

Intra-regional disputes were, for the most part, settled amicably during the period 1900-1929. International arbitration either resolved or defused disputes between the United States and Mexico, Nicaragua and Honduras, Venezuela and Great Britain, and Peru and Chile. Brazil made notable territorial gains in diplomatic negotiations with France, Great Britain, the Netherlands, and its contiguous Spanish American sister republics.

1889

October 2. **The First International Conference of American States met in Washington.** Sponsored by Secretary of State James G. Blaine, the conference was attended by all the Latin American countries except the Dominican Republic. Topics discussed included United States proposals for an inter-American customs union and the principle (known as the Calvo Doctrine) that resident aliens should not receive preferential treatment in host countries. A treaty providing for the arbitration of inter-American disputes was signed but failed ratification. The principal concrete achievement of the conference was the creation of the International Union of American Republics, which was to be represented in Washington by the Commercial Bureau of the American Republics (reorganized and renamed the Pan American Union in 1910). The conference marked the beginning of the modern Pan American movement.

1895

July 20. **Secretary of State Richard Olney asserted United States supremacy in the Western Hemisphere in a note to the British government.** The note was provoked by a Venezuelan dispute with Great Britain over its boundary with British Guiana (see Bolivarian Republics, 1887). When the British ignored repeated Venezuelan requests for arbitration, Olney intervened. On the basis of the Monroe Doctrine he argued that United States interests would be adversely affected by European intervention in the hemisphere, where the United States was "practically sovereign" and where "its fiat is law upon the subjects to which it confines its interposition." Great Britain rejected the validity of the Monroe Doctrine but eventually agreed to arbitration. Olney's note is usually regarded as evidence of growing United States pretensions to hegemony over Latin America.

1901

October 22. **The Second International American Conference met in Mexico City.** There the Latin American states became parties to the Hague Convention of 1897, for the pacific settlement of international disputes.

November 18. **By the second Hay-Pauncefote Treaty,** Britain granted the United States the sole right to construct, control, and fortify an interoceanic canal across the Colombian department of Panama. The first Hay-Pauncefote Treaty (February 1900) had stipulated that the United States not fortify the canal. It failed to gain approval in the United States Senate because of opposition to the non-fortification clause.

1902

June 28. **The Spooner Act, directing United States president Theodore Roosevelt to conduct negotiations with Colombia for a canal across Panama,** was signed by Roosevelt.

1904

December 6. **The Roosevelt Corollary of the Monroe Doctrine** was announced by United States President Theodore Roosevelt, following his nation's intervention in affairs of the Dominican Republic. In his annual message to the American Congress, Roosevelt announced that the United States would exercise police power where "wrong-doing or impotence" in sister republics of the hemisphere required it.

1906

August 23. **The Third International Conference of American States met at Rio de Janeiro.** While United States delegates to the conference were conciliatory, conferees, angered over United States "gunboat diplomacy" in the Caribbean, endorsed two sets of principles espoused by Argentine diplomats Carlos Calvo and Luis María Drago. The Calvo Doctrine held that as national sovereignty is inviolable, resident aliens do not enjoy the right to have their own nations pressure host governments on their behalf. The Drago Doctrine held that because public debts secured internationally are contracted by the sovereign power of the state, those debts constitute a special kind of obligation and armed force should be ruled out as a means of collecting them.

1910

July 12. **The Fourth International American Conference was held at Buenos Aires.** Delegates to that meeting strove to avoid controversy, and adjourned having done little more than adopt the name Pan American Union for their association.

1914-18

The outbreak of World War I interrupted commercial links with Europe, producing a time of hardship in most of Latin America. By war's end the United States emerged as the region's dominate force and single greatest trading partner.

After the United States declared war on Germany (April 6, 1917), Brazil, Cuba, Haiti, and all of Central America, save for El Salvador, did likewise. The Dominican Republic, Ecuador, Peru, Bolivia, and Uruguay suspended diplomatic relations with Germany. Mexico, El Salvador, Colombia, Venezuela, Argentina, Uruguay, Chile, and Paraguay remained neutral.

1919

April. **Ten Latin American nations signed the Treaty of Versailles, thereby becoming original members of the League of Nations:** Bolivia, Brazil, Cuba, Guatemala, Haiti, Honduras, Nicaragua, Panama, Peru, and Uruguay. Ecuador signed but did not ratify the treaty. Most of the other countries joined soon after but found the League an unsatisfactory vehicle for their concerns, mainly because the United States failed to ratify the treaty and never joined. Several Latin American countries left the League, including Brazil, which withdrew in 1926.

1923

March 25. **The Fifth International American Conference met in Santiago, Chile.** In spite of generalized antagonism of the Latin American delegates toward the United States, conferees were able to endorse the Gondra Treaty for investigation of disputes between American states. Mexico boycotted the meeting in protest of United States failure to recognize its revolutionary government. Peru and Bolivia also refused to attend, in protest over their ongoing Tacna-Arica dispute.

1928

January 16. **The Sixth International American Conference met at Havana, Cuba.** U.S. president Calvin Coolidge and head of mission Charles Evans Hughes arrived inappropriately on a battleship, intent on defending the right of the U.S. to intervene in the affairs of other American states. Angry Latin American delegates challenged that assumption, forcing Hughes to defend the United States right of "interposition of a temporary character" to prevent Americans from being "butchered in the jungle." The meeting represented the first time that Latin Americans had debated such issues on anything approaching equal footing with the United States. Within five years Washington officially renounced interventionism.

December 17. **United States undersecretary of state Reuben J. Clark presented his memorandum on the Monroe Doctrine,** stating that while United States intervention in Latin American affairs was permissible under certain circumstances, it could not be justified by the Monroe Doctrine.

Mexico, Central America, and the Caribbean

After 1870 Liberal hegemony in Mexico and much of Central America was complete. Liberal governments vigorously promoted economic growth, along with improvement in the infrastructure needed to sustain it. In Mexico **Porfirio Díaz** presided over a long era of stability (1876-1911) during which the country registered great advances in the production of petroleum, copper,

and other minerals and commercial crops such as henequen, sugar, and coffee. In Central America coffee became the leading export. Liberal regimes were usually authoritarian, paying only lip service to constitutional prescriptions regarding free elections and political freedoms. Peasants gained little from the economic progress of the era, frequently experiencing increased labor demands and the loss of their lands to large estates.

The Mexican Revolution of 1910-17, and developments subsequent to the revolution's violent phase, produced profound changes in that nation and shocked elites in neighboring countries. Born of a political protest against the Díaz dictatorship, the revolution gradually took on characteristics of a genuine social upheaval. Institutionalized in 1917 in a national constitution pledging land and labor reform and subordinating private property to the public interest, the Mexican Revolution inspired reformers everywhere in Latin America.

Throughout the region the influence of the United States loomed ever larger after 1870. American capitalists invested large sums in Mexico's railroads and mines and in the sugar industry in Cuba and the Dominican Republic. United States capital also dominated the expanding banana industry of Costa Rica and Honduras. Cuba and Puerto Rico, restive under Spanish rule, developed ever closer commercial ties with the United States, while Cuba looked to Washington for aid in attaining its independence. The Spanish American War of 1898 ended Spanish control of Cuba and Puerto Rico but confirmed the preeminent role of the United States in the Caribbean. This role was further underscored by United States participation in Panama's secession from Colombia in 1903 and the construction of the Panama Canal.

Relations between the United States and Mexico were generally cordial during the Díaz era but cooled during the revolution. While Washington recognized the government headed by **Francisco I. Madero**, the United States ambassador, Henry Lane Wilson, detested the Mexican president and conspired in his downfall at the hands of **Victoriano Huerta**. President Woodrow Wilson refused to recognize Huerta and in 1914 ordered United States naval forces to occupy Veracruz in the hope of hastening his removal. The United States recognized **Venustiano Carranza** in 1915 after his triumph over his revolutionary rivals, but relations remained strained for more than a decade, mainly because of threats to United States investments in Mexico.

Mexican–United States relations improved notably during the late 1920s, with the appointment of Ambassador Dwight Morrow, and the visit of Charles Lindbergh in December 1927. Those were early manifestations of what would soon be termed the U.S. "Good Neighbor Policy."

Central American and Caribbean affairs continued to be powerfully influenced by the United States during the first three decades of the twentieth century. Both Cuba and Panama became American protectorates while United States troops occupied Haiti, the Dominican Republic, and Nicaragua at various times. As the 1920s progressed, however, the United States moved to end the practice of armed intervention in the region.

1871

April. **Successful Liberal revolution in El Salvador.** After forces under Santiago González routed the army of Francisco Dueñas at Santa Ana on April 10, the latter's government collapsed. González became president, beginning an era of Liberal dominance that lasted until 1944.

June 29. **Liberal triumph in Guatemala.** Liberals led by Miguel García Granados and **Justo Rufino Barrios** won a decisive victory at San Lucas Sacatepéquez, defeating Conservative forces under Vicente Cerna, who had succeeded to the presidency in 1865 upon the death of **Rafael Carrera**. García Granados now became provisional president of Guatemala.

November 8. **Porfirio Díaz rebelled against Benito Juárez.** Díaz had recently run for the presidency against **Juárez** and had been defeated. He now issued the Plan de La Noria, attacking Juárez for trying to perpetuate himself in power.

1872

July 18. **Death of Benito Juárez.** Mexico's long-serving president died of a heart attack. He was succeeded, as the constitution prescribed, by Sebastián Lerdo de Tejada, president of the Supreme Court. Lerdo was elected president for a four-year term in October 1872. The death of **Juárez** also put an end to the Noria revolt.

1873

March 22. **Slavery was abolished in Puerto Rico.** Abolitionists on the island had been dissatisfied with the Moret Law (1870), which provided for gradual abolition, and had pressed for an immediate end to slavery. This was granted by the short-lived first Spanish republic (1873-74). There were only about 29,000 slaves in Puerto Rico in 1873.

June 4. **Justo Rufino Barrios took office as president of Guatemala.** A Liberal autocrat, **Barrios** was strongly committed to economic development based on the expansion of coffee cultivation.

October 5. **Mexico's reform laws were incorporated into the constitution.** As a result, church and state were separated, marriage was made a civil contract, and religious corporations were forbidden to acquire real estate. Legislation enacted in 1874 prohibited religious instruction in public schools, the wearing of ecclesiastical attire in public, and the holding of religious services and ceremonies outside of churches.

October 31. **The *Virginius* affair.** The United States and Spain came close to war over this incident. The *Virginius*, a vessel flying the United States flag and carrying arms and supplies for Cuban insurgents, was seized by Spain off the coast of Cuba. After the ship was taken to Santiago de Cuba, fifty-three passengers and crewmen, many of them Americans, were speedily executed. The United States protested the seizure and the executions, but Spain defended its actions. It was eventually decided that the *Virginius* had no right to fly the American flag, and Spain paid $80,000 to the families of the dead Americans.

1876

January 1. **The Plan de Tuxtepec was proclaimed in Mexico.** The plan repudiated the government of Sebastián Lerdo de Tejada, who sought a second term as chief executive, and adhered to the principle of no re-election to the presidency. It also recognized **Porfirio Díaz** as head of the anti-Lerdo forces. In September 1876 Lerdo's position was weakened by the defection of José María Iglesias, president of the Supreme Court, who also rebelled. At Tecoac in Oaxaca state (November 16, 1876) Díaz decisively defeated federal forces supporting Lerdo. The latter stepped down and ensured Díaz's triumph over Iglesias by turning over the federal garrison in Mexico City to him. Díaz became president in 1877.

August 27. **Marco Aurelio Soto became president of Honduras.** Soto, a Liberal, promoted economic development and public education. Although he was close to Guatemala's **Justo Rufino Barrios**, in whose cabinet he had served, he resigned in 1883 after a dispute with Barrios.

1878

February 11. **The Pact of Zanjón ended Cuba's Ten Years' War.** This agreement reflected the failure of the Cuban insurgents to defeat the pro-Spanish forces of the island. The pact provided for limited self-government and for the freedom of slaves who had joined the rebel armies. Some insurgents refused to accept the agreement and attempted to renew the conflict in the "Little War" (Guerra Chiquita) in 1879.

April 9. **The United States recognized the Díaz government.** Although Great Britain and other countries had extended diplomatic recognition to the new Mexican regime, United States recognition was delayed because of problems along the Rio Grande border. Among the most serious from the United States perspective were incursions into Texas by Indians and cattle rustlers. On June 1, 1877, the Hayes administration authorized the U.S. military to pursue miscreants across the border, but the **Díaz** government replied that any invasion of Mexico by United States troops would be repelled by force. Díaz did send additional Mexican troops to police the border, and recognition was granted. Conditions along the Rio Grande gradually improved.

1879

October 23. **Etienne Felicité Salomon was elected president of Haiti.** His administration established the Banque National d'Haiti, which was financed by French capital, and engaged a French military mission. He also allowed foreigners to acquire land in Haiti despite the fact that this was forbidden by the constitution. He was forced out of power on August 10, 1888.

1880

January 1. **A French company began work on a canal in Panama.** Headed by Ferdinand de Lesseps, builder of the Suez Canal, the Compagnie Universelle du Canal Interocéanique based its effort on a concession acquired from the Colombian government in 1878. The United States frowned on the project, and President Rutherford B. Hayes stated that "the policy of this country is a canal under American control." The company faced many difficulties in constructing a sea-level canal across Panama, including disease, labor shortages, and malfeasance. Work was suspended in 1894. The rights and properties of the company were acquired by the United States in 1904.

January 30. **Slavery was abolished in Cuba.** The law passed by the Spanish parliament provided for an eight-year period of apprenticeship (*patronato*), during which the former slaves were to work for their owners. On October 7, 1886, however, complete abolition was decreed. By then many of the apprentices had gained their freedom through self-purchase and other means, and there were only about 25,000 persons still in bondage in Cuba.

December 1. **Manuel González was inaugurated as president of Mexico.** He succeeded **Porfirio Díaz**, of whom he was a long-time ally.

1882

September 1. **Ulises Heureaux became president of the Dominican Republic.** Nicknamed Lilís, Heureaux stepped down in 1884, returned to the presidency in 1887, and remained in power as a dictator until his assassination on July 26, 1899. His government encouraged infrastructure development, modernized the armed forces, and promoted production of sugar, cacao, and coffee.

1883

December 15. **Mexico enacted legislation for public lands.** A new law authorized private companies to survey public lands (*terrenos baldíos*). Companies were to receive up to one-third of the land surveyed and could sell it to settlers, though no individual was to receive more than 2,500 hectares (7,250 acres). The law was intended to encourage European immigration to Mexico. However, it served mainly as a vehicle by which speculators acquired large tracts of land. In addition, some landowners who could not prove title to their holdings sometimes saw them denounced as public lands.

1884

December 1. **Porfirio Díaz returned to the Mexican presidency.** Despite his earlier commitment to the principle of no re-election, **Díaz** remained the president of Mexico until he was forced from power in May 1911.

1885

March 12. **Bernardo Soto became president of Costa Rica.** A Liberal, Soto succeeded to the presidency upon the death of Próspero Fernández Oreamuno. Soto's administration is remembered for the achievements of his minister of education, Mauro Fernández, in expanding public education both at the primary and secondary levels.

March 1-April 28. **United States naval forces landed in Panama.** Hostilities erupted on the isthmus as part of a larger struggle between Colombian Liberals and Conservatives (see Bolivarian Republics, 1885). On March 31 Colón was destroyed by fire, an action attributed to Pedro Prestán, leader of the Liberal insurgents there. United States troops were landed in the city of Panama and Colón to protect the property of the Panama Railroad and keep the transit route open, as mandated by the Bidlack-Mallarino Treaty of 1846. But, as the authorities in Bogotá anticipated, the presence of United States forces had the effect of hurting the revolutionaries and helping the government.

April 2. **Guatemala's Barrios was killed in battle.** On February 28, 1885, **Justo Rufino Barrios** decreed the union of the five Central American states into a single republic with himself as supreme chief. The Honduran government supported Barrios's plan, but it was opposed by El Salvador, Nicaragua, and Costa Rica. As a result, Barrios invaded El Salvador, but his forces were defeated at Chalchuapa, and Barrios was mortally wounded. With his demise the projected Central American union also died.

1887

March 7-10. **The Autonomist party of Puerto Rico was established.** Organized at a convention in Ponce, the party sought local self-government for the island even as it remained under Spanish rule.

1889

February-October. **The Nicaraguan canal project.** Chartered by the U.S. Congress in

February 1889, the Maritime Canal Company undertook to build a trans-isthmian canal through Nicaragua on the basis of contracts signed with the Nicaraguan and Costa Rican governments in 1887-88. Work got under way in Greytown, Nicaragua, in October 1889 and continued for more than three years. Lack of funds halted operations, and the company, unable to raise additional capital because of the financial panic of 1893, went bankrupt. Efforts to obtain the financial backing of the United States government for the company proved unsuccessful, though the idea of a Nicaraguan canal remained popular in the United States.

November 7. **Crowds converged on San José, Costa Rica, to demand that presidential election results be respected.** The opposition candidate, proclerical José Joaquín Rodríguez, had won the first phase of balloting, but there were signs that the government might declare its candidate the winner. In response to the thousands of protestors, President Bernardo Soto promised that the election results would be honored and resigned. Rodríguez won the election, taking office on May 8, 1890. The peaceful transfer of power from one party to another on this occasion is considered a milestone in the development of Costa Rican democracy.

1892

January 2. **The Cuban Revolutionary party was established.** Founded by **José Martí** and other Cuban exiles in the United States, it was dedicated to ending Spanish control of the island and establishing a democratic republic.

October. **Mexican troops crushed Tomochic rebels.** Many residents of the small Chihuahua town of Tomochic had become followers of Teresa Urrea, a healer and mystic. Their leader, Cruz Chávez, launched a millenarian, egalitarian movement that was perceived as a threat by state and national authorities. After suffering a defeat at the hands of the rebels in September, government troops renewed their assault in October.

Tomochic defenders fought to the last man, becoming heroes in Mexican folklore. Meanwhile, Teresa Urrea had gone to the United States, where she continued faith healing and may have taken part in anti-**Díaz** activities.

1893

September. **José Santos Zelaya became president of Nicaragua.** A Liberal, he ended many years of Conservative domination of the country. He stimulated export agriculture and infrastructure development, though he governed in a dictatorial fashion. He eventually alienated the United States, which played a key role in his ouster in 1909.

1895

February 24. **Renewal of the Cuban war for independence.** The war began with a proclamation in the village of Baire, near Santiago de Cuba. Organized by the Cuban Revolutionary party, the insurrection spread to much of the island, inflicting great suffering on civilians and causing severe damage to the economy. The administration of Grover Cleveland (1893-97) soon came under pressure to intervene because of losses suffered by American property owners in Cuba. The reconcentration policy of the Spanish captain-general, Valeriano Weyler y Nicolau (1896-98), which forced the relocation of thousands of rural people, also produced an outcry in the United States.

1897

November 25. **Spain offered autonomy to Cuba and Puerto Rico.** The charter created legislative bodies on the islands and provided for local self-government in areas such as justice, education, and public works. The Spanish government acted in the hope of averting United States intervention in the Cuban insurrection, but Cuban revolutionary leaders rejected the charter, which left extensive powers in the hands of Spanish authorities. The charter was accepted in Puerto Rico, and the new government was inaugurated in 1898, just before United States troops occupied the island.

1898

United States war with Spain. After three years Spain had not been able to defeat the Cuban insurgents or appease them with offers of an armistice and autonomy. In the United States many continued to favor intervention on behalf of Cuba, which would mean war with Spain. Some hoped that a war with Spain would enable the United States to acquire Spanish territory. Two events early in 1898 helped propel the United States toward war: the publication (February 11) of the DeLôme letter, in which the Spanish minister to Washington spoke unflatteringly of President William McKinley, and the sinking (February 15) of the *U.S.S. Maine* in Havana harbor with the loss of 260 lives. Although the cause of the explosion that sank the *Maine* is still uncertain, many Americans blamed Spain. President McKinley asked Congress for authority to end the hostilities in Cuba. Congress granted his request (April 19) and also adopted the Teller Amendment disclaiming any United States intention of annexing Cuba. Spain responded by declaring war against the United States.

The United States defeated Spain with relative ease, occupying Cuba, Puerto Rico, the Philippine Islands, and Guam. The Treaty of Paris (December 10) provided for the end of Spanish sovereignty over Cuba and for the cession of Puerto Rico, Guam, and the Philippines.

October 2. **Manuel Estrada Cabrera was inaugurated as president of Guatemala.** He succeeded José María Reyna Barrios, a nephew of **Justo Rufino Barrios**, who had served from 1892 until his assassination on February 8, 1898. **Estrada Cabrera** remained in power until 1920.

1899

March 30. **The United Fruit Company was incorporated in New Jersey.** Combining the holdings of the Boston Fruit Company and of **Minor C. Keith**, the company quickly became the dominant force in the cultivation of bananas in Latin America and their marketing in the United States. By 1914 it owned or leased more than 1.2 million acres of land in Costa Rica, Guatemala, Colombia, Cuba, and other countries. It produced sugar and other crops as well as bananas, and controlled railroads, wharves, and radio communications in several countries. Because of the economic and political influence it wielded in Central America, the company was often controversial.

1900

April 12. **Puerto Ricans were granted civilian government through the Foraker Act.** The act postponed the granting of full United States citizenship to Puerto Ricans, who received their first appointed civilian governor on May 1.

August. **Opposition to Mexican dictator Porfirio Díaz** appeared in the form of the newspaper *Regeneración*, published in Mexico City by Jesús, **Ricardo**, and Enrique **Flores Magón**. Arrested and imprisoned for a year (1901), the brothers removed to the United States where they continued publication of their increasingly anti-Díaz newspaper first in San Antonio, Texas, and later in St. Louis, Missouri.

1901

February 21. **Cuba's constitution was adopted.** On June 12, it was modified by the so-called Platt Amendment, giving the United States veto power over Cuban treaties, the right to intervene for "the preservation of Cuban independence and the maintenance of a government adequate for the protection of life, property and individual liberties" on the island, and the right to establish coaling stations or naval bases there. Cubans protested the amendment, which nevertheless was adopted on the argument that without the change the United States would not allow Cuban independence.

December 31. **Tomás Estrada Palma was elected president of Cuba** in elections called by U.S. military governor General Leonard Wood.

1902

May 8. **Ascensión Esquivel took office as president of Costa Rica** after an election under a new voting system featuring secret ballot and universal male suffrage. Conservative party leader Cleto González succeeded him (1906-10), going on to serve two additional terms (1912-14, 1928-32). Liberal party leader Ricardo Jiménez served three

terms (1910-12, 1924-28, 1932-36). Except for the dictatorship of Federico Tinoco (1917-19), Costa Rica's politics were placid and democratic during the first three decades of the twentieth century. Other chief executives of the period were Alfredo González (1914-17), Julio Acosta (1919, 1920-24), and Juan Bautista (1919).

June. **At the Corinto Conference in Nicaragua, all Central American states except**

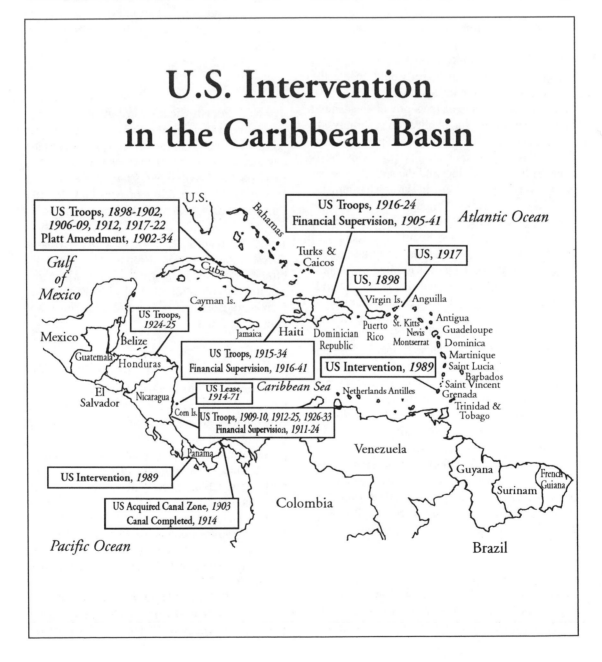

U.S. Intervention in the Caribbean Basin

Guatemala agreed to submit any disputes that might arise among them to a tribunal of Central American arbitrators.

December 21. **Nord Alexis became Haiti's president** following the death of incumbent P.A. Tirésias Simon Sam, and a brief civil war. Nord was succeeded by F. Antoine Simon (December 17, 1908).

1903

November 3. **Panamanian conspirators led by Manuel Amador Guerrero declared independence from Colombia.** The United States warship *Nashville*, which had reached Panamanian waters the previous day, protected the rebels from Colombian forces dispatched to the scene. The United States recognized Panamanian independence on November 6.

November 18. **The Hay–Bunau-Varilla Treaty, authorizing the United States to construct a trans-oceanic canal in Panama, was signed in Washington, D.C.** Philippe Bunau-Varilla, a chief stockholder and engineer of the French company originally contracted to build the canal, was instrumental in fomenting the Panamanian revolt of November 3. He concluded negotiations with United States Secretary of State John Hay prior to arrival of a Panamanian team sent to join the treaty deliberations. The document negotiated by Hay and Bunau-Varilla was more advantageous to the United States than the Hay-Herrán Treaty had been (see Bolivarian Republics, 1903). It awarded the United States virtual sovereignty over the canal zone (expanded to ten miles) in perpetuity and provided for a 10 million dollar payment and an annual payment of $250,000. The United States also guaranteed the independence of Panama, in effect making it a protectorate.

1905

February 7. **The United States and the Dominican Republic signed a treaty** providing for U.S. collection of Dominican customs. This extraordinary action was occasioned both by the pressure of foreign creditors and the political turmoil that had constantly afflicted the nation since the assassination of dictator Ulises Heureaux in 1899.

When the U.S. Senate refused to ratify the treaty, President Roosevelt put the agreement into effect anyway. A new treaty was approved in 1907. Ultimately, President Carlos Morales Lang Vasco was overthrown (January 12, 1906) by General Ramón Cáceres, who went on to govern the troubled nation until his assassination (November 19, 1911).

1906

June 2. **Mexican president Porfirio Díaz used troops to break the Cananea copper strike** following the governor of Sonora's request that 275 Arizona Rangers help him quell the conflict. Mexican workers at the United States-owned mine, located forty miles south of the Arizona border, protested working conditions and a salary scale favoring American miners doing comparable work. The commander of Mexico's rural police, Emilio Kosterlitzky, subsequently executed strike leaders.

July. **Anti-Díaz militants, led by the Flores Magón brothers, published the Liberal Party Plan, which advocated both political and social reform, including a minimum wage and shorter hours for workers.** Announced from the safety of St. Louis, Missouri, published in the newspaper *Regeneración*, the plan had little immediate impact upon Mexican affairs.

July. **The United States and Mexico mediated the struggle against Guatemalan dictator Manuel Estrada Cabrera**, and were later joined by Costa Rica. Honduras and El Salvador had aided Guatemalan refugees in the campaign against Estrada Cabrera. Mediation efforts were successful when all parties met aboard the *U.S.S. Marblehead*. In accord with the *Marblehead* Pact, all parties agreed to cease hostilities.

September 28. **Cuban president Tomás Estrada Palma resigned** following a Liberal revolt attending his re-election, and the failure of mediation by U.S. secretary of war William Howard Taft. Taft then called for American intervention under terms of the Platt Amendment to the Cuban constitution. President Theodore Roosevelt responded by appointing lawyer Charles Magoon governor of Cuba. Magoon was charged with imposing reforms and restoring democratic rule to the island. He did so by supervising a presidential election in 1908 that brought José Miguel Gómez to power (January 28, 1909).

1907

January 7. **Mexican troops fired on rebellious workers at the Río Blanco textile mill in the state of Veracruz.** Their strike broken, the workers were forced to sign a contract stipulating that they would pay for the depreciation of capital equipment. The incident heightened opposition to the **Díaz** government and strengthened the opposition Mexican Liberal party (Partido Liberal Mexicano, PLM), led by Enrique and **Ricardo Flores Magón**.

February. **Nicaragua's José Santos Zelaya invaded Honduras seeking to oust its president, Manuel Bonilla.** The latter was defeated at the Battle of Namasigüe (March 17-18) and was succeeded by Miguel Dávila. Bonilla returned to the presidency in February 1912 after United States mediation ended a revolution he had launched against Dávila with the help of banana entrepreneur Samuel Zemurray.

November 14-December 20. **A conference of Central American states, meeting in Washington, D.C., adopted treaties aimed at promoting peace and unity throughout the region.** One treaty provided that governments that came to power by force would not be recognized; the signatories also pledged that they would not interfere in each other's affairs. Another treaty created the Central American Court of Justice for the peaceful settlement of disputes. The court lasted until 1917 when it fell victim to a conflict over the Bryan-Chamorro Treaty.

1908

February 7. **Porfirio Díaz told American journalist James Creelman** that as Mexico was ripe for democracy, he welcomed the appearance of opposition political parties. Díaz also said that he

did not intend to stand for re-election in 1910. The dictator's remarks, which he later recanted, touched off a flurry of political activity prefacing Díaz's fall from power.

1909

February 1. **United States forces were withdrawn from Cuba** following inauguration of Liberal president José Miguel Gómez. Agitation against the Platt Amendment became a permanent feature of Cuban life, and grew more strident under Gómez's successor, Mario G. Menocal (1913-21).

December 16. **Nicaraguan president José Santos Zelaya was overthrown** by Conservatives aided by the United States. Three Conservative presidents served briefly: José Madriz (1909-10), José D. Estrada (1910-11), Juan J. Estrada (1911). At length Adolfo Díaz, who enjoyed United States support, was installed as president (May 9, 1911), going on to serve until 1917.

1910

March 1. **Panamanian president José Domingo Obaldía died**, setting into motion a political crisis over whether his successor, acting president Liberal Carlos A. Mendoza, should complete the former's term. But Mendoza's popular following, his coolness toward the United States, and his African features set United States chargé, Richard O. Marsh, against him. Pressure from Marsh, including the threat of the U.S. annexation of Panama, forced Mendoza to withdraw from the race. Elderly Pablo Arosemena was subsequently elected (inaugurated October 5), inspiring the remark that Panama was little more than an annex of the Canal Zone.

April. **Francisco I. Madero led an anti-reelection convention in Mexico City opposing the reelection of Porfirio Díaz.** Madero was nominated for the presidency and campaigned throughout the country until mid-June, when he was arrested. After Díaz was re-elected on June 21, Madero was released on bail in San Luis Potosí and fled to San Antonio, Texas, in early October.

October 5. **In San Antonio, Texas, Madero announced the Plan de San Luis Potosí,** setting November 20 as the date for a general uprising against the dictatorship. The revolt failed to materialize, although Pascual Orozco, **Francisco Villa,** and other Madero supporters staged localized uprisings in response to his call. **Porfirio Díaz** was inaugurated to another presidential term on December 1.

1911

February 14. **Madero entered northern Mexico and assumed leadership of revolutionaries in that region.** Over the ensuing months the revolution became generalized throughout the countryside.

May 10. **Mexican revolutionaries seized Ciudad Juárez.** Meanwhile **Emiliano Zapata** led a revolt of peasants in the southern state of Morelos. During March, U.S. president Taft mobilized 20,000 troops along the Mexican border and dispatched American warships to Mexican ports.

May 21. **The Treaty of Ciudad Juárez was signed between Madero and the Díaz government.** Under its terms **Díaz** would resign, leaving behind a caretaker government that would preside until new presidential elections were held. Díaz departed the country four days later.

August 2. **Haitian president Antoine Simon was overthrown and killed,** ushering in a period of political instability that witnessed six presidents in five years: Michel C. Leconte (1911-12), Tancrède Auguste (1912-13), Michel Oreste (1913-14), Oreste Zamor (1914), Joseph Davilmar Théodore (1914-15), Jean Vilbrun-Guillaume Sam (1915).

October 15. **Francisco I. Madero was overwhelmingly elected president of Mexico.** He was inaugurated on November 6.

November 19. **Dominican president Ramón Cáceres was assassinated.** He was succeeded by a parade of chief executives whose terms were brief: Eladio Victoria (1911-12), Adolfo Nouel y Bobadilla (1912-13), José Bordas (1913-14), Ramón Báez (1914), Juan I. Jiménez (1914-16), Francisco Henríquez y Carvajal (1916).

November 28. **Emiliano Zapata and other peasant leaders denounced Madero** for his refusal to announce massive land redistribution. They proclaimed the Plan de Ayala, under which large haciendas would be broken up and their lands distributed to the people.

1912

May–June. **Cuba's Independent Party of Color revolted** against President José Miguel Gómez's perceived betrayal of the black population through a 1909 law banning political parties based on race or religion. Poorly organized, and confined to Oriente Province, the uprising nevertheless provoked panic throughout Cuba. Spurred on by the landing of U.S. Marines at Daiquirí, the government crushed the *independentistas* and executed its leaders (June 1912).

July. **U.S. Marines entered Nicaragua to crush a Liberal revolt** that threatened to unseat U.S.-backed President Adolfo Díaz. Díaz's mandate was reconfirmed in a special election, held November 1912. United States involvement in the Nicaraguan civil war was significant in that it represented the first time the United States had intervened militarily to suppress revolution in a sister republic. Except for a brief six-month period in 1925-26, U.S. troops remained until 1933.

October 12. **Liberal Belisario Porras was inaugurated president of Panama,** introducing twenty years of physical progress in the country. Porras was succeeded in 1916 by Ramón Valdés (d. June 4, 1918), and went on to serve a second term (1920-24).

1913

February 9 18. **Movements to overthrow President Madero led to fighting in Mexico City.** During the turmoil, dubbed the "Tragic Ten Days," artillery battles raged in the heart of the city, as followers of former president **Díaz** fought to overthrow the **Madero** government. General **Victoriano Huerta**, in command of the federal forces defending Madero, changed sides and arrested Madero and other members of his government (February 18). The agreement between Huerta and the rebels was reached at the U.S. embassy. The United States ambassador, Henry Lane Wilson, was hostile to Madero. Under the agreement, Huerta became provisional president of Mexico.

February 11. **Carlos Meléndez was inaugurated president of El Salvador.** Scion of a powerful family, one of fourteen dominating the nation's coffee production and export, Meléndez served a second term (1915-19), and was succeeded in office by his brother Jorge, who served from 1919 to 1923. Coffee-rich El Salvador was a placid place up to 1931, when a sharp decline in the price of its chief export ushered in a period of military dictatorship.

February 22. **Francisco Madero and former Mexican vice president José María Pino Suárez, were murdered by henchmen of Victoriano Huerta.**

March 26. **Venustiano Carranza, governor of Coahuila, published the Plan de Guadalupe**, denouncing **Huerta** and his government, and proclaiming the formation of the Constitutionalist Army pledged to overthrow him. **Francisco "Pancho" Villa** joined Carranza. During subsequent months the Constitutionalists, aided by **Zapata** and his agrarian rebels in the south, moved against Huerta. Meanwhile, newly inaugurated U.S. president Woodrow Wilson recalled Henry Lane Wilson, and allowed armaments to enter the hands of those opposing Huerta.

May 20. **Conservative Mario G. Menocal was inaugurated Cuban president.** Closely linked to United States sugar interests, known for venality and corruption, Menocal amassed a personal fortune over two presidential terms.

1914

April 21. **The United States occupied the Mexican port of Veracruz,** claiming provocation by the dictator **Victoriano Huerta**. On July 15, Huerta was driven from power by Constitutionalist forces headed by **Álvaro Obregón** and **Venustiano Carranza**, the latter of whom became president (August 15). Carranza and Obregón then turned to oppose **Francisco Villa**, whose army controlled northern Mexico. President Wilson ordered the withdrawal of United States troops from Veracruz on November 23, 1914.

May–June. **The Niagara Falls Conference,** sometimes termed the ABC Conference, convened in Niagara Falls, Canada, to mediate hostility between the United States and Mexico. The former nation defended its action, while demanding the replacement of de facto president **Victoriano Huerta** by a provisional president. **Venustiano Carranza** refused to acknowledge the authority of the conference, and it accomplished little.

August 14. **The Panama Canal was opened to limited use** owing to persistent landslides. On July 20, 1920, the canal was dedicated and declared fully operational.

October 10-November 10. **The Aguascalientes Convention was held** for the purpose of reconciling disputes between **Carranza** and his rivals **Francisco Villa** and **Emiliano Zapata**. Carranza subsequently withdrew to Veracruz, from which city he began publishing a series of reform decrees. Villa and Zapata and their armies occupied Mexico City. Anarchy reigned over much of Mexico.

1915

April 6-15. **The forces of Carranza, commanded by Álvaro Obregón, fought and de-**

feated Francisco Villa at the battles of Celaya. Obregón, commanding the Constitutionalist forces, went on to defeat Villa a second time, in June, at León, causing Villa to withdraw northward, his forces decimated. Villa ceased to play an active role in the war against Carranza. **Emiliano Zapata** continued his campaign of land redistribution in southern Mexico.

July 27. **United States troops landed in Haiti to restore order,** one day after President Vilbrun-Guillaume Sam had ordered 167 political prisoners murdered and was in turn lynched. Philipe Dartiguenave became president (August 12) upon election by the National Assembly. He signed a treaty with the United States (September 16) formalizing the United States military presence there, restricting Haiti's right to increase its foreign debt, and prohibiting the government from reducing tariffs. The treaty was to be in force for ten years, and was subject to renewal. Succeeding Dartiguenave in 1922 was Louis Borno (1922-30).

1916

January 10. **Francisco Villa's troops murdered sixteen United States mining engineers** at Santa Isabel, in northern Mexico. **Villa** was protesting U.S. president Wilson's recognition of **Carranza** as president of Mexico the previous October.

February 18. **The United States ratified the Bryan-Chamorro Treaty with Nicaragua (1914),** giving the United States the exclusive right to lease naval bases on both the country's Pacific and Caribbean coasts, and to construct a trans-oceanic canal across the Central American nation. With one canal already opeative, the U.S. had no intention of building a second one, and this exclusive right precluded other world powers from doing so. Costa Rica, El Salvador, and Honduras protested before the Central American Court of Justice that the treaty violated their constitutional rights. The court found in their favor, but the United States and Nicaragua ignored the verdict. Nicaragua withdrew from the court, causing its collapse.

Emiliano Chamorro, who as Nicaraguan ambassador to the United States negotiated the treaty, was elected president with United States support (inaugurated January 1, 1917). Chamorro served until 1921, being succeeded by kinsman Diego Manuel Chamorro, who served for three years. The death of Diego Chamorro (October 12, 1923) made way for the caretaker regime of Bartolomé Martínez, who held office until Carlos Solórzano won the presidency in 1924.

March 9. **Francisco Villa led five hundred guerrillas across the United States border** to raid the town of Columbus, New Mexico. The Columbus Massacre, which claimed the lives of seventeen Americans, resulted in the dispatching of General John J. Pershing and 12,000 United States troops into northern Mexico (April 1916–February 1917) in fruitless pursuit of Villa.

November 1. **Conservative Mario G. Menocal was elected to a second term in Cuba,** thanks both to United States support and to increased prosperity produced by World War I. Charging electoral fraud, Liberal leader José Miguel Gómez raised the standard of revolt (February 10, 1917). The Liberal revolt failed when diplomatic notes were published stressing United States support for "legally established governments only."

November 29. **The Dominican Republic was occupied by United States troops** under command of Rear-Admiral H.S. Knapp, on order of Woodrow Wilson. That action was occasioned both by the refusal of newly elected President Francisco Henríquez y Carvajal to accept continued management of Dominican customs receipts by the United States, under terms of the 1907 United States–Dominican convention, and by the government's unauthorized public borrowing, in violation of the 1907 agreement. Knapp suspended Congress and, in his capacity as governor-general, appointed American naval officers to administer the nation. American administration of Dominican affairs lasted until September 1924.

1917

January 19. **The Zimmermann telegram was sent.** Named after Arthur Zimmermann, the

German foreign minister, the note was sent to the German minister in Mexico City. It proposed that Mexico take part in a joint campaign against the United States should the latter declare war on Germany. Mexico was promised the return of Texas, New Mexico, and Arizona. The **Carranza** government considered the proposal but ultimately rejected it as U.S.-Mexican relations had improved somewhat. Intercepted and decoded by the British, the telegram helped bring about the United States declaration of war against Germany in April 1917.

January 27. **Costa Rican president Alfredo González was overthrown** in a coup headed by Federico Tinoco, who failed to gain recognition by the United States. Tinoco went on to rule the country arbitrarily for two years.

February 5. **Mexico adopted a new constitution, born of the 1910 revolution.** The famous 1917 constitution, one of the most socially advanced in the world, provided for land reform, labor legislation, and protection of the national domain. **Venustiano Carranza**, who had presided over the constitutional convention, was elected president, going on to serve until his assassination in 1920.

March 2. **The Jones Act awarded territorial status to Puerto Rico,** and awarded United States citizenship to the island's people.

1919

April 10. **Emiliano Zapata was assassinated** on the hacienda of Chinameca, located in the charismatic leader's home state of Morelos. **Zapata** had become obnoxious to the government of President **Carranza** through his refusal to abide by its dictates.

August 12. **Costa Rican dictator Federico Tinoco left power, convinced that mounting opposition made his position untenable.** His brother, Minister of War Joaquín Tinoco, was assassinated two days earlier. Orderly political rule returned to the country with the election of Liberal Julio Acosta (December 9), who went on to govern until 1924. The succeeding regimes of

Ricardo Jiménez (1924-28), Cleto González (1928-32), and Ricardo Jiménez (1932-36) were uneventful.

October 30. **Haitian rebel leader Charlemagne Peralte was killed**, thus ending a year-long armed protest against the nation's occupation by the United States.

1920

April. **A Unionist movement in Guatemala produced the overthrow of long-time dictator Manuel Estrada Cabrera**, replacing him (April 8) with Carlos Herrera y Luna. Herrera and his supporters participated in a short-lived attempt to form a tripartite republic (with El Salvador and Honduras), formalized in a Pact of Union, June 17, 1921. Herrera was overthrown by the military shortly thereafter, and the union with El Salvador and Honduras ended. A succession of figurehead chief executives followed (José María Orellana, 1922-26; Lázaro Chacón, 1926-30; Baudillo Palma, 1930; José María Reyna Andrade, 1931). The Guatemalan army was the arbiter of national destinies throughout the 1920s.

April 23. **Under the Plan de Agua Prieta, Adolfo de la Huerta, Álvaro Obregón, and Plutarco Elías Calles joined forces against Venustiano Carranza**, whom they accused of dictatorial pretensions. **Carranza** was killed on May 21, while attempting to flee the country, and **Obregón** was elected president (September 5). With **Emiliano Zapata** assassinated and **Francisco Villa** in retirement, Obregón turned to the task of national reconstruction.

1921

May 20. **Alfredo Zayas was inaugurated president of Cuba,** following United States adjudication of the disputed election of 1920. While his regime was notoriously corrupt, Zayas managed to preserve national peace in the face of student militance, labor unrest, and an armed uprising led by members of the Veterans' and Patriots' Association. He was also able to moderate the influence of United States envoy General Enoch Crowder. Zayas remained Cuban president until 1925, when he ceded power to **Gerardo Machado**.

1923

January 13. **Religious strife flared in Mexico when President Álvaro Obregón** expelled papal representative Monsignor E. Filippi, after the priest took part in an elaborate outdoor religious ceremony in Guanajuato. Such celebrations were contrary to the Mexican constitution, and **Obregón** felt that Filippi's act of defiance should not go unanswered.

February 7. **New Central American treaties were signed.** As in 1907, the United States organized a conference of the five Central American states in Washington that led to the drafting of several treaties. The United States desire for stability was reflected in a ban on recognition of governments that had come to power by force even if they were later legitimated by elections. Another agreement imposed limitations on the size of Central American armies.

July 20. **Francisco "Pancho" Villa was assassinated** in Hidalgo del Parral, in northern Mexico, possibly on orders of President **Obregón** and perhaps because he was plotting with dissident Adolfo de la Huerta.

August 15. **The Bucareli Street Conference, initiated between United States and Mexican representatives,** concluded. The conference, which had lasted three months, dealt with demands that U.S. owners of lands seized be indemnified, and that U.S. companies not lose oil reserves in accord with the constitutional provision holding that such reserves were property of the Mexican nation. Mexico agreed to submit the land claims to arbitration, and further agreed not to apply the constitutional provision concerning oil reserves retroactively. In exchange for the

Mexican concessions, the United States formally recognized the **Obregón** administration.

December. **Civil war erupted in Mexico** owing to **Obregón**'s selection of **Plutarco Elías Calles** as his successor. Anti-Calles forces, rallying around their candidate Adolfo de la Huerta, fought government forces during late 1923 and early 1924. Obregón ultimately crushed the uprising of de la Huerta and his backers. With de la Huerta exiled and many of his supporters dead, Plutarco Elías Calles was elected Mexico's president and inaugurated December 1, 1924.

1924

June. **Tiburcio Carías Andino, Honduran caudillo and National party founder,** elected president a year earlier, was denied that office by Liberal party members who dominated the national Congress. United States mediation resulted in the accession to the presidency of Carías's running mate Miguel Paz Baraona (inaugurated February 1, 1925). The Liberals regained the presidency in 1929 under Vincente Mejía Colindres, who served until 1932.

September 18. **The last U.S. Marines departed the Dominican Republic,** and political power passed to Horacio Vásquez (inaugurated July 12). Vásquez signed a new convention with the United States that allowed him slightly more fiscal independence than had been the case under the 1907 accord. Corruption and political factionalism intensified after 1928, when Vásquez arbitrarily extended his term to six years. At length, in 1930, he was forced to resign in the face of opposition from his minister of the interior, Rafael Estrella Ureña, who enjoyed the tacit support of army commander **Rafael Leonidas Trujillo**.

October 1. **Roberto Chiari, hand-picked successor of Belisario Porras, was inaugurated president of Panama.** During his administration Chiari seized control of the Liberal party, blocking Porras's bid for re-election. When his term ended, he named his successor, Florencio H. Arosemena, who served until 1931.

1925

May 20. **Gerardo Machado was inaugurated Cuban president,** pledged to thoroughgoing reform. Leader of a revitalized Liberal party, he enjoyed initial popular support of a nationalist and progressive character. Machado was virtually unopposed during his first two years in office, a time of infrastructural improvement and modest prosperity. In 1928, Machado moved to establish a dictatorship, a move that soon foundered in the face of sharp economic decline following the onset of global depression in late 1929.

August. **The Communist party of Cuba (Partido Comunista de Cuba, PCC) was established.** The party was formed by several existing Marxist groups. Its first secretary-general, Julio Antonio Mella, was exiled to Mexico by **Machado** in 1927 and mysteriously assassinated there in 1929. The party opposed the **Grau** government in 1933. Legalized in 1938, the party supported **Fulgencio Batista**'s presidential candidacy in 1940, and two Communists joined his cabinet in 1942. It was renamed the Popular Socialist party in 1944.

August 4. **The last U.S. Marines left Nicaragua** following inauguration of Conservative Carlos Solórzano (January 1). But the Liberal-Conservative civil war resumed, leading to a return of U.S. Marines. Conservative leader Emiliano Chamorro ousted Solórzano and installed himself as president though he was soon replaced by Adolfo Díaz (1926). United States mediation (May 1927), through State Department official Henry Stimson, resulted in an agreement with Liberals, and Liberal army chief José María Moncada cooperated with U.S. troops in pacifying the countryside. Moncada won the 1928 contest (inaugurated January 1, 1929), going on to govern until December 1932. But Moncada's lieutenant, **Augusto César Sandino,** rejected the United States–supervised political arrangement and continued to promote guerrilla warfare in the countryside. Sandino, a hero of nationalists and anti-imperialists in his nation and elsewhere, withdrew to Mexico following Moncada's inauguration. Meanwhile, while Moncada accepted the command of Nicaragua's National Guard by United States officers, he worked to reduce United States influence in his country.

December 18. **The Mexican Congress ordered foreign oil companies to exchange their holdings for fifty-year concessions,** a dictate that stood in contradiction to the Bucareli Street accords of 1923. Foreign oil interests, especially those in the United States, protested the action.

1926

February. **Mexican church officials protested anticlerical provisions of the 1917 constitution,** in turn provoking President **Calles** to close church schools and convents and to expel foreign priests. Catholic laymen responded in July by organizing a consumer's boycott, and on July 31, the nation's priests closed their churches for what would extend to a three-year period. The "Cristero Revolt," as it came to be known, produced bloodshed in scattered parts of the nation as supporters of the church, and enemies of it, carried out terrorist acts. The conflict worsened the following year, with President Calles nationalizing church property and deporting foreign nuns and priests on February 11, 1927. Five months later 20,000 armed *cristeros* fought government troops in five west-center states.

1927

January 8. **Mexican president Calles indicated his willingness to submit the issues of land and oil, which threatened a break with the United States, to arbitration by the Hague Court.** Both countries subsequently moderated their positions, with the United States appointing the conciliatory Dwight W. Morrow ambassador to Mexico and Calles slowing the pace of land redistribution. In November 1927, the Mexican Supreme Court reaffirmed national ownership of the subsoil, but found unconstitutional the retroactive application of that principle.

1928

July 17. **Álvaro Obregón was assassinated one day after winning the Mexican presidency for a six-year term to begin on December 1.** The assassin, José de León Toral, a young zealot sympathetic to the Cristero cause, was arrested on the spot and later executed. Before the election the government had crushed a brief rebellion of anti-**Calles** and anti-**Obregón** military leaders who opposed both Obregón's candidacy and a Calles-supported constitutional amendment extending the presidential term to six years. The amendment also made it possible for a former chief executive, such as Obregón, to succeed himself following one intervening presidential term.

September 1. **Outgoing Mexican President Plutarco Calles pronounced his political "Testament,"** in which he declared the end of the era of caudillos. Calles went on to announce the formation of the vanguard National Revolutionary party (Partido Nacional Revolucionario, PNR), which would institutionalize the goals of the revolution. Earlier, Calles had named Emilio Portes Gil to serve as interim president until the successor to the assassinated **Álvaro Obregón** could be determined in an election to be held the following year.

1929

March. **Plutarco Elías Calles, as "Jefe Máximo" of the Mexican Revolution,** crushed a rebellion headed by elements opposed to his domination of the political arena. His rule behind the scenes is known as the Maximato (1928-34). Calles supported the mild-mannered Pascual Ortiz Rubio to serve out the five years remaining in the presidential term of the assassinated **Álvaro Obregón**. In the ensuing election, Ortiz Rubio prevailed in the face of a spirited campaign conducted by **José Vasconcelos**, the popular education minister who had served during Obregón's presidency. Ortiz Rubio took office February 5, 1930.

June 12-21. **The Mexican government and the Catholic Church reached a settlement of the religious crisis.** Under the *modus vivendi*, President Portes Gil disavowed any intention of persecuting the church and promised freedom of conscience. The Mexican bishops accepted the president's promises and ordered the Cristeros to lay down their arms and the priests to return to their churches. U.S. ambassador Dwight W. Morrow played an important role in negotiations leading to the settlement.

December. **Disorder in Haiti against United States dominance** led to a gradual lessening of the American presence there. An investigatory commission headed by W. Cameron Forbes convinced unpopular President Louis Borno to resign (April 1930). On November 18, 1930, the National Assembly elected Sténio Vincent to complete Borno's term.

Bolivarian Republics: Bolivia, Colombia, Ecuador, Peru, Venezuela

In the last three decades of the nineteenth century, civilian-dominated governments increasingly became the norm in the Bolivarian republics, and Liberal and Conservative parties competed for power. The ascendancy of Liberals usually meant curbs on the political and economic power of the Catholic Church; the conflict between church and state was especially bitter in Colombia and Ecuador.

Regardless of party affiliation, elites were unanimous in their support of continued economic modernization through railroad construction and export promotion. During this period, coffee emerged as Colombia's most important export while cacao production in Ecuador grew rapidly. Both Peru and Bolivia lost their nitrate-bearing provinces to Chile in the War of the Pacific (1879-83), but both countries remained important producers of minerals. In Bolivia tin supplanted silver as the main export. In Peru the production of lead, copper, and other minerals became significant, along with the cultivation of sugar and cotton on coastal plantations. After 1900 petroleum replaced coffee as Venezuela's leading export.

Economic modernization broadened and diversified society in the Bolivarian nations in the early twentieth century. Profoundly rural in 1870, they had all witnessed the beginnings of urbanization and industrialization by 1930. Public health improved significantly, especially in urban areas, as monies earned by exports were spent to improve drinking water and sewage treatment and to modernize medicine. The middle class expanded dramatically and a small proletariat took shape. This led to calls for social reform, drawing attention to what became known as the "social question." The urban population started demanding that politics, long the domain of ruling elites, become more democratic and socially concerned. New political parties emerged to challenge the hegemony of the traditional parties. They were generally antagonistic toward capitalism and the classist, frequently racist values pervading elite thought.

Relations between the Bolivarian republics and the United States were generally amicable during this period, though Colombians bitterly resented the American role in the secession of Panama in 1903. Substantial United States capital entered the region, especially after 1900, playing a major role in Venezuelan petroleum and Peruvian mining. Although relations among the Bolivarian nations were also generally amicable, Peru's relationship with Ecuador and Colombia was frequently strained because of border disputes in the Amazon region.

Bolivia suffered two major losses of national territory after 1870. It lost its Pacific littoral to Chile in the War of the Pacific and ceded Acre province to Brazil in 1903. These losses of territory, viewed as national disasters by Bolivians, had the effect of heightening tensions between Bolivia and Paraguay in the Chaco region. The Chaco dispute produced a border flare-up in 1928, which was temporarily resolved by an Act of Conciliation the following year.

1871

January 15. **Mariano Melgarejo lost power in Bolivia** after suffering a decisive military defeat in La Paz. Revolts of whites and Indians had erupted against him in late 1870 and had spread rapidly throughout the country. The new government was headed by Agustín Morales.

1872

August 2. **Manuel Pardo was inaugurated as Peru's first civilian president.** He was the candidate of the Civilista party, which wanted to end military domination of the government. The minister of war, Tomás Gutiérrez, and his three brothers, all army officers, tried to prevent Pardo's inauguration by deposing the outgoing president, José Balta, and seizing power. In the ensuing turbulence Balta was killed, but the plot was foiled as a Lima mob lynched Tomás Gutiérrez on July 26. Two of his brothers also died.

1874

August 6. **Bolivia and Chile signed the Baptista-Walker Martínez Treaty.** This treaty restated the provisions of an 1866 treaty setting the long-disputed boundary between Bolivia and Chile at 24° S. and providing that both countries would share in the proceeds of minerals extracted from territory lying between 23° S. and 25° S. In 1874 Bolivia also agreed not to raise taxes for twenty-five years on mineral exports belonging to Chilean nationals in the zone between 23° S. and 24° S. Bolivia's violation of this provision in 1878 was a major factor in the outbreak of war between the two countries.

1875

August 6. **Assassination of Ecuador's ruler. Gabriel García Moreno**, who had left the presidency in 1865, seized power in 1869. His repressive policies stirred unrest, which was fanned by the polemical writings of the exiled **Juan Montal-**

vo. A band of conspirators killed the dictator with machete blows and gunfire.

1876

February 21. **Aquileo Parra was declared president of Colombia.** Parra was elected to the presidency after an acrimonious campaign in which he was opposed by fellow Liberal **Rafael Núñez**, who had the backing of many Conservatives. So great was the division among Liberals that the Conservatives rose in rebellion against the Liberal-dominated government in July 1876 in the expectation that the followers of Núñez would join them or at least remain neutral. The Nuñistas remained loyal to the government, however, and the revolt was crushed by May 1877. Since many Catholic clergymen encouraged the uprising, the victorious Liberals exiled the four bishops deemed most culpable and enacted more anticlerical legislation.

September 8. **Liberal revolution in Ecuador.** Liberals led by Ignacio de Veintemilla launched a successful revolt against the government of Antonio Borrero y Cortázar, who had been elected president after the assassination of **Gabriel García Moreno**. After the defeat of Borrero, Veintemilla governed Ecuador until 1883.

1877

March 30. **The archbishop of Quito died by poison.** The death of Archbishop José Ignacio Checa y Barba occurred amid conflict over a series of anticlerical measures decreed by Veintemilla, who was widely blamed for the crime.

1879

Origins of the War of the Pacific. At the root of this conflict was Bolivia's tenuous grip on its mineral-rich Atacama Desert territories, which had increasingly come under the domination of Chilean settlers and businessmen. The immediate cause of the war, in which Bolivia and Peru were allied against Chile, arose out of Bolivian violations of the Baptista-Walker Martínez Treaty of 1874. In 1878 the administration of Hilarión Daza imposed a new ten-cent tax on nitrates exported by a Chilean-owned firm operating in the zone from which tax increases were barred by the treaty. When the company refused to pay the tax, the Bolivian government ordered the confiscation of its holdings. Bolivia responded to Chilean protests by asserting the legality of the tax and declared war on Chile (March 14, 1879). By that time Chilean troops had already seized the Bolivian port of Antofagasta (February 14, 1879).

Peru was drawn into the conflict as a result of a treaty of alliance (February 6, 1873) with Bolivia. The treaty called for the alliance to come into force in case of a threat to the territory of one of the signatories. In 1879 Chile asked for Peru's neutrality, but the latter chose to adhere to the treaty, and Chile declared war on Peru as well as Bolivia on April 5, 1879.

February 26. **Guzmán Blanco returned to power in Venezuela.** Having ruled Venezuela since 1870, **Antonio Guzmán Blanco** left for Europe after the inauguration of his chosen successor, Francisco Linares Alcántara (March 2, 1877). When Linares Alcántara died in 1878, the Congress showed hostility to Guzmán Blanco and ordered the demolition of statues that had been erected in his honor. Guzmán Blanco's supporters launched a successful revolution in protest, and he returned to Venezuela, where he was favorably received. He remained in the presidency until 1884.

Early battles of the War of the Pacific. Two important naval engagements gave Chile command of the sea. In an engagement on May 21, 1879, at the then-Peruvian port of Iquique the Peruvians sank the Chilean *Esmeralda*, a wooden warship, but suffered the loss of the larger of their two ironclads, the *Independencia*. Arturo Prat, commander of the *Esmeralda*, became a hero after he was killed during the battle. The other Peruvian ironclad, the *Huascar*, which was commanded by Miguel Grau, inflicted severe damage on Chilean shipping and coastal cities, but it was captured off Point Angamos on October 8, 1879. Grau was killed during the battle.

Meanwhile, after occupying Bolivia's coastal territories, the Chileans captured the Peruvian province of Tarapacá. As a result of these reverses, Daza was removed from power in Bolivia in December. When the president of Peru, Mariano Ignacio Prado, left the country to acquire armaments abroad, he was strongly censured, and Nicolás de Piérola was proclaimed dictator (December 23, 1879).

1880

April 8. **Rafael Núñez was inaugurated as president of Colombia.** Elected to the presidency amid renewed Liberal division, he had the support of the Independent Liberal faction and of many Conservatives. A partisan of greater governmental intervention in the economy, he successfully campaigned for the enactment of a protective tariff and the creation of a National Bank. **Núñez** also favored a more conciliatory policy toward the Catholic Church.

May 26-June 7. **Chilean forces captured Tacna and Arica.** In a series of hard-fought engagements, Chile defeated the armies of Peru and Bolivia and occupied Peru's nitrate-rich provinces. At this point Bolivian forces withdrew from the fighting, leaving prosecution of the war to Peru.

June 1. **The Bolivian Congress elected General Narciso Campero president of the republic.** Although begun during Bolivia's defeat in the War of the Pacific, Campero's administration marked the beginning of less arbitrary, more stable government in the republic. Campero was succeeded by Gregorio Pacheco (1884-88), a wealthy silver mine owner, who initiated the era known as the "Conservative Oligarchy" (1884-99).

1881

January 17. **Chilean troops entered Lima.** The Chileans occupied the Peruvian capital after fierce fighting in the nearby villages of Chorrillos and Miraflores. Piérola withdrew to the mountainous interior to try to organize resistance to the Chileans but resigned on November 28, 1881.

1883

July 9. **Guayaquil fell to enemies of Ignacio de Veintemilla, forcing him to flee Ecuador.** Both Liberals and Conservatives took part in the campaign against him, known as the War of the Restoration. For the next twelve years Ecuador was ruled by three civilian presidents: José María Plácido Caamaño (1883-88), Antonio Flores Jijón (1888-92), and Luis Cordero (1892-95).

End of the War of the Pacific. After the fall of Lima, General Andrés A. Cáceres waged a vigorous campaign against the Chileans but was decisively defeated at Huamachuco (July 10, 1883). The Treaty of Ancón (October 20, 1883) ended hostilities between Peru and Chile. Under the treaty Peru ceded the province of Tarapacá to Chile. Tacna and Arica were to remain under

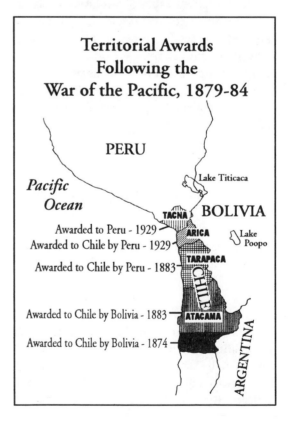

Territorial Awards Following the War of the Pacific, 1879-84

PERU

Pacific Ocean

Lake Titicaca

BOLIVIA

TACNA

ARICA

Lake Poopo

Awarded to Peru - 1929

Awarded to Chile by Peru - 1929

Awarded to Chile by Peru - 1883

TARAPACA

CHILE

Awarded to Chile by Bolivia - 1883

ATACAMA

Awarded to Chile by Bolivia - 1874

ARGENTINA

Chilean occupation for ten years, after which time a plebiscite to determine their fate was to be held. The plebiscite never took place. In 1929 the two countries divided the provinces, with Chile retaining Arica and Peru regaining Tacna. Bolivia and Chile signed a truce on April 4, 1884, but a peace treaty was not concluded until 1904. As a result of the war Bolivia lost its Pacific territories and became a landlocked nation.

1885

January–September. **Political transformation in Colombia.** Under the leadership of **Rafael Núñez**, who had been re-elected to the presidency in 1884, the Liberal regime established in the 1860s came to an end and the Conservatives were restored to power. Although Núñez was still identified with the Independent Liberal faction, his increasingly close ties with the Conservatives alarmed many other Liberals. After a Liberal uprising in the state of Santander in 1884 turned into a nationwide revolt, Núñez turned to the Conservatives for military assistance in defeating the rebels. Once the revolt had been put down, Núñez announced on September 10, 1885, that the Liberal-inspired constitution of 1863 had ceased to exist. In 1886 a new constitution was promulgated. Written in accordance with Conservative principles, it provided for a strong chief executive and the restoration of centralism, and of Catholicism as the religion of the nation. Núñez remained president until his death in 1894. During the 1884-85 revolution United States troops were landed in the Colombian state of Panama (see Mexico, Central America, and the Caribbean, 1885).

1887

February 20. **Venezuela severed diplomatic relations with Great Britain.** Venezuela had long been at odds with the British over its boundary with British Guiana (now Guyana). Initially, the dispute involved territory lying north and west of the Essequibo River. After the discovery of gold in the disputed region, the British extended their claims to include the mouth of the Orinoco River. The British ignored Venezuelan calls for arbitration, leading to the rupture in relations.

1888

June 29. **Juan Pablo Rojas Paúl was elected president of Venezuela.** Rojas Paúl had been endorsed by his predecessor, **Antonio Guzmán Blanco**, but he began to distance himself from the latter, then living in Europe. On October 26, 1889, statues of Guzmán Blanco were destroyed and his house was sacked while the government stood by. By 1890, when Rojas Paúl's term ended, Guzmán Blanco's influence in Venezuelan affairs had ended.

October 25. **Peru signed the controversial Grace Contract.** The administration of war hero Andrés A. Cáceres (1886-90) negotiated the contract with its foreign bondholders, to whom about $260 million was owed. Under its terms Peru was to satisfy its obligations to the bondholders by giving them control of Peruvian railroads for sixty-six years as well as other concessions. The bondholders in turn promised to expand and improve the railroads. Michael P. Grace, brother of the Irish-American entrepreneur **William R. Grace**, led the bondholders' committee that negotiated the contract. The contract, which was approved by the Peruvian Congress in 1889, enabled Peru to attract foreign investment again.

1895

June 5. **Liberal revolution in Ecuador.** After winning control of Guayaquil, the Liberals moved against the highland areas and won a decisive victory at Gatazo on August 14-15. **Eloy Alfaro**, leader of the revolution, would dominate Ecuadorian politics until 1912. Opposition to the proclerical regime of Luis Cordero had been exacerbated by the *Esmeralda* affair. In 1894, during the Sino-Japanese War, the *Esmeralda*, a Chilean cruiser, had been secretly purchased by Ecuador and immediately turned over to Japan.

September 8. **Nicolás de Piérola was inaugurated as president of Peru.** His election followed a popular uprising in 1894 against the second administration of Andrés A. Cáceres, who had reached the presidency by irregular means. The revolt was also a reaction against military domination of politics. Piérola was succeeded by another civilian, Eduardo López de Romaña (1899-1903).

1898

December 12. **Bolivia's Federalist War.** The conflict began after the Congress passed legislation making Sucre the permanent home of the national government. Liberal leaders in La Paz announced a federalist revolt against the administration of Severo Fernández Alonso. Led by General José Manuel Pando, the rebels defeated Fernández Alonso on April 10, 1899. The Liberals enlisted the aid of Indian peasants but when the latter attacked and killed whites and demanded the return of community lands, they were crushed. Pando's presidency (1899-1904) was the first in an era of Liberal domination in Bolivia (1899-1920). Federalism was not introduced, but La Paz became the de facto capital of the country.

1899

May 23. **Cipriano Castro's revolution of Liberal restoration. Castro** and his followers crossed the border from Colombia into Venezuela to begin a campaign that gave them control of Caracas by the end of October. Castro ruled Venezuela until 1908. He was the first of a series of presidents from Venezuela's Andean provinces.

October 3. **Arbitration award in Venezuela's boundary dispute with Great Britain.** The five-man panel gave British Guiana much of the disputed territory but assigned the mouth of the Orinoco River to Venezuela. The panel, which had no Venezuelan members, had been set up as a result of negotiations between the United States and Great Britain after Secretary of State Richard Olney demanded arbitration in a strongly worded note in 1895 (see International Developments, 1895). Venezuela was dissatisfied with the

award and continued to claim territory west of the Essequibo River.

October 18. **Liberal revolution in Colombia.** Liberals in eastern Colombia rebelled against the Conservative-dominated government, launching an insurrection that soon spread throughout the country and lasted until 1902. This revolution, known as the War of the Thousand Days, stemmed from Liberal resentment over their virtual exclusion from public office since the mid-1880s. Economic conditions were also poor because of the collapse of world coffee prices. The insurgents won an important victory at Peralonso near Cúcuta (December 15-16, 1899) but failed to exploit their advantage and move against Bogotá.

1900

May 11-26. **Conservatives triumphed as thousands died in Colombia's Battle of Palonegro** at a mountainous site 160 miles (256 km.) north of Bogotá. That contest proved to be the most deadly in the country's War of the Thousand Days, pitting members of the country's Liberal and Conservative parties against each other. On July 31 aged Colombian president Manuel A. Sanclemente was overthrown in a bloodless coup directed by members of a Conservative party faction whose members hoped their action would hasten peace talks with the Liberals. They placed their hopes in Sanclemente's replacement, Vice President José Manuel Marroquín. But Marroquín surprised them by pursuing the war with full vigor. The conflict raged sporadically for another two years. At length the Conservative government triumphed, but the nation was devastated.

1901

June. **Venezuela's La Libertadora revolution broke out.** Led by regional elites opposed to the centralizing measures of Liberal caudillo and president **Cipriano Castro**, the unsuccessful revolt dragged on until 1903.

1902

June. **Britain and Germany blockaded Venezuelan ports** (to February 1903), in an effort to force the payment of damage claims by Venezuelan dictator **Cipriano Castro**. The blockade, which Italy joined, was lifted following mediation by the United States. President Theodore Roosevelt did not believe the action violated the Monroe Doctrine provided that no acquisition of territory was involved. Roosevelt further opined that irresponsible Latin American nations should not attempt to hide behind the "protective petticoats" of the United States. The dispute was ultimately settled at the Permanent Court of Arbitration at The Hague in 1904.

November 21. **Colombian Liberal and Conservative generals signed a peace treaty ending the War of the Thousand Days.** They did so aboard the United States warship *Wisconsin*, off the coast of Panama. The previous month (October 24), Liberal general **Rafael Uribe Uribe** had signed a similar peace treaty with Conservatives (the Treaty of Neerlandia).

1903

March 17. **The U.S. Senate ratified the Hay-Herrán Treaty, which authorized construction of a trans-oceanic canal across the Isthmus of Panama**. Under terms of the treaty, completed January 22, the United States would administer a ten-kilometer (six mi.) zone embracing the canal. The treaty stated explicitly that Colombia would retain sovereignty over the zone. Other stipulations were that the United States would enjoy a renewable 100-year lease over the canal zone and would pay Colombia 10 million dollars, as well as $250,000 annually.

August 12. **The Colombian Senate voted down the Herrán-Hay Treaty**, explaining that it violated national sovereignty and that its financial terms were unacceptable. (For details on subsequent Panamanian independence see Mexico, Central America, Caribbean, 1903.)

1904

August 7. **Rafael Reyes was inaugurated president of Colombia** for a six-year term, ushering in that nation's first extended period of civil peace.

Reyes promoted modernization, encouraged the cultivation of coffee, and succeeded in linking the national capital, Bogotá, to the sea via a rail link to the Magdalena River port of Girardot (1907). His inability to work with Congress led him to suspend that body in 1908, going on to govern through a puppet assembly until 1909.

October 20. **Bolivia and Chile signed a treaty formally ending the War of the Pacific (1879-83).** By the treaty Bolivia ceded its coastal provinces to Chile, which agreed to build a railroad linking the port of Arica with the Bolivian capital, La Paz. Bolivia entered a period of political stability, with monies derived from tin exports. Liberal president Ismael Montes (inaugurated August 6, 1904) expended growing revenues derived from tin on ambitious public works programs. In 1906 Montes secured a large loan from a bank in the United States, and with it he completed Bolivia's internal rail links. Montes continued his expenditures on public works during his second term (1913-17). Fellow Liberal Heliodoro Villazón served as president from 1909 to 1913. World War I produced considerable disruption of the Bolivian economy.

1905

January 17. **Ecuador's anticlerical caudillo Eloy Alfaro entered the presidency for the second time,** succeeding his colleague Leonidas Plaza Gutiérrez (1901-5). During **Alfaro's** tenure national capital Quito gained access to the sea at the port of Guayaquil via a 288-mile rail link. Alfaro played a major role in the drafting of Ecuador's liberal constitution (1906), featuring guarantees of individual rights. While his term ended in 1911, Alfaro remained the supreme leader of his party until his assassination in 1912. After Alfaro's passing, a succession of Liberal presidents continued his policies of national modernization and encouragement of export crops, particularly cacao and bananas. Alfaro's successors were Leonidas Plaza (1912-16), Alfredo Baquerizo (1916-20), José Luis Tamayo (1920-24), and Gonzalo Córdova (1924-25).

1908

June 23. **The United States suspended relations with Venezuela**, owing to dictator **Cipriano Castro**'s reluctance to guarantee the safety of the lives and property of United States citizens. A month later (July 22), the Netherlands blockaded Venezuelan ports. Castro, in power since 1899, soon departed on a European tour.

September 24. **Augusto B. Leguía was elected president of Peru.** Leader of the Civilista party, **Leguía** dominated Peruvian politics for two decades. He sought foreign loans for purposes of national modernization and sponsored progressive legislation. Following Leguía's first term, three men occupied the presidency: Guillermo Billinghurst (1912-14), Oscar Raimundo Benavides (1914-15), José Pardo y Barreda (1915-19). Leguía won the presidency in 1919, going on to establish an authoritarian regime lasting until 1930.

December 19. **Venezuelan vice president Juan Vicente Gómez seized the presidency** in the absence of **Cipriano Castro.** **Gómez** was supreme in Venezuela until his death in 1935.

1909

January 4. **The Root-Cortés-Arosemena Treaties were signed.** The interrelated treaties were intended to normalize relations between Colombia and the United States and between Colombia and Panama in the wake of Panama's secession from Colombia in 1903. Panama and the United States ratified the treaties, but in Bogotá they touched off demonstrations against the increasingly unpopular **Rafael Reyes**, who resigned his presidency and departed the country (July 8). Jorge Holguín and Ramón González Valencia headed caretaker governments until national elections were held a year later.

1910

February 13. **Venezuelan dictator Juan Vicente Gómez was inaugurated president**, thus legitimizing his earlier seizure of the government.

August 7. **Carlos E. Restrepo, leader of Colombia's ephemeral Republican party, was inaugurated president.** Pledged to wean the citizenry from their historic attachment to the Liberal and Conservative parties, he built an impressive political movement made up of disaffected members of Colombia's two parties. Restrepo and his colleagues were ultimately unsuccessful in changing the political orientation of his countrymen. In 1914, Conservative José Vicente Concha won the presidency, going on to preside over Colombia during economic depression occasioned by World War I. He was succeeded by Conservative Marco Fidel Suárez, who served 1918-21.

1912

January 28. **Ecuadorian caudillo Eloy Alfaro was murdered** by a mob following his participation in a short-lived civil war. The war, touched off by the death of recently inaugurated president Emilio Estrada (December 1911), angered the public and produced demands for punishment of its chief perpetrator, **Alfaro.**

1914

Venezuela's Maracaibo oil fields entered production. Prudent management of the growing bonanza allowed dictator **Juan Vicente Gómez** to consolidate his political hold upon the nation.

April 19. **Victorino Márquez Bustillos became titular president of Venezuela,** in fact the creature of Juan Vicente Gómez. Late the previous year Gómez had provoked a political crisis when he announced his intention to extend his rule. He resolved the problem through the presidency of Márquez. Even though congress voted Gómez president for the period 1915-22, he allowed Márquez to occupy the chair as his deputy.

1919

January. **Regular air service was inaugurated in Colombia,** by planes of the Colombo-German firm SCADTA. That occurred simultaneously with the establishment of scheduled passenger and mail service in Europe and the United States.

January 13. **Workers and students in Peru carried out a general strike that paralyzed Lima and other cities.** Their action came near the end of the modernizing Civilista regime of José Pardo y Barreda, and marked the high point of a wave of work stoppages in protest of high inflation and lack of an eight-hour work day. The streets of Lima were the scene of bloody battles between workers and police, as Pardo y Barreda acted to break the work stoppage. The social turmoil of early 1919 in Peru marked the emergence of the socially progressive "Generation of 1919," the best-known member of which was **Víctor Raúl Haya de la Torre.**

July 4. **Backed by the military, former Peruvian president Augusto B. Leguía launched his *oncenio*,** an eleven-year period of authoritarian rule. Promising to "detain the advance of communism," he exiled leftists like the young **Haya de la Torre,** and crushed student demonstrations, notably those taking place during May 1923. He greatly strengthened the role of the state in national affairs through revision of the constitution (1920) and through the expansion of education and public works projects. While Leguía's paternalistic regime aimed at assimilating the nation's large Indian population, he did not hesitate to have the army crush an Indian uprising in the highlands during 1923.

Leguía had himself re-elected in 1924 and 1929. During his three terms he pursued a developmentalist policy featuring the recruitment of foreign loans whose monies were aimed at promoting the export of minerals and textiles. His foreign policy led to the favorable settlement of

border disputes with Colombia (1922, 1927) and settlement of the Tacna-Arica dispute with Chile in 1929.

1920

July 12. **Bautista Saavedra, member of Bolivia's new Republican party,** became president following the overthrow of unpopular José N. Gutiérrez. Saavedra was immediately confronted by an Indian uprising in the area of Lake Titicaca. He quickly crushed it, and in the process several hundred Indians lost their lives. Saavedra pursued national modernization through the contracting of foreign loans and favoring mining interests. He was succeeded in office by Hernando Siles (1926), who continued modernization efforts until 1930, when tin prices declined and foreign loans disappeared.

1921

November 11. **Colombian president Marco Fidel Suárez resigned in the face of charges of financial improprieties,** formulated by fellow Conservative **Laureano Gómez.** Contributing to Suárez's resignation was his support of ratification of the Thomson-Urrutia Treaty, which would regularize relations between Colombia and the United States (ratified by the U.S. Senate on April 12). On April 20, the Colombian Senate ratified the treaty, which provided a 25 million dollar indemnity for the loss of Panama. Interim President Jorge Holguín, who served until mid-1922, completed Suárez's term.

1922

March 24. **The Salomón-Lozano Treaty was signed.** The treaty defined the boundary between Colombia and Peru. Under its terms Colombia received the Leticia quadrilateral, an area of about 4,000 square miles, part of which bordered the northern bank of the Amazon River. In exchange Peru received territory south of the Putumayo

River. The opposition of some Peruvians to the treaty led to an attack on Leticia in 1932. Ecuador objected to Colombia's cession of the territory south of the Putumayo, which adversely affected its claims in its long-standing border dispute with Peru.

June 25. **Venezuela's puppet Congress voted Juan Vicente Gómez a second presidential term,** a post the dictator held until taking command of the national army in 1929.

August 7. **Colombian President Pedro Nel Ospina took office,** pledged to a series of measures aimed at national modernization financed by rising coffee revenues, foreign loans contracted principally in the United States, and the twenty-five million dollar United States indemnity. Ospina's term, and that of fellow Conservative Miguel Abadía Méndez, who succeeded him (1926-30), marked a time of unprecedented public spending in Colombia.

November 15. **Three hundred perished when police fired on strikers in Guayaquil, Ecuador.** Economic hardship arising from falling cacao prices had produced a general strike and mass demonstration that in turn sparked the slaughter of protesters.

1923

March. **Juan Vicente Gómez created the Venezuelan Petroleum Company,** which allowed him to control concessions granted to foreign petroleum companies. During Gómez's dictatorship, Venezuela produced some 70 percent of Latin America's oil exports.

June. **Bolivian miners struck the Uncia tin mine.** Favoring management, President Bautista Saavedra crushed the strike with such severity that dozens of miners and members of their families lost their lives.

1924

May 7. **Víctor Raúl Haya de la Torre founded Peru's APRA (Alianza Popular Revolucionaria**

Americana). He did so with several other Latin American students when in exile in Mexico.

1925

July 9. **General Francisco Gómez de la Torre overthrew Ecuador's president Gonzalo Córdova,** ending Liberal party domination of politics. Gómez de la Torre headed a three-man junta that turned the presidency over to Isidro Ayora (1926-31). During his term Ayora implemented statist policies aimed at enhancing cacao exports, Ecuador's chief money maker. He took steps to recognize and aid the emerging middle class and to formulate a labor code.

1928

February. **Venezuelan students protested the dictatorship of Juan Vicente Gómez. Gómez** responded by jailing the student leaders, among them twenty-year-old **Rómulo Betancourt**.

November–December. **Banana workers in United Fruit plantations on Colombia's Caribbean coast struck** for higher wages and better working conditions. Colombian labor leaders, notably the communists María Cano, the "Red Flower of Labor," and Ignacio Torres Giraldo, led the strike. On December 6, Colombian army troops fired into massed workers, killing more than a dozen. That set into motion a military sweep of the region during which other workers died and strike leaders were either imprisoned or driven into exile.

1929

March 6. **Ecuador's new constitution conferred citizenship on all literate Ecuadorians over twenty-one.** A subsequent election law (June 8, 1929) extended the right to vote and to hold office to all citizens, thereby enfranchising women. Ecuador was the first Latin American country to allow women to vote.

Southern Cone:
Argentina, Chile, Paraguay, Uruguay

Between 1871 and 1929, Argentina, Chile, and Uruguay experienced dramatic economic, social, and political change. Only Paraguay, slow to recover from its devastating war with Brazil, Argentina, and Uruguay (War of the Triple Alliance, 1864-70), lagged behind its neighbors in overall development. Chile, by contrast, decisively defeated Peru and Bolivia in the War of the Pacific (1879-83) and acquired from them territories rich in nitrates, then valuable for making fertilizer and explosives. (See Bolivarian Republics, 1879.)

The relative political stability of Argentina, Chile, and Uruguay and the liberal economic orientation of their elites encouraged rapid growth based on the expansion of exports. By 1914 the three nations had become major players in international commerce, supplying increasing quantities of minerals and foodstuffs to industrializing Western Europe. Chile supplied nitrates and copper; Argentina and Uruguay, meats, grains, and wool. Railroad construction and advances in shipping and communications made the export boom possible. Foreign, especially British, capital and technology also played a major role in spurring economic development. The extreme dependence of the Southern Cone nations on foreign capital and markets would have negative consequences as well. This was shown after World War I when markets for Chilean nitrates disappeared with the development of synthetic nitrates in Europe. The Great Depression of the 1930s would have an even greater impact because of the collapse of world commodity prices.

European immigration, mainly from Italy and Spain, was another important factor in the economic and social changes of the period, especially in Argentina. By 1914 about 30 percent of the Argentine population of 7.9 million was foreign born. Smaller but significant numbers of immigrants came to Uruguay and Chile as well. Immigrants to Paraguay were often Germans who settled in agricultural colonies. Elsewhere in the Southern Cone immigrants tended to move to the large cities, helping to account for the rapid growth of Buenos Aires, Montevideo, and Santiago.

Economic growth in the Southern Cone had profound political and social consequences. The middle class broadened and began demanding a voice in politics. In Argentina men of the middle sectors eventually gained control of government through the Radical Civic Union, representative and bastion of the rising middle class. In Chile the Radical party played a similar role. The process of political change was even more notable in Uruguay, where **José Batlle y Ordóñez** moved the nation toward social democracy.

Social progress lagged behind economic and political change. While the Southern Cone nations became more highly urbanized, many of their citizens remained impoverished and illiterate and were effectively excluded from the political process. But gradually the working class became more vocal, inspired by European social movements, notably the socialism and anarchism espoused by many European immigrants. By 1930 the "social problem" loomed ever larger in both Chile and Argentina.

Territorial disputes troubled the Southern Cone nations after 1871. Although Argentina and Chile reached agreement on their boundaries by 1902, differences between Chile and its former foes, Peru and Bolivia, continued long after the War of the Pacific. Differences also arose between Paraguay and Bolivia over the Gran Chaco, an arid region covering much of eastern Paraguay and extending into southeastern Bolivia.

Argentina, whose foreign policy consistently opposed the expansion of United States influence in Latin America, in fact took little interest in hemispheric affairs, pursuing a policy that was essentially isolationist. Early in the twentieth century its diplomats considered United States–led Pan Americanism to be injurious to Latin American sovereignty. Argentine leaders preferred viewing their nation as part of the European system.

1871

September 18. **Federico Errázuriz Zañartu took office as president of Chile.** During his administration the Liberal-Conservative Fusion that had brought him to power disintegrated because of Conservative opposition to proposed anticlerical legislation. In the event only a measure limiting the jurisdiction of ecclesiastical courts became law. Because of a constitutional amendment (1870) barring a president from being elected to two consecutive terms, Errázuriz was the first Chilean president to serve a single five-year term.

1875

January 15. **Military rule was established in Uruguay.** After disputed local elections produced disorder in Montevideo, military leaders removed President José Ellauri (1873-75). For the next fifteen years Uruguay was dominated by three military presidents: Lorenzo Latorre (1876-80), Máximo Santos (1882-86), and Máximo Tajes (1886-90). During this period the central government was strengthened, diminishing the influence of regional caudillos.

1879

April 6. **Argentina began its "Conquest of the Desert."** General **Julio A. Roca**, minister of war, led five divisions of troops in a systematic campaign to capture or disperse Indians occupying the territory south and west of the frontier of settlement. Erroneously labeled a desert, the region embraced 20,000 square miles lying south of the Río Negro and stretching from the Atlantic Ocean to the Andes Mountains. The approximately 20,000 Indians in the region were quickly defeated and some were placed on reservations. The newly acquired lands were organized into the territories of La Pampa, Neuquén, and Río Negro in 1884.

May 14. **Argentina returned Villa Occidental (renamed Villa Hayes) to Paraguay.** As a result of the War of the Triple Alliance, Argentina claimed all of Paraguay's Chaco region and occupied Villa Occidental, located on the western bank of the Paraguay River north of Asunción. Argentina retained that part of the Chaco lying between the Bermejo and Pilcomayo rivers, but an arbitral award by U.S. president Rutherford B. Hayes gave the northern section of the Chaco to Paraguay. Villa Occidental was renamed in his honor.

July 23. **Peru captured the Chilean war transport *Rimac*.** The *Rimac*, which was carrying men, horses, and armaments, was seized without resistance by the Peruvian ironclad *Huáscar* during the War of the Pacific (see Bolivarian Republics, 1879). As a result, there were widespread protests and rioting in Chile against the government and naval leaders. The cabinet of President Aníbal Pinto (1876-81) resigned, and the naval commander, Juan Williams Rebolledo, lost his post. He was replaced by Galverino Riveros.

1880

June 20-21. **Disturbances in Buenos Aires.** Fighting broke out between national forces and partisans of Carlos Tejedor, governor of the province of Buenos Aires. Tejedor had recently been defeated in a bid for the presidency by **Julio A. Roca**, but underlying the conflict was controversy over the future of the city of Buenos Aires, which was the capital of both the nation and the province. Tejedor and his followers feared that if the city was made into a federal district, as some proposed, its influence would decline and politics would instead be dominated by the interior provinces. The provincial forces were soon defeated, and Tejedor resigned as governor.

September 4. **The Paraguayan Congress elected Bernardino Caballero as president.** Associated with the faction that would organize the Colorado party in 1887, Caballero seized power after the death of President Cándido Bareiro (1878-80). During his administration (1880-86) Caballero promoted education, especially in Asunción, and encouraged immigration, and Congress authorized (1883, 1885) the sale of vast tracts of public lands.

September 21. **Buenos Aires was federalized.** Shortly before leaving office, President

Nicolás Avellaneda signed a law declaring Buenos Aires the capital of the nation and creating a federal district there. A new capital for Buenos Aires province was built at La Plata, founded in 1882. **Julio A. Roca** became president on October 12.

the past, no religious instruction was to be provided in public schools during school hours. Another piece of legislation provided for the creation of a civil registry for births, marriages, and deaths in the capital and territories. Many provinces adopted similar policies.

1881

July 23. **Argentina and Chile signed a treaty defining their boundaries.** The two countries had long been at odds over their Andean border as far south as 52° S. and over their conflicting claims in the Strait of Magellan and Patagonia. Serious differences arose as to the precise meaning of the sections of the 1881 treaty dealing with the Andean border south of 26° 52' 45". Another source of conflict was division of the region to the north known as the Puna de Atacama. The latter dispute was settled in 1899. King Edward VII of Great Britain acted as arbitrator in the former conflict, handing down an award in 1902 that divided the disputed territory between the two countries. In 1904 a bronze statue called the Christ of the Andes was erected in Uspallata Pass to celebrate the peaceful settlement of the conflict.

September 18. **Domingo Santa María took office as president of Chile.** In addition to ending the War of the Pacific (see Bolivarian Republics, 1879), his administration is noted for conflict between the state and the Catholic Church. In 1884 legislation was enacted providing for compulsory civil marriage and for registration of births, marriages, and deaths by the state. In addition, the Catholic Church lost its control over cemeteries. During Santa María's term the powers of provincial governors were reduced, and property qualifications for voting were ended.

1884

Educational reform and anticlericalism in Argentina. The Congress enacted legislation that provided for free and compulsory education for children from six to fourteen in the federal capital and national territories. However, in a break with

1885

August. **Chile engaged Emil Körner to modernize its army.** A German officer, Körner became subdirector of Chile's Military School and helped found a War Academy (1886) to offer scientific and technical instruction to officers. In 1891 he became chief of the General Staff. In the 1890s other German officers were brought to Chile while young Chilean officers were sent to Germany for further training. In the late nineteenth and early twentieth centuries, Argentina, Peru, and other countries undertook similar programs of military professionalization.

1887

July–August. **Formal organization of Paraguayan political parties.** Although two political factions arose after the War of the Triple Alliance, neither was organized as a political party until 1887. In July opponents of the administration of Patricio Escobar (1886-90) formed the Centro Democrático, renamed the Liberal party in 1894. The following month former president Bernardino Caballero and other government supporters established the Asociación Nacional Republicana, commonly known as the Colorado (Red) party. Few fundamental differences divided Liberals from Colorados, though the former had ties with Argentina and the latter with Brazil. The Colorados ruled Paraguay until 1904.

1888

November 19. **Chile's Radical party held its first convention.** The Radical party had originated in 1857 when it was founded by Liberals who objected to their party's fusion with Conservatives, but it was not formally organized until 1888. At the convention the delegates called for separation of church and state, noninterference by public officials in elections, and other reforms. Winning support from the middle classes, the party played an important role in Chilean politics from the 1860s through the 1960s.

1890

March 1. **Civilian government returned to Uruguay.** Julio Herrera y Obes, a Colorado, was elected president by Congress, ending fifteen years of rule by the military. Herrera had served in the cabinet of his predecessor, General Máximo Tajes, who began the transition to civilian rule.

July 26. **Revolution in Argentina.** Leandro Alem and other leaders of the newly created political movement Civic Union (Unión Cívica), aided by disaffected military personnel, launched an uprising against President Miguel Juárez Celman (1886-90). It occurred at a time of economic crisis, caused in part by the heavy indebtedness of the national and provincial governments and by excessive emissions of paper money. The rebels capitulated on July 29, but the president came under pressure from Congress and members of his own administration to resign (August 6). He was succeeded by Carlos Pellegrini (1890-92), who restored financial and political stability.

1891

January 1-August 29. **Civil war in Chile.** Conflict between President **José Manuel Balmaceda** and the Congress had arisen soon after he took office in 1886. His congressional opponents, who eventually became the majority, accused him of autocratic tendencies and of planning to impose a handpicked successor. These differences unfolded at a time when the powers of Chilean presidents had been eroded by custom and law while those of the Congress had increased. The crisis occurred when the Congress refused to pass an appropriations bill for 1891. On January 1, 1891, Balmaceda unconstitutionally declared that the current budget would remain in force. Thereupon the congressional majority announced the deposition of the president and, supported by the navy,

began an uprising against him. The insurgents gained control of Chile's northern provinces, where they could obtain nitrate revenues, and, with the help of German officer Emil Körner, began organizing a military force to confront the Chilean army, which had remained loyal to Balmaceda. A decisive revolutionary victory at Placilla (August 28) led to Balmaceda's resignation the following day. The triumph of the congressional forces marked the beginning of the Parliamentary Republic (1891-1920), an era characterized by presidential subordination to the legislature. Jorge Montt, a naval officer and leader of the anti-Balmaceda forces, became the first president of the new era (1891-96).

August. **Argentina's Radical Civic Union (Unión Cívica Radical) was born.** The formation of the UCR (often called the Radical party) grew out of a split in the Civic Union. As the presidential election of 1892 approached, the Civic Union nominated former president **Bartolomé Mitre** as its candidate. Controversy arose when Mitre agreed to become the candidate of the ruling National Autonomist party (Partido Nacional Autonomista) as well. Leandro Alem and other opponents of this agreement left the Civic Union, formed the UCR, and nominated Bernardo de Irigoyen for the presidency. Mitre withdrew from the contest, and Luis Sáenz Peña, backed by the National Autonomist party and the remnants of the Civic Union, became president (1892-95). Becoming a vehicle for the political aspirations of Argentina's middle class, the UCR rejected participation in an electoral process it deemed corrupt and unsuccessfully attempted revolution in 1893, 1896, and 1905. The first Radical president, **Hipólito Yrigoyen**, was elected in 1916.

October 16. **The *Baltimore* Affair.** A brawl in Valparaíso between Chileans and sailors from the *U.S.S. Baltimore* left two Americans dead and seventeen seriously wounded. The disturbance took place at a time of anti-American feeling in Chile because of the belief that the United States government and its minister, Patrick Egan, had been partial to the Balmacedistas in the recent civil war. The administration of Benjamin Harrison found the sailors blameless and accused the Chilean police of attacking the Americans. When the Chilean government disputed the American version and used undiplomatic language about Harrison, the United States issued an ultimatum and demanded an apology. Finding no support among its neighbors or European nations, Chile backed down and eventually paid $75,000 as compensation to the victims.

1897

March–September. **Upheaval in Uruguay.** Leaders of the Blanco party (now known as the National party) rebelled against the government of Juan Idiarte Borda (1894-97), a Colorado. The Blancos sought access to government positions, which were denied to them by the dominant Colorados. On August 25, 1897, President Idiarte Borda was shot to death by an assassin. His successor, Juan Lindolfo Cuestas (1897-1903), made peace with the insurgents on September 18. The agreement gave the Blancos control of six of Uruguay's nineteen departments and provided for minority representation in Congress.

1901

September 18. **Chilean president Germán Riesco was inaugurated,** signaling resurgence of that nation's Liberal party. Riesco, the third president of Chile's Parliamentary Period, 1891-1920, promoted economic modernization, especially in the country's northern nitrate zone. Riesco encouraged foreign, largely British, investment to the effect that over ten years' time most nitrate processing facilities were in British hands. He was followed in office by the like-minded Pedro Montt (1906-10), Ramón Barros (1910-15), and Juan Luis Sanfuentes (1915-1920).

1903

March 1. **Uruguay's Congress elected José Batlle y Ordóñez president,** prompting a civil war lasting eighteen months. Following victory by government forces, **Batlle** implemented social reforms of a liberal character. Legal and eco-

nomic rights were increased for women, public education and the organization of labor were promoted, and democracy was advanced through legislation prohibiting immediate succession by a sitting president.

1904

October 12. **Manuel Quintana of Argentina's dominant National Autonomist party (PAN) took office as president.** Quintana, elected by the old coalition headed by party leader **Julio Roca,** died in office (March 12, 1906), and was succeeded by José Figueroa Alcorta (1906-10) who, with the help of dissident PAN members, destroyed the coalition of provincial leaders through which Roca had dominated national politics for twenty-five years. Quintana was followed in office by Roque Sáenz Peña (1910-14) and Victoriano de la Plaza (1914-16), both of whom were members of the PAN.

December. **Paraguay's Colorado party,** which had presided over national recovery following the disastrous War of the Triple Alliance (1864-70), yielded power to the Liberals. President Juan A. Escurra (1902-4) vacated the presidency, making way for competing Liberals Cecilio Báez and Benigno Ferreira, who dominated Paraguay during an anarchic eight years that witnessed the accession of eight chief executives: Cecilio Báez (1905-6), Benigno Ferreira (1906-8), Emiliano González (1908-10), Manuel Gondra (1910-11), Albino Jara (1911), Liberato Marcial Rojas (1911), Pedro Peña (1912), Emiliano González (1912).

1911

March 1. **José Batlle y Ordóñez, inaugurated president of Uruguay for the second time,** pledged to continue the liberal social reforms that he had initiated during his first term (1903-7). He went on to promote new laws guaranteeing a minimum wage and state-backed accident insurance, and fiscal reforms centering on the foundation of a national bank. **Batlle** also promoted constitutional reforms and argued in favor of a plural executive system based on the Swiss model.

He was succeeded by Feliciano Viera (1915-19).

1912

February 13. **Argentina's Sáenz Peña Law was enacted.** Named after President Roque Sáenz Peña, it enfranchised all male citizens above the age of eighteen. The law, which provided for the secret ballot and minority party representation in Congress, and made voting compulsory, radically changed Argentine politics. With the reform, the burgeoning Argentine middle class entered that nation's political equation.

August 15. **Paraguayan caudillo Eduardo Schaerer assumed the presidency, bringing momentary political stability to the country** following ten years during which there were eleven chief executives. Schaerer brought Paraguay a brief time of political calm, during which he took statist measures to stimulate growth, such as the recruiting of government-backed foreign loans to improve ports and to create rail links with Argentina. He also pursued a policy of civil service reform. The climate of progress continued under Schaerer's successor, Manuel Franco (1916-19).

1916

October 12. **Hipólito Yrigoyen was inaugurated president of Argentina, representing the middle-class Radical Civic Union party (Unión Cívica Radical).** **Yrigoyen** went on to enact paternalistic political reforms, eliminate sources of power of the old Partido Autonomista Nacional, and govern in a highly personalist manner.

1918

June. **The University Reform Movement began at Argentina's University of Córdoba**, marking the appearance of students as a major force in Latin American political life. Among the students' demands were those calling for university autonomy, election of university administrators, and control of curriculum. Yrigoyen granted most student demands in October 1918. These reforms became a model for similar efforts for many other Latin American countries.

1919

January 7-14. **Buenos Aires's "Tragic Week" occurred,** a confused period of bloodshed and destruction of property pitting militant workers against poorly disciplined municipal police forces. Aggravating the situation was a widespread fear that labor leaders intended to emulate the recent Bolshevik Revolution in Russia. A struggle between Socialists, anarchists, and syndicalists for control of the labor movement followed. Anti-Semitic incidents also figured in the riots.

March 1. **Uruguay's new constitution went into effect.** Featuring a plural executive patterned on the Swiss model, it had been strongly promoted by President **Batlle y Ordóñez.** The document also featured universal male suffrage. The socially progressive *batllista* system continued under Presidents Baltasar Brum (1919-23), José Serrato (1923-27), and Juan Campisteguy (1927-31).

June 5. **The unexpected death of Paraguayan president Manuel Franco** coincided with a period of economic decline and political turbulence that witnessed three chief executives in as many years: José Montero (1919-20), Manuel Gondra (for a second time, 1920-21), Félix Paiva (1921).

November. **Fifty thousand unemployed nitrate workers demonstrated in Santiago, Chile,** in protest against hardship arising from a price collapse owing in part to the growing use of synthetic nitrates. Ten months earlier, in February 1919, fifteen unemployed sheep herders in southern Chile died in a clash with army troops.

1920

December 23. **Arturo Alessandri Palma was inaugurated as Chilean president,** following a hotly contested election. **Alessandri's** presidency ended the parliamentary period of Chile's history, and marked the beginning of unsettled politics owing to economic fluctuations and rising demand for social reform. In spite of his initial popularity with the masses, Alessandri found his proposals for church–state separation, an income tax, and a progressive labor code, thwarted by Congress.

1921

January. **The closing of a major nitrate mine in northern Chile produced a clash** between workers and police resulting in seventy-three deaths and many injuries.

October 29. **Factionalism within Paraguay's ruling Liberal party produced a rebellion** of the faction headed by Eduardo Schaerer. This in turn produced the resignation of President Manuel Gondra. The revolt became a civil war when members of the Colorado party moved to support Schaerer. At length the followers of Gondra prevailed, Schaerer fled the country, and Gondrista president Eligio Ayala was elected to a four-year term (June 1924).

1922

May. **Labor leader Luis Emilio Recabarren founded Chile's Communist party** (Partido Comunista de Chile) when he led his Socialist Workers party (Partido Obrero Socialista) into the Communist International.

October 12. **Marcelo Torcuato de Alvear was inaugurated to a six-year term as Argentina's president.** A member of the Radical party, Alvear placated the well-to-do, who had been unsettled by the populist style of **Hipólito Yrigoyen**. His independence from Irigoyen produced a split in the Radical party, with Alvear becoming leader of the anti-*personalista* faction, and Irigoyen leader of the *personalistas*.

1924

August 15. **Paraguayan president Eligio Ayala was inaugurated, having led the nation in a provisional capacity the previous year.** His administration was a progressive one marked by the passing of laws guaranteeing the minority Colorados representation in government. In 1926 Ayala implemented land reform that resulted in

the distribution of a quarter-million hectares to some 18,000 families.

September. **Ongoing economic difficulties brought military intervention in Chile.** A group of mainly junior army officers stepped into the political impasse between President **Arturo Alessandri** and Congress, which had refused to enact economic and political reforms sought by the president. At this time thousands were unemployed because of the decline of Chile's nitrate markets, while teachers and civil servants had gone unpaid for months because of falling government revenues. Yet the unsalaried Congress passed legislation providing remuneration for itself. On September 5, the officers presented Alessandri with a petition demanding passage of several reform measures, and he named an army general, Luis Altamirano, minister of the interior. Congress quickly passed the reform measures, but Alessandri, feeling intimidated by the officers, resigned on September 12. General Altamirano then became chief executive.

1925

January 28. **Young army officers, led by colonels Carlos Ibáñez and Marmaduke Grove, ousted the goverment headed by General Altamirano, whom they accused of betraying the reformist goals of the September 1924 movement.** They recalled President **Arturo Alessandri**, who convened a constitutional convention. Chile's new constitution, promulgated September 18, 1925, strengthened presidential powers at the expense of Congress, separated church and state, empowered the state to protect workers, and established the state's right to seize private property in the interest of the public good.

October 1. **Arturo Alessandri resigned his presidency as his term neared its end.** He did so because of conflict with the minister of war, **Carlos Ibáñez.** Emiliano Figueroa, a civilian politician, was elected president and took office on December 23, 1925, but was dominated by Ibáñez, who continued to sit in the cabinet.

1927

July 21. **Carlos Ibáñez del Campo took office as president of Chile.** Ibáñez initially became chief executive when the ineffective President Figueroa took a leave of absence and then resigned in May 1927. Ibáñez was elected president without opposition on May 22. As president, he undertook educational reform and embarked on an ambitious public works program financed by foreign loans. Onset of the Great Depression and definitive collapse of the nitrate market brought an end to Ibáñez's autocratic rule.

1928

April 1. **Seventy-six-year-old Hipólito Yrigoyen was elected to a second term as Argentina's president.** Said to be senile at the time of his election, Yrigoyen was incapable of national leadership. National affairs drifted, opposition to his presidency mounted, and he was overthrown in a military coup on September 6, 1930, as effects of the Great Depression began to be felt in Argentina.

August 15. **Paraguayan president José Patricio Guggiari was inaugurated.** Guggiari, a Gondrista member of the Liberal party, was confronted almost immediately by an outbreak of hostilities in the Chaco region. On December 5, 1928, a Paraguayan army officer attacked and destroyed a military post that the Bolivian army had placed on Paraguayan soil. As Paraguay's army was unprepared for war, Guggiari was forced to apologize for the incident and to agree to rebuild the post.

Brazil

In the two decades following the Paraguayan War (1864-70), Brazilian politics was dominated by three interrelated issues: debate over slavery, the growth of republican sentiment, and the increasing assertiveness of the military. The Free Birth Law of 1871 envisioned a gradual end to slavery but failed to satisfy critics of the institution. As Brazil moved toward the final abolition of slavery in 1888, coffee growers began to seek Europeans to replace slave workers. Thousands of immigrants—primarily from Italy, Portugal, and Spain—entered Brazil, settling mainly in São Paulo and the three states to the south.

Dissatisfaction with the monarchy developed after 1870 as the government seemed unable to meet the challenges associated with economic modernization, expansion of the middle classes, and urbanization. Members of the armed forces felt especially aggrieved after the Paraguayan War when the government decreed cutbacks in military spending and in other ways appeared to deny them the prestige and influence they felt they deserved. Many younger officers came under the influence of Comtian positivism, which offered a vision of order and progress in a republican setting. The positivist motto—Order and Progress—would be emblazoned on the flag of Brazil when it became a federal republic in 1889. The regime established by a new constitution of 1891, known as the Old or First Republic, lasted until 1930.

Under the republic, politics remained highly clientelist, dominated by a chain of power brokers reaching from local strongmen known as "colonels" (*coronéis*) up through state and national bureaucracies. Two states—São Paulo and Minas Gerais—came to dominate the federal government with the help of compliant chief executives in other states in the so-called "politics of the governors."

During the Old Republic popular participation in politics grew only slightly. Literacy was required for voting, yet the male literacy rate was only 19.1 percent in 1890 and 28.9 percent in 1920. Protests against elite domination of national affairs emerged sporadically after 1900, but they were easily handled by the military. Only endemic banditry in the back country, a few strikes led by a small labor movement, and quixotic uprisings by young army officers disturbed Brazil during the decades immediately preceding 1930.

In the decades following the establishment of the republic, Brazil reached its apogee as an exporter of primary products to the global market.

Coffee continued to lead in the ongoing export boom, augmented by other plantation crops, chiefly sugar and cacao, and by natural rubber. In the late nineteenth century exports of rubber gathered in Amazonia soared, but the boom ended after 1910, because of competition from rubber produced on Asian plantations. In spite of the vicissitudes of the global market, Brazil's exports pushed economic growth steadily ahead at 2.5 percent annually until the collapse of international trade in 1930.

Improvements in public health and continuing immigration doubled Brazil's population, making it 32 million by 1930. The city and hinterlands of São Paulo, center of the coffee industry, benefitted especially from economic growth, and the city became the site of the nation's incipient import-substituting industry.

Brazil enjoyed considerable diplomatic success during the First Republic. It added nearly 200,000 square miles to its national domain as a result of agreements with its neighbors: Argentina (1895), French Guiana (1900), Bolivia (1903), British Guiana and Ecuador (1904), Venezuela (1905), Dutch Guiana (1906), and Colombia (1907). Only in its negotiations with Uruguay (1909) did Brazil relinquish territory it had previously claimed. In 1905 Pope Pius X elevated the archbishop of Rio de Janeiro to the rank of cardinal, the first prelate in America to receive that honor.

During these years United States–Brazilian relations were especially cordial, thanks to the work of the **Baron Rio Branco**, Brazil's foreign minister from 1902 to 1912. In 1905 the United States diplomatic representative to Brazil was elevated to the rank of ambassador, the first in South America, and Brazil sent its first ambassador to the United States. United States–Brazilian friendship was underscored in 1906 when U.S. secretary of state Elihu Root traveled to Rio de Janeiro to attend the Third International Conference of American States. This was the first foreign trip ever made by a United States secretary of state while in office.

During late 1903–early 1904, Brazil pro-

moted the recognition of Panama by other Latin American republics, notably Chile and Mexico. In 1915, it helped mediate the dispute between Mexico and the United States. The Baron Rio Branco and **Joaquim Nabuco** championed the Monroe Doctrine. They viewed their nation as a diplomatic bridge between the United States and Spanish America.

1871

September 28. **Brazil enacted the Free Birth Law.** The law provided that children born to slave mothers would henceforth be free. However, they were to remain under the control of the mother's master until they reached the age of eight, when they could be released in return for a payment by the state to the master. Otherwise, they were to work for their master until the age of twenty-one. The law is also known as the Rio Branco law, after the prime minister at the time, the Viscount Rio Branco (José Maria da Silva Paranhos). Although the law meant that slavery would eventually become extinct, it failed to satisfy abolitionists.

1873

September 27. **Legal action was ordered against the bishop of Pernambuco.** Bishop Vital Maria Gonçalves de Oliveira of Pernambuco was the central figure in the most bitter church–state conflict during the empire. It began in 1872 when Bishop Vital placed under an interdict a lay brotherhood that had defied his order to expel members who were Masons. He later placed other brotherhoods in his diocese under an interdict for the same reason. Many prominent Brazilians, including Roman Catholic clergymen, were Masons, but Pope Pius IX had condemned the organization in an 1864 encyclical. Emperor **Pedro II**, however, had not given official sanction to the encyclical, a right which he claimed as patron of the church in Brazil. When the bishop refused to lift the interdict, the government initiated legal proceedings against him for violating the constitution and the civil code, and on February 2, 1874, he was sentenced to four years imprisonment. Bishop Antônio Macedo da Costa of Pará was similarly defiant and received the same sentence on July 1, 1874. The two bishops were pardoned in 1875, whereupon the papacy ordered that the interdicts be lifted. Although the state had apparently triumphed over the church, many devout Catholics lost their enthusiasm for the monarchy because of this episode.

1881

January 9. **A new electoral law was enacted.** Approved under the Liberal cabinet of José Antônio Saraiva, the legislation made elections for parliamentary deputies and senators direct. Prospective voters had to meet a relatively low income requirement, but it was very difficult to prove that one's income was adequate. Moreover, after the first registration, new voters would also have to meet a literacy requirement. As a result of the new law, the number of voters declined.

1888

May 13. **Brazil abolished slavery, becoming the last American state to do so.** Agitation over slavery intensified during the 1880s. Several provinces and municipalities ended slavery within their jurisdictions, and the Saraiva-Cotegipe law (1885) freed slaves over age sixty. Moreover, slaves were fleeing their plantations in large numbers. As a result, there was relatively little opposition in 1888 to the so-called "Golden Law," which freed approximately 750,000 slaves. Slaveowners received no compensation.

1889

March 1. **Miracle in Juazeiro, Ceará**. A woman who had received communion from Father Cícero Romão Batista fell to the ground, and the white communion wafer turned to blood, which was said to be the blood of Christ. The repetition of this incident soon brought many pilgrims to Juazeiro, even though the bishop of Ceará doubted the alleged miracle and partially suspended Father Cícero from the priesthood. The Vatican con-

demned the miracle in 1894. Over the years Juazeiro grew in population, and Father Cícero, who died in 1934, became an important political as well as religious leader in Ceará.

November 15. **End of the monarchy and proclamation of a republic.** Pedro II was deposed in a bloodless military coup led by Marshal **Manoel Deodoro da Fonseca** and supported by civilian republicans. The monarchy had alienated several important groups, such as Catholics offended by the imprisonment of two bishops in 1874 and landowners who received no compensation for their freed slaves in 1888. Military leaders were also resentful for what they considered the neglect of the armed forces after their victory in the Paraguayan War. Moreover, to many, especially evolving middle-class urban groups, the monarchy seemed an ineffectual anachronism. On November 16 Fonseca declared Brazil to be a federal republic.

1890

January 7. **Church and state were separated.** The provisional government headed by **Fonseca** also decreed full religious freedom for all sects in Brazil.

January 17. **A new banking decree contributed to a speculative boom.** Known as the Encilhamento, from a horse-racing term, the boom began under the last imperial government, which had moved to expand credit to landowners after the abolition of slavery. The 1890 decree, sponsored by Finance Minister **Rui Barbosa**, expanded credit further by creating three (later four) new banks of issue. This decree aggravated inflationary pressures and contributed to stock market speculation and a decline in the exchange rate for Brazil's currency. The Encilhamento ended in 1893, but the government's financial situation remained poor until the late 1890s.

1891

February 24. **Brazil's first republican constitution was promulgated.** The constitution provided for a federal form of government in which the central government retained extensive powers.

Literacy was required for voting. The assembly that wrote the constitution elected Marshal **Manoel Deodoro da Fonseca** president and transformed itself into Brazil's first republican Congress.

November 3. **Fonseca tried to establish a dictatorship.** After clashes with Congress, **Fonseca** dissolved it and declared a state of siege. The state governors generally supported his action, but there was opposition among civilians and some army officers, and the navy threatened to bombard Rio de Janeiro. In the face of this resistance, Fonseca resigned on November 23 and was succeeded by his vice president, Marshal **Floriano Peixoto.**

1893

February 2. **Rebellion in Rio Grande do Sul.** Federalists in Rio Grande do Sul rebelled against the governor, Júlio de Castilhos, and the state's constitution, which was strongly influenced by Comtian positivism and gave very strong powers to the governor. The insurgents conducted campaigns in the neighboring states of Paraná and Santa Catarina and received some support from federal army officers. But they did not have the support of the federal chief executive, **Floriano Peixoto.** Though the revolt was ultimately unsuccessful, it lasted for thirty-one months and produced 10,000 casualties.

September 5. **Rebellion in the navy.** Admiral Custódio de Melo and other officers, angered over what they perceived to be slights to the navy, demanded the resignation of **Floriano Peixoto,** but Admiral Luís Felipe Saldanha da Gama, who joined the rebels in December, supported a restoration of the monarchy. Naval rebels occupied Desterro (now Florianópolis), capital of Santa Catarina, but failed to coordinate their efforts with the Federalist insurgents of Rio Grande do Sul. The rebels' threats to bombard Rio de Janeiro were checked by foreign governments, especially the United States, which warned them not to interfere with commerce at the port. By June 1894 the naval revolt was over.

1894

November 15. **Prudente de Morais became the first civilian president of the republic.** Prudente José de Morais Barros, a former governor of São Paulo, is generally seen as a spokesman for the interests of the coffee growers of his state. His administration marked the beginning of the long domination of national politics by leaders from São Paulo and Minas Gerais.

1897

October. **Final assault on Canudos.** Canudos was a settlement in the state of Bahia, established in 1893 by a wandering holy man known as Antônio Conselheiro (Anthony the Counselor), who had roamed the backlands of northeastern Brazil repairing churches and cemeteries and preaching. He attracted as many as 25,000 followers to his millennial community at Canudos. When he attacked the republic, partly because the state had assumed control over the registry of births, marriages, and deaths from the church, outsiders concluded that Canudos was a hotbed of monarchism. In 1896-97 several expeditions of state and federal troops were sent to subjugate Canudos without success. Especially shocking was the rout of a 1,300-man force led by Antônio Moreira César in March 1897. The final campaign saw the surrender or death of nearly all of the defenders of Canudos. Conselheiro himself died, probably of dysentery, in September. The campaign against Canudos became the subject of the classic book *Os Sertões* (1902) by **Euclides da Cunha.**

November 5. **Assassination attempt on the president.** A soldier fired on President Prudente de Morais as he was reviewing troops who had returned from Canudos. The president escaped injury, but in the struggle to disarm the assailant the minister of war, Marshal Carlos Machado de Bittencourt, was stabbed to death. This incident was the climax of a period of tension marked by frustration over the long Canudos campaign and by a wave of invective directed against the president by a group of middle-class civilians and army officers known as Jacobins, who favored a more authoritarian, nationalistic government. President Morais now declared a state of siege and moved to curb Jacobins and other foes of his administration.

1898

November 15. **Manuel Ferraz de Campos Sales was inaugurated as president.** Campos Sales and his finance minister, Joaquim Murtinho, emphasized fiscal austerity in order to rehabilitate Brazil's finances after the inflationary era known as the Encilhamento. This effort was aided by a £10 million loan that Campos Sales had negotiated in London as president-elect; the lender had insisted on the adoption of a deflationary policy. Campos Sales, a Paulista like his predecessor, initiated the "politics of the governors" (*política dos governadores*), whereby the president and key governors made major decisions. This system remained in force until 1930.

1902

November 15. **Francisco de Paula Rodrigues Alves was inaugurated as president.** Under the Rodrigues Alves administration Rio de Janeiro was modernized, and through the campaign of **Dr. Oswaldo Cruz,** yellow fever, which previously had claimed 10,000 lives annually in the city, was eradicated.

1903

November 17. **Brazil gained possession of Acre province, ceded by Bolivia in the Treaty of Petrópolis.** During the previous year Brazilians had seized the territory to ensure their continued access to the natural rubber available there. In exchange for Acre, Brazil guaranteed Bolivia an eastward outlet to the sea via rail and river through its territory.

1904

November 10-14. **The government's decision to require smallpox vaccinations produced riots in** **Rio de Janeiro.** Origins of the demonstrations, which ultimately required intervention of the military, were complex. Members of the political opposition, seconded by leaders of the Positivist Church, initiated resistance to the vaccinations. Army officer and senator Lauro Sodré, a leader of the Center of Oppressed Classes, seized on the upset as an excuse to attempt a coup against the Rodrigues Alves government. Sodré was able to enlist the help of Rio's working class in his abortive revolt.

1906

March. **Brazil stabilized coffee prices through its "valorization" program,** involving government purchase and warehousing of the national coffee crop. The plan was devised at a meeting in Taubaté, São Paulo, attended by the governors of the three leading coffee-growing states (São Paulo, Rio de Janeiro, and Minas Gerais) and was later endorsed by the federal government. Thus it led other coffee-producing nations in the move toward controlling the production and sale of coffee.

November 15. **Afonso Augusto Moreira Pena was inaugurated president,** his election a result of the demand by political elites of Minas Gerais that a Mineiro succeed the Paulista Rodrigues Alves. Pena served until his death June 14, 1909. His term was completed by Nilo Peçanha (1909-10).

1908

March. **The Brazilian Labor Confederation (Confederação Operária Brasileira, COB) was established.** Uniting labor groups from São Paulo, Rio de Janeiro, and Pôrto Alegre, the COB had to contend with a weak and divided labor movement as well as with government repression. It published the pro-anarchist *Voz do Trabalhador.* The COB soon declined, but its leaders remained active in the anarchist movement through the 1920s.

1910

June 20. **The Indian Protection Service, under**

the directorship of **Cândido Mariano da Silva Rondon,** was authorized by President Nilo Peçanha. That action followed international protest against the abuse of Brazilian Indians, especially that voiçed at the XVI Congress of Americanists held in Vienna, Austria, 1908.

November 15.   **The inauguration of President Hermes da Fonseca, a *gaúcho* from Rio Grande do Sul,** marked the emergence of that southern state as a force in national politics, and the return of the military to politics. Hermes, a nephew of Marshal **Deodoro da Fonseca,** had served as minister of war under Afonso Pena. Rio Grande do Sul, along with politicians from several northern states, had triumphed through the new Conservative Republican party. The Rio Grande–led coalition turned back the civilist candidate **Rui Barbosa,** who had been supported by São Paulo and Bahia. Barbosa had generated excitement in the election through his criticism of excessive military influence in politics.

November-December.   **The "Revolt of the Chibata," led by Brazilian seaman João Cândido Felisberto,** highlighted the abuse of sailors by their officers. The rebellion, which consisted of two separate incidents, constituted the world's only mutiny in which an ordinary sailor commanded a squadron. The revolt ultimately produced reforms in the Brazilian navy.

1912

The Contestado social movement began in southern Brazil. Led by a healer and preacher known as José Maria (Miguel Lucena Boaventura), the movement took place in the Contestado region lying between the states of Paraná and Santa Catarina. The region was undergoing rapid change that disrupted existing patterns among the lower classes, who heeded José Maria's antirepublican rhetoric and millenarian promises. An attack (October 22, 1912) by state police against José Maria's followers was unsuccessful, though he was killed. Under one of his followers, the movement became based at a place called Taquaraçu, in Santa Catarina, and defied authorities until March 1916.

1914

November 15.   **The inauguration of Wenceslau Bras,** a mineiro, reflected the informal political arrangement between São Paulo and Minas Gerais, under which the two states alternately supported one another's presidential candidates. That agreement was known as *café com leite* (coffee with cream).

Brazil gained international prestige during Bras's administration and, after an initial economic downturn, the nation prospered. On October 26, 1917, Brazil declared war on Germany, becoming the only South American nation to do so. After the war Brazil further enhanced its standing in the international community by playing a leading role in the League of Nations.

1917

July. **Fifty thousand workers joined in a general strike in São Paulo,** an action representing the high point of labor militancy during 1917-20. As there was little improvement in working conditions following the many strikes of the period, Brazil's labor movement stagnated during the 1920s.

1919

July 28. **Epitácio da Silva Pessoa was inaugurated president,** following the death of Presidentelect Rodrigues Alves, who had been elected to a second term less than a year earlier. Pessoa was the first and only president from northern Brazil during the First Republic. He was challenged by **Rui Barbosa,** who had run for office in 1910 and 1914. **Barbosa** campaigned as an independent candidate pledged to labor reform. His good showing, with most of his votes coming from urban areas, reflected the growing political activism of Brazil's urban population.

1920

The *cangaceiro* (bandit) leader Virgulino Ferreira, known as Lampião, began his career, which involved depredations over much of

Brazil's Northeastern back country. Lampião's career ended with his death in 1938, a time when back-country banditry was ending in Brazil. Another of the legendary *cangaceiros*, Antônio Silvino, was active during 1897-1914.

1922

February. **Modern Art Week was inaugurated in São Paulo**, producing a cultural revolution in Brazil. Dubbing themselves "cannibals," avant garde artists and poets vowed to devour members of the Eurocentric art academies and to nationalize Brazilian art.

March 6. **Artur da Silva Bernardes, candidate of the São Paulo–Minas Gerais coalition, was elected president** in a contest pitting him against Nilo Peçanha, the candidate of a coalition of intermediate states led by Rio Grande do Sul, Pernambuco, Bahia, and Rio de Janeiro. The military leadership also supported Peçanha, which added a note of tension to the contest. Although Bernardes triumphed, and the army and the coalition of opposing states accepted the result, a sense of anger and frustration lingered, especially in Rio Grande do Sul and in military circles.

March 25-27. **The Brazilian Communist party (Partido Comunista do Brasil, PCB) was founded** by journalist Astrogildo Pereira and a group of disaffected former anarchists. The party's membership reached just 1,000 in 1929.

July 5. **Rebellious junior officers (*tenentes*, or lieutenants) seized Igrejinha Fort on Copacabana Beach in Rio de Janeiro,** thus initiating a series of uprisings against the government. Most of the rebels soon surrendered their weapons, though eighteen of them preferred to die fighting for their reformist cause. Later many of these *tenentes* had prominent public careers.

1924

July 5. **On the second anniversary of the Tenente Revolt in Rio de Janeiro, dissident army officers in São Paulo again raised the** standard of revolt. Other similar uprisings took place simultaneously in Sergipe and Amazonas. Driven from São Paulo by loyalist troops, the dissidents marched westward to Iguaçú Falls, where they joined another rebel, Captain **Luís Carlos Prestes**. Prestes went on to form the legendary "Prestes Column," which, pursued by police and troops, marched some 15,000 miles through the Brazilian back country before escaping and disbanding in Bolivia. Though few backlanders responded to Prestes's calls for revolt against the state, his flamboyant action came to symbolize popular defiance of the government. Prestes, called the "Knight of Hope," eventually joined the Brazilian Communist party.

1926

November 15. **Washington Luís Pereira de Souza was inaugurated president of Brazil.** While Washington Luís pursued policies pleasing to coffee-growing interests, he did little to address widespread discontent over elite domination of the political system and its reluctance to allow regions beyond the Rio-São Paulo-Minas Gerais triangle to share power.

Symbolic of the domination of national politics by narrowly defined coalitions of state political leaders—at the expense of any greater national vision—was the naming of the new president's cabinet. As in the case of previous administrations during Brazil's First Republic, cabinet members were chosen for their political connections rather than for their administrative competence. A case in point was Washington Luís's minister of finance, **Getúlio Vargas**. Vargas, who admitted to knowing nothing of finance, was appointed as a conciliatory gesture to the governor and political boss of Rio Grande do Sul, Antônio Borges de Medeiros.

1928

January 25. **Getúlio Vargas succeeded his mentor, Antônio Borges de Medeiros, as gover-**

nor of Rio Grande do Sul. Thus he positioned himself as candidate for the presidential election of 1930. **Vargas** soon became the symbol of dissatisfaction over the state of Brazilian politics.

June. **Paulo Prado's** *Portrait of Brazil: Essay on Brazilian Melancholy***, was published,** reflecting both the pessimism of educated Brazilians over their nation's immediate prospects, and their desire for thoroughgoing change.

1929

August 5. **Antigovernment forces in Congress launched the Liberal Alliance (AL),** which supported **Getúlio Vargas** as its candidate in the 1930 presidential contest. The AL was formed in part as a response to the decision of President Washington Luís to support fellow Paulista Júlio Prestes in the upcoming contest. In so doing he broke the tradition of alternating politicians from São Paulo and Minas Gerais in the presidency. Among the groups supporting the Liberal Alliance were those of the emerging middle class who opposed the coffee oligarchy and who wanted rapid modernization of the nation.

December 26. **A member of the Liberal Alliance shot and killed a supporter of the government during an altercation on the floor of Congress.** A product of the political tension attending the upcoming presidential contest, the killing was the first ever to take place there.

ECONOMIC NATIONALISM AND POLITICAL PROTEST
1930-1959

The Great Depression of the 1930s produced turmoil throughout Latin America. Widespread unemployment attended the collapse of export prices placing sudden and intense pressure on governments across the region. The experience convinced Latin Americans that their position in the global economy as suppliers of raw materials made them unacceptably vulnerable to economic downturns. This set them on a protectionist course featuring state encouragement of import substitution.

Economic hardship sharpened the perception that national affairs were in the hands of a political class that was at once inept and insensitive to the needs of ordinary citizens. Political protest, demand for more authentic representation of popular interests, and political experimentation characterized the middle decades of the twentieth century. In country after country old ruling cliques were swept away and new leaders experimented with institutional arrangements that were statist, eclectic, and in many cases military-dominated. The regimes that they created combined populist, corporative, Keynesian and socialist elements. Latin America's statist experiments of the 1930s were based on the perceived successes of Soviet vanguardism, Italian fascism, and democratic Keynesianism, as applied in the United States by President Franklin D. Roosevelt. Mexico's revolution provided a model that was yet closer at hand.

The strengthening of central government inevitably enhanced the power of the military. So too did World War II and the succeeding Cold War. Both conflicts brought Latin American leaders into intimate contact with the United States, the hemisphere's leader in the antifascist struggle during the 1930s and 1940s, and the world's preeminent anticommunist state after 1945.

The Cold War had a baleful impact on Latin America, especially upon democratic government.

Fears inspired by the advances of Marxism-Leninism in Central Europe and East Asia during the late 1940s, and United States insistence that regional leaders oppose communism at all costs, invigorated the conservative right and hindered the reformist left during the postwar years. Reformers, even the most democratic ones, were inevitably tarred with the brush of communism. Complicating the issue was the fact that small but vocal pro-Soviet communist movements became stronger in most nations south of the Rio Grande following World War II. Their presence frightened Latin American elites, causing them to oppose everything leftist, often to the extent of entrusting national destiny to the military. By the mid-1950s anticommunist military regimes existed in Cuba, the Dominican Republic, Guatemala, Honduras, El Salvador, Nicaragua, Venezuela, and Paraguay.

Latin American society modernized at an accelerating pace over the 1930-59 period, becoming more urban than rural by 1960. That change had the effect of improving the quality of life for most Latin Americans. Urbanization meant proximity to clean drinking water, improved health facilities, schools, and better-paying jobs. Thus Latin America's social indicators showed dramatic improvement between 1930 and 1960, and more people enjoyed significantly better living conditions than they had thirty years before.

International Developments

During 1930-60, the international relations of Latin American states passed through three distinct stages. First came markedly improved Latin–U.S. relations through the latter nation's implementation of its "Good Neighbor Policy," officially proclaimed in a 1933 speech by President Franklin D. Roosevelt. Through it the United States formally liquidated the "big stick" and "gunboat diplomacy" that had prevailed in the Caribbean and elsewhere at the turn of the century.

The rise of fascist dictatorships in Europe and Asia ushered in the second period, that of wartime collaboration between American states. Presided over by the United States, the hemisphere's dominant power, a structure of inter-American collaboration was forged through a series of meetings taking place before and during the war. All Latin American states save Argentina and Chile severed relations with the Axis powers between the Pearl Harbor attack of December 7, 1941, and early in 1943, going on to collaborate actively with the United States, especially through the supplying of raw materials to the war effort.

At war's end inter-American relations of the 1930-59 period entered their third stage, that colored by fears of communist expansion into the Americas. Most Latin Americans, leaders and ordinary citizens alike, opposed both communism and Soviet expansionism. They willingly supported United States leadership in the struggle to contain both. By the 1950s, however, many of them had come to resent United States insistence that they conform to a U.S.-inspired anticommunist policy that seemed unable to distinguish between democratic reformism and leftist subversion. As the decade of the 1950s drew to a close Latin Americans looked upon the United States with something less than trust and friendship. The uncertain state of relations between Latin American nations and their powerful neighbor to the north was underscored in 1958, when rioting students in two South American capitals disrupted the "good-will mission" of visiting United States vice president Richard Nixon.

Inter-American relations were generally pacific between 1930 and 1960. The Chaco War, fought by Paraguay and Bolivia (1932-35), was destructive of life, but did not spread beyond the war's immediate theater, a semi-desert zone known as the Gran Chaco. The Leticia conflict (1932-33), between Colombia and Peru, was of brief duration and was played out in the remote upper Amazon.

1933

December 3. **The Seventh International American Conference met at Montevideo, Uruguay,** and representatives of all republics of the hemisphere were present. At the meeting U.S. secretary of state Cordell Hull signed a convention barring intervention by any American state in the affairs of another. Other achievements of the meeting included the effecting of an armistice in the Chaco struggle between Paraguay and Bolivia, the strengthening and rationalization of peace machinery of the Americas, and the bettering of trade relations through a U.S.-led tariff-lowering initiative.

1936

January 3. **U.S. president Franklin D. Roosevelt articulated the Good Neighbor Policy toward Latin America in a speech before Congress,** saying "this policy of the 'good neighbor' among the Americas is no longer a hope—it is a fact, active, present, pertinent and effective." He reinforced his words in personal letters to all Latin American heads of state (January 30), in which he proposed that a special conference be held in Buenos Aires to consider the maintenance of peace in the Americas. Roosevelt's Good Neighbor Policy was, in essence, a pledge of nonintervention and noninterference in Latin America's domestic affairs.

December 1-23. **The Pan-American Conference for the Maintenance of Peace met in Buenos Aires,** where governments accepted for the first time the principle of consultation in the event conflict threatened. A convention was drafted coordinating existing treaties for the maintenance of peace. That the U.S. delegation, led by President Roosevelt, accepted less than the U.S. desire to make the Monroe Doctrine multilateral against foreign aggressors, served as evidence that Roosevelt's government intended to abide by its Good Neighbor Policy. The United States also made an even stronger commitment to the principle of nonintervention than it had at Montevideo.

1938

December 9. **The Eighth International American Conference convened in Lima, Peru,** and there it was agreed to proscribe the use of force as an instrument of foreign policy, to settle international differences by peaceful means and in keeping with international law, to abide by existing international agreements, and to extend inter-American intellectual and economic cooperation. There delegates adopted the Declaration of Lima, which reaffirmed the absolute sovereignty of the various American states and their determination to defend themselves against foreign intervention.

1939

September 23-October 2. **The First Inter-American Consultative Conference of Foreign Ministers met in Panama City.** There they proclaimed that the waters surrounding the Western Hemisphere to a distance of 300 miles (480 kilometers) constituted "sea safety zones," to be kept free from hostile acts by non-American belligerent nations. Delegates also issued a General Declaration of Neutrality of the American republics. The ministers also established a financial and economic committee charged with cooperation toward protecting their nations' economic and fiscal structures, to safeguard currency stability, and to develop industries and commerce.

1940

July 21-30. **The Second Inter-American Consultative Conference of Foreign Ministers met in Havana, Cuba,** and there they agreed to counter possible Nazi attempts to seize Dutch, Danish, and French colonies in the Americas following German occupation of those European nations. The Act of Havana provided that the American Republics, singly or jointly, should act as required to defend themselves from foreign aggression.

1942

January 15-28. **The Third Inter-American Consultative Conference of Foreign Ministers** met in **Rio de Janeiro** to formulate a response to the Japanese attack on the United States fleet at Pearl Harbor, Hawaii. On January 21, representatives from twenty-one American republics, voted to recommend the severance of diplomatic relations with the Axis powers. Earlier, between December 9, 1941, and the conference, many American states either declared war on, or broke relations with the Axis powers. Brazil and several others severed relations after the conference. Only Chile and Argentina continued relations with the Axis until 1943 and 1944, respectively.

1944

July 1-22. **Latin American nations attended the Bretton Woods Conference (the United Nations Monetary and Financial Conference),** where the postwar international economic order was established. The International Monetary Fund (IMF) and the International Bank for Reconstruction and Development (IBRD, or World Bank) were created at the meeting, and all Latin American states joined, Haiti and Argentina not until 1953 and 1956.

1945

February 21-March 8. **The Inter-American Conference on Problems of War and Peace Met in Mexico City.** Delegates approved the Act of Chapultepec, which provided for joint action to guarantee American states against aggression. The United States offered an "economic charter for the Americas," aimed chiefly at raising standards of living throughout the hemisphere. Another resolution was passed calling for quadrennial conferences of American states and the formation of an Organization of American States (OAS). A draft charter for the OAS was drawn up at a conference of foreign ministers convened in Rio de Janeiro, August 15–September 2, 1947.

April-June. **Twenty Latin American states, representing 39 percent of countries present, participated in organization of the United Nations.** Colombian foreign minister **Alberto Lleras Camargo** led Latin American delegates in insisting that the autonomy of the inter-American system be guaranteed. Thanks to their numbers, Latin American states were well represented in governing organs of the United Nations.

1947

September 2. **The Inter-American Treaty of Reciprocal Assistance was signed.** Drafted at a meeting near Rio de Janeiro, the treaty detailed the steps to be taken by American states in the event of armed attacks or other forms of aggression. It became operative in 1948.

1948

ECLA, the Economic Commission for Latin America, was created by the United Nations. Known in Latin America as CEPAL (Comisión Económica Para América Latina), the commission was headquartered in Santiago, Chile. Argentine economist **Raúl Prebisch** became its director in 1950.

April. **The Ninth International Conference of American States met in Bogotá, Colombia.** The chief item of business was approval of the charter of the Organization of American States (OAS). The charter established the Permanent Council, which became the executive body of the OAS. The Pan American Union became the secretariat of the new body. Three agencies were established within the OAS: the Inter-American Economic and Social Council, the Inter-American Council of Jurists, and the Inter-American Cultural Council. Head of the United States delegation George C. Marshall answered calls that his country increase its aid to Latin America by announcing an increase of $500 million in the allocation for Latin American loans through the Export-Import Bank.

Other actions taken by delegates were the establishment of an Inter-American Defense Board, and the declaration that "by its anti-democratic character and its interventionist tendency the political activity of international communism . . . is incompatible with the concept of American freedom."

1951

March 26-April 7. **The foreign ministers of twenty-one American republics met in Washington, D.C.** Under the urging of United States president Truman and his secretary of state, Dean Acheson, delegates agreed to strengthen the Inter-American Defense Board and to recommend that member states adopt legislation to prevent and punish subversive acts of international communism. Later in 1951, on December 13, the charter of the Organization of American States went into effect after Colombia ratified it.

1954

March 1. **The Tenth International Conference of American States opened in Caracas, Venezuela.** While Latin American states were chiefly concerned with economic issues, the United States's goal was to secure a declaration of opposition to communist penetration of the hemisphere. The United States was especially concerned about apparent communist influence in Guatemala. Eventually the United States secured a resolution opposing international communism—the Caracas Declaration— with seventeen nations approving, Guatemala disapproving, and Mexico and Argentina abstaining. Costa Rica boycotted the meeting to protest Venezuela's dictatorial president, **Marcos Pérez Jiménez**.

Latin American delegates proposed and then voted approval of a resolution calling upon industrialized nations to refrain from levying restrictions on the imports of raw materials, and for European nations to end colonialism in the Americas. The United States abstained.

1958

April 27-May 14. **U.S. vice president Richard Nixon was attacked by mobs during a good-will tour of South America.** Nixon was physically assaulted by mobs in Lima and Caracas, members of which opposed United States imperialism. There were no such incidents during Nixon's stops in Montevideo, Buenos Aires, Asunción, La Paz, and Bogotá.

1959

August 12-18. **The Fifth Inter-American Consultative Conference of Foreign Ministers convened in Santiago, Chile,** for the purpose of addressing the question of dictatorship in the hemisphere. While the ministers agreed, in the Declaration of Santiago, to censure dictatorial regimes, they condemned efforts to overthrow such regimes sponsored by other American states.

September 30. **Brazil, Argentina, Bolivia, Chile, Paraguay, Peru, and Uruguay** agreed to establish a South American free trade zone.

Mexico, Central America, and the Caribbean

Between 1930 and 1959 Mexicans worked to consolidate their revolution under aegis of their revolutionary party. The coincidence of their effort with Franklin Roosevelt's Good Neighbor Policy made that process a relatively benign one. Mexican-U.S. relations weathered the centralizing and statist measures of **Lázaro Cárdenas**, including Mexico's nationalization of foreign oil assets, and the two nations went on to cooperate amicably throughout the World War II and the Cold War eras.

If Mexico gained stability over the three decades following 1930, most of Central America and the Caribbean moved in the opposite direction. Most Caribbean states were torn by conflict and increasingly harsh political dictatorship. Guatemala, El Salvador, Nicaragua, Haiti, and the Dominican Republic ended the period under authoritarian regimes, giving them the aspect of quintessential "banana republics." Cuba, too, passed through a spell of traditional military dictatorship only to end under a radical revolutionary regime. **Fidel Castro**, who came to power early in 1959, embarked on a vigorously statist

and socialist course that either thrilled or frightened those who observed his progress.

1930

February 5. **Pascual Ortiz Rubio was inaugurated president of Mexico.** He went on to serve until September 4, 1932, when *jefe máximo* and Revolutionary party chief **Plutarco Elías Calles** forced his resignation for excessive independence in office. Ortiz was replaced by Abelardo Rodríguez (September 4), who completed Ortiz's four-year term.

February 23. **General Rafael Leonidas Trujillo overthrew Dominican president Horacio Vásquez.** Elected president soon after, **Trujillo** took advantage of a devastating hurricane in August 1930 to obtain dictatorial powers. Soon Trujillo decreed a series of government monopolies through which he began amassing vast wealth. In short order he made the nation his personal fiefdom. Meanwhile he maintained excellent relations with the United States. Only when his relations with the United States cooled late in his dictatorship did Trujillo loosen his grip on power, ultimately falling to assassins in 1961.

March. **A general strike paralyzed Cuba.** Plunging sugar prices coupled with generalized anger against dictator **Gerardo Machado** sparked the uprising, which produced a declaration of a state of siege nine months later. University students, who played an important role in opposition to Machado, were radicalized when two of them died during a demonstration (September 30). Resistance to Machado continued until he was overthrown in 1933.

1931

January 2. **Arnulfo Arias Madrid, leader of the secret organization Acción Comunal, seized the presidential palace in Panama and forced the resignation of President Florencio Arosemena.** A nationalist and a populist, the twenty-nine-year-old Arias engineered the election of his brother Harmodio to the presidency in 1932. The brothers went on to dominate Panamanian politics during the 1930s and 1940s. Their chief political goal was to remove control of the Panama Canal from the United States.

February 6-8. **General Jorge Ubico was elected president of Guatemala** thanks in large part to the confidence he inspired in the country's dominant social and economic groups. Minister of war during the administration of Lázaro Chacón (1926-30), **Ubico** had quelled popular discontent sprung from hardship brought by the Great Depression. His thirteen-year dictatorship was marked by harsh suppression of dissent. During the first year of his presidency he launched a vigorous anticommunist campaign culminating in the imprisonment of refugees from the unsuccessful leftist revolt in El Salvador and the execution of twelve communist leaders, one of them Honduran organizer Juan Pablo Wainwright. During 1934 he had several hundred political enemies executed on the pretext that they had plotted to assassinate him. Ubico went on to outlaw virtually all political and civic organizations.

While Ubico outlawed debt peonage, a traditional means of controlling Guatemala's 70 percent Indian population, he replaced it with an even more onerous form of *corvée* labor. Meanwhile he enhanced the power of landlords by legalizing violence employed in the protection of private property. Ubico also pursued a policy of cooperation with the United Fruit Company, granting generous land and tax concessions.

March 1. **Reformist president Arturo Araujo was inaugurated president of El Salvador**, pledged to a nine-point social program as well as to land reform. Depression-induced economic problems thwarted his good intentions, and his talk of social democracy produced opposition from the well-to-do.

December 2. **A military coup forced democratically elected leftist President Arturo Araujo into exile.** The military takeover strengthened the position of Salvadoran communists, whose political party had been founded a year earlier by **Farabundo Martí**. Araujo's vice president, General **Maximiliano Hernández Martínez**, was

named provisional president on December 5. At first the United States witheld recognition in keeping with the 1923 treaty that barred relations with governments that had come to power by irregular means. However, the other Central American governments recognized Martínez (being illegitimate and never knowing his father, Martínez always used his mother's and never his father's surname), and the United States followed suit in January 1934.

1932

January. **Members of the Salvadoran military executed some 10,000 citizens accused of complicity in or sympathy for an uprising of communist peasants.** The revolt, which began on January 22 in a mountainous region east of San Salvador, was organized by **Farabundo Martí**, who had founded the Salvadoran Communist party in 1930. The plot was discovered and Martí and two student accomplices were executed on February 1. Meanwhile the army and paramilitary groups rounded up and executed communists and noncommunists alike, many of the latter group people of Pipil Indian origin. The repression, known as La Matanza (The Massacre), was a watershed in Salvadoran history. It traumatized members of all social classes, who feared its recurrence. It also strengthened the regime of **Hernández Martínez**.

June 5. **Harmodio Arias was elected president of Panama.**

November 6. **Juan Bautista Sacasa won the Nicaraguan presidential election in a contest monitored by the United States.** One of his first acts was to pursue peace with dissident Liberal **Augusto César Sandino**, leader of the armed Ejército Defensor de la Soberanía Nacional de Nicaragua (EDSN).

1933

Depression-straitened Puerto Rico began receiving substantial amounts of aid from the administration of U.S. president Franklin D. Roosevelt.

Meanwhile pressure increased on the island for a redefinition of Puerto Rico's relationship to the United States.

January 2. **U.S. Marines departed Nicaragua.** One month later **Augusto César Sandino**, long-time leader of the nationalist resistance, signed an agreement by which his group, the EDSN, would surrender its arms in return for certain protections.

February 1. **Honduran National party leader Tiburcio Carías Andino was inaugurated president**, elected by a strong majority of the vote. His accession to power through democratic means ushered in fifteen years of authoritarian rule known as the Cariato. **Carías** faced rebellion by Liberal leaders and severe economic decline during his first year in power. He responded by crushing the Liberal uprising and adopting a policy of economic retrenchment. He curtailed the actions of labor organizations, censored the press, and had his term of office extended in the interest of peace. The Cariato gave Honduras its longest continuous period of political peace, though the country made little economic progress during these years.

June. **U.S. ambassador Sumner Welles negotiated with Cuban dictator Gerardo Machado, urging him to step down in the face of nation-wide opposition to his rule.**

July–August. **A strike of transportation workers in Cuba paralyzed the nation**, and, combined with United States pressure, moved the military to force President **Gerardo Machado** into exile. Carlos Manuel de Céspedes was named to replace him.

August. **Clashes between the Nicaraguan National Guard and the EDSN of Augusto César Sandino led to imposition of a state of siege.**

September 4. **Cuban president Céspedes was overthrown in a military coup led by Sergeant Fulgencio Batista.** Civilians soon joined the "sergeants' revolt," forming a revolutionary junta that on September 10 installed **Ramón Grau San Martín** as president. For one hundred days the Grau government passed nationalistic and socially progressive legislation, including a minimum wage and enfranchisement of women. The legislation frightened powerful groups within both Cuba and the United States. U.S. ambassador Sumner Welles termed this "government of a hundred days" "frankly communist," and used his influence to undermine it.

1934

January 15. **Cuban president Grau San Martín resigned.** The military withdrew its support from Grau after the United States refused to recognize his government. Moderate Carlos Mendieta was installed as president, and his government was quickly recognized by the United States. **Fulgencio Batista**, who had also withdrawn his support of Grau, remained a powerful presence in Cuban public life.

February 21. **Members of Nicaragua's National Guard, acting under orders of its commander Anastasio Somoza García, assassinated Augusto César Sandino.** Sandino, leader of the nationalist group EDSN, had just met, under a flag of truce, with Nicaraguan president Juan Bautista Sacasa. With Sandino's death the National Guard was able to destroy the remnants of the EDSN.

April. **Dominican dictator Rafael L. Trujillo spurred industrialization in his country** through the establishment of industrial parks and tax exemptions for foreign companies. In 1942 he altered the national constitution to encourage foreign investment. At the end of his dictatorship **Trujillo** had ownership in 80 percent of his nation's industrial concerns.

May 29. **The United States acceded to Cuban demands to abrogate the Platt Amendment.** Soon thereafter the United States and Cuba signed a reciprocal trade agreement favorable to Cuba.

July 2. **Lázaro Cárdenas, hand-picked candidate of Plutarco Elías Calles, was elected to a six-year term as president of Mexico. Cárdenas**, representative of the reform wing of

Mexico's Revolutionary party, quickly asserted himself against **Calles**. Cárdenas won the ensuing power struggle, ultimately exiling Calles (April 1936). Cárdenas then undertook a series of reforms of a populist, statist character. The new president sped land reform, ultimately redistributing some 18 million hectares (45 million acres), double that of his predecessors. The land was given as communally held *ejidos*. Cárdenas thus fulfilled a major goal of the revolution. He went on to vastly expand state power, pursuing a populist agenda.

August 6. **The United States withdrew its troops from Haiti,** thus ending a nineteen-year occupation of that country.

1935

March–May. **Cuban revolutionaries proclaimed a general strike,** which the government of Carlos Mendieta ruthlessly crushed. Strike leaders were killed, tortured, and driven into exile. The killing of strike leader Antonio Guiteras in May 1935 ended Cuba's revolution of 1933.

June 17. **Haiti adopted a new constitution that extended the term of President Sténio Vincent** to 1941.

December 12. **Cuban president José Barnet y Vinagres took office two days after the resignation of Carlos Mendieta.** Both were puppets of army commander **Fulgencio Batista**, as were presidents Miguel Mariano Gómez (1936) and Federico Laredo Brú (1936-40).

1936

February 23. **Two Puerto Rican nationalists killed Police Chief Francis Riggs.** The killing occurred at a time of heightened unrest sparked by Nationalist party leader Pedro Albizu Campos, and the two assassins were immediately killed at police headquarters. Albizu and other Nationalist leaders were subsequently convicted of sedition and imprisoned. Meanwhile, tension was exacerbated by the Tydings bill, which proposed to grant independence to Puerto Rico on terms highly disadvantageous to the island. In other incidents of January–February, police fired on rioters,

killing twenty-one and wounding over 150. As another consequence of the disorders, **Luis Muñoz Marín**, who until that time had been a chief dispenser of New Deal aid from the United States, lost much of his influence in United States political circles as a result of his refusal to condemn the Nationalists following Riggs's assassination.

February 25. **Mexico's Confederation of Mexican Workers (CTM) was founded by Vicente Lombardo Toledano**, an intellectual and socialist who enjoyed the support of President **Cárdenas**. The CTM and its rural counterpart, the National Peasant Federation (CNC), became two of the chief organizations supporting the national revolutionary party, reorganized along corporative lines in 1938 by President Cárdenas.

March 2. **The United States and Panama signed the Hull-Alfaro Treaty.** Named after Secretary of State Cordell Hull and the Panamanian foreign minister, Ricardo Alfaro, the treaty ended the United States protectorate over Panama, increased the annual payment to $436,000, and limited sales in Canal Zone commissaries to canal employees and their families. Another convention signed in 1936 provided for construction of a trans-isthmian highway. The U.S. War Department opposed both treaties, and they were not ratified by the U.S. Senate until 1939.

April 15. **The Honduran constitution was amended in order to allow President Tiburcio Carías to extend his term of office until 1943.**

May. **Dominican dictator Rafael L. Trujillo renamed the national capital Ciudad Trujillo.**

May 8. **Moderate León Cortés Castro became Costa Rica's president.** He had been elected on a platform stressing friendship with Germany (the greatest purchaser of Costa Rican coffee) but opposition to fascism. Neither the profascist Nationalist party nor the Communist party mounted a significant electoral challenge.

June 6. **Nicaraguan president Juan Bautista Sacasa resigned** in the face of national economic difficulties and a skillful campaign of opposition by **Anastasio Somoza**, leader of the

National Guard. An interim president was named, and national elections were scheduled for December 1936.

June 7. **Juan D. Arosemena was elected Panamanian president** following an electoral campaign tainted by fraud and violence. The hand-picked candidate of outgoing president Harmodio Arias, Arosemena continued the nationalistic and populist policies of Arias.

1937

January 1. **Having won the Nicaraguan presidential election the previous month, Anastasio Somoza García assumed office.** He would go on to dominate Nicaraguan life in dictatorial fashion until his assassination nineteen years later.

March 21. **The Palm Sunday Massacre took place in Ponce, Puerto Rico.** Shots were fired as Nationalists paraded in the city, leaving seventeen dead. Two policemen were also killed. It was unclear who fired the first shot, but the American Civil Liberties Union later blamed the violence on Nationalist fanaticism and extreme police brutality.

May 28. **Seventeen thousand Mexican oil workers struck,** demanding of the foreign-owned companies that employed them higher wages, better living and working conditions, and more social services. They returned to work in June, and two months later the nation's Labor Board found their demands meritorious, a finding later supported by the nation's supreme court. The oil companies refused the workers' demands, arguing both that they were excessive and that the Supreme Court decision supporting them was prejudicial.

June 23. **Mexico nationalized its railway system,** partially in response to strikes that had plagued national railroads over the previous two years. On May 1, 1938, President **Lázaro Cárdenas** placed the rail system under workers' control.

October 4. **Dominican dictator Rafael Trujillo "de-Africanized" the western portion of his country by slaughtering some 18,000 Haitians who had moved there.** The massacre was condemned throughout the Americas, and

moved Haitian president Sténio Vincent to request mediation by the United States. The Dominican Republic accepted responsibility for the atrocity and eventually (February 1938) agreed to pay $750,000 in compensation to families of the victims.

1938

January 19. **Mexico took measures to promote industry by increasing tariff rates to 200 percent on some imported products.**

March 18. **Mexico nationalized the holdings of seventeen foreign oil companies.** While President **Cárdenas,** who had signed the nationalization decree, was vilified in the United States and in Europe, he was supported by other Latin American leaders. Mexicans lionized him for standing up to the foreign-dominated oil industry. The United States government acknowledged Mexico's right to expropriate the industry, but demanded that the oil companies be compensated. After negotiations, in 1941 the American companies accepted a valuation of approximately $24 million plus interest. The expropriation led to a rupture of diplomatic relations between Mexico and Great Britain. When relations were restored in 1947, Mexico agreed to pay about $130 million to compensate British-owned oil companies. The expropriated properties were turned over to the state-owned Petróleos Mexicanos (PEMEX).

June. **Lázaro Cárdenas completed his reorganization of Mexico's Revolutionary party,** the PRN, along corporative lines, renaming it the Party of the Mexican Revolution (Partido de la Revolución Mexicana), or PRM. In accord with his reform, PRM members and candidates were grouped by occupation: labor, agricultural, popular, and military. While Cárdenas's successor, Manuel Ávila Camacho, removed the military from the structure of the government party, the principle of political representation by occupational corporation remained a feature of Mexican politics.

July 22. **Luis Muñoz Marín founded Puerto Rico's first modern political party, the Popular Democratic party, PPD (Partido Popular Democrático).**

1939

January 20. **El Salvador's authoritarian constitution of 1939 went into effect.** Highly statist in character, initiated by the dictator **Maximiliano Hernández Martínez**, it gave the central government the exclusive right to regulate public services, to promote small business, and to protect labor. It also granted military courts jurisdiction over civilians charged with rebellion and extended the presidential term from four to six years.

March 23. **A constituent assembly in Nicaragua approved a new constitution and re-elected Anastasio Somoza García to a second presidential term**, extending his rule to 1947.

September 16. **Mexican Conservatives Manuel Gómez Morín and Efraín González Luna founded the National Action Party, or PAN (Partido de Acción Nacional),** which went on to become the chief opposition party to the semi-official PRM.

December 23. **The Honduran parliament extended the presidency of Tiburcio Carías to 1949.**

1940

May 8. **Official candidate Rafael A. Calderón Guardia was inaugurated president of Costa Rica**, after winning 90 percent of the popular vote. The outbreak of World War II forced Calderón to break with his pro-German mentor León Cortés. Forming a popular front government with the Communists and enjoying support of the United States, he struck at Germans residing in Costa Rica. Calderón was succeeded in 1944 by his hand-picked candidate, Teodoro Picado, who went on to support the Allied war effort, enjoying the support of the Catholic Church, the Communists, and the United States. The mid-1940s was known in Costa Rica as the "era of the enemy alliances."

June 1. **Arnulfo Arias won presidential elections in Panama,** having employed violence and fraud to ensure his victory. Unseated in a coup a year later, Arias had time to impose a new constitution upon the nation.

July 1. **A Cuban constitutional convention completed work on a document that was both statist and socially progressive.** Labor, especially, benefited through provisions mandating an eight-hour work day, mandatory collective bargaining, and a minimum wage.

July 7. **Official candidate Manuel Ávila Camacho won the Mexican presidency,** handily defeating Juan Andreu Almazán, candidate of the conservative PAN party. Much more conservative than **Cárdenas**, Ávila Camacho slowed reform and strove to improve relations with the United States. He was especially active in arresting Nazi agents and sympathizers who, during the early 1940s, hoped to use Mexico as a base of operations. Ávila promoted national industrialization through the Nacional Financiera, a government-owned lending agency charged with granting loans to industry.

July 14. **Fulgencio Batista was elected Cuban president in a contest pitting him against Ramón Grau San Martín.** During his four-year term Batista sponsored a range of progressive social legislation. At the onset of World War II, he allied Cuba closely with the United States.

November 5. **Charismatic Puerto Rican leader Luis Muñoz Marín's new Popular Democratic party (PPD) made a strong showing in national elections,** going on to carry **Muñoz** into the presidency of Puerto Rico's Senate a year later.

1941

January 2. **Panamanian president Arnulfo Arias imposed a populist and racist constitution upon the nation** that at once enfranchised women and removed the rights of citizenship from West Indians and Asians. In 1941 the **Arias** administration established a social security system. In keeping with its nationalist orientation, it also introduced paper currency to replace the U.S. dollar and ordered businesses to use Spanish in their topmost signs. Widely judged to be quasi-fascist, the new charter also extended the presidential term to six years.

February 15. **By the Trujillo-Hull Treaty, the United States ceased direct collection of Dominican customs duties.** Thanks to the fact that Dominican customs were disbursed by the National City Bank of New York, that nation's debt was paid off by July 1947.

March. **Guatemalan students launched a campaign of opposition to the dictator Jorge Ubico,** going on to plot secretly against him. Among them was future president Julio César Méndez Montenegro.

May 15. **Elie Lescot was elected president of Haiti.** Unwilling to dispense patronage to members of the growing black middle class, and openly partial to the mulatto elite to which he belonged, Lescot was overthrown in a military coup in January 1946.

October 9. **Ricardo Adolfo de la Guardia, Panamanian minister of justice, deposed the president Arnulfo Arias** while the latter was visiting a mistress in Cuba, alleging that **Arias** had violated the terms of his own constitution. Arias had alienated the United States by refusing to permit the arming of Panamanian-flag vessels. He spent the remainder of World War II in exile, while de la Guardia collaborated fully with the Allied war effort.

December 10-11. **Mexico severed relations with Japan, Germany, and Italy** in response to the Japanese attack on Pearl Harbor.

1942

January. **Mexico and the United States established a Joint Defense Commission** through which the former country would assist the war effort through cooperation at the economic level.

May 28. **President Ávila Camacho informed the Mexican Congress that a "state of war" existed between Mexico and the Axis powers.** He took this action after the sinking of

two Mexican oil tankers by German submarines (May 14 and 24).

1944

March 1. **Salvadoran dictator Maximiliano Hernández Martínez instructed Congress to extend his term in office** through constitutional amendment. That action crystallized opposition against him, which culminated when a section of the officer corps staged a revolt that was subdued with difficulty by the national guard. A firing squad executed the ringleaders. His action outraged both the military and the population at large, and led to the call for a general strike on May 5. The strike produced the resignation of Hernández Martínez in favor of his colleague General Andrés I. Menéndez. The fall of Hernández Martínez ushered in a period of greater political openness.

June 1. **Ramón Grau San Martín was elected president of Cuba** to the delight of most voters who anticipated that he would provide them an enlightened, progressive administration. Sadly, **Grau**'s term was both corrupt and repressive, as was that of his successor Carlos Prío Socarrás (1948-52). Cuban disillusionment was personified by Eduardo Chibás, a former supporter of Grau. In 1947 he broke with Grau, going on to lead opposition to the Authentic party of Grau and Prío Socarrás. When Chibás committed suicide (August 5, 1951), a power vacuum was created that helped bring the 1952 coup of **Fulgencio Batista**.

June 22. **Accusing university students of promoting Nazi-fascist ideas, Guatemalan dictator Ubico withdrew constitutional guarantees and tightened military rule over the country.** That touched off a series of strikes that in turn led to secret formation of the National Renovation party (PRN). When railroad workers paralyzed transportation on June 21, the ailing Ubico announced his intention to yield power to a military triumvirate headed by Federico Ponce. **Ubico** departed Guatemala on July 1.

August. **Guatemalan leftists formed the Confederation of Guatemalan Workers (CTG),** which by 1950 dominated all other labor organizations in the country.

August 4. **An agreement was signed authorizing the temporary emigration of Mexican agricultural workers to the United States.** The U.S. Farm Security Administration contracted for the workers, who were given guarantees regarding wages and working conditions. About 200,000 of these *braceros* were employed in the United States during World War II.

October 20. **Violence instigated by Guatemalan junta leader Federico Ponce touched off an uprising that returned popular government to the country.** Students supported by younger military officers, among them **Captain Jacobo Arbenz Guzmán**, seized control of the capital and, with the help of the foreign diplomatic corps, formed a civil-military junta. The junta ruled until March 1945 when elected president **Juan José Arévalo** assumed office.

October 21. **Members of the Salvadoran military fired on students celebrating the recent overthrow of Guatemalan dictator Ubico.** That produced a preemptive coup against President Menéndez by General Osmin Aguirre. Aguirre went on to vigorously repress civil dissent, ultimately imposing a military candidate of his own choosing for the upcoming January 1945 presidential election.

November 7. **Puerto Rico's Popular Democratic party (PPD) swept elections on the island**, thus becoming its principal political party. Four years later it conveyed its founder and president, **Luis Muñoz Marín,** into the governorship of the island.

December 15. **Juan José Arévalo was elected president of Guatemala**. Arévalo was a socialist who promised a regime of psychological and moral liberation for his country.

1945

Guatemala's liberal constitution of 1945 took effect. The document was modeled on the Mexican constitution of 1917.

January 14-16. **Presidential elections in El Salvador gave victory to General Salvador Castañeda Castro, friend of the recently deposed dictator Maximiliano Hernández Martínez.** Castañeda presided over four years marked by pervasive anticommunism amid economic recovery founded in the rebound of coffee prices.

June 15. **Enrique Adolfo Jiménez was inaugurated president of Panama**, and immediately faced opposition from **Arnulfo Arias**, whose unsuccessful coup attempt (December 1945) earned him a one-year prison term. Meanwhile a constituent assembly drafted a new constitution returning the presidential term to four years, mandating progressive social and labor provisions, and emphasizing racial justice.

1946

January 11. **A Haitian military triumvirate headed by Paul Magloire ended the presidency of Elie Lescot,** ushering in a period of intense political activity during which the black majority seized political control from the mulatto minority. Dumarsais Estimé was elected president in May 1946.

July 7. **Miguel Alemán was elected president of Mexico.** Alemán vigorously continued his predecessors' promotion of industrialization even as he took steps to increase agricultural production. He changed the name of the semi-official government party to the Institutional Revolutionary party, or PRI (Partido Revolucionario Institucional). Yet another of his projects was construction of a new national university on the outskirts of Mexico City. His last years in office were plagued by well-substantiated charges that he, family members, and friends had helped themselves to public funds.

1947

February 2. **Leonardo Argüello was elected Nicaraguan president to succeed Anastasio Somoza.** But on May 26, **Somoza** removed Argüello, who had attempted to weaken Somoza's power base in the National Guard. The dictator installed his aged uncle, Victor Román y Reyes, as interim president, a move that angered U.S. president Truman. The United States did not recognize the government of Román y Reyes until April 30, 1948. By that date Costa Rica and several other Latin American nations had already done so.

December 16. **Guatemalan president Arévalo and Costa Rican dissident José Figueres signed the "Caribbean Pact,"** whose stated goals were overthrowing dictatorial government in Central America and creating a democratic union of Central American states, and whose implicit goal was to unite the region under Guatemalan leadership.

1948

February 11. **The Communist party was outlawed in Haiti,** as the government of Dumarsais Estimé took increasingly repressive measures against all opponents of his regime. In order to foster nonradical and *"folkorique"* social movements, Estimé drew upon the services of **François Duvalier,** his secretary of state for labor and public health. Along with writer Lorimer Denis, a founder of the Afrocentric Griots group, Duvalier worked to cultivate a more sympathetic approach to the Vodun religion, arguing that Vodun was the highest expression of Haitian spirituality.

March 1. **Costa Rica's Congress annulled the February 8 presidential election,** which was won by antigovernment candidate Otilio Ulate Blanco over the official candidate Rafael A. Calderón Guardia. Ulate was the candidate of a moderate coalition opposing the leftist Calderón.

March 11. **Revolution erupted in Costa Rica** in response to annulment of the recent presidential election. Planter and politician **José Figueres Ferrer** headed the uprising, which by early April had surrounded the national capital.

April 19. **José Figueres emerged as leader of Costa Rica's ruling junta,** which replaced President Teodoro Picado. The transition of power followed a brief civil war in which **Figue-** res's forces were joined by troops associated with the Caribbean Legion. The junta, deemed that of the "Second Republic," ruled until November 1949. During its time in power the junta replaced the national army with a civil guard, outlawed the Communist party, and moved to promote the development of power resources. Most important of the junta's actions was its calling of the plebiscite through which Costa Rica's constitution of 1949 was drafted. A rigorously democratic document, it enfranchised women and established an electoral tribunal as a fourth branch of government. The document had a social democratic and statist thrust, declaring the social function of property, nationalizing the banking system, and allowing state intervention in the economy.

May 9. **Panamanian elections pitted Arnulfo Arias against Domingo Díaz Arosemena.** Díaz won the contest, whose outcome was powerfully influenced by chief of the National Police, **José Antonio Remón.** Thus the National Police consolidated its role as arbiter of civilian politics during the 1940s and afterward.

October 10. **Juan Manuel Gálvez, handpicked candidate of Honduran caudillo Tiburcio Carías, won a six-year presidential term.** While **Carías** continued to maintain an active role in politics, Gálvez exercised a degree of autonomy while in the presidency. He undertook a series of modernization measures financed through the nation's first taxes on income and upon the fruit companies, Honduras's largest industries.

October 10. **Carlos Prío Socarrás was inaugurated president of Cuba,** going on to serve an undistinguished four-year term. While subject to charges of ineptitude, Prío did manage to reduce the corruption that had become rampant under his predecessor, **Grau San Martín.**

November 2. **Luis Muñoz Marín was elected Puerto Rico's governor.** Muñoz, who dominated the island's politics until the 1960s, announced his "Operation Bootstrap" program, aimed at industrializing the island, in his inaugural address. Favoring commonwealth status for Puerto Rico, rather than outright independence from the United States, Muñoz played a key role in ensuring that the island would retain organic ties with the United States

December 10. **Costa Rican exiles under the command of dissident Rafael Calderón, supported by Nicaraguan dictator Anastasio Somoza,** invaded Costa Rica from Nicaragua. Failing to defeat forces supporting the junta headed by **José Figueres**, the forces withdrew and Calderón exiled himself to Mexico.

December 14. **Salvadoran president Salvador Castañeda was overthrown in "the majors' coup"** by younger officers angered by the president's personalism and inattention to military prerogatives. The principal figure in the coup, Colonel Oscar Osorio, went on to form a semi-official and military-dominated Revolutionary Party of Democratic Unification (PRUD), which strove to lessen the repressiveness of earlier military regimes. The PRUD, and its attending military junta, led by Oscar Osorio, dominated Salvadoran politics for the ensuing decade.

1949

July 18. **Colonel Francisco Arana was assassinated in Guatemala.** Arana's death was part of a struggle within the military pitting conservative supporters of the old regime against a left-leaning faction whose most prominent member was Minister of Defense **Jacobo Arbenz Guzmán.** Arana's death touched off a military revolt--the twentieth in **Arévalo**'s administration--but it was quickly suppressed by loyal forces.

September 28. **Guatemala's Communist party was founded.** The clandestine party grew out of an earlier organization, the Guatemalan Democratic Vanguard, formed in 1947. The party was renamed the Guatemalan Labor party (Partido Guatemalteco del Trabajo, PGT) in December 1952, shortly before it was legalized.

November 8. **Costa Rican president Otilio Ulate Blanco took office**, as the nation returned to civilian rule following eighteen months under leadership of a revolutionary junta. He instituted a program of fiscal austerity while implementing significant reforms. Notable among them was establishment of a state-owned banking system. A

strong anticommunist, he ruthlessly impeded leftist organization of working-class groups.

November 25. **The illness of Domingo Díaz Arosemena produced a period of political confusion that ultimately returned Arnulfo Arias to the presidency of Panama.** Arias's autocratic and often violent second term, along with his attempt to reinstate the racist 1941 constitution (May 1951), led to his removal from office through impeachment.

1950

May 10. **Haitian president Dumarsais Estimé was overthrown by a military coup led by Colonel Paul Magloire** in a last-ditch attempt of the nation's elite to maintain control over the black majority. Magloire served in a desultory fashion until overthrown six years later.

May 21. **Anastasio Somoza García returned to the Nicaraguan presidency.** His rule of the country assured, **Somoza** bent to the task of national modernization. Nicaragua's economy had remained stagnant until mid-century, its real GDP per capita the second lowest in Latin America. Somoza encouraged agro-exports, especially cattle and cotton, to the effect that between 1949 and 1970 the economy grew faster than that of any other nation in Central America. Rewards of the economic transformation were unevenly distributed, with members of the Somoza family, their friends and associates benefiting disproportionately.

July 3. **The U.S. Congress approved Public Law 600, laying the foundation for a new Puerto Rican government.** The law was adopted "in the nature of a compact," so that Puerto Ricans might draft a constitution and establish a government of their own choosing. Despite the opposition of independence supporters, the law was approved in a referendum on August 3, 1950. Nationalist violence, including an attempt to assassinate President Truman on November 2, 1950, led to the jailing of Pedro Albizú Campos.

November 10-12. **Jacobo Arbenz Guzmán was elected president of Guatemala**, handily defeating Miguel Ydígoras Fuentes, who had served as public works director under **Jorge Ubico**.

1951

May 10. **Rioting in Panama led to the ouster of Arnulfo Arias,** who was attacked after voiding the constitution of 1946 and reinstating the 1941 charter. On May 25 the National Assembly convicted him of abuse of power.

June. **Central American delegates to the fourth meeting of the U.N. Economic Commission for Latin America (ECLA) proposed the integration of the Central American economies.** Between 1952 and 1958, plans were made to implement the proposal. A treaty calling for the gradual establishment of a Central American common market was signed in 1958 by Guatemala, El Salvador, Honduras, and Nicaragua. The agreement was operationalized two years later.

1952

March 3. **Puerto Ricans, by popular vote, ratified their first constitution.** Subsequently, on approval of the U.S. Congress, the island's governor, **Luis Muñoz Marín**, declared Puerto Rico to be a state in free association with the United States (an *estado libre asociado*), meaning that it would be fully autonomous in internal affairs, but would share citizenship with the United States

March 10. **Cuban army commander Fulgencio Batista overthrew President Prío Socarrás,** going on to rule the island in an increasingly despotic way for the following seven years. Under his administration Cuba became the vacation mecca for tens of thousands of American tourists, while sugar, most of which was destined for the United States market, earned 70 percent of export revenue. **Batista** and his clique benefited disproportionately from the economic boom amid growing anger over his venality and arbitrariness.

May 11. **Former national police chief José A. Remón won the Panamanian presidential election** with about half the votes cast, though the opposition charged fraud. During his administration the Colón Free Zone was created, and the National Police was strengthened and converted into a quasi-military National Guard. **Remón**'s principal achievement was negotiating a new canal treaty with the United States.

June 27. **Guatemalan president Arbenz signed an agrarian reform law** aimed at redressing the nation's highly regressive pattern of land tenure. Among the lands targeted for expropriation were 15 percent of the 1.6 million acres (650,000 hectares) owned by the United Fruit Company. The legislation was criticized by members of the Guatemalan elite, who pointed to it as proof of the president's radicalism. The U.S. government also viewed the reform as pernicious, for it was applauded by Guatemalan communists.

July 6. **Adolfo Ruiz Cortines was elected president of Mexico.** Staid candidate of the semi-official PRI, Ruiz provided prudent and honest leadership during his six years in office. He attempted to restrain government spending and, while he devalued the peso in early 1954, was praised for his handling of the national economy.

1953

February 25. **The Guatemalan government informed the United Fruit Company of a plan to expropriate, with compensation, 15 percent of its landholdings,** or about 247,000 acres (100,000 hectares). That action, along with evidence of growing communist influence in the government of **Jacobo Arbenz**, led the United States, through its recently established Central Intelligence Agency (CIA), to initiate plans to overthrow Arbenz. By late 1953 the CIA had denominated its anti-Arbenz campaign "Operation Success."

July 26. **Cuban opponents of Batista, led by Fidel and Raúl Castro, failed to seize the Moncada army barracks in Santiago.** Just 61 of some 170 rebels survived the attack, among them the Castro brothers. At his trial, **Fidel Castro** delivered a lengthy defense that he closed promising "History will absolve me." He served a nineteen-month prison term and was freed May 15, 1955.

July 26. **Women voted for the first time in the Costa Rican presidential contest won by José Figueres**, leader of the new social democratic National Liberation Party (PLN). Figueres was an activist president who raised taxes in order to fund social programs, implemented protective tariffs to encourage small industries, promoted legislation improving labor benefits, and provided for state ownership and management of the social service program of the United Fruit Company. While the economy boomed and diversified under Figueres's administration, his ambitious programs made him subject to charges of corruption as well as to accusations that he was a socialist.

1954

January 29. **The Guatemalan government charged Nicaragua and other Latin American states with planning an invasion of the country.** At that moment, the exiles Carlos Castillo Armas and Miguel Ydígoras were in fact planning an invasion of Guatemala from Honduras.

April. **Honduran banana workers went on strike against the United Fruit Company.** Communists were blamed for instigating the strike, as the banned Honduran Communist party had been revived just days earlier. President Juan Manuel Gálvez arrested the strike leaders and forced workers to elect more moderate representatives. Gálvez, now siding with the workers, forced United Fruit to agree to raise the wages of its Honduran workers (July 9).

June 18. **Carlos Castillo Armas and Miguel Ydígoras Fuentes launched an invasion of Guatemala.** Armed in part by the Central Intelligence Agency, they met only light resistance from a national army that refused to defend the Arbenz regime. On June 27, Arbenz resigned his presidency and fled the country.

July 8. **Carlos Castillo Armas became head of the military junta named to rule Guatemala.** A subsequent plebiscite (October 1954) formalized his rule, which continued until his assassination in 1957.

August 10. **Guatemalan President Castillo Armas issued a "political statute"** authorizing military rule of the country, abolished the liberal 1945 constitution, outlawed the Communist party, and banned all printed matter deemed subversive. While the new government did not repeal all of the progressive social legislation of the previous ten years, it in effect restored to power and protected coffee planters and other landholders, as well as foreign capitalists and their subsidiaries.

November 1. **Fulgencio Batista was elected president of Cuba.** His only opponent, former president **Ramón Grau San Martín**, had withdrawn from the contest, protesting that the election was rigged.

December 6. **Julio Lozano Díaz assumed dictatorial power in Honduras.** He took this action amid efforts in Congress to block the accession of Liberal Ramón Villeda Morales, who had won a plurality of the vote in recent elections.

1955

January. **Costa Rican dissident Rafael Calderón Guardia, in exile since his abortive invasion of 1948**, again entered national territory from neighboring Nicaragua in an effort to unseat his enemy, President **José Figueres**. Again he was supported by Nicaraguan dictator **Anastasio Somoza**. As had been the case seven years earlier, the invasion was abortive, serving only to enhance the image of Figueres, who prevailed upon the Organization of American States to establish a buffer zone between Costa Rica and Nicaragua.

January 25. **The Eisenhower-Remón Treaty was signed.** In addition to increasing the annuity paid by the United States to Panama to $1,930,000, the treaty made several concessions relating to the Canal Zone and canal employment. For example, Panama gained the right to tax the income of Canal Zone employees who were Panamanian citizens. In addition, a memorandum attached to the treaty stated that the United States would seek equal pay scales for U.S. and Panamanian employees in the Canal Zone and offer equal employment opportunities in the zone. Shortly before the signing of the treaty, President **Remón** was assassinated in the city of Panama (January 2, 1955).

July 7. **Freed from prison the previous May, Fidel Castro departed Cuba for Mexico,** where he organized a revolutionary movement in association with **Ernesto "Che" Guevara** and others.

August. **The Organization of Central American States (ODECA) was formalized.** Originating in an October 1951 meeting of Central American ministers, the body went on to establish, in 1958, the Central American Common Market (CACM), in collaboration with the U.N. Economic Commission for Latin America (ECLA).

1956

March 4. **José María Lemus was elected to a six-year presidential term in El Salvador.** An associate of the military junta leader Oscar Osorio, Lemus took advantage of high coffee prices and a buoyant economy to relax controls that the military had long imposed upon the civilian population. His presidency ended on an unsuccessful note, when the declaration of martial law in early 1960 resulted in his overthrow in October 1960.

September 21-29. **Nicaraguan dictator Anastasio Somoza García was assassinated** following his indication that he intended to extend his presidency. Somoza was shot in León, Nicaragua, and died a week later at a hospital in the Panama Canal Zone. Control of the nation by the Somoza family continued, however, when sons of the murdered dictator, Luis and Anastasio, took over as acting president and commander of the National Guard, respectively.

October 1. **Ernesto de la Guardia took office as president of Panama.** De la Guardia's four-year term was marked by increasing turbulence as anti-U.S. sentiment escalated.

October 21. **A bloodless coup forced Honduras's authoritarian president Julio Lozano from office.** A day later all political factions endorsed a caretaker military junta that governed until a constituent assembly was elected the following year.

November 25. **Fidel Castro, Che Guevara, and seventy-nine colleagues departed Mexico, launching their invasion of Cuba.** Traveling from Yucatán, Mexico, in the ship *Granma*, they were engaged by troops of **Fulgencio Batista.** Sixty-nine of the attackers died, but those who survived, including Fidel and Raúl Castro and Ernesto "Che" Guevara, fought their way to safety (December 1) in the Sierra Maestra mountains, in eastern Cuba.

December 12. **Haiti's military command staged a coup against the unpopular Paul Magloire.** A period of political turmoil ensued, during which a number of leaders, both civilian and military occupied the presidency. At length, elections were held (September 1957) and **François Duvalier** was elected.

1957

January-May. **Fidel Castro and his followers strengthened their guerrilla force in the mountains of eastern Cuba.** During January and May Castro's troops won victories against members of the Rural Guard. Meanwhile, *New York Times* correspondent Herbert L. Matthews reached **Castro** and reported favorably on the revolutionaries. With the help of Matthews, Castro appealed to the United States (May 20) to cease supplying armaments to the **Batista** dictatorship.

February. **Luis Somoza Debayle formalized his presidency in Nicaragua** through an election that was widely regarded as fraudulent. Opposition leaders imprisoned prior to the election included newspaper editor Pedro Joaquín Chamorro. In spite of the inauspicious beginning of his regime, Luis Somoza presided over a relatively benign period in national history. During his six-year term (1957-63) the economy prospered and free speech was protected for the most part.

July 26. **Guatemalan president Carlos Castillo Armas was assassinated,** ushering in a period of political turmoil. At length the army stepped in and organized elections for January 1958. Castillo's co-conspirator in the 1954 coup against **Jacobo Arbenz**, Miguel Ydígoras Fuentes, won that contest.

September 22. **A Honduran constituent assembly was elected in which the followers of Liberal party leader Ramón Villeda Morales won a majority.** Chosen as president the following November, Villeda went on to supervise the drafting of a new constitution that granted both a high degree of autonomy for the military and the right of the military to intervene in politics in the event of a constitutional crisis. Villeda Morales presided over continued economic modernization in Honduras, featuring rapid growth in manufacturing. His tenure was interrupted in 1963, when the armed forces stepped in to replace him.

October 22. **François Duvalier was inaugurated president of Haiti.** He went on to establish a tyranny over the island, remaining in power until his death in 1971. While his politics were populist in style, **Duvalier** did little to improve the lot of the masses.

1958

March–April. **The revolutionary struggle in Cuba intensified** when in March the United States suspended arms shipments to the government of **Fulgencio Batista** and, on the seventeenth of that month, **Fidel Castro** proclaimed "total war" against the island's government. Meanwhile Castro's forces established revolutionary fronts in numerous parts of the island. With suspension of arms to the Cuban army, its loyalty to Batista lessened. Revolutionary sentiment increased throughout the island.

March 2. **Miguel Ydígoras Fuentes was inaugurated president of Guatemala.** He governed the country until removed from office in a military coup of March 31, 1963.

May 8. **Conservative Mario Echandi Jiménez was inaugurated president of Costa Rica,** replacing liberal **José Figueres.** The alternation in office between conservatives and liberals continued, with liberal Francisco José Orlich, representing the National Liberation party, winning in 1962, and conservative José Joaquín

Trejos, of the National Union party, winning the 1966 contest.

July 6. **Adolfo López Mateos, candidate of the semi-official PRI, was elected president of Mexico** with some 90 percent of the popular vote.

December 9. **Cuban dictator Batista refused to step down in favor of a caretaker regime.** Former U.S. ambassador William D. Pawley had, in a meeting with **Batista**, offered the dictator safe haven in the United States in exchange for Batista's resignation.

December 31. **Fulgencio Batista fled Havana in the face of a generalized advance of revolutionary forces headed by Fidel Castro.**

1959

January 1-3. **Revolutionary forces under the command of Fidel Castro secured control of Cuba.**

February–March. **Striking railway workers were severely repressed by the Mexican government.** Thousands of strikers were arrested, and their leader, Demetrio Vallejo, was sentenced to a long prison term. Suppression of the strike issued in a period of relative calm in Mexico, as the interests of major social groups were successfully reconciled at high political levels.

February 16. **Fidel Castro assumed office as Cuban prime minister, following the resignation of José Miró Cardona.** The first postrevolutionary Cuban president was Manuel Urrutia. After Urrutia was forced to resign in July 1959, Osvaldo Dórticos Torrado assumed the presidency, a largely ceremonial post, which he held until 1976. Meanwhile, military trials of **Batista** supporters had begun. Approximately 600 prisoners had been executed by the time the trials ceased in May 1959.

February 19-20. **Mexican president López Mateos and U.S. president Eisenhower met to finalize arrangements for construction of the Amistad dam** on the Rio Grande near Ciudad Acuña, Coahuila, and Del Rio, Texas.

April 15. **Fidel Castro visited the United States.** During his trip he assured Americans that his revolution was not communist. The failure of President Eisenhower to meet with Castro and the fact that the United States did not offer economic aid are sometimes said to have intensified Castro's anti-Americanism.

April 24. **Armed Cubans and Panamanians staged an abortive invasion of Panama.** The small force was organized by Roberto (Tito) Arias, son of former president Harmodio Arias. It surrendered one week after reaching Panama.

May 17. **An agrarian reform law was promulgated in Cuba.** It provided for the expropriation of landholdings in excess of 30 *caballerías* (approximately 1,000 acres). Nearly all of the land seized was converted to state farms.

June. **Dominican exiles invaded their country in an attempt to unseat the dictator Rafael L. Trujillo.** Sponsored by **Fidel Castro**, the invaders were easily defeated by the Dominican army. Yet the expedition set into motion sympathetic movements that Trujillo crushed with utmost severity.

July 12. **Honduras's National Police were unsuccessful in their attempt to overthrow Liberal president Ramón Villeda Morales.** Right-wing elements in the police force believed that Villeda was not vigorous enough in his control of domestic leftists. Villeda responded by organizing a Civil Guard subject to presidential control. That body soon found itself clashing with the police and the army, a fact contributing to Villeda's overthrow (October 1963).

October 19. **Cuban revolutionary leader Huber Matos resigned as military commander of Camagüey province,** warning **Fidel Castro** of a "communist problem" within the 26 of July Movement that had unseated **Fulgencio Batista**. The following day Castro arrested Matos, imprisoning him for the next two decades. By late November most liberals and moderates had resigned their leadership positions in Castro's government. These events marked the turning point in Cuban internal and international politics.

November 3. **Rioting ensued after Panamanian students entered the Canal Zone to raise the Panamanian flag there.** On December 1, President Eisenhower stated that there should be some "visual evidence of [Panama's] titular sovereignty" over the zone, but it was not until September 1960 that he announced that the two flags would fly together in one place in the zone.

Bolivarian Republics: Bolivia, Colombia, Ecuador, Peru, Venezuela

The quality of life in the Bolivarian republics improved dramatically between 1930 and 1960, continuing the trend of the first three decades of the century. Life expectancy increased as levels of infant mortality declined, literacy rose and diet improved, all in rhythm with rising rates of urbanization. By the seventh decade of the twentieth century Colombia and Venezuela were 50 percent urban. In Ecuador, Peru, and Bolivia some 40 percent of the citizenry lived in towns and cities.

The movement from countryside to city was in part a consequence of government development policy. In 1930, each of the Bolivarian republics was heavily dependent upon revenues earned through the sale of minerals and agro-exports on world markets. When those markets collapsed during the Great Depression, and when flows of international trade were interrupted by World War II, Andean leaders erected protective tariffs and encouraged import substitution. Factories dedicated to the manufacture of textiles and other consumer goods proliferated, drawing increasing numbers of rural dwellers to higher-paying jobs.

As economies diversified and as populations became more urbanized, Andean peoples grew increasingly aware of the world beyond their mountains. Modernization and its appurtenances gave international events an immediacy that could not but impinge on national affairs. Populations once accepting of traditional, frequently authoritarian governance began demanding a more meaningful role in politics. Struggles for political power, often violent ones, were thus characteristic of the 1930-59 interval in Andean America.

Three international conflicts troubled the Bolivarian nations during the middle decades of the twentieth century. In 1932, Peru and Colombia clashed briefly over possession of the Amazonian village of Leticia. That same year Bolivia engaged Paraguay in the destructive Chaco War. Early in the following decade Peru made good on its long-standing threat to seize Amazon territory claimed by neighboring Ecuador.

During the interval between 1930 and 1959, the United States powerfully influenced foreign policies of the Bolivarian nations. United States influence, seconded by an essential like-mindedness concerning Axis aggression, combined to make the Andean nations and the Americans close allies during the Second World War. While Bolivarian leaders were less receptive to U.S. leadership during early years of the Cold War, they became more so as **Fidel Castro's** success heartened and invigorated the anti-establishment.

1930

January 30. **Colombian elections brought that nation's Liberal party to power for the first time in forty-eight years.** Triumphing over a divided Conservative party, Liberal president Enrique Olaya Herrera went on to grapple with depression-induced difficulties. The triumphant Liberals promised to speed modernization and reduce influence of the church. Olaya's chief task was coping with falling government revenues and sharply increased rates of unemployment produced by the global depression. His task became easier when the Leticia War (1932-33) allowed him to stimulate the economy through extraordinary military spending.

May 28. **A military coup toppled Bolivian president Hernando Siles,** who had tried to extend his term by reason of the depression-induced economic crisis. A caretaker government presided until national elections (January 1931) brought conservative Daniel Salamanca to the presidency.

August 25. **Peru's modernizing but corrupt and dictatorial President Augusto Leguía** was overthrown by Colonel Luis Sánchez Cerro. Fourteen months of political turmoil followed; at the end of that period Sánchez Cerro was elected president in an election that many said was fraudulent (October 11, 1931). Sánchez defeated **Víctor Raúl Haya de la Torre,** leader of the radical APRA (Alianza Popular Revolucionaria Americana) party.

1931

March 5. **Daniel Salamanca was inaugurated president of Bolivia** amid social unrest and economic crisis caused by collapsing tin prices.

August 25. **Ecuador's president Isidro Ayora resigned and fled the depression-racked nation.** Economic hardship and political turbulence moved apace for the next two years, at one point causing the savagely fought Four Days' War (August 28-31, 1932) between factions of the Liberal and Conservative parties. The bloodshed moved Liberals and Conservatives to agree on a series of transitional presidents and, ultimately, a presidential election (December 1933). That contest, won by the charismatic **José María Velasco Ibarra,** resulted in a regime that did not last a year. Taking office September 1934, Velasco declared himself dictator eleven months later, claiming that a Liberal-socialist bloc in Congress had hobbled his government. The military responded by overthrowing Velasco (August 21, 1935) and ruling until it handed power to a constituent assembly in mid-1938.

1932

June 15. **Bolivian forces occupied a Paraguayan military outpost, or *fortín*, at Lake Pitiantuta in the Chaco region disputed by Bolivia and Paraguay.** The Paraguayans recovered the outpost in mid-July, and Bolivian retaliation touched off the Chaco War, a bloody conflict lasting three years and costing some 50,000 Bolivian and 35,000 Paraguayan lives. Bolivia was labeled aggressor in the conflict that eventually led to the overthrow of President Daniel

Salamanca (November 1934) and a cease-fire (June 1935). While the war was exceedingly destructive to the interests of both countries, which it nearly bankrupted, it was especially so for Bolivia, which lost most of the Gran Chaco and suffered long-term political instability as a result of its military humiliation.

July. **Violence erupted in Trujillo, Peru.** On July 7, Apristas captured the city of Trujillo on Peru's northern coast, long an Aprista stronghold. As the armed forces fought successfully to retake the city a few days later, Aprista militants killed several dozen military prisoners. In reprisal the armed forces executed hundreds of Apristas suspected of taking part in the uprising. This episode is often seen as having created bitter enmity between the Peruvian military and the Aprista party.

September 1. **Peruvians seized the village of Leticia in the Colombian Amazon,** touching off the Leticia War. The Peruvian aggressors, sponsored by rubber and sugar entrepreneurs who had lost land in territory ceded to Colombia, were supported by President Sánchez Cerro. While the war caused an outpouring of patriotic fervor in Colombia, it did little to arouse the Peruvian citizenry. In February 1933 a Colombian naval expedition moved against the Peruvian forces. Two months later (April 30) Sánchez Cerro was assassinated by an Aprista.

1933

April 30. **Oscar Benavides assumed the presidency of Peru following the assassination of Luis Sánchez Cerro.** Benavides, who had served as Peru's president during 1914-15, continued his predecessor's struggle against the mass-based APRA party of **Víctor Raúl Haya de la Torre.** Combining repression with paternalism, Benavides sponsored social legislation through the Ministry of Welfare, established in 1935. He also returned Leticia to Colombia. When his candidate failed to win the presidency in 1936, Benavides extended his term until 1939.

1934

August 7. **Liberal Alfonso López Pumarejo was inaugurated president of Colombia,** characterizing his regime as one of "Revolution on the March." At the center of the **López** reforms stood an agrarian reform law featuring forced government purchase of large estates and a loan program allowing tenant farmers to purchase small farms. López also increased public spending on health and education, and encouraged organized labor. In addition, the constitution was amended (1936) to allow universal male suffrage, limit property rights, and reduce the role of the Catholic Church in public education. His actions split the Liberal party and alienated Conservatives.

November 27. **Bolivian president Daniel Salamanca was placed under arrest** by a rebellious military high command, moving the deposed president to remark that it was the first military operation they had carried out successfully. Salamanca was replaced by his vice president, José Luis Tejada Sorzano, who ruled until his own resignation in March 1936.

1935

June 12. **The Chaco War ended when Bolivia and Paraguay agreed to a cease-fire.** At that moment both nations were near bankruptcy, their internal politics in disarray. The final peace effected three years later left Paraguay in possession of most of the disputed territory, which was discovered not to contain valuable hydrocarbons.

December 17. **The death of Venezuelan president Juan Vicente Gómez** brought to the fore his minister of war, Eleázar López Contreras, who served as president until 1941. López kept tight rein on the army, as well as upon labor and incipient political parties, while spending monies earned through petroleum exports on social programs.

1936

May 17. **Bolivian president Luis Tejada resigned in the face of a general strike.** The strikers subsequently supported a military junta headed by Colonel David Toro, which agreed to meet labor demands. Toro, announcing his creation of a "socialist republic," created a Department of Labor, effected a minimum wage, and nationalized the holdings of Standard Oil.

1937

July 13. **Bolivian junta leader David Toro was replaced by Lieutenant Colonel Germán Busch**, a hero of the Chaco War. A man of humble origins, Busch was lionized by the common people, who regarded him as the leader most likely to prevail against powerful mining interests.

1938

June–October. **Clashes along the Peruvian-Ecuadorian border** led the latter nation to request mediation of the conflict by other Latin American states. The Peruvian incursions were in part a function of political turbulence in Ecuador. From August 1938, when President Alberto Enríquez transferred power to Manuel María Borrero, to June 1940, Ecuador had four chief executives.

July 21. **The signing of an agreement formally establishing peace between Bolivia and Paraguay** brought the Chaco War to a definitive end.

August 7. **Liberal Eduardo Santos was inaugurated president of Colombia.** Representing the moderate wing of his nation's dominant party, Santos went on to slow the reform initiated by his predecessor, **Alfonso López.**

1939

January 8. **Liberal police in Colombia fired on a Conservative political rally in the village of Gachetá.** The Gachetá Massacre, as it came to be known, resulted in seventeen deaths. More importantly, it led Conservative opposition leader **Laureano Gómez** to announce a policy of "Intrepid Action," under which Conservative civilians would arm themselves against the police, most of whom were Liberals.

April 24. **Bolivian president Germán Busch declared himself dictator** and proceeded to

govern the nation by decree. Two months later he attacked the mining companies, ordering them to deposit their earnings in the Central Bank, which Busch had recently placed under state control. Drafted without prior consultation, the president's decree proved unworkable. Busch committed suicide August 23, 1939, and was succeeded by General Carlos Quintanilla, representing a more conservative faction of the Bolivian military.

October 22. **Manuel Prado y Ugarteche was elected Peru's president.** Prado, the handpicked candidate of outgoing president Oscar Benavides, went on to serve a six-year term during which modernization picked up thanks to a strengthening economy. World War II brought heightened demand for Peruvian raw materials. The most notable achievement of Prado's first term was his building of schools throughout the Peruvian Sierra.

1940

January 11. **Carlos Arroyo del Río was elected Ecuador's president**, defeating Conservative Jacinto Jijón y Caamaño and **José María Velasco Ibarra**. Within a year of taking office Arroyo was forced to cope with a Peruvian attack (May 1941) that ultimately cost Ecuador half of its national domain.

1941

January 25. **Bolivian politician Víctor Paz Estenssoro founded the MNR (Movimiento Nacional Revolucionario),** which would, over the ensuing decade, lead a successful campaign to lessen the power of the nation's tin mining companies. **Paz** is believed to have authored the abortive 1939 decree requiring mining companies to deposit their profits in a state bank.

May–July. **Peruvian forces invaded Ecuador**, routing the defenders and establishing control over a major portion of that nation's Amazonian territory. A state of war existed between the two countries until January 1942, when foreign ministers attending the consultative conference in Rio de Janeiro prevailed on the Ecuadorian delegate to renounce some 200,000 square kilometers (124,000 sq. miles) of its Amazon watershed to Peru.

May 6. **Venezuela's Congress elected Isaías Medina Angarita to a five-year presidential term.** Medina was the hand-picked successor of López Contreras. More democratically minded than his predecessor, Medina sponsored a number of social and political reforms during his four years in office. Among them were an extension of the vote to women, the introduction of Venezuela's first income tax law, a requirement that foreign oil companies pay increased royalties, and sponsorship of an agrarian reform law. Medina was overthrown in September 1945.

September 13. **Venezuela's Democratic Action party, Acción Democrática (AD), was formed by activists and intellectuals**, among them **Rómulo Betancourt** and novelist **Rómulo Gallegos**. Advocating direct presidential election, it became the chief source of opposition to President Medina Angarita.

1942

January. **Young Venezuelan army officers, among them Marcos Pérez Jiménez and Carlos Delgado Chalbaud, formed the secret, nationalistic Patriotic Military Union (Unión Patriótica Militar, UPM).** Their goal was to make the military an active force in national modernization.

August 7. **Liberal Alfonso López Pumarejo was inaugurated as Colombia's president for the second time.** He attempted to renew his popular reform program of 1934-38, but charges of political corruption, leveled by Conservative opposition leader **Laureano Gómez**, made the second **López** administration an ineffectual one. López resigned a year short of completing his term (August 1945), leaving fellow Liberal **Alberto Lleras Camargo** to serve until mid-1946.

December 21. **The Catavi Massacre occurred when Bolivian soldiers opened fire on peaceful demonstrators at the Catavi tin mines, killing hundreds.** The violence occurred during a strike for higher wages and union recognition. The events at Catavi weakened the government of Enrique Peñaranda, who was overthrown a year later.

1943

March 13. **New oil legislation was enacted in Venezuela.** The law substantially increased the government's share of oil company profits. In exchange, the companies received new forty-year concessions.

December 20. **Major Gualberto Villarroel overthrew Bolivian president Enrique Peñaranda.** Leader of younger, progressive officers, and backed by the MNR, Villarroel went on to encourage labor organization and peasant activism. Villarroel (labeled a fascist by the United States government) was overthrown and lynched three years later (July 21, 1946).

1944

May 28. **A popular uprising in Guayaquil, Ecuador, supported by troops from that city's military garrison**, set into motion a nation-wide movement that unseated President Carlos Arroyo del Río. A coalition uniting leftists and conservatives agreed to invite **José María Velasco Ibarra** to head a new government. Velasco took office on May 31, but soon struck at his left-wing supporters. Economic deterioration during 1946-47 weakened Velasco's position, causing his overthrow in 1947.

July. **Colombian president Alfonso López Pumarejo was seized in a brief and abortive military coup.**

1945

June 10. **Liberal and Aprista forces combined to elect José Luis Bustamante president of Peru.** Postwar inflation, along with the growing stridency of the new president's Aprista supporters, led Bustamante to appoint anti-Aprista General **Manuel Odría** minister of government and police (January 1947). An abortive Aprista uprising of February 1948 set into motion events leading to Odría's unseating of Bustamante in September 1948.

October 17-18. **Leaders of Venezuela's Patriotic Military Union and the Democratic Action party (AD, Acción Democrática), deposed President Medina Angarita.** For the succeeding three years, known as the *trienio*, a seven-man council led by **Rómulo Betancourt** governed the nation. The council forced foreign petroleum companies to place profit sharing on a fifty-fifty basis, and patronized the new oil workers' union, Fedepetrol. A new constitution was approved on July 5, 1947, and AD leader **Rómulo Gallegos** was elected president on December 14, 1947.

1946

January 13. **Venezuela's Social Christian party was formed.** Rafael Caldera and others first formed a committee, Comité de Organización Política Electoral Independiente (COPEI), to prepare for upcoming elections. In 1948 the committee became the Social Christian party (though it often continued to be known as COPEI).

May 4. **Conservative Mariano Ospina Pérez won the Colombian presidency** in a contest that saw Liberals split their vote between dissident **Jorge Eliécer Gaitán** and party regular Gabriel Turbay. Ospina pledged to govern in coalition with the Liberals. **Gaitán**, a populist who aroused great enthusiasm among poorer Colombians in Bogotá and elsewhere, went on to assume leadership of the Liberal party.

July 21. **Bolivia's president, Gualberto Villarroel, was hanged from a lamppost after a mob stormed the presidential palace.** Although his administration, which was backed by the MNR, implemented several reforms, including the abolition of unpaid labor by peasants to landowners, his authoritarian methods aroused opposition. In 1947 he was succeeded by Enrique Hertzog; after the latter's resignation in 1949, the vice president, Mamerto Urriolagoitía, became president.

1947

August 23. **Ecuador's military overthrew President Velasco Ibarra**, but stepped aside allowing Congress to appoint Carlos J. Arosemena to complete **Velasco**'s term.

December. **Some 14,000 Colombians died in Liberal-Conservative fighting over the course of 1947.** Sources of the bloodshed included traditional political hatreds, the 1946 election of minority president Mariano Ospina Pérez, and the lack of effective state control in many of the regions affected.

1948

January 17. **Liberal-Conservative bloodshed in the northern department of Santander del Norte forced Colombian president Mariano Ospina Pérez to declare a state of siege there.**

Thousands of Liberals fled to neighboring Venezuela.

February 15. **Social democrat Rómulo Gallegos was inaugurated Venezuelan president**, and set about implementing reforms that included land expropriation with compensation and an income tax on oil companies.

April 9. **Colombian Liberal party leader Jorge Eliécer Gaitán was assassinated in Bogotá.** A riot followed in Bogotá (*el bogotazo*) when enraged followers of the populist leader, supported by police, most of whom were Liberals, attempted to overthrow the government of Conservative president Mariano Ospina Pérez. Some 1,400 died in the rioting, which destroyed several dozen blocks of downtown Bogotá, and which had lesser echo in other parts of the nation. Colombia's army quickly restored order in Bogotá and elsewhere.

June 6. **In Ecuador's first popular elections since 1940, moderate liberal Galo Plaza Lasso became the nation's chief executive. Plaza**, the son of President Leónidas Plaza (1901-5, 1912-16), served a four-year term marking the beginning of a twelve-year period of political stability and economic prosperity in Ecuador. From the late 1940s through the ensuing decade, banana exports earned revenues that Plaza and his successors, **Velasco Ibarra** (1952-56) and Camilo Ponce Enríquez (1956-60), were able to invest in economic and social infrastructure. The banana boom also had the effect of redistributing Ecuador's population, drawing settlement from interior mountains toward the coast. This in turn increased political pluralization, depriving the clergy and the Conservative party of domination.

October 29. **Manuel Odría overthrew Peruvian president José Luis Bustamante**, paving the way for a dictatorship, dubbed the *ochenio*, lasting until 1956. The most notable feature of **Odría**'s administration was his harsh control of the Apristas, especially of the movement's leader **Víctor Raúl Haya de la Torre**. In 1949 Haya sought refuge in the Colombian embassy in Lima, where Odría forced him to remain until 1954. Odría took steps to strengthen Peru's economy by encouraging foreign investment, resuming payment of the national debt, and easing currency controls. In order to placate the masses Odría placed his wife, María Delgado, in charge of a social program featuring the building of schools, low-cost housing, and public clinics.

November 24. **Venezuelan president Rómulo Gallegos was ousted in a military coup.** Viewed as excessively radical by the military, **Gallegos** was removed after refusing an ultimatum from the armed forces demanding changes in policy. A three-man junta was formed, made up of Carlos Delgado Chalbaud, **Marcos Pérez Jiménez**, and Luis Felipe Lloveda Páez. After Delgado's assassination (November 13, 1950), the junta was reorganized and preparations made for elections.

December 31. **Over the course of 1948, political bloodshed in Colombia, pitting Liberals against Conservatives, resulted in more than 43,000 deaths.**

1949

June 5. **Colombia's Liberal party won congressional elections in a contest marred by escalating political violence.** Sporadic, bloody clashes between Liberals and Conservatives in the countryside were duplicated in the national Chamber of Representatives when, on September 8, gunfire erupted leaving a Liberal representative dead and another mortally wounded.

November 9. **Colombian president Mariano Ospina Pérez suspended Congress when he learned that its Liberal majority intended to impeach him.** Liberals resorted to the measure because of their fear that the hated Conservative leader **Laureano Gómez** would become president in an election in which their party members could not participate owing to violence against them by Conservative police. On November 25, Liberal leaders called for electoral abstention and a general strike.

November 27. **Laureano Gómez** was elected Colombian president in a contest in which only

Conservatives voted. Meanwhile, Liberals began forming antigovernment guerrilla units in the eastern *llanos* and other parts of the nation.

1950

June. **Colombia adopted the Currie Plan for integrated national development.** Named for its originator, Lauchlin Currie, an economist employed by the World Bank, the plan called for commercialization of agriculture and further construction of import-substituting industry. Colombia was a favored recipient of World Bank aid because of its tradition of prudent macroeconomic management and its consistent rate of economic growth. The staunch anticommunism of Colombian leaders also made international aid agencies, and their chief patron, the United States, favorably disposed to aid Colombia.

August 7. **Conservative Laureano Gómez was inaugurated president of Colombia** during a time of growing violence in outlying parts of the nation. National police units, by then comprised almost entirely of Conservatives, and the national army clashed repeatedly with Liberal guerrillas, some 2,500 of whom were under arms in the eastern *llanos*, while another 2,000 fought elsewhere in the country.

December 31. **More than 50,000 Colombians died during 1950, victims of Liberal-Conservative strife known as *La Violencia*. This was the greatest number killed in one year in fighting that over eighteen years (1947-1965) claimed nearly 200,000 lives.**

1951

May 6. **Exiled MNR leader Víctor Paz Estenssoro polled nearly half of the votes cast in Bolivia's presidential election.** Since he had not won a majority, the final decision was to be made by Congress but before it could act, President Urriolagoitía resigned (May 16) in favor of a military junta. The new government, headed by Hugo Ballivián, annulled the election.

1952

April 9. **Hernán Siles Zuazo and Juan Lechín, leaders of Bolivia's National Revolutionary party (MNR) during the exile of party head Víctor Paz Estenssoro, overthrew the military junta headed by Hugo Ballivián.** Thus began the Bolivian Revolution of 1952. **Paz Estenssoro** returned to assume the presidency and, together with Siles, dominated politics in Bolivia for the following twelve years. While the revolutionaries were unable to break the power of the military in politics, they did bring about profound social changes. Chief among them were the mobilization and enfranchisement of the mass of the population, the nationalization of the Big Three tin-mining companies, the return of land to peasants who had lost their holdings over the previous century, and the launching of major economic development programs. The nationalist program of Paz Estenssoro and his colleagues drew inspiration from the Mexican Revolution of 1910-20.

August 31. **Ecuadorian leader José María Velasco Ibarra was inaugurated to his third presidential term.** It would be the only one of his five presidencies whose full term he would complete.

December 2. **Marcos Pérez Jiménez was proclaimed interim president of Venezuela.** When early returns in an election for members of a constituent assembly indicated that the promilitary Independent Electoral Front (FEI) was losing, news reports were suspended. After **Pérez Jiménez** was named president, an FEI victory was declared. The constituent assembly elected him president for a five-year term on April 13, 1953.

1953

June 13. **Colombian army commander Gustavo Rojas Pinilla, supported by a dissident faction of the Conservative party, overthrew President Laureano Gómez.** In the months following **Rojas**'s accession to power, thousands of Liberal guerrillas laid down their arms and returned to civilian life.

1955

April. **Colombian dictator Gustavo Rojas Pinilla declared a mountainous region southwest of Bogotá a Zone of Military Operations, and sent the army to pursue rebellious peasants there.** Inhabitants of the region had not given up their arms when **Rojas Pinilla** came to power. The fact that some of them were communists heightened fears that the peasants represented a potential danger to national sovereignty. Meanwhile adverse public reaction to the military campaign undermined support for Rojas and hastened his fall.

1956

February 5. **In Colombia's Bull Ring Massacre, henchmen of dictator Gustavo Rojas Pinilla killed 8 and injured 112 spectators** who had failed to shout "vivas" to the dictator.

June 16. **Manuel Prado was elected to a second term as Peru's president.** The early years of his administration were tranquil, thanks in large part to his legalization of the APRA party during his first year in office. But APRA's accommodation with the government splintered the party, making for growing political instability in Peru. That fact, coupled with continued economic fluctuation, weakened Prado's hand and forced him to the right. Conservative Pedro Beltrán, named prime minister in mid-1959, effectively ran Peru until December 1961, when he resigned to prepare for the 1962 presidential election.

June 17. **Hernán Siles and Juan Lechín were elected president and vice president of Bolivia.** High inflation and food scarcity induced Siles to cut back on social programs under instruction of the International Monetary Fund and the United States government. In January 1957, Siles accepted an IMF stabilization plan that required balancing the national budget by ending food subsidies, limiting wage increases, cutting spending on public projects, and creating a single currency exchange rate. While those actions were relatively successful, they weakened the MNR by sending its left wing into opposition to Siles.

July 24. **Colombian Conservative leader Laureano Gómez, then exiled in Spain, and Liberal leader Alberto Lleras Camargo, signed the Pact of Benidorm,** under whose terms Liberals and Conservatives sought to unseat the dictator **Rojas Pinilla** and explore routes toward equitable power sharing.

August 31. **Ecuadorian Conservative Camilo Ponce Enríquez was inaugurated,** having won office with just 30 percent of the vote. His effectiveness was limited owing both to the narrowness of his victory and to the end of the boom in banana exports. Declining exports and increasing unemployment troubled the last years of his term.

December 31. **During 1956, renewed violence in Colombia resulted in the loss of more than 11,000 lives.**

1957

May 6-10. **Opponents of Colombian dictator Gustavo Rojas Pinilla declared a nation-wide general strike. The strike and simultaneous popular demonstrations forced Rojas from office (May 10).** Those events were set into motion by the dictator's increasing repression and use of violence against his opponents, coupled with official corruption and poor management of fiscal affairs, along with his inability to end La Violencia. Precipitating his fall was **Rojas's** illegal extension of his term in office through 1962.

December 1. **Colombians approved through plebiscite a power-sharing arrangement under which the Liberal and Conservative parties would share power equally for a period of twelve years,** later extended to sixteen years. Under the arrangement, called the National Front, each party would alternate the presidency and other public posts.

1958

January 1. **An abortive military uprising in Venezuela, and growing civilian anger over his**

authoritarian rule, forced Marcos Pérez Jiménez into exile (January 23). A caretaker military regime headed by Wolfgang Larrazábal governed until elections were held late in the year.

May 13. **During a good-will tour to Venezuela, U.S. vice president Richard Nixon was threatened by angry mobs.** U.S. president Eisenhower ordered U.S. Marines and paratroopers to Caribbean bases in the event they should be needed to protect Nixon.

August 7. **Alberto Lleras Camargo was inaugurated Colombian president** under terms of the National Front agreement. One of Lleras's first tasks was to attack La Violencia, which had claimed well over 100,000 lives since 1947. Thanks to his campaign aimed at breaking up gangs of *violentos*, deaths through La Violencia declined from over 11,000 in 1956 to fewer than 2,000 in 1963, the last full year of Lleras's administration.

October 31. **Venezuelan political leaders agreed, in the Pact of Punto Fijo, to abide by the results of the upcoming presidential election.** Rómulo Betancourt of the social democratic AD party, Jóvito Villalba of the left-wing URD, and **Rafael Caldera** of conservative Christian democratic COPEI thus set the stage for Venezuela's transition to democracy.

October. **Deposed dictator Gustavo Rojas Pinilla returned to Colombia** to mount a campaign against the power-sharing National Front.

December 7. **Rómulo Betancourt won the Venezuelan presidential election, obtaining 49 percent of the votes cast.** He went on to rule with equanimity, moderating his earlier stridency. He was especially accommodating to his old rival, conservative **Rafael Caldera** of the Social Christian party (COPEI). Meanwhile a new tax law raised the nation's share of oil profits to 65 percent.

1959

June 3-4. **Economic hardship in Ecuador caused riots in Guayaquil** that the government crushed with indiscriminate force. At least a thousand civilians died at the hands of police who had been instructed to shoot to kill. The decline of Ecuador's agro-export model continued into the following decade, with negative impact on political stability.

December. **Peasant unrest in Bolivia's Cochabamba brought General René Barrientos to prominence.** Barrientos, who had participated in the 1952 revolution, supervised a Military-Peasant Pact that ended warfare between peasant militias. Barrientos's rise presaged the return to military rule in Bolivia in the mid-1960s.

Southern Cone:
Argentina, Chile, Paraguay, Uruguay

The global depression of the 1930s affected nations of the Southern Cone to varying degrees. Underdeveloped Paraguay, many of whose citizens lived at a subsistence level, was little troubled by the economic downturn. Uruguay and Argentina likewise did not suffer unduly from the collapse of international trade, for they enjoyed favored positions within protected British and Western European commercial systems. Chile, on the other hand, dependent on the export of copper, felt depression-induced hardship more than any other American nation.

All Southern Cone countries experienced political turbulence during the years between 1930 and 1959. There was widespread disillusionment with liberal democracy, which over the preceding century had frequently been honored in the breach by willful elites practiced at winking at the procedural niceties of the democratic process. This in turn heightened interest in new, antiliberal political movements emanating from Europe. Nazism, fascism, falangism, socialism, and communism all offered alternatives to liberal democracy. Consequently, Southern Cone nations, whose ties with Central Europe and Italy were closer than elsewhere in Latin America, witnessed the appearance of left- and right-wing political parties during the 1930s.

During the 1930s popular front governments periodically united disparate political movements to rule for brief periods of time. By the 1940s, however, authoritarian regimes asserted themselves in Paraguay and Argentina. In the latter nation caudillo **Juan D. Perón** drew on populist wellsprings to create a powerful political movement supported by both the military and organized labor. Paraguayan authoritarianism, which by the 1950s found its ultimate expression in **Alfredo Stroessner**, drew its strength chiefly from the military.

Chile and Uruguay fared better politically. Uruguay continued in the social democratic tradition of **José Batlle y Ordóñez**, by the 1950s becoming Latin America's most admired nation for the tenacity of its democracy and because of its advanced social legislation. Chile's progress was less placid, through it was admired for its relatively tranquil politics.

International relations among Southern Cone nations were stable during 1930-59. For a brief time following the military takeover of June 1943, the generals who presided over Argentina threatened to embark on imperialistic adventures. But in the end they did little more than tighten economic links with Paraguay, continuing a policy that Argentine leaders had pursued during and after the Chaco War. Uruguay and Chile continued to maintain their traditional coolness toward larger, wealthier Argentina.

During World War II, Argentina led Southern Cone nations in resisting Allied pressure to declare war on Germany. Along with Paraguay and Chile, Argentina had long-standing economic ties with Central Europe. The region had affective ties with Central Europe, for Germans had immigrated to the Southern Cone in considerable numbers. Italians had also immigrated to Argentina in large numbers. For those reasons an ongoing theme of World War II diplomacy was the United States–led attempt to dampen Nazi and fascist influence in the Southern Cone. Meanwhile Argentina blasted the North Americans for meddling in her affairs and in those of Paraguay.

All Southern Cone nations suffered economic stagnation in the postwar period. Inflation ad-

vanced and with it unemployment, while import substitution ran its course. Those difficulties, coupled with the perception that Latin American affairs did not stand high on the global postwar agenda, gave a certain cogency to anti-U.S. and anti-imperialist critiques. As the 1950s ended, peoples of the Southern Cone were divided. On one hand they wanted to integrate themselves fully into the political and economic system led by the United States. Yet on the other they had reason to resent their categorization as Third World nations whose economic woes were trumpeted from 1959 onward by **Fidel Castro**.

1930

September 6. **Retired Argentine general José F. Uriburu drove President Hipólito Yrigoyen from office**, ushering in fifty years of political turbulence whose chief feature was authoritarian rule by the military. Uriburu's coup was founded in **Yrigoyen**'s inept rule as well as divisions in his Radical party, in the nation's straitened economic condition, in the failure of Yrigoyen's middle-class supporters to rally to his defense, and in the ongoing hostility of Conservatives toward Yrigoyenismo. An admirer of Benito Mussolini's corporatist form of government, Uriburu hoped to reform Argentina's constitution along corporatist lines. But his plan was unpopular with his Conservative supporters, who forced him to call elections for November 1931. That contest, a product of "patriotic fraud" between Conservatives, anti-Yrigoyen Radicals, and Socialists, brought Agustín P. Justo to the presidency.

1931

March 1. **Colorado Gabriel Terra was inaugurated president of Uruguay.** A follower of **José Batlle y Ordóñez**, Terra soon allied himself with the conservative Blanco party, assumed moderate dictatorial rule (March 1933), and established a new constitution (1934) returning presidential governance to the nation. Terra controlled organized labor and devalued the peso in order to promote beef exports. Presidential elections of 1938 resulted in the victory of Terra's brother-in-law, Alfredo Baldomir.

July 27. **Chilean president Carlos Ibáñez resigned under pressure** of a citizenry shocked by the economic collapse of their nation. Over the preceding two years Chilean raw material exports had fallen by 88 percent, the national budget was halved, and Chile defaulted on its substantial foreign debt. Prior to the onset of the depression, **Ibáñez** had borrowed heavily abroad to finance a range of public programs.

Political turmoil attended the departure of Ibáñez. Nine men served as chief executive between mid-1931 and late 1932. Among them was the colorful air force commander Marmaduke Grove Vallejo, who proclaimed a short-lived Socialist Republic. In December 1932 **Arturo Alessandri**, the "Lion of Tarapacá," was elected to a second presidential term.

October 23. **Members of the Paraguayan presidential guard fired on students protesting the weakness of President José P. Guggiari.** Eleven died and many more were wounded. Guggiari had no role in the incident, but left the presidency temporarily. He was succeeded on August 15, 1932, by fellow Liberal Eusebio Ayala.

December. **Recently inaugurated Uruguayan president Gabriel Terra entered into a pork-barrel pact (*pacto de chinchulín*) with the opposition Blanco party.** Under terms of the agreement minority parties would be represented on the governing boards of all public corporations. That politicized public enterprises, ultimately leading to excessive patronage and expenditures.

1932

February 20. **Augustín P. Justo was inaugurated Argentine president** thanks to a pact between members of the Conservative party (recently renamed the National Democrats), members of the anti-**Yrigoyen** faction of the Radical party, and the Independent Socialists.

Known as La Concordancia, the agreement defined the parameters of Argentine politics for the ensuing decade. Even though the Concordancia was denounced as anti-democratic, it marked one of the most productive periods in Argentine history. Under Justo and his successor Roberto Ortiz (1938-42), extensive public works projects were completed, advanced labor legislation passed, and extensive subsidized low-cost housing built.

June 15. **The Chaco War began when Paraguayan and Bolivian troops clashed** at Lake Pitiantuta, located in the central part of the semi-desert Gran Chaco. Both nations had long-standing claims to the territory that were intensified by hopes that it contained oil deposits. Paraguayan colonel José Félix Estigarribia soon emerged as the conflict's hero, waging an offensive campaign that eventually drove the more numerous Bolivians, under the command of German national Hans Kundt, from defensive fortifications. (For additional detail see Bolivarian Republics, June 1932.)

December 24. **Arturo Alessandri Palma was inaugurated Chilean president.** During his six-year term **Alessandri** exercised prudent leadership over a nation slowly recovering from economic decline. The fiscal conservatism of Alessandri and finance minister Gustavo Ross, coupled with the president's tight control of political militants on both the left and right, made the second Alessandri presidency unpopular though successful.

1933

March 31. **Uruguayan president Gabriel Terra established a temporary and moderate dictatorship** (a *dictablanda*) for the purpose of reorganizing the government. His principal measure was abolition of the nation's plural executive, created in the 1919 constitution of **José Batlle y Ordóñez**. A Colorado, Terra acted with the support of Luis Alberto de Herrera, leader of the conservative Blanco party.

April 19. **Chilean Marxist groups united to form the Socialist party** in the wake of the failed hundred-day Socialist Republic of Marmaduke Grove Vallejo. That party went on to play a key role in establishing the Popular Front that elected Pedro Aguirre Cerda president of Chile in 1938.

May. **Argentina and Britain signed the bilateral Roca-Runciman Pact** under which Argentina would not levy tariffs on British manufactures and Britain would give preference to Argentine grain and beef. The agreement benefited Argentina in two ways. First, it helped that nation emerge quickly from the Great Depression, since agro-exports did not decline precipitously. Second, it forced nations such as the United States to locate manufacturing installations in Argentina. Thus Argentina was able to continue its building of import-substituting industry. Argentine nationalists, however, were outraged by the agreement.

1934

June. **Chilean soldiers killed one hundred peasants who protested their removal from frontier lands they had invaded** on the upper Bío-Bío River. This action underscored President **Alessandri's** reluctance to launch a significant program of land reform.

1935

June. **Young Argentine Radical party members organized FORJA (Fuerza de Orientación Radical de la Juventud Argentina), a nationalist and anti-imperialist group.** Supplied motive force by the book *Argentina and the British Empire: Links in a Single Chain* (1935) by Rodolfo and Julio Irazusta, FORJA became a leader in the opposition to the oligarchic, liberal-developmentalist Concordancia. Anti-Semitism also formed part of FORJA's nationalist critique.

June 12. **Paraguay and Bolivia agreed on a cease-fire that effectively ended the Chaco War.** (For additional information see Bolivarian Republics, June 12, 1935).

1936

February 17. **Paraguayan war hero Rafael Franco overthrew Eusebio Ayala,** who became unpopular over the course of the Chaco War. Franco came to power at the head of an amorphous movement of nationalists, socialists, and corporatists united only in their dislike of the discredited Liberal party. Franco and his followers, who became known as Febreristas, went on to create a revolutionary program informed by Soviet communism, Italian fascism, and Spanish corporatism. Their government survived until August 1937.

1937

August 13. **Paraguay's Liberals were restored to power through a military coup that toppled the Febrerista government of Rafael Franco.** Three ephemeral Liberal regimes followed the coup, and at length the Liberals settled on Chaco War hero José Félix Estigarribia as their candidate in the April 1939 presidential election.

1938

February 20. **Roberto M. Ortiz was inaugurated Argentine president.** Elected in a fraud-ridden campaign three months earlier, Ortiz was candidate of the Concordancia movement. As a lawyer of middle-class origins who had made a fortune working for British railway interests, Ortiz was scorned by members of the nationalist movement.

June 19. **Alfredo Baldomir was inaugurated president of Uruguay,** replacing Gabriel Terra, who had served two terms. A return to prosperity in Uruguay during 1941 allowed Baldomir to end his predecessor's alliance with the conservative Blanco party and, in 1942, to dismantle the centralizing 1934 constitution, creating a State Council of members drawn from all but the Communist party.

September 5. **Chilean Nazis briefly occupied government buildings in Santiago before being routed by government troops** with a loss of sixty-six lives. When the sixty-one survivors were executed after surrendering, **Carlos Ibáñez,** whom the Nazis were backing in the ongoing presidential election, withdrew from the race and endorsed Pedro Aguirre Cerda, candidate of the Popular Front. Ibáñez hoped thereby to weaken the government's candidate, Gustavo Ross.

October 25. **Pedro Aguirre Cerda was elected Chilean president at the head of a Popular Front coalition** that brought together left-wing factions, including members of the nation's Socialist and Communist parties. Popular with the people, he followed a moderate reformist course while ignoring demands of Marxist supporters that he allow agricultural workers to unionize. He nevertheless brought Marxists into his government, one of whom, **Salvador Allende Gossens,** served as his minister of health. Aguirre died in office (November 25, 1941), and Gerónimo Méndez Aranciba completed his term.

1939

August 15. **Chaco War hero José Félix Estigarribia was inaugurated president of Paraguay** and, responding to a strong mandate for change, commissioned the drafting of a new constitution patterned on Brazil's corporatist charter of 1937.

November. **A devastating earthquake in Chile led President Aguirre Cerda to found the National Development Corporation, CORFO (Corporación de Fomento).** Financed by a range of taxes, especially on the national copper companies owned largely by U.S. corporations, CORFO invested in infrastructural improvements and encouraged import-substituting industry, both public and private.

1940

July. **Illness forced Argentine president Roberto Ortiz to transfer power to Vice President Ramón Castillo.** Castillo became president when Ortiz resigned in June 1942. A hidebound conservative sympathetic to the Axis cause, Castillo was unpopular both at home and abroad.

September 7. **Popular Paraguayan president Jóse Félix Estigarribia died in a plane clash,** upon which his war minister Higinio Morínigo assumed the presidency. Morínigo quickly established a dictatorship that endured until his overthrow some seven years later.

1941

January. **Chile's Popular Front formally disbanded.**

April 17. **Paraguayan dictator Higinio Morínigo crushed an attempted Febrerista revolt.** One year later he outlawed the Liberal party.

1942

January. **Argentina's failure to denounce the Axis at the Pan-American Conference in Rio de Janeiro earned it the enmity of the United States, which labeled the Southern Cone nation "fascist" and "pro-Axis."**

February 21. **Uruguayan president Alfredo Baldomir postponed upcoming presidential elections, dissolved Congress, and called for a constitutional plebiscite.** The resulting document restored normal functioning of Uruguay's highly democratic electoral system, in effect ending the Colorado-Blanco (liberal-conservative) power sharing mandated in the 1934 constitution. With acceptance of the new charter Baldomir is said to have remarked "We have the costliest electoral system on the continent, but it is cheaper than revolution."

April 2. **Juan Antonio Ríos Morales was inaugurated Chilean president,** issuing in a period of moderate rule and steady economic progress. Dying in office (June 27, 1946), he was succeeded by Alfredo Duhalde (1946) and Juan A. Ibarren (1946).

1943

January 20. **Chile severed diplomatic relations with Germany, Italy, and Japan,** despite the reluctance of president Juan Antonio Ríos, who complained that the Allies could not guarantee his nation's safety from Japanese attack.

February 14. **Higinio Morínigo won a second term, unopposed, as Paraguayan president.** The campaign was carried out under a climate of press censorship and political oppression.

March. **Argentine army officers formed the secret United Officers Group, GOU (Grupo de Oficiales Unidos).** Led by General Pedro Ramírez, General Edelmiro Farrell, and Colonel **Juan D. Perón**, the group's aims were to promote economic competition with Brazil, reform of the nation's corrupt political system, and enhance the Argentine military. The nationalistic GOU was intensely anticommunist as well as antiliberal and anti-Semitic.

March 1. **Uruguayan president Juan José Amézaga was inaugurated.** Economic prosperity returned during the administration of Amézaga, and Uruguay developed a tariff-protected manufacturing sector. Good labor relations were maintained during the 1940s through wage councils comprised by labor, management, and government. Uruguay's *consejos de salarios* reflected a populist, corporatist trend in the reconciliation of class conflict.

April. **Argentine president Ramón Castillo broke the Concordancia pact by nominating an unpopular arch-conservative to succeed him.** His insistence on sugar planter Robustiano Patrón Costas over Buenos Aires governor Rodolfo Moreno prompted his overthrow two months later.

June. **Paraguayan dictator Higinio Morínigo became his nation's first head of state to pay an official visit to the United States.** During his visit he was awarded an honorary degree by Fordham University, part of a United States effort to ensure Paraguayan support during the war. During the war Paraguay received extraordinary amounts of American aid, most of which was effectively expended on road-building, communications, and other infrastructural improvements.

June 4. **Argentine army officers, acting through the GOU, overthrew President Ramón Castillo and installed themselves in power.** Over the ensuing three years the nation was headed, successively, by three members of the military junta: Arturo Rawson (1943), Pedro Pablo Ramírez (1943–44), and Edelmiro Farrell (1944–46).

October 27. **Colonel Juan D. Perón was made head of the National Department of Labor**, and was given the task of organizing nonleftist labor unions supportive of the government. The following month President Pedro Ramírez made **Perón** a member of his cabinet, having given the Department of Labor cabinet status. Upon assuming the new post, Perón stated his intent to foster labor harmony while extending social justice to workers.

December. **Argentina angered the United States when it recognized the regime of Major Gualberto Villarroel in Bolivia.** No other Latin American regime had recognized Villarroel, a social activist whom the United States had labeled a fascist.

December 31. **The Argentine government issued decrees dissolving political parties, establishing compulsory religious instruction in public schools, and regulating the press.** The decrees reflected the increasingly authoritarian tendencies of the Ramírez government.

1944

January 26. **Argentina severed relations with the Axis powers under pressure from the United States,** setting into motion events leading to the resignation of President Ramírez (February 25) and the accession of his vice president, Edelmiro Farrell. Farrell relinquished his post as minister of war to **Juan D. Perón**, who set out to strengthen the military. In July Perón became Argentine vice president when army officers chose him over General Luis Perlinger, the interior minister.

August–September. **The United States imposed economic sanctions on Argentina.** Despite Argentina's severance of diplomatic relations with the Axis, the U.S. government was convinced that its leaders had pro-Nazi sympathies. As a result, Argentine assets in the United States were frozen, U.S. exports to Argentina were restricted, and Argentine ports were declared off limits to U.S. vessels.

1945

March 27. **Argentina declared war on Germany and Japan**, thus ensuring itself admission to the United Nations.

October 9-17. **Juan D. Perón was stripped of posts in the government of President Edelmiro Farrell.** Argentine officers, concerned over Perón's increasing power and angry over his public liaison with entertainer Eva Duarte, forced him to resign his offices on October 9 and arrested him on October 12. On October 17, however, thousands of Argentine workers massed in downtown Buenos Aires to demand his release. Perón's captors, intimidated by the crowds, released him, and he appeared on the balcony of the Casa Rosada, the presidential palace, to announce his presidential candidacy. Thus, Perón emerged from the crisis stronger than ever.

October 22. **Juan D. Perón married Eva Duarte**, a radio celebrity with whom he had lived since mid-1944, and who had played a leading role in organizing the October 17 demonstration that freed him from prison. **Eva Perón** became wildly popular with *peronistas*, and played an important role in her husband's government.

1946

February 24. **Juan D. Perón won the Argentine presidential election** in the face of strong opposition from the Unión Democrática, a coalition joining members of the Radical, Conservative, Communist, and Socialist parties. **Perón**'s campaign received an unexpected boost from U.S.

assistant secretary of state Spruille Braden, a former ambassador to Argentina, who had angered the public through his political meddling. Shortly before the contest the U.S. Department of State had issued a "Blue Book" accusing **Perón** of having created a "Nazi-Fascist state."

November 3. **Chilean left-wing Radical party leader Gabriel González Videla was inaugurated president** at the head of a coalition joining Liberals, Communists, and Radicals. González, who had won by a plurality, soon broke with his Communist supporters when, under pressure from the United States, he expelled them from his cabinet (1947), outlawed their party (1948), and severed relations with the Soviet Union and other communist nations. González Videla continued his predecessor's moderate policies, promoting middle-class interests and import substitution.

November 24. **Paraguayan dictator Higinio Morínigo completed a program of political liberalization** by revoking a 1940 ban on political activity and bringing members of the Colorado and Febrerista parties into his cabinet. Meanwhile he jailed pro-Argentine and anti-American politicians associated with the right-wing Frente de Guerra group.

1947

January. **President Juan D. Perón established his control over the Argentine General Labor Confederation (CGT, Confederación General de Trabajo)**, following the resignation of that group's secretary-general, Luis Gay.

March–August. **Leftist Febrerista supporters of former President Rafael Franco attacked the government of Higinio Morínigo.** A bloody civil war followed, during which Morínigo's forces were reinforced both by the Colorado party and Argentine president **Juan Perón**. Distinguishing himself during the contest was Lieutenant Colonel **Alfredo Stroessner**, one of few army officers to support Morínigo.

August 2. **Luis Batlle Berres was inaugurated Uruguayan president** following the death of recently elected Tomás Barreta. The election of Batlle Berres, a nephew of the famous **José Batlle** y **Ordóñez**, coincided with a benign moment in Uruguay's history. High prices for the nation's agro-exports and a successful program of import substitution, along with its democratic tradition, made Uruguay the envy of other Latin American states. Uruguay's fame was enhanced in 1952, when a new constitution restored the plural executive. Thus, at a time when many Latin American states labored under dictatorial regimes, Uruguay was governed by committee.

December. **Argentine president Juan D. Perón proclaimed the Peronist party (Partido Peronista), which replaced the Partido Laborista and other groups that had backed his election.** The Peronist party was renamed the Justicialist party (Partido Justicialista) after his ouster in 1955.

1948

August 15. **Juan Natalicio González replaced Higinio Morínigo as president of Paraguay.** González, who had controlled the country since the civil war of the previous year, was supplanted a year later in a coup led by fellow Colorado party member Federico Chaves.

1949

March 15. **A new Argentine constitution was approved,** making possible consecutive presidential re-election, establishing state ownership of natural resources, extending new rights to workers and to the population, and enfranchising women.

September 10. **Federico Chaves became Paraguayan president**, going on to hold that office until overthrown in 1954. During that period Chaves strengthened Paraguay's relations with Argentina.

1951

April 11. **Argentina's Congress approved a bill expropriating the newspaper *La Prensa*.** The government of Juan Perón now had a virtual state monopoly over the mass media.

August 22. **Eva Perón's followers urged her to run for the vice presidency.** She was proposed as **Juan Perón**'s running mate by Argentina's labor confederation, but her candidacy was opposed by the armed forces and probably by Perón himself. Already ailing from the cancer that would kill her the next year, she gave an equivocal answer to a mass meeting on August 22, but she renounced the candidacy on August 31. She died on July 26, 1952.

November 11. **Juan D. Perón was re-elected president of Argentina**. He defeated the Radical party candidate, Ricardo Balbín, by a vote of 4.7 million to 2.4 million.

1952

March 1. **Andrés Martínez Trueba became Uruguay's chief executive officer under the nation's new collegial executive**, the Consejo Nacional de Gobierno (CNG), mandated by the new constitution. While the unique political arrangement was viewed favorably abroad, it was criticized by most Uruguayans, who saw it as encouraging clientelism. The mandating of minority party representation on governing boards, dating from the 1931 pork-barrel pact, swelled the budgets of public corporations to unacceptable levels. As Uruguay's program of import substitution had run its course by the 1950s, and inefficiency in its agricultural sector brought economic stagnation, the renewal of collegial governance and its tendency toward administrative inefficiency and costliness only hastened Uruguay's decline.

May. **Worsening economic conditions led the Argentine government to impose a wage and price freeze** that remained in force for two years. Excessive government spending coupled with a steady erosion of the value of Argentine exports necessitated the action.

June. **The Argentine Congress, dominated by *peronistas*, proclaimed the doctrine of *justicialismo*, a corporatist approach to politics that it made national law.** Justicialism was a corporatist doctrine under which interest groups were granted legal guarantees and benefits in exchange for their cooperation with the government. Over the course of 1952, *peronistas* brought labor, professional groups, and education within the corporatist structure.

September 4. **Chileans elected the popular Carlos Ibáñez president.** But the aged Ibáñez was unable to address the nation's rampant inflation and political fragmentation. While he did temporarily reduce inflation, his measures produced recession. Ibañez's term drew to a close in 1958 amid generalized protest over his failed economic program.

1953

April. **Rioting Peronists in Buenos Aires looted and burned businesses of anti-Peronists.** The government subsequently jailed its critics.

September. **Argentina's economy improved thanks to the government's new willingness to moderate statism and protectionism**, especially in the area of foreign investment. Earlier in the year foreign auto companies were allowed to invest in Argentina. In a speech of September 17, President **Juan D. Perón** invited foreign oil companies to invest in his nation. Perón's speech was part of his Third Position policy, through which he proclaimed Argentina's nonalignment in the Cold War. That in turn was aimed at achieving better relations with the United States.

1954

May 5. **A revolt in Paraguay brought to power Colorado politician Epifanio Méndez Fleitas and General Alfredo Stroessner.** In July **Stroessner** was elected president, thus initiating a rule that would extend to 1989. Stroessner built his regime on control of the army and the Colorado party, and strengthened it through a vocal anticommunism that won him support from the United States. Unparalleled economic prosperity during the 1950s also favored Stroessner, who went on to consolidate his control of all aspects of public life.

1955

June 16. **Peronist mobs attacked Catholic churches.** Following an abortive naval revolt, Peronist supporters vandalized and burned Catholic churches in Buenos Aires. The government exiled two high clergymen who protested, and the Vatican excommunicated **Perón**. Although Perón and other military leaders of the 1940s had had good relations with the church, tension developed in 1954, at least partly because of clerical opposition to the regime's efforts to spread *justicialismo* as Argentina's official doctrine. As a result, religious education in public schools (reintroduced in 1943) was abolished, and divorce and prostitution were legalized.

August 24-September 4. **Sixty thousand Chilean government employees struck for higher wages**, forcing President **Ibáñez** to promise salary increments.

September 19. **Juan Perón resigned his presidency and fled Argentina.** Perón's action was prompted by barracks revolts in several Argentine cities. Subsequent to his flight (September 19), a four-man junta was formed that appointed General Eduardo Lonardi provisional president. Two months later the junta ousted Lonardi and installed General Pedro Aramburu in his place. In the interim (October 5) a Peronist uprising occurred, prompting dismissal of the Peronist-dominated Supreme Court.

October. **Paraguayan president Alfredo Stroessner engineered reunification of the Colorado party**, in the process weakening the power of his chief rival, Epifanio Méndez Fleitas. One year later (October 1956) **Stroessner** exiled Fleitas, an action allowing him to impose anti-inflationary measures opposed by Fleitas. Meanwhile Congress approved the Defense of Democracy law, authorizing the government to arrest anyone considered communist. The law extended the state of siege indefinitely.

November 13. **General Pedro Aramburu was appointed interim president of Argentina** by the military junta that had overthrown **Juan D. Perón**. Aramburu embraced the austerity plan presented to him by economist **Raúl Prebisch** (January 1956), and repealed much Peronist legislation. Aramburu promised a return to civilian rule within two years.

1956

June 10. **Troops loyal to the Argentine military junta smashed an uprising among Peronist troops.** Twenty-seven of the rebels were executed.

October. **Paraguayan president Alfredo Stroessner met Brazilian president Juscelino Kubitschek at Iguaçú Falls to plan a "Friendship Bridge" over the Paraná River.** When completed nine years later, the bridge linked the Paraguayan and Brazilian road systems, giving the former nation access to the Atlantic port of Paranaguá, where Paraguay had enjoyed free-port privileges since 1956.

November. **Left-wing Chilean parties joined to form the Popular Action Front (Frente de Acción Popular, FRAP).**

1957

June. **A general strike in Argentina, followed by a second one the following month**, indicated the ongoing power of the Peronist labor movement.

July. **Chile's National Falange and Conservative Social Christian party united to form the Christian Democratic party.** Led by **Eduardo Frei**, the party grew rapidly and was seen as a reformist alternative to Chile's Marxist parties.

September 23. **An Argentine constituent assembly abolished the nation's corporatist, Peronist constitution of 1949, reinstating the constitution of 1853.**

December 27. **Paraguay agreed to accept 150,000 Japanese immigrants in exchange for a $12 million loan.**

1958

January. **Paraguayan exiles formed the 14th of May guerrilla movement**, which subsequently launched several abortive invasions of their nation.

February 9. **Alfredo Stroessner won an uncontested second term to the Paraguayan presidency.**

February 22. **Arturo Frondizi was elected Argentine president** in the first such contest held since 1951. Frondizi, who won because he had secretly agreed with the exiled **Juan Perón** to legalize the Justicialist party four years after his inauguration, was overthrown in a military coup (1962) before he could carry out his promise. He was backed by a faction of the Radical party, the Intransigent Radical Civic Union. Frondizi's accommodation with the Peronists, and his own leftism, which antagonized the military, diminished his popularity and had the effect of negating the positive economic measures that he took early in his presidency.

May. **President Alfredo Stroessner crushed a general strike called by the Paraguayan Labor Confederation (Confederación Paraguaya de Trabajadores, CPT).** Stroessner subsequently expanded the emergency powers granted him during the strike and used them to control both domestic opposition to his regime as well as that of Castroite insurgents.

August 5. **The Chilean Communist party was legalized.**

September 4. **Jorge Alessandri won the Chilean presidency by a plurality.** Coming in second was **Salvador Allende** of the left coalition FRAP. Third in the voting was **Eduardo Frei**, representing the Christian Democrats. Alessandri was a fiscal conservative who reduced inflation and government debt.

November 30. **Economic stagnation in Uruguay brought the first defeat of the ruling Colorado party in ninety-three years.** One of the Blancos's first acts was to invite the International Monetary Fund to help supervise trade liberalization. While IMF reforms did not create hardship for the masses, dissatisfaction increased.

1959

January. **Argentine president Arturo Frondizi accepted an austerity plan proposed by the**

International Monetary Fund. Luxury imports were restricted, the peso devalued, and rigid exchange rates scrapped, consumer subsidies eliminated, wage increases discouraged. Two months later, Frondizi's new finance minister, Álvaro C. Alsogaray, undertook the privatization of state-owned industries.

March. **Fidel Castro received enthusiastic receptions in the capitals of Argentina, Uruguay, and Brazil.** Many in those nations applauded his anti-imperialism and his revolutionary success.

April 1. **Bowing to political pressure, Paraguayan president Stroessner lifted martial law, declared amnesty for all political exiles, and announced plans to hold free elections.**

May 28. **Paraguayan police arrested rioting students and two members of the opposition** *democrático* **faction of the Colorado party.** Subsequent criticism led **Stroessner** to reimpose the state of siege, to arrest *democrático* leaders, and to purge their supporters in the army.

Brazil

The 1930 to 1959 interval was pivotal for Brazil. During those decades labor and the middle class emerged as political forces capable of defending their interests before old political elites. The Revolution of 1930, which brought **Getúlio Vargas Dornelles** to power, marked the end of the oligarchic Old Republic period (1889-1930), during which the leaders of two states, São Paulo and Minas Gerais, monopolized political power and influence.

Brazil ended its dependence on coffee as its chief export in the years after 1930. The Great Depression hastened that process, at the same time heightening economic nationalism and moving Brazilians to step up their drive for economic self-sufficiency. By 1960 they were successful to the extent that Brazilian industry met the nation's basic consumer needs save for capital equipment and some consumer durables.

The years 1930 to 1961 comprised the era of Getúlio Vargas. Not a member of the coffee oligarchy, but, rather, a *gaúcho* from the southern

state of Rio Grande do Sul, Vargas dominated the nation directly during 1930-45 and 1950-54. Between 1946 and 1950 Brazil was governed by Vargas's long-time minister of war, Eurico Dutra, and between 1956 and 1961, by **Juscelino Kubitschek**, the candidate of Vargas's Social Democratic party.

Vargas came to power at a moment when political leaders throughout Latin America and the Western world were voicing mistrust of a democratic process dominated by political elites not representative of the population at large. Like many of his contemporaries, Vargas informed his search for political alternatives to elite-ridden formal democracy through study of the corporative and authoritarian models currently in vogue in Italy and Germany, and in several other European nations. He experimented with corporative mechanisms as a means of reconciling capital and labor. But in so doing he gave voice to groups not previously represented through the spurious democracy of the Old Republic.

Getúlio Vargas imposed authoritarian rule upon Brazil, especially during 1937-45, when he proclaimed his dictatorial Estado Novo regime. During his tenure he dealt firmly with extremists on both the left and the right, always with the support and approval of the nation's military.

During the 1930s and 1940s, Vargas steered a middle course in international affairs. Through the early years of World War II, he insisted that Brazil remain on good terms both with democratic Britain and the United States, and with fascist Italy and Germany. Only in 1942 did he bow to geopolitical reality and national self-interest and align Brazil fully with the Allied powers.

After World War II, Brazil very much supported United States–led Cold War initiatives. First under Dutra, then again under Vargas and his successor Kubitschek, Brazil pursued an anticommunist policy that held its domestic left firmly in check. Throughout the 1930 to 1959 period, Brazil's military played a moderating role in national affairs, enabling the nation's leaders to stay the course of nationalistic, state-directed progress toward economic self-sufficiency.

1930

March 1. **Júlio Prestes was elected president of Brazil in a hotly contested election pitting him against Getúlio Vargas Dornelles, candidate of the Liberal Alliance (AL),** a coalition representing many disaffected middle-class and urban groups. Outgoing president Washington Luís had nominated Prestes, a fellow Paulista, as his successor. The nomination of Prestes and his subsequent election angered the powerful coffee-producing state of Minas Gerais, whose leading politicians had, over years of the Old Republic (1889-1930), alternated the Brazilian presidency with São Paulo. Complicating matters further was the global depression, which led to 67 percent deflation and reduced exports by more than a third.

May. **The government further angered opposition groups by refusing to seat Liberal Alliance members from several states** when Congress convened.

July 26. **The murder of prominent Liberal Alliance member João Pessoa, who had served as Getúlio Vargas's vice presidential running mate** five months earlier, shocked Brazilians and set into motion plans for revolution.

October 3. **A revolt broke out aimed at preventing the presidency of Júlio Prestes.** Led by members of the Liberal Alliance, along with members of the *tenente* movement (see Brazil, 1922, 1924, and 1931), the uprising originated in Rio Grande do Sul in the south, Paraíba in the north, and Minas Gerais. The revolt spread rapidly, and on October 24, a military junta forced Washington Luís from office.

November 3. **Junta members presented the presidential sash to Getúlio Vargas.** That act symbolized the end of Brazil's Old Republic, the political leaders of which had proven themselves unable to meet the demands imposed by urbanization, modernization, and swelling nationalism. The events of November 3, 1930, also ushered in the era of **Getúlio Vargas**. Vargas would go on to serve first as provisional president (1930-34), then

as constitutional president (1934-37), next as dictator (1937-45), and again as constitutional president (1951-54).

November. **Getúlio Vargas established the Ministry of Labor, Industry, and Commerce** through which he implemented his attempt to reconcile the demands of labor and capital, in keeping with his corporative political vision. Through the new ministry, both labor and management were forced to join government-regulated unions whose disputes would be settled in special labor courts (established 1934).

1931

February. **Leaders of the radical *tenente* movement formed the Third of October Club** as a means of institutionalizing their influence upon the **Vargas** government. The *tenentes*, young officers who had attempted to bring revolution between 1922 and 1926, wanted Vargas to strike at entrenched political and economic interests, to promote modernization and political centralization, and to strike a nationalist pose. They also promoted government support of advanced social legislation. Highly important during the early years of the Vargas regime, their radicalism led to their loss of influence over the course of the 1930s.

March. **A decree authorized the Labor Ministry to enroll factory workers in state-controlled unions.** Over the ensuing decade a half-million workers were enrolled in some 800 such bodies.

April. **An Education Ministry was established** and charged with reforming all levels of national education. A second national university was established in 1934, and a third in 1938.

July. **Getúlio Vargas established the National Coffee Department** in accord with the recommendation of a British financial mission. Through the new department Brazil destroyed large quantities of warehoused coffee, and acted to discourage expansion of coffee acreage. Over its first decade the agency supervised the destruction of some 60 million bags of coffee. National economic diversification soon ended coffee's economic preeminence.

1932

February 24. **President Vargas promulgated a new electoral code lowering the voting age to eighteen and extending the vote to women.** While liberal in many respects, the code continued the literacy requirement.

July–October. **Paulistas staged a constitutionalist revolt against the Vargas government,** charging that the president was acting unconstitutionally and in a dictatorial fashion. **Vargas** had precipitated the uprising by sending the radical *tenente* João Alberto to replace the state's elected governor. The uprising ended after three months of desultory fighting. Vargas did not exact vengeance on the rebels, doing little more than exiling two of their leaders. Furthermore, he promised the Paulistas a quick return to constitutional rule.

1933

April 23. **Fascist leader Plínio Salgado held the first parade of Green Shirts, members of his new Integralist party, in São Paulo.** Viewed as a curiosity by most Brazilians, the Integralists, organized a year earlier, adopted as their slogan "God, Country, and Family." Militantly nationalist, xenophobic, anti-Semitic, and antiliberal, the Integralists advocated an "integral" authoritarian state.

1934

July 16. **A new constitution was placed in effect.** It provided for extension of the vote to all literate Brazilians eighteen and older, and increased the power of the central government at the expense of the states. The document also drew upon corporative principles. One-sixth of the new Chamber of Deputies was chosen by indirect vote

of professional associations, divided between employers and employees.

July 17. **Getúlio Vargas was elected to a four-year presidential term by the constituent assembly.**

1935

March. **The National Liberation Alliance (ANL) was formed,** bringing together the Communist and other left-wing groups in a popular front organization. Among its goals were the ending of Brazil's foreign debt payments, nationalization of all companies, land distribution, and "the liberation of Brazil from imperialistic slavery." **Luís Carlos Prestes,** clandestinely in the country, was named its honorary president.

July 5. **Luís Carlos Prestes, popularly known as the Cavalier of Hope, called for the overthrow of Vargas and for establishment of a popular revolutionary government.** His action was conceived in Moscow and formed part of a Soviet offensive against Brazil as a client of the United States. **Vargas** responded to **Prestes's** call by outlawing the ANL. That led communists in Natal, Recife, and Rio de Janeiro to stage bloody uprisings (November 23–26), known in Brazilian history as the *intentona.* The government declared martial law and ordered the arrest of **Prestes,** going on to outlaw the Communist party (1937).

1936

March 5. **Luís Carlos Prestes was arrested following a lengthy search.** He accepted full responsibility for the communist revolt. Subsequently placed on trial (August 1936), he was sentenced to a seventeen-year prison term and his wife, a German Jew, was deported to Germany where she later died in a concentration camp. The arrest of **Prestes** was part of a generalized anticommunist campaign that included mass arrests and the torture of prisoners.

1937

September 30. **Minister of War Eurico Dutra announced discovery of the fanciful Cohen Plan, detailing a projected communist takeover of Brazil.** Concocted by Integralistas, the plan was seized upon by the government as a pretext for establishing a dictatorship two months later.

November 10. **Getúlio Vargas suspended democratic government, saying that Brazil was under attack by communist subversives.** The following month he outlawed all political parties and proceeded to govern by decree until overthrown in a military coup of 1945. In a radio speech following his action, **Vargas** presented an authoritarian, corporative constitution to the nation. He proclaimed liberal and individualistic democracy to be a failure and at an end in Brazil, and the collectivist and harmonious era of the Estado Novo, or "new state," to be at hand. Vargas further centralized power in the national government and pursued a nationalistic, military-supported program of industrialization. While Vargas had promised to submit his 1937 constitution to a plebiscite, he never did so, ruling by decree.

December 31. **Getúlio Vargas outlawed the use of special uniforms, flags, songs, and insignia by "political intermediaries" supportive of the Estado Novo.** His message was aimed at the Integralistas of Plínio Salgado.

1938

January. **Vargas closed all Nazi party centers operating in southern Brazil and decreed that German schools operating there adopt Luso-Brazilian names and employ Portuguese as the language of instruction.**

May 10-11. **Integralists and their supporters attempted a putsch against the Estado Novo.** A number of the attackers were killed and their leaders subsequently arrested. The founder of the Integralist movement, Plínio Salgado, professed his loyalty to the Estado Novo and said he was not involved in the plot. He was, nevertheless, exiled to Portugal.

1939

March 9. **Brazil negotiated a series of favorable financial agreements with the United States.** Brazil intended to use the aid to further industrialization schemes, and the United States hoped the aid would make Brazil less reliant on German trade and assistance.

December. **Growth in national industrial production was estimated at above 6 percent over the period 1924-39.** Forty-five percent of Brazil's industry was located in the state of São Paulo.

1940

January 1. **Getúlio Vargas announced a five-year plan of economic development** featuring the building of a steel mill and the development of hydroelectric power.

1941

August. **Sixty mostly German- and Italian-language newspapers were closed,** pursuant to the government's Brazilianization program.

1942

January 28. **Brazil severed diplomatic and trade relations with the Axis nations.**

March 3. **A Brazil–United States pact was signed** through which the United States guaranteed purchase of Brazilian coffee, cacao, and other primary products and allocated the shipment of chemicals and machinery to Brazil.

March 12. **Getúlio Vargas ordered the confiscation of funds belonging to Axis citizens residing in Brazil,** an action taken following the sinking of the ship *Cairu* by a German submarine.

May–August. **German submarines sank numerous Brazilian ships,** prompting Brazil and the United States to establish a joint defense board.

August 22. **Brazil declared war on Germany and Italy.** Since the rupture of diplomatic relations, nearly 700 lives had been lost through the sinking of Brazilian ships by German submarines.

1943

November 10. **War-induced inflation led Vargas to decree nation-wide salary increases** ranging between 10 and 85 percent.

1944

June–September. **Some 25,000 Brazilian troops were sent to join Allied armies fighting in Italy.**

1945

February 28. **Responding to pressure to end his dictatorship, Vargas signed a decree calling for federal and state elections, including the election of a president.** The date for presidential balloting was later set for December 2, 1945; state elections were to be held May 6, 1946.

April. **Vargas freed Luís Carlos Prestes and proclaimed amnesty for 563 political prisoners.** He also renewed relations with the Soviet Union, legalized the Communist party, and allowed the return of political exiles

April 7. **Opponents of Vargas organized the National Democratic Union, UDN (União Democrática Nacional).** Meanwhile, **Vargas** founded two parties of his own, the Brazilian Labor Party, PTB (Partido Trabalhista Brasileiro) and the Social Democratic Party, PSD (Partido Social Democrático), representing his two most important constituencies.

May. **Luís Carlos Prestes reorganized the Brazilian Communist party (PCB, Partido Comunista Brasileiro),** which went on to elect one senator and fourteen deputies during its two years of legal existence.

June. **Prestes and fellow Communist Francisco Julião organized peasant leagues** charged with supporting PCB candidates in upcoming elections. Thousands of peasants were mobilized prior to suppression of the leagues in 1947.

October 29. **Getúlio Vargas resigned his presidency,** designating Chief Justice José Linhares his replacement until presidential elections could be held. **Vargas's** action was prompted by popular dismay over the suggestion that he might renege on a promise to hold elections in December. Army leaders pressured Vargas into stepping down; chief among them was his long-time supporter General Eurico Gaspar Dutra.

December 2. **General Eurico Dutra was elected to a five-year presidential term.**

1946

January 31. **Eurico Dutra was inaugurated president.** One of his first acts was to preside over drafting of a constitution that supplanted the corporative documents of 1934 and 1937. Among the new constitution's leading features were a provision denying the executive the right to issue decree-laws, and another allowing the government to outlaw antidemocratic parties. Dutra's economic policy was founded on continuing import substitution and increasing planning activities of the central government.

April–June. **The Volta Redonda steel works began to operate.** Formally known as the Companhia Siderúrgica Nacional, the plant was Brazil's first major steel enterprise. It was state-owned and financed in part by a $20 million loan from the U.S. Export–Import Bank that was made during World War II in competition with an offer from Germany. The plant is located in Volta Redonda in the Paraíba Valley of Rio de Janeiro state.

1947

January 19. **Growth of the Communist party was reflected in state-level elections.** Communist gains, coupled with party leader **Luís Carlos Prestes's** remark that in the event of war between the USSR and Brazil his party would support the Soviets, angered many Brazilians.

May 1. **The Communist party was declared illegal by a three-to-two vote of the Superior Electoral Tribunal.** Six months later **Luís Carlos Prestes,** writer **Jorge Amado,** and other legislators were expelled from Congress. Meanwhile steps were taken to reduce Communist influence in labor unions.

October 20. **Brazil broke diplomatic relations with the Soviet Union** after Soviet newspapers criticized the Dutra regime as "related to the fascism of Hitler."

1948

February. **Congress granted President Dutra the power to control imports.** That action was prompted by the rapid loss of reserves and the advance of inflation, both prompted by the revival of international trade following the war.

1949

August 2. **The Advanced War College (Escola Superior de Guerra) was founded.** Established with the aid of a U.S. military mission, the ESG offered courses on national security and economic development to officers and businessmen, civil servants, and other civilians. Graduates of the ESG played a prominent role in the military governments of the 1960s.

1950

October 3. **Getúlio Vargas won the presidential election** thanks in large part to the hope that since Eurico Dutra had been unable to control inflation, perhaps the former dictator could.

1951

January 31. **Getúlio Vargas took up his presidential duties,** pledged to bring inflation under control and to advance state participation in strategic economic sectors. But conditions were such that he could not control rapid increases in

the cost of living. His problems were complicated by a severe drought in the Northeast. Meanwhile several of **Vargas**'s close advisors enriched themselves at public expense.

December 31. **In his end-of-year address Vargas blamed foreign investors for illegally contributing to Brazil's ongoing economic problems** through excessive remittances of profits. He accused his predecessor of protecting "foreign-inspired trusts," and promised to limit remittances abroad.

1952

March 15. **Brazil and the United States signed a military aid pact** aimed at coordinating policies in the anticommunist struggle. Communists protested the agreement, launching a variety of antigovernment activities.

April. **The National Bank for Economic Development, BNDE, was organized.** The bank became the principal source of long-term financing in Brazil.

1953

June. **In a cabinet shuffle Vargas named João Goulart minister of labor.** Suspecting that **Goulart,** a long-time **Vargas** confidant, intended to emulate Argentina's **Perón** and turn workers into shock troops of the administration, members of the press and the military stepped up their criticism of the government.

October 3. **Petrobrás was created.** The new corporation, Petróleos Brasileiros, was given a monopoly of most sectors of the petroleum industry, including the development of deposits and refining. In keeping with the nationalist sentiments of the day, stock in Petrobrás could be held only by state entities and by Brazilian firms and individuals.

1954

May 1. **Vargas announced a 100 percent in-**

crease in the minimum wage. The president's announcement was the culmination of a struggle between partisans of economic austerity and those like **João Goulart** who favored populist, pro-labor policies. Vargas dismissed Goulart from his post as minister of labor in February, only to align himself with the populists by decreeing a wage increase along the lines advocated by Goulart.

August 1. **Appearing at the Jockey Club in Rio de Janeiro, Vargas was booed by members angered by corruption within his official circle and by his inability to slow the inflation** that had reached 100 percent in three years' time. Journalist Carlos Lacerda, political rival of the president's son, Lutero Vargas, increased the tempo of his attacks.

August 5. **Carlos Lacerda was wounded in an assassination attempt that left air force Major Rubens Vaz dead.** An investigation established that a member of the presidential guard had carried out the attack. There were widespread calls for **Vargas**'s resignation.

August 24. **Compelled to resign by the military, Getúlio Vargas committed suicide.** He left behind a note in which he blamed his action on "forces and interests which work against the people." Vice President João Café Filho completed Vargas's term, presiding over presidential elections fourteen months later.

1955

July 14. **The Institute of Advanced Brazilian Studies (ISEB, Instituto Superior de Estudos Brasileiros) was established.** Intensely nationalistic, the institute supported development policies of soon-to-be-president **Juscelino Kubitschek**. Over the following nine years the institute became split over the issue of whether capitalist or socialist development models should be followed. At length left-wing academics triumphed, leading to the institute's dissolution by the military in 1964.

October 3. **Juscelino Kubitschek, candidate of the two political parties founded by Getúlio Vargas, the PSB and the PTB, won the presi-** dential contest. **Vargas** protégé **João Goulart** won the vice presidency. On November 11, top military officers staged a "preventive coup" against Acting President Carlos Luz, who had vowed to deny **Kubitschek** the presidency.

1956

January 31. **Juscelino Kubitschek was inaugurated president, promising "fifty years of progress in five."** A proponent of planning and development, he concentrated national investment in Minas Gerais, São Paulo, and Rio de Janeiro. There he deemed the preconditions for self-sustained growth to exist. According to W.W. Rostow's development theory, a successfully developed economic zone would propel the entire nation into development. Another of Kubitschek's projects was that of relocating the national capital away from the coast as a means of drawing population inland. During his term industrial production in Brazil increased 80 percent, while per capita GDP grew at better than 4 percent per year. Foreign investment was encouraged by Kubitschek, and major hydroelectric projects were launched. At the same time the president was criticized for neglecting education and agriculture, and for slighting the poorer, predominately rural states.

1957

April. **Ground was broken for the new national capital of Brasília.**

1958

May 28. **President Juscelino Kubitschek, writing to U.S. president Eisenhower, proposed "Operation Pan America,"** involving inter-American economic and political cooperation. Kubitschek's suggestion was embraced by Eisenhower and, subsequently, by U.S. president Kennedy who, three years later, launched the Alliance for Progress.

July. **The Brazilian national soccer team won the World Cup**.

1959

January. **The Development Superintendency of the Northeast, SUDENE (Superintendência do** **Desenvolvimento do Nordeste) was established**. Designed to promote development in the nation's impoverished Northeast, the agency was directed by noted economist Celso Furtado. While SUDE-NE did not achieve all of its goals, it was successful in alleviating the poverty in Brazil's most backward region.

REVOLUTIONARY MOVEMENTS AND ECONOMIC DEVELOPMENT 1960-1989

During the 1960s and 1970s the power of the Marxist-Leninist vision, bolstered by the success of the Cuban Revolution, produced revolutionary movements throughout Latin America. Where such movements appeared, states acted decisively to crush them; human rights suffered as a result. National militaries were the worst violators, for in quashing those advocating violent overthrow of the status quo they paid little attention to niceties such as extending due process to those arrested. The guerrillas' record was often no better, for they kidnapped and killed when they thought it would promote their ends. Throughout the Cold War years Latin American governments, whether democratically elected or dictatorial, enjoyed ongoing aid from the United States in combatting the revolutionary left.

While Cold War struggles took center stage from 1960 through 1989, important social processes were silently at work. During those thirty years, quality-of-life indicators such as the infant mortality rate, per capita GDP, and educational level improved steadily. And continued rapid movement from country to city made Latin America one of the world's most urbanized regions by 1989. Meanwhile Latin America passed through distinct economic phases. During the 1960s and 1970s, states took an active role in pushing the import substitution process to completion. The larger nations, Brazil, Mexico, and Argentina, moved on to the next stage of industrialization, gaining the ability to manufacture consumer durables such as automobiles. They often did so through the formation of state-owned enterprises financed by extensive international borrowing. Meanwhile they achieved greater efficiencies and economies of scale through regional integration. But by the 1980s events conspired against state-led industrialization. Global recession contributed to Mexico's debt crisis and plunged most Latin American nations into an economic slump.

Markets for their exports dried up, state revenues shrank, and servicing of the foreign debt grew onerous. Most nations were forced to accept painful austerity measures, often imposed by the International Monetary Fund (IMF).

The economic shocks of the 1980s hastened Latin America's search for new ways to achieve development and stability. Nations of the region sought to expand markets through regional trade associations. They also moved away from protectionism, and embraced economic liberalism. State-owned enterprises were privatized, government-funded social programs cut back, and restrictions on trade and other forms of economic activity eased. Business recovered and, starting in Chile, showed signs of unprecedented vigor. Critics pointed out that in a setting of unfettered capitalism social inequalities intensified. But their voices were drowned out in the generalized rush to open markets.

International Developments

The Cold War and Latin America's struggle to promote economic growth dominated the international scene from 1960 through 1989. The United States was important in both those areas.

As the world's dominant economic power and chief promoter of capitalism and democracy, the United States aggressively led Latin America in isolating communist Cuba from the hemispheric community after 1960. That leadership was exercised both diplomatically, through the Organization of American States and other international bodies, and militarily. This was especially the case in Central America and the Caribbean. In South America the United States provided strong support to governments, democratic and nondemocratic alike, as they fought domestic Marxist-Leninist guerrillas.

Anxious to ease the deprivation that was thought to benefit Marxism-Leninism, the United States launched the Alliance for Progress in 1961, and encouraged international lending agencies such as the International Monetary Fund and World Bank to extend significant amounts of development aid to Latin America. A decade later Latin American governments borrowed petrodollars to fund social programs and development projects. But the economic downturn of the 1980s plunged the debtor economies into crisis. Negotiations between debt-ridden states and international bankers, especially the IMF, became an ongoing feature of Latin American affairs during the 1970s and 1980s.

A third variety of international negotiations involved the exploration of ways to expand intra-regional trade. While a number of regional trade agreements were initiated in the 1960s, they did not enjoy exceptional success until late in the 1980s.

1960

February 18. **The Latin American Free Trade Association (LAFTA) was established by the Treaty of Montevideo.** Its goal was to expand intra-Latin American trade, which had fallen from an 11 to a 6 percent share of total global trade over the preceding decade. Eleven nations ultimately ratified the agreement: Argentina, Brazil, Chile, Peru, Paraguay, Uruguay, Mexico, Venezuela, Colombia, Ecuador, and Bolivia. It aimed at creating a customs union by 1973, but its movement toward that goal was slow. The 1973 oil price rise was especially divisive, as it drove a wedge between oil-exporting Venezuela, Ecuador, and Mexico, and other members of LAFTA. Four years earlier, in the 1969 Caracas Protocol, LAFTA members had voted to extend the deadline for achieving free trade to the year 1980. While falling short of its goal, LAFTA did stimulate trade among Latin American states.

August 20-29. **OAS foreign ministers took action against the Dominican Republic**. Meeting in San José, Costa Rica, the foreign ministers recommended a break in diplomatic relations and the imposition of limited economic sanctions. This extraordinary action, the first of its kind in inter-American history, was prompted by an OAS report accusing the **Trujillo** regime of flagrant violations of human rights and by evidence of Dominican complicity in an assassination attempt against the president of Venezuela, **Rómulo Betancourt**. In January 1961 the OAS Council expanded the economic sanctions against the Dominican Republic.

At San José the foreign ministers refused to support United States demands for collective action against Cuba. They merely adopted a resolution that, without mentioning Cuba by name, condemned extra-continental intervention in the Western Hemisphere, including efforts by the Sino-Soviet bloc to exploit conditions there.

September 5-12. **A meeting of the OAS Committee of Twenty-One, held in Colombia, produced the Bogotá Act,** under whose terms the United States would make $500 million in social-development loans available to Latin American countries.

October 1. **The Inter-American Development Bank (IDB) began operation.** Chartered in December 1959 by the United States and nineteen Latin American nations, the bank was capitalized by shares subscribed by the member states. Diminution of United States support for the bank in the early 1970s led to broadening of the bank's resource base through the admission of Canada, Japan, and European nations to membership. By 1992 the bank had forty-two members. Over its first thirty-five years the bank issued more than 2,000 loans totaling some $60 billion, most of which funded projects involving agriculture, energy, industry, transportation, public health, education, science, technology, urban development, and the environment.

1961

February. **The Agency for International Development (AID) was created by the United States government** in order to unify that nation's international aid programs. A major early thrust of AID was in Latin America and the Caribbean under the Alliance for Progress. AID programs were aimed at reducing poverty and increasing democratic governance.

August 17. **The charter of the Alliance for Progress was signed by all OAS members except Cuba at Punta del Este, Uruguay.** Their action was in response to a proposal for enhanced inter-American cooperation made by U.S. president John F. Kennedy (March 1961). Under the agreement the United States committed $20 billion to Latin America, a sum to be invested to further economic growth, democratization, social programs, and military counterinsurgency operations. Half the sum promised by Kennedy was ultimately forthcoming, though the monies were unevenly distributed by the countries that received them. Enthusiasm for the Alliance waned over the 1960s. Only seven of nineteen Latin American nations achieved the 2.5 percent annual growth in GDP projected in the charter of the Alliance for Progress, and by decade's end military coups had occurred in several nations. As the Alliance for Progress was ostensibly aimed at forestalling communist advances in Latin America, the program was perceived as less important by the 1970s, when the revolutionary threat diminished. During the 1970s, the program was quietly abandoned.

1962

January 22-31. **At Punta del Este OAS foreign ministers voted 14-1 to expel Cuba from the inter-American system for being a Marxist-Leninist regime,** incompatible with the democratic principles of the organization. OAS members went on to vote an arms embargo against Cuba. Mexico, Ecuador, Brazil, Bolivia, Argentina, and Chile abstained from the initial vote, and Mexico voted against in the final vote.

July–September. **The International Coffee Agreement was negotiated at the United Nations.** Signed by coffee-producing and -consum-ing countries, it tried to stabilize world prices for coffee by matching supply with demand. Another goal was to increase coffee consumption. The agreement collapsed in 1989.

1964

July 21-26. **The Ninth Consultative Meeting of foreign ministers of the OAS, held in Washington, D.C., voted (15-4) to declare Cuba guilty of aggression and intervention in Venezuelan affairs, and called upon members to sever diplomatic relations with Cuba.** Mexico, Chile, Uruguay, and Bolivia opposed the vote. By December 1964, all OAS member states save Mexico had broken relations with Cuba.

1965

May. **OAS ministers agreed to dispatch a peace-keeping force to the Dominican Republic,** to support U.S. troops who had invaded to crush a possible communist takeover there. This marked the first time an armed OAS mission intervened in a domestic dispute in a member state. Bowing to United States pressure, all member states save Mexico, Ecuador, Peru, Chile, Uruguay, and Venezuela voted for the measure, which led to creation of the Inter-American Peace Force.

1966

January 3-15. **The first Tri-Continental Conference of Asian, African, and Latin American Revolutionary Solidarity met in Havana, Cuba.** Delegates from about 100 countries attacked United States policies in Vietnam and expressed support for world revolution. The Organization of Latin American Solidarity (OLAS) was established to promote revolution throughout the region.

1967

February 14. **The Treaty of Tlatelolco, or Treaty for the Prohibition of Nuclear Weapons**

in Latin America, was signed in Mexico City. Initiated by Latin American presidents during 1962-63, the accord was a multilateral agreement not to manufacture, receive, store, or test nuclear weapons.

February 27. **Members of the Organization of American States signed the Buenos Aires Protocol, amending the OAS charter.** One revision included replacement of the inter-American conference, which was supposed to meet every five years, with a General Assembly to meet annually. Another incorporated the Inter-American Commission on Human Rights within the OAS structure. At a subsequent OAS meeting held at Punta del Este, Uruguay (April 12-14), the presidents of member states pledged themselves to increasing Latin American economic integration and exports, and improving rural living conditions and agricultural productivity.

August. **The Organization of Latin American Solidarity (OLAS) met in Havana, Cuba.** The makeup of the delegations and the resolutions adopted reflected tensions between Cuba on the one hand and the Soviet Union and Latin American Communist parties on the other. Contrary to the Soviet position, the delegates stressed the primacy of armed struggle in ousting Latin American regimes, and were critical of the Soviet Union for supporting Latin American governments that the delegates deemed repressive.

1968

August. **The Conference of Latin American Bishops (CELAM) embraced liberation theology.** Meeting in Medellín, Colombia, CELAM adopted the activist theology preached by Peruvian priest Gustavo Gutiérrez and other theologians. According to Gutiérrez, Roman Catholics must actively participate in the struggles of Latin America's poor. Gutiérrez and the bishops were inspired by the pronouncements of Vatican II (1962-65), and by the militancy of left-wing social reformers throughout the region. That liberation theology drew upon certain aspects of Marxist theory made it vulnerable to criticism from sup-

porters of the status quo. Tensions over this issue surfaced at the next bishops' meeting, in Puebla, Mexico, in 1979.

1969

December. **The Inter-American Foundation (IAF) was created by the United States government to promote Latin American development through the funding of nongovernmental organizations (NGOs).** A perceived failure of the Alliance for Progress to promote significant social development during the 1960s led to creation of the IAF. By the mid-1990s, the IAF had sponsored some 5,000 grassroots development projects in twenty-six countries.

1975

July 29. **OAS foreign ministers voted to allow freedom of action in relations with Cuba.** Sixteen nations (including the United States) voted in favor of the resolution, 3 (including Chile, Paraguay, and Uruguay) voted no, and 2 (Brazil and Nicaragua) abstained. The resolution did not revoke the exclusion of Cuba from the OAS, but permitted countries to conduct their relations with Cuba as they saw fit. By 1975 several countries including Peru, Argentina, Colombia, and Venezuela, had reestablished relations with Cuba.

1980

August 12. **In the Montevideo Treaty, signatories of the 1960 LAFTA pact changed the name of their organization to Latin American Integration Association (ALADI).** But their effort to achieve regional economic integration collapsed in 1982 as a result of that year's debt crisis. By 1984 most intra-regional trade (84 percent) was conducted on the basis of bilateral agreements. The Montevideo Treaty also endorsed bilateral agreements with countries from outside Latin America.

1984

September 3. **The Vatican and liberation theology.** The Vatican issued a document condemning economic injustice in Latin America and supporting liberation theology. The document, however, rejected Marxism as a tool of analysis. Soon afterward Leonardo Boff, a Brazilian Franciscan and prominent exponent of liberation theology, was interrogated in Rome about his writings and was later formally sanctioned. During the papacy of John Paul II, Vatican leaders moved in general to weaken the influence of clerics who favored liberation theology.

1989

The Inter-American Development Bank (IDB) sponsored formation of the Inter-American Investment Corporation (IIC). Funded by IDB members, the IIC lent to private enterprise.

Mexico, Central America, and the Caribbean

The 1960s and 1970s were a time of political ferment in Central America and the Caribbean. **Fidel Castro**'s success in resisting United States efforts to crush his revolution excited radical reformers who dreamed of emulating him and leading their respective countries to socialism. Meanwhile the United States exerted a powerful influence in the Caribbean region, determined as it was to forestall further defections to the communist camp. The United States systematically opposed every movement of leftist savor. The Dominican Republic, Nicaragua, Guatemala, and El Salvador were all scenes of bloody Cold War struggles.

Only Mexico, whose revolution had occurred a half-century earlier, was relatively calm (though Mexico, too, witnessed short-lived guerrilla movements during the 1960s and 1970s). Mexico remained on good terms with both the United States and Cuba, thereby lending a degree of stability to an otherwise stormy Middle America.

The revolutionary threat eased by the late 1980s. Everywhere save Cuba, peoples of the Caribbean considered ways of getting on in a world dominated by market forces and the powerful nations that revered those forces. The United States attempted to ease that process by expanding the list of duty-free products that Caribbean and Central American nations could ship to the United States (in the Caribbean Basin Initiative of January 1984).

1960

February 13. **Cuba signed a trade agreement with the Soviet Union,** leading U.S. president Eisenhower to authorize CIA training of Cuban exiles for invasion of the island (March 17). In late June **Fidel Castro** expropriated U.S.-owned oil refineries when they refused to process Soviet crude, causing Eisenhower to cancel Cuba's sugar quota (July 6). Cuba responded by expropriating all United States property on the island (August 7–October 24), to which the United States responded by prohibiting most exports to Cuba.

August. **Conditions grew increasingly chaotic in the Dominican Republic, following condemnation of the Trujillo regime by the OAS.** Héctor Trujillo, **Rafael Trujillo**'s brother and figurehead president for eight years, stepped down (August 2) and was succeeded by Vice President **Joaquín Balaguer**. Rafael remained in charge, however, and stepped up repression of those who opposed him, having many tortured and murdered. The rape and murder of the three Mirabal sisters by Trujillo's soldiers (November 25) heightened domestic outrage against the dictator.

October 1. **Roberto Chiari was inaugurated president of Panama.** The son of a former president and the candidate of a four-party coalition, the National Opposition Union, he was elected to a four-year term on May 8. On September 21 a Panamanian flag was permanently raised in the Canal Zone alongside the United States flag.

October 26. **Unpopular Salvadoran president José María Lemus was arrested and exiled** by a reform-minded, prodemocratic faction within the military. A civilian-military junta supplanted him until it too was overthrown by conservative officers led by Lieutenant Colonel Julio A. Rivera, whose Party of National Conciliation (PCN) ruled the country for eighteen years (under Colonels Rivera, 1961-67; Fidel Sánchez, 1967-72; Arturo Molina, 1972-77; and General Carlos Romero, 1977-79). While the national army controlled both the PCN and national elections, the party's existence permitted the military to argue that their country possessed the accoutrements of formal democracy. During the 1960s and 1970s, the status quo, led by the coffee-exporting elite, supported military rule. Radical social reform was quelled by a paramilitary organization known as ORDEN, founded in 1964 ostensibly to fight communism.

November 8. **Governor Luis Muñoz Marín led his Popular Democratic party (PPD) to a sweeping victory in Puerto Rican elections.** The Republican Statehood party (PER) increased its share of the vote to 32 percent, while the Independence party (PIP) won slightly over 3 percent.

November 13. **Guatemalan president Ydígoras Fuentes personally led troops in putting down an uprising of nationalist army officers** who wanted to stop Cuban exiles and the American CIA from operating on Guatemalan soil. Lieutenants Marco Antonio Yon Sosa and Luis Augusto Turcios Lima subsequently fled into exile, but soon returned to eastern Guatemala where they organized the Rebel Armed Forces (FAR). The left-revolutionary guerrilla fought an ongoing civil war with the Guatemalan army for the ensuing thirty-five years. During the 1960s and 1970s the status quo was supported by the coffee-exporting elite that had traditionally stood behind the military.

November 21. **Guillermo Ungo, José Napoleón Duarte, and six others formed El Salvador's Christian Democratic party.** The party formed a loyal opposition to the military-dominated PCN, participating in but never winning power during the eighteen years of PCN dominance.

December 12. **All Central American nations except Costa Rica signed, under ECLA tutelage, the General Treaty of Central American Economic Integration.** The ambitious agreement provided for immediate regional free trade in all except a small number of products. It also called for the creation of a common market in five years' time, and provided for establishment of institutions that included the Central American Bank for Economic Integration. The treaty was a successor to earlier agreements (June 2, 1958), which initiated the process of economic integration.

1961

January 3. **The United States and Cuba severed diplomatic relations.**

February 27. **Ernesto "Che" Guevara became minister of industry in Cuba.** Along with Cuban premier **Fidel Castro**, **Guevara** favored state ownership and direction of the means of production to further the equitable distribution of food and manufactured goods. The two leaders rejected economic management giving precedence to market forces, insisting that economic life center upon moral rather than material incentives. Their attempt to create an industrialized command economy funded by ever-increasing sugar production fared poorly.

April 14. **President Luis Somoza personally dispatched CIA-trained Cuban exiles, en route to southern Cuba, from Puerto Cabezas, Nicaragua.** Somoza and Guatemalan president Miguel Ydígoras Fuentes collaborated with the Americans in preparing the operation.

April 15-17. **U.S.-supported dissidents bombed and then invaded south-central Cuba, at the Bay of Pigs.** An air strike on April 15 failed to destroy Cuba's air defenses and gained

Central America

MEXICO

Belmopan

BELIZE

GUATEMALA

HONDURUS

Guatemala

Tegucigalpa

San Salvador

EL SALVADOR

NICARAGUA

Managua

Lago de Nicaragua

Caribbean Sea

Pacific Ocean

COSTA RICA

San José

Panama

PANAMA

COLOMBIA

unfavorable international attention, leading President Kennedy to cancel a second air strike scheduled to coincide with the landing at the Bay of Pigs. The invasion failed, and **Fidel Castro** subsequently allowed the United States to ransom 1,180 surviving attackers with medical and other supplies. On April 18, Soviet leader Nikita Khrushchev denounced the invasion and promised aid to Cuba.

May 22. **François Duvalier was inaugurated to a second term as Haitian president** following an election in which he was the only candidate. Within two years of his 1957 election Duvalier had crushed all opposition to his regime through use of his fearsome militias known as the *tontons macoutes.* He made good use of black nationalism and appeals to the poor through promotion of the Afro-American religion Vodun. Throughout his dictatorship there were incessant attempts to overthrow him, all of which failed. Not long after securing Haiti's vote for expelling Cuba from the OAS, the United States suspended aid to the Caribbean nation.

May 30. **Dominican dictator Rafael L. Trujillo was assassinated** while being chauffeured through the outskirts of Ciudad Trujillo. The American CIA approved the dispatch of weapons to his killers, but they were not delivered.

June 3. **The Central American Common Market (CACM) became operative** when Guatemala, El Salvador, and Nicaragua ratified the organization's enabling treaty (of December 1960). Honduras and Costa Rica subsequently ratified the document. Trade within Central America grew rapidly during the 1960s, increasing sevenfold by 1967. During the decade regional economic growth averaged 5.8 percent. That progress was interrupted in 1969 by a war between El Salvador and Honduras, and subsequently by economic and political crises of the 1970s and 1980s.

July. **Nicaraguan Tomás Borge and two companions founded the Sandinista National Liberation Front (FSLN, Frente Sandinista de Liberación Nacional)**, whose goal was overthrow of the **Somoza** dynasty. Borge and his colleagues, Carlos Fonseca and Silvio Mayorga, had fought the Somoza regime during the 1950s, all three

suffering exile. Borge had earlier visited Cuba where he sought the aid of **Fidel Castro**.

November 20. **Trujillo family members fled the Dominican Republic** after their bid for power was foiled by the appearance of U.S. warships. OAS sanctions against the Dominican Republic were lifted on January 4, 1962, after **Joaquín Balaguer** agreed to step down as head of the Council of State that was governing the country.

December 2. **Fidel Castro proclaimed that he was a Marxist-Leninist.** Later that month his minister of industry, **Ernesto "Che" Guevara**, announced a five-year development plan, founded in assistance from the Soviet Union and Communist Bloc nations.

1962

February 4. **Fidel Castro issued the Second Declaration of Havana, calling for Marxist**

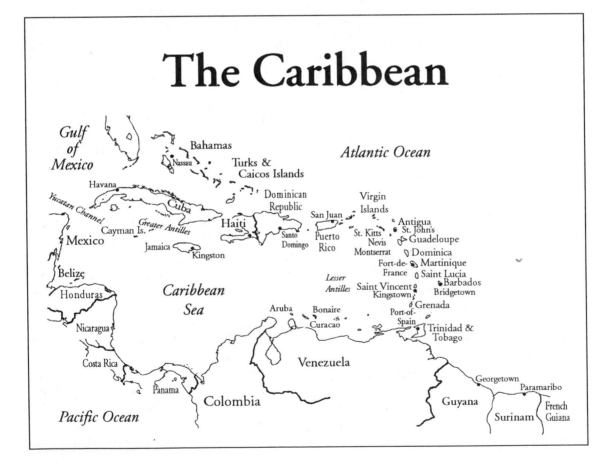

The Caribbean

revolution in Latin America. He went on to sponsor Marxist-Leninist groups in Bolivia, the Dominican Republic, Nicaragua, Panama, Venezuela, Colombia, and elsewhere.

September 26. **The Honduran Congress enacted an agrarian reform law**, thus reducing the appeal of the radical peasant union FENACH. President Ramón Villeda, who since his term began in 1957 had advocated moderate social reform, promoted his programs with aid from the Alliance for Progress. In spite of his close collaboration with the United States, his plan for land reform unsettled commercial banana interests who encouraged the army to unseat him.

October 22. **U.S. president Kennedy demanded the withdrawal of Soviet missiles from Cuba**, going on to quarantine the island (October 23). Two days later the United States and the Soviet Union accepted U.N. acting secretary-general U Thant's offer to mediate the dispute. On October 28 the Soviets agreed to remove the missiles and the United States agreed to end its naval blockade and promised not to invade Cuba. The United States also pledged to remove missiles from Turkey. Information made available by Russia in the 1980s and 1990s revealed that the Soviet Union had deployed in Cuba twenty-four SS-4 missile launchers equipped with nuclear warheads with a range of approximately 1,000 miles. Sixteen SS-5 missile launchers were under construction, awaiting delivery of nuclear missiles and warheads with a range of 2,500 miles. Tactical nuclear weapons, to be used in the event of a United States invasion, were also deployed in Cuba.

December 20. **Juan Bosch was elected president of the Dominican Republic** in the first such contest held there since 1924. Bosch, leader of the Dominican Revolutionary Party (PRD), attempted to establish social democracy in his country. His advanced social program, which included laws secularizing education, raising taxes on business, and reducing the power of the military, alienated the nation's most powerful interests. He lost the support of the United States when he moved to establish diplomatic relations with Cuba.

1963

March 30. **Guatemalan president Miguel Ydígoras Fuentes was overthrown in a revolt** led by his defense minister, General Enrique Peralta Azurdia. Peralta and his supporters feared both the communist guerrillas and the impending return of former president **Juan José Arévalo**. Peralta occupied the presidency until 1966.

April–May. **Haitian dictator François Duvalier's security force, the *tontons macoutes*, fought to preserve the regime** against groups that turned to terrorism upon learning that **Duvalier** would not step down when his constitutional term ended. When he learned that the United States was aiding Haitian exiles, Duvalier intensified repression. The United States suspended diplomatic ties (May 17), but by June 1964, Duvalier was powerful enough to have himself named "President for Life."

May 1. **René Schick Gutiérrez, a Somoza family confidant, took office as president of Nicaragua,** thanks to a law enacted by political modernizer Luis Somoza requiring that a president not succeed himself. Schick's term was relatively peaceful. He died in office in 1966 and was succeeded by Lorenzo Guerrero Gutiérrez.

July 18. **Mexico and the United States settled the Chamizal border dispute,** which had troubled Mexican-U.S. relations for fifty years.

September 25. **The Dominican military overthrew President Juan Bosch in a bloodless coup.** A military-backed three-man civilian junta governed the country until 1965. The United States briefly suspended diplomatic relations after the coup.

October 3. **A military coup removed Honduran president Ramón Villeda** when his Liberal party nominated Modesto Rodas Alvarado for the upcoming presidential contest. Rodas had promised to reduce the power of the army once in office. General Oswaldo López Arellano succeeded Villeda, going on to rule until 1971. The United States briefly suspended diplomatic relations after the coup.

December. **The U.S. backed Central American Defense Council (CONDECA), a regional** defense force aimed at forestalling communist guerrilla movements, was formed by Guatemala, Honduras, El Salvador, and Nicaragua. Costa Rica rejected membership. A creature of the U.S. military, CONDECA later collapsed but was revived in 1983 by Guatemala, El Salvador, and Honduras to coordinate strategy against the Sandinista government of Nicaragua during the 1980s.

1964

January 9-11. **Flag riots took place in Panama**. Disturbances broke out after the governor of the Canal Zone authorized the flying of the U.S. and Panamanian flags together in sixteen places in the zone and the lowering of the U.S. flag elsewhere. As American students, supported by their parents, tried to prevent the lowering of the U.S. flag in front of Balboa High School, Panamanian students arrived, hoping to raise their flag there. In the ensuing scuffle, the Panamanian flag was torn, and widespread rioting erupted. Hundreds were injured, and twenty-seven persons—23 Panamanians and 4 American soldiers—were killed. President Chiari, whose government was faulted for failing to halt violence in Panama City and Colón, suspended diplomatic relations with the United States. But negotiations soon got under way that eventually led to new Panama Canal treaties.

December 1. **Gustavo Díaz Ordaz was inaugurated to a six-year presidential term in Mexico**. A conservative from Puebla who had served as secretary of the interior *(gobernación)* under Adolfo López Mateos, Díaz lacked the charisma and popularity of his predecessor. He ruled with an iron hand, maintaining PRI supremacy in spite of periodic challenges of the conservative PAN party. Mexico's crisis of legitimacy began during the administration of Díaz Ordaz.

1965

April 24. **Civil war broke out in the Dominican Republic** after the ruling junta was ousted in a military coup. Civilian and military supporters of deposed president Juan Bosch, calling themselves

Constitutionalists, tried to seize power but met resistance from anti-Bosch officers. U.S. president Lyndon Johnson, claiming that the Constitutionalists had been infiltrated by communists, intervened (April 28), sending 23,000 U.S. troops to oppose the revolutionaries. An Inter-American Peace Force, made up mainly of Brazilians, also entered the Dominican Republic, and the OAS joined the United States in seeking an end to the conflict. An OAS committee headed by Ellsworth Bunker devised an agreement acceptable to all factions (August 31), and elections were scheduled for the following year.

May. **Mexico introduced a border industrialization program**. The government announced that it would allow duty-free importation of materials and components to be assembled and later exported, provided that they remained in bond while in Mexico. The program took advantage of a 1962 provision in the United States tariff stating that products assembled abroad from United States components might enter the United States with duties levied only on the value added. Established in part to create employment after the end of the *bracero* program in 1964, the new measures were initially limited to a 30-kilometer (18-mile) section along the border, but were later extended to other sections of Mexico. The new factories, known as *maquiladoras*, proliferated with the fall of the Mexican peso during the 1980s. By the mid-1990s more than 2,000 of the plants existed, employing more than 500,000 Mexicans.

October. **The Cuban Communist party (Partido Comunista de Cuba, PCC) was established**. The party was an outgrowth of two earlier groups—the Integrated Revolutionary Organizations (1961) and the United Party of the Socialist Revolution (1963)—which had merged Cuba's first Communist party (then known as the Popular Socialist party), **Fidel Castro**'s 26th of July Movement, and the Revolutionary Student Directorate. Castro became the first secretary of the Politburo, the party's chief policymaking body. The party did not hold its first congress until 1975.

November 17. **PRI president Carlos Madrazo was fired by Mexican leader Díaz Ordaz**. The action illustrated Díaz's intent to thwart Madrazo's plan to democratize the PRI and to lessen the president's control over it.

1966

June 1. **Joaquín Balaguer was elected president of the Dominican Republic, defeating Juan Bosch by a 57 to 39 percent margin.** Bosch claimed fraud, but international observers found no serious irregularities in the election. Re-elected in 1970 and 1974, **Balaguer**'s first three presidencies were years of prosperity in the Dominican Republic. The nation received infusions of U.S. aid, and the United States paid top prices for Dominican sugar. Meanwhile Balaguer consolidated his position by either crushing or co-opting the PRD opposition.

July 1. **Julio César Méndez Montenegro was inaugurated Guatemala's president, the first civilian president since Juan José Arévalo (1945-1951).** Méndez, a reformist candidate, was supported by leftist guerrillas who hoped he would provide them a democratic opening. Such opening did not take place, and civil war raged in rural Guatemala during the latter 1960s. Led by Colonel Carlos Arana Osorio, the Guatemalan army practiced scorched earth tactics characterized by massive human rights violations and the murder of thousands of rural-dwelling civilians accused of abetting the guerrillas.

1967

February 5. **Anastasio Somoza Debayle was elected president of Nicaragua. Somoza**, who had recently resigned as head of the National Guard, defeated Fernando Agüero of the Conservative party. In January some forty persons died during demonstrations protesting anticipated fraud in the election. Somoza stepped down in 1972, but again sought the presidency in 1974.

July 23. **A plebiscite on the status of Puerto Rico was won by the pro-Commonwealth PPD party, following strenuous campaigning by party founder Luis Muñoz Marín.** The PPD won over 60 percent of the vote, while the pro-statehood PER won 39 percent. After the vote statehood advocate Luis Antonio Ferré Aguayo

organized the new pro-statehood party, the New Progressive party (PNP). The PNP went on to win gubernatorial elections in 1968, 1976, 1980, 1992, and 1996. Meanwhile the PPD, under the leadership of Rafael Hernández, Colón ruled in 1972-76 and 1984-92.

1968

March. **Fidel Castro announced his "revolutionary offensive" against private property in Cuba** when he ordered nationalization of all private enterprise not previously under state control. With that action only black-market private enterprise remained on the island.

September. **Mexican revolutionary Lucio Cabañas founded the Revolutionary September 23rd League**, a peasant organization active in the state of Guerrero. Cabañas died in a clash with the military in 1974.

October 2. **The Tlatelolco Massacre took place in Mexico City.** Police and soldiers fired on demonstrators in the Plaza of Three Cultures in the Tlatelolco district of Mexico City, killing at least 300. The events that culminated in the massacre began in July with charges of brutality against riot police who had been summoned to quell a fight among high school students. University students and others soon became involved in strikes and demonstrations, and their demands took on an antigovernment character, as seen on August 27, when an estimated 500,000 marched to the Zócalo, or main square, of Mexico City. The Díaz Ordaz administration responded by ordering the occupation of the National University, which touched off a wave of violence. The protests were especially embarrassing because they occurred as the government prepared to host the Olympic Games in Mexico City in October. The relatively small rally on October 2 was initially peaceful, and there is disagreement as to whether snipers or the police fired the first shots. The government's use of massive force, however, and the heavy loss of life discredited the regime, though the Olympic Games proceeded smoothly.

October 11. **Lieutenant Colonel Omar Torrijos Herrera and other officers of Panama's National Guard overthrew President**

Arnulfo Arias just three days into his third presidency. **Torrijos** consolidated his dominance by exiling his chief military rival in 1969, and, two years later, having himself declared "Maximum Leader" of the nation. He did so through the 1972 constitution, one allowing a figurehead president but granting Torrijos dictatorial authority.

1969

March. **Tension along Honduras's border with El Salvador increased** when the former nation's agrarian reform institute ruled that land grants would be restricted to native-born Hondurans, and that Salvadoran squatters would be expelled. At the time some 300,000 undocumented rural migrants resided in Honduras.

July 14-18. **El Salvador and Honduras fought the Football War,** so called because it was precipitated by a regional soccer competition. The Salvadoran army entered Honduran territory to protect Salvadoran citizens, who were being violently ejected by the Honduran army. The Salvadorans were quickly forced, under United States and OAS pressure, to withdraw from Honduran soil. The war had important implications and consequences. Apart from causing some 2,000 deaths, it destroyed the Central American Common Market and exacerbated social and political tensions in densely populated El Salvador. The returning migrants intensified hardship at lower levels of society resulting in increased calls for land reform.

1970

March 1. **Carlos Arana Osorio, supported by the military-dominated Democratic Institutionalist party, won a plurality in Guatemala's presidential election.** He was proclaimed president-elect by the Congress on March 22, and took office July 1. Nicknamed the Butcher of Zacapa, allegedly an organizer of the White Hand (La Mano Blanca) death squad, he contin-

ued the war against rural guerrillas, which intensified over the decade. The civil war ultimately claimed the lives of some 100,000 Guatemalans. Subsequent to Arana Osorio's term, two other high-ranking soldiers occupied the presidency, both elected over Christian Democratic party candidates in fraud-ridden contests: General Kjell Laugerud García (1974-78) and General Romeo Lucas García (1978-82).

May 8. **José Figueres Ferrer was inaugurated to a second term as Costa Rican president.** In an effort to stimulate the economy, **Figueres** established trade and diplomatic relations with the Soviet Union, and also invited fugitive financier Robert Vesco to conduct operations in the country. Figueres was succeeded in office by PLN co-founder Daniel Oduber Quirós (1974-78).

July 26. **In a speech to the nation, Cuban leader Fidel Castro admitted failure in the economic sphere.** He made specific reference to the inability of the island's sugar industry to harvest 10 million tons in 1970. Although a record 8.5 million tons were produced, the massive effort to reach the 10 million ton figure disrupted the economy.

December 1. **Luis Echeverría Álvarez was inaugurated to a six-year term as Mexican president.** **Echeverría**, secretary of the interior under Díaz Ordaz, was expected to govern the nation in the conservative and authoritarian manner of his predecessors. But he surprised Mexicans with his populism and economic nationalism. Echeverría created 761 new state-owned enterprises during his term, raising the total to 845. By 1976 the state's contribution to gross domestic product went from 8 to 12.5 percent. He steered an independent course in foreign policy, promoting Third World causes and frequently opposing U.S. foreign policy initiatives.

1971

April 21. **Haitian dictator François Duvalier died,** leaving the nation poorer than when he came to power fifteen years earlier. Rapid population growth coupled with deforestation and erosion solidified Haiti's status as the hemisphere's poorest nation. **Duvalier** arranged for his son, Jean-Claude "Baby Doc" Duvalier, to succeed him.

June 6. **Ramón E. Cruz took office as president of Honduras.** The inauguration of Cruz, a civilian and the candidate of the National party, marked the end of nearly eight years of military domination. He was ousted, however, on December 4, 1972, in a military coup led by General Oswaldo López Arellano.

June 10. **Paramilitary forces attacked students in Mexico City,** allowing President **Echeverría** to sack their commander, head of the Federal District Alfonso Martínez. The move strengthened Echeverría's control of the ruling PRI party.

1972

February 20. **Salvadoran Christian Democratic leader José Napoleón Duarte was denied the presidency in what came to be called "the stolen election."** Colonel Arturo Molina, winner of the contest, subsequently exiled both **Duarte** and his running-mate, social democrat Guillermo M. Ungo. The disputed contest heightened political tensions in El Salvador, leading members of the opposition to form guerrillas. Political violence escalated during Molina's presidency and during that of his successor, General Carlos Romero.

March. **Salvadoran dissidents formed the People's Revolutionary Army (ERP),** dedicated to overthrowing their nation's military-dominated government through force. Two years before, other revolutionaries had formed the Farabundo Martí National Liberation Front.

November 15. **Haitian "President for Life" Jean-Claude Duvalier consolidated his power** when he dismissed and exiled Luckner Cambronne, a leading member of the council of state created by his father, **François Duvalier.** The younger Duvalier pursued economic modernization in a desultory way, and eased political repression. His marriage to mulatto divorcée Michele

Bennett displeased the nation's anti-mulatto black majority. The dictator's wife, from a wealthy commercial family, angered Haitians with her extravagant ways.

December 23. **Cuba and the Soviet Union signed an agreement postponing for fourteen years all payments on loans from the USSR.** The pact, signed during a visit by **Fidel Castro** to Moscow, reflected Cuba's increasingly close relations with the Soviet Union. In July 1972, Cuba was formally admitted to the Council for Mutual Economic Assistance (COMECON), the Soviet bloc's economic community.

December 23. **As many as 20,000 died, and 300,000 were left homeless, when an earthquake destroyed Managua, Nicaragua.** The disaster had important political consequences. National Guard commander **Anastasio "Tachito" Somoza** appropriated most relief monies and supplies sent from abroad, heightening anger over his venality.

1973

September 17. **Mexican industrialist Eugenio Garza Sada was killed in a kidnapping attempt in Monterrey.** This incident, coupled with a wave of other kidnappings by leftist groups, worsened relations between President **Echeverría** and the business community.

1974

December 1. **Anastasio Somoza was inaugurated to a second term as Nicaraguan president.** His decision to assume direct control of the nation resulted in formation of an umbrella opposition group, the UDEL (Unión Democrática de Liberación), led by Pedro Joaquín Chamorro. One of the few groups excluded from the UDEL was the Marxist FSLN.

1975

March 31. **"Bananagate" scandal in Honduras.** General Oswaldo López Arellano, who had ruled Honduras since 1972, was deposed after it was charged that he and other officials had taken large bribes from United Brands (successor to the United Fruit Company). The bribes were linked to the government's cancellation of a new tax on banana exports. The head of United Brands, Eli Black, who was implicated in the scandal, committed suicide on February 3, 1975.

November 10. **Mexico voted in the United Nations to equate Zionism with racism**. In the UN General Assembly Mexico voted for a resolution declaring Zionism to be "a form of racism and racial discrimination." The resolution passed, but most other Latin American countries voted against it or abstained. In retaliation, U.S. Jewish groups organized a tourist boycott of Mexico early in 1976. Mexico's vote is generally seen as part of a campaign by President **Echeverría** to curry favor with the Third World nations of Asia and Africa to enhance his chances of being named UN secretary- general.

1976

February 4. **A devastating earthquake in Guatemala, coupled with the government's ineffective response to the tragedy, increased dissatisfaction with military rule**. More than 20,000 were killed, and more than 1 million left homeless as a result of the earthquake, which measured 7.5 on the Richter scale.

February 15. **Cuba's new constitution was approved in a plebiscite**. Marxism-Leninism was declared the state ideology and the PCC the only legal political party. A council of ministers became Cuba's highest political body. The council was headed by **Fidel Castro**, who became president of Cuba.

August 31. **President Echeverría announced that the Mexican peso would be devalued**. Echeverría was reluctant to oversee the first devaluation since 1954, but was forced to take this step because rising inflation and massive capital flight made defense of the peso difficult to sustain despite heavy borrowing by the government.

September 16. **The U.S. Federal Tax Reform Act exempted Puerto Rican–based compa-** nies from income taxes on business and passive investment income. The act led to the establishment of pharmaceutical and other high-tech industries on the island, which by the 1980s accounted for half of Puerto Rico's employment in manufacturing.

November 19. **Outgoing president Echeverría nationalized 250,000 acres of agricultural land in northwestern Mexico**, announcing that he would give it to peasants who had recently invaded it. Critics labeled the president's move a ploy to gain favor in the face of his poor management of national finances.

December 1. **José López Portillo was inaugurated to a six-year term as Mexican president**. Capitalizing on high petroleum prices and the discovery of large oil deposits near Veracruz, López Portillo made Mexico the world's fourth exporter of petroleum by 1981. Meanwhile he borrowed heavily abroad and spent lavishly on public projects. Graft and corruption abounded in the heady economic atmosphere.

1977

June 2. **Cuba and the United States announced that they would open interest sections in each other's capitals**. United States diplomatic and consular officials were to be housed in the Swiss embassy in Havana, and those of Cuba in the Czech embassy in Washington. This agreement occurred during a brief period of improved relations during the administration of President Jimmy Carter.

September 6. **The United States and Panama signed two new canal treaties**. The first document, the Panama Canal Treaty, terminated all previous treaties, recognized Panamanian sovereignty over the canal and the zone, and provided for U.S. operation of the canal until December 31, 1999, at which time Panama would assume complete control. The Treaty Concerning the Permanent Neutrality and Operation of the Canal stated that it shall at all times be open to peaceful transit by the ships of all nations. An appended statement of understanding (October 14, 1977) provided that each nation may defend the canal against threats to its neutrality. The treaties were controversial in the United States and barely won ratification by the U.S. Senate in 1978.

September 19. **Nicaraguan president Somoza, under pressure from U.S. president Carter, restored constitutional rule to his country.** That action touched off a flurry of political activity among anti-Somoza groups.

1978

January. **Thousands of Cuban troops were reported to be in Ethiopia to help that nation repel troops from United States–supported Somalia.** Those soldiers joined 36,000 others sent in 1975 to assist the Soviet-supported government in Angola, fighting a civil war against United States–financed insurgents. Cuba confirmed the presence of the troops in Ethiopia in March.

January 10. **Crusading Nicaraguan journalist Pedro Joaquín Chamorro was assassinated by a henchman of the Somoza dictatorship.** The act had the effect of strengthening, broadening, and moderating the Sandinista National Liberation Front (FSLN). Many of those previously associated with Chamorro's non-Marxist UDEL coalition, including his widow, **Violeta Barrios de Chamorro**, joined forces with the left-wing, anti-**Somoza** guerrilla FSLN.

March 5. **General Romeo Lucas García won a plurality in Guatemala's presidential election.** Another candidate, former president Enrique Peralta Azurdia, charged fraud in the balloting, which attracted less than 40 percent of the electorate. Congress declared Lucas García the winner on March 13; he took office on July 1.

May 8. **Rodrigo Carazo Odio was inaugurated president of Costa Rica**, carried to victory by a reformist Unidad coalition. Falling coffee prices and general economic decline, coupled with his support of Nicaraguan exiles, discredited his political movement and paved the way for a return to power of the National Liberation Party (PLN) in 1982.

May 16. **Antonio Guzmán won the Dominican presidency** after U.S. president Jimmy Carter prevailed upon **Joaquín Balaguer** not to extend his term in office. Guzmán went on to vastly expand the Dominican public sector, allowing members of his family to misappropriate public funds. He committed suicide shortly before the end of his term (July 3, 1982). President-elect and fellow PRD member Salvador Jorge Blanco took office on August 16. It was Jorge Blanco's task to reduce the nation's staggering foreign debt, something he did reluctantly by acceding to IMF austerity demands. By the end of his term in 1986, he had met with some success.

May 29. **Farmers in the village of Panzos in western Guatemala were massacred by army troops while protesting a government development program that threatened their lands.** Months earlier, President Kjell Laugerud had launched a development program in lands bordering densely populated Indian communities, aimed at benefiting petroleum, nickel, and agri-business interests.

July 25. **Puerto Rican police killed two young radicals at Cerro Maravilla, a mountain near Ponce.** Questions about the police account of the killings persisted, and in 1983 it was revealed at Puerto Rican Senate hearings that the two men were shot after they had surrendered. Ten police officers were convicted in 1983 on federal charges of perjury and conspiracy to obstruct justice.

August 22. **Sandinistas led by Edén Pastora seized the National Palace in Managua** The seizure humiliated President **Somoza** and led to extensive publicity for the Sandinista cause and the release of political prisoners, among them Marxist **Daniel Ortega Saavedra**.

1979

July 17-19. **Anastasio "Tachito" Somoza fled Nicaragua as Sandinista forces approached Managua.** The dictator's National Guard disintegrated and fled before the FSLN advance, which began on May 29. On July 19, victorious Sandinistas, led by **Daniel Ortega** and **Violeta Barrios de Chamorro**, entered the capital. The

Sandinista Front went on to establish a governing junta that included Ortega, Barrios de Chamorro, and others. Socialist in orientation, the FSLN launched massive literacy, public health, and agrarian reform programs once in power. After 1980, U.S. hostility toward the new regime hobbled Sandinista reform efforts.

October 15. **Junior military officers overthrew Salvadoran president Carlos Romero,** moved to do so by escalating national violence and popular anger with the hidebound PCN regime. The change of government did little to calm political tensions, as El Salvador slipped into a civil war that soon claimed a thousand lives per month.

November. **Cuba and Grenada signed an airport agreement.** The airport, with its planned 9,000-foot runway, was a source of concern to the Reagan administration, which believed it would be used for military purposes rather than for tourism. The United States was alarmed by the close ties between the government of Maurice Bishop, who had seized power in Grenada on March 13, 1979, and Cuba, which provided extensive economic and military assistance. After Bishop was ousted and killed by leftist military foes, the United States invaded the island (October 25, 1983).

1980

March 18. **Mexican president López Portillo launched a program to increase agricultural production,** the first such initiative in twenty-five years. The program was moderately successful, though Mexico continued to import 10 million tons of food annually. Meanwhile, national unemployment stood at 25 percent, with underemployment running to 50 percent of the work force.

March 24. **Salvadoran archbishop Oscar Romero was murdered while saying mass in a hospital chapel.** An outspoken critic of human rights violations in his country and of United States aid to the nation's ruling junta, Romero fell to a death squad assassin with links to the national army. During 1980 death squads took many additional lives, including those of reformist political leader Enrique Álvarez and five associ-

ates (November) and those of three American nuns and a lay worker (December). Because of widespread abuses by the Salvadoran army and right-wing death squads, U.S. aid to Salvadoran governments remained a controversial topic in Washington throughout the 1980s.

April–September. **Some 125,000 Cubans migrated to Florida in the Mariel boatlift,** joining more than 200,000 Cubans who had previously departed the island for the United States (160,000 through a United States–Cuban program, 1965-73). When U.S. president Carter announced that his country would accept all Cuban refugees, **Fidel Castro** released thousands from prisons and mental hospitals, allowing them to join the exodus from the northern port of Mariel. While the "boatlift" was seen as a brilliant move by Castro and an error by Carter, the Cuban leader was moved to spur food production by permitting the formation of farmers' markets between 1980 and 1986.

April 19-22. **Moderates Violeta Barrios de Chamorro and Alfonso Robelo resigned from Nicaragua's ruling junta** in response to the Sandinista leadership's establishment of ties with Cuba and the Soviet Union, and to their decision to postpone elections for five years. Relations with the United States worsened during 1980, and became hostile with the inauguration of Ronald Reagan as U.S. president early the following year.

October. **Five Salvadoran leftist groups united to form the Farabundo Martí National Liberation Front, FMLN (Frente Farabundo Martí para la Liberación Nacional).** That action marked the beginning of a civil war that over six years cost 70,000 lives. On January 10, 1981, the FMLN failed in its "final offensive" to topple the government, leading to a protracted rural-based program of guerrilla warfare. Some 8,000 FMLN members subsequently confronted the 50,000-man national army in a contest that was inconclusive.

1981

June 6. **PEMEX head Jorge Díaz Serrano resigned in a dispute over oil pricing.** A few days earlier, in response to an oil surplus in world markets, Díaz Serrano had announced a cut in the price of Mexican crude. But other officials in the López Portillo administration, led by cabinet minister José Andrés Oteyza, objected to this step for nationalistic and political reasons. After Díaz Serrano's resignation, the price cut was partly rescinded, but the result was a cancellation of contracts and a drop in oil exports. In August the price was reduced again. The fall in world oil prices aggravated Mexico's economic difficulties.

July 31. **Panamanian leader Omar Torrijos died in a plane crash**, leaving a power vacuum in the country that was soon filled by National Guard intelligence chief **Manuel Noriega**.

September. **El Salvador's National Republican Alliance (ARENA, Alianza Republicana Nacional) was formed by former army officer Roberto D'Aubuisson.** While ARENA received its chief financial support from large property owners who opposed land reform, and its founder was a right-wing extremist with links to the nation's death squads, ARENA enjoyed considerable popular support. It became El Salvador's leading political party in 1989.

November. **U.S. president Reagan authorized covert CIA action in support of Nicaraguan "Contras,"** many of whom were former members of the National Guard who had fled to Honduras. That action followed by four months Edén Pastora's defection from Sandinismo. Pastora established his own anti-Sandinista guerrilla in Costa Rica. There was much opposition to providing military aid to the Contras in the U.S. Congress, which voted in 1982 and 1984 to cut off such aid. It was later restored.

November 29. **Honduran Liberal Roberto Suazo Córdova was elected president,** succeeding Policarpo Paz García, who left office surrounded by rumors of his involvement in drug trafficking. Suazo proceeded to collaborate with the United States by allowing the U.S. military to supply Nicaraguan Contras on Honduran soil. When military commander Gustavo Álvarez Martínez was dismissed by Suazo, and subsequently plotted to assassinate the president, U.S.

authorities arrested him in Miami. Suazo was succeeded by José Azcona Hoyo (1986-90), who presided over a continued U.S. military buildup.

December. **Massacre in El Salvador.** During an offensive against leftist guerrillas, Salvadoran army troops killed several hundred civilians in and around the village of El Mozote in Morazán province. Because the troops involved had received training by United States advisors, reports of the massacre by United States journalists raised questions in Washington. Both Salvadoran and American officials, however, denied that a massacre had occurred.

1982

February 3. **Responding to charges of official corruption, Haitian dictator Jean-Claude Duvalier made former World Bank official Marc Bazin his finance minister.** While Bazin was soon removed from his post, the United States and foreign lending agencies continued funding the impoverished nation. Meanwhile Haitians left the nation in great numbers. By the early 1980s some 200,000 of them lived in the Dominican Republic, and 500,000 in the United States.

February 18. **Mexico allowed the peso to float.** Although President López Portillo had promised on February 5 to defend the peso "like a dog," a massive outflow of the country's foreign reserves and other problems made the step necessary. The peso quickly dropped from 26 to 45 to the dollar, but economic difficulties continued.

March 23. **Retired army officer José Efraín Ríos Montt seized power in Guatemala.** He acted in response to popular anger over a fraudulent election conducted by outgoing President Romeo Lucas García, as well as by the recent unification of leftist guerrillas under the National Guatemalan Revolutionary Unity (URNG) group. Ríos Montt went on to mount a major counterinsurgency campaign that reduced the level of guerrilla activity but produced thousands of civilian deaths and drove an estimated million Guatemalans, most of them living in the heavily

Indian western highlands, into exile in Mexico. Ríos Montt's challenge to the military establishment led to his overthrow in mid-1983.

May 8. **Luis Alberto Monge Álvarez was inaugurated Costa Rican president.** Pledging to stem the nation's economic crisis, he imposed an IMF-crafted austerity plan that included reducing the large public bureaucracy and curtailing social programs. His task was made difficult by an influx of refugees from the Nicaraguan civil war, and by United States pressure that forced him to tolerate *contra* bases on Costa Rican soil.

July 30. **Panamanian president Aristides Royo, placed in power five years earlier by General Omar Torrijos**, resigned under pressure of the National Guard, by then dominated by General **Manuel Noriega**. Royo was succeeded by Ricardo de la Espriella.

August. **Economic crisis in Mexico.** Serious economic problems—including a large public sector deficit, continuing capital flight, and a foreign debt of about $80 billion—precipitated a crisis in mid-August. On August 12, the government suspended principal payments on the foreign debt and closed all foreign exchange markets. The next day Finance Minister Jesús Silva Herzog flew to Washington where a multi-billion-dollar rescue package was crafted, involving loans, loan guarantees, and credits from the International Monetary Fund and various governments. Mexico's private creditors also agreed to a three-month moratorium on principal payments from Mexico. In September, President López Portillo nationalized the country's Mexican-owned private banks and imposed extreme exchange controls. These moves only aggravated economic problems, and the exchange controls were soon eased.

December 1. **Miguel de la Madrid was inaugurated to a six-year presidential term in Mexico.** A technocrat who had campaigned on a platform to end fraud and corruption, he directed his government to prosecute several of those who had enriched themselves at public expense. Meanwhile he pursued a program of fiscal austerity coupled with a shift toward economic liberal-

ism that moved Mexico away from statism and protection. These changes were supervised by his finance minister, **Carlos Salinas de Gortari**, one of whose charges was to keep Mexico from defaulting on its massive national debt, which grew to $105 billion by the late 1980s and whose servicing consumed half the national budget. De la Madrid and his cabinet were unable to control inflation, which averaged 100 percent annually during his presidency. Real wages fell by 50 percent during his term, and population growth continued at high levels. De la Madrid's neoliberalism split the governing party, causing leftist PRI members to challenge the political establishment in 1988. During his term, de la Madrid promoted political reforms whose effect was to enhance the electoral prospects of opposition parties.

1983

August 8. **Guatemalan defense minister Oscar Mejía overthrew President Ríos Montt**, whose evangelical Protestantism and threat to powerful economic interests made him obnoxious to the military. Pressured by his own military, and by the United States, Mejía called for the drafting of a new constitution (1984-85) and for presidential elections (late 1985).

August 12. **Manuel Noriega consolidated his hold on Panama by becoming head of the National Guard.** He ruthlessly repressed all opposition until driven from power by the United States six years later. Basing his power in the National Guard, which he renamed the Panamanian Defense Force, **Noriega** engaged in a number of unethical and/or illegal activities, not the least of which was his brokering of illegal drug shipments between Colombia and the United States.

1984

January 1. **The Caribbean Basin Initiative (CBI)**, a U.S.-funded twelve-year program conceived in early 1982 by the Reagan administration, went into effect. Aimed at stimulating the economies of Caribbean Basin nations through a range of incentives, the CBI brought significant new investment to Costa Rica and the Dominican Republic. Cuba and Nicaragua, alluded to as "communist-ruled countries," were excluded from the program.

April 23-25. **Riots in the Dominican Republic.** More than 100 Dominicans were killed in rioting that broke out after President Salvador Jorge Blanco imposed austerity measures demanded by the International Monetary Fund. When Jorge Blanco took office in August 1982, the Dominican Republic was deeply in debt, and he was forced to accept IMF conditions to obtain a $600 million loan. Violence erupted shortly after the government announced price increases for food and oil.

May 4. **Christian Democrat José Napoleón Duarte won the Salvadoran presidency.** Supported by both a war-weary population and the United States, **Duarte** defeated challenger Roberto D'Aubuisson of the ARENA party by a 54 percent to 46 percent margin in a runoff election. Duarte attempted to end the civil war during his five-year term, becoming a signatory to the Arias Peace Plan in 1987, but to little avail. His inability to revive a flagging economy and his failure to control corruption within his party, complicated by his ill health, disillusioned Salvadorans with both Duarte and his party.

May 10. **CIA mining of Nicaraguan harbors was condemned by the International Court of Justice.** The Reagan administration's hostility toward the leftist Sandinista government intensified the following year (May 1985) when the United States embargoed trade with Nicaragua.

September 21. **Nicaraguan junta head Daniel Ortega signed the first draft of the Contadora peace agreement**, drawn up by representatives of Mexico, Panama, Colombia, and Venezuela. The negotiators had begun deliberations a year earlier, on Contadora island, off the coast of Panama. The agreement proved unacceptable to other Central American nations,

and was modified through negotiations extending to 1987.

October 11. **Panamanian president Nicolás Ardito Barletta took office**, having won in a contest pitting him against **Arnulfo Arias**. Placed in power by army commander **Manuel Noriega**, Ardito Barletta was removed from office a year later when he authorized an investigation into the murder of Dr. Hugo Spadafora, a critic of the Panamanian military, whose decapitated body was found September 14, 1985. Ardito Barletta was succeeded by Eric Delvalle.

November 4. **Daniel Ortega handily won a six-year presidential term in Nicaragua**, going on to centralize economic planning and to authorize work on a new constitution. Meanwhile the Sandinista leader cultivated good relations with the Soviet Union in order to offset enmity of the United States, chief sponsor of the Contra rebels. By 1987 the civil war had cost Nicaragua an estimated 40,000 lives and up to $4 billion. Sixty-two percent of the nation's budget was devoted to military expenditures.

1985

February. **U.S. drug enforcement agent Enrique Camarena was tortured and murdered in Mexico**, touching off an investigation that linked high-ranking Mexican officials with the crime. The Camarena case troubled Mexican-U.S. relations for nearly a decade.

September 19. **An earthquake leveled extensive areas of Mexico City, leaving some 10,000 dead.** Slow government response to the disaster, coupled with its economic impact, heightened dissatisfaction with the regime of President de la Madrid.

December 1985–July 1986. **Mexico was hard hit by a fall in oil prices** that reduced per-barrel price from $23.70 to $8.90. President de la Madrid responded by continuing his austerity program and accelerating the process of selling, closing, and merging the 1,155 state-owned enterprises that had existed when he took office in 1982.

December 8. **Marco Vinicio Cerezo Aréva-lo was elected Guatemalan president in a runoff election, becoming the first civilian to hold that office since 1970.** Cerezo, the nation's first Christian Democratic president, faced a panoply of problems ranging from civil violence and crime to deteriorating economic conditions. Declining prices for exports coupled with a large public debt led to currency devaluation. That in turn increased hardship at all save the highest levels of society, a fact reflected by endemic work stoppages, especially by government employees. A friend of business, and responding to the global trend toward privatization, Cerezo sold several state-owned businesses, most importantly the national airline. Meanwhile he pursued an austerity plan that increased the gap between rich and poor but did little to improve the economy. Cerezo's greatest successes were in foreign affairs. He was instrumental in helping end the Nicaraguan civil war and in facilitating dialogue between the Salvadoran government and the FMLN guerrillas, and he helped both establish the Central American Parliament and increase Central American economic integration.

1986

February 7. **Dictator Jean-Claude "Baby Doc" Duvalier fled into exile**, leaving Haiti's government in the charge of a six-man council headed by Lieutenant General Henri Namphy.

May. **Cuban premier Fidel Castro lashed out at directors of state enterprises for capitalist tendencies**, going on to denounce the profit motive as injurious to communist society. He redoubled his effort to combat market forces in Cuba by prohibiting the farmers' markets that had existed since 1980. Meanwhile Cuba announced its suspension of principal and interest payments on its foreign debt, which had climbed to $6 billion.

May 8. **Oscar Arias Sánchez was inaugurated to a four-year term as Costa Rican president**. He quickly established himself as leader of the Central American peace process. **Arias** also enjoyed success in reducing Costa Rica's national debt.

May 16. **Seventy-nine-year-old Joaquín Balaguer, now blind, narrowly won a fifth term as president of the Dominican Republic.** To revive the nation's crumbling economy the new president launched a large public works program that included an immense monument commemorating the quincentenary of **Columbus**'s voyage. Meanwhile, social and economic conditions continued to deteriorate.

July 24. **Mexico joined the General Agreement on Tariffs and Trade (GATT)**, and proceeded to embark on trade liberalization. Nonpetroleum exports increased from $3 to $5 billion over the ensuing twelve months.

1987

June 1. **Robert Díaz Herrera retired as chief of staff of the Panamanian Defense Force (PDF).** He publicly accused **Manuel Noriega**, PDF commander, of several crimes, including fraud in the 1984 election and organizing the assassination of opposition leader Hugo Spadafora. He also accused Noriega of conspiring with the United States government to cause the death of **Omar Torrijos**, which he said had not been an accident. Three days of violent protests in support of Díaz led President Delvalle to decree a state of emergency in July.

August 7. **The Arias Peace Plan was signed by presidents of the five Central American nations.** Also known as Esquipulas II, for the Guatemalan village where negotiations were conducted, the Arias Plan brought cloture to a peace process initiated by the Contadora Group (Mexico, Panama, Colombia, and Venezuela) in 1983. Aimed chiefly at ending the Nicaraguan civil war, the Arias Plan established a framework for peace and democratization throughout Central America. It provided for a cease fire, committees of conciliation, the return of political exiles, free elections in all Central American countries, and the monitoring of elections by international observers. Warmly applauded in most quarters, the Plan led to the award of the 1987 Nobel Peace Prize to its author, Costa Rican president **Oscar Arias Sánchez**.

November 28-29. **Armed supporters of exiled Haitian dictator Jean-Claude Duvalier unleashed a wave of terror that halted elections.** As armed gangs attacked polling stations, churches, and other targets with impunity, the government of Lieutenant General Henri Namphy canceled the planned election. At least thirty persons died in the violence. On November 29, the United States suspended all nonhumanitarian aid to Haiti. Controversial balloting on January 17, 1988, resulted in the election of a civilian, Leslie Manigat, but he was ousted in a June 1988 coup led by Namphy, who established a military government.

December. **"Solidarity Pacts" in Mexico froze wages and prices**, adding to the hardship of middle and lower classes.

1988

April 1. **A cease-fire went into effect between Nicaragua's Sandinista government and Contra rebels**. Eleven months later (February 1989), at the third meeting of Central American presidents under the Arias Plan, arrangements were made for disbanding the Contras in exchange for advancing Nicaraguan presidential elections to November 1990.

July 6. **Carlos Salinas de Gortari won a six-year presidential term** in a heated election pitting him against **Cuauhtémoc Cárdenas**, son of former president **Lázaro Cárdenas**, candidate of the leftist National Democratic Front. Representing the conservative PAN party was Manuel Clouthier. Salinas won with 50.4 percent of the vote, though Cárdenas, with 31.1 percent, claimed that Salinas won the presidency through fraud. **Carlos Salinas** was a Harvard-educated economist wedded to economic liberalism. He continued the privatization policy of his predecessor, selling

most remaining state-owned enterprises during his term. His entering into the NAFTA free trade pact with the United States and Canada was the foremost act of his administration. While Salinas promised to open Mexico's political system, opposition parties had little success campaigning against government-financed candidates of the Institutional Revolutionary party (PRI).

September 11. **Armed thugs attacked St. Jean Bosco Church in Port-au-Prince, killing 13 and wounding 70.** They did so during a service led by the activist priest **Jean-Bertrand Aristide**, a proponent of liberation theology. An international outcry resulted, leading to the overthrow of military governor Henri Namphy, and his replacement by former Duvalier supporter General Prosper Avril. The events of late 1988 in Haiti signaled the collapse of military discipline and the rise of paramilitary groups lacking any known central command. Growing anarchy brought down the Avril regime in early 1990.

1989

Members of the Mexican left formed the Democratic Revolutionary party (PRD, Partido Revolucionario Democrático) following the strong showing of **Cuauhtémoc Cárdenas** in the 1988 presidential contest. The party was an amalgam of left-wing PRI members and the Mexican Communist and Socialist parties.

March 19. **ARENA candidate Alfredo Cristiani decisively won the Salvadoran presidency**, placed in office by an electorate angered by political corruption, exhausted by political violence, and fearful of the extreme left.

May 10. **Panamanian dictator Manuel Noriega annulled the presidential contest when it became clear that U.S.-supported opposition candidate Guillermo Endara had won.** Subsequently **Noriega** installed a puppet president whom the United States government refused to recognize.

July 2. **Ernesto Ruffo Appel of the conservative PAN was elected governor of the Mexican state of Baja California Norte.** This was the first time in the modern history of Mexico that the victory of an opposition gubernatorial candidate had been recognized.

July 13. **Cuban hero General Arnaldo Ochoa Sánchez and three other high military officers were executed in Cuba for embezzlement and drug trafficking.** Ten other military officers and interior ministry officials received long prison sentences after trials in June. The incident may have been aimed at removing rivals to the leadership of **Fidel Castro**.

November 11. **The FMLN launched a major offensive in San Salvador and several provincial towns.** The Cristiani government responded forcefully to the offensive, which cost an estimated 2,500 lives by early December. On November 16, six Jesuit priests, their housekeeper, and her daughter were murdered at the University of Central America in San Salvador. The priests had been proponents of reform and critics of human rights abuses in El Salvador. In January 1990 five soldiers and four officers of the Salvadoran army were arrested for the crime.

December 20. **Some 12,000 U.S. troops invaded Panama, captured and imprisoned Manuel Noriega.** This action occurred after Panamanian officers failed to unseat **Noriega** in a U.S.-sponsored coup attempt (October 13). The Americans then installed Guillermo Endara, who served as president until 1994. While most Panamanians approved of the U.S. action, Latin Americans elsewhere deplored it.

Bolivarian Republics: Bolivia, Colombia, Ecuador, Peru, Venezuela

The Bolivarian nations presented a diverse picture in 1960. Colombia had just ended a spell of military dictatorship and was governed by the Liberal-Conservative National Front. Venezuela, too, had emerged from ten years of military rule, and was on the verge of making great strides thanks to its oil wealth. In Ecuador, Peru, and Bolivia, the military continued to play a promi-

nent role in national government. Peru's military was especially important in national development during the 1960s and 1970s, finally handing power over to civilians during the economic crisis of the 1980s.

Fidel Castro's socialist experiment captured the imagination of radical reformers throughout the Bolivarian nations, inspiring them to launch their own guerrilla movements. During 1960-89, revolutionary guerrillas appeared in Venezuela, Colombia, Peru, and Bolivia.

The global recession of the 1980s brought extreme hardship to oil-exporting Venezuela and Ecuador. Those two countries, along with Peru and Bolivia, found their economic difficulties intensified by the need to service substantial foreign debt contracted during the borrowing frenzy of the 1970s. Among the Bolivarian nations, only Colombia avoided suspending debt repayment and suffering the imposition of painful IMF-directed austerity programs during the trying years of the 1980s. Venezuela, Ecuador, Peru, and Bolivia were forced to slash social programs in order to avoid bankruptcy.

From the 1980s onward, Colombia, and to a lesser degree Bolivia and Peru, suffered a range of problems arising from their citizens' participation in the illegal drug trade. While it enriched the few who engaged in it, illegal narcotics had a vastly corrupting effect on public institutions. Drug wars claimed thousands of lives, especially in Colombia, from the 1980s onward.

The Bolivarian countries completed import substitution during the 1960s, and began moving away from inward-looking development and relatively closed economies. By the 1980s, they had begun lowering tariffs and exploring ways to increase trade among themselves and the world. The late 1980s found them giving new life to their free trade association, LAFTA.

1960

June 6. **José María Velasco Ibarra won the Ecuadorian presidency.** His victory coincided both with the collapse of Ecuador's agro-export model and with political militancy drawing inspiration from **Fidel Castro**'s Cuban Revolution.

Velasco Ibarra adopted a militant anti-Americanism during the first year of his term, leading to his ouster in November 1961 and his replacement with Vice President Carlos J. Arosemena. The military ruled Ecuador either directly or indirectly until 1979.

June 24. **Venezuelan president Rómulo Betancourt was injured in an assassination attempt ordered by Dominican dictator Trujillo.** The OAS subsequently sanctioned the Dominican Republic.

August 6. **Víctor Paz Estenssoro began his second term as Bolivia's president.** Paz, founder of the dominant MNR party and leader of the 1952 revolution, assumed a moderate stance during his four-year term. He acceded to United States pressure to keep the left in check, eventu-

ally expelling his vice president, Juan Lechín, from his post. Lechín went on to conspire with the military, which overthrew Paz late in 1964.

September. **Venezuela joined Iran, Iraq, Kuwait, and Saudi Arabia in forming the Organization of Petroleum Exporting Countries (OPEC).** Earlier that year the government had formed the Venezuelan Petroleum Company (CVP), having authority to broaden national control over the oil industry.

1961

January 23. **Venezuela adopted a new constitution sanctioning social democracy and political centralization.**

October. **Colombian physician Tulio Bayer**

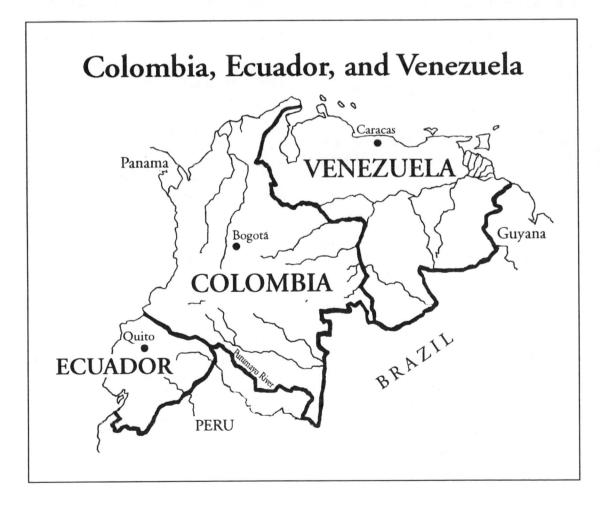

Colombia, Ecuador, and Venezuela

and Castroite guerrilla **Ramón Larrota launched a short-lived revolution in the eastern *llanos*.** While the Colombian army easily quashed the uprising, the guerrilla presence in numerous parts of the country led Conservative leader Álvaro Gómez Hurtado to denounce (November 29) what he called communist "independent republics" (small enclaves located in remote Andean fastnesses).

November 11. **Venezuela broke diplomatic relations with Cuba,** and later voted to expel Cuba from the OAS. Earlier that year **Rómulo Betancourt** had forced communists from his Acción Democrática party. This led Domingo Alberto Rangel and others to form the Movement of the Revolutionary Left (MIR), which helped form the revolutionary Armed Forces of National Liberation (FALN) two years later.

December 13. **Colombia's agrarian reform law was passed,** leading to the foundation of that nation's agrarian reform institute, INCORA. U.S. president Kennedy and his wife were on hand when the reform law was signed by President **Alberto Lleras.** Agrarian reform being one of the chief goals of the U.S. Alliance for Progress, Colombia thus positioned itself to become Latin America's second greatest recipient of aid through the program.

1962

May 6. **Conservative Guillermo León Valencia was elected Colombia's second president under the power-sharing National Front.** In so doing he withstood the challenge of Alfonso López Michelsen, a dissident Liberal whose splinter Liberal Revolutionary party (MRL) claimed Castroite inspiration. It was under Valencia that the Violencia was ended by the Colombian army. Symbolic of that fact was the death of Teófilo Rojas ("Chispas"), the most notorious perpetrator of Violencia, January 23, 1963, at the hands of an army patrol. Official estimates placed the number of Colombians killed by him at 525.

July 18. **Peru's military dismissed President Manuel Prado.** The military acted after APRA leader **Víctor Raúl Haya de la Torre** won a narrow plurality in a recent presidential election (June 10). Since he had not won the required one-third, Congress was to decide the winner. Perceiving that the military would not permit his accession, Haya de la Torre withdrew, throwing his support to the third-place finisher, former dictator **Manuel Odría.** When the armed forces learned of this agreement, they removed Prado and pledged to hold new elections in a year.

1963

June 9. **Fernando Belaúnde Terry won Peru's presidency, defeating APRA leader Haya de la Torre and Manuel Odría.** During his administration, Belaúnde attempted to carry out land reform, but his effort was thwarted by Congress. He enjoyed greater success in stimulating industrial growth, though he did so by pursuing statist policies that overburdened the economy. Belaúnde financed increased government spending in part by tripling Peru's foreign debt, leading him to declare a 44 percent currency devaluation in 1967. Meanwhile he expanded military prerogatives to combat guerrilla insurgency in the highlands. Peasants there and in coastal plantations had begun responding to radical appeals once agrarian reform failed.

July 11. **A three-man military junta formally assumed power in Ecuador,** replacing President Carlos J. Arosemena, who was accused of alcoholism and of ignoring the communist threat. The new government pursued a policy of import substitution financed principally through the contracting of foreign loans.

December 1. **Venezuelans elected Raúl Leoni to the presidency.** In October and November the FALN embarked on a wave of terrorism in an unsuccessful effort to block the contest. Leoni, a co-founder of Acción Democrática with **Rómulo Betancourt,** continued his predecessor's nationalist, reformist, and internationalist policies.

1964

May. **The Colombian army drove communist guerrillas from their enclave of Marquetalia,**

located 150 miles southwest of Bogotá. A follow-up campaign in September 1965 drove the guerrillas from a second enclave, into the Caquetá region of southeastern Colombia. In May 1966, the guerrillas, under the leadership of Manuel Marulanda Vélez ("Tiro Fijo"), constituted themselves as the Fuerzas Armadas Revolucionarias de Colombia (FARC). Later that year the Colombian Communist party endorsed the "simultaneous roads to socialism" strategy, which called for supporting both guerrilla warfare and participation in democratic politics.

November 4. **Charismatic military leader René Barrientos Ortuño overthrew Víctor Paz Estenssoro just three months into Paz's third presidency.** Barrientos's coup represented a continuation of the rightward drift in Bolivian politics. An election in June 1966 overwhelmingly ratified Barrientos's seizure of power.

1965

January 7. **Colombia's second major communist guerrilla force, the Cuban-trained Army of National Liberation (ELN), initiated activities** when it briefly seized a village north of Bogotá.

December. **Peru's Castroite Army of National Liberation (ELN) was defeated in a clash with army forces.** The movement's leaders, who began a revolt four months earlier, were either killed or imprisoned.

1966

February 15. **Revolutionary priest Camilo Torres Restrepo died during a skirmish with the Colombian army.** Despairing of effecting change through peaceful means, he had recently joined the ELN.

August 7. **Liberal Carlos Lleras Restrepo was inaugurated Colombia's third president under the power-sharing National Front.** Under Lleras Colombia undertook reforms guaranteeing that the nation would continue to enjoy economic stability. Among them were adoption of the "crawling peg" method of currency inflation that benefited the export sector, as well as a move away from protectionism. A constitutional reform (1968) strengthened presidential control over fiscal affairs. While encouraging industrialization and consolidation of the national market, Lleras spurred export diversification through participation in the Andean Pact. In 1967, Lleras also sponsored the National Association of Peasants (ANUC), which enlisted some 30 percent of Colombia's rural population prior to its dismantling during the 1970s.

November 3. **Ernesto "Che" Guevara arrived in Bolivia hoping to launch a revolution there.** But peasants failed to respond to his message partly because of cultural differences with **Guevara**'s band, many of whom were Cubans, and partly because President René Barrientos had worked to cultivate peasant support. **Guevara**'s presence became known by April 1967, prompting operations by the Bolivian army, supported by members of the U.S. Special Forces. In October 1967 Guevara was captured and executed.

December 14. **Venezuelan troops occupied the campus of Venezuela's Central University.** President Raúl Leoni thus defied leftist students who had taken advantage of the university's autonomous status. Ongoing student protest led to the institution's temporary closing a year later.

1967

May 25. **Ecuador's sixteenth constitution was promulgated.** It allowed the creation of numerous autonomous state agencies and increased regional autonomy at the expense of the central government.

1968

August 18. **Peru signed an agreement with the International Petroleum Company (IPC).** Under the agreement, IPC, a subsidiary of Standard Oil of New Jersey, was to turn over to Peru a large oil field at La Brea-Pariñas that had originally been acquired by irregular means. Concessions to the company, however, and charges that it would pay for crude oil in Peruvian soles rather than U.S. dollars, made the agreement extremely controversial. Along with poor economic conditions, it was a major factor in the overthrow of President Belaúnde in October.

September 16. **José María Velasco Ibarra was inaugurated Ecuador's president for the fifth time.** His last presidency coincided with political turmoil in the country. **Velasco** increasingly sought conservative support, suspending the constitution in mid-1970.

October 3. **A radical nationalist military revolt in Peru ended the presidency of Belaúnde and ushered in the seven-year regime of General Juan Velasco Alvarado.** Velasco pushed through a program featuring land reform and the nationalization of major industries: banking, petroleum, mining, agriculture, and the media. He seized privately owned sugar plantations on the coast and converted them to cooperative farms, while mandating land distribution in the highlands. Meanwhile he sought to enlist lower-class backing through his National System for Support of Social Mobilization (SINAMOS). His aim was to harmonize society through the pursuit of corporative mechanisms. His paralytic stroke in 1973 and the nation's economic decline hobbled Velasco's program. Industrial production declined, the balance of payments became unfavorable, inflation increased, and the national debt grew.

December 1. **Christian democrat Rafael Caldera Rodríguez won the Venezuelan presidency.** Longtime leader of the COPEI party, **Caldera** won the contest with 29 percent of the vote. He went on to extend national control over petroleum reserves, and in 1973 nationalized natural gas deposits. Caldera exerted leadership in international Christian democracy, and surprised opponents and supporters alike by establishing diplomatic relations with the Soviet Union (1970). He also lifted the ban on Venezuela's Communist party. His action was greeted by a diminution of revolutionary action in the countryside, especially after he renewed his nation's ties with Cuba and asked the OAS to end its sanctions on that country. Espousing noninterventionism and ideological pluralism, Caldera's government likewise later recognized the **Pinochet** regime in Chile. During Caldera's tenure Venezuela joined the Andean Pact (1973).

1969

April 27. **Bolivian president René Barrientos died in a helicopter crash.** His death ushered in a period of political instability during which three army officers ruled, the last of whom was the leftist and anti-American Juan José Torres.

May 26. **The Andean Pact was signed by five nations.** It was created largely in response to dissatisfaction with the Latin American Free Trade Association (LAFTA). Under terms of the agreement, Colombia, Ecuador, Peru, Bolivia, and Chile were to integrate their economies and implement an industrial policy (Venezuela joined the pact in 1973, and Chile withdrew in 1976). The Andean Pact also called for creation of a customs union. While it initially brought substantial increases in trade, old protectionist tendencies soon re-emerged. Disparities in the levels of economic development of member states made them reluctant to substantially lower their high tariffs. The economic shocks of the 1980s intensified protectionism. In 1987, member states revised their integration schedule.

1970

April 19. **Conservative Misael Pastrana won the Colombian presidency in a close race with former dictator Gustavo Rojas Pinilla.** Critics claimed that **Rojas**, leader of the populist ANAPO party, lost the election through fraud engineered by **Carlos Lleras Restrepo**. While Rojas's movement grew weaker thereafter, disgruntled *anapistas* subsequently formed the M-19 guerrilla group. Between 1974-90, the M-19 staged a series of spectacular actions protesting the exclusionary politics of the National Front.

May 31. **A massive earthquake struck northern Peru.** Measuring 7.7 on the Richter scale, it killed approximately 70,000 and injured 140,000 others. Hardest hit was Yungay, a provincial capital in Ancash department.

1971

January 11-19. **Ecuador seized U.S. tuna boats.** Ecuador seized and fined the boats for fishing within the 200-mile zone it regarded as its territorial waters. At that time the United States recognized only a 12-mile territorial limit and suspended military sales and assistance to Ecuador on January 18. Ecuador continued to seize U.S. tuna boats, as did Peru and Chile, both of which also claimed a 200-mile zone. In 1974 the United States accepted a 200-mile economic zone for coastal states, and in 1975 created a 200-mile fishing zone in waters off its own coasts.

August 19-22. **Colonel Hugo Banzer Suárez overthrew Bolivian president Juan José Torres after fighting in which more than 120 persons were killed. Banzer** went on to surprise observers of the Bolivian political scene by ruling longer than any other chief executive of the twentieth century, thanks to good economic conditions during the 1970s. Banzer carried out significant public works projects during his term, as well as increasing food production and diversifying exports. During Banzer's tenure Bolivia became the principal supplier of coca leaves to the hemisphere's manufacturers of cocaine. By the end of the decade the Bolivian military was heavily involved with the nation's drug mafia.

1972

February 15. **Ecuadorian president Velasco Ibarra was removed by the military.** Armed forces chiefs took the action when **Velasco Ibarra** refused to cancel the upcoming presidential election which they feared would be won by populist Assad Bucaram. Ecuador then entered a period of formal military rule lasting to 1979. General Guillermo Rodríguez Lara announced that his government would be both revolutionary and nationalistic, committed to attacking poverty and achieving rapid industrialization. The years of military rule coincided with great change in Ecuadorian society. Urbanization doubled, going from 20 to 40 percent, foreign investment in import-substituting industry increased rapidly, and revenue earned through oil exports funded expansion of the public sector.

1973

December 9. **Carlos Andrés Pérez, candidate of Acción Democrática (AD), won the Venezuelan presidency.** When **Pérez** entered the presidency Venezuela stood as one of Latin America's most fortunate nations. Petroleum prosperity had enabled it to double its GDP between 1958 and 1972. Per capita GDP was second only to Argentina's, and soon exceeded that of the Southern Cone nation. Negatively, Venezuela's strong currency hindered nonpetroleum exports, and heavy government spending increased the foreign debt to $8.4 billion (up from $1.2 billion in 1958). The country's economic situation improved dramatically as Pérez began his presidency. The Arab oil boycott pushed the price of oil from $2.01 per barrel to $14.26 by January 1975 (and to $29.40 in 1982). Awash in cash, Venezuela continued to spend lavishly, nationalizing the iron industry in 1975 and the petroleum industry in 1976. Graft and corruption accompanied the bonanza. At the end of Pérez's term, Venezuela's Congress found him guilty of permitting political corruption.

1974

August 7. **Liberal Alfonso López Michelsen became president following his victory in Colombia's first competitive election since implementation of the National Front accord.** The resurgence of guerrilla activity led López to impose a state of siege in June 1975. Forty percent inflation intensified labor militancy, which peaked in a general strike of September 1977.

1975

January 1. **Venezuela announced the nationalization of the iron ore industry.** The industry was controlled by two U.S. firms, which were to receive $101 million in compensation.

February 5-6. **Disturbances in Lima.** After a strike by police (Civil Guards) was crushed by the army, thousands looted stores and set fire to hotels, offices, and the headquarters of SINAMOS, an agency created to mobilize support for the government. At least 100 persons were killed in the rioting, which the government blamed on APRA. The disturbances indicated President Velasco's weakening grip and foreshadowed his removal.

August 29. **President Juan Velasco Alvarado of Peru was deposed by fellow officers.** Removal of the ailing leader marked the end of the first phase of the military revolution of 1968. He was succeeded by General Francisco Morales Bermúdez, who followed a more centrist course and began to dismantle some of the post-1968 reforms.

November 13. **Ecuador's Rodríguez Lara was confronted by a general strike** in support of increased wages. The nation's oil boom had ended, and severe inflation increased labor militancy. Members of the business community lobbied for the removal of Rodríguez, whom they accused of statism and "underhanded communism." On January 11, 1976, Rodríguez was replaced by a military junta, which implemented an austerity program that included a wage freeze. To help combat these problems the government sought foreign loans.

1976

January 1. **The Venezuelan petroleum industry was nationalized.** The oil properties owned by foreign companies were turned over to a state enterprise called Petróleos de Venezuela. The companies were to receive about $1 billion for their holdings, and continued to be involved in petroleum production in Venezuela.

March–April. **Peruvian president Morales embraced fiscal reforms and moved to curtail work stoppages.** In March he agreed to meet key demands of United States creditors. They included a 44 percent currency devaluation, the lifting of restrictions on foreign investment, and the sale of companies nationalized subsequent to 1968. In April he outlawed strikes in export

industries. U.S. banks reciprocated with a $400 million emergency loan.

1977

October 17. **Ecuadorian troops fired on workers protesting low wages and spiraling inflation.** Generalized discontent with military rule moved Ecuador's junta to speed the transition to civilian rule.

December 28. **Miners' wives began a hunger strike in La Paz, Bolivia.** Their demands included the removal of troops from the mines and amnesty for all political focs of the government of **Hugo Banzer**, who had recently announced that he would not seek the presidency in upcoming elections. The women won the support of other opponents of the regime, which granted most of their demands in January. The hunger strike weakened the government and opened the floodgates of political activity. After an election (July 9, 1978) marred by fraud, Banzer was ousted in a military coup.

1978

May. **Nation-wide unrest in Peru attended a new round of government austerity measures mandated by the IMF.** When a general strike was called (May 22-23), President Morales Bermúdez deported union leaders, journalists, and politicians. Elections for a constituent assembly, originally scheduled for June 4, took place July 18. APRA won 37 of the 100 seats, and **Víctor Raúl Haya de la Torre** was named president of the assembly.

June 4. **Liberal Julio César Turbay Ayala won the Colombian presidency in a contest marked by high abstention.** When guerrilla attacks intensified during his term, Turbay gave the army a free hand in anti-guerrilla operations. Amid an outcry over human rights violations, the M-19 staged a daring theft of army weapons (1979) and seized the Dominican embassy in Bogotá (1980). These incidents never threatened government stability, though they underlined popular dissatisfaction with a political system dominated by Colombia's traditional parties.

December 3. **The Venezuelan presidential election was won by COPEI's Luis Herrera Campins.** Herrera was forced to preside over Venezuela's economic decline. The collapse of oil prices coupled with a large public sector and costly state-owned companies (79 state-owned and 176 mixed enterprises) produced inflation and capital flight. As economic uncertainty increased under Herrera Campins, Venezuela continued to assert itself diplomatically. In 1982 Venezuela supported Argentina's claim to the Falklands/Malvinas Islands (in opposition to the United States), and a year later joined with Colombia, Panama, and Mexico in forming the Contadora Group. Meanwhile Herrera Campins strongly supported fellow Christian Democrat, El Salvador's **José Napoleón Duarte.**

1979

July 12. **Peru approved a new constitution providing for a powerful presidency and a highly centralized government.**

August 10. **Reformer Jaime Roldós Aguilera became Ecuador's president** at the head of the coalition Concentration of Popular Forces (CFP). With his inauguration a new constitution entered into force, notable chiefly in that it extended the franchise to illiterates.

1980

May 17. **Peru's Shining Path guerrilla movement launched its People's War.** On the eve of Peru's first presidential election since 1963, Shining Path guerrillas broke into the town hall of an Andean village, took ballot boxes and voting lists, and burned them in the town square. Founded in 1970 by Abimael Guzmán, the group embraced Maoist principles. Its members challenged the national government by assassinating local political officials and destroying public property. Over the ensuing twelve years, violence associated with the Shining Path movement resulted in 26,000 deaths and $24 billion in damages, as well as the flight of up to 600,000 residents of regions affected by the violence.

May 18. **Fernando Belaúnde Terry won a second term as Peru's president**, replacing General Francisco Morales Bermúdez. Inaugurated on July 28, Belaúnde hoped to stimulate economic growth through neoliberal policies, all the while maintaining his predecessor's austerity initiative. Meanwhile he devoted public monies to grandiose public works programs in the Amazon region. While enjoying some initial success, Belaúnde's program was frustrated by the global recession and by a clientelistic administrative style that invited corruption. In addition, the onset of the warm Pacific current known as El Niño disrupted fishing and agriculture during 1982-83. As the public debt grew, GDP declined by 1 percent in 1982, and by 12 percent a year later. Half of Peru's population fell into poverty as the crisis deepened.

June 29. **Members of the Bolivian left elected MNR founder Hernán Siles Zuazo president.** Siles was a popular figure who had been denied the presidency on two previous occasions (1978 and 1979) by the military. The army again intervened (July 17), when General Gabriel García Meza seized power on behalf of the nation's drug mafia. Dubbed the "cocaine coup," the overthrow of Siles ushered in one of the most corrupt and brutal regimes in Bolivian history.

1981

January 28-February 2. **Hostilities erupted between Ecuador and Peru.** Fighting broke out over disputed territory in the Cordillera del Condor mountains. The region was part of the territory assigned to Peru in the 1942 Rio Protocol, which Ecuador repudiated in 1960. A cease-fire was soon declared, but another skirmish occurred on February 20.

May 24. **Ecuadorian president Jaime Roldós died in an airplane crash.** He was succeeded by Vice President Osvaldo Hurtado. By this time Ecuador had entered a period of economic decline resulting from falling oil prices and a high foreign debt. Budgets were slashed and the currency devalued. Real wages fell, and unemployment rose, reaching 40 percent by 1984.

August 4. **Bolivia's military expelled and exiled President García Meza** following international outcry over human rights abuses committed during his regime, and over his open involvement in the drug trade. At that moment Bolivia entered a period of severe financial decline.

December. **Colombian illegal drug cartel members formed the paramilitary group Muerte a Secuestradores (MAS),** after members of the M-19 guerrilla group kidnapped the daughter of a cartel member. During the 1980s nonleftist, mostly rural-dwelling Colombians, most of whom were large property owners, responded to guerrilla formation by organizing self-defense and paramilitary groups.

1982

August 7. **Conservative populist Belisario Betancur Cuartas was inaugurated as Colombian president.** **Betancur** had campaigned on the promise that he would improve living conditions of Colombia's poor and that he would offer amnesty to the nation's guerrillas. His peacemaking effort was frustrated when neither the M-19, FARC, nor ELN guerrillas came to terms with the government; he had better luck with international peace-making: Colombia played a leading role in the Contadora Group, which helped resolve the Nicaraguan civil war. Betancur's administration began during an economic downturn that reduced national growth to a mere 1 percent during 1981-82 (down from 6 percent annually between 1961 and 1981). The decline was temporary, as Colombia soon resumed rapid growth thanks to prudent handling of its foreign debt, major discoveries of petroleum in the eastern plains, and the export of steam coal through a joint venture with Exxon. Monies earned through the sale of illegal drugs contributed an additional 2-3 percent to GDP.

October 5. **The Bolivian Congress elected Hernán Siles Zuazo to the presidency.** The armed forces, discredited and determined to turn power over to civilians, summoned the Congress

elected in 1980, which was dominated by Siles supporters. Siles attempted five economic stabilization plans during his term, all of which failed, partly because of the opposition of organized labor.

1983

February 18. **On Venezuela's "Black Friday," President Herrera Campins halted the free market in the bolívar** (long valued at 4.5 to the United States dollar) and imposed monetary controls. A sharp drop in the value of the bolívar soon followed. Meanwhile the IMF pressed Venezuela for austerity measures that included ending a range of government subsidies.

December 4. **Jaime Lusinchi won the Venezuelan presidency.** A member of Acción Democrática, Lusinchi had the unenviable task of coping with his nation's accelerating economic slide brought about by falling oil prices. Since the previous year Venezuela had registered a negative growth rate, as foreign investment there ceased. In February 1986, Lusinchi signed an agreement with foreign creditors by which he agreed to devote up to 45 percent of government revenue to debt service.

1984

May 6. **Neoliberal León Febres Cordero won a runoff for the Ecuadorian presidency.** He pledged to reduce government economic controls and to promote growth of the private sector. His dictatorial style alienated many Ecuadorians, and ongoing deterioration of the economy further weakened his mandate. When a 1987 earthquake damaged the country's principal oil pipeline, Febres declared a moratorium on external debt payment.

December. **Peru's struggle against Shining Path guerrillas intensified as President Belaúnde granted the army carte blanche** in its campaign against them. Human rights abuses abounded on both sides, and the civil war captured global attention. Meanwhile another another left-wing guerrilla, the Tupac Amaru Revolutionary

Movement (MRTA, Movimiento Revolucionario Tupac Amaru), had begun activity. The group's chief leader, Víctor Polay, patterned his organization on the Cuban model. While MRTA lacked the size and ferocity of Shining Path, it too carried out acts of urban terrorism and maintained a stronghold in the Huallaga Valley.

1985

June 1. **Alan García was declared president-elect of Peru.** The first Aprista to become president, García won 48 percent of the vote in balloting on April 14, and avoided a run-off after Marxist Alfonso Barrantes, who had come in second, withdrew. A charismatic politician of thirty-six, García was successful during the first two years of his term. The GDP increased by 8.75 percent and inflation fell. Meanwhile García defied the international banking community by suspending most payments on the national debt, and he demonstrated his independence from the United States through vocal support of Nicaragua's Sandinista government. He pleased human rights activists by sacking high-ranking army officers accused of killing peasants in highland emergency zones. But García's popularity did not survive his presidency. Human rights violations increased from mid-1986 onward, and his economic iconoclasm brought Peru down by 1988. At decade's end, García's failures stimulated a colloquy around Peru's "ungovernability." The president himself contributed to the acceptance of that vision through his speeches against bureaucratic centralism.

August 6. **Víctor Paz Estenssoro was inaugurated president of Bolivia for the fourth time.** In balloting on July 14, he had won 26.4 percent of the vote, behind former president **Banzer** with 28.6 percent. However, **Paz**'s allies controlled the newly elected Congress, which named him president. He soon enacted one of the continent's most draconian economic stabilization programs. He slashed social programs and all other public expenditures, dismantled the state mining company, sharply reduced economic protection, and encouraged the relocation of unemployed tin miners to lowland agricultural zones. The economic liberalism of Paz returned economic stability to Bolivia, a condition welcomed by both small farmers and middle-class urban dwellers. By so thoroughly reversing his populist and statist philosophy of the 1950s, Paz Estenssoro illustrated a flexibility rare in Latin American revolutionary leaders. In exchange for substantial United States aid, Paz granted that nation broad powers to combat Bolivia's illegal drug trade.

November 7. **Colombia's M-19 guerrillas seized the nation's Supreme Court building in hopes of forcing concessions from President Belisario Betancur.** Hours later army units attacked and destroyed the building. More than one hundred died in the incident, including half of Colombia's Supreme Court justices and all of the M-19 attackers. Meanwhile a new political party appeared in Colombia, the Patriotic Union (UP). The political arm of the communist FARC guerrillas, the UP attempted to enter national politics. Enemies of the FARC murdered some 1,100 UP members between 1985-89.

November 13. **A mud slide in Colombia took the lives of some 25,000 people.** The disaster was occasioned by volcanic activity in the Nevado del Ruiz, which liquefied the mountain's snowcap. At length the lake formed by the mountain's activity rushed down the mountainside, mixing with topsoil as it went, and burying the town of Armero, located on the plain below.

1986

May 25. **Liberal Virgilio Barco won the Colombian presidency** as drug-related violence, terrorist attacks by the leftist guerrillas and right-wing death squads rose to unprecedented levels.

June 18-19. **Some 250 Peruvian convicts, most members of Shining Path, died when the army stormed three prisons that they had seized.** That act marked a sharp upturn in human rights violations in the country.

July. **Bolivian president Víctor Paz Estenssoro invited U.S. troops to assist his nation's army in eradicating the country's** cocaine laboratories in Operation Blast Furnace.

1987

July 28. **President Alan García shocked Peruvians by proposing to nationalize all banks in the country.** Congress supported him, approving a bank nationalization bill. That move produced a private-sector backlash having strong antistatist and neoliberal aspects. Novelist **Mario Vargas Llosa** was the initial beneficiary of anti-García sentiment. Within two years he mounted a strong presidential campaign at the head of a libertarian, center-right coalition.

1988

August 10. **Rodrigo Borja, who had narrowly lost to Febres Cordero four years earlier, became Ecuador's president.** Borja, candidate of the populist Democratic Left party (ID), took office amid popular enthusiasm and hope that he would improve the nation's straitened economy. But despite majority support in Congress, Borja was forced to impose a limited austerity program that included currency devaluation and a mix of tax increases. Meanwhile he resisted World Bank measures that included eliminating public subsidies, firing public employees, and privatizing state enterprises. His moderation won him friends neither on the left nor the right, and had the effect of heightening the fragmentation of Ecuador's political system. A key source of his difficulty lay in a foreign debt that had grown from $500 million in 1975 to $11 billion in 1989.

December 4. **The Venezuelan presidency was won for a second time by AD leader Carlos Andrés Pérez,** in part on the promise that he would lead the nation back to the prosperity that attended his 1974-79 presidency.

1989

February 27-March 1. **Riots swept Venezuela when Carlos Andrés Pérez announced new austerity measures that included a sharp increase in bus fares and gasoline prices.** The decree touched off days of rioting and looting that the president answered with force. About 300 died before order was restored. The incident shook the self-confidence of Venezuelans.

August 6. **Jaime Paz Zamora was inaugurated as Bolivia's president.** In balloting on May 7, Paz had come in third but was chosen president by Congress after forging a strategic alliance between his leftist MIR party and the conservative ADN movement of former president **Hugo Banzer**. In spite of his leftist credentials, Paz Zamora continued the neoliberal policies of his predecessor, distant relative **Paz Estenssoro**.

August 18. **Popular Colombian politician Luis Carlos Galán was assassinated** while campaigning for the upcoming presidential contest. Galán fell victim to henchmen sent by drug lords whom he had threatened with extradition to the United States if elected. The assassination was but one of many marking the Colombian state's struggle against members of that nation's drug cartels. Meanwhile Colombia's economy remained robust, having averaged 5.3 percent growth over the preceding fifteen years (as compared with Latin America's average of 3.3 percent).

November 12. **Peru's municipal elections were won by the conservative, anti-statist Democratic Front,** whose candidate in the upcoming presidential contest was **Mario Vargas Llosa**. The Shining Path waged a month-long campaign of terrorism to disrupt the elections.

Southern Cone: Argentina, Chile, Paraguay, Uruguay

There was a degree of uniformity in Southern Cone affairs during the interval 1960 through 1989. Early in the 1960s, civilian regimes, generally of a liberal, reformist character, attempted to extend the social safety net in a setting of economic stagnation resulting from exhaustion of the protectionist, import-substitution model. Popular dissatisfaction grew, a process accelerated by political militants who damned the status quo as hopelessly bourgeois and beyond redemption.

Advocating a radical redistribution of wealth as prescribed in the writings of Karl Marx, they moved to abolish the existing order through armed revolution. **Fidel Castro**'s Cuban Revolution provided them the example of how that should be done.

Southern Cone revolutionaries were few in number, most of them of a middle class that had grown and flourished as a consequence of national modernization. Young and idealistic, freed by education and relative affluence to pursue revolutionary solutions to social problems, they alarmed members of the middle and upper classes, two groups comprising a substantial majority of the citizenry by the century's seventh decade. None were more alarmed than members of national militaries, most of whom were rabidly anticommunist. Disposed to defend the status quo and convinced that Castroite revolutionaries posed a real threat to national stability, the military asserted itself. First in Argentina, then in Uruguay and Chile, the army rose up to impose dictatorial "national security states" whose chief goal was to rid society of the leftist threat. Thus during the early 1970s, civil government was suspended and the left virtually liquidated in "dirty wars" pitting national military establishments against a relatively few poorly armed revolutionaries and, in many cases, their friends, relatives, and sympathizers. The result was the tragic decimation of a generation of young radical activists.

The Southern Cone's military dictators were generally inept in national economic management. An exception was Chile's **Augusto Pinochet**, who, rather than attempting to make economic policy himself, turned that chore over to free-market ideologues who reversed the statism and protectionism that had prevailed throughout the region since the 1930s. Chile's government economists slashed tariffs, encouraged foreign investment, sold state-owned enterprises, deregulated business, and cut social programs with revolutionary zeal. Their jettisoning of the welfare state ideal was especially painful to disadvantaged groups, whose living standard declined sharply. But the middle and upper classes prospered. By the latter 1980s, Chile enjoyed economic growth unequaled in its history. As the 1980s ended, all Southern Cone governments rushed to emulate Chile's example. Meanwhile, with the Cold War at an end, nations of the Southern Cone returned to democratic rule. That was even the case in Paraguay, the South American nation least familiar with democratic governance.

1960

Paraguay's foreign exchange reserves fell to their lowest point since the 1947 civil war, in spite of an IMF stabilization plan imposed early in the regime of **Alfredo Stroessner**. Yet the dictator soon reversed Paraguay's decline by encouraging foreign investment, international borrowing, and the initiation of a variety of public works programs. As a result GDP rose an average of 4.6 percent per year during the 1960s, and 11 percent between 1977 and 1980. As economic activity increased, inflation rose steadily, reaching 28 percent in 1979. Meanwhile Stroessner cultivated good relations with Brazil and Argentina, a policy that further promoted national growth.

March. **Argentina's President Arturo Frondizi capitulated to the wishes of his military, instituting the Conintes plan, which assigned control of the antiterrorist struggle to the armed forces**. Under the plan civilians could be tried in military courts. Seven months later (October) the military accused Frondizi of tolerating the presence of communists in national universities.

November 3-7. **Workers protested limits on wage increases imposed by Chilean president Alessandri**, prompting a wave of strikes during which two died. Workers eventually received a 15 percent increase.

December. **Thanks to an IMF stabilization plan, Argentina's economy rebounded, posting a 7 percent increase in GDP.** Meanwhile the nation continued import-substituting economic modernization through foreign investment. Argentina remained one of the continent's most protected economies, with tariffs averaging 131 percent (slightly lower than Brazil's, on a par with Chile's, slightly higher than Colombia's).

1962

March 29. **Argentine president Arturo Frondizi was forced to resign by the military**. Frondizi had antagonized military leaders by meeting with **Ernesto (Che) Guevara** (August 1961) and by ordering Argentine abstention in the vote to exclude Cuba from the OAS (January 1962). The immediate cause of his downfall was the strong showing of Peronist candidates in recent provincial and congressional elections at a time when many officers were opposed to a Peronist comeback. Frondizi was succeeded by Senate President José María Guido and by Radical Arturo Illia, who was elected president in 1963.

August. **The Chilean Congress launched a modest land reform program** by passing legislation leading to the formation of CORA (Corporación de Reforma Agrícola).

December. **Raúl Sendic and other Uruguayan leftists formed the revolutionary National Liberation Movement, known as the Tupamaros**. Dismayed by his inability to organize sugar cane workers in northeastern Uruguay, and convinced that democratic politics did not facilitate radical change, Sendic and his colleagues laid plans for mounting an urban guerrilla movement centered in Montevideo.

1964

September 4. **Christian Democrat Eduardo Frei Montalva won Chile's presidential election**, defeating **Salvador Allende**, candidate of the left-wing Popular Action Front (FRAP). Fearing a victory by the left, Chilean conservatives had supported **Frei**, as had the United States. Frei made good on his promise to pursue agrarian reform, to implement social programs aimed at benefiting the poor, and to move toward nationalizing the nation's copper industry. But as his term drew to a close economic problems forced Frei to scale back the reform effort. Meanwhile politics grew increasingly polarized as the left

mounted an aggressive campaign to place Salvador Allende in the presidency.

1965

March 7. **Eduardo Frei's Christian Democrats decisively won congressional elections**. The Chistian Democrats won 82 of 147 seats in the Chamber of Deputies, an unusually strong showing for a single party in Chile's multi-party system.

June. **Paraguay and Brazil inaugurated the friendship bridge over the Paraná River**. The bridge linked the road systems of the two countries, allowing Paraguay access to Brazil's Atlantic port of Paranaguá. At the same time the two countries discussed collaborating on the Itaipú Hydroelectric Project, aimed at constructing the world's largest dam (construction begun 1968).

1966

January 25. **The Chilean Congress passed legislation outlining the Frei administration's policy of "chileanization" of the copper industry**. The principal mines were owned by two United States firms, Kennecott and Anaconda, which sold a majority interest to the government. The Frei administration also wanted to increase copper production.

June 28. **Proclaiming "the Argentine Revolution," General Juan Carlos Onganía replaced Arturo Illia as the nation's leader**. Continued Peronist strength coupled with renewed inflation prompted the military takeover. **Onganía**'s term enshrined the doctrine of "national security" as a guiding principle. This doctrine featured authoritarian rule by the military as guarantor of moral and spiritual values. Onganía's regime, which attempted to control inflation through wage freezes, was unpopular.

November 27. **Uruguayan voters approved return to a presidential form of government**. The change marked the end of a twelve-year experiment with collegial government.

1967

March 1. **Oscar Gestido, representing the right wing of the Colorado party, was inaugurated Uruguayan president.** Upon his death nine months later, Gestido was succeeded by his vice president, Jorge Pacheco Areco. Economic and political crises greeted the little-known Colorado conservative. Pacheco met both through the imposition of a limited state of siege that continued to the end of his administration in 1973.

July 16. **Chile's president Frei signed land reform legislation** providing for the distribution of large holdings and the encouragement of cooperative farms.

1968

February. **Uruguay negotiated stand-by credit with the IMF, contingent on budgetary cutbacks.** Inflation fell as a result of the measure and the nation began a modest economic recovery.

August. **Uruguay's Tupamaro guerrillas launched an offensive against the government of Jorge Pacheco**, kidnapping members of Pacheco's administration and publicizing the government's shortcomings. The level of Tupamaro activity increased during 1970 when the group kidnapped and executed U.S. official Daniel Mitrione.

1969

March 1. **Chile's Christian Democrats lost in nation-wide congressional elections**, losing their majority in the Chamber of Deputies.

May 17-18. **Young Chilean Christian Democrats formed the United Popular Action Movement (MAPU)**, the following year joining the Popular Unity (UP) coalition that supported **Salvador Allende**'s presidential campaign. At the same moment, middle-class college students in the Castroite Movement of the Revolutionary Left (MIR) launched a series of bank robberies to finance their activities. While eschewing formal participation in Chilean politics, they too supported the Allende candidacy.

May 29-30. **Leftist students and workers seized downtown Córdoba, Argentina, in what was termed** *el cordobazo.* Their action was the most significant of a group of similiar uprisings in Argentine cities, all in protest of the autocratic rule of General **Juan Carlos Onganía**.

June 30. **Augusto Vandor, leader of the conservative wing of the Peronist General Labor Confederation (CGT), was assassinated, probably by the Peronist Montoneros**, a guerrilla group that became active during the late 1960s.

October 21-22. **Military rebellion took place in Chile.** Units led by General Roberto Viaux seized control of the Yungay and Tacna regiments. Although they were protesting low pay and poor working conditions in the army, they were also concerned about a possible leftist victory in the 1970 elections. After the rebels surrendered, their leaders were convicted of insubordination. This revolt is known as *el tacnazo*.

1970

May 29. **Former Argentine president Pedro Aramburu was kidnapped by Montonero guerrillas.** The Montoneros, left-wing Peronists, blamed Aramburu for the execution of Peronist officers after an abortive rebellion in 1956 and for secretly removing **Eva Perón**'s embalmed cadaver from Argentina. The kidnapping demonstrated the weakness of President **Onganía**, who was deposed on June 8 by the military and replaced by General Roberto M. Levingston. Aramburu's body was found on July 16.

September 4. **Socialist candidate Salvador Allende won a plurality in Chile's presidential election.** The candidate of a coalition known as Popular Unity (UP), he led with 36.5 percent of the vote, followed by former president **Jorge Alessandri** and Christian Democrat Radomiro Tomic. Since **Allende** had not won a majority, the issue had to be decided by Congress, where he was declared president on October 24 with Christian Democrat support. It was later revealed that the U.S. government and the International Telephone and Telegraph Company and other firms had spent over $1 million to prevent an Allende victory. On October 25, army commander René Schneider died of wounds suffered in a kidnap attempt by right-wing officers angered by his refusal to support an anti-Allende coup.

November 3. **Salvador Allende Gossens took office as Chile's president.** Allende's socialist program met with some success during his first year in office. His government nationalized 134 enterprises from key industrial and commercial sectors, agrarian reform was greatly accelerated, and state-sponsored programs distributed free food to Chile's neediest citizens. Meanwhile GDP increased by 7.7 percent and unemployment fell. But by late 1971 those positive economic trends reversed. Private capital fled the country, and a hostile United States government withdrew its aid, used its influence to halt IMF and World Bank loans to Chile, and authorized the CIA to spend $8 million in assisting anti-government forces. The combination of lavish spending by Allende's government coupled with domestic and international opposition devastated Chile's economy. Foreign reserves were soon exhausted and the government reduced to inflating the money supply.

1971

March 26. **General Alejandro A. Lanusse was installed as president of Argentina.** Amid mounting guerrilla violence and labor unrest, he promised an early return to civilian rule.

June 8. **The assassination of Chilean Christian Democratic politician Edmundo Pérez by leftists** increased political polarization and intensified the climate of anger and fear.

July 11. **Chile's copper mines were nationalized after Congress unanimously approved a constitutional amendment providing for their takeover.** The amendment authorized compensation to mine owners, but the government claimed that the owners owed back taxes.

September. **The Tupamaro guerrillas declared a truce with Uruguay's government** preceding the elections of November 28, 1971. Their action was a show of support for a recently

created (March 1971) leftist Frente Amplio coalition, which united the nation's Communist, Socialist, and Christian Democratic parties, as well as Zelmar Michelini's Colorado splinter List 99 party. The Frente won 18 percent of the vote in the November election. Meanwhile Tupamaro founder Raúl Sendic escaped from prison during a massive jail break on September 6, 1971.

November 10. **Fidel Castro traveled to Chile on a state visit.** Salvador Allende later stopped in Cuba in December 1972, at the end of a two-week foreign tour.

1972

March 1. **Juan María Bordaberry assumed Uruguay's presidency following an election widely regarded as fraudulent.** Conservative and authoritarian, Bordaberry, who presided over the destruction of the Uruguayan left, remained in power until 1976.

April 14. **Uruguay's Tupamaro guerrillas ended their truce with the government,** going on to stage eleven assassinations of police and military officials whom they accused of membership in death squads. The government declared a state of siege and undertook a merciless extermination of the Tupamaros. Symbolizing the Tupamaros' demise was the capture of Raúl Sendic, who remained in prison for the ensuing twelve years.

August 15-22. **A bloodbath occurred in Trelew, Argentina,** after twenty-five imprisoned Montoneros and other guerrillas broke out of a maximum security prison. They reached an airport in nearby Trelew, from which six escaped to Chile. The remaining nineteen were captured and kept at a naval base in Trelew, where sixteen were killed and the others wounded, supposedly in an escape attempt. The killings provoked demonstrations and exacerbated tensions in Argentina.

September 12. **Paraguayan dictator Alfredo Stroessner's henchmen raided the Catholic University during an antigovernment rally.** Their action was part of a government campaign against reformist priests involved in *conscienti-*

zación of the masses, a program aimed at instilling antiregime, anticapitalist consciousness in the Paraguayan population. Harassment of the activist priests continued through the decade, eventually destroying the *conscientización* movement.

October 10. **Chilean truck owners called a nation-wide strike in protest of Salvador Allende's socialist policies.** Shopkeepers and other middle-class groups soon joined them. The strike, one of 2,474 taking place during 1972, was especially damaging to the national economy. A similar work stoppage took place the following June. Meanwhile, radical "people's power" *(poder popular)* groups attempted to break the strike through spontaneous organization of *cordones industriales*, working-class groups pledged to keeping factories in operation. An extension of the strike was the "March of the Empty Pots," a nonviolent action by upper and middle-class housewives in December.

November. **Juan Perón visited Argentina** from exile in Spain in an attempt to unify his divided Justicialist party. He remained in Argentina until December 14. The following day it was announced at a convention of the Justicialist party that Héctor J. Cámpora was his choice to run for president in elections scheduled for March 1973.

1973

February. **Uruguay's military initiated a progressive takeover of civil government** through formation of a National Security Council (COSENA), which usurped powers normally exercised by the president. The closure of Congress on June 27 by President Bordaberry marked the beginning of a military dictatorship. Within two years some 7,000 opponents of the government had been arrested, 200 of them subsequently murdered and buried clandestinely. The military retained Bordaberry as president until 1976. A succession of figurehead presidents followed until 1981, when General Gregorio Álvarez was appointed to lead the government until 1984.

March 4. **Salvador Allende's UP coalition won 43.4 percent of the vote in Chilean congressional elections,** an increase over its 1970

showing. The opposition coalition, known as the Democratic Confederation, retained its congressional majority, but failed to win the two-thirds majority needed to impeach **Allende**.

March 11. **Peronist Héctor J. Cámpora was elected Argentine president amid growing chaos and institutional breakdown.** Inaugurated May 25, Cámpora remained in office forty-nine days before being forced to step down, as **Juan Perón** returned to run in new presidential elections called for September 1973.

April. **Uruguay's government announced a neoliberal five-year plan** featuring the lessening of government economic intervention while working to control inflation. The plan was moderately successful, as Uruguay enjoyed steady though unspectacular growth through the remainder of the decade.

June 20. **Bloody disorders attended Juan Perón's return to Argentina.** Among the estimated 2 million supporters who awaited **Perón** at Ezeiza Airport were Montoneros and members of the left-wing Peronist Youth. As Perón's plane approached, gunfire erupted causing numerous deaths. There are conflicting accounts as to the origins of the violence, but it may have been provoked by right-wing Peronists. Perón's airplane was diverted to another airport. The next day he gave a speech in which he indicated his opposition to the Peronist left.

June 29. **Tanks and armored vehicles attacked Chile's Defense Ministry and Presidential Palace.** Loyal troops soon crushed the revolt, the first effort by the Chilean military to overthrow an elected government in forty-two years.

August 22. **By an 81 to 47 vote the Chilean Chamber of Deputies declared Salvador Allende's socialist program unconstitutional and illegal, and invited the military to defend the constitution.**

September 11. **Chilean Army Commander Augusto Pinochet Ugarte led the overthrow of Salvador Allende's government.** As many as 5,000 Chileans, most of them **Allende** supporters, died in the fighting of that day (Allende among them) or were killed over succeeding weeks during what the military declared a "state of internal war." A Junta del Gobierno, comprised of heads of the army, air force, and navy, was formed and proceeded to assume control of all branches of government. The Chilean coup proved to be the bloodiest military takeover in the history of twentieth century Latin America.

September 23. **Juan D. Perón won 62 percent of the vote in Argentina's presidential election.** His wife, María (Isabel) Martínez de Perón, was elected his vice president. They took office on October 12.

1974

June 26. **General Augusto Pinochet assumed the Chilean presidency** after the junta issued a decree naming him chief of the nation for an indefinite period. **Pinochet** also remained army commander while the air force, navy, and police chiefs were given legislative and advisory powers. Earlier the junta had announced its intent to rejuvenate the nation morally and to extirpate Marxism.

July 1. **Isabel Perón became Argentine president upon the death of her husband Juan D. Perón.** Thus she became the first female chief executive in Latin American history. But her term was not successful. Inflation spiraled out of control, reaching 335 percent during 1975, beef exports dropped sharply, and guerrillas assassinated business leaders and members of the military. Meanwhile, the president's chief advisor, José López Rega, organized a right-wing terrorist group that he dubbed the Argentine Anticommunist Alliance (AAA).

1975

April 14. **The appointment of Sergio de Castro as Chile's economic minister marked the ascendance of economic liberalism in the Andean nation.** A proponent of University of Chicago economist Milton Friedman's free market, monetarist views, de Castro went on to slash government spending and reduce government regulation of the economy, sell government-owned

enterprises, open the nation to foreign investment, and reduce tariffs. The turn to economic liberalism marked a radical departure from the structuralist, statist, import-substitution model followed throughout Latin America since the 1930s. De Castro's actions all but eliminated inflation over ten years' time, and stimulated an economic boom in foreign investment and in the export of raw materials and foodstuffs. By the latter 1980s, the free market experiment was seen as responsible for an "economic miracle" in Chile. Negatively, the new economic policy led to a reconcentration of income, high rates of unemployment, and the dismantling of many social programs created over the preceding half-century. The lot of the poor worsened during the mandate of Chile's new economic policymakers, dubbed "the Chicago boys."

1976

March 24. **General Jorge Videla led a coup that replaced Argentina's president Isabel Perón.** The military's principal activity during its first three years in power was to liquidate the revolutionary threat. It did so with great brutality, in what became known as the Dirty War, a conflict having its origins in the *cordobazo* of 1969. By 1979 some 10,000 citizens, many of them not guerrillas but rather tarred through suspected association with them, had died after being seized, tortured, and murdered by members of the police, military, or death squads. Subsequently buried clandestinely, they became known as *los desaparecidos* (the disappeared). The Dirty War traumatized Argentine society.

September 21. **Chilean agents assassinated former Allende ambassador and cabinet member Orlando Letelier in Washington, D.C.** Letelier had conducted lobbying activities against **Pinochet**'s military regime in Chile. A U.S. citizen, Ronni K. Moffitt, was also killed by the car bomb. Four Cuban exiles and a U.S. citizen who had lived in Chile were eventually convicted of the crime. For years United States authorities sought the extradition of three Chilean officers accused of masterminding the plot. One surrendered to U.S. agents in Brazil, and two were convicted in Chile in 1993.

1978

June 25. **Argentina's victory in the World Cup, which it hosted, helped distract the country from the Dirty War, which neared its end.**

December 22. **War between Argentina and Chile was averted** thanks to intervention by the Vatican. At issue was control of the Beagle Channel.

1980

September 11. **Chileans approved a new constitution.** The document provided for an eight-year transitional period during which **Augusto Pinochet** would remain president. Voters would then decide whether he was to continue in office for another eight years. Although two thirds of the voters approved the constitution, critics faulted the way balloting was conducted.

November 30. **Uruguayan voters rejected a constitution backed by the military that would have increased military power vis-à-vis civilian authorities.** The effort failed when the citizenry defeated the proposal by a 58 percent to 42 percent margin. With that defeat, opposition to the dictatorship grew more vocal, becoming so as the regime's experiment with pre-announced currency devaluations failed. By the early 1980s Uruguay confronted declining GDP, falling real wages, and 66 percent inflation (1984).

December. **The Paraguayan Campesino Movement (MCP) was founded.** Claiming membership of some 10,000 families by 1987, it was the country's largest mass organization. MCP's goal was to protect the interests of the landless and smallholders threatened by the advance of capitalist agriculture.

1981

November. **A severe economic downturn forced Chile's government to intervene** in four banks and four financial companies on the brink of bankruptcy. The crisis deepened the following year, when GDP fell by more than 14 percent.

December 29. **General Leopoldo Galtieri assumed control of the Argentine government**, supplanting General Roberto Viola, who had succeeded General Jorge Videla the previous March. Prompting Galtieri's takeover were Viola's ill health and an economic downturn bringing high inflation and economic recession.

1982

April 2. **Argentina invaded the Falkland (Malvinas) Islands, thereby provoking war with Britain.** The Falklands, seized by Britain in 1833, had been claimed by Argentina since that time. Britain resisted the attack, and by June 4, reclaimed the islands. Nearly 1,000 lives, most of them Argentine, were lost in the conflict. Popular reaction against loss of the Falklands War, and against military rule itself, coupled with the poor economic situation, soon forced Galtieri to call elections for 1983. Diplomatic relations between Argentina and Britain were restored in 1990.

November 5. **Paraguay and Brazil completed the Itapú Hydroelectric Project on the Paraná River.** The dam generated electricity sufficient to meet Paraguay's needs, as well as supplying electric power to a large portion of southern Brazil. With its completion Paraguay entered into an economic recession whose impact was sharpened by a 30 percent annual inflation rate and compounded by global recession. Meanwhile President **Alfredo Stroessner** refused to devalue Paraguay's currency, angering manufacturers and exporters.

1983

January. **Argentina and the International Monetary Fund (IMF) negotiated a stand-by agreement through which $3.7 billion was lent to meet short-term needs.** A combination of war and global recession drove the nation close to bankruptcy. In 1982 Argentina had suffered 310 percent inflation, and its fiscal deficit stood at 14 percent of GDP.

March. **Members of Chile's proscribed political parties, the church, and the nation's interest associations issued a Democratic Manifesto** calling for monthly "days of national protest" against the **Pinochet** dictatorship. While **Pinochet** initially resisted the protests, he soon entered conversations concerning Chile's transition to democracy.

October 30. **Raúl Alfonsín led his Radical party to a surprise victory over the Peronists in Argentine elections.** The discredited military thus allowed a return to civilian rule. Alfonsín struggled to stabilize the economy and to prosecute military officers who had committed human rights abuses during the Dirty War. He was more successful in the latter endeavor than he was in the former.

1984

August 3. **Uruguay's Naval Club Pact cleared the way for a return to civilian government.** Under the pact elections would be held in November as scheduled, the 1967 constitution would be reinstated, and the military's National Security Council (COSENA) would serve the new government in an advisory capacity.

October 30. **Opponents of the Pinochet government launched a nation-wide work stoppage.** The stoppage was the culmination of more than a year of demonstrations seeking an early return to democracy. Several bombs exploded, and the government staged repressive operations in Santiago shantytowns. On November 6, it declared a state of siege that was not lifted until June 1985.

November 25. **Julio María Sanguinetti won Uruguay's presidential election**, thus returning the nation to constitutional rule after a dictatorship lasting eleven years. He entered office March 1, 1985. Sanguinetti enjoyed moderate success in macroeconomic management, aided by falling oil prices and an easing of the global recession. The nation's falling GDP was reversed through his encouragement of exports, and, during 1986-87, increased by a cumulative 17 percent. Meanwhile real wages increased and unemployment declined.

1985

April–December. **Trials in Argentina found top-ranking members of the military guilty of human rights abuses.** Previously, a presidential commission had documented 8,906 cases of death or disappearance of victims of the Dirty War. Former presidents Jorge Videla and Roberto Viola were sentenced to lifetime house arrest and seventeen years of house arrest, respectively. Other officers were sentenced to long terms in prison, or to house arrest. Videla, Viola, and six other officers were pardoned in 1990 by President **Carlos Menem**, as was Montonero leader Mario Firmenich, who had been jailed since 1984.

June. **Argentine president Alfonsín launched the Austral Plan, aimed at stabilizing the economy.** The plan featured balancing the national budget, freezing wages and prices, and monetary reform. While the plan was initially successful, inflation rebounded as Alfonsín neared the end of his term.

December. **Uruguayan president Sanguinetti's freeing of 250 former Tupamaro guerrillas angered the military.** While the president had extended amnesty to all military involved in the early-1970s war against the guerrillas, Sanguinetti secured a law (December 1986) exonerating the military for offenses committed during the dictatorship. The law was approved by a 57.5 percent vote in a plebiscite of April 1989.

1986

September 7. **Left-wing guerrillas carried out an assassination attempt against dictator Augusto Pinochet,** who escaped with light injuries. The act dramatized **Pinochet**'s contention that only his rule stood between social order and revolutionary violence. The following day Pinochet imposed a state of siege and declared a "war against Marxism."

1987

April 15-17. **Argentine army officers in Córdoba and Buenos Aires rebelled against President Raúl Alfonsín, demanding that he halt trials of** officers accused of human rights abuses. To that time legal action had been taken against more than 300 officers accused of crimes committed during the Dirty War. Following a massive out-pouring of public support for Alfonsín, the rebels laid down their arms. Alfonsín agreed in turn to limit trials to high-ranking officers. The April 1987 revolt was the most serious of three taking place against Raúl Alfonsín.

1988

October 5. **In a national plebiscite Chileans voted against allowing Augusto Pinochet a presidential term during 1989-97.** After a vigor-ous campaign by a seventeen-party coalition led by the Christian Democrats and the Socialists, about 54 percent of the voters rejected **Pinochet**'s continuation in office. According to the 1980 constitution, elections were to be held in 1989, and Pinochet was to step down on March 11, 1990.

1989

February 3. **Paraguayan dictator Alfredo Stroessner was overthrown months short of celebrating his thirty-fifth year in power.** **Stroessner**'s protégé, General Andrés Rodríguez, headed the coup, which had been anticipated since the mid-1980 split in Paraguay's Colorado party, the dictator's political arm. When the faction closest to **Stroessner** proposed elevating the dictator's eldest son, a homosexual, to the presi-dency, Rodríguez and other army officers, who disliked **Stroessner**'s son, seized the initiative and exiled both **Stroessner** and his son.

May 1. **Paraguayans overwhelmingly elect-ed General Andrés Rodríguez to a four-year presidential term** on the promise that he would restore democracy. He surprised many by keeping his word, allowing the return of exiles, freeing the press, and purging Stroessner cronies from public office. Himself one of those favored by former dictator Stroessner, Rodríguez had amassed a per-sonal fortune of $1 billion through a variety of government-favored business ventures, some of which involved illegal activities, notably alleged participation in the international narcotics trade.

May 14. **Peronist Carlos S. Menem was elected president of Argentina.** Winning about 48 percent of the vote, he defeated Radical candi-date Eduardo Angeloz and Álvaro Alsogaray of the Democratic Center Union. **Menem**'s victory was partly the result of public anger over Argen-tina's worsening economic problems.

July 8. **Argentine president Alfonsín trans-ferred power to Carlos S. Menem, marking the first time in sixty years that one democratically elected president was succeeded by another.** Alfonsín stepped down six months before his term ended owing to the nation's near economic col-lapse. Food riots broke out the previous month, and inflation ran at better than 100 percent per month. **Menem**, who had campaigned on a populist platform, quickly reversed his position. He announced that he would combine political liberalism and fiscal austerity. He began privatiz-ing the nation's massive public sector and revers-ing long-standing statist economic measures.

November 26. **Center-right Blanco party leader Luis Alberto Lacalle Herrera won Uru-guay's presidency.** Pledged to the privatization of state-owned enterprises, and promising to invigorate a national economy that had stagnated under the last two years of his predecessor's administration, Lacalle became the first Blanco elected during the twentieth century.

December 14. **Christian Democrat Patricio Aylwin Azócar, leader of a broad anti-Pinochet coalition, triumphed in Chile's presidential election.** Inaugurated March 1990, **Aylwin** went on to establish a coalition government.

Brazil

During the interval 1960 through 1989, Brazil lurched toward fulfilling the prediction that it would become a major world power. With a population of more than 150 million in 1990, and a diversified economy that produced a range of exports, from coffee and textiles to automobiles and light aircraft, Brazil played an increasingly important role in hemispheric affairs. Furthermore it weathered political turmoil during the 1960s, going on to complete a successful transition from military to civilian government by the late 1980s. All the while quality-of-life indicators steadily improved. Average life expectancy increased from fifty-two to sixty-seven years between 1960 and 1990; per-capita GDP more than doubled; 71 percent of Brazilians had potable water in their homes by 1990, whereas just 31 percent had the same thirty years earlier; the percentage of the potential electorate casting votes in national elections jumped from 24 percent to 55 percent over that interval.

Yet in many senses Brazil remained a glass half-empty. The nation endured twenty-one years under military rule (1964-85), during which the gap between rich and poor widened appreciably as military presidents bent their efforts toward industrializing the nation. Severe regional disparities were not addressed. While 80 percent of Brazilians had achieved literacy in 1990, levels of illiteracy ran as high as 60 percent in rural parts of the Northeast. An inadequate educational system burdened the nation with a work force half of which possessed less than a fifth-grade education.

Brazil thus presented a contradictory picture of change—and lack of it—over the interval 1960-89. Like its sister republics of the Southern Cone, Brazil approached the ninth decade of the century with a citizenry reeling from economic instability even as it remained hopeful that new, democratically elected leaders, might improve their lot as well as that of the nation.

1960

February 23. **U.S. president Eisenhower arrived in Brasília to begin a goodwill tour of South America.**

April 21. **President Juscelino Kubitschek formally inaugurated the new national capital of Brasília.**

1961

January 31. **Former mayor of São Paulo Jânio Quadros was inaugurated president,** with former Vargas labor minister **João Goulart** as his vice president. Popular with voters, to whom he had promised an activist, reformist presidency, Quadros proposed to give Brazil an independent foreign policy that would make it a leader of nonaligned Third World nations.

August 19. **President Quadros decorated Ernesto "Che" Guevara with the Order of the Southern Cross, Brazil's highest honor,** as part of his strategy of raising the nation's international profile and demonstrating its independence from the United States.

August 25. **Hoping to pressure Congress into granting him expanded power, Jânio Quadros tendered his resignation.** The ploy misfired when Congress accepted his offer. The recently organized General Labor Command (CGT) subsequently organized a general strike in support of the accession to the presidency of **João Goulart**.

September 7. **Populist nationalist and former leader of the Brazilian Labor party (PTB) João Goulart was inaugurated president.** Goulart assumed office in spite of opposition from the nation's military leadership, who suspected him of communist sympathies, as well as from the conservative-dominated Congress that, five days earlier, had amended the constitution so as to expand congressional power vis-à-vis the president.

1962

February 16. **Leonel Brizola, popular governor of Rio Grande do Sul, leader of the radical wing of the PTB, and brother-in-law of João Goulart, nationalized the U.S. company ITT (International Telephone and Telegraph).** The action delighted nationalists and members of the working class, though it displeased most members of the business establishment.

1963

January 6. **Brazilians voted to restore a presidential system to their nation,** following a congressional action of September 2, 1961, that had given the nation a quasi-parliamentary regime as a means of curbing presidential power.

September 12. **Enlisted men of the marines, air force, and navy, seeking support from the radical left, staged an uprising in Brasília** and briefly seized Congress. They were protesting a Supreme Court decision barring them from holding elective office. President **Goulart** neither supported nor denounced the action.

1964

March 13. **João Goulart moved decisively to the left.** At a giant rally in Rio de Janeiro, he signed decrees nationalizing private oil refineries and providing for expropriation of underutilized lands near federal installations. He also promised to propose other reforms to Congress, such as the extension of the suffrage to illiterates and enlisted men.

March 19. **Conservative opponents of Goulart's reforms staged a March of the Family with God for Liberty in São Paulo.** The size of the protest, which drew some 500,000 marchers, demonstrated the extent of middle-class opposition to Goulart.

March 26-29. **More than 1,000 sailors and marines revolted in Rio de Janeiro.** The mutiny occurred after the navy minister, Admiral Sílvio Mota, ordered the arrest of a sailor active in organizing an enlisted men's union. Goulart responded to the crisis by dismissing Mota and appointing a successor who promptly ordered a full amnesty for the mutinous sailors. Goulart's action seemed a direct assault on military discipline and strengthened the hand of officers plotting against the regime.

March 31-April 4. **The armed forces unseated João Goulart, ushering in twenty-one years of military rule in Brazil.** Coup leaders termed their movement the "Brazilian Revolution," which they insisted had rescued the nation from mob rule. Moderate and conservative Bra-

zilians praised the action, as did the United States, whose ambassador termed the takeover "the single most decisive victory for freedom in the mid-twentieth century."

April 9. **The new military government issued the First Institutional Act,** which expanded powers of the president at the expense of the legislature and judiciary. The ruling junta went on to name General Humberto Castelo Branco to the presidency. Castelo Branco, a moderate who held power until 1967, opened Brazil to foreign investment in order to make the country self-sufficient in consumer durables. He also pursued economic stabilization by freezing wages and prices, reducing the money supply, and improving the balance of payments. Meanwhile he controlled leftists and nationalists. Castelo Branco called some 9,000 persons before military courts on charges of subversion and corruption, expelled fifty-five leftist legislators from Congress, and deprived former presidents **Goulart**, Quadros, and **Kubitschek** of their political rights. He pursued a pro–United States foreign policy, supporting that nation's Cold War initiatives.

1965

October 27. **President Castelo Branco promulgated Brazil's Second Institutional Act,** dissolving political parties and providing for election of the president and vice president by Congress. President Castelo Branco took this action under pressure from military hardliners angry over opposition successes in recent state elections. Soon afterward two new parties were formed: the pro-government Aliança Nacional Renovadora (National Renovating Alliance, ARENA) and the opposition Movimento Democrático Brasileiro (Brazilian Democratic Movement, MDB).

1966

February 5. **Castelo Branco further strengthened his hand through the Third Institutional Act, which ended the popular election of state governors and mayors of state capitals.**

December 3. **President Castelo Branco launched Operation Amazônia,** an effort to develop that vast region of Brazil. The Superintendency for Development of Amazônia (SUDAM) was established to coordinate the program, and a free zone was set up in Manaus to encourage industrial production.

1967

The National Indian Foundation (FUNAI) was established to rectify corruption in the Indian Protection Service (SPI).

January 24. **A new constitution was promulgated.** It greatly enhanced presidential powers and those of the federal government over the states. It also provided for the election of the president by an electoral college made up of Congress and state delegates. The constitution was substantially amended on October 17, 1969, to further expand executive power.

March 15. **General Artur da Costa e Silva became Brazil's president.** The new president eased restrictions imposed by his predecessor, and indicated willingness to restrict the activities of foreign business in the country. Costa e Silva's tolerance, and the death of former president Castelo Branco (July 1967), heightened militancy on both the left and right. Critics of the regime became more vocal in demanding an end to military rule, clerics **Helder Câmara** and Bastos d'Ávila demanded social democracy, and students launched numerous demonstrations. Those on the right pressured military hardliners to impose tighter restrictions.

1968

December 13. **Artur da Costa e Silva issued the Fifth Institutional Act, which effectively established a military dictatorship.** Immediate cause of his action was congressional rejection of a presidential request to lift the parliamentary immunity of a senator who had criticized human rights abuses by the military. The new Institutional Act allowed the president to shut down Congress, suspend the political rights of citizens for ten years, and end the mandate of elected officials. A wave of arrests followed. Among those imprisoned were Carlos Lacerda and **Juscelino Kubitschek**, who had united to form an antidictatorial front.

The government went on to resume its program of economic development, which had increased economic growth to an unprecedented 11 percent during 1968, a level that would be maintained through 1974. Known as Brazil's "economic miracle," the 1968-74 period witnessed constant expansion of the industrial sector, especially in the area of auto production, the nation's leading economic sector. There was a notable diversification of exports. Ambitious state-sponsored economic development projects also spurred growth. The government embraced a policy of financing economic development through foreign borrowing, at the same time restricting the activity of trans-national corporations (TNCs). While the policy reduced TNCs' share of local assets from 27 percent to 9 percent (1969 to 1984), it saddled Brazil with the world's largest foreign debt.

1969

August 29. **Artur da Costa e Silva suffered a debilitating stroke.** The top military leaders distrusted the civilian vice president, Pedro Aleixo, and bypassed him to set up an interim government headed by the army, navy, and air force ministers.

September 4. **U.S. ambassador Charles Burke Elbrick was kidnapped.** The kidnappers were members of two leftist groups—National Liberating Action (ALN) and MR-8—who demanded the release of fifteen political prisoners. When the government complied with this demand and the plane carrying the fifteen was on the runway, there were efforts to prevent its departure by naval personnel outraged over the government's apparent surrender to the leftists. Elbrick was released the same day (September 7). Meanwhile, institutional acts enacted on September 5 authorized the government to exile Brazilians considered dangerous to national security and restored the death penalty in certain instances, including subversion. Carlos Marighela, founder of the ALN, was shot to death in São Paulo in November 1969.

October 8-9. **The army high command chose security chief Emílio Garrastazú Médici to be president** when it became clear that Costa e Silva would not recover from his illness. Congress, where ARENA had a majority, elected Médici president on October 25. Over the first four years of his presidency Médici combatted the nation's urban guerrillas, ultimately removing them from the national scene, committing massive human rights violations in the process. A Brazilian amnesty committee later documented the deaths of 170 of those arrested during his regime.

1970

June. **President Médici announced the National Plan of Integration (PIN).** The plan was intended to secure Brazil's possession of Amazônia and to provide land for settlers from the impoverished and drought-ridden Northeast, who were to be aided by a new National Institute of Colonization and Agrarian Reform (INCRA). The plan began with construction of the Transamazonian Highway, a 3,000-mile road stretching from the Atlantic to the Peruvian border.

1974

March 15. **General Ernesto Geisel was inaugurated president,** taking office as rising petroleum prices ended the nation's "economic miracle," and as opposition to military rule heightened. **Geisel** responded with a policy of mild political liberalization dubbed *distensão* (decompression) that first became apparent in November 1974, when he allowed an open election in which the left-coalition Brazilian Democratic Movement (MDB) made considerable gains. Fearing a resurgence of the left, Geisel subsequently slowed political liberalization. During his term Geisel broadened Brazilian foreign policy by improving relations with emerging economic powers Japan and West Germany, as well as with South Africa, Israel, and Taiwan. He also launched a commercial and cultural program of outreach to Lusophone Af-

rican nations Angola, Mozambique, and Guinea-Bissau.

1975

June 27. **Brazil signed an agreement with German suppliers to purchase up to eight nuclear reactors.** The United States was opposed to the transaction because the technology to be provided would enable Brazil to build nuclear weapons. United States pressure against Germany and Brazil failed to undo the deal, though safeguards to ensure that nuclear energy would only be produced for peaceful purposes were incorporated into the agreement.

1977

April 1. **President Geisel suspended Congress when MDB members refused to pass a government-sponsored judicial reform bill.** The president then decreed a series of constitutional amendments, known as the "April package," designed to enhance the strength of the progovernment ARENA party. One measure provided for election of all state governors and one-third of the federal senators by state electoral colleges. The Congress was reconvened on April 13.

November. **Two thousand businessmen called on the government to resume its policy of political liberalization.**

1978

May 12. **Auto workers at a Swedish-owned factory in São Paulo launched a sit-down strike.** The movement spread to other factories in the area, eventually involving 500,000 workers. The auto workers, who belonged to the Metalworkers' Union, eventually received a wage increase. The strike, the first serious labor stoppage in ten years, brought visibility to the head of the union, Luís Inácio da Silva (nicknamed Lula).

July. **Eight prominent industrialists petitioned the government to increase democracy in Brazil** as a route to greater social and economic justice. President **Geisel** responded by stepping up his liberalizing *distensão*. Shortly before leaving office he ended censorship, reinstated habeas corpus for political detainees, and abolished the Fifth Institutional Act, which had authorized the dictatorship.

1979

March 13. **Members of the Metalworkers' Union struck for higher wages in São Paulo.** When the strikers refused to return to work, the government removed Lula and other union leaders. The strikers remained firm, however, supported by Catholic activists, students, and the MDB. In April the workers received a wage increase; the ousted leaders were also reinstated. A forty-one-day strike in April 1980 was unsuccessful.

March 15. **General João Baptista Figueiredo became president**, going on to accelerate the political liberalization begun by his predecessor. Within four months of taking office he announced his intention to restore democracy to Brazil, further proposing amnesty for those accused of political crimes over the previous eighteen years. Figueiredo's program became known as that of *abertura* (opening), which set into motion the process ending military control of the nation.

November 30. **Legislation revamping the party system was enacted.** The measure was devised by the government to encourage the formation of several new parties and thereby weaken the opposition. Soon afterward ARENA was reorganized as the Partido Democrático Social (Social Democratic party, PDS), and the MDB as the Partido Movimento Democrático Brasileiro (Brazilian Democratic Movement party, PMDB). Among the other parties formed was the Partido dos Trabalhadores (Workers' party, PT), led by Luís Inácio (Lula) da Silva.

1980

November. **Political *abertura* continued when Congress passed a constitutional amendment reintroducing the direct election of state gover-** nors and federal senators. Military hardliners resisted the move, going so far as to bomb several public buildings in protest. The provision went into effect two years later.

1982

November 15. **The opposition PMDB swept national elections, assuming control of the Chamber of Deputies and winning gubernatorial contests in the nation's three most populous states.**

December 2. **Brazil began talks with the International Monetary Fund on proposed loans of more than $5 billion.** Brazil needed the loans to refinance its foreign debt of more than $80 billion. Brazil's problems were owed in part to a decline of more than 8 percent in export earnings in 1982, the first such decline since 1967. To obtain the loans, Brazil agreed to several austerity measures, such as reduction of the public sector deficit and the phasing out of subsidies. A severe recession, coupled with inflation, followed.

1984

April 25. **Congress narrowly defeated a constitutional amendment allowing direct election of the president in 1985.** The campaign for the *diretas* mobilized millions of Brazilians throughout the country, and though unsuccessful, demonstrated a rising popular demand for a greater voice in government.

1985

January 15. **Brazil's electoral college elected Tancredo Neves president.** Neves, the first civilian elected president since 1961, won 480 of 686 votes. The victory of Neves, candidate of the PMBD, was assured when he also won the support of a dissident faction of the PDS. Neves had campaigned on the promise to introduce long-overdue social reforms to Brazil. Over two decades of military rule the distribution of wealth had worsened to the point that social inequality was greater in Brazil than in any other major nation—50 percent of the population shared 10 percent of national wealth, while 1 percent enjoyed 17 percent.

March 15. **Vice President elect José Sarney became president of Brazil following the illness of Tancredo Neves.** The seventy-five-year-old Neves underwent emergency surgery on March 14 and died April 25. Sarney's presidency was marked by severe inflation (80 percent per month by 1989) compounded by economic stagnation and a budget deficit equaling nearly 5 percent of GDP. By the end of his term some 50 percent of the population lived in some degree of poverty.

1988

September 3. **A new constitution was created that enhanced congressional power as well as that of the judiciary, and reduced presidential power.** While criticized as confused and amorphous, the document contained a number of socially progressive features.

December 22. **Francisco (Chico) Mendes was murdered in a remote village in Acre state.** Mendes had become internationally known for his efforts on behalf of rubber workers whose livelihood was threatened by the deforestation of Amazônia and the spread of cattle ranching. His murderers, members of a ranching family, were sentenced to lengthy prison terms in 1990. They escaped in February 1993.

1989

December 17. **Fernando Collor de Mello won the presidency,** defeating Workers' party candidate Luís Inácio (Lula) da Silva by a 43 percent to 38 percent margin. As governor of Alagoas, he had criticized President Sarney and promised to rid public administration of corruption. Collor was the first president to be elected by direct popular vote instead of by the electoral college

system introduced by the military regime. Meanwhile Brazilians dubbed the ten years just completed as their "lost decade."

The Southern Cone

DEMOCRACY AND NEOLIBERALISM
1990-1999

Latin America entered the post-Cold War period at peace and with democratic regimes in place throughout the region. Meanwhile, Latin Americans turned away from statism and protectionism and exhibited a new openness toward the global economy. In the new climate of economic liberalism national budgets were trimmed, subsidies and social programs eliminated, and state enterprises sold to private-sector buyers, both domestic and foreign. Consequently, economic growth accelerated and inflation fell, most notably in Brazil and Argentina, two nations afflicted with chronic inflation.

But economic reform weighed heavily on the poor and lower middle class and tended to widen the gap between rich and poor. The sale of state-owned companies increased unemployment, as did cuts in government spending, and domestic industry was often hurt by imports. The region also continued to be burdened by the large foreign debts contracted in the 1970s and 1980s. It was also vulnerable to economic fluctuations originating elsewhere.

Latin America thus presented a mixed picture at the end of the twentieth century. Its prospects for economic growth were better than at any time since mid-century, but stubborn structural problems, such as generally low levels of education, lingered. Nevertheless, Latin Americans were inclined to approach the new century with guarded optimism. A survey taken in 1996 found that 61 percent of Latin Americans backed democracy as the best form of government, but only 27 percent indicated satisfaction with the way democracy functioned in their countries. In short, Latin Americans' new openness to the outside world and toward one another inspired at least as much hope as trepidation.

International Developments

Two themes dominated inter-American relations during the 1990s. The first was a renewed interest in regional economic integration, sparked by the example of the European Community. Mexico joined the United States and Canada in crafting the North American Free Trade Association (NAFTA), and in southern South America, Argentina, Brazil, Paraguay, and Uruguay followed suit with their Southern Cone common market (Mercosur, or Mercosul in Portuguese). The second theme was the effort to reshape inter-American associations in accordance with international realities after the Cold War. However, the Organization of American States, its membership augmented by the admission of Canada, Suriname, and the English-speaking states of the Caribbean, was now playing a relatively minor role in the settlement of disputes, while the United Nations was more visible.

1990

June 27. **U.S. President George Bush announced his Enterprise for the Americas Initiative.** Through that program the United States offered debt-restructuring aid to Latin American nations and pledged to work toward the establishment of a free trade zone embracing the entire hemisphere. In addition, he proposed to create a new fund, to be administered by the Inter-American Development Bank, to encourage private investment in the region.

1991

June 4. **Delegates to the 21st General Assembly of the Organization of American States in Santiago, Chile, signed a declaration expressing a commitment to democracy and to the renewal of the inter-American system.** A resolution adopted on June 5 called for an immediate meeting of the OAS Permanent Council in the event of a coup in one of the member nations.

July 18-19. **The first Ibero-American summit was held in Guadalajara.** It was attended by the presidents of the Latin American countries as well as by the president and prime minister of Portugal and king and prime minister of Spain. The concluding declaration affirmed the historical and cultural ties among the Iberian nations of the Old and New Worlds and called for closer political and economic cooperation. The summit reflected the closer relations between the two regions that developed after the restoration of democracy to Spain and Portugal in the 1970s and their entry into the European Union. Similar summits were held annually throughout the 1990s.

1994

December 9-11. **The United States hosted the Summit of the Americas in Miami, the first such gathering since 1967.** All of the hemisphere's heads of government attended, with the exception of Cuba's **Fidel Castro**. Delegates agreed to a timetable for creating a hemispheric free trade zone by 2005. They also endorsed the defense of democracy and human rights, protection of the environment, the alleviation of poverty, attacks on corruption and the illegal drug trade, and increased responsibilities for the OAS and the Inter-American Development Bank.

1997

The appearance of the warm ocean current known as El Niño was felt in much of Latin America. Its effects ranged from heavy rains and flooding in Peru, Bolivia, Brazil, and other countries to drought in Mexico and Central America. The severity of Hurricane Pauline, which battered the southern Pacific Mexican states of Oaxaca and Guerrero on October 8-9, was also attributed to El Niño. The effects of El Niño continued into 1998, as hurricanes and storms raged from Mexico to the Andean Republics.

1998

April 18-19. **Thirty-four Western Hemisphere leaders met in Santiago, Chile, and agreed to begin negotiations on the Free Trade Area of** **the Americas, that was supposed to be in force by 2005.** Hemisphere leaders had agreed on the creation of a free trade area at their first summit in 1994, but little was accomplished after that. Moreover, U.S. influence had waned because of the Clinton administration's failure to obtain "fast-track" authority from Congress to negotiate trade pacts. The United States was also criticized for its trade embargo on Cuba, the only Western Hemisphere nation not invited to the summit.

1999

June 28-29. **Thirty-three Latin American and Caribbean leaders and thirteen representatives from the European Union met in Rio de Janeiro and agreed to begin negotiations on achieving free trade by 2005.** But EU reluctance to free farm trade hindered progress. During 1990-98 Latin American imports from the EU increased by 164 percent, while the region's exports to the EU grew by only 29 percent. Success in expanding Latin American-EU trade was believed to hinge on the fate of trade liberalization talks scheduled in the World Trade Organization's Millennium Round of global trade negotiations set for November 1999.

Mexico, Central America, and the Caribbean

Two events made Mexico the center of hemispheric and world attention during the 1990s. First, in 1994 that nation joined Canada and the United States to form the world's most extensive free trade area, the North American Free Trade Association (NAFTA). Second, in the same year Mexico's sudden decision to devalue its currency plunged the nation into an economic downspin whose impact was felt throughout Latin America as nations as far away as Argentina experienced a loss of investor confidence.

Mexico's economic problems were accompanied by a sharp decline in popularity of the long-dominant Institutional Revolutionary party (PRI).

Dissatisfaction with the party's economic performance, along with reports of rampant corruption in official circles, produced gains for opposition parties. Despite the easing of the economic crisis by 1997, the political future remained clouded.

Central America entered a time of relative political calm during the 1990s though economic prosperity remained elusive. The end of the Cold War, which helped end long-standing guerrilla insurgencies in the region, also had the effect of causing Central America to fade from view as a region of global concern. Economic stagnation, aggravated by high poverty rates and problems arising from the international drug trade, condemned Central America to the status of a regional backwater.

Cuba and Haiti remained Caribbean trouble spots. The former nation remained at odds with the United States as it attempted to recover from the loss of its eastern European trading partners. Haiti found it difficult to maintain peace amid the hemisphere's most grinding poverty, this despite U.S.-led international pressure that restored democratic rule in 1994.

1990

January 27. **Rafael Leonardo Callejas Romero was inaugurated as president of Honduras.** Elected by a faction of the National party, Callejas pursued a neoliberal economic policy favored by national and international business interests.

February 25. **Violeta Barrios de Chamorro won a surprise victory in Nicaragua's presidential contest.** The widow of slain journalist Pedro Joaquín Chamorro, she ran as the candidate of a fourteen-party coalition, the United National Opposition (UNO), defeating the incumbent, **Daniel Ortega** of the FSLN, by a substantial margin. The United States, which had long opposed Ortega, lifted its five-year-old trade embargo against Nicaragua in March.

April 25. **Violeta Barrios de Chamorro was inaugurated as Nicaragua's president.** As a gesture of conciliation, she retained General Humberto Ortega, a Sandinista and brother of **Daniel Ortega**, as chief of the armed forces, but her decision produced controversy within the UNO. Another problem was the poor state of the Nicaraguan economy as a result of Sandinista mismanagement and the recent civil war between the U.S.-backed Contra rebels and the Sandinista government. Only in 1993 did Nicaragua's economy begin to rebound.

May 8. **Costa Rica inaugurated a new president, Rafael Calderón Fournier, of the Social Christian Unity party.** The son of a former president, Calderón entered office pledged to reducing Costa Rica's fiscal deficit and privatizing government-owned enterprise while maintaining the nation's extensive social welfare network. Calderón's austerity measures rendered him and his party unpopular. Meanwhile, crime began to be a serious problem in what had traditionally been one of Latin America's most peaceful nations.

May 16. **Incumbent President Joaquín Balaguer was reelected president of the Dominican Republic, narrowly defeating his old rival, Juan Bosch.** Bosch's charges of fraud brought a recount, which confirmed Balaguer's victory in June. He was inaugurated on August 16 amid social unrest because of government austerity measures.

June 9. **The body of Michael DeVine, an American resident of Guatemala, was found near his inn in the department of Peten.** He had been kidnapped the day before by gunmen dressed in military uniforms. On December 21, 1990, the United States cut off military aid to Guatemala, partly because of suspected military involvement in his killing. In 1996 Colonel Julio Roberto Alpírez, a Guatemalan officer with ties to the Central Intelligence Agency, was accused of ordering the murders of DeVine and of Efraín Bámaca, a guerrilla leader married to a U.S. citizen.

June 10. **The United States and Mexico agreed to move toward discussion of a free-trade pact.** The agreement was reached during a visit of President **Carlos Salinas** to Washington.

September. **Mexico's PRI, meeting in party convention,** adopted reforms aimed at making it more democratic and less subject to corruption. One reform mandated the holding of primary elections to select state and local candidates.

December 2. **Guatemalan soldiers killed fourteen peasants in Santiago de Atitlán** during a protest march of unarmed townspeople at a local military barracks. The killings contributed to the suspension of U.S. military aid to Guatemala on December 21.

1991

January 6. **Jorge Serrano Elías won the Guatemalan presidency in a runoff election.** He had come in second in the first round of balloting on November 11, 1990, but won the runoff by a large margin. Voter turnout in both elections was extremely low.

February 7. **Jean-Bertrand Aristide was inaugurated president of Haiti.** A Roman Catholic priest and proponent of liberation theology, he had been elected on December 16, 1990, in Haiti's first democratic election, winning more than 60 percent of the vote. He was opposed by the army and by supporters of the Duvalier dictatorship.

July 16-18. **The 10th summit of Central American presidents met in San Salvador.** This was the first time that Panama was included as a full participant. The presidents approved a treaty creating a Central American parliament and agreed to end tariffs on agricultural products by June 1992. The parliament (Parlacén) was established on October 28, 1991, but only Guatemala, El Salvador, and Honduras joined.

September 30. **Haitian General Raoul Cedras ousted President Jean-Bertrand Aristide.** The coup was followed by a cessation of U.S. aid and refusal to recognize the new ruling junta and by President Aristide's request that the United Nations help restore democracy to Haiti. On October 7-8 the National Assembly, pressured by the military, declared Haiti's presidency to be vacant and installed Supreme Court Justice Joseph Nerette as interim president.

December 12-13. **At their 11th summit, Central American presidents tooks steps to strengthen regional economic integration.** Reforms were made to the charter of the Organization of Central American States (ODECA), and the System of Central American Integration (SICA) was established to ensure the implementation of decisions taken at summit meetings.

1992

January. **Long-standing agrarian policy was altered by an amendment to article 27 of the Mexican constitution.** The new policies were proposed by President Salinas in November 1991 in an effort to boost agricultural productivity. *Ejidos,* which occupied more than half of Mexico's arable lands, could now be alienated, and Mexico's obligation to distribute land was ended. Landowners who made improvements to their property no longer faced expropriation. At the same time an amendment to article 130 of the constitution ended restrictions on churches.

January 16. **A peace agreement between the government of El Salvador and leftist insurgents of the FMLN was signed in Mexico City.** Provisions of the agreement included a cease-fire, the disarming of guerrillas and their incorporation into legal political parties, the restructuring of the Salvadoran armed forces and a reduction in their size, and the establishment of a truth commission to investigate human rights abuses.

October 6. **A huge lighthouse honoring Christopher Columbus was inaugurated in Santo Domingo to celebrate the five hundredth anniversary of the navigator's landing on Hispaniola.** President **Joaquín Balaguer** was criticized for spending an estimated $25 million on the monument. Pope John Paul II visited the Dominican Republic during the quincentenary celebrations.

October 16. **Guatemalan Indian activist Rigoberta Menchú Tum was awarded the Nobel Peace Prize.** She had fought against government-sponsored seizures of Indian lands during the 1970s. Following the death of her father during a peasant takeover of the Spanish embassy in Guatemala City in 1980, she fled to Mexico. She had publicized the cause of Guatemala's indigenous peoples through the widely-read English translation of her autobiography, *I, Rigoberta Menchú: An Indian Woman in Guatemala* (1983). However, anthropologist David Stoll challenged its accuracy and authenticity in his controversial *Rigoberta Menchú and the Story of All Poor Guatemalans* (1998).

November 3. **Pedro Rosello of the New Progressive party (PNP) was elected governor of Puerto Rico.** The PNP, which favored statehood for the island, also won control of the legislature. Rossello defeated Victoria Munoz Mendoza of the Popular Democracy party (PPD).

1993

March 20. **El Salvador's National Assembly, dominated by members of President Alfredo Cristiani's ARENA party and other rightist groups, voted an amnesty for those who had committed human rights abuses during the recent civil war.** The vote came six days after a UN-sponsored truth commission issued a report blaming most abuses on Salvadorian security forces. The first prisoners to be released as a result of the amnesty were two army officers who were serving 30-year sentences for the murder of six Jesuits in 1989.

May 25. **Guatemalan President Jorge Serrano suspended the constitution and dissolved Congress amid mounting discontent with his policies.** Protests led by political, business, and civic leaders led the army to remove Serrano on June 1. Congress subsequently elected the respected Ramiro de León Carpio to serve the remainder of Serrano's term.

June 23. **A UN trade embargo against Haiti went into effect.** The embargo, approved by the Security Council on June 16, barred the sale of oil and arms to Haiti and was imposed because of the refusal of its military to restore ousted President Aristide to power. The foreign bank accounts of Haiti's leaders were also frozen. The embargo was suspended in August after an agreement had been reached in July for the return of Aristide by October 30.

July 15. **Cuba announced that it was lifting the ban on the holding of the U.S. dollar and other foreign currencies by Cuban citizens.** The move was seen as an effort to increase foreign currency reserves and to curb the black market in dollars. Further liberalization of the economy was decreed on September 9, when the government allowed certain workers, such as mechanics and taxi drivers, to sell goods or services directly to the public.

August 19. **Former Nicaraguan Contras (now known as re-Contras) seized nearly forty hostages, including several legislators, in a village north of Managua and demanded that President Barrios de Chamorro dismiss army chief Humberto Ortega and other officials.** In retaliation, Sandinistas stormed the Managua offices of the UNO on August 20 and captured thirty-four conservative political figures. All the hostages were released August 25 after their captors had been promised immunity from prosecution and their grievances relayed to the government.

October 11. **A Haitian mob prevented the landing of U.S. and Canadian troops in Port-au-Prince.** The noncombatant forces had been sent to Haiti to help implement the July agreement for President Aristide's return. The collapse of the agreement prompted the UN to reimpose economic sanctions on October 19 while the United States barred all exports to Haiti except for food and medicine.

November 14. **Puerto Ricans voted to retain commonwealth status, narrowly defeating a statehood initiative.** Returns showed that 48.4 percent of the electorate endorsed the status quo while 46.2 percent favored statehood. The pro-independence vote was 4.4 percent. The outcome of the vote was affected by fear of the independence movement and of the prospect of paying federal taxes should statehood become a reality. Peripheral issues were the movement within the United States to promote English as the national language and loss of the island's Olympic teams should statehood be attained.

1994

January 1. **The North American Free Trade Agreement (NAFTA), linking Mexico, Canada, and the United States, went into effect.** The agreement aimed at eliminating tariff and other barriers to trade among the three countries over a period of fifteen years. A draft agreement had been concluded on August 12, 1992; after side agreements on labor rights, environmental protection, and import surges were reached, it was approved by the legislatures of the three countries.

January 1. **The Zapatista National Liberation Army (EZLN) launched a revolt in Chiapas, Mexico's poorest state.** The uprising was prompted by peasant demand for land, by declines in earnings for the state's main sources of income (timber, coffee, cattle, and corn), and by federal neglect of the region. The government declared a unilateral cease-fire on January 12. Talks began soon afterward and continued despite a brief government offensive in Febuary 1995. In February 1996 the government reached an agreement with EZLN leaders, promising to recognize the autonomy of Mexico's Indians and their right to multicultural education. Later that year, however, the EZLN called off further peace talks on the grounds that the government had failed to honor existing agreements. Talks resumed in November 1998 but ended with no progress.

January 27. **Carlos Roberto Reina was inaugurated president of Honduras, having led his Liberal party to victory in November 1993 on a platform pledging "moral revolution."** As president, Reina struggled to lessen the power of the army and to reduce human rights abuses.

March 23. **PRI presidential candidate Luis Donaldo Colosio was shot to death as he left a rally in Tijuana, Mexico.** The assassin confessed and was convicted by prosecutors, but many questions about the killing remained unanswered.

April 24. **Armando Calderón Sol, candidate of the ARENA party, won El Salvador's presidency in a runoff election.** He defeated Rubén Zamora, candidate of a leftist coalition, by a wide margin. Calderón took office June 1.

May 8. **José María Figueres took office as president of Costa Rica.** The son of former president **José Figueres** and candidate of the National Liberation party (PLN), he narrowly defeated Miguel Angel Rodríguez of the ruling Social Christian Unity party. Figueres pledged to improve social conditions, which had worsened under his predecessor's austerity policies, but he was unable to improve national economic performance significantly.

May 8. **Ernesto Pérez Balladares was elected president of Panama.** The candidate of the Democratic Revolutionary party (PRD), the party associated with **Omar Torrijos** and **Manuel Noriega**, he won about one third of the vote. Mireya Moscoso, widow of former president **Arnulfo Arias**, came in second with about 29 percent of the vote. Pérez Balladares took office September 1.

May 16. **Dominican President Joaquín Balaguer claimed an election victory over José Francisco Peña Gómez, candidate of the Dominican Revolutionary party (PRD).** The ballot count was suspended on May 19, and when it was resumed on May 24, **Balaguer** was declared the winner by a slim margin. Balaguer took office on August 16, but continuing attacks on the legiti-

macy of his victory led him to agree to cut his term short by two years.

July–August. **President Fidel Castro allowed thousands of Cubans to leave the island for the United States in small boats.** The departures were attributed both to growing austerity in Cuba and to anti-Castro radio broadcasts from the United States. On August 19 U.S. President Clinton announced the suspension of a twenty-eight year policy allowing Cuban refugees to become legal residents after reaching the United States. He further announced that Cuban "boat people" would be intercepted at sea and interned at the Guantanamo naval base. Castro halted the exodus when the United States agreed (September 1994) to accept at least 20,000 refugees annually. By that time some 21,000 Cubans had been intercepted by the U.S. Coast Guard. They were eventually admitted to the United States.

August 21. **Ernesto Zedillo Ponce de León was elected president of Mexico.** Named as the PRI's candidate after the assassination of Luis Donaldo Colosio, **Zedillo** won 50.1 percent of the vote in what was generally considered a fair election with few irregularities. Diego Fernandez de Cevallos of PAN won 26.8 percent of the vote, and **Cuauhtémoc Cárdenas** of the PRD came in third with 17 percent.

September 19. **Three thousand U.S. troops arrived in Haiti following the agreement of Lieutenant General Raoul Cedras to return power to Jean-Bertrand Aristide.** Cedras's action followed conversations, backed by the threat of force, conducted with U.S. representatives Jimmy Carter, Senator Samuel Nunn of Georgia, and former chief of staff Colin Powell.

September 28. **José Francisco Ruiz Massieu, the second highest official in Mexico's PRI, was shot to death.** The gunman was apprehended and sentenced to a fifty-year prison term in 1995.

October 15. **President Jean-Bertrand Aristide returned to Haiti.** Army commander Cedras had resigned his post and left the country five days earlier. **Aristide** confronted many severe problems, including high unemployment and an economy that had declined by thirty percent since 1991.

December 20. **President Zedillo, who had been inaugurated on December 1, devalued the Mexican peso and plunged the nation into economic crisis.** His action was seen as a necessary but belated response to Mexico's slow economic growth and large trade deficit. Aided by loans and loan guarantees from the United States and other sources, the government devised a recovery plan based on the adoption of austerity measures, such as cuts in government spending. As a result, unemployment and economic hardship for the poor and middle classes soared.

1995

January 15. **Dissident members of Nicaragua's FSLN formed the Sandinista Renewal Movement.** Led by Sergio Ramírez, a former vice president, the dissidents were critical of what they considered the authoritarian and extreme positions of party head **Daniel Ortega.**

February 12. **Mexico's PRI suffered a major defeat as it lost the governorship of the important state of Jalisco to the National Action party (PAN) candidate, Alberto Cárdenas Jiménez.** The PAN also triumphed in Guanajuato on May 28 and retained the governorship of Baja California Norte on August 6.

February 28. **Raúl Salinas, brother of former president Carlos Salinas, was arrested.** Raúl was accused of massive financial irregularities and of masterminding the murder of José Francisco Ruiz Massieu. The arrest further damaged the image of **Carlos Salinas**, already tarnished by the economic crisis of December 1994, who left Mexico for voluntary exile abroad. On January 21, 1999, Raúl Salinas was convicted of ordering the assassination and sentenced to a fifty-year prison term, later reduced to 27 ½ years.

June 10. **The Cuban government confirmed that it had arrested fugitive American financier Robert Vesco, wanted in the United States for fraud and cocaine trafficking.** Cuba,

which had granted him asylum in the early 1980s, accused him of being an agent of "foreign special services." On August 26 he was sentenced to a thirteen-year prison term.

June 25. **State police killed seventeen peasants in Mexico's Guerrero state.** The peasants, members of the Southern Sierra Campesino Organization, were en route to a rally of the opposition Democratic Revolutionary party. The incident produced much criticism of the police, five of whom were murdered, probably in retaliation, on July 7. As a result of the controversy, Governor Rubén Figueroa Alcocer was forced to step down in March 1996.

1996

January 7. **Alvaro Arzú won Guatemala's presidency in a runoff election with fifty-one percent of the vote.** A former mayor of Guatemala City and candidate of the center-right National Advancement party (PAN), he defeated Alfonso Portillo Cabrera of the rightist Guatemalan Republican Front. Arzú took office on January 14. One of his first acts was to dismiss members of the armed forces accused of human rights abuses, including Colonel Julio Roberto Alpírez.

February 7. **Jean-Bertrand Aristide turned over the Haitian presidency to René Préval.** The candidate of **Aristide's** Lavalas coalition, Préval was more moderate than his precedessor. He promised to privatize state enterprises and abolish seven ministries in order to secure loans from the World Bank and the International Monetary Fund.

February 24. **Cuban air force jet fighters shot down two small aircraft piloted by members of an exile group, Brothers to the Rescue.** All four crewmen were killed. The aircraft had been searching for Cuban rafters, but the group had previously dropped anti-Castro leaflets over Havana. Cuban officials maintained that the aircraft had violated Cuban air space and had ignored warnings, but the incident outraged many in the United States. As a result, Congress passed the Helms-Burton bill, signed on March 12, which punished foreign companies that invested in Cuba. The United States also tightened its own sanctions on Cuba.

June 28. **A new guerrilla group appeared in Guerrero, Mexico.** About fifty armed guerrillas interrupted a memorial ceremony for the seventeen peasants killed in 1995. The guerrillas, who claimed to be members of the Marxist Popular Revolutionary Army (ERP), killed at least thirteen persons on August 28-29 in incidents in the states of Guerrero, Oaxaca, and Mexico.

June 30. **Leonel Fernández won the Dominican presidency in a runoff election.** He narrowly defeated José Francisco Peña Gómez of the PRD, who had led in the first round of voting on May 16. Fernández, candidate of the Dominican Liberation party (PLD), had the support of incumbent President **Joaquín Balaguer**, who suggested during the campaign that Peña Gómez, a black of Haitian origin, would unite the Dominican Republic with Haiti if elected. Fernández took office on August 16.

October 20. **Nicaraguans elected Arnoldo Alemán president.** A rightist former mayor of Managua, Alemán won about 51 percent of the vote, defeating FSLN candidate and former president **Daniel Ortega**, who received 38 percent. Both candidates endorsed free-market policies though Alemán reminded voters of Ortega's past socialist orientation. Alemán took office on January 20, 1997.

November 5. **Pedro Rosello was reelected governor of Puerto Rico**, winning 51 percent of the vote to defeat Héctor Luis Acevedo of the Popular Democratic party. During the campaign, Rosello, of the pro-statehood New Progressive party, promised to work for a binding plebiscite in 1998 to settle the question of the island's status.

November 14. **Mexican President Zedillo's plan to reform electoral politics was eviscerated in the Chamber of Deputies.** PRI deputies, who had a majority, pushed through amendments that restricted the right of opposition parties to form coalitions, raised limits for government expenditures on elections, and impeded the access of opposition candidates to the media. The deputies' action was attributed to internal division within the party and to recent PRI losses in municipal elections.

December 29. **The Guatemalan government and leftist guerrillas signed a peace agreement.** Talks between the government and the guerrilla group, the UNRG, had begun in 1990 and were stepped up by President Arzú, who met with guerrilla leaders in Mexico City soon after taking office. Provisions of the agreement included demobilization of the guerrillas and their incorporation into civil society, reduction of the armed forces by one third, and the protection of the culture and languages of Guatemala's indigenous people. Prior to the signing of the agreement the National Assembly passed an amnesty law covering soldiers and guerrillas who had committed human rights abuses.

1997

June 9. **Haitian Premier Rosny Smarth resigned** to protest the alleged rigging of recent legislative elections (April 6) by supporters of former president **Jean-Bertrand Aristide**, who was expected to seek another presidential term in 2000. Smarth supported President Rene Préval's economic austerity plan, which was opposed by Aristide and his followers. President Préval named Eric Pierre as premier on July 25, but he was rejected by the Chamber of Deputies, as were other nominees. The impasse continued until January 1, 1999, when Préval announced that he would rule by decree.

July 6. **Opposition parties gained a majority in the Mexican Chamber of Deputies.** Although the ruling Institutional Revolutionary party (PRI) remained the largest party in the 500-seat chamber, the Democratic Revolutionary party (PRD) won 129 seats, the National Action party (PAN) 122 seats, and two smaller parties 14. This was the first time in Mexico's modern political history that the PRI had failed to win a congressional majority. The PAN also won three of six contested governorships. **Cuauhtémoc Cárdenas**, candidate of the PRD, was elected governor of the Federal District, the first time the position was filled by popular election.

October 17. **The remains of Ernesto "Che" Guevara were laid to rest in Cuba.** The revolutionary hero's remains had recently been discovered in a Bolivian mass grave.

December 22. **Gunmen killed forty-five persons, including fifteen children, in the Mexican state of Chiapas.** The killings took place in Acteal, a Tzotzil Indian village. The victims were believed to be supporters of the Zapatista rebels active in Chiapas since 1994. On July 19, 1999, twenty persons convicted of taking part in the massacre were each sentenced to thirty-five years.

1998

January 21. **Pope John Paul II arrived in Cuba in the first such visit since the 1959 revolution of Fidel Castro.** The pope was received enthusiastically by Cubans. While on the island, he criticized the U.S. embargo on trade with Cuba. Following the pope's visit, officials released several dozen "prisoners of conscience," thereby honoring a request by the pope to President **Castro**.

January 27. **Carlos Roberto Flores Facussé was inaugurated as president of Honduras.** A member of the center-right Liberal party, Flores had defeated Alba Nora Gunera of the National party by a wide margin in balloting on December 30. Upon taking office, he pledged to combat crime and poverty during his administration. In 1999 constitutional reforms reasserted civilian authority over the military.

February 24. **Cuba's National Assembly elected Fidel Castro to another five-year presidential term.** Castro's brother Raúl was reelected first vice president, and five other vice presidents were also reelected.

March 3. **Daniel Ortega, former president of Nicaragua and leader of the Sandinista party (FSLN), was publicly accused by his thirty-year-old stepdaughter of sexually abusing her when she was a child.** The stepdaughter, Zoilamérica Navarez, was the daughter of **Ortega's** longtime companion, Rosario Murillo, and had been adopted by Ortega. Navarez filed formal charges against Ortega on May 27, but he claimed immunity from prosecution as a member of Nicaragua's National Assembly. His supporters maintained that the charges were politically motivated and reelected him head of the FSLN on May 23.

April 26. **A Roman Catholic bishop, Juan Gerardi Conedera, was found dead in Guatemala City.** The seventy-five-year Gerardi, head of the human rights office of the archdiocese of Guatemala City, had recently published a report critical of the human rights record of the armed forces during the recent civil war. On July 22 the Roman Catholic priest who discovered the body, Mario Orantes Nájera, was arrested for the crime, but he was released on February 17, 1999.

May 8. **Miguel Angel Rodríguez Echeverría was inaugurated president of Costa Rica.** The candidate of the Social Christian Unity party, he narrowly defeated José Miguel Corrales of the PLN in balloting on February 1, 1998.

July 5. **Mexico's Democratic Revolutionary party (PRD) won the governorship of Zacatecas, its first statehouse victory.** In balloting elsewhere the Institutional Revolutionary party (PRI) won the governorships of Durango and Chihuahua, reclaiming the latter from the National Action party (PAN), which had gained control in 1992. In elections on August 2 the PRI retained the governorships of Veracruz and Oaxaca, but lost Aguascalientes to the PAN. The winning candidate in Veracruz was Miguel Alemán Velasco, son of former president **Miguel Alemán**.

July 21-22. **Three Salvadoran National Guardsmen sentenced to thirty years in prison for the 1980 rape and murder of four U.S. churchwomen were paroled.** A judge ordered their release under a new law aimed at reducing prison overcrowding. Two other Guardsmen convicted of the same crime remained in prison.

August 10. **Panmanian voters soundly rejected a constitutional amendment that would have allowed President Ernesto Pérez Balladares to serve a second consecutive term.** Under the constitution that went into effect in 1972, ten years must elapse before a president can be reelected.

September 21-24. **Hurricane Georges battered the Greater Antilles.** Puerto Rico alone suffered more than $2 billion in damage, while 600 died in Puerto Rico, Hispaniola, and Cuba. The Dominican Republic was also hard hit.

October 14. **The United Nations General Assembly approved by its largest majority yet a resolution calling on the United States to end its trade embargo against Cuba.** While 157 countries voted for the nonbinding resolution, only two—the United States and Israel—voted no; 12 countries abstained. The annual votes began in 1992.

October 24-November 1. **Hurricane Mitch devastated Honduras and Nicaragua and caused extensive damage in other Central American countries and Mexico.** More than 10,000 died, most because of floods and mudslides occasioned by torrential rains. The hurricane was one of the most powerful ever recorded in the Caribbean.

December 1. **The Cuban government announced that December 25 would be permanently reinstated as a holiday.** The celebration of Christmas was halted in 1969 on the grounds that workers were needed for the sugar harvest. On December 31, thousands of Cubans celebrated the fortieth anniversary of the triumph of the revolution. In a speech in Santiago on January 1, 1999, **Fidel Castro** reaffirmed his commitment to the revolution, which he said had barely begun.

December 13. **Puerto Ricans voted to continue their commonwealth relationship with the United States.** In a non-binding referendum 45.5 percent cast votes in favor of statehood while 50.2 percent voted "none of the above," a choice indicating support of commonwealth status.

1999

February 7. **Mexico's Democratic Revolutionary party (PRD) won the governorship of Baja California Sur** while the Institutional Revolutionary party (PRI) retained the Guerrero statehouse amid charges of fraud and vote-buying. In elections on February 21, the PRI also retained control of Quintana Roo and Hidalgo.

February 25. **Guatemala's independent Historical Clarification Commission (also known as the Truth Commission) issued its report on the recent civil war.** Set up under the 1996 peace accord, the commission concluded that the army was responsible for 90 percent of the approximately 200,000 deaths that occurred during the conflict. On March 10, while visiting Guatemala, President Clinton apologized for past U.S. support of military governments there.

March 7. **Francisco Flores Pérez was elected president of El Salvador.** Flores, of the ruling National Republican Alliance (ARENA) received 52 percent of the vote while Facundo Guardado of the Farabundo Martí Liberation Front (FMLN) came in second with about 29 percent. Voter turnout in the election was less than 40 percent. After taking office on June 1, Flores announced emergency measures to combat crime and revive the economy by reducing the fiscal deficit and raising agricultural production.

May 2. **Mireya Moscoso, widow of Arnulfo Arias, was elected to succeed Ernesto Pérez Balladares as president of Panama.** The candidate of the Arnulfista party, Moscoso won 45 percent of the vote, defeating Martín Torrijos, son of **Omar Torrijos** and candidate of the ruling Democratic Revolutionary party (PRD), by about 7 percentage points. High unemployment and a poverty rate estimated at 36 percent contributed to the victory of Moscoso, who ran a populist campaign.

November 7. **Francisco Labastida won the first national primary to be held by Mexico's ruling party, the PRI.** Labastida, a former minister on the interior (gobernación), would probably face Vicente Fox of the PAN and Cuauhtémoc Cárdenas of the PRD in the July 2000 presidential election.

Bolivarian Republics: Bolivia, Colombia, Ecuador, Peru, Venezuela

During the 1990s the Bolivarian republics moved forward with free-market economic reforms aimed at making their economies more competitive internationally. Foreign investment was encouraged, stimulated by the selling of state-owned enterprises. These measures were accompanied by successful attempts at lowering government spending and reducing inflation. But the economic reforms had a steep social cost as massive layoffs and cuts in government subsidies increased human suffering throughout the region.

Meanwhile, the illegal narcotics trade troubled life in Colombia, Peru, and Bolivia. Drug traffickers corrupted public officials and violently attacked those whom they deemed a threat to their operations. These nations also found themselves under growing pressure from the United States to cooperate in drug interdiction and eradication programs. The United Nations reported in July 1999 that coca cultivation had decreased substantially in Bolivia and Peru, but had increased in Colombia, still the primary source of cocaine.

By the 1990s all of the Bolivarian republics enjoyed democratic rule, although Peru's **Alberto Fujimori** seemed intent on prolonging his government well into the next century. Colombia's long-standing guerrilla insurgency grew worse over the decade, invigorated by an escalating flow of monies earned through participation in the illegal drug trade. Thus, as the decade approached its end, the Bolivarian republics presented a mixed picture of social malaise amid democratic government and a generally brightening economic picture at the macroeconomic level.

1990

February 15. **The presidents of the United States, Bolivia, Colombia, and Peru signed the Cartagena Declaration.** The document pledged greater coordination and intensified efforts to reduce the consumption, trafficking, and production of cocaine. To realize these goals, U.S. President Bush promised to ask Congress for additional aid for the three Andean countries to enable them to cope with the social and economic costs of coca eradication.

May 27. **Liberal Cesar Augusto Gaviria won Colombia's presidential election.** The campaign manager of Liberal candidate Luis Carlos Galán, who was assassinated in 1989, Gaviria won 48 percent of the vote; Álvaro Gómez Hurtado, a former Social Conservative who had formed the National Salvation Movement, won 24 percent. Two other presidential candidates were killed during the campaign, probably by drug traffickers or rightist paramilitary groups: Bernardo Jaramillo Ossa of the leftist Patriotic Union and Carlos Pizarro León Gómez, leader of the M-19 movement, which had reached a peace accord with the government in March. Antonio Navarro Wolff, who replaced Pizarro as the M-19 candi-

date, won 13 percent of the vote and joined Gaviria's cabinet.

June 10. **Alberto Fujimori was elected president of Peru in a runoff election, defeating novelist Mario Vargas Llosa by a substantial margin.** In the first round of voting on April 8, **Fujimori**, candidate of a new party called Cambio 90, was a strong second-place finisher behind **Vargas Llosa**, who had campaigned on a platform of free-market reforms. The APRA candidate came in third, and the party supported Fujimori in the runoff. The Shining Path attempted to disrupt both elections.

July 28. **Alberto Fujimori was inaugurated president of Peru.** On August 8, despite campaign pledges to the contrary, he introduced an austerity program known as "Fujishock," which raised the price of gasoline, ended subsidies on basic foodstuffs, and allowed the currency to float. Under Carlos Boloña, named economy and finance minister early in 1991, a broad neoliberal program was adopted that featured the privatization of state-owned enterprises, the liberalization of trade, the encouragement of private investment, and the firing of state employees.

1991

January. **Cholera Epidemic in Peru.** The first case of the highly contagious disease, which had not been seen in Peru since the 1880s, was reported in the port city of Chimbote. The epidemic quickly spread to Ecuador, Colombia, and other countries. Approximately 500,000 cases were eventually reported, 80 percent of them in Peru. About 4000 persons died.

July 4. **Colombia adopted a new constitution that replaced its 1886 charter.** The document provided for minority-party representation in Congress, popular election of departmental governors, ongoing investigation of human rights abuses, and prohibition of the extradition of native-born Colombians. The latter provision had moved Medellín drug cartel leader Pablo Escobar to surrender to Colombian authorities (June 1991). Leaders of the Cali cartel similarly submitted to incarceration because of the non-extradition provision.

1992

February 4.   **Venezuelan President Carlos**

Andrés Pérez narrowly avoided assassination in a conspiracy involving some ten percent of the nation's armed forces.   The plotters, calling themselves the Bolivarian Revolutionary Movement, protested government corruption and its austerity program.   Their leader, Lieutenant

Peru and Bolivia

Colonel Hugo Chávez Frías, spent twenty-six months in prison and launched a political movement upon being pardoned in 1994.

April 5. **Peru's president Alberto Fujimori assumed emergency executive powers and dismissed the national Congress** in the face of that body's opposition to his proposed anti-terrorist legislation and his economic program. While the move produced criticism abroad and a temporary suspension of U.S. aid, it was highly popular with Peruvians. A coalition backing **Fujimori** won a majority in elections on November 22 for a constituent congress.

June 9. **Víctor Polay Campos, head of Peru's Tupac Amaru Revolutionary Movement (MRTA), was captured in a Lima suburb.** He had been captured in 1989 but had escaped a year later. The MRTA was Peru's second largest guerrilla movement.

July 22. **Colombian drug kingpin Pablo Escobar, head of the Medellín cartel, escaped from incarceration** as he was about to be transferred to a military prison. He went on to wage a campaign of terror against the government that did not end until he was killed by police in December 1993. Control of Colombia's narcotics industry now passed to the Cali cartel.

July. **Nine students and a professor from La Cantuta University near Lima, Peru, were abducted and murdered.** On February 22, 1994, nine members of the armed forces were convicted of the crime, but they were amnestied in 1995.

August 10. **Moderate conservative Sixto Durán Ballén took office as president of Ecuador.** He had been elected in runoff balloting on July 5, defeating businessman Jaime Nebot Saadi. In accordance with his campaign promises, on September 3 Durán Ballén issued an economic reform package that cut public spending, devalued the currency, and called for privatization of state-owned enterprises. The package produced many protests, including a general strike on September 23.

September 12. **Peruvian police captured Shining Path leader Abimael Guzmán and several of his key subordinates.** The left-wing

movement was severely weakened by his arrest. On October 7 Guzmán was sentenced to life in prison by a secret military court.

November 27. **Air force units bombed Venezuela's presidential palace, and military officers and leftist civilian allies launched an abortive coup attempt.** More than three hundred persons died, many of them looters and pro-coup demonstrators as well as prisoners killed in an escape attempt from a prison near La Guaira.

1993

May 20. **Venezuela's Supreme Court ruled that there were sufficient grounds to prosecute President Carlos Andrés Pérez for embezzlement and misappropriation of $17 million.** Congress suspended the president's powers, a move made permanent on August 31, and named Ramón J. Velásquez to serve the remainder of Pérez's term. In 1996 Pérez, who had been in prison and under house arrest since 1994, was convicted of mismanaging government funds and sentenced to twenty-eight months in prison.

June 9. **MNR candidate Gonzalo Sánchez de Lozada was elected president of Bolivia.** With thirty-four percent of the vote, he defeated thirteen other candidates, including former president **Hugo Banzer Suárez**. Since no candidate won a majority, Congress had to make the final choice, but with the withdrawal of Banzer on June 9, Sánchez de Losada's victory was assured. Taking office on August 6, he continued the austerity measures of his predecessors.

October 31. **Peruvians narrowly approved a new constitution giving their nation a more highly centralized and presidential government with a unicameral legislature.** The document also cleared the way for President **Alberto Fujimori** to seek a second consecutive term.

December 5. **Venezuelans elected Rafael Caldera to a second presidential term.** The 77-year-old former president had been expelled from COPEI in June and ran as the candidate of several small leftist parties, won a thirty percent plurality. He blasted his AD and COPEI opponents as

"IMF-package candidates," promising a lessening of austerity measures mandated by the international agency.

1994

February 2. **Rafael Caldera took office as president of Venezuela amid a severe banking crisis.** On January 17 the government assumed control of Banco Latino, the country's second-largest commercial bank, to prevent its collapse. In the ensuing panic the government was forced to bail out twelve other banks in 1994.

June 13. **Ecuadorian Indians began demonstrations against a new agricultural development law which they claimed limited their rights to land and water.** Thousands of Indians blocked highways and prevented the delivery of food and other products to cities. The law was amended on July 7 to guarantee the property rights of indigenous peoples. The episode reflected the increasing militancy of Ecuador's Indians, who were represented by an umbrella group, Confederation of Indigenous Nationalities of Ecuador (CONIE), established in 1990.

June 19. **Ernesto Samper was elected president of Colombia in a runoff election.** A Liberal, he narrowly defeated Andrés Pastrana of the Social Conservative party. Two audiotapes suggesting that Samper's campaign had received money from the Cali drug cartel were made public in late June. Samper took office on August 7.

1995

January 26. **Hostilities broke out between Peru and Ecuador over disputed territory in the Cordillera del Condor range.** A cease-fire went into effect on February 4, and on February 17 a pact was signed aimed at demilitarizing the territory in question. About fifty deaths resulted from the fighting.

April 9. **Peru's President Alberto Fujimori was reelected to a second five-year term.** He won 64 percent of the vote against former United National secretary-general Javier Pérez de

Cuéllar, who received about 22 percent. **Fujimori's** supporters also won a narrow majority in the unicameral Congress. The president's popularity was buoyed by a sharp decline in political violence since 1992 and by an economic growth rate of 12.4 percent during 1994. On August 23, 1996, the Congress approved an interpretation of the 1993 constitution that would enable Fujimori to seek a third term in 2000.

August 6. **Colombian police captured Miguel Rodríguez Orjuela, co-leader of the Cali drug cartel.** Following his apprehension only one of seven top Cali cartel members remained at large. The cartel reputedly controlled eighty percent of the cocaine smuggled into the United States.

1996

January 27. **Colombian President Ernesto Samper was accused of knowingly accepting large contributions from drug traffickers during his 1994 campaign.** The accusation was made by his former campaign manager and defense minister, Fernando Botero—son of the world famous artist of the same name—who had been arrested in August 1995 for illegal enrichment. Congress exonerated the president on June 12, but many demanded Samper's resignation, including the vice president, Humberto de La Calle, who stepped down on September 10.

March 1. **The U.S. government decertified Colombia as a nation in compliance with international anti-drug principles.** The decertification deprived Colombia of U.S. aid and threatened economic sanctions. On July 11 the United States revoked the visa of President Ernesto Samper, saying that he had knowingly accepted $6 million from the Cali drug cartel during his 1994 campaign.

March 10. **The Andean Community was formed at a summit attended by the presidents of Bolivia, Colombia, Ecuador, Peru, and Venezuela.** Replacing the Andean Pact of 1969, it was designed to emulate the European Union and produce more coordinated economic policies.

July. **Thousands of coca farmers living in Colombia's Amazonian departments of Guaviare, Caquetá, and Putumayo protested the government's eradication of their illegal crops, covering some 125,000 acres.** In August the Putumayo growers agreed to voluntarily reduce their cultivation of coca in exchange for increased financial compensation. Deliberations with growers in Caquetá were halted on August 23, when the army fired on crowds in the departmental capital of Florencia, killing four.

July 7. **Ecuadorians elected Abdala Bucaram to the presidency in a runoff election.** He won about fifty-four percent of the vote, defeating Jaime Nebot Saadi, who had led Bucaram in the first round of voting on May 19. The nephew of populist leader Assad Bucaram and brother-in-law of the late Jaime Roldós, Abdala Bucaram waged a populist campaign but adopted neoliberal measures upon his inauguration on August 10.

August 30-September 2. **Leftist FARC guerrillas launched attacks in Colombia's Putumayo and Guaviare departments, killing more than 50 soldiers and capturing another 60.** The attacks were believed to be a response to government coca eradication and other anti-drug efforts since the FARC derived substantial sums from the protection of coca fields and drug facilities. In September another guerrilla group, the ELN, blew up several oil pipelines. The FARC seized ten marines in Chocó department on January 16, 1997. Meanwhile, paramilitary groups began kidnapping and assassinating relatives of FARC and ELN guerrilla leaders, causing several others to flee Colombia.

October 11. **Bolivia signed an agreement providing for its entry into Mercosur,** the Southern Common Market, as of January 1, 1997. Bolivia became an associate member.

December 17. **Members of the Túpac Amaru Revolutionary Movement (MRTA) seized more than 600 hostages at the Japanese ambassador's residence in Lima.** By mid-February 1997 only 72 hostages remained in captivity, but the government continued to refuse the captors' principal demand that imprisoned MRTA members be released.

1997

February 6. **Ecuador's Congress removed President Abdala Buccaram on grounds of "mental incapacity."** His austerity program had angered the citizenry, which accused him of betraying his promises to follow a populist agenda. Conservative Fabio Alarcón, president of the Congress, was selected to replace him and won endorsement in a referendum on May 25.

April 22. **Peruvian troops stormed the Japanese ambassador's residence killing all 14 Tupac Amaru guerrillas who had held 72 hostages since December 17, 1996.** One hostage died during the operation and two soldiers were killed.

June-July. **Workers, students, professional groups, and others staged protests against what they considered the increasingly authoritarian tendencies of President Alberto Fujimori.** The protests occurred after the legislature, dominated by **Fujimori** supporters, dismissed three members of the Constitutional Tribunal who blocked his efforts to run for a third term. Tensions also arose over charges aired on a television station (July 13) that the intelligence services had secretly wiretapped the telephone conversations of prominent Peruvians. The Peruvian citizenship of the Israeli-born station owner was revoked the same day. Critics now questioned Fujimori's citizenship, suggesting that he had not been born in Peru but in Japan.

August 5. **Bolivia's Congress elected General Hugo Banzer president for a five-year term.** Banzer, who had served as president in 1971-78, received 115 votes in the Congress, while the second-place finisher, Juan Carlos Durán, got 30. The vote by Congress was necessary because no candidate won an absolute majority in national elections in June.

October 26. **Approximately 49 percent of Colombia's registered voters cast ballots in departmental and municipal elections despite efforts by leftist guerrillas to sabotage the voting.** As a result of the violence unleashed by the FARC and ELN, which included the murder or kidnapping of many candidates, numerous office-seekers withdrew from the race, and balloting was canceled in many towns. While rural voters abstained from voting, turnout was high in major cities.

1998

February 10. **Peru's Supreme Court ruled that President Alberto Fujimori could run for a third consecutive term.** While Peru's constitution bars three-term presidencies, the court held that Fujimori was exempt from the provision because he was already in office when the constitution was adopted in 1993.

February 26. **The United States government granted Colombia conditional certification for its drug-fighting efforts under a national security waiver.** This action came after the Colombian Congress lifted a six-year ban on the extradition of drug traffickers. However, extradition would not be applied retroactively.

March 2. **Colombia's FARC guerrillas defeated an elite army mobile brigade, killing 73 and taking 46 prisoners.** The loss of life was the worse since Liberal guerrilla Guadalupe Salcedo ambushed and killed 99 soldiers in 1953. The action, occurring in the remote Amazonian department of Caquetá, was the eighth in a series of army reverses beginning April 16, 1996, when a combined FARC-ELN force ambushed an army convoy in southern Colombia, killing 30 and wounding 15. Estimates placed combined guerrilla forces at 15,000, and the national army at 33,000.

May 12. **Political assassinations continued in Colombia as left-wing extremists killed retired general Fernando Landazábal Reyes.** Landazábal's assassination was apparently in response to the murders several weeks earlier (April 16 and 18) of María Arango and Eduardo Umaña Mendoza, lawyers sympathetic to the left. As Landazábal's assassination took place, right-wing paramilitary forces assaulted the village of Puerto Alvira in Meta department, whose residents were said to be sympathetic to the FARC

guerrillas. The two hundred heavily armed men, members of the Colombian United Self-Defense Forces (Autodefensas Unidas de Colombia, AUC), executed fourteen peasants, including a six-year-old child.

June 21. **Andrés Pastrana Borrero won the Colombian presidency in a runoff election.** Pastrana, a member of the Conservative party, defeated the Liberal party's Horacio Serpa, winning 50.3 percent of the vote to Serpa's 46.3 percent. Before taking office on August 7, Pastrana met with FARC guerrilla leader Manuel Marulanda Vélez in talks aimed at ending the decades-old civil war.

July 12. **Jamil Mahuad Witt defeated Alvaro Noboa for the Ecuadorian presidency in a runoff election.** Mahuad, former mayor of Quito and the candidate of the Popular Democracy party, took 51 percent of the vote, while Noboa, of the Roldosista party, won 49 percent. Mahuad took office on August 10.

September 27. **The progovernment majority in Peru's Congress voted down a proposal to hold a referendum on President Alberto Fujimori's plan to seek a third presidential term.** A petition with over a million names seeking such a referendum had been presented to the National Electoral Authority in July.

October 26. **Peru and Ecuador signed a peace treaty settling their fifty-six-year-old territorial dispute.** Peru's president, Alberto Fujimori, and Ecuador's Jamil Mahuad Witt signed the treaty, which had been drafted by Argentina, Brazil, Chile, and the United States. The treaty reaffirmed Peruvian control of a disputed 48-mile tract along the Amazonian border between the two countries. They agreed to demilitarize the area and create two national parks there. Ecuador was also given access to the Amazon River and ownership of a one-square-mile outpost atop the Cordillera del Condor, where several Ecuadorian soldiers were buried after a 1995 clash with Peru.

December 6. **Former lieutenant colonel Hugo Chávez Frías won the Venezuelan presidency with fifty-six percent of the vote.** He overwhelmingly defeated Henrique Salas Romer, who received forty percent. Salas was supported by both the Democratic Action party and COPEI, and his defeat demonstrated the collapse of these parties, which had dominated Venezuelan politics since 1958. A populist who led a failed coup attempt in 1992, Chávez promised to end corruption and return Venezuela to good economic health. His Patriotic Front coalition also fared well in congressional and gubernatorial elections.

1999

February 2. **Hugo Chávez Frías took office as president of Veneuzela.** He immediately called for the election of an assembly to draft a new constitution, a proposal overwhelmingly approved by voters on April 25.

May 6. **Colombian President Andrés Pastrana formally resumed peace talks with the FARC guerrillas**, meeting FARC leader Manuel Marulanda Vélez for the first time since he took office. Few concrete steps toward peace resulted from the meeting. In January Pastrana had gone to the same southern town, San Vicente del Caguán, to begin peace talks, but Marulanda Vélez failed to appear, citing security concerns. Colombia's other major guerrilla group, the ELN, broke off peace talks on February 16. Meanwhile, both leftist groups and the rightist self-defense force, the AUC, continued to commit acts of violence. In January the AUC killed some 150 persons, alleged FARC sympathizers. In March the FARC killed three U.S. citizens in northeastern Colombia. The ELN highjacked an Avianca airplane in April and kidnapped 143 churchgoers in a Cali suburb on May 30.

May 26. **Colombian defense minister Rodrigo Lloreda Caicedo resigned because of his belief that President Pastrana had made too many concessions to the guerrillas.** He had previously criticized Pastrana's decision (November 7, 1998) to withdraw troops from a large area of Caquetá and Meta departments, giving de facto recognition of FARC control over the region. Peace talks, scheduled to resume on July 19, were again called off after the FARC launched a major offensive in several departments, presumably in

order to enhance its bargaining position. The turmoil had an adverse effect on the economy as the GDP fell by 4.8 percent during the first quarter of 1999, the steepest quarterly decline in twenty years. Negotiations were resumed in October.

August 25. **A crisis developed when Venezuela's constituent assembly issued a decree denying the Congress the right to pass laws or to meet.** The assembly was dominated by supporters of President Hugo Chavez.

August 27. **President Jamil Mahuad of Ecuador reached an agreement with the International Monetary Fund aimed at relieving that nation's economic difficulties.** The crisis was due partly to severe problems in Ecuador's banking sector and a foreign debt of $13 billion. The agreement called for an IMF loan of $500 million.

Southern Cone: Argentina, Chile, Paraguay, Uruguay

With democratic transition complete throughout the Southern Cone nations by 1990, civilian leaders occupied themselves with advancing free-market reforms over the remainder of the decade. They worked to reduce the state's role in the economy, mainly by selling publicly owned enterprises to private, often foreign, interests. One result was a sharp fall in inflation, most strikingly seen in Argentina, a country long plagued by hyper-inflation. But the region's political leaders were not unopposed in their programs of economic liberalism. Workers and middle sector groups protested cuts in social programs and subsidies, as well as the high unemployment rates accompanying economic reforms. Another important aspect of economic reform was the establishment of a regional trade pact with Brazil (Mercosur).

1990

March 11 **Christian Democrat Patricio Aylwin assumed office as Chile's president, becoming that nation's first democratically elected chief of state since 1973.** Former dictator **Augusto**

Pinochet retained considerable power, however, since he was to remain army commander. **Aylwin** also continued the highly effective neoliberal reforms initiated under Pinochet. During Aylwin's administration Chileans enjoyed low unemployment and inflation in the single-digit range.

December 3. **Thirteen died in an unsuccessful army revolt against Argentine President Carlos Menem.** The nation's Supreme Council of the Armed Forces meted out lengthy sentences to the leaders of the revolt. The government also announced plans to reduce the size of the armed forces and privatize economic enterprises controlled by the military.

1991

March 20. **Argentine Economy Minister Domingo Cavallo launched a convertibility plan aimed at reducing hyper-inflation, which reached a peak of 20,266 percent in 1990.** The plan of the Harvard-trained economist involved pegging Argentina's peso to the dollar and requiring that the domestic money supply be backed by hard-money reserves. The plan was successful and reduced inflation to a mere four percent within a year. Cavallo's program was but one of President **Menem**'s economic reforms, which also included privatization of the nation's large public sector and opening the nation to private, especially foreign investment.

March 26. **The Treaty of Asunción was signed, committing Argentina, Brazil, Paraguay, and Uruguay to form a Southern Common Market (Mercorsur).**

1992

June 20. **A new Paraguayan constitution was approved.** Replacing a charter promulgated in 1967, it reduced presidential powers and banned reelection of the president.

December 13. **Uruguayans voted over-**whelmingly to repeal key sections of a privatization law passed in 1991.** The referendum did not affect all planned privatizations, but it was argued that the size of the vote in favor of repeal—seventy-two percent—represented a rejection of the Lacalle administration's economic policies and a vote in favor of Uruguay's welfare state.

1993

May 9. **Paraguayans chose businessman Juan Carlos Wasmosy to be president, the first**

elected head of state in over fifty years. Was-mosy, a Colorado, took office on August 15, promising to continue free-market reforms.

November 12. **The former head of Chile's intelligence service (DINA), retired General Manuel Contreras, received a seven-year prison sentence for masterminding the 1976 assassination of Orlando Letelier, Salvador Allende's foreign minister.** A second former DINA official was sentenced to a six-year term. Chile's Supreme Court upheld their sentences in 1995.

December 11. **Chileans elected Christian Democrat Eduardo Frei Ruiz-Tagle to a six-year presidential term.** Frei, son of former president Eduardo Frei Montalva, headed the left-of-center Coalition for Democracy, winning approximately 58 percent of the vote. He defeated Arturo Alessandri Besa, candidate of a right-wing coalition, who received 24 percent. Frei took office on March 11, 1994.

1994

August 24. **A new Argentine constitution modifying the 1853 charter was promulgated.** It included provisions for the direct election of the president for a four-year term with one reelection permitted and for runoff elections should no presidential candidate receive at least forty-five percent of the vote. The constitution also reaffirmed Argentine sovereignty over the Malvinas (Falkland Islands).

November 27. **Former president Julio María Sanguinetti of the Colorado party was narrowly elected president of Uruguay with about 32 percent of the vote.** He defeated candidates of the conservative Blanco (National) party and of a leftist coalition including the Broad Front (Frente Amplio), each of whom won about 31 percent. Sanguinetti was sworn in on March 1, 1995.

1995

January 1. **Mercosur came into force, linking Argentina, Brazil, Paraguay, and Uruguay in a common market.** Tariffs were ended on most goods traded among the four partners and a common external tariff was adopted on goods from outside the region.

May 14. **Carlos Menem was reelected president of Argentina.** Winning about 50 percent of the vote, he defeated José Octavio Bordón of the center-left coalition Frente del País Solidario (Frepaso), who won 29 percent, and Horacio Massaccesi of the UCR, or Radical party, who won 17 percent. **Menem** began his second term on July 8.

December 15. **An agreement was signed providing for closer economic ties between Mercosur and the European Union.** Called the EU-Mercosur Interregional Framework Agreement, it sought gradual liberalization of trade between the two blocs with the goal of introducing full free trade by 2005.

1996

April 22-25. **Crisis in Paraguay.** A crisis was touched off when General Lino César Oviedo refused President Wasmosy's order to resign because of his political activities. Fearful of a military coup, Wasmosy then offered to name Oviedo defense minister if he would resign. Thousands of Paraguayans demonstrated in support of Oviedo's removal and later expressed outrage over the president's offer of the defense ministry. On April 25 President Wasmosy announced that he was withdrawing his offer to Oviedo, who was arrested in June but continued to pursue his presidential candidacy.

July 26. **Argentina's economy minister, Domingo Cavallo, resigned.** Cavallo, a supporter of neoliberal economic reforms, clashed with President Menem over proposed new cutbacks in middle-class subsidies which were opposed even by sectors of the ruling Peronists. Cavallo was succeeded by Roque Fernández, also a supporter of neoliberalism. Proposed changes in the labor laws led to a 36-hour general strike on September 26-27. Having been adversely affected by Mexico's financial crisis of late 1994, Argentina remained in recession, with unemployment in May 1996 estimated at 17.1 percent.

October 1. **Chile joined Mercosur as an associate member.** In this capacity Chile could maintain external import duties lower than those of the other members.

November 18. **Chile and Canada signed a free trade pact to go into effect in June 1997.** The agreement provided for the removal of tariffs on eighty percent of the trade between them. It was hoped that the agreement would pave the way for Chile to enter NAFTA, an idea derailed after Mexico's financial crisis of late 1994.

December 8. **Uruguayans approved constitutional reform.** Approved by a narrow 50.2 percent of the voters, the reform ended the electoral system (*ley de lema*) which allowed each party faction to present its own slate of candidates for the presidency and other elective offices, with the victor being the candidate with the most votes from the party with the most votes. President Sanguinetti and other supporters of the constitutional reform hoped that it would lessen party factionalism and increase the coherence of party platforms.

1997

May. **Protests took place in Jujuy, Santa Fe, and other Argentine provinces.** Demonstrators often erected roadblocks to show their unhappiness over high levels of unemployment and over the government's austerity policies, particularly plans to privatize state-owned industries. In response the government promised to increase spending on social programs.

September 22. **Lino Oviedo narrowly won the Colorado party's presidential primary in Paraguay.** However, President Juan Carlos Wasmosy, a Colorado, stated that he would not support Oviedo in the May 1998 election as he considered him a danger to Paraguayan democracy.

October 26. **An opposition alliance defeated the governing Peronista party in Argen-**

tine congressional elections. The alliance, made up of the centrist Radical party and the center-left coalition Frepaso, won approximately 46 percent of the vote to the Peronists' 36 percent. The balloting was to fill half the seats in the 257-member lower chamber of Congress.

1998

March 11. **General Augusto Pinochet was sworn in as a Chilean senator for life,** a privilege extended to former presidents under the 1980 constitution. The previous day he had resigned as head of the armed forces. His presence in the Senate sparked protests from other legislators and street demonstrations in Santiago and Valparaiso.

May 10. **Raúl Cubas Grau of the ruling Colorado party was elected president of Paraguay, defeating Domingo Laíno of the opposition Democratic Alliance coalition.** A wealthy businessman and engineer, Cubas was considered a stand-in for retired general Lino César Oviedo, who was barred from seeking the presidency by Paraguay's electoral tribunal. Though jailed for leading a coup attempt in 1996, Oviedo won the Colorado presidential primary in 1997 and remained popular. Cubas freed Oviedo soon after taking office on August 15.

July 14. **Former Argentine president Jorge Videla was indicted on charges of child abduction.** The indictment grew out of a probe of illegal adoptions and seizures of children of victims of Argentina's "dirty war" of the 1970s. Several other retired officers were arrested on similar charges over the next six months.

July 21. **Argentine president Carlos Menem ended his efforts to seek a third presidential term.** He had previously stated that he would run again despite an explicit constitutional ban on such a move. **Menem's** campaign had drawn criticism from former Radical president Raúl Alfonsín and from members of his own Peronist party, including presidential hopeful Eduardo Duhalde, governor of Buenos Aires province. Despite this, Menem supporters in the Peronist (Justicialista) party continued to seek ways of securing him another term.

October 16. **Former Chilean dictator Agustín Pinochet was arrested in London.** Pinochet, in Great Britain for medical treatment, was placed under arrest at the request of Spanish authorities, who charged him with genocide and terrorism and sought his extradition. On October 8, 1999, a British magistrate ruled that Pinochet could be extradited to Spain.

1999

March 28. **President Raúl Cubas Grau of Paraguay resigned.** He was forced to step down amid a political crisis caused by the assassination of Vice President Luis María Argaña Ferrero, an opponent of Cubas and retired general Lino Oviedo. Senate president Angel González Mucchi was sworn in as Cubas's successor. Both Cubas and Oviedo fled into exile.

October 24. **Fernando de la Rúa was elected president of Argentina.** A Radical and candidate of the center-left Alliance coalition, De la Rúa defeated Peronist Eduardo Duhalde, winning about 49 percent of the vote.

October 31. **Socialist Tabaré Vázquez of the leftist coalition Broad Front (Frente Amplio) won a plurality** of 38.5 percent in the first round of Uruguay's presidential election. Colorado Jorge Battle came in second with 31.3 percent and would face Vázquez in a runoff on November 28.

Brazil

Brazilians began the 1990s by inaugurating their youngest president in history—40-year-old Fernando Collor de Mello—only to see him discredited and removed from office in a corruption scandal. In 1994 **Fernando Henrique Cardoso** was elected, his reputation enhanced by a successful stint as finance minister, during which he managed to tame Brazil's hyper-inflation. As president, Cardoso continued the privatization of state-owned enterprises begun by Collor and labored to reduce government spending and the debt burden of both the national and state governments. During this period Brazil welcomed foreign investment as never before and moved toward trade liberalization, most notably through the trade agreement called Mercosur (see South-

ern Cone). Despite the brightening economic picture, millions of Brazilians remained mired in poverty.

1990

March 15. **On the day of his inauguration President Collor imposed an austerity package aimed at curbing an inflation rate estimated at eighty-five percent a month.** Key features included an eighteen-month freeze on large bank accounts, tax increases, an end to many subsidies, and a plan for privatization of state-owned enterprises. The plan failed to control inflation and instead produced a recession.

1991

February 1. **A new anti-inflation plan went into effect.** Dubbed Collor II, it included wage and price controls in an another unsuccessful effort to control inflation.

December 13. **Brazil and Argentina concluded an agreement giving each country the right to inspect the other's nuclear installations under the auspices of the International Atomic Energy Agency.** The two countries had the most advanced nuclear technology in Latin America, but plans for military uses were abandoned with the restoration of civilian rule in the 1980s. Neither country had ratified the Tlatelolco treaty (1967), which created a nuclear-free zone in Latin America.

1992

May. **President Collor was implicated in an influence-peddling scheme coordinated by Paulo Cesar Faria, his close associate and former campaign finance manager.** The accusations of corruption were initially made by the president's younger brother, Pedro. Fernando Collor's first economy minister, Zélia Cardoso de Mello, was also implicated.

December 29. **President Collor resigned the presidency as senators were beginning to vote on articles of impeachment drawn up by the Chamber of Deputies.** Despite his resignation, the Senate found him guilty of corruption and barred him from public office for eight years. In 1994 he was tried before the Supreme Federal Tribunal for corruption but was acquitted because of insufficient evidence. Collor was succeeded by the vice president, Itamar Franco.

1993

May 20. **President Franco named Fernando Henrique Cardoso finance minister.** Over the next six months Cardoso introduced a series of measures to curb inflation and cut government deficits. They included tax increases, efforts to reduce public spending and tax evasion, and the eventual introduction of a new currency.

1994

July 1. **Brazil's new currency, the real, was introduced.** Part of **Cardoso's** economic stabiliza-tion program, the currency was to be pegged to the U.S. dollar, and the government pledged to curb the money supply. Meanwhile, the monthly rate of inflation had fallen dramatically since Cardoso's accession as finance minister.

July 17. **Brazil won the World Cup, defeat-ing Italy 3-2 in an overtime game.** Brazil had previously won the World Cup in 1958, 1962, and 1970.

October 3. **Ferdinand Henrique Cardoso was elected president.** Running as the candidate of the Brazilian Social Democratic party (PSDB), he won 54 percent to 27 percent for his chief rival, Luís Inácio (Lula) da Silva of the Workers' party

(PT). Cardoso took office on January 1, 1995.

1995

November 8. **The Senate voted for a constitutional amendment to end the forty-two-year monopoly of Petrobrás in the petroleum industry.** The Chamber of Deputies had acted in June. Private companies, both foreign and domestic, would now be able to contract with Petrobrás for exploration, drilling, distribution, and refining of petroleum.

1996

April 17. **At least nineteen peasants were killed in the northern state of Pará as state police attempted to end a road blockade organized by the Landless Workers Movement (MST).** The organization had been involved in numerous land invasions in several states.

1997

June 5. **President Cardoso signed a constitutional amendment allowing presidents, governors, and mayors to serve two consecutive terms.** The amendment would enable Cardoso to seek reelection in 1998.

1998

July 29. **The Brazilian government sold its controlling interest in Telebrás, the national telephone company, in Brazil's largest privatization to date.** The auction of the 12 holding companies into which Telebrás had been divided

netted approximately $19 billion. Opponents of the sale tried unsuccessfully to block it through demonstrations and appeals to the courts.

October 4. **Fernando Henrique Cardoso was elected to a second presidential term, winning a majority of the votes and avoiding a runoff.** Cardoso won approximately 53 percent of the vote while his leading opponent, Luís Ignácio (Lula) da Silva of the Workers' party (PT) won about 32 percent. The election was held at a time of growing turmoil brought on by the economic crisis in Asia. As foreign investors withdrew their money from Brazil, **Cardoso** agreed to a range of cost-cutting financial reforms in exchange for a $41.5 billion bailout from the International Monetary Fund. Despite the agreement, economic difficulties persisted into 1999.

1999

January 13-15. **The government devalued the real and allowed it to float freely.** The government was responding to a crisis triggered when the governor of Minas Gerais, former president Itamar Franco, announced a 90-day moratorium on payment of the state's debt to the federal government. Rio Grande do Sul declared a similar moratorium. The government also responded by barring the two states' access to foreign credit while the World Bank froze loans to them. The government later made concessions to these and other states.

May 2. **Petrobrás, the state petroleum enterprise, lost its monopoly over fuel imports in another important step toward deregulation of the oil industry.** Foreign and domestic firms would now be able to import and sell oil freely.

Part II

Topical Chronology

SOCIETY

Population

c. 1500

The Indigenous Population. Experts generally agree that the Western Hemisphere was populated by people from Asia, but there is disagreement over the time of the first arrivals, though there is evidence that it was at least 10,000 years ago. Over the centuries hunters and gatherers in the region now known as Latin America learned to cultivate crops and developed a sedentary or semi-sedentary way of life. In some areas societies with complex polities and economic systems arose. At the time of their initial contact with Europeans these areas of "high civilization" were the Nahua- and Zapotec-speaking zones of central and southern Mexico; the Maya regions of the Yucatán peninsula and parts of Central America; and Andean South America, much of which was dominated by the Incas. Other important peoples included the Arawak of the Caribbean islands; the Muisca (also known as Chibcha), who inhabited highland areas of modern Colombia; and the Tupinambá of coastal Brazil.

There has long been debate over the size of the indigenous population around 1500. One school asserts that Latin America was densely populated, especially the areas of high civilization. S. F. Cook and Woodrow Borah, for example, calculated a population of about 25 million for central Mexico in 1519. The population of Andean South America is considered to have been lower than that of central Mexico, but some estimate more than 30 million for the entire region. Noble David Cook has posited a population of nearly 9 million for the territory included in modern Peru. Although the current consensus supports the idea of a relatively large population in 1500, many dissenters argue for a smaller population.

c. 1500-1810

Demographic Disaster and Recovery. There is no doubt that the native Americans—called Indians by Europeans—suffered a drastic decline in the decades after the arrival of the Spanish and the Portuguese. Because of disagreement over the size of the precontact population, there is also disagreement over the extent of the decline. Since most scholars agree that by the early seventeenth century there were fewer than a million native Americans left in central Mexico, those who accept estimates of very large numbers in 1500 logically argue for catastrophic declines in the sixteenth century. The decline would have been enormous in relation to an estimated population of 25 million in 1519, but far less so if a much lower initial figure were accepted. Patterns of decline are evident everywhere throughout Spanish and Portuguese America in the sixteenth and seventeenth centuries, though the rate of decline varies from place to place. Although many Indians died from warfare, overwork, and abuse by European settlers, the principal reason for their decline was the introduction of diseases previously unseen in the Western Hemisphere, notably smallpox, measles, and typhus. (See Science and Medicine.) In the islands of the Caribbean, Indians virtually disappeared, but elsewhere their numbers began to increase after 1650.

Africans were present in the New World from the early sixteenth century, initially being brought to the colonies from Spain or Portugal by their masters or employers. By 1550 slaves were being imported directly from Africa, and the traffic continued throughout the colonial period. People of African origin could be found in all the colonies, but they were most numerous in the Caribbean islands, northern South America, and especially Brazil, which received more than 2 million Africans by 1810.

European immigration to the colonies was made up largely of Spaniards and Portuguese and probably did not total 2 million during the entire colonial period. Although reliable figures are not available, women accounted for a substantial minority of Spanish immigrants, who came mainly from Andalusia, Extremadura, and other parts of the kingdom of Castile. Miscegenation occurred from the beginning in all the colonies and produced a large population of mixed racial ancestry, consisting of *mestizos* (of white and Indian ancestry), mulattoes (of white and black ancestry), and many other permutations. It has been estimated that the population of the Spanish American colonies in 1800 totaled approximately 13.5 million, of whom 45 percent were Indians, 33 percent were mixed bloods of all kinds, 18 percent were white, and 4 percent were black. The population of Brazil at the same time was about 2 million, of whom two-thirds were blacks and mulattoes; whites accounted for 29 percent, and Indians for 5 percent.

c. 1810-1990s

Population Trends in the New Nations. Latin America's population grew relatively slowly during the first century of independence. Despite high fertility rates, malnutrition and poor sanitation and health care kept mortality rates high, especially in the early nineteenth century.

Public officials sought to increase population growth in order to stimulate economic development and to prevent foreign encroachments on unoccupied national territory. European immigration was seen as a desirable means of achieving these ends and of "whitening" the local population with the admixture of a "superior" race. While all governments favored immigration, Europeans were attracted primarily to Argentina, Brazil, and Uruguay. Approximately 6.5 million Europeans, most from Italy and Spain, arrived in Argentina between the mid-1850s and 1930, though only about half became permanent residents. Between 1884 and 1933 Brazil received nearly 4 million immigrants, mainly from Portugal, Italy, and Spain. About 1 million immigrants, mainly Italians and Spaniards, arrived in Uruguay between 1836 and 1926. Cuba and Chile were also important destinations for European immigrants. Substantial numbers of immigrants from Germany, Russia, France, and the British Isles also moved to Latin America during these years.

Although European immigrants were always preferred, Peru and Cuba imported Chinese workers in the mid-nineteenth century, and approximately 250,000 Japanese settled in Brazil between 1908 and 1963. The years between 1870 and 1950 also saw the arrival of Middle Eastern immigrants, mainly Christians from Syria, Lebanon, and Palestine, who were known as *turcos* because they initially carried Turkish passports. In the early decades of the twentieth century, the construction of the Panama Canal and the development of banana plantations on the relatively uninhabited Caribbean coast of Central America led to the importation of thousands of workers from Jamaica, Barbados, and other West Indian islands. During the nineteenth century internal migration was of significance in some countries as a result of the settlement of sparsely populated frontier areas. The populations of Sonora, Tamaulipas, and other northern Mexican states grew during the Porfirian era (1876-1911) as a result of railroad construction and the development of mining and other industries in the region. Continuing a process begun in the late colonial period, settlers from the Colombian province of Antioquia moved into new lands to the south and southwest. Meanwhile, Brazilian coffee growers were fanning out from São Paulo in search of virgin lands.

Population Trends since 1930. In the decades after 1930 the most striking trend was a "population explosion" in most countries, principally in the years 1940-70. Although foreign immigrants entered Argentina, Brazil, Cuba, and Venezuela in considerable numbers after 1930, the principal reason for population growth was the drop in mortality rates throughout Latin America. Starting in the late nineteenth century, improvements in public health, such as the eradication of yellow fever and the provision of pure water in urban areas, cut infant mortality rates dramatically and increased life expectancy. Fertility rates remained high, however, except in Argentina and Uruguay and to a lesser extent in Chile and Cuba.

A second notable phenomenon of the post-1930 period was the intensification of internal migration. In some countries settlers continued to flow to relatively undeveloped areas;

in Brazil, for example, Mato Grosso, Goiás, and Amazônia attracted ranchers, miners, and other entrepreneurs as well as peasants fleeing the impoverished Northeast. The principal characteristic of internal migration, however, was the flow of people from rural areas to cities both large and small, which generally grew more rapidly than the population as a whole. This influx was due to several factors: improved transportation and communications links between the countryside and the city, rural poverty, the perception that urban life offered greater economic and social opportunities, and dislocations caused by political violence.

The conditions that created this rural exodus also contributed to substantial emigration from one Latin American country to another or to the United States or Europe. After World War II the prospect of better job possibilities brought thousands of Colombians to Venezuela, and Bolivians to Argentina. Mexican emigration to the United States, which first increased substantially during the revolutionary decade 1910-20, accelerated after 1940. Puerto Ricans left the island for the mainland in large numbers between 1946 and 1964, the outflow totaling some 60,000 a year during the 1950s. In addition to the immigrants from these and other countries, attracted to the United States for economic reasons, others felt compelled to flee their homelands for political reasons, notably the many Cubans who left in opposition to the **Castro** regime, more than 200,000 in 1960-62 alone, and the Guatemalans, Salvadorans, and Nicaraguans who sought to escape civil strife in their countries during the 1970s and 1980s.

After 1970 a new era in Latin American demographic history could be discerned as the rate of population growth began to decline. This decline had already occurred in Argentina, Uruguay, Chile, and Cuba, but was now evident in Brazil, Colombia, Costa Rica, and other countries where falling mortality rates were now accompanied by falling fertility rates. (See Table 1.) The decline in fertility was due to numerous factors, including improvements in the educational and economic levels of women and a greater willingness and ability to limit births,

especially on the part of urban women of the middle and upper classes. In addition, governments as well as private entities began to encourage family planning, which in effect meant birth control. In Colombia, for example, where the population was growing at the high rate of approximately 3.2 percent a year in the 1960s, the administration of **Carlos Lleras Restrepo** launched a successful program of official support for family planning, which had reduced the annual rate of increase to less than 2 percent by the early 1990s. In Brazil a private organization, the Brazilian Society of Family Welfare (BEMFAM), was established in 1967 to encourage family planning at a time when the government still adhered to a pronatalist position. Despite declining fertility and rates of population growth since the 1970s, the population of Latin America continued to grow more rapidly than that of the United States or Europe.

Table 1

Total Fertility Rates in Selected Countries*

Country	1950-55	1980-85
Argentina	3.2	3.4
Brazil	6.2	3.8
Chile	4.9	2.6
Colombia	6.7	3.9
Costa Rica	6.7	3.5
Cuba	4.0	2.0
Dominican Republic	7.5	4.2
Guatemala	7.1	6.1
Mexico	6.7	4.6
Peru	6.9	5.0
Uruguay	2.7	2.8
Venezuela	6.5	4.1

*The total fertility rate indicates the average number of children a woman will have during her child-bearing years.

Source: *Statistical Abstract of Latin America*, vol. 29.

Race

c. 1500-1750

Colonial Policies and Attitudes. The European conquerors of America were extremely conscious of presumed racial differences and assigned individuals to hierarchical categories based on race. At the same time factors besides racial ancestry, such as skin color, legitimacy of birth, and wealth, might affect an individual's racial classification. Both Spaniards and Portuguese perceived Indians as constituting a distinct racial and ethnic entity. In Spanish law, they were considered perpetual minors and wards of the state. In the Spanish colonies only Indians paid tribute to royal officials, and only they were subjected to forced labor under the *encomienda* and *repartimiento* systems. The Spanish crown attempted to segregate Indian communities and to create a República de Indios with only limited contact with Europeans and others. Although these efforts ultimately failed, most Indians in the Spanish colonies continued to live in their own communities governed by Indian officials who were sometimes descended from the pre-Columbian nobility and were accorded special privileges, such as exemption from tribute payments and the right to bear arms.

The Spanish crown forbade the enslavement of Indians in the mid-sixteenth century, although the practice persisted mainly in remote sections of the empire. The Portuguese authorities also attempted to limit Indian slavery, though with less success. In both Spanish America and Brazil, therefore, chattel slavery came to be limited to Africans and their descendants. Some slaves were able to win their freedom through flight and manumission by owners, but principally through self-purchase. As a result, by 1810 there were large numbers of free persons of African ancestry in all the colonies. In Spanish America as in Brazil, free blacks and mulattoes were discriminated against and were barred from higher education, public office, the priesthood, and many guilds. *Mestizos* also faced discrimination and, with mulattoes and other mixed bloods, were known as *castas*.

c. 1750-1850

Race in the Age of Revolution. By the end of the eighteenth century barriers against *mestizos* and mulattoes were breaking down, and members of these groups were able to enroll in universities, hold public office, and engage in other activities from which they were theoretically barred. Indian restiveness could be seen in the great Andean revolt begun in 1780 by **Túpac Amaru II**, a descendant of the Inca nobility. The most dramatic and far-reaching racial protest in the Western Hemisphere in the late eighteenth century was the slave revolt in the French sugar-growing colony of Saint-Domingue (now Haiti), where black slaves represented 90 percent of a total population of some 500,000. Led for a time by **Toussaint L'Ouverture**, the blacks eventually drove out most of the surviving whites and ended French rule over the colony.

The wars for independence in Spanish America seriously eroded or ended formal racial distinctions that discriminated against non-whites. Indian tribute was abolished, though the financial needs of new governments sometimes delayed this action. Although **Simón Bolívar** and other leaders were initially reluctant to move against slavery, that institution was ultimately weakened by the new governments. They ended their participation in the international slave trade and moved to abolish slavery itself, usually through a gradual process. Of those countries with substantial numbers of slaves, Colombia abolished slavery in 1851 and Venezuela and Peru in 1854. Brazil and Cuba, however, continued to import African slaves and retained slavery for many more years. In fact, the percentage of slaves in Cuba's population rose significantly during the late eighteenth and early nineteenth centuries after Spain liberalized regulations governing the importation of slaves; meanwhile, the island was turning increasingly to sugar cultivation partly because of the collapse of the industry in Saint-Domingue.

1850-1888

Abolition of Slavery in Cuba and Brazil.

Slavery was perceived to be vital to the economies of both Cuba and Brazil. The latter imported approximately 1.5 million slaves between 1800 and 1850 despite having signed a treaty with Great Britain in 1826 pledging to end its participation in the slave trade by 1830. The Spanish government signed similar treaties with the British with little immediate effect. At mid-century, however, largely as a result of British pressure, both Cuba and Brazil moved to cut off the importation of slaves from Africa.

Several factors, including the growth of domestic antislavery sentiment and the global condemnation of slavery, led to the gradual abolition of slavery in Cuba and Brazil. In 1870, facing the rebellion in Cuba known as the Ten Years' War, the Spanish government enacted the Moret Law, which provided that children born of slaves would be born free. In 1880 the government abolished slavery but decreed an eight-year period of tutelage for the former slaves that was cut short in 1886. Meanwhile, slavery was abolished in Puerto Rico, also a Spanish possession, in 1873. Brazil also enacted a "free birth" law in 1871, but abolitionist sentiment continued to grow, as did resistance by the slaves, until complete abolition was decreed in 1888.

Race Relations in the Twentieth Century. Although laws distinguishing among racial groups disappeared in the early nineteenth century, nonwhites—especially Indians and blacks—continued to face discrimination. In some countries vagrancy laws and laws requiring labor on public works were enforced only against Indians. In Cuba, blacks felt that their contributions to the independence struggle of the 1890s had not been adequately recognized and in 1908 formed the Independent Party of Color (PIC). A law (1910) outlawing parties based on race and an unsuccessful insurrection in 1912 brought about the party's demise. Supporters of the Cuban Revolution of 1959 have credited it with promoting racial equality on the island. Brazil has depicted itself as a racial democracy in the twentieth century, but discrimination persisted against blacks and dark-skinned mulattoes, who were likely to live in poverty and were relegated to

the most menial occupations. Moreover, elites continued to view "whitening" through miscegenation and European immigration as a desirable goal through the 1940s, in effect treating the black presence as an undesirable element.

In the early decades of the century the movement known as *indigenismo,* or Indianism, arose in Mexico and in other countries with a large Indian population. Supporters of the movement pointed to the poverty and exploitation experienced by most Indians in these countries and sought reforms to improve their condition, usually by assimilating them more fully into the mainstream culture. Indianism was an important element of the Mexican Revolution of 1910 and was the basis for some of the reforms of the 1920s and 1930s, such as greater attention to rural education and the revival of communal landholding. In Peru **José Carlos Mariátegui** advocated the establishment of a socialist society based on the Inca model. The APRA party, founded in 1924 by **Víctor Raúl Haya de la Torre**, also promoted Indianist causes and used the name Indoamerica to refer to Latin America. In Mexico, as elsewhere, *indigenismo* had a strong cultural component that exalted the achievements of pre-Columbian peoples and the traditions and folklore of contemporary Indians. **Diego Rivera** and other Mexican artists presented positive depictions of indigenous life, past and present, in their paintings and murals, and Carlos Chávez used native musical instruments in several of his compositions. Another by-product of the movement was the Indianist novel, which portrayed the oppression of Indians by white and mestizo landowners and government officials. (See Literature.) After 1950, however, *indigenismo* came under attack as being ineffective and paternalistic. Some also concluded that the emphasis on the integration of the Indian into the mainstream society devalued indigenous cultures and was at bottom racist. Others argued that the problems faced by Indians were not due primarily to their race or ethnicity but to their poverty, thereby likening them to similarly situated people of other races. Meanwhile, the number of people who could be considered Indians by virtue of their culture continued to be substantial in several countries, accounting for 12.4 percent of the Mexican population in the late 1970s, 37 percent in Peru, and more than 59 percent in Guatemala and Bolivia. By the end of the century new grassroots Indian groups had emerged which campaigned, often successfully, for bilingual education programs and the representation of indigenous groups in legislative bodies. In 1992 Rigoberta Menchú, a Maya woman from Guatemala, won the Nobel Peace Prize in recognition of her work on behalf of Indian peasants victimized by threats to their lands and government counterinsurgency programs.

Brazil's African heritage, often seen as a handicap by whites, underwent reevaluation in the 1930s by **Gilberto Freyre** and other intellectuals, who viewed it as a positive force. During this same period blacks formed organizations to press for an end to discrimination in employment, housing, and places of public entertainment. The Brazilian constitution of 1946 barred racial discrimination, and in 1951 the Brazilian Congress passed a law that imposed penalties for discrimination in public places on the basis of color or race. However, neither measure had much effect. Racial consciousness among blacks intensified in the 1970s spurred in part by the U.S. civil rights movement and by the independence movements in Portuguese Africa. The relaxation of political controls by the military government in the mid-1970s encouraged the formation of numerous groups committed to studying and improving the condition of Brazilian blacks, such as the Institute for Research in Black Culture in Rio de Janeiro and the United Black Movement Against Racial Discrimination.

Women

Women in Pre-Columbian Society. The "high civilizations" of Mesoamerica and Andean South America in 1500 assigned distinctive roles to men and women, with the latter carrying on mainly domestic tasks while warfare and public life were the province of men. Thus, when a boy was born in Aztec Mexico, a tiny shield, bow, and arrows were placed in his fist; a baby girl received miniature tools for spinning and weaving and a broom. Among the Aztec, however, the lives of some women had a public dimension, for they served as priestesses, sold food in public markets, and were employed as healers and midwives.

At the same time, standards of appropriate sexual behavior differed greatly for men and women. Aztec and Inca nobles and rulers were permitted to take concubines in addition to their principal wives, but no such right was accorded women regardless of their rank. Women often received more severe punishments than men for transgressions of various kinds. Among the Aztecs, only fornication with a married woman was defined as adultery, with the death penalty being imposed on both parties. An Inca woman who killed her husband was executed regardless of the cause. The penalty imposed on a man who killed his wife depended on his rank and the reason for his action; if the wife had been guilty of adultery, he would go free.

c. 1500-1850

Sex and Gender in the Colonial and Early National Periods. A prominent feature of the conquest era was the often forcible subjugation of Indian women by Spanish and Portuguese men. Many European men formed liaisons with indigenous women which rarely ended in marriage, though fathers often acknowledged the children born of these unions. A well-known example is that of **Malinche**, who was both interpreter and mistress to **Hernán Cortés**. Although he did not marry her, she later became the wife of another Spaniard. Spanish men preferred to marry Spanish women, who soon began arriving in the colonies in substantial numbers. In Brazil, by contrast, the number of Portuguese women always remained small. There were also relatively few women among the African slaves imported into the colonies, though female slaves were more likely to attain freedom than men.

The stereotype of the secluded Iberian woman is inaccurate, especially for women of the lower economic strata. Indian and black women who lived in urban areas were often employed as domestic servants or earned their living as food vendors, midwives, or healers. Spanish or Portuguese women were less likely to be employed, but might manage large properties, especially if they were widowed. During the early colonial period some Spanish women held *encomiendas*. (See also Religion.)

Single women and widows had greater freedom than married women, who were under the tutelage of their husbands in matters relating to their children and property. But a husband could not alienate his wife's dowry without her permission; she could also accumulate property during the marriage and make a will without his consent. According to Iberian law, property was divided equally between sons and daughters with few exceptions.

Marriage was indissoluble. The Catholic church required the full consent of both parties for a marriage to be valid, and annulments were occasionally sought on the grounds that consent had been coerced. Other grounds for annulment, which rendered a marriage invalid, included impotence and consanguinity. Some women petitioned the ecclesiastical authorities for a separation, charging their spouses with desertion, failure to provide, or physical abuse. However, many couples in the colonies dispensed with marriage altogether, living in free unions.

Women sometimes took a direct part in public affairs, albeit under male direction. Inés Suárez, the mistress of **Pedro de Valdivia**, was his most trusted advisor and took an active role in the defense of Santiago, Chile, when it was attacked by Indians in 1541 during his absence. Micaela Bastidas, the *mestizo* wife of **Túpac Amaru II**, was an important leader and strategist during the great Andean rebellion he launched, and she was executed alongside him in 1781. Women became more visible during the Spanish-American wars of independence. They made their homes available to antiroyalist plotters, made financial contributions to the cause of independence, or served as nurses, spies, or combatants. Policarpa Salavarrieta (1795-1817) was executed in Bogotá by the Spanish authorities because of her intelligence-gathering activities. During the so-called Reconquest by Spain, many other women suffered execution, imprisonment, or confiscation of their property for their work on behalf of independence. Despite their contributions, there was little change in women's actual or legal status in the decades after independence. Girls received greater access to schooling, but this was the continuation of a trend evident in the late colonial period based on the Enlightenment belief that an educated woman would make a better wife and mother.

1850-1990s

Expanding Opportunities and the Dawn of Feminism. The rapid pace of socioeconomic change in most Latin American countries after 1850 was accompanied by change in the opportunities afforded women, at least those of the middle and upper classes, notably in Argentina, Chile, Uruguay, Brazil, Cuba, and Mexico. Women gained admission to state-supported secondary and teacher-training (normal) schools and to universities; the first women medical doctors and lawyers in the region appeared in the 1880s. Though domestic service remained the principal form of female employment, some women found work in factories, offices, and retail establishments.

Professional women and schoolteachers were at the forefront of feminist movements, which got under way around 1900 in Argentina, Mexico, and other countries. Encouraged by the progress of women in Europe and the United States, feminist organizations usually pressed for improved educational and employment opportunities for women, civil equality for married women, and legislation establishing divorce. Activist women from Latin America, the United States, and Europe gathered in Buenos Aires in 1910 for the first International Feminist Congress, which approved a platform calling for suffrage, divorce, and improved protection for working women and children. Progress on these goals was halting at best. In 1926 the Argentine Congress enacted landmark legislation that allowed married women greater control of their earnings. Uruguay (1907), Mexico (1915), and Cuba (1918) made divorce possible during this period, but the persistence of the double standard is illustrated by the Mexican law's ban on a woman's remarriage until more than three hundred days had elapsed after the divorce. In addition, many governments enacted protective legislation that prohibited night-time work for women and children, limited the number of hours they might work, and barred them from occupations considered dangerous, such as mining. In 1934 Cuba provided for paid maternity leave for pregnant workers (though excluding domestics), while that country's constitution of 1940 outlawed discrimination by sex.

Many women also sought the right to vote, and suffragist organizations were established in several countries. In 1922 Bertha Lutz (1894-1976), who had earned a degree in biology at the Sorbonne, founded the Brazilian Federation for Feminine Progress (FBPF) to seek the ballot, a goal attained ten years later. Suffrage had been decreed earlier in Ecuador (1929), and the remaining countries followed, including Cuba (1934), Argentina (1947), and Mexico (1953). The last country to take this step was Paraguay (1961).

Late Twentieth-Century Trends. The revival of feminism in the United States and Europe during the 1960s was duplicated in Latin America. New women's groups arose to protest the continuing inequality of women in the work place and in public life and to seek reform in many areas. Working-class women who did not necessarily consider themselves feminists became active in associations where they sought improved health care and municipal services for their neighborhoods. Women were also active in the struggle against the military dictatorships of the 1960s and 1970s in Brazil, Chile, and other countries. In Argentina mothers of victims of the military regime of the 1970s demonstrated in the main square of Buenos Aires to demand information about the fate of their children; in 1979 they formed the Association of the Mothers of the Plaza de Mayo, which became internationally known and pressed for the prosecution of military leaders after civilian

government had been restored. During these years women met regularly at a series of conferences called Encounters (Encuentros), beginning in Bogotá in 1981.

National and local governments were somewhat responsive to women's concerns, such as improved day-care facilities and the physical and sexual abuse of women. Several countries enacted divorce legislation, among them Brazil (1977) and Argentina (1987). The issue of women's reproductive freedom was debated, but nontherapeutic abortions remained illegal throughout the region, except for Cuba. Many women resorted to illegal abortions, however.

Women entered the work force in larger numbers, though the percentage of gainfully employed women lagged behind that of Western Europe and the United States. They remained concentrated in low-paying service occupations, although a few women gained distinction in business, the media, and other nontraditional fields. Women were also being appointed or elected to public office in larger numbers. Some were close relatives of prominent male political figures, such as Isabel Perón, who succeeded to the presidency of Argentina after the death of her husband, **Juan Perón**, in 1974, and **Violeta Barrios de Chamorro**, who was elected president of Nicaragua in 1990. Others were without such ties, among them Luiza Erundina de Souza, who was elected mayor of São Paulo in 1988.

Women and the Cuban Revolution. Before the revolution, Cuban women had numerous guarantees in law, if not always in reality; they were well represented in the labor force, and fertility was low. After 1959 revolutionary leaders sought to increase women's participation in the labor force and in general mobilize women in support of the revolution. To achieve this goal, the Federation of Cuban Women (FMC) was established in 1960 under the leadership of Vilma Espín (b. 1930), an anti-Batista activist in the 1950s and the one-time wife of Raúl Castro, Fidel's younger brother. The FMC took a leading role in the government's early literacy campaigns and in efforts to improve the health of women and children. By 1980 it had more than 2 million members.

After 1960 women's presence in the work force increased substantially, though they tended to be employed in traditional fields, such as service (e.g., restaurant and retail workers), health, and education. Women's representation in governmental organs also increased somewhat, and in 1986 Espín became the first woman to serve on the Politburo of the Cuban Communist party. In 1991 she was removed, and three younger women were appointed, constituting 12 percent of Politburo membership. Complaints over the heavy burden borne by working wives led to the inclusion of a provision in the 1975 Family Code making husbands and wives equally responsible for housework and child care.

Urban Development

Urbanism in Pre-Columbian America. Urbanization already had a long history in Mesoamerica and Andean South America when the Spaniards arrived in the early sixteenth century. An important urban center in South America was Tiahuanaco (Tiwanaku), near Lake Titicaca in modern Bolivia, whose influence extended far beyond its immediate environs. The city, which flourished from about 400 to 1200, comprised a ceremonial-administrative center surrounded by residential areas; its population probably surpassed 20,000. On the northern coast of Peru, Chan Chan, the capital of the Chimú empire, was founded about 850. Covering an area of nearly ten square miles, it contained palace-like compounds known as *ciudadelas* that were probably the residences of Chimú rulers as well as residential areas for lesser elites and commoners. According to legend, Cuzco, the Inca capital, was founded about 1200 by the first Inca, Manco Capac. When **Francisco Pizarro** entered the city in 1533, it contained some 4,000 residences as well as palaces and temples built of stone megaliths.

Scholars have disagreed over whether the major sites of the Classic period in Mesoamerica were merely ceremonial centers lacking a permanent population or cities in the conventional sense, with the latter view now dominant. One of the largest such cities, Tikal in northern Guatemala, is characterized by temple-pyramids, some of which date back to the third century, and residential sites scattered over twenty square miles. Its approximate contemporary in central Mexico, Teotihuacán, probably had a population of more than 150,000 at its height in the sixth century. Dominated by three large pyramid complexes, the city also contained many apartment compounds that housed officials, soldiers, merchants, artisans, and farmers who cultivated outlying fields. After the decline of Teotihuacán in the eighth century, the city of Tenochtitlán arose nearby, serving as the capital of the Aztec empire. Aztec legend relates that it was founded in 1325 by the Aztecs, who had been told by their god Huitzilopochtli to build a city upon the site where they saw an eagle sitting atop a cactus (*tenochtli*) with a serpent in its mouth. Tenochtitlán was located on an island in Lake Texcoco and linked to the mainland by causeways. In the center of the city was a Sacred Precinct containing palaces and the temples of Huitzilopochtli and other gods; around it were four residential-administrative districts housing a population that probably totalled 125,000 in 1519. (See Art and Architecture.)

c. 1500-1870

Cities in Early Latin American History. The urban traditions of Spain and Portugal and the nature of the conquest led to the early establishment of cities in the Indies. By 1620 nearly two hundred cities had been founded in the Spanish colonies. In some instances Spaniards created municipalities on the site of pre-Columbian cities. Mexico City, for example, was founded on the ruins of Tenochtitlán. Elsewhere, new cities were established, such as Lima (1535). Royal ordinances of 1573 offered detailed instructions for the establishment of cities and directed founders to consider climate, wind direction, and the availability of water, among other points, in choosing sites and laying out streets. Spanish cities in the colonies were usually designed on a gridiron plan around a central plaza.   Along the sides of the plaza were concentrated the cathedral and other public buildings, including the *cabildo*, which housed the city government.   Coastal cities, especially those in the Caribbean and northern South America, such as Havana and Cartagena, were vulnerable to attack by foreign enemies and were heavily fortified.   After Henry Morgan, the English bucaneer, sacked and burned Panama City in 1671, a new city was built at a more defensible location nearby.   After the first capital of Guatemala, the city now known as Antigua, was severely damaged by an earthquake in 1773, a new capital was built on the site of modern Guatemala City. A few other Spanish cities were founded in the eighteenth century, notably Montevideo (1724), which owes its creation to the Spanish-Portuguese struggle for control of the Banda Oriental (the future Uruguay).   Buenos Aires, founded in the sixteenth century, grew rapidly during the late 1700s partly as a result of the government's liberalization of trade, which greatly increased its exports; in 1776 it became the capital of the new viceroyalty of the Río de la Plata.   Urban life was less developed in Brazil than in the Spanish colonies, and its cities were smaller and less systematically planned. The two most important cities were Salvador or Bahia (1549), which served as the first colonial capital, and Rio de Janeiro (1565), which became the capital in 1763.

With the achievement of independence by the 1820s, the former viceregal capitals and other administrative centers generally became capitals of the new nations. In Costa Rica, San José, which had been founded in the mid-eighteenth century, supplanted the colonial capital, Cartago, in 1834. Managua, only a village at the end of the colonial period, was named the capital of Nicaragua in 1858 after decades of rivalry between León, the colonial capital, and Granada. The names of some cities were changed or modified to honor heroes of the recent conflict, as in the case of Valladolid, Michoacán, in Mexico, renamed Morelia in honor of native son **José María Morelos.**

c. 1870-1990s

Urban Growth in an Era of Change. Economic development in the late nineteenth and early twentieth centuries brought many changes to Latin American cities as a result of the construction of railroads and port facilities, the expansion of banking and financial institutions, and the creation of light industry.   As a result, the percentage of the population living in cities increased substantially. Improvements were made in the quality of urban life with the introduction of trolley lines, illumination by electricity, and the provision of pure water and sewerage.   Health improved with the eradication of yellow fever and other diseases in the early twentieth century. (See Science and Medicine.)   City governments undertook urban beautification projects, creating monumental boulevards evocative of contemporary Paris. In Mexico, for example, the emperor Maximilian began an urban renewal project that was continued in the 1870s.   Its centerpiece was a boulevard modeled on the Champs Elysées, and called Paseo de la Reforma.

Foreign immigrants in particular gravitated to urban centers and made up a large proportion of the population of such cities as Buenos Aires and São Paulo.   In 1909 the Federal District comprising Buenos Aires and its suburbs had a population of 1.2 million, of whom about 45 percent were immigrants. São Paulo, founded in the 1550s, grew relatively slowly until the nineteenth century, when it became the center of Brazil's coffee industry and a major manufacturing site. The growth of Monterrey in northern Mexico also dates from the late nineteenth century, when it became an important railroad hub and the home of important industries, notably Cervecería Cuauhtémoc (1890). This era also saw the foundation of Belo Horizonte (1897), capital of the Brazilian state of Minas Gerais. Meanwhile, a few cities that had been important administrative and commercial centers during the colonial period declined; among them may be cited Popayán, Colombia, and Sucre (previously known as La Plata and Chuquisaca), Bolivia.

Urban Expansion since 1950. Latin American cities experienced extremely rapid growth in the decades between 1950 and 1980. The population of Mexico City, for example, grew from 3.1 million in 1950 to 13.8 million in 1980. This explosive growth was the result partly of natural increase but mainly of rural-to-urban migration. Millions of peasants escaped unpromising conditions in the countryside and flocked to cities large and small in search of better lives for themselves and their children. But the new factories and businesses arising in and around urban areas could not provide adequate employment for all, and many recent arrivals were underemployed as street vendors and casual laborers. For women, domestic service was the most likely source of employment. Recent migrants often lived in newly formed shantytowns on the city's outskirts or other undesirable areas far from their place of work. Initially lacking basic services, shantytowns usually became permanent communities as settlers acquired title to their plots and improved their dwellings. Meanwhile, middle- and upper-class residents were moving to new developments far from the old residential districts in the city center. The proliferation of buses, taxicabs, and private automobiles to provide transportation for the burgeoning population contributed to massive traffic jams and severe air pollution in Santiago de Chile, Mexico City, and other urban areas.

Latin American cities continued to grow after 1980, though at a somewhat slower rate, and by the end of the century most people in the region could be classified as urban. The Mexico City metropolitan area, which embraces some 500 square miles, had a population near 16 million in 1995. São Paulo's population was approximately 16.4 million. Both Mexico and Brazil contain other large cities, among them the latter's new capital, Brasília, inaugurated in 1960. Elsewhere one primate city absorbed much of the country's population while other cities lagged behind. This was true of Argentina, for example, where the

Buenos Aires metropolitan area, with some 11 million people in 1995, accounted for more than one-third of the country's population while the second and third largest cities, Córdoba and Rosario, each had only about 1 million inhabitants.

Science and Medicine

Science and Medicine in Pre-Columbian America. Of the indigenous inhabitants of the New World, the peoples of Mesoamerica are considered to have reached the highest attainments in science, especially in astronomy and calendrics, which were employed to predict the future, record historical and mythical events, and to regulate the agricultural cycle. Wide use was made of the fifty-two-year calendar round, which comprised two interrelated cycles. The first consisted of 260 days (formed of thirteen numbers and twenty named days); the second, which approximated the solar year, consisted of eighteen named months of twenty days and ended with an unlucky period of five days. Each day in the 260-day cycle had its counterpart in the latter year and would not be repeated until fifty-two years of 365 days had elapsed. A few people, including the Maya of Yucatán, also used the Long Count, which was based on a 360-day cycle called a *tun* and its multiples, the *katun* of twenty *tuns*, or 7,200 days, and the *baktun* of twenty *katuns*, or 144,000 days. The Maya also devised a sophisticated mathematical system of place value notation. The system was vigesimal, running 1, 20, 400, and so forth. Figures were designated by dots and bars.

Pre-Columbian sites in Mesoamerica, as well as extant books, or codices, reveal an intense interest in the movements of celestial bodies. The city of Teotihuacán, for example, seems to have been designed to harmonize with the position of the sun and certain stars. At Chichén Itzá, the post-Classic Maya site in Yucatán, the building known as the Caracol was apparently an observatory with openings in the walls and roof to allow astronomers to observe the movements of the planets and the stars. The Mayan pictorial manuscript known as the Dresden Codex contains tables showing the movements of Venus as well as tables indicating that the Maya could predict solar eclipses.

The Andean people's lack of a system of writing has inhibited understanding of their astronomical skills. It is known, however, that the Inca observed and named many stars, and are believed to have erected towers along the Cuzco skyline to observe the solstices and equinoxes. The Inca appear to have used a lunar calendar.

Pre-Columbian America was free of many of the diseases that afflicted the Old World, but its people suffered from tuberculosis, hepatitis, and encephalitis, as well as ailments peculiar to certain regions, such as Chagas's disease (American trypanosomiasis). Intestinal parasites were also common. Syphilis was once believed to have originated in America, but this belief is now generally discredited.

Medicine and treatment combined science, religion, and magic. It was believed that illness was produced by the gods, by magic, or by evil spirits; healers might use divination to diagnose maladies, and treatment might include offerings to the gods or magical operations. However, healers also prescribed bloodletting, plasters, sweat baths, and a wide range of herbal remedies that were used as febrifuges, purgatives, emetics, and sedatives.

Medicine and Public Health in Colonial Latin America. The Europeans who arrived in the New World in the sixteenth century brought with them diseases previously unknown in America, such as smallpox, measles, and typhus, which decimated native populations in a series of epidemics that affected people of all ranks. (See Population.) Smallpox apparently made its first appearance in Santo Domingo in December 1518 or January 1519. It is believed to have been brought to Mexico by a stricken servant of **Pánfilo de Narváez** in 1520 and killed Cuitláhuac, who briefly succeeded **Moctezuma** as Aztec emperor. Smallpox was soon carried to South America, where it claimed the life of the Inca emperor

Huayna Capac in about 1525. The subsequent introduction of the African slave trade was followed by the arrival of yellow fever, which appeared in Barbados, Cuba, Yucatán, and other places in the Caribbean in the late 1640s. The northeast coast of Brazil experienced an outbreak in 1686-94. The deadly variety of malaria known as *Plasmodium falciparum* is also believed to have been brought from Africa. Since the mosquitoes that carry yellow fever and malaria cannot survive in cold climates, these diseases inflicted the greatest damage on Europeans and Indians living in tropical lowland areas. In the seventeenth century the pulverized bark of the Andean genus of evergreen trees known as *cinchona* began to be used in Peru to reduce fever and quickly gained favor as a means of preventing or curing malaria. In 1742 the Swedish botanist Linnaeus named the genus after the countess of Chinchón, wife of a seventeenth-century viceroy of Peru, who was said to have been cured of malaria after taking the powdered bark, though the story is apocryphal.

The first European physician to come to America was Diego Álvarez de Chanca, who sailed on **Christopher Columbus**'s second voyage in 1493. In the colonies, as in Spain, medical practitioners included physicians who had received university training like Álvarez de Chanca, as well as "empirical" healers such as surgeons, bleeders, barbers, bonesetters, and midwives, who had acquired their expertise through apprenticeships. Indigenous healers (*curanderos*) also remained active. Public officials attempted, with limited success, to regulate practitioners through the institution of the *protomedicato*. In 1646 the crown ordered the establishment of a three-man tribunal in Mexico City that was authorized to examine university-trained physicians as well as other practitioners and pharmacists. In Lima a single *protomédico* was responsible for licensing medical professionals.

Academic instruction in medicine began at the University of Mexico with the creation of a chair in medicine in 1578. Additional chairs were established in 1598 and 1621, the latter being a chair of anatomy and surgery. A separate Royal

School of Surgery began operations in 1770. The first chair in medicine at Lima's University of San Marcos was established in 1634. Universities in Quito, Havana, and other cities in the Spanish empire also trained physicians and surgeons. In Brazil, however, professional medical training was not available until the nineteenth century. During the sixteenth and seventeenth centuries medical students in the Spanish colonies read the works of the ancient authorities Hippocrates and Galen and of the eleventh-century Arab physician Avicenna, but locally produced treatises, such as *Tractado brebe de medicina* (1592) by Agustín Farfán (1532-1604), frequently recommended indigenous therapies.

Hospitals were founded throughout the Spanish colonies by religious orders, public officials, and private donors. Some hospitals were designed to care for the sick of both sexes, both Spaniards and Indians. Among these was the Hospital de la Concepción de Nuestra Señora, established in Mexico City in 1521 by **Hernán Cortés**, which attended to poor patients. Other hospitals took care only of Indians or received patients suffering from specific diseases, such as leprosy or syphilis. In Brazil a hospital was founded in Bahia in 1549, becoming known as the Hospital of Saint Christopher in the seventeenth century. This and other hospitals in that colony were administered by a lay brotherhood, the Santa Casa da Misericórdia.

In the late eighteenth century medicine and health care in colonial Latin America experienced change as a result of the interest in science and reform associated with the Enlightenment. Traditional texts were replaced or supplemented by recent works by European physicians such as Hermann Boerhaave and William Cullen. There was also greater interest in clinical medicine, and a chair in this field was created in Mexico City in 1796. In Lima, Hipólito de Unánue (1755-1833) became an advocate for medical reform, pressing successfully for the creation of an "anatomical amphitheatre" at the Hospital of San Andrés so that students might observe demonstrations on human cadavers. He also organized a series of clinical lectures on specific diseases and

conditions which were given there in 1794-95. In 1811 Unánue achieved another goal with the establishment of a new medical school in Lima, the College of San Fernando.

By this time physicians and public officials had become aware of the importance of sanitation and quarantine in averting or mitigating outbreaks of contagious diseases. In Mexico City the **Conde de Revillagigedo**, viceroy from 1789 to 1794, strove to improve public health in a variety of ways, from requiring leashes for ferocious dogs to improving the collection and removal of garbage and excrement. Such measures had only limited effect, and epidemics continued to rage in major cities. By 1780 inoculations against smallpox were being administered in the colonies, though many people resisted the practice. In 1803 the Spanish government despatched a large expedition under Francisco Xavier Balmis to its American colonies and the Philippines in an effort to vaccinate the population against smallpox. During the long sea voyage the vaccine fluid was preserved through the inoculation in relays of boys taken from Spanish orphanages. The main body of the expedition visited the West Indies, Mexico, and the Philippines, while branch expeditions traveled to South America, reaching Chile and the Río de la Plata. Thousands were vaccinated as a result.

Science in the Sixteenth and Seventeenth Centuries. The earliest scientific work by Europeans in the Indies came out of their experiences in the New World environment and often had utilitarian ends. In 1570 King **Philip II** ordered his court physician, Francisco Hernández (c. 1517-1587), to go to Mexico to study the medicinal qualities of native plants. Hernández and his team of painters, scribes, and herbalists traveled extensively throughout the country, quizzing native doctors about the curative power of plants. He was also interested in the potential industrial uses of plants. In 1590 **José de Acosta**, a Jesuit who had spent approximately fifteen years in Peru, published *Historia natural y moral de las Indias*, in which he attempted to correct ancient beliefs in physical geography which the discovery of America had shown to be false. He argued, for example, that, contrary to Pliny, the equatorial regions are habitable and speculated on how the New World came to be populated by plants and animals before the arrival of Europeans. He also offered detailed descriptions of flora and fauna unique to the Indies.

During the seventeenth century scientific endeavor in Latin America was little affected by the Copernican theory and the scientific revolution under way in Europe. The gifted Mexican astronomer, mathematician, and man of letters **Carlos Sigüenza y Góngora** read the works of Galileo, corresponded with European scientists, and condemned superstition. While many in Mexico City were alarmed by a solar eclipse in 1691, he thanked God for the opportunity to study it with his quadrant and telescope. The previous year he had published *Libra astronómica*, in which he refuted the widespread belief that comets were harbingers of disaster. Another colonial polymath, Pedro de Peralta (1663-1743), observed lunar eclipses in Lima, communicating his findings to the French Academy of Sciences, and published yearly almanacs setting forth the movements of the planets and making astronomical predictions. Little scientific work was done in Brazil during this period, except by two men active during the period of Dutch rule over much of the colony (1630-54). Wilhelm Piso, a physician from Leiden, studied tropical diseases and the therapeutic powers of native plants, being the first European to prescribe *ipecacuanha* as a cure for dysentery. The German naturalist Georg Marggraf gathered many specimens of plants and animals and made astronomical and meteorological observations. His notes were posthumously published by his friend Johannes de Laet in *Historia Naturalis Brasiliae* (1648), the first scientific study of the colony.

Science in the Late Colonial Period. The accession of the Bourbon dynasty to the Spanish monarchy in 1700 reinvigorated scientific activity in the colonies, especially during the reign of **Charles III** (1759-88). Scientists and intellectuals increasingly rejected traditional authorities, such as Aristotle, who relied mainly on deduction to reach their conclusions, and embraced the theories of Copernicus, Newton, and other modern scientists. In Peru Cosme Bueno (1711-1798) began to teach Newtonian physics at Lima's University of San Marcos in 1758, and the new science prevailed at the Real Convictorio de San Carlos, founded in 1774 to replace the colleges of the expelled Jesuits. Adherents of the older paradigms remained powerful, however, as the Spanish botanist and mathematician José Celestino Mutis (1732-1808) discovered when he aroused the wrath of the Dominican order by defending Copernicus's heliocentric theory in Bogotá in the 1770s. Colonial scientists also took pains to communicate their findings to foreign institutions and to convey them to local communities through periodical publications, such as the *Gazeta de Literatura de México* (1788-1795), founded by José Antonio de Alzate (1737-1799), considered a pioneer of scientific journalism, and the *Semanario de la Nueva Granada* (1808-11), founded by **Francisco José de Caldas**. During this period scientific work frequently reflected an embryonic American nationalism. This could be seen in the efforts of the Quito physician Eugenio Espejo (1747-1795) and others to refute the contention of some European scientists that the New World climate produced animals that were weaker and generally inferior to their European counterparts.

Scientific investigation in the Spanish colonies was greatly furthered by a series of European expeditions authorized by the government to undertake research in various fields. Contact with expedition members acquainted colonial scientists with recent discoveries and lessened their sense of isolation and inferiority. The earliest expedition (1735-44) brought ten French scientists to Ecuador, where they proposed to measure an arc of the meridian at the equator to help determine the dimensions of the earth. Led by Charles-Marie de la Condamine, the expedition was accompanied by two Spanish naval officers, **Jorge Juan** and **Antonio de Ulloa**, who went on to distinguished careers. At the conclusion of the expedition, la Condamine sailed down the Amazon River to its mouth and brought home the first rubber samples ever seen in Europe. Louis Godin, another member of the expedition, remained in South America for thirty years.

Expeditions organized by the Spanish government emphasized scientific investigation for practical purposes. The study of botany remained a favored field of government-sponsored research: it promised economic returns through the discovery of useful plants and was unlikely to challenge religious orthodoxy. Several botanical expeditions of the late eighteenth century focused on different parts of the empire, usually studying animal life, astronomy, and other fields in addition to botany. Hipólito Ruiz and Antonio Pavón spent a decade (1777-87) traversing the interior of Peru, Bolivia, and Chile. They brought back to Spain a herbarium of dried specimens and 124 live plants for the Royal Botanical Garden in Madrid. In 1783 José Celestino Mutis, who had arrived in Bogotá in 1760, was named head of an eighteen-man botanical expedition that studied thousands of plants in what are now Colombia and Ecuador. A by-product of the expedition was the establishment (1803) in Bogotá of the Royal Astronomical Observatory, of which Caldas was made director. In 1787 Martin Sessé, an Aragonese physician, headed an expedition that studied plant and animal life in Mexico, Guatemala, and other parts of the viceroyalty of New Spain, with the assistance of a young Mexican naturalist, José Mariano Mociño (1757-1820). From 1789 to 1794 Alejandro Malaspina, an Italian-born officer in the Spanish navy, led an ambitious scientific and geopolitical expedition that gathered information on the institutions and peoples of Spain's colonies as well their natural resources. It did botanical research along the coasts of South America and sailed along the Pacific coast of Central and North America as far north as Nootka Sound. It amassed nearly 16,000 dried specimens of plants, grasses, mosses, algae, and fungi. Thaddeus Hanke, a Bohemian scientist who joined the expedition in Chile, settled in Bolivia, where he remained until his death in 1817.

In keeping with the utilitarian goals of the crown, Fausto de Elhuyar, a Spanish scientist trained in Germany and known as the discoverer of tungsten, was appointed director of a newly created School of Mines in Mexico City in 1792. Elhuyar's work in Mexico earned the praise of the most distinguished scientist to visit the Americas in the late colonial period, **Alexander von Humboldt**. During his extensive travels (1799-1804) in the company of the French naturalist Aimé Bonpland, Humboldt conducted scientific research and attained penetrating insight into the economic and social condition of the Spanish colonies. Equally important, he raised the self-esteem of colonial scientists and helped them establish contacts with one another and their European counterparts.

Brazil also experienced a quickening of scientific activity in the late eighteenth century, partly as a result of reforms introduced by the **Marquês de Pombal** at Coimbra University, where many Brazilians studied. Alexandre Rodrigues Ferreira (1756-1815), a native of Bahia, made a detailed study of the flora and fauna of Amazonia between 1783 and 1792. José Mariano da Conceição Velloso (1742-1811), a Franciscan born in Minas Gerais, collected and classified more than 1,500 plants in the captaincy of Rio de Janeiro, which he described in his *Flora Fluminensis* (1825). **José Bonifácio de Andrada e Silva** was a prominent mineralogist in Europe before returning to Brazil, where he played a leading role in the independence movement.

Latin American Science since Independence. Scientific activity in the Spanish American colonies was crippled as a result of the wars of independence. Many scientists became personally involved in the conflict. A few, such as **Francisco José de Caldas**, lost their lives while others were permanently drawn into politics or diplomacy. The loss of financial support from Spain was also damaging at a time when the new republics suffered from fiscal penury. Chronic political instability during the first half-century following independence also inhibited the development of enduring programs for scientific education and research. At this time scientific inquiry was likely to be pursued, if at all, in connection with education in medicine and engineering.

After 1870 the economic development and

political stability experienced by most countries created conditions more conducive to scientific enterprise. The dissemination and widespread acceptance of the ideas of Auguste Comte, Charles Darwin, and Herbert Spencer also fostered the creation of new educational institutions and programs that emphasized science. In Mexico, for example, the curriculum of the National Preparatory School, founded in 1869 under the leadership of Gabino Barreda (1818-1881), was organized in accordance with Comte's hierarchy of sciences, beginning with mathematics and including astronomy, physics, chemistry, and biology. Instruction at Brazil's military academy, reorganized and renamed the Escola Politécnica in 1874, was similarly influenced by Comtian positivism. Among the adherents of evolution was the noted Argentine geologist and paleontologist Florentino Ameghino (1854-1911), who discovered more than 6,000 species of fossil mammals. He is also remembered for his efforts to prove that human beings had originated in America. During this period many new scientific and technically oriented institutions were established throughout the region, such as Mexico's National Observatory in Tacubaya in 1878 and the School of Mines in Medellín, Colombia, in 1887.

Latin American science remained heavily dependent on foreign training and personnel as well as imported theories. The field of geology in Brazil, for example, was developed by Americans, such as Charles F. Hartt, who headed a short-lived Imperial Geological Commission in the mid-1870s, and Orville A. Derby, who in 1906 became the first director of Brazil's Geological and Mineralogical Service. In Argentina, the first three directors—Benjamin Gould, John M. Thome, and Charles D. Perrine—of the important observatory founded in Córdoba in 1871 came from the United States. Medellín's School of Mines was modeled on the Mining College of the University of California, where its founders, **Pedro Nel Ospina** and his brother Tulio, had studied. In other fields European influence was more pronounced. Modern physics was introduced to the scientifically oriented University of La Plata in Argentina in 1909 by the German

Emil Bose, a specialist in electro-chemistry; he was succeeded in 1914 by Richard Gans, an authority on the theory of magnetism. Miguel Fernández, who had been trained in Germany, introduced Mendelian genetics at La Plata in 1915.

After World War I the Rockefeller Foundation's work in public health and medical education (see below) also led it to support scientific research, thereby strengthening the influence of U.S. scientific models. In Brazil, for example, between 1940 and 1970 the foundation contributed an estimated $1.4 million to research and education in the natural sciences in addition to its expenditures in public health and medicine. The Rockefeller Foundation also assisted the work of Bernardo A. Houssay (1887-1971), who in 1919 was appointed head of the University of Buenos Aires's department of physiology, which he converted into an Institute of Physiology. When Houssay was forced out of the university for political reasons in the 1940s, the foundation and other private sources financed a new Institute of Biology and Experimental Medicine. In 1947 Houssay won the Nobel Prize in physiology (shared with Carl F. and Gerty T. Gori) for his work on the role of the pituitary gland in carbohydrate metabolism. Luis F. Leloir (1906-1987), Latin American's second Nobel Prize winner in science, joined the Institute of Physiology in 1934. He was awarded the prize in chemistry in 1970 for his work on the processes by which carbohydrates are broken down into simple sugars.

Latin American physicists, especially in Brazil, also gained distinction in the twentieth century. Starting in the 1930s, physicists at the University of São Paulo, led by the Russian-born Gleb Wataghin, conducted important research on cosmic rays. Wataghin's work was continued by César Lattes, who was part of an international team that discovered the meson-pi particle in 1947 at the Bolivian astrophysical laboratory in Chacaltaya. In Mexico Manuel Sandoval Vallarta (1899-1977) also did work on cosmic rays.

By the mid-twentieth century the scientific community in several countries had attained sufficient size and influence to form organizations to encourage scientific research and values. Among these were the Brazilian Society for the Progress of Science (SBPC, 1948) and the Venezuelan Association for the Progress of Science (AsoVAC, 1950). Meanwhile, governments became more conscious of the role of science in promoting economic development and supported the formation of national research councils. Brazil's National Research Council (CNPq), founded in 1951, initially worked to develop a nuclear power capability in that country, but the program foundered. By contrast, Argentina's National Atomic Energy Commission (CNEA, 1950) played a major role in the development of an autonomous nuclear power industry, including the construction of nuclear reactors and facilities for the enrichment of uranium. The nuclear program went forward despite the emigration of many Argentine scientists during the political upheavals of the 1960s and 1970s. Brazil's CNPq was more successful in sponsoring the scientific and technological training required for the creation of an indigenous computer industry, which employed some 16,000 persons in 1983. In 1975 the CNPq was enlarged and renamed the National Council of Scientific and Technological Development; it later came under the jurisdiction of a newly created Ministry of Science and Technology.

Despite increased commitment to scientific research by governments, businesses, universities, and other institutions, scientific productivity in Latin America remained relatively low, though it was increasing by the end of the twentieth century. In 1983 Latin America accounted for 1.1 percent of the world's scientific literature; by 1991 Latin America's share had risen slightly to 1.4 percent. Most publications originated in only a few countries: Argentina, Brazil, Chile, Mexico, and Venezuela.

Medicine and Public Health after Independence. The turmoil engendered by the wars of independence disrupted health care services, which suffered further from the political instability and economic disarray that afflicted many countries during the first post-independence decades. Even so, new medical facilities were

founded, as in Brazil (1808), where the future **João VI** established chairs for instruction in surgery and anatomy in Bahia and Rio de Janeiro; chairs in obstetrics and pharmacy were added later. In 1827 the faculties were reorganized as medical schools in accordance with contemporary French models. Elsewhere, as in Mexico City (1833), medical schools were reorganized or rebuilt.

At this time the incidence of smallpox was limited by continued use of vaccination, but yellow fever and malaria still raged. After a long hiatus yellow fever reappeared in Brazil in 1849, killing more than 7,000 in Bahia and Rio de Janeiro, and remained a serious problem for the rest of the century. Yellow fever epidemics occurred in cities in many other countries, including Buenos Aires, where more than 10,000 died in a six-month period in 1871. Asiatic cholera made its first appearance in Latin America in the 1830s and devastated the region in the 1850s. Tuberculosis also became a significant problem in the nineteenth century.

Latin Americans continued to go abroad for medical training, while foreign physicians, especially from France, were often invited to staff medical facilities. Foreign physicians also set up individual practices in the region. Latin American doctors emulated European practitioners and adopted important discoveries, such as the use of anesthesia in surgery, the introduction of antisepsis, and the germ theory of disease. Although Latin Americans were primarily consumers of European medical science, there were some efforts at original research. Starting in the mid-1860s physicians in Bahia, Brazil, conducted important research on hookworm and its causes, which they associated with poor hygienic conditions. In 1881 the Cuban doctor **Carlos J. Finlay** correctly identified the *Aedes aegypti* mosquito as the carrier of yellow fever. Typically, however, the findings of Latin American physicians gained little recognition abroad.

The economic and social changes experienced in Latin America in the late nineteenth century brought greater attention to the need to improve public health and control epidemic diseases as well as the respiratory and intestinal ailments that accounted for most of the region's deaths. During this period the urban population not only grew but was often concentrated in densely packed and unsanitary slums that facilitated the transmission of disease. As a result, governments made efforts to provide pure water and sewerage and improve garbage collection, at least in central city districts. In Cuba and Panama the American physicians Walter Reed and William C. Gorgas virtually eliminated yellow fever by successfully testing Finlay's ideas and taking steps to eradicate the *Aedes aegypti* mosquito. Their efforts entailed military-style operations that called for the fumigation of houses to kill mosquitoes, control of mosquito breeding grounds, and isolation of suspected cases. In Brazil, **Oswaldo Cruz**, who became head of the federal department of public health in 1903, conducted similarly successful campaigns against yellow fever and bubonic plague. However, in 1904 a program of compulsory vaccination against smallpox met with fierce resistance in Rio de Janeiro from those who objected to its obligatory nature and from opponents of the government and was therefore only partially successful. As a result, a 1908 outbreak of smallpox in Rio de Janeiro took 9,000 lives.

In 1909 Carlos Chagas (1879-1934), Cruz's colleague at the research institute named after Cruz, announced the discovery of a new disease, American trypanosomiasis, which he had encountered after finding a pathenogenic trypanosome in an insect called the *barbeiro*. Many people in South America still suffer from this ailment, which is also known as Chagas's disease. Another important Brazilian research center was the Instituto Butantã, established in São Paulo in 1899, which became known for its work on the biochemistry of snake venom.

After World War I the International Health Board of the Rockefeller Foundation became active in Brazil, Mexico, Ecuador, Peru, Colombia, and other Latin American countries. In both Ecuador and Peru, for example, it provided funding and technical expertise to help

local medical authorities carry out campaigns against yellow fever. In Guayaquil local fish that ate mosquito larvae were used for the first time, a practice repeated during an anti–yellow fever campaign in the northern coastal region of Peru in 1921. In Colombia and other countries the Rockefeller Foundation also took part in efforts to eliminate hookworm and to improve education in the health sciences. Present in Brazil from 1916, the foundation gave major support to the new Faculty of Medicine of São Paulo, which was organized in accordance with American principles of medical education. The foundation also assisted the Oswaldo Cruz Institute.

Medicine and Health Care since 1930. Medical education continued to expand throughout the region, and many new medical schools were established under both public and private auspices. In Mexico alone the number of medical schools increased from nine at the beginning of the century to fifty-nine by the early 1990s. While the number of medical school graduates rose, doctors tended to be concentrated in large cities while rural areas suffered from shortages of medical personnel. Health care was available through social security systems and other public institutions as well as through private resources, but many people lacked access to medical facilities because of poverty or place of residence.

Latin Americans' health improved during the period, as can be seen in the relatively high figures for life expectancy (see Table 2). However, many problems remained. Infant mortality was high in most countries for several reasons, including the inadequate prenatal care available to poor women and the continuing high incidence of intestinal diseases (see Table 3). Millions of people in Mexico, Brazil, and other countries lived in areas at risk for malaria transmission. Also worrisome was the return of the *Aedes aegypti* mosquito, which had supposedly been eradicated in the 1950s and 1960s. Besides carrying the yellow fever virus, this mosquito is also known to transmit dengue fever and the potentially fatal dengue hemorrhagic fever, both of which appeared in Cuba, Venezuela, Brazil, and other countries in the 1980s and

1990s. The return of yellow fever also seemed likely.

Latin America's first cholera epidemic since the nineteenth century began in Peru in January 1991 and spread to neighboring countries. More than 500,000 cases were reported in Peru alone in 1991-92, but the fatality rate remained low for several reasons, including prompt recognition of the disease and effective public information campaigns.

An important agency in the promotion of public health is the Pan American Health Organization (PAHO), which was established in 1958 but traces its origins to the Pan American Sanitary Bureau founded in 1902. It is part of the Organization of American States and is also the Regional Office for the Americas of the World Health Organization. In association with national governments and nongovernmental groups, PAHO has been active in numerous areas. After World War II it played a major role in mosquito eradication through the use of DDT. More recently, important spheres of action have included water supply, sanitation, and immunization of children against polio, measles, and other diseases.

Medicine in Cuba since 1959. Although Cuba's pre-revolutionary medical system was relatively well developed, changes introduced after 1959 are generally considered to have greatly improved the provision of health care to the entire population. Efforts were made to increase the number of medical school graduates, who after 1965 became employees of the state. As a result, the number of inhabitants per physician decreased from 1,252 in 1965 to 231 in 1990. An extensive system of polyclinics was set up to provide a range of services in a given region and to serve as teaching hospitals for primary care students. By 1989 there were 420 polyclinics and 263 hospitals on the island. Emphasis was also placed on preventive programs, such as inoculation against communicable diseases and improved nutrition for infants and children. One result of the new programs was a decline in infant mortality, which was only 9.9 per 1,000 live births (first year of life) in 1993. By the 1990s, however, Cuba's economic difficulties were believed to be affecting

the health sector, which was suffering from a lack of basic medicines and supplies.

Table 2

Life Expectancy at Birth in Selected Countries, 1993

Argentina	71.4
Brazil	66.4
Chile	72.1
Colombia	69.4
Costa Rica	76.3
Cuba	75.7
Dominican Republic	67.6
Guatemala	66.6
Mexico	70.4
Peru	64.8

Source: *USAID*.

Table 3

Infant Morality in Selected Countries, 1993*

Argentina	28.5
Brazil	55.9
Chile	16.8
Colombia	36.7
Costa Rica	13.5
Cuba	9.9
Dominican Republic	55.8
Guatemala	47.7
Mexico	34.7
Peru	74.9

*Estimated number of deaths in children under age one per 1,000 live births.

Source: *USAID*.

POLITICS AND GOVERNMENT

The Pre-Columbian Period

c. 1492 C.E.

Government among the native Americans mirrored the different worlds of their respective cultures and responded to their very different requirements—from the great empires of the sedentary Aztec and Inca civilizations to the more modest groupings of the nomadic bands that traversed the northern reaches of Mexico and the southern extensions of South America. More complex nucleation marked the first. Empires by definition require more elaborate administrative structures and generate more control mechanisms than do the demographically weak nomadic groups. For the latter, government necessarily has to be very limited or the very essence of its survival and durability—its mobility and adaptability—is put at risk with the excess baggage of too much structure.

While native American civilizations and cultures had evolved over centuries and even millenniums, the more complex, imperial ones, had a differentiated social structure characterized by rulers, nobles, and commoners. Among the Aztecs these were the *tlatoque* (singular, *tlatoani*), *pipiltin*, and *macehualtin*, respectively. The last of these worked for and paid tribute to the *tlatoque*, who ruled over a specific district or city-state. Among the *macehualtin* were semi-free/semi-"serf" individuals on whom the burden of work fell more heavily and whose labor obligations and residence could be reassigned. The main function of the *pipiltin,* or nobility, was to collect the tribute from which they and the *tlatoque* lived. Tribute could be in the form of labor and/or agrarian and artisan products.

The Aztecs expanded far beyond their modest sedentary beginnings in their capital, Tenochtitlán, in the valley of Mexico, where they had taken up residence after migrating from the north. In league with two other city-states, Texcoco and Tlacopán, they conquered the valley and expanded out over the surrounding mountains. They ruled in central and much of southern Mexico in a political construct historians label as an "empire" but which was loosely organized and still in the process of consolidation when the Spanish arrived. Most of the *tlatoque,* or rulers, who administered the empire were from the ranks of the warrior elite who had successfully led the Aztec expansion. At the top was a council of four military commanders who advised the supreme *tlatoani* or emperor, who himself had been a member of the council prior to his selection. Previously this "election" involved the approval of Texcoco and Tlacopán and other allied city-states, but in 1502, when **Moctezuma II** was chosen, a narrow circle of the Tenochtitlán *tlatoani*'s family made the decision.

Religion and government went hand in hand, and each validated and infused the other, but the preponderance of power was in the hands of the military and not the religious elite. Nevertheless, full-time priests had important roles and had recast the past by reconfiguring myths and rituals, so that Aztec imperial rule was seen as a historical necessity. Some of this had a life of its own and accounts for the Aztec preoccupation with human sacrifice. Human sacrifice was believed to sustain the cosmos and keep it from being consumed by fire. It was thought that the blood of sacrificial victims kept the sun from standing still and propelled it across the sky so that life would continue. The Aztec vision of the world was so gloomy that their allies and enemies had reasons to defect to the Spanish, whose cosmology was much more benign.

The Inca called their empire Tawantinsuyu, the Land of the Four Quarters. Their capital, Cuzco, was at the intersection of these divisions. At the top of Inca hierarchy was the Sapa Inca, or "emperor," and the noble families of pure Inca blood, which perhaps totaled no more than 1,800 families. All key administrative positions in the empire—military, political, and religious—were staffed by pure-blooded Inca, probably never more than 500 adult males. Other administrative positions went to favored peoples, the Hahua Inca, those who were Inca by adoption. Below this provincial nobility were ethnic rulers who had accepted Inca overlordship willingly and who were left in place to rule their people as long as they followed Inca leadership. Family members, especially those who would eventually succeed in power, were sent to Cuzco to learn Quechua and Inca ways.

At the bottom of the polity were the *hatunruna,* or "households," who were organized into larger units of 10, 50, 100, 500, 1,000, 5,000, and 10,000 households, each one with its official administrator. A fixed amount of labor from these units was set aside for the state, which employed the labor in producing artisan goods and cultivating lands from the radically different ecological zones that are characteristic of the Andes. The purpose was to provide for the elite and the administrators of the state apparatus and

Spanish American Colonial Territorial Divisions

Viceroyalty of New Spain
Guadalajara
Mexico
Guatemala
Santo Domingo

Viceroyalty of Peru
Panama
Santafé
Quito
Lima
Charcas
Chile

to make sure that everyone would have access to the products and commodities they did not themselves produce or that were in short supply. Historians tend to describe this exchange in benign terms as a reciprocal relationship with mutual obligations, but there were unquestionably forced appropriations of labor, services, goods, and peoples on the part of the Inca. Much of this appropriation was found in the indigenous rotary draft system of labor known as the *mita*. These labor drafts not only involved producing artisan goods and cultivating lands but serving in military campaigns and construction projects. The Inca also assigned people to full-time state service, such as *yanacona*, men who tended the royal llama herds or worked the royal coca fields.

In summary, the imperial civilizations of the Aztec and the Inca had polities that approximated the monarchies of Western Europe. The governing class was a nobility—hereditary in the case of the Inca and increasingly so, but still warrior-based, for the Aztec. Both ruling classes were in a state of flux when the Spanish arrived. Conquest obligated both to incorporate subject peoples into the ruling elite, the Inca more so than the Aztec. Both forged alliances and brought subject peoples into the empire through marriage. Inca Quechuanization was far more thoroughgoing and deliberate than Aztec Nahuatlization, reflecting the Inca elite's narrower demographic base but seemingly more generous sharing of power. Both made tribute demands on their subjects. Both had special categories of people whose labor was at the service of the elite or state.

In other parts of the New World native Americans shared some characteristics of the Aztec and Inca. In the Caribbean the *caciques*—an Arawak name that the Spanish carried with them to the mainland and that became synonymous throughout Latin America with a native American leader—were hereditary rulers. The Spanish referred to the great ones as "kings" and to those of second rank as chiefs of districts. Below them were the *nitaínos* or nobility, whom the Spanish equated with nobles and who were exempted from certain obligations. Then came the commoners, and at the bottom were the

naborías, a category of unfree individuals who have been variously described as lifetime servants, serfs, or slaves. But native Americans of the Caribbean lacked overarching unifying imperial structures, tribute, and forced labor mechanisms.

In the Cordillera Oriental of what is today Colombia, the Muisca were on the verge of state formation when Spanish arrival interrupted the process in 1536. A critical mass of ever larger numbers, greater social complexity, more efficient tribute mechanisms, and greater political control—centered on two rulers, called the *Zipa* at Bogotá and the *Zaque* at Tunja—probably made urban growth, state consolidation, and expansion inevitable. But while the Muisca had definitely moved farther toward state control than their Caribbean counterparts, they far from equaled the Aztec and Inca achievement. Curiously absent from the Muisca experience was the unfree worker category of *naborías* of the Caribbean, and the state-dedicated *yanacona* laborer of the central Andes.

Elsewhere, native American government was less elaborate and more egalitarian, more in tune with societies that were less socially stratified. Invariably people were organized along tribal lines, usually with a council of male elders making most of the decisions. They frequently met on a daily basis and were often only loosely commanded by their chiefs. Intertribal relations varied considerably but often involved deadly feuds.

Wherever the Iberians appeared they used the native American political and social structures to their own advantage, sometimes infiltrating the tribal networks and becoming valued members of the native American communities. Native Americans never thought of themselves as such, but rather as separate and distinct peoples, so that the Iberians were frequently not viewed as threats but as potential allies against enemies. This accounts for much of the Iberian success. When the Spanish conquered the Aztec and Inca empires, they did not do away with all native American political institutions and figures. They found it useful to leave the local elite in place. They even sanctioned rump Inca emperors as a way to improve their own governance. They were especially adept at using and adapting native American political traditions, such as the tribute and labor mechanisms like the *mita*, for delivering goods and services. This cannibalization of another's political system and its successful grafting onto their own was part of the legacy of the Reconquest of the Iberian Peninsula from the Moors. This process had much to do with the political success of the Iberians in the New World.

The Colonial Period

1492-1807

Introduction to Colonial Government. Iberian government and political institutions in colonial Latin America rested on legacies going back to the European Middle Ages when rule was with few exceptions monarchical and validated ritually by church authority and by reference to the Bible and Roman law as known through Justinian's Code. Outstanding Spanish monarchs included **Isabella** of Castile, **Charles V**, and **Philip II.** Later monarchs rarely had the will or the disposition to govern personally. They were psychologically or, in the case of the impotent **Charles II** (1665-1700), biologically incapable of ruling. They turned the business of government over to their court favorites (the *privado* or *valido*) whose strictly personal agenda of family aggrandizement accelerated the decline of Spanish power. With the change from the Habsburg to the Bourbon dynasty at the beginning of the eighteenth century, Spanish fortunes improved, especially during the reign of **Charles III**, and historians frequently refer to these changes collectively as the Bourbon Reforms.

Portugal had similar ups and downs. Its best rulers, Manuel I (1495-1521) and João III (1521-57), came early and marked the apogee of Portuguese power. Portugal and Spain shared the same fate when Spanish monarchs ruled both empires from 1580 to 1640. When Portugal rebelled in 1640, its independence from Spain did not revive its fortunes. In the seventeenth and eighteenth centuries, with the exception of Pedro II (1683-1706), Portuguese monarchs were generally frivolous and incompetent. The insane

Maria I (1777-1816) dismissed the **Marquês de Pombal**, Portugal's greatest state minister (1750-77). His restructuring paralleled and even anticipated that of the Bourbons, and historians generally refer to these changes as the Pombaline Reforms.

Early Structures and Policies. As both the Portuguese and the Spanish expanded into the Atlantic, they created administrative structures to oversee the mechanics of organizing and financing their costly maritime expeditions down the coast of Africa or across the Atlantic. Trading or commercial houses were established and assigned these functions. Monarchs were trying to minimize their outlay and risk by having great lords and merchants organize and fund the expansion. The crown was to share in any profits. The boundary between the state and private sectors was not clearly defined. Later, if results were promising enough, the crown went to the expense of creating institutions of a more political nature.

The best known of these Iberian trading houses was the House or Board of Trade (Casa de Contratación) created by Spain in 1503 to oversee and exploit the possibilities of its recently discovered lands in the New World. It was based in southern Spain at Seville, Castile's wealthiest city, to take advantage of the latter's money and expertise. None of the overseas expeditions launched by the Spanish was an exclusively royal undertaking, and a trading house was a convenient mechanism to attract and to control the resources necessary for a successful undertaking as well as to ensure that the crown's interests were protected. Seville was also conveniently close enough to Spain's Atlantic ports to oversee the operation. While probably initially conceived as an exclusively royal trading house, the Casa de Contratación quickly became dominated by an elite group of merchants based in Seville who tended to monopolize Spain's commerce with the New World. Its role was to oversee the provisioning of the fleets, the licensing of who could go to the New World, the registering of American treasure, and the keeping of essential accounts and records.

While the Spanish had only one trading house, the Portuguese had several, most of which antedated Spain's and were probably modeled on those of the Italian city-states whose merchants were very active in the Iberian Peninsula. The Casa de Ceuta appeared as early as the 1430s. In 1445 another was established at the port of Lagos on the southern coast of Portugal to oversee the developing trade in the south Atlantic. The Casa da Guiné appeared a short time later, also at Lagos, but was eventually moved to Lisbon and expanded to include São Jorge da Mina on the Gold Coast. The Casa dos Escravos (House of Slaves) appeared in 1486 to monopolize the trade in African slaves and was eventually attached to the Casa da Guiné e Mina. The Casa da Índia was established at Lisbon in 1501 after Vasco da Gama and **Pedro Álvares Cabral** returned from their expeditions to India. In the course of the sixteenth century these trading houses went through several reorganizations and reappeared under various names, including Casa da Guiné e Índia; Casa da Mina e Índias; and Casa da Guiné, Mina e Índia. Whatever trade with Brazil the crown wanted to control, which was minimal at first, was overseen by one of these entities.

The object of Portuguese government was to hold, protect, and supply the key links in its far-flung empire and extract a profit from the spice trade with the Far East. This strategy precluded the conquest and acculturation of the native population in the hinterland beyond the enclave and coincided with Portugal's small demographic base. Portuguese government was very limited and did not initially amount to much more than what was contained in its trading houses and *feitorias* (fortified trading posts overseas). While Spain had only one trading house, it eventually did have several *consulados*, officially organized merchant groups or guilds that had a semi-monopoly over certain aspects of trade and commerce in some markets. The distinction between private and royal interests was not clear cut. Nevertheless, Spanish political institutions controlled the House of Trade in Seville and the various *consulados* that came into being over the course of the colonial period. The House of Trade and *consulados* had commercial rather than political functions. The Portuguese, on the other hand, frequently had no overarching administrative structures that controlled their trading houses and *feitorias*, and the latter two had both commercial and political functions.

Differences between Portuguese and Spanish government in the New World grew out of their two very different traditions of expansion and empire building. Simply put, the Portuguese traded, while the Spanish exploited the lands and peoples conquered. One was a maritime trading empire, the other extractive. There were important similarities in certain particulars, but once the two empires had a critical mass, trading characterized the Portuguese while extraction and consumption distinguished the Spanish. Over time, as the center of gravity shifted from Asia to Brazil, the Portuguese empire came to resemble its Iberian counterpart. Also from 1580 to 1640, when they had the same rulers, the Portuguese imitated the Spanish in many of their imperial practices and adopted some of the latter's governmental institutions.

In theory Spain was made up of several kingdoms, each one with different laws and customs but, with the accession of **Charles V**, ruled by the same monarch. On the other hand, Portugal was a single entity whose overseas colonies were an extension of the kingdom of Portugal and were ruled directly. Spain's monarch was advised by a series of councils that were organized territorially—Castile (1480), Aragon (1494), Indies (1524), Italy (1555), Portugal (1582), and Flanders (1588)—and functionally by those processes that cut across territoriality—Inquisition (1483), Military Orders (1495), Crusades (1509), War (1517), State (1522), and Finance (1523).

The creation of the Council of the Indies in 1524 gave Spain's New World colonies a separate administration in the motherland, long before Italy and Flanders had theirs. Even though New Spain's silver mines and Peru's riches had not yet been discovered, enough wealth had already been generated to raise Spanish expectations to the point that they thought it was worthwhile to invest in a centralizing administrative agency. Having power delegated to it by the monarch to act in his name made the Council far more than an advisory body. Its power was administrative, legislative, and judicial and, unless the monarch personally overturned its decisions, it was the supreme authority for Spain's New World colonies. Administratively it nominated all higher officials, presented all prelates, and organized the fleets, expeditions of discovery, financial systems, church activities, and the appropriate treatment of the native Americans. Legislatively it drafted and issued laws, directives, regulations, and other provisions for government. Judicially it was the court of last instance in important civil cases.

Portugal never institutionalized control over Brazil to the same degree as Spain did in the authority it gave to the Council of the Indies over its American colonies. Portugal's monarchs ruled through the trading houses and the separate agreements they had made with different individuals. From the beginning Portuguese centralization was very piecemeal, tentative and almost always inconclusive. Financial reforms in 1516 resulted in the creation of three treasurer supervisors (*vedores da fazenda*) who scrutinized activities overseas. These officials evolved into three formal financial committees or boards (*mesas*) and by 1578 into one treasury board (*mesa da fazenda*) that was split again into three committees in 1584.

With the union of the two crowns of Portugal and Spain in 1580 there was a tendency to model Portuguese administration on that of Spain, and councils of the Treasury (Conselho da Fazenda) and of India (Conselho da Índia) were created in 1591 and 1604, respectively, but incipient nationalism and bitter rivalries with long-standing government agencies in Portugal brought about the suppression of the latter in 1614. It was really not until 1642-43, after Portugal broke away from Spain, that it imitated the Spanish and created an entity dedicated strictly to colonial affairs, the Overseas Council (Conselho Ultramarino). Up until this time activities dealing with Brazil were never handled separately but were lumped together with those from Asia and Africa, usually India, Mina, Guinea, and the islands of São Tomé and Cape Verde.

With the Habsburg-Bourbon dynastic change at the beginning of the eighteenth century, Spain placed authority over its colonies in the hands of an individual colonial minister of state rather than a council. In 1714 the newly created Secretary of the Marine and of the Indies took over the most important responsibilities of the Council of the Indies, which continued to function but was much reduced in power and authority. With control over the colonies in the hands of a minister rather than a committee, Spain gradually pursued a more activist policy in the New World whose collective results are known as the Bourbon Reforms. The most important minister in terms of impact was **José de Gálvez**. In Portugal empire-wide changes also occurred when the **Marquês de Pombal** assumed control over the entire government as secretary of state for foreign affairs and war (1750-77), but again, the Portuguese tended to administer their overseas colonies directly as an extension of the kingdom of Portugal rather than as a separate colonial entity like the Spanish.

Viceroys and Viceroyalties. In the New World, Spain opted rather quickly for the same kind of regal/conciliar government with which Spaniards were familiar in the motherland. Standing in for the monarch was the viceroy, and advising, working with, or acting in his place was the tribunal known as the *audiencia*. The viceroy was president of the *audiencia* and in addition had the responsibilities and powers of initiative associated with those of a governor, captain-general, and superintendent of finance. These included overseeing and implementing a wide range of measures associated with government, military affairs, and financial matters. He was also vicepatron of the church.

The first viceroy in the New World was **Christopher Columbus**, who acquired the hereditary title as part of the agreement he signed with the crown in 1492. In 1511 his son Diego was confirmed in the title, but differences soon arose over the extent of his powers. After his death in 1526, crown officials proceeded to define his office of viceroy as a royally domesticated institution.

In the first two centuries only two viceroyalties were created, New Spain in 1535 and

Peru in 1543. The first embraced Mexico, the Philippines, Central America, the Caribbean, and the Venezuelan coast; the second oversaw Panama and most of South America. A third one, New Granada, was carved out of northern South America in 1717 and again in 1739 after being suppressed in 1723 for financial reasons. It initially included Quito (Ecuador), New Granada (Colombia), and Venezuela, with Panama added in 1739. A fourth viceroyalty, Río de la Plata, appeared in 1776 and embraced most of modern-day Bolivia, Paraguay, Uruguay, and Argentina, thus significantly reducing the importance of the viceroyalty of Peru. There were sixty-one viceroys in New Spain, forty-one in Peru, fourteen in New Granada, and eleven in Río de la Plata.

In the sixteenth and seventeenth centuries, Spanish viceroys tended to be members of the high nobility; **Antonio de Mendoza**, the first viceroy of New Spain (1535-50), and **Francisco de Toledo**, in Peru (1569-81), were outstanding examples of their class and their achievements. In the eighteenth century viceroys tended to be experienced military and naval officers who had apprenticed in other parts of the Indies. Viceroys were almost always peninsulars, with only 4 of the 127 total being born in the New World. A substantial number of the viceroys were generals and bishops, with clerics supplying fifteen, eleven in New Spain alone. Viceroys received large salaries intended to be commensurate with their regal position—8,270 to 13,787 pesos in New Spain and 27,574 in Peru in the sixteenth century; 27,574 pesos in New Spain and 41,360 in Peru in the seventeenth century; and 60,000 pesos in both in the eighteenth century. Other benefits probably allowed them to double even these princely sums and maintain courts equal to those of European kingdoms. While the viceroy's term in office was legally fixed at three years in 1629, the average tenure was six years throughout the colonial period. Some viceroys were continued long beyond their assigned term, and others had no stated limit in their appointment. Nevertheless, all could be recalled or suspended at any moment by the king or the Council of the Indies.

In spite of their considerable powers and imposing presence, viceroys found the effectiveness of their authority limited in theory and practice for the following reasons:

1. The king or Council of the Indies made all the important appointments in America, so that the viceroy had only limited control over those subordinates whose tenure and authority had already been fixed in Spain.

2. The king or council also tended to macromanage colonial affairs, so that everything from general policy to mundane matters had already been spelled out for the viceroy.

3. Viceroys shared power with their *audiencias*. They did not have a totally free hand in most matters, and none in judicial cases before the *audiencia*.

4. Finally, while the ocean between the viceregal capital and the mother country enhanced a viceroy's independence, the formidable geography between the capital and distant provinces limited his power over his subordinates.

In frontier areas or provinces not easily managed by the viceroy, the Spanish government appointed captains-general and governors. Captains-general were far more important and tended to be little viceroys in everything except salary and prestige. Their appointments were usually for eight years. Where they governed—in the Philippines, Chile, New Granada, Venezuela, Guatemala, Santo Domingo, Cuba, Charcas, and Quito—they acted with great independence, although the latter two had less autonomy and depended more directly on the viceroy of Peru or New Granada. They usually concerned themselves with colonizing schemes, economic development projects, defense, and an extension of royal power and authority in new regions. This frequently involved warfare with native Americans who had not yet accepted Spanish acculturation and overlordship. In the Caribbean the administration of captains-general and governors was even more focused on military matters, but it was more defensive and oriented toward resisting the attacks of the Dutch, French, and English.

Consistent with its more decentralized and less structured imperial bureaucracy, Portugal did not create a viceroy for Brazil until the eighteenth century, relying on governors-general instead. Portugal finally raised Brazil, like its Asian colonies, to viceregal status in 1720. The first governor-general, **Tomé de Sousa**, (1549-53), represented Portugal's first sustained attempt to take control of its American possession. It charged him with overseeing and asserting royal authority over the donatary captaincies, with Pernambuco exempted, that had been parceled out to important subjects in the 1530s. The headquarters of the governor-general and of royal government in Brazil was established at Salvador da Bahia in 1549 and remained there until 1763, when the viceregal capital was transferred to Rio de Janeiro. From 1621 to 1652 and from 1654 to 1772 Brazil was divided into two states, with the northern captaincies of Maranhão and Pará being separated from Salvador into the Estado do Maranhão e Grão-Pará.

The governor-general or viceroy of Brazil theoretically had far-reaching powers over administrative, military, fiscal, and commercial matters; presided over the *relação*, the Portuguese colonial equivalent of the Spanish *audiencia*; and made land grants and government and church appointments. However, the realities of Brazil's geography undermined most attempts at control and centralization. Given the difficulties in sea transportation along the Brazilian coast—the contrary winds and currents—it was often easier for each region to communicate directly with Portugal than with the governor-general or viceroy in Salvador or in Rio.

Provincial Administration. At the provincial level, the Spanish governed through governors, *corregidores*, and *alcaldes mayores*. In a few areas some governors approached the power and importance of a captain-general, and the latter was sometimes both captain-general and governor, thus enhancing the military powers of the former office and the administrative powers of the latter. Nevertheless, in practice the distinction was not clear cut and both tended to assume a wide range of military, administrative, judicial, and fiscal functions for the orderly advancement of royal authority as well as the enhancement of their private purse. Captains-general usually served for

eight years and governors for five, but some governors had indefinite or even lifetime appointments in recognition of their private initiative and investment in the conquest of their province.

Corregidores and *alcaldes mayores* were usually a step below governors in importance, but in Peru some *corregidores* were synonymous with governors. In New Spain *alcaldes mayores* were the norm rather than *corregidores*. The responsibilities and functions of both were similar and paralleled those of a governor but at a less important geographical level. They usually worked closely with the local *cabildos*, or town councils, administered justice in the first instance, and organized provincial life and government. Peninsulars usually served for five years while New World-born appointees were in office for only three. Viceroys could make interim appointments of one or two years.

There were *corregidores* and *alcaldes mayores de españoles* and *de indios*, that is, of both the Spanish and native American communities. In those areas formerly associated with the rule of the Inca, the *corregidor de indios* was a highly sought-after position even if the appointee had to wait seven to ten years to occupy it. The Spanish paid thousands of pesos for these positions because of the enormous profits to be made from the native Americans. The *corregidor* had a monopoly over the forced sale of merchandise (*reparto de mercancía*) in the native community at greatly inflated prices. The practice also existed in Mesoamerica but was much more widespread in areas once associated with Inca rule—a manifestation of the thorough-going centralization the Inca had carried out during their reign. The *corregidor* had simply appropriated the delivery system of the Inca and, usually in league with the local *kuraca* (chief), directed the native American community's labor toward acquiring a monetary surplus that was then appropriated in exchange for overpriced merchandise.

The original purpose of the *corregidor de indios* had been to shield the native American community from the more exploitative practices of the *encomendero*. The job of the *corregidor de indios* was to collect the tribute of the native Americans, organize their labor obligations, and administer justice. These functions tended to be common to all *corregidores* and *alcaldes mayores de indios*. In places where the native community was not as highly organized or as disciplined as in Peru, there was less of a surplus and fewer forced sales of merchandise, and, as a result, the *corregidor de indios* was not as sought-after a position.

In the eighteenth century one of the most important of the Bourbon Reforms was the introduction of a new provincial administrator, the intendant, who was to combine in his position the powers and functions formerly associated with the local governors, *corregidores*, and *alcaldes mayores,* whose posts were now suppressed. But his powers were really much more extensive, approaching those of a captain-general. He could, for example, correspond directly with Madrid on fiscal and military matters and bypass the viceroy in many instances. His generous salary of 5,000-8,000 pesos and presumed superior training and education were supposed to lead to a more activist but rational and efficient administration and bring in more revenue.

The reform first appeared in Cuba in 1764, and when judged a success by **José de Gálvez**, it was introduced in Río de la Plata, Venezuela, Chile and Peru, and New Spain in 1782, 1783, 1784, and 1786, respectively. There were twelve intendants in New Spain, eight in Peru and Río de la Plata, two in Chile, and one in both Venezuela and Cuba. Revenues increased dramatically. In Río de la Plata and New Spain, where twelve intendants had replaced over two hundred local officials, the growth was especially impressive. Nevertheless, the increase may have resulted from other factors. Revenues were up significantly in the late colonial period in New Granada, where the intendants were never introduced because of the Comunero Rebellion of 1780-82. It is also important to note that intendants needed local officials to carry out their directives, and thus a group of new petty bureaucrats called *subdelegados* appeared on the scene. They were poorly paid and looked suspiciously like the old *corregidores* and *alcaldes mayores* in both their functions and performance.

The introduction of the intendancy system heightened regionalism in Spanish America by placing the powers and functions of many local officials in the hands of a single regional bureaucrat who now had jurisdiction over a major region. This laid the structural basis for much of the federalism that followed in the nineteenth century, setting the stage for centralist-federalist controversies. The geographical boundaries of the intendancies in New Spain, for example, paralleled those of many of the present-day states of Mexico Chiapas, Puebla, and Veracruz, for example—or the modern nation-states of Central America—Honduras, Costa Rica, Nicaragua, and El Salvador.

Portuguese administration in the New World at the provincial level was far less structured and substantive than its Spanish counterpart. The wealth generated by Brazil was never of the same order or magnitude as that of New Spain or Peru, and the revenues were never enough to put very many agents of the central government at the provincial level. In fact even in the capital of Salvador da Bahia government looked very provincial. Coming out with **Tomé de Sousa**, the first governor-general, were only two royal officials—an *ouvidor-geral* (chief magistrate) who was to oversee judicial matters, and a *provedor-mor da fazenda* (chief overseer of the exchequer) who was to manage treasury matters. They carried instructions and powers different and separate from those of the governor-general. They were to inspect all the donatary captaincies and put in place the structure necessary to carry out justice and collect the monarch's revenue. In general, there was no separate set of laws or administration from what already existed in Portugal. The governor-general's powers and prerogatives were detailed in the Ordinances of the Kingdom of Portugal (Ordenações do Reino). Those of the *ouvidor* and *provedor* were spelled out in similar peninsular instructions that were common to the kingdom of Portugal.

The *Audiencia*. The conciliar feature of Iberian government in the New World was reflected in its high courts. For the Spanish these were the *audiencias,* and for the Portuguese the *relaçãos.* The *audiencia* was modeled on a Castilian prototype. Under Isabella and **Ferdinand** there were two, one at Granada that had jurisdiction south of the Tagus River and another at Valladolid with jurisdiction north of the river. These were strictly law courts. In the New World, however, the *audiencia* was much more than a court of law and came to have extensive administrative, political, and military functions as well as judicial ones. *Audiencias* acted much as the councils did in Spain, that is, as advisory and ruling bodies for the monarch, or in the case of the New World, for his stand-in, whether viceroy, captain-general, or governor. The *audiencias* came into existence as the Spanish empire expanded. They also disappeared when areas declined in importance, failed to meet expectations, or fell victim to administrative consolidation.

The first *audiencia* in the New World was Santo Domingo. It was created in 1511 as a royal counterweight to the pretensions of **Christopher Columbus**'s son Diego, who was confirmed in his title of viceroy in the same year. Other *audiencias* that were formed in the New World replicated the same general functions—advisory, governing, and judicial—as those acquired by Santo Domingo in its initial period from 1511 to 1526. New Spain received the second *audiencia* in 1528, located in Mexico City. South America received its first functioning *audiencia* at Lima in 1544, and a second one—New Granada—at Santa Fe de Bogotá in 1549-50. *Audiencias* were also established in Panama, Central America, Guadalajara, Manila, Charcas (modern Sucre, Bolivia), Quito, Santiago (Chile), Buenos Aires, Caracas, and Cuzco. In general terms, the individual *audiencias* were the forerunners of most of the modern nation-states of the Hispanic world, that is, the Philippines, Mexico, Panama, Venezuela, Colombia, Ecuador, Peru, Bolivia, Chile, and Argentina, while those at Santo Domingo and Guatemala included the geographical boundaries of what some political idealists had hoped would be the separate nation-states of the Caribbean and Central America.

The most important *audiencias* were the viceregal ones of New Spain and Peru. There were two levels of prestige among nonviceregal *audiencias,* the higher being that of those whose president was not a lawyer but a captain-general, resulting in greater independence from the viceroy in Mexico City or Lima. In this category were Bogotá, Panama, Chile, and Santo Domingo, while Quito and Charcas, even when given a governor and captain-general in the seventeenth century, came under the closer supervision of the viceroy in Lima, as did the *audiencia* of Guadalajara in its relationship with the viceroy in Mexico City.

Membership on the *audiencia* included a president, generally four to eight *oidores* or judges, depending on the importance of the *audiencia* and the time period, a *fiscal,* and minor officials. The most important member was the president. In Mexico City and Lima this was the viceroy, who also carried the titles of captain-general and governor, as was the case in New Granada when it had a viceroy in the eighteenth century. Elsewhere, such as Panama, Santo Domingo, or Chile, or New Granada in the seventeenth century, the president would be the governor or captain-general or both where those offices existed. Where they did not, such as Quito or Charcas during much of the colonial period, the president was a *letrado,* that is, a lawyer, with a law degree from a university, as was the case with all the *oidores.* If the president, even if he was viceroy, was not a *letrado,* he could not vote in judicial decisions, only *oidores* could.

The second most important official was the *fiscal,* who was the junior *oidor* in the early colonial period but a separate officer later. His importance came from the summary reports or briefs that he produced for the *audiencia* outlining the main issues and facts of law on the basis of which decisions would be rendered. The *fiscal* was the royal attorney who represented the crown's interests, especially monetary ones, as the name implied, as well as those of special groups, like the native Americans, for whom the monarch felt a special obligation. The *fiscal* had no vote in cases in which the crown was a party, but in others he could cast the deciding vote in the instance of a tie. Nevertheless, he always had a voice in the deliberations, and his briefs outlined the main issues of law to be decided.

In the larger *audiencias* in Mexico City and Lima there were separate chambers for criminal and civil cases. After 1542 only civil cases involving more than 10,000 pesos could be appealed to Spain to the Council of the Indies.

Audiencias operated in an administrative and legislative capacity in addition to their judicial function. They helped regulate different aspects of urban and provincial life. Individual *oidores* served on different *juntas,* or committees, involving such diverse subjects as ecclesiastical and fiscal matters and mining and native American affairs. They served as probate judges, inspectors of fleets and armadas, and judges of commercial disputes arising from the *consulados,* or merchants' associations, that by the end of the colonial period existed in Mexico City, Lima, Caracas, Guatemala, Buenos Aires, Havana, Cartagena, Santiago, Guadalajara, and Vera Cruz. They might be dispatched to distant provinces on a *visita,* that is, to inspect the regional government, to organize mining operations, to carry out a census of the native Americans, or to assign them their tribute and labor obligations. Their findings were frequently issued as reports that today inform historians' conclusions about life in Spanish America in the colonial period.

Letrados served indefinite terms until they died in office or were retired. The salary of a president of the *audiencia* generally ran from 4,800-8,200 pesos while those of the *oidores* went from 2,000 to 3,400 pesos. Sometimes they remained in one *audiencia* for years on end, rising from *fiscal* or junior to senior *oidor* or even to the presidency. Sometimes they moved to other *audiencias,* going from less desirable ones to Mexico City or Lima or even in a few instances to the Council of the Indies. The *letrados* who staffed the *audiencias* were career bureaucrats whose similar education and government service gave them a certain professionalism and esprit de corps that formed the basis for much of the success and some of the failures of Spanish imperial administration.

The *Relação.* A high court for Brazil, the *relação,* which was similar to the Spanish *audiencia,* was created and located at Salvador da Bahia in 1609. It served as an appeals court from those decisions made by the *ouvidores* in the individual captaincies. Before this, all appeals had to go to Portugal, a process that was very expensive and which favored the wealthy. The court had ten judges, or *desembargadores,* and the requirements for service and the restrictions on their activities paralleled those for the *oidores* on Spanish *audiencias.* It is not clear whether the initiative for the creation of the *relação* came from the Portuguese or from the Spanish, whose king also ruled Portugal and its empire from 1580 to 1640. Whatever the case, the *relação* had a rocky beginning and was abolished in 1626, perhaps because the Dutch had temporarily occupied Salvador da Bahia (1624-25), and the *relação* had not acquitted itself well. Supposedly it had suspended the very laws that were necessary to raise troops for the defense of the colony. There were also complaints about the judges' venality. But the fundamental reason may have been the opposition of the powerful. What is clear, however, is that in spite of its defects, once the Portuguese got clear of the Spanish and had the Dutch occupation of Brazil almost ended, they saw the wisdom of restoring the *relação* and did so in 1652. The Portuguese established a second *relação* at Rio de Janeiro in 1751, foreshadowing the latter's choice in 1763 as the new viceregal capital.

While the historiography on the *relação* is in general weak and uninformative, recent scholarship has shown that of the 168 judges who served between 1609 and 1751, about 20 percent got permission to marry local women and ten judges were Brazilian born. One fundamental difference from the Spanish system was that the king of Portugal could and did overturn decisions. In the Portuguese system decisions made in the Brazilian *relação* did not necessarily establish a precedent that restrained the monarch, as seemed to be the case in the Spanish system.

Municipal Government. The conciliar feature of Iberian government at the local level was the town council—the *cabildo* or *ayuntamiento* for the Spanish and the *senado da câmara* for the

Portuguese. The town council usually worked hand-in-hand with the leading district official of the area, ordinarily the *corregidor* or *alcalde mayor* for the Spanish and the *capitão-mor* (captain), *provedor*, and *ouvidor* for the Portuguese, unless the town was also a capital city, in which case the official could be the viceroy, captain-general, or governor. But at times there were bitter disputes between the town council and the district official. Ideally the council provided basic infrastructure like roads, sanitation, jails, and markets; regulated prices; prevented fraud in the town market; prosecuted criminal activity; and oversaw the orderly functioning of local life within the town's jurisdiction, which included the surrounding countryside up to the next town's jurisdiction. The most important officials in the Spanish town councils were the councilors (*regidores*) and the magistrates (*alcaldes ordinarios*); the Portuguese had similar officials. The *regidores* arrived at a consensus position, and the *alcaldes ordinarios* executed the decisions of the council, enforced law and order, and decided civil and criminal cases in the first instance. *Regidores* usually had permanent seats on the council, while *alcaldes ordinarios* served for only one year, although after a few years, they could be reelected.

In the initial discovery and conquest periods, *regidores* were usually picked, sometimes even before the town's foundation, by the organizing captain of the conquering expedition, so that many of the first *regidores* in New Spain, Peru, and southern Colombia, for example, had been selected by **Hernán Cortés**, **Francisco Pizarro**, and **Sebastián de Belalcázar,** respectively. During the reign of **Charles V** (1516-56) additions of *regidores* to the town council were frequently made by specific license granted by the monarch or the Council of the Indies. Under **Philip II** (1556-98) the practice of selling the position of *regidor* became widespread, so that by the end of his reign many of these proprietary positions could be passed on to one's heirs for a confirmation fee. As a result, many town councils were in the hands of these hereditary members. The town council usually represented the entrenched interests of the local creole elite,

ordinarily the leading landowners, although in capitals, mining cities, or major ports the number of *regidores* who were miners or merchants increased. In Buenos Aires, for example, most of the *regidores* were peninsular merchants. But in most places creole landowners dominated.

The town councils were not representative nor democratic. Some were very active, but others were moribund institutions on which no one wanted to serve. As a general rule, Brazilian town councils were more active and independent than their Spanish American counterparts. The more thoroughgoing centralization of Spanish imperial administration and the more numerous officials at the various levels seem to have preempted many of the activities and much of the independence of Spanish town councils. For the Portuguese, on the other hand, there was less central authority and their town councils filled more space at the local and district level. The result was more dynamic and active town councils in Brazil than in Spanish America, though sometimes the anemic character of the latter became transformed in periods of great conflict or tension. This was especially the case during the onset of the wars of independence when the membership of some councils was opened up (*cabildo abierto*) to all important citizens. They became the nuclei of revolutionary activity and represented some of the first attempts at self-government by popular will.

Role of the Catholic Church. One of the distinguishing characteristics of Iberian government in the New World during the colonial period was the vital role played by the Catholic church. The division between church and state that has since become such an operative feature of modern government was not the case in the colonial period. Church and state were one. In exchange for royal patronage and funding of missionary activity and church construction in newly conquered lands, the pope had signed away his control in the so-called *patronato real* (Spanish) or *padroado real* (Portuguese), so that all bishops, archbishops, and members of cathedral chapters were appointed by the monarch or royal officials. Rome had no direct contact with the American church. The pope had to go through the Council of the Indies for Spanish America and the Mesa da Consciência e Ordens for Brazil. Royal officials erected dioceses and parishes, approved the dissemination of papal bulls, regulated and collected ecclesiastical revenues, governed the church, and even carried out ecclesiastical reform.

At every level of Iberian government in the New World church officials validated the system and were an integral part of the government. In many instances church officials served as viceroys, *oidores*, and governors. Monarchs found them to be useful umpires, and pressed them into service as authority figures to speak out and regulate the performance of secular officials. The administrative structures of the church paralleled those of the secular government. The ecclesiastical counterpart of the viceroy, captain-general, and governor was the archbishop and bishop; the equivalent of the *audiencia* was the cathedral chapter; the complement of the town council and *corregidor* or *alcalde mayor* was the parish priest and his parish council, sodality, and choir groups. Religious and secular power validated one another at all levels. It was one of the great strengths of Iberian government in the New World. (See also Religion.)

Investigative Mechanisms. The Spanish and Portuguese institutionalized two official processes to limit abuses, solve administrative problems, and issue performance reports on individual officials. The first, the Spanish *visita* or the Portuguese *devassa*, was an official inspection tour that could range over an entire viceroyalty or concentrate on a single province or region. It was usually secret and unannounced until the *visitador* or inspector appeared on the scene. His appearance meant that there was a serious problem perceived by higher authorities that needed to be investigated and remedied. Whether dispatched by the Council of the Indies or the local *audiencia* the *visitador* had wide-ranging powers of investigation and action. One of the most famous *visitas* was that of **José de Gálvez** whose tour (1765-71) of New Spain as *visitador general* resulted in a wide array of changes throughout the Spanish empire collectively known as the Bourbon Reforms. As a

follow-up came the visita to New Granada of Juan Francisco Gutiérrez de Piñeres that provoked the Comunero Revolt of 1781.

The second mechanism used to promote administrative efficiency, the Spanish *residencia* or the Portuguese *residência*, involved a general review of one's performance at the end of one's term in office. As a general rule all higher officials—viceroys, *oidores*, captains-general, governors—and most second rank administrators—treasury officials, *corregidores*, *alcaldes mayores*—went through the review. In the most important cases an incoming viceroy or *oidor* or an official passing through to another jurisdiction usually served as the *juez de residencia*, or review judge. Like the *visitadores*, they had wide-ranging powers of investigation and action. In both procedures rival camps of witnesses usually appeared to testify for and against those being investigated. There were ways to short-circuit the process and to reach an agreement with investigating officials, and the powerful who had court connections could also annul or weaken any punishment or sentence. Nevertheless, both mechanisms were strong deterrents to malfeasance in office, and sometimes resulted in heavy fines, confiscation of property, imprisonment, and permanent banishment from public service or from a particular region.

The Iberian system of government showed great initiative early on and great resiliency throughout the colonial period. It was a shrewd mixture of private initiative (embodied in the military-conqueror-entrepreneur), government oversight, and spiritual glue at all levels that allowed Spain and Portugal to succeed where other New World empires failed. If there was a weakness, it was the mixing of public and private to the extent that government officials functioned as gate keepers, rather than as umpires, and charged for opening the gate. A significant amount of corruption did permeate the administrative structure and left a legacy of government intervention for private gain that endures to the present day. Also, the separation of powers principle that is seen as the very basis of modernity—whereby the executive, legislative, and judicial branches of the government perform only their respective functions—was not an operative feature of the Iberian system. Spanish and Portuguese colonial bureaucrats often performed all three. Nevertheless, Spain and Portugal succeeded in their colonial empires in the New World where everyone else, except for the English, failed.

Both Spain and Portugal got a head start on the other European powers in the New World. Their acculturation of the native Americans through conquest and conversion gave them a demographic superiority over their European rivals. This initial advantage of position and numbers allowed Spain and Portugal to resist most challenges over the next three hundred years. Only in isolated places—Belize, the Guianas, the southwestern United States, some Caribbean islands, and the Malvinas (Falkland Islands)—were the Iberians ever successfully dislodged. It was not until the seventeenth century that other European powers—the French, English, and Dutch—were able to establish permanent settlements in the New World, but only in North America and the Caribbean. The bulk of Spain and Portugal's subject population, sufficiently acculturated to Iberian ways, remained intact. This Iberian demographic superiority in the New World effectively withstood the challenges and blandishments of others until the independence movement of the early nineteenth century definitively broke Iberian ascendancy in the New World. The governmental measures employed helped both Spain and Portugal fashion the greatest empire up to the early modern period and to keep it for three hundred years.

The Independence Era

1808-1825

Spain's colonial rule was remarkably successful. It lasted three hundred years, and was marked by stability if not efficiency. Over those centuries there were few overt protests against metropolitan domination of civil affairs. When the independence era began in 1808, owing to Napoleon Bonaparte's removal of the royal family from Spanish soil, most Spanish Americans perceived their struggle as that of returning the king to his throne.

Early leaders turned to institutions of colonial governance to direct their first hesitant steps toward self-rule. They met in *cabildos abiertos*, emergency open meetings with medieval antecedents, when events on the Iberian Peninsula interrupted direct monarchical control of politics. Gradually, however, a spirit of independence emerged throughout Spain's vast American empire, plunging it into an extended period of tumult.

Portuguese America was more fortunate, its transition to independence easy, even benign. Brazilians welcomed the Portuguese royal family to their shores in 1808, after the House of Braganza and its court had been driven from Lisbon by Napoleonic armies late in 1807. The people of Brazil were thus spared the uncertainty and confusion that attended the displacement of monarchical rule in Spanish America. When King **João VI** at last departed Brazil in 1821, he left his son, Prince Regent Pedro, behind. A year later Pedro declared Brazil's independence and soon thereafter accepted the title **Pedro I**, becoming the country's emperor. Brazil existed as a constitutional monarchy until 1889.

Elsewhere, Latin America's transition to independence was often bloody. The process ran from Haiti's violent slave revolt led by **Toussaint L'Ouverture** and **Jean-Jacques Dessalines**, to the military campaigns of **Miguel Hidalgo y Costilla** and **José María Morelos** in Mexico, to those of **Simón Bolívar** in northern South America, and those of **José de San Martín** in the Southern Cone. Spanish America emerged from its wars of independence ravaged and exhausted. In that setting those who survived set about the arduous task of self-government. The attainment of independence, moreover, still left unresolved controversies over the boundaries of the new nation-states and over the relationship of provinces to the central authority.

Political Tumult in the New Republics

1826-1870

Vast and scantily populated, Latin America experienced a half-century of political instability following independence. At the end of that period it was clear that if the region were to progress, national leaders must find some way to achieve political accommodation.

Constitutions and Presidents. With the notable exceptions of Mexico, which briefly experimented with monarchy under **Agustín de Iturbide**, and Brazil, which began its national life as a constitutional monarchy, Latin American states adopted constitutional, presidential systems following their wars of independence. While the statesmen who drew up Spanish America's first constitutions were guided by Spain's Cádiz constitution of 1812, they were more strongly influenced by the 1789 U.S. constitution. Thus, they separated governmental power into three branches: the executive, the judicial, and the legislative. Most legislatures were bicameral, their representation determined in a way similar to that practiced in the United States. Most Latin American constitutions contained statements of individual rights similar to those enumerated in both the U.S. charter and the French constitution of 1791. An initial debate centered on the relative merits of federal versus centralized systems. While centralized systems were preferred, there were notable federalist experiments in several nations. Early constitutions also preserved the status of Catholicism as the state religion. In spite of their attempt to achieve a balance of power among the branches of government, the executive branch inevitably emerged supreme over the legislative and judicial. Whether gaining power

via election, or through extra-legal means, Latin America's presidents tended to be strong, often arbitrary rulers.

1826

Simón Bolívar's Bolivian Constitution. The Liberator prescribed a system whose president held lifetime tenure, selected his own vice president, was immune from impeachment, and freely convened and adjourned legislatures. There was also a three-man Council of Censors holding lifetime tenure, whose duty was to promote civic virtue. The constitution was modified in 1831 and abrogated in 1834.

1833

Chile's longest-lived constitution. Strongly influenced by the nation's foremost politician, **Diego Portales**, the document was in force until 1925. It provided for a highly centralized system under the leadership of a powerful president elected for a five-year term; until 1871 he could serve a second consecutive term. Voting and the holding of public office were restricted to literate, property-owning men. During the 1890s presidential power was reduced and Chile adopted a modified parliamentary system.

1853

Argentina's first successful constitution. The document owed its principal features to the ideas of the U.S. constitution, as adapted to Argentine realities by the statesman **Juan B. Alberdi**. It provided for a federal system and separation of powers, guaranteed individual freedoms, encouraged European immigration, and liberalized trade by abolishing interprovincial tariffs and nationalizing the Buenos Aires customshouse.

1857

Mexico's liberal constitution enacted. Incorporating major features of the 1855-56 reforms instituted by **Benito Juárez** and others, the document established a federal republic in which personal freedoms enjoyed thoroughgoing protection. Special church and military courts were abolished, and individual land holding was favored over corporate land holding. Trade restrictions, both internal and international, were lifted to encourage economic growth.

1863

Colombia's Rionegro constitution. The document provided for a federal system of nine sovereign states and a weak central government whose president served a nonrenewable two-year term. States were given the right to organize armies and to trade freely in armaments. Complete freedom of speech was guaranteed.

Caudillos and Caudillo Rule. The man on horseback, the caudillo, was a constant feature of nineteenth-century Latin American history. The wars of independence had helped ambitious men achieve upward mobility and had schooled them in the art of leadership. And the political and economic disarray afflicting postindependence Latin America provided fertile ground for their rise. Skill in the field and force of personality were usually sufficient to make caudillos supreme in local or regional politics, and at the national level as well. Not all caudillos were military men. Paraguay's Dr. **José Gaspar de Francia** demonstrated that one could rule absolutely through a mix of charisma, intelligence, and ruthlessness. Few nations experiencing extended periods of caudillo rule benefited from the experience. But that was the price paid for achieving nationhood at a time when Latin Americans had little tradition of self-rule, lived in a region remote from the world's economic heartland, and were overwhelmingly unlettered and impoverished.

1829-52

Rosas of Argentina. Juan Manuel de Rosas won the admiration of Argentines during the 1820s, when he used a gaucho militia to quell political tumult in Buenos Aires province. In 1829 the legislature of Buenos Aires elected him provincial governor and voted him extraordinary powers; from that point until his overthrow in 1852, he ruled with an iron hand. Rosas used secret police and military might to control enemies and to force conservative, xenophobic rule upon the nation.

1830-47

Páez of Venezuela. José Antonio Páez, a hero of the wars of independence, led Venezuela in its break with the Gran Colombian federation in 1829. For decades he relied on his personal prestige and the loyalty of a cowboy militia, the *llaneros*, to support his state-building activities. Páez was one of Spanish America's more benign and successful caudillos.

1833-55

Mexico's Santa Anna. Antonio López de Santa Anna dominated Mexican politics through the army and by playing national leaders off against one another. The Age of Santa Anna was one of tumult and bloodshed for Mexico, a time during which the nation lost half its territory to the United States.

1838-65

Guatemala's Rafael Carrera. José Rafael Carrera's power rested in his influence over the traditional masses of rural Guatemala. In 1837-40 he fought Guatemalan Liberals and **Francisco Morazán**, who was trying to preserve the Central American Federation created in 1824. His 1852 concordat with the Vatican was the first between the Holy See and an independent Latin American state.

1864-70

Mariano Melgarejo of Bolivia. One of Latin America's most brutal caudillos, **Mariano Melgarejo** ruled Bolivia in association with his mistress Juana Sánchez. Owing to his misrule

Bolivia later lost significant portions of its national territory.

Liberalism and Liberal Parties. Latin American political liberalism had its origins in the Enlightenment and the French Revolution. Fathers of the independence movement, **Antonio Nariño, Simón Bolívar,** and **Miguel Hidalgo,** were liberals in that they championed republicanism and individual rights, and opposed monarchy. A slightly younger generation of liberals, **Francisco Paula de Santander** and **José María Morelos** among them, were staunch defenders of the rule of law, constitutional government, and the separation of powers. Liberals were also likely to be supporters of federalism. The single greatest unifying element among Latin American liberals was their desire to weaken the influence of the Roman Catholic church in order to open their countries to new and progressive tendencies. The church–state issue, more than any other aspect of liberal ideology, divided Latin Americans and set in motion the formation of their first political parties: Liberals and Conservatives. (See also Religion.) Those two parties appeared throughout Latin America during the middle decades of the nineteenth century. They received special motive force from the revolutionary movements sweeping Europe during 1847 and 1848. By the 1850s and 1860s Liberal parties were ascendant in many Latin American nations.

1837

Brazil's Liberal Party. Initially opposed to predominant Conservative influence during the regency of **Dom Pedro II**, it promoted export agriculture and greater regional autonomy. After the political crisis of 1868, it called for the abolition of slavery, direct elections, separation of church and state, and reduction of the crown's role in politics. In 1870 radical Liberals formed the Republican party.

1840

Venezuela's Liberal party was formed in opposition to the supporters of **José Antonio Páez**, who were dubbed *godos* (Goths). Antonio Leocadio Guzmán, father of **Antonio Guzmán Blanco** and a founder of the party, used the pages of his newspaper, *El Venezolano*, to propound its goals, which included the abolition of slavery and universal male suffrage.

1848-49

Colombia's Liberal Party. Colombian Liberals enacted wide-ranging reforms during the administrations of Presidents José Hilario López (1849-53) and José María Obando (1853-54). They remained the dominant force in nineteenth-century Colombian politics until 1885. Among their reforms were the extension of voting to all adult males, approval of free public education, abolition of slavery, expulsion of members of the Jesuit order, reduction of the presidential term to two years, imposition of a system of extreme federalism, adoption of *laissez faire* economic policies, and encouragement of export agriculture.

1849

Chile's Liberal Party. José V. Lastarria (1817-88) and others founded the party, which dominated national politics during the period 1871-91. Liberals unhappy over the Liberal-Conservative fusion of the 1850s formed the important Radical party in 1857.

1855

The Beginning of Mexico's Liberal Reform. Mexican revolutionaries, led by the liberal **Benito Juárez** and others, launched La Reforma, which was anchored by the anticlerical Ley Juárez (1855) and the Ley Lerdo (1856), aimed at democratizing land holding though it failed to achieve that goal. Mexico's liberal reforms were articulated in the constitution of 1857.

1856

Nicaraguan Liberals and William Walker. Liberal parties in Central America were discredited as a result of the Nicaraguan party's acceptance of help from the American mercenary. **Walker** helped Nicaraguan Liberals triumph over Conservatives in 1855, made himself president in 1856, and was executed by Honduran Conservatives in 1860.

1878

Ecuador's Liberal Radical Party. Organized by Ignacio de Veintemilla, the party's chief task was completion of church–state separation. The Liberal Radicals dominated Ecuadorian politics until 1944. Earlier in the nineteenth century Ecuadoran Liberals were followers of **Vicente Rocafuerte** and **Juan Montalvo**.

1887

Paraguay's Liberal Party. Gaining power early in the twentieth century, the party was marked by its commitment to laissez faire economic policies.

Conservatism and Conservative Parties. As in Europe, Latin American political conservatism was born in reaction to practices seen as destructive of society and proper social relationships, which Conservatives viewed as properly hierarchical and inegalitarian. Conservatives thus opposed Liberals' abolition of *fueros*, or traditional privileges, and what they viewed as the revolutionary threat produced by Liberal "social leveling." In practice, however, Conservatives and Liberals generally followed similar economic policies. While Conservatives were frequently of old and monied families, the chief bond uniting party members was religion. Most Conservatives were confessing Roman Catholics who regarded the church both as society's chief moral force and as its preponderant institution. For them, Liberal attacks on church prerogatives were wrong in every sense, to be countered at any cost.

1830-47

Conservative Dominance in Venezuela. Venezuela's Conservative party took shape during

the first presidential term of **José Antonio Páez** (1831-35). It also supported the presidencies of José María Vargas (1835-36) and of Carlos Soublette (1837-39, 1843-47).

1836

Mexican Conservatism. Conservative aspirations were reflected in two short-lived constitutions. The Siete Leyes (Seven Laws) of 1836 converted the states into departments whose governors would be appointed by the president. The president was to be elected indirectly for an eight-year term and could be reelected. The constitution also provided that Catholicism would be the only religion permitted and guaranteed the *fueros*, or special privileges, of the clergy and the armed forces. The Bases Orgánicas of 1843, drafted by a junta of notables handpicked by **Antonio López de Santa Anna**, contained similar provisions. Like its 1836 predecessor, it limited the right to vote and to hold office to men who met financial qualifications. Some Conservatives also promoted the notion that for their nation to achieve political stability, a European prince of royal blood must rule.

1837

Brazil's Conservative Party. The party emerged simultaneously with the nation's Liberal party. Its mainstay were large coffee- and sugar-exporting interests who opposed restrictions on slavery or the slave trade, yet it was Conservative ministries that were responsible for the principal antislavery measures enacted in Brazil. Brazilian Conservatives also supported a strong monarchy and opposed federalism. They dominated the cabinets of Emperor **Pedro II.**

1844-65

Conservative Guatemalans and Dictator Rafael Carrera. Members of Guatemala's Conservative elite supported Carrera, who held sway over the nation's Indian majority. During Carrera's rule the church was highly influential, and mechanisms of the colonial social order were maintained.

1848

Colombia's Conservative Party. Founded by José Eusebio Caro and Mariano Ospina Rodríguez, Colombian Conservatives organized to combat the Liberal reform program in force at the time. They were critical of Liberal attacks on the church, and what they saw as that party's demagogic appeals to the urban lower classes. Colombia's Conservatives ruled sporadically until 1885, when they established political control lasting to 1930.

1854

Conservatives and Liberals in Nicaragua. The Conservative defeat of Liberals moved the latter to briefly gain power through the aid of U.S. filibuster **William Walker**. Walker's defeat in 1857 won the Conservatives popularity that ensured them control of national politics until 1893.

1878

First National Convention of Chile's Conservative Party. Chilean conservatives controlled Chilean politics after 1830, when they triumphed over liberal forces at the Battle of Lircay. The party split in the 1850s when the Nationals broke away, and the Conservatives joined the Liberals in a fusion that lasted until the 1870s. When the nation's Liberal party gained political advantage, Chilean conservatives formally founded their party.

1883

Ecuador's Conservative Party Constituted. While Conservative political factions had existed since the 1830s, and the party was triumphant during the regime of **Gabriel García Moreno** (1861-75), its formal organization was forced by the Liberals' chartering of their party in 1878.

Elite Accommodation and Progress

1870-1930

The Ideology of Elite Accommodation. After mid-century Latin American leaders moved away from the idealism that had inspired their early spate of constitution-writing and liberal state-making. They became convinced that progress could be achieved if they gave order precedence over freedom, and if they approached problem-solving scientifically. Thus Latin America could hope to achieve the level of progress enjoyed by Western Europe and the United States. The ideology they shared was positivism, based in the writings of French philosopher Auguste Comte. Comte instructed in his *Cours de philosophie positive* (1830-42) that the social organism progressed through three stages, culminating in the triumph of scientific attitudes, a stage he called "positive politics." According to Comtean doctrine, the duty of leaders was to ensure a climate of order, within which progress could achieve full flower. Positivism was especially influential in Mexico, Brazil, Chile, and Central America.

Turn-of-the-century writers refined Comte's organic vision of human society, focusing upon race and environment as determining factors in cultural evolution. European theories of racial and cultural determinism were readily accepted by Latin American elites. It seemed logical to them that their mixed-race populations, deemed inferior by racial theorists, and their tropical and broken terrains, held up as hindrances to nation-building by geodeterminists, played a large role in their backwardness. Latin America's small political elite internalized positivist and deterministic ideas and adapted them to unique national needs.

1867

Gabino Barreda's *Civic Oration*. Barreda, commissioned by **President Benito Juárez** to reorganize Mexican education, called for reforming school programs to eliminate speculative thinking, to encourage an entrepreneurial and scientific spirit among Mexicans, and to train social engineers who would aid industrialists in achieving economic progress.

1874

José V. Lastarria's *Lessons in Positive Philosophy*. The Chilean intellectual and politician argued that liberty and authority are relative, and he advocated what he termed "responsible authoritarianism."

1878-85

Justo Sierra's *La Libertad*. Through his newspaper, the Mexican intellectual **Sierra,** and his colleagues, who became known as the *científicos*, promoted a new, positivist liberalism, which called for strong government and economic development.

1889

Positivist Slogan "Order and Progress" Emblazoned on Brazil's Flag. Brazilian positivists supported the overthrow of Emperor **Pedro II** in 1889 and establishment of the republic. Their leader, **Benjamin Constant de Magalhães**, is said to have coined the slogan.

1892

Mexican Positivists' Liberal Union Manifesto. Signed by **Justo Sierra**, Francisco Bulnes, and others, the movement promoted a third term for President **Porfirio Díaz**, as well as fiscal reforms aimed at stimulating foreign investment.

1902

Rebellion in the Backlands. In this famous study of the Brazilian military campaign against the rebel backland city Canudos, author **Euclides da Cunha** employed positivist analysis in reporting the city's destruction in 1897.

1903

Nuestra América. The most important book of Argentine positivist Carlos O. Bunge, it interpreted Latin American political instability as a function of the region's inferior mixed-blood peoples.

1912

A Positivist Critique of Mexico's Liberal 1857 Constitution. In *La constitución y la dictadura*, jurist and novelist Emilio Rabasa criticized the 1857 document as hindering national development through the restriction of presidential power.

1915

Formation of the Argentine Race by José **Ingenieros**. The Argentine positivist argued that European immigrants, being more fit to inhabit temperate zones, inevitably and properly triumphed over the region's Indian inhabitants.

1919

Democratic Caesarism. Venezuelan writer Laureano Vallenilla Lanz argued that democratic leveling necessitated dictatorial rule in Latin America.

1928

Questions on the Progress of Colombia. Conservative politician **Laureano Gómez** drew upon ethno-deterministic scholarship to deliver a negative assessment of his country's mixed-blood population and its tropical environment. He termed Colombia "a kind of hothouse culture" demanding intelligent political leadership.

Elite Rule and National Progress. During the late nineteenth century fewer than 20 percent of Latin Americans dictated the political affairs of their respective nations. They constituted a political elite, distinguished from their fellow citizens by education, economic self-sufficiency, and urban residence. The remaining 80 percent of the population was typically an unlettered rural peasantry living outside the money economy, having little impact upon national affairs other than through ritualized voting in elections managed at the national level, and serving as foot soldiers in periodic civil wars. Within such settings the upper strata of society directed politics as they chose. Having reconciled earlier disputes by mutual acceptance of the positivist slogan "Order and Progress," Latin American elites dictated the style and pace of national development. Around the turn of the century they began to integrate their region into the economic system of the capitalist West, thus ensuring their countries access to monies required for national modernization.

Because of their overwhelming desire for political stability and economic progress, Latin America's modernizing elite gave short shrift to public welfare. As a result most Latin Americans entered the twentieth century poor, uneducated, and in ill health. A substantial majority of Latin Americans were illiterate in 1910, and even in the region's wealthiest nation, Argentina, half of all rural dwellers could neither read nor write. Infant mortality over most of the region ran to 50 percent; in rural Argentina three out of ten infants died before their first birthday. Urban labor typically worked seven-day, seventy-seven-hour weeks; received low wages; and enjoyed no insurance from accident, illness, or layoff. By the early twentieth century Latin Americans had ample reason to criticize elite-dominated politics. Many of them consequently began a search for alternatives to what they perceived as a bankrupt political system.

New Political Movements and Tendencies. During the last decades of the nineteenth century and the first decades of the twentieth, Latin American political elites and counter-elites began experimenting with ways of addressing failures in the dominant liberal-republican model. Some of their approaches were reformist, and others revolutionary, borrowed wholly or in part from movements that appeared earlier in Europe. Yet others were largely autochthonous, sprung from visceral anger over social injustice.

Liberal Reformism. Short-lived attempts to solve national problems through moderate, progressive, liberal alternatives were made in both Mexico and Colombia during the first decade of the twentieth century. In 1909 **Francisco I. Madero** launched a movement to establish liberal democracy in Mexico. Despairing of the prospects for peaceful political change, he then turned to revolution and became president in 1911. Madero's assassination in 1913 ended his movement. Colombia's Republican party, founded in 1909, joined Liberal and Conservative moderates who wished to reduce the level of partisanship in national politics. While Republican leader Carlos E. Restrepo won the presidency in 1910, his supporters soon abandoned him, rejoining the Liberal and Conservative parties.

Anarchism and Anarchosyndicalism. Anarchists and anarchosyndicalists appeared in most Latin American countries during early years of the twentieth century, especially in Argentina, Uruguay, and Brazil, which attracted many immigrants from southern Europe, where these movements flourished. The former advocated destroying the state and replacing it with communal society. One of Latin America's best-known anarchists, Mexican **Ricardo Flores Magón**, was forced from his country in 1904, and later died in a United States prison. Anarchosyndicalism aimed at destroying the state through the general strike carried out by trade unions. The failure of general strikes in Chile, Argentina, Brazil, and other countries during the second decade of the century, and the appearance of Communist parties after 1917, severely weakened anarchosyndicalism.

Socialism. Utopian socialists appeared in several Latin American nations during the mid-nineteenth century. The most notable of them was Chilean Francisco Bilbao (1823-1865), who, in 1850, enrolled as many as six thousand in his ephemeral Society of Equality. The Argentine Socialist party appeared in 1896 and maintained an active presence in that country through the 1930s. Other Socialist parties, likewise founded by European immigrants, appeared in Uruguay (1910) and Chile (1912). But since they advanced their redistributionist philosophy through normal political channels, rather than through revolutionary action, they had only a small following among the working class. Thus socialist success was tempered by the rise of anarchosyndicalism and communism. During the 1920s most of the region's Socialist parties were subsumed by emergent communism. In Chile, however, socialism experienced gains during the 1930s and 1960s. In 1970 long-time Socialist leader **Salvador Allende** was elected president of Chile.

Communism. Communism spread rapidly in Latin America following formation of the Third International in 1919. Parties were established in Argentina (1918), Mexico (1919), and Brazil (1922). The Uruguayan Socialist party and the Chilean Socialist Workers' party joined the International during 1920 and 1922, thereby becoming Communist parties. Cuba organized its Communist party in 1925, and by decade's end virtually all Latin American nations possessed Communist parties. Early twentieth-century Communists led uprisings in several nations. Notable among them were Brazil's **Luís Carlos Prestes**, and Colombia's labor leaders María Cano and Ignacio Torres Giraldo. Communist growth slowed in 1928, when members were directed, at the Communist International's Sixth Congress, to establish independent labor unions. Although Communist-dominated unions throughout the region joined to form the Latin American Trade Union Confederation in 1929, their exclusivism cost them the support of many leftists who rejected direction from Moscow.

Indigenismo. *Indigenismo*, or Indianism, appeared in Latin America during the second decade of the twentieth century. Some of the movement's proponents, found chiefly in Peru and Mexico, favored integration of the Indian into the mainstream of society; others sought the solution of political, economic, and social problems in their countries' Indian heritage. Leading

Peruvian *indigenista* intellectuals and politicians were **José Carlos Mariátegui** and **Víctor Raúl Haya de la Torre**. The former used communal Incan practices to justify his call for socialist revolution in Peru. Similarly, Haya de la Torre found sufficient virtue in American Indian culture to warrant exchanging the name Latin America for Indoamerica. Through his APRA party, organized in 1924, Haya advanced an *indigenista* agenda through the 1960s. Among Mexico's leading proponents of *indigenismo* were anthropologists Manuel Gamio and Moisés Sáenz. Through their influence and that of many other Mexican reformers, that nation designed rural education programs to meet the needs of Indians, and its 1917 constitution legalized communal land holdings. This formed the basis for restoration, during the 1920s and 1930s, of Indian *ejidos* lost over the preceding period of liberal domination. (See also Race.)

Radical Agrarianism. A sense of injustice over the loss of communal lands during the time of **Porfirio Díaz** and the reluctance of **Francisco I. Madero** to move resolutely on land reform moved Mexican revolutionary **Emiliano Zapata** to formulate his Plan de Ayala, demanding immediate and thoroughgoing land reform, in late 1911. His revolutionary repatriation of lands to smallholders and communities in his home state of Morelos between 1911 and his death in 1919 served to inspire later land reformers throughout Latin America.

Nationalist Anti-imperialism. Latin Americans, especially in the Caribbean Basin, chafed at their status as client states or near-colonies of more powerful nations. Thus nationalist anti-imperialism formed a political constant in anti–status quo political movements that transcended ideology. Cuba's **José Martí** and Nicaragua's **Augusto César Sandino** were political leaders whose popularity rested in their refusal to subsume their nationalism to any overarching ideology. A chief architect of Cuban independence from Spain, Martí gave his life in 1895 during a new attempt to liberate the island.

Sandino likewise died not long after waging a heroic campaign to rid Nicaragua of the U.S. troops who occupied it almost continuously between 1912 and 1933. Both men stand as paramount heroes in their respective countries.

Corporatism. Corporative political organization, having deep roots in Latin American governance,

was widely employed as an antidote to individualizing, pluralistic liberalism. Through corporative formulas governments recognize or call into existence functional groups for the dual purposes of controlling and favoring them. Thus Mexico's 1917 constitution singled out labor in its famous Article 123, granting workers special treatment within the new national system, all the

Guerrilla Movements from 1955

while tying their interests to those of the government. Corporative organizational principles later figured prominently in the organization of Mexico's ruling revolutionary party. While political corporatism enjoyed its great popularity during the 1930s, it was widely discussed in Latin America during the 1920s. Brazil's José Oliveira Viana presaged later advocates of corporatism when he called for strong central government that would interact closely with interest groups.

Strengthening National Government

1930-1959

In 1930 Latin America was a profoundly different place than it had been six decades earlier. Two generations of rule by progress-minded elites, along with a long spell of relative peace, had allowed the region to become integrated into the economic system of the industrializing West. Lucrative exports had enriched society in a way never before known. Consumer culture became a reality, urbanization moved apace, and by the fourth decade of the century Latin America possessed a vigorous and growing middle class and a small but vocal proletariat. Those developments suggest why onset of the depression produced major political changes. Suddenly an energized and empowered citizenry, its interests harmed by the economic downturn, demanded a greater voice in the direction of national affairs.

The dimensions of that movement for political change became manifest in months following the onset of the depression. Governments across Latin America fell in quick succession as the men directing them admitted to impotence before the painful economic decline. Three kinds of state-strengthening regimes typically emerged to replace the old elite-dominated political systems: populist-corporative, democratic, and dictatorial. Only Mexico escaped political turmoil; its citizens had renovated their political system through the long revolutionary process beginning in 1910.

Models for Reform. Leaders seeking solutions

for the sudden loss of faith in the political system reflected on earlier models of reform. Mexico's populist, nationalist revolution of 1910-20 was highly suggestive to them. Of special interest was that country's 1917 constitution, the most advanced national charter of its time, containing extensive social guarantees. The social and political reforms of Uruguay's **José Batlle y Ordóñez** were also an object of study. Between 1903 and 1915, Batlle had made Uruguay one of the region's most progressive, admired nations. Likewise, Chile's **Arturo Alessandri**, supported by a progressive military, had been successful in answering the demands of new social groups, most notably organized labor, during years prior to the Great Depression. Farther afield, Russia's 1917 revolution and the subsequent regimes of Lenin and Stalin proved instructive. The fascist regimes of Benito Mussolini, Antonio de Salazar, and José Antonio Primo de Rivera were studied by Latin Americans of authoritarian and statist temperament. Finally, the interventionist state prescribed by English economist John Maynard Keynes influenced the thinking of liberal-minded reformers.

State Strengthening Through Populism and Corporatism. Latin America's three largest nations, Brazil, Mexico, and Argentina, achieved fundamental reform through populist movements that swept aside the old regimes. There were notable populist movements in other countries as well. Populism drew support chiefly, though not exclusively, from urban middle- and working-class constituencies. Populist politicians were usually charismatic leaders who championed society's dispossessed and all others who felt themselves denied adequate voice in government. They favored nonrevolutionary solutions to social and political problems, usually choosing to empower their followers through corporative mechanisms that bound their interests to those of the government. Populist leaders were also nationalists, given to strengthening their countries' economies through industrialization. They likewise favored strong militaries, and frequently founded their regimes upon military support.

1930-45

Getúlio Vargas and Corporative Populism in Brazil. Brazilians angry over the monopoly of power exercised by coffee-producing São Paulo and Minas Gerais bore **Getúlio Vargas** to power through a revolutionary movement. Accordingly, Vargas moved decisively to empower labor and middle-sector groups. He achieved that goal through courts having authority over labor–management disputes and government-organized and -controlled labor unions. Middle-class Brazilians were extended political representation on the basis of occupational groups. Meanwhile, the activities of political opponents were strictly limited, and revolutionary communist and fascist groups proscribed. Vargas did not institutionalize his corporative mechanisms, but his populism, exercised through protégés, remained important in Brazilian politics to the mid-1960s.

1930-70s

Peruvian Populism: Víctor Haya de la Torre. The young **Haya de la Torre** founded his continent-wide, anti-imperialist APRA movement in Mexico in 1924, establishing it in Peru six years later. While Haya's APRA appealed to "oppressed movements and classes" throughout Latin America, it was active principally in Peru. Haya's radical oratory and his sometimes violent followers centered in urban Peru, struck fear into the hearts of those whom the Apristas labeled oligarchs. APRA's enemies thus denied Haya the presidency for forty years. Yet APRA, through its demands for statist, redistributionist, and reformist policies, influenced government policy through the 1980s.

1934-40

The Reforms of Mexican President Lázaro Cárdenas. **Cárdenas** became Mexico's most popular president of the postrevolution period by championing the interests of ordinary citizens. After breaking the power of caudillo **Plutarco Elías Calles**, he launched a massive program of land redistribution to communal *ejidos*. He favored farmers and workers and sponsored their unions, rendering them quasi-official entities. Cárdenas reorganized the revolutionary party along corporative lines in 1938, defining party affiliation in terms of the member's occupational group. He effectively wedded interests of the nation's revolutionary party, renamed the Institutional Revolutionary party (PRI) in 1946, to those of the state.

1946-55

The Populist Authoritarianism of Juan D. Perón. Perón won power thanks to the support of Argentine labor. He dominated organized labor, and in 1947 formed the Peronist (Justicialist) party. Perón formalized his control of politics in a statist constitution that decreed national ownership of natural resources, extended voting to women, and granted extensive rights to workers. His Justicialist party incorporated occupational groupings that bound the interests of labor to the state.

1953-57

Colombia's Rojas Pinilla. General **Gustavo Rojas Pinilla** emulated Argentina's Perón during his time as Colombia's president (1953-57). Rojas founded a state welfare agency, placing his daughter at its head. His lieutenants formulated a corporative political philosophy reminiscent of Perón's Justicialism. During the 1960s Rojas won wide support in urban Colombia through his mass-based, multi-class ANAPO party, and in 1970 narrowly lost the presidential election. Anapismo declined as a political force following the death of Rojas in 1975.

State Strengthening Through Liberal Reformism and Social Democracy. Many Latin Americans never lost faith in the egalitarian promise standing at the core of early nineteenth-century liberalism. Through the decades of elite accommodation, when the issue of economic development overshadowed liberalism's social message, ideological liberals continued to believe that social justice could be achieved through democratic, reformist means. During the early twentieth century nonrevolutionary socialism also gained adherents in Latin America. Those variants of democratic reformism, frequently difficult to distinguish from one another, served as vehicles of change in countries stretching from the Southern Cone to Central America.

1934-38

Colombia's "New Deal." Colombia's Liberal party returned to power in 1930, and under President **Alfonso López Pumarejo** sponsored reforms that were popular with a broad cross-section of the citizenry. López and the dynamic young group of activists who surrounded him defused social unrest and wedded a majority of Colombians to his party through agrarian, tax, and educational reforms. His programs extended the vote to all adult men, weakened church–state ties, and increased the state's power to intervene in domestic politics and economics.

1938-46

Moderate Reform in Democratic Chile. After the initial shock of economic depression, Chile emerged as Latin America's most stable and democratic country. Radical, Communist, and Socialist parties integrated nonelite sectors into politics, and during the Popular Front (1938-41) enacted legislation favoring middle- and working-class interests.

1930s-50s

Batllist Uruguay. Along with Chile, Uruguay stood as one of Latin America's favored republics. Thanks to the socially advanced programs of President **José Batlle y Ordóñez** (1903-07 and 1911-15), which cemented national consensus, Uruguay was spared the political turmoil suffered by most other Southern Cone nations. Economic well-being allowed a revival of Battlism during the post–World War II period. At that moment Uruguay stood as one of the world's most admired nations, earning the nickname "the Switzerland of South America."

Dictatorial Negation of Reform. The same pressures for state-strengthening and the reform of elite-dominated political institutions were present in Latin America's smaller, less developed nations. There the collapse of world trade during 1929-31 devastated economies dependent on the export of sugar, coffee, bananas, and the like. But owing to low levels of social differentiation—especially the lack of a significant middle class and urban proletariat—and widespread poverty among the rural peasantry, traditional elites often successfully resisted change. They typically relied on military strongmen to defend the status quo, becoming adept at winning U.S. aid for the purpose of silencing reformers whom they invariably tarred as communists. Thus, the Central American states except for Costa Rica and Panama fell under the sway of long-lived dictatorships: **Jorge Ubico** in Guatemala (1931-44), **Maximiliano Hernández Martínez** in El Salvador (1931-44), **Tiburcio Carías Andino** in Honduras (1933-48), and **Anastasio Somoza García** in Nicaragua (1936-56). In the Dominican Republic, **Rafael Leonidas Trujillo** ruled directly or indirectly for more than thirty years (1930-61).

Foreign Political Influences from 1930 Through World War II. Its importance as a supplier of raw materials and its strategic location made Latin America ever more important to the world's leading countries. The United States, its European allies, and enemies, all vied in expanding their influence throughout the region during the turbulent 1930s and the years of World War II. Their attentions made a significant impact upon political thought and policy.

The United States. By 1930 U.S. policymakers

had abandoned gunboat diplomacy in favor of that of the Good Neighbor. The United States worked successfully over the decade to draw Latin America into regional peace-keeping and self-defense pacts, which were formalized in Montevideo in 1933 and in Buenos Aires three years later. In a 1939 Panama City meeting, the United States led Latin American states in proclaiming Western Hemisphere neutrality. A year later, in Havana, Cuba, the United States likewise enlisted Latin American support in countering Nazi attempts to seize Dutch and French colonies. Following the December 1941 attack on the U.S. naval base at Pearl Harbor, most Latin American nations either declared war on Germany and its allies or broke relations with them. Only Argentina and Chile remained neutral for a time.

From the late 1930s through World War II the United States encouraged Latin American nations to strike at domestic interests supportive of fascist Italy and Nazi Germany. The governments of many countries responded by confiscating German property and placing German nationals and right-wing militants under surveillance. Colombia, for example, went so far as to intern German nationals in a concentration camp near Bogotá. Leaders not vocally committed to the Allies were tarred as pro-Nazi; two of them, **Arnulfo Arias** of Panama and Gualberto Villarroel (1908-1946) of Bolivia, were overthrown as a consequence. The United States also imposed economic sanctions against the Argentine government because of the allegedly pro-Axis sentiments of its leaders and its failure to sever diplomatic relations with the Axis until 1944. Meanwhile the United States tolerated and even supported authoritarian rulers who supported the Allied war effort. Notable among them were **Trujillo** of the Dominican Republic and **Somoza** of Nicaragua. The United States winked at the authoritarian practices of Brazil's **Getúlio Vargas**, while rewarding his support with substantial military and economic aid.

At war's end the United States pressured Latin American states for a return to democratic practice. That helped bring about notable though brief democratic and reformist regimes in Guatemala and Venezuela, as well as an enduring move to democratic governance in Puerto Rico. Brazil's Vargas also relinquished power after fifteen years of rule, and Nicaragua's Somoza allowed a political associate to be elected president.

The USSR and the Communist International. Latin American Communists closely followed dictates of the Comintern during the 1930s and 1940s. The 1936 Comintern directive to form popular front regimes with other progressive groups enabled Chilean Communists to help Pedro Aguirre Cerda win the presidential contest of 1938. Mexican Communists exercised a certain influence through their support of **Lázaro Cárdenas** during 1934-40, as did Cuban Communists, who supported **Fulgencio Batista** during the late 1930s and early 1940s. The Comintern directive that Latin American Communists denounce World War II as an imperialist struggle proved counter-productive. But reversal of the directive following the Nazi invasion of the USSR in 1941 enabled them to regain lost popularity. Thanks to their support of the Allied war effort, Latin America's Communists constituted the dominant force in Latin America's labor movement by 1946.

Fascism. Brazilian fascists organized during 1932, calling themselves Integralists, and adopting symbols and rituals copied from Italian fascism. Their Chilean counterparts formed a Nazi party shortly thereafter. Both constituted antiregime fringe groups, and they were united in their antiliberalism and anti-Semitism, as well as in their nationalism and admiration for authoritarian rule in the style of Mussolini and Hitler. While both movements planned to seize power by force, they were thwarted late in the 1930s. Brazil's **Getúlio Vargas** made Integralism illegal in 1937, and Chile's **Arturo Alessandri** crushed the *nacistas* following their failed coup attempt of 1938. Mexican fascists joined the counter-revolutionary Sinarquista group in 1937, which disappeared as a viable political movement following defeat of the Axis in 1945. Elsewhere in Latin America, fascist movements became integrated into other popular movements, such as **Peron**'s Justicialism in Argentina and **Víctor Paz Estenssoro**'s National Revolutionary Movement (MNR) in Bolivia. Throughout Central America, the Caribbean, and northern South America, fascist movements were quashed by national governments aided and encouraged by U.S. military and diplomatic missions.

The Interventionist State and Cold War Politics

1960–1989

Political parties representing middle- and working-class interests were increasingly successful during the 1950s, 1960s, and 1970s. The growing strength of Christian Democratic, social democratic, socialist, and populist parties was in part a function of an expansion of the electorate. This in turn was owed both to the enfranchisement of women and to rapid urbanization that concentrated the electorate near centers of political power. Nontraditional parties also profited from the quickening modernization that heightened social complexity and made the middle class a powerful political force for the first time in history.

The state steadily increased its size and reach after mid-century in response to demands that it provide a variety of new social services. The drive to complete industrialization also made for a more interventionist state. Foreign aid played its role in state-strengthening. U.S. assistance became abundant after 1961, when **Fidel Castro**'s embrace of Marxism-Leninism stirred fear of widespread communist revolution. Governments were urged to use those monies for land reform, improved public health and education, and social services. Borrowed capital was also used to create a large number of public enterprises. By the late 1980s employment by the state had quintupled, running to between 10 and 20 percent of total employment throughout the region, more than double the rate of public employment in Western

Europe and the United States.

As Latin American states grew larger and richer, they became unwieldy and riddled with corruption. Their weaknesses became all the more apparent during the 1980s. Known as Latin America's "lost decade," the eighties witnessed economic downturns aggravated by sharp increases in energy costs. Large public debt, excessive economic protection, and spiraling inflation heightened the perception that fundamental political reform was necessary.

Fidel Castro's sponsorship of guerrilla insurgencies after 1961 set into motion a cycle of military coups extending through the 1960s into the 1970s. Brazil and Southern Cone nations established bureaucratic-authoritarian regimes on their way to neutralizing the leftist threat. Cold War tensions eased during the 1980s, making possible a restoration of democratic rule. Yet ongoing economic woes led to mounting criticism of Latin America's public sector. By 1990 a retreat from statism was under way.

Emergent Political Parties and Movements. There was a broadening of the political spectrum after mid-century. In most cases parties dominant during the nineteenth century joined the new groups or disappeared altogether. The principal exceptions were Colombia, where the Liberal and Conservative parties continued to hold sway, and Uruguay, where the Colorados and Blancos (National party) continued to dominate political life.

Christian Democratic Parties. Middle-class Roman Catholics found a nonrevolutionary means of pursuing social reform through Christian Democracy. Sprung from social teachings of the church dating from the 1891 papal encyclical *De Rerum Novarum*, Christian Democracy became a significant political force after mid-century. Venezuela's Social Christian party (also known as COPEI) was established in 1946; its founder, **Rafael Caldera**, was elected president in 1968. Other important Christian Democratic parties were established in Chile (1957), El Salvador

(1960), and Guatemala (1964). Mexico's National Action party (PAN), founded in 1939 in opposition to the policies of the **Cárdenas** administration, later adopted some Christian Democratic positions.

Social Democratic Parties. Advocating redistribution of wealth through democratic means, the social democratic movement became important in several Latin American nations. Under the leadership of its founder, **Luis Muñoz Marín**, Puerto Rico's Popular Democratic party (PPD) effected important changes in the island's economy and political status in the 1940s and 1950s. Founded in 1941, Venezuela's Acción Democrática (AD) held power briefly (1945-48). It came to power after the fall of dictator **Marcos Pérez Jiménez** in 1958 with the election of **Rómulo Betancourt**, who introduced agrarian reform and other redistributive policies. Costa Rica's National Liberation party (PLN) was formally organized in 1951 but grew out of the 1948 revolution. As president (1953-58), PLN founder **José Figueres** greatly increased the state's role in the economy and obtained better terms for Costa Rica from the United Fruit Company. The Dominican Revolutionary party (PRD) was founded in 1939 by Juan Bosch, whose presidential term was cut short by a military coup in 1963. The party elected candidates to the presidency in 1978 and 1982, but they disappointed expectations for reform.

Movements of the Revolutionary Left. Left-wing revolutionary guerrilla movements appeared in most Latin American countries following **Fidel Castro**'s Cuban Revolution of 1959 and his call for the formation of Marxist-Leninist guerrillas in 1962. **Ernesto "Che" Guevara**'s book *Guerrilla Warfare* (1960) served as a handbook for revolutionaries in the 1960s, showing how rural bases, or *focos*, could become a springboard to victory. Some groups received the support of their local Communist party, but it was not always forthcoming. All such movements, save for the one established in Nicaragua, were unsuccessful in emulating Castro's success.

1953-56

Cuban revolutionary **Fidel Castro conceived his July 26 Movement while imprisoned on the Isle of Pines.** He succeeded in driving dictator **Fulgencio Batista** from the island in 1959. During 1961-62 he began promoting Marxist-Leninist revolution throughout Latin America.

1961

Nicaragua's **guerrilla movement, the Sandinista National Liberation Front (FSLN), was organized, gaining power through the revolution of 1979.** Its leader **Daniel Ortega** headed the Sandinista government until 1990.

1962

Guatemala's Rebel Armed Forces (FAR) was established. In 1982 it united with three similar groups to form the National Guatemalan Revolutionary Unity, which remained active until the mid-1990s.

Uruguay's urban guerrilla group, the Tupamaros, was organized. Named after the eighteenth-century rebel **Túpac Amaru II**, it remained active until the early 1970s.

1963

Venezuela's guerrilla group, the Armed Forces of National Liberation (FALN), was formed. It included military officers who had taken part in unsuccessful rebellions against the government of **Rómulo Betancourt** in 1962 as well as militants belonging to the Venezuelan Communist party and a leftist offshoot of the AD, the Movement of the Revolutionary Left (MIR). It remained active until its members accepted an amnesty offered by the government of **Rafael Caldera** (1969-74).

1964

Colombia's Revolutionary Armed Forces of Colombia (FARC) was organized. It remained active throughout the remainder of the century.

1965

Colombia's guerrilla Army of National Liberation (ELN) began operations and remained active through the 1990s.

1969

Chile's Movement of the Revolutionary Left (MIR) was organized. It was composed mainly of middle-class students who supported armed struggle in contrast to the electoral strategies of the traditional leftist parties. The MIR undertook bank robberies and other armed actions in 1969-70, but suspended these activities before the election of 1970. It never joined the UP coalition that supported **Salvador Allende**, but continued to present itself as an alternative force for revolutionary change.

1970

Peru's Maoist Shining Path (Sendero Luminoso) guerrilla movement was begun by Abimael Guzmán. It became active in 1980.

1970

El Salvador's guerrilla Farabundo Martí Popular Liberation Force was established. In 1980 it joined with four similar groups to form the Farabundo Martí National Liberation Front (FMLN). It remained active until 1991.

1970

Argentina's urban guerrilla group, the Montoneros, began operations. The Montoneros emerged from within the Peronist Youth movement after the *cordobazo* of 1969. Its leaders had ties to militant Catholic groups and were also influenced by the ideas of Ernesto "Che" Guevara. They favored dramatic actions, such as the kidnapping and murder of former president Pedro Aramburu in 1970.

Retreat from Statism: Latin America's Lost Decade. Latin America's public sector had expanded rapidly during the thirty years after 1950. High petroleum prices during the 1970s had allowed Venezuela, Mexico, and Ecuador to add many new government programs. Adoption of the militaristic "national security" doctrine in Brazil and the Southern Cone during the 1960s and 1970s, likewise paved the way for similar growth in government budgets. Where petroleum sales did not finance state expansion, foreign borrowing did. During the 1970s banks in the United States and Europe were awash in petrodollars, money deposited there following the sharp increase in oil prices after 1973.

Signs of trouble began to appear in the late 1970s. Inflation rose to alarming levels in many countries. An accompanying decline in oil revenues forced the firing of government workers, setting off protests in oil-exporting Ecuador, Venezuela, and Mexico. Intensifying the region's economic woes was an economic recession that spread through the developed world during the late 1970s and early 1980s, which brought a sharp drop in Latin American export earnings. Suddenly it became impossible for Latin American states to service their crushing debts. Mexico's brief suspension of debt payments in 1982 touched off panic in world financial markets. Brazil, Peru, Argentina, and other countries found themselves in a similar situation.

Latin America's debt crisis sounded the death knell for populist statism. Foreign lenders demanded that governments institute austerity measures. Throughout the region millions of state employees lost their jobs, subsidies for food and fuel were ended, and several hundred state-owned companies were closed or sold to the private sector. Meanwhile inflation heightened the misery of ordinary people and national economies foundered. Across Latin America citizens demanded relief.

Neoliberalism, Democracy
and the Issue of Reform

1990–1999

The 1990s witnessed a major shift in the way political leaders throughout Latin America perceived the role of the state. Rapid economic growth in anglophone America, Western Europe, and Asia, coupled with Latin America's economic stagnation, convinced them that their region must open itself to global market forces. In so doing they reversed many of the statist, interventionist policies that had been in force for a half-century or more.

Latin Americans were ambivalent about their leaders' rush to embrace neoliberalism, especially in countries such as Mexico and Argentina, where the abandonment of protection and shrinkage of the state were especially damaging to middle-class interests. The retreat from statism focused new attention upon the need to strengthen public institutions. In the face of popular dissatisfaction with every facet of the public sphere, national leaders and institutions were challenged to make good on the promise of democratic governance.

Neoliberal Politics. Latin America's shift to neoliberalism was forced by internal and external factors. Internally, the retreat from statism was hastened by a pervasive belief that political elites were corrupt as well as incompetent. Cases of egregious public corruption abounded. Within a span of five months (December 1992–May 1993), Brazil's President Fernando Collor de Mello and Venezuela's **Carlos Andrés Pérez** were removed from office for financial improprieties. Mexico's **Carlos Salinas** was likewise accused of massive corruption shortly after he left office in 1994, and Peru's ex-president Alan García took refuge abroad to avoid prosecution for crimes he allegedly committed while in office.

External factors were pivotal to the political reorientation. International lending institutions, foremost among them the International Monetary Fund, demanded that debtor nations slash government programs and enact a range of reforms. Meanwhile Latin American leaders began turning to export-driven development models, spurred by the examples of Korea and Taiwan, and during the latter 1980s they observed the failure of the Soviet Union's statist experiment, as well as the striking economic opening of the People's Republic of China. Closer at hand, Chile served as a case study of successful neoliberal reform. Since the late 1970s that country had, by minimizing state intervention in the economy, achieved a level of fiscal health that made it the envy of most Latin American nations.

These factors led to a dramatic abandoning of inward-looking statism early in the 1990s. In Mexico, President Carlos Salinas accelerated his nation's economic opening by joining Canada and the United States in the North American Free Trade Agreement. **Carlos Menem** in Argentina, **Alberto Fujimori** in Peru, and **Fernando Henrique Cardoso** in Brazil all won popular support by bringing inflation down to manageable levels, opening national borders to foreign trade, and streamlining government. The leaders of virtually all other Latin American states undertook similar neoliberal reforms.

Middle-Class Democracy. By 1990, the military had returned to its barracks. Democracy prevailed over most of Latin America. As the filling of top political offices through elections became routinized, constitutions were increasingly amended to allow for immediate presidential succession. Thus the popular Peruvian president **Alberto Fujimori** could be elected to a second five-year term in 1995, and Argentine president **Carlos Menem** won a second term in 1995. Brazil's **Cardoso** was reelected in 1998.

Another trend was voter dissatisfaction with defects in national institutions, foremost among them political institutions. Similarly, Latin Americans expressed a great lack of confidence in the church, the military, the media, and their labor unions. Thus the electorate was increasingly willing to turn on public officials whom they perceived as ill-serving or deceiving them. In early 1997 Ecuadorians supported congressional removal of their eccentric President Abdala Bucaram after just five months in office. And when Argentines perceived that President **Carlos Menem**'s reforms had become harmful to their interests, they forced him to soften them and to fire their chief architect, Domingo Cavallo.

The most striking examples of mounting public anger over maladministration occurred in Mexico and Venezuela. In Mexico, near-universal discontent over incompetent handling of public finances during 1994 led to stunning electoral defeats for the semi-official Institutional Revolutionary party (PRI) as voters flocked to the Democratic Revolutionary party of **Cuauhtémoc Cárdenas** and to the National Action party (PAN). In 1997, the PRI lost control of Mexico's lower house for the first time. In Venezuela, voters' disgust over corruption and declining living standards because of low oil prices led them to abandon the parties that had dominated politics since 1958, Acción Democrática and COPEI. This trend was shown most dramatically in the landslide presidential victory (1998) of Hugo Chávez Frías, a former army officer who had tried to overthrow President **Carlos Andrés Pérez** in 1992.

The Challenge of Institutional Strengthening. At century's end Latin America's great challenge lay in strengthening its political institutions. Governments lacked credibility with the public. Cronyism and clientelism weakened bureaucracy, and corruption was rife at the highest levels of administration. Tax collections ran at only half the rate of those in the world's leading nations and regressive taxation was the norm. Research increasingly showed that if Latin American states were to advance they must both improve the efficiency of government and upgrade the quality of public goods such as law enforcement, the protection of private property, and the providing of services in the areas of health, public welfare, and education.

ECONOMIC DEVELOPMENTS

Economic Ideas

Prior to 1492

Indigenous America. The peoples of America's most highly evolved states, the Inca and Aztec, expressed their economic ideas through religious teachings, legal codes, and moral exhortations. Citizens of those empires carried out economic tasks mindful of the need to placate the gods and to render their assigned share to their rulers. The Inca collected taxes in the form of foodstuffs and manufactures, and those were distributed among the nobility, the priesthood, and the citizenry at large. The Aztec, too, demanded taxes in the form of tribute from subject tribes.

A majority of pre-Columbian Americans were subjects of neither the Inca nor Aztec, nor of any other centralized state. Rather they were members of thousands of tribes and bands, most of them numbering fewer than a thousand. Tribal peoples, many of them hunter-gatherers, viewed the fruits of the earth as communal property. They shared the proceeds of productive activity with relative equality.

Most economic exchange took place at the level of barter, though gold, cacao, tobacco, beads, seashells, and other objects frequently served as mediums of exchange. Markets in principal Aztec and Inca cities were places where a wide variety of goods were exchanged. Luxury goods, precious stones and metals, and exotic plants and animals were objects of long-distance trade. But except in Mesoamerica and Andean South America, intertribal hostility and geographic barriers limited such trade.

1492-1700

Bullionism and Mercantilism. Spanish and Portuguese conquest of the New World sprang from nation-state consolidation. Political theorists such as the Florentine Niccoló Machiavelli (1469-1527) and the Frenchman Jean Bodin (1530-1596) stressed the supremacy of states and their rulers.

Economic theorists of the day equated the nation with the individual merchant, positing that a soundly managed nation, like a well-managed private enterprise, sold more than it purchased and always earned a surplus of hard currency. The teaching that a successful nation accumulates ever-increasing stores of gold and silver was known as "bullionism," a term popularized in the writings of Englishman Thomas Mun (1571-1641).

Spain became the object of bullionist envy during its "Golden Century," the sixteenth. Gold and an immense quantity of silver flowed from the New World into Spanish coffers. Substantial amounts of bullion continued to flow from the Americas to Spain and Portugal during the ensuing two centuries as well.

Mercantilism, the notion of strict control of trade and commerce, was the economic philosophy of European nation-states from the sixteenth through the eighteenth centuries. Not a self-conscious school of thought, mercantilism was rather a collection of seemingly self-evident principles that guided the policymaking of politicians, statesmen, and merchants during those three centuries. Its key tenets were most cogently set out in the writings of Jean Baptiste Colbert (1619-1683), economic advisor to French monarch Louis XIV. Colbert argued that commerce must be conducted within the borders of the nation and its dependencies, with trade balances ever favoring the mother country. Thus it was incumbent upon colonial dependencies to develop their economies in harmony with their respective mother countries, never competing directly with them.

Spanish mercantile policy was formulated by the Council of the Indies, established in 1524, which worked closely with the Casa de Contratación (Board of Trade). The two bodies regulated trade and formulated trade policy for Spain throughout the colonial period. Portuguese economic policy was set by the Casa da Índia, founded in 1501. (See also Politics and Government.)

1700-1808

Bourbon and Pombaline Reforms. Economic ideas underwent gradual liberalization over the course of the eighteenth century. The change of dynasty in Spain bringing the House of Bourbon to the throne resulted in economic reforms that eased long-standing constraints on trade between Spain and colonial ports. Similar trade liberalization occurred in Portugal through the actions of Sebastião José de Carvalho e Mello, the **Marquês de Pombal**, who shaped economic policy between 1750 an 1777.

Spanish and Portuguese Americans began to mount their own challenges to mercantilism late in the eighteenth century. Creole intellectuals formed discussion groups called "economic societies of friends of the country," and through them sought ways to stimulate growth and rationalize economic policy. Such reformist initiatives inevitably brought them into conflict with entrenched economic interests both at home and on the Iberian Peninsula, but also whetted desires among colonists for greater economic freedom. In New Spain the forward-thinking creole priest **Miguel Hidalgo y Costillo** first ran afoul of colonial authorities when he violated mercantilist agricultural restrictions during the first decade of the nineteenth century.

1808-20s

Mercantilism Supplanted by Free Trade. The coming of independence made possible the rapid supplanting of the mercantilist ideology imposed upon Latin America over most of the colonial period. As independence was achieved creole economic elites rushed to expand commerce with the industrializing nations of Western Europe. During the eighteenth century Spanish statesmen and intellectuals such as José del Campillo y Cossío and Pedro Rodríguez (Conde de Campomanes) had urged economic reform, and the crown responded with a series of decrees (1765-89) liberalizing trade within the empire. It

was the upheaval of the independence era, however, accompanied by penetration of Latin American markets by European and North American merchants, that encouraged local elites to become advocates of free commerce with non-Latin nations.

1830s-70s

The Triumph of Economic Liberalism. As the nineteenth century progressed and Latin American states achieved stability, national leaders embraced economic liberalism in accordance with prevailing European models. Especially influential were the ideas of Adam Smith, which Latin Americans absorbed through the writings of his French interpreter, Jean Baptiste Say (1767-1832). Accordingly, they fought to end colonial-era restrictions on economic liberty. Among their chief goals were the removal of church-held lands from mortmain and the division of Indian communal landholdings. Still, the dominant elites were not rigidly wedded to *laissez faire* principles. They accepted tariffs as necessary both for raising revenue and protecting infant industry. Around mid-century, debates over economic policy commonly found Conservatives advocating high tariffs to promote industrial growth—most leaders were familiar with Alexander Hamilton's 1791 argument in favor of protection—and Liberals advocating free trade along the lines spelled out by Adam Smith. In Mexico, by way of example, Conservative **Lucas Alamán** supported a regime of protective tariffs, while Liberal José Luis Mora favored policies geared toward trade stimulation.

1870s-1920s

Export Booms and the Doctrine of Comparative Advantage. During the latter nineteenth and early twentieth centuries Latin Americans found ample justification for adopting an export-driven economic strategy. Industrializing Europe paid high prices for the region's raw materials, lending credence to free trade doctrines holding that the surest route to national wealth was through exploiting natural economic endowments. For Latin American countries that meant a range of minerals and agricultural products. David Ricardo's doctrine of comparative advantage was a compelling one for economic planners. According to Ricardo, when nations traded those products that they produced most expeditiously, importing other nations' most abundant products, trade would flourish and all countries would profit. As Latin America's raw materials enjoyed favorable terms of trade during the latter nineteenth century, few economic elites questioned the wisdom of exchanging their nations' raw materials in exchange for European manufactured products.

Across Latin America finance ministers like Mexico's José Limantour, who served from 1892 to 1911, placed their nations on sound financial footing through raw material exports. At the same time the region's larger nations took initial steps toward industrialization. They were moved to do so both by the evident prosperity of industrialized Western Europe and by the arguments of theorists such as the German Friedrich List.

1930-45

Inward-looking Development I: Global Depression, Economic Nationalism, Keynesianism, and the Impact of World War II. From the Great Depression through World War II, Latin America moved toward state-led, inward-looking development. Four factors combined to increase government intervention in economic affairs, largely to the end of lessening dependence on exports and building an import-substituting industrial base. First was the shock produced by the collapse of international trade in 1930, second was the rise of economic nationalism, third was the popularity of Keynesian economics, and fourth was the impact of World War II.

Widespread unemployment, political protest, and deflation set Latin American states scrambling to lessen dependence on exports and to substitute domestic manufactures for those previously imported. Those trends were given

dynamic impetus by popular demand that governments lessen their economic dependence upon foreign economic interests. States such as Mexico under **Lázaro Cárdenas** (1934-40) and Brazil under **Getúlio Vargas** (1930-45) employed corporative approaches to promote state intervention in economic affairs. Others, such as Colombia under **Alfonso López** (1934-38) and Chile under **Arturo Alessandri** (1932-38), increased state spending along lines outlined in writings of British economist John Maynard Keynes.

Latin America's import-substituting industrialization (ISI) was spurred by World War II. As supporters of the Allied war effort, states of the region benefited from the transfer of industry and technology from the United States, which at war's end played a hegemonic role in the hemisphere.

1945-70

Inward-looking Development II: Structuralism and Dependency Theory. The postwar period, particularly the 1950s and 1960s, was dominated by the thought of Argentine economist **Raúl Prebisch**, whose economic analysis became known as "structuralism." Prebisch and his followers, among them Brazilian Celso Furtado and Chilean Aníbal Pinto, argued that deteriorating terms of trade doomed the world's less-developed "periphery" nations to unequal exchange with industrialized Europe and the United States—the industrialized "center." Only through industrialization, aided by selective protection and state intervention in the economy, could Third World nations end their unequal relationship with rich nations. Prebisch also advocated the formation of international free trade zones aimed at expanding the market for regional products.

During the 1960s structuralist assumptions were modified by Marxist scholars who formulated what became known as dependency theory. These scholars interpreted Latin American underdevelopment as a function of historic exploitation of Third World peoples by a metropolitan economic elite. They argued that foreign and domestic elites acted in concert to enrich the core and to impoverish the periphery. They opposed the operation of transnational corporations in Latin America, and advocated the development of nationally owned industry to serve the domestic market. Radical *dependentistas* such as André Gunder Frank argued that the grip of dependency could be broken only through socialist revolution. Moderates like Brazilian **Fernando Henrique Cardoso** believed that economic dependency could be lessened through reformist means.

1970-90s

Outward-looking Development: Return to the Liberal Model. By 1970 Latin America had exhausted the possibilities of further economic expansion through ISI development. The problem of economic stagnation was compounded by sharp increases in petroleum prices followed by an attempt to finance continued development through foreign borrowing and deficit spending. By the end of the decade most Latin American nations were deeply in debt and entering a decade that would be marked by global economic recession. Economic planners sought new ways to spur growth.

The striking economic success of Asian nations that had embraced an export-driven strategy following World War II, coupled with exhaustion of the import-substitution model, drove Latin Americans to begin liberalizing their economies by the late 1970s. That process began in Chile, where **Augusto Pinochet** encouraged the implementation of neoliberal policies under direction of economists known as the "Chicago Boys" for their adherence to the monetarist teachings of Milton Friedman, under whom they had studied at the University of Chicago. Chile's economic planners slashed tariffs, welcomed foreign investment, and sold state-owned enterprises to buyers from the private sector. Chile's monetarists accepted low inflation at the expense of high unemployment. When their programs drastically lowered Chile's inflation and produced high rates of economic growth, other states embraced neoliberal policies. By the 1990s

economic planners were following the strategy of Harvard University management specialist Michael Porter, who taught that economic factors must be carefully managed to achieve maximum efficiency.

At the end of the twentieth century Latin American leaders returned to the creation of regional free trade associations. They were moved to do so chiefly by the example of the European Union. Mexico joined Canada and the United States in launching the North American Free Trade Association on January 1, 1994. Meanwhile Southern Cone nations moved to implement their own free trade association, Mercosur.

The Economic Life of Pre-Columbian America

c. 1492 C.E.

Pre-Columbian Native American economies were varied, running from the highly-evolved and complex ones of Mesoamerica and Andean South America, to those of the Amazonian Xingu tribes who were hunter-gatherers having few material possessions. Millions of indigenous peoples inhabited the Americas, forming an intricate cultural mosaic.

In spite of their diversity and notwithstanding their varied achievements, indigenous Americans shared factors in common that collectively placed them at a material disadvantage when coming into contact with Europeans. Their ten millennia of isolation from other world regions had hindered their advance, and the nature of their own geography had slowed cultural diffusion among them. Desert separated Mexico and Central America from North America, and the jungles of the Darien cut off Central Americans from the continent that lay to the south. Indigenous peoples living in South America were separated from one another by the Andes mountains and the Amazon jungle, to mention but two of that continent's natural barriers to cultural exchange.

Thus geographic impediments helped ensure relatively late domestication and slow dispersion of plant species needed to support large sedentary populations. The scarcity of domesticated animals further slowed cultural advance. Nor had the native Americans moved beyond the most rudimentary metallurgy by 1492. There was no widely dispersed writing system or lingua franca, except within Mesoamerica and the Inca empire, and a majority of Native Americans were innumerate. All these factors help explain why the technological and economic attainments of America's indigenous peoples, while notable in their own right, paled before those of European invaders.

The Circum-Caribbean. The islands of the Caribbean and the coastal regions of present-day Costa Rica, Panama, Colombia, and Venezuela were densely populated by many indigenous groups. Notable among them were the Arawak-speaking Taino and Caribs of the Greater and Lesser Antilles. Caribs also inhabited extensive portions of the mainland, along with the more localized Talamanca of Costa Rica, Tairona of Colombia's coastal region, and Quimbaya and Muisca of the interior highlands. All were tribal peoples having chiefs, priests, and commoners. They possessed distinctive art and architecture, and were agricultural societies with permanent settlements. Thanks to social differentiation it was possible to assess commoners a portion of their production for the support of tribal elites.

Along with handicrafts for daily use, native peoples of the circum-Caribbean manufactured high-quality textiles, refined salt for trade and tribal use, and mined gold and emeralds. Owing to the abundant alluvial gold of coastal rivers, several tribes achieved excellence in gold-working. That was particularly the case of the Quimbaya and Muisca of highland Colombia, who specialized in creating finely crafted ornaments through the lost wax method.

Lively trade was conducted, especially among Carib peoples of coastal and riverine areas. Periodic trade fairs were held, especially along the Orinoco River, where members of many tribes gathered to harvest turtle eggs and to exchange goods. Other locations favored for regional trade gatherings included the Isthmus of Panama,

highland Colombia, and the Colombo-Venezuelan *llanos.*

Trade goods included strings of snail shells (*quiripa*), used as a medium of exchange. Along with luxury goods, including gold, emeralds, and fine textiles, slaves constituted valuable trade items. The warlike Caribs were the region's chief slave traders.

Mesoamerica. The Aztec (Mexica) empire dominated central Mexico at the end of the pre-Columbian era. While the Aztec language, Nahuatl, served as a lingua franca, the region was home to other advanced cultures, such as the Tarascans and Zapotec.

The high level of social organization among central Mexican peoples enabled them to achieve considerable economic diversification. Their farmers grew a wide variety of crops, many of them irrigated. Basic food crops included maize, beans, squash, and chili. Fish from lakes, rivers, the Pacific and Caribbean also figured in the diet. Domesticated animals included the turkey and the dog.

Considerable economic specialization existed within the Aztec empire. For example, some villages were designated producers of pottery, others did stone cutting and work with precious stone, and others textile production. Mining was carried out in some areas, though most metal-work was in basic metals for decorative or religious purposes. Aztec craftsmen were skilled lapidaries. Craftsmen exercised quality control through a guild-like structure.

Local and long-distance trade figured prominently in the lives of the central Mexican peoples. The Aztecs recognized sixty-nine categories of traders, some of whom were female, defined by their specialty. Valued trade goods included textiles, slaves, gold, cacao, and tobacco. Woven mantles, gold, and cacao served as mediums of exchange.

Merchants controlled standards and administered markets. Taxes were assessed citizens of the Aztec empire, so identified through their clan identity. Tribute was demanded of subject peoples. It ran from foodstuffs and handicrafts, to luxury items, to slaves destined for personal service or religious sacrifice.

In contrast to central Mexico, there was no dominant empire among the Maya-speaking peoples of the Yucatán peninsula, Guatemala, and other parts of Central America in the early sixteenth century. Most commoners in the numerous Mayan city-states were maize-growing peasants. Merchants, however, engaged in substantial trade both by land and by sea. Products from highland areas such as jade, obsidian, and quetzal feathers were exchanged for goods from lowland areas, such as textiles, pottery, slaves, honey, and cacao.

Along the coast of the modern Mexican state of Tabasco were port cities that functioned as commercial entrepôts visited by merchants from central Mexico, Yucatán, and other parts of Mesoamerica. The local people spoke mainly Chontal Maya, but Nahuatl was also widely used. Trade items included manufactured goods such as clothing, pottery, and jewelry as well as feathers, jade, and other raw materials. Cacao, a major product of the zone, was another important trading commodity. Local merchants, known as Putuns, also traveled extensively by canoe.

The Central Andean Highlands. Pre-Columbian America's most extensive civilization was that of the Inca. Stretching some three thousand miles along a north-south axis, the Inca empire incorporated many tribal groups, including the numerous Aymara people. Native America's most noted architects and engineers, the Inca unified their empire through an extensive highway system linking major population centers from present-day Ecuador well into Chile and Argentina.

Central Andean peoples domesticated and consumed a wide variety of tubers, most importantly the potato, which existed in many varieties. One key to their political success lay in their ability to warehouse foodstuffs for communal distribution in times of famine. Especially important was their technique of freeze-drying potatoes and other tubers.

Owing to the verticality of their terrain, peoples of the Central Andes carried out lively trade in foodstuffs between lowland and highland areas. To ensure a variety of foods the Inca sent subject peoples to form agricultural colonies at lower elevations. There, maize, many varieties of beans and squash, coca, and cacao were cultivated and distributed throughout the empire. While human porters transported much freight along Andean highways, the Inca possessed extensive herds of llama that they used both for food and as pack animals. The llama also provided wool and hides, and a technique was developed for drying and storing llama meat, known as *charqui*.

Inca leaders did not assess taxes or tribute, but rather obligated their subjects to physical labor. Known as the *mita*, and defined as specified labor assigned on a periodic basis, the levy was integral to the Inca political and economic achievement. Commoners, male and female alike, were assigned tasks running from the provisioning of soldiers of the empire, to constructing and maintaining highways and dwellings for the nobility and priesthood. Others were assigned the task of gathering naturally occurring forest products and exotic animals.

Those living within the Inca empire were skilled potters and weavers. Ceramics were colorful and artistic, and fabrics woven of wool from llama and alpaca were highly valued and traded far beyond the empire. Gold, silver, copper, and other minerals were mined and fashioned into objects used for decorative, religious, or ceremonial purposes. These products and many others were traded throughout the Inca empire.

Native Peoples of the Southern Cone. The Araucanians (or Mapuche) were the principal tribal group of central and southern Chile. Fiercely independent, the Araucanians successfully resisted threats from without through their ability to join together in bands, tribes, and confederations when forced to do so. Thus they rejected inclusion in the Inca empire. The Araucanians lived in semi-sedentary kinship groups, practiced agriculture, and created artisanal products, most notably textiles.

The Guaraní, who lived in the upper Platine region east of the Paraná and Paraguay rivers, were the Southern Cone's other notable tribal group. Semi-sedentary like the Araucanians, they cultivated maize, squash, beans, and peanuts, but moved frequently in search of fertile land. Unlike the Araucanians, they sought alliances to help them resist enemies, particularly the war-like Payaguá Indians living along the Paraguay River.

Other major Southern Cone groups were migratory hunter-gatherers. They included the Diaguita of northern Argentina, and the Tehuelches (also known as Patagones), who inhabited the plains of Argentina east of the Andean cordillera. Both groups hunted and herded the llama, and cultivated maize, squash, and beans. Their principal manufacture was a maize-based beer, which they consumed in quantity.

Native Peoples of Brazil. The Indians of Brazil were preliterate and innumerate. While skillful in creating crafts for domestic use and personal decoration, they worked largely in ephemeral materials gathered from the forests in which they lived. Brazil's leading tribe was the fierce Tupí, who inhabited most of the coastal region. The Tupí were semi-sedentary, had no domesticated animals and few personal possessions. Their society was communal, and their artisanal production limited to baskets, hammocks, and cookware made of clay or wood. That was much the case with Amazonian tribes such as the Xingu and the Manau, as well as with tribes of the Brazilian plateau, among them the Bororo and Goiá.

Economic Development During the First Two Centuries of Spanish and Portuguese Rule

1492-1700

The Spanish and Portuguese crowns exploited their American possessions in terms of mercantile assumptions. The experience was a heady one for them in that their colonies were the world's leading producers of gold and silver bullion during the more than three centuries that they held sway over the New World. Mercantilist restrictions on trade were rigid in Spanish America and to a slightly lesser degree in Portuguese America through the first two centuries of colonial rule. They eased somewhat during the eighteenth century.

Adventurers from Spain moved quickly through the Caribbean, and through North, Central, and South America during the decades following 1492. Their search for gold and silver was amply rewarded. Aztec and Inca rulers heaped treasure at their feet, and their descendants labored in rich mines discovered in Peru, Mexico, and New Granada (modern Colombia). Settlement was slower in Brazil, where the Portuguese encountered no high Indian civilizations, and where precious metals were not discovered until the end of the seventeenth century.

Latin America's earliest economic development took place in hinterlands of Peruvian and Mexican mining centers, as well as those of viceregal capitals, principal ports, and other important towns and cities. Over the first two centers of colonial rule in Spanish America, Peru's economic axis extended from Lima to the mines of Upper Peru, with important subsidiary arms extending southward into Argentina and Chile, and northward to Quito. Over time the economic sphere of Mexico (New Spain as it was known in colonial times) came to embrace the Caribbean and Central America. Meanwhile, important sites of gold mining developed in New Granada, in Andean northern South America. Brazil's earliest settlements hugged the coast, the most significant of them being along the northeast, where the chief economic activity was sugar growing.

1492-c. 1550

Acquiring the Treasure of the Indies. Spanish adventurers avid for gold and silver fell upon the Indies. Small deposits of gold were discovered in the Greater Antilles during the first decade of colonization, and during 1505-8 Juan de la Cosa removed significant amounts of gold from the Urabá region of northern South America. But it was not until the Aztec conquest of 1519-21, and that of the Inca during the 1530s, that significant wealth was discovered. The distribution of Aztec and Inca treasure by **Hernán Cortés** and **Francisco Pizarro** established America as a place where riches could be had for the taking. Less successful treasure-hunting expeditions included those of Juan Díaz de Solís, who dubbed the estuary draining southern South America Río de la Plata (river of silver); **Francisco Vázquez de Coronado**, who vainly sought seven cities of gold in the deserts of the southwestern United States; **Gonzalo Pizarro**, who sought gold and cinnamon in the Amazon watershed; and **Gonzalo Jiménez de Quesada**, who engaged in a fruitless search for "the gilded man," or El Dorado (1569-72).

1500-1600

From Dyewood to Sugar in Brazil. Brazil's first settlers found little of commercial interest and no high Indian civilizations. At first they bartered with the native Tupí for brazilwood, from which a red dye was extracted. But soon sugar cultivation became the colony's leading economic activity. The first shiploads of sugar departed Brazil in 1526. By 1550 some forty ship-loads of sugar, the product of fifty mills, were sailing from Pernambuco. By 1620 approximately 40 million pounds of sugar were flowing to Europe each year from Brazil's *engenhos* (sugar mills).

1503-c. 1700

Institutions and Mechanisms of Spanish American Economic Control. Spain's principal organ for enforcing economic policy in the Americas was the Casa de Contratación (the Board of Trade), established in Seville in 1503. The Casa's chief task was to enforce mercantile regulations and to encourage the flow of bullion and other products from America to the mother country. It also oversaw the shipment of Spanish manufactures to the Americas. Additionally, the Casa supervised tax collection, judged trade-related disputes, and generally protected the crown's economic interests in Spain's colonial empire.

Closely associated with the Casa de Contratación was Seville's merchant guild, the *consulado*. Merchant members of the *consulado* were given exclusive right to trade with the Americas. In exchange they worked closely with the Casa.

Spain restricted all trade to certain monopoly ports, thus helping ensure that mercantilist restrictions would be honored. All American trade was cleared through the port of Seville (until 1717, when the port of Cádiz took its place). Ships departing Seville were required to deliver their goods at the American ports of Veracruz, Nombre de Dios or Portobelo in Panama, and Cartagena in New Granada. Havana was designated a monopoly port late in the sixteenth century, going on to become the preeminent point of trans-shipment in the Americas.

After 1523, when foreign enemies such as the Englishman Francis Drake and the Dutch Piet Heyn, began to prey on Spanish commerce, a fleet system was implemented to protect the flow of cargo. Protected by an armada, two fleets sailed from Spain each year, one destined for Veracruz and the other for Nombre de Dios or Portobelo. They were then united in Havana, and from there were escorted back to Spain. The fleet system prevailed well into the eighteenth century.

The crown also regulated trade between Mexico and the Philippines, a Spanish possession in the 1560s. By the late sixteenth century galleons of up to 2,000 tons were sailing annually between Acapulco and Manila, sending silver and a few other American products to the Orient in exchange for luxury goods including Chinese silk and porcelain, Japanese lacquerware, Indian fabrics and gemstones, and spices and precious stones from the Philippines and other South Asian regions. Though fears of excessive bullion loss led the crown to limit Asian trade, illegal commerce with the region continued throughout the colonial period. A consequence of the Manila trade was exploration of the coast of California. Returning galleons put in along the California coast to resupply ships' stores.

Portuguese Overseas Control. Portugal's Casa da Índia, established 1501, exercised control over that country's overseas possessions. The Casa was a customshouse, the crown's own trading company, and the supervisor of crown monopolies. Located in Lisbon, it also supervised the licensing and provisioning of overseas expeditions. In 1509 King Manoel I (1495-1521) reorganized the Casa, adding tax collection to its duties as well as refining its code of trade regulation. In 1591 a treasury council was added to the body.

Portuguese overseas administration was less rigorous than Spain's. Until 1580 individuals not associated with merchant guilds, and the ships of other countries, were allowed to trade between Portugal and its overseas possessions.

1540s-c. 1650

Early Mining Booms. The native American treasure that first inflamed Spanish appetite for gold and silver was quickly exhausted. So too were the Antillian gold mines, worked out between 1541 and the early 1560s. Thus succeeding waves of immigrants scoured the countryside searching for new deposits of precious

metals. Their diligence was quickly rewarded. From the mid-sixteenth century well into the seventeenth rich deposits of silver and gold were discovered, increasing European silver and gold reserves by 50 and by 5 percent respectively. Between 1560 and 1685 some 30,000 tons of silver bullion was extracted from American mines. The most notable early silver strike was at Potosí in Upper Peru (Bolivia). The Potosí mine, a veritable mountain of silver, yielded 60 million troy pounds of the precious metal by the end of the colonial period. By 1600 other silver mines opened at Oruro, also in Upper Peru, and Castrovirreina in Lower Peru. Soon thereafter other silver mines were discovered in Chile.

Mexican silver production, which ultimately became preeminent in the Americas, increased more slowly than that of Peru. Mines there began production in the mid-sixteenth century in Zacatecas, Pachuca, Guanajuato, and San Luis Potosí.

The process of silver extraction was significantly enhanced with the use of a mercury-

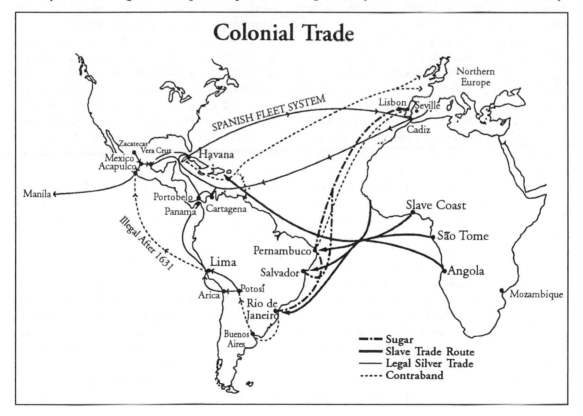

Colonial Trade

based amalgamation process, introduced to Mexico in 1556 and to Peru in 1571. The 1563 discovery of the Huancavelica mercury mine near Lima ensured supplies of that mineral to supplement production at Almadén, Spain.

Spanish America's most productive gold mines were located in New Granada (Colombia), first in the middle and upper Magdalena River Valley, and subsequently in the regions of Antioquia and El Chocó.

1540s-1700

Mining-driven Economic Growth in Peru and Mexico. Mines were the engines of economic growth in early colonial Spanish America. While their operation was supervised from viceregal capitals Lima and Mexico City, it was revenue from the mines that generated the wealth that fueled the bureaucratic apparatus. The mining strikes of the mid-sixteenth century set off silver rushes that quickly swelled populations. Potosí grew from 3,000 in the 1540s to 120,000 by 1680, becoming America's largest city during the seventeenth century.

Mining generated a plethora of economic activities. Thousands of draft animals, especially mules, were needed to transport ore, bullion, and supplies. Thus ranching centers developed at lower elevations to supply the animals, especially in Salta and Tucumán in northwestern Argentina. Foodstuffs flowed in from all areas. High value-added foods were grown in suitable regions immediately peripheral to the mines. Grazing lands were more distant, with animals herded to urban areas for slaughter. A host of artisanal manufactures were made in town and countryside to meet the myriad needs of the mines and those whose livelihoods were related to mining.

Manufacturing was carried out in *obrajes*, workshops specializing in consumer nondurables, particularly textiles. In Peru scores of *obrajes* sprang up in Cajamarca, Cuzco, and Trujillo. By the early seventeenth century Quito and Tucumán became centers of *obraje* production. Each of those manufacturing centers generated its own peripheral zone of agricultural production and animal husbandry. Thus by the early seventeenth

century Peru had become a far-flung, loosely integrated economic region whose commerce flowed over land and sea, and across routes spanning thousands of miles. Distant Chile became part of the system following a 1687 earthquake that disrupted Peruvian grain supplies. Chile soon sent Lima regular shipments of grain, copper, and other products.

The viceroyalty of New Spain developed in similar fashion. Silver mining again drove expansion, but at a more moderate pace. A less mountainous terrain allowed for more diverse agricultural production. The better land in proximity to centers of population was given over to the production of fruits and vegetables, olive orchards, and dairy herds. More distant lands were put into production of maize and wheat, while lands in outlying areas were devoted to ranching, and the growing of maguey plants for pulque production. As in Peru, *obraje*-produced goods were sold in towns and cities. New Spain enjoyed easier access to Spain than did Peru. That, along with its ever-increasing silver production, helped it surpass Peru in wealth and importance in the late colonial period.

By the early seventeenth century New Spain had become the center of an integrated regional economy. The kingdom of Guatemala sold livestock, cacao, cochineal, and indigo in Mexico City, Puebla, and Veracruz in exchange for *obraje* manufactures, especially textiles. Cuba sent cattle to Mexico in exchange for wheat. Mexico threatened to bring Peru into its commercial orbit when trade between the ports of Callao and Acapulco increased during early decades of the seventeenth century. But the crown closed that route in 1631 out of fear that it would increase bullion loss to Asia.

1502-c. 1700

Labor in Spanish America and Brazil. Labor was first acquired in Spanish America through the *encomienda*, an institution of Iberian origin that granted the labor and tribute of a specific group of Indians to a conqueror or other deserving Spaniard, who thereby became an *encomendero*. *Encomiendas* might be bequeathed for one or more generations. Early colonial administrators freely allotted Indian labor to Spanish settlers. The first example of such allocation occurred on the island of Hispaniola, when Governor Nicolás de Ovando parceled out Taíno Indians to Spanish settlers. As the Aztec and Inca empires fell to the Europeans, **Cortés** and the **Pizarros** assigned *encomiendas* ranging from thousands of tributaries to important lieutenants, down to one or two to ordinary soldiers. The *encomienda* was technically not slavery, but it was subject to the same abuses as outright slavery, which was banned by the crown for Indians in the mid-sixteenth century and persisted only in Chile and other frontier zones. Early Spanish settler and cleric **Bartolomé de las Casas** was so angered over the high mortality among *encomienda* Indians on Hispaniola that he devoted his life to attacks on the institution. His campaign at length led to the crown's effort to restrict *encomienda* grants in the New Laws of 1542. In addition, the crown was wary of encouraging the rise of a powerful *encomendero* class in the Indies. There was so much opposition to the New Laws in the Indies that they could not be enforced, though *encomenderos* were increasingly barred from exacting labor from their charges. By the end of the sixteenth century, however, the institution had lost much of its utility owing to sharp declines in Indian populations through disease and abuses by *encomenderos.*

Another institution, a labor levy called the *repartimiento* (also known as the *mita* in Peru, and *cuatequil* in Mexico), became the chief device for allocating Indian labor from the 1560s onward. Similar in many ways to labor drafts under the Inca, *repartimientos* were the allocation of male Indians to Spanish colonists by the state. Recipients of *repartimientos* were obligated to feed, clothe, and house their Indian workers, as well as pay wages, and were allowed to work them for a period of several months. The practice of physical removal of Indians from their homes for extended periods of time, and their transportation to frequently distant work sites, produced high rates of mortality.

By the latter sixteenth century free labor had begun to emerge throughout both Spanish and Portuguese America. A few of such workers were Indians and freed slaves. Most, however, were the mixed-blood progeny of Europeans and Indians or Africans. Those *mestizos* (*mestiços* or *mamelucos* in Portuguese) received wages, though many of them were self-employed, working as craftsmen, yeoman farmers, and manual laborers in a host of occupations.

While race mixture steadily peopled Brazil with mixed-bloods, Portuguese settlers satisfied their initial labor needs through enslavement of native peoples. As in Spanish America, churchmen, notably Jesuit **Antônio Vieira**, worked to end Indian enslavement. But although Portuguese monarchs were sympathetic, they were unable to end the practice. Tens of thousands were enslaved during the sixteenth and seventeenth centuries by *mameluco*-led expeditions originating in São Paulo.

African slave labor became the norm on sugar plantations of northeast Brazil. Slaves first appeared on the sugar estates in 1538, and by 1600 their number had reached 50,000. That number equaled Brazil's Portuguese and mixed-blood population.

1492-c. 1700

Land in Spanish and Portuguese America. In both Spanish and Portuguese America, land was liberally granted to well-placed men who agreed to colonize it. The Portuguese crown first established the donatory system through which enormous tracts were awarded to important national figures. But that system of grants resulted in little colonization and was abandoned in 1549 when Captain-General **Tomé de Sousa** reached Brazil. The colony's first captain-general was instructed to liberally award land to any Portuguese citizen willing to settle it. De Sousa's land grants formed the basis of the colony's sugar industry, based in the *fazendas* of northeastern Brazil.

The crown of Castile claimed dominion over land in Spanish America. It made large grants to leaders of early expeditions who in turn allocated portions of them to their followers. Indian communities had lands set aside for their use.

Lands were also awarded to private persons by viceroys and other administrative agents of the crown in America. While the crown reserved ownership of subsoil resources, it liberally extended usufruct of them, subject only to payment of 20 percent of profits deriving from mining, the *quinto real*; but the so-called 'royal fifth' was quickly reduced to 10 percent or less.

By the seventeenth century a mixed pattern of landholding had emerged, becoming complex around major mining sites, administrative capitals, and manufacturing centers. Proximity to markets determined land use. Labor-intensive agricultural activities on high-priced land prevailed close to population centers while ranching took place on more distant *estancias*.

Since economic growth drove up land values, the securing of clear land titles became increasingly important. The crown had thwarted efforts of the first settlers to turn their grants of *encomiendas* into petty empires. But as time passed descendants of the conquistadores found ways of securing title to land through purchase, inheritance, or usurpation. First in 1591, and again in 1601, 1643, and 1674, title verification was conducted through a process known as *composición*. In all cases *composición* coincided with times of rising land prices caused by increased economic activity.

Problems of Credit and Finance. During the entire colonial period Spanish and Portuguese America suffered from the lack of both a banking system and any reliable means of exchange. Mints were established early in both Mexico (1536) and Peru (1568), but could not maintain standard coinage. The shaving of coins invariably robbed them of their face value. Meanwhile officials of the crown and foreign merchants adeptly drained hard currency from the Americas via taxes, especially through a sales tax known as the *alcabala*. The hoarding of gold and silver also increased the scarcity of specie.

Individuals were driven to find alternate means of exchange. Forms of currency included cacao beans, coca leaf, measures of textiles, flasks of wine, and other high-value, portable items. Often they were forced to resort to barter.

Loans from European banking houses could sometimes be had, but invariably at high rates of interest. Among the elite, transfers of dowry served as a kind of banking mechanism, while merchants commonly lent money among themselves. Monasteries and other institutions associated with the Catholic church were another major source of credit, especially to landowners. One modest but ongoing source of capital was from immigrants to the Americas, many of whom arrived bearing investment capital. Yet in spite of their best efforts, Latin Americans were unable to overcome the limitations imposed upon them by mercantilist fiscal policy.

1600-1700

Economic consolidation in the seventeenth century. The seventeenth century was a time of economic consolidation in Spanish and Portuguese America. Trade settled into predictable patterns. Shipments of bullion remained key, but other products gained importance in trans-Atlantic trade. They included dyes for Europe's textile industry; leather and cordage for freight; luxury consumer goods such as sugar, cacao, and tobacco; and medicinal products such as cinchona bark for the treatment of malaria. Among the items moving from Europe to America were blooded stock for breeding, armaments, fine textiles, wine and olive oil, tools and machinery made of iron and other refined metals.

Brazil's growth slowed during the seventeenth century. Sugar prices fell sharply during the 1620s, and during the following decade the Dutch seized the colony's chief sugar-growing region. When the Dutch were driven out in 1654, they transferred newfound sugar-growing skills to the Caribbean. Exports from Caribbean "sugar islands" acted to prolong Brazil's economic stagnation until the gold rush of the 1690s.

Illegal trade became an increasingly important feature of economic life in Spanish and Portuguese America during the seventeenth century. Neither Spain nor Portugal was capable of satisfying the demand for consumer goods among their American subjects. Market pressures led to the diversion of growing amounts of bullion to illegal commerce. During the 1670s Spain established customshouses in Salta and Tucumán in an attempt to halt the flow of illegal trade with Brazil. Portugal countered by establishing the town of Colônia do Sacramento on the north shore of the Plata estuary, and from it conducted a lively traffic in contraband goods. Thus goods from northern Europe made their way into the hands of Spanish Americans in exchange for Peruvian silver.

Eighteenth Century
Economic Development and Reform

The eighteenth century was a time of population expansion and economic quickening in both Europe and Latin America. Population increase in both places heightened European demand for American products and aided Latin America in meeting that demand. Technological advance also sped the economic growth. Ships became larger and faster, and a host of mechanical inventions heralded the coming industrial age.

Two exciting events ushered in the new century: gold was discovered in Brazil, an event that altered both colony and mother country; and in Spain the Hapsburg dynasty ended and was succeeded by the French House of Bourbon. The influx of Brazilian gold stimulated economic growth in Europe. Spain's House of Bourbon displayed absolutist and reformist attitudes that in time brought substantial economic change to Spanish America.

The Enlightenment ideas percolating through Europe brought economic reform. In Spain enlightened despots and their ministers introduced wide-ranging changes in their American possessions. In Portugal it was the royal minister, the **Marquês de Pombal**, whose mid-century reforms had great bearing on his country's most profitable colony, Brazil.

Over the century peripheral parts of Spanish America grew in importance. They included the greater Río de la Plata region, northern South America, and Central America.

Economic Maturation and Growth in Spanish America. Economic growth in eighteenth-century Spanish America was rooted partly in the area's demographic recovery. High birthrates led to the colonization of virgin lands, as in New Granada where during the late 1700s Antioquian colonists began moving into a broad expanse of the central Andean cordillera lying south of Medellín. By 1800 Spanish America's population approached 14 million, making it a third more populous than Spain. The most populous colony was Mexico, which had close to 5 million inhabitants in 1793. During the course of the eighteenth century Mexico also became the most prosperous colony, mainly because of the expansion of silver production as a result of improved technology and the discovery of new mines. Accordingly, silver production rose from approximately 3.25 million pesos in 1700 to about 27 million pesos by 1804. Meanwhile, silver production in the viceroyalty of Peru languished. It reached a nadir in 1700-20, but even after it began to increase at mid-century, the output of Peru's mines did not approach that of Mexico's.

Spanish America's population growth was also mirrored in the expansion and deepening of regional economies. The cultivation of labor-intensive and lucrative foods such as wheat, fruits and vegetables, and dairy products, continued to drive up land prices around population centers. Thus regional economies continued to grow as less remunerative sorts of agriculture were pushed into more remote areas. The late eighteenth century was attended by the appearance of large cattle-producing *estancias* in northern Mexico, eastern Colombia and Venezuela, southern Brazil and Uruguay, and in the Argentine pampa. Argentina soon exported salted meat to Brazil and the Caribbean for consumption by slaves. Both Central America and Venezuela emerged as producers of cacao, indigo, and tobacco. Tobacco was also an important Mexican product, as were cochineal dye and sugar. By 1800 Cuba was increasingly important as an exporter of cattle and sugar, and Havana had become Spanish America's leading port.

1693-c. 1808

Brazil's Golden Age. Brazil was more lightly populated than Spanish America, possibly having fewer than 1 million inhabitants at the beginning of the eighteenth century. Slightly more than a century later, in 1808, its population stood at just 2.4 million. Half of all Brazilians were slaves.

A major shift in population occurred after the discovery of gold in Minas Gerais, located in the colony's south-central region. Soon from five to six thousand gold hunters were arriving in Minas Gerais annually, many of them from northeastern sugar-growing regions. Half of the new arrivals were slaves. The gold rush reinvigorated the flow of slaves from Africa to Brazil, and made the colony the single greatest destination of slaves in the Americas. The strikes continued through the early eighteenth century. In 1718 gold was discovered in Cuiabá, and in 1734 far inland in Mato Grosso. During the 1720s diamonds were discovered in Minas Gerais, and a diamond district was established there in 1734.

Brazilian mines produced 80 percent of all gold mined during the eighteenth century. From the 1730s through the 1760s ten tons were taken annually from alluvial and subterranean deposits, dropping to five tons annually toward the end of the century. Some effects of the bonanza were negative. Portugal allowed national industry to decline during the 1700s, preferring to purchase manufactures abroad, principally from England. That practice caused it to enter the nineteenth century with a stagnant and underdeveloped economy. It also rendered both Portugal and Brazil highly dependent upon England.

But the mining rush had a significant effect upon the physical growth of Brazil. It drew population away from the coast where it had been concentrated for two centuries, sending it into the colony's vast interior. As had been the case in Peru and New Spain, vigorous economies quickly sprang up around the mines. As in most mineral rushes, greater fortunes were made through selling goods to miners than by searching out gold and diamonds. And as had been the case in Spanish America, backland ranches sprang up to provide cattle, horses, and mules for the mines.

Brazil's mineral rush played a vital integrative role for the colony. The fact that the mines were two hundred miles inland forced the creation of roads linking the mining district to Rio de Janeiro and São Paulo. The same process linked the sugar-growing Northeast to the gold and diamond fields. Meanwhile the vastly dispersed inland estates became linked to one another and to the mining districts through trails extending along the frontier for many hundred miles. Inland Brazil thus became linked by rustic highways extending as far south as Spanish territory, to the distant Banda Oriental (Uruguay) and Río de la Plata. By the end of the century Brazil possessed a vast though lightly populated inland ranching frontier running from Maranhão in the far north to the Plata estuary in the south. Livestock and hides were traded all along its nearly 2,000-mile extension (along with smuggled gold and diamonds), calling into existence what has been called Brazil's "age of leather." *Yerba mate*, the strong mineral-rich tea grown in Paraguay and northeastern Argentina, was traded northward into Brazil. More easily transported than other frontier products, *yerba mate* also served as a medium of exchange.

Yet another product of Brazilian frontier expansion was settlement of the colony's far south, the region of Rio Grande do Sul. Contiguous with the Banda Oriental of the Río de la Plata, the *riograndenses* developed a gaucho culture like that of Uruguay and Argentina. Because Rio Grande enjoys a temperate climate, it supported the growing of wheat and other temperate-climate crops.

Economic Reform. The dynastic change bringing the House of Bourbon to the Spanish throne ushered in an era of reform. Spain's Bourbon monarchs, especially **Charles III** (1759-88), were imbued with a spirit of absolutism, but they also possessed a rationalist turn of mind leading them to reexamine colonial policy with an eye to streamlining and modernizing colonial administration. Their measures were known collectively as the Bourbon Reforms. They began with institutions of governance, in 1714 replacing the conciliar system of the Hapsburgs with a ministry system. The Council of the Indies thus became the Ministry of Marine and Indies, a body more directly controlled by the crown. In 1790 the Casa de Contratación was abolished. Colonial jurisdictions were also modernized. A new viceroyalty, that of Nueva Granada, was created in 1717 (soon abolished and reestablished in 1739), followed some decades later by that of Río de la Plata (1776). In part because of a desire to appropriate Jesuit wealth, Charles III suppressed the religious order throughout the empire in 1767.

A concerted effort to improve tax collection throughout Spanish America began in the 1760s. Newly created officials (intendants) with extensive powers were sent to America and charged with increasing crown revenues at the regional level. They did so with considerable success. Growing economic prosperity and the urgency of levying war-related taxes also worked to increase revenues. But so too did trade-enhancing measures such as the reduction of ad valorem duties to 6 percent.

Early in the century the crown attempted to increase trade and lessen smuggling through the formation of monopoly trading companies. In 1714 it chartered the Honduras Company, in 1728 the Caracas Company, in 1740 the Havana Company, and in 1758 the Santo Domingo Company. Only the Caracas Company achieved notable success in stimulating trade and development. Those experiments with mercantile companies were prompted by English and Dutch successes with monopoly companies organized during the seventeenth century.

The inroads of contraband and the disruptions caused by the War of the Spanish Succession (1701-13) led to the decline of the fleet system by 1750, though occasional fleets sailed to New Spain until 1789. Meanwhile, the crown was moving toward a policy of free trade within the empire. Nine Spanish ports were declared free to trade with the Caribbean in 1765. The same privilege was extended to Louisiana in 1768 , to Campeche and Yucatán in 1770, to ports in New

Granada during 1776-77, and to all of Spanish America save New Spain and Venezuela in 1778. By 1790 Spanish merchants were allowed to trade freely everywhere in Spanish America.

Eighteenth-century economic quickening was also reflected in the formation of new *consulados* in regions that earlier were economically undeveloped peripheral regions. Between 1793 and 1795 *consulados* were established in Caracas, Guatemala City, Buenos Aires, Havana, Cartagena, Santiago de Chile, Veracruz, and Guadalajara, which testified to their economic emergence.

Spain's Bourbon Reforms had their counterpart in the measures taken in Portugal by the **Marquês de Pombal**. The energetic Pombal governed Portugal from 1750 to 1777, implementing sweeping changes to tighten political administration at home and in the colonies. In 1755 a Board of Trade was created to stimulate Portuguese industry, and the Royal Treasury was reformed in 1761 to improve revenue collection. Brazil, Portugal's most important foreign possession, also figured prominently in his plans. Among Pombal's Brazilian reforms were measures to tighten tax collection and to restrict trade in contraband. He instituted quality controls for sugar in order to increase exports of that commodity (though it was the disruption of sugar supplies during the American, French, and Haitian revolutions that revived Brazil's sugar industry).

Like the Spanish, Pombal rechartered monopoly companies to the end of invigorating trade to northern Brazil. His model was the earlier Company of Brazil (1649), which had been formed under the urging of Jesuit Father **Antônio Vieira**. In 1755 Pombal chartered the Company of Grão Pará and Maranhão, which was given exclusive right to trade in northern Brazil and to import slaves there. Four years later he authorized the Company of Pernambuco and Paraíba, for trade to the northeastern coastal region. The suppression of the Jesuit order in 1759 allowed Pombal to seize its substantial holdings in Brazil.

Two of Pombal's reforms were especially important. His movement of the colony's capital from Bahia to Rio was intelligent given the increasing movement of population southward. His encouragement of new crops in the south—indigo, rice, and especially coffee—heralded a singularly important economic development.

In spite of Pombal's reforms, Brazil's economy was stagnant during the latter eighteenth century. The effect of declining Brazilian gold production could not be reversed by reforms dictated in Portugal. Mercantile restrictions, such as a 1785 ban on Brazilian textile production, reinforced the colony's dependence on Portugal and, by extension, on England, patron of the Portuguese crown.

The Bourbon and Pombaline economic reforms were designed primarily to benefit Spain and Portugal. But in that they quickened economic activity throughout Latin America, their overall impact upon the region was positive.

Economic Developments

1808-1850

Latin America ended Iberian economic domination between 1808 and 1825. The struggle for independence, which had significant origins in colonial-era mercantilist restrictions, and which extended to 1825, disrupted the economy of much of Spanish America. Mines flooded, labor supplies diminished, real property was destroyed, and capital fled. The sharp declines of 1810-25 were followed by economic stagnation extending to mid-century.

But economic decline was not universal during Latin America's independence and early national periods. British merchants and entrepreneurs appeared in port cities of Brazil and Argentina as early as 1808, seeking markets for their manufactures and raw materials and foodstuffs. During the second quarter of the century, North American imports began to appear in some markets, especially Cuba and Mexico. Among the economic bright spots were Chile, where mining produced significant export earnings after 1830, and Cuba, where slave-

produced sugar earned high revenues for Spain's remaining American colony. Elsewhere, however, slow growth was the rule. Mexico, Central America, and much of Andean America suffered the combined impact of political upset, insufficient sources of investment capital, and inadequate ports and highways. While the early phase of industrialization in Europe made for favorable terms of trade for Latin American exports, the flow of raw materials was hindered by poor roads and ports, and by political instability. Until mid-century most of the region was characterized by parochial markets supplied by artisanal manufactures.

1808-1825

The End of Mercantilist Restrictions and British Influence. During the period 1808-9 Brazilian and Argentine ports were opened to world commerce, followed in 1818 by Chile, and in 1821 by Peru. Initially it was British merchants who took advantage of the opening. Between 1809 and 1811 the British supplied 35 percent of all foreign imports to the region. During the second decade of the century British imports were evenly divided between those sold in Brazil and those sold in Spanish America. Trade treaties negotiated in 1810 granted Britain preferential treatment in Brazilian commerce, a condition that endured until 1844. Elsewhere the British negotiated similar trade agreements in exchange for recognition of the new nations.

Exports. Spanish America began to expand commercially during the 1830s and 1840s. In 1834 Venezuela ended restrictions on contractual agreements, with the result that coffee exports grew rapidly. By 1840 coffee represented 40 percent of Venezuelan exports. Guano accounted for over half of Peru's exports by mid-century. During the 1840s Chile became a major silver exporter. Cuba, which remained a Spanish colony, held its position as the region's major sugar exporter. In the Río de la Plata region wool and salted meat produced in plants called *saladeros* became important exports. Meanwhile, by 1830 coffee had overtaken sugar as Brazil's leading export.

Fiscal Constraints on Industry and Government. Scarcity of investment capital severely hindered economic growth in the decades following independence. Capital fled the region during the decades of warfare. While there was a brief enthusiasm for Latin American government bonds during the early 1820s, high rates of default on bond issues closed that source of lending. Commercial banks were weak or nonexistent, and neither domestic nor foreign investors dared risk financial commitment to Latin America. There was little development of industry prior to mid-century, though the quantity of raw material exports did invigorate artisanal production in many areas. Shut out of international capital markets, Latin American governments were forced to rely heavily upon tariffs for the generation of revenue. Colombia, for example, which abolished the *alcabala* (sales tax) in 1836, and eliminated the tobacco monopoly in 1850, supplied half of all government revenues through customs revenues, raised chiefly through taxes on foreign imports.

Labor Supply, and the Ending of Slavery and Caste Distinctions. Except in Cuba and Puerto Rico, which remained under Spanish control, the wars of independence sundered social relations, which in turn produced a shortage of labor in many places. The new liberal and egalitarian ideology of independence brought laws abolishing slavery (Chile, 1823; Central America, 1824; Mexico, 1829) or freeing children born to slave women (Chile, 1811; Argentina, 1813; Gran Colombia, 1821; Peru, 1821). The abolition of legal discrimination against members of the black, mixed-blood, and Indian populations occurred gradually over the decades following independence. This had the effect of helping to intensify economic stagnation during the 1830s and 1840s, for it freed bound workers. The great exceptions were Brazil and Cuba, where thousands of slaves were imported over the first half of the nineteenth century in defiance of international treaties. Agriculture there, notably sugar cane and coffee production, enjoyed spectacular increases as a result.

Domestic Manufactures and Internal Trade and Commerce. Low levels of productivity and high levels of inefficiency characterized Latin American manufactures in the postindependence period. Most goods were produced through cottage industry or in primitive and labor-intensive workshops (*obrajes*) where goods of high quality were sometimes produced but whose unit cost was high. Handicrafts supplied most consumption needs, owing to the general scarcity and relatively high cost of imports. Very few countries attempted to import modern manufacturing techniques, Mexico being the most notable case. Prior to mid-century the state sponsored creation of a modern textile industry, employing protection, import taxes, and a state-supported bank to pay for equipment. Generally there was little consensus for state encouragement of the nonexport manufacturing sector in the decades following independence.

Latin America's Export Boom

1850-1929

By mid-century most Latin American leaders were convinced that the way to national prosperity lay in the export of foodstuffs and raw materials. Europe and the increasingly industrialized United States offered premium prices for Latin American exports, and foreign capitalists were eager to invest in the railroads, highways, and ports required to speed the flow of foods, minerals, and nonfood agricultural products to foreign markets.

Thanks to such encouragement there was steady increase in the flow of Latin American exports to Europe and the United States from the 1850s through the 1920s. While World War I sharply curtailed exports for a time, trade rebounded during the postwar period, reaching unprecedented levels in the years prior to 1930. Latin America's tropical exports enjoyed excellent terms of trade, surpassing those of the region's chief temperate-zone exports, wheat and cattle. Monies earned through exports freed local investors from dependence on foreign capital sources. Meanwhile real wages increased modestly, from 10 to 25 percent from the 1870s to the 1920s. National economies became monetized during the period, stimulating the growth of rural and urban middle classes.

Until the Great Depression, Latin American leaders were optimistic about their export-driven economy. Politics had stabilized following the dislocations of the independence era and the period of *caudillismo* and civil war between Liberals and Conservatives. They were generally satisfied with Latin America's role in the international economy, convinced that as the doctrine of comparative advantage instructed, their region properly exchanged its raw materials for manufactured goods.

Incipient modernization was manifest throughout the region. Export revenues paid for improved sanitation and drinking water, bringing marked improvement in public health for all social groups. Social diversification moved apace, spurred by growing economic complexity. Nondurable consumer goods, notably processed foods and simple manufactures, began to be produced in most countries. The countryside around towns and cities was increasingly the home of yeoman farmers dedicated to supplying foodstuffs to the growing number of urban dwellers.

Economic change gave rise to social movements, especially among urban workers. Labor organization occurred throughout Latin America during the first decades of the twentieth century, though its gains were modest owing to low levels of urbanization and industrialization. It was in Mexico where the costs of Latin America's insertion into the global economy became most apparent. In 1910 peasants displaced by the move to commercial agriculture were among those who rose in revolt against a government that had failed to address their grievances.

But up to 1930 few Latin Americans saw the Mexican Revolution as anything more than an isolated event. Elites considered Argentina the nation to be emulated. That Southern Cone leader witnessed the transformation of domestic agriculture during its decades of extraordinary export of grain and meat to European markets. By 1930, Argentina had an industrial base, a vigorous

middle class, and pretensions to world leadership. It stood as a paramount example of Latin American progress through raw material exports.

1850-1914

Latin America's Leading Exports by Country. Argentina was the region's leading exporter. With only 10 percent of Latin America's population, it shipped 30 percent of all exports, chiefly wheat, corn, and meat, by 1900. Uruguay, too, supplied meat to the European market, though wool was its principal export.

Coffee was the chief export of Brazil, accounting for more than 80 percent of the world supply by 1901. Coffee accounted for more than 50 percent of export revenues in Venezuela, Nicaragua, El Salvador, Guatemala, and Haiti by the turn of the century. Although coffee produced less than half of Colombia's export revenue in 1914, vast plantings were under way at that time. By 1930 Colombia had become the world's second coffee exporter after Brazil, earning some 70 percent of its export revenue by that commodity.

Bananas were the leading export of Honduras, Panama, and Costa Rica. Sugar was the chief export of Cuba and Puerto Rico, while both sugar and cacao dominated exports in the Dominican Republic.

Tin accounted for 72 percent of Bolivian exports, while nitrates and copper represented 78 percent of Chilean exports (71 percent and 7 percent respectively). Forty-six percent of Mexican export revenues were earned by silver and copper (30 percent and 10 percent respectively) in 1901.

Among the larger nations, Peru's exports were best diversified at the end of the nineteenth century, with 22 percent earned by copper, 15 percent by sugar, and the remainder by a range of tropical products including rubber, quinine, and dye woods.

Economic Growth and Per Capita Earnings from Exports. By the eve of World War I, export-driven economic growth was more than double the rate of population increase (3.9 percent as opposed to 1.5 percent). That resulted in satisfactory levels of employment and modest wage increases across the region, with Argentina and Chile showing the highest rates of growth and lowest levels of unemployment. Colombia, Peru, Costa Rica, and El Salvador also experienced significant export-led growth, as did Mexico up to the outbreak of its 1910 revolution.

Latin America's export earnings were $20 per capita on the eve of World War I. That was one-quarter of British-dominion export earnings, but equivalent to those of the United States. Cuba and Argentina led Latin American exporters, with per capita earnings through exports above $60.

Principal Trade Partners for Exports and Imports. Between 1850 and 1914 Britain bought better than half of all Argentine, Chilean, Bolivian, and Peruvian exports; Germany was Uruguay's best customer; and France purchased a majority of Venezuelan, Haitian, and Ecuadorian exports. Elsewhere by 1914 the United States was the chief consumer of Latin American exports.

By 1914, Mexico and nations of the Caribbean and Central America bought more than half of their imported goods from the United States. Meanwhile South American countries purchased half or more of their imports from Britain and Germany. In terms of products, Great Britain was the region's chief supplier of textiles, Germany and France supplied luxury items, and the United States was Latin America's main vendor of agricultural and mining equipment.

Land, Labor, and Urban–Rural Ratios. Significant areas of land were opened to commercial agriculture during the 1850-1914 interval. In Mexico the state did so through the break-up of Indian *ejidos* (communal landholdings) and the seizure of church properties. In Argentina the military swept Indians from the southern pampa in the "conquest of the desert" in 1879. In Colombia expanses of the Andean cordillera were colonized by coffee farmers. Everywhere, however, the concentration of landownership, typically affecting the best portions of national terrain, acted as a drag on agricultural productivity.

Improvements in public health stimulated population growth. In the Southern Cone, especially Argentina and Uruguay, immigration also contributed to the increase. In 1914, 90 percent of Latin Americans lived in rural areas, except in Argentina where some 30 percent of the population was urbanized.

Capital. Banking remained underdeveloped throughout most of the region. Owing to the absence of national banking systems, foreign banks were the most successful financial institutions. But even they were limited as a majority of the citizenry remained outside the money economy. Save for Argentina, per capita circulation of bank notes averaged between $4 and $5 across the region. Foreign investment, both direct and portfolio, was relatively modest, save in Argentina, Brazil, Chile, Cuba, and Mexico, and amounted to approximately $8.5 billion in 1914. Investment capital in the form of loans originated in Britain, except in Mexico, Central America, and the Caribbean, where U.S. investment predominated. Foreign direct investment was significant as well. British capital played a major role in railroad construction in Argentina and Brazil, while U.S. investors were dominant in Mexico until 1908, when the government acquired control of the principal lines.

Foreigners also invested heavily in mining during the late nineteenth and early twentieth centuries. The Guggenheim interests were active in Mexican and Chilean mining, and the American colonel William Greene established the large Cananea Consolidated Copper Company in Sonora, Mexico. After 1900 foreign oil men developed Mexico's petroleum industry, notably the American Edward L. Doheny and the British businessman Sir Weetman Pearson. By the mid-1920s large foreign companies, such as Royal Dutch/Shell and Standard Oil of New Jersey (now Exxon), were beginning to exploit Venezuelan deposits. Agricultural production generally remained in the hands of Latin Americans, but in Central America the United Fruit Company and other American firms dominated the banana industry. By 1920 American corporations produced more than half of Cuba's sugar. In addition, Germans produced sugar in Peru and established coffee plantations in Guatemala. German and French investors were also prominent in the manufacture of consumer goods, such as beer and textiles.

Internal Economic Change. Prior to World War I the largest part of Latin America's labor force was involved in domestic agricultural production for the home market. Whether peons working on haciendas, or frontier settlers, agricultural workers were largely outside the money economy and not engaged in mechanized farming.

In spite of Latin America's rural character, foodstuffs accounted for some 20 percent of imports prior to World War I. That discouraged the expansion of agricultural production for domestic consumption, sending it into decline in some countries. Population growth aggravated the situation, as it dampened incentives to increase production through mechanization. Thus while the export boom and resulting flow of hard currency stimulated national economies, they did not modernize the large domestic-use agricultural sector.

Manufacturing remained modest save in Argentina, Mexico, and Brazil, as most national elites maintained an ideological commitment to raw material exports as instructed by the doctrine of comparative advantage. Lack of domestic markets and transportation infrastructure for domestic trade were also formidable barriers to internal economic development. Additionally, foreign manufactures were cheaper and of better quality than those made domestically. Thus, by 1914, 75 percent of Latin American manufactures were of only the most basic sort: foods, textiles, and clothing. There was no significant trade among Latin American nations either, owing to the same array of factors hindering internal commerce.

By 1914, Latin America's economic leaders—Argentina, Uruguay, and Chile—enjoyed income levels of between $400 and $500 per capita GDP (which, nevertheless, was less than half that of fellow raw material exporters Canada, Australia, and New Zealand). Sugar- and coffee-exporting Cuba and Puerto Rico possessed per capita GDPs of between $400 and $350,

respectively. The per capita GDPs of most other republics were in the $100-$200 range, reflecting the combined impact of political instability and economic underdevelopment.

1914-18

The Impact of World War I. The single most important consequence of World War I was to consolidate the U.S. economic presence in Latin America. Germany was immediately replaced by the United States as a capital equipment supplier, and the U.S. superseded the British in all markets save those in southern South America. From 1913 to 1927, U.S. trade to Latin America increased by 80 percent; and by the latter 1920s some 60 percent of all Mexican, Central American, and Caribbean trade, both import and export, was conducted with the United States. The general effect of that shift was to intensify Latin America's economic dependence and to delay its abandoning of the export model.

Suspension of the gold standard in 1914 had an immediate negative impact upon finance. National currencies grew unstable and inflated. European loans dried up, and many previously issued were recalled. Until U.S. lenders replaced those in Britain and continental Europe, Latin American governments were forced to finance their own debt. The sharp reductions in tariff revenues, through which governments earned a major portion of their monies, intensified their penury. Most governments slashed public spending, throwing thousands who derived their incomes directly or indirectly from the government out of work. Meanwhile a beleaguered citizenry found its money buying less as prices rose and the cost of imported goods soared. Thus World War I had the effect of increasing hardship at all levels of society, which in turn produced social unrest. That was especially the case in urban areas where labor became more vocal. Workers staged general strikes in Rio de Janeiro in 1917, and in Lima in 1919. In 1919 Buenos Aires was shaken by seven days of rioting, and soldiers fired on demonstrating workers in downtown Bogotá. War-induced social dislocations were less severe in Central America and the Caribbean, owing to their proximity to U.S. markets.

Domestic manufacturing was not greatly stimulated by the war. While the conflict sharply reduced importation of foreign products, economic hardship shrunk demand for domestically produced goods. Another limiting factor was the unavailability of the capital equipment required to expand production.

Even as it failed to stimulate generalized growth of Latin American industry, the conflict worked to reinforce regional dependence on raw material exports. Venezuelan petroleum, Chilean nitrates, and Bolivian tin were in increasing demand as the war progressed, often commanding bonanza prices. Countries exporting nonstrategic raw materials were less fortunate. Coffee-exporting Brazil and Colombia, for example, suffered declines in their terms of trade of up to 50 percent.

1919-29

Weakening of the Export Model. Economic developments during the immediate postwar period illustrated the increasing weaknesses of the export model. The region experienced a sharp depression during 1920-21 brought on by a collapse in export prices. Hardship spread through the export sector and was followed by the outflow of foreign exchange, a fall in the money supply, sharp reductions in imports, declines in government revenue, and a fall in the value of national currencies. Those dislocations both underlined Latin America's continued vulnerability before external economic shocks and the underdeveloped state of national financial institutions. In Cuba, for example, sugar prices skyrocketed after the war, producing a frenzied boom known as the "dance of the millions." The collapse of prices in late 1920 caused an economic crisis.

Latin American states made a concerted effort to strengthen both their currencies and their banking systems during the early 1920s. The middle and upper classes demanded financial stability, resulting in a return to the gold standard in most places. As fiscal reform was a

prerequisite to the renewal of foreign lending, governments sought advice from foreign advisors, most notably from North American economist Edwin Kemmerer. Among the nations hosting missions headed by Kemmerer, who became known as "the Money Doctor," were Mexico, Guatemala, Colombia, Ecuador, Peru, Bolivia, and Chile. Along with endorsing the gold standard as a means of curbing inflation, Kemmerer helped establish central banks in the republics seeking his advice. He also proposed mechanisms for improving fiscal control, such as the creation of national comptrollers and the regular auditing of national accounts. Kemmerer was less successful in convincing Latin Americans to reform their system of taxation. As a result, some 60 percent of taxes continued to be derived from import and export duties, while less than 5 percent came from taxes on income and property. Consequently, while the economic reforms of the 1920s were significant, they proved too timid to insulate Latin American from fluctuations in export markets.

The rise to economic dominance by the United States worked to Latin America's disadvantage in several ways. Southern Cone exporters suffered because their grains and cattle were not competitive in U.S. markets. Meanwhile Argentina and Uruguay found the British market increasingly restricted because of that nation's policy of imperial preferences. Global investment, a portion of it even originating in Latin America, flowed into the United States, only to be returned to Latin America in the form of abundant loans. While the bulk of those monies was invested in railroads, highways, and other such infrastructure, significant portions of the loans were squandered. The United States thus encouraged excessive borrowing in its sister republics, a phenomenon dubbed the "dance of the millions" by Colombian politician **Laureano Gómez**.

Also contributing to the slowing of Latin America's export boom was the greater integration of Central European economies into those of industrialized Western Europe. This both lessened Europe's dependence upon Latin America's raw materials and contributed to a stagnation of prices.

Technological advances worked to the disadvantage of certain exports. The development of synthetic nitrates in years following the war devastated Chile's nitrate industry, a blow only partially softened by improvements in copper extraction. Some exports suffered sharp declines owing to new competition. Between 1901-10 and 1931-40 plantation-grown natural rubber from Asia reduced Brazilian rubber exports by more than 50 percent, while plantation-grown African cacao provided stiff competition to Brazilian, Ecuadorian, and other Latin American exporters.

Only Brazil, Chile, and Uruguay registered significant departures from the export model. Brazil had maintained high coffee prices through its valorization program, begun in 1906 and reinstated in 1920. Revenues generated through coffee exports, coupled with a loose money policy and tariff protection, stimulated significant industrial growth in the state of São Paulo. Chile, thanks to high nitrate earnings during the war years and to equally high copper earnings following the collapse of nitrate demand, built an industrial base that enabled it to manufacture 80 percent of its nondurable consumer goods by 1929. Uruguay created its manufacturing base thanks to taxes levied on its agricultural sector, an innovation of the social democratic regime of **José Batlle y Ordóñez**.

These examples notwithstanding, export trade continued to dominate Latin American economies at the end of the 1920s. In Argentina, industrial leader in 1929, only 19.5 percent of GDP was generated through manufacturing. Uruguay's proportion was 15.6 percent, Chile's 12.6 percent, Brazil's 12.5 percent, and Mexico's 11.8 percent. Meanwhile 30 percent of revenues generated throughout the region came from traditional exports, and combined revenues earned through exports and imports ran between 50 percent and 60 percent of GDP. Moreover, the top three exports earned better than 50 percent of GDP in a majority of Latin American nations on the eve of the Great Depression. Latin American nations clearly remained subject to vicissitudes of the global market in 1929.

Inward-looking Development: The Shift to Import-Substituting Industrialization

1930-1969

The contraction of international trade touched off by the New York stock market crash of late 1929 encouraged Latin American leaders to develop ways of shielding their nations from the vicissitudes of the global market. Over the decade of the 1930s and on through the years of World War II, leaders worked to construct an industrial base in their respective countries. In the process they created their countries' first integrated national markets.

Developing import-substituting industry (ISI) became avowed national policy during the postwar years. Commitment to ISI growth continued to guide the efforts of economic planners through the 1960s. Only when ISI development had been pushed to maximum limits did Latin America's leaders return to export-driven economic strategies.

1930-38

Toward Inward-looking Development. Latin American exports suffered sharp declines in both price and quantity between 1929 and 1932. Mineral-exporting Bolivia and Chile were hardest hit, the latter nation witnessing an 83 percent fall in the purchasing power of its exports. As the world price of sugar fell from 2.18 cents per pound in 1928 to less than a penny in 1932, Cuba experienced economic turmoil that weakened support for dictator **Gerardo Machado**. Partly in response to the crisis, the U.S. Congress enacted the Jones-Costigan Act (1934), which allotted a share of the U.S. market to Cuba and other foreign sugar producers. Countries trading nonmineral exports and having some diversity of product, or developing significant new exports, were less severely affected. Among those were Argentina, Brazil, Ecuador, Peru, and Central America. Least harmed by the global depression was Venezuela, whose petroleum was in constant demand throughout the decade. Regionally, however, prices of exports fell by nearly two-thirds between 1928 and 1932.

The disruption of international trade played havoc with national finances. As currencies deflated, debt service became onerous; nor were there new loans available to help meet payments. As most currencies were tied to the gold standard, countries witnessed an accelerating flight of their international reserves, raising the specter of national insolvency.

Economic planners took a number of steps to avert fiscal disaster. Most of them removed their countries from the gold standard within two years of the trade collapse and instituted exchange controls aimed at fiscal stabilization. They restricted imports through quotas and tariffs and suspended foreign debt payments, though no country repudiated its debt. Instead most announced their intention to resume interest payments in the near future, while effecting repayment schemes, often involving the issuing of government bonds. Only oil-rich Venezuela escaped depression-induced hardship. That nation paid off its foreign debt prior to the death of dictator **Juan Vicente Gómez** in 1935. Argentina avoided default thanks only to extraordinary measures taken by itself and its principal creditor, Great Britain.

Both manufacturing and nonexport agriculture benefited from the downturn in international trade. At the same time export prices soon rebounded as international tensions increased over the decade and nations stepped up purchases of strategic materials. Thus, following brief initial hardship Latin American exports registered a 6.3 percent annual increase between 1932 and 1939 (save in Argentina and Mexico, where exports stagnated). Export earnings continued to provide the muscle for growth in import-substituting industry (ISI) and import-substituting agriculture (ISA). For that reason the Great Depression did not lead to significant structural change in Latin America.

To offset negative effects of the trade collapse, national leaders encouraged import-substituting industrial growth in a variety of ways. They raised tariff barriers and discouraged imports through foreign exchange rationing and currency devaluation. For those reasons industry grew 7 percent annually in Latin America between 1932 and 1939. Nations enjoying the best rates of growth had an industrial base in place at the depression's onset: Argentina, Brazil, Mexico, Chile, Peru, Colombia, and Uruguay. Consumers played their role by increasing purchases of domestic manufactures during the decade, encouraged to do so by the scarcity of imports and their high prices.

Processed foods and textiles were the most common Latin American manufactures during the 1930s, though consumer durables, chemicals, metals, and paper products made their appearance in Argentina, Brazil, and Mexico. Still, at the end of 1939 industrial concerns remained small, averaging just 20-25 workers per establishment. And industry's contribution to GDP was modest, running between 9 percent and 18 percent everywhere save Argentina, where it totaled 22.7 percent. In dollar terms, manufactured goods reached $122 per capita in Argentina in 1939, $84 in Uruguay, and $77 in Chile. While those figures were low in comparison with the world's leading industrialized nations, they considerably surpassed Peru's $29, Brazil's $24, and Colombia's $17. Worker productivity was low throughout Latin America. Antiquated equipment, low levels of electrification, poor capitalization of plants, and poorly educated work forces contributed to low productivity, even in industry leader Argentina, where labor produced at just 25 percent the U.S. average.

State intervention in the economy was not yet the rule in Latin America. Most industrial firms were privately owned, and governments only indirectly encouraged industrialization. Among the exceptions was Argentina, which gave exclusive control of new oil fields to a state enterprise, Yacimientos Petrolíferos Fiscales (YPF), in 1922. Uruguay embarked on a statist course during the 1920s. Bolivia and Mexico nationalized their petroleum industries in 1937 and 1938, respectively.

Central American and Caribbean nations made significant gains in the development of import-substituting agriculture during the 1930s, lacking as they did the prerequisites for ISI growth. Elsewhere ISA made gains as part of the generalized quickening of domestic economies following the initial trade contraction of 1929-32. ISA development was particularly fast in the hinterlands of rapidly growing urban areas. Rising land prices there forced the cultivation of higher value-added crops. Thus the fortunes of ever-larger numbers of peasants were linked to those of urban dwellers, having the effect of bringing them into the money economy.

Incipient industrialization called for infrastructural improvements. Highway construction was widespread, as was the expansion of electric generating capacity. Air transportation likewise developed rapidly, especially in the Andean nations. Airlines operating in Colombia, for example, logged more than a million miles in 1939.

For these reasons Latin America did not suffer exceptional depression-related hardship in the years following 1932. Its initial inward-turning was positive, as reflected in an annual 5 percent increase in GDP throughout the region during 1932-39. The overall effect of the Great Depression was to loosen the link between national economies and the export model. Most nations enacted modest fiscal reforms during the 1930s, replacing export-related taxes with direct ones on sales, incomes, and land.

The 1930s was a transitional decade in terms of the shift from the export model to that of inward-looking development. Latin America's quick recovery from the depression enhanced the reputations of national economic planners—Argentine central bank director **Raúl Prebisch**, for example. Inflation remained low in spite of loose money policies, allowing domestic consumers to purchase locally produced manufactures. The Great Depression had the positive effect of stimulating domestic economies across Latin America.

1939-45

The Impact of World War II. The impact of World War II upon Latin America's economy was twofold: it led to great strengthening of U. S. economic penetration of the region, and it brought the state more prominently into economic management and planning than at any previous time. Flowing from those changes, and of growing significance at war's end, were increasing nationalism and a desire to moderate U.S. influence through import substitution.

When hostilities began in 1939 some two-thirds of Latin American trade was with nations other than the United States (30 percent with Great Britain and Europe, 6 percent with sister republics, and 32 percent with Asia and other world regions). With onset of the war, trade with continental Europe ceased (14 percent of the total); and that conducted with Britain declined from 16 percent to 13 percent of the total. By 1941, the United States consumed 54 percent of Latin America's exports and provided 62 percent of its imports. The overall trade share enjoyed by the United States stood at 54 percent in 1941 and 49 percent in 1945.

Latin America rallied to the Allied cause as the war unfolded. By early 1943 all nations save Argentina had severed diplomatic and commercial relations with the Axis powers or had declared war on them. They first pledged their economic cooperation with the Allies at the Inter-American Conference in Panama, in September 1939. That meeting led to the establishment of agencies whose goal was to enhance Latin America's ability to contribute its raw materials and manufactures to the war effort. An Inter-American Development Commission was established to stimulate the flow of strategic materials to U.S. industry, and to encourage industrial growth within Latin America. Steps were taken to provide U.S. financial aid and expertise in currency stabilization. By 1945, the United States had extended over $271 million in loans to Latin America, chiefly through the Export-Import Bank (established 1934) and the Lend-Lease program. The greatest single project funded by those loans was Brazil's Volta Redonda steel mill, whose construction began in 1941 and was completed in 1946. The United States also led in promoting price stabilization of coffee and other tropical exports and in developing intra-regional trade. The Inter-American Coffee Convention, effected in 1941, ensured markets and favorable prices to all coffee-producing states.

While inter-American economic cooperation stopped short of the establishment of a regional customs union, bilateral agreements nearly tripled trade among Latin American states between 1939 and 1945 (from 9 percent to 25 percent).

Between 1939 and 1945 the region's industry grew at an annual rate of 5.7 percent, with significant expansion in the area of semi-durable consumer goods. Such growth was especially notable in Argentina, Brazil, Chile, Mexico, Venezuela, and Colombia, where steel, chemicals, cement, plastics, rubber, and petrochemicals were manufactured in increasing quantity. Joint ventures with U.S. firms contributed to that growth, which brought a small capital goods industry into existence by war's end. In those six republics industry grew 7 percent annually during the interval 1939-45.

State intervention in the economy became ever more important as the war progressed. The rapid industrial growth coupled with agricultural stagnation (agriculture expanded a mere 0.6 percent annually in the six nations that led in industrial growth) sped urbanization at a time of significant inflation. The cost of living doubled during the war years as government spending grew and the price of imported goods escalated. By the mid-1940s labor unrest was a constant feature of Latin American life.

As foreign exchange poured in and as high prices for imported goods combined to increase inflation (12.6 percent annually between 1939 and 1945), governments attempted to slow price increases through a range of measures. These included price freezes, multiple exchange rates, reduction of disposable income through direct taxes, and forced purchase of government securities.

While World War II worked to the benefit of Latin America's economy, it left nations with overvalued currencies. In 1945, when the war ended, exports entered a period of stagnation. The war-time boom had increased income disparities even as it left a majority of the citizenry unable to protect incomes from inflation. That provided a further imperative for governments to remain active in the economic sphere. So too did the widespread perception that Latin America's position within the global economy was steadily worsening.

1945-60

The Apogee of Inward-looking Development. A number of problems presented themselves to Latin American policymakers following 1945. They perceived that with the return to peace their resource-rich region was suddenly less important to the United States and its allies. And while the United States spent billions of dollars to rebuild Europe, no Marshall Plan was forthcoming for Latin America. At the 1945 Inter-American Conference on Problems of War and Peace, held in Mexico City, Latin Americans heard only platitudes about improving their living standards. Meanwhile the reopening of world markets hurt raw material exports, even as the return of European products to markets won during the war years drove out inferior Latin American manufactures (Argentina, for example, had moved into the South African market). Overvalued currencies also harmed exports. While the Korean conflict briefly invigorated the export sector, and high coffee prices benefited producers of that commodity, prices were generally stagnant during the 1950s.

As exports languished (they increased just 2 percent between 1950 and 1955), imports boomed, doubling between 1945 and 1948. That caused Latin American nations to quickly exhaust foreign exchange reserves built up during the war. Inflation consequently surged, particularly in the larger states.

Most disappointing to Latin American leaders was an international economic climate that seemed prejudiced against their interests. As early as the 1944 Bretton Woods meeting, it was clear that trade liberalization would become the chief goal of developed nations in the postwar period. Over the protests of Latin American delegates to the meeting, such as Colombian finance minister **Carlos Lleras Restrepo**, Bretton Woods conferees put into place mechanisms aimed at liberalizing world trade. Among them were the International Monetary Fund (IMF), the World Bank, and the General Agreement on

Tariffs and Trade (GATT). The GATT, which became operational in early 1948, was aimed at reducing tariffs world-wide. But Latin Americans did not see free trade as benefitting them. Only Brazil, Chile, and Cuba initially ratified the agreement; Uruguay, Peru, Haiti, and the Dominican Republic became unenthusiastic GATT members during the 1950s.

By 1950 most Latin American economists embraced the thesis of Argentine economist **Raúl Prebisch**, which held that the region's traditional raw material exports suffered progressive erosion in terms of trade vis-à-vis the manufactured goods of industrialized countries. The "Prebisch thesis," as it came to be known, was popularized through the Economic Commission for Latin America (ECLA), established by the United Nations in 1948 and headed by Prebisch between 1949 and 1963. It called for the construction of import-substituting industry (ISI) and the creation of diverse, self-sufficient economies not dependent upon exports. So persuasive was the Prebisch thesis, which also called for thoroughgoing structural reform, that it dominated economic thought in Latin America throughout the 1950s and remained powerful into the 1960s and beyond.

Latin America's most industrially advanced nations, Argentina, Brazil, Chile, Uruguay, Mexico, and Colombia, vigorously pursued import substitution during the 1950s. As a result of that strategy they registered a 6.6 percent annual rate of industrial growth during the 1950s, and a 5.1 percent annual increase in GDP over the same period (5.3 percent annually for 1950-81). Those figures, coupled with rising nationalism and the radical statist example of Cuba after 1959, also worked to make inward-looking growth the guiding paradigm for development everywhere in Latin America by 1960.

For ISI development to be successful, Latin America's six most industrialized states were forced to expand their intermediate and heavy industry. By 1949 they already produced between 80 percent and 88 percent of their own consumer goods. But moving to higher levels of manufacturing was costly, and generally beyond their reach. Foreign loans were scarce during the 1950s, and Latin American nations continued to bear the onus of depression-era loan defaults. Thus they turned to multi-national corporations (MNCs) for help in achieving industrialization. MNCs were happy to comply, for they were guaranteed captive markets for their products. By the 1960s multi-nationals were ensconced in areas providing high returns on investment: chemicals, manufacturing geared to extractive industry, and food processing. Meanwhile domestically owned industry concentrated in lower-return enterprises.

The rapid development of heavy industry resulted in a burst of peripheral spin-offs. A host of new products appeared in domestic markets, especially surrounding the steel and chemical industries. The effect was thus to broaden and diversify the economies of leaders in ISI development. Societal impact included a sustained transfer of labor from agriculture to industry. By the 1960s a growing proportion of labor was also entering the service sector.

Latin America's rejection of the export model in favor of an inward-looking one had the consequence of isolating it from the global economy in two ways, first through creating barriers to imports, and second by causing deterioration of the export sector.

Protection took many forms. States of the region imposed quantitative restrictions, adopted multiple exchange rates, imposed licensing requirements, and threw up administrative obstacles to trade. But the tariff was the favored means of discouraging imports. By 1960 tariffs averaged 105 percent in the six most industrialized nations, a level ten times that of duties imposed by member states of the European Economic Community. Latin America's duties were the highest ever imposed by industrializing nations.

The inward-looking strategy brought about a sharp decline in exports. Whereas in 1950 exports accounted for 17.2 percent of GDP in the region's six most industrialized nations, they totaled just 8.9 percent in 1960. Latin America's global trade share consequently slipped from 13.5 percent in 1946 to 4.4 percent in 1975.

Export decline was not as severe in the smaller nations during the late 1940s and 1950s. Perceiving large-scale industrialization to be beyond their reach, and put off by Bolivia's failed attempt to implement the strategy during the 1940s, they concentrated on intensifying and diversifying exports. Cuba significantly upped its sugar production, as did Ecuador its banana cultivation. Venezuela did the same with petroleum. Among the successful diversifiers was Peru, which became a major exporter of fish and fish meal. Bolivia entered into significant export of natural gas; Paraguay initiated cotton and soybean export; and Central American nations greatly increased the production of cotton and cattle for export. The Dominican Republic and other countries were able to expand sugar exports to the United States after the latter nation awarded them shares of Cuba's sugar allotment after 1960. Because of their initial reluctance to adopt the inward-looking strategy, Latin America's smaller nations increased their share of trade from one-third to one-half of the regional total between 1945 and 1960. But by the latter year they too began to embrace the ISI strategy.

Latin America's inward-looking economic strategy boasted successes at its apogee in 1960. It had brought significant intermediate and heavy industry to the region, as well as satisfactory rates of economic growth. The regional economy at large expanded at a 5.1 percent annual rate between 1950 and 1960, and the economies of several nations exceeded that: Venezuela's grew at an annual rate of 7.6 percent, Brazil's at 6.8 percent, Mexico's at 6.1 percent, and Colombia's at 5.5 percent. Economic expansion also brought social diversification. Most importantly, it swelled the middle class to half or more of the total Latin American population.

But inward-turning had its negative consequences, not the least of which was to marginalize Latin America from the postwar boom in international trade. Protection bred inefficiency, resulted in high costs, and reduced productivity. Protected industries produced goods that were both more costly and of lower quality than those available in the global market. Reliance on MNCs for advanced technology resulted in the loss of significant profits, a problem aggravated by the tendency of MNCs to minimize tax payments through transfer pricing

and to generally take advantage of their protected status. And as the new industries tended to be import intensive, they did little to save foreign exchange. Thus states of the region faced ongoing balance-of-payment problems during their inward-looking phase. This in turn created inflationary pressure, touching off debates between monetarists, who urged fiscal restraint and trade liberalization, and structuralists, who pointed to production bottlenecks, especially in the area of agriculture, as the source of inflation and slow economic growth.

By 1960 all Latin American states were involved in inward-looking development in spite of its many drawbacks. Yet the limited size of national markets, aggravated by widespread poverty, constrained economic growth in ways that became increasingly apparent. This moved economic planners, foremost among them ECLA's **Raúl Prebisch**, to promote market expansion through international economic integration.

1960-1980

Trade Expansion Through Regional Economic Integration. Latin American economic planners began advocating the formation of regional free trade zones during the latter 1950s. ECLA recommended it in 1956, and formation of the European Economic Community (EEC) in 1958 gave the idea motive force. In 1959 **Raúl Prebisch** published *The Latin American Common Market*, in which he likened the highly protected markets of Latin American states to "watertight compartments." He went on to compare the products of regional industry unfavorably with similar products available in global markets. Meanwhile economic planners had seen a steady decline in intra-regional trade over the decade, from 11 percent during 1953-55, to 6 percent in 1961. These were leading factors in Latin America's formation of regional associations during the 1960s.

1960

The Treaty of Montevideo and the Latin

American Free Trade Association (LAFTA).
Meeting in Montevideo, Uruguay, in 1960, seven
Latin American states agreed to establish a free
trade area by the year 1972. Led by the Southern
Cone nations Argentina, Uruguay, Chile, and
Paraguay, along with Brazil, Bolivia, and Mexico
(later joined by Colombia, Peru, Venezuela, and
Ecuador), Latin American nations agreed to
follow GATT guidelines in reducing trade barriers
through ongoing negotiation. Initially their
progress toward that goal was good. Intra-
regional trade doubled, to 12 percent of total trade
by the mid-1960s. But soon the rate of integration
slowed, reaching just 20 percent by 1980. A
range of problems hindered progress: among them
were defects in the Treaty of Montevideo;
inadequate land, sea, and air links between
member states; and a range of
structural—particularly fiscal—constraints. Most
daunting was the ongoing opposition of domestic
manufacturers who wanted to continue enjoying
the benefits of captive domestic markets.

The LAFTA agreement was revised in 1968
through the Protocol of Caracas. Efforts were
made to smooth financial impediments to trade,
and the deadline for achieving tariff reduction was
extended to 1980. LAFTA did succeed in
increasing the proportion of manufactures in
intra-regional trade from 10 percent in 1960 to 46
percent in 1980 (meanwhile trade in food products
fell from 41 percent of the total in 1965 to 25
percent in 1980). Yet overall results were
disappointing, as member states continued facing
logistical and fiscal constraints to intra-regional
trade and, most importantly, the resistance of
domestic interests to lower tariffs.

1960

The Central American Common Market. In
1960 El Salvador, Guatemala, Honduras, and
Nicaragua signed the General Treaty for Central
American Integration, which served as the basis of
the Central American Common Market (CACM),
joining El Salvador, Guatemala, Honduras, and
Nicaragua (Costa Rica joined in 1963). The
agreement called for immediate free trade in 95
percent of listed goods, the removal of tariff

barriers by 1966, formation of a customs union,
industrial integration, and creation of a monetary
union.

CACM enjoyed some success during the
1960s, as exports within the community rose to 28
percent of the total. Ninety-six percent of
manufactured exports were exchanged within the
community by 1970. Yet a range of problems
moderated the success of CACM. Honduras, for
example, which exported mainly agricultural
products to other CACM members, soon had an
unfavorable balance of trade with them. The most
severe blow to CACM, however, was the 1969
Soccer War between El Salvador and Honduras,
which crippled the agreement. The debt crisis of
the 1980s further reduced intra-regional trade to
14 percent of total trade. It drove trade in
manufactures down from 85 percent of the total in
1980 to 69 percent in 1986. Additionally, civil
war involving Nicaragua, Honduras, El Salvador,
and Costa Rica hurt trade between CACM
members.

1969

The Andean Pact. Through the Cartagena
Agreement of 1969, Bolivia, Chile, Colombia,
Ecuador, and Peru (Venezuela joined in 1973)
agreed to create a framework for further
liberalizing trade among themselves. While
remaining members of LAFTA, they hoped to
speed economic integration in ways not
envisioned by the broader accord. Specifically,
they hoped to establish a customs union through
their Common External Tariff, which they agreed
to implement over the course of the 1970s.
Although Chile withdrew from the pact in 1973,
the remaining members managed to increase their
exchange of manufactures from 24 percent to 36
percent by 1980.

1980s

The Caribbean Basin Initiative. The Caribbean
Basin Initiative (1984) represented an effort of the
United States to further isolate and weaken the
economies of Cuba and Nicaragua, while
stimulating those of surrounding states. It

involved providing duty-free access to the United States of specified imports, especially those of a nontraditional character.   The initiative had limited impact as many of the listed items were already covered by existing agreements. It thus increased inter-regional trade by only 15 percent. Thanks to the initiative, however, Colombia, Costa Rica, and the Dominican Republic developed significant new exports for the U.S. market, especially in cut flowers, electronics, and fish products.

From State-led Development to Liberal Reform

1970-1999

During the 1970s states played a more active role in the economic sector than ever before. They did so principally through foreign borrowing, the larger nations, especially, Brazil, Mexico, and Argentina, becoming heavily indebted in order to achieve industrial deepening (investment in increasingly sophisticated and efficient productive capacity). Such deepening was aimed at pushing these nations toward greater self-sufficiency in the manufacture of capital equipment, and toward expanding their range of manufactured consumer durables. Smaller states, too, tried to go beyond limits of import-substituting, inward-looking development by developing new exports and increasing traditional ones. States both small and large took advantage of globalization by establishing export-processing zones where unskilled workers assembled labor-intensive manufactures.

The combined effect of global recession and foreign debt caused Mexico to default on its debt in 1982, sending all of Latin America into decline. Economic growth virtually ceased throughout the region as monies paid for debt service soared. Governments cut back on social programs, causing a worsening of social indicators and heightened human suffering.

Around 1990 circumstances dictated yet another shift in economic strategy. Turned away from protectionism and statism as neoliberal strategies regained favor among economic planners. Across the region states took steps to reduce tariffs and other forms of protection. They began dismantling costly social programs, selling state-owned enterprises, and streamlining the public sector. Those actions were prompted by public dismay over the economic declines of the 1980s and government's seeming inability to halt them.

Economic health returned to Latin America during the early 1990s. Inflation fell sharply. Meanwhile foreign investment poured in as governments privatized the large public sector and abolished restrictions on foreign capital. The corresponding increases in GDP rivaled those of the 1950-82 period. There was also renewed interest in strengthening exports through regional integration.

Late in the decade the region's economic reforms attracted international attention. Chile's privatized social security system became an object of study in the United States. Economic woes in the Asian Pacific moved leaders of the "Asian Tigers" to study Latin American economic management.

At the end of the twentieth century Latin America's economy presented a mixed picture. Inflation was reduced; macroeconomic indicators, and social indicators continued to improve. Yet the region remained the world's most unequal in terms of the distribution of economic benefits. Poverty there ran from 20 percent in the better-off nations of the Southern Cone, to 50 percent or better in Bolivia, Nicaragua, and Haiti. Elsewhere it averaged 40 percent of the total population. There is widespread agreement that Latin America's prevailing challenge is as much political as economic: to find institutional ways of distributing economic gains downward through the social structure.

1970-82

State-led Development. A variety of factors caused Latin American countries to sharply increase their level of economic involvement during the 1970s. The press of international events during the 1940s had heightened state economic involvement in support of the inter-American war effort. Following the war, and through the 1950s and 1960s, ECLA orthodoxy held that states must lead in fostering import-substituting growth. But by the late 1960s the easy phase of import substitution had been

International Economic Integration

Alaska

Canada

United States

Atlantic Ocean

Mexico

Belize
Jamaica
Guatemala
El Salvador
Nicaragua
Honduras
Costa Rica
Panama

St. Kitts and Nevis**
Antigua and Barbuda**
Montserrat**
Dominica**
St. Vincent**
St. Lucia**
Barbados*
Grenada**
Trinidad and Tobago*

Pacific Ocean

Venezuela
Guyana
Colombia
Ecuador

Peru
Brazil

Bolivia
Paraguay

Chile***
Uruguay
Argentina

Symbol	Name	Description
ALADI		Latin American Association for Development and Integration
	Andean Group (Also members of ALADI)	
CACM		Central American Common Market
CARICOM		Caribbean Community
MERCOSUR and ALADI		Southern Common Market
NAFTA		North American Free Trade Area
NAFTA and ALADI		

*   Member of CARICOM
**   Member of CARICOM and OECS
        (Organization of Eastern Caribbean States)
*** Former member of the Andean Group

achieved over much of the region. Brazil, for example, produced 99 percent of its consumer goods, 91 percent of its intermediate goods, and 87 percent of its capital goods. It was clear that if costly economic deepening were to occur, it must be promoted by the national government.

Domestic politics played their role in the turn to statism. Economic nationalism grew markedly after **Fidel Castro** made Cuba socialist. While other Latin American heads of state rejected Castro's Marxism, they were forced leftward by his example, soon mounting land reform programs and scrambling to raise living standards through a variety of public programs. Labor and the left approved of such activism, and so too did national militaries and the private sector. The former perceived economic self-sufficiency as furthering national security, while the latter liked bidding for state contracts within a noncompetitive environment.

Economic penetration by multinational corporations (MNCs) also spurred state activism. By the 1960s multinational corporations had come to dominate key areas of production—autos, chemicals, machine tools—especially in the larger nations. They controlled 40 percent of Mexican manufacturing, as well as 36 percent of that country's 400 largest enterprises. Twenty percent of Brazil's largest companies, and 50 percent of manufacturing capital were also foreign-owned.

The MNCs valued their position in Latin America's highly protected markets. They charged high prices for products uncompetitive in international markets. And they had no incentive to make the sort of costly capital investment needed to achieve industrial deepening in the larger states.

To free themselves from the cloying embrace of MNCs, Latin American nations pursued continued economic development during the 1970s with borrowed capital. Export earnings were not sufficient to finance such industrial expansion owing both to the noncompetitiveness of regional exports and to the fact that traditional raw material exports had declined during the postwar period. Petrodollars flowed into Latin America following the oil shocks of 1973 and 1978-79, and were used to finance a spate of nationalizations, purchases of MNC assets, and formation of state-owned enterprises (SOEs). Favored targets of nationalization included extractive industries, banks, and utilities. The lion's share of borrowed monies went to a handful of countries that invested them in leading-sector industries: autos, steel, and machine tools in Brazil; petroleum in Mexico and Venezuela; and heavy industry in Argentina. Most of those enterprises were state-owned. At the height of statism during 1979-82, Mexico had 1,155 SOEs and Brazil 654. Peru and Venezuela carried out extensive nationalization and established hundreds of SOEs, as did Chile prior to the fall of **Salvador Allende** in 1973.

Public sector spending in Latin America rose from 10 percent of GDP in 1970, to 25 percent in 1980. In Brazil, Argentina, Peru, and Venezuela it jumped from the 25-35 percent range early in the decade to 50-60 percent ten years later. Economic domination by the state was most pronounced in Venezuela, where by 1974 central government revenue amounted to 34.5 percent of GDP, triple that of either Brazil or Mexico at that time.

During the 1970s the SOEs' share of markets and assets across the region rose from 28 percent to 50 percent, while the share of locally owned firms remained little changed. Thus the growth of SOE market share took place at the expense of MNCs. In Brazil, for example, between 1969 and 1984, the total of markets and assets controlled by MNCs fell from 27 percent to 9 percent.

The debt-led growth of the 1970s and early 1980s served its purpose in larger states, which directed their public firms to contract with local domestic suppliers. Thus they promoted the development of a wider industrial economy. Brazilian SOEs supplanted nearly all private sector capital investment during that time; meanwhile the state influenced industrial policy through its Development Bank System (BNDES). That entity had its counterpart in Mexico's Nacional Financiera and Chile's CORFO.

By 1980 Brazilian SOEs absorbed half the output of privately owned companies. Some 65 to 75 percent of capital goods consumption was from state firms. In that regard they provided vital motive force to local industry. Between 1968 and 1974 Brazil's state-led "economic miracle" produced an 11 percent annual rate of growth, resulting in a tripling of GDP between 1965 and 1980. Negatively, most of those gains were distributed upward through society, benefitting the middle and upper classes and largely bypassing the poor.

There were similar though less spectacular economic advances elsewhere in Latin America. This was especially the case in Mexico, where the government promoted the nation's automobile industry. By the latter 1980s Mexico exported 2.5 million auto engines to the United States. The more industrialized nations, among them Argentina and Colombia, witnessed significant increases in manufactured exports. Brazil led in that category with manufactures totaling 37 percent of exports by 1980.

During the 1970s several nations successfully followed the Taiwanese model in establishing or expanding export-processing zones. The Dominican Republic and Haiti took advantage of low domestic labor costs to attract assembly plants, chiefly from the United States. As a result, manufactures increased from 3 to 24 percent of exports in the former country, and from 8 to 59 percent in the latter one.

Earlier experiments in encouraging manufacturing through tax abatement included Panama's Free Zone, in the city of Colón, established in the 1950s; the Manaus Free Trade Zone in northern Brazil, established in 1967; and the *maquiladora* zone along Mexico's border with the United States, dating from the late 1960s. By 1994 Brazil's free trade zone in Manaus contained three hundred factories producing a range of manufactured goods, including motorcycles and television sets. Colón's duty-free zone specialized in the assembly of electronic devices and clothing. Mexico's *maquiladoras* increased significantly during the period 1983-93, presaging that country's entry into the North American Free Trade Agreement with the United States and Canada in 1994.

Latin America thus achieved excellent rates of economic expansion during the 1970s (though there were exceptions, poorly managed Peru being

the most notable). The regional GDP grew between 4 and 5 percent annually over the decade (with Brazil's average annual growth of 6.8 percent between 1950-81 leading all others). Over the 1970s investment in machinery and equipment increased 8 percent annually. The rate of capital accumulation in 1981 was nine times that of 1950.

1973-1982

Debt-led Growth. Latin America's growth during the 1970s and early 1980s was fueled by an extraordinary pool of capital that became available during the decade. Thanks to those monies countries were able to promote development even when easy import-substituting expansion was no longer possible and when exports languished. Foreign loans were also used to underwrite costly social programs at a time of strident popular demand for increased state activism on behalf of the poor. States also used loans to fund improvements in national infrastructure.

Negatively, Latin America increased its foreign debt from $21 billion in 1970 to $328 billion in 1982. That placed the region in the paradoxical situation of having taken on the debt to increase economic self-sufficiency and improve the quality of exports, while mortgaging earnings through such improvements into the foreseeable future. And exports were sufficient to service the foreign debt only as long as they enjoyed healthy demand and adequate price.

Loan monies first came in the form of eurodollars administered through the branches of private banks that had proliferated during the postwar period. Then the oil shocks of 1973 and 1978-79 put vast amounts of capital into circulation. Awash in petrodollars, private banks lent to Latin American governments lavishly and with few restrictions. Anxious to lend, they set interest rates lower than those prevailing in Latin America, and this made borrowing all the more attractive.

Eighty percent of lending during the 1980s was from private banks, and most monies were lent to the larger countries. Thus Brazil's foreign debt jumped from $5 billion in 1970 to $50 billion in 1980. Mexico's rose from $7 billion in 1972 to

$58 billion in 1982. Forty percent of Mexican loans went to the state oil company PEMEX, which had confirmed the discovery of large new petroleum reserves in the early 1970s.

By the latter 1970s Latin America's smaller nations had also contracted substantial loans, especially Venezuela, which secured them with its large oil reserves. As debt mounted, interest payments rose accordingly. Between 1960 and 1970 Latin America's debt service had consumed 18 percent of export earnings each year. By 1976 that figure stood at 26 percent, and between 1977 and 1981 it rose to 43 percent. In 1982 debt servicing consumed an unsustainable 59 percent of export earnings. Clearly the policy of debt-led development had been pursued beyond the bounds of prudence.

1982-90

Economic Stagnation and Retrenchment. When Mexico declared itself unable to service its foreign debt in August 1982, panic spread through international financial markets. At that moment the amount loaned to Latin American governments by New York City's largest banks far exceeded their capital. The nine largest U.S. banks had a loans/capital ratio of 180 percent. Of that figure Latin American states had borrowed as follows: Mexico, 50 percent; Brazil, 46 percent; Venezuela, 26 percent; Argentina, 21 percent; Chile, 12 percent. They and other heavily indebted states struggled to meet their debt payments over the course of the 1980s amid global economic stagnation.

Factors underlying the debt crisis of the 1980s included a tight money policy in the United States that raised interest rates to unprecedented levels during the late 1970s and early 1980s, forcing that nation into recession during 1980-82. The U.S. economic downturn, along with new protectionist policies there and in Europe, sharply reduced the purchase of Latin American exports. Stiff inter-debtor competition also contributed to debtor state difficulty in generating enough foreign exchange to service foreign loans. All those factors accounted for the fact that between 1974 and 1986, terms of trade for Latin America and other less developed nations declined 60 percent.

In August 1982 international lending institutions abruptly ceased funding to Latin America, an action pushing solvent but debt-burdened nations like Brazil, Argentina, Chile, and Venezuela close to illiquidity. At that point the United States government, led by the directors of its Treasury and Federal Reserve system, turned to the International Monetary Fund (IMF) for help in rescheduling Latin America's debt. Serving as an intermediary between Latin American governments and private banks, the IMF forced the banks to issue new loans that were used to pay interest in arrears. While that action allowed Mexico to resume debt service and helped other states continue interest payments, it increased Latin America's foreign debt outstanding from $328 billion in 1982 billion to $432 billion in 1990.

IMF intervention in the Latin American financial crisis came at a high price. The international financial institution demanded massive, painful economic adjustments. During 1985-87, the World Bank joined in the debt repayment effort, lending $29 billion to help cushion the effects of adjustment. At length, during 1987-89, banks accepted a plan of U.S. Treasury secretary James Baker, through which governments purchased low-interest bonds in exchange for bank discounting of debt outstanding. In 1989 yet another round of international lending enabled debtor nations to buy back further-discounted portions of their debt, thus allowing them to escape onerous IMF-imposed austerity plans.

Economic decline and sharp increases in human suffering characterized Latin America's "lost decade" of the 1980s. Owing to the high level of cooperation among private banks, the IMF and World Bank, and U.S. and European governments, Latin American debtors were forced to reimburse debt holders a larger proportion of their GDP than Germany paid to the victors of World War I. The region's largest nations were those most injured by events of the 1980s, ending the decade economically stagnant and burdened with growing debt. Per capita GDP stood 8 percent lower in 1990 than it had been in 1980.

Argentina, Bolivia, Haiti, Guatemala, Nicaragua, Peru, and Venezuela suffered a better than 2 percent annual decline in GDP between 1981 and 1989. Among the larger nations, only Colombia, which did not indebt itself heavily, experienced positive economic growth.

Latin America's lower and middle classes bore the brunt of the economic downturn. Between 1980 and 1990 real wages fell by one-third. In Mexico they fell 44 percent. Peru, Argentina, Nicaragua, and Venezuela also experienced hyperinflation, which destroyed the value of wages. Economic stagnation drove urban unemployment to 8 percent and underemployment to 33 percent.

1990s

Neoliberal Reform. At the end of the 1980s Latin American leaders knew that thoroughgoing reform was needed to jolt the region out of its economic decline. They were broadly agreed that populist statism must yield to economic liberalism. In many ways this represented a return to the thinking of a hundred years earlier. They acted to open domestic markets by liberalizing trade and encouraging foreign investment of all sorts. The sale of SOEs accelerated the influx of foreign capital, as did the passing of new laws protecting property, both foreign and domestic. Meanwhile states adopted frequently painful fiscal discipline. Currencies were allowed to approach real exchange rates, public spending was slashed, and tax reforms implemented. Restoration of the banking sector to private ownership helped rebuild the confidence of domestic and foreign business interests. Accordingly, domestic savings began to increase and stock markets boomed.

Chile had led the way in reform during the mid-1970s and 1980s, and by the end of the latter decade had succeeded in sharply reducing inflation. Other countries followed suit generally with good results. Argentina, which entered the 1990s suffering from hyperinflation, implemented its "convertability plan" in 1991, pegging its currency to the dollar. While carried out at enormous sacrifice, in that it raised peso costs for

domestic manufacturers, reducing consumption, and thus driving up unemployment, the plan cut inflation to single digits by late in the decade. Other nations enjoyed similar results, and by the late 1990s annual rates of inflation were under 10 percent in all but three countries of the region.

By late in the 1990s, Chile, Mexico, Argentina, and Peru had pushed neoliberal reforms the farthest. Brazil, Uruguay, Colombia, Venezuela, Bolivia, Peru, Ecuador, Costa Rica, El Salvador, Panama and the Dominican Republic had also liberalized their economies, though at a more sedate pace. Honduras, Nicaragua, and Paraguay had attempted to do so, but struggled against political and structural obstacles. Although Cuba maintained its commitment to the command economy, it too began to allow limited private enterprise and to welcome foreign investors.

The Mexican peso crisis of late 1994 and 1995 sent shock waves across the region, dampening growth in many countries, particularly in Argentina. But by 1997 the region had recovered, and was registering 4.5 percent growth in GDP. Restructured enterprises registered sharp increases in labor productivity.

Privatization of SOEs had contributed to the improvement of economic indicators. By way of example, one public sector Argentine steel-maker employing 51,000 workers registered $6 billion in losses during 1982-91. During 1997, having reduced its work force by 45,000, it registered a $2 billion profit.

By 1997, some 300 state-owned firms had been sold—94 in Brazil, 55 in Argentina, 53 in Peru, and 35 in Mexico, and dozens more in other countries. Privatizations in Brazil had totaled $27 billion in 1997, but were expected to yield an additional $65 billion by 1999. Major privatizations included Mexico's telephone company, which became Telmex, and the Argentine state oil company, YPF. The largest privatizations took place in Brazil, where the government sold its controlling interests in the Rio Doce Valley Company (CVRD), a huge mining complex, in 1997, and in Telebrás, the national telephone company, in 1998.

1990s

Renewed Regional Integration. There was renewed interest in regional economic integration during the 1990s. This trend began in Mexico, where in the mid-1980s business and political leaders began strengthening ties with the United States, first through encouragement of *maquiladoras*, or assembly plants, especially after 1984. In 1986 the nation's leaders made Mexico a member of GATT (which became the World Trade Organization in 1995) and pushed the nation's foreign trade to 14 percent of GDP by 1990. This success also led them to embrace the North American Free Trade Agreement (NAFTA), which began operation in 1994.

Near the end of the decade pro-NAFTA forces could point to an 18 percent annual increase in *maquiladora* production after 1994, as well as a jump in joint ventures with U.S. firms, especially in the area of textiles. It also resulted in a doubling of car and truck exports over 1994-97, as Mexico became an attractive North American manufacturing center. Meanwhile the Mexican auto industry became completely integrated with those of the United States and Canada. NAFTA also encouraged U.S. retailers such as Wal-Mart to form joint ventures in Mexico. Unlike the *maquiladoras*, they used local inputs, and also promoted the sale of Mexican-made products in their U.S. stores. Post-NAFTA joint ventures also led to improved quality, service, and delivery of products to Mexican consumers, as well as lower prices. They also forced Mexican firms to improve the quality of their products.

Critics of NAFTA found fault with its effect of promoting further growth of *maquiladoras*. They point out that few of the materials assembled in *maquiladoras* originate in Mexico, meaning that the plants are not integrally linked to the nation's economy. As the plants make use of unskilled, mostly female labor, and offer little opportunity for advancement or progress beyond minimal wage levels, they do not offer the benefits of traditional factories. That complaint notwithstanding, *maquiladoras* accounted for more than 50 percent of all Mexican manufactures by the late 1990s (up from 37 percent in 1989).

Anti-NAFTA forces in Mexico further pointed out that as Mexico's economy was just one-twentieth that of the United States, the agreement rendered their country little more than an economic appendage of its northern neighbor. Meanwhile their counterparts in the United States, coming from organized labor and the green movement, damned the accord as causing job loss and contributing to pollution.

Friends of liberal trade policy in the United States and elsewhere faulted NAFTA as having an indirect negative impact upon U.S. trade policy. By the late 1990s NAFTA's critics had been so effective in laying U.S. economic woes at the door of the agreement that they managed to slow the pace of regional integration. Thus President Bill Clinton was unable to expand the pact to include Chile after his failure to win "fast-track" negotiating authority from Congress in 1997. An April 1998 hemispheric summit in Santiago de Chile made little progress in creating Clinton's Free-Trade Area of the Americas (FTAA).

During 1990-96 Brazil, Argentina, Uruguay, and Paraguay succeeded in deepening their economic integration. During 1990-96 their mutual trade rose from $4 billion to $17 billion, buoyed in 1995 by formalization of the customs union Mercosur. Mercosur pursued a policy of "open regionalism" during the 1990s, featuring tariff-lowering, movement toward establishment of common external tariffs, and preferential trade agreements with nonmember neighboring states. During 1996 the Mercosur states conducted 1.5 percent of world trade (as compared to 18.7 percent by NAFTA's members). They also strengthened ties with the European Union and, during 1996-97, accepted Chile and Bolivia as associate members. But Chile's full membership became problematic in late 1997, as Mercosur's four full members increased their common tariff to 15 percent while Chile was reducing its to 8 percent. At the end of the decade, economic recession within Latin America and the growing strength of anti–free trade forces throughout the Americas suggested that Mercosur's immediate progress would be slow.

Excluded from NAFTA, Central American

nations launched an ambitious plan to coordinate microeconomic reforms in late 1995. Their leaders agreed to meet on a regular basis in pursuit of a common agenda embracing deregulation; attracting foreign investment; and linking electric grids, telecommunications, and highways. Fruits of renewed Central American economic reform included the selection of Costa Rica as the site of Intel's new $300 million silicon-chip factory. That took place in part because Costa Rica was the only Latin American country to sign the World Trade Organization agreement eliminating barriers to trade in information technology.

Renewed Central American cooperation paved the way for important economic developments during the 1990s. By the end of the decade 60 percent of exports from the region's "industrial heartland"—Guatemala, El Salvador, and Costa Rica—consisted of *maquiladora*-produced goods and nontraditional agricultural products. Especially important in that development was Asia-Pacific direct investment. South Korean companies operated 180 *maquilas* in Guatemala alone at the end of the 1990s.

1990s

Continuing Obstacles to Economic Progress. At the end of the 1990s Latin America's economy presented a mixed picture. The depression of the 1980s and ill effects of Mexico's peso collapse were surmounted. Acceptable levels of economic growth had been achieved. And most importantly, inflation seemed to be under control. National leaders appeared to be committed to the construction of modern, efficient, administrative states. Yet daunting obstacles remained to be overcome before Latin American states could contemplate achieving full development. The region remained vulnerable to the whims of foreign investors, as demonstrated by the flight of capital from Brazil in late 1998 and 1999. Especially intractable were the interrelated problems of institutional weakness and unequal human development.

A leading impediment to economic development in Latin America was the traditional weakness of central governments. Although central governments there traditionally attempted to monopolize power, leaving regions with little local autonomy, especially in the area of revenue-raising, at the same time they remained fundamentally weak, in some cases to the extent of being unable to exercise police control over national terrain. Taxes remained regressive while levels of tax collection were among the world's lowest. Labor law tended to be archaic, serving a minority of workers and leaving the majority unprotected. Commercial codes, too, tended to be insufficient. A rising level of violence against people and property served as another drag on economic growth. In 1997, for example, Latin America's murder rate stood at 20 per 100,000 population, double that of the United States. In El Salvador and Colombia the murder rates for 1997 reached an appalling 140 and 90 per 100,000, respectively.

Business analysts from OECD countries faulted Latin American entrepreneurs for an over reliance on cheap labor and abundant natural resources. During much of Latin America's inward-looking phase few members of the business elite attempted to gear their activities to the demands of a sophisticated world marketplace. Most of Latin America's largest private businesses were hierarchical, inward-looking family conglomerates. Only in recent times, thanks in part to the recent economic reforms and their encouragement of joint ventures, had the insular quality of Latin American business culture begun to change. Higher education was offering increased training in the field of business. Brazil's top business school, the Fundação Getúlio Vargas, established a modern MBA curriculum in 1993. During the late 1990s major Latin American firms began recruiting graduates from business schools at home and abroad.

The underdevelopment of its human capital was the foremost economic impediment confronting Latin America. At the end of the twentieth century 40 percent of the population lived in poverty, and 15-20 percent in extreme poverty. The only mitigating aspect of this otherwise gloomy picture was a World Bank prediction that with continued economic growth the percentage of poor in Latin America would shrink to 30 percent during the twenty-first century. Still, the absolute number of poor, 165 million in 1996, would continue to rise owing to population increase. At the end of the 1990s the proportion of poor in Latin America's six principal regions ran as shown in Table 4.

Table 4

Percent of Poor in Latin America

Region	Poverty	Absolute Poverty
Central America	60%	36%
Andean America	44%	25%
Caribbean	38%	19%
Brazil	35%	23%
Mexico	26%	17%
Southern Cone	10%	5%

Source: *The World Bank, 1998.*

Analysts link Latin American poverty to inadequacy in the area of education. At the end of the 1990s average education there barely exceeded five years, as compared to better than twelve years in the United States and Canada, and above eleven years in Western Europe. More importantly, Latin Americans possessed two fewer years of education on average than the citizens of other countries at similar levels of economic development. Comparative test scores for the year 1996 revealed that Latin American children scored 30 percent lower on average than children in the developed OECD nations. While OECD nations spent 3.7 percent of their GDP on education, and the world average expenditure was 2.9 percent, Latin America's was just 2.4 percent.

Education goals set at the 1994 Summit of the Americas included the providing of universal primary education for children, and secondary education for at least 75 percent of youth. By 1998, 85 percent of all children received primary education and 46 percent of youth attended secondary school. Twenty percent of secondary school graduates attended college. Primary school enrollment was under 45 percent in Bolivia, El Salvador, Honduras, and Nicaragua, and under 18 percent in Haiti.

Unemployment and underemployment loomed as yet another structural constraint to regional economic progress. Late in the 1990s unemployment ran at better than 7 percent, while more than one-third of the population was underemployed. Many of those in the latter category were self-employed, working in the informal economy and in micro-enterprises. In 1992, 54 percent of the nonagricultural work force was determined to be in the informal economy, a 14 percent rise over 1980. Most micro-enterprises, and virtually all parts of the informal economy, failed to provide adequate living wages for individuals working in them.

The 1980s depression, and Mexico's sharp decline during 1994-95, combined to worsen the economic standing of Latin America's poor. Whereas the ratio of wealth controlled by the top 20 percent of the population, as compared to that owned by the bottom 20 percent, stood at 15:1 in 1982, it had increased to 22:1 in 1995. That widening gap between rich and poor, in what historically has been the world's most economically unequal region, had lessened support for structural reform on behalf of the poor. And to the extent that Latin America's inequality persisted, it acted as a drag on economic progress. Prospects for economic growth in Latin America were good at the end of the 1990s. But nations there needed to strengthen political and economic institutions and reduce the size of their underclass if they hoped to some day join the ranks of developed market economies.

CULTURE

Religion

Pre-Columbian Religion. Although all the indigenous peoples of the New World had systems of religious belief, the deities, rituals, and cosmogony of many societies still remain unclear. More is known about the religion of the peoples of the areas of high civilization in Mesoamerica and Andean South America than some others, but even in these cases information is limited, especially about the practices of early cultures in those regions. Scholars are dependent on archaeological remains and on Spanish and Portuguese sources that describe religious practices and beliefs in existence at the time of the initial encounter with Europeans.

The religion of the peoples of Mesoamerica, especially the Maya and those of central Mexico, exhibited certain uniformities, such as a belief in cyclical creation and destruction and the identity of church and state. The chief god of the Maya was Itzamná (Lizard House), who was the patron of learning and the inventor of writing. Other deities included his consort Ix Chel (Lady Rainbow), who was the goddess of weaving, medicine, and health, and the *chacs*, or rain gods. Maya priests were the custodians of learning and ritual, which was based on the permutations of the calendar, especially the 260-day sacred count.

At the time of the Spanish conquest, Huitzilopochtli (Hummingbird on the Left), the hero-god of the Aztecs or Mexica, had been transformed into the principal deity of central Mexico, absorbing aspects of the ancient war and sun gods of the region. Central to his worship was the belief that the sun required the blood of sacrificial victims, who came from the ranks of war captives. Another important deity was Quetzalcoatl (Feathered Serpent), who was associated with creativity and fertility. In the post-Classic era he was also worshipped by the Maya of northern Yucatán, who called him Kukulcán.

In Andean South America the supreme deity was Viracocha, the creator. The principal god of the Incas was Inti, the sun god and progenitor of the royal dynasty. He was served not only by a male priesthood but also by the Virgins of the Sun, women dedicated to lives of chastity and service. There were also many *huacas*, or sacred shrines, inhabited by spirits to whom gifts and sacrifices had to be offered.

1493-1577

Establishment of the Catholic Church in the New World. About a dozen members of the clergy accompanied **Christopher Columbus** on his second voyage to the Indies in 1493, and many others arrived later. In 1511 bishoprics were created for Hispaniola and Puerto Rico. By the mid-sixteenth century bishoprics had been established in other colonies, including Panama (1524), Mexico City (1525), Cartagena (1533), and Lima (1541). Dioceses in the Spanish colonies were initially subject to the archbishop of Seville, but Mexico City, Lima, and Santo Domingo became archbishoprics in 1546. Clergymen arrived in Brazil soon after the visit of **Pedro Cabral** in 1500, but the church grew slowly there. The diocese of Bahia was founded in 1551, and that of Rio de Janeiro in 1577.

Royal Patronage and the Catholic Church. The kings of Spain and Portugal exercised great power over the Catholic church in the New World. The Spanish crown derived its power from papal bulls, especially those issued in 1493, 1501, and 1508. The crown assumed the responsibility of supporting the church in the colonies and of encouraging the conversion of the Indians. In exchange, the crown (and its representatives) obtained the right to collect ecclesiastical taxes and to appoint bishops and other clerics to positions in the Indies. In addition, royal approval was required for the construction of churches and for the publication in the New World of papal pronouncements. The kings of Portugal wielded similar power over the church in Brazil.

c. 1500-1610

The Religious Orders and Early Missionary Activity. The Spanish and Portuguese crowns entrusted the task of proselytizing among the indigenous populations to the various religious orders that comprised the regular clergy, so called because they followed a *regulum*, or rule. There were Franciscans on Hispaniola before 1500, but missionary work on the island was carried on mainly by the Dominicans. **Bartolomé de las Casas**, the historian and protector of the Indians, became a Dominican in 1523. Organized missionary activity in Mexico began with the arrival of twelve Franciscans in 1524, followed by contingents of Dominicans and Augustinians. Dominicans and Franciscans arrived in Peru at an early date, but the disturbed state of the colony initially hindered their efforts. In Brazil, the Society of Jesus was by far the most important religious order. Six Jesuits led by **Manuel da Nóbrega** came to the colony with **Tomé de Sousa** in 1549, and nine more arrived six years later. Jesuits arrived in Peru in 1568 and in Mexico in 1572.

Because members of religious orders were usually the first clerics in a colony, they often assumed duties normally performed by members of the secular clergy, that is, priests active in the world (*seculum*), such as being in charge of parishes and serving as bishops. **Juan de Zumárraga,** the first bishop of Mexico, was a Franciscan. As the colonies matured, the secular clergy increasingly displaced the regulars in these roles. To carry out their work, early missionaries lived in indigenous communities, learned native languages, and prepared catechisms and hymnals in them. In frontier areas, Franciscans, Jesuits, and other orders established missions where Indians lived under their exclusive control. The most famous of these were the missions established by the Jesuits among the Guaraní of what is now Paraguay, Argentina, and Brazil, starting in 1610.

Contemporary accounts indicated that missionaries baptized millions of Indians in a relatively short period of time, and there has long been debate over the nature of Indian conversions. The Indians often continued to worship their old gods in secret and, if discovered, often were severely punished. When Maya idols were found in Yucatecan caves in 1562 and it was reported that Indians were combining human sacrifice with Christian ritual, the Franciscan missionary **Diego de Landa** jailed and tortured nearly five thousand to get at the truth. On the other hand, members of religious orders, such as las Casas and the Jesuit **Antônio Vieira,** frequently protected Indians from the rapacity of European settlers. Writings by missionaries such as Landa and **Bernardino de Sahagún** were also responsible for preserving valuable information about indigenous history and culture.

Female Religious in the Colonies. Latin America's first convent was La Concepción, established in Mexico City about 1550. The first nunnery in Lima, La Encarnación, was founded in 1561. Many other convents were founded, often by women, in these and other Spanish American cities throughout the colonial period, though the number of nuns grew at a slower pace during the eighteenth century. The first nunnery in Brazil--Santa Clara do Destêrro in Bahia--was not founded until 1677, and the number of nuns in Brazilian convents always remained relatively small.

Colonial women became nuns because they had a religious vocation, because suitable marriage partners could not be found, or because the prospect of marriage was unappealing. The celebrated Mexican poet Sor **Juana Inés de la Cruz** fell into the last of these categories. Since admission to a convent usually required a substantial dowry, only white women from affluent families were likely to become nuns. However, in 1724 a nunnery for Indian women was established in Mexico City, and mestizo women occasionally became nuns as well. In addition to nuns, convents, especially those that did not follow a strict rule, housed many other female inhabitants, ranging from infants to students to slaves. Since nuns governed themselves, with some supervision from male clerics, and managed real estate, schools, and businesses, convent life offered women an unusual degree of autonomy.

The Inquisition. Tribunals of the Holy Office of the Inquisition were established in Mexico City and Lima in 1571 and in Cartagena in 1610. The primary task of the inquisitors and their agents was to preserve religious orthodoxy. To achieve this end they investigated people accused of practicing Judaism or Protestantism. As recent Christians, Indians were not under the jurisdiction of the Holy Office, and cases of idolatry among them were handled by other clergymen. Other offenses subject to the Inquisition included sorcery, blasphemy, and bigamy. In addition, the Inquisition was authorized to prevent the publication or importation of books considered injurious to faith and morals. Persons found guilty were expected to express repentance, often in public, and underwent punishment inflicted by the secular authorities. Those who refused to repent might be executed.

No inquisitorial tribunal was ever established in Brazil, but agents of the Lisbon tribunal were active in the colony. On three occasions— 1591-95, 1618-20, 1763-69—inquisitorial visitors were dispatched from Portugal to investigate reports of religious and moral failings. Those accused in Brazil were sent to Portugal for trial.

Economic and Social Role of the Church. The Catholic church was the primary provider of education and social services in colonial Latin America. The religious orders operated schools in monasteries and convents, and the Dominicans and Jesuits played leading roles in secondary and university education. Clergymen also directed hospitals, orphanages, and other charitable institutions.

Funds for support of the church and its social and educational functions came from various sources. The crown collected several ecclesiastical taxes, of which the most important was the tithe, levied on agricultural products and livestock. Pious laypeople frequently donated or bequeathed funds or property to church bodies for philanthropic purposes or to support priests who

were to say masses on their behalf after their death. As a result, the religious orders and other ecclesiastical corporations acquired large amounts of urban and rural real estate, which also contributed to their support. The Jesuits were especially noted for their productive estates, encompassing large tracts of land and employing many workers, including African slaves.

1759-67

Expulsion of the Jesuits. In an age when European monarchs attempted to assert royal authority over competing institutions, the kings of Portugal and Spain resented the wealth and influence of the Jesuits. They were also disliked by many laypeople and members of other religious orders. In 1759 the **Marquês de Pombal**, chief minister of King Joseph I, suppressed the order in the Portuguese empire. The pretext was the alleged complicity of some Jesuits in a plot to assassinate the king, but many believe that the expulsion of the Jesuits from Brazil was mainly due to Pombal's desire to confiscate their extensive properties there. Approximately 600 Jesuits were expelled. King **Charles III** suppressed the order in Spain and its colonies in 1767 after Jesuits were accused of instigating recent antigovernment riots in Madrid. More than 2,000 Jesuits were expelled from the Spanish colonies. The expulsion order produced rioting in Mexico.

Jesuit properties were auctioned off to laypeople with the crown retaining the proceeds, and the Jesuits' missions and educational institutions were turned over to other orders. The expelled Jesuits moved to Italy, remaining there even after Pope Clement XIV suppressed the order in 1773. Francisco Javier Clavijero (1731-1787), a Mexican-born Jesuit exiled to Italy, wrote *Historia antigua de México* (1780-81), in which he praised his native country and criticized those who disparaged the New World.

1810-40

The Catholic Church and Independence. Leaders of the Spanish-American independence movements were generally supportive of Catholicism, and many American-born priests supported the anti-Spanish cause, among them the Mexicans **Miguel Hidalgo** and **José María Morelos**. By contrast, members of the upper clergy, who tended to be Spaniards, were usually royalists.

Because of Spanish pressure, the papacy was reluctant to acknowledge Spanish-American independence. In 1824 Pope Leo XIII issued an encyclical exhorting the bishops and archbishops of Spanish America to remain loyal to the king. However, in 1827 Pope Leo began to fill the many bishoprics that had fallen vacant since the start of the conflict. His successor, Gregory XVI, formally recognized the independence of New Granada (modern Colombia) in 1835, and recognition of the other republics soon followed.

The first constitutions of the new republics retained Catholicism as the state religion, and the new governments sought to assert the rights of patronage over the church that Spain had enjoyed. But the papacy rejected their claim that patronage was an attribute of sovereignty, though it often accepted state nomination of bishops, whom it confirmed. In general, the disappearance of Spanish authority in the former colonies brought the clergy more directly under papal authority. In Brazil the constitution of 1824 established Catholicism and asserted the right of patronage, which was vigorously upheld by the emperors.

c. 1840-1930

Conflicts Between Church and State. Throughout Latin America there were clashes of varying degrees of intensity between state and church, especially when political leaders of a Liberal orientation gained control of governments. Liberals usually attempted to curb the economic power of the church, offer greater religious freedom to non-Catholics, secularize public education, and in general reduce the influence of the church over the population. Clerics and devout laypeople opposed such measures because of religious conviction and because of a belief that a strong church was a source of stability. Their position was strengthened by the Syllabus of Errors issued by Pope Pius IX in 1864, which condemned liberalism. Since clerics often publicly supported the Conservative foes of Liberals, they were also attacked for improper interference in politics.

Church–state conflict was most bitter in Mexico, Colombia, Ecuador, Venezuela, and Guatemala. Where Liberals triumphed, the church was usually forced to divest itself of its real estate, religious orders were suppressed, religious instruction was prohibited in public schools, religious freedom for all sects was decreed, and civil marriage was introduced. By contrast, in Colombia, where Conservatives regained control of the government in the mid-1880s, Catholicism was declared to be the religion of the nation, religious instruction was made mandatory in public schools, the church was given the freedom to own property, and marriage according to the Roman Catholic rite was for all practical purposes the only form of matrimony recognized by the state.

Although the church suffered as an institution because of Liberal reforms, Catholicism retained its powerful hold on the masses. Conflict gradually diminished by the end of the nineteenth century, and several countries decreed the separation of church and state, among them Brazil (1891) and Chile (1925). Acrimony resurfaced in Mexico as a result of anticlerical provisions in the constitution of 1917, which banned outdoor religious ceremonies, denied churches any role in primary education, and prohibited criticism of the constitution or public officials by ministers. Catholic protests over the constitution led to clerical closure of the churches and an unsuccessful uprising by Catholic rebels known as *kristeros* (1926-29).

1930-90s

From Catholic Action to Liberation Theology. Catholic Action associations of lay people were founded in Latin America after 1930. Like their European counterparts, their purpose was to reinvigorate Catholicism and to defend it from liberalism and communism. Although many Catholic Action leaders adopted extreme conservative positions on the political and social issues of the day, some in Chile, Brazil, and other countries embraced Catholic teachings supportive of democracy and social change, taking part in the formation of Catholic labor unions and Christian Democratic parties. By the 1960s many members of the clergy had become extremely concerned about the plight of the poor while others expressed criticism of dictatorships in Argentina, Venezuela, and the Dominican Republic. The Conference of Latin American Bishops (CELAM), founded in Rio de Janeiro in 1955, adopted progressive positions from its inception.

During the 1960s forces both within the church and external to it combined to intensify clerical concern for the poor and oppressed. Encyclicals by Pope John XXIII and Pope Paul VI and the decrees of Vatican Council II (1962-65) emphasized the obligations of the church to the poor, criticized capitalism, and softened the traditional hostility of the church toward Marxism. In Latin America the Cuban Revolution and the Alliance for Progress turned minds to agrarian reform and other issues of development, while dependency theory gained currency among academics and intellectuals. Catholic thinkers such as the Peruvian priest Gustavo Gutiérrez and the Brazilian Franciscan Leonardo Boff devised an interpretation of Christianity that viewed Jesus Christ as a liberator of the oppressed from poverty and injustice. A few clerics even took up arms in support of Castroite revolutionary movements. Among them was Camilo Torres, a Colombian priest who joined the Army of National Liberation (ELN) and was killed in combat in 1966.

The impact of liberation theology could be seen at the second meeting of CELAM in Medellín, Colombia, in 1968. The bishops present adopted a document that urged drastic change in existing socioeconomic structures, stated that without justice there could be no peace, and pledged to promote *concientización*, a form of education aimed at encouraging the poor to become aware of the structural causes of their plight. To facilitate this work grassroots organizations called Christian base communities were established in Brazil, El Salvador,

Nicaragua, and other countries. Although many bishops and archbishops, such as the Brazilian **Hélder Câmara**, endorsed the positions adopted at Medellín, others remained aloof, especially in Mexico, Argentina, and Colombia. At the third CELAM meeting, in Puebla, Mexico, in 1979, the bishops took a more moderate position, though reaffirming their concern for the poor. Meanwhile, Catholic clerics and lay activists played a leading role in opposing right-wing military dictatorships in Brazil, Chile, and Central America. In 1980 Archbishop **Oscar Romero** of El Salvador, an outspoken critic of human rights abuses by the government, was murdered while saying mass.

Late Twentieth-Century Developments. Under Pope John Paul II, the Vatican expressed concern about Marxist influences on liberation theology and about apparent tendencies among some clerics to create a people's church in opposition to the official church. In the mid-1980s the Vatican imposed travel and speaking restrictions on Boff. However, it continued to endorse an overriding commitment to the poor. Other issues of concern to Catholics in the late twentieth century were the rapid growth of other Christian denominations in Latin America and the shortage of priests in the region. In Brazil, for example, there were 8,708 Catholics per priest in 1995, and in Mexico, 6,804 Catholics per priest; the United States had one priest per 1,117 Catholics in 1995. Another trend was the severance of all ties between the state and the Catholic church. For example, the Colombian constitution of 1991, which replaced that of 1886, ended state support of Catholicism and put all churches on equal footing.

Afro–Latin American Religions. Syncretistic folk religions of partly African origin have survived in countries where a large portion of the population is descended from African slaves, notably Haiti, Cuba, and Brazil. These religions usually incorporate elements of Christianity, such as the identification of Roman Catholic saints with spirits or deities of West African origin. Another common feature is the invocation of these spirits by priests, mediums, or worshippers who are in turn possessed by the spirits and speak in their voices.

Vodun, a name derived from the Dahomeyan word for spirit, is widely practiced in Haiti. In Cuba the Spanish term *santería* is used to designate several African-based religions, the most important of which has Yoruba roots. It continued to gain adherents after the 1959 revolution and was subsequently introduced to the United States and other countries where Cuban exiles settled.

There are several Afro-Brazilian religions. Candomblé, also of Yoruba origin, is considered the most traditional and is practiced mainly in the Northeast by persons of African descent. Umbanda appeared in the 1920s in Rio de Janeiro state and is also influenced by pre-Columbian indigenous religion and by Spiritism, which gained adherents in Brazil after the writings of the French Spiritist Allen Kardec were introduced in the 1850s. Umbanda attracts persons of all races and classes and has spread to Argentina and Uruguay.

Protestantism. Since the residence of non-Catholics in colonial Latin America was forbidden, Protestant religions were not introduced until the nineteenth century. The first Protestants in Latin America were American or European residents or immigrants who brought their religion with them. German immigrants to southern Brazil, for example, were often Lutherans. Starting in the 1920s Mennonite colonies were established in Paraguay, Mexico, and other countries. Organized missionary activity began about 1850 with the arrival of missionaries from mainline churches in the United States and Great Britain. Liberal political leaders such as **Benito Juárez** of Mexico and **Justo Rufino Barrios** of Guatemala often welcomed Protestant missionaries, whom they considered allies in their efforts to weaken the Catholic church. Conversely, devout Catholics opposed the Protestant presence. Fundamentalist "faith missions" became active in the twentieth century, especially after World War II. As late as 1960, however, Protestantism was an insignificant force in the region as a whole.

Starting in about 1960, the number of Latin American Protestants increased dramatically, with the most substantial growth being experienced among Pentecostals. During this period Pentecostal churches in the United States, such as the Assemblies of God, expanded their efforts in Latin America, though missionaries were increasingly being replaced by native-born religious leaders. The growth of Pentecostalism has been attributed to several factors, including the shortage of Catholic priests and the dislocations accompanying rapid socioeconomic change and, in some countries, civil war. Although reliable figures are difficult to obtain, the countries with the largest percentage of Protestants in their population are believed to be Guatemala, Brazil, and Chile. Also noteworthy has been the growth of the Mormon church, which counted nearly 3 million adherents in Latin America in the early 1990s.

Jews in Latin America. Both Spain (1492) and Portugal (1496) expelled from their domains Jews who refused to undergo baptism. Spain also barred the emigration of converted Jews (New Christians) and their descendants to the Indies, but many found ways to settle there nonetheless. There was also a substantial New Christian population in Brazil. New Christians who secretly practiced Judaism were often targets of the Inquisition. The most notorious case was that of Luis de Carvajal the Younger, nephew of the governor of Nuevo León in Mexico, who was condemned as a relapsed heretic and burned at the stake in 1596.

After independence a small number of Western European Jews settled in Latin America, but it was not until the late nineteenth century that large numbers of Jewish immigrants arrived, mostly from Eastern Europe and settling mainly in South America. Between 1881 and 1942, over 200,000 Jews entered Argentina; about 70,000 settled in Brazil. The increased Jewish presence provoked periodic outbreaks of anti-Semitism, especially in Argentina, such as attacks on Jews during the Semana Trágica of 1919. By the early 1980s there were probably fewer than 500,000 Jews in Latin America, half of them in Argentina;

Brazil, Mexico, and Uruguay also had significant Jewish populations. Little growth was expected because of low birth rates among Jews, intermarriage with non-Jews, and emigration.

Education

Pre-Columbian Education. Most native American children received instruction from their parents in the skills and arts they would need as adults. Such schools as did exist were designed mainly to prepare young men for the priesthood or warfare. Among the Aztecs, the sons of commoners were sent to schools called *telpochcalli*, where they were trained as warriors. These schools also had sections for girls, and both boys and girls attended schools where they learned ceremonial songs and dances. Sons of the nobility and selected commoners attended schools called *calmecac*, which were attached to the major temples. Here they were prepared for the priesthood or for high public office. Noble girls also attended these schools, where they were instructed in embroidery. According to **Diego de Landa**, Maya priests in Yucatán were responsible for training future priests in ritual, calendrics, writing, mathematics, and astronomy. Unmarried youths lived in communal houses, where they received instruction in warfare.

The sons of Inca nobles and conquered leaders were educated in a school in Cuzco, learning about Inca religion and history and the use of the *quipu*, an Andean mnemonic device. Especially attractive girls were selected to be "chosen women," sometimes termed "Virgins of the Sun," and were educated in "convents" in provincial capitals. They were taught domestic skills, weaving, and religion. Others were taken as secondary wives by Inca nobles; a few were sacrificed at important ceremonial occasions. Such sacrifice was believed to ensure them eternal bliss in their afterlife.

c. 1525-1750

Schools and Universities in the Early Colonial Period. In the Spanish colonies, as in Brazil, the Roman Catholic clergy played a major role in education at all levels. They operated elementary and secondary schools known as colleges or *colegios*, and often served as university professors. Among the earliest educational institutions established in the Spanish colonies were schools for the instruction of Indians. The Franciscan lay brother Pedro de Gante (c. 1480-1572) founded the school of San José in Mexico, which offered elementary education to Indian boys as well as training in music and crafts. The College of Santa Cruz de Tlatelolco near Mexico City, founded in 1536, served the sons of Indian nobles and offered higher education, including courses in Latin, rhetoric, logic, and philosophy. In general, however, efforts on behalf of Indian education were limited, and schooling was reserved mainly for whites and mestizos.

Children learned their first letters from tutors or in schools run by the religious orders or by laypeople. The Jesuits founded secondary schools in important cities, such as the Colegio de San Pablo in Lima (1568), which served as the preparatory school for students planning to enter the university. Here boys learned Latin, Greek, scriptures, theology, logic, and philosophy, and upon completion of their studies, received bachelor's degrees. Universities, modeled on those of Spain, offered courses of study leading to advanced degrees in theology, law, and medicine.

Santo Domingo claims to be the site of the first university in the Western Hemisphere because of a papal bull in 1538 elevating a Dominican school there to university rank. But this institution did not function as a genuine university or admit lay students until the seventeenth century. In 1551 the crown authorized the establishment of universities in Mexico City and Lima. Classes at the University of Mexico began in 1553, but the University of San Marcos in Lima languished until the 1570s when Viceroy **Francisco de Toledo** provided it with adequate funds. Universities were established in other colonial cities, including Bogotá (1563), Chuquisaca (modern Sucre, 1624), Guatemala City (1676), and Havana (1712).

Because of the sparse population and rural character of colonial Brazil, education was less developed there than in Spanish America, and the role of the Jesuits was even more important. In 1554 **Manuel da Nóbrega**, an early Jesuit missionary, opened a school for Portuguese orphans and Indians near the site of modern São Paulo; it was moved to Rio de Janeiro in the 1560s. The Jesuits also founded numerous colleges in Brazil, but no university was ever established. Students might prepare for the priesthood in the colony, but those who sought careers in medicine or law had to go to Portugal to complete their studies.

c. 1750-1850

Changes under the Bourbons and in the Early National Period. The accession of the Bourbon dynasty in Spain, coupled with the influence of Enlightenment ideas regarding education and the importance of useful knowledge, brought change to schools at all levels in the late eighteenth century. The crown encouraged the establishment of free primary schools by both municipalities and the clergy, and the education of girls received greater attention than before. The expulsion of the Jesuits in 1767 disrupted education in colleges and universities, but these institutions were reinvigorated by the introduction of courses incorporating recent advances in science and mathematics and placing greater emphasis on observation and experiment. (See Science and Medicine.)

The leaders of the newly independent nations favored the expansion of education, but their efforts were hampered by the internal turmoil and poor financial condition of most of the republics. Even so, the number of boys and girls enrolled in public and private primary schools increased substantially. Elementary curricula were similar to those of the late colonial period, except that education in citizenship was introduced. In the 1820s Mexico and other countries experimented with the mutual instruction method devised by the Englishman John Lancaster in the late eighteenth century. Under this method older students instructed younger students in material imparted by a master teacher, who could thus reach a large number of students. The Lancasterian method also emphasized discipline and obedience.

During this period national universities were founded in Argentina (1821), Uruguay (1833), Chile (1842), and other countries. In Brazil the lack of higher education was remedied by the establishment of colleges of medicine in Bahia (1808) and Rio de Janeiro (1810); law schools were established in São Paulo and Olinda in 1827. The prestigious Colégio Dom Pedro II was founded in Rio de Janeiro in 1837.

c. 1850-1990s

Modernization and Educational Expansion. The political stability and economic growth that occurred in most Latin American countries after 1850 created conditions conducive to educational development as leaders sought to create a citizenry capable of participating in the new socioeconomic order. In Argentina **Domingo F. Sarmiento**, as director of education in Buenos Aires province (1856-61) and president (1868-74), created many new public schools, including kindergartens and *colegios*, and fostered numerous reforms. By the start of the twentieth century Argentina's educational system was considered the best in Latin America; about two-thirds of its population was literate in 1914. Other countries lagged behind. In Mexico, though the number of children enrolled in public primary schools more than tripled between 1878 and 1907, only 29 percent of the population over twelve was literate in 1910.

The growth of public elementary schooling was accompanied by the establishment of teacher training (normal) schools, the first of which was founded in Chile in 1842. Students at these schools were often women, who increasingly came to dominate elementary teaching. Starting in the 1880s in Chile, Mexico, and Brazil, women gained admission to higher education throughout the region, but female literacy levels and educational opportunities remained inferior to those of men in most countries.

By 1900 many intellectuals and students believed that Latin America's universities were not meeting the needs of their rapidly changing societies. This sentiment found expression in a reform movement begun by students at the

University of Córdoba, Argentina, in 1918. Student demands included political autonomy, or self-government, for universities; student participation in university governance; voluntary class attendance; and the establishment of extension programs for workers. Students in Córdoba and other Argentine universities won approval of their demands in 1918, and the movement spread to other countries with some success. During this period many students, faculty, and administrators were highly politicized and often clashed with government leaders. Students were prominent in opposition to the dictators **Juan Vicente Gómez** and **Gerardo Machado** in Venezuela and Cuba, respectively, and national universities in both countries were shut down for several years. Public universities predominated during this period, though a few private universities were founded, sometimes under Roman Catholic auspices, such as the Jesuit Universidad Iberoamericana (1943) in Mexico City. Business leaders were responsible for the establishment in 1943 of the Instituto Tecnológico de Monterrey, Mexico.

Late-Twentieth-Century Trends in Education.
After 1950 Latin American governments invested heavily in education, but found it difficult to keep pace with rapid population growth. By the end of the century nearly all children had access to elementary education and basic literacy was widespread (see Table 5). Literacy campaigns for adults and other nontraditional programs gained favor in some countries, and governments were pressed to offer bilingual education to indigenous children. Educational reformers such as the Brazilian Paulo Freire advocated methods of instruction that would awaken the children of the poor to the reasons for their condition and help them find remedies. During this period the gap between male and female educational attainments narrowed significantly and in some countries disappeared.

There was also substantial growth in the numbers attending secondary institutions. In 1960, only 37 percent of young people aged 12-17 were enrolled in school; by 1980 the percentage had increased to 61, though there were wide disparities among countries. Enrollments in universities also mushroomed, and public

universities suffered from shortages of full-time faculty and inadequate library and laboratory facilities. Students frequently dropped out or spent years completing degrees. However, efforts to tighten admission standards or raise fees at public universities usually brought strong protests. University students remained highly politicized, especially those in the social sciences and humanities, often embracing leftist political causes. In Mexico City, secondary and university students were in the vanguard of protests that culminated in the Tlatelolco massacre of October 2, 1968. In Peru the Maoist group Shining Path was founded at the University of San Cristóbal de Huamanga in impoverished Ayacucho department. Its founder, Abimael Guzmán, was a professor of education at the university and recruited many followers there.

One response to the political and financial problems of the public universities was a proliferation of private institutions, funded by Roman Catholic or business groups or by international institutions, such as the Ford Foundation. Enrollment at these institutions, which appealed to members of the upper and upper-middle classes, grew dramatically, accounting for 39 percent of university students by 1975.

Table 5

Illiteracy in Selected Countries, 1995*

Country	Percent
Argentina	3.8
Brazil	16.7
Chile	4.8
Colombia	8.7
Costa Rica	5.2
Dominican Republic	17.9
Guatemala	44.4
Mexico	10.4
Peru	11.3
Venezuela	8.9

*Adult illiterates as percentage of those 18 and over.

Source: *Inter-American Development Bank.*

Art and Architecture

Pre-Columbian Art. The artifacts of pre-Columbian America were once displayed exclusively in museums of anthropology and natural history. In the late nineteenth century, however, European artists and intellectuals began to value the aesthetic qualities of the handiwork of "primitive" peoples, including those of the Western Hemisphere. Much of this work is now considered art worthy of exhibition on an equal footing with the painting and sculpture of "advanced" civilizations.

The artistic legacy of the civilizations of Mesoamerica and Andean South America is especially rich. The peoples of central Mexico and the Maya regions of southern Mexico and Central America excelled in the construction of cities with impressive temples and other buildings, especially during the Classic period (150-900 C.E.). Major sites distinguished for their monumental architecture include Teotihuacán near Mexico City, Monte Albán in Oaxaca, and Tikal in northern Guatemala. Uxmal, located in northwestern Yucatán, is noted for its long, elaborately decorated buildings, such as the House of the Governor and the Nunnery Quadrangle. The most characteristic structures of Chichén Itzá in northern Yucatán, such as the Castillo and the ball court, date from the post-Classic period and resemble those of the Toltec center of Tula in central Mexico. At the Maya site of Bonampak in Chiapas, Mexico, well-preserved murals portray scenes of warfare and offer insight into Maya society of the late Classic period. Murals at Cacaxtla, a site in the Mexican state of Tlaxcala that flourished from about 650 to 950, have been widely known only since the mid-1970s. The largest mural depicts the aftermath of a battle as jaguar soldiers prepare to sacrifice captives dressed as birds. Painted on another mural are corn and cacao plants and an old man with a merchant's backpack.

In addition to the superb stone carvings that decorated buildings and stelae, the artistic legacy of pre-Columbian Mesoamerica includes outstanding works of sculpture in the round. The earliest known examples are the colossal human heads and other basalt figures associated with the Olmec culture, which flourished along the Gulf of Mexico c. 1,000-400 B.C.E. The Olmecs also produced small but exquisite figurines carved of jade. Distinguished examples of Maya sculpture include two stucco heads found in the Temple of the Inscriptions at Palenque and a limestone standard-bearer found in the Venus Platform at Chichén Itzá and notable for the individualism with which the figure is represented. The latter site has also yielded numerous examples of the *chacmool*, a human figure in a distinctive reclining position placed at the front entrance of temple buildings. The Aztec, who dominated central Mexico at the time of the Spanish conquest, were also superb carvers in stone, creating fearsome figures, such as an eight-foot-high rendering of the goddess Coatlicue as well as a stone offering vessel in the shape of an eagle in which every feather is skillfully carved. The Aztec were skilled metal-workers and wood-carvers as well. Few examples remain of another Aztec art, the making of feather pictures (*amentecayotl*).

The archaeological site of Chavín de Huántar in northern Peru contains the earliest monuments of Andean South America, dating to 900-200 B.C.E. Representations of jaguars, hawks, serpents, and other animals are carved into structures at the site in a style that spread far beyond Chavín de Huántar. Another site noted for its stone megaliths is Tiahuanaco, located in modern Bolivia and probably built c. 100–725 C.E. The Inca, latecomers to the region, were extraordinarily skilled in stonemasonry, as can be seen in surviving structures in their capital, Cuzco. Overlooking the city is the fortress of Sacsahuamán, notable for its three great walls built of enormous stones.

The Paracas culture (c. 800 B.C.E.–100 C.E.) of the southern coast of Peru produced fine textiles of wool and cotton which were used for mortuary purposes and were well preserved in the desert environment of the area. They are notable for their rich coloring and elaborate yet harmonious designs. The Nazca culture (c. 370 B.C.E.–540 C.E.) of the same region is noted for its polychrome slip clay pottery and for its large desert drawings. The Moche culture (c. 100 B.C.E.–540 C.E.) is noted for its ceramics, which provide realistic portraits of individuals as well as scenes of daily life. The Moche also created ornaments of gold and other metals. The Tairona, Muisca, and Quimbaya cultures in what is now Colombia also produced outstanding ceramic pieces and gold work.

c. 1500-1810

The Colonial Period. The art and architecture of colonial Latin America reflects the European forms, styles, and iconography introduced by Spain and Portugal to the New World. On occasion the requirements of the new environment and the emergence of native artists and artisans produced modifications in European models. Throughout the period churches and other religious buildings dominated architecture, starting with the construction of monasteries in the mid-sixteenth century. In Mexico these establishments usually consisted of a single-nave church with an adjoining convent and an enclosed courtyard and open chapel in front. Their design and decoration embraced a variety of styles—Gothic, Renaissance, and Mudéjar (Moorish-Christian). An important early church in South America is San Francisco in Quito. Completed in 1575, it is noteworthy for its symmetrical facade in a late Renaissance style and for its superb interior. After 1650 church construction reflected the influence of the Baroque. An outstanding South American example is the Compañía Church (1651-58) in Cuzco, notable for its unity of style. In Mexico an ultrabaroque style (also known as Churrigueresque) became prevalent in the eighteenth century and can be seen in the Church of Santa Prisca (1751-58) in Taxco. The introduction of classicism to Spanish America was signaled by the establishment (1785) of the Academy of San Carlos in Mexico City. The Spaniard Manuel Tolsá (1757-1816), named director of the school in 1798, was a talented architect and sculptor, famous for his Palacio de Minería in Mexico City and his monumental bronze statue of Charles IV in the garb of a Roman emperor, but more remembered as "El Caballito" for its majestic equestrian representation than for the regal grandeur of its rider who was a mediocre king.

Brazilian architecture closely followed European models. An outstanding example of the baroque is the Church of São Pedro dos Clérigos in Recife, begun in 1728. A more exuberant style was adopted for churches constructed in Minas Gerais after the discovery of gold there. The outstanding practitioner in this style was Antônio Francisco Lisbôa, nicknamed **O Aleijadinho**, whose architectural masterpiece is the Church of São Francisco de Assis (1766-94) in Ouro Preto. A gifted sculptor, Lisbôa produced pulpits, altars, and other objects related to church architecture. His best-known work of sculpture is a group of twelve prophets he created in soapstone (1800-5) for the Church of Bom Jesus de Matosinhos in Congonhas do Campo.

Colonial painters concentrated on religious subjects but also produced portraits and scenes of historical events. Baltasar de Echave Orio (c. 1558–c. 1620), a native of Spain's Basque country, helped introduce to Mexico a Mannerist style based on Flemish and Italian models. Becoming Mexico's leading painter, he founded a dynasty of artists including his son, Baltasar de Echave Ibía, and his pupil, Luis Juárez. By the early eighteenth century, a distinctive Mexican style can be discerned. Although the influence of Murillo and other contemporary painters is apparent, the work of Mexican artists such as the mestizo Miguel Cabrera (1695-1768) exhibits nuances of color and composition unique to Mexico. Cabrera painted religious scenes but is also noted for his portraits and for paintings depicting racial mixture in Mexico.

In South America Diego Quispe Tito (c. 1611-1681), an Indian working in Cuzco, reinterpreted European models, as in his *Holy Family* (1680), based on a Flemish engraving of the Vision of the Cross. The painters of the Cuzco School of the late seventeenth and eighteenth centuries also created a peculiarly New World style through their unique renderings of religious figures, such as virgins evocative of Byzantine icons who were depicted in resplendent attire and with pyramidal contours. Also distinctive were paintings of archangels dressed in lavish secular garb and carrying muskets.

c. 1800-c. 1990s

Art in the Independent Nations. The attainment of independence brought little immediate change in art and architecture. The new nations continued to value European training and to import foreign artists and architects and created academies to impart artistic traditions. The first post-independence academy of fine arts was established in Brazil in 1826 under the direction of Jean-Baptiste Debret (1768-1848), one of a team of French artists and craftsmen invited to Brazil in 1816. The academy's neoclassical building was designed by another member of the group, Auguste-Henri-Victor Grandjean de Montigny (1776-1850). A Venezuelan academy was founded in the mid-1830s; others were established elsewhere during the remainder of the century.

In architecture neoclassical design long remained dominant, as seen in the façade of the cathedral of Buenos Aires, designed by the Frenchman Próspero Catelin and completed in 1823. French influence is also evident after 1850 in urban beautification projects which took the Paris of Baron Haussmann as a model, such as the creation of several new monumental avenues in Rio de Janeiro starting in 1903. By the end of the century neoclassicism was being replaced by other styles, as in the Italianate central post office in Mexico City (1902-4)—the work of Adamo Boari, who also designed the Palace of Fine Arts, begun in 1905 but not completed until the 1930s.

The painting of historical scenes, in accordance with academic models, was an important feature of nineteenth-century art, with subjects from Latin American history becoming increasingly popular. An outstanding early example is *Columbus Before the Spanish Sovereigns* (1850), painted by the Mexican Juan Cordero (1822-1884) while he was studying in Rome on a scholarship. In Mexico scenes based on pre-Columbian themes, such as José María Obregón's *The Discovery of Pulque* (1867),

reflected an embryonic Indianism, though this painting, like others in this vein, suggests classical antiquity as much as ancient Mexico. Other artists turned to depiction of episodes from the struggle for independence, as in Arturo Michelena's realistic *Miranda in La Carraca* (1896). Meanwhile, the Uruguayan Juan Manuel Blanes (1830-1901) painted scenes of more recent historical events, such as *Paraguay: Image of Your Desolate Country* (1880), portraying the ravages of the Paraguayan War (1864-70), and *Review of Río Negro by General Roca and His Army* (n.d.)

Paintings emphasizing local color (*costumbrismo*) and the picturesque proved another fertile field in the nineteenth century. Significant contributions were made by foreign artists, such as Debret and Johann Mauritz Rugendas (1802-1858), a Bavarian who made numerous drawings, water colors, and paintings during his extensive travels throughout Latin America. A gifted Mexican *costumbrista*, José Agustín Arrieta (1802-1874), created still-lifes and arresting portraits of regional types, such as *The Man from the Coast* (n.d.) and *The Chinaco and the China* (n.d.), which evoke Dutch genre painting. Also transcending the genre are *The Violinist* (1899) by the Brazilian José Ferraz de Almeida Júnior (1850-1899) and the romanticized gauchos painted by Juan Manuel Blanes in *Dawn, Dusk, Early Morning* (n.d.), and *Early Evening* (n.d.).

The Mexican José María Velasco (1840-1912) was the ablest practitioner of landscape painting, which attracted few artists. His sweeping vistas of the Valley of Mexico are distinguished by their mastery of color and perspective. Graphic art is exemplified above all by the work of the prolific Mexican printmaker **José Guadalupe Posada**, whose illustrations for broadsides recorded sensational events with a satirical edge. Especially noteworthy are the *calaveras*, broadsides sold on the Day of the Dead (November 2), whose skeletal figures evoke humanity's universal fate.

Twentieth-Century Art and Architecture. In about 1920 Latin American architecture began to be influenced by modernism, especially the International Style associated with Le Corbusier, which was often employed in the large urban projects characteristic of the era. By 1945, however, architects had moved away from strict adherence to functionalism and were increasingly incorporating native and traditional elements into their buildings.

Le Corbusier's ideas probably had their greatest impact in Brazil through the designs of its two leading architects, Lúcio Costa (1902-1998) and **Oscar Niemeyer**. In 1936 Le Corbusier himself came to Brazil as a consultant on the planned Ministry of Education and Public Health in Rio de Janeiro, which was designed by Costa, Niemeyer, and other architects. Notable features of the building include horizontal louvers to shield glass windows against the tropical sun and ceramic tile decorations painted by **Cândido Portinari**. Costa and Niemeyer's most celebrated collaboration was the design of Brasília, the country's new federal capital. Costa contributed the overall design, or pilot plan, which suggested an airplane. Government buildings were located on the fuselage while the wings were devoted to residential housing. Brasília proved controversial from the day of its inauguration in 1960. Critics found the city dehumanizing and claimed that its layout created traffic bottlenecks and made it inhospitable to pedestrians. Moreover, although Costa envisioned a city that would house people from all classes, Brasília soon became ringed by satellite communities that eventually housed the majority of the Federal District's population.

Latin America's first large-scale urban development project was El Silencio (1941-43) in Caracas, Venezuela, designed by Carlos Raúl Villanueva (1900-1976). Villanueva completed other major projects in Caracas, such as the University City built during the 1950s. Its 2,600-seat auditorium, or Aula Magna, is noted for its remarkable ceiling, decorated with brightly colored stabiles by the sculptor Alexander Calder. Another major University City project was designed in Mexico City in 1946-54 by a group of architects led by Mario Pani. Juan O'Gorman (1905-1982) designed the project's Central Library, the exterior of which he decorated with

four mosaic murals. In Mexico, the Spanish-born Félix Candela (1910–) became known for his use of thin shell vaulting made of reinforced concrete, as in the capital's Church of the Miraculous Virgin (1954) and the Bacardi bottling plant in Cuatitlán (1963).

Latin American painting in the twentieth century continued to be shaped by international art movements, but many painters were committed to the creation of work that would reflect the region's culture and society. Impressionism and post-impressionism made their influence felt only at a relatively late date. The Venezuelan Armando Reverón (1889-1954) is noted for a series of seascapes he painted after moving to the coastal town of Macuto. These nearly white canvases convey the impression of light that unites all the colors of the spectrum. Pedro Figari (1861-1938) devoted himself to painting after a distinguished career as a lawyer in his native Uruguay. Influenced by the work of Edouard Vuillard, Figari painted in a seemingly naive style, creating scenes of a rural way of life that had already disappeared.

Brazil's multi-faceted Modern Art Week of 1922 stimulated an era of artistic renewal, in which painters combined modernist approaches with an emphasis on nationally oriented subjects, especially involving Indians and blacks. The best-known Brazilian artist of the period is Tarsila do Amaral (1886-1973), who studied in Paris with Fernand Léger and André Lhote. Her paintings *Black Woman* (1923) and *Abaporu* (1928) are distinctive for their Brazilian themes as well as for their abstract forms and vivid colors.

The most influential Latin American art movement of the twentieth century was Mexican muralism, which emerged during the 1920s as a by-product of the revolution of 1910. The "Big Three" muralists—**Diego Rivera, José Clemente Orozco**, and **David Alfaro Siqueiros**—sought to create an art that would not only be Mexican in subject matter but would also be accessible to the masses because of its location on the walls of public buildings. For nearly fifty years these artists as well as many lesser-known figures created murals in Mexico City, Guadalajara, and other Mexican cities. Painted in fresco and other media, the murals usually presented historical episodes or scenes of Mexican life and folklore in a figurative style that contained echoes of the artists' exposure to European art of the past and present. The Mexican movement attracted much interest internationally and encouraged a resurgence of muralism in the United States, often under the aegis of New Deal federal arts programs. In Brazil, **Cândido Portinari** became noted as a muralist, particularly for his ceramic murals. At the Church of St. Francis of Assisi in the Belo Horizonte suburb of Pampulha, he created an exterior mural in blue and white tiles depicting scenes from the life of the saint.

The Mexicans' interest in the Indian had special resonance in Andean South America, where many artists used indigenous subjects in their paintings, sometimes pointing to their oppression in contemporary society. The Peruvian José Sabogal (1888-1956) was a leader of this school. His best-known work is a portrait of a dignified Indian functionary, *The Indian Mayor of Chincheros: Varayoc* (1925). *The Strike* (1940) by the Ecuadorian Oswaldo Guayasamín (1919–) combines Indianism with social protest. Portinari also demonstrated his concern for Brazil's destitute, as in the three paintings of the Refugee Series (1944), which show the effects of Northeastern drought on the poor of that near-arid region.

European avant-garde movements such as cubism and surrealism had their Latin American disciples. Rivera himself painted numerous canvases in a cubist style while living in Europe from 1906 to 1921. Roberto Matta Echaurren (1911–), a native of Santiago, Chile, who settled permanently abroad, was identified with surrealism, as can be seen in *Invasion of the Night* (1941) and *A Grave Situation* (1944), before being expelled from the movement in the late 1940s. When André Breton, a leading surrealist spokesman, visited Mexico in 1938, he detected affinities with surrealism in the paintings of **Frida Kahlo**, which offer interpretations of her life experiences in a pictorial context that is clearly Mexican. While living in Paris, the Cuban Wilfredo Lam (1902-1982) was also associated with surrealism but came under the influence of

Picasso as well, as is evident in his *Light of Clay* (1950). After returning to Cuba in 1941, Lam began to produce canvases allusive of Afro-Cuban *santería*. The Mexican Rufino Tamayo (1899-1991) also incorporated the modernist vision into his work after moving to New York in 1926, as in *Lion and Horse* (1942), which is evocative of Picasso's *Guernica*. Although Tamayo spurned the highly politicized themes favored by many Mexican muralists, his choice of color and themes and his modeling of the human figure reveal his Mexican roots.

Nonfigurative art attracted many painters, starting with the Uruguayan Joaquín Torres-García (1874-1949), who became associated with Mondrian and other constructivist artists while living in Europe. But he also incorporated pre-Columbian artistic conventions in his geometric *Indoamerica* (1938) and the colors and shapes of ancient Peruvian pottery in *Constructive Art with Large Sun* (1942). The influence of Mondrian is also evident in *Coloured Lines* (1950) of the Venezuelan Alejandro Soto (1923–) and his 1950s series of "colourhythms," in which colored forms painted in Duco are arranged in parallel vertical lines. The Brazilian Lygia Clark (1920-1988) began her career by painting rigorously abstract works, such as *Relief Painting with Yellow Square* (1957), but later turned to sculpture, creating a series of *Bichos*, or Animals, in metal in the 1960s.

As the twentieth century drew to a close, Latin American painters remained preoccupied with the problem of creating art that would be reflective of the culture and circumstances of the region without marginalizing themselves from international trends and concerns. Among the most prominent were the Mexican Alberto Gironella (1929-1999) and the Uruguayan José Gamarra (1934–), whose work reinterpreted history and myth. The Colombian **Fernando Botero** acquired an international reputation for his painting and sculptures, dominated by obese figures that satirized pillars of Latin American society. Meanwhile, the discussion and exhibition of all kinds of art in Latin America was facilitated by the proliferation of museums and galleries throughout the continent and by the sponsorship of foundations, private firms, and the Pan American Union's Division of Visual Arts. From its inception in 1951 the São Paulo Biennial became an important venue for the exhibition of contemporary art from Latin America as well as from other regions.

Music

Pre-Columbian Music. No pre-Columbian musical composition has survived, but Spanish chroniclers and archaeological evidence indicate that music was an integral part of ceremonies associated with religion and warfare, which were also accompanied by singing and dancing. Although string instruments were apparently not known, the region was rich in wind and percussion instruments. In central Mexico, the principal percussion instruments were the *teponaztli*, which resembled a covered wooden barrel with incisions on the top and bottom, and the *huehuetl*, related to the modern kettledrum. Wind instruments included conch shell trumpets and flutes of various sizes made of clay, bone, and conch. Instruments used in Andean South America included the *antara*, a ceramic panpipe, and the *quena*, a vertical clay flute.

Music in Colonial Latin America. Sixteenth-century missionaries quickly realized that music would be an effective tool in the conversion of the Indians. Accordingly, they composed hymns in indigenous languages and trained Indians to sing church music. Music was taught to Indian children in the school founded near Mexico City in the 1520s by the Franciscan lay brother Pedro de Gante, and in 1530 a small choir trained there began to sing in Mexico City's new cathedral. In Brazil, the Jesuit **Manuel da Nóbrega** offered musical instruction to Indians in Salvador (Bahia) soon after the foundation of the city in 1549.

Sacred music dominated musical life throughout the colonies as organs were introduced and chapelmasters composed polyphonic masses, Magnificats, motets, and other pieces. Outstanding composers of the colonial period included Francisco López Capillas (c. 1615-1673), chapelmaster of Mexico City's cathedral; José de Orejón y Aparicio (1706-1765), chapelmaster of the cathedral of Lima; and José Mauricio Núñez

García (1767-1830), who was appointed chapelmaster of the Royal Chapel by the Prince Regent **João** after his arrival in Brazil in 1808.

In the seventeenth and eighteenth centuries the *villancico*, a song to be sung in churches on religious holidays, became popular in Mexico. The poet-nun Sor **Juana Inés de la Cruz** wrote the words to many *villancicos* sung in the cathedrals of Mexico City, Puebla, and Oaxaca. A few of her villancicos are partly in Nahuatl, the indigenous language of central Mexico.

During the eighteenth century theatres were built in the major cities for the staging of operas and related Spanish forms, such as the *zarzuela*, in which dialogue is usually spoken. Concerts and operas were also presented in viceregal palaces. *La púrpura de la rosa* (1701), composed by the Spanish-born Tomás de Torrejón y Velasco (1644-1728) and based on a play by the Spanish poet Pedro Calderón de la Barca, was the first opera to be written and produced in the New World. It was commissioned by the viceroy of Peru in honor of King Philip V's eighteenth birthday. *La Parténope* (1711) by the Mexican Manuel de Zumaya (c. 1678-1756) was the second opera to be staged in the colonies and the first to be written by an American-born composer.

c. 1820-1910

Italian Opera and Salon Music. During the nineteenth century Italian opera played a major role in the musical life of the Latin American nations. European impressarios and artists presented the operas of Rossini, Donnizetti, Verdi, and other Italian composers while Latin Americans who essayed their own operatic compositions were guided by Italian models. The Mexican Melesio Morales (1838-1908) wrote several operas, the most notable of which, *Ildegonda* (1866), was performed successfully in Florence three years after its Mexico City premiere. Aniceto Ortega (1823-1875), a medical doctor by profession, wrote *Guatimotzin* (1871), which was distinctive not only because of its nationally oriented theme--the conquest of Mexico--but also because it incorporated pre-Columbian elements into its predominantly Italian style. The role of an Aztec princess was performed by Angela Peralta (1845-1883), a soprano known as "the Mexican nightingale," who sang successfully in Europe before forming her own opera company in Mexico. The leading operatic composer of nineteenth-century Latin America was Antônio Carlos Gomes (1836-1896), a native of São Paulo who lived much of his life in Italy. His most successful opera was *Il Guarany* (1870), which premiered at La Scala in Milan and was based on the romantic novel, *O Guarani*, by José de Alencar. Arturo Berutti (1862-1938) composed several operas based on the history and folklore of his native Argentina, among them *Pampa* (1897), about the legendary gaucho Juan Moreira created by the writer Eduardo Gutiérrez.

In addition to operas, Latin American composers produced many short pieces, such as polkas, waltzes, mazurkas, and marches, similar to those current in Europe. *Sobre las olas* (1891), a set of five waltzes by the Mexican Juventino Rosas (1868-1894), gained international popularity. Symphonies and chamber music were performed by native and foreign artists, but Latin Americans composed few works in these genres in the nineteenth century. Meanwhile, private individuals and governments founded institutions to offer instruction in musical performance and composition, such as the Imperial Academy of Music and National Opera, established in Brazil in 1857. In 1866 the Mexican Philharmonic Society established a conservatory that became the National Conservatory of Music in 1877, when the government assumed responsibility for its support. New theatres were also built, among them Montevideo's Teatro Solís (1856), now the oldest opera house in Latin America. Inaugurated in 1908, the Teatro Colón in Buenos Aires, with 3,500 seats, was the largest in the region.

1910-1990s

Art Music in the Twentieth Century. The most important development in the first decades of the century was the emergence of composers committed to creating music that would reflect its Latin American origins rather than merely duplicating European models. Music composed in this vein usually contained allusions to folk and popular music and sometimes employed indigenous instruments. Although several nineteenth-century composers, such as the Brazilian Alberto Nepomuceno (1864-1920), were proponents of musical nationalism, the movement flourished mainly after 1910. The most prominent composer with a nationalist orientation was **Heitor Villa-Lobos**, who integrated Brazilian folk music into many of his works. During the 1920s and 1930s the Mexican Carlos Chávcz (1899-1973) combined Mexican folk music with modernist styles in *H.P.* (*Caballos de Vapor*) (1932), *Sinfonía India* (1935), and other compositions, though he also wrote many non-nationalist works, such as the *Sinfonía de Antígona* (1933). Other nationalist composers include the Mexicans Manuel María Ponce (1882-1948) and Silvestre Revueltas (1899-1940), the Cubans Amadeo Roldán (1900-1939) and Alejandro García Caturla (1906-1940), the Argentine Carlos López Buchardo (1881-1948), and the Chilean Pedro H. Allende (1885-1959).

After 1950 composers continued to subscribe to musical nationalism, but they also turned increasingly to atonality, serialism, aleatory techniques, and other contemporary styles. The outstanding composer of the era was Alberto Ginastera (1916-1983), a native of Buenos Aires, who is remembered for his *Cantata por América Mágica* (1961), three operas—*Don Rodrigo* (1964), *Bomarzo* (1967), and *Beatrix Cenci* (1971)— and many other works.

Folk and Popular Music. During the colonial period a rich body of folk music and dance arose in Latin America, based mainly on Iberian and African traditions. This music was the source of much of the region's commercialized popular music of the twentieth century. The appeal of the latter often transcended national boundaries and reached far beyond Latin America.

In Mexico, the broad genre known as the *son*, dating back to the colonial period, combined music with song and dance in a rhythm alternating between 3/4 and 6/8 time. There are many variants, notably the *huapango*, associated with Veracruz and other sections of eastern Mexico and performed by ensembles consisting of harps, violins, and guitars of different types. The courtship dance known as the *jarabe* (literally "syrup") and now associated mainly with Jalisco also originated during the colonial period, when it was condemned as immoral by the Inquisition. The *corrido*, a narrative song sung to a simple melody played on a guitar, probably dates from the seventeenth century. It flourished in northern Mexico, especially during the revolution of 1910, and remained popular well into the twentieth century. The *canción ranchera*, which typically describes an unhappy romance, is normally sung to the accompaniment of a mariachi ensemble of trumpets, violins, bass guitar (*guitarrón*), *vihuela*, and guitar. The form was popularized by the singers Jorge Negrete (1911-1953) and Pedro Infante (1917-1957), who became hugely successful film stars in Mexico. During the mid-twentieth century the *bolero*, a Cuban adaptation of a Spanish form, also gained great popularity in Mexico and other Latin American countries. One of the most successful *boleros* was "Solamente una vez" by the prolific Mexican composer Agustín Lara (1900-1970).

Syncopation and reliance on percussion instruments are often typical of folk and popular music in regions marked by strong African cultural influences, such as the Caribbean islands and Brazil. An important Cuban dance was the *habanera*, played in a moderate to slow 2/4 time. Its origins can be traced to the European *contradanza*, a line dance introduced to the island about 1800, supplemented by native Afro-Cuban rhythms. In about 1880 the *danzón*, a couple dance also originating in the *contradanza*, gained popularity. Twentieth-century dance forms of partly African origin include the Cuban *son*, rumba, and mambo, and the Dominican *merengue*. Salsa music, which is derived in part from the *son* and the rumba, began its ascendancy after 1960. Another popular dance form, the *cumbia*, native to the Caribbean coast of Colombia, is apparently of Spanish origin.

The *lundu*, a song and dance derived from Angola, appeared in Brazil during the colonial period. In the dance, a circle of spectators surrounded a pair of dancers who tapped their feet, swayed their hips, and touched their navels. By the late eighteenth century songs in *lundu* style had appeared, the music being played in 2/4 time.

The *lundu* was probably the source of the samba, Brazil's most popular twentieth-century dance form. Music for the samba, which emerged in the early 1900s, is usually written in 2/4 time and is played on drums and other percussion instruments, guitar, and the four-string *cavaquinho*. Bossa nova, which spread throughout the world in the 1960s, derives its rhythmic elements from the samba but is also characterized by highly syncopated guitar playing and shows the harmonic influence of American jazz. Antônio Carlos Jobim (1927-1994) was a leading composer of bossa nova music, including the internationally known "Garota de Ipanema" ("The Girl from Ipanema," 1962).

The Argentine tango originated as a dance in the working-class districts of Buenos Aires in the late nineteenth century and is believed to be derived from the Cuban *habanera* and an Argentine dance form called the *milonga*. Though intially disdained by Argentine elites, it attained international popularity about the time of World War I. Tango music was performed by ensembles—at first quartets, later twelve-man bands—in which the *bandoneón* (related to the accordion) was the central instrument. **Carlos Gardel** became the most celebrated performer of the tango song, which emerged about 1920.

Hybridism became a principal feature of Latin American music during the latter twentieth century. Brazil's "new samba" reflected the influence of U.S. jazz traditions, even to the extent of incorporating the complex structures of Charles Mingus and John Coltrane. Caetano Veloso of Brazil's Northeast broadened popular music with his Tropicalism, mixing Brazilian forms with music from Anglo America, especially English neo-rock-and-roll. Meanwhile foreign artists brought Latin elements into their own music. Musicians of Andean Peru and Bolivia created *chicha*, which combined Andean melodies having strong Amerindian antecedents with Afro-Caribbean rhythms. *Chicha* thus became an Andean variant of salsa.

By the end of the twentieth century Latin American music transcended its region. Its melodies and rhythms were ensconced in "world music," and its varied traditions familiar and appreciated on all continents. Immigration spread that dissemination. Puerto Ricans traveled northward bringing *plenas*, with their tropical lyrics, and the Afro-Caribbean *bomba*, giving them place beside Latin rhythms in the urban eastern United States. Mexican immigrants made *rancheras* standard musical fare throughout the U.S. Southwest and California. *Rancheras* became hemispheric favorites. Telling emotional, usually mournful tales of lost love, they were played everywhere in Hispanic South America, from the northern Andes to the Southern Cone.

Early Books and Printing

Pre-Hispanic Books. The Maya, the Mixtecs, and the native peoples of central Mexico produced books that recorded matters related to ritual, divination, astronomy, history, and genealogy. The books were made of rectangular strips of animal hide or paper produced from bark. Scribes painted pictographic, ideographic, and phonetic signs on the strips, which were sewn together and folded like a screen. Fewer than twenty pre-Hispanic books, now known as codices, have survived. Similar books were also produced after the conquest.

1539

First Printing Press in the Western Hemisphere. **Juan de Zumárraga**, the first bishop of Mexico, encouraged the establishment of a printing press in Mexico City to produce catechisms, dictionaries, and other works needed for the conversion of the Indians. In 1539 Juan Pablos, a native of Brescia, Italy, set up a printing press in Mexico City as the agent of Juan Cromberger, a printer in Seville. The first book printed in the Western Hemisphere--*Breve . . . doctrina christiana en lengua mexicana y castellana*, a bilingual catechism--appeared the same year. The first printing press in the viceroyalty of Peru was established by an Italian, Antonio Ricardo, who had previously worked in

Mexico City. His first publication (1584) was probably a four-page pamphlet, *Pragmática sobre los diez días del año*, announcing the adoption of the Gregorian calendar in Europe. Printing presses were established in Puebla in 1640, in Guatemala City in 1660, and in most of the other Spanish colonies in the eighteenth century. Approximately 25,000 titles were printed in Spanish America by 1825. A printing press functioned briefly in Rio de Janeiro in 1747, but a permanent press was not established in Brazil until 1808, probably with equipment that arrived with the royal family.

Literature

Pre-Hispanic Literature. The advanced civilizations of Mesoamerica and Andean South America created a rich body of literature consisting mainly of lyric and religious poetry and prose narratives. Most surviving indigenous works were transmitted orally and were recorded after the Spanish conquest by native or European chroniclers, such as **Bernardino de Sahagún** and **Garcilaso de la Vega**. Several poems are attributed to Nezahualcóyotl (r.1431-1472), king of Texcoco in central Mexico. The outstanding work of pre-Hispanic literature is the pictographic *Popol Vuh*, which relates the creation myths and history of the Quiché Maya of Guatemala. It was first reduced to writing in the mid-sixteenth century. This manuscript, now lost, was recopied with a Spanish translation in the early eighteenth century by Francisco Ximénez, a Dominican priest in Chichicastenango, Guatemala.

The Quiché Maya were also the creators of the most important surviving drama of the pre-Hispanic era. Called the *Rabinal Achí*, it dramatizes an encounter between the title character and his captive, the Quiché Man. The piece appears to be entirely of pre-Hispanic origin, but was not recorded until the mid-nineteenth century.

c. 1500-1600

Discovery and Conquest. As Spaniards

encountered the lands and peoples of America, they were moved to describe their actions and reactions in chronicles, which constitute the earliest post-Conquest narratives. **Hernán Cortés** recounted the conquest of Mexico in five letters to the king, *Cartas de relación* (1519-36), but the outstanding narrative in this vein is **Bernal Díaz del Castillo's** *Historia verdadera de la conquista de la Nueva España* (*True History of the Conquest of New Spain*, 1632). Of the many chroniclers who discuss the history and cultures of pre-Hispanic America, perhaps the most celebrated is **Garcilaso de la Vega**, the Peruvian *mestizo*. His principal writings—*La Florida del Inca* (*The Florida of the Inca*, 1605) and *Comentarios reales. . . de los Incas* (*Royal Commentaries*, 1609, 1616-17)—are generally believed to combine history and fiction. Alonso de Ercilla y Zúñiga (1533-1594) wrote *La Araucana* (1569-89), an epic poem in thirty-seven cantos. It narrates the conflict between the Spanish invaders of southern Chile and the Araucanian Indians, who are portrayed sympathetically.

c. 1600-1750

The Baroque Era. The complex imagery and verbal conceits associated with European baroque literature can also be found in much of the writing of Spanish America and Brazil after 1600. Bernardo de Balbuena (1561?-1627), who emigrated to Mexico as a child, is remembered mainly for his long poem, *La grandeza mexicana* (1604), which glorified Mexico City and is an example of embryonic creole nationalism. The two major lyric poets of the era were Sor **Juana Inés de la Cruz** and Juan del Valle y Caviedes (1645?-1697?). Sor Juana, generally considered the outstanding literary figure of colonial Spanish America, produced poetry and dramatic works on both religious and secular themes. She is also remembered for an intellectual autobiography, *Respuesta a Sor Filotea* (1691), in which she argued in favor of the education of women. Caviedes, a Spaniard who settled in Lima, is known for his satirical poems that attack the foibles and misdeeds of physicians, prostitutes,

and other social types. Although the polymath **Carlos Sigüenza y Góngora** wrote poetry, his literary reputation rests mainly on *Los infortunios de Alonso Ramírez* (*The Misadventures of Alonso Ramírez*, 1690), a fact-based picaresque tale considered a forerunner of the Latin American novel.

The settlement of Brazil occurred later than that of the Spanish colonies, and significant literary production did not begin until the seventeenth century, when two writers stand out. Gregório de Matos (1636-1695) was noted for his satiric and erotic poetry, which led to his banishment from Brazil. **Antônio Vieira** is considered the greatest Portuguese writer of the baroque era for his sermons and other prose works.

c. 1750-1880

Neoclassicism and Romanticism. The neoclassical forms and modes of discourse prominent in eighteenth-century Europe reached the colonies and found expression in the poetry of Venezuelan **Andrés Bello** and the Ecuadorian José Joaquín Olmedo (1780-1847), best known for "La victoria de Junín" (1826) lauding **Simón Bolívar**'s exploits at the famous battle. In 1816 the Mexican journalist and man of letters José Joaquín Fernández de Lizardi (1776-1827) published *El periquillo sarniento*, translated into English as *The Itching Parrot* (1942). Considered the first genuine novel of Latin America, it combines the adventures of its picaresque hero with the author's moralistic commentary.

Three poets—the Brazilians José Basílio da Gama (1740-1795) and Tomás Antônio Gonzaga (1744-1810) and the Cuban José María Heredia (1803-1839)—exemplify the transition from neoclassicism to romanticism in the early nineteenth century. Gama's long poem in blank verse, *O Uruguai* (1769), presents the Indians of the Jesuit missions in the mold of Rousseau's noble savages. Gonzaga is remembered mainly for *Marília de Dirceu* (1792-1812), lyrics dedicated to his young fiancée. Heredia's "Niagara" is an ode in which the poet expresses melancholy as he contemplates the mighty falls yet finds hope for renewal.

Romanticism emerged in Latin America during the early post-independence period when writing in all genres flourished. This literature was marked not only by the emphasis on emotion and imagination characteristic of the movement but also by a strong sense of identification with local landscapes. Romantic poets of Spanish America include **Esteban Echeverría**, whose long narrative poem "La cautiva" (1837) celebrates the Argentine landscape, and **José Hernández**, whose *Martín Fierro* (1872) and *La vuelta* (1879) are laments for the Argentine gaucho beleaguered by the forces of change. In 1836 Domingos José de Magalhães (1811-1882) published *Suspiros poéticos e saudades*, considered the first important work of Brazilian romanticiscm. The poetry of Antônio Gonçalves Dias (1823-1864) is distinctive for his exaltation of the Indian and his love for Brazil, evident especially in his "Canção do Exílio."

Brazil's leading romantic novelist was José de Alencar (1829-1877), who extolled the Indian as well as the beauty of his native land in *O Guarani* (1857) and *Iracema* (1865), both of which recount love affairs between Indians and whites. **Joaquim Maria Machado de Assis**, considered Brazil's greatest literary figure, was initially influenced by romanticism, but his major novels defy easy categorization.

The Cuban **Gertrudis Gómez de Avellaneda** wrote in several genres, but is best known for her antislavery novel, *Sab* (1841). Other romantic novelists of Spanish America include José Mármol (1817-1871) and Jorge Isaacs (1837-1895). Iin his novel *Amalia* (1851), Marmol, an opponent of **Juan Manuel de Rosas**, contrasts the refinement of the dictator's foes with the brutality of his supporters. With its star-crossed lovers and brilliant depiction of life and nature in Colombia's Cauca Valley, Isaacs's *María* (1867) is the epitome of the romantic novel. *Facundo* (1845) by **Domingo F. Sarmiento**, while not a work of fiction, partakes of romanticism with its portrayal of the Argentine pampa and the types who inhabited it. **Juan Montalvo** and **Ricardo Palma** were also distinguished prose stylists of the era.

c. 1880-1920

Realism and Naturalism. In the late nineteenth century much Latin American fiction began to reflect the unsentimental examination of quotidian reality that was characteristic of many contemporary European novels. A few novelists were also swayed by the deterministic view of human existence developed by Emile Zola and other naturalists. Novels of realism and naturalism often probed the social and economic issues that loomed large in an era of significant change in Latin America.

Aves sin nido (*Birds Without a Nest*, 1889), the best-known novel of Peruvian writer **Clorinda Matto de Turner**, exhibits some romantic traits but offers a realistic depiction of the exploitation of Indians by white officials and priests. The Colombian Tomás Carrasquilla (1858-1940) described provincial life in *Frutos de mi tierra* (1896) and Spanish colonial society in *La marquesa de Yolombó* (1928). The Uruguayan Eduardo Acevedo Díaz (1851-1921) wrote *Ismael* (1888) and other historical novels dealing with the gaucho. Another Uruguayan, Florencio Sánchez (1875-1910), the leading playwright of the period, treated the problems of tenement dwellers in *Nuestros hijos* (1907). Earlier plays, such as *M'hijo el dotor* (1903) and *La gringa* (1904), deal with the impact of immigration and the conflict between traditional and modern values.

Several novelists produced works shaped by naturalism. The leading Brazilian representative of this school was Aluísio Azevedo (1857-1913), who attacked racial prejudice in *O mulato* (*Mulatto*, 1881) and offered a pessimistic view of tenement life in *O cortiço* (*A Brazilian Tenement*, 1890). Other writers inflenced by naturalism include the Argentine Manuel Gálvez (1882-1962), who explored social problems in numerous novels, including *La maestra normal*

(1914) and *Nacha Regules* (1919), and the Mexican Federico Gamboa (1864-1939), noted especially for *Santa* (1903).

c. 1880-1920

Modernism in Spanish America. The poets and other writers to whom the term modernist is applied took part in a movement of literary renovation initially influenced by the French Parnassians and symbolists. Modernists were distinguished by their quest for formal innovation, by their luxuriant, sensuous imagery, and by their frequent choice of exotic themes. Among the precursors of the movement were the Cubans **José Martí** and Julián del Casal (1863-1893), the Colombian José Asunción Silva (1865-1896), and the Mexican Manuel Gutiérrez Nájera (1859-1895), who founded the influential literary journal *Revista Azul* (1894-96).

The towering figure of modernism is **Rubén Darío** of Nicaragua, whose collections *Prosas profanas* (1896) and *Cantos de vida y esperanza* (1905) set the pattern for the movement. The latter, considered his best book, also reflected a new appreciation for Spanish culture and suspicion of the United States in the wake of the Spanish-American War. Also prominent was the Argentine Leopoldo Lugones (1874-1938), who moved from the modernism of *Los crepúsculos del jardín* (1905) to simpler images and forms in *Las horas doradas* (1922). Although he was an essayist, **José Enrique Rodó** is usually included among modernist writers. The novel *La gloria de Don Ramiro* (1908) by the Argentine Enrique Larreta (1873-1961) is considered the finest expression of modernism in prose. The Mexican man of letters **Alfonso Reyes** was initially influenced by modernism but quickly found his own aesthetic voice.

c. 1920-45

Post-Modernism and the Vanguard in Spanish-American Poetry. During the second decade of the twentieth century, global and regional events strongly affected Latin American cultural life as well as its politics and economy. The Mexican Revolution of 1910 and American interventionism in the Caribbean stirred cultural nationalism throughout the region, as did World War I, which seemed to show the bankruptcy of European institutions. Yet many Latin Americans were quick to embrace new European forms of literary expression, such as futurism and Dadaism.

Many poets continued, at least initially, to adhere to the modernist approach but probed their inner lives more fully and paid greater attention to the Latin American context. The Mexican Ramón López Velarde (1888-1921) is remembered for his poems of romantic love and physical passion and for "La suave patria" (1921), his "muted epic" celebrating Mexico. Several important women poets emerged in the post-modernist era, among them the Chilean **Gabriela Mistral**, the Uruguayan Juana de Ibarbourou (1895-1979), and the Argentine Alfonsina Storni (1892-1938), noted for her protests against male-dominated society, as in "Hombre pequeñito" (1918). Afro-Caribbean themes and folklore are prominent in the work of the Puerto Rican Luis Palés Matos (1898-1959) and the Cuban Nicolás Guillén (1902-1989).

More directly influenced by the European avant-garde was the Chilean Vicente Huidobro (1893-1948), who devised *creacionismo*, a literary theory that espoused modernity and experimentation. In *Trilce* (1922) the Peruvian César Vallejo (1892-1938) employed an idiom of dislocation and isolation to express his view of the human condition. The early poetry of **Jorge Luis Borges** and **Pablo Neruda** also shares characteristics of the Latin American vanguard.

Modernism in Brazil. Brazilian modernism was a multi-faceted movement in all the arts that developed after São Paulo's Modern Art Week of February 1922. While modernist poets differed from one another, in general they stressed the importance of writing on native themes in Portuguese as spoken in contemporary Brazil. They also embraced freedom and innovation in form. The leading exponent of Brazilian modernism was Mário de Andrade (1893-1945), whose collection *Paulicéia desvairada* (1922) exhibits the movement's characteristic traits. His novel *Macunaíma* (1928) uses folklore to chart the life course of its protagonist, called in the subtitle "a hero without any character." Other poets of the modernist school were Jorge de Lima (1893-1953) and Carlos Drummond de Andrade (1902-1987).

c. 1920-90s

Regionalist Fiction. An important current in Latin American literature after 1920 was the exploration of contemporary life and culture in unique local settings and situations. The best-known manifestations of this trend are the novels and other prose narratives produced in the wake of the Mexican Revolution. The leading example of the genre is **Mariano Azuela**'s novel *Los de abajo* (*The Underdogs*), which was first published in 1915 but failed to gain recognition until the mid-1920s. Also notable are *El águila y la serpiente* (*The Eagle and the Serpent*, 1928) by Martín Luis Guzmán (1887-1976), an autobiographical narrative of the author's experiences in the revolution, and *Ulises criollo* (1935), the first volume of the five-volume autobiography of **José Vasconcelos**.

Many novels of this period attacked the exploitation of the Indian and explored the future of indigenous identity, often on the basis of the author's first-hand knowledge. Major works in this vein are *Huasipungo* (1934) by the Ecuadorian Jorge Icaza (1906-1978); *El Indio* (1935) by the Mexican Gregorio López y Fuentes (1897-1966); *Yawar Fiesta* (1941) by the Peruvian José María Arguedas (1911-1969); and *El mundo es ancho y ajeno* (*Broad and Alien Is the World*, 1941) by the Peruvian Ciro Alegría (1909-1967). *La vorágine* (*The Vortex*, 1924) by the Colombian José Eustacio Rivera (1888-1928) is notable for its jungle setting and for its portrayal of the mistreatment of rubber workers there. The novels of **Rómulo Gallegos** are also rooted in the environment of his native Venezuela.

An offshoot of Brazil's Modern Art Week was the appearance of a group of novelists whose books dealt with the distinctive yet impoverished region known as the Northeast. They included Graciliano Ramos (1892-1953), who is noted as much for his psychological insight as for his

concern about social conditions in the Northeast; José Lins do Rego (1901-1957), who traced changes in the sugar industry; Raquel de Queiroz (1910-), who addressed feminine education and adolescence in *As três Marias* (*The Three Maries*, 1939); and **Jorge Amado**, whose *Terras do sem-fim* (*The Violent Land*, 1943) is set in the cacao-growing zone of Bahia.

Latin American Literature since 1945. In the second half of the twentieth century Latin American writers were extraordinarily productive in all genres and received greater international recognition than ever before. This was reflected in the fact that five Latin Americans were awarded the Nobel Prize for literature: **Gabriela Mistral**, 1945; **Miguel Ángel Asturias**, 1967; **Pablo Neruda**, 1971; **Gabriel García Márquez**, 1982; and **Octavio Paz**, 1990. Latin American writings continued to be affected by foreign literary trends, but now the style of its best-known practitioners began to be emulated abroad as well.

In addition to Neruda and Paz, distinguished poets of the period include the Cuban José Lezama Lima (1910-1976), also noted for his novel *Paradiso* (1966), and the Chilean Nicanor Parra (1914-), whose "antipoems" point out the absurdity of human existence in a detached, ironic style. Drama also flourished during this period. The most important playwright was probably the Mexican Rodolfo Usigli (1905-1979), author of *Corona de sombra* (1943), based on the lives of Maximilian and Carlota, and *El gesticulador*, first performed in 1947, which condemns Mexico's political culture.

It was, however, Latin American fiction that attained the greatest distinction after 1945. **Jorge Luis Borges** won acclaim for his meticulously crafted short stories, including the collections *Ficciones* (1944) and *El Aleph* (1949). Agustín Yáñez (1904-1980) is best known for his novel *Al filo del agua* (*The Edge of the Storm*, 1947), a compelling psychological portrait of a Mexican village on the eve of the revolution of 1910. *El reino de este mundo* (*The Kingdom of This World*, 1949) by the Cuban Alejo Carpentier (1904-1980) is a tale of the Haitian Revolution combining fiction and history. It is considered an early example of a work shaped by "magical realism," a term referring to the blending of the real and the fantastic supposedly characteristic of Latin American society.

The term was applied to the works of numerous authors, including **Borges, Miguel Ángel Asturias**, and **Gabriel García Márquez**, whose *Cien años de soledad* (*One Hundred Years of Solitude*, 1967) became an international best-seller. The decade of the 1960s was notable for the publication of so many other outstanding novels that critics spoke of a "boom" in Latin American literature. Among them may be mentioned *La muerte de Artemio Cruz* (*The Death of Artemio Cruz*, 1962) by **Carlos Fuentes** and *La ciudad y los perros* (*The Time of the Hero*, 1962) by **Mario Vargas Llosa**. *Rayuela* (*Hopscotch*, 1963) by the Argentine Julio Cortázar (1914-1984) is innovative in language and structure, the latter designed to mimic a game of hopscotch. *Tres tristes tigres* (*Three Trapped Tigers*, 1967) by Guillermo Cabrera Infante (1929–) depicts pre-revolutionary Havana nightlife in a vernacular style marked by puns and wordplay.

João Guimarães Rosa (1908-1967) and Clarice Lispector (1925-1977) are among the most highly regarded post-modernist Brazilian writers. The former's masterpiece is *Grande sertão: Veredas* (*The Devil to Pay in the Backlands*, 1956), a monologue by a one-time outlaw tormented by his past. *A maça no escuro* (*The Apple in the Dark*, 1961) and other novels by Lispector portray the isolation and uncertainty of modern life.

The Press

1722-1820

Early Newspapers and Periodicals. Latin America's first newspaper was the *Gaceta de México*, an eight-page monthly that appeared from January through June 1722. Its founder was a clergyman, Juan Ignacio María de Castorena,

who later became bishop of Yucatán. A second newspaper with the same name appeared from 1728 to 1739. Other early newspapers were established in Guatemala (1729) and in Lima (1743). The first daily newspaper was the *Diario de Lima* (1790-93). Brazil's first newspaper, *Gazeta do Rio de Janeiro*, appeared in 1808. The *Mercurio Peruano* (1791-75), a biweekly periodical published in Lima, contained articles designed to improve the economy of the viceroyalty of Peru and the education and health of its people. The *Semanario del Nuevo Reino de Granada* (1808-11), founded by **Francisco José de Caldas**, was an early journal of science and other useful information. Several factors shortened the lives of these and other early periodicals: the limited number of subscribers, shortages of paper, and the occasional censorship of governmental and ecclesiastical officials.

The upheaval caused by the independence movement of the early nineteenth century put an end to Caldas's *Semanario*, but newspapers proliferated during this period, serving to disseminate the aims of the revolutionaries and record their triumphs and defeats. Among such newspapers were the short-lived *Despertador Americano* (1810-11), organ of **Miguel Hidalgo**'s movement in Mexico; *La Gaceta de Buenos Aires* (1810-21), initially edited by **Mariano Moreno**; and *La Aurora de Chile* (1812-14), edited by the Chilean priest and revolutionary Camilo Henríquez.

The Nineteenth-Century Press. Once independence had been achieved, newspapers continued to be founded in national and provincial capitals, usually in support of specific political leaders or parties. Limited in circulation because of continuing high rates of illiteracy in most countries, newspapers offered national and international news as well as fiction and poetry to their readers. The oldest surviving newspaper in Latin America is Brazil's Diário de Pernambuco, founded in Recife in 1825. *El Mercurio*, established in 1827 in Valparaso, Chile, by Pedro Félix Vicuña, is the oldest continuously published newspaper in the Spanish-speaking world. In 1880 it was acquired by Agustín Edwards, who began a Santiago edition in 1900. Lima's *El Comercio*, founded in 1839, came under the control of the Miró Quesada family in 1876. Two Buenos Aires newspapers trace their origins to the mid-nineteenth century: *La Prensa*, established in 1869 by José Gainza Paz, and *La Nación*, founded in 1870 by ex-president **Bartolomé Mitre**. Other long-lived newspapers include *O Estado de São Paulo*, founded in 1875 with the name *A Provincia de São Paulo*; *El Espectador*, established in Medellín, Colombia, in 1887 by Fidel Cano but now published in Bogotá; and *Jornal do Brasil*, founded in Rio de Janeiro in 1891.

During the second half of the century a few publishers launched less politically oriented newspapers that relied more heavily on advertising and paid circulation than their predecessors. Chile's *El Ferrocarril* (1855-1911) was the first newspaper to be supported mainly by advertising. Aided by a government subvention, Mexico City's *El Imparcial*, established in 1896 by Rafael Reyes Spíndola, was sold for a penny, cheaper than other newspapers. It quickly acquired a large circulation and introduced innovations like sponsorship of sporting events and raffles. In Mexico, as in other countries that experienced economic growth in the late nineteenth century, the number of newspapers increased, rising from 202 in 1884 to 1,571 in 1907.

Another trend of the era was the establishment of periodicals by and for women. These newspapers and reviews usually urged improved educational opportunities and other reforms so that women might become better wives and mothers. Other topics addressed included the progress of women in other countries, the rights of married women, and the sexual double standard. Among such periodicals were *La Camelia* (Buenos Aires, 1852); *O Jornal das Senhoras* (Rio de Janeiro, 1852-55); *O Sexo Femenino* (Rio de Janeiro, 1873-76); *La Mujer* (Bogotá, 1878-81); and *La Mujer Moderna* (Mexico City, 1904-08).

1900-1990s

The Twentieth-Century Press. Despite the popularity of radio and television, the print media continued to play a major role in the political and cultural life of Latin America. However, the circulation of elite newspapers often lagged behind that of tabloids and other more popularly oriented newspapers. Important newspapers founded after 1900 include *El Universal* (Caracas, 1909), *El Tiempo* (Bogotá, 1911), *Excelsior* (Mexico City, 1917), *Novedades* (Mexico City, 1934), and *El Norte* (Monterrey, 1938). Magazines of news and commentary are published in several countries. Among them are *Caretas* (Lima, 1950), *Veja* (Brazil, 1968), *Resumen* (Caracas, 1973), *Somos* (Argentina, 1976), *Hoy* (Chile, 1977), and *Proceso* (Mexico, 1977). In some cases, leading newspapers and magazines have become part of large media empires. The Globo Group of Brazil, for example, includes *O Globo*, a major Rio de Janeiro daily, as well as radio stations and the TV Globo network.

The leading news agency in Latin America is United Press International (formerly United Press), which established its dominance in the 1920s. Dependence on UPI and other foreign agencies, such as the Associated Press and Agence France Presse, has led to periodic efforts to establish alternative sources of international news. One of the more successful is Inter-Press Service, founded in 1964 by Latin America and European journalists.

No professional training for journalists existed in Latin America until the mid-1930s, when programs were established in Argentina (1934), Brazil (1935), and Mexico (1936). Through the auspices of UNESCO, the International Center of Advanced Studies in Communications for Latin America (CIESPAL) was established in Quito in 1959. It quickly became a center for journalism education and communications research for the region.

Press Censorship and Intimidation of Journalists. Throughout Latin American history authoritarian or dictatorial governments have attempted to control the press either by preventing the publication of objectionable stories or by penalizing newspapers and journalists after the appearance of such articles. This type of action has been taken by populist governments, such as **Juan Perón**'s in Argentina in the 1950s, and military regimes of both the right and the left. In 1951 Argentina's Peronist-controlled Congress expropriated *La Prensa*, which had been critical of the government. It became a trade union tabloid until it was returned to its owners after the fall of Perón. A similar fate befell *El Comercio* of Lima, which was seized in 1974 by the left-leaning administration of General Juan Velasco Alvarado and turned over to the National Agrarian Federation. Government supporters defended this action as an effort to promote press freedom, which they said had never existed in Peru, where a small group of wealthy families dominated the media. Several other newspapers were expropriated during the Velasco administration but were later returned to their original owners. In 1976 Julio Scherer García, the editor of Mexico City's *Excelsior*, was ousted in an internal coup believed to have been orchestrated by President **Luis Echeverría**, of whom the newspaper had been critical. Scherer and many of his colleagues at *Excelsior*—Vicente Leñero, Enrique Maza, Carlos Marín, Froylán López Narváez—went on to establish and staff *Proceso*, Mexico's leading muckraking weekly and implacable foe of its national powerbrokers.

Many other measures have been used to ensure friendly press coverage or forestall criticism. Governments have put journalists on the payroll or have acquired newspapers. Government control over newsprint has also been used to punish unfriendly newspapers. In 1935 the Mexican government established a monopoly over the manufacture and importation of newsprint, Productora e Importadora de Papel, S.A. (PIPSA), which was occasionally used as a tool for regulating the press before being privatized by the administration of **Carlos Salinas de Gortari**. In view of such hazards, many publishers and journalists have frequently practiced self-censorship to avoid giving offense.

In numerous instances violence has been directed at press critics of governments. A notorious case was the assassination in 1978 of Pedro Joaquín Chamorro, a long-time critic of dictator **Anastasio Somoza García** and editor of *La Prensa* of Managua. Chamorro's death was attributed to supporters of the dictator and galvanized the anti-Somoza opposition.

Journalists have been targeted by nongovernment groups as well. Several journalists are believed to have been murdered in Peru during the 1980s by the Maoist Shining Path. In 1986 Guilllermo Cano, editor of Bogotá's *El Espectador*, noted for its antidrug campaigns, was murdered, probably by drug traffickers. In 1989 a bomb destroyed the offices of the newspaper.

Post-Revolutionary Cuba. After **Fidel Castro**'s accession to power in 1959 and the establishment of a socialist regime, all newspapers and magazines came under state ownership. The leading newspaper, *Granma*, was named after the yacht on which Castro sailed from Mexico to Cuba in 1956. It was established in 1965 by the merger of *Hoy*, the organ of Cuba's Popular Socialist (Communist) party, and *Revolución*, the organ of Castro's 26th of July Movement. The agency Prensa Latina was established in 1959 to provide international news to Cuban media and to supply Cuban news to other Latin American countries.

POPULAR CULTURE

Radio and Television

Latin Americans embraced radio and television when the two electronic media appeared on the scene in 1920 and 1950, respectively. They rightly saw in the new means of communication proof of their cultural and material advance. But most of all the public loved those media for their entertainment value and for the way radio, and later television, liberated them from the monotony and isolation that afflicted their lives. Some 80 percent of Latin Americans lived in rural areas when radio and television appeared. At century's end radio and TV were constant companions of most Latin Americans. Through satellite transmission of television and an abundance of AM, FM, and short wave radio stations they are both linked to the greater world and made inextricably a part of it.

1920-39

Radio's Early Years. Latin America's first radio transmitter began operation in 1920, in Buenos Aires. Its audience consisted of only a few families lucky enough to own receivers. Over the ensuing months similar halting experiments with radio took place in Mexico, Brazil, and elsewhere. Progress in establishing the new medium was slow at first, as illustrated by the attempt to bring radio to Colombia. In 1924 President **Pedro Nel Ospina** authorized purchase and installation of a German-made radio transmitter. But that nation's first radio station did not become operational until 1929, three years after Ospina had left office.

Politicians and educators were among the first to make use of radio. Mexico's **José Vasconcelos** installed one of his country's first transmitters at the Ministry of Education in 1924. During the following decade, President **Lázaro Cárdenas** used radio to promote ideals of the revolution by way of two transmitters installed in offices of the National Revolutionary party. Radio played a role in Brazil's presidential campaign of 1930, and again in 1932, when radio broadcasts were used to

rally supporters of **Getúlio Vargas** during the constitutionalist revolt of that year.

Governments and politicians were initially able to control the use of radio. During the 1930s and 1940s Brazil's Vargas censored it, and the Colombian government restricted radio frequencies through licensing requirements. Colombia's first radio transmitters were owned by the nation's Liberal and Conservative parties, who counted virtually the entire citizenry among their members. During the 1930s and 1940s Colombians throughout the nation avidly listened to broadcasts of heated political debates conducted in national and departmental legislatures.

By the 1930s commercial stations had come to dominate Latin America's air waves. By then networks in the United States, the Columbia Broadcasting System (CBS) and the National Broadcasting System (NBC), had established links with broadcasters in Cuba, Mexico, and Brazil, helping make those countries regional leaders in the new communication technology. Thanks to their links with the United States, stations there possessed the most modern transmitters available. Furthermore, those corporate alliances were innovative in the sense that they were among Latin America's first transnational corporate alliances not of an extractive character.

Radio's success accelerated consumerism. The Radio Corporation of America (RCA), owner of NBC, advertised its radios and record players throughout Latin America. Soon every family was convinced that its home was incomplete unless it boasted both phonograph and radio. Other companies, such as Proctor and Gamble, promoted laundry products through radio dramas called *novelas*. The *radionovelas*, patterned on soap operas in the United States, achieved such popularity in Cuba that they were soon being exported to other Spanish-speaking nations.

1940-60

The Golden Age of Latin American Radio. By the 1940s radio had established itself at the center of a vigorous entertainment industry giving employment to writers, announcers, and artists as well as a host of support staff and technicians. Receivers sold by the tens of thousands and companies such as RCA, Phillips, and Philco fed consumer demand through advertisement on affiliated stations. Radio popularized the music of **Carlos Gardel**, helping make the Argentine tango popular around the world. Commercial interests associated with radio achieved synergy in the entertainment field by signing local entertainers to record contracts, and then encouraging stations to broadcast the records. Radio listenership thus increased as did sales of records and record players. It was through an RCA audition that the career of Brazilian entertainer **Carmen Miranda** was launched. Her recordings, popular first in Latin America and then in the United States and Europe, propelled her to stardom on stage and screen.

Beyond those whose livelihoods were directly dependent upon radio broadcasting, thousands of others sold and serviced radios and transmission equipment. Meanwhile public infatuation with the medium ran unabated. When inclement weather threatened to delay delivery of a plane load of new Philco radios at the height of Colombia's Christmas shopping season during 1945, citizens living in the national capital rushed buses and autos to the city's airport where they illuminated the runway with their headlights, ensuring the precious cargo's safe arrival.

During World War II radio proved itself a powerful propaganda tool. Over the course of the conflict nations supportive of the allied war effort aired programs developed in the United States at the Office of the Coordinator of Inter-American Affairs (OCIAA). Nations that cooperated with the OCIAA were rewarded through receipt of technical assistance that notably improved the quality of their transmissions.

By mid-century radio was a well-established and significant force in Latin American life. Transmitters beamed programs into remote corners of all nations. The medium thus played a significant role in nation-building (though in some cases radio's power was revealed in negative ways, as in Colombia in 1948, when incendiary broadcasts produced bloodshed and nearly toppled

the country's democratically elected government).

Radio also helped establish affective links among Latin Americans regardless of nationality. Musical styles once largely the patrimony of individual nations—the Mexican *ranchera*, the Brazilian samba, the Argentine tango—became the cultural patrimony of all, thanks to radio broadcasts of popular artists. Taped *radionovelas*, whether produced in Mexico, Cuba, or Brazil, developed loyal followings everywhere they were aired. And radio news programs created from wire service reports kept Latin Americans informed of national, hemispheric, and global events with an immediacy that could not be attained through the print media.

The Advent and Growth of Television

Television appeared in Latin America at mid-century, its spread emulating that of radio in some respects. Proximity to the United States and the character of a given country's commercial relations with the U.S. had much to do with television's early history in individual nations. In 1950 Mexico was the first Latin American nation to establish commercial television. It was the world's sixth country to do so. Elsewhere television's growth was fitful. Economic nationalists were reluctant to allow the easy import of foreign-made hardware, while populist and left-wing leaders insisted that television play a public service role. In some places censorship and government regulation dampened growth of the new medium. Still by the 1960s popular pressure forced governments, save for that in Marxist Cuba, to ease such impediments and restrictions. This made possible the rapid growth of commercial television.

The 1960s were characterized by a proliferation of "canned" programs produced in the United States and dubbed in Mexico for Spanish-speaking audiences. During the 1970s governments attempted to lessen U.S. influence by encouraging local programming and extending regulation of television. By the 1980s, however, the medium's commercial power, technological advances in the industry, and the impulse toward privatization combined to free television from the kind of government controls that had hindered its early growth.

1950-1970s

U.S. Influence, State Attempts at Control, and Growth of Commercial Television. When Mexico initiated commercial television in 1950, its first stations were affiliates of the U.S. networks CBS and NBC. Their most popular programs were those produced in the United States and dubbed into Spanish. Mexico thus became the point of entry for the U.S.-based programming that dominated Latin American television during the 1960s and 1970s. By the end of the 1960s nearly one-third of all programming consisted of dubbed U.S. programs, a figure that increased to one-half by the end of the 1970s. Meanwhile, 60 to 80 percent of news broadcasts were taken from U.S. wire services.

The dominance of U.S.-derived programming was largely a function of slow development of Latin American domestic television from the 1950s through the 1970s, which had much to do with the unsettled politics in the region during the thirty years following 1950. During those decades South America was swept first by populist and revolutionary movements followed by a spell of military rule. Such upheavals conspired to make canned U.S. imports far superior to locally produced programs.

Argentina provides an example of the unfortunate impact of political turmoil upon the nascent television industry. Until 1955 that nation was ruled by **Juan Perón**, who censored all media and permitted the operation of just one television channel. When Perón was overthrown, followers of his who had run the nation's radio and television system were fired. That devastated the broadcast industry. When Perón returned to power in 1973, he also removed many key media personnel and went on to nationalize the television industry. Thus, by the latter 1970s Argentine television stood in disarray, and the nation possessed just three poorly functioning channels.

The statist and nationalist impulse hobbled broadcasting in other nations as well. Cuba, where commercial radio had flourished during the 1940s and 1950s, saw a thoroughgoing nationalization of both radio and television following **Fidel Castro**'s 1959 revolution. When Colombian television was inaugurated by dictator **Gustavo Rojas Pinilla** in 1954, it was proclaimed a public service. Chilean television originated on college campuses during the 1960s and was dedicated to service in the political struggles of that era. Populist regimes appearing in Venezuela and Peru during the 1970s moved to nationalize television there (though in Venezuela, where commercial, U.S.-affiliated commercial stations had become well established, the nationalization decree of President **Carlos Andrés Pérez** was never fully enforced.)

In spite of the political turbulence attending Latin American television's first thirty years, commercial interests steadily gained ground. Such was the case in Brazil during the twenty years of military rule following 1964. While it censored the media, military governments also took steps to encourage its growth. Thanks to such encouragement Brazil's TV Globo had become one of the world's largest networks by the late 1970s.

Investors in commercial television, both domestic and foreign, pursued their interests along lines defined earlier in radio. The U.S. American Broadcasting Company (ABC) expanded into the Latin American market through the Central and South American networks CATVN and LATINO. The U.S.-based media conglomerates CBS, NBC, and Time-Life affiliated with national networks such as PROARTEL in Argentina and PROVENTEL in Venezuela.

Privately-owned television remained dominant in Mexico, even in the face of government attempts to expand public television at its expense during the 1970s. To combat the threat to its interests, that nation's two largest networks combined to form the media conglomerate Televisa in 1973. Strong support of Televisa within the ruling Institutional Revolutionary party enabled the new entity to beat back the reform attempts of Presidents **Luis Echeverría** and **José López Portillo**.

1980s to the Present

The Globalization of Television and Radio. Latin American television grew and diversified during the 1980s. That growth was founded first in progressive deregulation, beginning in Chile during the 1970s and spreading to other countries during the ensuing decade. Abetting deregulation, and to an extent making it inevitable, were technological advances that transnationalized and diversified television. By the mid-1980s, for example, Latin Americans spent nearly one-third of their viewing time watching rented or personally owned video tapes. Meanwhile satellite and cable transmissions vastly expanded the number of channels available. The leading television networks in Brazil and Mexico, the fourth and fifth largest in the world, operated their own satellite transmitters, and also provided viewers programming bought from a variety of other satellite news sources, such as PanAmSat, CNN International, and TNT Latin America. Viewers across the region also had ready access, via satellite transmission from Europe and North America, to programs running the gamut from sports events to X-rated films.

Radio enjoyed robust if less spectacular growth during the 1980s and 1990s. In larger urban areas an array of AM and FM stations offered programming for every taste. Stations targeted every musical preference and offered programming geared to the interests of every conceivable constituency.

The late-twentieth-century globalization of broadcasting brought an unprecedented expansion of Latin American–produced television into non–Latin American markets. *Telenovelas*, especially those produced in Brazil, won audiences across Europe and as far afield as East Asia. Higher-quality productions became available to global audiences thanks to the appearance of made-for-TV films based upon novels of award-winning writers such as **Gabriel García Márquez**. Mexico's Televisa was a leader in providing Spanish-language programming to North America, offering thousands of hours of programming to audiences there.

At the end of the twentieth century Latin American radio and television are fully integrated parts of the global information network. The extraordinary growth of those media, in much less than a century, had revolutionized communication there, having incalculable impact upon the minds and personalities of people throughout the region.

Cinema

1896-1929

The Era of Silent Film. Latin America's moving picture era began in 1896, when agents of the French Lumière brothers traveled to Mexico, Argentina, and Brazil. There they filmed public monuments and notable local figures, and exhibited their work to the delight of audiences. The new medium proved exceedingly popular. Within a few years there were several hundred cinemas operating in Mexico alone. The public flocked to them to watch locally shot documentary footage, as well as newsreels depicting events taking place in Europe and the world. The new technology gave rise to a host of new professions. Among them was that of the peripatetic projectionist who toured the countryside demonstrating the new invention to an astonished citizenry.

At the outset all feature films shown in Latin American were imported from Europe and the United States. French and Italian productions predominated during early years of the twentieth century, but they were supplanted by U.S. features during and after World War I. Hollywood never again ceded its supremacy in the Latin American market. U.S. stars Rudolph Valentino and John Barrymore, Greta Garbo and Mary Pickford had loyal followings everywhere in Latin America. Film reviews became a standard feature of magazines and newspapers, and within a few years specialized film journals appeared in several nations.

The new medium enthralled Latin Americans. Movie theaters stood as palpable symbols of the material progress that had long eluded them. Through film they were offered glimpses of foreign lifestyles about which they had only dreamt. Members of the movie-going public closely followed the careers of film idols, anxiously awaiting arrival of their new productions. Woe to the theater- owner whose presentation of Hollywood's latest offering was lacking in any detail. Switched reels, imperfect film copies, or the malfunction of projection equipment could touch off a riot resulting in the destruction of movie house property.

Attendance at new film openings became a regular high point in the life of Latin American cities. Well-to-do families watched from private boxes, dressed in their Sunday finery. Bolivian man of letters Alcides Arguedas remarked on the phenomenon during a visit to Bogotá in 1928: "Colombians have a new god. His name is Charlie Chaplin."

Early Latin American film-making was chiefly documentary. Mexico's revolution was a favorite topic during the second decade of the century, as were short features of important public and social events. By the 1920s documentary film-makers were entertaining audiences with scenes of Bolivian tin miners, young women rolling cigars in Cuban factories, horse races and sporting events, ships loading coffee at Brazilian ports, gaming casinos in Havana, and curiosities such as the Cuban man who could cover much of his face with his lower lip.

Locally produced feature films began appearing by the 1920s. They were produced by Mexican, Argentine, and Brazilian film-makers, and several of them were popular enough to rival foreign imports. *La banda del automóvil gris* (*The Grey Car Gang*, 1919) is considered Mexico's best silent film. Produced and directed by Enrique Rosas, it recounts the activities of a contemporary criminal gang in Mexico City. Argentine José Agustín Ferreyra directed several films set in the working-class neighborhoods of Buenos Aires. His *La muchacha de Arrabal* (1922) was notable because of its accompaniment, tango music played by a theater orchestra. Brazil's earliest film director of note was Humberto Mauro, whose early films included the romance *Braza dormida* (*Dying Embers*, 1928).

1929-49

From the Advent of Sound Through the War Years. When sound-film appeared in 1929, Hollywood briefly made Spanish-language movies featuring personalities like Argentine tango singer **Carlos Gardel**. It soon became clear, however, that audiences would continue to attend U.S.-made films, subtitled and having English dialogue. Such films dominated 80 to 90 percent of movie screens, along with a smattering of European offerings.

By the 1930s, Latin America's Spanish-language film-making was centered in Mexico and Argentina. Meanwhile Portuguese-speaking Brazil had developed a more modest film industry serving its own domestic market.

Mexico's strength in movie-making rested in its studio-produced *charro* productions, starring singing cowboys such as Tito Guizar and Jorge Negrete. Fernando de Fuentes's *Allá en el Rancho Grande* (*Out on the Rancho Grande*, 1936), which became the most popular of that genre, was seen by audiences across Latin America. The *charro* film, which had much in common with U.S. cowboy musicals produced during the same era, took a comedic form during the 1940s. Its quintessence was the Alberto Gout production *Cuando viajan las estrellas* (1942), starring Jorge Negrete.

Fernando de Fuentes emerged as Mexico's most noted director during the 1930s, winning acclaim first for two evocations of the revolution, *El compadre Mendoza* (*Godfather Mendoza*, 1933), and *Vámonos con Pancho Villa* (*Let's Go With Pancho Villa*, 1935), both of which depict ethical dilemmas presented by the traumatic national event. De Fuentes won acclaim in 1943 with his *Doña Bárbara*, based on the novel of Venezuelan **Rómulo Gallegos**.

Mexico's film industry flourished during World War II thanks in part to that country's friendship with the United States. During that era of good neighborliness, Hollywood was encouraged to share its technical expertise with

Mexican film-makers. Dolores del Río and María Félix starred in numerous films during the period, and were joined in the mid-1940s by Argentine actress Libertad Lamarque. Mariano Moreno, known as **Cantinflas**, won international acclaim with *Ahí está el detalle* (*That's the Thing*, 1940), his first full-length feature. Meanwhile films having urban settings were produced with growing frequency. Director Ismael Rodríguez produced the melodramas *Nosotros los pobres* (*We the Poor*, 1947) and its sequel, *Ustedes los ricos* (*You the Rich*, 1948).

While Mexico's film industry boomed in the 1930s, enjoying a "golden age" during the 1940s, Brazil's cinematographic community produced little of note during either decade. Portuguese-language films were not marketable in Spanish America, forcing Brazil's principal production company, Atlântida, into production of low-budget, unsophisticated burlesque comedies called *chanchadas*. A few Brazilian films did win recognition during the 1930s, among them *Alô, Alô Brazil* (1935) and *Alô, Alô Carnaval* (1936), featuring recording star **Carmen Miranda**. Late in the decade the Vera Cruz film company was formed in an effort to raise the quality of Brazilian film, but of its eighteen productions only Lima Barreto's *O cangaceiro* (1953) was sufficiently popular to defray production costs.

The failure of Vera Cruz left sophisticated Brazilian viewers little incentive to patronize national productions. Despite a law requiring the screening of three nationally made films per year, the nation managed fewer than twenty new releases annually throughout the 1940s. Meanwhile Mexican production reached 107 films in the year 1949.

Argentina's film industry suffered during the war years. The United States restricted sale of film stock to Argentine film-makers, owing to their nation's wartime neutrality. Government censorship further dampened artistic endeavor. One bright spot during the 1940s was Luis César Amadori's *Dios se lo pague* (*May God Reward You*, 1948), a drama set in Buenos Aires, which received international acclaim.

1950-70

The New Cinema. During the 1950s and 1960s a generation of socially committed film-makers emerged throughout Latin America. Usually on the political left, they wanted to use film's mass appeal to raise consciousness of social ills, and of economic and cultural imperialism. The New Cinema movement, known in Brazil as Cinema Novo, was in part a reaction against studio-produced movies in the *chanchada* tradition, having little or no social message. At first the founders of New Cinema formed film clubs and discussion groups, and some, like Argentine Fernando Birri, Cuban Julio García Espinosa, and Colombian **Gabriel García Márquez** studied film-making abroad. There they became steeped in Italian neorealism and the French New Wave.

Brazilians were prominent in New Cinema. Among its best-known directors were Glauber Rocha and Nelson Pereira dos Santos. Rocha published a manifesto in 1954, titled "An Aesthetic of Hunger," calling for the creation of films depicting national social problems, especially those of poverty and inequality. Glauber Rocha's *Deus e o diablo na terra do sol* (*Black God, White Devil*, 1964) and Pereira dos Santos's *Vidas secas* (*Barren Lives*, 1963; based on Garciliano Ramos's classic novel), set in Brazil's drought-ravaged Northeast, were landmarks of Cinema Novo film-making. Dealing with the misery of peasant farmers, they were sobering critiques of the region's unequal land distribution.

Brazilian film-makers were forced to soften their criticism during the military repression of the latter 1960s and early 1970s. They did so by turning to allegory, as in Glauber Rocha's controversial and personal *Terra em transe* (*Land in Anguish*, 1966), and by making historical films, as in Pereira dos Santos's treatment of an early-sixteenth-century French colonist who ran afoul of the primitive Tupí Indians, *Como era gostoso o meu francês* (*How Tasty Was My Little Frenchman*, 1971).

Argentina's leading proponents of New Cinema were Fernando Birri and Fernando Solanas. Their works were more strident than those of their Brazilian counterparts, reflecting Argentina's high degree of political polarization during the postwar decades. The deteriorating political situation there ultimately drove most practitioners of socially conscious film-making into exile, but not before Argentina produced several major contributions to the New Cinema. Two of the most notable were Leopoldo Torre Nilsson's *La casa del ángel* (*The House of the Angel*, 1957), which explored urban decadence and bourgeois hypocrisy, and Fernando Solanas's *La hora de los hornos* (*The Hour of the Furnaces*, 1966-68), which blasted neocolonialism and U.S. cultural imperialism.

The New Cinema movement stimulated feature film production in parts of Latin America that had previously produced only documentaries. Bolivian Jorge Sanjinés was a leader among a small group of directors who appeared in the Andean nations during the 1950s and 1960s. Sanjinés's most famous work was *Yawar Mallku* (*Blood of the Condor*, 1968), which effectively explored themes of genocide and cultural imperialism. Colombia's most notable contribution to New Cinema was *Chircales* (*Brick Makers*, 1968-72), directed by Marta Rodríguez and Jorge Silva. A social documentary, it illustrated the wretched lives of brick makers living on the outskirts of Bogotá.

Mexico's film industry, geared to popular tastes and enjoying patronage of the national government, was well established by the 1950s. For those reasons, counter-elite film-makers made a smaller impact there than elsewhere. One notable exception was Spanish expatriate Luis Buñuel, who became a naturalized Mexican citizen in 1949 and directed twenty films there between 1946 and 1964. Especially influential in the New Cinema movement were *Los olvidados* (*The Young and the Damned*, 1950), *El bruto* (*The Brute*, 1952), *Viridiana* (1961), and *Simón del desierto* (*Simon of the Desert*, 1964). Throughout his years in Mexico. Buñuel was hampered by twenty-one-day shooting schedules and small budgets. In 1964 Mexican director Alberto Isaac made *En este pueblo no hay ladrones*. That film was notable in being the first of **Gabriel García Márquez**'s short stories adapted to film.

The New Cinema did not produce many notable works in Cuba. Cuba's film industry was in its infancy during the 1950s. That country's 1959 revolution did, however, give powerful impetus to the New Cinema movement throughout Latin America. Within Cuba the government pressed film-makers into service to the revolution. It did so by patronizing and controlling their work through the Cuban Institute of Cinematographic Art and Industry (ICAIC), founded in 1959. Most ICAIC efforts were directed toward documentary productions during the 1950s and 1960s. Near the end of the latter decade two acclaimed features were produced, Humberto Solás's *Lucía* (1968) and *Memorias del subdesarrollo* (*Memories of Underdevelopment*, 1968), directed by Tomás Gutiérrez Alea. While many members of the film community sympathized with the revolution's goals, Cuban directors chafed under its ideological rigidities. Within that setting the ICAIC attempted to allow Cuban film-makers a degree of artistic license. Thus Gutiérrez Alea's *Memorias*, a bittersweet drama about a middle-aged intellectual far from zealous in his support of the revolution, was very much in the spirit of the New Cinema.

Latin America's New Cinema movement was pivotal to the region's film industry. Born of nationalism and anti-imperialism, and in the resolve of the progressive-minded to heighten awareness of social inequality, it liberated Latin American cinema from the embrace of formulaic low-budget movies geared to a general audience.

1970 to the Present

Recent Latin American Cinema. During the century's last three decades, and despite enthusiasm generated by the New Cinema, Latin American film-makers saw no relief in their struggle for market share against U.S. and European feature film. Cinema devotees were willing to stand in line for hours to see a highly-touted Hollywood release, but they rarely did so for domestically-produced features that were few in number and lacked the advertising budgets and distribution networks of major U.S. productions.

During the 1970s and early 1980s statist

political regimes intervened to aid film production. National film institutes appeared in most larger countries, making a significant impact there. But they proved ephemeral, falling prey to the economic hard times of the 1980s. The popularity of radio, television, and, by the 1980s, video tape rentals also worked to the detriment of domestic film-makers. Yet to its credit Latin America consistently produced notable films throughout the century's final decades, increasingly through international collaborative ventures. And before their disappearance the national film institutes had helped create film industries in countries where none had existed previously.

Colombia encouraged the making of documentaries and short features through its institute FOCINE, mandating that they be shown prior to feature presentations. Luis Ospina, Ciro Durán, and Jorge Ali Triana emerged as leading Colombian directors during the 1970s. Ospina's *Pura sangre* (*Pure Blood*, 1982) and Triana's *Tiempo de morir* (*Time to Die*, 1985) won critical acclaim, as did Sergio Dow's *El día que me ama* (*The Day You Love Me*, 1986) and Sergio Cabrera's 1993 feature *La estrategia del caracol* (*The Strategy of the Snail*).

Venezuelan and Peruvian film institutes encouraged feature-film making. By the 1980s and '90s important works had begun to appear in those countries. Peru's Francisco Lombardi gained international recognition with his *La ciudad y los perros* (*The City and the Dogs*, 1986). So too did Miguel Pereira with *Boca de lobo* (*The Mouth of the Wolf*, 1988), and Alberto Durant with *Alias, La gringa* (1991). Venezuelan director Fina Torres won the Camera d'Or at Cannes with *Oriane* (1985). Other notable Venezuelan films included Román Chalbaud's *Cuchillos de fuego* (*Flaming Knives*, 1990) and Luis Alberto Lamata's historical drama *Jericó* (1991).

During the 1980s and 1990s Latin American directors began exploring new subjects and themes. Slavery was the subject of Cuban director Sergio Giral's *El otro Francisco* (*The Other Francisco*, 1973) and Tomás Gutiérrez Alea's *La*

última cena (*The Last Supper*, 1976) as well as of Brazilian Carlos Diegues's *Xica* (1976) and *Quilombo* (1984).

Other films took up the theme of women in Latin American society. Early examples were *Lucía* (1968) and *Retrato de Teresa* (*Portrait of Teresa*, 1970) of Cuban directors Humberto Solás and Pastor Vega, respectively. A later one was *La Tigra* (*The Tigress*, 1990) of Ecuadorian Camilo Luzuriaga. Many of the best portrayals of women were by female directors. Notable among them were Suzana Amaral's [Brazil] (*Hour of the Star*, 1985) and María Navarro's [Mexico] *Danzón* (1991). Argentine director María Luisa Bemberg emerged as Latin America's leading feminist director with *Señora de nadie* (*No One's Woman*, 1982), *Camila* (1984), *Miss Mary* (1986), *Yo, la peor de todas* (*I, the Worst of All*, 1990), and *De eso no se habla* (*We Don't Talk About It*, 1993). Luis Puenzo's 1986 drama *La historia oficial* (*The Official Story*), about the adoption of a child whose parents were killed during Argentina's Dirty War, won the Oscar for Best Foreign Film in 1986. Laura Esquivel's feminist novel *Como agua para chocolate* (*Like Water for Chocolate*) was adapted for the screen by Alfonso Arau in 1991. It went on to become the highest-grossing Latin American film ever shown in the United States.

Homosexuality was the theme of Jaime Hermosillo's [Mexico] comedy *Doña Herlinda y su hijo* (*Doña Herlinda and Her Son*, 1985) and Hector Babenco's [Brazil] *Kiss of the Spider Woman* (1985). Cuban director Tomás Gutiérrez Alea's *Fresa y chocolate* (*Strawberry and Chocolate*, 1994) was notable for its sensitive portrayal of homosexuality and political intolerance in contemporary Cuba.

Latin American cinema had gained maturity and complexity over the course of the 1980s. Hector Babenco's *Pixote* (1981) provided an unsentimental though disturbing view of street children from the slums of São Paulo. Eliseo Subiela's *El hombre que miraba al sudeste* (*The Man Facing Southeast*, 1988), a highly constructed film open to multiple readings, stands as an example of how modern Latin American cinema has been able to produce semiotically interesting films with relatively low budgets.

Collaborative ventures were increasingly common during the 1980s and 1990s. Growth of the Latin American population in the United States and the emergence of Latino stars increased the demand for films dealing with Latino issues. Notable productions included Gregory Navas's *El Norte* (1984), depicting the plight of Guatemalan Indians immigrating illegally to the United States, and Robert Young's *Ballad of Gregorio Cortez* (1982), starring Edward James Olmos as the celebrated outlaw. Olmos promoted and starred in *Stand and Deliver* (1988), directed by Ramón Méndez, depicting a gifted teacher of Chicano youth in Los Angeles. Olmos also co-starred, with Raúl Julia and Sonia Braga, in *The Burning Season* (1994), directed by John Frankenheimer, on the life of Brazilian political activist Chico Mendes. U.S. actor Robert Redford directed Brazilian star Sonia Braga in *The Milagro Beanfield War* (1988), a celebration of Latino culture in New Mexico.

European film-makers collaborated with Latin American counterparts in the production of notable cinema. Brazilian-Italian cooperation produced *Gabriela* (1983), starring Sonia Braga and Marcello Mastroianni. *Oriane*, cited above, resulted from Venezuelan-French collaboration; *Sugar Cane Alley* (1984), which depicted Caribbean plantation culture during the 1920s, was a French-Martiniquian production.

Three well-received Brazilian films of the latter 1990s reflected collaboration of European and U.S. studios. *Four Days in September* (1997), directed by Bruno Barreto, dramatized the 1969 kidnapping by leftist students of U.S. ambassador to Brazil, Charles Burke Elbrick. Carlos Diegues, who had earlier directed *Gabriela*, again cast Sonia Braga in the starring role in *Tieta of Agreste* (1997), also based on a novel by **Jorge Amado**. In 1998 Fernanda Montenegro was acclaimed for her role in *Central Station*, directed by Walter Salles. The film depicts the odyssey of a woman and an orphan boy traveling from Rio to Brazil's Northeast.

Spanish television joined with the Cuban-based Foundation for Latin American Cinema to produce numerous made-for-television films based on short stories of **Gabriel García Márquez**. Among them were *Letters from the Park* (1988), directed by Tomás Gutiérrez Alea; *Fable of the Beautiful Pigeon Fancier* (1988), directed by Ruy Guerra; *The Summer of Miss Forbes* (1988), directed by Jaime Hermosillo; and *A Very Old Man with Enormous Wings* (1988), starring and directed by Fernando Birri.

Several Cuban directors made films while living in the United States, among them Orlando Jiménez Leal's *El Super* (1980). *Nobody Listens* (1988), directed by Jiménez Leal and Jorge Ulla, and *Bitter Sugar* (1996), of Leon Ichaso, denounced censorship, repression, and poor living conditions in Castro's Cuba.

Cinema in Latin American was both diverse and international at the end of the twentieth century. The forces of globalization had strengthened it by making greater resources available to talented directors, even those living in countries lacking established film industries. This ensured the region and the world a consistent flow of high-quality cinema. At the same time, film-makers in Brazil, Mexico, and Argentina maintained modest though constant production of low-budget movies for the general public. Known as *porno-chanchadas* in Brazil, they were heavy on sex and violence. Such films passed quickly to television and video. The relative vigor of Latin American cinema at century's end, coupled with the fact that it offered culturally authentic works to a movie-going public whose numbers were rapidly approaching a half-billion, boded well for its ongoing growth and development.

Spectator Sports and Athletics

Latin America has been the home of spectator sports since pre-Columbian times, when Mesoamerican Indians played a ball game combining aspects of basketball, handball, and soccer. The ruins of elaborate stone stadiums, where Mayan and Aztec elites watched the ball game, are scattered across Central America and southern Mexico.

Bullfighting came to the New World with the Spanish conquest, and became a feature of life in several countries. Most major cities of Mexico, Venezuela, Colombia, and Peru, where bullfighting has been most popular, possess their *plazas de toros* (bull rings). There are also bull rings in smaller towns and cities, often rustic affairs similar to rodeo corrals seen in the southwestern United States. The sport of bullfighting remained a principal public entertainment in Latin America throughout the colonial and early national periods. It was a part of major festivals and celebrations for the first four centuries of Latin American history.

European and North American sports were introduced to Latin America during the nineteenth century, becoming popular over the course of the twentieth. The first decades of the twentieth century witnessed a proliferation of athletic clubs organized by members of the local elite. Such clubs, which sprang up in national as well as provincial capitals, emphasized tennis, field hockey, polo, and cycling, most being patterned upon British models. Codes of behavior and proper conduct stressed physical conditioning as integral to the formation of virtuous and upstanding citizens. Proper young men and women, and their parents as well, participated in competitions as an outgrowth of club membership. The sporting clubs soon evolved into country clubs whose membership often included the nation's leading citizens.

By the latter twentieth century country club membership had become common among members of the middle class. *Clubes campestres* dotted the outskirts of towns and cities, offering playing fields, tennis and basketball courts, and swimming pools, often for modest fees. Large companies and public corporations built similar facilities for the use of their employees. Most offered soccer fields, tennis and basketball courts, and swimming pools. Some possessed racquetball courts, bowling alleys, and golf courses, all for use by company employees.

Physical education for both male and female students formed part of school curricula by the mid-twentieth century. Basketball, volleyball, and *microfútbol* (soccer played in reduced space) were played in school patios throughout Latin America. Schools outside urban areas invariably possessed

soccer fields, while the more expensive private high schools sometimes had their own swimming pools, as well as facilities for track and field events.

By the end of the twentieth century Latin Americans of every class had discovered the joys of athletics and simple physical exercise. Factory workers played pickup soccer during lunch hour, soccer was played continuously on weekends in parks and other public spaces, and devotees of that sport played in soccer clubs and semi-professional leagues. Ordinary people jogged, performed aerobics, and participated in court games available to them through membership in athletic clubs.

As with athletics, modern spectator sports gained popularity during the twentieth century. That process was a function of urbanization, increased leisure time among the citizenry, and increasing affluence among the popular classes. Latin Americans were primed for spectator sports even before they made their appearance. They knew of the popularity of sports in the United States and Europe, and had long followed them via newspaper reports and, by the 1920s, telegraph transmissions. In 1927 fans all over Latin America stood for hours before telegraph offices receiving reports on the Dempsey–Tunney fight.

Soccer (*fútbol* in Spanish America, *futebol* in Brazil) quickly emerged as the region's preeminent spectator sport. By the 1930s professional leagues existed in every country, and during that decade it became a point of high national pride when a country's team qualified to play in the World Cup. Virtuoso players such as Brazil's **Pelé** and Argentina's Diego Maradona were considered national treasures. They commanded immense salaries and the adulation of fans. Professional team ownership became part of the cachet of fabulously wealthy Colombian drug czars. A World Cup playoff game helped spark war between El Salvador and Honduras in 1969.

Latin American soccer teams have commanded respect of the international soccer community throughout the twentieth century. During the 1920s both Brazil and Mexico hosted international tournaments in that sport. The first World Cup was won by Uruguay in 1930, which also hosted the event. Uruguay won for a second time in 1950. Argentina also won the World Cup twice (1978, 1986), and Brazil did it an unprecedented four times (1958, 1962, 1970, 1994).

Baseball became popular in countries of the Caribbean Basin after the residents of port cities observed off-duty U.S. sailors playing pitch-and-catch at dockside. As in the case of soccer, baseball's appeal rested in the relative simplicity of its equipment and in its egalitarian character. And as with soccer, Latin Americans of the circum-Caribbean embraced the sport with a fervor that elevated many of them to the highest professional level. **Roberto Clemente**, Orlando Cepeda, Fernando Valenzuela, and Sammy Sosa were but four of many Latin American players who became preeminent in the U.S. "big leagues." It was noted that Miami's divided and contentious Latin American community became unified just once: during 1997, when the city's professional baseball team, the Florida Marlins, won the World Series. The team's starting lineup was made up of players who haled from several countries of the Caribbean Basin.

Professional cycling is a popular sport in Latin America, especially in the Andean countries. Young men of modest means can be seen training on mountain highways, hoping to win a place on one or another corporate-sponsored team. Individual countries hold annual races sending competitors over some of the world's most grueling highways. Latin Americans invariably figure in cycling's premier event, the Tour de France.

At the end of the twentieth century most of the world's major spectator sports, and a number of minor ones as well, were practiced throughout Latin America. Athletes from Argentina, Brazil, and Cuba routinely harvest medals in Olympic basketball, boxing, tennis, and a host of other sports. Auto racing was popular in many countries, especially in Brazil, whose Emerson Fittipaldi gained international fame through his skill in Formula One events. World-class tennis players from Latin America included Pancho Segura from Ecuador, Pancho González from Mexico, and Gabriela Sabatini from Argentina. Boxing world champions included Pascual Pérez of Argentina, Roberto Durán of Panama, and Vicente Rondón of Venezuela. Professional jai alai flourishes in Mexico (where it is called *frontón*), and in some parts of the United States and the Caribbean.

During the 1980s the electronic media, particularly satellite television, vastly increased the viewing of spectator sports in Latin America. From that decade onward Latin American sports fans followed European professional soccer teams as well as those of their own countries. The same was true for baseball. Satellite television enabled millions of Latin American viewers to follow compatriots playing baseball in the U.S. big leagues. Meanwhile, many more became fans of U.S. professional basketball. Thanks to modern communication, Michael Jordan became a role model in many Latin American homes. International television linkages won followings for nontraditional sports as well. British rugby and North American football were but two examples.

Part III

300 Notable Figures of Latin American History

Acosta, José de (1540-1600), Jesuit historian. Born in Medina del Campo, Spain, Acosta became a Jesuit at a young age. He came to the New World in 1571 and lived fourteen years in Peru and one in Mexico and then returned to Spain in 1587. His *Historia natural y moral de las Indias (The Natural and Moral History of the Indies)* was published in Seville in 1590. In it he denied that the Indians were one of the Lost Tribes of Israel. He was the first writer to suggest that the Indians had migrated to the New World from the Old over a land bridge that connected the two. He argued that the Indians had lived in the New World for a long time, adapted to their environment, and developed their unique civilization and culture without the intervention of others. As such his book is considered to be a precursor of the more rationalist historical works that would follow. His history does posit a providential Christian design in the unfolding of events.

Alamán, Lucas (1792-1853), Mexican statesman and historian, considered the outstanding Conservative spokesman of his generation. Born in Guanajuato, Alamán was the son of wealthy and socially prominent parents. Of a scholarly bent, he received an excellent education, including study at Mexico City's School of Mines in 1812-13. From 1814 to 1820 he lived in Europe, where he traveled extensively and continued his studies. Upon his return to Mexico, he was elected to represent his native province in the Spanish Cortes. Arriving in Spain in 1821, he became an advocate for home rule even as Mexico's independence was being achieved. After returning to Mexico, he served as minister of the interior and foreign relations in the first republican governments (1823-25) and in the administration of Vice President Anastasio Bustamante (1830-32), when he warned of American threats to Mexican sovereignty in Texas and founded an industrial development bank, the Banco de Avío. Alamán and other members of the Bustamante administration were later attacked for complicity in various misdeeds, including the capture and execution of **Vicente Guerrero**, but he denied the charges. He held numerous other posts in subsequent years, including that of minister of the interior and

foreign relations (1853) under **Antonio López de Santa Anna**. Over the years Mexico's political disorders had convinced him of the folly of federalism and made him a proponent of a strong, highly centralized government. He favored state support of the Roman Catholic church, not only because he was a devout Catholic but also because he regarded it as the only institution that linked all Mexicans. A supporter of economic expansion, he created the Ministry of Development, Colonization, and Industry in 1853. Alamán is also remembered for his historical writings, notably his five-volume *Historia de Méjico* (1849-52), a sweeping account of Mexico's independence movement and recent history from a Conservative perspective.

Alberdi, Juan Bautista (1810-1884), Argentine political thinker and writer. A native of Tucumán, Alberdi was educated mainly in Buenos Aires but received a law degree from the University of Córdoba in 1834. Back in Buenos Aires, he, along with **Esteban Echeverría** and other young intellectuals, became part of the Generation of 1837. Although he wrote a sympathetic portrait of the dictator **Juan Manuel de Rosas** in *Fragmento preliminar al estudio del derecho* (1837), he was forced to flee into exile the following year. Alberdi would spend most of his life abroad, initially in Uruguay and, after a trip to Europe, in Chile. After the fall of Rosas, he supported the Argentine Confederation led by **Justo José de Urquiza**, from whom he accepted a diplomatic assignment to the United States and Europe and obtained recognition of the new confederation from several foreign governments. He did not go back to Argentina until 1879, after he had been elected to Congress, and returned to Europe in 1881.

Alberdi's most important work is *Bases y puntos de partida para la organización política de la República Argentina* (1852), whose influence can be seen in the constitution of 1853. In his discussion of the kind of government that would best suit Argentina's needs, he endorsed federalism but favored a strong chief executive. He believed that foreign trade and investment were vital to Argentine development, as was European immigration. This belief underlies his most famous aphorism: *gobernar es poblar* ("to govern is to populate"). He also supported religious tolerance as a means of attracting immigrants to Argentina.

Aleijadinho, O (Antônio Francisco Lisbôa; 1738?-1814), Brazilian mulatto sculptor and architect. Born illegitimate in Villa Rica do Ouro Prêto, Minas Gerais, to Manuel Francisco Lisbôa and a slave, *O Aleijadinho* (the Little Cripple) was probably Latin America's greatest colonial sculptor. Enormously prolific, he designed and produced works for many *mineiro* churches; the most important were São Francisco in Ouro Prêto and São João do Rei, Nossa Senhora do Carmo in Sabará, and Bom Jesus de Matosinhos in Congonhas. The last alone has sixty-seven wooden life-sized figures and twelve stone statues. Incredible as it may seem, a debilitating disease left him painfully crippled, and he executed some of his most famous works with chisel and mallet strapped to his atrophied and shriveled hands. His extraordinary talent pushed the late-arriving European art styles of baroque and rococo to unparalleled heights in Brazil after they had been supplanted in Europe.

Alemán Valdés, Miguel (1900-1983), Mexican president. Miguel Alemán was born in the state of Veracruz and bore the name of his father, who later achieved the rank of general in the revolution of 1910-20. The younger Alemán attended schools in Mexico City, ultimately earning a law degree at the National University in 1928. He worked for the federal government in various capacities until 1936, when he won the governorship of Veracruz. That paved the way for his rapid rise within Mexico's semi-official party. Manuel Ávila Camacho, the party's candidate for the 1940-46 presidential term, chose Alemán to manage his campaign. After winning, Ávila made Alemán his interior minister, and in 1946 selected him to become presidential candidate for the 1946-52 period. Alemán duly won the contest, becoming only the second civilian to hold the presidency since **Francisco I. Madero**, and the first to do so under the party's new name of Institutional Revolutionary party (PRI). The chief achievement of Alemán's presidency was to complete Mexico's process of import substitution, encouraging industrial development through protective tariffs and government loans. His pro-business stance set into motion three decades of significant economic growth. Alemán borrowed heavily from the Export–Import Bank of the United States to boost agricultural production. Those monies were spent in bringing land into production through irrigation. The national constitution was modified to protect the owners of commercially viable land holdings from expropriation. Loans from private U.S. banks helped modernize PEMEX, the national petroleum company, allowing it to double production. Other monies were used to construct a new and modern campus for the national university, a modern highway system, and infrastructure for the development of Acapulco as a resort. At the end of his term Alemán and his colleagues were blamed for massive theft of public monies. Such allegations would henceforth follow outgoing PRI regimes through the remainder of the century, save for that of Alemán's immediate successor, Adolfo Ruiz Cortines.

Alessandri Palma, Arturo (1868-1950), twice Chilean president. Educated as a lawyer, Arturo Alessandri served eighteen years in Chile's Congress (1897-1920), becoming a leading contender for president in 1920. He headed a coalition opposing the conservative elite that had dominated politics up to that time. His gift for oratory and aristocratic appearance won him a following among the popular classes, who dubbed him the Lion of Tarapacá, for the nitrate-producing region that he represented. His rise coincided with economic hardship attending the post-war collapse in nitrate prices. Narrowly elected on a platform promising administrative decentralization, reform of tax and labor laws, separation of church and state, and enlarged presidential power, Alessandri at length turned to the army to help him prevail over a Congress loath to pass his reforms. But the army usurped Alessandri's power, forcing him into an exile (September 1924) lasting until dissident officers, led by **Carlos Ibáñez**, recalled him in early 1925. Reform continued under civil-military rule, though power clearly rested in the hands of Ibáñez. Alessandri resigned his presidency (October 1925), and resumed his exile, becoming a leader of the anti-Ibáñez opposition. In 1932 he was elected to a six-year presidential term.

The second Alessandri administration was nearly as turbulent as his first. Faced by political unrest on the left and right, and forced to grapple with problems attending the Great Depression, he abandoned his earlier populism. He and his finance minister, Gustavo Ross, maintained fiscal austerity, restoring the nation's economic health by the end of his term. In spite of that success, Alessandri angered Chileans through his harsh suppression of political dissidents. His refusal to meet demands of the left and his bloody suppression of a Nazi uprising in 1938 alienated many who had previously supported him. Chileans elected Allesandri to the Senate twice during the 1940s, a tribute to one who had given the nation effective if controversial leadership during two turbulent moments in national history.

Alessandri Rodríguez, Jorge (1896-1986), Chilean president, industrialist, son of **Arturo Alessandri Palma**. Trained as a civil engineer, Jorge Alessandri held no major political post until he served as President Gabriel González Videla's minister of finance (1947-50). Alessandri became the presidential candidate of Chilean conservatives in 1958, narrowly defeating the candidate of the left, **Salvador Allende**, by a 32 to 29 percent margin. Christian Democrat **Eduardo Frei** was third with 20.5 percent. Moderates welcomed the electoral result, as Alessandri promised to address national economic problems through financial constraint and belt-tightening and through encouragement of private enterprise and foreign investment. Yet in spite of his efforts the economy stagnated as inflation moved apace. Worsening agricultural yields moved Alessandri to launch Chile's first major agrarian reform, aimed at putting unused latifundia into production. He took Chile into the Latin American Free Trade Association as part of his program to boost exports. Staunchly anti-communist, Alessandri

severed Chile's diplomatic relations with Cuba shortly before leaving office in 1964. Jorge Alessandri was a popular president in spite of his failure either to meaningfully stimulate the economy or to improve the lot of the beleaguered lower and middle classes. His reputation for honesty and moderation led conservatives to make him their candidate in the 1970 presidential contest. Alessandri lost the election to Socialist **Salvador Allende** by a single percentage point. As Allende won by a plurality, it was the Chilean congress that ultimately chose him over Alessadri.

Alfaro Delgado, José Eloy (1842-1912), Ecuadorian president. Eloy Alfaro was born near the Pacific coast in the village of Montecristi, the fifth child of a Spanish merchant father and an Ecuadorian mother. In early manhood he became inspired by the ideals of revolutionary liberalism, and vowed to sever Ecuador's ties with the Catholic church and to defeat the Conservative party and its paladin **Gabriel García Moreno**. He began his political career in 1862, kidnapping the Conservative governor of his home province. He led uprisings against the government of García Moreno in 1865 and 1871, and suffered numerous exiles over his decades as a guerrilla leader. A good businessman, heir to a hat-making business, and married into a wealthy Panamanian family, Alfaro spent his family's fortune to fund his revolutionary activities. His passionate dedication to his cause won him fame throughout the continent. Among his supporters were Liberal notables **Juan Montalvo**, from his own country, Colombian **Rafael Uribe Uribe**, and Cubans **José Martí** and **Antonio Maceo**. Alfaro at last achieved success when political scandal and Conservative division brought the Liberal party to power in what is termed Ecuador's Bourgeois Revolution of 1895 for the support it drew from coastal commercial interests. Alfaro was called from Panama to extinguish the last vestiges of Conservative power. He was elected president following his successful campaign. His presidency was marked by an attack on church prerogatives, the expulsion of foreign clergy, and freeing of Indians from the head tax—all under aegis of a new constitution. He also linked Quito and Guayaquil by rail, a project completed in 1908. Alfaro's fatal flaw lay in his inability to relinquish power. After grudgingly allowing his hand-picked successor, General Leonidas Plaza, to succeed him in 1901, he seized the presidency from Plaza's successor, Lizardo García, in 1905. A constituent assembly legitimized that act a year later. Following his second presidency, which ended in 1911, he again attempted to seize power by force of arms. In early 1912 he was arrested and imprisoned in Quito. On January 28, a mob dragged him from his cell and lynched him.

Allende Gossens, Salvador (1908-1973), president of Chile and a founder of the Chilean Socialist party. A medical doctor by profession and a committed socialist, Salvador Allende was elected to the Chamber of Deputies in 1937, and served as minister of health (1939-42) in the Popular Front government of Pedro Aguirre Cerda. Thereafter he served in the Senate from 1945 to 1969. Allende ran for president in 1952, gaining 5.4 percent of the vote. In 1954, his Socialist party joined the Communists to form the Popular Action Front (FRAP). Allende was the coalition's presidential candidate in 1958, when he narrowly lost to **Jorge Alessandri**, and in 1964, when he lost by a substantial margin to **Eduardo Frei**. Allende won the 1970 presidential contest by a narrow plurality, thanks to a split between conservatives and Christian Democrats. In that contest Allende represented the new Popular Unity coalition, made up of Socialists, Communists, and four small non-Marxist parties. During his first year in office Allende vastly increased spending on social and public works programs, while imposing price controls and expropriating unproductive large land holdings. He fully nationalized Chile's copper mines, along with scores of other industries. Allende celebrated his successful first year in office by hosting **Fidel Castro** in a state visit. Chile's economy worsened during 1971. Inflation rebounded and agricultural production declined, as government land confiscations continued and widespread land invasions took place. Capital fled the country, and a decline in copper prices further accelerated the downturn. Allende's actions galvanized the opposition. Christian

Democrats joined with the conservative National party, and both received financial support from the United States, whose president, Richard Nixon, vowed to unseat Allende. Late in 1972, the opposition staged a crippling employers' strike, forcing Allende to halt the nationalization of small and intermediate industry. Early in 1973, the opposition increased its congressional majority. Conditions in Chile worsened over the first half of 1973. Inflation soared and consumer goods became scarce. Employers organized strikes, while members of the political opposition called for military intervention. Troops loyal to the government put down a coup attempt in June 1973. But within two months anti-Allende forces within the military gained the upper hand. That was reflected in Allende's unwilling appointment of General **Augusto Pinochet** as acting commander in chief early in September 1973. Soon thereafter, on September 10, Pinochet demanded the president's resignation. Allende refused, and with troops besieging the presidential palace, committed suicide the following day. The military remained in control of Chile during the following sixteen years.

Almagro, Diego de (1475?-1538), conqueror of Peru and Chile. Almagro was born illegitimate in Almagro, New Castile, Spain. He arrived in the Indies in 1514 and participated in early conquest activities in Panama, becoming an associate of **Francisco Pizarro**. The two planned and participated in three expeditions to Peru (1524, 1526, 1531), but Almagro was increasingly bypassed and remained the odd man out. He was still on the Isthmus of Panama when Pizarro and his men captured the Inca emperor **Atahualpa**. He missed the division of Atahualpa's treasure, the largest booty taken by the Spanish during the conquest. In 1535 he organized an expedition to Chile from Cuzco. He and his followers underwent great hardship. They struggled back to Cuzco in 1537 just as the Inca siege against the forces of Pizarro had been lifted. Embittered at his lack of honors and riches, he plunged Peru into a civil war. He occupied Cuzco and imprisoned the Pizarro brothers, Hernando and Gonzalo, but after the latter escaped he freed the former on condition that he return to Spain. Hernando reneged and soundly defeated Almagro in the Battle of Salinas and had him executed in 1538. Almagro's illegitimate mestizo son, Diego the Younger, returned the favor when his followers assassinated the Pizarro clan leader, Francisco, in Lima in 1541.

Alvarado y Mesía, Pedro de (1485?-1541), leader in the conquest of Mexico, Central America, and Ecuador. Born in Badajoz, Extremadura, Spain, Alvarado came to the New World about 1510. He was **Hernán Cortés**'s chief lieutenant in the conquest of Mexico. His red hair earned him the Nahuatl nickname of "Tonatiuh" (the Sun). The Spanish used his distinctive appearance to psychological advantage to intimidate the Indians by prancing him around on a lathered-up steed outfitted with clanging bells. Brave, cruel, and impetuous, he lacked Cortés's astuteness, subtlety, and foresight. Cortés left him in charge in the Aztec capital of Tenochtitlán when he dashed out to resist forces sent from Cuba. But Alvarado was alarmed by Indian rituals and precipitated a massacre, which in turn produced an Aztec uprising and then Spanish flight from the city with great loss of life and treasure. In 1523 Cortés entrusted him with the conquest of Soconusco, Guatemala, and El Salvador. Here he carved out a place for himself and dominated the region until his death. His marriage to Francisca de la Cueva in 1527 brought him into the ranks of the high Spanish nobility and neutralized charges against him of wrongdoing. Her death in 1528 in Veracruz on the way to Guatemala led him to marry her sister Beatriz over a decade later in order to preserve the ongoing political relationship. After Alvarado's death his mestizo daughter Leonor married Beatriz's brother, Francisco de la Cueva, to keep the Guatemalan inheritance in the family. Alvarado was always decamping to other fronts and leaving family members in charge. Hearing of the great wealth in Peru, Alvarado helped outfit 500 Spaniards and 2,000 Indians and transported them to Quito (1533-34), where he reached an agreement with **Diego de Almagro** to leave the men and materiel in exchange for 100,000 gold pesos. In 1541, outfitting his fleet to cross the Pacific to the Spice Islands, he made port in

Jalisco, Mexico. There he encountered the viceroy of New Spain, **Antonio de Mendoza**, engaged in putting down the Mixtón Indian revolt (1540-41). Alvarado agreed to participate and lost his life after a horse fell on him.

Amado, Jorge (1912–), Brazilian novelist. Jorge Amado grew up on a cacao plantation near the city of Ilhéus, in the state of Bahia. Completing a law degree in 1937, he became active in the Brazilian Communist party, ultimately winning a seat in the Chamber of Deputies (1945-47). While Amado published a biography of **Luís Carlos Prestes** in 1942, his forte was fiction. He began his writing career during the 1930s, producing four novels set in the area of Bahia, the most notable of which, *Terras do sem-fim* (1943), translated into English as *The Violent Land*, depicted the ruthlessness of that region's land barons. Amado traveled abroad in 1947, after the Communist party was declared illegal. His polemical *O mundo da paz* (1950) and *Os subterráneos da liberdade* (1954) won him the Stalin International Peace Prize in 1954. Returning to Brazil in 1955, he began writing the earthy novels, set both in urban and rural Bahia, that won him fame. *Gabriela, cravo e canela* (*Gabriela, Clove and Cinnamon*, 1958) was his first international best seller, and was followed by *Dona Flor e seus dois maridos* (*Dona Flor and Her Two Husbands*, 1966), *Tereza Bautista* (1972), and *Tieta* (1977). Each novel portrayed strong women who struggled against the unfairness and hypocrisy of bourgeois, male-dominated society. But as works written with humor and affectionate evocation of place, they were much more than populist morality tales. Brazil's African heritage figures prominently in Amado's later novels, particularly in *Tenda dos milagres* (*Tent of Miracles*, 1969), whose focus is the Afro-Brazilian religion of Candomblé and its easy co-existence with Brazilian Roman Catholicism in the popular classes. While the carnality of his later novels make Amado a controversial writer, he remains Brazil's most popular and best-known modern novelist.

Anchieta, José de (1534-1597), Spanish Jesuit missionary in Brazil. Born in Tenerife, Canary

Islands, Anchieta joined the Jesuits as a lay brother in 1551, while at the University of Coimbra, and took his last vows as a priest in 1577. He arrived in Brazil in 1553, taught at the Jesuit school in São Paulo, and laid the basis for the Jesuit educational system in Brazil. Called the "Apostle of Brazil" for his missionary work, he learned various Indian languages and worked with government officials to reduce the Indians to settled communities (*aldeias*) under the control of the Portuguese. He was the Jesuit provincial of the southern province from 1578 to 1587. His letters and reports for the period 1554 to 1594 constitute one of the chief primary sources for our knowledge of sixteenth-century Brazil.

Andrada e Silva, José Bonifácio de (1763-1838), Brazilian scientist and statesman, known as the patriarch of Brazilian independence. A native of Santos, José Bonifácio studied law at the University of Coimbra in Portugal. He then traveled extensively in Europe, studying mineralogy and metallurgy at the University of Freiburg and discovering several species of minerals in Sweden. After returning to Portugal, he was named professor of metallurgy at Coimbra.

He returned to Brazil in 1819 after an absence of thirty-six years and, with his two younger brothers--Martin Francisco and Antônio Carlos--became active in the turbulent political life of the era. In January 1822 he submitted to the future **Pedro I** a petition from São Paulo condemning Portuguese efforts to recolonize Brazil and urging him to remain in Brazil. A few days later Pedro appointed him minister of the kingdom and foreign affairs. Bonifácio endorsed Pedro's declaration of independence from Portugal on September 7, 1822, and agreed with his desire to end the African slave trade, but clashed with the emperor over his and his brothers' attacks on Portuguese soldiers and residents. His proposals for agrarian reform also alarmed conservatives. José Bonifácio resigned from the cabinet in July 1823 and was exiled, along with his brothers, when Pedro dissolved the constituent assembly a few months later.

José Bonifácio returned to Brazil in 1829 and was reconciled with Pedro, who appointed him

tutor to his son, the future **Pedro II**, when he abdicated in 1831. He was dismissed as tutor in 1833 after being accused of plotting to restore Pedro I to the throne but was absolved at a subsequent trial.

Arbenz Guzmán, Jacobo (1913-1971), Guatemalan soldier and president. Jacobo Arbenz graduated from the military Escuela Politécnica in Guatemala City in 1935 and entered the army that year. In July 1944 he joined in the overthrow of **Jorge Ubico,** and three months later, with fellow major Francisco Arana, led the "October revolution" that ousted conservative General F. Ponce Vaides, who headed the junta that replaced Ubico. By late 1944, Arbenz was a member of Guatemala's ruling civil-military triumvirate. He went on to serve as defense minister during the administration of **Juan José Arévalo** (1945-51). Throughout Arévalo's term, Arbenz, a socialist, vied with Francisco Arana to stand as the regime's presidential candidate in 1950. Arana's assassination in July 1949 cast a shadow over Arbenz's candidacy, but it ensured him victory in the November 1950 presidential election. Inaugurated in early 1951, Arbenz dedicated himself to the reform of Guatemala's agricultural system, in which 19 percent of farmers controlled 87 percent of the land. He encouraged agrarian unionism, extended credit to small farmers, and promoted rural cooperatives. In 1952, he announced the keystone of his program, an agrarian reform law that would expropriate, with compensation, 2.7 million acres of unused arable land, from some 1,000 plantations, making it available to landless peasants. Arbenz's friend and confidant, José Manuel Fortuny, a founder, in 1949, of the Guatemalan Communist party, played an important role in drawing up the plan. The U.S.-owned United Fruit Company was especially hard hit by the expropriation. Threatened with loss of 400,000 of its 550,000 acres, the company's owners complained that they were to be reimbursed at a fraction of the land's value (Arbenz had based reimbursement on United Fruit's declaration of the land's value on tax returns). Arbenz's program, his nationalism and outspoken anti-Americanism, and the fact that Communists figured among his official circle, set into motion plans for his overthrow. United Fruit and the U.S. government conspired with domestic dissidents to destabilize his regime. The Arbenz government was denounced as Communist, while the recently formed U.S. Central Intelligence Agency armed a small band of dissidents led by Colonel Carlos Castillo Armas and General Miguel Ydígoras Fuentes. The arrival of a shipment of Czechoslovakian armaments at Puerto Barrios set the overthrow of Arbenz into motion. On June 18, 1954, a "Liberation Army" headed by Castillo Armas, and supported by the CIA, moved into Guatemala from neighboring Honduras. Failing to enlist the support of his own military, Arbenz resigned (June 27) and fled the country. He lived in exile until his death.

Arévalo Bermejo, Juan José (1904-1990), Guatemalan president. Juan José Arévalo graduated from normal school in 1922 and subsequently took a job with Guatemala's Ministry of Education. He traveled to Argentina in 1931, in protest of General **Jorge Ubico**'s election to the presidency. Graduating from college there in 1934, he taught school in Argentina until Ubico's fall in 1944, when leaders of the civic-military junta that replaced the general called Arévalo home. He won the December 1944 presidential election by a large margin, and assumed office March 1945. The new president proclaimed his a "teacher's revolution." He guaranteed the protection of extensive civil rights stipulated in a new constitution, modeled on Mexico's 1917 charter; he also initiated unprecedented programs of a social democratic character that included a social security system, state-supported medical services, and a labor code guaranteeing the right to strike and to bargain collectively. Arévalo continued Ubico's highway-building program, but reversed the dictator's favored treatment of foreign investors and domestic landowners. This angered members of both groups, especially when Arévalo's Congress passed a law requiring that the holders of idle land rent it to peasants. Arévalo's social activism, and the perception that he favored the left (diplomatic relations were established with the Soviet Union in 1945), subjected his regime to a succession of

military revolts. His vision was in fact left-liberal, democratic, and internationalist: he promoted the cause of Central American union and formulated an antidictatorial pact for the region with Costa Rican dissident **José Figueres** (December 1947). At the same time he worked to limit advances of the left, with the help of his anticommunist army chief, Colonel Francisco J. Arana. But by 1949 Arana was rumored to be plotting a coup against Arévalo and the president's left-wing defense minister, **Jacobo Arbenz**, Arana's rival for the presidency in 1950. Arana's assassination in July 1949 sullied the reputations of both Arévalo and his defense minister. Arbenz, who was implicated in the killing, succeeded Arévalo in 1951. Juan José Arévalo remained influential in Guatemalan politics after leaving office, though he lived abroad until the 1980s. His brief and furtive return in March 1963 prompted the "preventive coup" in which right-wing members of the military overthrew President Miguel Ydígoras Fuentes. Three years later, with the return to civilian rule, he became Guatemala's ambassador-at-large. Arévalo became a prominent critic of United States policy in Latin America during his exile. He gained stature with the publication of *The Shark and the Sardines* (1961) and *Anti-Kommunism in Latin America: An X-Ray of a Process Leading to a New Colonialism* (1963).

Arias Madrid, Arnulfo (1901-1988), Panamanian president. Arnulfo Arias was trained as a physician at Harvard Medical School. Politics was, however, his first love. In 1930 he joined a nationalist organization called Acción Comunal and soon assumed its leadership. He overthrew President Florencio Arosemena in 1931 and promoted the election of his brother Harmodio to the presidency of Panama in 1932. During the 1930s Arias served in his brother's administration, and in that of President Juan D. Arosemena (1936-40). Arias was elected president in 1940, going on to promote racist and xenophobic policies that included stripping citizenship from Panamanians of West Indian and Asian origin. A populist, he extended the vote to women and instituted a social security system. He also created a system of secret police and extended the presidential term from four to six years through a constitution drafted during 1941. Arias was deposed by his minister of justice, Adolfo de la Guardia, in October 1941, an action supported by the United States, which feared that he harbored pro-Axis sympathies. Arias lost the 1948 presidential contest, but regained the office in 1949, when President Domingo Díaz Arosemena resigned because of ill health. He reintroduced his 1941 constitution and dissolved Congress and the supreme court. He was removed from office in May 1951. Arias unsuccessfully campaigned for president in 1960 and 1964. He won the 1968 contest, but was soon overthrown in a coup led by Lieutenant-Colonel **Omar Torrijos**. In 1984 he ran for the presidency again, being defeated by Nicolás Ardito Barletta, who was backed by **Manuel Noriega**. After his death followers created the Arnulfista party of Panama. Its candidate, his widow, Mireya Moscoso, garnered 29 percent of the vote in losing the 1994 presidential election, but was successful in 1999.

Arias Sánchez, Oscar (1940–), Costa Rican president. Oscar Arias was the son of politically active and well-to-do parents. He attended primary and secondary school in San José, and took a degree in economics and law at the University of Costa Rica (1963). He earned a master's degree in political science at the London School of Economics in 1967, returning home to teach at the University of Costa Rica (1968-69), and to serve as secretary and economic advisor to President **José Figueres Ferrer** (1970-72). Arias then returned to Britain to complete doctoral studies in political science at the University of Essex (1974). He served as economic advisor to President Daniel Oduber Quirós (1974-78), and helped direct the National Liberation party (PLN). Arias became the party's general secretary in 1979, represented the PLN in the National Assembly, and served in the administration of President Alberto Monge (1982-86). He led a generational revolt within PLN (1985), winning the party's presidential nomination, and then the general election (1986). While Arias improved Costa Rica's economy and reduced the national debt, his great success came on the international front. He asserted himself

against the United States, prevailing upon that nation to remove bases of the Nicaraguan Contras from Costa Rican soil. He worked to bring Central American leaders together to discuss ending guerrilla insurgencies in Nicaragua, El Salvador, and Guatemala. His effort was rewarded in August 1987, in the village of Esquipulas, Guatemala, where Central American presidents signed an accord that eventually brought peace to the region. Widely known as the Arias Peace Plan, it earned Oscar Arias the 1987 Nobel Peace Prize.

Aristide, Jean-Bertrand (1953–), Haitian Catholic priest and president. Jean-Bertrand Aristide, the younger of two children, was born in the southern coastal village of Port-Salut. His widowed mother soon moved her family to Port-au-Prince, where she enrolled her children in a parochial school run by the Salesian order. Jean-Bertrand began studying for the priesthood in 1974. In 1979 he was awarded a bachelor's degree in psychology from the Haitian national university, and went on to study abroad in Jerusalem, Egypt, Italy, and Britain, until 1982, when he returned to Haiti for his ordination. His first church was St.-Jean-Bosco, located in a Port-au-Prince slum. Aristide's sermons against social injustice quickly won him a devoted following among the city's poor, but shocked his superiors and angered dictator Jean-Claude Duvalier. The Salesians again sent Aristide abroad, to Montreal, where he spent another three years in theological study. He returned home in late 1985, in time to take part in protests that forced Duvalier from power, February 7, 1986. Returned to his pastorate at St.-Jean-Bosco, he soon became outspoken in support of the *dechoukaj* movement, dedicated to the violent elimination of Haiti's murderous *tontons macoutes*. That, and his ministry to the poor, in the idiom of liberation theology, led to a September 11, 1988 attack on St.-Jean-Bosco by *tontons macoutes*, which left eleven parishioners dead and seventy injured. While the attack led to the overthrow of military ruler Henri Namphy and caused Aristide to suffer a nervous breakdown, it did not dissuade the Salesians from expelling him from their order December 15, 1988. Aristide suffered another nervous breakdown in 1989, but recovered in 1990, going on to win Haiti's first free election in December 1990, with an overwhelming 67 percent of the vote. He had campaigned on a platform promising improved education for the poor, an end to political violence, and land reform. Inaugurated January 1991, Aristide was removed in a military coup seven months later. He sought exile in the United States, at length signing the Governors Island Accord (July 1993), by which he could resume his presidency. He returned to Haiti in October 1994, but was forced to effect structural economic reforms that limited his populism. Aristide presided over presidential elections in late 1995, and transmitted power to René Préval of his Lavalas party. He remained a significant force in Haitian politics.

Artigas, José Gervasio (1764-1850), leader of the independence movement in Uruguay (then known as the Banda Oriental). Born in Montevideo to a landowning and military family, Artigas engaged in a variety of rural activities as a youth, possibly including cattle rustling and smuggling. In 1797 he enlisted in a militia known as the Blandengues, created by the Spanish authorities to combat banditry and protect frontier settlements against Indian attack. Early in 1811 he joined the independence movement launched the previous year in Buenos Aires and defeated Spanish forces at Las Piedras (May 18, 1811). However, when a Portuguese invasion of Uruguay led the Buenos Aires junta to sign an armistice (October 20, 1811) with the Spanish viceroy in Montevideo, Artigas rejected it and crossed the Uruguay River into Entre Ríos province with his army and 4,000 civilian followers. By this action Artigas demonstrated not only his popular support but also his determination to reject subordination by Buenos Aires as well as by Spain. After British pressure forced the Portuguese to withdraw from the Banda Oriental in 1812, Artigas returned and had gained control of the entire province by 1815. By now he had emerged as a champion of provincial autonomy in opposition to the centralizing tendencies of Buenos Aires and became "protector" of a Federal League embracing the Banda Oriental and the provinces of Santa Fe, Entre Ríos, Córdoba, Corrientes, and Misiones. For the Banda Oriental

he proposed the distribution of idle and royalist lands to blacks, Indians, and poor whites. He welcomed British merchants to Uruguayan ports but sought to protect domestic industries.

Artigas's fortunes declined after the Portuguese again invaded the Banda Oriental in 1816. In January 1817 he surrendered Montevideo to them but waged a guerrilla war in the interior until he suffered a decisive defeat at Tacuarembó on January 22, 1820. Meanwhile, the Federal League had disintegrated as the leaders of Santa Fe and Entre Ríos fought their own successful war against Buenos Aires and then turned against Artigas. On September 5, 1820, he crossed the Paraná River, seeking asylum in Paraguay, where he remained until his death. Despite the setbacks he experienced, Artigas is considered the father of Uruguay's emergence as an independent state, while the federalism he espoused eventually became the basis of Argentine national organization. Because of his concern for the poor, he is also seen as a democratic populist.

Asturias, Miguel Ángel (1899-1974), Guatemalan writer and Nobel Prize laureate. Born to well-to-do parents, Miguel Ángel Asturias received his early education in Guatemala City and earned a law degree at the University of San Carlos (1923). Proud of his Mayan ancestry and angered by the historic ill-treatment of Guatemala's Indian majority, he wrote his law school thesis on social problems of the Indian. He began post-graduate study in political economy in London, but soon shifted his interest to Mayan culture, first working at the British Museum and then at the Sorbonne. In Paris he worked with anthropologist Georges Raynard, going on to publish, in Spanish, the Mayan sacred book *Popol Vuh* (1925) and the prose poem *Leyendas de Guatemala* (1930). Asturias returned to Guatemala in 1933. For a time he worked for the government newspaper *El Liberal Progresista*, and later produced a radio news program, among whose collaborators was **Jacobo Arbenz**. The fall of dictator **Jorge Ubico** in 1944 allowed Asturias to publish *El Señor Presidente* (1946), based on the career of Guatemalan strongman **Manuel Estrada Cabrera**. The novel, a satire employing surrealism and magical realism, was acclaimed as the best parody of the archetypical Latin American dictator. Its author was lauded as the region's leading "new novelist." During the presidencies of **Juan José Arevalo** and **Jacobo Arbenz** (1945-54), Asturias served in diplomatic capacities. He published the fantastical *Hombres de maiz* (*Men of Maize,* 1949) during that period. Considered his best work, the novel anticipated many themes of the late-twentieth century Latin American novel and influenced the work of **Jorge Luis Borges**, Alejo Carpentier, and Arturo Uslar Pietri. Among his later works was a trilogy depicting the plight of workers on Central American banana plantations, *Viento fuerte* (*Strong Wind,* 1950); *El papa verde* (*The Green Pope,* 1954); and *Los ojos de los enterrados* (*The Eyes of the Buried,* 1960). In 1956 he published short stories treating the overthrow of President Jacobo Arbenz, *Weekend in Guatemala,* and, in 1963, the anti-imperialist novel *Mulata.* In 1966 Asturias was named ambassador to France by President César Méndez Montenegro. That same year he was awarded the Lenin Peace Prize; in 1967 he received the Nobel Prize for literature. Asturias resided in France until his death.

Atahualpa (1498?-1533), Inca ruler (1525?-32) when the Spanish conquered Peru. Atahualpa came to power in a contested succession against his half brother Huascar after his father, **Huayna Capac,** died suddenly from a smallpox epidemic that swept the empire ahead of the Spanish. The civil war that ensued was winding down when the Spanish captured Atahualpa at Cajamarca on November 16, 1532. Atahualpa, fearing the Spanish would replace him and govern through Huascar, arranged for the latter's execution. Atahualpa and his retinue had gone out to meet the Spanish, never imagining they would be attacked and taken prisoner. In trying to win his freedom, Atahualpa filled a spacious room once with 13,420 pounds of 22 1/2-carat gold and twice with 26,000 pounds of silver that had streamed in from throughout the empire at his command. This "miracle" at Cajamarca made the 168 Spaniards present rich beyond compare and gave credence to the rags-to-riches dreams of Spaniards coming to the New World. Atahualpa's continued presence made some Spaniards like **Diego de Almagro** nervous, and they moved to kill him while opponents to this regicide like **Hernando de Soto** and **Hernando Pizarro** were away. Atahualpa was judged guilty of murdering his half brother Huascar and of planning a revolt against the Spanish. "Converted" to Christianity by the priest Vicente de Valverde, Atahualpa was garroted rather than burned. Myths of Atahualpa's return and the expulsion of the Spanish continued to haunt the Andes and proved to be a troublesome legacy.

Ávila, Pedro Arias de (Pedrarias Dávila; 1440?-1531), Spanish conqueror, governor of Panama (1514-26) and of Nicaragua (1527-31). Born in Segovia, Spain, to a prominent noble family, Pedrarias had had an distinguished military career against the Moors in Granada (1482-92) and in North Africa (1508-11) when at the age of seventy-four he was made governor of Panama. Rumors of a great sea to the south and complaints against **Vasco Núñez de Balboa** led the crown to appoint the more renowned Pedrarias. He was ordered to relieve Balboa and bring him to justice. News of Balboa's great discovery of the Pacific Ocean in 1513 came only after Pedrarias had sailed for Panama. Balboa's exoneration during the official inquiry and his popularity with his men fed Pedrarias's jealousy. The crown's growing appreciation of Balboa's achievements put Pedrarias further on guard. In spite of betrothing his daughter to Balboa, Pedrarias had him arrested on trumped up charges of treason, tried, and executed him in 1519. While Pedrarias was in the twilight of his career, the shadow he cast was a long and dark one. With his brutality and frantic search for gold and slaves, he ended the goodwill Balboa had established with various Indian groups. Pedrarias had eliminated a popular figure who had already probably located the source of much of the gold that would later pour out of Colombia. Also Balboa had made plans to build ships to go south in search of "Biru," as the Indians called it. Pedrarias inherited these projects. He failed to exploit the Colombian possibilities but did lend support to **Francisco Pizarro**'s expeditions to Peru. He also helped organize the conquest of Nicaragua and was made governor in 1527. He died there in León at the age of ninety with a career that a contemporary chronicler summed up as "the wrath of God."

Aylwin Azócar, Patricio (1918–), Chilean president and a founder of the Chilean Christian Democratic party. In the 1950s Aylwin presided over the Catholic progressive National Falange party, which merged with the Social Christian Conservative party to form the Christian Democratic party in 1957. The combined parties went on to constitute Chile's major political party. Aylwin initially supported the military coup that unseated socialist **Salvador Allende** (September 11, 1973). But soon he became a leader of the democratic opposition to dictator **Augusto Pinochet**. Following the death of **Eduardo Frei Montalva** (1982), Aylwin headed the Christian Democrats. During the presidential contest of 1989, he forged a broad coalition led by his and the Socialist parties; as its candidate, Aylwin decisively defeated the candidate put forward by Augusto Pinochet. Inaugurated March 1990, Patricio Aylwin benefited from the effects of his predecessor's economic policy. When he left office in early 1994, Chile's inflation and unemployment rates were Latin America's lowest, and poverty rates were in decline. That prosperity had allowed him to devote tax revenues to new social programs. Throughout his administration Aylwin struggled to assert himself against Augusto Pinochet, who continued to exert great influence over public life. Especially thorny was the problem of prosecuting human rights abuses committed during the former dictator's sixteen-year tenure. Aylwin's most notable victory in that regard was the sentencing to jail of the officers behind the assassination of former foreign minister Orlando Letelier in 1976. Patricio Aylwin's transmission of the presidency to his successor, Eduardo Frei Ruiz-Tagle, in early 1994, completed Chile's transition to democracy.

Azuela, Mariano (1873-1952), Mexican novelist. Born in Jalisco and trained as a physician, Mariano Azuela became an early supporter of

Francisco I. Madero in the latter's attempt to overthrow the dictator **Porfirio Díaz**. By 1910 he had published *María Luisa* (1907) and two other novels. Azuela was a political leader in Jalisco during Madero's presidency (1911-13); in 1914 he joined Villista forces in their unsuccessful contest with the Carrancistas. Forced to flee north, he wrote *Los de abajo* (*The Underdogs*), which first appeared in serial form in a Spanish-language newspaper in El Paso, Texas, in 1915. Rediscovered in the mid-1920s and regarded as the greatest novel of the Mexican Revolution, it portrays a band of peasant revolutionaries who do not know why they fight and reflects Azuela's disillusionment with the revolution. Moving to Mexico City in 1916, he went on to chronicle what he perceived to be failures and betrayals of the revolution in works such as *Las moscas* (*The Flies*, 1918) and *Domitilo quiere ser diputado* (1918). While Azuela's later works did not achieve the fame or power of *The Underdogs*, he remained a respected member of Mexico's literary establishment throughout his career.

Balaguer, Joaquín (1907–), Dominican president. Joaquín Balaguer was born to a well-to-do family in Villa Bosono. Educated at private schools, he went on to take law degrees in both Santo Domingo and Paris. He became involved in politics in 1930, when he joined the Patriotic Citizens Coalition, which helped overthrow President Horacio Vásquez. Balaguer caught the eye of president-then-dictator **Rafael L. Trujillo**, who succeeded Vásquez in the presidency. Over the next thirty-one years Balaguer served as Trujillo's ambassador, education minister, vice president, and president. He published several scholarly works during the Trujillo years, among them *La política internacional de Trujillo* (1941) and *Historia de la literatura dominicana* (1956). After Trujillo's fall he published *Entre la sangre del 30 de mayo y la del 24 de abril* (1983), an account of Dominican events from Trujillo's assassination in 1961 to the revolution of 1965; and *Memorias de un cortesano de la "era de Trujillo"* (1988). Balaguer was president when Trujillo was killed in May 1961. Between that time and the election of Juan Bosch in December

1962, he played a key role in helping thwart the dictatorial ambitions of Trujillo's son and brothers. He was also instrumental in the lifting of OAS sanctions imposed following the Trujillo-inspired attempt on the life of Venezuelan president **Rómulo Betancourt**. Balaguer lived in the United States from late 1962 to 1966, a time of political unrest, civil war, and foreign intervention in his country. During that time he founded the Reformist party (Partido Reformista, PR), drawing its leadership from Trujillo's old Partido Dominicano. He returned home to decisively defeat Juan Bosch in the presidential election of June 1, 1966. He won reelection in 1970 and 1974. Over his first three terms Balaguer made use of massive U.S. aid and the revenues from high sugar prices to crush a left-wing guerrilla insurgency and to coopt opposition groups through the dispensation of patronage. After 1978 he resumed leadership of his Reformist party, using it to help him win another trio of presidential contests: 1986, 1990, 1994. But during his final stints as chief executive, Balaguer's failing health matched his country's economic decline. Domestic and foreign pressure forced him to cut short his sixth term in August 1996.

Balboa, Vasco Núñez de (1475?-1519), conqueror and first European discoverer of the Pacific Ocean. A native of Jerez de los Caballeros, Extremadura, Spain, Balboa came to the Indies in 1501. Fleeing creditors on Hispaniola, he threw his lot in with a Spanish group on the mainland near the Gulf of Urabá (Colombia). The settlement was in disarray from hostile Indian attacks. Although just a common soldier, Balboa argued for a resettlement farther west. With his advice followed, the settlers' situation improved. Support for Balboa as their leader also grew, and eventually the nominal authorities, Diego de Nicuesa and Martín Enciso, were expelled. Balboa's rise was a clear example of the career of a caudillo, a leader whose legal basis is tenuous but whose power rests on charisma and the support of the masses. Balboa knew he had to produce if he was going to stay on top. His accomplishments were three. First, he made the colony self-sufficient by forging alliances with nearby Indian groups against their enemies in

exchange for food and labor. Second, he traveled up-river south into the interior of Colombia and identified the probable sources of gold production, which he hoped to return to at a later date. Third, he traced down the reported great body of water and became the European discoverer of the Pacific Ocean in 1513. He also gathered a fortune in gold, pearls, and slaves. He did all of this without losing a single man, a rare accomplishment. Complaints against Balboa from those expelled came before royal officials in Spain. They dispatched the well-connected, high-born **Pedrarias (Pedro Árias de Avila)** to bring Balboa under control. After he arrived in Panama in 1514, Pedrarias's jealousy of the upstart grew even though he betrothed his daughter to Balboa. In 1519 he arrested his prospective son-in-law, tried him on spurious charges, and when he was found guilty, had Balboa decapitated.

Balmaceda Fernández, José Manuel (1840-1891), president of Chile (1886-91). Balmaceda was born in Santiago to a prominent family. He entered public life at an early age, serving as secretary to **Manuel Montt** at the Lima conference of 1864. In 1878 he was named minister to Buenos Aires and helped keep Argentina neutral during the War of the Pacific. Appointed minister of foreign relations in the administration of Domingo Santa María (1881-86), he successfully steered Chile to diplomatic victory in negotiations to end the war. In 1886 he was elected president with the support of the Liberal, National, and Conservative parties.

As president, Balmaceda launched an ambitious public works program that included expansion of the railroad and telegraph systems, construction of bridges, and provision of potable water to cities. Educational facilities were also expanded. Needing funds for his program, Balmaceda favored increased output of nitrates, Chile's leading export, from which the government derived large revenues. Since the producers sometimes found it in their interest to curtail production, Balmaceda clashed with them, especially John Thomas North, an Englishman who with his partners controlled about 25 percent of Chile's output. The government also sought to end the monopoly rights of a railroad controlled by the North interests. Because of his conflict with North, Balmaceda is sometimes seen as a champion of Chilean nationalism who resisted foreign economic domination.

Balmaceda also clashed with the Chilean Congress, which had assumed greater powers over the past decades and accused the president of arbitrary conduct. The result was an eight-month civil war beginning in January 1891. After the defeat of his forces, Balmaceda, who had taken refuge in the Argentine embassy, shot himself to death on September 19, 1891, the day after his term ended.

Banzer Suárez, Hugo (1926–), Bolivian president. Hugo Banzer began his military career just as the Bolivian Revolution took place in 1952. Despite his refusal to join the victorious Nationalist Revolutionary Movement (MNR), and notwithstanding reductions in the size of the military following the revolution, Banzer managed to retain his commission. He supported the 1964 coup that ousted MNR founder **Víctor Paz Estenssoro**, serving briefly as minister of education under René Barrientos. Subsequently he directed the Colegio Militar. Banzer opposed populist military ruler Juan José Torres (1970-71), suffering exile following a failed coup attempt in early 1971. Seven months later Banzer did overthrow Torres thanks to help from the army's conservative faction, the MNR, and the right-wing Socialist Falange party (FSB). Between 1971 and 1974 Banzer headed a popular front government with the MNR and the FSB. When the coalition disintegrated in 1974, he found new political allies in the private sector and went on to form his own Nationalist Democratic Action party (ADN) in 1979. He placed third in the 1980 presidential election, but won the 1985 contest with a 28.6 percent plurality. Unable to win election in the Congress, Banzer instructed supporters to vote for runner-up Víctor Paz Estenssoro. Banzer played presidential kingmaker once again, in 1993, when he supported first-place finisher Gonzalo Sánchez of the MNR, enabling Sánchez to claim the presidency. Hugo Banzer represented a stabilizing, conservatizing force in Bolivian politics, but he

was subject to charges that he profited from Bolivia's illegal cocaine trade during the 1970s and 1980s and that he had ruled in a dictatorial fashion. He was elected to another presidential term in 1997.

Barbosa de Oliveira, Rui (1849-1923), Brazilian statesman and jurist. A native of Salvador, Bahia, Barbosa was educated as a lawyer. In 1879 he became a parliamentary deputy, becoming known as an opponent of slavery. Originally a Liberal, he later supported the republican cause and became minister of finance in the provisional government established after the fall of the monarchy. In this capacity he was credited by some with stimulating industrial development but was blamed for encouraging the wave of inflation and speculation known as the Encilhamento. He also played a principal role in drafting the constitution of 1891.

An Anglophile and a proponent of English liberalism, Barbosa strongly criticized the government of **Floriano Peixoto** for militarism and violations of civil liberties. After a stay in Argentina and England, where he defended the naval insurgents of 1893-94, he returned to Brazil in 1895 and represented Bahia in the Senate for many years. In 1907 he distinguished himself at the Second International Peace Conference in The Hague as a champion of the juridical equality of all states. In 1910, supported by the state governments of Bahia and São Paulo, he unsuccessfully sought the presidency in opposition to Marshal Hermes da Fonseca, who was backed by Minas Gerais and Rio Grande do Sul. Waging a vigorous campaign, he excoriated military influence in government and advocated establishment of the secret ballot and the expansion of federal power over the states. He made another unsuccessful bid for the presidency in 1919.

Barbosa was a founder of the Brazilian Academy of Letters in 1908 and its president until 1919. He was also noted for his erudition and command of languages, his vast private library, his oratorical skills, and his many writings, which fill more than 150 volumes.

Barrios, Justo Rufino (1835-1885), Guatemalan

president (1873-85). Barrios was born to an affluent family in western Guatemala. He was educated in Guatemala City, becoming a notary public. He also managed his family's properties, including a plantation along the Mexican border. In 1871 he joined the Liberal leader Miguel García Granados in a successful revolution against Vicente Cerna, who had succeeded long-time Conservative president **Rafael Carrera** upon the latter's death in 1865. García Granados went on to become president while Barrios served as commander of the military district of Los Altos.

Barrios succeeded to the presidency in 1873 and was reelected in 1880. He is remembered as the architect of the modernizing Liberal regime that dominated Guatemala until 1944. His administration emphasized the expansion of coffee cultivation and the improvement of the nation's infrastructure, authorizing construction of railroads to link Guatemala's ports with the interior. Considering the Catholic church an obstacle to modernization, he launched an anticlerical campaign that suppressed religious orders, nationalized church properties, and made marriage a civil contract. He also promoted educational reform. However, Barrios's policies brought little benefit to Guatemala's indigenous majority. Indian peasants faced increasing pressure on their land and especially their labor as Barrios strengthened the institution of debt peonage and revived forced wage labor (*mandamientos*).

In 1882 Barrios settled a boundary dispute with Mexico, surrendering Guatemalan claims to Soconusco, but he repudiated the Wyke-Aycinena Treaty of 1859, which acknowledged British sovereignty over Belize. He attempted to revive Central American union, but found support only in Honduras. To pursue his ambition, he invaded El Salvador but was mortally wounded in battle at Chalchuapa (April 2, 1885).

Barrios de Chamorro, Violeta (1929–), Nicaraguan president. Born to wealthy landowning parents, and educated at private schools in Managua, Violeta Barrios married newspaper editor Pedro Joaquín Chamorro in 1950. From the 1950s through the 1970s, she supported her politically prominent husband in his effort to overturn the **Somoza** dictatorship. But she did not otherwise involve herself in politics. That changed after Pedro Joaquín Chamorro's assassination in January 1978, an act that produced massive protests and hastened the fall of **Anastasio Somoza Debayle**. Violeta de Chamorro actively supported the insurrection against Somoza, going on to join a five-person junta that governed after July 1979. She resigned from that body in mid-1980, in protest of policies of the socialist Sandinista National Liberation Front (FSLN), which effectively controlled the government. Throughout the 1980s she criticized the FSLN through the newspaper *La Prensa*, which she directed after her husband's death. In early 1990 she was the surprise victor over FSLN leader **Daniel Ortega** in a presidential contest that saw her representing a fourteen-party coalition. Violeta Chamorro inherited an economy devastated by a civil war that had cost 60,000 lives during the 1980s alone and had driven additional tens of thousands from the country. At first her efforts to revive the economy were hobbled by the United States, which withheld aid, claiming that the Marxist FSLN was influential in her government. This forced her to adopt stringent measures to reverse Nicaragua's economic decline. She was able to do so by 1993, and when she left office in 1997 the country enjoyed 4 percent economic growth. Chamorro was also able to reduce inflation to single digits and to refinance the nation's staggering foreign debt. Still her program drove unemployment to above 70 percent, and left approximately that percentage of Nicaraguans in poverty.

Batista y Zaldívar, Fulgencio (1901-1973), Cuban president and dictator. Fulgencio Batista was born in Oriente province to poor parents. He joined the army at age twenty, reaching the rank of sergeant thanks to his skill in typing and shorthand. Batista gained prominence when he led a "sergeants' revolt" against the army command on September 4, 1933, and a day later helped organize the junta that took power following the resignation of President Carlos de Céspedes. When the regime of provisional president **Ramón Grau San Martín** failed to win U.S. recognition,

Batista, by now a colonel and army chief of staff, ousted Grau in January 1934. Between 1934 and 1940 he ruled the nation behind a succession of figurehead presidents. In 1940 Batista ran for and won the presidency in a contest pitting him against Grau San Martín. His four-year term coincided with unparalleled wartime prosperity. While graft and corruption were features of his regime, he gave the nation a relatively benign and productive administration characterized by infrastructural improvement and ready sale of the nation's sugar crop. After his term, Batista moved to Florida, where he lived for four years. He returned to Cuba after his election to the Senate in 1948 and began advancing his candidacy for the 1952 presidential contest, but seized power in a military coup. He easily toppled unpopular President Carlos Prío Socarrás in March 1952, going on to rule under martial law through 1958. The Batista regime grew more repressive as time passed, becoming infamous both at home and abroad. Through the first half of the decade Batista was successful in controlling the opposition underground, as when his forces crushed a July 26, 1953, attack on an army barracks, led by the young lawyer **Fidel Castro**. For a time he placated the United States, having himself elected president in late 1954 voting that opposition parties boycotted. Batista's rule weakened rapidly after 1956 when left-wing followers of Fidel Castro launched a guerrilla war against the regime. In March 1957, Batista narrowly escaped death in a bombing carried out by followers of Prío Socarrás. When Batista's forces failed to defeat the guerrillas in a mid-1957 military operation, and the United States withdrew support from him in 1958, his fate was sealed. On December 31, 1958, Fulgencio Batista and leading members of his government fled Cuba despite the presence of some 3,000 guerrillas led by Fidel Castro. Batista lived out his final years in Spain.

Batlle y Ordóñez, José (1856-1929), political journalist and twice president of Uruguay. José Batlle y Ordóñez, often called the father of modern Uruguay, was the son of a former president, Lorenzo Batlle (1868-72), and a life-long militant in his nation's liberal Colorado party. While in his twenties Batlle y Ordóñez studied in Europe, first at the Sorbonne and then at the Collège de France. At first he embraced the collectivist, spiritual philosophy known as Krausism (for K.C.F. Kraus), but was soon won over to the social democratic philosophy that made headway in Europe during the 1880s. Returning to Uruguay in 1886, Batlle threw himself into politics. That year he founded *El Día*, an organ of the Colorado party, and participated in an uprising against the caudillos Lorenzo Latorre and Máximo Santos. In 1893 he was elected to the Chamber of Deputies, and in 1896 to the Senate, in both instances as leader of the Colorado popular and anti-oligarchic faction. In 1903 he won a four-year presidential term thanks to the backing of a Colorado–Blanco party coalition in the General Assembly. Immediately he was forced to contend with a revolt of Blanco dissidents that lasted eighteen months. Triumphing in that contest, Batlle launched a reform initiative featuring the most advanced labor and social legislation ever seen in Latin America. When the program stood complete, at the end of Batlle's second presidential term (1911-15), and through Uruguay's 1919 constitution, it legalized labor's right to strike, shortened the workweek, established pension funds and accident insurance for workers, expanded women's rights, legalized divorce, abolished the death penalty, separated church and state, expanded public education, established state stores where consumers could purchase goods at subsidized prices, and worked to give the nation a more progressive tax system. Batlle was an economic nationalist who both encouraged industrialization through economic protection and achieved the nationalization of meat-packing, banking, transportation, communications, and utilities. While Batlle worked to modernize Uruguay's all-important ranching sector and promoted land reform, he did not challenge commercial ranching or its system of dependent labor.

One of Batlle's most unusual reforms, drawn from his study of the Swiss political system during a second period of study and travel in Europe (1907-11), resulted in Uruguay's experimenting with a plural executive, or *colegiado*, which was featured in Uruguay's 1919 constitution (and a second time, in the 1952 constitution). Even though that Batlle's reforms did not enfranchise women or depart from the nation's tradition of indirect democracy, they met resistance from many quarters. Subsequent Colorado leaders slowed reform, and the depression of the 1930s forced suspension of many government programs. José Batlle y Ordóñez nevertheless left a powerful imprint upon Uruguayan politics and society. The social democratic impulse that he championed, known as Batllismo, influenced national politics over most of the twentieth century.

Belalcázar, Sebastián de (Benalcázar; 1490?-1551), conqueror of southern Colombia. Born in Belalcázar, Córdoba, Spain, as Sebastián Moyano, he took the name of his hometown like many others fleeing their humble past. Belalcázar began his social climb in Panama where he joined **Vasco Núñez de Balboa** in 1513. *Encomendero* there in 1519 and first *acalde* in León, Nicaragua, in 1523, Belalcázar had accumulated enough wealth to participate as a captain in **Francisco Pizarro**'s third expedition to Peru in 1531. He was at Cajamarca when the Inca emperor **Atahualpa** was captured (1532) and participated in the division of his great treasure. Sponsoring expeditions and moving north away from the control of the Pizarros, he aided in the founding of Quito (1534), Guayaquil (1535), and Cali and Popayán (1536). In 1538 he reached the Sabana de Bogotá and the Chibcha civilization in eastern Colombia, but the expeditions of **Gonzalo Jiménez de Quesada** and **Nicolás Féderman** had already arrived. The three traveled together to Spain in 1539 to settle their rival claims. Belalcázar came away with the governorship of Popayán for life, his three mestizo children legitimated, and his son married to the daughter of a Spanish noble. Forced by the viceroy **Blasco Núñez de Vela** to participate in the civil wars in Peru against the Pizarros, he ended up on the losing side at the battle of Añaquito in 1546 but was allowed to return to his governorship in southern Colombia. There he successfully defended his rule against all challenges from 1536 until 1550, when he was sentenced to death for the execution (1546) of Jorge Robledo, whom he

caught trespassing on his territory. He was on his way to Spain to appeal this sentence when death overtook him in Cartagena.

Belgrano, Manuel (1770-1820), leader in Argentina's independence movement. A native of Buenos Aires, Belgrano studied there and in Spain. In 1794 he was named secretary of the *consulado*, or merchants' guild, of Buenos Aires. After the French invasion of Spain and the imprisonment of **Ferdinand VII**, Belgrano initially supported a plan to seek independence by means of a constitutional monarchy under Carlota Joaquina, Ferdinand's sister, who had recently arrived in Brazil with her husband, the future **João VI**. With the failure of this plan, Belgrano became active in the movement that led to the deposition of the viceroy in May 1810, and he became a member of the junta established on May 25, 1810. Despite his lack of military experience, he was given command of a small expedition sent to Paraguay to force its submission to Buenos Aires but was defeated in two engagements in 1811 as the Paraguayans moved to assert their independence from both Spain and Buenos Aires. He won victories over Spain at Tucumán (September 24, 1812) and at Salta (February 20, 1813) but was defeated later in 1813 at Vilcapujio and Ayohuma, both in Upper Peru (modern Bolivia), by the Spanish general Joaquín de la Pezuela. At the congress of Tucumán in 1816, he advocated a formal declaration of independence from Spain as well as the creation of a constitutional monarchy, preferably under an Inca prince.

Bello, Andrés (1781-1865), Venezuelan man of letters, educator, and legal scholar. Bello was born in Caracas to parents descended from Canary Island immigrants. After receiving a bachelor's degree in 1800 from the University of Caracas, he became an assistant to the captain-general of Venezuela. He was still employed by the government in 1810 when the captain-general was deposed, but he continued to profess loyalty to the imprisoned **Ferdinand VII**.

On June 9, 1810, with **Simón Bolívar** and a third man, he left Venezuela for London, where they hoped to obtain British assistance for the new

Caracas junta. Bello remained in England until 1829. During this period he assisted diplomats from Chile and Gran Colombia and co-edited three short-lived journals: *El Censor Americano* (1820), *Biblioteca Americana* (1823), and *Repertorio Americano* (1826-27). While in London he also wrote his two best-known poems, which are based on classical models. In "Alocución a la Poesía" (1823), he invites "divine Poetry" to abandon Europe for America and goes on to describe the natural beauty and fecundity of Latin America and to extol the heroes of the independence movement. "Agricultura" (1826) praises rural life and depicts the impact of the recent revolutions on the fertile lands of the tropics.

In 1829 Bello moved to Chile, where he spent the remainder of his life and made many contributions to the intellectual life of the new nation. A moderate who avoided the extremes of liberalism and conservatism, he became an influential advisor to Chilean governments and was elected senator in 1837. He was the editor of the official government newspaper, *El Araucano*; published treatises on international law (1832) and Spanish grammar (1847); and drafted a civil code for Chile (1855). In 1843 he became the first rector of the University of Chile, a position he held until his death.

Betancourt, Rómulo (1908-1981), Venezuelan president. Rómulo Betancourt was born near Caracas and educated in the Venezuelan capital. He was an organizer of the 1928 student festival that turned into a protest against dictator **Juan Vicente Gómez** and led to Betancourt's exile. Betancourt studied and worked in a number of Latin American countries during the intervening seven years. From 1931 to 1936 he was active in Costa Rica's Communist party. He returned home following Gómez's death in 1935, and launched Organización Venezolana and the Partido Democráta Nacional, which headed opposition to the government of President Eleazar López Contreras. When López suppressed leftist groups, Betancourt went into hiding and fled the country in 1939, traveling first to Argentina and then to Chile. He returned in 1941 to found Acción Democrática.

Dissatisfaction with President Isaías Medina Angarita (1941-45) brought Betancourt and his colleagues into an alliance with a faction of disgruntled army officers headed by **Marcos Pérez Jiménez** during 1945. A civil-military coup overthrew Medina in October 1945. Betancourt headed a seven-man junta that governed for the following three years—a time known in Venezuela as the *trienio*. Far-reaching reforms were enacted: peasant unions were organized; land reform, begun under Medina, was expedited; universal suffrage was decreed; and a constituent assembly was elected. The body wrote a new constitution guaranteeing civil rights, protecting labor's right to strike, and recognizing the social function of property. On February 15, 1948, Betancourt transmitted power to AD candidate **Rómulo Gallegos**, overwhelming victor in the presidential contest of December 14, 1947. Gallegos continued Betancourt's reforms, quickly pushing through a tax on petroleum companies that more than doubled government revenue. But within ten months Gallegos, Betancourt, and all other AD leaders were driven into a ten-year exile by the coup of Marcos Pérez Jiménez. Betancourt lived in Cuba, Puerto Rico, and Costa Rica during that time, all the while attacking Pérez. When the dictatorship ended in January 1958, he returned to Venezuela and a year later was elected to a five-year presidential term. During his presidency Betancourt was confronted by economic recession, a communist guerrilla insurgency, and an assassination attempt (June 1960) that injured him seriously. In spite of those difficulties he was able to continue democratic reforms initiated during the *trienio*, most notably through the social democratic 1961 constitution. Betancourt courted foreign corporations in an effort to industrialize Venezuela. He also invested heavily in health and education programs, and resumed agrarian reform. When his term ended Betancourt traveled abroad, returning in 1973 to support **Carlos Andrés Pérez** in his successful presidential bid. Betancourt, regarded as the father of Venezuelan democracy, remained politically active until his death.

Betancur Cuartas, Belisario (1923–), Colombian president. Belisario Betancur, the second of twenty-two children, was born to a modest farm family in rural Antioquia. He attended school in Medellín, ultimately taking a degree in law from the Universidad Bolivariana (1947), and traveling to Europe and the United States for additional study. Betancur became politically active while in his twenties. A Conservative *laureanista* (follower of **Laureano Gómez**), he served in the assembly of Antioquia (1945-47), and worked for Conservative newspapers in Medellín and Bogotá. During the **Rojas Pinilla** dictatorship he was jailed briefly for his political activities on behalf of the exiled Gómez. Betancur served as labor minister under President Guillermo León Valencia (1962-66), and later managed the Bogotá publishing house Tercer Mundo. He ran unsuccessfully for president in 1970 and 1978, serving as ambassador to Spain from 1979 to 1981. Betancur won the 1982 presidential election on a platform promising housing and education for the poor. His term began auspiciously with the creation of a peace commission to supervise the surrender of guerrillas who accepted his amnesty offer. But the peace talks broke down within two years, and in November 1985, M-19 guerrillas seized the Palace of Justice in downtown Bogotá. The bloody denouement, in which the army stormed the building, traumatized Colombians. Betancur was more fortunate in international affairs, playing a significant role in the Contadora peace process. He also helped return the nation to good economic health, in part through the signing of a favorable contract with Exxon for exploitation of the nation's El Cerrejón coal fields.

Bolívar, Simón (1783-1830), Venezuelan military leader and statesman known as the Liberator, who led the movement to free northern South America from Spanish rule. Born in Caracas into Venezuela's creole aristocracy, Bolívar was orphaned at the age of nine. Having moved to Spain in 1799, he married the daughter of a nobleman and returned to Venezuela, only to see his bride die less than a year later. During a second trip to Europe, he read widely in the works of the Enlightenment, observed the coronation of Napoleon I in 1804, and is said to have vowed in Rome to

free Spanish America from colonial rule.

After returning to Venezuela in 1807, he supported the ouster of Spanish officials in 1810 and the declaration of independence in 1811. By 1813 he had become the acknowledged leader of Venezuela's fight for independence and later extended his anti-Spanish campaign to New Granada (Colombia) and Ecuador. In 1821 he was chosen president of Gran Colombia, composed of Venezuela, New Granada, and Ecuador. In 1824 he was given dictatorial powers in Peru. Once the last Spanish forces in South America had been defeated, however, he experienced political setbacks. In 1826 **José Antonio Páez** launched a secessionist movement in Venezuela, and in New Granada Bolívar was attacked for dictatorial tendencies. Ailing and depressed, he surrendered all his offices and was en route to voluntary exile in Europe when he died in Santa Marta, New Granada.

Never a democrat, Bolívar became more conservative over time, as can be seen in the constitution (1826) he wrote for the republic of Bolivia, which provided for a lifetime president. He was also an internationalist who favored the union of Gran Colombia, Peru, and Bolivia in a single nation. Despite his failures, Bolívar is considered one of the major figures of Latin American history and the supreme national hero of Venezuela.

Borges, Jorge Luis (1899-1986), Argentine writer. During his lifetime Jorge Luis Borges was at once his nation's most widely known man of letters and the Argentine literary establishment's most visible critic of the country's authoritarian tradition. Born in Buenos Aires of wealthy parents, he was educated in Europe. Returning to Argentina in 1921, Borges helped popularize avant-garde literary styles, notably ultraism, a form of prose poetry that rejected formal literary canons in favor of rhythmic patterns and images. His favored literary form was the short story, through which he explored the absurdity of the human condition and the impossibility of understanding reality. For Borges the individual's search for meaning was akin to being lost in a circular labyrinth having no center. Borges published widely in literary journals such as *Proa*, which he helped found in Buenos Aires in 1924. The publication of *Ficciones* (1944) and *El Aleph* (1949) won him a wide readership and invitations to teach and lecture throughout Europe and the Americas. An outspoken critic of the dictator **Juan D. Perón**, whom he satirized in several of his stories, and of Argentine popular culture, Borges was forced to spend major portions of his career abroad. In 1961 he shared the Formentor Prize with French playwright Samuel Beckett. The denseness, ambiguity, and philosophical bent of his prose have attracted and influenced generations of writers, particularly in North America and France.

Botero, Fernando (1932–), Colombian painter and sculptor. Fernando Botero was born in Medellín, where he received his primary and secondary education. Early indication of his passion for art came when he scandalized teachers at his Jesuit high school with frank articles on Picasso and Dalí. After working as illustrator for the Medellín newspaper *El Colombiano*, he traveled to Europe and studied at the Academy of San Fernando in Madrid and at the Academy San Marco in Florence. He subsequently worked and exhibited in France, Italy, Mexico, Colombia and the United States. Botero's unique "inflated" figures began to win critical acclaim during the 1950s. His *La Camera degli sposi* won the grand prize at Colombia's Ninth Salon of Art in 1958, critic Marta Traba describing it as "disconcerting upon first contact . . .[it is] as anti-Baroque as anti-classical, as anti-expressionist as anti-abstract." Between 1958 and 1960 Botero taught at the Academy of Fine Arts in Mexico City, and in 1960-61 at Colombia's National University. He won a Guggenheim award in 1960 and moved to New York City where he lived until 1973. Ordinary scenes from Colombian village life, often in a humorous vein—such as grossly endomorphic prostitutes dancing with their equally obese clients—are favored subjects in Botero's paintings. Yet social satire and irony also figure in his work, as in the painting *Obispos muertos* (*Dead Bishops*, 1957). By the 1980s Botero had achieved international acclaim. From the 1960s he

produced sculpture in bronze, marble, and synthetic materials, usually massive figurative works treated in his unique pneumatic style. Some dozen of them were exhibited in New York and in Paris along the Champs Élysées during 1994.

Boyer, Jean-Pierre (1776-1850), president of Haiti (1819-43). A native of Port-au-Prince and a mulatto, Boyer was an officer under **Toussaint L'Ouverture** during the turmoil that gripped the French colony of Saint Domingue in the 1790s. However, in 1799 he allied himself with the mulatto general André Rigaud in his conflict with Toussaint and, after Rigaud's defeat, left for France. He returned to Saint Domingue early in 1802 with the French forces sent by Napoleon to subdue the colony, but eventually joined **Alexandre Sabès Pétion** and other mulattoes in the successful campaign to expel the French. During the era of Haiti's division, he was the secretary of Pétion, who ruled the south, and commander of the Presidential Guard. After Pétion's death in 1818, he was declared president for life. When **Henri Christophe**, who ruled the north, killed himself in 1820, Boyer moved successfully to reunite the country under his leadership. In 1822 he invaded Santo Domingo, which had recently declared its independence from Spain, and annexed it to Haiti. In 1825 he secured French recognition of Haitian independence but at a heavy price, for he agreed to give preferential treatment to French goods and to pay an onerous indemnity of 150 million francs (reduced to 60 million in 1838). Meanwhile, commercial agriculture stagnated despite the introduction (1826) of a rural code intended to restore forced labor. During Boyer's administration the distinctions between Haiti's mulatto elite and black masses grew sharper as the former monopolized government and trade, while the latter could look only to the army for upward mobility. A revolt forced Boyer to flee Haiti on February 13, 1843. He spent the remainder of his life in Jamaica and Paris.

Bucareli y Ursúa, Antonio María (1717-1779), governor and captain-general of Cuba (1766-71) and viceroy of New Spain (1771-79). Born into a noble family in Seville, Spain, Bucareli joined the military and served with distinction in a variety of administrative positions. He took command in Cuba after the English occupation (1762-63) and eased the colony back into a Spanish harness, rebuilding the military fortifications as well as directing a general economic recovery. Sent to Mexico as viceroy to oversee the reforms suggested by the *visitador* **José de Gálvez**, Bucareli undertook a thorough reorganization of the colony's defenses, rebuilding coastal fortifications, creating militia units, strengthening the northern *presidios* (forts), and dispatching an expedition to Alaska. He was an efficient and honest bureaucrat, considered by some to be New Spain's best viceroy in the eighteenth century. He advised against the introduction of Gálvez's system of powerful regional bureaucrats or intendants. With revenues increasing and no major problems on the horizon during Bucareli's administration, the intendancy system was not put into place until 1786.

Bulnes Prieto, Manuel (1799-1866), president of Chile (1841-51). A native of Concepción, Bulnes took part in the wars of independence as a youth. Later he led campaigns against the Araucanian Indians and against the Pincheiras, brothers who led a notorious bandit gang. In 1838 President Joaquín Prieto, Bulnes's uncle, put him in command of Chilean forces in the war against the Peru–Bolivia Confederation. His decisive victory over the confederation army at Yungay (January 20, 1839) made him a national hero and led to his election to the presidency.

As president, Bulnes governed in accordance with the Conservative principles dominant at the time. His two five-year terms were productive and relatively tranquil. Numerous educational institutions were established, including the University of Chile and a normal school for the training of teachers, the first in Latin America. In 1843 Bulnes dispatched an expedition to assert Chilean sovereignty over the Strait of Magellan. Chile's first railroad, linking Copiapó and Caldera, was begun, and a contract signed for construction of a line between Santiago and Valparaíso.

Bulnes's last years as president were marred by intensified political agitation. The Liberal opposition demanded greater political freedom and an end to government interference in elections. The Liberals were also strongly opposed to **Manuel Montt**, the Conservative candidate selected to succeed Bulnes. When a Liberal revolt occurred just before Montt took office, Bulnes took command of the government forces and defeated the rebels at the Loncomilla River (December 8, 1851).

Cabeza de Vaca, Álvar Núñez (1490?-1564), explorer and writer. Born in Jerez de la Frontera, Andalusia, Spain, Cabeza de Vaca was treasurer on the ill-fated **Pánfilo de Narváez** expedition to Florida in 1528. Shipwrecked, he was one of only four who survived; they spent eight years walking west, where they finally met a party of Spaniards in northern Mexico. They did not die thanks to the good will of various Indian tribes and to their own success as shamans. Later Cabeza de Vaca was made governor of Río de la Plata (1540-45), but this too ended badly. He was shipped home to Spain in chains after a rebellion ended his command. He is best remembered for his written account of his incredible adventure. A pirated edition entitled *Naufragios* (*Castaways*) appeared in 1542; an approved edition appeared in 1555 along with his *Comentarios*, about his South American experiences. In *Naufragios* he described how the Europeans lose their innocence and are reduced to savagery and cannibalism. It is the Indians and their civilization and culture that teach them how to survive in a moral way.

Cabot, Sebastian (1474?-1557), navigator. Born in Bristol, England, or Venice, Italy, Sebastian was the son of John Cabot, who explored the coast of North America for Henry VII, the king of England. Sebastian was made chief cartographer to the Council of the Indies and was put in charge of an expedition in 1525 to go to the Far East via South America. Upon arriving at the Río de la Plata, he explored upriver on the Paraná and Paraguay rivers in search of supposed riches instead of continuing on to the Pacific. When he arrived in Spain empty-handed in 1530, he was exiled to Africa for two years. Later he was restored to his position as chief cartographer, but he died in England.

Cabral, Pedro Álvares (1467/8-1520?), Portuguese explorer. Born in Belmonte, Portugal, Cabral was the commander of the fleet of thirteen ships and 1,200 to 1,500 men chosen to follow up Vasco da Gama's successful voyage to India (1498). Swinging westerly way out into the Atlantic to avoid the doldrums and catch the wind and currents that would bring them around the southern tip of Africa, they arrived on the Brazilian coast (presently the state of Bahia) on April 22, 1500. Cabral took possession in the name of the king of Portugal, dispatched one of the ships home with the news, and continued on to India, returning to Lisbon in late July of 1501.

Caldas, Francisco José de (1768-1816), Colombian scientist. Caldas studied mathematics and physics in his native Popayán but was forced by his father to complete legal studies in Bogotá. Pursuing his scientific inquiries in an unsympathetic environment, he independently discovered in 1801 that the boiling point of water varies with atmospheric pressure and used this insight to construct a hypsometric thermometer for measuring altitude. In 1801-2 he became acquainted with the European scientists **Alexander von Humboldt** and Aimé Bonpland, who provided valuable information on recent developments in astronomy and botany. In 1802 he joined New Granada's Botanical Expedition, devoting himself to plant geography and the study of cinchona species. In 1806 he became director of a new astronomical observatory in Bogotá. From 1808 to 1811 he published the *Semanario del Nuevo Reino de Granada*, a weekly (later monthly) periodical which he used as a vehicle for disseminating useful scientific data related to the viceroyalty.

Caldas's scientific work was disrupted by the start of the independence movement in 1810 and the subsequent internal conflicts among the rebellious provinces. Caldas edited the *Diario Político* (1811), a record of political events, but

was occupied mainly as a military engineer with the pro-independence forces. When the Spaniards temporarily regained control of New Granada in 1815-16, he was captured and, though he pleaded for clemency, was executed in Bogotá on October 29, 1816.

Caldera Rodríguez, Rafael (1916-), Venezuelan president. Rafael Caldera was educated in Caracas and attended the city's Central University, where he specialized in labor law. During his first year in college, 1934, he participated in the Congress of Catholic Youth in Rome, where the Christian Democratic movement was founded. In 1936 he established the conservative National Student Union (UNE), which opposed the secular and social democratic Venezuelan Student Federation. In 1938 he formed the Electoral Action party, and in 1942 merged it with another conservative group under the name National Action. Meanwhile he taught labor law as a university professor. Caldera served briefly as attorney general in the junta headed by **Rómulo Betancourt**, which overthrew President Isaías Medina Angarita in October 1945. But he resigned in protest of Betancourt's social democratic agenda and in 1946 formed the Comité de Organización Política Electoral Independiente (COPEI), also known as the Social Christian party. He ran unsuccessfully as COPEI's presidential candidate in 1947. In 1958 he led COPEI in helping create a government of national union, following the overthrow of dictator **Marcos Pérez Jiménez**. He ran unsuccessful presidential campaigns in 1958 and 1963, but won Venezuela's top office in 1968. Caldera's first presidency coincided with a wave of nationalist enthusiasm, fed by rising petroleum prices. Those factors enabled him to extract new concessions from foreign oil companies, to obtain legislation requiring reversion to the state of oil properties once their concessions expired in 1983, and to nationalize Venezuela's natural gas deposits. His opposition to OAS sanctions against Cuba created a favorable climate for negotiation with Castroite guerrillas, who agreed to end their insurgency.

Because he was elected president with a small plurality and ruled with the help of shifting coalitions in Congress, Caldera was able to espouse a policy of ideological pluralism. Thus he could both reestablish ties with Cuba and recognize the **Pinochet** regime in Chile. Caldera also took Venezuela into the Andean Pact. In 1993 he ran for a second term on a populist platform sufficiently radical to have him expelled from COPEI. He won the presidency on December 5 through the support of several left-wing parties, pledging not to subject Venezuelans to painful austerity measures mandated by the International Monetary Fund. When he began his term in January 1994, Caldera was faced with falling living standards and near collapse of the nation's banking system. He found himself forced, amid steadily eroding popularity, to endorse many of the harsh IMF measures supported by his predecessor, **Carlos Andrés Pérez**.

Calles, Plutarco Elías (1877-1945), Mexican revolutionary leader and president (1924-28). Born in Guaymas, Sonora, Calles was the illegitimate son of Plutarco Elías, a member of one of the state's leading families, but adopted the surname of his stepfather. He worked at various jobs--schoolteacher, bookkeeper, hotel manager, and police chief in Agua Prieta--before joining the fight against **Victoriano Huerta** in 1913 under the leadership of **Álvaro Obregón**. From 1915 to 1919, as governor of Sonora, Calles encouraged education and agrarian reform and launched anticlerical and antialcohol campaigns. With Obregón and fellow Sonoran Adolfo de la Huerta, he broke with President **Venustiano Carranza** in 1920 and later served as interior secretary (*gobernación*) under Obregón.

During his presidential term Calles continued programs of land distribution and educational expansion begun by his predecessor. He also advanced the interests of the Regional Confederation of Mexican Workers (CROM), a labor group whose head, Luis N. Morones, served as secretary of industry, commerce, and labor. Other highlights of Calles's administration were the establishment of the Bank of Mexico (1925) and the promotion of road-building and irrigation projects. Calles clashed with the Catholic hierarchy over the anticlerical provisions of the 1917 constitu-

tion, and his determination to enforce them precipitated the closing of the churches by priests and the Cristero uprising against the government (1926-29). Calles's seeming radicalism initially led to strained relations with the United States, but the arrival of Ambassador Dwight Morrow in 1927 brought substantial improvement.

The six-year period following the assassination of Obregón in 1928 is known as the Maximato because of the acknowledgement of Calles as "maximum chief" while three other men--Emilio Portes Gil, Pascual Ortiz Rubio, and Abelardo Rodríguez--served in the presidency for short periods. In 1929 Calles brought together existing political parties and revolutionary leaders in a new organization, the National Revolutionary party (PNR), renamed the Institutional Revolutionary party (PRI) in 1946. Calles endorsed the selection of **Lázaro Cárdenas** as the PNR presidential candidate for the term beginning in 1934, apparently in the belief that the latter would bow to his dictates. Once Cárdenas was inaugurated, however, his efforts to reignite revolutionary change produced conflict with Calles, who by now had adopted a more conservative outlook. Calles lost the ensuing contest and was forced to leave Mexico in 1936. He was allowed to return in 1941.

Câmara Pessoa, Hélder (1909-1999), Brazilian archbishop. Hélder Câmara was ordained in 1931, and worked five years as a parish priest in his hometown of Fortaleza, in Brazil's impoverished Northeast. His anticommunism moved him to become active in the right-wing Integralist movement during the 1930s, and during the 1940s, having been transferred to Rio de Janeiro, he became active in Catholic Action, which promoted social reform along non-Marxist lines. During the war years he spent increasing time working in Rio's *favelas*, or slums, sponsoring a variety of social programs through the Saint Sebastian Crusade, which he founded. In 1952 Câmara was named auxiliary bishop of Rio, and later that year he founded the National Conference of Brazilian Bishops (CNBB). His work with the poor, and his increasing outspokenness on their behalf, won him growing popularity, and even an invitation to serve, in 1960, as running mate of presidential candidate Jânio Quadros. In 1964 Câmara was appointed archbishop of Olinda and Recife. While he supported the coup that unseated leftist president **João Goulart** (1964), he became vocal against military violations of human rights following the "coup within the coup" of December 1968. Câmara's criticism of military excesses, coupled with his attacks on government economic programs that vastly increased the gap between rich and poor, earned him persecution at the hands of right-wing forces, who labeled him "Castro in a cassock." It also won him a Nobel Peace Prize nomination in 1970, and the support of Brazil's Roman Catholic hierarchy. The Brazilian church had in fact endorsed Câmara's stand on behalf of liberation theology even before the religious movement gained world-wide notice at the August 1968 meeting of the Conference of Latin American Bishops in Medellín, Colombia. Earlier in 1968, Câmara had issued a pastoral letter in which he blasted oppression of the poor by capitalism and imperialism. One of Brazilian Roman Catholicism's most progressive leaders, Hélder Câmara retired in 1985.

Cantinflas (Mariano Moreno; 1911-1993), Mexican comedic film star. Born in Mexico City, Mariano Moreno briefly attended Mexico's National University, but soon found his calling in entertainment. He developed a stage persona not unlike Charlie Chaplin's Little Tramp. Mexicans quickly fell in love with Cantinflas, whose apparently inept but canny and street-wise character inevitably triumphed over the more powerful and sophisticated after first reducing them to dithering ineffectuality. Cantinflas began as a carnival performer, moving on to become a mainstay of the Mexican film industry. His bit part in the 1936 *No te engañes corazón* won him more substantial roles in *Así es mi tierra* (1937) and *Águila o sol* (1937). *Ahí está el detalle* (1940), in which he had the starring role, won him a national following and ensured his film career. He ultimately starred in more than thirty films, usually portraying the innocuous character who, hilariously, always triumphs in the end. Cantinflas played leading roles in two Hollywood films, the Academy Award–winning *Around the World in Eighty Days* (1956) and the less-well-received *Pepe* (1960).

Caramurú (Diogo Álvares e Correia; ?–1557), Portuguese adventurer in Brazil. Born in Viana do Castelo, Portugal, he lived among the Tupinambá from about 1509 to 1511. He may have been a sailor shipwrecked near the site of the future Salvador, Bahia. The Tupinambá called him Caramurú, or Man of Fire, because of his expertise in the use of firearms. He acculturated quickly and integrated into Indian society easily, correctly assessing the strength and weaknesses of the various indigenous groups. He eventually served as a bridge and an all-purpose local advisor to the Portuguese who began to arrive in the area around Salvador, Bahia.

Cárdenas del Río, Lázaro (1895-1970), Mexican revolutionary leader and president (1934-40). Cárdenas was born in Jiquilpan, Michoacán, to a middle-class family. After working as a tax clerk, town jailer, and printer, he joined the campaign against **Victoriano Huerta** in 1913 and fought in the numerous struggles that followed, attaining the rank of division general in 1928. The same year he became governor of Michoacán, where he pursued a reformist course despite taking leaves of absence to serve as head of the National Revolutionary party (PNR) and as interior secretary (*gobernación*). He had long been an ally of **Plutarco Elías Calles**, who backed him as the PNR presidential candidate in 1934. Despite the certainty of his election, Cárdenas campaigned strenuously. Once installed as chief executive, he moved out of the presidential residence in Chapultepec Castle into more modest quarters and continued to travel extensively throughout the country. During his first eighteen months in the presidency, Cárdenas's encouragement of strikes by organized labor brought him into conflict with Calles and his followers. The latter also supported anti-Catholic activities, which Cárdenas concluded would be detrimental to the reformist policies he favored. Calles lost the ensuing battle and was forced into exile in April 1936.

Over the next two years Cárdenas reinvigorated the revolutionary agenda. He undertook a massive program of agrarian reform, affecting approximately 45 million acres, which was based on the landholding community known as the *ejido* rather than on private ownership. On March 18, 1938, he announced the expropriation of the country's foreign-owned petroleum industry after a long dispute between the companies and the oil workers' union. The president's action created tensions with the American and British governments; agreements regarding compensation were reached in the 1940s after sometimes acrimonious negotiations. Meanwhile, the oil properties had come under the control of a state-owned enterprise, Petróleos Mexicanos (PEMEX). In 1938 the president oversaw a restructuring of the PNR, which was renamed the Party of the Mexican Revolution (PRM) and organized on the basis of four functional sectors: labor, agrarian, military, and popular. The labor sector was comprised mainly of the Confederation of Mexican Workers (CTM), a new labor organization formed in 1936. The National Peasants' Confederation (CNC), made up of *ejido* farmers, was the main component of the agrarian sector.

The economic and social dislocations caused by these and other changes led Cárdenas to adopt a more centrist position in the last two years of his term. He feared polarization, which might threaten the achievements of his administration and lead to a civil war, as was occurring in Spain. (Cárdenas was a strong supporter of the Spanish Republican government.) As a result, he selected a moderate, Manuel Ávila Camacho, to succeed him in 1940. After he left the presidency, Cárdenas served as secretary of defense during World War II and often spoke out on public issues, usually embracing leftist causes. He remains a popular figure, remembered for his integrity and concern for ordinary Mexicans. His son, **Cuauhtémoc Cárdenas**, became the first popularly elected mayor of Mexico City in 1997.

Cárdenas Solórzano, Cuauhtémoc (1934–), Mexican politician. Born in Mexico City, Cuauhtémoc Cárdenas is the son of Mexico's most popular twentieth-century president, **Lázaro Cárdenas**. He was educated in Mexico City, and took a degree from the National School of Engineering in 1957. He conducted post-graduate study in France and Germany during 1957-58, returning home to private practice during the 1960s. Over the following decade Cárdenas occupied a variety of appointive posts, except during 1976 when he served briefly in the national Senate. In 1980 he won the governorship of Michoacán as candidate of the semi-official Institutional Revolutionary party (PRI). He served in that post until 1986.

Between 1986 and 1988 Cárdenas, who shared his father's populist, statist bent, worked to reform the PRI and Mexican politics generally. In 1988 he broke with the PRI to become presidential candidate of a left-wing coalition, the National Democratic Front, challenging PRI candidate **Carlos Salinas de Gotari**. Losing to Salinas, he went on to help found the Partido Revolucionario Democrático (Democratic Revolutionary party, PRD) a year later. In 1994 he ran for president as the PRD candidate, losing to PRI candidate **Ernesto Zedillo Ponce de León**. In elections of July 1997 a coalition of PRD and PAN (National Action party) candidates won a majority of the seats in the lower house of the national Congress. At the same time Cárdenas won the mayoralty of Mexico City in the first-ever election to that post. Inaugurated December 1997, he announced plans to reduce crime, pollution, and political corruption in the national capital. As holder of Mexico's second most visible elective office, he was well positioned for a run in the 2000 presidential contest.

Cardoso, Fernando Henrique (1931–), Brazilian social scientist and president. Fernando Cardoso taught sociology at the University of São Paulo until the military coup of 1964. Shortly thereafter he joined the staff of the Economic Commission for Latin America (ECLA) in Santiago, Chile, where he made major contributions to dependency theory. Through his works, most importantly *Dependency and Development in Latin America* (1979), with Enzo Faletto, he argued that class interests cut across the center–periphery spectrum rendering unlikely the emergence of any independence-minded national bourgeoisie. He also equated the decline of populist politics in Latin America with the completion of import-substituting industrialization. Cardoso returned to Brazil in 1968, and worked to end the military dictatorship there. He took advantage of the relaxation of military rule to help found the Brazilian Social Democratic party (PSDB) in 1988. Following the resignation of President Fernando Collor de Mello (May 1993), Cardoso was named finance minister of new president Itamar Franco. His program of economic stabilization, the Real Plan, so successfully cut inflation that Cardoso won the 1994 presidential election, decisively defeating Workers' party candidate Luís Inácio da Silva. During his first term (1995-99), Cardoso worked to reform the nation's civil service and pension systems, and to shrink the public sector through the sale of state-owned enterprises. His success in doing so, while restraining inflation, made him the most popular Brazilian president in recent memory. After the constitution was amended to allow him a second four-year term, Cardoso won reelection in October1998.

Carías Andino, Tiburcio (1876-1969), Honduran president. The son of a Liberal general, Tiburcio Carías entered politics in 1903 as a supporter of National party founder and president, Manuel Bonilla. He went on to lead the Nationalists after Bonilla's death in 1913. Although Carías won the 1924 presidential election, Liberal opponents denied him office. He lost to a Liberal in the 1928 presidential contest, but triumphed in the election of 1932. Upon taking office Carías was confronted by a sharp decline in banana exports owing to the Great Depression. The nation's chief revenue-earner was then ravaged by sigatoka disease, and hurricanes devastated banana plantations. The combined impact was a fiscal crisis to which Carías responded by imposing austerity measures. A Liberal revolt in 1932 and political ferment in neighboring Guatemala, El Salvador, and Nicaragua led him to sharply curtail labor and restrict freedoms of speech and the press. Control of the military guaranteed his continuance in power to 1943 (authorized in the new 1936 constitution). In 1939 Congress extended Carías's term

to 1948, causing critics to characterize his regime—widely termed the Cariato—as one of *continuismo*. During the World War II Carías staunchly supported the United States and its allies. When the war ended he made clear his intent to relinquish power in 1948. The 1944 overthrow of dictators **Maximiliano Hernández Martínez** in El Salvador and **Jorge Ubico** in Guatemala may have stiffened his resolve to do so. When Carías left office both the army and the National party stood as dominant forces in Honduran politics.

Carranza, Venustiano (1859-1920), Mexican revolutionary leader and president (1917-20). Carranza was born in comfortable circumstances in the northern state of Coahuila. He began his political career in 1887 by serving as municipal president (mayor) of Cuatro Ciénagas, his home town, and held several other offices before 1910. A supporter of **Francisco I. Madero** in the early stages of the Mexican Revolution, he was serving as governor of Coahuila at the time of Madero's ouster by **Victoriano Huerta**. Carranza disavowed Huerta in the Plan of Guadalupe (March 26, 1913), which pledged the restoration of constitutional rule. Carranza was recognized as the First Chief of the Constitutionalist Army in the ensuing civil war, but, after the defeat of Huerta in 1914, his authority was challenged by **Francisco Villa** and others. As armed conflict between Carranza's foes and supporters broke out, he cultivated agrarian and labor support by pledging reforms in these areas. By late 1915, thanks to the military prowess of **Álvaro Obregón**, Villa had been defeated, and Carranza's government received de facto recognition from the United States. Relations remained strained, however, especially after Villa's attack on Columbus, New Mexico, in March 1916 and President Woodrow Wilson's dispatch of troops across the border to pursue the *villistas*. Clashes between Mexicans and the U.S. troops brought the two countries to the verge of war, which was averted partly because of American belief that such a conflict would benefit Germany. Under Carranza, Mexico remained neutral during World War I and, though he occasionally appeared to lean toward Germany, he resisted the overtures of the Zimmermann telegram.

Meanwhile, a new constitution, more radical than the moderate draft prepared by Carranza, had been promulgated in February 1917, and he was elected president the following month. As chief executive, Carranza evinced little inclination to carry out constitutional provisions aimed at benefiting peasants and workers, and he is often seen as a traitor to the populist aspirations of Mexico's revolutionaries. His reputation was also tarnished by the assassination of **Emiliano Zapata** in 1919. Many, however, praise Carranza as a staunch nationalist who successfully resisted U.S. pressures.

As his term drew to a close, Carranza endorsed as his successor a virtually unknown civilian, Ignacio Bonillas, while the popular Obregón emerged as an opposition candidate. A dispute between Carranza and the governor of Sonora, Adolfo de la Huerta, led the latter to repudiate the president in the Plan of Agua Prieta (April 23, 1920); Obregón also supported de la Huerta. As Mexico's powerful military embraced the plan, Carranza fled the capital by train, hoping to reach Veracruz. Forced to abandon the train, he found himself in the village of Tlaxcalatongo, Puebla, where he was treacherously attacked and killed (May 21, 1920).

Carrera, José Rafael (1814-65), Guatemalan head of state (1844-48, 1851-65). Of indigenous ancestry, Carrera was born in Guatemala City in modest circumstances. In 1832, after a stint in the army of the Central American Federation, he settled in the town of Mataquescuintla, where he was a swineherd. By the late 1830s he had emerged as a leading opponent of the Liberal reformers who dominated the government in the Guatemalan capital and of **Francisco Morazán**, head of the federation. In 1840 Carrera's decisive defeat of Morazán in Guatemala City marked the end of the federation. Carrera was now the dominant figure in what would become the independent republic of Guatemala. Prior to 1850 he worked with Liberals as well as Conservatives, but after

defeating Liberal revolutionaries from Guatemala and neighboring states, he allied himself permanently with Guatemala's Conservatives. He was chosen president in 1851, and in 1854 was named president for life.

As president, Carrera signed a concordat (1852) with the Vatican, giving the Catholic church a privileged position. He maintained friendly relations with Great Britain, which won Guatemalan acknowledgment of its sovereignty over Belize in the Wyke-Aycinena Treaty of 1859. Carrera also contributed substantial forces to the Central American army that defeated **William Walker** in 1857. During his administration the *consulado*, a colonial institution akin to a Chamber of Commerce that was revived in in 1839, developed ports on the Pacific, especially San José, which was linked by road to the capital.

Carrera's regime was often denounced as a military dictatorship that did little to advance education or the overall development of Guatemala and meddled in the internal affairs of neighboring countries. However, his American biographer, Ralph Lee Woodward, Jr., and others now argue that, despite its failings, Carrera's government followed a paternalistic policy toward Guatemala's Indian peasantry that protected their land and culture, both of which would come under attack after his death. Carrera designated his close associate, Vicente Cerna, as his successor, but the latter was ousted by Liberals in 1871.

Castilla, Ramón (1797-1867), general and president of Peru (1845-51, 1855-62). Of Spanish and indigenous ancestry, Castilla was born in Tarapacá to a family of modest means and he had little schooling. In 1816, while living in Chile, he joined the Spanish army and fought against the supporters of independence. After being captured in the Battle of Chacabuco, he was taken to Buenos Aires, where he was freed. He returned to Spanish service in Peru, but joined the patriot forces in 1822. He was wounded at the Battle of Ayacucho.

Castilla played a prominent role in Peru's early political upheavals. He opposed the Peru–Bolivia Confederation of **Andrés Santa Cruz** and commanded a cavalry division at the

Battle of Yungay in 1839. He was a member of Agustín Gamarra's cabinet from 1839 to 1841 and was taken prisoner at the Battle of Ingavi, which ended Gamarra's effort to annex Bolivian territory to Peru.

Castilla became president of Peru in 1845 after emerging as the dominant leader in a successful revolt against the government of Manuel Ignacio Vivanco. He returned to power in 1855 after deposing his successor, José Rufino Echenique. Although Castilla had received the support of Peruvian Liberals in his campaign against Echenique, he later moved toward a more moderate position, as can be seen in the constitution of 1860. Castilla's administrations coincided with a boom in guano exports. Government revenue generated by guano was used for infrastructure improvements, but mainly benefited landed and mercantile elites. Regarded as Peru's most distinguished nineteenth-century statesman, Castilla died while trying to unseat Mariano Ignacio Prado.

Castro, Cipriano (1858-1924), Venezuelan president and dictator. Castro was born to middle-class parents in the Andean state of Táchira. He attended secondary school in the Colombian town of Pamplona, where he came under the influence of local Liberals. After his return to Venezuela, he became an advocate of Liberal reform and took part in local and national politics. In the early 1890s he went into exile in Colombia after he took up arms in support of President Raimundo Andueza Palacio, who was forced to leave office in 1892. On May 23, 1899, Castro and a band of sixty men crossed the border into Venezuela to launch what he called the Liberal Revolution of Restoration (Revolución Liberal Restauradora); he easily defeated the forces of President Ignacio Andrade and entered Caracas in October.

The revolution's motto was "New Men, New Ideals, New Methods," but few positive measures can be attributed to Castro's nine years in power. His tenure marked the beginning of a long ascendancy of leaders from Táchira in national politics. His regime can also be seen as a transitional one between the era of regional caudillos who domi-

nated politics in the nineteenth century and the modernizing, more highly centralized administration of his successor, **Juan Vicente Gómez.** Castro is probably best known for his dispute with foreign creditors, which led to a blockade of Venezuelan ports in December 1902 by Great Britain, Germany, and Italy. The dispute was eventually settled by arbitration. Conflict over the claims of American citizens soured relations with the United States, and diplomatic ties were briefly ruptured in 1906 and 1907. In November 1908, his health weakened by a sybaritic lifestyle, Castro left Venezuela to seek medical treatment in Europe. He left Gómez, then vice president, in charge, but the latter seized power for himself on December 19, 1908. Efforts by Castro to regain power failed, and he died in Puerto Rico.

Castro Ruz, Fidel (1926–), Cuban president and Communist party leader. A native of Oriente province, Fidel Castro was the third of seven children born to Ángel Castro, a Spanish immigrant who had prospered in Cuba, and Lina Ruz, his second wife. He attended private schools and later entered the University of Havana, where he earned a law degree in 1950. Castro was passionately involved in politics while in high school and college. During 1947 he shot a fellow student during an argument, and the same year plotted the overthrow of dictator **Rafael Trujillo** of the Dominican Republic. In April 1948 he attended a meeting of socialist youth in Bogotá, Colombia. During a riot attending the assassination of Liberal party leader **Jorge Eliécer Gaitán**, Castro joined Liberal mobs attempting to overthrow the government of Conservative president Mariano Ospina Pérez. He joined the nationalist and anti-imperialist Ortodoxo party in 1947 and ran for Congress as an Ortodoxo candidate in 1952. But his political ambitions were frustrated by the coup of **Fulgencio Batista** (March 10, 1952). On July 26 of the following year, Castro led a failed attempt to storm the Moncada army barracks in Santiago. He survived the attack but was jailed and subsequently given a fifteen-year prison sentence. At his trial he eloquently defended himself, uttering a phrase that later became famous: "History will absolve me." Freed in May

1955, Castro traveled to Mexico, where he organized a force to invade Cuba. On December 2, 1956, he and eighty-one other revolutionaries landed at the southeastern part of the island, where they were were attacked by an army detachment. In fighting that followed, all but nine invaders were killed or captured. Castro, his brother Raúl (b. 1931), **Ernesto "Che" Guevara**, and six others fled into the Sierra Maestra mountains. They remained there for twenty-one months, building a fighting force that ultimately numbered 3,000 men and women and was recruited from all sectors of the population, especially from peasants and small landowners from Oriente province. During that period the guerrillas withstood a large-scale army offensive (June 1957). In April 1958, Castro concluded a united front agreement with other anti-Batista groups, and prepared to march out of his mountain stronghold. He did so August 1958, making steady progress against a dispirited Cuban army. By January 1, 1959, his troops had driven Batista and his government from the island. Within a week, Castro's July 26th Movement was in control of Cuba. Castro soon replaced provisional president Manuel Urrutia with the loyal Osvaldo Dorticós, and assumed the title of prime minister, which he held until 1976. That year, in accordance with Cuba's new constitution, he became president by virtue of his position as head of the Council of State, whose members are chosen by the National Assembly.

Castro began implementing revolutionary social and economic reforms once ensconced in power. First he launched an agrarian reform that by 1963 had converted 70 percent of agricultural land into state-owned farms. Within two years he had nationalized all banks and industry on the island, placing the latter under the direction of his minister of industry, **Che Guevara**. His massive confiscation of private property alienated the United States, which ended trade with Cuba in 1960, severed relations with the island six months later (January 1961), and sponsored an armed attack on the island in April 1961. The abortive Bay of Pigs invasion of April 15-17 enhanced Castro's reputation while forcing him into a close alliance with the Soviet Union. Castro proclaimed

himself a Marxist–Leninist late in 1961, and privately invited the Soviets to arm Cuba with nuclear weapons. The ensuing Cuban Missile Crisis of October 1962 was resolved only after the United States agreed never again to invade Cuba, and the Soviets promised to withdraw their weapons. Castro's revolution, and his successes against the United States, won him immense popularity around the world, especially in less developed countries—and particularly among Latin American revolutionaries. Young Marxist–Leninists strove to emulate his example by forming *castrista* guerrilla groups in most countries of the region. Meanwhile Castro offered them training and supplies.

During the 1970s Castro moved to streamline state machinery, moving away from the highly personalized leadership he and his lieutenants had provided earlier—leadership that he admitted had devastated Cuba's economy. Meanwhile, the economy continued to suffer, both from effects of the U.S. embargo and from Castro's dogged effort to supplant the profit motive through an imperfect process of centrally planned resource allocation. Living standards declined precipitously, save in the areas of education and health care, moving the dictator to allow some 125,000 Cubans to depart the island in September 1980 (the Mariel boatlift). Living standards plummeted again following collapse of the Soviet Union in 1991, forcing Castro to allow limited private enterprise.

Fidel Castro continues as Cuba's supreme leader at century's end. His prestige has remained high among those who admired his ability to turn back every effort of the United States to defeat him. Yet many have criticized him for depriving Cubans of fundamental freedoms in order to safeguard his revolution and for impoverishing them in the process. As Castro ages he preserves his image as a brilliant politician and a charismatic leader of global stature. Thanks to his reforms, Cubans have enjoyed relatively high standards of health and education in spite of their poverty.

Caxias, Duque de (Luís Alves de Lima e Silva; 1803-1880), Brazilian military leader and statesman. Descended from a long line of distinguished officers, Caxias was educated at the Military School in his native Rio de Janeiro. He first gained distinction for his efforts to preserve the territorial integrity and stability of the Brazilian empire by crushing revolts in Maranhão, Rio Grande do Sul, and other provinces in the 1840s. In 1841 he was named Baron of Caxias, after the name of a town in Maranhão. In 1852 he commanded the Brazilian forces that defeated the Argentine dictator **Juan Manuel de Rosas** at the Battle of Caseros. In 1867-68 he succeeded **Bartolomé Mitre** as commander-in-chief of the Allied forces in the Paraguayan War, resigning this post in January 1869 soon after the occupation of Asunción. Shortly afterward the emperor conferred on him the title of duke; he was the only duke not related to the royal family. A Conservative, Caxias served in the Senate from 1845 until his death and as prime minister on three occasions: 1856-57, 1861-62, and 1875-78.

Charles II (1661-1700), king of Spain (1665-1700) and last Spanish Hapsburg ruler. Charles was a biological misfit whose inability to produce an heir set off the War of the Spanish Succession (1700-13). Nicknamed "El Hechizado" (the "Bewitched" or "Possessed") because of his epileptic fits and seizures, Charles was a living symbol of how far Spain had declined in the seventeenth century. Further loss of territory and alienation of royal power marked his reign. Most power was in the hands of aristocratic cliques, although Charles did designate Philip of Anjou as his successor and thereby started a European-wide war led by those who did not want Bourbons on the thrones of both France and Spain.

Charles III (1716-1788), king of Spain (1759-88). The fifth child of Philip V (1700-46), Charles had a quarter-century of experience as king of Naples and Sicily (1734-59) when he succeeded his brother Ferdinand VI (1746-59) as king of Spain. He is seen as the best of the Spanish Bourbons of the eighteenth and nineteenth centuries and is considered one of the "enlightened despots" of Europe. Imbued with ideas of progress and administrative reform, he surrounded himself with leading lights of the Spanish Enlightenment like

Count Campomanes and Gaspar Melchor de Jovellanos and chose as his ministers outstanding individuals such as the Marquis of Esquilache and the counts of Aranda and Floridablanca. Spanish absolutism reached its height during his reign and can be seen in his foreign policy, anticlericalism, and administrative reforms. He fought two wars against the English. In the first he lost Florida (1763) but gained Louisiana. In the second he recovered Minorca and Florida (1783). He supported the expulsion of the Jesuits (1767) and limitations on the other religious orders. Great strides were taken in restructuring the tax and administrative system so that it was more efficient and less corrupt. There were negative consequences like rebellions in Peru (1780-81) and New Granada (1781). Overall the most substantial changes were the new intendancy system and free trade within the empire.

Charles V (1500-1558), king of Spain (1516-56) as Charles I and emperor of the Holy Roman Empire (1519-56) as Charles V. The grandson of **Isabella I** and **Ferdinand II** and of the emperor Maximilian I, Charles was heir to a vast empire running from the New World to Central Europe, but he failed to consolidate his inheritance. His policy of containing the French and stopping the spread of Protestantism in Germany and of Islam in the Mediterranean saddled Spain with a policy and a legacy that would lead to its evident decline by the seventeenth century. Charles ruled through a system of stand-in kings or viceroys and administrative councils. Each kingdom was a separate entity with its distinct customs and laws. There never was a united Spain much less an empire with one set of laws. The government and function of the Indies within the empire took on its main outlines during the reign of Charles with the creation of the Council of the Indies (1524) and the viceroyalties of New Spain (1535) and Peru (1543) and the discovery of the main sources of precious metals. While the gold and silver of the Indies would never equal the bullion production of Charles's Old World possessions until after his reign, they were an ever larger percentage of the total and were important to Charles's ability to wage war. Charles's divestiture of his empire in favor of his brother Ferdinand I and his son **Philip II,** with the former as emperor and the latter as king of Naples, Milan, the Netherlands, Spain, and the Indies, left Europe with the Austrian and Spanish Hapsburgs.

Christophe, Henri or Henry (1767-1820), revolutionary leader and ruler in Haiti. Christophe was born on the island of Grenada. Probably free since birth, he went to sea as a cabin boy and was later employed in the kitchen of a hotel in the French colony of Saint Domingue. In 1779, with troops from the French West Indies, he took part in an unsuccessful campaign to dislodge the British from Savannah during the American Revolution. He returned to the Saint Domingue hotel, eventually becoming its manager.

In 1790 Christophe and other black volunteers joined white militia in opposing the mulatto rebel Vincent Ogé. By the mid-1790s, however, he had become the ablest lieutenant of **Toussaint L'Ouverture**, who assigned him to the North Province, where he attempted to revive the plantation economy by a state-directed system of forced labor known as *fermage*. He initially resisted Napoleon's attempt to reconquer Saint Domingue but reached an accommodation with the French on April 25, 1802. However, he soon rebelled against them and, after the independence of Haiti was declared by **Jean-Jacques Dessalines** in 1804, was given command of the north. After Dessalines's assassination in 1806, Christophe was recognized as president of a new Haitian republic, but conflict with **Alexandre Pétion** led to the creation of a separate state in the north, of which Christophe was proclaimed king on March 26, 1811.

As King Henry, Christophe established an authoritarian regime. Order was maintained by the Royal Corps of Dahomets, made up of blacks brought directly from Africa. For defense against enemies, he built the massive citadel at La Ferrière at an elevation of 3,100 feet above sea level. A rural code prescribed strict discipline for plantation workers, who received one-fourth of the total yield. Though barely literate himself, Christophe valued education highly and, as a result of his contact with British abolitionists,

brought English teachers to Haiti. In mid-August 1820, as military conspirators were plotting against him, Christophe suffered a cerebral hemorrhage that paralyzed his right side. On October 8, 1820, he committed suicide, according to tradition, with a silver bullet.

Claver, San Pedro (1580-1654), Spanish missionary among African slaves in Colombia. Born in Verdú, Catalonia, Claver became a Jesuit in 1602. He arrived in Cartagena in 1610 but studied at Tunja in the interior until 1615 when he returned to the coast. He was ordained in Cartagena in 1616. His life's work was to meet the slave ships that arrived in Cartagena where their human cargo were resold and dispatched to various destinations in South and Central America. He baptized the slaves and ministered to their needs. He had black translators versed in African languages who facilitated his work. Known as the Apostle of the Negroes, he was beatified by Pius IX in 1851 and canonized by Leo XIII in 1888. Many schools, organizations, and groups in the United States and Latin America are named after him.

Clemente Walker, Roberto (1934-1972), Puerto Rican baseball player. Roberto Clemente's talent was such that the Brooklyn Dodgers drafted him before his twentieth birthday, making him one of baseball's first African-American players. Brooklyn traded him to the Pittsburgh Pirates in 1955, and he spent the remainder of his career with that team. Clemente compiled a lifetime .317 batting average, collected over 3,000 base hits, won four league batting titles, and twelve Golden Gloves. He was named the National League's Most Valuable Player in 1966, selected World Series MVP in 1971, and voted National League All Star Team member twelve times. When, on December 23, 1972, an earthquake devastated Managua, Nicaragua, Clemente collected an airplane load of relief supplies destined for earthquake survivors. He died when the plane crashed approaching Nicaragua, December 31, 1972. His death moved baseball's All Star Committee to conduct a special election in 1973, by which Clemente was elected to the sport's Hall of Fame.

Cochrane, Thomas Alexander (tenth Earl of Dundonald) (1775-1860), Scottish admiral, noted for his services to the cause of Latin American independence. The eldest son of the ninth earl of Dundonald, Lord Cochrane had a brilliant career in the British navy during the French revolutionary and Napoleonic wars. Later he was elected to Parliament but lost both his seat and his naval commission after being implicated in a securities fraud that led to his being jailed for a year. In 1817 he accepted an invitation to head the navy of newly independent Chile. In February 1820 he captured Valdivia, Spain's strongest naval base in the Pacific. Later that year he escorted the army that sailed from Chile to liberate Peru under the command of **José de San Martín**. However, he quarreled with San Martín over strategy and financial matters, and in 1821 left Peru to harry Spanish shipping in the Pacific. In 1823 he became first admiral of the Brazilian navy, successfully effecting the departure of a Portuguese squadron from Bahia and Maranhão. In 1824 he helped defeat the rebellious provinces that formed the Confederation of the Equator. Back in Europe, he supported the cause of Greek independence against the Turks and rejoined the British navy in 1832.

Coelho Pereira, Duarte (?-1553 or 1554), Portuguese naval commander and first donatary captain of Pernambuco (1534-53/54). Even though he was illegitimate, Coelho became a *fidalgo* and a member of the king's household in 1521 on the basis of his exploits in the Far East, where he first traveled in 1509. In the 1530s he continued to make a name for himself in the king's diplomatic service and as fleet commander in the Atlantic from the Azores to the African fortress at São Jorge de Mina. Further rewards came, and in 1534 he was one of the twelve awarded proprietary captaincies in Brazil. Pernambuco was the choicest of the lot with its fertile soil, good port, closeness to Portugal, and settlement already in place. Coelho did not squander the opportunity. He brought order to the troubled colony, kept the French at bay and hostile Indians in their place, and promoted miscegenation with friendly tribes. More importantly he transformed the economic basis of colonial life in Brazil. Under his direction sugar replaced brazilwood as the most important commercial activity and became the model for future Portuguese success in Brazil. By 1542 he was reporting to the king on the growing amount of sugar cane planted and the large *engenho* (sugar mill) that was about to go on line and the need for black slaves from Africa. By 1550 five sugar mills were in operation and many others were being built. With the great silver discovery at Potosí (1545) by the Spanish and the growing importance of sugar in Brazil, the Portuguese crown decided that direct royal rule would offer more benefits. As of 1548 government policy was to replace the donatary captains with royal officials, a move bitterly opposed by Coelho. He died in Portugal while protesting restrictions on donatorial prerogatives.

Columbus, Christopher (**Cristoforo Colombo**, 1451?-1506), Genoese explorer. Various members of Columbus's family were involved in the Genoese wool trade whose network reached the main commercial centers of Western Europe. As part of this system, Columbus had gone to sea at an early age and sailed the Mediterranean and Atlantic with an ever widening experience that ranged from the Aegean to Ireland, England, Madeira, the Canary Islands, and the coast of Africa as far south as modern Ghana. In the 1470s he settled in Lisbon and married into a prominent Italian–Portuguese family. His skill and study convinced him that Asia was no more than 2,400 nautical miles from the Canary Islands—actually it is more than 10,500—and could be reached by sailing west. He presented his project to various personages in Portugal, France, and Spain, but the considerable expense involved, political considerations, and other priorities deterred interested sponsors. But the fall of Granada in 1492 brought together the right circumstances and a summons from Queen **Isabella**. An agreement was signed with the crown sponsoring a western voyage and with Columbus getting noble status and the title of viceroy over any discovered lands. The first voyage of three ships with a crew of about ninety sailed from Palos in southern Spain on August 3, 1492. It began with a shake-down cruise to the

Canaries. There improvements, repairs, and resupply and good weather made them ready for a quick crossing in thirty-six days. They made landfall at Guanahani, one of the Bahama islands, that historic October 12, 1492, and changed the course of history. The trip home with six captive Indians took them to the Azores, Lisbon, and Palos, a journey of fifty-eight days. Exactly what had been discovered still had to be determined, but Spanish officials moved immediately to back up their claims. Columbus's second voyage (1493-96) was a full-scale colonization effort composed of seventeen vessels and 1,200 settlers, but the third (1498-1500) and fourth (1502-4) were more modest ventures of only six and four ships, respectively. Disenchantment with the advances Columbus could bring to the project grew. While his initial discoveries had been fundamental and he had explored the coastline of Cuba and of Central America from Honduras to Panama and detected the Orinoco River, Spanish settlers had revolted, Indians had been enslaved, and reports accused him of bad government. Part of the problem was that Columbus came from an Italian–Portuguese maritime tradition that emphasized trade and commerce from fortified coastal enclaves, while the Spanish or Castilian tradition was of conquest, settlement, government, and acculturation of the conquered population. Also, Columbus, contrary to what was increasingly evident to all, adamantly maintained that his discoveries were in the Far East. While the crown continued to allow him to explore, as of 1499, with the appointment of Francisco de Bobadilla, officials other than Columbus had higher authority in the New World. Columbus died in Spain some eighteen months following his fourth voyage. He spent his last months in a vain attempt to gain money and honors that he claimed had been promised him by Ferdinand and Isabella.

Coronado, Francisco Vázquez de (Vázquez de Coronado, Francisco; 1510-1554), explorer. Coronado was born into an important Spanish noble family in Salamanca. He came to Mexico in 1535 as part of the entourage of **Antonio de Mendoza**, the first viceroy. As Mendoza's protégé, Coronado quickly accumulated land and

power. Named to Mexico City's *cabildo*, he married the daughter of Alonso de Estrada, the royal treasurer, and then was made governor of New Galicia in western Mexico in 1539. This was the place from which to organize an expedition to the north to check out the location of Cíbola, the rumored city of great wealth. It was no accident that the viceroy Mendoza then chose him to lead the expedition. Spaniards, 336 strong, and 1,000 Indians moved out in 1540, traversing Sinaloa, Sonora, Arizona, New Mexico, and the panhandles of Texas and Oklahoma before deciding that the rumored wealth was a mirage. Dispirited, with nothing to show for their efforts except Pueblo Indians and buffaloes, they turned around in Kansas and retraced their steps. The exodus from New Galicia had weakened the Spanish presence there, and the resulting Indian revolt led to the Mixtón War (1540-41), which the viceroy had to put down personally. Little wonder that when Coronado reappeared in Mexico City in 1542, Mendoza refused to meet with him. The initial promise of a successful career had faded, and he died a broken man in Mexico City. The Coronado trek also marked the end of the great expeditions of exploration and conquest from Mexico.

Cortés, Hernán (Fernando, Hernando; 1484?-1547), conqueror of Mexico. Born in Medellín, Extremadura, Spain, Cortés came to the New World in 1504 with some legal training at the University of Salamanca. He functioned briefly as a notary on Hispaniola, and then participated in the conquest of Cuba, where he acquired an *encomienda* and several gold mines. In 1518 he was chosen by Diego Velázquez, the governor of Cuba, to lead an expedition to the Mexican Gulf Coast to explore and trade but not to colonize. Nevertheless, once there, Cortés quickly expanded the goals of the mission and convinced its participants of the larger possibilities. He bypassed the authority of Velázquez by establishing a town with a *cabildo* (town council) and put it directly under the control of the king. He astutely named it La Villa Rica de la Vera Cruz, boldly asserting its wealth and calling on the powers of the "True Cross" to bless his undertaking. He convinced his men to include in the ship he was despatching to

Spain not only the king's share of the booty, but theirs as well, as a gift to the crown. With the problem of his rebellion against Velázquez seemingly finessed, Cortés could now begin his march on the Aztec empire. With his young Indian mistress **Malinche**, barely fifteen, translating and divulging the mysteries of the Indian world, Cortés had a ready and apt associate to point out danger and to counteract Aztec stratagems. He defeated the Tlaxcalans, mortal enemies of the Aztecs, and won them over to his side, convincing them their future lay with the Spaniards. With his Tlaxcalan allies in tow, he entered Tenochtitlán on November 8, 1519. The Aztec capital was built in the middle of Lake Texcoco and could be reached only by causeways and canoes. At the very center of Aztec power and might the best strategy seemed to be an old one, and the emperor **Moctezuma II** was taken hostage and made to issue Spanish orders. A new danger appeared when Velázquez sent out a force under **Pánfilo de Narváez** to take back control. Cortés split his forces, leaving **Pedro de Alvarado** in charge in the capital, and marched out and surprised Narváez's larger force at midnight in a rainstorm. Hanging several of Velázquez's closest supporters and co-opting the rest, Cortés marched back to Tenochtitlán, now in full-scale revolt. Rushing into the capital to lift the siege against Alvarado's beleaguered forces, Cortés then had to abandon it on that fateful "Noche Triste," July 1, 1520, with great loss of life and accumulated booty and treasure. He retreated to Tlaxcala where its people helped him rebuild. He ordered up the component parts for a fleet of ships, which he had hauled over the mountains, assembled, and launched on Lake Texcoco where they overpowered Aztec canoes. He then cut the water and food supply and starved Tenochtitlán into submission. Cortés sent out various expeditions to the west and south to consolidate the conquest. The revolt of one of his most trusted captains, Cristóbal de Olid, in Honduras in 1524, spurred Cortés on his most difficult campaign (1524-26) across Tabasco, Yucatán, Guatemala, and Honduras with marginal results other than the execution of Olid. The great achievement had been the taking of Tenochtitlán. Thus ended the most singular and dramatic of all the conquests in the New World.

The Aztec empire was too great a prize for one person, and Cortés was not given a government position commensurate with his achievements. Nevertheless, while in Spain in 1529 he was made the marquis of the Valle de Oaxaca with 23,000 tributaries, well over 100,000 subjects, with rights of tribute, justice, and administration—a princely grant equal to the holdings of the grandees of Spain, an honor never bestowed again in the New World. Upon his return to New Spain in 1530, he clashed with the *audiencia* for exceeding his allotted 23,000 tributaries by 300 percent. After 1535 he was outranked in prestige in the colony by the new viceroy, the grandee **Antonio de Mendoza**. Back in Spain by 1540, complaining over his treatment to the absent emperor **Charles V** away in Germany, Cortés grew tired of waiting for vindication. He was making plans to return to the land of his success when death overtook him in 1547 in a village near Seville. With an ambiguous legacy as the destroyer and creator of Mexico, Cortés and his achievements have weighed heavily on the Mexican psyche. The first republican government after independence ordered his bones destroyed although they were concealed successfully by the Mexican historian **Lucas Alamán**.

Cosío Villegas, Daniel (1898-1976), Mexican historian, man of letters, and founder of cultural institutions. Born in Mexico City, Cosío Villegas graduated from the National School of Jurisprudence in 1925 but had little interest in practicing law and took advantage of the opportunity to study economics at Cornell University, the London School of Economics, and other foreign institutions. Upon his return to Mexico, he helped found the National School of Economics. He also launched a major publishing house, the Fondo de Cultura Económica, and the quarterly journal *El Trimestre Económico*, both of which he headed from 1934 to 1948. While serving as Mexican chargé d'affaires in Lisbon during the Spanish Civil War, he arranged for the emigration to Mexico of many Spanish intellectuals. The Casa de España, which was created as a center for their activities, was transformed in 1940 into El

Colegio de México, an important institution for research and advanced study in history and the social sciences. Cosío Villegas was closely associated with the Colegio de México from its inception, serving as its president from 1957 to 1963.

Beginning in 1948, Cosío Villegas oversaw the production of the ten-volume *Historia moderna de México* (1955-72). He himself wrote five volumes of the history, which traces the political, diplomatic, social, and economic development of the country from 1867 to 1910. In 1951 he founded *Historia Mexicana*, which quickly became Mexico's leading historical journal, and served as its editor until 1961. Cosío Villegas's last major historical undertaking was the direction of the twenty-three-volume *Historia de la revolución mexicana*, which began publication in 1979. He was also a prolific essayist and political analyst noted for his incisive commentaries on contemporary Mexico.

Cruz, Juana Inés de la (1648 or 1651-1695), Mexican poet and writer and colonial Latin America's greatest intellectual. Born illegitimate in San Miguel de Nepantla near the capital of Mexico, Juana Inés de Asbaje y Ramírez was a child prodigy. She was taken to the viceregal court at the age of five where her intellectual talents developed and astounded observers. Spurning marriage proposals, she entered a Carmelite convent in 1667 and definitively settled in two years later as Sor (Sister) Juana Inés de la Cruz at the Convent of San Jerónimo, where she had a library of books and time to study and write. She wrote poetry, plays, and essays. She clearly had mastered the literary genres of the Spanish-speaking world as well as contemporary scholastic and scientific knowledge. Her range went from ancient classical philosophers and church fathers to Renaissance figures and perhaps even to René Descartes. Whether discussing theological or philosophical questions or writing poetry her approach was highly original and had ever more complex levels of meaning and movement toward resolution or contemplation of a paradox. Often New World themes emerged and challenged Spanish stereotypes and presumptions, and her voice became that of creoles, Indians, blacks, and

women. In several instances in response to males she presented a strong defense of women and of her life in the pursuit of knowledge. She was called "the tenth muse" and "the new American phoenix." As a woman she necessarily defended what she was and the essence of her gender. Little wonder that she has became a symbol of feminism. Sor Juana stands out as a compelling counterpoint to the male-dominated society of her time and raises questions as to what would have been achieved if a different set of standards and values had reigned. She died during a plague ministering to her sister nuns.

Cruz, Oswaldo Gonçalves (1872-1917), Brazilian physician and epidemiologist. A native of São Luís do Paraitinga in São Paulo state, Cruz studied medicine in Rio de Janeiro; from 1896 to 1898 he received additional training at the Pasteur Institute in Paris. Upon returning to Brazil in 1899, he joined the staff of the Serum Therapy Institute of Manguinhos in Rio de Janeiro, which had been founded to provide vaccines and serum to combat an outbreak of bubonic plague in the port city of Santos. Cruz became head of the institute in 1902, and in 1903 he was named director of the federal health department by President Francisco de Paula Rodrígues Alves, who wished to rid Rio de Janeiro of yellow fever, smallpox, and other diseases as part of his campaign to modernize the city. Cruz's efforts against yellow fever were successful, though many objected to the intrusive nature of the operation. Opposition to a planned program of compulsory vaccination against smallpox was more intense and contributed to an abortive revolt against the government. Cruz offered his resignation, which was refused, but the campaign against smallpox was only partially successful. After 1909 he devoted himself to the institute, which had been renamed in his honor and became a leading center for the study of infectious and parasitic diseases.

Cuauhtémoc (1494?-1525), the last Aztec ruler and the leader of the resistance against the Spanish after they had been driven from Tenochtitlán, the Aztec capital on July 1, 1520. A nephew of the emperor **Moctezuma II**, he wed the emperor's daughter, later baptized as Isabel Moctezuma, the widow of Cuitlahuac, Moctezuma's short-lived successor and Cuauhtémoc's immediate predecessor. She later married three Spaniards in succession, thus demonstrating the legitimacy of imperial succession and the power and claims therein contained that both Aztecs and Spaniards sought in this match. When Cuauhtémoc was chosen as the new leader at the age of twenty-five, the Aztecs were already prostrate from a smallpox epidemic and very quickly thereafter succumbed to a lack of food and water, the onslaught of **Hernán Cortés** and the Tlaxcalans, and the defection of auxiliaries and allies. His capture and the Spanish belief that he knew the location of hidden treasure led to his torture in which the Spanish greased his feet and held them over open flames. Revealing nothing, he continued as a prisoner and was made to accompany Cortés on his expedition to Honduras, which departed from Mexico City in 1524 to put down the Cristóbal de Olid revolt. Cuauhtémoc's continued presence disturbed the Spanish and made them fearful of a possible Indian uprising. The hardship of the Honduran march further unstrung the Spanish and led them to hang Cuauhtémoc for "treason" during Lent of 1525. Vanquished in life but ever present as a symbol of native resistance to the Spanish conquest, Cuauhtémoc has become a rallying cry for Mexican nationalism in the nineteenth and twentieth centuries and is celebrated in opera, in the naming of children, and in the imposing statue at the intersection of Insurgentes and Paseo de La Reforma, Mexico City's two most important avenues.

Cunha, Euclides da (1866-1909), Brazilian engineer and journalist, known mainly for his book *Os Sertões* (1902), translated into English as *Rebellion in the Backlands* (1944). Cunha entered Brazil's military academy in 1886, but was dismissed for displaying republican sentiments and began writing for newspapers. He was able to complete his military studies after the fall of the monarchy but resigned from the army in 1896, later being employed as a civil engineer. In 1897 the newspaper *O Estado de São Paulo* assigned him to cover a military campaign against the town of Canudos, inhabited by followers of a holy man known as Antônio Conselheiro (Anthony the Counsellor). Cunha kept a diary of his experiences, published posthumously as *Canudos: Diário de uma espedição* (1939). He later served on a commission that delineated the boundary between Brazil and Peru in Amazônia. On August 15, 1909, he was mortally wounded in a duel with a man he believed to be his wife's lover.

Os Sertões is regarded as one of Brazil's greatest books. It combines geography, sociology, history, and fiction as it recounts Conselheiro's career, government assaults on Canudos, and the heroic resistance of its defenders. Cunha vividly describes the physical environment of the semi-arid backland where Canudos was located as well as its impoverished inhabitants. Cunha depicted them as primitive specimens of humanity but was critical of the government's brutality toward them. *Os Sertões* made literate Brazilians aware of the disparities between the country's urban centers and its backward rural areas and was an immediate success.

Darío, Rubén (Félix Rubén García Sarmiento, 1867-1916), Nicaraguan poet, short-story writer, and journalist. Recognized during his lifetime as the leading contemporary poet of the Hispanic world, Darío was the outstanding practitioner of the literary style known as modernism, which was characterized by verbal richness and rhythmic experimentation. Born in Metapa (now Ciudad Darío), he was raised mainly by a great-aunt and her husband. He was a precocious youngster who steeped himself in Spanish and French literature and began writing poetry before he reached his teen-age years. From 1886 to 1889 he lived in Chile, where he wrote for a Santiago newspaper, *La Época*, and published an important collection of poems and short stories, *Azul* (1888). After several years in Central America, he visited Spain as a member of the Nicaraguan delegation that traveled to that country to celebrate the four hundredth anniversary of **Christopher Columbus**'s birth. During his short stay Darío became acquainted with prominent Spanish writers and critics and won their praise. While in Cartagena, Colombia, on the return trip to Nicaragua, he visited the Colombian president, **Rafael Núñez**, who arranged for him to be named Colombian consul-general in Buenos Aires. Darío lived in the Argentine capital for five years (1893-98), serving as Colombian consul until Núñez's death and contributing to *La Nación* and other newspapers. In 1896 he published *Prosas profanas*, which is distinctive for its formal innovation and the musicality of its verse. From 1899 to 1907 Darío lived in Europe, mainly in Spain and France. His third major collection, *Cantos de vida y esperanza* (1905), is more directly personal and introspective than its predecessors. It also celebrates Latin America and its Spanish heritage, as in the well-known poem "A Roosevelt." He returned to these themes in another celebrated poem, "Canto a la Argentina."

Darío returned to a hero's welcome in Nicaragua in 1907 and was named minister to Spain by President **José Santos Zelaya**, a post which he held until 1910. Darío spent most of his remaining years in Europe, but the ailing poet returned to Nicaragua in November 1915 and died in León on February 6, 1916. In addition to his poetry and stories, he published several collections of essays and newspaper articles, including *España contemporánea* (1901), *Tierras solares* (1904), and *Opiniones* (1906), as well as a memoir, *La vida de Rubén Darío* (1915).

Dessalines, Jean-Jacques (1758-1806), Haitian revolutionary leader and emperor (1804-6). Dessalines was born a slave in northern Haiti while it was still the French colony of Saint Domingue. In the 1780s he became the slave of a free black, whose floggings are said to have contributed to the extreme brutality later displayed by Dessalines. During the upheavals that racked Saint Domingue in the 1790s, he became one of the chief lieutenants of **Toussaint L'Ouverture** and played a major role in the defeat of the mulatto general André Rigaud in 1799-1800. Along with Toussaint, he submitted to the French forces that occupied Saint Domingue in 1802 and was incorporated into the French army. However, the capture of Toussaint, the atrocities of the French, and their apparent intention to restore slavery led Dessalines to rise in revolt, emerging as the leader of the black and mulatto forces that expelled the French in 1803. On January 1, 1804, he declared the independence of Haiti. He initially assumed the title of governor-general for life, but was proclaimed emperor and crowned on October 8, 1804. Meanwhile, he had ordered the extermination of most of the remaining whites in Haiti. In February 1805 he invaded Santo Domingo, then held by French and Spanish troops, but was repulsed. On May 20, 1805, he promulgated Haiti's first constitution as an independent nation. It decreed that Haiti was to be known as a black nation and prohibited land ownership by whites. The following year a revolt in the south led to the ambush and murder of the emperor near Port-au-Prince on October 17, 1806.

Dias, Henrique (1600?-1662), Brazilian black military leader in the war against the invading Dutch. The renewal of hostilities between Spain and the Netherlands and the formation of the Dutch West India Company in 1621 led to concerted attacks on the Portuguese part of the Spanish empire by the Dutch. Their occupation of Bahia (1624-25) and Recife (1630-54) led to an Atlantic-wide struggle in which over 20,000 died in Brazil alone. Dias, like others, was caught up in the conflict and had to choose sides. When he elected the Portuguese in 1633, he was literate and a free black, probably never having been a slave. His small company eventually grew to more than three hundred men of color. He became a master guerrilla fighter and a shrewd tactician, using his knowledge of the local terrain to maximum advantage. He helped defend Bahia (1638), recover territory in Alagoas (1639) and Pernambuco (1645-46), take a Dutch fort in Rio Grande do Norte (1647), and capture Olinda (1648) and finally Recife (1654). As early as 1639 he had been granted the title of "Governor of All Creoles, Blacks, and Mulattoes." Received at the Portuguese court in 1656, he secured freedom for all those slaves who had served under him and the formal constitution of his military unit. Ever since, black militia forces in Brazil have been called "Henriques."

Díaz, Porfirio (1830-1915), president and dictator

of Mexico (1877-80, 1884-1911). Of Spanish and indigenous ancestry, Díaz was born in the city of Oaxaca to a family in modest circumstances and lost his father by the age of three. With the help of a relative, he was able to study at the local seminary but decided on a career in law instead of the priesthood. A Liberal, Díaz was named subprefect of Ixtlán after the Ayutla Revolution. He took up arms during the War of the Reform and became a national hero because of his military exploits during the French intervention. He played a crucial role in the Mexican victory over the French at Puebla on May 5, 1862, and commanded the troops that captured Mexico City in 1867. He rebelled unsuccessfully after being defeated by **Benito Juárez** in the presidential election of 1871. Rebelling with greater success in 1876, he dominated Mexican politics for the next thirty-four years.

Díaz's admirers justified his long tenure in the presidency by pointing to the impressive economic development of the era. With the help of foreign capital, the railroad system grew from about 400 miles of track in 1876 to 15,000 in 1911, mining and commercial agriculture made great gains, and the petroleum industry got under way after 1900. Critics of the regime argued that Mexico's peasants, comprising the majority of the population, gained little from these changes. The government's restrictions on the press and the manipulation of elections also drew censure, as did its alleged surrender to foreign interests.

As the presidential election of 1910 approached, economic difficulties, stemming partly from the adoption of the gold standard in 1905 and the U.S. Panic of 1907, produced unrest. Although Díaz stated in the Creelman interview of 1908 that he would retire in 1910, he decided to seek another term. Díaz's decision to retain the incumbent vice president, the unpopular Ramón Corral, also proved controversial given the president's great age. These events precipitated the Mexican Revolution of 1910, which led to Díaz's resignation on May 25, 1911. He died in Paris.

Díaz del Castillo, Bernal (1495?-1584), soldier and chronicler of the conquest of Mexico. Born in Medina del Campo, Spain, Díaz came with

Pedrarias **(Pedro Arias de Ávila)** to Panama in 1514. He participated in Francisco Hernández de Córdoba's expedition to Yucatán (1517), **Juan de Grijalva**'s exploration along the Mexican Gulf Coast (1518), and **Hernán Cortés**'s conquest of Mexico (1519-22), all of which were launched from Cuba under the direction of the governor, Diego de Velázquez. Much of what is known about these linked and ever-expanding dramas is based on Díaz's *Historia verdadera de la conquista de la Nueva España* (*True History of the Conquest of New Spain*). Begun in the 1550s, completed in 1568, but not published until 1632, it is the eye-witness account of the clash of two great civilizations. Traditionally it has been viewed as an unvarnished relation from the ranks in contrast to the elegant and flowery account of Cortés's secretary, Francisco López de Gómara. The latter also makes his master a Renaissance man, alone responsible for the success of the conquest, while Díaz underscores the contribution of the group as a whole. More recent scholarship has suggested that Diaz's prose is just as elegant and as lofty as Gómara's and that its real purpose was a defense of the *encomendero* class against the attacks of the great defender of the Indians, **Bartolomé de las Casas**. Certainly Díaz was not as poor as he claimed, and while he got no *encomiendas* in Mexico—Cortés probably excluded him for being too close to his enemy, Governor Velázquez—he received several in Guatemala.

Duarte de Perón, María Eva (1919-1952), second wife of Argentine president **Juan D. Perón**. Eva Duarte was the fifth illegitimate child of Juan Duarte and Juana Ibarguren. At age fifteen she traveled to Buenos Aires where she eventually became a successful actress. She met Colonel Juan D. Perón, a widower, in January 1944 at a benefit for victims of a recent earthquake and soon became his mistress. Eva Duarte devoted herself to enhancing the reputation of her consort. When Perón's military rivals imprisoned him, she helped organize the mass demonstration (October 17, 1945) leading to his release. Eva Duarte married Juan Perón a week later, and four months later Argentines elected Juan Perón their president. Eva Perón devoted the rest of her life to strengthening Peronism. She was remarkably successful in appealing to the nation's poor, who admired her for escaping poverty and who loved her for making their cause her own. Through her Social Aid Foundation Eva Perón distributed massive amounts of public assistance to the poor. She championed women's rights, playing a major role in the 1947 enfranchisement of Argentine women, and going on to head the Peronist Women's party. In late 1947 she undertook her "Rainbow Tour" of European capitals, promoting the interests of Argentina and of her husband. In August 1951 Peronists demanded that she stand as their vice presidential candidate in the upcoming election, but were thwarted by the military. By this time Eva Perón's health was in decline, and in September she was diagnosed with an incurable cancer. Her death in 1952 coincided with and contributed to the weakening of Peronism. So powerful was her hold upon the nation's imagination that anti-Peronists spirited her embalmed body away from Argentina in 1955, not permitting its return until 1971. Eva Perón remains a controversial, even mythic figure in Argentina.

Duarte Fuentes, José Napoleón (1925-1990), Salvadoran president. José Napoleon Duarte was born in San Salvador to upper-middle-class parents. In June 1944 he became a student leader in demonstrations that toppled dictator **Maximiliano Hernández Martínez**. Several months later he entered the University of Notre Dame, graduating in 1948 with a degree in civil engineering. Returning to San Salvador he worked and started a family, but did not involve himself in politics. In early 1960, however, Duarte was invited to join a Christian Democratic discussion group. Soon he joined with others to constitute the Salvadoran Christian Democratic party. Four years later he became the mayor of San Salvador, and in February 1972 the Christian Democrats joined with two other parties of the left to back Duarte as their presidential candidate. While Duarte clearly won the contest, an electoral commission overturned it, declaring Colonel Arturo Molina the victor. Younger officers launched an abortive coup against Molina, and during the upset Duarte was jailed, beaten, and expelled from the country. He

spent seven years in Venezuela, returning in October 1979 after the overthrow of President Carlos Romero by reform-minded junior officers. In March 1980, Duarte joined the ruling military-civilian junta, and in November he became its president. From that position he attempted, with little success, to control left- and right-wing violence that had plunged El Salvador into civil war. On May 4, 1984, Duarte won the presidency, thus becoming El Salvador's first civilian chief executive since 1931. His term was not a successful one. Ongoing civil war claimed thousands of lives and devastated the nation's economy. While the United States gave massive aid to El Salvador, most of it was military, rather than humanitarian, in character. A 1984 attempt to reach a peace accord with Marxist FMLN guerrillas failed, and by 1988 the guerrillas were sabotaging dams, bridges, and electric generators. In October 1986, an earthquake devastated San Salvador, killing 1,000 and leaving 400,000 homeless. The near collapse of El Salvador's economy forced Duarte to introduce austerity measures that cost him popular support. One bright spot was his signing of the Arias Peace Plan in 1987, though his term expired before it bore fruit. In 1988 he was diagnosed with terminal cancer. Duarte's term ended amid charges that his regime was riddled with corruption and inefficiency. A final redeeming moment came in March 1989, when Duarte transmitted power peacefully to another elected civilian, Alfredo Cristiani.

Duvalier, François (1907-1971), Haitian president and dictator. François Duvalier was born into Haiti's black (*noir*) middle class. He attended school in Port-au-Prince and entered the École de Médecine there, graduating in 1934. He practiced medicine during the 1930s and 1940s, becoming known for his public health research in the treatment of tropical diseases. During the 1940s he worked with an antimalaria campaign conducted in Haiti by the U.S. Army, and was subsequently awarded a one-year public health scholarship to Michigan State University. Duvalier entered politics during the 1946 presidential campaign, supporting a party formed by *noiriste* candidate Daniel Fignolé. Dumarsais Estimé, another pro-black candidate, won the contest and appointed Duvalier his undersecretary of labor. Meanwhile Duvalier became active in the Griots group, an organization that celebrated Haiti's African heritage, especially *vodun*, the African-based religion practiced by a majority of Haiti's poor. Following the 1950 overthrow of Estimé by Colonel Paul Magloire, who favored Haiti's mulatto elite, Duvalier actively opposed Magloire. In late 1956 he participated in the general strike that led to Magloire's overthrow, and went on to campaign for and win a four-year presidential term (September 1957). Duvalier, by then widely known by his nickname "Papa Doc," entered office amid hopes that he would improve the lot of Haiti's poor. But instead he concentrated on crushing opponents in the military, the private sector, and organized labor. He did so through the use of secret police known as *cagoulards* (hooded men) and a personal militia dubbed *tontons macoutes* (bogeymen). Duvalier brought the Catholic church to heel, expelling priests who spoke against him, using the pretext that they were leftist subversives. For a time his avowed anticommunism placated the United States. In 1961 he had himself reelected president in a contest that he thoroughly subverted. When his second term drew to a close in 1963, and there appeared bitter opposition to his continuance in power, Duvalier unleashed a wave of terror that appalled the world. All the while he maintained a base of support within the black under-class, especially in rural areas, by exploiting his support for *vodun*. The Kennedy administration withdrew the U.S. ambassador and cut off aid, but U.S.-Haitian relations improved under President Lyndon Johnson. In June 1964 Duvalier had himself declared president-for-life and redoubled his repressive acts. His rule remained unchallenged until his death. His nineteen-year-old son, Jean-Claude Duvalier (Baby Doc), inherited the title "president-for-life," ruling Haiti until 1986.

Echeverría, Esteban (1805-1851), Argentine poet and political writer. A native of Buenos Aires, Echeverría spent five years in Paris (1825-30), where he became acquainted with the writings of Victor Hugo and other romantic authors. After returning to Argentina, he wrote several works of poetry, notably *Elvira, o la novia del Plata* (1832) and *La cautiva*, published in the collection *Rimas* (1837). *La cautiva*, about a white woman captured by Indians, is notable for its description of the Argentine landscape and is considered the first important work of Argentine romanticism.

Echeverría is also known for his political activism as a leader of the so-called Generation of 1837 and founder (1838) of the Asociación de Mayo, which was modeled on the Young Italy movement of Mazzini. Its program, which appeared under the title *Dogma socialista* in 1846, shows the influence of Saint Simon and other contemporary thinkers and sought the gradual introduction of political democracy to Argentina. By the late 1830s Echeverría had become an opponent of the dictatorship of **Juan Manuel de Rosas**, whom he attacked in his most celebrated work, the short story "El matadero" (The Slaughterhouse), first published in 1871. The story compares Buenos Aires under Rosas to a slaughterhouse and shows the unhappy fate of a high-minded Rosas foe at the hands of the brutal plebeians who were the dictator's strongest supporters. After becoming involved in an unsuccessful revolt against Rosas in 1839, Echeverría was forced to flee to Uruguay, where he remained until his death.

Echeverría Álvarez, Luis (1922–   ), Mexican president. Luis Echeverría was born in Mexico City and graduated from the National University with a degree in law (1945). His marriage to the daughter of a prominent state politician ensured his political career. Echeverría went on to hold important positions in the ruling Institutional Revolutionary party (PRI) and the national government, ultimately serving as secretary of the interior (*gobernación)* under President Gustavo Díaz Ordaz (1964-70). He won the 1970 presidential election as the official candidate of the PRI, despite his never having previously held elective office. While in office Echeverría projected a populist image styled on that of celebrated President **Lázaro Cárdenas**. Taking office amid an economic downturn, he expanded the number of state-owned enterprises to more than seven hundred, and expanded social services in what he called a program of "shared development." He liberally employed populist rhetoric, proclaiming himself a leader in the struggle against economic colonialism. While privately courting U.S. capital, he pursued a foreign policy displeasing to Washington, one advocating an end to the Cuban embargo and favoring socialist regimes throughout the world. Despite his efforts, Echeverría's presidency was not successful. He angered PRI members by filling high party and government posts with his followers, he alienated the business community by publicly rebuking it and confiscating privately held lands without prior warning, and he tightened government control over the news media. His liberal borrowing and spending policies quintupled Mexico's foreign debt, forcing austerity measures at the end of his term. When Echeverría's term ended public dissatisfaction with the ruling PRI stood at an historic high. Echeverría subsequently served Mexico abroad in diplomatic capacities. He returned to Mexico City in 1979 to direct a private international studies institute.

Estrada Cabrera, Manuel (1857-1924), Guatemalan president and dictator. Estrada Cabrera was born in Quetzaltenango, the natural son of a food vendor. Despite his poverty, he became a lawyer and held various municipal and provincial posts before being named to the cabinet of President José María Reyna Barrios in 1892. Having been named first *designado*, or presidential alternate, in 1897, he succeeded to the presidency after the assassination of Reyna Barrios in 1898. He was subsequently elected to four presidential terms.

As president, Estrada Cabrera adhered to the economic policies associated with Guatemalan Liberals. He favored the country's coffee interests and encouraged U.S. investment, which rose from $6 million in 1897 to $40 million by 1920. In 1912 **Minor C. Keith** was able to obtain a monopoly over railroad transportation in Guatemala by forming the International Railways of Central America. Meanwhile, Estrada Cabrera had created a brutal and corrupt dictatorship in which he

wielded power virtually alone.

Increasingly isolated in his later years, Estrada Cabrera suffered from diabetes and drank heavily. In April 1920 an opposition coalition called the Unionist party led a successful effort to remove the president, who was declared insane by the National Assembly on April 8. There was some resistance from his supporters, but Estrada Cabrera surrendered on April 14.

Féderman, Nicolás (1505 or 1509-1542), conqueror in Venezuela and Colombia. Born Nikolaus Federmann, probably in the free imperial city of Ulm, this German came to participate in the conquest as a result of loans made by the Welsers to **Charles V**. This commercial group acquired the right to conquer and settle Venezuela. Féderman was the most able of the Germans sent out to implement the terms of the concession. In command briefly (1530-31) in Coro, Venezuela, Féderman was banished for exceeding his authority. Upon his return to Augsburg (1532) he composed a report for his German employers in which he called attention to the riches and commercial possibilities of Venezuela, all with an eye toward obtaining an expedition under his command. Féderman's *Indianische Historia*, as the report was entitled upon its later publication, convinced the Welsers to sponsor the expedition. The Council of the Indies named him governor of Venezuela. Back in Coro by 1535, Féderman and Jorge Espira (Georg Hohermuth) planned a two-stage conquest of the Chibcha (Muisca) civilization of highland Colombia where reports located El Dorado. The former was to proceed west and then up the Magdalena River while Espira was to go southwest across the *llanos*, or plains. The plan went amiss when Féderman found his way blocked by a rival group of Spaniards at Santa Marta and had to return, while Espira found nothing of value after three years of great hardship and barely made it back in 1538. In the interval news had arrived announcing a forthcoming *residencia* or judicial review. Since these rarely turned out well, Féderman quickly struck out in the general direction of Espira's route, but they crossed without ever meeting. Féderman kept the Andes in sight as he crossed the *llanos*. When he encountered gold among the Indians, he turned west toward its presumed source and ascended the Andes only to discover that the Chibchas had already been conquered—**Gonzalo Jiménez de Quesada** and his expedition had arrived two years earlier (1537). A short time later the expedition from Popayán of **Sebastián de Belalcázar** also appeared. The three rivals faced off on the Sabana de Bogotá but decided to journey together to Spain where higher authorities could determine the merits of each conquistador. Féderman and his men had brought badly needed horses, armament, and supplies, and they were able to sell these at great profit. Most of Féderman's men stayed and helped found and settle many of the early towns of highland Colombia. In Flanders by 1540 Féderman argued with the Welsers over the financial accounting of the expedition and suddenly found himself in jail and abandoned. To get his case moved out of their stronghold, Féderman accused the Welsers of defrauding the Spanish crown. Since the Council of the Indies wanted the Welsers out of Venezuela and needed this incriminating witness, they surreptitiously transported him to Valladolid, Spain, where he gave damning testimony against his former employers. He was under house arrest when he died unexpectedly. The Welsers let their Venezuelan concession lapse with the royal bankruptcy in 1557.

Ferdinand II (1452-1516), king of Aragon (1479-1516), Castile and León (1474-1504), Sicily (1468-1516), and Naples (1504-16). Ferdinand's secret marriage to **Isabella of Castile** (1469) and his wife's succession to the throne brought civil war to the Iberian Peninsula in 1474. Ferdinand's astute diplomacy, military management, and succession in Aragon allowed the royal couple to prevail. Ferdinand supported Isabella's policy of reestablishing royal authority and of religious and ethnic conformity, which led to the establishment of the Inquisition (1480), the crusade against the kingdom of Granada (1482-92), and the expulsion of the Jews (1492). While Ferdinand was co-ruler in Castile, Spain was not united. Each kingdom was ruled as a separate unit with its separate laws, traditions, and institutions intact. When Isabella

died in 1504, Ferdinand was forced to retire to Aragon while his daughter Juana and her husband Philip, the archduke of Austria, assumed control of Castile. To protect his kingdom, Ferdinand concluded an agreement with France, Aragon's traditional enemy, and married Germaine de Foix, the niece of the French king. Philip's death in 1506 and Juana's madness threatened Castile with the return of chaos, and Castilians were delighted to have Ferdinand back as administrator of Castile from 1510 until his death in 1516. Ferdinand's rejection of a political or administrative union of the two crowns set the pattern for separate kingdoms under one ruler no matter how many new kingdoms were added. The new possessions were the fruit of Ferdinand's long-term diplomacy of marrying his children into the various royal families of Europe. The result was to take Spain far afield as Ferdinand's grandson **Charles V** succeeded not only to the Indies, Sicily, Naples, the Netherlands, Aragon, Navarre, and Castile but also became emperor of the Holy Roman Empire. The fruit of the New World went to sustain an empire that was not Iberian and whose ruler was not even Spanish. Ferdinand's more limited goals had always been to protect Aragon, which meant containing the French, dominating the western Mediterranean, and making war on Islam and the Turks. These goals were also expanded into imperial commitments that consumed much of the New World's precious metal production.

Ferdinand VII (1784-1833), king of Spain (1808, 1814-33). The son of Charles IV and María Luisa of Parma, Ferdinand became the hero of Spaniards unhappy with Spain's alliance with France after 1795. The blame for this unpopular policy fell upon the chief minister, Manuel Godoy, who was believed to be the queen's lover. As a result of the Treaty of Fontainebleau (1807), which provided for Franco-Spanish dismemberment of Portugal, more than 100,000 French troops had entered Spain by March 1808. Rioting in Aranjuez on March 17, 1808, led to Godoy's fall from power and Charles's abdication. Ferdinand had been secretly currying favor with the French ruler, Napoleon I, and believed that the latter would support his accession to the throne. Napoleon, however, had decided to end Bourbon rule over Spain. Having brought the royal family to the French town of Bayonne, Napoleon prevailed on Ferdinand and Charles to surrender their rights and installed his brother Joseph as king of Spain. For the next six years Ferdinand was kept under guard in France.

These events touched off an anti-French insurrection in Spain and rebellion against the Spanish authorities in the American colonies, where creole leaders claimed that Ferdinand's captivity had temporarily dissolved the dynastic tie that bound them to Spain. Ferdinand was able to assume the Spanish throne in 1814. During his captivity a *cortes*, or parliament, had drafted a liberal constitution (1812), but it was rejected by Ferdinand, who restored absolutism. Meanwhile, as the colonies moved toward independence, some of Ferdinand's advisers urged a policy of conciliation and the introduction of free trade and other reforms. The king, however, remained convinced that the colonies could be subdued by force. After a military revolt in 1820, he was compelled to accept the constitution, but in 1823 a French army invaded Spain and enabled him to regain his former powers. He was succeeded by his three-year-old daughter, Isabel II, who ruled until 1868.

Figueres Ferrer, José (1906-1990), Costa Rican president. José "Pepe" Figueres was born in rural Costa Rica to Spanish immigrant parents. After graduating from high school in San José, he traveled to the United States where he studied independently for four years. He returned to Costa Rica in 1928, married to a U.S. citizen, and spent thirteen years engaged in commercial farming. In 1941 he became active in the new Center for the Study of National Problems. A year later he was forced into a two-year Mexican exile after publicly criticizing President Rafael Calderón Guardia. While in Mexico he founded an exile organization dedicated to opposing the region's dictators. It later became known, somewhat fancifully, as the Caribbean Legion. When Figueres returned to Costa Rica in 1943, he was hailed by antigovernment factions. He went on to assume leadership of a newly formed political group, Democratic Action, which took the lead in opposing Calderón

Guardia's hand-picked successor, President Teodoro Picado (1944-48). When in March 1948 Costa Rica's Congress annulled the election of apparent victor Otilio Ulate, and declared Rafael Calderón Guardia president-elect, Figueres declared civil war. At the end of an armed contest lasting six weeks he drove Picado and Calderón Guardia into exile. For the next eighteen months Figueres headed a governing junta that carried out reforms of a social democratic character, chief among them nationalization of Costa Rican banks and levying a 10 percent tax on wealth. A constituent assembly drafted a new constitution, notable in that it abolished the national army and extended the vote to women. During the Otilio Ulate presidency (1949-53), Figueres helped found the National Liberation party (Partido Liberación Nacional, PLN). He ran for president as PLN candidate in 1953, emerging with 65 percent of the vote.

During his presidency (1953-58), Figueres greatly expanded government power, establishing semi-autonomous agencies in areas such as electric power, insurance, and banking. He also introduced government planning, directing private-sector activity through subsidies and selective taxation. He established state-supported programs in the area of social welfare, and encouraged import substitution through economic protection. His negotiations with the United Fruit Company, through which that enterprise increased its remission of profits to Costa Rica from 15 to 42 percent, set the pattern for such negotiations in other banana-exporting Latin American nations.

Figueres won international acclaim through his criticism of authoritarian rulers **Rafael Leónidas Trujillo**, **Marcos Pérez Jiménez**, **Fulgencio Batista**, and **Anastasio Somoza García**. During his first presidency he offered sanctuary to victims of those dictators, among them Dominican politician Juan Bosch, and Venezuelans **Rómulo Betancourt** and **Carlos Andrés Pérez**. His was the only nation to boycott the Tenth International Conference of American States in Caracas. In the late 1950s he aided **Fidel Castro**'s insurgency. Figueres was a major Latin American supporter of U.S. President John F. Kennedy's Alliance for Progress during the

1960s. He won a second presidency in 1970, with 53 percent of the vote. Reduced congressional support made his second term less noteworthy than his first, and his attempt to spur economic development through involvement with fugitive financier Robert Vesco besmirched his reputation. Figueres renewed diplomatic relations with the Soviet Union in 1971, and led in the drive for international sanctions against air piracy. Costa Ricans honor José Figueres as the leader most important in helping them solidify their democratic tradition. His son, José María Figueres, became president of Costa Rica in 1994.

Finlay, Carlos Juan (1833-1915), Cuban physician and medical researcher. Of Scottish and French ancestry, Finlay was born in Puerto Príncipe (now Camagüey) and studied at the Jefferson Medical College in Philadelphia, receiving his medical degree in 1855. After his return to Cuba, he practiced general medicine and ophthalmology and began to study the causes of yellow fever. In 1881 he announced to the Cuban Academy of Medico-Physical and Natural Sciences his conclusion that the infection had to be carried by an agent, and that the vector was the *Culex fasciatus* mosquito (now known as the *Aedes aegypti*). Over the next seventeen years Finlay performed numerous experiments to test his theory and published his findings, but they were generally ignored both in Cuba and abroad. After the Spanish-American War, Dr. Walter Reed demonstrated the validity of Finlay's ideas as U.S. officials sought to prevent the spread of yellow fever among American soldiers in Cuba. Cuban nationalists later complained that Finlay's contribution to the eradication of this feared disease had been unjustly overlooked, and worked, with some success, to win him the recognition he deserved. Finlay served as Cuba's chief health officer from 1902 to 1909.

Flores, Juan José (1800?-1864), president of Ecuador. Flores was born in modest circumstances in Puerto Cabello, Venezuela, and received little formal education. He initially supported the royalists in Venezuela's independence struggle but soon switched sides, attaining the

rank of colonel in the patriot forces in 1821. In the late 1820s **Simón Bolívar** conferred upon him supreme military and civil authority in Ecuador, then part of the tripartite nation of Gran Colombia. Meanwhile, his marriage (1825) to a member of a prominent Quito family had cemented his relations with the local elite, and when Ecuador seceded from Gran Colombia in 1830, Flores was named president of the new republic. In 1834 a revolt led by **Vicente Rocafuerte** ended with an agreement whereby Flores pledged to step down at the end of his term and support the accession of Rocafuerte as his successor. Returning to the presidency in 1839, Flores faced severe financial difficulties and clashed with the Catholic clergy over his assertion of the right of patronage over the church and his effort to reform monastic orders. The clergy were also offended by several provisions of a new authoritarian constitution drafted under Flores's initiative in 1843. The constituent assembly elected Flores to a third presidential term on March 31, 1843, but clerical discontent and controversy over proposed taxes contributed to a revolt that led to his resignation on June 17, 1845.

Flores now traveled to Europe, where he attempted to realize a plan he had long harbored: the establishment of a monarchy in Ecuador and possibly Peru and Bolivia as well. He obtained the financial backing of Spain, which was to provide a prince, and began recruiting an expeditionary force there and in Ireland. Three British vessels were also acquired. However, publicity about the enterprise produced complaints from Spanish American governments, and the British government ordered the seizure of the three ships in November 1846. Spain also ended its support.

Flores spent the years 1847-60 in fruitless efforts to regain power in Ecuador. He returned to Ecuador in 1860 to command the forces of **Gabriel García Moreno**, who was attempting to assert his control over the country and repel a Peruvian invasion. After a successful military campaign, Flores remained loyal to García Moreno, whose conservative views he shared. Flores's son, Antonio Flores Jijón, served as president of Ecuador from 1888 to 1892.

Flores Magón, Ricardo (1874-1922), Mexican journalist, considered an ideological precursor of the Mexican Revolution. The second of three sons, Ricardo Flores Magón was born in Oaxaca and educated in Mexico City. He entered law school, but dropped out to pursue a journalistic career in opposition to the dictator **Porfirio Díaz**. In 1900, he and his brother Jesús (b. 1872) founded the newspaper *Regeneración*, dedicated to criticism of Díaz. In 1901, he and like-minded activists organized the First Liberal Congress, which condemned the growing influence of the church and the government's suppression of civil liberties. Before the year ended Flores Magón had been jailed and his newspaper closed. After his release in 1902, he worked for another opposition journal, *El Hijo del Ahuizote*, suffering ongoing harassment by government agents. Banned from journalistic activity in 1904, Flores Magón and his brother Enrique (b. 1877) relocated to San Antonio, Texas, and then in 1905 to St. Louis, after a Díaz-dispatched assassin to San Antonio failed in his attempt on their lives. They resumed publication of *Regeneración*, clandestinely circulating it in Mexico where it was blamed for instigating the Cananea strike of 1906. In July 1906 Flores Magón's Liberal party issued a far-reaching program of political and economic reform and later that year launched several abortive uprisings in Mexico. In 1907 Flores Magón was arrested in Los Angeles and jailed until 1910 for conspiring to violate U.S. neutrality laws. Meanwhile, he had become an anarchist, and when the Mexican Revolution began, he refused to cooperate with **Francisco I. Madero**, whom he considered insufficiently radical. Some of his followers began a revolt in Baja California, but he remained in the United States, ran afoul of the 1917 Espionage Act, and was incarcerated. He died in the federal prison at Ft. Leavenworth, Kansas.

Fonseca, Manoel Deodoro da (1827-1892), Brazilian army officer and first president of the republic (1889-91). A native of Alagoas, Fonseca became a professional army officer and distinguished himself during the Paraguayan War (1864-70), attaining the rank of colonel. He was promoted to brigadier general in 1874 and to marshal in 1884. Extremely popular within the army, he became a spokesman for officers who felt that the monarchy lacked proper appreciation for their services and who wished to air their complaints in public. In 1887 he was chosen president of the new Military Club, which had been founded by politically active officers.

Not a member of the republican movement, Fonseca was initially drawn into a conspiracy aimed at removing the prime minister, the Viscount Ouro Preto, but on November 15, 1889, he disavowed the monarchy and announced the establishment of the republic. He became provisional president in the new, predominantly military government. On February 25, 1891, the assembly that had approved Brazil's new constitution elected him president by 129 votes to 97 for Prudente Morais de Barros, a civilian.

As president, Fonseca, accustomed to immediate obedience in the army, found it difficult to deal effectively with civilian politicians. His conflicts with Congress resulted in his imposition of a dictatorship on November 3, 1891, but military and civilian opposition soon arose. Suffering from poor health and perceiving the strength of the opposition, he resigned on November 23, 1891. Hermes da Fonseca, president from 1910 to 1914, was his nephew.

Francia, José Gaspar Rodríguez de (1766-1840), Paraguayan dictator, known as El Supremo. Francia was born in Asunción, the son of a militia officer. In 1785 he received a doctorate in theology from the highly respected University of Córdoba. After teaching theology at the Royal College and Seminary of San Carlos in Asunción, he practiced law and held several municipal offices. He assumed an increasingly prominent role as Spanish authority waned in Paraguay, becoming identified with the cause of independence from Buenos Aires as well as from Spain. In 1813 he was appointed one of two consuls who were to alternate in power, and in 1814 he was named Supreme Dictator of the Republic. In 1816 this title was conferred in perpetuity.

During his twenty-six years of absolute rule Francia crushed Paraguay's Spanish and creole elite and encouraged miscegenation. The power of the Catholic church, another possible source of opposition, was curbed, and the *cabildos*, or municipal councils, of Asunción and Villa Rica, Paraguay's second largest town, were suppressed. Paraguay's foreign foes were kept at bay while a self-sufficient economy developed, based partly on the production of extensive state-owned lands. Francia gained notoriety in Europe because of his detention of foreigners, especially the celebrated French botanist Aimé Bonpland, who was abducted in 1821 and not permitted to leave Paraguay until 1831. Despite Francia's repressiveness, modern historians credit him not only with providing stability and efficient administration but also with preserving the independence of Paraguay and bequeathing his successors an egalitarian, homogeneous nation.

Frei Montalva, Eduardo (1911-1982), Chilean president and co-founder of Chile's Christian Democratic party. Frei became interested in politics during his student years at Catholic University in Santiago. There he was active in the Association of Catholic Students, representing that organization at an international conference in Rome in 1934. While in Rome, and during subsequent travel and study in France, he became steeped in the socially progressive ideas of Jacques Maritain and other Catholic moral philosophers. Their teachings provided the ideological basis for European Christian Democracy. Returning to Chile, Frei led like-minded conservatives in founding the National Falange, a movement advocating social activism guided by Roman Catholic precepts. His reformist stance led him to break with the hidebound Conservative party in 1938, turning the Falange into a party whose leadership he assumed during the 1940s. In 1946, Frei joined the cabinet of Gabriel González Videla as minister of public works. Later he represented Santiago in the Senate. In 1957, Frei, **Patricio Aylwin**, and others founded the Chilean Christian Democratic party. Frei then used the party to mount an unsuccessful bid for the presidency in 1958. He became Chile's first Christian Democratic president in 1964, a time when national politics were becoming radicalized by the example of Cuba's communist revolution. Centrists and

conservatives, intimidated by growing radicalism in Chilean politics, gave Frei a 56 percent margin over **Salvador Allende**, who represented a leftist coalition. During his presidency Frei sought agrarian and tax reform and "Chileanization" of the copper industry. His efforts met with initial success in spite of congressional opposition. But during the last year of his tenure, 1970, the economy stagnated and inflation increased, both to the detriment of living standards. Meanwhile his party became divided when its more radical members rebelled against Frei's leadership, going on to name their own candidate for the 1970 election. While Eduardo Frei left office a popular president, his moderate reformism fell victim to the intense polarization of Chilean politics. His last years were spent in opposing the two men who succeeded him in the presidency, **Salvador Allende**, and **Augusto Pinochet**, and in working to reunite Christian Democrats. His son, Eduardo Frei Ruiz-Tagle, was elected president of Chile in 1993.

Freyre de Mello, Gilberto (1900-1987), Brazilian historian. Gilberto Freyre grew up in Recife and attended Baylor and Columbia universities (1918-22) in the United States. While at Columbia he was galvanized by Franz Boas, whose lectures challenged racist theories in vogue at the time. The German-born anthropologist criticized racial determinism, stressing rather the impact of environment upon society. Returning to Brazil, Freyre devoted himself to dispelling racist myths; following Boas he argued that it was culture and environment that shaped Brazil and its people, and that miscegenation had played a positive integrative role in forming the nation. Freyre came to national attention when, in 1926, he organized the First Brazilian Congress of Regionalism. Joining his voice with others of Brazil's "Generation of 1922" (among them **Cândido Portinari**, **Heitor Villa-Lobos**, and **Oscar Niemeyer**), he called for national cultural awakening. Freyre's first major work, *Casa grande e senzala* (*The Masters and the Slaves*, 1933), created a sensation. It treated Brazil's slave-based plantation society of colonial times, arguing that African peoples and their culture left a powerful imprint upon national life. His *Sobrados e mucambos* (*The Mansions and the Shanties*) followed in 1936, extending his sociocultural analysis into the nineteenth century. It, too, presented a positive view of Brazilian race relations, portraying Brazilian slavery as more benign than that practiced in Spanish and Anglo-America. Freyre's first two books were especially influential in the United States, where they figured in the rise of comparative studies of slavery and race relations. At mid-century the United Nations chose Brazil as the setting of a major study of race relations, largely as a consequence of Freyre's pioneering work. His *Ordem e progresso* (*Order and Progress*, 1959), completed his analysis of processes leading to the dissolution of Brazilian patriarchy. Freyre's call to extend comparative analysis to Portugal's African colonies, through what he termed "Lusotropicology," was not embraced by the scholarly community. During the last decades of his life he published two novels set in Brazil's Northeast: *Dona Sinhá e o filho padre* (*Mother and Son*, 1964), and *O outro amor do Dr. Paulo* (1977). Freyre entered public life in the 1940s, ultimately serving as Brazil's representative to the United Nations in 1949. He was active in the ARENA political coalition during the 1960s and 1970s. Brazil's most noted twentieth-century historian was awarded an honorary British knighthood in 1971.

Fuentes, Carlos (1928–), Mexican writer. The son of a diplomat, Carlos Fuentes was born in Panama and attended school in the United States, Chile, and Switzerland. He earned a law degree at the National University of Mexico in 1955, subsequently entering Mexico's foreign service. He published his first book in 1954, *Los días enmascarados*, short stories on contemporary Mexico revealing the influence of **Octavio Paz**'s *Labyrinth of Solitude*. Publication of his 1958 novel, *La región más transparente* (*Where the Air Is Clear*), placed Fuentes in the vanguard of a new generation of Latin American writers. While that book continued the theme of corrupted revolutionary ideals, its urban setting reflected the changing reality of Mexican society, and that of Latin America at large. *La muerte de Artemio Cruz* (*The Death of Artemio Cruz*, 1962), the labyrinthine meditation of a dying and corrupted revolutionary hero, was seen as completing the cycle of fictional works exploring failures of the Mexican Revolution. Fuentes celebrated the "boom" in Latin American literature in his critical work *The New Latin American Novel* (1969). In his later novels he reached beyond Mexico to treat European settlement of the Americas, most notably in his epic *Terra Nostra* (1975). Fuentes continued in Mexico's diplomatic service throughout his literary career. He has played a leading role in advancing understanding of Latin America through the electronic media. In 1992 he scripted and narrated *The Buried Mirror*, a film series concerning the European discovery of America and its high Indian civilizations.

Fujimori Keinya, Alberto (1938–), Peruvian president. Alberto Fujimori was born four years after his Japanese parents immigrated to Peru. Though reared in humble circumstances, he was able to earn an agricultural engineering degree at the National Agricultural University (UNA) and a master's degree in mathematics in the United States, at the University of Wisconsin-Milwaukee. Fujimori joined the UNA faculty upon his return to Peru, ultimately becoming the school's president. During the 1980s he hosted a television talk show, and in 1989 took the lead in organizing a broad-based, populist political movement called Cambio 90. Promising to end Peru's economic disarray and combat left-wing violence, he won (June 1990) a surprising 56.5 percent of the popular vote in a runoff election against novelist **Mario Vargas Llosa**. Once in power Fujimori launched a neoliberal economic reform so extreme that it was dubbed "Fujishock." Government budgets were slashed, hundreds of state-owned enterprises sold, subsidies ended, and thousands of public workers fired. Import controls were dropped and foreign investment was recruited. The success of those measures was quickly apparent, most notably in the area of inflation, which dropped from 7,000 percent in 1990, to the low double digits in 1994. In April 1992, Fujimori suspended Congress when it refused to extend his power to act against Communist guerrillas. His *autogolpe* (self-coup), as it came to be known, paved the way for virtual elimination of the Shining Path and Tupac Amaru (MRTA) guerrillas through the capture and imprisonment of their principal leaders, particularly Shining Path founder Abimael Guzmán (September 1992). During 1993 Fujimori presided over the drafting of a new constitution that expanded presidential power, authorized a second, consecutive five-year presidential term, and established the death penalty for terrorists. In April 1995, Fujimori was reelected with 64 percent of the vote, besting former United Nations secretary-general Javier Pérez de Cuéllar. While Peru's economic growth was less striking during the latter 1990s than it had been over the first half of the decade, Alberto Fujimori's popularity remained high. He was lauded for his handling of a lengthy hostage crisis involving seizure of the Japanese embassy by Tupac Amaru guerrillas (December 1996–April 1997). However, his efforts to seek a third term in 2000 produced much controversy.

Gage, Thomas (1602?-1656), English Dominican friar and author of the rabidly anti-Spanish *The English-American and His Travail by Sea and Land . . .* (1648). Gage spent much of his life swimming against the current and fleeing from authority figures. Born into a Catholic English family that had suffered persecution, Gage was educated abroad in France and Spain by Jesuits. Repudiating his mentors, Gage became a Dominican instead in Jerez, Spain, in 1625, which resulted in his disinheritance by his pro-Jesuit father. Beginning an unforgettable voyage to the New World as the Dominican missionary Tomás de Santa María, Gage began to write of his experiences as he traveled the Caribbean to Veracruz and then down to Guatemala. After a decade he grew tired of Guatemala and requested a transfer, which the Dominicans denied, whereupon he fled the confines of monastery life. Traveling the length of Central America to Panama he wrote of the arrival of the Spanish treasure fleet at Portobelo in 1637 and described the fairs where New World gold and silver were exchanged for Old World merchandise. Back in England, via Spain, by 1638, Gage converted to Anglicanism

and became fanatically anti-Catholic. The publication of his travel account was a sensation in England. The English finally had an eye-witness account from one of their own who had actually lived in the heart of the Spanish empire. His prose gave renewed life to the Black Legend of Spanish cruelty, bigotry, and ignorance. To this stereotype Gage gave some pro-English nationalistic flourishes. In spite of these limitations Gage had a keen eye for observation, and his description of the flora and fauna, crops, commerce, and the economy and society of Mexico and Central America is an important primary source, especially for the neglected seventeenth century. In 1655 he accompanied the British expedition that attacked Hispaniola and captured Jamaica, where he later died.

Gaitán, Jorge Eliécer (1898-1948), Colombian politician. Jorge Eliécer Gaitán was born in Botogá to lower-middle-class parents. Educated in law at the National University, he did postgraduate work in criminal law in Rome. Success in the courtroom and fiery antigovernment speeches following the massacre of banana workers by army troops in 1928, earned him fame. Gaitán was a Liberal maverick, and a splendid orator whose populist message won him a worshipful following among the urban poor, especially in Bogotá. He held a number of appointive and elective posts during 1930-46, years of Liberal party dominance, serving as labor and education minister under Presidents **Alfonso López Pumarejo** and Eduardo Santos. In the early 1930s he founded a short-lived political party, the National Union of the Revolutionary Left (UNIR), but failed to make it an entity uniting urban and rural poor against the Liberal and Conservative parties, which Gaitán accused of being dominated by an oligarchy. Gaitán's 1946 presidential candidacy split the Liberal party, allowing Conservative Mariano Ospina Pérez to win the contest. For two years after his loss Gaitán led the dispirited Liberal party. On April 9, 1948, he was assassinated by a lone gunman who was lynched on the spot. The crime sparked a riot during which downtown Bogotá was destroyed (*el bogotazo*), and which had similar but less devastating echo throughout the nation. Gaitán's assassination had profound repercussions for Colombia: it heightened dissatisfaction with democratic politics, giving impetus to the tradition of armed resistance to government that has been a feature of Colombian politics to the present day.

Gallegos, Rómulo (1884-1969), Venezuelan novelist and president. Rómulo Gallegos was born and educated in Caracas. At first he studied law in the capital's Central University, but decided to devote his life to writing and teaching. Among Gallegos's students were **Rómulo Betancourt** and Raúl Leoni. In 1909 he helped found the literary magazine *La Alborada*, and ten years later edited the journal of culture and literature *Actualidades*. In 1929 he published his fourth novel, by far his most famous, *Doña Bárbara*. Through that work, along with *Cantaclaro* (1934) and *Canaima* (1935), he demonstrated his conviction that civilization, in the form of Western culture and capitalist development, would help Venezuela transcend primitive *caudillismo*. Gallegos published six other novels, coming to be known as Latin America's foremost "novelist of the land." He entered politics in 1931, winning a seat in the national Senate. But he chose to exile himself in Spain (1931-35) rather than serve in the puppet assembly of dictator **Juan Vicente Gómez**. Returning to Venezuela following the death of **Gómez** in 1935, Gallegos helped form the prodemocracy Organización Venezolana and served briefly as education minister to President Eleazar López Contreras. In 1941 he ran unsuccessfully for president as candidate of the recently organized Acción Democrática party, losing to General Isaías Medina Angarita. Six years later, following Medina's overthrow and the three-year rule of a junta headed by Rómulo Betancourt, Gallegos again ran for president. Although he won 75 percent of the vote, going on to launch a variety of popular social programs, he could not placate the military, who feared his populism and his social democratic leanings. On November 24, 1948, Gallegos was overthrown in a coup headed by Colonel **Marcos Pérez Jiménez**. He spent the following ten years in exile, returning home a national hero in 1958.

Gálvez, José de (1720-1787), Spanish statesman. Born into the lower nobility in Macharavialla, near Málaga, Gálvez studied law at the University of Salamanca. He had a flourishing legal practice in Madrid when he was appointed *visitador* to New Spain in 1765. This wide-ranging inspection tour lasted six years, during which time Gálvez thoroughly reorganized tax collection and accounting procedures, sacking some officials and jailing others. He instituted the tobacco monopoly and moved trade from Mexican to Spanish merchants. He cut the price of mercury, stimulated investment in silver mining, and increased precious metal production significantly. He improved the defensive perimeter of the northern frontier and put down Indian disorders in Sonora and Chihuahua. His physical collapse forced his return to Spain in 1771, whereupon he took his place on the Council of the Indies to which he had been appointed in 1767. He was made minister of the Indies in 1776 and applied the same *visita* or inspection-tour techniques he had undertaken in New Spain to other parts of the empire. His *visitadores* to Peru and New Granada provoked the Túpac Amaru rebellion (1780-81) and the Comunero Revolt (1781). Farther south, the new viceroyalty of Río de La Plata was established (1776) at Buenos Aires. Gálvez's support for the American Revolution (1776-83) checked English expansionism in North America, won back Florida, strengthened Spanish Louisiana, and ended the English presence on the Mosquito Coast and Darién. He pushed for an empire-wide financial and accounting restructuring along the same lines he had undertaken in New Spain with the addition of powerful regional officials, the intendants, as the workhorses of the new reforms. Many of these changes created significant tension—some historians argue they brought dynamic change while others suggest they caused sterile division—throughout the empire. Whatever the case, the new intendancy system did promote regionalism and supplied the basis for nineteenth century federalism. In spite of his reforming tendencies Gálvez took care of his relatives and placed many of them in high bureaucratic positions.

García Márquez, Gabriel (1928–), Colombian writer and Nobel Prize laureate. Gabriel García Márquez was born and attended primary school in the town of Aracataca, near Colombia's Caribbean coast. He attended high school near Bogotá, and briefly studied law at the National University. During his early years he worked as a journalist, first for *El Espectador*, and, after it was closed by dictator **Gustavo Rojas Pinilla**, for newspapers in Europe and in Venezuela. In 1955 he published his first novel, *La hojarasca* (*Leaf Storm*), and six years later the well-received novela *El coronel no tiene quien le escriba* (*No One Writes to the Colonel*), a melancholy tale about a retired army officer. Other novels and short stories followed, including *Los funerales de la Mamá Grande* (*Big Mama's Funeral*, 1962), a parody of the elites found in every back-country Colombian village. It was during his residence in Mexico—sometimes referred to as an exile forced by the writer's left-wing political views—that García Márquez wrote his great novel *Cien años de soledad* (*One Hundred Years of Solitude*, 1967). Set in a region not unlike the one in which the author grew up, it tells, in highly subjective fashion, the folly of Colombian history, focusing especially on the country's nineteenth-century civil wars. It combines humor, eroticism, pathos, and absurdity, giving them a setting that is at once peculiarly Colombian and, metaphorically, pan–Latin American. Called by critics both a metaphor for the human condition and a recounting of humankind's decline from a state of nature into the corruption and alienation of modern life, *Cien años de soledad* quickly became an international best seller, helping to earn its author the Nobel Prize for Literature in 1982. Some have called it the greatest novel of the twentieth century. One of the work's most notable features is its "magical realism," the blending of the real and the fantastic. The technique has had a significant influence upon writers in Latin America and elsewhere. Other novels followed, notably *El otoño del patriarca* (*Autumn of the Patriarch*, 1975), whose central figure is a parody of the Latin American dictator. García Márquez turned to historical fiction during the 1980s and 1990s, publishing *El amor en los tiempos del cólera* (*Love in the Time of Cholera*, 1985), set in turn-of-the-century Cartagena; and *El general en su laberinto* (*The General in His Labyrinth*, 1989), describing the last days of Simón Bolívar. García Márquez has produced a steady stream of nonfiction works during his career. One of his most recent, *Noticias de un secuestro* (*News of a Kidnapping*, 1996), recounts the 1993 kidnapping of the author's friend Maruja Pachón.

García Moreno, Gabriel (1821-1875), president and dictator of Ecuador (1861-65, 1869-75). A native of Guayaquil, García Moreno studied law at the University of Quito. His marriage (1846) into a prominent Quito family boosted his political career. Although he initially evinced Liberal inclinations, two sojourns in Europe during the 1850s led him to embrace a staunchly Conservative philosophy. He rose to power during a tumultuous period (1859-61) that saw Ecuador divided between warring factions in Quito and Guayaquil and facing a Peruvian invasion. During this power struggle he proposed making Ecuador a French protectorate and continued his overtures to Napoleon III until 1863.

Named president in 1861, García Moreno stepped down in 1865 but undermined his two successors and seized power in 1869. Noted for his devotion to the Catholic church, he signed a concordat with the Vatican (1862) which provided that all education was to conform to Catholicism and gave bishops the power to censor books. The constitution of 1869 established Roman Catholicism as the sole religion of Ecuador and made Catholicism a requirement for citizenship. He gave Catholic religious orders control of the educational system, which expanded considerably, especially during his second term. García Moreno is also remembered for constructing a vital wagon road between Quito and Guayaquil and for beginning Ecuador's first railroad.

García Moreno treated opponents harshly. Among his most famous critics was **Juan Montalvo**. The latter's diatribes against the dictator influenced the assassins who mortally wounded him shortly after his reelection to the presidency in 1875.

Garcilaso de la Vega, El Inca (1539-1616), Peruvian writer and historian. Born in Cuzco as Gómez Suárez de Figueroa to the Spanish captain Sebastián Garcilaso de la Vega and the Inca princess Chimpu Ocllo, he was called El Inca to distinguish him from his father and to underscore his Indian heritage. When his father married a rich Spaniard, he, his mother, and the other children were forced to leave home. Nevertheless, the terms of his father's will did provide him with an annual living. In 1560, a year after his father's death, he traveled to Spain and came under the patronage of his uncle, Alonso de Vargas. He briefly did battle in Granada (1568-70) to put down the Morisco rebellion. In the early 1590s he moved to Córdoba and began to interact with a group of Spanish writers and intellectuals. He translated Leon Hebreo's *Diálogos de amor*, and it was published in Madrid in 1590. In 1605 his first history appeared, *La Florida del Inca* (*The Florida of the Inca*). In it he detailed the problems experienced by the ill-fated expedition of **Hernando de Soto** as it trekked across the southeastern part of the United States. His evocative prose demonstrated a talent for the dramatic rendering of history, which if not always accurate, certainly made for more interesting reading than the standard accounts attempted by chroniclers. For his next project Garcilaso de la Vega drew on the experience of growing up in Peru during the conquest and on what he could remember of the Inca past. *Comentarios reales de los Incas* (*Royal Commentaries of the Incas*) was published in Córdoba in 1609, and the second part, covering the Spanish conquest through the execution of Túpac Amaru (1572), appeared a year after his death as *Historia general del Perú (General History of Peru)*. It was widely read and admired throughout Europe by contemporaries for its engaging prose and obvious literary merit. It revealed that people of Indian heritage could write as well as Europeans. As a primary source, it is fundamental for information on the Inca past and the Spanish conquest. Nevertheless, Garcilaso de la Vega often embellished the record, especially when contrasting the Incas against other Indian cultures, and he saw Peruvian history as a unilinear progression, in three stages, from barbarism to civilization: Before the Incas there was a dark, savage Indian past. With the Incas came civilization and the beginning of natural law. With the Spanish came Christianity and the culmination of civilization. The process paralleled the European vision of history as it moved from paganism to Judaism and the Old Testament and the Romans to the New Testament and the spread of Christianity.

Gardel, Carlos (1890-1935), Argentine singer and popular idol throughout Latin America. Born in Toulouse, France, Gardel was the natural son of a domestic servant who took him to Argentina in 1893. He was raised in a working-class district of Buenos Aires, where he began his singing career. In 1913 he joined forces with José Razzano, a Uruguayan singer, and the duo enjoyed considerable success singing traditional and contemporary songs in theatres and making phonograph records and radio broadcasts. Gardel struck out on his own in 1925 after Razzano's voice failed, and he gained even more fame as a soloist, especially as a singer of tangos, some of which he composed himself. Charming and hard working, he was described as a fine baritone with an excellent sense of rhythm and the ability to penetrate deeply into the meaning of each song. Among his best-known tango recordings are "La cumparsita" by Gerardo Hernán Matos Rodríguez, "Yira yira" by Enrique Santos Discépolo, and "Adios muchachos" by Julio Sanders and César Vidani.

Gardel performed to great acclaim in Spain and France and before Spanish-speaking audiences in New York. In the early 1930s he made several Spanish-language films for Paramount, which spread his reputation throughout Latin America. In 1935 he was touring the Caribbean and northern South America when he was killed in Medellín, Colombia, after the airplane on which he was a passenger failed to take off and collided with another aircraft.

Geisel, Ernesto (1908-1996), army officer and Brazilian president. Ernesto Geisel spent most of his career in the Brazilian army, which he entered at age seventeen. He served in the Brazilian Expeditionary Force during World War II (1944-

45), and attended the U.S. Army General Staff College afterward, going on to help found Brazil's Superior War College. In 1955-56 he was in charge of an oil refinery in São Paulo belonging to Petrobrás, the state oil monopoly, and from 1957 to 1961 he represented the War Ministry on the National Petroleum Council. From 1969 to 1973 he was the head of Petrobrás. Elevated to the presidency in 1974, Geisel relaxed the state's apparatus of repression in response to growing demands that Brazil return to democracy. In a policy of *distensão* (relaxation), Geisel dismantled the special security units formed during the late 1960s, and began lifting restrictions on civil liberties. A nationalist, Geisel worked to strengthen ties with Germany, Japan, and Luso-phone Africa, all in order to establish distance between his nation and its principal ally, the United States. In office during the sharp increase in world petroleum prices, Geisel launched programs aimed at lessening Brazil's dependence on imported oil. In late 1977 he withstood a challenge of hard-line army officers to the *distensão* policy. He resolved it by temporarily closing Congress and firing his army minister. In 1979 Geisel relinquished power to General João Baptista Figueiredo, who continued Brazil's transition to democracy through the policy known as *abertura* (opening).

Gómez, Juan Vicente (1857-1935), Venezuelan president and dictator. Juan Vicente Gómez was born in the western state of Táchira, the natural son of a rancher. He attended school in the city of Cúcuta in nearby Colombia. By early middle age Gómez was a well-established rancher in the region with a taste for political intrigue. He lost his possessions in 1892 and fled to Colombia after joining the failed campaign of **Cipriano Castro**, also from Táchira, to support the continuation in power of President Raimundo Andueza Palacio. Returning to Venezuela two years later, he rebuilt his fortune and by 1899 was ready to support another uprising, Cipriano Castro's successful "Revolution of Liberal Restoration." Once in power Castro appointed Gómez to important posts, naming him governor of the Federal District (1899) and Táchira (1900), army comman-

dant (1902), and vice president (1903). In 1908, Cipriano Castro's dissolute lifestyle forced him to seek medical treatment in Europe, leaving Gómez acting president. Once the dictator reached his destination, Gómez declared himself president, holding power almost continuously until his death twenty-seven years later.

Juan Vicente Gómez was one of Latin America's most long-lived dictators; but unlike many others he was an efficient administrator who left his nation better off than when he first assumed its leadership. His first task was to break the power of regional caudillos, something he did by professionalizing the army. He sent promising officers abroad for advanced training, and invited German, Italian, and French military missions to instruct Venezuelan troops. He reversed Cipriano Castro's xenophobic, abrasive foreign policy, especially regarding the United States. When it was discovered that Venezuela possessed rich petroleum reserves he gave foreign oil companies free rein in exploiting them. Thus Venezuela began exporting crude oil in 1914, within fifteen years becoming the world's greatest petroleum exporting nation. While Gómez was not loath to spend a portion of the nation's vast petroleum earnings on friends and family—among them his scores of natural children—he invested large sums in infrastructural improvements, especially in a national highway system. Gómez's rule was authoritarian: he brooked no interference in his affairs, and used a secret police force to quash all dissent. He did not hesitate to jail or exile political enemies. But Gómez's economic policies made the nation prosperous and won him the support of most citizens. When he died, Venezuela stood ready to progress under a generation of democratic-minded leaders.

Gómez, Máximo (1836-1905), revolutionary leader in Cuba. Gómez was born in comfortable circumstances in Baní in the Dominican Republic. After fighting Haitian invaders and suffering losses in a civil war in 1866, he settled in Bayamo, Cuba. When the Ten Years' War began in 1868, he joined the insurgent forces as a sergeant, rapidly rising in rank as he demonstrated his ability as a strategist of guerrilla warfare.

Gómez favored taking the war into the sugar-producing provinces of western Cuba in order to disrupt the economy and encourage slaves to join the revolution. Civilian leaders of the revolution were ambivalent about Gómez's proposal, and it was not until January 1875 that he crossed the fortified line known as the *trocha*, which Spain had erected to protect the west. However, divisions among the insurgent leaders and the arrival of Spanish reinforcements weakened the revolutionary effort and led to the Treaty of Zanjón (1878) and the suspension of hostilities. In exile in Central America and the United States, Gómez remained committed to the cause of Cuban independence in association with **Antonio Maceo** and **José Martí**, who organized the Cuban Revolutionary party in 1892. Having been named military chief of the revolutionary forces in 1893, Gómez returned to Cuba on April 11, 1895, to renew the struggle. He again waged guerrilla warfare against the Spaniards, advocating a "scorched earth" policy and invasion of the west, which was undertaken in October 1895. Gómez welcomed U.S. entry into the conflict in 1898, though it meant that he and the other Cuban military chiefs would be sidelined. He refused to seek the presidency in 1901, asserting "men of war for war, and those of peace for peace."

Gómez Castro, Laureano (1889-1965), Colombian president. Laureano Gómez was born in Bogotá to middle-class parents. Jesuit educated, he took an engineering degree at Colombia's National University. Upon graduation a Jesuit mentor asked him to edit the proclerical newspaper *La Unidad*, which he did for seven years (1909-16). It soon became apparent that Gómez was an eloquent and vehement defender of church prerogatives and all things Conservative. From 1911 onward he represented the right wing of his party in representative assemblies, at first in the Chamber of Deputies and later in the Senate. During his early years he collaborated with the Liberal party, especially with his contemporary **Alfonso López Pumarejo**, in harassing the Conservative party hierarchy. Moderate Conservative Marco Fidel Suárez (1918-21) resigned his presidency following a fiery Gómez indictment of his shortcomings. Gómez served as Colombia's minister to Argentina (1923-25), and as public works minister during the administration of **Pedro Nel Ospina**. Between 1928 and 1931, he lived in Europe, and near the end of his stay served as minister to Germany. Returning to Colombia, he led Conservatives in opposing Liberal presidents who held power between 1930 and 1946. He founded a newspaper, *El Siglo*, and through its pages rallied his followers against the government. In 1939, after the killing of seventeen Conservatives by Liberal police, he encouraged party members to arm themselves against Liberals. It was Gómez who led the campaign that drove Alfonso López from the presidency in 1945, and it was he who engineered the Conservative return to power in 1946 through the successful candidacy of Mariano Ospina Pérez. Gómez fled to Spain after the assassination of Liberal caudillo **Jorge Eliécer Gaitán** in 1948, and from there launched his own presidential campaign, presenting himself as the man who would save the nation from international communism acting through the Liberal party. He returned in 1949, winning the presidency amid Liberal abstention and escalating political violence. Inaugurated in August 1950, Gómez exercised power for fifteen months before ill health forced him to step aside in favor of President-designate Roberto Urdaneta Arbeláez. Colombia's Violencia reached its greatest heights during Gómez's presidency. Consequently there were few achievements during that period, save for the drafting of a new (and abortive) corporative constitution having elements in common with similar experiments by **Getúlio Vargas** of Brazil and **Juan D. Perón** of Argentina. Gómez lived in Spain following the coup of General **Gustavo Rojas Pinilla** on June 13, 1953. While there he met with Liberal envoy **Alberto Lleras Camargo** to draft the National Front agreement under which Colombia was governed between 1958 and 1974. Gómez returned to Colombia in 1957, and lived in Bogotá until his death.

Gómez de Avellaneda, Gertrudis (1814-1873), Cuban writer. Born in Puerto Príncipe (now Camagüey), she was the daughter of a Spanish naval officer who died in 1823. Nicknamed Tula, she was well educated by tutors, among them the poet José María Heredia, and began writing as a child. In 1836 she traveled with her mother and stepfather to Spain, where she would spend most of her adult life. She soon won acclaim for her literary works while leading an unconventional personal life that included the birth of an illegitimate child who died in infancy. Her first marriage (1846) ended with her husband's death four months later. In 1855 she married a prominent army officer and returned to Cuba with him in 1859. After his death in 1863, she moved back to Spain, where she died.

Gómez de Avellaneda's literary production reflects the romanticism dominant during her early career, though her fiction also possesses realist traits. Her large body of lyric poetry includes the well-known sonnet "Al partir," written upon her departure from Cuba in 1836, and a companion piece, "La vuelta a la patria," written upon her return twenty-three years later. Her novel *Sab* (1841), set in Cuba, is notable for its condemnation of slavery. Her second novel, *Dos mujeres* (1842), raises questions about the institution of marriage. Gómez de Avellaneda also won success as a dramatist, an unusual feat for a woman in her day. She wrote sixteen full-length plays, among them the comedy *La hija de las flores* (1852) and *Baltasar* (1858), based in part on the biblical books of Daniel. Despite her popular and critical successes as a writer, she was rejected for membership in the Royal Spanish Academy in 1853 solely because of her sex. Her writings often refer to the subjugation of women, whom she likened to slaves in *Sab*.

González Prada, Manuel (1844-1918), Peruvian writer. Though born into a wealthy and aristocratic Lima family, González Prada early became an enemy of wealth—and of the Peruvian political and social establishment generally. The War of the Pacific (1879-83), which he protested by closeting himself inside the family estate, convinced him that his country's leadership was hopelessly venal and inept, and that nothing in Peru's Hispanic past merited preserving. He spent the remainder of his life advocating overthrow of the state and its recreation along uncorrupted,

indigenous lines. A prolific writer, author of twenty-one books, González Prada was a modernist who advocated literary invention and economy of style. In 1891 he established a group called Círculo Literario to promote his views. During 1892-98 he traveled and studied in Europe, a period during which he both embraced philosophical anarchism and accepted notions of biological determinism. In his *Páginas libres* (1894), González Prada equated Peru's distress with a pernicious Hispanic heritage that saddled the nation with a pestilential, diseased body politic. Returning home, he persisted in calling for violent overthrow of the state, most importantly in his *Horas de lucha* (1908). Near the end of his life he inspired the young with the rallying cry "old men to the tomb, young men to work!" González Prada became director of Peru's National Library in 1912, following the retirement of **Ricardo Palma**. During his remaining years he conducted an influential salon attended by younger men, whom he moved to action by his calls for revolution. The most important among them were **José Carlos Mariátegui** and **Víctor Raúl Haya de la Torre**.

Goulart, João Belchior Marques (1918-1976), Brazilian president. Born in Rio Grande do Sul, João Goulart was from a ranching family having political ties to **Getúlio Vargas**. When Vargas resigned the presidency and returned to Rio Grande do Sul in 1945, Goulart became his aide and a leader of the Brazilian Workers' party (PTB) in the state. Following his reelection in 1950, Vargas named Goulart head of the PTB. Goulart's ties to labor strengthened when his sister married working-class champion Leonel Brizola, in 1952. Goulart was named Vargas's labor minister in 1953, but soon resigned in a dispute over economic policy. Goulart became president of the PTB following the suicide of Getúlio Vargas, and in 1955 ran successfully for Brazil's vice presidency with **Juscelino Kubitschek**. He won the vice presidency a second time in 1960, in the election that brought Jânio Quadros to the presidency. The populist and reform-minded Quadros had not been in office eight months when he resigned in protest of a conservative-dominated Congress that had denied his reforms. Quadros's action threatened to plunge Brazil into civil war, for many viewed Goulart as a dangerous radical. At length a compromise was worked out through which Goulart could become president (September 7, 1961), but with reduced powers. Once in office he promoted nationalization of foreign-owned industry, pursued a foreign policy designed to strengthen ties with communist-bloc nations, and promoted land reform and other programs aimed at benefiting the nation's poor. His radicalism alienated important constituencies, both within Brazil and abroad. At length, in March 1964, the military ousted Goulart, who fled to Uruguay where he remained until his death.

Grace, William Russell (1832-1904), Irish-born entrepreneur in Peru and founder of W. R. Grace & Co. Grace sailed to Peru in 1851 and joined a firm of ship chandlers in Callao, becoming a partner by 1854. During Peru's guano boom he prospered by sending storeships to the Chincha Islands, from which guano was extracted. In 1866 Grace settled permanently in New York but continued his business ventures in Peru, where his younger brother Michael acted as his representative. In 1871 he launched W. R. Grace & Co. in New York, with Michael and Charles R. Flint as partners. Over the years the firm came to play a major role in the Peruvian economy, engaging in commerce and sugar cultivation and refining, and acting as Peru's agent during the War of the Pacific (1879-83). After the war Michael devised a controversial plan to enable Peru to reestablish its credit by ceding to existing bondholders control of the country's railroads for sixty-six years and making other concessions. Meanwhile, William had become the first Roman Catholic to be elected mayor of New York in 1880; he was elected to a second two-year term in 1884. After William's death of pneumonia on March 20, 1904, the Grace enterprises remained under the control of family members. In addition to its extensive Peruvian operations, W. R. Grace & Co. operated a shipping line to South America begun in 1882, owned a half interest in the Panagra airline, and manu-

factured textiles and other products in several countries. By the end of the twentieth century, however, the company was no longer active in Latin America.

Grau San Martín, Ramón (1887-1969), Cuban president. Born to well-to-do parents, Grau San Martín was a physician and faculty member at the University of Havana. He became an early opponent of President **Gerardo Machado**, suffering exile as a result. By 1931, he was involved in the clandestine, anti-Machado ABC society. Two years later he and other members of that group cooperated with U.S. Ambassador Sumner Welles in the latter's successful campaign to force Machado's resignation (August 12, 1933). Less than a month later (September 4) Grau, along with Sergeant **Fulgencio Batista**, who had led a revolt against Machado's successor, Carlos Manuel de Céspedes, formed part of a five-man ruling junta. Within a week Grau had been named provisional president of Cuba. A nationalist and social democrat, Grau enacted a vigorous reform program. During his brief tenure he abrogated the hated Platt Amendment to the Cuban constitution, and instituted a range of reforms that protected and encouraged labor, set agrarian reform into motion, and extended the vote to women. But Grau's socially advanced program angered Sumner Welles, who branded it "communistic" and blocked U.S. recognition of the government. Grau was forced from office on January 4, 1934. He spent the next decade opposing a series of puppet presidents installed by Fulgencio Batista, and, in the presidential contest of 1940, Grau lost to Batista himself. In 1934 Grau and other social democrats had formed the Auténtico (Authentic) party, dedicated to upholding the ideals of national hero **José Martí**. He campaigned under the Auténtico banner in 1940, and again, successfully, in 1944, winning the presidency in a contest pitting him against Carlos Saladrigas, the candidate backed by Batista. The second Grau San Martín presidency was a bitter disappointment to members of the Auténtico party, and to Cubans generally. Graft and corruption ran rampant as members of the victorious party monopolized government posts and helped themselves to public monies. Grau himself ended his term with a fortune in excess of a hundred million dollars. His successor, Carlos Prío Socarrás, a co-founder of the Auténtico party, was equally corrupt and inept. The failure of Grau and Prío facilitated the return to power of Fulgencio Batista in 1952.

Grijalva, Juan de (1489?-1527), conqueror who first learned of **Moctezuma** and the Aztec empire. Born in Cuéllar, Segovia, Spain, Grijalva was a nephew of **Pánfilo de Narváez** and of Diego de Velázquez, governor of Cuba, all veterans of the conquest of Cuba and future actors in the Mexican drama. Grijalva is remembered chiefly for being outfitted in 1518 by Velázquez with an expeditionary force for exploration and commerce along the Mexican Gulf coast and reporting the existence of a great empire of wealth and riches farther inland. Meeting Indian resistance, Grijalva lacked the daring and imagination to go after the prize and returned to Cuba where a furious Velázquez turned to the less timorous **Hernán Cortés**, who not only outmaneuvered the Aztecs but Velázquez as well.

Guaman Poma de Ayala, Felipe (1535?-1615?), indigenous interpreter, chronicler, and defender of Indian rights. Probably born in San Cristóbal de Suntunto, Ayacucho, Peru, Guaman Poma lived in Cuzco and Ayacucho. Educated in the Spanish language and a native speaker of Quechua, he served as an interpreter in the Spanish campaign (1568-71) against native religious practices. He also appears in various legal records defending Indian land rights, for which he was expelled from Ayacucho (1600) and his home town (1611). In protest he presented the viceroy a 1,200 page "letter" for the king of Spain as *Nueva crónica y buen gobierno* (1615), describing the "real" pre-Columbian and colonial life of the Indians, so that Spaniards could learn and would not forget and the king would reform bad Spanish government. Forgotten and unknown until discovered in the Royal Danish Library in Copenhagen in 1908, it is only recently that scholars have begun to appreciate its significance. They now rank it with **Garcilaso de la Vega**'s *Royal Commentaries* as

one of the most important extant indigenous accounts of the Andean past.

Guerrero, Vicente (1783-1831). Mexican insurgent leader and president (1829-30). Of mixed-race ancestry, Guerrero was born in the state now named after him. In 1810 he joined the forces of **José María Morelos** in southern Mexico. After the latter's execution in 1815, Guerrero remained in the field, being named commander-in-chief of the southern army in 1818. He collaborated with **Agustín de Iturbide** in drafting the pro-independence Plan de Iguala, but broke with Iturbide after he became emperor.

After Iturbide's abdication in 1823, Guerrero was a leader in the York rite Masonic lodges that espoused liberal, anti-Spanish policies in contrast to the more conservative elite-dominated Scottish rite lodges. He was a presidential candidate in 1828 but won fewer votes than the secretary of war, Manuel Gómez Pedraza. Guerrero's supporters refused to accept the outcome and launched a series of revolts that led Gómez Pedraza to abandon his claim to the presidency. Early in 1829 Congress named Guerrero president. During his short term, which was marred by the irregularity of his accession, Congress passed legislation aimed at expelling Spaniards from Mexico, and a Spanish expeditionary force briefly occupied Tampico but was defeated by **Antonio López de Santa Anna**. Slavery was also abolished. Efforts by Treasury Secretary Lorenzo Zavala to introduce a progressive income tax and other new levies aroused criticism. In December 1829 a military revolt led to Guerrero's ouster and the installation of the vice president, Anastasio Bustamente, as chief executive. While leading a resistance movement in the south, Guerrero was captured by a ruse and executed in Oaxaca.

Guevara, Ernesto "Che" (1928-1967), Argentine revolutionary. Che Guevara was born in Rosario to middle-class parents. He attended school there, and at age seventeen entered medical college in Buenos Aires. He interrupted his studies in late 1951 to spend eighteen months traveling throughout South America conducting field research on leprosy. After graduating as a surgeon in 1953, he again left Argentina, at length reaching Guatemala, where he did volunteer work for the government of President **Jacobo Arbenz** (1951-54). Guevara made his way to Mexico after the fall of Arbenz, there meeting **Fidel Castro** in 1955. On December 2, 1956, he fought his way into the Sierra Maestra mountains alongside Castro and other members of the revolutionary July 26 Movement. By then he had become, with Castro's brother Raúl, one of the revolutionary leader's chief lieutenants. It was Guevara and Raúl Castro who led guerrilla forces into Havana January 1, 1959. The handsome and charismatic Argentine went on to become a key member of the regime that replaced dictator **Fulgencio Batista**. He carried out a number of diplomatic missions for the Castro government, and on December 11, 1964, addressed the General Assembly of the United Nations as head of the Cuban delegation. Guevara was a leading theoretician of Marxist revolution in Third World countries, as well as of socialist economic development. In 1960 he published his influential *Guerrilla Warfare*, which taught would-be revolutionaries to operate on the basis of small, highly mobile rural guerrilla units called *focos*. Between 1959 and 1961, Guevara supervised nationalization of Cuba's banking industry. In 1961 he became Fidel Castro's minister of industry, going on to direct an ultimately disastrous attempt to industrialize the island. As one who believed that centralized planning would make market mechanisms unnecessary, Guevara placed the state in charge of all economic activity, going so far as to demonetize the national economy. In 1965, when it was apparent that his economic policies were unworkable, Guevara was removed from his ministerial position and allowed to concentrate on fomenting revolution outside Cuba. He traveled to central Africa where he spent time with Congolese rebels, and returned to Havana in 1966 to plan a guerrilla operation in Bolivia. In November 1966 he rendezvoused with a score of colleagues in rural southern Bolivia, and began campaigning early the following year. The group's presence was detected in March 1967, and within weeks it was hotly pursued by Bolivian army units supported by U.S. military advisors. Most of Guevara's force

died in an ambush on October 8, 1967. Guevara himself was captured and executed a day later. His body was secretly buried, but his remains were discovered in 1997 and sent to Cuba. He continues to be an inspiration to Marxist revolutionaries, as well as a cult figure among the youth of Latin America and elsewhere.

Guzmán, Nuño Beltrán de (1485?-1558), conqueror of western Mexico. Born to a noble family in Guadalajara, Spain, Nuño de Guzmán was a partisan of Diego de Velázquez, governor of Cuba, and an avowed enemy of **Hernán Cortés** and his followers. As governor of Pánuco (1527) he encroached on their territory; as president of New Spain's first *audiencia* (1528-31), he confiscated their wealth, redistributed their *encomiendas*, and jailed many; as conqueror (1529) and governor of New Galicia, he ravaged the Indian civilizations of western Mexico. Noted for his corruption and extreme cruelty, he was a plague on both Spaniards and Indians. Even though this negative picture has come down to us from the followers of Cortés, it appears to be true. Arrested by the second *audiencia* in 1537, he was remitted to Spain. He endured virtual house arrest at the royal court in Valladolid where he was kept on a short leash for the rest of his life.

Guzmán Blanco, Antonio (1829-1899), Venezuelan president. Guzmán Blanco was the son of Antonio Leocadio Guzmán (1801-1884), founder of Venezuela's Liberal party. After studying law, he spent several years as a diplomat in the United States. He returned to Venezuela to take part in the Federal War and negotiated the Treaty of Coche (1863), which ended the war. The dominant figure in the administration of Juan Falcón, he traveled to Europe to negotiate a loan for Venezuela and improved the administration of the country's finances.

Guzmán Blanco served as president of Venezuela on three occasions: 1870-77, 1879-84, 1886-88. Although his methods were authoritarian and he used his office for personal gain, he is remembered as a modernizer who sought to remold Venezuela along the lines of the more advanced societies he had observed on his foreign travels. He lessened the economic and spiritual power of the Catholic church, promoted public education, and embarked on many public works projects, such as highway and railroad construction and the improvement of port facilities. In 1883 he sponsored a lavish ten-day commemoration of the centenary of **Simón Bolívar**'s birth, thereby encouraging the cult of the Liberator. Guzmán Blanco was himself acclaimed "Illustrious American, Regenerator of Venezuela" by the Venezuelan Congress in 1873. Guzmán Blanco left for Europe before the end of his last presidential term, expecting to influence events from abroad. However, his chosen successor, Juan Pablo Rojas Paúl (1888-90), soon asserted his independence and ignored Guzmán Blanco's instructions. Guzmán Blanco remained in Europe until his death.

Haya de la Torre, Víctor Raúl (1895-1979), Peruvian politician. From a middle-class provincial family, Haya de la Torre attended high school and studied law in his home town of Trujillo (1915-17), completing his studies in Lima (1917-20). He first won fame as a leader of Peru's university reform movement, serving as president of the nation's Student Federation (1919-20). When President **Augusto Leguía** closed public universities following student demonstrations, Haya established the González Prada Popular Universities, named for the anarchist intellectual whose salon he had earlier attended, **Manuel González Prada**. Jailed and then exiled because of his opposition to the Leguía dictatorship, Haya traveled to Mexico at the invitation of education minister **José Vasconcelos**. While in Mexico, he founded the American Popular Revolutionary Alliance (APRA), which he hoped would become Latin America's first international political party. APRA was dedicated to anti-imperialism, socialism, and the mobilization of oppressed peoples throughout what Haya called Indoamerica. While APRA never became the regional force that Haya had envisioned, it did become Peru's most important political party of the twentieth century. During the late 1920s Haya traveled and studied in Europe, while there publishing *El anti-imperialismo y el APRA* (1928), a volume calling

for the overthrow of the ruling class and its replacement by Indians, peasants, workers, and the middle class. Haya returned to Peru after Leguía's fall, going on to lose the 1931 presidential contest to Luis Sánchez Cerro. Claiming fraud, Apristas staged an uprising that resulted in Haya's jailing. Freed following Sánchez Cerro's assassination (1933), Haya lived in hiding until 1945, when he emerged to help elect President José Luis Bustamante y Rivero. APRA lost influence during Bustamente's administration, and in 1948 attempted to gain power through force. That prompted the military coup of General **Manuel Odría**, October 1948. Between 1949 and 1954 Haya sought asylum in the Colombian embassy in Lima. He traveled and lectured abroad subsequent to that time, returning to Peru to campaign for APRA candidates in national elections, and to run unsuccessfully for the presidency in 1962 and 1963. While Haya's political ambitions were consistently thwarted by the military, he was throughout his long life the peerless leader of Peru's first mass-based political party.

Hernández, José (1834-1886), Argentine poet and journalist, best known as the author of the epic poem *Martín Fierro* (1872, 1879). Hernández had little formal education and spent much of his youth in the pampas of Buenos Aires province, where he became a skilled horseman and acquired extensive knowledge of the culture and language of the gauchos whom he would immortalize in his poem. After the fall of the dictator **Juan Manuel de Rosas** in 1852, Hernández fought in the federalist armies that resisted the centralizing aims of Buenos Aires. In 1856 he began to write for *La Reforma Pacífica*, a newspaper that sought the incorporation of Buenos Aires province into the Argentine Confederation. After a decade working as a government official and writing for provincial newspapers, he returned to Buenos Aires, where he founded *El Río de la Plata* in 1869. In this short-lived newspaper Hernández advocated provincial autonomy and equitable treatment of the poor. However, his support for Ricardo López Jordán, the assassin of **Justo José de Urquiza**, forced him to close the newspaper and to go into exile in Brazil and Uruguay. He returned to

Argentina permanently in 1875 and prospered in business. From 1879 until his death he served in the provincial legislature of Buenos Aires.

The first part of his poem, *El gaucho Martín Fierro*, is a first-person narrative in which a gaucho troubador (*cantor*) relates his transformation from a self-respecting family man and rural worker into a hunted outlaw. In the sequel, *La vuelta de Martín Fierro*, the title character is reunited with his sons and offers advice on the incorporation of the gaucho into modern Argentine society. The poem is considered an outstanding example of an Argentine literary genre that celebrated the gaucho's independence and way of life, viewing him as the quintessential Argentine, even as authentic gauchos were being marginalized by the forces of modernization.

Hidalgo y Costilla, Miguel (1753-1811), Mexican priest remembered as the initiator of Mexico's independence movement. Hidalgo was raised on an hacienda in Guanajuato of which his father was manager. He studied at the College of San Nicolás in Valladolid (now Morelia), receiving a bachelor's degree in theology in 1773. In 1778 he was ordained a priest. He taught at the college and served briefly as its rector before being removed for reasons that are still not fully known.

In 1803 he was assigned to the parish of Dolores in Guanajuato, where he worked to improve the lives of his parishioners by encouraging various economic enterprises, such as bee keeping and a pottery factory. Hidalgo, who was known for his unorthodox political and religious views, also became involved with Ignacio Allende, a militia officer, and others who wanted to sever Mexico's ties with Spain. On September 16, 1810, he rang the church bells of Dolores and called upon the townspeople to rise against the Spanish authorities. He attracted many Indian and mestizo followers, to whom he appealed by raising the standard of the dark-skinned Virgin of Guadalupe. His forces soon captured Guanajuato, Valladolid, and other cities, and Hidalgo was recognized as chief commander of the movement. His goals are not entirely clear, but he was committed to the end of Indian tribute and the abolition of slavery. However, his inability to control his undisciplined forces not only produced conflict with Allende but also alarmed creoles, who feared that an Hidalgo victory would bring a social revolution harmful to their interests. After Spanish forces inflicted a series of reverses, notably at Calderón, Hidalgo fled northward. He was captured in Coahuila and executed on July 30, 1811. Despite his failures, Hidalgo occupies a prominent place in the Mexican pantheon because of his early support for independence and his identification with the lower classes. September 16 is Mexico's principal national holiday.

Hostos y Bonilla, Eugenio María de (1839-1903), Puerto Rican man of letters and educator. Born in a suburb of Mayagüez, Hostos studied at a secondary school in Bilbao, Spain, and at the law school of the University of Madrid. He left Spain in 1869, disappointed by the failure of the new republican government to grant autonomy to Puerto Rico and Cuba. Meanwhile, he had published a novel, *Peregrinación de Bayoán* (1863), in which he condemned Spain's misrule over its Caribbean colonies. During the next decade he traveled extensively in Latin America, promoting the cause of Cuban and Puerto Rican independence. While in Lima, he also wrote newspaper articles condemning the exploitation of Chinese labor in Peru, and in Chile he advocated the admission of qualified women to higher education. From 1879 to 1888 he lived in the Dominican Republic, where he founded that country's first teacher-training (normal) school and in general worked to reform and modernize its educational system. Difficulties with the government of Dominican dictator Ulises Heureaux led him to move to Chile, where he also devoted himself to education and was professor of constitutional law at the national university. With the start of the Spanish-American War in 1898, he traveled to the United States and Puerto Rico, initially hoping that the island would obtain its independence but later urging the prompt establishment of a civilian government and the granting of autonomy. In 1900 he returned to the Dominican Republic and served as inspector general of public education until his death. Hostos's collected works, published in 1939, total twenty volumes. Among his best-known writings are a long essay on *Hamlet* (1873) and *Moral social* (1888), in which he presented a guide for ethical living in modern society.

Huayna Capac (Huayana Capac; 1488?-1525?), Tahuantinsuyu or Inca "emperor." Under his undisputed rule the Inca empire expanded to its maximum extent although Huayna Capac's conquests were modest in comparison with those of his predecessors. His continued absence from Cuzco, the official and religious center and capital of the empire, and his preference for residing in what today is Ecuador, created tensions and led to the development of a court that rivaled Cuzco's. His sudden death from a smallpox epidemic advancing ahead of the Spanish left a clouded succession and led to a civil war between his sons, the half-brothers Huascar and **Atahualpa**. Their struggle left the empire deeply divided just at the moment the Spanish appeared on the scene and changed the course of history.

Huerta, Victoriano (1854-1916), Mexican army officer and dictator (1913-14). The son of a *mestizo* and his Indian wife, Huerta was born in modest circumstances in Jalisco but gained admission to Mexico's military academy and became a professional officer, reaching the rank of brigadier general in 1901. During the counterrevolutionary outbreak known as the Ten Tragic Days (February 1913), President **Francisco I. Madero** ignored advice and put Huerta in command of federal troops defending his government. On February 18 Huerta joined the anti-Madero rebels in a pact signed at the U.S. embassy that made him provisional president of Mexico. The murder of Madero on February 22 permanently besmirched Huerta's administration.

Many Mexican political leaders endorsed Huerta's accession to power, but he faced mounting opposition from Constitutionalist forces led by **Venustiano Carranza**. President Woodrow Wilson was also hostile to Huerta; he recalled U.S. ambassador Henry Lane Wilson and occupied the port of Veracruz (April 21, 1914) in a transparent effort to weaken the Mexican ruler. As president, Huerta supported reformist programs but governed ruthlessly. In the end he was unable to repel the Constitutionalist army and resigned on July 15, 1914. In June 1915 Huerta was preparing to launch a new revolt with German financial backing when he was arrested by U.S. officials in Texas. He was kept at Fort Bliss in San Antonio and died of cirrhosis of the liver in El Paso.

Humboldt, Alexander von (1769-1859), Prussian geographer and naturalist. Influenced by the rationalist spirit of the Enlightenment, the Spanish crown and its leading ministers supported various scientific missions to the New World some of whose participants and even leaders were foreigners. Securing the permission and the recommendation of the Spanish crown, Humboldt and his scientific companion, the Frenchman Aimé Bonpland, arrived in Venezuela in 1799, laden with the latest scientific instruments for measuring and quantifying the New World according to the standards of the time. His five-year trip through Venezuela, New Granada, Quito, Lima, and New Spain produced a wealth of data (60,000 specimens of flora alone) and duly impressed local officials and scientists who shared with Humboldt their own findings and even official reports. The contacts Humboldt made on this trip served him well when he returned to Europe, as correspondence poured in for the rest of his life updating him on this or that finding. Out of this came Humboldt's masterpieces, the *Voyage aux régions équinoxiales du Nouveau Continent (Travels to the Equinoctial Regions of the New Continent*; 34 vols., 1805-34), *Essai politique sur le royaume de la Nouvelle Espagne (Political Essay on the Kingdom of New Spain*; 3 vols., 1811-12), *Essai politique sur l'île de Cuba (Political Essay on the Island of Cuba*; 2 vols., 1826) as well as many other publications. Humboldt's findings showed that Spanish America was not as unenlightened as European contemporaries believed. Humboldt's trip was like a breath of fresh air for those New World intellectuals whose work was now further stimulated. Creoles gained confidence in themselves and in their homelands on the eve of independence. Humboldt's works are still read with profit today for their social commentary and often unparalleled statistical information, especially on the production of precious metals.

Ibáñez del Campo, Carlos (1877-1960), army officer and twice president of Chile. Carlos Ibáñez gained prominence while serving on a military mission to El Salvador (1903-9), during which he took part in a battle against Guatemalan troops. In 1920 President **Arturo Alessandri** named him director of the Cavalry School in Santiago. Along with senior officers he helped break the deadlock between reform-minded Alessandri and conservative-dominated Congress in 1924. Early in 1925 it was Ibáñez who, along with junior officers, assumed control of the ruling junta and recalled Alessandri from exile. Though Alessandri and Ibáñez worked together in the cause of reform, friction between the two men led the president to resign in October 1925. Ibáñez easily won the presidency in 1927. During his first term (1927-31) he borrowed heavily abroad to finance social programs and improvements in national infrastructure. He also presided over settlement of the long-standing Tacna-Arica dispute with Peru. Onset of the Great Depression ended the president's programs and produced widespread hardship. Chile's economic decline sharpened anger over Ibáñez's authoritarianism, leading him to resign in 1931. Returning to Chile following a brief exile, he allied himself with the political right. That association, and his propensity to military intrigue, were enough to deny him the presidency in 1938 and 1942. But Cold War fears, along with social, economic, and political turmoil following World War II, worked to Carlos Ibáñez's advantage. He won the 1952 presidential election with a substantial plurality. His success lay in his image as a strong paternal figure, his use of mystical and nationalist appeals, and his promise to end political corruption. While continued political and economic turbulence, and his advanced age, made his second presidency unsuccessful, Carlos Ibáñez left office one of Chile's more popular chief executives.

Isabella I (1451-1504), Spanish queen of Castile and León (1474-1504). Isabella came to the throne in a disputed succession that plunged the Iberian Peninsula into a civil war. Portugal and some of the Castilian nobles fought her and her husband, the future **Ferdinand II** of Aragon (1479-1516). She had refused to honor an agreement to marry Alfonso V, king of Portugal, and instead wed Ferdinand in 1469. The latter's succession in Aragon and the Treaty of Alcáçovas in 1479 brought an end to the civil war and allowed the two monarchs to work in tandem to bring peace and order to their two realms and to reestablish royal authority. This project involved greater religious and ethnic conformity. Isabella established the Inquisition in 1480 and launched the war against the Moorish kingdom of Granada in 1482. Its fall ten years later and the expulsion of the Jews in the same 1492 cleared the way for Isabella to support **Christopher Columbus**'s plan to sail west to get to the Far East. The terms of the Treaty of Alcáçovas had established the South Atlantic along the coast of Africa as exclusively Portuguese, except for the Canary Islands, and so the only route open to the Spanish had to be to the west. The subsequent discovery of the New World opened a new frontier where the Reconquest could begin anew. Isabella's religious fervor and sense of destiny carried over into the New World where her conquistadors replicated the Castilian tradition of the Spanish Reconquest that involved the conquest, settlement, government, and acculturation of the conquered peoples. To Isabella's credit she did forbid Columbus's enslavement of the Indians. Certainly "La Católica," as she was called, appeared more "Catholic" than the great Borgia pope, Alexander VI (1492-1503), who signed away to the monarch of Castile all ecclesiastical control (patronage)—including appointments—in Granada, the Canary Islands, and the New World.

Iturbide, Agustín de (1783-1824), Mexican army officer and emperor (1822-23). Iturbide was born to a wealthy creole family in Valladolid (now Morelia). He joined the militia as a youth and from 1810 to 1816 fought against anti-Spanish insurgents, rising to the rank of colonel. In 1816 accusations of financial irregularities led to the loss of his command. Having returned to active duty in 1820, he devised the Plan de Iguala (February 24, 1821), which repudiated Spanish rule but promised social and political stability under a constitutional monarchy. The plan quickly won adherents throughout Mexico and was endorsed by the newly arrived Spanish captain-general, Juan O'Donojú.

Iturbide became Mexico's first monarch on May 18, 1822, but he was unable to cope with the country's serious financial problems and with political opposition in the press and in Congress, which he dissolved on October 31, 1822. By early 1823 republican movements were spreading throughout the country, and Iturbide resigned on March 19. He was exiled to Europe, where he began making plans for a return to Mexico, unaware that he had been declared a traitor and outlaw. He landed near Tampico in July 1824 but was soon captured and executed. Iturbide had achieved independence for Mexico but lacked the legitimacy and political skills to govern successfully.

Jiménez de Quesada, Gonzalo (1509?-1579), conqueror of Colombia. Born in Córdoba, Spain, to a family of Jewish origin that moved to Granada, Jiménez and his father were lawyers. In 1535 the New World beckoned, especially after an adverse legal decision left the family ruined financially. Jiménez joined the large expedition headed for the Indies led by Pedro Fernández de Lugo, the long-time governor of the Canary Islands and recently appointed governor of Santa Marta. With the requisite legal training Jiménez was able to fill various judicial and administrative positions and by default became a key figure in the new colony, now overburdened with too many Spaniards, not enough food, and growing dissatisfaction. An expedition to the interior to carry off the excess was a way out and might find the rumored El Dorado. Suddenly, not yet twenty-eight, without New World experience or training, Jiménez was put in command. Departing Santa Marta on April 5, 1536, the expedition struggled up the Magdalena River and began the ascent into the highlands. The climate and geography took their toll on the greenhorns and only 200 of the original 670 Spaniards entered the Eastern Cordillera near Vélez almost a year later. Once there

however they gathered up 200,000 pesos in gold and 1,815 large emeralds and conquered the Chibchas (Muiscas), the largest and most important Indian civilization in Colombia. Jiménez parceled out Indians in *encomiendas*, founded the city of Santafé de Bogotá, and named the new kingdom New Granada after his home province. Two years later rival expeditions from Coro, Venezuela, and Popayán led by **Nicolás Féderman** and **Sebastián de Belalcázar** appeared. The clever Jiménez convinced the two they should all travel together to Spain and settle their differences before royal authorities while his brother Hernán remained in charge in Bogotá. Even though Jiménez was not allowed to govern the newly conquered kingdom, he did emerge with an annual salary of 2,000 ducats and a permanent seat on Bogota's *cabildo* (town council). As the senior figure and spokesman for the conquistadors, Jiménez represented their interests and wrote several works, of which only *El epítome* (1547) and *Antijovio* (1567) survive. Reliving his youthful success and seduced by the rumors that El Dorado lay to the east, Jiménez got permission to head up another expedition. Of the 300 Spaniards and 1,500 Indians that descended the Eastern Cordillera in 1569 and traversed the vast *llanos* (plains) that stretched toward the Amazon basin, only 50 of the Spaniards and 30 of the Indians made it back three years later. Nevertheless, in 1574 Jiménez was putting down Indian revolts in the Central Cordillera near Mariquita where he died at the age of 70, some say 80, in 1579, afflicted with leprosy.

João VI (1767-1826), king of Portugal (1816-26). After the death of his father, Pedro III, in 1786 and the mental derangement of his mother, Queen Maria, João became ruler in her name, being appointed regent in 1799. He was married to a Spanish princess, Carlota Joaquina, in 1785, but the union was not happy. In late 1807, as a French army was approaching Lisbon, João, Carlota, Maria, and other members of the royal family sailed to Brazil, along with some 10,000 courtiers, artisans, and servants, and a British escort.

The arrival of the royal family in Rio de

Janeiro in March 1808 marked the beginning of Brazil's progress toward independence. In 1808 João opened Brazilian ports to the ships of all friendly nations and lifted restrictions on manufacturing in the colony. He introduced the printing press to Brazil on a permanent basis and established several educational and cultural institutions, including two medical schools and an academy of fine arts. In 1815 he proclaimed Brazil to be a kingdom equal to Portugal. He took this action because of the anomalous situation created by his continued residence in Brazil even after the expulsion of the French from Portugal. In 1816 João became king of Portugal upon the death of his mother.

João returned to Portugal in 1821 in an attempt to assert his royal powers after liberal revolutionaries there convened a *cortes*, or parliament. Before leaving, he is said to have his advised his older son, the future **Pedro I**, whom he left behind as his deputy, to seize the crown of Brazil if independence became inevitable. In Portugal João found himself caught between the forces of liberalism and champions of absolutism, who were led by his younger son, Miguel.

Juan y Santacilia, Jorge (1713-1773), Spanish scientist and naval officer. Born in Novelda, near Alicante, Spain, Juan received an excellent education at the new naval academy (Guardia Marina) in Cádiz. He and **Antonio de Ulloa** were chosen to accompany the French expedition (1735-44) to Quito to effect measurements at the equator. Both were accomplished scientists who personified the best of the new technical training being given to Spanish officers and who represented the rationalist and scientific values associated with the Enlightenment. Their four-volume *Relación histórica del viage a la América meridional* (*Voyage to South America*) appeared in 1748. A year later their secret report to the crown detailed the generalized fraud, corruption, and inefficiency of Spanish administration in the Indies. It was published for the first time in 1826 in England as the anti-Spanish *Noticias secretas de América* (*Discourse and Political Reflections . . .*). In Spain Juan continued his scientific work and his employment as a technical advisor and trouble-shooter for the crown, improving the mercury mines at Almadén, the sea walls at Cartagena, and the arsenal at El Ferrol.

Juárez, Benito (1806-1872), president of Mexico (1858-72). In Mexico Juárez is usually regarded as the embodiment of nineteenth-century liberalism and of national resistance to foreign aggression. He was born in San Pablo Guelatao in Oaxaca, the son of Zapotec parents. Orphaned by the age of four, he eventually made his way to the state capital, where he was befriended by a Franciscan lay brother who sponsored his education. Juárez considered the priesthood but studied law instead, being admitted to the bar in 1834.

Juárez's political career began with his election to the city council of Oaxaca in 1831. He later served in the state legislature and in congress. Elected governor of Oaxaca in 1848, he proved an honest and effective administrator of a moderate Liberal orientation. However, he fell afoul of **Antonio López de Santa Anna**, who exiled him after coming to power in 1853.

After the triumph of Liberalism in the Ayutla Revolution, Juárez was named minister of justice in the cabinet of the provisional president, Juan Álvarez, and drafted the Ley Juárez (1855), which limited the jurisdiction of military and ecclesiastical courts to criminal cases. In 1857 he was elected president of the supreme court, making him first in line to succeed President Ignacio Comonfort, who resigned in January 1858 after a Conservative counterrevolution. In the ensuing War of the Reform (1858-61), Juárez established his capital at Veracruz, where he supported strongly anticlerical measures in 1859. Soon after returning to Mexico City in 1861, Juárez was forced to flee by the French intervention. He moved first to San Luis Potosí, then to Chihuahua, and finally to El Paso del Norte (now Ciudad Juárez).

With the restoration of the republic in 1867, Juárez's government turned to reorganizing the educational system and improving Mexico's finances. His unsuccessful efforts in 1867 to amend the constitution to strengthen the presidency led to accusations that he was bent on dictatorship. His reelection campaigns in 1867 and 1871 produced similar charges. After his death, however, Juárez came to be seen as major national hero, and in 1906 the centenary of his birth was elaborately celebrated throughout the country.

Kahlo, Frida (1907-1954), Mexican painter. The daughter of a German Jewish photographer and his Mexican wife, Kahlo was one of the first women to attend the National Preparatory School. Her studies ended in 1925 after a serious traffic accident that permanently impaired her health. She began painting during her convalescence and received the encouragement of **Diego Rivera**, whom she married in 1929. Both Kahlo and Rivera had extramarital affairs, and they divorced in 1939. They remarried in 1940, however, and Kahlo remained devoted to her husband. Like Rivera, she was a member of Mexico's Communist party.

Kahlo's paintings are intensely personal, revolving around her relationship with Rivera, her physical suffering, and her inability to bear children. They also reflect her strong commitment to her Mexican identity, as in *My Nurse and I* (1937), in which she depicts herself as an infant with an adult's head, at the breast of an Indian woman whose massive contours evoke pre-Columbian art. Her work also has affinities with surrealism. Although she was overshadowed by the internationally celebrated Rivera, in 1938 she made her first important sale to the American actor Edward G. Robinson, who purchased four paintings, and had a one-woman exhibition in New York; the surrealist writer André Breton arranged another show in Paris in 1939. Her fame grew after her death, and she was the subject of a motion picture, *Frida, naturaleza viva* (1984). The house where she was born and died, in the Mexico City suburb of Coyoacán, is now a museum.

Keith, Minor Cooper (1848-1929), American entrepreneur in Central America. Born in Brooklyn, New York, Keith was a nephew of railroad promoter **Henry Meiggs**. In 1871 Meiggs signed a contract with the Costa Rican government for the construction of a railroad linking San José

with the Caribbean coast at Puerto Limón. Meiggs turned the contract over to Minor's older brother, Henry Meiggs Keith, who invited Minor to join him in Costa Rica. When Henry Keith left Costa Rica in 1873, Minor took over the railroad project, which he completed in 1890. Meanwhile, he had married Cristina Castro Fernández, a member of one of Costa Rica's leading families, and had launched several other enterprises in that country. The most important of these was the large-scale cultivation and export of bananas, which he shipped to New Orleans and other American cities. Keith also acquired banana lands in Panama and Colombia. In 1899 he joined his interests with those of the Boston Fruit Company to form the United Fruit Company, which quickly came to dominate the banana industry in Latin America. Keith served as vice president of the company but became less active in its affairs after 1912. In that year he merged Guatemala's railroads into a single company, International Railways of Central America, which was closely linked to UFCO.

Kubitschek de Oliveira, Juscelino (1902-1976), Brazilian president. Juscelino Kubitschek, of Czech descent, graduated from medical school in 1927, after which he traveled to Europe for further study (1927-30). Shortly after beginning practice in Belo Horizonte, he became physician to Minas Gerais state troops sent to quell the 1932 revolt against **Getúlio Vargas**. Thus he caught the attention of Benedito Valadares, governor of Minas Gerais, who made him his secretary. Two years later Kubitschek won a seat in the national Congress (1934-37), returning to private practice upon that body's suspension. Three years later he was named mayor of Belo Horizonte. Enthusiastic and energetic, Kubitschek drew upon modern urban planning theory to modernize the city, at one point hiring Brazil's most famous architect, **Oscar Niemeyer**, to construct an entire new neighborhood. When democracy was restored in 1945, Kubitschek became a founding member of the Social Democratic Party (PSD), going on to win election as a PSD representative to the body that drafted the 1946 constitution. He served as a federal deputy (1946-50), and won the governorship of Minas Gerais in 1951. During his term (1951-55), Kubitschek lavished state monies on highways and electric power generation. PSD candidate for the presidency in 1955, with Vargas protégé **João Goulart** as his running-mate, he won by a small plurality in a bitterly contested race. Kubitschek and Goulart took office thanks only to timely intervention by the military. During his term (1956-61), he presided over rapid economic growth in Brazil. Promising "fifty years' progress in five," he invited massive foreign investment in heavy industry, and borrowed abroad to fund infrastructure improvement. Brazil enjoyed an extraordinary 7 percent annual growth during his term. By 1960 the nation was able to meet half its heavy industry needs, and it completed the import substitution phase of economic development. Kubitschek's crowning achievement was the construction of Brasília, a futuristic national capital located 600 miles inland. While Kubitschek's visionary programs captured world attention for Brazil, they also left the country heavily indebted and subject to spiraling inflation. Kubitschek's plan to run for a second term was thwarted by the 1964 military coup. Following a brief voluntary exile, 1965-67, he returned to help create a democratic anti-government opposition. He died in a 1976 traffic accident. Juscelino Kubitschek was the incarnation of postwar Brazilian confidence and economic nationalism. Brazilians honor him as a man who took their nation far toward realizing its historic claim to greatness.

Landa, Diego de (1524-1579), Franciscan missionary and historian of the Maya. Born in Cifuentes, Old Castile, Spain, Landa came to the Yucatán in 1549. There he participated in the conversion of the Maya, making a great effort to learn their language and culture. His labor was rewarded with the discovery that they had not really converted but had maintained their traditional religion. He became convinced that they were idolaters secretly practicing human sacrifice under the guise of Catholic rites. In 1562 he launched a full-scale investigation as inquisitor and imprisoned and tortured more than four thousand. At least 170 committed suicide or died

from the ordeal. Finally realizing his rush to judgment of collective guilt and punishment was endangering Spanish rule, he sought closure in a great *auto de fe* (act of public faith) on July 12, 1562, in which the survivors were pardoned. Complaints forced him to return to Spain in 1564 where he successfully defended himself and wrote *Relación de las cosas de Yucatán* (*A History of the Things of the Yucatán*). First published in 1864, his analysis of Maya civilization is one of the chief sources of their early history. He was one of the first Europeans to offer an explanation of the meaning of their glyphs. In his haste to convert the Maya he destroyed many of their temples and texts. Ironically, his effort to document his arguments led him to preserve some of these, which are now the main sources for understanding their pre-Columbian past. Landa returned to the Yucatán in 1573 as bishop and died there seven years later.

Las Casas, Bartolomé de (1474-1566), Dominican missionary, bishop, and human rights advocate. Born into a merchant family in Seville, Spain, Las Casas formed a lifelong friendship with a Taíno Indian boy his father had brought back from the New World in 1498. In 1502 Las Casas himself traveled to the Indies where he helped his family in various mercantile activities. His interest in Indians, their languages, and culture grew. He returned to Spain and went on to Rome where he was ordained a priest on March 3, 1507. Back in Hispaniola by 1510, he joined the ongoing conquest of Cuba where he preached and converted the Indians. In 1514 he stunned Spanish settlers by condemning the *encomienda*. He argued that the Indians would freely convert and did not need the tutelage of *encomenderos*. Appalled by the rapid decline of the Indian population, he made his way to the Spanish court and preached against a system that allowed this to happen. Trying to put into practice his belief that Indians could be governed without force, he got royal permission to establish such a community in Venezuela in 1520. It failed. He joined the Dominicans (1523) in response to their earlier condemnation (1511) of the *encomienda* and his crisis of conscience. His reputation and influence at court grew and had an effect. The resulting New Laws (1542) benefitted the Indians and severely restricted the *encomenderos*. Although the crown suspended much of the offending legislation in response to *encomendero* protests and outright rebellion in Peru, at least the principle of reducing *encomendero* power in a piecemeal fashion became part of the royal program. Las Casas was made bishop of Chiapas in 1544. His moralizing there and in Mexico City got him recalled by the Council of the Indies (1547). In 1550 **Charles V** ordered the two sides to debate their respective positions. Juan Ginés de Sepúlveda, one of Spain's great jurists and humanists, represented the opposition and took three hours to present his case that the cultural and moral inferiority of the Indians justified Spanish warfare against them. Las Casas had spent a lifetime campaigning against Spanish mistreatment and in favor of Indian rationality. He took five days. His arguments are detailed in his massive *Historia de las Indias* (written 1520-61) and *Apologética historia sumaria* (written in the 1550s), but it is his widely reprinted, propagandistic *Brevísima relación de la destrucción de las Indias* (*The Devastation of the Indies: A Brief Account*, 1552) that has galvanized readers ever since. Las Casas's arguments brought the Spanish court to a standstill, gave form and substance to the Spanish theory of government and international law, and supplied ample ammunition for those fomenting the "Black Legend" of Spanish wrong-doing. The ensuing historiographical debate has now lasted almost half a millennium.

Lautaro (c. 1532-1557), leader of Chile's Araucanian Indians. Lautaro was about ten years old when captured by Spaniard **Pedro de Valdivia**, who took the boy to Santiago, a stockaded settlement founded in 1541. It was Valdivia's plan to Europeanize Lautaro and use him to assist in the pacification of his tribe, the war-like Araucanians. But Lautaro had other ideas. The young captive spent his five years as stableboy studying the Spaniards and their horses, all the while evolving strategies for defeating them. Around 1547 Lautaro escaped and returned to his people. At the time Valdivia was in Peru helping put down the revolt of **Gonzalo Pizarro**.

When Valdivia returned to Chile he hoped to quickly subdue the Araucanians. At first it seemed that he might do so. In 1550 he founded Concepción and in 1552 Valdivia and Villarica, deep in Araucanian territory. But Araucanian resistance stiffened. Lautaro had by that time emerged as a leader thanks both to his valor and to his understanding of the enemy and their war horses. Lautaro taught the Araucanians to lure the Spanish into narrow defiles where mounted soldiers were vulnerable to lateral assault. The Araucanians soon counter-attacked, destroying the Spanish stockade at Tucapel in mid-1553. In ensuing warfare Lautaro had the satisfaction of capturing and executing Valdivia, on December 25, 1553. There followed an Araucanian counter-offensive that drove the Spanish from settlements in southern Chile, including Concepción, which they destroyed twice, February 1554 and December 1555. Lautaro and his followers fought Valdivia's replacement, Francisco de Villagra, during 1556-57. It was in April of the latter year that Lautaro was killed at the Battle of Peteroa.

Europeans could not but admire the Araucanians and their leader Lautaro. Spanish poet Alonso de Ercilla praised both in his epic poem *La Araucana* (1569-89), one of the New World's first literary works. Independence heroes **José de San Martín** and Carlos de Alvear honored the Araucanian chieftain's memory when, in 1812, they named their secret revolutionary organization the Lautaro Lodge.

Lavalleja, Juan Antonio (1784-1853), Uruguayan military leader, remembered as the initiator of his country's fight for independence. Lavalleja was born into a ranching family. Starting in 1811, he fought against Spanish rule in Uruguay and later supported the campaigns of **José Gervasio Artigas** against the ambitions of Buenos Aires and Portugal in the region. From 1818 to 1821 he was a prisoner in Brazil. On April 19, 1825, he and thirty-two companions crossed the Río de la Plata from Argentina into Uruguay to launch a war of liberation against the Brazilian forces that had occupied the province since 1821. With **Fructuoso Rivera**, he won a major victory over the Brazilians at Sarandí (October 12, 1825), after which the Argentine government accepted the Uruguayans' invitation to incorporate their province into the United Provinces (as Argentina was then called). Lavalleja now became a general under Argentine command in the Cisplatine War against Brazil (1825-28). However, with the collapse of the Argentine government in 1827, Lavalleja took command of the forces opposing Brazil and assumed dictatorial powers in Uruguay, which became an independent nation in 1828.

Lavalleja served briefly as provisional president in 1830 but was outmaneuvered by Rivera, now his chief rival, who became Uruguay's first constitutional president. He twice (1832, 1834) rebelled unsuccessfully against Rivera. In later years Lavalleja became associated with the forces of Manuel Oribe and **Juan Manuel de Rosas** as they jockeyed for dominance in the Río de la Plata. After the fall of Rosas in 1852, he was invited to join a triumvirate with Rivera and Venancio Flores, but died soon afterward.

Leguía, Augusto (1863-1932), Peruvian businessman and president. From a well-to-do provincial family, Leguía devoted the first half of his life to private business concerns. During the 1890s he was an important promoter of Peruvian agricultural exports, notably sugar, cotton, and rubber, and of railroad construction. Leguía entered politics in 1903, becoming finance minister to Presidents Manuel Cándamo and José Pardo. Elected president in 1908, he attempted to give Peru an activist administration geared to advance economic development. But entrenched interests in Congress, controlled by his own Civilista party, blocked his major initiatives. When his term ended Leguía traveled to Europe, living mainly in London. He returned to Peru in 1919, during a time of social turmoil touched off by a sharp postwar economic recession. Capitalizing on Civilista disarray, he campaigned for and won the presidency under a reform banner. When a Civilista-controlled Congress tried to keep him from taking office, Leguía rallied support from the military. He subsequently suspended Congress, purged Civilista office-holders, and decreed a number of reforms that included an eight-hour day for labor and recognition of Peru's indigenous peoples through the declaration of a national holiday in their honor. He addressed concerns of the nation's rapidly expanding middle class through an elaborate employment code. Leguía's principal aim was to speed economic development in Peru by boosting agricultural and mineral exports. To do so he borrowed extensively abroad, expending those monies on ports, railroads, and highways. While Leguía's program did speed modernization, it produced charges of cronyism and corruption that sullied his reputation. He engineered his own reelection in 1924 and 1929, amid growing outcry against his autocratic and increasingly corrupt rule. The collapse of Peru's export economy in 1930 produced his speedy overthrow in a coup led by Lieutenant Colonel Luis Manuel Sánchez Cerro. Augusto Leguía died in prison two years later.

Lleras Camargo, Alberto (1906-1990), Colombian president. Alberto Lleras Camargo was born in Bogotá to a middle-class family, and was educated in the Colombian capital. He earned a politics degree at the Universidad Externado, soon thereafter becoming a journalist at Colombia's leading newspaper, *El Tiempo*. Lleras Camargo served as Liberal party secretary (1930-33) and as **Alfonso López Pumarejo**'s government minister (1936-38), and helped draft López's extensive program of social and political reform. He promoted López's faction of the Liberal party in the pages of *El Liberal*, a newspaper that he founded in 1938, and served as president (1945-46), following López's resignation. Lleras Camargo served as secretary-general of the Organization of American States (1948-54), and became the first rector of the University of the Andes in 1955. During 1956-57 he played a major role in crafting the Liberal–Conservative power-sharing pact known as the National Front, under which Colombia was governed between 1958 and 1974. He became the nation's first president under the National Front agreement. During his four-year term he had major success in reducing the number of deaths caused by La Violencia, the largely rural Liberal–Conservative conflict that had claimed nearly 200,000 lives since 1945. Colombia's GDP expanded at some 5.5 percent annually under his prudent administration. Lleras Camargo returned to journalism following his presidency. He founded the international news magazine *Visión*, which he edited until his retirement in 1978.

Lleras Restrepo, Carlos (1908-1994), Colombian president. Carlos Lleras Restrepo was born in Bogotá and attended school there. He studied law at Colombia's National University, and gained early prominence as a leader of student demonstrations against Conservative president Miguel Abadía Méndez (1926-30). He played an active role in politics after 1930, first serving in the Chamber of Representatives and then as finance minister in the administrations of **Alfonso López Pumarejo** and Eduardo Santos. A self-taught economist, Lleras Restrepo headed Colombia's delegation to the Bretton Woods Conference in 1944. He turned his formidable energies to private concerns, especially banking, following Liberal defeat in the 1946 presidential election, though he did retain his Senate seat. After President Mariano Ospina Pérez suspended Congress and declared a state of siege in late 1949, Lleras Restrepo helped organize armed Liberal self-defense groups in Colombia's eastern *llanos*. He was driven into exile in 1952, but returned two years later. Reelected to the Senate in 1958, he helped win passage of the Agrarian Reform Law of 1962. Lleras Restrepo became Colombia's third National Front president in 1966. The first chief executive in two decades not to govern against the backdrop of La Violencia, he went on to give Colombia an extraordinarily fruitful administration. His more important achievements included a constitutional reform increasing state authority over economic policy, planning, and budgetary matters. He issued a 1967 decree-law reforming monetary policy and strengthening the nation's central bank. That, and related measures, helped Colombia move from an import-substitution model to one that encouraged exports. Lleras promoted agrarian reform during his term, and created a union for agricultural workers. He promoted the Andean Common Market, and worked to moderate the influence of both the United States and transnational corporations in Colombian affairs. After his presidency Lleras Restrepo remained politically active, though he failed to win Liberal support for a 1974 presidential bid. From the 1970s to the time of his death he directed the influential political magazine *Nueva Frontera*.

López, Carlos Antonio (1792-1862), president of Paraguay (1844-62). López was one of eight children of a creole shoemaker and his *mestizo* wife. He was able to attend the Royal College and Seminary of San Carlos in Asunción and later took up the practice of law. He married Juana Paula Carillo, who bore him five children. The eldest, **Francisco Solano López**, succeeded his father in 1862.

López avoided the attention of the dictator **José Gaspar de Francia** by spending most of his time at the family ranch near Olivares. After Francia's death in 1840, López was named one of two consuls who were to rule for a three-year term. In 1844 a national Congress elected him president; he was reelected in 1854 and in 1857.

As president López retained many of Francia's policies, but he lessened Paraguay's isolation and embarked on a program of modernization. Under López education expanded somewhat, and the first Paraguayan newspapers were established. Agriculture flourished, and exports of *yerba mate*, tobacco, and other products increased. Argentina recognized Paraguayan independence in 1852, and diplomatic relations were subsequently established with Great Britain, France, and other countries. Foreign merchants, technicians, and educators entered the country in substantial numbers. William K. Whytehead, an Englishman, was named chief engineer of Paraguay and put in charge of an arsenal and a shipyard as well as construction of the country's first railroad. A German team built a telegraphic network. In 1855 the López government became embroiled in a dispute with the United States when the U.S.S. *Water Witch* defied an order closing Paraguayan waterways to foreign warships and was fired upon by shore batteries at Itapiru. One U.S. seaman was killed. López is regarded as a benevolent despot who left his son a prosperous, well-integrated nation.

López, Francisco Solano (1826-1870), president and dictator of Paraguay (1862-70). López's rule is closely identified with the War of the Triple Alliance (1864-70), which cost him his life and ravaged his country. The eldest son of **Carlos Antonio López**, Francisco was groomed for leadership from an early age. At eighteen he was named commander of a 4,000-man force sent to Argentina to assist the foes of **Juan Manuel de Rosas** in an unsuccessful effort to unseat him. Despatched to Europe in 1853 as minister plenipotentiary, he conducted negotiations with the governments of Great Britain, France, Spain, and the Vatican, and arranged for the firm of J. & A. Blyth to act as general agent for Paraguay in acquiring military equipment, recruiting technicians, and selling Paraguayan exports. In Paris he met Elisa Alicia Lynch, a young Irish woman separated from her French husband. She followed López to Paraguay in 1855 and eventually bore him five children.

Named vice president shortly before his father's death, he was declared president for a ten-year term. López's presidency was dominated by the war against Brazil, Argentina, and Uruguay, which he began in protest of Brazilian intervention in Uruguay's internal affairs. In 1868, as the prospects of a Paraguayan victory diminished, López unleashed a wave of repression against hundreds of alleged conspirators that resulted in dozens of deaths. Victims included his two brothers and two brothers-in-law. As the Allied forces occupied Paraguayan territory, López waged a desperate guerrilla campaign that ended only when he was killed by a Brazilian cavalry unit. López is remembered by some as a national hero and defender of the rights of small states against the ambitions of great powers. Others see him as a megalomaniac who squandered the lives of thousands of his countrymen and destroyed the prosperous nation bequeathed to him by his father.

López Pumarejo, Alfonso (1886-1959), Colombian president. Alfonso López was the son of banker and coffee exporter Pedro A. López. Educated in Colombia, England, and the United States, he spent his early years working in family enterprises. He became active in politics following the Liberal triumph in 1930, becoming minister to London in the administration of President Enrique Olaya Herrera (1930-34). López won the presidency in 1934, going on to launch his Revolution on the March, a reform program so wide-ranging as to be likened to Franklin D. Roosevelt's New Deal. Stressing that property has a social function, López undertook land reform aimed at breaking up large coffee farms and unused private holdings, and selling them to small holders. López also weakened church–state ties. Other reforms included the enfranchisement of all adult males and the streamlining of bureaucratic procedures, especially regarding tax collection. Conservatives, led by **Laureano Gómez**, passionately opposed the flood of Liberal legislation. They especially criticized the firing of Conservative office-holders, down to and including local police forces—a traditional feature of Colombian politics following any shift in political power. López won reelection in 1942; but furious Conservative opposition, financial scandals, and a brief kidnapping of the president by rebellious soldiers during 1944, led him to resign. After transmitting power to President-designate **Alberto Lleras Camargo**, López served two years as Colombia's representative to the United Nations (1946-48). Although retired from politics, he continued to play an important role in national life. During the 1950s he worked to end the bloody Liberal–Conservative strife known as La Violencia that had claimed thousands of lives annually since 1945. He was a principal actor in the bipartisan accord known as the Frente Nacional (National Front), which helped end La Violencia. Alfonso López Pumarejo is considered the most prominent public figure in twentieth-century Colombian history. His son, Alfonso López Michelsen, served as Colombian president from 1974 to 1978.

L'Ouverture, Toussaint (1743-1803), Haitian revolutionary leader. There is uncertainty about the details of Toussaint's early life, but he was apparently born a slave on the Bréda plantation in the North Province of what was then the valuable French colony of Saint Domingue. He became a coachman and veterinarian on the plantation and had acquired his freedom by 1791. In August of that year, as France and Saint Domingue were gripped by internal upheaval, the colony's slaves, who comprised approximately 90 percent of the population, launched a massive rebellion. Toussaint joined the rebels some time afterward, serving as a physician and secretary to the leader Georges Biassou. In February 1793 Toussaint, along with Biassou and several others, gave his allegiance to Spain, which controlled the adjacent colony of Santo Domingo and was at war with the French republic. By now Toussaint was becoming known as L'Ouverture, perhaps because of his ability to find an opening wherever he went. He conquered substantial amounts of territory in northern Saint Domingue for Spain, but in May 1794 he rejoined the French, who had recently abolished slavery in their possessions. Over the next few years he established his ascendancy over Saint Domingue, being recognized as division general and lieutenant-governor by 1797. He forced the evacuation of invading British forces in 1798 and defeated the mulatto chieftain André Rigaud in 1799-1800. In 1801 he extended his sway over Santo Domingo, which had been ceded to France by the Treaty of Basel in 1795.

Although nominally subordinate to France, Toussaint was in fact master of Saint Domingue, and a constitution drafted in 1801 made him governor-general for life with the power to choose his successor. The constitution also abolished slavery, though Toussaint established a system of compulsory labor in order to revive the ravaged economy. He also welcomed the return of white planters. However, Napoleon Bonaparte, now in power in France, was determined to reassert French control over Saint Domingue and dispatched a large force to the colony under the command of his brother-in-law, General Charles-Victor-Emmanuel Leclerc. After initial resistance, Toussaint reached an accommodation with Leclerc, but the latter distrusted him and seized him by a ruse on June 7, 1802. He was imprisoned in a fortress in the French Alps, where he was found dead on April 7, 1803. Neither Leclerc, nor his successor, Donatien-Marie-Joseph de Vimeur Rochambeau, was able to effect the reconquest of Saint Domingue, which became Haiti in 1804. Toussaint, therefore, is recognized as the founder of the nation; he is also a symbol of black liberation from oppression.

Maceo, Antonio (1845-1896), Cuban revolutionary leader, known as the "Bronze Titan." Maceo was born in Oriente province in eastern Cuba, the son of a Venezuelan-born free black and his light-skinned wife, who was also free. At the age of sixteen Antonio became a muleteer, transporting produce and tobacco to market. After the start of the Ten Years' War in 1868, he joined the Cuban insurgents and soon distinguished himself for his courage and mastery of guerrilla tactics, attaining the rank of brigadier general by June 1872. However, his successes aroused the hostility of conservatives in the insurgent camp who accused him of trying to create a black republic on the island, a charge that he vehemently denied.

Maceo rejected the Treaty of Zanjón, which ended the war, and left Cuba on May 10, 1878. Except for a short visit to Cuba in 1890, he spent the subsequent years in exile, mainly in Central America and the United States, as he plotted with **Máximo Gómez** and **José Martí** to renew the struggle for independence. He returned to Cuba on March 31, 1895, soon after the resumption of the war. He initially operated in Oriente, where he was military chief, but later moved westward. On January 22, 1896, his forces reached Mantua, the westernmost town on the island. Meanwhile, he continued to reject charges that he favored blacks and was unenthusiastic about possible U.S. intervention in the conflict. He was killed in a skirmish with Spanish troops near Havana on December 7, 1896.

Machado, Gerardo (1871-1939), Cuban president. Gerardo Machado was a businessman who had fought against Spain in the civil war of 1895-98. Active in the Liberal party, he served as mayor of Santa Clara, and, in 1924, won the presidency as successor to Liberal hero José Miguel Gómez (1859-1913). As president he sponsored public works projects, including a highway running the length of the island. At the end of his first term he altered the constitution allowing for extension of his rule in the face of public outcry. When the Great Depression caused sugar prices to plummet, opposition to the *machadato* escalated. Machado responded by solidifying his support among the Liberal and Conservative parties, while harshly controlling the opposition. Anti-Machado ferment increased sharply in 1931, with formation of the secret ABC society, a group uniting the disaffected middle class, labor, and students. By 1933 the organized opposition harassed the government via strikes, terrorist acts, and even a clandestine radio station. Machado responded with repressive tactics that included the assassination of opposition leaders. Perceiving that Cuba had entered a revolutionary state, U.S. President Franklin D. Roosevelt appointed Sumner Welles U.S. ambassador to Cuba, instructing him to seek a peaceful resolution of the crisis. Welles's pressure and a massive general strike fatally weakened Machado's position. On August 12, 1933, the army demanded and received Machado's resignation. That same day the dictator fled into exile, leaving Cuba in hands of a provisional government soon dominated by military strongman **Fulgencio Batista**.

Machado de Assis, Joaquim Maria (1839-1908), Brazilian novelist, poet, and short story writer, considered the country's greatest man of letters. Machado de Assis was born in a poor district of Rio de Janeiro. His father was a black house painter, his mother a Portuguese woman who died when her son was very young. An epileptic with little formal education, he worked in printing establishments until he secured employment with the Ministry of Agriculture in 1873. Meanwhile, he had published short stories, poetry, and a novel *Ressurreição* (1871). These and other early works reflect the influence of the romanticism dominant in Brazil at the time.

His writings after 1880 are characterized by greater maturity, stylistic innovation, and psychological depth. The novel *Memórias póstumas de Bras Cubas* (1881) is the autobiography of a deceased narrator who recounts his erotic adventures. It has been translated into English under the titles *Epitaph of a Small Winner* and *The Posthumous Memoirs of Bras Cubas*. Machado's masterpiece, *Dom Casmurro* (1899), is also a memoir whose narrator is convinced that his late wife betrayed him with his best friend. Other outstanding works by Machado include the novels *Quincas borbas* (*Philosopher or Dog?* 1891) and *Esaú e Jacó* (*Esau and Jacob*, 1904) and the short story collections *Histórias sem data* (1884) and *Várias histórias* (1896).

Madero, Francisco Indalecio (1873-1913), Mexican revolutionary leader and president (1911-13). The scion of a wealthy and politically influential family from the state of Coahuila, Madero took courses in business and agriculture in the United States and France. After returning to Mexico, he became convinced that the country's ills were attributable largely to the absence of political democracy. When **Porfirio Díaz** indicated in 1908 that he would not seek another presidential term, Madero wrote a book, *La sucesión presidencial en 1910* (1909), in which he called for political reform. Díaz's change of mind led Madero to challenge the dictator himself as the candidate of the Anti-Reelectionist party. He was arrested, shortly before the election, but was able to escape to San Antonio, Texas, in October 1910. By now convinced that Díaz could be removed only by force, he issued the Plan de San Luis Potosí (October 5, 1910), which disavowed the president and called for a revolt against the regime.

After the fall of Díaz, Madero was elected president and took office on November 6, 1911. However, **Emiliano Zapata** and others attacked him for his timid approach to land distribution. He was also opposed by those on the right, such as Félix Díaz, nephew of the dictator, and General Bernardo Reyes, both of whom rebelled unsuccessfully against the government. Their plotting while incarcerated led to the anti-Madero revolt known as the Tragic Ten Days (February 1913). The betrayal of Madero by General **Victoriano Huerta** brought about the president's resignation and his murder on February 22, 1913. Madero thus became a martyr to the cause of the Mexican Revolution. Stanley Ross, his American biographer, called him an "apostle of Mexican democracy," but others fault him for failing to undertake basic socioeconomic reform.

Magalhães, Benjamin Constant Botelho de (1836-1891), Brazilian educator, republican leader, and positivist theorist. Winning an imperial scholarship, the humbly born but precocious Magalhães (popularly known as Benjamin Constant, after the French political philosopher whose namesake he was) received military training and eventually served with distinction in the Paraguayan War of 1864-70. After his retirement from active duty at the rank of major, Constant won further recognition as a professor at Brazil's military academy. A fervent positivist, he taught that his country could progress socially and economically only if it first achieved order. In so doing Brazil must become a republic, ridding itself of antiquated social institutions, chief among which were slavery and monarchy. Brazil's ruler was Constant's patron and admirer, Emperor **Pedro II**. Maintaining close ties with the military, whose interests he defended, Constant urged Marshall **Deodoro da Fonseca** and others to overthrow the emperor. That goal was achieved on November 15, 1889, in a bloodless coup. Provisional President Fonseca named Benjamin Constant his minister of war. Dying just before Fonseca's election as Brazil's first president, Constant was denied the pleasure of hearing Congress proclaim him "founder of the republic," and of seeing the positivist slogan "order and progress" emblazoned upon the new national flag.

Malinche, La (Doña Marina; Malintzin; 1504?-1527?) Aztec Indian woman, translator and consort of **Hernán Cortés**. Sold into slavery as a child owing to the untimely death of her father, to her mother's remarriage, and to her stepfather's refusal to rear the child of another, Malinche passed into the possession of Mayan-speaking Totonac Indians living on Mexico's Gulf Coast. The Totonacs, hoping to placate Spanish soldiers under command of Cortés, who reached their village in March 1519, gave Malinche and other slave women to the interlopers. She was one of twenty Indian women presented to Cortés when he

landed on the Gulf Coast in 1519. After they were baptized, Cortés parceled the women out among his officers with Malinche going to Alonso Hernández Portocarrero. She was barely fifteen. When Portocarrero departed for Spain, she became Cortés's mistress and a key player in the unfolding drama of the conquest of Mexico. Intelligent and fluent in two chief Indian languages of Mexico, Nahuatl (Aztec) and Mayan, Malinche, baptized Doña Marina by the Spaniards, became Cortés's interpreter as he made his way toward the Aztec capital of Tenochtitlán, in the Valley of Mexico. With the repatriation of the Spaniard Gerónimo de Aguilar, who had been living among the Maya as a result of being shipwrecked eight years earlier, the expedition now had an experienced translator. With Malinche they not only got someone versed in Aguilar's Mayan dialect but a native speaker of Nahuatl, the language of the Aztecs. She also quickly learned the language of her new masters. More importantly she revealed the mysteries of Aztec polity, psychology, and cosmology to the Spanish and advised and saved them from fatal traps, such as **Moctezuma**'s planned massacre of them at Cholula. She was a fortuitous trump card in Cortés's successful march on the Aztec empire. Her usefulness to the invaders is suggested in Aztec drawings depicting La Malinche as equal in stature to Cortés. Without her help Cortés might have failed in his conquest of the Aztec Empire. In 1522 she bore Cortés a son, Martín Cortés, one of the first *mestizos* (mixed-blood persons) born on the American mainland, who was later legitimated and taken to Spain at the age of five, and who served as a page to the future **Philip II** and died fighting the Moriscos in Granada. Malinche accompanied Cortés as an interpreter on his expedition to Honduras from 1524 to 1526, in the course of which Cortés arranged for her marriage to a lieutenant, Juan Jaramillo, in 1524. She bore Jaramillo a daughter, María, in 1525. She died very young, not yet twenty-four, probably of smallpox, in Mexico City. Four centuries after her death, nationalistic Mexicans seized upon the historical Malinche, turning her name into an epithet—*malinchismo*—designating one who slavishly serves foreigners to the detriment of one's own people. Her legacy today is a complex, ambiguous, ultimately confused, mix of misogynist nationalism that defines *malinchismo* as the tendency to prefer foreign to Mexican ways.

Mariátegui, José Carlos (1894-1930), Peruvian journalist, Marxist essayist, Indianist, romantic nationalist, and political activist. Born into an impoverished lower-middle-class family, Mariátegui worked as a newspaper typesetter upon completing his primary schooling. In 1918, he embraced socialism. A year later he traveled to Europe on a government scholarship, returning in 1923 a committed Marxist. In 1926 he founded the socialist journal *Amauta*, and two years later published *Siete ensayos de interpretación de la realidad peruana (Seven Interpretive Essays on the Peruvian Reality)*, in which he predicted capitalism's imminent demise and counseled Peruvians to return to their Inca heritage, which he idealized and mythicized as communal and classless. In 1929 the Comintern condemned his ideas as not sufficiently in tune with Marxism-Leninism. Mariátegui countered that Marxist-Leninist solutions did not fully accord with the Peruvian reality. He reasoned that by returning to Inca values Peru could achieve communism without having to experience capitalist industrialism. Mariátegui embraced fellow socialist **Víctor Haya de la Torre**'s characterization of Latin America as "Indoamerica," a region whose Indian and mixed-blood peoples were exploited and oppressed by the developed, Caucasian West. Mariátegui broke with Haya and his APRA party in 1927, becoming a founder of the Peruvian Socialist party in 1928. Though he died prematurely, a victim of cancer, Mariátegui's legacy was an enduring one for Latin American revolutionary socialists.

Martí, Agustín Farabundo (1893-1932), Salvadoran Communist party founder. Martí was the son of a small farmer who reared him to be critical of the country's domination by a handful of land-owning families. He studied law at the National University, and in 1920 took part in strikes called by El Salvador's nascent labor movement. This led to his expulsion from college and his exile,

following which he traveled to Guatemala and Mexico, meeting with leaders of the left in both countries. In 1925, while living in Guatemala City, Martí formed the Central American Socialist party, which he hoped would unite the isthmus under social democratic rule. He returned to El Salvador in 1928, but was soon exiled to Nicaragua. There he met guerrilla leader **Augusto César Sandino** and for a time served as his secretary. By the late 1920s, Martí had become a convinced Trotskyite. He continued his travels during 1929-30, at length reaching San Francisco and making contact with socialist organizations there. The year 1930 found him back in El Salvador, where he founded that nation's Communist party. The January 1931 election of reform President Arturo Araujo hampered Martí's organizational activities. However, Araujo's overthrow in a military coup late that year convinced leftist intellectuals and peasants that the time was ripe for Marxist revolution. Martí and his followers set January 22, 1932, as the date for an uprising against the regime of General **Maximiliano Hernández Martínez**. But the the plan was discovered and its ringleaders arrested. Martí and two of his colleagues were executed on February 1, 1932. By that time the revolution had been crushed with great loss of life.

Martí y Pérez, José Julián (1853-1895), Cuban revolutionary leader and man of letters. The son of Spanish immigrants, Martí was born in Havana and attended a secondary school where he was influenced by the principal, poet Rafael Mendive, who was imprisoned for his anti-Spanish activities. At the age of sixteen Martí himself was jailed for co-authoring a seemingly disloyal letter, but he was soon banished to Spain. He continued his studies at universities in Madrid and Zaragoza, receiving degrees in philosophy and letters and in law. Forced to leave Spain after the overthrow of the republic in 1875, Martí spent the next three years in Mexico and Guatemala. In Mexico he contributed to the *Revista Universal*; wrote a play, *Amor con amor se paga*, which was staged in 1875; and met his future wife, Carmen Zayas Bazán, the daughter of a Cuban émigré. In Guatemala he was a professor at the normal school.

Martí returned to Cuba after the end of the Ten Years' War, but soon ran afoul of the authorities and was again banished. After a brief stay in Venezuela, he settled in New York in 1881 and remained there until 1895.

While living in New York, Martí supported himself with various jobs, including work as a translator and correspondent for the New York *Sun* and South American newspapers. Above all, he dedicated himself to the renewal of the Cuban independence movement, making speeches, raising funds, and founding the Cuban Revolutionary party in 1892. By early 1895 he had chartered three yachts and acquired arms with which to initiate an uprising in Cuba, but federal authorities in Fernandina, Florida, detained the vessels and seized the arms on January 14. Despite this setback, Cuban insurgents launched the revolt on Febrary 24. Martí traveled to the Dominican Republic, where he joined **Máximo Gómez**, the military chief of the movement, with whom he landed in Cuba on April 11, 1895. On May 19 Martí was killed in an engagement with Spanish troops, thereby becoming a martyr to the cause of Cuban independence.

As a literary figure, Martí is remembered mainly for three volumes of poetry: *Ismaelillo* (1882), dedicated to his absent son, *Versos sencillos* (1891), and *Versos libres* (1913). Because of their visionary qualities and remarkable imagery, they are considered early examples of modernist verse. Martí is also remembered for his essays, many of which vividly describe people, places, and events in the United States—for example, Ralph Waldo Emerson, Coney Island, and the Haymarket riot. He admired many aspects of U.S. society and culture but was wary of the imperialistic designs of the United States in Latin America. As Cuban nationalism grew in the 1920s and 1930s, Martí became the subject of a cult that has survived the vicissitudes of Cuban politics, and he remains the country's supreme national hero. Since he never drafted a detailed compendium of his political and economic beliefs, he could be claimed as an ally by people of differing ideologies. In general, however, he was a humanist who sympathized with workers and opposed racial discrimination. Martí also saw

himself as a spokesman for what he called "our America" and became a well-known and respected figure throughout Latin America.

Martínez, Maximiliano Hernández (1883-1966), Salvadoran soldier and president. Maximiliano Hernández Martínez attended military school in Guatemala City and entered the Salvadoran army in 1899. He impressed superiors during a 1906 border conflict with Guatemala, and by 1919 had advanced in rank to brigadier general. A talented officer, he taught at the Salvadoran Military Academy during the 1920s. Martínez (of illegitimate birth, and never legally recognized by his father, Hernández Martínez used only his mother's surname) was elected vice president in elections of early 1931, and served for eleven months with President Arturo Araujo. When Araujo's reform program led junior officers to overthrow him in December 1931, Martínez outmaneuvered them and had himself declared president. The coup moved Communist party leader **Agustín Farabundo Martí** to organize an uprising for January 22, 1932. The plot was discovered, and Martí arrested and then executed (February 1, 1932). Fearing intervention by U.S. Marines, Martínez dispatched troops to crush the rebels. In the slaughter that followed more than ten thousand peasants died, most of them innocent highland Indians. Martínez resisted United States and Guatemalan pressure to step down, and in early 1934 the U.S. recognized his regime. Later that year he had himself elected president, going on to serve until 1944. Some building of roads and public buildings took place during his term, though he did little to promote economic development beyond encouraging coffee exports. His forte lay in his ability to control dissent in the name of a rigid anticommunist policy. Salvadorans chafed under his rule, finally forcing him into exile through a May 1944 general strike.

Matto de Turner, Clorinda (1852-1909), Peruvian novelist, journalist, and advocate for Indians and women. Born near Cuzco, she left boarding school at an early age to look after her widowed father and two brothers. In 1871 she married Joseph Turner, an Englishman; his death in 1881 left her in straitened economic circumstances. Meanwhile, she had begun her literary career in 1876 when she founded *El Recreo*, a weekly magazine published in Cuzco. In 1884 she published *Tradiciones cuzqueñas*, a collection of tales and sketches modeled on the work of **Ricardo Palma**. In 1889 she was named editor of the prestigious Lima journal *El Perú Ilustrado*, but she was dismissed two years later after a seemingly sacrilegious story by a Brazilian writer appeared in the journal. She was also excommunicated by the Catholic church.

In 1889 she published her first and best-known novel, *Aves sin nido* (*Birds Without a Nest*), an early example of the *indigenista* genre. Set in the fictitious Andean town of Killac, the novel attacks the exploitation of Indians by the local priest and public officials. The novel also condemns sexual misconduct by the clergy. Her two other novels, *Indole* (1891) and *Herencia* (1895), develop similar themes. Besides campaigning for improvement in the life of Peru's Indians, she also sought greater educational opportunities for women and their intellectual and economic emancipation. An ally of two-time president Andrés Cáceres, she was forced to leave Peru when he was overthrown in 1895. She settled in Buenos Aires, where she continued to write and became editor of the literary journal *El Búcaro Americano*.

Mauá, Visconde de (Irineu Evangelista de Souza; 1813-1889), Brazilian entrepreneur. Mauá was born in modest circumstances in Rio Grande do Sul. At the age of thirteen he began working for an English importing firm and was made a partner seven years later. At twenty-four he was named manager of the firm. Mauá visited England in 1840 and was impressed by its industrial development, which he hoped to see duplicated in Brazil. Over the next three decades he became Brazil's most important capitalist, promoting or investing in myriad enterprises. However, his espousal of economic liberalism sometimes produced criticism from traditionalists. In 1846 he acquired an iron foundry and shipyard in Rio de Janeiro, where he built seventy-two ships, some of which were employed in a shipping company he

created to navigate the Amazon River. The foundry also produced lamps used in a gas-lighting company he owned in Rio de Janeiro. He was deeply involved in banking, establishing the Bank of Brazil (1851) and the banking firm of Mauá, MacGregor & Cia (1854), which had branches in Argentina and Uruguay as well as Brazil. He also built Brazil's first railroad, a ten-mile line inaugurated in 1854 that linked Guanabara Bay with Petrópolis. This achievement brought him the title of baron. He was elevated to the rank of viscount in 1874 after a company he founded with an English partner successfully laid a submarine cable from Brazil to Europe.

By the mid-1870s Mauá was facing financial difficulties, partly as a result of losses suffered during the building of the São Paulo Railway and the accession of his political foes in Uruguay. In 1878 he was forced to declare bankruptcy. He spent his remaining years managing a small investment house.

Meiggs, Henry (1811-1877), American railroad builder in Chile and Peru. A native of Catskill, New York, Meiggs began his career in the lumber business. In 1849 he moved to San Francisco, where he engaged in real estate speculation; he was forced to flee in 1854 after amassing enormous debts and being exposed as a forger. Settling in Chile, he undertook completion of a railroad line between Santiago and Valparaíso, only one-third of which had been built in 1857. He finished the work in 1863 and used part of his profits to erect a palatial residence in Santiago. He also undertook other railroad projects in Chile. In 1868 he went to Peru, where he signed a contract with the government of President Pedro Diez Canseco to build a railroad from Arequipa to Mollendo. After José Balta became president in August 1868, Meiggs committed himself to the construction or completion of another six railroad lines. The Arequipa line was inaugurated in 1871, but elsewhere Meiggs encountered difficulties. A planned railroad between Callao and La Oroya involved extremely difficult terrain while many workers succumbed to illness. The most serious problems proved to be financial as the Balta government, gripped by railroad fever, borrowed recklessly to finance Meiggs's projects. In August 1875, facing bankruptcy, the administration of Balta's successor, Manuel Pardo, suspended work on the railroads. Meiggs was trying to resume work on the railroads when he died. **Minor C. Keith**, co-founder of the United Fruit Company, was his nephew.

Melgarejo, Mariano (1820-1871), Bolivian dictator. A native of the department of Cochabamba, Melgarejo was a *mestizo* of illegitimate birth. He embarked upon a military career as a teenager and took part in the Battle of Ingavi (1841) as well as numerous revolts. In December 1864 he led a successful military uprising against the regime of José María Achá, governing for the next six years as provisional president and dictator.

Generally considered the worst of Bolivia's nineteenth-century rulers, Melgarejo was notorious for his heavy drinking and dissolute personal life. He lacked a strong base of support but received the backing of the country's silver-mining interests during much of his tenure, which coincided with an influx of foreign capital. In 1866 he approved a treaty with Chile that conceded many of the latter's territorial claims by setting the northern boundary between the two countries at 24° S. and providing for joint exploitation of the nitrate-rich region lying between 23° S. and 25° S. A treaty with Brazil in 1867 granted that nation some 40,000 square miles of Bolivian territory in exchange for the right to navigate Brazilian rivers to the Atlantic. Melgarejo also began an assault on the lands of Indian communities with an 1866 degree that declared them to be state property and required occupants to purchase titles within sixty days or face the loss of their lands. After Melgarejo was forced from power in 1870 by military plotters and an Indian insurgency, the lands lost by the 1866 decree were temporarily restored to indigenous communities. Melgarejo was killed in Lima on November 23, 1871, by his son-in-law, who was also a brother of his mistress, Juana Sánchez.

Mendoza, Antonio de (1490/94-1552), count of Tendilla, viceroy of Mexico (1535-49) and Peru

(1551-52). As the first viceroy in the New World and as the king's alter ego, Mendoza set the standard by which other viceroys have been patterned and judged. He worked in tandem with the *audiencia* of Mexico and their respective roles paralleled those of the king and his councils. As a member of the high Spanish nobility, Mendoza projected a presence that gave stability and respect to royal government in New Spain. He kept the *encomenderos* in their place, put down the Indian uprising in western Mexico known as the Mixtón War (1540-41), withheld implementation of the New Laws (1542), and worked with the church in developing educational, cultural, and social services appropriate to a great kingdom.

Mendoza, Pedro de (1487-1537), Spanish commander and founder of Buenos Aires (1536). Born in Guadix, Granada, Mendoza was entrusted with a large expedition of eleven ships carrying more than 2,000. Intended to cut off Portuguese expansion to the south and to repeat the Peruvian miracle, the expedition was a disaster for the participants. With no precious metals, Buenos Aires was no Peru and the nomadic Indians of the pampas refused to be held in *encomienda*. The Spanish nearly starved to death. Many opted to return to Spain in 1537, even if empty-handed, at least with their lives intact, although Mendoza died at sea. Those who stayed abandoned Buenos Aires (1541) and moved 1,000 miles up river to Asunción, Paraguay, where the semi-sedentary Guaraní Indians could be subjugated.

Menem, Carlos Saúl (1930–), Argentine president. Carlos Menem was born to Syrian immigrant parents in La Rioja province, entering politics there in 1955 and winning elective office on the Peronist (Justicialist) party ticket. In 1973 he was elected governor of La Rioja, but was removed from power and jailed during the purge of Peronists that occurred in 1976. Following his release from prison in 1980, Menem was elected Peronist governor of La Rioja in 1983 and again in 1987. He became the Justicialist party's presidential nominee in 1989, going on to defeat the Radical party candidate in that contest. As president he jettisoned Peronist favoritism toward labor and the military, as well as its policies of state intervention in the economy and protectionism. Menem's currency reform enjoyed unprecedented success, reducing inflation to single digits in three years' time. He opened Argentina to foreign investment, sold many state-owned enterprises, helped create the regional free trading bloc Mercosur in 1991, and heightened Argentina's participation in United Nations peace-keeping operations. His slashing of government budgets and his control of labor brought charges that Menem had betrayed Peronist principles. Yet the general population praised his success in managing the economy. In 1993 the rival Radical party endorsed his plan to amend the constitution allowing a second presidential term. Carlos Menem was reelected to a second four-year term in May 1995. Economic recession during the latter 1990s resulted in a wave of strikes and a lessening of his popularity.

Miranda, Carmen (1909-1955), Brazilian singer and actress. Born near Oporto, Portugal, Carmen Miranda (Maria do Carmo Miranda da Cunha) immigrated to Rio de Janeiro with her parents in 1910. She left school at fifteen, and worked in sales until 1930, when RCA Victor invited her, along with other amateurs, to make a test record. The record became a hit and launched her career. During the 1930s she made nearly 300 recordings for Victor, most of them sambas; starred in two films, *Alô, Alô Brasil* (1935) and *Alô, Alô Carnaval* (1936); and, with her sister Aurora, also a performer, made nine Latin American tours. In 1939 Broadway producer Lee Schubert invited her to New York, where she performed immensely popular theater and night club routines with her samba band. During World War II, as the spirit of Good Neighborliness with Latin America intensified, North Americans embraced the flamboyant star as their symbol of Brazil. Twentieth Century Fox signed her to star in musicals (*Down Argentine Way*, 1940; *Weekend in Havana*, 1941; *That Night in Rio*, 1941) in which she invariably sang and danced sambas, costumed in gaudy carnival outfits topped by headdresses adorned with tropical fruits—stylized versions of the dress of Bahian market women. The best of Carmen

Miranda's Fox musicals, in which she often co-starred with Alice Faye and Cesar Romero, was *The Gang's All Here* (1943), directed by Busby Berkeley, an extravaganza featuring showgirls performing dance routines while holding gigantic bananas. In 1947 she starred with Groucho Marx in *Copacabana*. During the 1950s Carmen Miranda appeared in nightclubs and on television. She died of heart failure following a performance on the Jimmy Durante show, the victim of overwork, a failed marriage, and abuse of barbiturates. She had long battled depression caused in part by her rejection by members of Brazil's cultural elite.

Miranda, Francisco de (1750-1816), promoter of Spanish-American independence. The son of a Spanish merchant and militia officer, Miranda was born and educated in Caracas. In 1772 he traveled to Spain, where he purchased a commission in a Spanish infantry company, and later fought in North Africa and in campaigns in Florida and Barbados during the American Revolution. In 1782, while stationed in Cuba, Miranda, by now a colonel, was accused of smuggling and other irregularities. To avoid punishment, he fled to the United States, thus beginning twenty-five years of travel there and throughout Europe. Between 1785 and 1789 he visited England, Holland, Prussia, Austria, Italy, Turkey, Sweden, and Russia, where he became a favorite of Catherine the Great. In 1792-93 he commanded a division in the French revolutionary army but was later imprisoned and ordered to leave France.

By the mid-1780s Miranda had become an ardent supporter of Spanish-American independence and devoted himself to efforts to enlist the support of foreign governments in achieving that goal. Back in the United States in 1806, he failed to get official backing for his projects but organized a private expedition that reached Venezuela and captured the city of Coro. However, contrary to Miranda's expectations, the inhabitants did not join him, and the expedition failed. In 1808 the British government was prepared to send an expeditionary force to help liberate Spanish America, but the French invasion of Spain in that year and the deposition of **Ferdinand VII** converted Spain from an enemy into an ally of Great Britain, and the expedition was canceled. These events had repercussions in the colonies, where local leaders removed Spanish officials and set up government juntas, as occurred in Caracas on April 19, 1810. Miranda returned to Venezuela in December and assumed a leading role in the revolutionary movement. He argued successfully in favor of an outright declaration of independence but was chagrined over the adoption of a federalist constitution for the new republic. In April 1812 he was made commander-in-chief of the army and given dictatorial powers as royalist forces under General Domingo Monteverde were making gains. The loss of Puerto Cabello to the royalists and other reverses led Miranda to sign a treaty (July 25, 1812) with Monteverde surrendering Venezuela to the Spaniards. **Simón Bolívar** and other patriot leaders considered this an act of treason and in turn took steps that led to Miranda's capture by the royalists. He was eventually transported to Spain, where he died in the prison of La Carraca on July 14, 1816.

Mistral, Gabriela (Lucila Godoy Alcayaga; 1889-1957), Chilean poet and Nobel laureate. Gabriela Mistral was born Lucila Godoy into a lower-middle-class family in rural Chile. Introspective and melancholy by nature, she chose as subjects of her poetry the weak and humble, especially women and children, along with life's mundane pleasures and her nation's natural setting. Between 1912 and 1922, she taught school in rural Chile, all the while publishing her poetry in newspapers and magazines, first in Chile and later throughout the Spanish-speaking world. Mistral first came to national attention in 1914, when she won a national poetry contest with three "Sonnets of Death," dealing with a lost love who later committed suicide. Spanish literary critic Federico de Onís brought her wider attention by sponsoring her first book, *Desolación* (1922). The volume incorporated the passionate "Sonnets," and verse written in a postmodernist style. Late in 1922 Mistral went to Mexico at the invitation of **José Vasconcelos** to aid him in his program of educational reform. By then a popular and established poet, Mistral spent the rest of her

life abroad, serving Chile as a consular representative in Europe and the Americas, and as guest lecturer at universities in the United States and elsewhere. Throughout her travels she wrote poetry and carried on voluminous correspondence. In 1924 she published *Ternura*, a collection of cradle songs for children, and in 1938, *Tala*, an evocation of rural Chilean landscapes written in a colloquial voice. Her most characteristic work, *Tala* was poorly received in Chile, a fact that heightened her sense that as a woman and one of mixed-blood ancestry, her work could never receive a fair reading among the creole literati of her native country. Her sense of despair deepened in 1943 when a beloved adopted son committed suicide. Receipt of the Nobel Prize for Literature in 1945 lifted her spirits, though only briefly. Mistral's last book, *Lagar*, containing poems of grief and loss, was published in 1954. One of Latin America's most original poets, her work stands as a unique evocation of Andean, *mestizo* America.

Mitre, Bartolomé (1821-1906), Argentine statesman, historian, and president (1862-68). Because of its opposition to the dictatorship of **Juan Manuel de Rosas**, the family of Mitre was exiled to Uruguay in the 1830s. There he was active in the anti-Rosas movement; he also lived in Bolivia and Chile. In 1851 Mitre returned to Argentina to take part in the final campaign against Rosas, which ended in his flight in 1852. He supported the separation of Buenos Aires province from the Argentine Confederation, but in contrast to those who favored a permanent withdrawal, he hoped to see its incorporation on favorable terms. After holding cabinet posts in the provincial government during the 1850s, Mitre was elected governor of Buenos Aires province in 1860. By defeating **Justo José de Urquiza** at the Battle of Pavón in 1861, he was able to bring the province into the nation, now known as the Argentine Republic, and became president for a six-year term in 1862. As president, Mitre promoted education and economic development, but spent much of his time as commander-in-chief of the forces of the Triple Alliance during the Paraguayan War (1864-70). Mitre sought the presidency again in

1874 but was defeated by Nicolás Avellaneda. Refusing to accept defeat, Mitre and his supporters launched an unsuccessful revolt, after which he was jailed and court-martialed but quickly pardoned by Avellaneda. Unhappy with the course of events under President **Julio A. Roca**, elected in 1880, and his successor, Miguel Juárez Celman, Mitre helped organize an opposition group, the Civic Union, which chose him as its presidential candidate in 1891. Mitre, however, reached an accommodation with the ruling party and became its candidate as well after he agreed to drop his original running mate. As a result of the ensuing furor, the Civic Union was split, and Mitre withdrew from the presidential contest.

In 1870 Mitre founded *La Nación*, which remains one of Argentina's leading newspapers. He was also a distinguished historian, whose most important works--*Historia de Belgrano y de la independencia argentina* (1876-77) and *Historia de San Martín y de la emancipación sudamericana* (1887-90)--laid the foundations of the historiography of Argentine independence.

Moctezuma II (Montezuma, Motecuhzoma; 1466?-1520), Aztec ruler (1502-20) when **Hernán Cortés** led the Spanish into the capital Tenochtitlán in 1519 and carried out the conquest of Mexico. Moctezuma's poignant legacy is that of a ruler of an "empire" of upward of 20 million who allowed a small band of Spaniards to take him prisoner and make off with a prize demographically and geographically larger than Spain: high drama of the first magnitude. This was no ordinary cacique, but the ruler of a vast state that stretched from central Mexico to the Gulf Coast and south toward Guatemala, the loss of which has fascinated the imagination. Explanations advanced have depicted Moctezuma as deeply religious, vacillating, and awe-struck by the Spaniards and their shrewd leader Cortés, who Moctezuma thought was a returning God, thus fulfilling indigenous myths about a second coming. Given the obvious similarities with Christian beliefs, much of this may be apocryphal and the product of the victor's need to explain one of the great events of history in terms Europeans could understand. What is known is that Moctezuma did

enlarge his empire through conquest, as had his predecessors, moving east into Puebla and Veracruz and south into Oaxaca, but he failed to subdue the Tlaxcalans, traditional enemies of the Aztecs. On his initial march from Veracruz into the interior, Cortés obtained the allegiance of the Tlaxcalans, gained entrance to Tenochtitlán, took Moctezuma prisoner, and neutralized Aztec allies. Spanish sources say Moctezuma died from a stoning by his own people, while Indian sources declare the Spanish killed him.

Montalvo, Juan (1832-1889), Ecuadorian man of letters. Montalvo was born in Ambato and educated in Quito before taking up diplomatic posts in Europe in 1857. Returning to Ecuador in 1860, he founded the magazine *El Cosmopólita* (1866-69). Because of his opposition to the dictator **Gabriel García Moreno**, he moved to Ipiales, Colombia, where he wrote *La dictadura perpétua* (1874), attacking the regime. After García Moreno's assassination in 1875, Montalvo is said to have exclaimed: "My pen killed him!" He returned to Ecuador but soon became critical of García Moreno's successors and again left the country. In 1880-82 he published the *Catilinarias*, vitriolic attacks on Ignacio Veintemilla, Ecuador's new Liberal ruler. From 1881 until his death he lived in Europe. A partisan of liberal democracy, Montalvo is remembered mainly for his polemical writing, but he was also admired as a literary stylist, particularly in *Siete tratados* (1882-83), a collection of essays, and *Capítulos que se le olvidaron a Cervantes* (1895), a novel.

Montesinos, Antonio de (d. c. 1530), first European to denounce mistreatment of native Americans. Montesinos was a member of the first group of Dominicans sent to Hispaniola in 1510. At that time a substantial portion of the island's native Taíno Indian population had already died from disease and from abuse at the hands of Spanish colonists. Montesinos was horrified by the suffering he saw, and by the evil effects of the system of Indian labor allotment known as the *encomienda*. Thus in his Christmas sermon of 1511 he shocked all in attendance, among them the island's largest holders of *encomiendas*, with a blistering indictment of them and of the crown's Indian policy. "You are in mortal sin . . . for the cruelty and tyranny you use in dealing with these innocent people," he said. "Are these not men? Have they not rational souls? Are you not bound to love them as you love yourselves?" he continued. The Christmas homily so angered the friar's listeners that many of them stormed from the church. Montesinos responded by refusing them the rite of communion.

Discontent over Montesinos's campaign on behalf of the Taíno quickly reached Spain. King **Ferdinand** ordered Governor Diego Columbus to discipline the priest and others of his order who supported him. In late 1512 Montesinos was recalled to Spain by his Dominican superiors. He took advantage of his return to personally lay his case on behalf of the Indians before the crown. Montesinos was not allowed to return to America, and he died in obscurity.

Montesinos's actions had two important consequences. First, on December 27, 1512, the crown approved the Laws of Burgos, which aimed at ending the worst abuses of *encomienda*. Second, his arguments helped convince fellow Dominican **Bartolomé de las Casas** to renounce his own *encomienda* and to begin the campaign that ultimately made him colonial Latin America's most effective defender of Indian rights.

Montt, Manuel (1809-1880), president of Chile (1851-61). Montt studied at the Instituto Nacional, a state-supported institution for secondary and higher education, and went on to become its rector in 1835. He held several cabinet posts in the first administration of **Manuel Bulnes**, including that of public instruction, and was responsible for several important advances in education, such as establishment of the National University.

Assuming the presidency amid a civil war, Montt proved to be an able and energetic chief executive committed to conservatism and the preservation of order. His first five-year term occurred during an economic boom fueled by growth in Chilean exports to the gold fields of California and Australia. During his administration railroad construction continued, and the telegraph and gas lighting were introduced. Important reforms included the abolition of entailed estates (*mayorazgos*) and the promulgation of a new civil code drafted by **Andrés Bello**. Montt also promoted foreign immigration.

Montt's second five-year term was marked by political turmoil and by conflict with the Catholic church. As a result of a clash between the administration and Archbishop Rafael Valentín Valdivieso in 1856, Montt's political supporters divided into two camps. Proclerical elements joined the opposition in a Conservative-Liberal fusion while the president's supporters formed the National party in 1857, also known as the Montt-Varista party because of the president's close ties with Antonio Varas, who was Montt's choice to succeed him in 1861. In 1859 a major revolutionary outbreak occurred. Although it was unsuccessful, Varas withdrew from the presidential race, and Montt was succeeded by José Joaquín Pérez (1861-71). After leaving the presidency, Montt headed the supreme court and represented Chile at the Lima conference of 1864.

Morazán, Francisco (1792-1842), Liberal leader and president of the Central American Federation (1830-34, 1835-39). Morazán was born in modest circumstances in Tegucigalpa, Honduras. His paternal grandfather was a Corsican who had emigrated to the West Indies. Morazán first rose to prominence in Honduras, one of the five component states of the Central American Federation created in 1824. In 1827 he became chief executive of Honduras, having identified himself with the forces of liberalism in the region. Over the next year he led an army of Honduran, Salvadoran, and Nicaraguan Liberals in a successful campaign against Conservatives dominant in Guatemala and the federal president, Manuel José Arce, forcing the surrender of Guatemala City on April 12, 1829. Morazán and the Liberals, now in charge, adopted strongly anticlerical policies, expelling nearly three hundred clerics and seizing the property of religious orders in Guatemala. Morazán was elected president of the federation in 1830; he was named to a second term in 1835 after the death of his successor. Morazán's presidency and the federation itself were undermined by regional jealousies, especially resentment over the preponderance of Guatemala. In addition, the anticlerical decrees and other Liberal policies introduced by Morazán's allies, such as Manuel Gálvez in Guatemala, created much acrimony. By 1838 **Rafael Carrera** had emerged as the leader of Conservative forces in Guatemala and proceeded to inflict a series of military defeats on Liberals in Guatemala and on Morazán, scoring a decisive victory with the capture of Guatemala City in March 1840. Meanwhile, the federation had disintegrated as the various states had gone their own way. After a period of exile in Panama and Peru, Morazán landed in Costa Rica in 1842 in an effort to restore the federation. He seized power there but was soon ousted and executed by a firing squad (September 15, 1842).

Morelos y Pavón, José María (1765-1815), Mexican priest and revolutionary leader. Morelos was born in Valladolid (now Morelia), Michoacán, the son of a *mestizo* carpenter. He worked on an uncle's hacienda and as a muleteer before studying for the priesthood. After his ordination in 1797, he was assigned to several impoverished, undesirable parishes. In 1810 he offered his services to **Miguel Hidalgo**, who ordered him to conduct military operations against the royalists in southern Mexico. From 1810 through 1813 Morelos and his forces won control of a large amount of territory stretching from Acapulco to Oaxaca in southern Mexico and embracing parts of Puebla and Veracruz as well.

In 1813 Morelos convoked a congress which met in Chilpancingo, Guerrero, and proclaimed Mexico's independence from Spain (November 6, 1813). On October 22, 1814, the congress, now meeting in Apatzingán, Michoacán, promulgated Mexico's first constitution, which retained Roman Catholicism as the state religion but abolished slavery and distinctions among racial groups. The constitution never went into effect as royalist troops led by Viceroy Félix Calleja scored a series of victories against Morelos and his followers in 1814 and 1815. Morelos himself was captured and executed on December 22, 1815. After his death, Mexico's insurgents continued to wage

guerrilla war against the royalists until independence was achieved in 1821. Despite his failures, Morelos is remembered as a champion of socioeconomic reform, like Hidalgo, but as an abler military and political strategist. In addition to his native city, the state of Morelos, established in 1869, is named after him.

Moreno, Mariano (1778-1811), leader in Argentina's independence movement. Born in Buenos Aires to a government official, Moreno studied theology and law in Chuquisaca (now Sucre, Bolivia), where he was exposed to the writings of Montesquieu and other thinkers of the French Enlightenment and wrote a dissertation condemning exploitation of the Indians. After his return to Buenos Aires in 1805, he was employed as legal counsel to the high court, or *audiencia*. In 1809 he penned a well-known memorial addressed to the viceroy, Baltasar Hidalgo de Cisneros, in which he advocated legalization of trade with Great Britain. Writing on behalf of the landowners and merchants of Buenos Aires, he argued that free trade would encourage exports and increase government revenue. Later that year limited trade with neutral and friendly nations was authorized.

After the deposition of the viceroy in 1810, Moreno became one of two secretaries in the new governing junta, which was headed by Cornelio de Saavedra. During this period he edited the junta's newspaper, *La Gaceta de Buenos Aires*, laid the foundations of Argentina's National Library, and edited a Spanish translation of Rousseau's *Contrat social* (omitting passages hostile to religion). However, Moreno clashed with Saavedra over the role to be played by provincial representatives in the junta and resigned his position. He died while en route to England on a diplomatic mission. Because of his cosmopolitan views and support of free trade and the interests of Buenos Aires, he is considered a precursor of the Unitarian party.

Mosquera, Tomás Cipriano de (1798-1878), Colombian general and president. Mosquera was born in Popayán to an aristocratic family. An older brother, Joaquín, served briefly as president in 1830 and as vice president in 1833-35. A younger brother, Manuel José, was archbishop of Bogotá in 1835-53. Tomás saw service as an officer in the patriot forces during the wars of independence and distinguished himself for his loyalty to **Simón Bolívar** in the internal disputes that gripped Gran Colombia in the late 1820s. After several years in Peru, Europe, and the United States, Mosquera served in Congress and as minister of war. He commanded government forces during the War of the Supremes (1839-42) and acquired a reputation for harshness toward his foes. Succeeding his son-in-law, Pedro A. Herrán, in the presidency, Mosquera gave Colombia an administration (1845-49) notable for innovation and reform: tariffs were reduced, steps were taken to end the state's tobacco monopoly, and steam navigation was permanently introduced to the Magdalena River.

After running unsuccessfully for the presidency in 1856, Mosquera became governor of the state of Cauca in 1858. Although he had always been linked to the Conservative party, in 1860 he disavowed the Conservative president, Mariano Ospina Rodríguez, and led a successful revolt against him with the support of the Liberal party. As provisional president, he issued a series of controversial anticlerical decrees that divested the Catholic church of its property, suppressed religious orders, and in general asserted government control over the clergy. In 1863 delegates to the constitutional convention of Rionegro elected him president for a one-year term, and he was elected in 1866 to serve a full two-year term. The dominant Liberals had always distrusted Mosquera because of his Conservative antecedents and reputation for arbitrary behavior. Their suspicions were confirmed when he clashed with Congress and ordered its closure on April 29, 1867. On May 23, 1867, Liberal plotters removed him from the presidency. After a period of exile in Peru, he served as governor of Cauca (1871-73) and as senator from that state (1876-77).

Muñoz Marín, Luis (1898-1980), Puerto Rican governor. Luis Muñoz Marín was the son of Puerto Rican political leader **Luis Muñoz Rivera**. He received his early education in the United States, during the years that his father edited the

Puerto Rico Herald in New York City (1901-4), and served as the island's commissioner in the U.S. House of Representatives (1910-16). Muñoz Marín attended college in the United States and remained there through the 1920s, a period during which he contributed articles and poetry to the *Nation*, the *New Republic*, and the *American Mercury*. During the 1920s he supported Puerto Rican independence, and was affiliated with the island's Socialist party. But by 1931 had returned home to play an active role in Liberal party politics. Until 1936 he was highly successful in securing U.S. aid for Puerto Rico through his contacts in the government of Franklin D. Roosevelt. He lost much of that support, however, in months following the February 23, 1936, assassination, by two Puerto Rican nationalists, of the island's police chief, Francis Riggs. Muñoz angered the United States when, after perpetrators of the murder were lynched by U.S. nationals while in police custody, he refused to condemn the men who had shot Riggs.

In 1938, Muñoz founded the Popular Democratic party (PPD, Partido Popular Democrático). The PPD soon dominated Puerto Rican politics. Its supporters made Muñoz Puerto Rico's first democratically elected governor in 1948, reelecting him to the post in 1952, 1956, and 1960. During that time Muñoz pursued two chief initiatives: first, he worked to industrialize the island through a program called Operation Bootstrap (Operación Manos a la Obra); second, he promoted Puerto Rican commonwealth status within the U.S. federal system (as opposed to outright independence or statehood). Through Operation Bootstrap, Puerto Rico achieved significant industrialization, chiefly through tax incentives to mainland companies that moved to the island. He was able to proclaim Puerto Rico an Associated Free State (Estado Libre Asociado) of the United States in 1952, following ratification of the island's first constitution. Sixty percent of Puerto Ricans endorsed his call for continuance of commonwealth status in a plebiscite held in July 1967 (as opposed to 39 percent voting for statehood). Muñoz Marín remained active in Puerto Rican politics until his death.

Muñoz Rivera, Luis (1859-1916), Puerto Rican political leader and journalist. Born in Barranquitas, Muñoz Rivera began his political career in the mid-1880s and was a founder of the Autonomist party in 1887. In 1891 he founded a newspaper, *La Democracia*, in Ponce, in which he urged political autonomy for Puerto Rico. To achieve this goal, he favored forming an alliance with a Spanish monarchist party, the Liberal Fusionists, who were led by Práxedes Mateo Sagasta. Muñoz Rivera's stand split the Autonomists but bore fruit late in 1897 when Sagasta, recently named prime minister, issued a charter granting autonomy to Puerto Rico. Muñoz Rivera became secretary of justice and government in the new regime, but its existence was cut short by U.S. occupation of the island in 1898.

With the establishment of American rule over the island, Muñoz Rivera pressed for self-government and was critical of the Foraker Act of 1900, which subordinated the elective lower house of the legislature to the appointed governor and Executive Council. In 1901 he moved to New York, where he established the *Puerto Rico Herald*, a bilingual newspaper, to promote the island's interests. Back in Puerto Rico in 1904, he formed the Unionist party, which soon came to dominate island politics. From 1910 to 1916 Muñoz Rivera served as Puerto Rico's resident commissioner in Washington. Although he died before the Jones Act of 1917 was signed, he supported the legislation, which conferred U.S. citizenship upon Puerto Ricans and replaced the Executive Council with an elected Senate. Muñoz Rivera's son, **Luis Muñoz Marín**, would continue his fight for self-government. Also noted as a poet, Muñoz Rivera published two collections, *Retama* (1891) and *Tropicales* (1902).

Murillo Toro, Manuel (1816-1880), president of Colombia (1864-66, 1872-74). Murillo was born in modest circumstances in Chaparral, Tolima. After obtaining a law degree in 1836, he became an activist in the embryonic Liberal party, fighting in the War of the Supremes (1839-42) and later editing the *Gaceta Mercantil*, a newspaper in Santa Marta. He served as secretary of finance during the administration of José Hilario López (1849-53) and, after an unsuccessful bid for the presidency in 1856, as president (governor) of the state of Santander (1857-59). During this period Murillo was a leader of the Gólgota faction of the Liberal party and advocated an extreme form of *laissez faire*, arguing that governments should play no role in infrastructure development or even education.

Murillo supported the rebellion (1860) of **Tomás Cipriano de Mosquera** against the administration of Conservative Mariano Ospina Rodríguez. After serving as Colombian minister in Washington, he was elected to a two-year presidential term during which he made conciliatory gestures toward the Catholic church and accepted Conservative control of the important state of Antioquia. By 1872, when he again became president, he had modified some of his earlier views and urged government support for railroad construction. He also believed that government action was sometimes needed to assist disadvantaged members of society. He remained an influential Liberal strategist until his death, often attacked as the head of a corrupt political "oligarchy" inhospitable to new men and new ideas.

Nabuco, Joaquim (1849-1910), Brazilian abolitionist, diplomat, and man of letters. Nabuco was born in Recife to parents of distinguished lineage. He attended the prestigious Pedro II College in Rio de Janeiro and later studied law, receiving his degree in 1870. During the next few years he traveled and served Brazil as a diplomat in Washington and London (1876-78). After the death of his father, a prominent Liberal statesman, in 1878, Nabuco began his own political career, winning election to the lower house of parliament. Nabuco spoke in favor of religious liberty and political reform, but he became known above all for his abolitionist views. In 1880 he was a cofounder of the Brazilian Anti-Slavery Society and, while living in London, wrote *O Abolicionismo* (1883), a condemnation of Brazilian slavery. After his return to Brazil, he continued his anti-slavery activism in parliament and in the press until 1888, when slavery was finally abolished. Nabuco retired from public life after the overthrow of **Pedro II**, to whom he was devoted; he was also doubtful about the benefits of a republic. During this period he dedicated himself to writing and produced a biography of his father, *Um estadista do império* (1888-89) and an autobiography, *Minha formação* (1900). He later became reconciled to the republican system and in 1900 accepted the position of minister to London. In this post he was occupied mainly with the defense of Brazilian claims in a boundary dispute with British Guiana. Nabuco considered the arbitral award (1904) by the king of Italy a defeat for Brazil. In 1905 he went to Washington as Brazil's first ambassador to the United States, playing an important role in the subsequent warming of relations between the two countries. He died in Washington.

Nariño, Antonio (1765-1823), Colombian precursor of independence. Born in Bogotá of a prominent family, Nariño first gained notoriety in 1794 after he translated and printed about one hundred copies of the French Declaration of the Rights of Man. Fearful of the consequences of his action, he destroyed many of the copies and tried to hide books by Voltaire and other forbidden authors in his library. Despite these efforts, he was found guilty of treason and sedition in 1795. While en route to exile in Africa, he jumped ship in Spain and, failing to get his sentence reversed in Madrid, traveled to France and England, where he met **Francisco de Miranda** and other anti-Spanish plotters. He returned to New Granada (modern Colombia) in 1797 and surrendered to authorities, apparently in the belief that he would receive clemency, but he was kept in confinement until 1803.

Nariño was again incarcerated when the independence movement began in 1810, but he was freed and named president of Cundinamarca province in 1811. In this position he espoused centralist principles in opposition to those who envisioned the new republic as a loose confederation of provinces. In the ensuing armed conflict Nariño was initially successful but was captured by royalists in Pasto in 1814 and sent to Spain. Released after the liberal revolt of 1820, he returned to New Granada to preside over the open-

ing of the Congress of Cúcuta in 1821. His last years were marred by quarrels with **Francisco de Paula Santander** and his allies.

Narváez, Pánfilo de (1478/80-1528), soldier in Jamaica, Cuba, Mexico, and Florida. Born in Valmanzano, Segovia, Spain, Narváez was a close associate of Diego de Velázquez, the governor of Cuba, and participated in the conquest there from 1510 to 1514. He is best remembered for being supplied by Velázquez with men, horses, and armament sufficient to arrest **Hernán Cortés** for rebellion. After arriving on the Mexican Gulf Coast in 1520, he tried to divide Cortés's Tlaxcalan allies and to undermine his authority over **Moctezuma**. Cortés met the challenge through enticements and a midnight attack that surprised Narváez's superior forces. Narváez lost an eye to a pike thrust but not his life. Put in charge of an expedition to Florida in 1528, he landed near Tampa Bay. Indian attacks and illness reduced his group's numbers and led them to construct ships to try to sail along the coast toward Mexico. Narváez disappeared on one of the ships. Only four others, including **Álvar Núñez Cabeza de Vaca**, survived the shipwrecks, and they spent eight years of traveling on foot to reach Spanish outposts in northern Mexico.

Neruda, Pablo (Neftalí Reyes; 1904-1973), Chilean poet, Nobel laureate. Pablo Neruda was one of Latin America's most prolific poets, publishing more than fifty volumes of verse over a half century's time. Between 1928 and 1936, the Chilean government appointed him to consular posts in several Asian and European nations. During that period he published several acclaimed books of verse in the modernist style, among them his *Veinte poemas de amor y una canción desesperada* (*Twenty Love Poems and a Song of Despair,* 1924), celebrating a favored theme: his love of women. The powerful cycle of poems *Residencia en la tierra* (*Residence on Earth,* 1933-35) reflects his loneliness and unhappiness while in the Far East and offers a bleak vision of the human condition. In 1936 Neruda lost his consular posting in Madrid because of his sympathy for the Republican cause. His *Las Furias y las* *penas* (1936) and *España en el corazón* (1937) reflect both his partisanship in the Spanish conflict and his hatred of fascism. During World War II he joined the Communist party and went on to serve in the Chilean Senate (1945-48). While in Peru in 1943 he was inspired to write one of his most celebrated poems, "Las Alturas de Machu Picchu" ("The Heights of Machu Picchu," 1947). Neruda lived in exile between 1949 and 1953, forced out of Chile by its anticommunist government. During that period he wrote *Canto general* (1950), a poem in epic style recounting Latin America's history from a Marxist perspective, which earned him the Stalin Peace Prize. The poet's period of greatest literary creativity occurred between his return to Chile in 1953 and his death in 1973. His last twenty years were marked by his publication of some twenty volumes of poetry laced with humor and celebrating everyday things, and his publication of a play and a prose autobiography, *Confieso que he vivido: memorias (Memoirs,* 1974). In 1971 he received the Nobel Prize for Literature. Pablo Neruda was Latin America's best-known twentieth-century poet. In his passion for life, his celebration of love, and his advocacy of radical social change, he stands as the region's most representative modern poet.

Niemeyer Soares Filho, Oscar (1907–), Brazilian architect. Born in Rio de Janeiro into a monied family, Oscar Niemeyer entered Brazil's National School of Fine Arts at age twenty-three. There he began his long association with school director Lúcio Costa, serving on Costa's staff after graduation in 1934. Niemeyer's commitment to modernism deepened when that movement's leader, Le Corbusier (Charles-Édouard Jeaneret), visited Brazil in 1936. Niemeyer's brilliance and inventiveness soon won him major commissions, first to design, with Costa, Brazil's Ministry of Education in Rio (1937) and the Brazilian Pavilion for the 1939 World's Fair. During the 1940s Niemeyer continued his experimentation in wedding local traditions and materials with modernist conventions (frequently referred to as Brazil's "New Architecture," a term coined in 1930 by Lúcio Costa). A notable example of that vision was Niemeyer's Church of St. Francis of Assisi,

near Belo Horizonte (1943), which integrates plastic and architectural forms and features a tile mural by **Cândido Portinari**. Early in the 1950s he helped design the United Nations Building in New York, and a decade later played a major role in planning and constructing Brazil's new national capital, Brasília. Niemeyer supervised a team of sixty architects who worked from the rough plan of Lúcio Costa, refined in the pages of Niemeyer's architectural journal *Módulo* (after Le Corbusier's 1949 book of the same title). He personally designed the presidential residence, the Congress building, and the city's cathedral, a structure of sweeping concrete buttresses evoking an immense flower opening to the heavens. The project was completed in a remarkable two years' time. For the next forty years Niemeyer, by then acknowledged as one of the world's leading architects, designed public and commercial buildings in Brazil, Europe, the Middle East, and North Africa. Throughout his long career Niemeyer set the standard in architectural form and imagination, fully justifying colleague Walter Gropius' characterization of him as the "Bird of Paradise" of the architectural world.

Nóbrega, Manoel da (1517-1570), Jesuit missionary to Brazil. A member of the Portuguese nobility, Manoel da Nóbrega was educated at the universities of Salamanca and Coimbra. He joined the Society of Jesus in 1544, and in 1549 was selected to head the first Jesuit mission to Brazil. He arrived in Bahia along with the colony's first governor, **Tomé de Sousa**. De Sousa and Brazil's other early governors relied heavily on the Jesuits, especially in pacifying and Christianizing the Indians. To that end Nóbrega initiated the policy of gathering Indians into villages called *aldeias*. He did so chiefly to protect them from enslavement by settlers. The *aldeias* were also paternalistic and utopian communities where the Indians were catechized, taught Portuguese as well as their own languages, and instructed in useful skills. Meanwhile the Indians grew crops for sustenance and sale. Nóbrega's *aldeias* became models for all other Jesuit missionaries in Brazil.

In 1553 Nóbrega was named provincial of

Brazil; that same year he traveled south to São Vicente where he established a high school at the village of Piratininga, the present site of São Paulo. The school was not only one of Brazil's first, but was notable for jointly educating the children of Indians and Portuguese. In 1556 Nóbrega returned to Bahia, and four years later was relieved of his duties as provincial. He then turned to the task of expelling French settlers from their colony on Guanabara Bay, established in 1556 and called Antarctic France. He was especially disturbed by the presence of Huguenots among the French settlers. Nóbrega had the satisfaction of seeing Governor **Mem de Sá** disperse the French in 1560. He went on to help found Rio de Janeiro in 1565, and to establish a high school there two years later. He directed the school until his death.

Manuel da Nóbrega was an academic who wrote the first scholarly books on Brazil. In his *Informação das terras do Brasil* (1550) and *Diálogo sobre a conversão do gentio* (c. 1556), he praised the colony as an earthly paradise and criticized the Portuguese for their pillaging of the land and its people. His views and works influenced his younger Jesuit colleague, **José de Anchieta**, and seventeenth-century Jesuit notable **Antônio Vieira**.

Noriega Moreno, Manuel Antonio (1936–), Panamanian dictator. Humbly born, Manuel Noriega attended public school in Panama and military academy in Peru, graduating in 1962. He entered the National Guard, and received additional training at the U.S. Army School of the Americas in Panama. A close associate of **Omar Torrijos**, Noriega helped suppress a revolt against Torrijos in 1969. As a result he was placed in charge of military intelligence. Following the death of Torrijos in 1981, Noriega established control over the National Guard by mid-1983. Once in control of that body, which he renamed the Panamanian Defense Force (PDF), he proceded to set government policy through it, ruling from behind the scenes through a succession of puppet presidents. He lavishly rewarded friends and supporters, while he exiled, jailed, and killed opponents. Panama's strategic location enabled him to help Colombian drug czars transport cocaine to the U.S. market. Meanwhile Noriega accepted monies from the U.S. Drug Enforcement Agency, supposedly for helping its agents stem the flow of illegal drugs northward. He was also paid by the U.S. Army and the Central Intelligence Agency for assisting in their transport of weapons to Nicaragua's right-wing Contra rebels. At the same time he expedited the shipment of weapons from left-wing sources to El Salvador's FMLN guerrillas. Perhaps the most profitable of Noriega's activities lay in exploitation of Panama's lax banking laws to help illegal drug interests launder their immense profits. Noriega's own drug trafficking led to his indictment by the U.S. Department of Justice in 1988. The United States then imposed economic sanctions on Panama, and strengthened them after May 1989, when Noriega annulled national elections. In October 1989, the United States sponsored an abortive coup against Noriega. Two months later, on December 20, 1989, some 12,000 U.S. troops invaded Panama and captured Noriega. He was tried for drug trafficking in a U.S. court, convicted, and sentenced to a forty-year term in a federal prison. His sentence was reduced to thirty years in March 1999.

Núñez, Rafael (1825-1894), Colombian statesman. The son of an army officer, Núñez was born in Cartagena and educated there, receiving a law degree in 1844. Having moved to Panama to take up a minor post there, he married (1852) the sister-in-law of a powerful Panamanian politician, through whose influence he was able to win a seat in Congress. A Liberal, Núñez became secretary of finance in the cabinet of Provisional President **Tomás C. de Mosquera** after the latter's defeat of the Conservative government of Mariano Ospina Rodríguez. In this capacity he is considered the intellectual author of the decree (1861) expropriating the real estate of civil and ecclesiastical corporations. From 1863 to 1874 Núñez lived abroad, first in the United States, where he worked as a correspondent for Latin American newspapers, and later in France and England, where he held consular posts. Upon his return to Colombia, he ran unsuccessfully for the presidency in 1875 but won election to a two-year term starting in 1880. Meanwhile, he had divorced his first wife and married Soledad Román in a civil ceremony in 1877, actions that produced controversy in staunchly Catholic Colombia.

By 1880 Núñez's years of exposure to American and European society and his observation of conditions in Colombia had led him to modify many of his earlier, conventionally Liberal views. He now believed that under the constitution of 1863 the federal government was too weak to ensure stability and that the state should actively encourage economic development. He also questioned the wisdom of strongly anticlerical policies adopted by his fellow-Liberals in the late 1870s. As president, Núñez obtained legislation creating a national bank and a protective tariff. However, his views and his developing rapport with the Conservatives aggravated division within the Liberal party. During his second presidential term (1884-86) his Liberal foes rebelled against his government, only to see him turn to the Conservatives for assistance in crushing the insurgents. With the backing of the Conservatives and his remaining Liberal supporters, Núñez oversaw the writing of a new constitution (1886) that restored centralism, made Catholicism the state religion, and greatly enhanced the powers of the presidency. Núñez became titular president under the new charter but remained in retirement in Cartagena. Most Liberals condemned Núñez as an apostate who had betrayed his party, but to Conservatives and other supporters, he was the "Regenerator" who saved Colombia from anarchy and atheism. Núñez was also a man of letters who wrote poetry and the words of the Colombian national anthem. His newspaper articles were collected in *Ensayos de crítica social* (1874) and the seven-volume *Reforma política en Colombia* (1944-50).

Núñez de Vela, Blasco (?-1546), first viceroy of Peru. Núñez de Vela had been the crown's *veedor* (inspector) in charge of maintaining Castile's military apparatus in a ready state. He administered this efficiently and effectively without the usual corruption. He was seen as a no-nonsense, practical bureaucrat who would improve the moral

tone of the government of the increasingly chaotic Peru. But he was a moralizing disaster. Charged with enforcing the New Laws of 1542, which significantly reduced the power of the *encomendero* class, he arrived in Peru in 1544 and applied them like an avenging angel. He was intransigent, petty, unwilling to take advice from potential allies, and he alienated everyone. He assassinated the royal *factor* (business agent) in a fit of rage; he was then arrested and was being shipped off to Spain when he convinced the ship's captain to land him on the northern Peruvian coast. By now there was a full-scale rebellion against royal government with **Gonzalo Pizarro** as the leader. Somewhat chastened by the turn of events, Núñez de Vela tried to rally support, but rebel forces defeated and killed him at Añaquito near Quito on January 18, 1546.

Obregón, Álvaro (1880-1928), Mexican revolutionary leader and president (1920-24). Born in Sonora, Obregón was the youngest of eighteen children and lost his father at an early age. He had little formal education and worked at a variety of jobs before acquiring (1906) a tract of land in Huatabampo, Sonora, where he began to grow chick peas. In 1911 he was elected municipal president (mayor) of Huatabampo.

Obregón did not take part in the anti-Díaz campaign of 1910-11, but he defended the government of **Francisco I. Madero** against the rebellion of Pascual Orozco in 1912. His military ability brought him a major role in the Constitutionalist campaign against **Victoriano Huerta**. In the subsequent internecine conflict among the victorious Constitutionalists, he sided with **Venustiano Carranza** in the latter's struggle against **Francisco Villa**. By using barbed wire and the trench warfare tactics then being employed in Europe, he defeated Villa at the Battle of Celaya in April 1915. He inflicted another major defeat on Villa at the Battle of León (June 1915), during which his right arm was blown off by an artillery shell. With the triumph of Carranza, Obregón served as secretary of war but resigned on May 1, 1917, ostensibly to return to private life. However, on June 1, 1919, he announced his presidential candidacy, emerging as the leading opponent of the civilian favored by Carranza and as the champion of dissatisfied agrarian and labor interests. In April 1920 he joined with the governor of Sonora, Adolfo de la Huerta, in a successful revolt against Carranza and was later elected president for a four-year term beginning on December 1, 1920.

As president, Obregón steered a moderate, pragmatic course as he pursued stability and consolidation of revolutionary gains. He oversaw a substantial acceleration of agrarian reform, with approximately 10 million acres being distributed during his term. His administration is also associated with the educational reforms and artistic renaissance encouraged by his secretary of education, **José Vasconcelos**. Although unsympathetic to Roman Catholicism, he failed to enforce the anticlerical provisions of the constitution of 1917, except in the case of Monsignor Philippi, the apostolic delegate who was expelled in 1923 after participating in an outdoor religious ceremony banned by the constitution. In 1923 Obregón won American recognition of his government by pledging not to move against U.S.-owned oil properties if they had been exploited by "positive acts" before 1917. Obregón also worked successfully to limit the influence of Mexico's powerful military class and to centralize authority in the presidency.

When Obregón selected **Plutarco Elías Calles** as his successor, Adolfo de la Huerta led an unsuccessful revolt in 1923-24. During the Calles administration the constitution was amended to permit Obregón's reelection as president. He won reelection in 1928, but before he could take office he was assassinated (July 17, 1928) by a young man described as a religious fanatic, who was later executed.

Ocampo, Victoria (1890-1979), Argentine essayist, publisher, and patron of the arts. Victoria Ocampo's privileged upbringing and literary bent brought her into contact with many of Europe's leading writers. One of them, José Ortega y Gasset, urged her to turn her wealth to the service of poetry and literature. In 1931 she complied by founding the review *Sur*, in company with writers Waldo Frank and Eduardo Mallea. Her journal became widely read throughout the Americas and Europe, helping popularize the work of Latin American writers such as **Pablo Neruda**, **Gabriela Mistral**, and **Jorge Luis Borges**. A proponent of literary universalism, Ocampo's *Sur* regularly published pieces by writers such as Rabindranath Tagore, Albert Camus, and Aldous Huxley. During the 1930s she became active in women's issues through the Unión de Mujeres Argentinas, which she helped found in 1936. A vocal critic of fascism and all forms of authoritarian rule, Ocampo suffered persecution during the regime of **Juan D. Perón**, once serving a brief prison term for her opposition to the dictator. Equally critical of revolutionary Marxism, she was tarred by the left as an elitist oligarch. Yet friends of the arts honored her contribution as both a publisher and writer. The author of twenty-six volumes of essays, she became the first female member of the Argentine Academy of Literature. In 1967 Harvard University awarded her an honorary doctorate in humane letters.

Odría, Manuel Apolinario (1897-1974), Peruvian dictator. Manuel Odría attended military school in the town of Chorrillos, and joined the army in 1919. He received advanced training in Peru and the United States, and, as a lieutenant colonel, gained fame during the 1941 invasion of Ecuador. He served as minister of government to President José Luis Bustamente y Rivera (1945-48), but resigned in protest of APRA influence in Bustamente's administration. When APRA instigated an insurrection of troops stationed in Callao, Odría overthrew Bustamente (October 29, 1948) and carried out savage repression of APRA. His eight-year rule, known as the *ochenio*, coincided with economic prosperity stimulated in part by the Korean War. Odría was an economic liberal who encouraged foreign investment geared toward enhancing exports, especially of minerals. He resumed payment of Peru's foreign debt, in suspension since 1931. The dictator emulated his contemporary, **Juan Perón** of Argentina, in cultivating support among the nation's urban poor. He extended public services to Lima's slums, and put his wife in charge of a new state welfare agency. Widespread opposition to his rule, coupled with economic decline following the Korean War, moved Odría to step aside for a popularly elected president in 1956. He then formed his own party, the Odriísta National Union, whose strength lay in the urban poor. In 1962 he allied himself with former enemy **Víctor Raúl Haya de la Torre** in an unsuccessful attempt to regain the presidency through democratic means. Odría and his party played a significant role in national politics until the military coup of 1968.

O'Higgins, Bernardo (1778-1842), leader of Chile's war for independence and supreme director (1817-23). Born in Chillán, O'Higgins was the natural son of Ambrosio O'Higgins, a native of Ireland who rose in Spanish service and became viceroy of Peru (1796-1801). Although Bernardo saw little of his father, the latter enabled him to acquire a good education. From 1795 to 1801 he lived in England, where he became acquainted with **Francisco de Miranda**, who converted him to his anti-Spanish views. After returning to Chile he took possession of an hacienda inherited from his late father.

   With the start of the independence movement in 1810, O'Higgins offered his services to the revolutionaries. However, he often came into conflict with José Miguel Carrera, who was named dictator in 1812. In October 1814 the Chilean forces suffered a major defeat at the hands of the royalists at Rancagua, and O'Higgins was forced to flee to Argentina. There he became an officer in the army that **José de San Martín** was organizing for the liberation of Chile and Peru. Returning to Chile, he won a decisive victory at Chacabuco (February 12, 1817) and was named supreme director a few days later.

   As supreme director he founded schools and an orphanage, reestablished the National Library, and completed a canal that opened up lands south of Santiago for agriculture. He also organized a military and naval expedition to combat the royalists in Peru under San Martín. However, he antagonized the Chilean aristocracy by abolishing titles of nobility and proposing to end entailed estates (*mayorazgos*). Some considered him overly autocratic while others thought him some-

what foreign because of his Argentine connections. He resigned under pressure in 1823 and left for Peru, where he spent the rest of his life.

Olivares, Conde-Duque de (Gaspar de Guzmán y Pimental; 1587-1645), Spanish statesman and chief minister (1622-43) of Philip IV (1621-65). When the inexperienced Philip suddenly came to the throne at the age of sixteen and found himself with the awesome responsibility of managing a world empire, he turned to Olivares as his head of household to help him rule. As the king's *privado*, or *valido*, or favorite, Olivares quickly became the chief minister and dominated the Spanish government for over two decades. A contemporary rival and equal to the French statesman Cardinal Richelieu, Olivares tried to reform the Spanish government and set Spain once again on a course toward the greatness and achievements of **Philip II** (1556-98). Olivares continued the war against the Netherlands that evolved into the Thirty Years' War (1618-48) and fought the French in northern Italy (1628-31), both traditional objectives of Spanish policy. Part of Olivares's reform program was an attempt to raise further revenue and to redistribute the weight away from the overburdened and overtaxed Castilians. This was his Unión de Armas project (1626). In trying to get non-Castilian subjects to make a greater contribution in men and money, Olivares hoped to bring about greater unity, spread the burden more equitably, and break down some of the provincialism of the individual Spanish kingdoms. Various attempts failed. Olivares's final ploy was to get Catalonia to contribute by basing Spanish troops there, but this brought about the Catalan revolt (1640-52) and the loss of Portugal and its empire in 1640. Olivares resigned discredited. His whirlwind activity and high-minded reform lay stillborn and in ruins, fatally flawed like previous Spanish policy by being overreaching, overcommitted, and overspent. During Olivares's term the New World saw the introduction of taxes on stamped paper (*papel sellado*), salt, and office holders (*media anata*) that reflected his philosophy of taxing everyone, especially the two estates that had long escaped most taxation, the nobility and the clergy.

Onganía, Juan Carlos (1914-1995), Argentine president. Juan Carlos Onganía prepared for his army career at the National Military College, eventually rising to the position of chief of staff. In August 1962, he led the army's legalist (*azul*) faction in crushing a rebellion of that body's anti-Peronist *colorado* faction, which had demanded the imposition of military rule. Dismissed as army chief by President Arturo Illia in late 1965, Onganía became instrumental in the coup that unseated Illia in June 1966. Onganía assumed the presidency soon afterward, announcing his intent to lead an "Argentine Revolution" of corporatist character. He suspended political parties, strictly controlled labor unions, and sent troops to occupy university campuses. For a time his measures met with popular approval. His economic stabilization plan of 1967-69 reduced inflation and encouraged foreign investment. But Onganía's authoritarianism, coupled with increasing labor and student militance, and the appearance of revolutionary guerrillas, set into motion events that ended Onganía's presidency. Early 1969 was marked by a wave of strikes and student protests that came to a head in May with the seizure of Córdoba by workers and students (*el cordobazo*). That unrest, along with a wave of assassinations carried out by leftist rebels, led the military to remove Onganía in June 1970. By attempting to govern above politics, Juan Carlos Onganía had furthered the erosion of parties and organized labor. He thus furthered the advance of left- and right-wing extremist groups.

Orellana, Francisco de (1511?-1546), commander of the first European descent of the Amazon River. Born in Trujillo, Spain, Orellana participated in the conquest of Peru. He accompanied **Gonzalo Pizarro** to Quito where they organized an expedition to find El Dorado or the "Land of Cinnamon." Orellana was second in command. With close to 180 Spaniards and 4,300 Indians, they left Quito in 1541, crossed the Andes and descended to the Amazon basin but began to run out of food and supplies. With a makeshift brigantine built, Pizarro dispatched Orellana downstream to find and return with supplies within twelve days. Departing on Decem-

ber 26, 1541, with fifty-seven men, Orellana did not find an Indian village with food for eight days. Unable to get back up the swift-flowing river in the allotted time, he continued downriver. Little did they know they would navigate the course of the Amazon River, a voyage of epic proportions. They did not reach the Atlantic Ocean until August 26, 1542, eight months later. They had seen hundreds of hostile Indian groups along the banks, reportedly fought women warriors, hence the term Amazon, and assumed there were untold riches further inland. They had established the enormous dimensions of the interior of the South American land mass. Orellana returned to Spain and was licensed (1544) to conquer the explored area. With a new wife, Ana de Ayala, and four ships, two of which sank in the Atlantic crossing, they returned to the Amazon. Going upriver and not finding food exhausted their resources. Orellana got the "fevers" and died in his wife's arms. The survivors finally made it to the island of Margarita off the Venezuelan coast.

Orozco, José Clemente (1883-1949), Mexican painter, regarded, with **Diego Rivera** and **David Alfaro Siqueiros**, as one of the three "great ones" of the muralist movement of the 1920s and 1930s. Born in Jalisco, Orozco was raised in Mexico City. While studying in the National Preparatory School, he lost his left hand in an accident. After completing a course in agriculture, he enrolled in the Academy of Fine Arts in 1906. In 1914 he followed Gerardo Murillo (Dr. Atl), the academy's director, to Orizaba, where he had a firsthand view of the Mexican Revolution. His earliest works, biting political cartoons and drawings and water colors of prostitutes and young girls, brought him little recognition.

His first murals, painted in fresco at the National Preparatory School during the mid-1920s, offer a somber, even tragic representation of the recent revolution as well as an ambivalent portrayal of the Spanish conquest. In 1927, facing a bleak future in Mexico, he traveled to the United States, where he received mural commissions at Pomona College, the New School, and Dartmouth College. The Dartmouth murals, a depiction of New World civilization in which

Quetzalcoatl is assigned a central role, are considered among his finest. His masterpiece is generally considered to be a series of frescoes painted in the Hospicio Cabañas in Guadalajara in 1938-39. Here he portrayed the evolution of Mexican history in its beneficent and malign aspects as well as the despotisms of the twentieth century. Human creativity is represented by a man of fire in the cupola. Orozco also painted murals in the Palace of Fine Arts in Mexico City, the Governor's Palace in Guadalajara, and other sites, and produced approximately five hundred easel paintings.

Ortega Saavedra, Daniel (1945–), Nicaraguan revolutionary and president. Daniel Ortega was born to middle-class parents who had, during the 1940s, actively opposed the dictatorship of **Anastasio Somoza García**. After briefly studying for the priesthood, he entered high school in Managua. There, in 1961, he became active in the Nicaraguan Patriotic Youth organization. A year later he briefly enrolled in Managua's University of Central America, but concentrated on leading student protests against the government of Luis Somoza Debayle. In 1963, Ortega joined the recently formed Marxist Sandinista National Liberation Front (FSLN or Sandinistas). One year later he was arrested in Guatemala for illegal political activity, and deported to Nicaragua where he was tortured and then released. Ortega was arrested for bank robbery in 1967, and sentenced to an eight-year prison term. He remained in jail until freed in a December 1974 hostage-for-prisoner swap. Within months he became a member of the FSLN directorate, where he promoted the view that the Marxist group must form tactical alliances with non-Marxists to expedite overthrow of the dictator **Anastasio Somoza Debayle**. His view prevailed, and the Sandinistas went on to lead a broad coalition that drove Somoza from Nicaragua in mid-1979. Ortega became the dominant Sandinista leader following the revolution, and in 1984 was overwhelmingly elected to a six-year presidential term. Land reform and improvements in health and education were priorities of the new government. Ortega sought aid from socialist nations, notably the Soviet Union and Cuba, and aligned Nicaragua with the Socialist International. But the new regime's socialism won the enmity of the United States, which boycotted Nicaraguan goods, blocked World Bank loans, financed a counter-revolutionary insurgency—the Contras—and went so far as to mine the nation's principal harbor (May 1984). U.S. opposition to Ortega and the Sandinistas crippled government reform efforts and devastated Nicaragua's economy. While U.S. enmity lessened late in the 1980s, especially after Ortega signed the Arias Peace Plan (February 1987), it had an enduring effect. Hyperinflation and plummeting national production and living standards, coupled with an unpopular draft law, caused Ortega to lose the 1990 presidential election to **Violeta Barrios de Chamorro** by a 55 percent to 41 percent margin. While Ortega led Sandinista representatives in the National Assembly during the 1990s, he failed to capture the presidency in October 1996, losing to conservative Arnoldo Alemán. In 1998 he was reelected head of the FSLN despite charges of sexual abuse brought against him by his stepdaughter.

Ospina, Pedro Nel (1858-1927), Colombian president. Pedro Nel Ospina was born in Bogotá, in the presidential palace, the son of President Mariano Ospina Rodríguez (1856-61). He grew up in Guatemala, where his family relocated after his father's overthrow. Later he attended the University of California, where he took an engineering degree. Upon his return to Colombia he engaged in entrepreneurial activities running from coffee cultivation and export, to mining and manufacturing. He lent active support to establishing the National School of Mines, founded in 1887. More significantly, he launched the Antioquian textile industry through his establishment of a plant near Medellín in 1906. Ospina was also active in public affairs, serving in Congress during the 1890s and commanding troops during the War of the Thousand Days (1899-1902). Elected president in 1922, he effectively promoted the nation's economic development, establishing a central bank, recruiting foreign loans, and investing the 25-million-dollar Panama indemnity in improvements to highways and port facilities. Ospina modernized the national budgetary process and created the office of national comptroller. He was also instrumental in establishing the National Federation of Coffee Growers in 1927.

Páez, José Antonio (1790-1873), Venezuelan patriot leader and president. Páez was born in Barinas province, the son of a minor official, and grew up virtually illiterate. After killing a man in a fight, he fled to Venezuela's *llanos*, or plains region, where he worked as a ranch hand and later acquired cattle of his own. Emerging as the commander of an army of *llaneros* (plainsmen) during the struggle for independence, he acknowledged the leadership of **Simón Bolívar** in 1818. Páez distinguished himself at the decisive battle of Carabobo (June 24, 1821) and was immediately promoted to the rank of general-in-chief. With the organization of the tripartite nation known as Gran Colombia, Páez was named commanding general of the department of Venezuela. Like other Venezuelans, he resented the authorities in Bogotá and rebelled against the government in 1826-27, thereby accelerating the disintegration of Gran Colombia. In 1831 he became Venezuela's first president, initiating the era known as that of the Conservative Oligarchy and ruling on behalf of the landowners and merchants of Caracas and the north-central region of the country. By this time Páez had become a wealthy landowner himself, acquiring plantations and ranches throughout Venezuela.

Páez left the presidency in January 1835. When the so-called Revolution of the Reforms broke out a few weeks later against his successor, José María Vargas, Páez took command of the government forces and crushed the insurgents, who were based in eastern Venezuela. Páez served a second presidential term (1839-43), but saw his influence wane in the 1840s as Liberalism gradually grained ascendancy. In February 1848 he rose unsuccessfully against the regime of José Tadeo Monagas and was forced to leave Venezuela. After nearly a decade of exile in the United States and travel in Europe and Latin America, Páez returned to Venezuela for a few months in 1858-59 and again in 1861. In September 1861

he was made supreme civil and military commander of the centralists opposing federalist insurgents in the Federal War, but he was soon compelled to yield power to the latter. He left Venezuela in 1863, settling in New York, where he wrote his autobiography (1869) and where he died on May 7, 1873.

Palafox y Mendoza, Juan de (1600-1659), bishop of Puebla (1640-54) and viceroy of Mexico (1642). Born in Fitero, Navarre, Palafox studied law at Salamanca and quickly moved up the ecclesiastical and royal bureaucracy and became a member of the Council of the Indies. He was appointed *visitador general* (chief inspector) of Mexico in 1639 with extensive powers. A reform-minded regalist with a mystical vision that the Hapsburgs were destined to lead Christendom, Palafox worked to increase royal power and authority. He sacked the reigning viceroy for being too close to the Portuguese, hunted down crypto-Jews with an Inquisition-driven campaign of persecution, took parishes out of the hands of the regular orders and turned them over to the secular clergy, built fifty new churches, two seminaries, endowed one with his personal library of 5,000 volumes, and finished the cathedral of Puebla. He then took on the Jesuits by denying their claimed exemption from paying tithes on their landed estates. While this controversy was not settled in Palafox's favor until a century later in 1753, the Jesuits were 15,000 strong, and Palafox had upset too many entrenched interests. He suddenly found himself appointed bishop of Osma (in Soria) and was forced to return to Spain. His recall showed just how far decentralization and the loss of royal power had gone. Local elites and various interest groups now had control over much of the royal government.

Palma, Ricardo (1833-1919), Peruvian politician and man of letters. Born in Lima to well-to-do parents, Ricardo Palma became active in Peru's mid-century liberal movement. He fled to Chile after joining an abortive 1860 revolt against caudillo **Ramón Castilla**. From Chile he traveled to Europe where, after Castilla left the presidency (1862), he served as Peruvian consul in London,

Paris, and Venice. Palma returned to Lima to serve as secretary to President José Balta (1868-72). He went on to serve three Senate terms. During the 1870s, Palma wrote for the Lima newspaper *La Prensa*, often against the new Civilista party, and frequently as chronicler of well- and little-known events of Peru's past. In 1881, at Peru's nadir in the War of the Pacific (1879-83), he helped defend Lima against the Chileans. After the Chileans withdrew from Lima, he was asked to replace the collection of the National Library, which had been destroyed during the occupation. Palma was so aggressive in collecting books and manuscripts that he became widely known as "the begging librarian."

Ricardo Palma's fame rests in his newspaper pieces, published collectively between 1893 and 1896 under the title *Tradiciones peruanas*. Consisting of vignettes from Peruvian history, the *Tradiciones* have never been out of print. Witty and frequently ironic in tone, they mark their author as one of Latin America's premier *costumbrista* (folkloric) writers. Among Palma's other works is *Papeletas lexicográficas* (1903), in which he argues that words of Spanish-American origin ought to be accepted by Spanish lexicographers.

Paz, Octavio (1914-1998), Mexican poet, essayist, and Nobel Prize laureate. Octavio Paz was born near Mexico City, into a literary family. He graduated from Mexico's National University in 1937 with a degree in law. That same year he helped found a school for workers in Yucatán, and attended a congress of antifascist writers hosted by the Spanish government. That experience, coupled with the Nazi-Soviet pact of 1939, led Paz to renounce Marxism and embrace literature as way of linking intellectualism and political activism. In 1938 he founded the vanguardist literary journal *Taller*, and published his first book of verse, *El hijo pródigo*, in 1943. In that volume he explored the theme of art's redemptive power in the face of revolutionary betrayal. During 1944-45, he studied in the United States on a Guggenheim grant. In 1950 he published *El laberinto de la soledad (The Labyrinth of Solitude)*, a celebrated meditation on the Mexican psyche and cultural identity, and in 1951 *¿Águila o sol?*, a collection of verse advancing the poet's contention that pre-Columbian beliefs remain strong in Mexico albeit beneath Western forms. The latter volume reveals the influence upon Paz of surrealist poet André Breton. Between 1952 and 1968, the poet served Mexico in varied diplomatic capacities, most notably as ambassador to India and Japan. Paz published numerous works during that period, among them *El arco y la lira* (*The Bow and the Lyre*, 1956), a critical examination of poetry's role in history and society; and *Piedra del sol* (1957), a surrealistic reevaluation of Mexican history and myth. Paz resigned his Indian ambassadorship in 1968 to protest the Mexican government's massacre of student demonstrators. He went on to hold prestigious lectureships in Europe and the United States, while he continued his outpouring of poetry and prose. In 1990 Paz received the Nobel Prize for Literature in recognition of both his work and of his great influence upon Mexican and Latin American poetry. During the 1990s he continued to dominate Mexican cultural politics through his avant-garde literary magazine *Vuelta*.

Paz Estenssoro, Víctor (1907–), four-time president of Bolivia. Víctor Paz Estenssoro had just completed university training in law and economics when called to serve as an officer in the Chaco War (1932-35). Following the war he joined middle-class critics of his country's backward social and economic system. Paz served as housing minister in 1937 during the brief presidency of progressive Colonel David Toro, going on to help draft Bolivia's socialist 1938 constitution. In 1940 Paz was elected to the Chamber of Deputies, and a year later founded the National Revolutionary Movement, or MNR. His indictment of the government in 1942, following the Catavi Massacre, won the MNR a mass following and Paz Estenssoro the post of minister of finance in the progressive administration of Major Gualberto Villarroel, who overthrew conservative general Enrique Peñaranda in 1943. Paz resigned that post in 1946, not long before rioting students lynched Villarroel. He fled the country during the conservative reaction that ensued.

Paz Estenssoro returned to Bolivia after the MNR-led revolution of 1952 and assumed the presidency for a four-year term. During that period he carried out reforms that included nationalization of the tin mines, sweeping land reform, expansion of the electorate from 7 percent to 100 percent of adult Bolivians, and reorganization of the army. Winning a second term in 1960, he undertook modernization of the tin mines and colonization of the eastern lowlands. His third presidency (1964) was cut short by a military coup. Paz returned to Bolivia in 1971, following the coup of Colonel **Hugo Banzer**. But he suffered exile three years later following a break with Banzer. Paz returned to Bolivia in 1978 to assume leadership of the MNR. He placed second in the presidential contests of 1979 and 1980. Though he was runner-up in the 1985 presidential contest, the winner, Hugo Banzer, threw his support to Paz, who was subsequently elected president by Congress. Paz's fourth term began during a severe and extended economic crisis featuring hyperinflation. He attacked it through his New Economic Policy, of a neoliberal character. Over four years Paz privatized many state enterprises, including the tin mines, encouraged private investment, and opened the country to foreign investment. That reversal of his earlier statism was the most thoroughgoing of any of his political contemporaries. When Paz left office in 1989 he enjoyed popularity unique among Bolivian heads of state. Bolivia enjoyed low inflation, renewed economic growth, and the prospect of continued democratic governance.

Pedro I (1798-1834), emperor of Brazil (1822-31). Pedro was the older of the two surviving sons of **João**, prince regent and heir to the throne of Portugal, and his Spanish wife, Carlota Joaquina. In 1807 he accompanied his parents and the Portuguese court when they sailed for Brazil to escape the invading forces of Napoleon I. In 1817 Pedro married Leopoldina, daughter of the emperor of Austria, who bore him six children, including the future **Pedro II**; she enjoyed great popularity in Brazil until her death in 1826. However, Pedro was unfaithful to her, and in 1822 he established a liaison with the Brazilian-born

Domitila de Castro. In 1829 he married Amélia von Leuchtenburg, a member of Bavaria's royal family.

Meanwhile, João had become king and returned to Portugal in 1821 in order to preserve his throne after a liberal uprising in 1820. Pedro remained behind in Brazil as prince regent. When the Portuguese Cortes, or parliament, demanded that he return to Europe, **José Bonifácio de Andrada** and others protested against Portugal's apparent intention to reduce Brazil to its former status as a colony. As a result, Pedro declared (January 9, 1822) that he would remain in Brazil, thereby becoming a rallying point for the rapidly growing forces that favored independence. Encouraged by José Bonifácio and Leopoldina, Pedro declared Brazil's independence from Portugal on September 7, 1822, and was proclaimed emperor.

Though liberal minded, Pedro distrusted democracy and dissolved Brazil's constituent assembly. He appointed a council of state that drafted a constitution, promulgated on March 25, 1824, which gave him strong powers as hereditary chief of state. As emperor, Pedro came under increasing criticism, especially for his handling of foreign affairs. Critics complained of his acceptance of onerous financial conditions in exchange for Portuguese and British recognition of Brazil's independence. In addition, in 1828 Brazil was forced to surrender the Cisplatine province occupied in 1816, which became the independent republic of Uruguay. His antipathy to slavery and his use of European mercenaries also alienated many Brazilians. Above all, he came to be distrusted because of his Portuguese birth and deepening involvement in Portuguese affairs after the death of João in 1826. Pedro renounced the Portuguese throne in favor of his seven-year-old daughter Maria; his younger brother, Miguel, was to act as regent during her minority and later marry and rule jointly with her. However, Miguel was declared king by Portuguese conservatives and a civil war ensued. Tensions between native-born Brazilians and Portuguese and challenges to his imperial prerogatives led Pedro to abdicate on April 7, 1831. Leaving for Europe, he led a successful campaign against Miguel and secured the Portuguese throne for Maria. He died of tuberculosis on September 24, 1834.

Pedro II (1825-1891), emperor of Brazil. Pedro was the Brazilian-born son of **Pedro I** and his Austrian empress, Leopoldina, who died in 1826. After his father's abdication and return to Portugal in 1831, he was placed under the tutelage of **José Bonifácio de Andrada** until the latter's dismissal in 1833. José Bonifácio was succeeded as tutor by the Marquês de Itanhaén, who was assisted by a Carmelite friar, Pedro de Santa Mariana. Young Pedro proved an apt pupil: intelligent, obedient, and studious. Amid continuing political turmoil, pressure arose, mainly among Liberals, for curtailment of the period of Pedro's minority. In July 1840 he agreed to assume the reins of government and was crowned the following year. In 1843 he was married to Teresa Cristina, daughter of the king of Naples. Usually described as plain and less intellectually oriented than her husband, she bore him four children. Two sons died in infancy, and a daughter in 1871. The surviving daughter, Isabel, married the Comte d'Eu, a grandson of Louis Philippe of France, in 1864.

As he matured, Pedro increasingly asserted the extensive powers granted him by the constitution of 1824. Though some historians see him as overly conservative and traditional, he is generally credited with preserving political stability in Brazil, encouraging economic modernization, and moving toward the abolition of slavery. He traveled extensively in Europe (1871-72, 1876-77) and visited the United States in 1876.

After 1870, however, Pedro and the monarchy came under increasing attack as anachronisms. His dismissal of the Zacharias cabinet in 1868 infuriated many Liberals and contributed to the emergence of republican sentiment. Republicanism also grew among army officers who felt unappreciated by the government after the Paraguayan War (1864-70). The lack of a male heir and the unpopularity of the Comte d'Eu also weakened the monarchy. Meanwhile, Pedro was in poor health and went to Europe in mid-1887, remaining abroad until August 1888. After the proclamation

of a republic on November 15, 1889, Pedro and the royal family left for Europe. He died in Paris.

Peixoto, Floriano Vieira (1839-1895), president of Brazil (1891-94). Born to a modest family in Alagoas, Peixoto became a professional soldier and served with distinction during the Paraguayan War (1864-70). In 1889 he was raised to the rank of marshal and made adjutant general of the army. On November 15, 1889, he played a key role in the overthrow of the monarchy by refusing to attack rebellious troops. In 1891 the constituent assembly elected him vice president of the new republic by a wide margin.

Succeeding to the presidency after the resignation of the president, **Manoel Deodoro da Fonseca**, Peixoto deposed the state governors who had backed Fonseca's imposition of a dictatorship on November 3, 1891. As chief executive, Peixoto confronted rebellions in the state of Rio Grande do Sul and in the navy, the latter of which had monarchical tendencies. He was also opposed by some civilians, such as **Rui Barbosa**, who was critical of continuing military dominance in politics. On the other hand, Peixoto had the support of middle-class urban nationalists known as Jacobins and of civilian leaders in São Paulo, who provided crucial assistance in crushing the insurgents in Rio Grande do Sul and in the navy. Some of Peixoto's supporters favored his retention of power beyond the expiration of his term, but he stepped down on November 15, 1894, in favor of Prudente de Morais Barros, a civilian from São Paulo. He is remembered as the "iron marshal" and as the "consolidator of the republic."

Pelé (Edson Arantes do Nascimento; 1940–), Brazilian soccer player. Born in Minas Gerais, the son of a minor league player, Edson Arantes do Nascimento showed early virtuosity while playing street soccer, or *peladas*, winning the nickname Pelé. He was barely a teenager when recruited to train with the São Paulo professional team Bauru. Soon he was acquired by the Santos Football Club, for which he played his first professional game at age sixteen, in 1956. Pelé was asked to join the Brazilian national team, and in 1958 led Brazil to its first World Cup championship. His brilliance in the 1958 competition, during which he scored six goals, made him a global celebrity. Pelé remained with Santos during subsequent seasons, and also figured in Brazil's 1962 and 1970 World Cup victories. In 1974 he left Santos to play with the New York Cosmos of the North American Soccer League, for three years helping popularize soccer in the United States. At the end of his career, in 1977, Pelé had amassed more than 1,300 career goals. Subsequently he appeared in films and otherwise capitalized upon his fame. A Brazilian national institution, Pelé was one of the best ever to play the world's most popular sport.

Pérez, Carlos Andrés (1922–), Venezuelan president. Carlos Andrés Pérez was only nineteen when, as a delegate to the first convention of Acción Democrática (AD), he helped found the party in 1941. There the charismatic and eloquent young man caught the eye of the AD leader, **Rómulo Betancourt**. Pérez served as Betancourt's secretary when the latter headed Venezuela's ruling junta (1945-48). During the regime of **Marcos Pérez Jiménez** (1952-58), he and Betancourt collaborated in opposing the dictator from exile. Carlos Andrés Pérez served as interior minister to Betancourt (1959-64), going on to lead AD until his own presidential victory in 1973. Pérez's five-year term coincided with swelling government revenues thanks to increased oil prices and foreign borrowing. Thus he was able spend large sums on public improvements and social programs and to nationalize the nation's petroleum reserves in 1976. Pérez conducted an activist foreign policy during his first presidency. He urged Third World nations to form commodity cartels, encouraged Nicaragua's Sandinista rebels in their struggle against the dictator **Anastasio Somoza**, and supported Panama's effort to win control of the Panama Canal. Pérez won a second term in 1988, becoming the first person to do so. In spite of evidence that widespread corruption had occurred during his first term, Venezuelans hoped Pérez could return them to their earlier prosperity. They were mistaken. One of the new president's first acts was to accept an IMF-directed austerity program that touched off riots throughout the nation (February 1989). But he

stayed the course, massively devaluating the currency, privatizing state-owned enterprises, and slashing social programs. Meanwhile evidence of corruption resurfaced, and on May 20, 1993, the supreme court handed down an indictment against the president. A day later the Senate removed him from office. Pérez was subsequently sentenced to two years of house arrest. When released in September 1996, he vowed to clear his name and announced formation of a new anti-establishment party, the Movement for Openness and National Participation.

Pérez Jiménez, Marcos (1914–), Venezuelan dictator. Marcos Pérez Jiménez was born in the state of Táchira, graduated from the Escuela Militar in Caracas (1934), and received advanced training in Peru. In 1944 he organized the revolutionary Patriotic Military Union and conspired with **Rómulo Betancourt**, **Rómulo Gallegos**, and other members of the Acción Democrática party (AD) to overthrow President Isaías Medina Angarita. Rather than including Pérez in the seven-man junta that ruled Venezuela for the following three years, Betancourt, who headed the body, sent him abroad on a lengthy diplomatic mission. That moved Pérez to conspire against Betancourt and Acción Democrática, overthrowing the party's first elected president, Rómulo Gallegos, just ten months into his presidency (November 24, 1948). In 1950 Pérez assumed the presidency of the military junta that had replaced Gallegos, following the kidnapping and murder of its leader, Colonel Carlos Delgado Chalbaud. Two years after that he seized definitive power when it appeared that the opposition Democratic Republican Union would win control of a new constituent assembly. Pérez Jiménez went on to establish one of Latin America's most repressive dictatorships. He had political opponents exiled, jailed, and murdered, while enriching himself and his friends with public monies. At the same time he won favor among the urban poor through lavish expenditures on public works programs. He also encouraged the development of heavy industry and the commercialization of agriculture. But by late 1957 his heavy-handed rule had antagonized so many interests that a broad coalition of groups forced him from office and into exile in January 1958. Pérez was extradited from the United States in 1963, tried, and convicted in 1968 of misuse of government funds. He was sentenced to four years' imprisonment, but since he had been jailed since 1963, he was freed and went to Spain. While Pérez Jiménez remained popular in some quarters, especially in poor neighborhoods of Caracas, he was, as a convicted felon, constitutionally barred from further political activity.

Perón, Juan Domingo (1895-1974), thrice president of Argentina (1946–55, 1973–74). Juan Perón was born in modest circumstances on a ranch in Buenos Aires province. He attended the national military academy in 1911, going on to enter the army as a second lieutenant in 1913. The affable and athletic Perón was a good soldier, popular with his peers and his superior officers and with men in the enlisted ranks as well. A successful course of study at the Superior War School (1926-29) earned him appointment to the army general staff in 1929. Between 1931 and 1936 he taught at the Superior War School, while publishing several books that revealed his nationalism and belief in political centralism and state intervention in the economy. Between 1936 and 1941, he served abroad, most notably as military attaché to Rome, where he studied the authoritarian, nationalistic regime of Benito Mussolini at first hand. Perón returned to Buenos Aires in 1941, joining the GOU (Grupo de Oficiales Unidos), an association of nationalist officers dedicated to promoting Argentine interests and opposing involvement in World War II on the side of the Allies. The GOU led in the overthrow of President Ramón Castillo in June 1943. Perón steadily increased his power after the coup. Sensing the political potential of Argentina's under-represented popular classes, he quickly made himself their champion. In October 1943 he was named head of the Secretariat of Labor and Social Welfare, and early the following year assumed leadership of the war ministry. In 1944 Perón added the national vice presidency to his titles. By 1945 he enjoyed unrivaled popularity among the nation's workers. On October 9, 1945,

the army suddenly stripped Perón of power and imprisoned him on October 12. But five days later a massive Buenos Aires demonstration, orchestrated by labor leaders and Perón's consort Eva Duarte, frightened the military into releasing him unconditionally. Perón then resigned from the army, launched a presidential campaign at the head of his nascent Peronist party, and went on to win the February 1946 contest.

Perón acted decisively to redistribute political and economic power during his first term in office (1946-51). He institutionalized labor's political power through the Peronist party (renamed the Justicialist party in 1947), and in a corporative 1949 constitution. He enfranchised women in 1947 and organized their vote on his behalf through formation of the Peronist Women's party headed by his wife, **Eva Duarte de Perón**. Perón pursued his populist agenda by spending Argentina's substantial financial reserves on social programs and nationalization of the national rail system and other foreign-owned enterprises. Workers' wages and quality of life improved significantly as a result of those measures. But the price controls that Perón imposed to finance his social programs harmed agricultural interests. Agricultural exports consequently declined sharply. Cash surpluses quickly disappeared and were replaced by significant debt. By 1950, inflation had eroded many of the earlier gains, which in turn eroded support for Perón. The growing authoritarianism of his regime both alienated supporters and energized the opposition. Resistance to his rule increased in 1951 when, under terms of the 1949 constitution, he won a second presidential term in a violence-marred campaign. Perón's closing of the opposition daily *La Prensa* in 1951, and the heightened persecution of his political opponents, produced an abortive coup attempt later in the year. The death of his wife Evita, who was revered by Peronists and who served him as a strategist, deprived him of a valued ally. The nation's economic difficulties forced Perón to adopt austerity measures during 1953. By early 1954 the church had joined the anti-Peronist opposition. Opposition to the dictatorship peaked during mid-1955. In September of that year the army stepped in to force Perón from office and into exile.

Perón's exile lasted until mid-1973. But Peronism remained strong during that interval, directed by leaders who received their orders from Perón. Meanwhile Argentina languished under a succession of civilian and military regimes. In May 1973 Peronist Héctor Cámpora was elected president amid intense excitement that Juan Perón would soon return. Perón did return to Argentina in mid-1973, whereupon Campora resigned the presidency and called for new elections. Perón won his third term with an impressive 62 percent majority. His third wife, Isabel Martínez de Perón, was elected vice president. Inaugurated in October 1973, Perón proved unable to control the forces dividing both Argentina and the Peronist party. Juan Perón died after ten months of ineffectual rule (July 1, 1974). His wife succeeded him but was removed by the military in March 1976. Peronism remained strong in Argentina for the ensuing two decades, a legacy of the man who empowered his nation's popular classes.

Pétion, Alexandre Sabès (1770-1818), Haitian revolutionary leader and president (1807-18). Pétion was born in Port-au-Prince, the son of a Frenchman and a free mulatto woman. Though trained as a goldsmith, he entered the militia at the age of eighteen. He was initially a supporter of **Toussaint L'Ouverture,** but in 1799 allied himself with the mulatto general André Rigaud and left Saint Domingue after the latter's defeat. He returned to Saint Domingue early in 1802 with the French expedition under General Charles-Victor-Emmanuel Leclerc that attempted to subdue the rebellious colony. However, in October 1802 Pétion joined **Jean-Jacques Dessalines** and **Henri Christophe** in their successful campaign against the French.

After the death of Dessalines, Pétion proclaimed Christophe as president of the new republic of Haiti but drafted a constitution that severely limited presidential powers. As a result of the ensuing conflict, Haiti was divided into two states, with Christophe ruling in the north and Pétion in the south. First chosen president in 1807, Pétion was named president for life in 1816. Beginning in 1809, he initiated a program of land distribu-

tion to army officers and soldiers that created a nation of peasant small-holders but harmed productivity and led to falling exports. Pétion is also remembered for offering asylum in 1815-16 to **Simón Bolívar**, whom he asked to free the slaves in Spanish America.

Philip II of Spain (1527-1598), king of Spain (1556-98), Naples and Sicily (1554-98), and Portugal (1580-98) and ruler of the Netherlands (1555-98). While Philip was determined to consolidate and extend Spanish power, royal government, and religious orthodoxy and was called the "Prudent" king for his diligent work habits, direct administration, and bureaucratic control, his reign must be viewed as a failure. His policies committed Spain beyond available resources and ultimately set the stage for its decline in the seventeenth century. More gold and silver from the Indies and new taxes, especially in Castile, increased his revenues threefold during his reign and allowed him to survive four bankruptcies (1557, 1560, 1575, and 1596), defeat the Turks at Lepanto (1571), conquer Portugal (1580) and add her empire to his, launch the Spanish Armada (1588), contain the French, and fight continuous rebellion in the Netherlands as of 1566. Under his leadership Spain was the preeminent European power, but the moment was fleeting. In a continuous search for more revenues that would bring a definitive closure that never came, Philip sold off government offices and alienated vast areas of royal control for the temporary benefits of immediate income. This "go-for-broke" policy ultimately left Spain bankrupt and lacking in the resources necessary to maintain her power. In the Indies, government officials brought conquistadors and *encomenderos* under royal control, organized labor systems, and put in new district magistrates (*corregidores*) and taxes, such as the *alcabala* (sales tax), but at the same time the crown sold off administrative offices and tax collection sometimes several generations into the future. This Janus-like policy left vast areas of the New World in the hands of local elites and became the basis for a regionalism that continues to the present day.

Philip V (1683-1746), first king of Spain (1700-24; 1724-46) from the house of the Bourbons. Born in Versailles, France, Philip was the grandson of Louis XIV and was made heir to the throne of Spain by the childless **Charles II** (1665-1700). Philip's accession provoked the War of the Spanish Succession (1700-13). Other European powers feared having Bourbons as kings of both Spain and France. Philip's victory allowed for an empire-wide restructuring that laid the foundations for Spanish absolutism and the century-long changes known as the Bourbon Reforms. Catalonia and Valencia, having chosen the wrong side in the war, lost their special privileges, and, except for Navarre and the Basque provinces, every region in Spain was subject to the same laws and taxes. Other significant changes included having ministers in charge rather than councils, substituting French military organizational principles for Spanish ones, and collecting taxes with greater efficiency. In the latter case revenues more than doubled from 5 million pesos to 11.5 by 1711. Philip's second wife, Elizabeth Farnese of Parma, however, embroiled her husband in dynastic wars in Italy that slowed reform. Philip's own mental illness and religious predilections led him to abdicate in 1724 in favor of his sixteen-year-old son, Louis, but with the latter's death, he once again assumed the throne. Philip was served by able ministers like José de Patiño (1727-36) and the Marquis de la Ensenada (1743-54), aristocrats of merit, but the grandees were excluded from high office. In the New World, in addition to the above reforms, captains-general took over some of the functions of the viceroys, formal trading groups like the Caracas Company imitated French, Dutch and English mercantilism, and individual sailings of registered ships gradually replaced the convoy system.

Pinochet Ugarte, Augusto (1915–), Chilean army officer and president. A native of Valparaíso, Pinochet was a career military officer. During the 1950s and 1960s he taught at national war colleges in Chile and Ecuador, and in 1968 published a popular text on geopolitics. At the time of **Salvador Allende**'s inauguration, Pinochet was an influential member of the army's large conservative, anticommunist faction. When General Carlos Prats, a member of the army's moderate wing, became minister of the interior in October 1972, Pinochet assumed the post of acting commander-in-chief. He headed the military junta that assumed power following Allende's overthrow on September 11, 1973, going on to rule Chile for sixteen years, the first six by fiat, and the latter ten under a constitution adopted in 1980.

Pinochet and his supporters carried out their promise to eliminate the Marxist left from Chilean politics. Pursuant to the authoritarian Doctrine of National Security, they jailed and executed many supporters of the previous government and drove others into exile. In the early years Pinochet enforced his rule through a secret police known by the acronym DINA, dissolved in 1977.

Early in his regime Pinochet placed Chile in the vanguard of Latin American economic liberalism. He allowed free market economists to open Chile to foreign investment while privatizing hundreds of state-owned enterprises. Although the measures resulted in renewed concentration of wealth and were subject to criticism on other counts, they had the effect of lowering inflation and prices and causing Chile's economic growth to surpass that of all other Latin American nations. Latin America's economic recession of the early 1980s galvanized anti-Pinochet forces. Early 1983 was marked by mass protests in favor of a return to democratic rule. By the mid-1980s even the United States, formerly Pinochet's staunchest foreign supporter, opposed his dictatorship. On October 5, 1988, Chileans rejected the dictator's bid to extend his term for an additional eight years. Accordingly he approved presidential elections for the following year. Pinochet left the presidency in late 1990, but he retained control over the army and great influence in national politics. In March 1998 he stepped down as armed forces commander and entered the Chilean Senate. On October 16, 1998, while in London for medical treatment, he was arrested and held for extradition to Spain, where he was charged with genocide and other crimes.

Pizarro, Francisco (1478?-1541), conqueror of

Peru. From Trujillo, Extremadura, Spain, Francisco was the illegitimate son of a minor noble. He came to the Indies in 1502 and became an experienced veteran in Darién and the Isthmus of Panama serving with Alonso de Ojeda, Martín Enciso, **Vasco Núñez de Balboa**, and Pedrarias (**Pedro Arias de Ávila**). He was already in his middle forties and early fifties when he helped organize and lead the three expeditions to Peru (1524, 1526, 1531) that ended with the capture of **Atahualpa** at Cajamarca in 1532. Two years later the Spanish melted down 13,420 pounds of 221/2-carat gold and 26,000 pounds of silver. After the crown's *quinto real* (royal fifth) was subtracted, Pizarro and his three brothers got 24 of the 218 shares of this fabulous wealth. Becoming master of Peru was a more complex problem. An Inca revolt at Cuzco and a civil war with the followers of **Diego de Almagro** took their toll. A group of disappointed Almagrists assassinated Pizarro in Lima in 1541.

Pizarro never really had time to take control and enjoy his prize. He did pass out *encomiendas* and establish cities, among them Lima, the administrative capital of Peru, on the northern Peruvian coast, since Cuzco, the Inca capital, was too high and isolated at 11,000 feet. At the time of Pizarro's death Peru was still a divided and chaotic land where another two decades would be needed for peace to descend on Spanish society.

Pizarro, Gonzalo (1506?-1548), conqueror of Peru and leader of the rebellion against royal authority. Gonzalo was the illegitimate half-brother of **Francisco** and the youngest of the Pizarro brothers. He was at Cajamarca when **Atahualpa** was captured (1532) and shared in the division of the Inca's great treasure. Courageous if somewhat impetuous, he showed promise in the Inca siege of Cuzco. Francisco was preparing him for a leadership role in Peru and in 1540 made him governor of Quito from where he led an expedition to the Amazon. When he and a few men reappeared ghost-like in Quito in 1542, after being given up as lost and dead, it only enhanced his reputation as a fearless leader. Learning of Francisco's assassination (1541) and resentful at being excluded from government—the terms of

Francisco's will would have made him governor of Peru and heir apparent—he was the obvious choice for other malcontents to rally around. When the new viceroy, **Blasco Núñez de Vela,** arrived and tried to enforce the New Laws that would have curtailed the power of the *encomenderos*, rebellion broke out. Gonzalo seized the opportunity, and entered Lima in 1544 as commander of the rebel forces. Núñez de Vela was packed off to Spain but escaped on the way and formed an army. In the ensuing battle at Añaquito in 1546 Gonzalo defeated and executed the viceroy. The crown responded with the appointment of the cleric Pedro de la Gasca as president of the *audiencia* of Lima with full authority to change the offending laws and to reach a settlement. Gasca adroitly suborned many of the followers of Pizarro. When the final engagement took place in 1548, Gonzalo's army evaporated, with many throwing down their arms and joining the other side. Gonzalo was executed along with forty-nine other leaders the next day.

Pizarro, Hernando (1503?-1578), conqueror of Peru. Born in Trujillo, Extremadura, Spain, Hernando was the only legitimate son of the Pizarro brothers' father, Captain Gonzalo Pizarro. With an acceptable birth, education, and military training he had social and political contacts in Spain that served his half-brother **Francisco** well. He helped negotiate the agreement that put the latter fully in command of the third expedition (1531) that resulted in the capture of **Atahualpa** at Cajamarca (1532) and the division of the Inca's treasure. In 1534 he oversaw the transport to Spain of the king's share. He returned to Peru in 1535. There he got caught in the Inca siege of Cuzco and distinguished himself militarily. Just as the siege was lifted, the forces of the disgruntled **Diego de Almagro** occupied the city and imprisoned him. Released when he promised to return to Spain, he quickly gathered an army and defeated Almagro at the Battle of Salinas (1538) and then ordered the latter's execution. Back in the Iberian Peninsula by 1539, he was imprisoned by the Council of the Indies when charges were brought against him by the followers of Almagro. As Peru descended into a civil war led by his brother

Gonzalo, the crown found it prudent to keep him in prison, where he stayed until 1561. Nevertheless, he continued to oversee Pizarro interests in Spain and in Peru through his business agents. He was well attended in prison, fathered several children from various women, and married (1551) the *mestiza* daughter of Francisco in order to keep the family fortune intact. His investments paid off, and he built a sumptuous house on the main square of his hometown, Trujillo. His was one of the richest families in Extremadura.

Plaza Lasso, Galo (1906-1987), Ecuadorian president and statesman. The son of two-time Ecuadorian president Leonidas Plaza Gutiérrez (1901-5, 1912-16), Galo Plaza Lasso was born in New York City at a time when his father served as ambassador to the United States. Plaza Lasso attended college in the United States, briefly serving as attaché in Ecuador's Washington, D.C., embassy (1929-30). He managed the family estates until elected mayor of Quito in 1936. Subsequently he served as his nation's minister of defense (1938-40) and as ambassador to the United States (1944-46). He held a Senate seat between 1946 and 1948, and in 1948 won the presidency at the head of a ticket supported by Liberals and independents. Plaza Lasso went on to become Ecuador's first chief executive in twenty-eight years to complete his term. He gave Ecuador solid if unspectacular leadership, bending most of his efforts to helping make bananas the nation's principal export. Although Plaza Lasso remained influential in national politics until his death, the locus of his political activity was international (save for an unsuccessful presidential bid in 1960). During the early 1950s he served as a United Nations envoy on peace-keeping missions in Lebanon, the Congo, and Cyprus. In 1957-58 he headed the U.N. Economic Commission for Latin America (ECLA) committee charged with drafting the plan for the Latin American Free Trade Area (LAFTA). In 1968 Plaza Lasso became secretary-general of the Organization of American States. Remaining in that post until 1975, he worked to increase U.S. economic ties in Latin America. He also attempted to effect U.S. rapprochement with Cuba.

Pombal, Marquês de (Sebastião José de Carvalho e Mello; 1699-1782), Portuguese statesman and José I's chief minister (1750-77). Born into the lower nobility and educated in law at the University of Coimbra, Pombal served as Portugal's ambassador to Great Britain (1739-45) and emissary to Austria (1745-49) where he saw firsthand the great changes that were going on abroad. Anxious for Portugal to adopt Enlightenment ideals of rationalism and progress, he pushed a wide-ranging program of innovation and change when he became chief minister. Known today as the Pombaline Reforms, they paralleled and in many cases antedated, and were more thoroughgoing than, the Spanish Bourbon Reforms although they lacked the anticreole thrust of the latter. They were, for example, decidedly more anticlerical. The Jesuits were expelled from the Portuguese empire in 1759 with 670 departing Brazil alone. Their properties were auctioned off and their schools occupied. The Mercedarians met the same fate in the mid-1760s. Greater centralization and control over Brazil were promoted. The Junta do Comércio (Board of Trade) was created in 1755, the Erário Régio (Royal Treasury) in 1761, and separate Juntas da Fazenda (Boards of Treasury) for each of the captaincies in 1767. The viceregal capital was moved from Bahia to Rio de Janeiro in 1763; a second Relação (High Court) had already been established there in 1751. Economic changes were also significant. Inspection boards were created in 1751 to improve the competitiveness of Brazilian sugar and tobacco. Monopoly trading companies were created in 1755 and 1759, and the fleet system was terminated in 1766. While Pombal's quarter-of-a-century rule failed to arrest the decline in Brazil's gold production, his nationalistic program of regalism, enlightened despotism, and economic reform brought new structures and sense of purpose to Brazil. Made Conde de Oeiras in 1759 and Marquês de Pombal in 1769, he was stripped of his power by the new monarch, Maria I, in 1777.

Ponce de León, Juan (1460-1521), conqueror, first governor of Puerto Rico (1509-11), and explorer of Florida. Born in Santervás de Campos, Valladolid, Spain, Ponce de León went to Puerto

Rico in 1508. Under his leadership the Indians were distributed in *encomienda* and brutally worked in the gold-bearing river beds and streams. Soon one of the richest men in the Caribbean, he looked farther afield for other conquests. With license to conquer to the north, he traversed the Bahamas and the east and west coasts of Florida in 1513. Returning with colonists in 1521, he was wounded by hostile Indians and died in Cuba.

Porres, San Martín de (1579-1639), Peruvian mulatto saint. Born in Lima, Porres was the illegitimate son of Juan de Porres, a knight in the Order of Calatrava, and Ana Velázquez, a black servant from Panama. Unrecognized at first, Porres was later taken to Guayaquil by his father, educated there, and then returned to Lima when his father was appointed governor of Panama. He worked with surgeons, barbers, and herbalists and learned the rudiments of healing. He became a Dominican lay helper at fifteen and a professed lay brother at twenty-three. Known for his charity and humility, visionary experiences, and especially for his curative powers, he seemed to possess some inner knowledge or power, for which reason people were drawn to this socially marginal individual. When he died, the viceroy and the archbishop personally carried his casket. He was beatified in 1837 and canonized in 1962.

Portales, Diego (1793-1837), Chilean statesman, considered the creator of the Conservative regime that dominated the country for decades after 1830. Portales was born to a prominent creole family. Rejecting the priesthood or a legal career, he became a businessman. After the deaths of his wife and infant son, he went to Peru, where he established a partnership with José Manuel Cea. In 1824 the firm acquired from the Chilean government the tobacco, playing card, and liquor monopoly, which gave it the exclusive right to sell these items in Chile. The cancellation of the monopoly in 1826 propelled Portales into Chile's political arena, where he allied himself with the Conservative faction known as *pelucones*, or bigwigs, because of their aristocratic lineage.

By now Portales was convinced that Chile required a strong, competent, and highly centralized government that would guarantee order and stability. Portales never sought the presidency, but as a cabinet member he dominated the administrations of José Tomás Ovalle (1830-31) and Joaquín Prieto (1831-41). The constitution of 1833 reflected his views.

Portales resigned from the cabinet in 1832 and served briefly as governor of Valparaíso. He sought to make this port the most important on South America's Pacific coast. Portales returned to Prieto's cabinet in 1835 amid renewed political turmoil, but soon turned his attention to foreign affairs. He perceived the creation of the Peru–Bolivia Confederation by **Andrés Santa Cruz** in 1836 as a threat to Chile's commercial interests and supported the declaration of war (December 28, 1836) against the confederation. The war was not popular, and numerous conspiracies arose against the government. Portales himself was the victim of a mutinous regiment, which seized him at Quillota. He was shot to death a few days later.

Portinari, Cândido Torquato (1903-1962), Brazilian painter. Cândido Portinari was born in rural São Paulo to an Italian immigrant family. Early manual labor on coffee plantations sensitized him to the lot of the poor and inspired him to make them themes of his later work. His talent won fifteen-year-old Cândido a scholarship to study at the National Fine Arts School in Rio de Janeiro. There he came into contact with members of Brazil's Modernist "Generation of 1922," among them architect **Oscar Niemeyer** and composer **Heitor Villa-Lobos**. They collectively declared their cultural independence from European forms. Portinari was also influenced by the Mexican muralists **Diego Rivera**, **José Clemente Orozco**, and **David Alfaro Siqueiros**. A scholarship awarded him in 1928 allowed Portinari to study in Europe, where he was further influenced by cubism.

Like others of his generation, Cândido Portinari drew heavily on national themes. He painted canvases and worked in tile, but his best-known pieces are his murals. Portinari's first international recognition came in 1935, when his canvas *Coffee* won an award at the International Exposition of the Carnegie Institute in Pittsburgh. During the later 1930s he decorated Brazil's Ministry of Education building in Rio with murals depicting scenes from Brazilian history. They won him a commission to paint historical murals, *Discovery of the New World*, at the Hispanic Foundation of the Library of Congress in Washington, D.C. During the 1940s he collaborated with Oscar Niemeyer, most notably in decoration of the Church of St. Francis of Assisi near Belo Horizonte. During the late 1940s he executed paintings and murals on historical themes, and illustrating the ravages of drought in Brazil's Northeast. During the 1950s Portinari painted the panels *War* and *Peace* at the United Nations building in New York City. He died in 1962, victim of the heavy metals used in his paints.

Posada, José Guadalupe (1852-1913), Mexican printmaker. Born in Aguascalientes, Posada began his career in his native city and in León. In 1888 he moved to Mexico City, where he opened a small shop near the main square, or Zócalo. Many of the prints he produced were for Antonio Vanegas Arroyo, a publisher of broadsides, religious items, and other printed works for the poor people of the capital. Many of Posada's illustrations, usually made by etching on a zinc plate later dipped in acid, depicted religious figures or commented on current events, but the best known are *calaveras*, scenes of skeletons produced for the Day of the Dead (November 2), which deftly satirized the powerful and the pretentious. Posada was little known in his lifetime, but his work was discovered in the 1920s by the Franco-Mexican artist Jean Charlot, who saw him as a forerunner of the artistic renaissance the country was then experiencing. Since then Posada has been hailed as a Mexican Daumier, whose bold lines and acerbic wit brilliantly captured the popular culture of his day.

Prebisch, Raúl (1901-1986), Argentine economist. Raúl Prebisch graduated from the University of Buenos Aires in 1923, and taught there for more than twenty years (1925-48). He managed Argentina's new Central Bank from 1935 to 1943.

Prebisch's fame as Latin America's leading economist rests in his critique of classical economics, specifically the notion of comparative advantage, which holds that nations should specialize in the economic activity for which they are best suited. Prebisch argued that industrialized countries occupied the "center" of the world economy, and less industrialized ones the "periphery." Such a system benefited the former and worked to the detriment of the latter, who were forced to buy ever more expensive manufactured goods with ever cheaper exports (thereby suffering deterioration of terms of trade). Prebisch inferred that industrialized nations advocated free trade principles but violated them in practice. He argued that peripheral Latin America must follow a policy of "inward development" through state-led industrialization and protection. His ideas, which contributed to "dependency analysis," gained acceptance throughout the less-developed world during his years (1949-63) as director of the United Nations Economic Commission for Latin America (ECLA). Between 1964 and 1969, Prebisch served as secretary-general of the United Nations Conference on Trade and Development (UNCTAD). Among his more important books are *Introducción a Keynes* (1947), *Change and Development: Latin America's Great Task* (1971), and *Capitalismo periférico: crisis y transformación* (1981).

Prestes, Luís Carlos (1898-1990), Brazilian political leader. Born in Rio Grande do Sul, Prestes graduated from military school at age twenty. In 1924, on the anniversary of the 1922 Tenentes Revolt, he became one of numerous Brazilian junior-grade officers who rebelled in protest against the corrupt and repressive Old Republic. Unlike his peers, he refused to surrender, instead leading some 1,000 revolutionary troops on a three-year trek through the hinterlands. The odyssey made Prestes a folk hero, earning him the sobriquet "The Cavalier of Hope." At length the Prestes Column, as it came to be known, hotly pursued by the army, disbanded and its members escaped into Bolivia. Prestes traveled to the Soviet Union where he worked in the Comintern until his return to Brazil in 1935. There he helped lead the National Liberation Alliance in a failed attempt to overthrow the government of **Getúlio Vargas**, an act that cost him nine years' imprisonment. Upon his release in 1945, Prestes collaborated with Vargas in the war effort, reorganized the Brazilian Communist party (PCB), and won election to the Senate. When Vargas's successor, Eurico Dutra, purged Congress of its Communist members and outlawed the PCB in 1947, Prestes went into hiding, periodically calling for overthrow of the government. He returned to public life in 1956, during the administration of **Juscelino Kubitschek**. After the military coup of 1964, Prestes returned to hiding. But by then he called for a democratic transition to socialism, a stance that led PCB militants to publicly reject his leadership. Prestes denounced them and departed Brazil. He returned in 1979, following the proclamation of political amnesty. A factionalized PCB proceded to strip him of his post as party secretary-general. Prestes spent his last years campaigning on behalf of populist politician and labor leader Leonel Brizola.

Remón Cantera, José Antonio (1908-1955), Panamanian president. José Antonio Remón attended the Mexican Military Academy and joined the Panamanian National Police in 1931. In 1947, when he became commander of the force, he possessed a national reputation as a result of his energetic modernization and strengthening of that body. He created his own political party in 1951, a year later winning the presidency at its head. Remón carried his energy and organizational skill into Panama's top elective office, improving national administration in a host of ways. He initiated public works programs, built clinics and schools, and expanded the National Police (renamed the National Guard), thanks in part to his assessment of a national income tax and improvement in tax collections. Remón promoted economic development and established the Colón free trade zone. Although he limited the freedom of labor unions and political parties, he was praised for his honesty. His most notable achievement was his renegotiation of the 1903 Hay–Bunau-Varilla Treaty. Through the Remón-

Eisenhower Treaty of 1955, payments to the government from the Panama Canal Commission were greatly increased. The treaty also ended discriminatory pay scales for Panamanians working in the Canal Zone and won Panama the right to tax salaries earned there by Panamanians. Remón was assassinated in January 1955.

Revillagigedo, Conde de (Juan Vicente de Güemes-Pacheco y Padilla; 1740-1799), viceroy of New Spain (1789-94). Born in Havana, Cuba, Revillagigedo grew up in Mexico while his father was viceroy there (1746-55). Imbued with the modernizing tenets of the Enlightenment, Revillagigedo helped to implement some of the more controversial features of the Bourbon Reforms: a new system of regional administration centralized in the hands of a regional bureaucrat (the intendant), a revamped system of finance and taxation, a more open trading system, and a reorganized and much reduced local militia but with an increased military presence of Spanish soldiers. This restructuring upset entrenched interests, opened the way for others, and created significant tensions within the kingdom. Many of the political controversies of the nineteenth century—the centralist–federalist struggles and the increased militarization of society—sprang from these reforms. Less controversial were Revillagigedo's road-building campaigns, regularization of the mail service, support for primary schools, patronage of the arts, refurbishment of the viceregal capital, and improvements in public health.

Reyes, Rafael (1850-1921), Colombian president. Born in the village of Santa Rosa de Viterbo, north of Bogotá, Rafael Reyes made his fortune through commercial ventures, especially quinine and rubber extraction, in Colombia's Amazon jungles. He fought on the side of the Conservative government in the civil war of 1885, afterward serving President **Rafael Núñez** as an envoy to Europe. He again defended the government in the civil war of 1895, afterward again traveling to Europe as minister to France. In 1901 he represented Colombia at the Second International American Conference in Mexico City. Elected president in 1904, he soon suspended Congress and governed the nation through a puppet assembly until 1909, a period known in Colombian history as the *quinquenio*. Reyes set Colombia's modernization into motion, reestablishing the nation's credit abroad and encouraging foreign investment, most notably by the United Fruit Company, which established banana plantations on the north coast. He encouraged infant industry through protective tariffs, and built highways and railroads. Although a Conservative, he won Liberal support by guaranteeing minority representation in Congress. He also worked to improve diplomatic links with the United States, suspended as a result of the secession of Panama. That strategy led to his downfall. In March 1909 he submitted three bilateral treaties to his constituent assembly—the Root-Cortés-Arosemena accords, which would have normalized relations between Colombia and the United States and Panama. The proposal touched off student demonstrations that convinced Reyes to relinquish power. In July 1909 resigned his presidency and departed for Europe. He returned to Colombia in 1919, and resided there until his death.

Reyes Ochoa, Alfonso (1889-1959), Mexican intellectual and diplomat. Alfonso Reyes was born in Monterrey, the son of General Bernardo Reyes. He was a prominent member, with Antonio Caso, Pedro Henríquez Ureña, Martín Luis Guzmán, and **José Vasconcelos**, of the Ateneo de la Juventud (1909-14). While his peers in the Ateneo strove to interpret Mexico and to celebrate its uniqueness, Reyes, a humanist with a passion for Greek culture, attempted to fix the nation's place within greater Western civilization. That became an integrating theme running through his substantial and multifarious literary production. Following his father's death during the 1913 overthrow of President **Francisco I. Madero**, and his rejection of **Victoriano Huerta**'s offer to become the usurper's personal secretary, Reyes left Mexico for what stretched to an absence of twenty-five years. He spent 1914-26 in Spain and France, conducting research at Madrid's Centro de Estudios Históricos and serving in varied diplomatic capacities. Among his publications

during that period were *Visión de Anáhuac* (1917), concerning Spain's historic perception of Mexico, and *Ifigenia cruel* (1924), an autobiographical play treating his self-imposed exile. Between 1927 and 1938 he served as Mexico's ambassador to Argentina and Brazil. Throughout his time there he published poetry, plays, and critical essays, as well as translations and anthologies of European writing. In 1939 he returned home to head the Casa de España, renamed the Colegio de México in 1940. In 1941 he received national and international recognition for his *La crítica en la edad ateniense*. While Reyes's admirers throughout the Hispanic world regularly promoted his candidacy for the Nobel Prize, he did not gain wide recognition beyond Latin America until publication in the United States of *The Position of America and Other Essays* (1950).

Rio Branco, Barão do (José Maria da Silva Paranhos Júnior; 1845-1912), Brazilian diplomat and foreign minister. Born in Bahia, Rio Branco was the oldest child of the Visconde do Rio Branco (1819-1880), the imperial diplomat and statesman best known as the author of the Free Birth Law (1871), which envisioned the gradual abolition of slavery. Though trained as a lawyer in Recife, the younger Rio Branco was deeply interested in Brazilian history and diplomacy. He entered the foreign service at the age of thirty-one, serving as consul in Liverpool from 1876 to 1891. He received the title of baron in 1888. Rio Branco first distinguished himself for his effective advocacy of Brazilian claims in boundary disputes with Argentina over the Misiones territory (1893-95) and with France over French Guiana (1898-1900). While serving as minister to Germany, he was named foreign minister in 1902. In the latter post, which he held until his death, he oversaw the peaceful settlement of boundary disputes with Bolivia, Peru, and other countries. All together, his efforts resulted in the addition of approximately 342,000 square miles to the national domain.

Rio Branco is also remembered for his efforts to enhance the international prestige of Brazil, especially in Latin America, and to develop a close relationship with the United States. In 1905 the two countries elevated the top diplomat in their respective capitals to the rank of ambassador. Rio Branco was also a supporter of the Pan American movement, which held its third international conference in Rio de Janeiro in 1906.

Rivadavia, Bernardino (1780-1845), Argentine statesman. Rivadavia was born in Buenos Aires to a wealthy Spanish merchant and his Argentine wife. He himself married the daughter of a former viceroy and became prominent as a lawyer and merchant and as a defender of Buenos Aires during the British invasion of 1806-7. In 1811-12 he was secretary of the triumvirate that ruled Buenos Aires and later traveled extensively in Europe, where he became an admirer of the English philosopher Jeremy Bentham. From 1821 to 1824 he served as minister of government and foreign affairs in the administration of Martín Rodríguez, governor of Buenos Aires province. In this capacity he initiated numerous reforms, including the establishment of the University of Buenos Aires and the Beneficent Society, which was given responsibility for all schools and other institutions serving women and girls. He also attempted to limit the economic and political power of religious orders and the Catholic church as a whole. He welcomed British trade and investment and introduced the practice of granting long-term leases on public lands. Since the renters eventually acquired ownership of huge tracts of public land, this measure has often been criticized. In 1826 he was named president of the United Provinces of the Río de la Plata, but his centralist constitution aroused provincial opposition while his plan to make the city of Buenos Aires the federal capital was resisted by local federalists who did not want the province to lose control of the city's revenues. His government was also attacked for signing a treaty that in effect ceded the Banda Oriental (the future Uruguay) to Brazil. Rivadavia resigned the presidency in June 1827 and spent most of his remaining years in Spain. He is remembered as a founder of the Unitarian party, whose leaders were committed to free trade and the introduction of European immi-

grants and European ideas and institutions. To many, this cosmopolitan vision seemed elitist and unpatriotic.

Rivera, Diego (1886-1957), Mexican muralist and painter. A native of Guanajuato, Rivera studied at Mexico City's Academy of Fine Arts. From 1907 to 1921 he lived in Europe, where he was strongly influenced by cubism. Upon his return to Mexico, he led the mural movement that filled public walls with frescoes celebrating national culture and history, especially the revolution of 1910. A lifelong Marxist-Leninist, he joined Mexico's Communist party in 1922. In 1929 he married **Frida Kahlo**, who also became a well-known painter.

Between 1923 and 1928 he created in the Ministry of Education a series of frescoes depicting Mexican labor and festivals and illustrating three *corridos*, or revolutionary songs. In 1925-26 he painted another set of frescoes for a new agricultural school in Chapingo. Often considered his masterpiece, these murals portray Mexico's agrarian revolution and the fecundity of the earth. Rivera also painted several murals in the United States, notably a paean to science and technology at the Detroit Institute of Arts (1932-33). A mural he began in New York's Rockefeller Center was destroyed in 1934 after he refused to remove a portrait of Lenin, which he had placed in a prominent location. He later recreated the mural, *Man at the Crossroads*, in Mexico City's Palace of Fine Arts. Other important murals by Rivera can be found in the Cortés Palace in Cuernavaca and in the National Palace and the Diego Rivera Museum, both in Mexico City. He was also an accomplished easel painter. Many of his best-known canvases, such as *Woman Grinding Maize* (1924) and *Flower Day* (1925), portray Mexico's indigenous culture.

Rivera, Fructuoso (c. 1784-1854), Uruguayan patriot leader, president, and founder of the Colorado party. Rivera was born near Montevideo to a landowning family. Starting in 1811, he took part in the anti-Spanish struggle as a lieutenant of

José Gervasio Artigas. He also opposed the ambitions of Buenos Aires to rule Uruguay and those of the Portuguese, who invaded the province in 1816. After the Portuguese victory at Tacuarembó in 1820, however, he did not follow Artigas into exile but surrendered to the Portuguese and was made commander of their forces in Uruguay. In 1825, when **Juan Antonio Lavalleja** launched his anti-Portuguese uprising, Rivera, apparently by prearrangement, allowed himself to be captured. Although his relations with Lavalleja became strained, Rivera distinguished himself in the campaigns that led to the emergence of Uruguay as an independent state in 1828.

Rivera took office as Uruguay's first president on November 6, 1830. Although he handed power to his successor, Manuel Oribe, in 1834, he soon concluded that the latter was bent on eroding his power base in the countryside and rose in revolt in July 1836. It was during the ensuing conflict that the forces of Oribe and Rivera began wearing blue and red emblems that became associated with Uruguay's fledgling parties, the Blancos and Colorados. Oribe was forced to step down in October 1838, and Rivera began a second presidential term on March 1, 1839. The conflict between the two men continued, however, becoming part of a larger struggle as Oribe sought assistance from **Juan Manuel de Rosas** in Buenos Aires while Rivera had the support of anti-Rosas exiles in Montevideo, which was besieged by Oribe (1843-51). Great Britain, France, and Brazil also intervened on behalf of the anti-Rosas forces. Defeated at the battles of Arroyo Grande (December 6, 1842) and India Muerta (March 27, 1845), Rivera was forced to flee to Brazil. He returned to Uruguay in 1846, but his attempt to enter into negotiations with Oribe led his fellow Colorados in Montevideo to decree his banishment to Brazil in 1847. After the fall of Rosas in 1852, Rivera was asked to join a ruling triumvirate with Lavalleja and another Colorado leader, Venancio Flores, but he died while en route to Montevideo. Rivera is considered a typical caudillo, or strongman, of early nineteenth-century Latin America, effective as a military leader but less successful in the role of chief executive.

Roca, Julio Argentino (1843-1914), president of Argentina (1880-86, 1898-1904). Born in Tucumán province to an upper-class family, Roca completed his formal education at the age of sixteen. Embarking on a military career, he fought on behalf of the Argentine Confederation at the battles of Cepeda (1859) and Pavón (1861). He later fought in the Paraguayan War (1864-70). In 1879, by now a general and minister of war in the cabinet of President Nicolás Avellaneda, Roca led the so-called "conquest of the desert," which was aimed gaining control of lands south of the Río Negro. In 1880 he sought the presidency as a spokesman for the interests of the interior provinces as opposed to those of Buenos Aires. After his election, partisans of the losing candidate and governor of Buenos Aires, Carlos Tejedor, staged an unsuccessful revolt. The city of Buenos Aires was federalized before Roca took office on October 12, 1880. Despite his provincial antecedents, Roca was committed to national integration; he also encouraged foreign investment and immigration as means of stimulating economic development. Nicknamed El Zorro ("the fox"), the wily politician molded the dominant National Autonomist party (PAN), which ruled Argentina until 1916, into an effective coalition representing Argentina's landed interests.

In 1886 Roca installed his brother-in-law Miguel Juárez Celman as his successor, but the latter was forced to resign in 1890 in the midst of a financial and political crisis. Though the PAN was somewhat weakened as a result, Roca was able to engineer the election of Luis Sáenz Peña for the presidential term beginning in 1892. During Roca's second term an uproar arose over a plan to consolidate the national debt by obtaining a foreign loan secured by Argentine customs duties. Roca was forced to declare a state of siege and withdrew his support for the plan. His term was also marked by tension stemming from a boundary dispute with Chile, which was resolved by arbitration in 1902. His influence waned after the death of his successor, Manuel Quintana, in 1906 and the accession of Vice President José Figueroa Alcorta, a Roca foe.

Rocafuerte, Vicente (1783-1847), Ecuadorian statesman. Born in Guayaquil to an aristocratic family, Rocafuerte was educated at home and in schools in Madrid and Paris. After returning to Ecuador in 1807, he was elected as a deputy to the Cortes, or parliament, created by the liberal Spanish constitution of 1812, but the Cortes was dissolved soon after Rocafuerte took his seat in 1814. He spent most of the subsequent years in Europe and the United States, where he wrote a book (1821) in praise of American political institutions. At the request of Mexican friends he also wrote an attack on the monarchy of **Agustín de Iturbide**. While in Mexico, he was persuaded to join a diplomatic mission to England (1824-29) and helped obtain British recognition of Mexico. Back in Mexico, he was active on behalf of liberal causes but was forced to return to Ecuador in February 1833. There he was elected to Congress and soon clashed with **Juan José Flores**, who ordered his arrest and exile. While en route to exile, however, he accepted leadership of an armed revolt against Flores. In mid-1834 Rocafuerte became Flores's prisoner, but continuing rebel successes led Flores to make peace with the insurgents and in effect to install Rocafuerte in the presidency.

As president (1835-39) Rocafuerte sought to improve education, modernize the economy, and reform the fiscal system, but his efforts met with bitter opposition and little was accomplished. At the conclusion of his term he became governor of Guayas province. Although he initially worked in harmony with Flores, who was again president, he denounced the authoritarian constitution of 1843 written under Flores's direction and attacked the latter as an upstart and tyrant. After Flores's ouster in 1845, Rocafuerte served as president of the Senate and represented Ecuador in Lima, where he died.

Rodó, José Enrique (1871-1917), Uruguayan essayist and journalist. José Enrique Rodó won fame throughout the Spanish-speaking world following publication of his essay *Ariel* in 1900. Rodó's thesis was that Latin America possessed a superior form of civilization rooted in its peoples' inherent spirituality and idealism. Those qualities

had enabled them to reject "Jacobite tyranny" that destroyed social harmony by leveling society and, ultimately, destroying culture. The antithesis of Rodó's Ariel was, as in Shakespeare's *The Tempest*, Caliban, a vulgar, earth-bound creature incapable of spiritual greatness. Readers interpreted Rodó's Caliban as symbolizing the United States, a country whose people were blinded by materialism and rendered incapable of spiritual greatness through the leveling effect of democracy. Rodó's fame earned him two terms in Uruguay's General Assembly (1902-5, 1908-14), where he represented the Colorado party. Meanwhile he continued to publish collections of his erudite polished essays: *Liberalismo y jacobinismo* (1906); *Motivos de Proteo* (*The Motives of Proteus*, 1909); and *El Mirador de Próspero* (1913). Rodó's *Ariel* captured the imagination of a generation of young, traditionminded Latin Americans intimidated by the emergence of an aggressive and bumptious United States and made uneasy by the first signs of working-class movements in their midst. Emergence of Latin America's "social problem" soon rendered the elitist "arielist" notions superfluous. Rodó did not outlive *arielismo*. He died of an illness contracted in Sicily, where he had gone to cover World War I for Montevideo newspapers.

Rojas Pinilla, Gustavo (1900-75), Colombian soldier and president. Rojas Pinilla graduated from normal school in his hometown of Tunja (1917), going on to attend the Colombian Military Academy in Bogotá. He began his military career in 1920, but interrupted it to earn an engineering degree at Tri-State College in Angola, Indiana in the United States (1927). He worked in Colombia as a civil engineer until 1932, when he resumed active military service during the Leticia crisis. As commander of the Third Brigade, headquartered in Cali, he acted expeditiously to quell rioting provoked by the assassination in Bogotá of Liberal caudillo **Jorge Eliécer Gaitán**. Rojas achieved the rank of general in 1949, and in 1950 was named commander of the military forces. During 1950-51 he served as Colombian delegate to United Nations peace-keeping forces. On June 13, 1953, Rojas, supported by moderate Conservatives, overthrew President **Laureano Gómez**. His action was initially applauded by Colombians. Political violence decreased sharply, and record coffee prices brought economic well-being. But Rojas's mismanagement of public affairs, his growing authoritarianism, a decline in coffee prices, joint Liberal-Conservative opposition to his rule, and a resurgence in political conflict (La Violencia) combined to force his resignation May 10, 1957. Rojas returned from self-imposed exile in 1959, and was subsequently deprived of his political rights in a Senate trial. In 1961 he founded a personalist, populist political party, the National Popular Alliance (ANAPO), which steadily gained power over the ensuing decade. Rojas narrowly lost the 1970 presidential election to Conservative Misael Pastrana Borrero, amid charges of fraud on the part of outgoing president, **Carlos Lleras Restrepo**. ANAPO declined as a national political force following the death of Rojas Pinilla.

Romero, Oscar Arnulfo (1917-1980), Salvadoran archbishop. Oscar Romero was humbly born in Ciudad Barrios. He entered San Miguel Seminary in 1931, so impressing his superiors that he was sent on to the National Seminary in San Salvador (1937), and thence to Gregorian University in Rome, where he was ordained in 1942. Romero served as parish priest in Ciudad Barrios until the 1960s, thereafter beginning a rapid ascent through the church hierarchy. He was named monsignor in 1967 and bishop of Santiago de María in 1974. In 1977 he became archbishop of El Salvador. Up to that time Romero's ministry had been a rather conservative one. But his rise coincided with the growth of social activism among the Salvadoran priesthood, as well as with increasing attacks on religious workers by right-wing paramilitary groups. The murder of Father Rutilio Grande in early 1977 transformed Romero and his message. The new archbishop displeased the nation's military rulers when he boycotted the inauguration of President Carlos H. Romero in mid-1977. He infuriated them during 1978 and 1979 by denouncing human rights violations by army and paramilitary groups. In February 1980, the same month he was nomi-

nated for the Nobel Peace Prize by the British Parliament, he preached that insurrection was justified in the face of tyranny. On March 23, in a widely reported sermon, Romero implored soldiers not to fire upon unarmed civilians. One day later he was assassinated as he celebrated mass in San Salvador. Romero's murder heightened international awareness of the fratricidal conflict raging in El Salvador and made him a symbol of principled resistance to tyranny.

Rondon, Cândido Mariano da Silva (1865-1958), explorer and advocate for Brazilian Indians. Born in Matto Grosso, Rondon studied at the Military School in Rio de Janeiro. There he was exposed to positivist principles in classes taught by **Benjamin Constant de Magalhães**, coming to embrace that philosophy's doctrine of progress. In 1890 Rondon was sent on an expedition to map and explore Brazil's vast interior, particularly uncharted portions of the Amazon territory, and to construct telegraph lines there. In the course of his work he became intrigued by the region's diverse Indian population, and committed to protecting it from abuse by white and mixed-blood Brazilians. That, coupled with his positivist-inspired conviction that the Indians could be integrated into national life, set Rondon upon his course as Brazil's foremost defender of its Indian peoples. Thanks to his activities Brazil established the Indian Protection Service (SPI) in 1910, and named Colonel Rondon its director. The SPI gained international recognition under Rondon's leadership. Its acculturation methods were held up as models of their time. And the pledge taken by SPI agents, "die if need be, but never kill," was universally admired, notably so by Theodore Roosevelt, whose Amazonian expedition of 1913-14 was guided by Rondon. While Rondon and his agency did not achieve notable success in protecting Brazil's Indians from encroaching civilization, they were applauded for their good intent. Two years before Rondon's death the nation recognized his contribution by renaming Guaporé Territory, in the center-west, Rondônia, in his honor.

Rosa de Lima, Santa (Rosa de Santa María; St.

Rose of Lima; 1586-1617), first American saint. Born into a modest family in Lima, Peru, as Isabel de Flores, Rosa joined the third order of the Dominicans at the age of twenty. Fasting and self-inflicting corporal penitence, she was able to go into trances and had visions of a mystical union with God. She cared for the sick, was thought capable of performing miracles, and was revered as a holy woman. Her fame and following grew and coincided with a deepening American awareness that their religious experience and identity were separate from those of their Iberian counterparts. She was beatified in 1668 and canonized in 1671. She is the patron saint of Lima, America, and the Philippines.

Rosas, Juan Manuel de (1793-1877), governor of Buenos Aires province (1829-32, 1835-52) and dictator of Argentina. The scion of a landowning family, Rosas had little education and married at the age of twenty. His wife, Encarnación Ezcurra (d. 1838), and his daughter Manuela (1817-1898) were important political associates. As a young man, he acquired immense tracts of land in the Buenos Aires frontier and became a wealthy rancher. He entered politics in 1820 as a supporter of Argentine federalism, but his primary concern was protection of the interests of Buenos Aires province and especially of its ranchers. In 1829 he was elected governor of the province with dictatorial powers; he returned to power in 1835 with similar authority. Although Buenos Aires was linked to the other provinces only in a loose confederation, Rosas was able to dominate much of the country until a coalition of domestic and foreign foes brought about his ouster in 1852.

Despising the principles of political democracy and liberty, Rosas provided order in a region that had known near-anarchy since independence. He used terror to stifle dissent, and dozens were executed by the military, the police, and the Sociedad Popular Restauradora, a Rosista political club. Support for the regime was shown by the wearing of red ribbons proclaiming death to Rosas's foes. Thousands fled Buenos Aires, going mainly to Montevideo, where Rosas tried to install friendly regimes. Rosas enjoyed support among the lower classes of the province, but they gained little from the regime. His defiance of France and Great Britain in the 1830s and 1840s made him a hero to nationalists. Rosas admired the British, however, and after he was forced from power, he settled in Southampton, England.

Sá, Mem de (1500?-1572), third governor-general of Brazil (1557-72). He increased the presence of royal government, established bureaucratic and fiscal control, and brought about economic development. While he restricted the enslavement of the Indians, he did pacify those around Salvador da Bahia and supported the Jesuit plan of settling them into *aldeias* (villages). Farther south he wiped out the French colony (1565-67) in Guanabara Bay and founded Rio de Janeiro.

Sá e Benavides, Salvador Correia de (1602-1681), Portuguese naval commander. Born in Cádiz, Spain, Sá was the son of Martim de Sá, governor of Rio de Janeiro (1602-8; 1623-32), with whom he traveled and learned about Brazil and his military craft. He participated in the defense of Bahia against the Dutch in 1624 on his third trip to Brazil. Made admiral of Río de la Plata in 1627, governor of Rio de Janeiro in 1637, administrator of the São Paulo and Santos mines in 1639, a member of the Overseas Council in Lisbon in 1644, convoy commander in 1645, and governor and captain-general of Angola in 1647, he was a major figure in the Portuguese empire of the South Atlantic. His crowning achievement was the taking of Luanda and Benguela from the Dutch in Angola in 1648. Known mainly for his naval exploits, he had success on land as well, having led pacification campaigns against the Indians in the Paraguayan Chaco and in Tucumán (Argentina) in the 1630s.

Saavedra Lamas, Carlos (1878-1959), Argentine diplomat, statesman, and Nobel Peace Prize winner. After teaching law at the University of Buenos Aires (1903-12), Saavedra Lamas entered politics serving as minister of justice and public service (1914-16) in the administration of President Victoriano de la Plaza. During the 1930s he collaborated in the conservative Concordancia movement that governed following the overthrow of **President Hipólito Yrigoyen**. Between 1932 and 1938, he served as foreign minister under President Agustín P. Justo. Saavedra Lamas captured world attention during the 1930s, both for his efforts to end the Chaco War (1932-35), and for his leadership at the Seventh International Conference of American States (1933) held at Montevideo. There he presented what came to be known as the Saavedra Lamas Anti-War Pact, which outlawed wars of aggression among American states. His fame as a statesman reached its peak in 1936, the year he received the Nobel Peace Prize. At the Inter-American Conference for the Maintenance of Peace (December 1-23), U.S. secretary of state Cordell Hull embraced the Saavedra Lamas Anti-War Pact. That action, along with U.S. president Franklin Roosevelt's promise that his country would be a "good neighbor" to Latin American states, crowned the Argentine diplomat's leadership of Latin American states in resisting U.S. unilateralism in hemispheric affairs. Saavedra Lamas retired from public life in 1938, going on to serve as rector of the University of Buenos Aires (1941-44).

Sáenz de Thorne, Manuela (1797-1856), mistress and confidant of **Simón Bolívar** and political activist in her own right. Sáenz was born in Quito, the natural daughter of parents of Spanish ancestry. In 1817 she married an Englishman, James Thorne, who was twice her age, and moved with him to Lima. An ardent supporter of the cause of independence, she met Bolívar in 1822 while she was visiting Quito. Separating from her husband, she became Bolívar's companion and advisor in Peru and later joined him in Bogotá. There she saved his life on September 25, 1828, when she warned him of the arrival of would-be assassins and enabled him to escape by leaping from a window. As Bolívar's political fortunes waned, her public defense of his policies created controversy, and she was forced to leave Colombia after his death in 1830. Barred from Ecuador as well, she settled in Paita, Peru, where she lived in poverty but remained in contact with **Juan José Flores** and other old Bolivarians.

Sahagún, Bernardino de (1499 or 1500-1590),

Franciscan missionary and ethnographer. Born in Sahagún, Spain, Bernardino de Ribeira or, as he was called, Bernardino from Sahagún, arrived in Mexico in 1529. He came to believe he would never truly convert and thus educate the Indians unless he learned their language and culture. Imbued with the humanism of the Renaissance he saw the process as a dialogue between the two cultures, and although he never doubted the superiority of Christianity and the necessity of eradicating paganism, his intellectual journey to understand the other side reached sophisticated levels of comprehension. He helped establish and taught in the Colegio of Santa Cruz, in Tlatelolco, where sons of the Aztec elite were taught Spanish, Latin, and Nahuatl. With their help Sahagún worked to recover the Indian past and to leave a written record of Aztec civilization as well as their view of the Spanish conquest. To understand their cultural underpinnings was for him a necessary step on the road to their true conversion. The result was the *Historia general de las cosas de Nueva España* (*A General History of the Things of New Spain*), sometimes called the Florentine Codex for the place in Italy where it was preserved. Presented in fourteen books with parallel columns of Nahuatl and Spanish it was an encyclopedic compendium of what was known about the Aztec world and is still one of the main sources for our understanding of that realm and how it came to pass. It was first published in 1829-30 in Mexico.

Salinas de Gortari, Carlos (1948–), Mexican president. Carlos Salinas was born in Mexico City, where he attended private schools. He took an economics degree at the National University in 1971, and earned a doctorate in political economy at Harvard University in 1978. During 1979-81 he worked in the national Office of Planning and Budget, which at the time was directed by Miguel de la Madrid. When de la Madrid became president in 1982, Salinas was named director of the budget office. In that capacity he supervised a neoliberal reform program featuring privatization of state-owned enterprises and the recruitment of foreign industry, especially in the duty-free *maquiladora* zone along the U.S. border. Salinas launched his candidacy for the presidency in 1987, and in mid-1988 with 51 percent of the vote defeated **Cuauhtémoc Cárdenas**, leader of a left-wing coalition opposed to neoliberalism, who got 31 percent. Many subsequently claimed that Cárdenas was deprived of the presidency through election fraud. Salinas continued his predecessor's neoliberal program, selling most remaining state-owned companies and amending the constitution to allow for privatization of communal *ejido* farms. In 1988 he proposed to U.S. president-elect George Bush the abolition of trade restrictions between Mexico and the United States. He had the satisfaction of seeing Canada, the United States, and Mexico joined in the North American Free Trade Agreement (NAFTA) at the end of his presidency.

While Salinas had promised Mexicans that he would democratize politics, the PRI machine frustrated his efforts. Salinas reached the heights of popularity in November 1993, when the U.S. Congress approved the NAFTA accord. But he suffered a reversal of fortune over the course of 1994. During early January, Zapatista guerrillas in southern Mexico proclaimed their armed opposition both to the federal government and the NAFTA agreement. On March 23, the reform-minded PRI candidate Luis Donaldo Colosio, favored to win the approaching presidential election, was assassinated. In December, shortly after President **Ernesto Zedillo Ponce de León** took office, the economy collapsed as a result of poor economic management on the part of Salinas. Large amounts of short term notes held abroad came due, and even though the United States helped with bridge loans, the peso lost half of its value in less than a month. Those blows, coupled with allegations of rampant corruption during his term in office, particularly involving his brother Raúl, ruined Salinas's reputation and ended his candidacy to become secretary-general of the United Nations. He fled Mexico in early 1995, at length settling in Ireland, a country from which he could not be extradited to face charges of financial impropriety.

Sandino, Augusto César. (1895-1934), Nicaraguan revolutionary. Augusto César Sandino was the natural son of a peasant mother and a middle-class father. He attended school in his native village of Niquinohomo. In 1920 he was forced to flee Nicaragua after shooting a man in a fight, and spent six years in Honduras and Tampico, Mexico. Sandino returned to Nicaragua in 1926, and joined Liberal general José María Moncada in opposing the government of Conservative Emiliano Chamorro. When Henry L. Stimson, President Coolidge's personal representative, brought about a settlement between Liberals and Conservatives (May 1927), Sandino refused to lay down his arms. Rather, he declared his force the Defending Army of National Sovereignty (EDSN) and began attacking both U.S. troops in Nicaragua and those of Adolfo Díaz, a U.S. favorite who became president late in 1926. Sandino reduced the intensity of his attacks following Moncada's inauguration as president January 1, 1928. At length he traveled to Mexico, remaining there eleven months (June 1929–May 1930). He resumed command of the ESDN upon his return and increased attacks on U.S. forces. Meanwhile, his relationship with the established parties remained ambivalent, for they preferred to negotiate withdrawal of the foreigners. The November 1932 election of Liberal general Juan Sacasa and the withdrawal of U.S. marines convinced Sandino to end his insurgency. On February 2, 1933, he agreed to lay down his arms in exchange for the promise of autonomy within his former zone of operations and permission to keep a body guard. The government agreed to those provisions, but soon the National Guard, under the command of **Anastasio Somoza García**, violated them by attacking former EDSN members. In early 1934 Sandino met with Sacasa at the presidential palace, under guarantee of safe conduct. Upon leaving the meeting he and three companions were seized by Somoza henchmen, taken to the outskirts of Managua, and murdered. The National Guard subsequently wiped out all vestiges of the EDSN presence in highland Nicaragua. But Sandino remained a hero to Nicaraguan nationalists. In 1961 Nicaraguan revolutionary leftists gave his name to their Sandinista National Liberation Front. They seized power in 1979, and ruled the nation throughout the ensuing decade.

San Martín, José de (1778-1850), Argentine leader in the independence movement of Spanish South America. Born in Yapeyú in what is now Corrientes province, San Martín was the son of a Spanish army officer who was transferred to Spain in 1785. He joined the Spanish army in 1789 and fought in several engagements in the subsequent conflict with France. He left Spain in 1811, ostensibly to travel to Lima, but made his way to Buenos Aires instead. By now he was committed to the cause of Spanish-American independence and founded a quasi-Masonic organization called the Lautaro Lodge to further the patriot cause. Having been made a lieutenant colonel in the Argentine army, he defeated a Spanish force that had sailed up the Paraná River and landed at San Lorenzo near Rosario (February 3, 1813). The following year he was named governor of Cuyo province, where he devoted himself to organizing an army that would strike at the heart of Spanish power in Peru. He was convinced that only an attack on Peru by way of Chile would permanently end Spanish rule in South America. In this enterprise San Martín was aided by the arrival in Argentina of **Bernardo O'Higgins** and other Chilean exiles. He supported the formal declaration of independence from Spain issued by the congress of Tucumán on July 9, 1816, as well as a proposal to establish a monarchy under an Inca prince. San Martín remained an adherent of constitutional monarchy throughout his public career.

San Martín left Cuyo at the head of an army of 5,000 men in January 1817 and, after crossing the Andes, defeated the Spanish at Chacabuco on February 12, 1817. After the final triumph of the patriot forces in Chile at Maipú (April 5, 1818), he began preparations for the campaign against Peru. In August 1820 his army of approximately 4,500 Chileans and Argentineans sailed for Peru aboard a fleet of twenty-four vessels commanded by the British admiral **Thomas Cochrane**. Negotiations with the royalists for a peaceful settlement in Peru failed, but they evacuated Lima, and San Martín was able to enter the city unopposed. He declared the independence of Peru on July 28, 1821, and after being named protector of the new nation, he decreed an end to forced labor by Indians and the gradual abolition of slavery.

Since the royalists continued to control Andean Peru, San Martín's campaign remained unfinished. In July 1822 he met with **Simón Bolívar** in Guayaquil. The details of this celebrated encounter are not known, but after its conclusion San Martín decided to allow Bolivar to prosecute the war against the royalists. He resigned as protector and left Peru, where he had been under attack for his delay in confronting the royalists. In 1824 he traveled to Europe, where he remained for the rest of his life, except for a short trip to Uruguay in 1828. He kept abreast of events in Argentina, however, and bequeathed his sword to **Juan Manuel de Rosas**, whose stand against the French in 1838 he admired.

Santa Anna, Antonio López de (1794-1876), Mexican military and political leader. Born in Jalapa, Veracruz, Santa Anna joined a royalist infantry regiment as a junior officer in 1810. After an assignment in northern Mexico, he was transferred in 1815 to his native province, where he proved effective in pacifying pro-independence insurgents. In 1821, however, he supported the independence plan formulated by **Agustín de Iturbide**. For the next thirty years Santa Anna would be the most influential actor in Mexican politics, being named president on numerous occasions. Despite his defeats and disgrace, Mexicans were sufficiently impressed by his charisma and military skills to look to him for leadership in periods of crisis.

After playing a prominent role in the campaign that led to Iturbide's abdication in 1823, Santa Anna became a national hero in 1829 when he defeated a Spanish expedition that briefly occupied Tampico. He was elected president in 1832 but initially remained at his hacienda, Manga de Clavo, near Veracruz, while the vice president, Valentín Gómez Farías, acted as chief executive in Mexico City. The Liberal vice president's policies alienated both the clergy and the military and soon brought Santa Anna out of retirement, and the offensive measures were repealed. Santa Anna commanded Mexico's forces in the war for Texas independence and suffered a humiliating defeat at the Battle of San Jacinto, which was followed by his capture two days later. He regained his military luster in 1838 by repulsing a French force that attacked Veracruz during the Pastry War. During the fighting he was wounded in the left leg, which was amputated below the knee.

Santa Anna again served as president from 1841 to 1845 and then was exiled, only to be restored to power in 1846 after the start of the war with the United States. After the battle for Mexico City, he named an interim president as he left the capital to continue the war. However, discontent over his military failures led to the loss of his military command on October 7, 1847. In 1848 he went into exile again, spending the next five years in Jamaica and Colombia. Santa Anna occupied the presidency for the last time in 1853-55. Governing autocratically, he curtailed press freedom, dissolved Congress, and imposed centralism on the country. His sale of land south of the Gila River to the United States for $10 million (the Gadsden Purchase) proved very controversial. Forced from power by the Ayutla Revolution, he lived in Colombia and the Danish West Indies. He was allowed to return to Mexico in 1874.

Santa Cruz, Andrés (1792-1865), Bolivian military leader and statesman. Born in La Paz, Santa Cruz was the son of a Spanish official and a wealthy Indian woman. He fought in the royalist army at the start of the independence movement but joined the patriot forces in 1821. In 1823 he attempted to liberate Bolivia, then known as Upper Peru, by occupying La Paz and Oruro and defeating the royalists at Zepita. However, he was unable to retain control over the region, and Bolivia did not become independent until 1825. Elected president of Bolivia in 1828 after the resignation of **Antonio José de Sucre**, Santa Cruz took office on May 20, 1829. During his decade as Bolivia's chief executive, he proved to be an effective administrator who promulgated new civil and commercial codes and established numerous schools and cultural institutions. He reduced mining taxes and attempted to protect the domestic textile industry and to develop Cobija,

Bolivia's only undisputed port. Despite his efforts, the economy grew little, and government revenues stagnated. As a result, he devalued the country's silver peso and restored Indian tribute, abolished by **Simón Bolívar** in 1824-25, guaranteeing the Indians possession of their communal landholdings for ten years.

Santa Cruz had long been interested in Peru, of which he had been president in 1826-27, and harbored the idea of uniting it with Bolivia. In 1836, taking advantage of internal turmoil in Peru, he created the Peru–Bolivia Confederation, of which he became protector. The creation of the confederation was opposed by Agustín Gamarra and other Peruvians and by Argentina and Chile, which viewed it as a strategic and economic threat. An Argentine force and a Chilean expedition were both defeated in 1837. The Chileans' second and larger expedition, led by **Manuel Bulnes**, had greater success, inflicting a decisive defeat on Santa Cruz at Yungay on January 20, 1839. The confederation now collapsed, and, though he made abortive efforts to regain power in Bolivia, Santa Cruz's political career was also at an end. He eventually settled in France, where he died.

Santander, Francisco de Paula (1792-1840), leader of the independence movement in Colombia and president (1832-37). Santander was born in Cúcuta in northeastern Colombia (then called New Granada), the son of a well-to-do landowner. He was completing his legal studies in 1810 when the independence movement began, and he joined the patriot forces. As General Pablo Morillo reestablished Spanish rule in 1816, Santander, by now a colonel, retreated to the eastern plains region of Casanare. There he helped organize the campaign led by **Simón Bolívar** that brought the liberation of New Granada at the Battle of Boyacá on August 7, 1819. In 1821 he was elected vice president of Gran Colombia (made up of New Granada, Venezuela, and Ecuador) and governed the new nation in the absence of the president, Bolívar; both he and Bolívar were reelected to their respective posts in 1826. A conscientious and able administrator, Santander pursued a generally liberal course, encouraging education and moving to curb the influence of the Catholic church. He also insisted on maintaining the powers of patronage over the church previously enjoyed by the kings of Spain. After Bolívar returned to Gran Colombia in November 1826, his relations with Santander became strained. Santander and his supporters resented Bolívar's lenient treatment of the rebellious **José Antonio Páez** of Venezuela and objected to Bolívar's increasingly authoritarian tendencies. When an unsuccessful attempt was made on Bolívar's life on September 25, 1828, Santander was accused of complicity, though the charges were never substantiated. He was exiled and spent the years 1829-32 in Europe and the United States.

After the disintegration of Gran Colombia, the assembly that drafted a constitution for the new republic of New Granada elected Santander provisional president in 1832. Elected to a four-year term in 1833, he followed a somewhat less liberal course than as vice president of Gran Colombia, but he continued to promote education, especially at the primary level. However, he earned criticism for his harshness toward military conspirators captured in a foiled plot to overthrow the government in 1833. At the end of his term he surrendered the presidency to José Ignacio de Márquez, though he had preferred another candidate, José María Obando. Santander was elected to the Chamber of Deputics, where he led the opposition to Márquez until his death. In Colombia Santander is remembered as the "man of laws" because of his fidelity to constitutional norms and as the progenitor of the Liberal party, which was organized by his followers in the 1840s.

Sarmiento, Domingo Faustino (1811-1888), Argentine man of letters, educator, and president (1868-74). Sarmiento was born in the western province of San Juan to parents who were poor but had distinguished ancestors and relatives. Largely self-taught, he identified at an early age with the centralizing, cosmopolitan tenets of Argentine liberalism and became an opponent of the dictator **Juan Manuel de Rosas**, governor of Buenos Aires province, who dominated much of the country. As a result, Sarmiento was twice forced into exile in Chile. During his second residence there (1841-

45) he achieved prominence as a journalist and was named director of Chile's new normal, or teacher-training, school, the first in Latin America. During this period he also wrote his most celebrated work, *Civilización y barbarie: vida de Juan Facundo Quiroga* (1845). Usually known as *Facundo*, the book defies classification as it combines biography, history, sociology, and fiction. It is ostensibly a study of a regional chieftain, Facundo, but it is also an attack on the Rosas regime. The book is notable for its description of the Argentine pampa and its gaucho inhabitants, whom Sarmiento equated, along with Facundo and Rosas, with the forces of barbarism. In 1845 Sarmiento traveled to Europe on a study mission for Chile. He was unimpressed by France, Italy, or Spain but found much to praise in Switzerland and Germany. He was most enthusiastic about the United States, where he met the educator Horace Mann, whose wife, Mary, translated *Facundo* as *Life in the Argentine Republic in the Days of the Tyrants; or, Civilization and Barbarism* (1868).

Sarmiento returned to Argentina in 1851 to take part in the final campaign against Rosas, but he considered **Justo José de Urquiza**, who defeated Rosas at the battle of Caseros, to be just as much a barbarian as the fallen Rosas and went back to Chile. He returned to Argentina in 1856 when he was named director of schools for the province of Buenos Aires. From 1862 to 1864 he was governor of his native province. When Ángel Vicente Peñaloza (nicknamed "El Chacho"), a chieftain of La Rioja province, rebelled against the federal government, Sarmiento hunted him down; he was decapitated and his head displayed on a pike. Sarmiento denied ordering the execution, but President **Bartolomé Mitre** quelled the controversy by dispatching Sarmiento as minister to the United States. Elected president in 1868, Sarmiento oversaw the end of the Paraguayan War, during which his only son was killed, and strove to implement the liberal agenda by welcoming immigrants, expanding education, and developing the railroad system. He made peace with Urquiza in 1870 and persecuted the latter's assassin, Ricardo López Jordán.

After his retirement from the presidency,

Sarmiento held various offices, including that of superintendent of education in Buenos Aires province (1879-82), but devoted himself mainly to his writings, which fill fifty-three volumes. Among the better known are the travel account *Viajes en Europa, Africa i América, 1845-47* (1849-51) and the memoir *Recuerdos de provincia* (1850). Sarmiento is sometimes seen as a self-promoter and egotist, dubbed "Don yo" ("Mister I") by his enemies; his contempt for the Argentine masses and frequently high-handed methods of governance are also criticized. Nevertheless, he remains a towering figure in nineteenth-century Argentine politics and letters.

Sierra Méndez, Justo (1848-1912), Mexican intellectual, educator, and historian. Born in Campeche, Sierra was the son of Justo Sierra O'Reilly (1814-1861), a Yucatecan jurist and man of letters. His maternal grandfather, Santiago Méndez, dominated Yucatecan politics from 1833 to 1857. The younger Sierra was educated in Mexico City, completing his legal studies in 1871. Meanwhile, he had begun his literary career in 1867 by publishing a poem in the newspaper *El Globo*, of which he became an editor. In 1878 Sierra and several associates founded *La Libertad*, a newspaper that expressed the views of a new generation of positivist Liberals who, like himself, spurned violent political upheaval and favored a pragmatic, evolutionary approach to national development. In 1880 he became a member of Congress, and in 1892 played a leading role in a national Liberal convention that, while accepting the reelection of **Porfirio Díaz**, called for political and administrative reform. In 1894 he was appointed to the supreme court.

Eventually, however, Sierra's work in education overshadowed his other achievements. He began teaching history in the National Preparatory School in 1877, and in Congress, in the press, and in two national education conferences (1889, 1890) he advocated a variety of reforms, such as a requirement that primary schooling be made compulsory. In 1901 he was named undersecretary of education and in 1905 became head of a newly created cabinet-level department of education. In this capacity he oversaw the reorganiza-

tion of higher education, with the establishment (1910) of the National University, to which the preparatory school and a new School of Advanced Studies were attached. Among the most notable of Sierra's historical writings are the magisterial *Evolución política del pueblo mexicano*, (*The Political Evolution of the Mexican People*), which first appeared in 1900-2 as part of a multi-volume work supervised by Sierra, and *Juárez, su obra y su tiempo* (1906), written in collaboration with Carlos Pereyra to refute an attack on **Benito Juárez** by Francisco Bulnes. After the start of the Mexican Revolution of 1910, Díaz obtained the resignation of Sierra and the other members of his cabinet in March 1911. Sierra returned to teaching at the preparatory school until Díaz's successor, **Francisco I. Madero**, named him minister to Spain, where he died.

Sigüenza y Góngora, Carlos de (1645-1700), Mexican priest and intellectual. Born in Mexico City, Sigüenza y Góngora won the competition in 1672 for the chair of mathematics and astronomy at the University of Mexico. From this position and intellectual establishment he wrote Baroque poetry in the style of Luís de Góngora—his mother's relative—defended the Copernican system, argued that comets were not a divine curse but a natural phenomenon, and increasingly came to champion American and Mexican perspectives and values. He took great pride in his native city as the viceregal and intellectual capital of Spanish America. A budding creole identity and sense of *patria* were evident. He was a defender of Aztec civilization and culture and collected pre-Columbian manuscripts and codices but had reservations about the Indian masses as revealed in his first-hand report on the Mexico City riots of 1692. His *Los infortunios de Alonso Ramírez* (*The Misadventures of Alonso Ramírez*, 1690) as a "captivity story" broke new ground in the picaresque genre. Today he is seen as a precursor of the Mexican Enlightenment and Mexican nationalism.

Silva Xavier, Joaquim José da (Tiradentes; 1746-92), participant in the regional conspiracy for Brazilian independence known as the Inconfidência Mineira. Born in Minas Gerais, Tiradentes (the "tooth-puller"), as he was called from the trade skills he picked up from his godfather, a dentist, was socially the least important of the plotters. While his Portuguese-born father had been a gold miner and a member of the city council of São João do Rei, Tiradentes was orphaned and put in the care of his brother, a priest. His lack of success as a muleskinner and gold miner and his minor officership in the military contrasted sharply with the status and position of the other plotters. The conspiracy itself originated in 1788-89 in one of the many self-improvement societies of regional intellectuals that sprang up throughout Spanish and Portuguese America in the late colonial period. This particular group was dissatisfied with the more rigorous collection of taxes on gold and the precipitous decline in precious metal production that Minas Gerais had suffered. As the most vociferous of the plotters, the most socially marginal, and the one willing to assume sole responsibility, Tiradentes became a convenient scapegoat and was the only one executed. Over time Brazilian nationalism has transformed Tiradentes into a rallying symbol of national identity and opposition to colonialism.

Siqueiros, David Alfaro (1896-1974), Mexican painter and, with **José Clemente Orozco** and **Diego Rivera**, one of the three "great ones" of the mural movement of the 1920s and 1930s. A native of Chihuahua, Siqueiros studied at the Academy of Fine Arts in Mexico City and from 1919 to 1922 lived in Europe, where he was exposed to masterpieces of the past as well as new trends in art. He was a loyal Communist and political activist who fought on behalf of the Republicans during the Spanish Civil War and took part in an abortive assassination plot against Leon Trotsky during the latter's sojourn in Mexico (1937-40). From 1960 to 1964 he was imprisoned because of his criticism of the Mexican government and efforts on behalf of political prisoners.

As a muralist, Siqueiros was noted for his use of industrial pigments, sometimes applied with a spray gun, and for his efforts to create painted environments that would absorb viewers. An example of this approach is *Portrait of the Bour-geoisie* (1939-40), painted with pyroxylin on cement for the headquarters of the electricians' union in Mexico City. Other outstanding murals in Mexico City are *From the Dictatorship of Porfirio Díaz to the Revolution* (1957-65) in the National History Museum and *The March of Humanity* (1967-71) in the Polyforum. Siqueiros also painted many smaller works. Among the best known is *Echo of a Scream* (1937), with its chilling portrait of an abandoned child.

Somoza Debayle, Anastasio "Tachito" (1925-1980), Nicaraguan soldier and president. The son of **Anastasio "Tacho" Somoza García**, Tachito Somoza attended a military academy in Long Island, New York, and the United States Military Academy at West Point. Graduating in 1946, he returned to Nicaragua and became an officer in the National Guard. His father made him commander of the Guard in 1955. The younger Somoza retained that post for ten years, a period during which his father was assassinated (1956) and succeeded in the presidency (1956-63) by his elder brother Luis. Tachito Somoza resigned from the Guard in 1966 in order to run for the presidency in 1967. He duly won the election, continuing what became known as the "Somoza dynasty." Somoza Debayle continued his father's strategy of co-opting the opposition Conservative party by guaranteeing it a substantial minority of congressional seats. During his presidential term he tightened censorship and effectively used the National Guard to neutralize opposition groups, such as the recently formed Sandinista National Liberation Front (FSLN). Gains made by the opposition led Congress to suspend electoral politics in early 1972, at the end of Somoza's term. Congress invested executive and legislative power in a bipartisan triumvirate, and Somoza returned to his post as National Guard commander. A devastating earthquake in December 1972 served as Somoza's excuse for assuming power, declaring a state of siege, and going on to rule Nicaragua by decree. Opposition to his dictatorship, both legal and illegal, increased sharply thereafter. Somoza's misappropriation of supplies sent for earthquake relief, and a spectacular mass kidnapping conducted by the FSLN in

1974, further invigorated those who opposed him. U.S. president Jimmy Carter lent them his support after 1976. But it was the assassination, by the dictator's henchmen, of newspaper editor Pedro Joaquín Chamorro in January 1978 that galvanized the opposition and sped the dictator's downfall. The brutality employed by Somoza to retain power prompted a mid-1979 Organization of American States resolution calling for him to step down. A near-simultaneous armed offensive by a broad FSLN-led coalition drove Somoza from Nicaragua on July 17, 1979. He later found refuge in Paraguay, but was assassinated there by FSLN agents September 17, 1980.

Somoza García, Anastasio "Tacho" (1896-1956), Nicaraguan president and dictator. Anastasio Somoza García attended business school in the United States, returning to Nicaragua in 1919. His fluent English, winning personality, and marriage to a niece of Liberal general Juan Bautista Sacasa enabled him to launch a political career and brought him to the attention of U.S. officials, notably Matthew Hanna, the U.S. minister. In 1932 President-elect Sacasa named him director of the National Guard. Somoza went on to make it Nicaragua's most powerful institution as well as his personal police force. Through the Guard he carried out the murder of former guerrilla leader **Augusto César Sandino** in 1934, forced President Sacasa to step down in June 1936, and won the fraudulent presidential election of December 1936. Once in control of the nation, he amply remunerated his supporters, among whom were members of the well-paid national bureaucracy. Family and friends were awarded real estate confiscated from the dictator's enemies, including German residents who had their property seized in 1942. They also benefited from the proceeds of taxes that passed through the dictator's hands. Somoza curried favor with the United States. President Franklin D. Roosevelt hosted him in a state visit of 1939, yet the United States increasingly opposed Somoza's continuance in power, pressuring him, in 1947, to allow the election of a hand-picked presidential candidate. But the dictator removed him a short time later and replaced him with an aged relative. Somoza

García transformed Nicaragua's economy by encouraging commercial agriculture, especially cotton. He also recruited foreign capital and commercial franchises, always in such way as to reward family and friends. His clique so thoroughly controlled the nation that he often referred to Nicaragua as "my farm." Somoza's rule was not entirely self-serving. He had a labor code passed in 1944, an income tax in 1952, and in 1953 established a government planning institute. Somoza García was sanctioned by the Organization of the American States when he aided Costa Rican dissidents in an abortive attempt to overthrow the regime of President **José Figueres** in early 1955. When he secured the Liberal party nomination for yet another term as president the following year, he was mortally wounded by a young opponent (September 21, 1956). Luis Somoza (1922-67), his eldest son, succeeded him.

Soto, Hernando de (1496/97-1542), conqueror and explorer. Born in Villanueva de Barcarrota, Badajoz, Spain, Soto came with the Pedrarias (**Pedro Arias de Ávila**) expedition to Panama in 1514. He accumulated a substantial fortune in the Central American slave trade of Indians and contributed significantly to **Francisco Pizarro**'s third expedition (1531), which led to the conquest of Peru. As a principal captain at Cajamarca, he received 4 shares of the 218 of **Atahualpa**'s enormous treasure when it was melted down in 1534. Richer than ever, he booked passage to Spain in order to arrange his appointment as governor of Cuba and to clear the field for his great undertaking. His expedition left Havana in 1539, landed near Tampa Bay, and explored much of the southeastern United States, moving through parts of the modern states of Florida, Georgia, Alabama, Mississippi, Tennessee, and Arkansas; but Soto failed to repeat his earlier successes. The dreams of precious metals and great empires were illusions. Death caught Soto in Louisiana where his followers dumped his body in the Mississippi River to hide it from the Indians. The remaining survivors constructed makeshift boats and made it to Mexico after crossing the Gulf of Mexico.

Soto's ill-fated enterprise marked the end of the great expeditions of exploration and conquest from Cuba.

Sousa, Martim Afonso de (1500-1564), Portuguese navigator who commanded the first colonizing expedition to Brazil in 1531. With five ships, a force of over five hundred, and ample powers to appoint officials and give out land, Sousa founded Portugal's first town in the New World in 1532 at São Vicente in southern Brazil. The colony prospered because of its sugar production and mills and ties to investors in Lisbon and Antwerp. Pernambuco was the only other colony of the ten settled in the sixteenth century to replicate São Vicente's success. Sousa, along with his brother Pero Lopes de Sousa, received four of the fifteen donatary captaincies granted by royal officials between 1533 and 1535.

Sousa, Tomé de (1502?-1579), first governor-general of Brazil (1549-53). Sousa was illegitimate but of noble birth. He fought in Morocco and the Far East. His expedition to Brazil in 1549 of six ships with over one thousand, including six Jesuits and artisans, was intended to establish a royal presence and challenge the proprietary captaincies granted between 1533 and 1535. Sousa founded Salvador da Bahia in 1549, and it became the capital of Brazil. Sousa worked to establish and regularize royal government, and except for Pernambuco he personally inspected all the captaincies. He worked closely with the Jesuits in founding new towns and missions and building churches and schools.

Stroessner, Alfredo (1912–   ), authoritarian president of Paraguay. Alfredo Stroessner was born in rural Paraguay, the son of a German immigrant. In 1929 he entered the Military Academy in Asunción. Upon graduation he served with distinction in the Chaco War (1932-35). Stroessner progressed through the ranks, in 1940 becoming one of several junior officers to receive advanced instruction in Brazil. Four years later he was sent to study at Paraguay's Superior War School in recognition of his aid in crushing a coup attempt against President Higinio Moríni-

go. President Morínigo turned to Stroessner again in 1947, when supporters of former president Rafael Franco, reinforced by most of the military, declared civil war. Stroessner helped defeat the rebels, for which he was made commandant of artillery (1948). During 1948-54, Paraguay suffered political turmoil as leaders of the factionalized Colorado party fought for precedence. Stroessner prospered during those struggles (though he suffered a brief exile in 1948), ultimately winning promotion to commander of the army in 1951. The inability of Colorado leaders to resolve their disputes enabled Stroessner to seize power in May 1954. He ruled for the ensuing thirty-four years.

Alfredo Stroessner's dictatorship rested in the support he received from the army, the Colorado party, and the general population, as well as from the fact that he was highly organized and an indefatigable worker. Those strengths allowed him to establish a highly authoritarian regime. Stroessner exiled and jailed political opponents, and strictly controlled the press. His anticommunism won him favor in the United States, which extended him military and financial support. He also remained on good terms with the leaders of Argentina and Brazil, most of whom shared his methods and views. Another key to Alfredo Stroessner's success was his openness to foreign investment, a chief source of Paraguay's economic growth during the 1960s and 1970s. He contracted foreign loans for major construction projects and improvements in economic infrastructure. Those revenues enabled Stroessner to placate potential critics through the distribution of jobs and other forms of patronage. Meanwhile he did little to monitor smuggling, a traditional source of wealth in Paraguay. The twenty years of economic growth over which Stroessner presided both increased pluralism in Paraguay and accustomed citizens to a heightened level of physical comfort. Thus when global recession struck early in the 1980s, Stroessner's popularity plummeted. January 1989 found the Colorado party in disarray and the dictator attempting to have his unpopular eldest son succeed him. On February 3, the army intervened, removing Stroessner and forcing him to seek exile in Brazil.

Sucre, Antonio José de (1795-1830), Venezuelan general and president of Bolivia (1826-28). Born in Cumaná to a prominent family, Sucre joined the pro-independence forces of Venezuela as a teenager. In 1820 he became chief of staff to **Simón Bolívar**, who sent him to Guayaquil, Ecuador, to further the patriot cause there. His victory at the Battle of Pichincha in 1822 achieved the independence of Ecuador. In 1823 Sucre went to Lima as Bolívar's emissary to take charge of anti-Spanish operations in Peru. In December 1824 he commanded the patriot forces at the Battle of Ayacucho, which ended Spanish rule in South America. Early the next year he entered Upper Peru (modern Bolivia) to eliminate pockets of royal resistance and convened a constituent assembly that voted in favor of independence for the region instead of association with Argentina or Peru.

Named president of Bolivia in 1826, Sucre undertook an ambitious program of reform, but his efforts were impeded by the country's poor financial situation and resentment against him as a foreigner. He stepped down after an army mutiny in 1828 and returned to Gran Colombia. In 1829 he commanded a Colombian army that defeated Peruvian invaders at Tarqui. In 1830 he presided over a congress that met in Bogotá in an unsuccessful effort to prevent the disintegration of Gran Colombia. He was returning to his home in Ecuador when he was assassinated at Berruecos, near Pasto, Colombia, on June 4, 1830. The instigator of the crime has never been ascertained, but at the time suspicion fell on the Colombian leader José María Obando. Sucre is remembered as Bolivar's ablest and most loyal lieutenant. The Bolivian city previously known as Chuquisaca and La Plata was renamed in his honor. The Ecuadorian monetary unit is also named after him.

Toledo y Figueroa, Francisco de (1515-1582), viceroy of Peru (1569-81). Born in Oropesa, New Castile, Spain, the third son of the Count of Oropesa, Toledo had seen extensive military and diplomatic service in Europe when he was ap-

pointed viceroy in 1568. Peru was still a turbulent kingdom with free-wheeling *encomenderos*, governors, and bureaucrats, and it still faced an independent Inca state in Vilcabamba. Toledo imposed royal authority and reorganized Peru. It was never the same again. Much of the institutional framework of colonial Peru dated from the Toledean Reforms. On his arrival in 1569 Toledo undertook a thoroughgoing *visita*, or general inspection tour, that lasted five years and covered the major centers of the highlands—Huamanga, Arequipa, Cuzco, Potosí, and La Plata. The rigors of the reforms weighed most heavily on the Indian population. Toledo wiped out the independent state of Vilcabamba so thoroughly in 1571 that its location was lost until the twentieth century. He took its ruler, **Túpac Amaru**, the last Inca, to Cuzco and had him executed in the main plaza in 1572. Indian communities were forcibly resettled (*reducción*) and brought together for ease of control and tax collection. The rotary draft system of forced Indian labor known as the *mita* crystallized in its main form under Toledo's direction. A certain percentage of Indians and their families rotated in and out of their villages and returned from or headed for the mercury mines at Huancavelica and the mining operations at Potosí. Many traveled far distances and never returned to their communities. The infusion of labor pushed silver production to record heights, and Potosí became the main source of precious metal production until New Spain's mines overtook Peru's late in the seventeenth century.

Torrijos Herrera, Omar (1929-1981), Panamanian chief of state. Omar Torrijos attended public schools in Panama and a military academy in El Salvador. He entered the National Guard in 1949. On October 11, 1968, he led a colonels' revolt that removed from office recently inaugurated President **Arnulfo Arias**. Torrijos moved quickly to solidify his control of the country. He suspended Congress and the supreme court, outlawed political parties, occupied the national university, and exiled some 3,000 student dissidents. In 1972 he legitimized his rule through a new constitution that named him Maximum Leader of the Panamanian Revolution. A nationalist and a populist,

Torrijos made his prime goal that of bringing the Panama Canal under Panamanian control. He achieved it through the Carter-Torrijos Treaty, which stipulated December 31, 1999, as the date for U.S. transfer of canal ownership. Torrijos won widespread popular support for his regime through a series of far-reaching measures benefiting the nation's poor. He resumed land reform, and had laws passed protecting those who invaded vacant land; he extended new protections to labor, both rural and urban; and he expended large sums to construct low-cost housing, schools, and hospitals. To do so he contracted foreign loans that left Panama the world's most heavily indebted nation per capita. Torrijos projected his populism internationally, associating Panama with the non-aligned movement, opposing the U.S. embargo of Cuba, and championing the cause of Nicaragua's Sandinista rebels. Yet he remained on relatively good terms with the United States. During the latter 1970s he honored a U.S. request that he extend sanctuary to the exiled shah of Iran. In 1978, Torrijos institutionalized his regime through creation of a broad-based political party, the Democratic Revolutionary party (Partido Revolucionario Democrático, PRD). The PRD became Panama's leading party thanks in part to massive government patronage. Meanwhile Torrijos turned Panama into a major center of international banking, removing restrictions on foreign banks operating in the country and legalizing secret accounts. He was slowly restoring democratic practices to the nation when he died July 31, 1981, in a plane crash. Panamanians honor Omar Torrijos as their most notable national leader.

Trujillo Molina, Rafael (1891-1961), Dominican president and dictator. Rafael Trujillo was born near Santo Domingo to a middle-class family. He received a basic education in local schools, and worked at odd jobs until 1919. That year he joined the Dominican National Guard, recently established by U.S. forces who had occupied the country since 1916. When U.S. troops departed in 1924, he had earned the praise of U.S. officers who had trained the Guard, and achieved the rank of lieutenant colonel. President Horacio Vásquez named Trujillo commander of the Guard (later renamed the National Army) in 1927, hoping to ensure his support. But when the ailing Vásquez encountered political difficulties in 1930, Trujillo overthrew him. Intimidating rival candidates, Trujillo easily won the August 1930 presidential contest, going on to institute one of Latin America's most thoroughgoing modern dictatorships. He allowed but one political party, his own Partido Dominicano, and permitted no one other than his supporters to serve in Congress. Until 1952, he had himself regularly reelected president, save for the interval 1938-42, during which time he ruled through surrogates. During his years in power Trujillo amassed great wealth through his control of state monopolies, taxation, the nation's banking and insurance industries, and most other profitable enterprises. At the time of his assassination he, his family, and friends, controlled 80 percent of national industry and employed 45 percent of all Dominicans. Trujillo ruthlessly suppressed his enemies, whom he routinely tarred as communists. He was capable of great violence, as in late 1937, when he ordered the slaughter of some 18,000 Haitians living illegally on Dominican soil.

During his rule Trujillo modernized the nation. He initiated import substitution during the mid-1930s, and later in the decade ordered the construction of ambitious public works projects. As a staunch supporter of the Allied war effort, he ensured the country's economic prosperity during the 1940s, and in the immediate post-war period he earned continued, though grudging, support of the United States through his loudly proclaimed anticommunism. By the late 1950s, however, Trujillo's grip on power slipped. He angered some in the United States by ordering the kidnapping and murder of Dr. Jesús Galíndez, a Columbia University teacher who had criticized him. When Cuban and Venezuelan leaders **Fidel Castro** and **Rómulo Betancourt** sponsored an abortive attempt to overthrow him in June 1959, the dictator responded with a wave of terror. For many months afterward he had suspected enemies jailed, tortured, and murdered. His attempt to assassinate Rómulo Betancourt in June 1960 led the OAS to vote economic sanctions against the Dominican Republic. His soldiers' murder of the three young Mirabal sisters late in 1960 convinced many that Trujillo must be removed at any cost. The dictator was shot to death May 30, 1961. Trujillo's son and brothers attempted to retain power after the assassination, but were driven from the country through a U.S. show of force in November 1960.

Túpac Amaru (1554?-1572), the last Inca emperor (1571-72). Túpac Amaru, the third son of Manco Inca, succeeded to the position after his half-brothers Sayri Túpac and Titu Cusi. His leadership from the independent Inca state of Vilcabamba was brief. It and the appearance of an indigenous millenarian movement that denied the validity of Christianity and that foresaw the expulsion of the Spanish drew the close attention of **Francisco de Toledo**, the new viceroy (1569-81). He quickly moved against Vilcabamba and extinguished it and the Inca dynasty by executing Túpac Amaru in the main plaza of Cuzco before horrified Indians forced to witness the ritual. But the name of Túpac Amaru still resonates in the Andes and has lived on among various revolutionary groups from the eighteenth century to the present day.

Túpac Amaru II (José Gabriel Condorcanqui; 1738-1781), Peruvian leader of the Andean-wide rebellion of 1780-83. As a descendant of Inca royalty—in fact, of the last Inca **Túpac Amaru,** who had been executed by Viceroy **Francisco Toledo** in 1572—Condorcanqui was in line to inherit a *cacicazgo* (chieftainship of an Indian community) and received a Spanish education in Cuzco. In 1763, at the age of twenty-five, he became *cacique* of Tungasuca, Pampamarca, and Surimana. As an enterprising muleteer between Cuzco and the great silver mine at Potosí, he was familiar with much of Upper Peru (Bolivia). Both as head of his Indian community and in his travels to Potosí, he became increasingly aware of Spanish abuses against the Indians, and his social consciousness grew. He was especially outraged at the 200-year-old practice of forcing unwanted merchandise on Indian communities at three and

four times the ordinary price by Spanish *corregidores* often in league with co-opted *caciques*. He also resented the *mita* labor system that forced Indians to leave their villages and work in the silver mine at Potosí. He traveled to Lima in 1777 with authority from other *caciques* to seek a provincial exemption from the *mita*, but his petition fell on deaf ears even though the Bourbon reformer José Antonio de Areche was on the scene as a personal emissary of **José de Gálvez**, the Spanish minister of the Indies. Areche and Gálvez were more interested in raising new revenue to sustain Spain's support of the American colonies in their war of independence (1776-83) against Great Britain. In 1778, with rebellions already breaking out over new taxes and more rigorous collection, Condorcanqui returned to Upper Peru and planned his revolt. On November 4, 1780, adopting the name of his martyred ancestor, Túpac Amaru, he arrested the local *corregidor,* Antonio de Arriaga—already excommunicated by the bishop of Cuzco—judged him guilty of defrauding the Indians, and had him executed November 10, 1780. Using social issues as a rallying point, the rebels emancipated all slaves on November 16 and defeated the loyalists sent out from Cuzco two days later. As the revolt grew creoles and *mestizos*, who had significant grievances against Spanish officials, rethought their strategy and self-interest and began to have second thoughts about an Indian-dominated Peru. The week of January 2-9, 1781, saw Túpac Amaru II besieging Cuzco with over 40,000 partisans, but co-opted *caciques* came to the rescue and forced him to abandon the siege. His forces melted away. He was finally betrayed and captured on April 6, 1781, at Langui. He was taken to Cuzco where he was interrogated and tried and torn apart by four horses after being forced to watch the torture and execution of his wife and other family members. The social divisions of Peruvian society doomed the revolt and threw into high relief the political faultlines that still persist in Peru and Bolivia.

Ubico y Castañeda, Jorge (1878-1946), Guatemalan soldier and president. Jorge Ubico received his early education in the United States, returning to graduate from the military Escuela Politécnica in Guatemala City. He fought in a 1906 border conflict with El Salvador, was appointed military governor of two highland districts, and served as minister of war under President José M. Orellana (1922-26). In 1931 General Ubico won the presidency as candidate of the Liberal Progressive party. He launched a major highway-building project resulting in the construction of over 6,000 miles of roadway, including the highland Petén route into Mexico. He encouraged commercial agriculture, welcoming foreign capital to promote that goal. Thanks to his administrative frugality, Guatemala rapidly recovered from economic depression. Ubico ended Indian debt peonage, replacing it with an onerous vagrancy law that in effect required landless peasants to labor for up to six months annually on commercial farms. Throughout his thirteen-year rule Ubico brutally silenced dissidents, especially communists. His repressive measures increased following a spurious 1934 assassination attempt, which he used as a pretext for the execution of several hundred political enemies, as well as more than a dozen communists from El Salvador and Honduras who had sought refuge in Guatemala. He strictly controlled the press and radio, near the end of his rule giving vent to personal peculiarities such as the gratuitous dispensing of advice during rambling radio broadcasts. Opposition to his rule caused the dictator, then in ill health, to resign his office and depart Guatemala on July 1, 1944. Ubico died in exile.

Ulloa, Antonio de (1716-1795), Spanish scientist and naval officer. Born in Seville, Spain, Ulloa received an excellent education at the new naval academy (Guardia Marina) in Cádiz. He and **Jorge Juan y Santacilia** were chosen to accompany the French expedition (1735-44) to Quito to effect measurements at the equator. Both were accomplished scientists who personified the best of the new technical training being given to Spanish officers and who represented the rationalist and scientific values associated with the Enlightenment. Their four-volume *Relación histórica del viage a la América meridional* (*Voyage to South America*) appeared in 1748. A year later their secret report to the crown detailed the gener-

alized fraud, corruption, and inefficiency of Spanish administration in the Indies. It was published for the first time in 1826 in England as the anti-Spanish *Noticias secretas de América* (*Discourse and Political Reflections . . .*). Ulloa continued his scientific work and his employment as a technical advisor and trouble-shooter for the crown, serving as governor of the mercury operation at Huancavelica, Peru (1757-64), and of Spanish Louisiana (1766-68). He alienated colonists in both regions, especially the viceroy of Peru and the French residents of New Orleans.

Uribe Uribe, Rafael (1859-1914), Colombian political leader. Uribe Uribe was born on an hacienda in the state of Antioquia. He inherited his father's Liberal political views and, as a teenager, fought in support of the Liberal government during the Conservative revolution of 1876-77. Returning to school, he received a law degree in 1880. Uribe Uribe's career in politics was shaped by the fact that it occurred during an era of Conservative hegemony (1885-1930) when Liberals were generally excluded from public office. For this reason Uribe Uribe advocated the use of force to topple the Conservatives and played a commanding role in the War of the Thousand Days (1899-1902). However, the Liberals failed to overthrow the Conservatives, and Uribe Uribe agreed to lay down his arms in the Neerlandia treaty (October 24, 1902), after which he renounced violence as a means of political change. In the following decade he served in the Chamber of Representatives and the Senate and accepted diplomatic assignments from **Rafael Reyes**, for which he was criticized by other Liberals. He also differed from many Liberals by opposing the short-lived, bipartisan Republican Union. A man of great vigor and intellectual curiosity, he was a prolific writer and charismatic orator. He is credited with helping to move the Liberal party away from *laissez faire* and toward social democratic positions on economic issues. On October 15, 1914, he was hacked to death on the streets of Bogotá by two artisans who blamed him for their failure to find employment on government projects.

Urquiza, Justo José de (1801-1870), Argentine statesman. A native of Entre Ríos province, Urquiza became a wealthy rancher and businessman there and took an active part in the interprovincial struggles that dominated Argentine political life in the first decades after independence. A federalist, he became governor in 1841. Although he had a been a long-time ally of the dictator **Juan Manuel de Rosas**, he came to resent the economic stranglehold of Buenos Aires over his own and other interior provinces. He therefore joined other foes of Rosas and won a decisive victory over the dictator at the Battle of Caseros (February 3, 1852). Urquiza now favored the drafting of a constitution that would create a federal republic of which Buenos Aires would be the national capital. However, **Bartolomé Mitre** and other provincial leaders there distrusted Urquiza and were reluctant to surrender the city's revenues to the federal government. As a result, Buenos Aires boycotted the constituent congress convened by Urquiza in late 1852 and did not join the new Argentine Confederation it created. Elected president of the confederation in 1854, Urquiza attempted to stimulate trade and economic growth, but his efforts had only limited success because of the opposition of Buenos Aires. Urquiza's victory over Buenos Aires at the Battle of Cepeda (October 23, 1859) set the stage for the entry of Buenos Aires into the confederation, but mutual suspicion and political squabbles prevented final agreement. Both sides again resorted to force, with Urquiza, who had completed his presidential term in 1860, being put in command of the confederation army. At the Battle of Pavón (September 17, 1861), Urquiza unaccountably retired from the field. As a result, Buenos Aires entered the confederation on favorable terms. Urquiza, meanwhile, completed another term as governor of Entre Ríos (1860-64). On April 11, 1870, he and two of his sons were murdered by Ricardo López Jordán, who was embittered by Urquiza's behavior at Pavón and considered him a tool of Buenos Aires.

Valdivia, Pedro de (1500?-1553), soldier and conqueror of Chile. Born in Valle de la Serena, Badajoz, Spain, Valdivia fought in Flanders and Italy. He came to Venezuela in 1535, and in 1537 moved to Peru, where he helped in lifting the Inca siege against the Spanish trapped at Cuzco. He became **Francisco Pizarro**'s aide-de-camp and was a key infantry leader in the Pizarros's victory over **Diego de Almagro** at the Battle of Salinas in 1538. He then sold his rewarded *encomienda* and land to finance an expedition to Chile. Leaving Cuzco with thirteen Spaniards—with more joining up on the way—and 1,000 Indians, he founded Santiago (1541), and eventually La Serena (1544), Concepción (1550), Valdivia (1552), and Villarica (1552). Returning to Peru in 1547, he was caught in the civil wars and chose to support crown officials against the Pizarros. He had made the right decision. He kept his Chilean prize intact and was made governor and captain-general. He died in battle fighting the Araucanian Indians led by **Lautaro**.

Vargas, Getúlio Dornelles (1883-1954), Brazilian president (1930-45 and 1951-54). Born in Rio Grande do Sul to politically prominent parents, Getúlio Vargas was drawn early to public life. His formative years were spent under the tutelage of local Republican party boss Antônio Borges de Medeiros, who taught Vargas rigorous discipline even as he advanced the young man's political career. Between 1907 and 1909 Vargas worked as public prosecutor of Rio Grande do Sul, and between 1909 and 1922 served in the state legislature, save for the interval 1912-17, when he was expelled for expressing criticism of Medeiros. In 1923 Vargas won a seat in the national Congress, and in 1926 became finance minister of President Washington Luís. After winning the governorship of Rio Grande do Sul in 1928, following Borges de Medeiros's retirement, he was positioned to run for the presidency in 1930. A reform coalition called the Liberal Alliance supported Vargas, who was opposed by Julio Prestes, candidate of fellow Paulista Washington Luís. After Prestes won the contest on March 1, 1930, Vargas's supporters revolted. Their successes led the military to depose Washington Luís and to install Vargas as president on November 3, 1930. Vargas ruled Brazil for the ensuing fifteen years: first by decree, to mid-1934; then as elected president, 1934-37; and finally by fiat, 1937-45.

Getúlio Vargas, the affable politician from Rio Grande do Sul, was Brazil's most important political figure of the twentieth century. Upon taking power he broke the parochial domination of national affairs by state governments and gave the country a centralized administration. He modernized Brazil, nationalizing key industries and services, encouraging the growth of import substituting industry, strengthening export cartels, reforming and expanding Brazil's federal bureaucracy, and expanding presidential power. He promoted public education and welfare and empowered labor and the middle sectors while tightly controlling them through political reforms of corporative savor, especially during the time of the authoritarian Estado Novo, 1937-45.

As World War II approached Vargas wrung military and economic concessions from both the United States and Germany by playing one off against the other. When war began Vargas embraced the Allied cause. The United States responded with increased financial and military aid, and with directives to U.S.-based industry that it establish plants in Brazil. On October 29, 1945, Vargas was forced from office by the military, who demanded a return to democracy. Before resigning the presidency Vargas had established the Brazilian Labor party (PTB) and the Social Democratic party (PSD), which dominated national politics until 1964. Winning a Senate seat in 1945, Vargas marked time until 1950, when he ran for president as candidate of the PTB. He ran a strongly populist campaign, promising new benefits to workers and sanctions against exploitative elites, both domestic and foreign. Though Vargas's opponents tarred him as a demagogue, and warned that if elected he would establish a Peronist-style dictatorship, the *riograndense* defeated two opponents, taking 49 percent of the vote. But Vargas proved unable to dominate Brazil as he had earlier. Large wage increases to labor and stepped-up government spending, coupled with a stagnant economy, produced unprecedented criticism of Vargas. Newspaper editor Carlos Lacerda, a leader of the anti-Vargas National Democratic Union, blasted the president for his inability to reverse the nation's economic slide, and charged his regime with corruption. On

August 5, 1954, an assassination attempt against Lacerda failed but resulted in the death of an air force officer who accompanied him. When an investigation revealed the key plotter to be a member of Vargas's staff, military leaders demanded the president's resignation. Vargas refused the ultimatum and shot himself (August 24, 1954). The traditions of strong, centralized national government, nationalism, and populism, inculcated by Vargas over his long tenure, remained powerful forces in Brazil long after his passing.

Vargas Llosa, Mario (1936–   ), Peruvian novelist. Mario Vargas Llosa's happy childhood was interrupted by his parents' divorce, which resulted in his being sent to military school in Lima. His unpleasant experiences there provided the subject matter for his 1962 novel, *La ciudad y los perros* (*The Time of the Hero*), which became an international best-seller. A searing critique of machista culture in a setting of unequal power relationships, the work was publicly burned by the rector of the writer's alma mater. After taking an undergraduate degree at Lima's University of San Marcos, the writer attended graduate school in Spain, producing one of the earliest and finest doctoral dissertations on Colombian novelist **Gabriel García Márquez**. He subsequently spent time in Paris working in French radio and television. A popular lecturer, he received numerous invitations to teach at leading universities in Europe and the United States. Later best-sellers included *La casa verde* (*The Green House*, 1966), a critique of capitalism and materialism; and *Conversación en la catedral* (*Conversation in the Cathedral*, 1969), dwelling upon the violence and injustice suffered by Latin America's poor. Vargas Llosa's early novels are set in Peru and stand collectively as savage critiques of Peruvian life. They are meticulously crafted and often complex narratives treating the lives and hopes of ordinary people. Still they contain sufficient excitement and color to appeal to the general reader. By the 1980s Vargas Llosa extended his writing to include the historical novel, a notable example being *La guerra del fin del mundo* (*The War of the End of the World*, 1981), treating the Brazilian government's destruction, during the 1890s, of the rebellious backlands city of Canudos. A Marxist in his youth, Vargas Llosa experienced political metamorphosis in middle age. He rejected socialism and adopted a liberal, if not libertarian, stance. His commitment to political activism intensified during the 1980s. In November 1989, he led the conservative Democratic Front to victory in municipal elections, going on to run for Peru's presidency a year later. He won the first round of presidential voting, but lost in the final round (June 1990) to independent candidate **Alberto Fujimori**. He returned to Europe following his defeat and later took Spanish citizenship.

Vasconcelos Calderón, José (1882-1959), Mexican philosopher and man of letters. Born in Oaxaca, José Vasconcelos was educated in public schools in Yucatán, Mexico City, and Eagle Pass, Texas. In 1905 he graduated from the National University with a law degree. Vasconcelos entered public life when opposition to the dictatorship of **Porfirio Díaz** became intense. A member of the Ateneo de la Juventud (1909-14), he joined other intellectuals and artists, among them **Alfonso Reyes**, Pedro Henríquez Ureña, and Antonio Caso in criticizing the positivist philosophy dominant in official thinking, and exploring ways of creating an authentically Mexican culture. After 1910 he worked closely with **Francisco I. Madero**, leader of the revolutionary movement that drove Díaz from power in 1911. Vasconcelos spent much of the first decade of the revolution, 1910-20, in the United States, first representing Madero in Washington, D.C., and later in exile. President **Álvaro Obregón** made him rector of the National University (1920-21), and subsequently secretary of education (1921-24). That period defined an important moment in both the career of Vasconcelos and the evolution of modern Mexico. He secured an extraordinary budget for education, which he invested in a range of activities designed to raise the cultural level of the populace at large. He invited forward-thinking educators from abroad to help found schools for the rural and

urban popular classes, among them Chilean poet **Gabriela Mistral** and Peruvian student leader **Víctor Raúl Haya de la Torre**. He stocked classroom libraries throughout the nation with copies of the classics, and encouraged university reform throughout the continent by hosting an international student conference in 1921. And Vasconcelos commissioned painters such as **José Clemente Orozco**, **Diego Rivera**, and **Davíd Alfaro Siqueiros** to cover public buildings with murals celebrating the nation's history—especially its Indian heritage—as well as its revolution. A trip to Argentina and Brazil in 1922 led to his writing *La raza cósmica: misión de la raza iberoamericana* (*The Cosmic Race*, 1925), which celebrated the region's mixed-race heritage. A critic of .**Plutarco Elías Calles**, Vasconcelos headed an abortive and ultimately embittering presidential campaign against the National Revolutionary party candidate Pascual Ortiz Rubio in 1929.

The period 1929-40 found Vasconcelos in yet another exile, during which he published the first four volumes of his five-part autobiography—*Ulises criollo* (1935), *La tormenta* (1936), *El desastre* (1938), and *El proconsulado* (1939)—as well as *Bolivarismo y monroismo* (1934), illustrating differences in Anglo and Latin American culture. Vasconcelos moved to the right during the ideologically turbulent 1930s, his anti-Americanism leading him to advocate the superiority of Hispanic respect for hierarchy and social inequality. He returned to Mexico in 1940 and spent his remaining years as director of Biblioteca de Mexico. His last autobiographical volume was *La flama* (1959).

Velasco I ("The Elder"), Luis de (1511?-1564), second viceroy of Mexico (1550-64). Born in Carrión de los Condes, Palencia, Spain, Velasco had been viceroy of Navarre (1547-48) before he succeeded to the position in New Spain. He was a prudent and wise administrator and continued the policies of his predecessor, **Antonio de Mendoza**. He chipped away at *encomienda* power and privilege by implementing provisions of the controversial New Laws (1542). He made significant strides in abolishing Indian slavery. He developed frontier policy to protect the silver mines in the north. He founded the University of Mexico (1551) and made efforts to establish regular traffic between New Spain and the Philippines. He died in office. His son, **Luis Velasco II**, The Younger, was also viceroy.

Velasco II ("The Younger"), Luis de (1538-1617), viceroy three times, twice of Mexico (1590-95; 1607-11) and once of Peru (1596-1604), and president of the Council of the Indies (1611-17). Born in Carrión de los Condes, Palencia, Spain, Velasco came to New Spain with his father, **Luis Velasco The Elder**, who was also viceroy. Velasco The Younger helped uncover the Cortés Conspiracy in 1565. As viceroy in New Spain he made improvements in the defenses of the northern frontier, restructured textile production, and took steps to alleviate flooding in Mexico City. In Peru he made changes in the system of Indian labor in the textile industry, the mercury mines at Huancavelica, and the silver operations at Potosí. He was made the marquis of Salinas del Río Pisuerga in 1609.

Velasco Alvarado, Juan (1910-1977), Peruvian soldier and president. From a working-class background, Juan Velasco Alvarado enlisted in the army as a private at age nineteen. His energy and intelligence won him promotion, advanced training, foreign postings and, by 1959, elevation to the rank of brigadier general. On October 3, 1968, as army commander-in-chief, he led a coup that ended the presidency of Fernando Belaúnde Terry. While Belaúnde's administration had been a populist, reformist one, his inability to implement his programs in the face of congressional opposition, coupled with deepening economic crisis, moved the military to intervene.

Velasco Alvarado vastly increased the pace of reform within an authoritarian setting. A strident nationalist who embraced the dependency thesis of Argentine economist **Raúl Prebisch**, he restricted foreign investment in Peru while nationalizing a host of businesses and industries, most notably the U.S.-owned International Petroleum Company. Velasco believed that his government could lessen conflicts between capital and labor through corpo-

rative arrangements binding individual interests to the state. Thus he founded several peak associations (umbrella organizations linked to the government), the largest of which was the National Social Mobilization Support System (SINAMOS), which sought to integrate and mobilize peasants and workers. He mandated massive land reform that by the mid-1970s had redistributed to peasant cooperatives more than half of arable land in the highlands, as well as many hectares of coastal plantations devoted to export agriculture. He also sponsored the construction of low-cost housing in urban areas.

By late 1974 Velasco Alvarado had borrowed heavily to fund his programs. Meanwhile Peru had entered economic contraction during that year as exports dwindled and export prices slumped. Natural disasters, press censorship, inflation, and bureaucratic bungling also had eroded the initial popularity of Velasco and his regime. A wave of strikes and urban rioting ushered in 1975, but the president's ill-health made it difficult for him to address these problems vigorously. Velasco Alvarado was removed by his fellow officers in August 1975. A more moderate military regime followed. Velasco Alvarado died in Lima two years later.

Velasco Ibarra, José María (1893-1979), Ecuadorian president. José María Velasco Ibarra studied law in Quito, but chose journalism as his first career. Elected to Congress in 1932, he employed a powerful, affecting oratory that instantly won him fame. Within a year he was elected president of the Chamber of Deputies, and a year after that (1934) designated acting president by the Conservative party. Charging obstructionism by congressional Liberals and Socialists, Velasco suspended the constitution within months of assuming office. In 1935 he was overthrown by the military. After a nine-year Colombian exile (1935-44), he returned to lead Conservatives and Liberals in opposing the corrupt regime of Carlos Arroyo del Río. Velasco won a second presidential term in 1944, but grew increasingly autocratic, suffering another military coup in 1947. In 1952 he returned from Argentine exile to win a four-year presidential term. His most notable achievement was assertion of Ecuador's claim to a 200-mile off-shore territorial limit. Velasco's single complete term was otherwise undistinguished, for he was an extraordinarily inept administrator. When his term ended Velasco, who liked to be called "the National Personification," returned to Argentina, earning the additional sobriquet, "the Great Absentee." In 1960, he returned to campaign for president on an anti-U.S. platform, defeating pro-U.S. **Galo Plaza Lasso**. Velasco had seemingly found his metier in strident anti-Americanism. But that angered the military, prompting them to remove him from office once again. Following yet another Argentine exile (1961-66), Velasco returned to campaign for a fifth presidential term. He won the 1968 contest, employing populist appeals to win the middle- and lower-class urban vote. He suspended the constitution in 1970, prompting the military, which feared the growth of populism nation-wide, to send Velasco back to Argentina in 1972. Velasco Ibarra remained there until 1979, returning to Quito shortly before his death.

Vespucci, Amerigo (1454-1512), Italian navigator and cosmographer. Born in Florence, Vespucci came from a merchant family with extensive commercial and banking interests. Well-educated, early in his career he served as a secretary on a diplomatic mission to Paris (1481-83). Later he oversaw family business affairs in Italy and abroad, auditing, for example, accounts in Seville in 1489. It is through his extensive correspondence and reports that we have a record of his travels and voyages. In Spain when **Columbus** returned from the Indies in 1493, Vespucci could not but have been impressed with the preparations for the second voyage that required seventeen ships, 1,200 colonists, and extraordinary financial backing. On May 10, 1497, Vespucci himself set sail for the New World from Cádiz in an expedition of four ships in which he probably had invested. He recorded the experience in a diary that showed the expedition crossing the ocean from the Canaries to the Caribbean, where it probably moved up the Mexican Gulf Coast and on around Florida as far north as the Chesapeake Bay before arriving in Cádiz on October 15, 1498. A year

later in another expedition he again left Cádiz and touched the Canaries, but continued on farther south to the Cape Verdes before crossing the Atlantic and landing in southern Brazil on June 27, 1499, thereby discovering Brazil a full ten months before the Portuguese **Pedro Álvares Cabral**. Upon returning to Seville, he accepted an invitation to explore on behalf of the Portuguese King Manuel I. In May 1501 he joined an expedition that sailed out of Lisbon to the Canaries, down the African coast to Dakar before heading west and reaching Brazil. Looking for a southwest route to the Far East, his group continued down the Argentine coast eventually planting a flag in southern Patagonia not far from where Ferdinand Magellan would eventually pass the straits that bear his name. The return home brought them to Sierre Leone and the Azores before arriving in Lisbon in September 1502. Vespucci's fourth voyage (1503-4) took him out of Lisbon south to the Cape Verdes and Sierra Leone and then west across the Atlantic to Bahia and then south to São Vicente where they loaded brazilwood and returned to Portugal. With a wife and business associates in Seville, Vespucci relocated there in 1505, taking Castilian citizenship and settling in as the kingdom's *piloto mayor* (chief geographer), responsible for preparing and maintaining the master sailing charts. Vespucci's letter *Mundus Novus* to Lorenzo di Pierfrancesco de' Medici had trumpeted the existence of a new continent, and when Martin Waldseemüller published his map of the world April 25, 1507, the continent bore a version of Vespucci's first name, America. The power of the printed word immortalized a man whose exploits were no more than those of others now forgotten by posterity.

Vieira, Antônio (1608-1697), Jesuit missionary and writer. Born in Lisbon, Vieira arrived in Bahia, Brazil, in 1614 with his father, a minor government official. There he was educated by the Jesuits, joined their order in 1623, and became a priest in 1634. He studied Tupí and one of the Angolan languages in order to work among the Indians and black slaves, perhaps in remembrance of his mulatta grandmother. His fame as an educator, preacher, writer, and advocate for social causes grew. In 1641 he was chosen by the viceroy to go to Portugal to express the support of the colonists for the recently restored Portuguese monarchy. The new king, João IV, was impressed with his abilities and made him his royal confidant and court preacher. He was dispatched on various diplomatic missions to Amsterdam and Rome. He advised the king to curtail the Inquisition, to support New Christian investment in Brazil, and to transfer Pernambuco to the Dutch. He returned to Brazil in 1653 as superior of the Jesuit missions in the Amazon and fought against the colonists over their treatment of the Indians. Vieira had long argued that Portugal's destiny was to unite Christendom and that the highest religious calling was to work as a missionary in Brazil in counterdistinction to the idleness of many religious in Portugal. These liberal social thoughts, messianic views, and moralizing got him arrested and imprisoned for five years by the Inquisition beginning in 1663. Upon his release he traveled to Rome, where he convinced the pope to exempt him from the authority of the Inquisition and to suspend its activities in Portugal.

Vieira is considered by some to be the most outstanding cultural figure produced by Brazil or Portugal during the colonial period. His sermons were electrifying, and people formed long lines to enter the churches where he was to preach. His published sermons alone run to sixteen volumes. His prose was a model of dramatic elegance and clarity.

Villa, Francisco (Pancho) (1877-1923), Mexican revolutionary leader. Little is known with certainty about the early life of Villa, who was born Doroteo Arango in the northern state of Durango. He apparently was an hacienda peon, miner, and merchant as well as a cattle rustler, and settled in San Andrés, Chihuahua, shortly before the outbreak of the Mexican Revolution of 1910. He offered his support to **Francisco I. Madero** and took part in the capture of Ciudad Juárez on May 10, 1911. After the deposition and murder of Madero in 1913, Villa allied himself with the Constitutionalist forces under the nominal leadership of **Venustiano Carranza**. Named governor of Chihuahua on December 21, 1913, he financed his military campaigns by seizing the holdings of the state's large landowners. Villa's Division of the North played a major role in the defeat of **Victoriano Huerta**, but even before the latter's departure Carranza showed his suspicions of Villa by preventing the occupation of Mexico City by his forces. The ensuing conflict pitted Carranza and **Álvaro Obregón** against Villa and **Emiliano Zapata**. At the Battle of Celaya in April 1915 Villa fielded an army estimated at 25,000 men, but his horsemen's charges proved unavailing against the defensive tactics of Obregón. A second major defeat at León in May–June 1915 and the de facto recognition of Carranza's government by the United States the following October eventually crippled his movement and limited his field of operations to Chihuahua. Villa was indignant over recognition of Carranza by the United States, which he had courted and which had once seemed to view his movement with favor. On January 10, 1916, *villistas* murdered seventeen American engineers and technicians at Santa Isabel (now General Trías), Chihuahua, and on March 9, 1916, about five hundred *villistas* crossed the border to attack Columbus, New Mexico, killing seventeen soldiers and civilians and burning part of the town. In response, President Woodrow Wilson dispatched a large contingent of troops under General John J. Pershing into Mexico in an effort to capture Villa and destroy his armed followers. Neither goal was achieved, and the U.S. troops were withdrawn early in 1917.

After the ouster of Carranza in 1920, the provisional president, Adolfo de la Huerta, arranged for the retirement of Villa, who was given a 25,000-acre hacienda, Canutillo, in Durango. He remained there until he was shot to death in nearby Parral on July 20, 1923. Because it was presumed that he would have supported de la Huerta in the upcoming presidential contest, some suspected that Obregón, now president, and the candidate he favored, **Plutarco Elías Calles**, were implicated in the assassination. Villa was a colorful figure, regarded with awe and respect as well as fear by contemporaries such as the Mexican writer Martín Luis Guzmán and the American journalist John Reed, who gave him a prominent place in his book *Insurgent Mexico* (1914).

Villa-Lobos, Heitor (1887-1959), Brazilian composer and conductor. Born into a middle-class Rio de Janeiro family, Heitor Villa-Lobos received his first musical instruction from his father, an amateur musician, and other relatives. The death of his father in 1899 impoverished the family, causing twelve-year-old Heitor to move into the home of an aunt, a pianist, who instilled in him a love of Bach. That early influence, coupled with Villa-Lobos's fascination with the improvisional street musicians of Rio de Janeiro, the *chorões*, would play a profound role in his later work. Between ages eighteen and twenty-three he traveled extensively in Brazil, steeping himself in his country's musical traditions. One of his earliest compositions, a suite of seven *Songs of the Sertão* (1910), reflected his life-long fascination with Brazil's folk rhythms and melodies.

Villa-Lobos's formidable productivity brought him early critical attention, some of it negative, owing to his eclecticism and harmonic innovation, as well as his failure to follow European musical conventions. Yet his undeniable talent brought him increasing international attention and, ultimately, the support of Artur Rubinstein, upon whose 1923 recommendation the young Brazilian was invited to study in Paris. The seven years that Villa-Lobos spent in Europe were among his most productive. During that period he produced what would become his best-known work, his *Bacchianas brasileiras*, sixteen compositions running from orchestral works to those for single instruments, inspired by the music of Bach and Brazilian folk music. *Bachianas* captivated European music critics, winning Villa-Lobos invitations to present his music throughout the continent. Other fruits of his European stay were sixteen pieces based on children's songs, the *Cirandas* (1926), and *Rudepoema* (1921-26), dedicated to Artur Rubinstein.

Villa-Lobos returned to Brazil in 1930, and, at the invitation of the state of São Paulo and the federal government, he promoted music education and spoke in nationalistic terms on behalf of Brazil's varied musical traditions. In the post-war years his fame was such that he performed regularly in Europe and the United States, while continuing his compositional outpouring. During the last years of his life he turned to the writing of string quartets, considered among his finest works. Heitor Villa-Lobos's 3,000 compositions stand as a monument to Brazil's and Latin America's greatest twentieth-century composer.

Walker, William (1824-1860), American filibuster who led private military campaigns in Latin America and served briefly as president of Nicaragua. A native of Nashville, Tennessee, he was trained as both a doctor and a lawyer. In 1853 he invaded Baja California and Sonora with forty-five followers, ostensibly to protect the inhabitants from marauding Indians, and created a Republic of Sonora comprising both regions. Mexican resistance and the hostility of U.S. authorities led to the failure of this expedition.

In 1855 Walker went to Nicaragua with fifty-seven men at the invitation of Liberals who were trying to drive the rival Conservatives from power. After Walker captured the Conservative stronghold of Granada, the Conservatives came to terms, and he became army chief in a coalition government headed by Conservative Patricio Rivas. In July 1856 Walker himself became president. Meanwhile, Central Americans, led by Costa Rican president Juan Rafael Mora and aided by the British, joined forces to combat Walker, who they feared planned to annex Nicaragua to the United States. He also alienated Cornelius Vanderbilt by canceling the concession of the Accessory Transit Company, which Vanderbilt controlled, to transport passengers across the Nicaraguan isthmus. On May 1, 1857, Walker was forced to surrender to a U.S. naval officer. After an unsuccessful attempt to return to Nicaragua by way of Honduras in 1860, he was executed by a Honduran firing squad.

The Walker episode left a lingering distrust of the United States among Central Americans since his activities had had the support of many Americans, especially southerners, who applauded his legalization of slavery. He described his experiences in *The War in Nicaragua* (1860).

Yrigoyen, Hipólito (1852-1933), twice Argentine president and an early leader of the Radical party. Born in Buenos Aires province, the natural son of a blacksmith, Hipólito Yrigoyen entered public life thanks to the help of his uncle, Leandro Alem, a crusader against oligarchic domination of Argentine politics. Yrigoyen's personality was complex. Introspective and philosophic on one hand, he was also a practical politician given to plotting overthrow of the conservative regimes dominant at the time. In 1890, he joined the Civic Union, formed by Alem and **Bartolomé Mitre**, going on to participate in the Civic Union–led rebellion that drove President Miguel Juárez Celman from power (August 6, 1890). In 1890, the Civic Union split, with Alem and Yrigoyen forming the Radical Civic Union (UCR, Unión Cívica Radical), dedicated to ending elite rule at any cost. Yrigoyen became UCR leader in 1896, when Alem committed suicide following yet another failed attempt at revolution.

Yrigoyen emerged as paladin of Argentina's middle classes during the first decades of the twentieth century, a time of explosive economic growth and social diversification. When he and his movement failed to overthrow conservative President Manuel Quintana in 1905, Yrigoyen was forced to wait until political change allowed him to assume power through democratic means. Such change was not long in coming. An electoral reform of 1912 enfranchised native-born males above the age of eighteen, in effect swelling UCR ranks. Thus Yrigoyen won the 1916 presidential contest by a substantial plurality of votes. Once in office he pursued a prudent course, working to strengthen his party while placating conservatives and the church. But an opposition-controlled Congress thwarted his legislative initiatives, particularly his proposed tax on incomes aimed at reducing the nation's debt. Yrigoyen nevertheless managed to please both his middle-class and his nationalist followers by favoring the university reform movement, by creating a state petroleum enterprise, and by maintaining Argentine neutrality during World War I. Critics faulted him for personalism, flagrant intervention in provincial affairs, and his politicization of the military. The onset of economic depression during 1921, coupled with the president's inability to control economic cycles plaguing Argentina, ended his first term on a

negative note. The UCR split during the administration of Yrigoyen's hand-picked successor, Marcelo de Alvear. Yrigoyen soon moved to oppose Alvear, whose program of fiscal austerity involved firing many Yrigoyen appointees to public office. When the 1928 presidential election approached, Yrigoyen campaigned on a platform advocating both expanding state control over petroleum and opposition to the United States and the powerful Standard Oil Company. Reelected by a sizeable majority, Yrigoyen concentrated on easing the nation's debt burden. But the global depression that struck within a year of his inauguration rendered the administration's programs futile. As the depression deepened, UCR members deserted the party, while the political left and right united against him. At that moment the military, which had its own grievances, moved against the discredited president. On September 6, 1930, General José Uriburu overthrew and exiled him. Hipólito Yrigoyen died in 1933.

Zapata, Emiliano (1879-1919), Mexican revolutionary leader and champion of agrarian reform. Zapata was born into a peasant family in Anenecuilco, a village in the state of Morelos. He had little formal education but achieved local prominence as a defender of peasants whose lands were threatened by encroaching sugar plantations. In 1910-11 Zapata emerged as the leader of forces in Morelos opposing the regime of **Porfirio Díaz**, but after the triumph of the revolution he clashed with its chief, **Francisco I. Madero**, over the latter's reluctance to undertake agrarian reform. On November 11, 1911, Zapata issued the Plan de Ayala, disavowing Madero, who had recently taken office as president. Probably drafted by Otilio Montaño, a schoolteacher, the plan is notable for its concern for landless Mexicans and its commitment to land redistribution. After the demise of Madero, Zapata fought the government of **Victoriano Huerta**, taking his campaign to Guerrero and other states besides Morelos. With the disintegration of the anti-Huerta coalition in 1914, Zapata rejected the claims of **Venustiano Carranza** and allied himself with **Francisco Villa**, whom he met at Xochimilco on December 4, 1914, shortly after *zapatista* forces had entered

Mexico City. Zapata captured the city of Puebla in mid-December, but he soon withdrew to Morelos, where he initiated agrarian reform while continuing his resistance to the *carrancistas*. On April 10, 1919, Zapata was killed in an ambush planned by General Pablo González, Carranza's commander in the region. Surviving *zapatistas* endorsed **Álvaro Obregón**'s anti-Carranza movement of 1919-20 and dominated Morelos after he became president. Zapata himself became a mythic figure and an enduring symbol for advocates of Mexico's peasantry.

Zedillo Ponce de León, Ernesto (1951–   ), Mexican president (1994–2000). Ernesto Zedillo was born in Mexico City to lower-middle-class parents and raised in the northern border town of Mexicali. There he attended public elementary school, going on to win admittance to the National Polytechnic Institute in Mexico City. While there he worked part-time in the president's office of economic policymaking. At age nineteen he joined the Institutional Revolutionary party (PRI), shortly thereafter winning a scholarship to Yale University, where he received an M.A. in economics in 1977. In 1981 he earned a Ph.D. at Yale, writing a dissertation on Mexican government irresponsibility as a source of the nation's economic woes. Between 1981 and 1987, Zedillo held positions at the central bank and at a national economic adjustment agency. He joined the economic team of PRI presidential nominee **Carlos Salinas de Gortari** in 1987, becoming one of a group dubbed Salinas's "technocratic yuppie" advisors. President Salinas made Zedillo his education minister in 1992. Zedillo left the ministry in 1993 to manage the presidential campaign of PRI candidate Luis Donaldo Colosio. When Colosio was assassinated in March 1994, Salinas named Zedillo to replace him as PRI candidate. Zedillo won the presidential contest with about 50 percent of the vote, easily besting contenders from the conservative PAN party and the left-wing PRD. Inaugurated December 1, Zedillo was immediately confronted with economic crisis produced by peso devaluation and capital flight, as well as an armed insurgency of Mayan Indian rebels in southern Mexico. The country barely avoided bankruptcy during 1995, thanks to austerity measures and an emergency $20 billion loan provided by U.S. president William Clinton. Relative economic health returned in 1996, with Mexico enjoying 4 percent growth. Zedillo also faced obstacles in democratizing Mexico's PRI-dominated political system, but the outcome of July 1997 elections, in which the opposition parties made major gains, enhanced his credentials as a democratic leader.

Zelaya, José Santos (1853-1919), president and dictator of Nicaragua. A native of Managua, Zelaya came to power as a result of a Liberal uprising that began in León on July 11, 1893, and ended more than thirty years of Conservative rule in Nicaragua. A Liberal modernizer like other contemporary Central American rulers, he encouraged education, sought to lessen the influence of the Roman Catholic church, and promoted railroad construction and commercial agriculture. Although his tenure became increasingly arbitrary and he interfered in the affairs of Honduras and other neighboring states, his admirers remember him as a nationalist who challenged the pretensions of Great Britain and the United States. Between 1894 and 1904 he was able to incorporate into Nicaragua the Mosquito Coast (Mosquitia), where the British had maintained a protectorate despite an 1860 treaty acknowledging Nicaraguan sovereignty there. However, American and other foreign businessmen in the region resented Nicaraguan authority and looked to the United States to protect their interests. After the United States decided to build an interoceanic canal in Panama rather than Nicaragua, Zelaya sounded European and Japanese interest in a Nicaraguan canal, to the annoyance of the American government. Zelaya further antagonized the United States by mounting a successful campaign in 1907 to unseat the president of Honduras, Manuel Bonilla, thereby undermining stability in Central America. In 1909 Juan J. Estrada, Zelaya's governor in Bluefields on the east coast, rebelled against the government with the support of Nicaraguan Conservatives and the U.S. consul there. When Zelaya's forces captured and executed two American adventurers who were in the service of the rebels, U.S. secretary of state Philander Knox called Zelaya a "blot on the history of Nicaragua." In view of U.S. determination to bring about his ouster, Zelaya resigned in December 1909 and went into exile.

Zumárraga, Juan de (1468?-1548), Franciscan priest and first bishop (1528-47) and archbishop (1547-48) of Mexico. Born in Durango, Vizcaya, Spain, Zumárraga was chosen personally by the emperor **Charles V** as bishop of Mexico and dispatched there even before his consecration (1534). He opposed the rapacious first *audiencia* (1528-31), especially its president **Nuño Beltrán de Guzmán**, smuggled out reports to Spain, and reported personally to the emperor. With **Antonio de Mendoza** as the first viceroy and with the new second *audiencia*, Zumárraga became an integral part of a team effort that brought greater peace and stability to New Spain. While he was overzealous with his inquisitorial powers, presiding over 131 trials, he was inspired by the humanism of the Renaissance and brought Erasmian texts and the first printing press to Mexico and was a strong patron of education.

Selected Bibliography

General Works and Histories of Individual Countries or Regions

Bethell, Leslie. ed. *Cambridge History of Latin America.* 10 vols. Cambridge, Eng., 1984-95.

Burns, E. Bradford. *Latin America: A Concise Interpretive History.* 6th ed. Englewood Cliffs, NJ, 1994.

Bushnell, David. *The Making of Modern Colombia: A Nation in Spite of Itself.* Berkeley, CA, 1993.

Clayton, Lawrence A., and Michael L. Conniff. *A History of Modern Latin America.* New York, 1998.

Collier, Simon, Thomas E. Skidmore, and Harold Blakemore. *The Cambridge Encyclopedia of Latin America and the Caribbean.* 2nd ed. Cambridge, Eng., 1992.

Collier, Simon, Thomas E. Skidmore, Harold Blakemore, and William F. Sater. *A History of Chile, 1808-1994.* Cambridge, Eng., 1996.

Eakin, Marshall C. *Brazil: The Once and Future Country.* New York, 1997.

Ewell, Judith. *Venezuela: A Century of Change.* London, 1984.

Masterson, Daniel M. *Militarism and Politics in Latin America: Peru from Sánchez Cerro to Sendero Luminoso.* New York, 1991.

Meyer, Michael C., William L. Sherman, and Susan M. Deeds. *The Course of Mexican History.* 6th ed. New York, 1999.

Rock, David. *Argentina, 1516-1987: From Spanish Colonization to the Falklands War and Alfonsín.* rev. ed. Berkeley, CA, 1987.

Rogozinski, Jan. *A Brief History of the Caribbean: From the Arawak and the Carib to the Present.* New York, 1994.

Schoultz, Lars. *Beneath the United States: A History of U.S. Policy Toward Latin America.* Cambridge, MA, 1998.

Skidmore, Thomas E., and Peter H. Smith. *Modern Latin America.* 4th ed. New York, 1997.

Tenenbaum, Barbara, ed. *Encylopedia of Latin American History and Culture.* 5 vols. New York, 1996.

Williamson, Robert C. *Latin American Societies in Transition.* Westport, CT, 1996.

Woodward, Ralph Lee., Jr. *Central America: A Nation Divided.* 3rd ed. New York, 1999.

Pre-Columbian America

Clendinnen, Inga. *The Aztecs: An Interpretation.* Cambridge, Eng., 1991.

Coe, Michael D. *The Maya.* 5th ed. New York, 1993.

Davies, Nigel. *The Ancient Kingdoms of Peru.* London, 1977.

Rouse, Irving. *The Tainos: The Rise and Decline of the People Who Greeted Columbus.* New Haven, CT, 1992.

Iberian Expansion and Colonial Latin America: 1402-1803

Andrien, Kenneth J. *Crisis and Decline: The Viceroyalty of Peru in the Seventeenth Century.* Albuquerque, 1985.

Andrews, Kenneth R. *The Spanish Caribbean: Trade and Plunder, 1530-1630.* New Haven, CT, 1978.

Bedini, Silvio A., ed. *Christopher Columbus and the Age of Exploration: An Encyclopedia.* 2 vols. New York, 1992.

Black, Clinton V. *Pirates of the West Indies.* Cambridge, Eng., 1989.

Boxer, Charles R. *The Golden Age of Brazil, 1695-1750.* Berkeley, CA, 1962.

Boxer, Charles R. *The Dutch in Brazil, 1624-1654.* Oxford, Eng., 1957.

Boxer, Charles R. *The Portuguese Seaborne Empire, 1415-1815.* New York, 1969.

Burkholder, Mark A., and Lyman L. Johnson. *Colonial Latin America.* 3rd ed. New York, 1998.

Hanke, Lewis. *The Spanish Struggle for Justice in the Conquest of America.* Philadelphia, 1949.

Hemming, John. *The Conquest of the Incas.* New York, 1970.

Hemming, John. *Red Gold: The Conquest of the Brazilian Indians.* Cambridge, MA, 1978.

Israel, J. I. *Race, Class and Politics in Colonial Mexico, 1610-1670.* New York, 1975.

Kelsey, Harry. *Sir Francis Drake: The Queen's Pirate.* New Haven, CT, 1998.

Lynch, John. *The Hispanic World in Crisis and Change, 1598-1700.* Oxford, Eng., 1992.

Lynch, John. *Spain, 1516-1598: From Nation State to World Empire.* Oxford, Eng., 1993.

Phillips, William D., and Carla Rahn Phillips. *The Worlds of Christopher Columbus.* Cambridge, Eng., 1992

Sauer, Carl O. *The Early Spanish Main.* Berkeley, CA, 1966.

Simpson, Lesley Byrd. *The Encomienda in New Spain: The Beginning of Spanish Mexico.* rev. and enl. ed. Berkeley, CA, 1950.

Thomas, Hugh. *Conquest: Montezuma, Cortes, and the Fall of Old Mexico.* New York, 1993

Weber, David J., ed. *New Spain's Far Northern Frontier: Essays on Spain in the American West, 1540-1821.* Albuquerque, 1979.

The Struggle for Independence: 1804-1825

Fick, Carolyn E. *The Making of Haiti: The Saint Domingue Revolution from Below.* Knoxville, TN, 1990.

Graham, Richard. *Independence in Latin America: A Comparative Approach.* 2nd ed. New York, 1994.

Kinsbruner, Jay. *Independence in Spanish America: Civil Wars, Revolution, and Underdevelopment.* Albuquerque, 1994.

Lynch, John. *The Spanish-American Revolutions, 1808-1826.* New York, 1973.

Macaulay, Neill. *Dom Pedro: The Struggle for Liberty in Brazil and Portugal.* Durham, NC, 1986.

Masur, Gerhard. *Simón Bolívar.* Albuquerque, 1948.

Caudillos and Conflict: 1826-1869

Burns, E. Bradford. *The Poverty of Progress: Latin America in the Nineteenth Century.* Berkeley, CA, 1980.

Bushnell, David, and Neill Macaulay. *The Emergence of Latin America in the Nineteenth Century.* 2nd ed. New York, 1994

Costa, Emilia Viotti da. *The Brazilian Empire: Myths and Histories.* Chicago, 1985.

Davis, William Columbus. *The Last Conquistadores: The Spanish Intervention in Peru and Chile, 1863-1866.* Athens, GA, 1950.

Jones, Oakah L. *Santa Anna.* New York, 1968.

Lynch, John. *Argentine Dictator: Juan Manuel de Rosas, 1829-1852.* New York, 1981.

Shumway, Nicolas. *The Invention of Argentina.* Berkeley, CA, 1992.

Sinkin, Richard N. *The Mexican Reform, 1855-1876: A Study in Liberal Nation-Building.* Austin, TX, 1979.

Van Aken, Mark J. *King of the Night: Juan José Flores and Ecuador, 1824-1864.* Berkeley, CA, 1989.

Williams, John Hoyt. *The Rise and Fall of the Paraguayan Republic, 1800-1870.* Austin, TX, 1979.

Woodward, Ralph Lee, Jr. *Rafael Carrera and the Emergence of the Republic of Guatemala, 1821-1871.* Athens, GA, 1993.

Incipient Modernization and Social Change: 1871-1929

Albert, Bill. *South America and the First World War: The Impact of the War on Brazil, Argentina, Peru, and Chile.* Cambridge, Eng., 1988.

Bergquist, Charles. *Coffee and Conflict in Colombia, 1886-1910.* Durham, NC, 1978.

Brunk, Samuel. *Emiliano Zapata: Revolution and Betrayal in Mexico.* Albuquerque, 1995.

Hart, John M. *Revolutionary Mexico: The Coming and Process of the Mexican Revolution.* Berkeley, CA, 1987.

Katz, Friedrich. *The Life and Times of Pancho Villa.* Stanford, CA, 1998.

Klein, Herbert S. *Parties and Political Change in Bolivia, 1880-1952.* London, 1969.

Knight, Alan. *The Mexican Revolution.* 2 vols. Cambridge, Eng., 1986.

Love, Joseph L. *Rio Grande do Sul and Brazilian Regionalism, 1882-1930.* Stanford, CA, 1971.

Love, Joseph L. *São Paulo in the Brazilian Federation, 1889-1937.* Stanford, CA, 1980.

Macaulay, Neill. *The Sandino Affair*. Chicago, 1967.

McCreery, David. *Development and the State in Reforma Guatemala, 1871-1885*. Athens, OH, 1983.

Pérez, Louis A., Jr. *Cuba Between Empires, 1878-1902*. Pittsburgh, 1983.

Pérez, Louis A., Jr. *Cuba Under the Platt Amendment, 1902-1934*. Pittsburgh, 1986.

Rock, David. *Politics in Argentina, 1890-1930: The Rise and Fall of Radicalism*. Cambridge, Eng., 1975.

Ross, Stanley R. *Francisco I. Madero: Apostle of Mexican Democracy*. New York, 1955.

Sater, William F. *Chile and the War of the Pacific*. Lincoln, NE, 1986.

Vanderwood, Paul. *The Power of God Against the Guns of Government: Religious Upheaval in Mexico at the Turn of the Twentieth Century*. Stanford, CA, 1998.

Economic Nationalism and Political Protest: 1930-1959

Ameringer, Charles. *Don Pepe: A Political Biography of José Figueres of Costa Rica*. Albuquerque, 1978.

Bantjes, Adrian. *As If Jesus Walked on Earth: Cardenismo, Sonora, and the Mexican Revolution*. Wilmington, DE, 1998.

Becker, Marjorie. *Setting the Virgin on Fire: Lázaro Cárdenas, Michoacán Peasants, and the Redemption of the Mexican Revolution*. Berkeley, CA, 1996.

Fraser, Nicholas, and Marysa Navarro. *Eva Perón*. New York, 1980.

Gleijeses, Piero. *Shattered Hope: The Guatemalan Revolution and the United States, 1944-1954*. Princeton, NJ, 1991.

Henderson, James D. *When Colombia Bled: A History of the Violencia in Tolima*. University, AL, 1985.

Levine, Robert M. *Father of the Poor? Vargas and His Era*. Cambridge, Eng., 1998.

Page, Joseph. *Perón: A Biography*. New York, 1983.

Potash, Robert A. *The Army and Politics in Argentina, 1928-1945*. Stanford, CA, 1969.

Potash, Robert A. *The Army and Politics in Argentina, 1945-1962*. Stanford, CA, 1982.

Rock, David., ed. *Latin America in the 1940s: War and Postwar Transitions*. Berkeley, CA, 1994.

Sharpless, Richard E. *Gaitán of Colombia: A Political Biography*. Pittsburgh, 1978.

Skidmore, Thomas E. *Politics in Brazil, 1930-1964: An Experiment in Democracy*. New York, 1967.

Stein, Steve. *Populism in Peru: The Emergence of the Masses and the Politics of Social Control*. Madison, WI, 1980.

Walter, Knut. *The Regime of Anastasio Somoza, 1936-1956*. Chapel Hill, NC, 1993.

Zook, David H. *The Conduct of the Chaco War*. New York, 1960.

Revolutionary Movements and Economic Development: 1960-1989

Anderson, Jon Lee. *Che Guevara: A Revolutionary Life.* New York, 1997.

Balfour, Sebastian. *Castro.* 2nd ed. London, 1995.

Crabtree, John. *Peru Under García: An Opportunity Lost.* Pittsburgh, 1992.

Gorriti, Gustavo. *The Shining Path: A History of the Millenarian War in Peru.* Chapel Hill, NC, 1998.

Landau, Saul. *The Guerrilla Wars of Central America: Nicaragua, El Salvador, Guatemala.* New York, 1993.

McClintock, Cynthia, and Abraham Lowenthal, eds. *The Peruvian Experiment Reconsidered.* Princeton, NJ, 1983.

Pérez-Stable, Marifeli. *The Cuban Revolution: Origins, Course, and Legacy.* 2nd ed. New York, 1999.

Potash, Robert A. *The Army and Politics in Argentina, 1962-1973.* Stanford, CA, 1996.

Sigmund, Paul E. *The Overthrow of Allende and the Politics of Chile, 1964-1976.* Pittsburgh, 1977.

Skidmore, Thomas E. *The Politics of Military Rule in Brazil, 1964-1985.* New York, 1988.

Post-Cold War Challenges: 1990-1998

Castañeda, Jorge G. *Utopia Unarmed: The Latin American Left After the Cold War.* New York, 1993.

Clawson, Patrick L., and Lee W. Rensselaer, III. *The Andean Cocaine Industry.* New York, 1996.

Purcell, Susan Kaufman, and Riordan Roett, eds. *Brazil Under Cardoso.* Boulder, CO, 1997.

Purcell, Susan Kaufman, Riordan Roett, and Luis Rubio, eds. *Mexico Under Zedillo.* Boulder, CO, 1998.

Vargas Llosa, Alvaro. *The Madness of Things Peruvian: Democracy Under Siege.* New Brunswick, NJ 1994.

Society

Arrom, Silvia. *The Women of Mexico City, 1790-1857.* Stanford, CA, 1985.

Bowser, Frederick P. *The African Slave in Colonial Peru, 1524-1650.* Stanford, CA, 1973.

Conrad, Robert E. *The Destruction of Brazilian Slavery, 1850-1888.* Berkeley, 1972.

Conrad, Robert E. *World of Sorrow: The African Slave Trade to Brazil.* Baton Rouge, 1986.

Denevan, William M., ed. *The Native Population of the Americas in 1492.* 2nd ed. Madison, WI, 1992.

Gibson, Charles. *The Aztecs Under Spanish Rule: A History of the Indians of the Valley of Mexico.* Stanford, CA, 1964.

Hahner, June E. *Emancipating the Female Sex: The Struggle for Women's Rights in Brazil, 1850-1940.* Durham, NC, 1990.

Holloway, Thomas H. *Immigrants on the Land: Coffee and Society in São Paulo, 1886-1934.* Chapel Hill, NC, 1981.

Kandell, Jonathan. *La Capital: The Biography of Mexico City.* New York, 1988.

Knight, Franklin W. *Slave Society in Cuba During the Nineteenth Century.* Madison, WI, 1970.

Martín, Luis. *Daughters of the Conquistadores: Women of the Viceroyalty of Peru.* 1983.

Mattoso, Kátia M. De Queirós. *To Be a Slave in Brazil, 1550-1888.* New Brunswick, NJ, 1986.

Meade, Teresa A. *"Civilizing" Rio: Reform and Resistance in a Brazilian City, 1889-1930.* University Park, PA, 1997.

Miller, Francesca. *Latin American Women and the Search for Social Justice.* Hanover, NH, 1991.

Pineo, Ronn, and James A. Baer, eds. *Cities of Hope: People, Protests, and Progress in Urbanizing Latin America, 1870-1930.* Boulder, CO, 1998.

Pino, Julio Cesar. *Family and Favela: The Reproduction of Poverty in Rio de Janeiro.* Westport, CT, 1997.

Rout, Leslie B., Jr. *The African Experience in Spanish America, 1502 to the Present Day.* Cambridge, Eng., 1976.

Russell-Wood, A. J. R. *The Black Man in Slavery and Freedom in Colonial Brazil.* London, 1982.

Schwartz, Stuart B. *Sugar Plantations in the Formation of Brazilian Society: Bahia, 1550-1835.* Cambridge, Eng., 1989.

Scobie, James R. *Buenos Aires: From Plaza to Surburb, 1870-1910.* New York, 1974.

Smith, Lois M., and Alfred Padula. *Sex and Revolution: Women in Socialist Cuba.* New York, 1996.

Solberg, Carl E. *Immigration and Nationalism in Argentina and Chile, 1890-1914.* Austin, TX, 1970.

Stern, Steve J. *Peru's Indian Peoples and the Challenge of Spanish Conquest: Huamanga to 1640.* Madison, WI, 1980.

Politics and Government

Alden, Dauril. *Royal Government in Colonial Brazil, with Special Reference to the Administration of the Marquis of Lavradio, Viceroy, 1769-1779.* Berkeley, CA, 1968.

Burkholder, Mark A., and D. S. Chandler. *From Impotence to Authority: The Spanish Crown and the American Audiencias, 1687-1808.* Columbia, MO, 1977.

Delpar, Helen. *Red Against Blue: The Liberal Party in Colombian Politics, 1863-1899.* University, AL, 1981.

Graham, Carol. *Peru's APRA: Parties, Politics, and the Elusive Quest for Democracy.* Boulder, CO, 1992.

Hale, Charles A. *Mexican Liberalism in the Age of Mora.* New Haven, CT, 1968.

Hale, Charles A. *The Transformation of Liberalism in Late Nineteenth-Century Mexico.* Princeton, NJ, 1989.

Haring, Clarence H. *The Spanish Empire in America.* New York, 1947.

Henderson, James D. *Conservative Thought in Twentieth Century Latin America.* Athens, OH, 1988.

Liss, Sheldon B. *Marxist Thought in Latin America.* Berkeley, CA, 1984.

McDonald, Ronald H., and J. Mark Ruhl. *Party Politics and Elections in Latin America.* Boulder, CO, 1989.

Mainwaring, Scott, and Timothy Scully, eds. *Building Democratic Institutions: Party Systems in Latin America.* Stanford, CA , 1995.

Parry, John H. *The Audiencia of New Galicia in the Sixteenth Century: A Study in Spanish Colonial Government.* Cambridge, Eng., 1948.

Schwartz, Stuart B. *Sovereignty and Society in Colonial Brazil: The High Court of Bahia and Its Judges, 1609-1751.* Berkeley, CA, 1973.

Scully, Timothy R. *Rethinking the Center: Party Politics in Nineteenth- and Twentieth-Century Chile.* Stanford, CA, 1992.

Wiarda, Howard J., and Harvey F. Kline. *Latin American Politics and Development.* 4th ed. Boulder, CO, 1996.

Wickham-Crowley, Timothy. *Guerrillas and Revolution in Latin America: A Comparative Study of Insurgents and Regimes Since 1956.* Princeton, NJ, 1992.

Economics

Baer, Werner. *The Brazilian Economy: Growth and Development.* 4th ed. Westport, CT, 1995.

Bulmer-Thomas, Victor. *The Economic History of Latin America Since Independence.* Cambridge, Eng., 1995.

Bulmer-Thomas, Victor. *The Political Economy of Central America Since 1920.* Cambridge, Eng., 1987.

Cardoso, Fernando H., and Enzo Faletto. *Dependency and Development in Latin America.* Berkeley, CA, 1979.

Devlin, Robert. *Debt and Crisis in Latin America: The Supply Side Story.* Princeton, NJ, 1989.

Fisher, John R. *The Economic Aspects of Spanish Imperialism in America, 1492-1810.* Liverpool, 1997.

Greenfield, Gerald M., and Sheldon L. Maram, eds. *Latin American Labor Organizations.* New York, 1987.

Haber, Stephen M. *Industry and Underdevelopment: The Industrialization of Mexico, 1890-1940.* Stanford, CA, 1989.

Orme, William A., Jr. *Understanding NAFTA.* Austin, TX, 1996.

Thorp, Rosemary. *Progress, Poverty and Exclusion: An Economic History of Latin America in the Twentieth Century.* Baltimore, 1998.

Thorp, Rosemary, and Geoffrey Bertram. *Peru, 1890-1977: Growth and Policy in an Open Economy.* New York, 1978.

Culture

Ades, Dawn. *Art in Latin America: The Modern Era, 1820-1930.* New Haven, CT, 1989.

Arbena, Joseph L., ed. *Sport and Society in Latin America: Diffusion, Dependency, and the Rise of Mass Culture.* Westport, CT, 1988.

Barnard, Timothy, and Peter Rist, eds. *South American Cinema: A Critical Filmography, 1915-1994.* Austin, TX, 1998.

Béhague, Gerard. *Music in Latin America.* Englewood Cliffs, NJ, 1979.

Brown, Diana DeG. *Umbanda: Religion and Politics in Urban Brazil.* Ann Arbor, MI, 1986.

Collier, Simon. *The Life, Music, and Times of Carlos Gardel.* Pittsburgh, 1986.

Elkin, Judith Laikin, and Gilbert W. Merkx, eds. *The Jewish Presence in Latin America.* Boston, 1987.

Fane, Diana. *Converging Cultures: Art and Identity in Spanish America*. New York, 1996.

Foster, David William. *Mexican Literature: A History*. Austin, TX, 1994.

Fox, Elizabeth. *Latin American Broadcasting: From Tango to Telenovela*. Luton, Eng., 1997.

King, John. *Magical Reels: A History of Cinema in Latin America*. New York 1990.

Lever, Janet. *Soccer Madness: Brazil's Passion for the World's Most Popular Sport*. rev. ed. Prospect Heights, IL, 1995.

Lindstrom, Naomi. *Twentieth Century Spanish American Fiction*. Austin, TX, 1994.

Maier, Joseph, and Richard W. Weatherhead, eds. *The Latin American University*. Albuquerque, 1979.

Mainwaring, Scott. *The Catholic Church and Politics in Brazil, 1916-1985*. Stanford, CA, 1986.

Mason, Tony. *Passion of the People?: Football in South America*. New York, 1995.

Mecham, J. Lloyd. *Church and State in Latin America: A History of Politicoecclesiastical Relations*. rev. ed. Chapel Hill, NC, 1966.

Menéndez Alarcón, Antonio V. *Power and Television in Latin America: The Dominican Case*. New York, 1992.

Miller, Daniel R., ed. *Coming of Age: Protestantism in Contemporary Latin America*. Lanham, MD, 1994.

Mora, Carl J. *Mexican Cinema: Reflections of a Society*. rev. ed. Berkeley, CA, 1989.

Orme, William A., Jr. *A Culture of Collusion: An Inside Look at the Mexican Press*. Coral Gables, FL, 1997.

Ricard, Robert. *The Spiritual Conquest of Mexico*. Berkeley, CA, 1966.

Salwen, Michael Brian. *Radio and Television in Cuba: The Pre-Castro Era*. Ames, IA, 1994.

Salwen, Michael Brian, and Bruce Garrison. *Latin American Journalism*. Hillsdale, NJ, 1991.

Schwaller, John F. *Church and Clergy in Sixteenth-Century Mexico*. Albuquerque, 1987.

Shreiner, Claus. *Música Brasileira: A History of Popular Music and the People of Brazil*. New York, 1993.

Sinclair, John. *Latin American Television: A Global View*. New York, 1999.

Solé, Carlos A., and Maria Isabel Abreu, eds. *Latin American Literature*. 3 vols. New York, 1989

Traba, Marta. *Art of Latin America, 1900-1980*. Baltimore, 1994.

Vaughan, Mary Kay. *Cultural Politics in Revolution: Teachers, Peasants, and Schools in Mexico, 1930-1940*. Tucson, 1997.

Vaughan, Mary Kay. *The State, Education and Social Class in Mexico, 1880-1928*. DeKalb, IL, 1982.

Science and Medicine

Appel, John Wilton. *Francisco José de Caldas: A Scientist at Work in Nueva Granada*. Philadelphia, 1994.

Cook, Noble David. *Born to Die: Disease and New World Conquest, 1492-1650*. Cambridge, Eng., 1998.

Cueto, Marcos, ed. *Missionaries of Science: The Rockefeller Foundation in Latin America*. Bloomington, IN, 1994.

Engstrand, Iris H. W. *Spanish Scientists in the New World: The Eighteenth-Century Expeditions.* Seattle, 1981.

Lanning, John Tate. *The Royal Protomedicato: The Regulation of the Medical Professions in the Spanish Empire.* Ed. John J. TePaske. Durham, NC, 1985.

Stepan, Nancy. *Beginnings of Brazilian Science: Oswaldo Cruz, Medical Research and Politcy, 1890-1920.* New York, 1976.

INDEX

Names in **boldface** are contained in Part III, 300 Notable Figures of Latin American History

American Cinema, 417a
France, 417a
French New Wave, 414b
globalization and, 417b
Lumière brothers, 412b
Martinique, 417a
Mexico, 412b-414a, 415a
Mexican Revolution in, 413a
national film institutes, 416a
New Cinema, 414b-415b
silent film, 412b-413a
Spain, 417a
Venezuela, 416a
Cinema Novo. See New Cinema
Cisneros, Baltasar Hidalgo de,
102b-103a
Cisplatine War (1825-28), 109b,
125b
City planning. See Urban
development
Clark, Lygia, 397b
Clark, Ruben J., 138a
Claver, Saint Pedro, 451b
Clavijero, Francisco Javier, 386b
Clayton-Bulwer Treaty (1850),
115b
Clement XIV, pope, 33b, 386b
Clemente, Roberto, 419a, 451b
Cleveland, Grover, 142b
Clientelism, 346b
Clinton, William J., 276b, 280a,
381b, 552b
Coca cultivation,
Peru and, 281a
Bolivia and, 281a
Colombia and, 281, 285a
Cocaine trafficking, 281a
Coche, Treaty of (1863), 123b
Cochrane, Thomas, 107a, 452a,
533a
Coelho Pereira, Duarte, 93a,
452a-b
Coffee,
Inter-American Coffee
Convention (1941), 370b-
371a
coffee industry, 119b, 131a,
143b, 162a, 170b, 174b,
362b, 364b, 368a
Colbert, Jean Baptiste, 347b
Cold War. See Latin America,
1930-59; Politics and
government; individual

countries
Collor de Mello, Fernando, 269b,
291a, 345a, 446a
Collor de Mello, Pedro, 291b
Colombia,
agrarian reform law of 1961,
246a, 488a
Alliance for Progress, 246a
agriculture,
commercialization of,
203a
ANAPO (National Popular
Alliance), 248b, 339b, 529a
Andean Pact, 247b, 488a
anticlericalism, 502a, 506b-
507a
anticommunism, 203a, 204a,
473b
Antioquian colonization,
359b
Armero mud slide (1985),
253b
Army of National Liberation.
See ELN
AUC. See United Self-
Defense Forces
(Autodefensas Unidas
de Colombia)
aviation, 161a
Bananeras Massacre (1928),
162b, 468b
banking, 488a, 511b
bogotazo, el (April 9, 1948),
202a, 468b-469a
Botanical Expedition, 442a
Boyacá, Battle of (1819),
534b
Bull Ring Massacre (1956),
204a
Cali drug cartel, 281b,
284a-b
Cartagena Declaration
(1990), 281a
Catholic Church, 193b,
506b-507a, 535a
certification by U.S., 284b,
286a
civil war of 1876-77, 155a,
543b
civil war of 1885, 141b,
157a, 524b
civil war of 1895, 524a
civil war of 1899-1902,

158b-159a, 543b
cinema, 416a
coffee, 153b, 162a
communist guerrillas, 245b-
247a, 250b
Comunero Revolt (1781),
65b-66a, 327a-b, 469b
Congress of Cúcuta (1821),
504b
Conservative hegemony
(1885-1930), 543b
Conservative party, 121b,
122a, 123a-124b, 157a,
197a, 202b, 203b, 286b,
502a
constitution of 1832, 121a,
535a
constitution of 1863, 123b,
157a, 502a, 507a
constitution of 1886, 157a,
507a
constitution of 1991, 281b,
388b
Contadora Group, 252a,
439a
crawling peg currency
inflation, 246a
corporatism in, 473b
Currie Plan (1950), 208a
drug cartels, 254b
drug trafficking, 408b,
506a-b
economic liberalism, 331b,
503b
El Cerrejón, 439a
exports, manufactured, 378a
ELN (Ejército de Liberación
Nacional) guerrillas,
246a, 285a-287b, 344b
FARC (Fuerzas Armadas
Revolucionarias de
Colombia) guerrillas,
246b-247a, 253b, 284a-
287b, 343b-344a
Gachetá Massacre (1939),
199a
GDP (1980s), 380a
Gran Colombia, 106b,
119a-b, 120a-b, 330b,
464b, 502a
Great Depression (1929-30s)
and, 197a
Hay-Herran Treaty (1903),

DATE DUE

			PRINTED IN U.S.A.